Lecture Notes in Artificial Intelligence 3155

Edited by J. G. Carbonell and J. Siekmann

Subseries of Lecture Notes in Computer Science

Peter Funk   Pedro A. González Calero (Eds.)

Advances in Case-Based Reasoning

7th European Conference, ECCBR 2004
Madrid, Spain, August 30 - September 2, 2004
Proceedings

Series Editors

Jaime G. Carbonell, Carnegie Mellon University, Pittsburgh, PA, USA
Jörg Siekmann, University of Saarland, Saarbrücken, Germany

Volume Editors

Peter Funk
Mälardalen University, Department of Computer Science and Engineering
72123 Västerås, Sweden
E-mail: peter.funk@mdh.se

Pedro A. González Calero
Universidad Complutense de Madrid, Facultad de Informática
28040 Madrid, Spain
E-mail: pedro@sip.ucm.es

Library of Congress Control Number: 2004110637

CR Subject Classification (1998): I.2, J.4, J.1, F.4.1

ISSN 0302-9743
ISBN 3-540-22882-9 Springer Berlin Heidelberg New York

This work is subject to copyright. All rights are reserved, whether the whole or part of the material is concerned, specifically the rights of translation, reprinting, re-use of illustrations, recitation, broadcasting, reproduction on microfilms or in any other way, and storage in data banks. Duplication of this publication or parts thereof is permitted only under the provisions of the German Copyright Law of September 9, 1965, in its current version, and permission for use must always be obtained from Springer. Violations are liable to prosecution under the German Copyright Law.

Springer is a part of Springer Science+Business Media

springeronline.com

© Springer-Verlag Berlin Heidelberg 2004
Printed in Germany

Typesetting: Camera-ready by author, data conversion by Olgun Computergrafik
Printed on acid-free paper   SPIN: 11310648   06/3142   5 4 3 2 1 0

Preface

The 7th European Conference on Case-Based Reasoning (ECCBR 2004) was held from August 30 through September 2, at the Complutense University of Madrid, Spain. ECCBR was born in Aberdeen, UK (2002), after a series of European workshops held in Trento, Italy (2000), Dublin, Ireland (1998), Lausanne, Switzerland (1996), Paris, France (1994), and Kaiserslautern, Germany (1993). ECCBR is the premier international forum for researchers and practitioners of case-based reasoning (CBR) in the years interleaving with the biennial international counterpart ICCBR, whose 5th edition was held in Trondheim, Norway in 2003.

The CBR community has shown for years a deep interest in the application of its research to real-world problems. As a result, the first day of both ECCBR and ICCBR has been traditionally dedicated to presenting industrial CBR applications. ECCBR 2004 Industry Day was co-chaired by Mehmet Göker and Francisco Martín who invited professionals from different fields to describe their fielded CBR systems. The second day of the conference was dedicated to four workshops focusing on the following research interests: CBR in health sciences, explanation in CBR, computational creativity, and CBR applied to time series prediction. We are grateful to the Workshop Program co-chairs, Pablo Gervás and Kalyan Moy Gupta, for their efforts in coordinating these workshops, along with the individual workshop chairs and participants. Materials from the Industry Day and the workshops were published separately and can be obtained from the ECCBR 2004 website, http://www.idt.mdh.se/eccbr/.

This volume comprises the papers presented at the conference organized into three sections: two invited papers are followed by 31 research papers and 25 application papers. Especially relevant is the number of applied research papers in wide-ranging application areas, such as traffic control, Web search, music generation, object recognition, medicine, and software engineering. The quality of the submitted papers was unusually high this year, and of the total of 85 submissions, the program committee selected 24 papers for oral presentation and 32 papers for poster presentation. Papers presented as posters were classified by the reviewers to be more suitable for a limited interacting audience and three time slots of the conference were dedicated to poster sessions.

The chairs would like to thank all those who contributed to the success of ECCBR 2004. Particular thanks goes to all the program committee and additional reviewers without whose time and effort this volume of selected papers would not exist. We also wish to thank the invited speakers, Agnar Aamodt and Mehmet Göker, and all session chairs. A special thanks goes to Luis Hernández-Yáñez and Mercedes Gómez-Albarrán for local arrangements, Pablo Beltrán-Ferruz and Federico Peinado-Gil for preparing the proceedings, and Ning Xiong for his assistance in the paper selection process. Finally, we gratefully acknowledge the generous support of the sponsors of ECCBR 2004 and of Springer-Verlag for its continuing support in publishing this volume.

June 2004 *Peter Funk*
Pedro A. González Calero

Conference Chairs

Peter Funk Mälardalen University, Sweden
Pedro A. González-Calero Complutense University of Madrid, Spain

Industry Day Chairs

Francisco Martin School of Electrical Engineering and Computer Science, Oregon State University, USA
Mehmet H. Göker PricewaterhouseCoopers. Center for Advanced Research, San Jose, USA

Local Arrangements

Mercedes Gómez-Albarrán Complutense University of Madrid, Spain
Luis Hernández-Yáñez Complutense University of Madrid, Spain

Workshop Chairs

Pablo Gervás Complutense University of Madrid, Spain
Kalyan Moy Gupta NCARAI, Washington, DC, USA

Program Committee

Agnar Aamodt Norwegian University of Science and Technology
David W. Aha Naval Research Laboratory, USA
Klaus-Dieter Althoff Fraunhofer IESE, Germany
Paolo Avesani ITC-IRST, Italy
Ralph Bergmann University of Trier, Germany
Isabelle Bichindaritz University of Washington, USA
Enrico Blanzieri Università di Torino, Italy
Derek Bridge University College Cork, Ireland
Robin Burke DePaul University, USA
Susan Craw Robert Gordon University, UK
Pádraig Cunningham Trinity College Dublin, Ireland
Belén Díaz-Agudo Complutense University of Madrid, Spain
Boi Faltings EPFL Lausanne, Switzerland
Peter Funk Mälardalen University, Sweden
Mehmet H. Göker PricewaterhouseCoopers. Center for Advanced Research, San Jose, USA
Pedro A. González-Calero Complutense University of Madrid, Spain
Jacek Jarmulak Ingenuity Inc., San Jose CA, USA
David Leake Indiana University, USA
Brian Lees University of Paisley, UK
Lorraine McGinty University College Dublin, Ireland
Michel Manago Kaidara Software S.A., France

Bruce McLaren — University of Pittsburgh, USA
Ramon López de Mántaras — IIIA-CSIC, Spain
Cindy Marling — Ohio University, USA
David McSherry — University of Ulster, UK
Héctor Muñoz-Avila — Lehigh University, USA
Bart Netten — TNO TPD, The Netherlands
Petra Perner — Institute of Computer Vision and Applied Computer Sciences, Germany
Enric Plaza — IIIA-CSIC, Spain
Luigi Portinale — Università del Piemonte Orientale, Italy
Alun Preece — University of Aberdeen, UK
Francesco Ricci — ITC-IRST, Italy
Michael M. Richter — University of Kaiserslautern, Germany
Thomas Roth-Berghofer — University of Kaiserslautern, Germany
Rainer Schmidt — University of Rostock, Germany
Barry Smyth — University College Dublin, Ireland
Maarten van Someren — University of Amsterdam, The Netherlands
Jerzy Surma — Technical University of Wroclaw, Poland
Henry Tirri — University of Helsinki, Finland
Brigitte Trousse — INRIA Sophia Antipolis, France
Ian Watson — AI-CBR University of Auckland, New Zealand
Rosina Weber — Drexel University, USA
Stephan Wess — empolis knowledge management, Germany
David C. Wilson — University of North Carolina at Charlotte, USA
Nirmalie Wiratunga — Robert Gordon University, UK
Ning Xiong — Mälardalen University, Sweden

Additional Reviewers

Stefan Schulz — Technical University of Berlin, Germany
Ludger van Elst — DFKI-Kaiserslautern, Germany
Markus Nick — Fraunhofer IESE, Germany

Sponsoring Institutions

ECCBR 2004 was supported by the Spanish Ministry of Science and Technology, Musictrands, Kaidara Software, the Center for Advanced Research at PricewaterhouseCoopers, the Mälardalen University, Department of Computer Science and Engineering, and the Complutense University of Madrid, Departamento de Sistemas Informáticos y Programación.

Table of Contents

Invited Papers

Knowledge-Intensive Case-Based Reasoning in CREEK 1
    Agnar Aamodt

Designing Industrial Case-Based Reasoning Applications 16
    Mehmet H. Göker

Research Papers

Maintaining Case-Based Reasoning Systems:
A Machine Learning Approach.. 17
    Niloofar Arshadi and Igor Jurisica

JColibri: An Object-Oriented Framework for Building CBR Systems 32
    Juan José Bello-Tomás, Pedro A. González-Calero,
    and Belén Díaz-Agudo

Mémoire: Case Based Reasoning Meets the Semantic Web
in Biology and Medicine 47
    Isabelle Bichindaritz

Facilitating CBR for Incompletely-Described Cases:
Distance Metrics for Partial Problem Descriptions...................... 62
    Steven Bogaerts and David Leake

Dialogue Management for Conversational Case-Based Reasoning 77
    Karl Branting, James Lester, and Bradford Mott

Hybrid Recommender Systems with Case-Based Components 91
    Robin Burke

Measures of Solution Accuracy in Case-Based Reasoning Systems 106
    William Cheetham and Joseph Price

Representing Similarity for CBR in XML 119
    Lorcan Coyle, Dónal Doyle, and Pádraig Cunningham

An Analysis of Case-Base Editing in a Spam Filtering System 128
    Sarah Jane Delany and Pádraig Cunningham

A Case Based Reasoning Approach to Story Plot Generation 142
    Belén Díaz-Agudo, Pablo Gervás, and Federico Peinado

Explanation Oriented Retrieval 157
  Dónal Doyle, Pádraig Cunningham, Derek Bridge, and Yusof Rahman

Exploiting Background Knowledge when Learning Similarity Measures.... 169
  Thomas Gabel and Armin Stahl

Software Design Retrieval Using Bayesian Networks and WordNet........ 184
  Paulo Gomes

Case-Base Injection Schemes to Case Adaptation
Using Genetic Algorithms 198
  Alicia Grech and Julie Main

Learning Feature Taxonomies for Case Indexing 211
  Kalyan Moy Gupta, David W. Aha, and Philip Moore

Maintenance Memories: Beyond Concepts and Techniques
for Case Base Maintenance 227
  Ioannis Iglezakis, Thomas Reinartz, and Thomas R. Roth-Berghofer

Textual Reuse for Email Response 242
  Luc Lamontagne and Guy Lapalme

Case-Based, Decision-Theoretic, HTN Planning 257
  Luís Macedo and Amílcar Cardoso

Using CBR in the Exploration of Unknown Environments
with an Autonomous Agent 272
  Luís Macedo and Amílcar Cardoso

Ceaseless Case-Based Reasoning 287
  Francisco J. Martin and Enric Plaza

Explanation Service for Complex CBR Applications 302
  Rainer Maximini, Andrea Freßmann, and Martin Schaaf

Explaining the Pros and Cons of Conclusions in CBR................. 317
  David McSherry

Incremental Relaxation of Unsuccessful Queries 331
  David McSherry

Justification-Based Case Retention 346
  Santiago Ontañón and Enric Plaza

Case Retrieval Using Nonlinear Feature-Space Transformation 361
  Rong Pan, Qiang Yang, and Lei Li

Case-Based Object Recognition 375
  Petra Perner and Angela Bühring

Explanations and Case-Based Reasoning: Foundational Issues 389
  Thomas R. Roth-Berghofer

MINLP Based Retrieval of Generalized Cases 404
  *Alexander Tartakovski, Martin Schaaf, Rainer Maximini,
  and Ralph Bergmann*

Case-Based Relational Learning of Expressive Phrasing
in Classical Music 419
  Asmir Tobudic and Gerhard Widmer

CBRFlow: Enabling Adaptive Workflow Management
Through Conversational Case-Based Reasoning 434
  Barbara Weber, Werner Wild, and Ruth Breu

CASEP2: Hybrid Case-Based Reasoning System for Sequence Processing .. 449
  Farida Zehraoui, Rushed Kanawati, and Sylvie Salotti

Application Papers

Improving the Quality of Solutions in Domain Evolving Environments 464
  Josep Lluís Arcos

PlayMaker: An Application of Case-Based Reasoning
to Air Traffic Control Plays 476
  Kenneth R. Allendoerfer and Rosina Weber

Case-Based Collaborative Web Search 489
  Evelyn Balfe and Barry Smyth

Case Based Reasoning and Production Process Design:
The Case of P-Truck Curing 504
  Stefania Bandini, Ettore Colombo, Fabio Sartori, and Giuseppe Vizzari

An Architecture for Case-Based Personalised Search 518
  Keith Bradley and Barry Smyth

Quantifying the Ocean's CO_2 Budget with a CoHeL-IBR System 533
  *Juan M. Corchado, Jim Aiken, Emilio S. Corchado, Nathalie Lefevre,
  and Tim Smyth*

Development of CBR-BDI Agents: A Tourist Guide Application 547
  *Juan M. Corchado, Juan Pavón, Emilio S. Corchado,
  and Luis F. Castillo*

Improving Recommendation Ranking
by Learning Personal Feature Weights 560
  Lorcan Coyle and Pádraig Cunningham

Investigating Graphs in Textual Case-Based Reasoning 573
  *Colleen Cunningham, Rosina Weber, Jason M. Proctor, Caleb Fowler,
  and Michael Murphy*

A Case Study of Structure Processing to Generate a Case Base 587
  *Hector Gómez-Gauchía, Belén Díaz-Agudo,
  and Pedro A. González-Calero*

TempoExpress, a CBR Approach to Musical Tempo Transformations 601
  Maarten Grachten, Josep Lluís Arcos, and Ramon López de Mántaras

Case Acquisition and Case Mining for Case-Based Object Recognition 616
  Silke Jänichen and Petra Perner

Criteria of Good Project Network Generator and Its Fulfillment
Using a Dynamic CBR Approach 630
  Hyun Woo Kim and Kyoung Jun Lee

Integrated CBR Framework for Quality Designing
and Scheduling in Steel Industry 645
  Jonghan Kim, Deokhyun Seong, Sungwon Jung, and Jinwoo Park

RHENE: A Case Retrieval System for Hemodialysis Cases
with Dynamically Monitored Parameters 659
  *Stefania Montani, Luigi Portinale, Riccardo Bellazzi,
  and Giorgio Leonardi*

A Case-Based Classification of Respiratory Sinus Arrhythmia 673
  Markus Nilsson and Peter Funk

Fault Diagnosis of Industrial Robots Using Acoustic Signals
and Case-Based Reasoning 686
  Erik Olsson, Peter Funk, and Marcus Bengtsson

A Case-Based Approach to Managing Geo-spatial Imagery Tasks 702
  *Dympna O'Sullivan, Eoin McLoughlin, Michela Bertolotto,
  and David C. Wilson*

Analysing Similarity Essence for Case Based Recommendation 717
  Derry O'Sullivan, Barry Smyth, and David C. Wilson

Satellite Health Monitoring Using CBR Framework 732
  Kiran Kumar Penta and Deepak Khemani

Extending a Fault Dictionary Towards a Case Based Reasoning System
for Linear Electronic Analog Circuits Diagnosis 748
  Carles Pous, Joan Colomer, and Joaquim Melendez

Dynamic Critiquing 763
  James Reilly, Kevin McCarthy, Lorraine McGinty, and Barry Smyth

Using CBR for Semantic Analysis of Software Specifications 778
  Nuno Seco, Paulo Gomes, and Francisco C. Pereira

An Indexing Scheme for Case-Based Manufacturing Vision Development .. 793
  Chengbo Wang, John Johansen, and James T. Luxhøj

Feature Selection and Generalisation for Retrieval of Textual Cases....... 806
  Nirmalie Wiratunga, Ivan Koychev, and Stewart Massie

Author Index... 821

Knowledge-Intensive Case-Based Reasoning in CREEK

Agnar Aamodt

Department of Computer and Information Science
Norwegian University of Science and Technology (NTNU)
NO-7491 Trondheim, Norway
agnar.aamodt@idi.ntnu.no

Abstract. Knowledge-intensive CBR assumes that cases are enriched with general domain knowledge. In CREEK, there is a very strong coupling between cases and general domain knowledge, in that cases are embedded within a general domain model. This increases the knowledge-intensiveness of the cases themselves. A knowledge-intensive CBR method calls for powerful knowledge acquisition and modeling techniques, as well as machine learning methods that take advantage of the general knowledge represented in the system. The focusing theme of the paper is on cases as knowledge within a knowledge-intensive CBR method. This is made concrete by relating it to the CREEK architecture and system, both in general terms, and through a set of example projects where various aspects of this theme have been studied.

1 Introduction

A knowledge-intensive case-based reasoning method assumes that cases, in some way or another, are enriched with explicit general domain knowledge [1,2]. The role of the general domain knowledge is to enable a CBR system to reason with semantic and pragmatic criteria, rather than purely syntactic ones. By making the general domain knowledge explicit, the case-based reasoner is able to interpret a current situation in a more flexible and contextual manner than if this knowledge is compiled into predefined similarity metrics or feature relevance weights. A knowledge-intensive CBR method calls for powerful knowledge acquisition and modeling techniques, as well as machine learning methods that take advantage of the general knowledge represented in the system.

In the CREEK system [3,4,5], there is a strong coupling between cases and general domain knowledge in that cases are submerged within a general domain model. This model is represented as a densely linked semantic network. Concepts are inter-related through multiple relation types, and each concept has many relations to other concepts. The network represents a model of that part of the real world which the system is to reason about, within which model-based reasoning methods are applied. From the view of case-specific knowledge, the knowledge-intensiveness of the cases themselves are also increased, i.e. the cases become more "knowledgeable", since their features are nodes in this semantic network.

The focusing theme of this paper is cases as knowledge within a knowledge-intensive CBR method. This will be made concrete by relating it to the CREEK architecture and system, both in general terms, and through a set of example projects where various aspects of this theme have been studied. To give an initial hint at the main issue, Fig. 1 characterizes some aspects of CBR methods along what may be called the knowledge-intensiveness dimension. The early nearest-neighbour-based methods are at the one end of the scale, while the CREEK system is illustrated closer the other end. Some typical characterizations of knowledge-intensive CBR methods (right part) and knowledge-empty or knowledge-lean methods (left part), are listed.

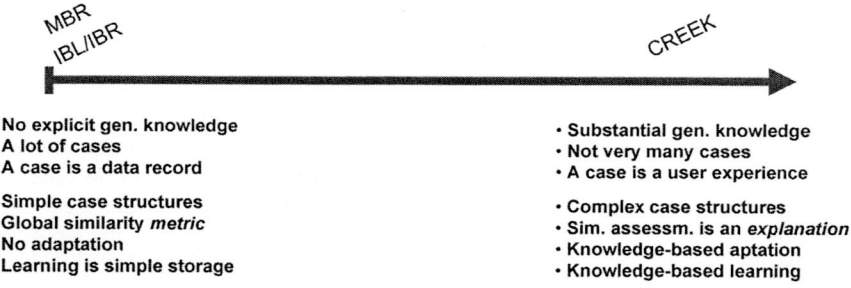

Fig. 1. The knowledge-intensiveness dimension of CBR methods

As Fig. 1 indicates, the notion of knowledge-intensiveness is not an either/or issue. CBR systems may be more or less knowledge-intensive. The meaning of the term "knowledge-intensive" may also vary, depending on what viewpoint to the concept of knowledge that an author or research group has. Further, when we look at the contents of a case, what some people refer to as knowledge may be referred to as information by others – or even as data. This is not surprising, since a data structure, such as a case, can serve several roles in a system. In order to get a better understanding of the concept of knowledge, as it is interpreted in CREEK, we will therefore start by clarifying what we see as the main distinction between knowledge, information, and data, related to the different roles a case may have. The next chapter defines the three terms from that perspective.

Explicit models of knowledge call for effective knowledge modeling methods and tools, both for manual model development and automated methods, i.e. machine learning. To support systems development within the CREEK architecture, some assumptions on the nature of knowledge modeling has been made, and an assisting tool has been developed to assist the knowledge modeling process. This is the topic of chapter 3. In chapter 4 the CREEK architecture and system is summarized, emphasizing knowledge content and how it is processed. Chapter 5 illustrates the architecture and system through a summary of recent and ongoing research projects. The paper is summarized and concluded in the final chapter.

2 What Is Knowledge in a CBR System?

There is, in general, no known way to distinguish knowledge from information or data on a purely representational basis. Attempts to make distinctions based on size or complexity are therefore likely to fail. Another option - and the one underlying the CREEK architecture - is to identify how and for what purpose the structures are used, i.e. what the various *roles* of data, information, and knowledge are in a case-based reasoning process. Their interpretation within the contexts they are applied, and by whom they are interpreted and applied, therefore become important. The latter aspect leads to the *frame of reference* problem of data, information, and knowledge [6], which is the problem of relating one of these entities to a subject of reference: Whose knowledge is it? For a discussion of this topic within the broader context of databases, information systems, and AI systems, see [7].

2.1 Data vs. Information vs. Knowledge

For any decision-making process, an environment is assumed in which a decision-making agent (i.e. a reasoning agent) receives input from and returns output to an environment external to it. In a simple set-up, the external environment is a user communicating through a terminal, and the decision-making agent is a terminal-based, advice-giving computer system. Within this context, the essential differences between data, information and knowledge are as follows (see Fig. 2).

Data are syntactic entities, i.e. uninterpreted characters, signals, patterns, and signs that have no meaning for the system (the subject of reference) concerned. Data are input to an interpretation process. Data become information after having been interpreted to give meaning. This is illustrated in Fig. 2 by the Data Interpretation arrow. Taking a human being as the subject of reference, a series of signals from a sensor, or the string "´Q)9§?8$%@*¨&/", is data to most of us, while "low interest rate", "increased blood pressure", and "the Gulf war" have meaning, and therefore are information. The meaning of these terms may be different for different systems (here: people), and it is each individual's knowledge about particular domains - and the world in general - that enable us to get meaning out of these data strings.

Information is interpreted data, i.e. data with meaning. It is the output from a data interpretation process, as just described. Once the data have been given an interpretation as information (an initial interpretation, at least), it is elaborated upon in order to be better understood, and in order to derive (infer) new information. This is illustrated by the Elaboration arrow in Fig. 2. Hence, information is input to this elaboration process, as well as output from it. The elaboration process is where the core decision-making processes take place. Often, in a real setting, elaboration and data interpretation processes are interleaved. Information is also the source of learning, i.e. the input to a learning process.

Knowledge is learned information, i.e. information that has been processed and incorporated into an agent's reasoning resources, and made ready for active use within a decision process. A widely shared view is that learning is the integration of new information into an existing body of knowledge, in a way that makes it potentially useful for later decision-making. New knowledge may also come from inference processes within the knowledge body itself. This is illustrated by the vertical and the semi-circular Learning arrows in Fig.2, respectively. Knowledge, then, is the output of a learning process, after which it becomes the internal resource within an intelligent system that enables the system to interpret data to information, to elaborate and derive new information, as well as to learn more (the gray lines in the figure).

Note that the term knowledge is used here in a very general sense. It does not distinguish between 'true' and 'believed' knowledge. This is different from the influential branch of philosophy in which the term knowledge is used exclusively for statements that are true in the world, and where belief is used if truth cannot be ascertained (e.g.

[8]). Other philosophical theories (e.g. [9]) have questioned this position, arguing that the logicist, or deductive-nomological philosophical view that lies behind that view is unable to explain major philosophical problems such as analogical reasoning, abduction, and scientific development.

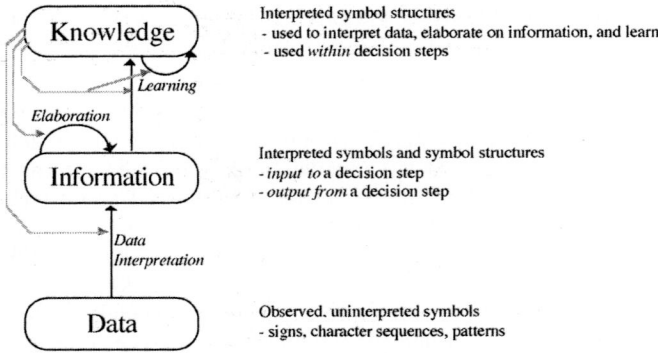

Fig. 2. The Data-Information-Knowledge model

2.2 Case Roles in CBR Systems

In Fig.1 some discriminating characteristics of knowledge-lean and knowledge-intensive methods were listed. CBR systems come in different shapes and fashions. From the above discussion, we see that in order for a system to reason, in the sense of interpreting data and deriving new information, it needs knowledge. Systems with no knowledge can do no reasoning in this sense. CBR systems that are placed at the left of the scale, will therefore typically be closer to information systems than knowledge-based systems. Note the peculiarity in that for an "information system", as the term is commonly used, a human being is assumed to be the subject of reference, i.e. it is information for the human interpreter (and data for the system). In a knowledge-based system, however, knowledge as well as relevant parts of the information is with respect to the system. Below, the three main roles of cases in various systems, corresponding to their role as data, information, or knowledge, are highlighted, in order to contrast the CREEK approach to others.

Cases as data for the computer system is the simplest mode, in which the system does not do case-based reasoning as such, but applies case-based methods for case indexing and retrieval. Since the system views cases as data only, it does not have knowledge of the items that describe case contents. The partial matching property of CBR is used to improve database retrieval by producing a ranked list of matching records rather than one exact match. The strength of computers as data managers and information handlers, where the frame of reference for information is the user, is combined with the strength of human beings for intelligent decision-making. Some types of help desk systems are examples.

Cases as information for the computer system implies that there is knowledge in the computer that is able to interpret and utilize case contents as information. If cases are information only – and not knowledge – the based-based methods must be of some other kind, such as model-based or rule-based. The characteristic of a case-based system of this kind is that a substantial part of the system's information is organized as cases.

Cases as knowledge for the computer system, is the case-based *reasoning* approach per se, i.e. the case base is not merely a source of information for the user, but a knowledge base that is actively used in the system's reasoning processes. The full flexibility of viewing a case as data, information, and/or knowledge is therefore available. Cases may be the only type of knowledge in such a system or they may be combined with other knowledge types - as in CREEK. These systems exhibit learning in the full sense, since they incorporate new cases in a way that makes them immediately ready to be used in the solving of new problems.

From these different case roles, we see that a case-based system architecture can facilitates a gradual transformation from a pure database or information system, to a full-fledged knowledge-based system. In this way a system will always have its data available in a non-generalized form, and their active use can be incrementally put into effect by adding interpretation and reasoning capabilities to the system as the use of the system identifies what active decision support users really want.

3 Knowledge Modeling

Along with Clancey [10], a knowledge-based system can be viewed as a qualitative model of that part of the real world that the system is to reason about. Knowledge modeling, then, becomes the whole process that starts with a real world task environment, through several steps realizes a (partial) model of it in a computer system, and maintains that model over time. The knowledge of a system will to some extend be biased by the methods through which that knowledge was acquired and represented. A brief description of the high-level knowledge modeling framework for CREEK systems is therefore given.

The knowledge modeling approach is based on the combination of a top-down driven, initial knowledge acquisition process, and a bottom-up modeling process represented by continuous learning through retaining problem solving cases. The objective of the initial knowledge modeling task is to analyze the domain and task in question, to develop the conceptual, mediating models necessary for communication within the development team, and to design and implement the initial operational and fielded version of the system. The knowledge maintenance task takes over where the initial knowledge modeling ends, and its objective is to ensure the refinement and updating of the knowledge model as the system is being regularly used. In Fig. 3 the two outer, rounded boxes illustrate these two top-level tasks of the knowledge modeling cycle. Within each of the two tasks, the major subtasks (rounded rectangles) and models (sharp rectangles) taken as input and returned as output from these tasks are shown. The modeling subtasks are indicated by their gray background. Arrows indicate the main flow of knowledge and information, and show the most important input/output dependencies between subtasks and models. As shown by the area where the two large boxes overlap, the conceptual knowledge model and the computer internal model are shared by subtasks of both initial knowledge modeling and knowledge maintenance.

A knowledge modeling cycle typically starts with a high level specification (e.g. functional specification) of the target computer system, at some level of detail. The resulting submodels are structured into a conceptual knowledge model. The knowledge is described at the knowledge level [11,12], where the emphasis is to capture the goal-directed behavior of the system, and to model knowledge content from the perspective of the application domain, without being constrained by implementational limitations. A common starting point is to identify the main categories of the three knowledge types: *Task knowledge*, *Method knowledge*, and *Domain knowledge*. Task knowledge models what to do, usually in a task-subtask hierarchy. Tasks are defined by the goals that a system tries to achieve. Method knowledge describes how to do it, i.e. a method is a means to accomplish a task (e.g. to solve a problem). Domain knowledge is the knowledge about the world that a method needs to accomplish its task. Examples are facts, heuristics, causal relationships, multi-relational models, and – of course – specific cases (see [13] for a more elaborate discussion on knowledge level modeling for CBR systems). The conceptual knowledge model forms the basis for designing and implementing the computer internal model, i.e. the knowledge model of the operating target system. This model is described at a level referred to as the symbol level, which deals not only with intentional knowledge content, but also with manipulation of symbols that represent knowledge in the computer.

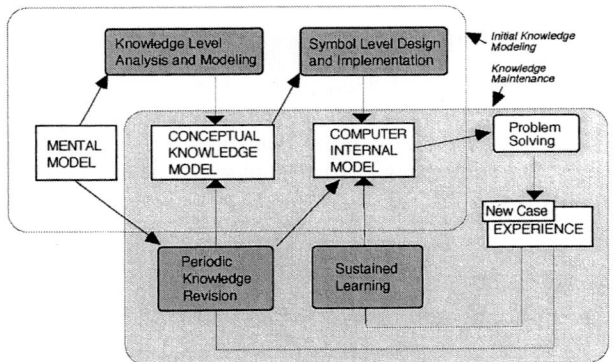

Fig. 3. The knowledge modeling cycle

The lower, partially overlapping box illustrates the main subtasks of knowledge maintenance. Knowledge maintenance starts when a system has been put into regular operation and use. The knowledge maintenance task has two optional subtasks as indicated in the figure. One is sustained learning, i.e. the direct updating of the computer internal model each time a new problem has been solved. The other is a periodic and more substantial revision process. As illustrated, this revision task may lead directly to the modification of the symbol level model (computer internal model), but it may also go through an update of the knowledge level model (conceptual knowledge model) first.

To assist in the top-down modeling parts of the cycle described, a knowledge modeling editor is used (Fig. 4). A CREEK system comes with a top-level ontology, part of which is shown in the figure, from which the higher-level parts of the domain model is grown. Concepts, relations, as well as cases, can be constructed and manipulated in flexible manners through a knowledge map interface (to the left) or a frame interface (right part of the figure). The knowledge representation in the topic of next chapter.

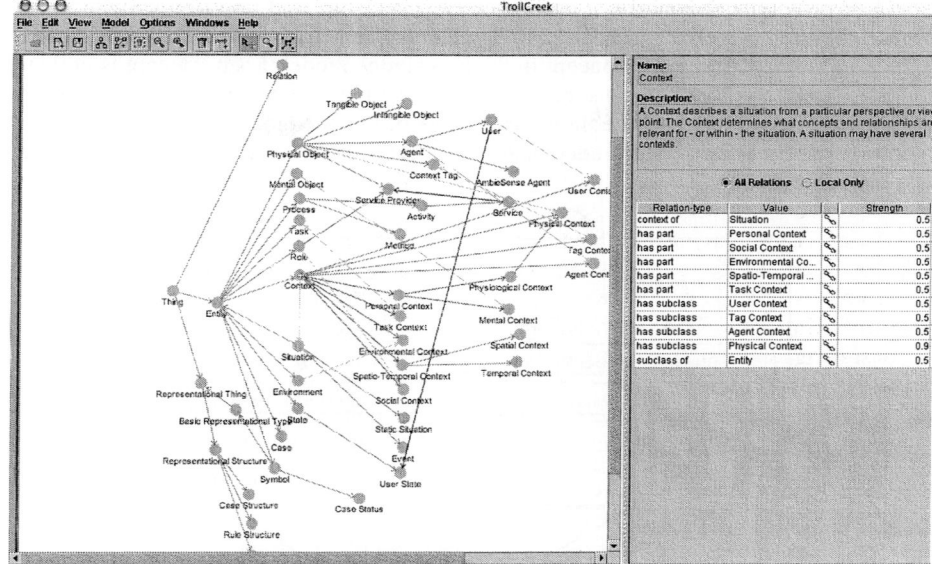

Fig. 4. The TrollCreek Knowledge Modeling Editor

4 The CREEK System

The CREEK system is an architecture for knowledge-intensive case-based problem solving and learning, targeted at addressing problems in open and weak-theory domains [14]. CREEK contains several modules integrated within a common conceptual basis: The General Domain Model (see Fig. 5). Each module represents a particular sub-model of knowledge. The main modules are the object-level domain knowledge model (real world entities and relationships), a strategy level model (for example a model of diagnostic problem solving), and two reasoning meta-level models, one for combining case-based and other types of reasoning, and one for combined learning methods. CREEK integrates problem solving and learning into one functional architecture.

Situation-specific experiences are held in the case base of solved cases. All the concepts are 'glued together' into a single, interconnected knowledge model. Diagnosis task concepts, for example, such as "symptom" and "diagnostic-hypothesis" (part of the diagnosis and repair strategy model), and learning task concepts, such as "case-indexing" and "failure-generalization" (part of the combined learning model), are defined within the same representation structure as general domain concepts like "appendicitis" and "fever", and case-related domains terms as "Patient#123456" and "current-radiation-dosage".

A knowledge model represented in CREEK is viewed as a semantic network, where each node and each link in the network is explicitly defined in its own frame. Each node in the network corresponds to a concept in the knowledge model, and each link corresponds to a relation between concepts. A concept may be a general definitional or prototypical concept, a case, or a heuristic rule, and describe knowledge of domain objects as well as problem solving methods and strategies. A frame represents a node in the network, i.e. a concept in the knowledge model. Each concept is defined by its relations to other concepts, represented by the list of slots in the concept's frame definition. Fig. 6 illustrates the three main types of knowledge in CREEK, a top-level ontology of generic, domain-independent concepts, the general domain knowledge, and the set of cases.

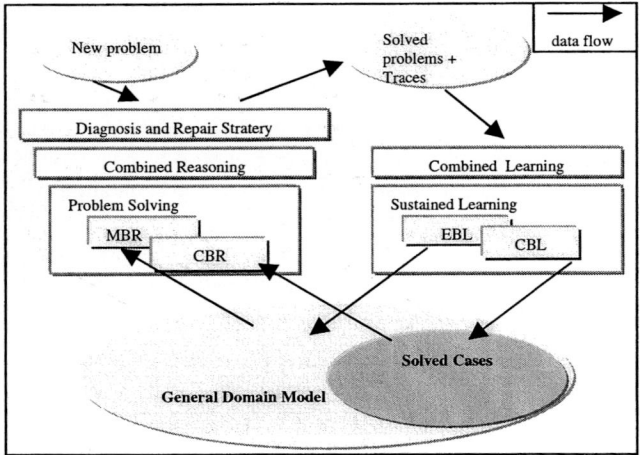

Fig. 5. The CREEK functional Architecture

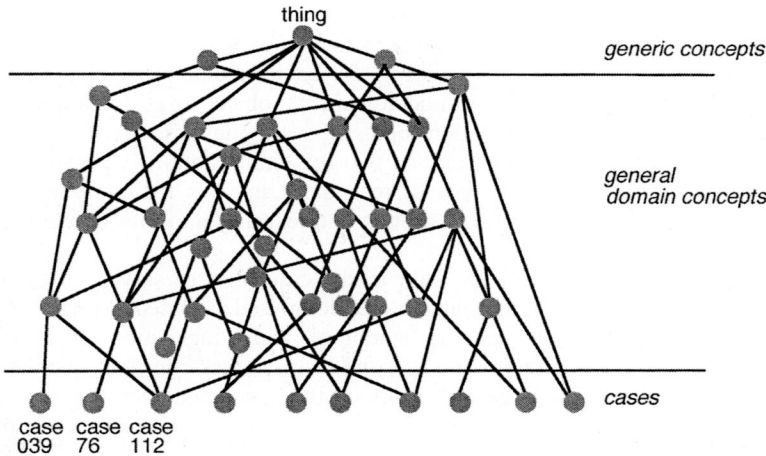

Fig. 6. Integrating cases and general knowledge

The case-based interpreter in CREEK contains a three-step process of 1) activating relevant parts of the semantic network 2) generating and explaining derived information within the activated knowledge structure, and 3) focusing towards and selecting a conclusion that conforms with the goal. This *activate-explain-focus* cycle, referred to as an 'explanation engine' [3], is a general mechanism that has been specialized for each of the four CBR tasks described in section 4, although the Revise task is not a system's task in CREEK. (see Fig. 7).

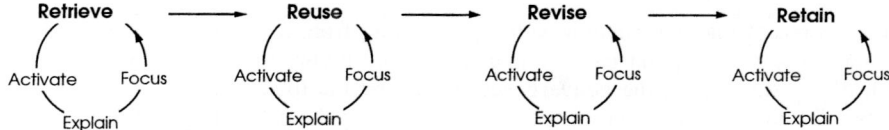

Fig. 7. The CBR process and the explanation engine

Similarity assessment is divided between the Activate and Explain steps of Retrieve. Activate first determines a relevant broad context for the problem, by spreading activation from goal concepts to relevant findings. Spreading-relations include general taxonomic ones, causal relations, associational relations, and application-specific relations. Only cases with activation strength above a certain threshold will be considered for further matching. The activation strength is based on the number of matched relations and their relevance factor, according the following formula [15]:

$$sim(C_1, C_2) = \frac{\sum_{i=1}^{n}\sum_{j=1}^{m} sim(f_i, f_j) * relevance\ factor_i}{\sum_{i=1}^{n} relevance\ factor_i}$$

C_1 and C_2 are cases, n is the number of findings in C_1, m is the number of findings in C_2, f_i is the ith finding in $C_{1,\ fi}$ the jth finding in C_2, and sim(f_1,f_2) is simply given as:

$$sim(f_1, f_2) = \begin{cases} 1 & if\ v_1 = v_2 \\ 0 & otherwise \end{cases}$$

The relevance factor is a number calculated by combining the predictive strength (related to degree of sufficiency) and importance (related to degree of necessity) of a feature for a case. Following Activate, Explain will then evaluate and attempt to improve the match between the input case and the activated cases. Only unmatched findings need to be explained, because the strength of the matched findings cannot be increased when they share the same value. Different explanation paths are combined [16], resulting in a matching strength for each activated case. The paths have convergence points, which are entities for which there exists an explanation path from the values of both findings. The strength of one such path is the product of the strength of each relation leading from the finding to the convergence point:

$$path\ strength(f, c) = \prod_{i=1}^{n} relation\ strength_i$$

There might exist one or more parallel paths from each finding to each convergence point. The formula below is a general formula for adding a new strength (S_{new}) to an old strength (S_{old}) to incorporate an additional explanation path:

$$parallel\ strength\ (S_{old}, S_{new}) = S_{old} + (1 - S_{old}) \cdot S_{new}$$

Thus, the total strength of all the paths leading from a finding f to a convergence point c, with n being the number of paths between f and c is computed after the following formula:

$$total\ path\ strength(f,c) = \sum_{i=1}^{n} parallel\ strength(path\ strength(f,c)_i, path\ strength(f,c)_{i+1})$$

The strength of one explanation path (eps) leading from a finding f1 to a finding f2 via the convergence point c, is computed by multiplying the total path strength for each of the findings to the convergence point, and the total explanation strength for the two findings (f1 and f2) is then computed by using the parallel strength formula:

$$eps(f_1, f_2, c) = total\ path\ strength(f_1, c) \cdot total\ path\ strength(f_2, c)$$

$$Explanation\ strength(f_1, f_2) = \sum_{i=1}^{n} parallel\ strength(eps(f_1, f_2, c_i), eps(f_1, f_2, c_{i+1}))$$

Here n is the number of convergence points between the findings, and c_i is the ith convergence point.

Focus makes the final selection of the best case or rejects all of them, normally based on the case with the strongest explanatory justification. It may adjust the ranking of the cases based on preferences or external constraints, such as resource or cost considerations related to applying or executing the solution in the real world. The explanatory power of the general domain model is also utilized in Reuse and Retain. This was implemented in the former Lisp-based version. So far our research related to the current Java-based version – called TrollCreek - has focused on the Retrieve step.

The general domain knowledge is assumed to be extensive enough to provide sufficient support to the case-based methods, but may also provide a back-up capability of problem solving on its own, if nor similar case is found. The general domain knowledge is typically built up by rather 'deep' relationships - for example a combination of causal, structural, and functional relations. It contains a simple model-based casual reasoning method, in addition to the basic inference methods of frame matching, constraint propagation, and plausible inheritance (see next chapter).

The TrollCreek tool allows running the case matching process at any time during system development. To illustrate, assume that we are on an oil rig in the North Sea. Drilling fluid losses have been observed, and the situation turns into a problem (so-called Lost Circulation). See the case description to the left in Fig. 8. TrollCreek produces first of all a list of similar cases for review of the user. Testing of Case LC 22 suggests that Case LC 40 is the best match, with case 25 as the second best, and with a matching degree of 45% - as shown in Fig. 9. Examination of these cases reveals that Case LC 40 and 25 are both of the failure type Natural Fracture (an uncommon failure in our case base). By studying Case LC 40 and 25 the optimal treatment of the new problem is devised, and a new case (Case LC 22) is stored in the case base (right part, Fig. 8).

The user can choose to accept the delivered results, or construct a solution by combining several matched cases. The user may also trigger a new matching process, after having added (or deleted) information in the problem case. The user can also browse the case base, for example by asking for cases containing one specific or a combination of attributes. Figure 4 shows parts of the explanation of why Case LC 22 is a problem of the type Natural Fracture. The interactive graph displays the part of the semantic network that was involved in the matching, either by direct or indirect (explained) matches. A textual explanation of an indirect match is also displayed, as shown to the middle right in Fig. 9.

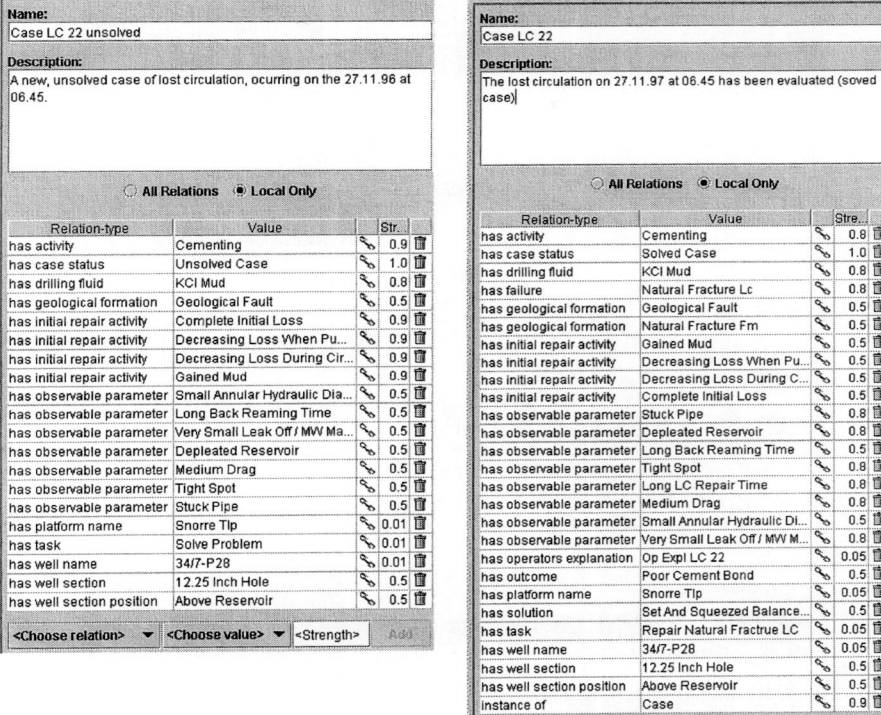

Fig. 8. Unsolved case (left) and the corresponding solved case (right) of Case LC 22

5 Recent and Ongoing Research

The transition to the Java platform, form Lisp, led us to make a revision of the knowledge representation and basic inference methods. An earlier idea of plausible inheritance as an inference method for semantic networks [14] was generalized and made into the core model-based inference method of CREEK [16]. The main principle is that inheritance is extended to be applicable to any pair of a relationship and a relation, as opposed to inheritance only along a subclass relation. A location relationship may be inherited along a part-of relation, for example – assuming that parts of things are in the same location as the thing itself. Fig 10. illustrates how an initial frame, "epidemic case #3", having a local subclass relationship with "bacterial epidemic", and a causal relationship with "dirty water", inherits additional relationships (the R_i set at the lower right), through as set of inheritance rules (the I set at the lower left).

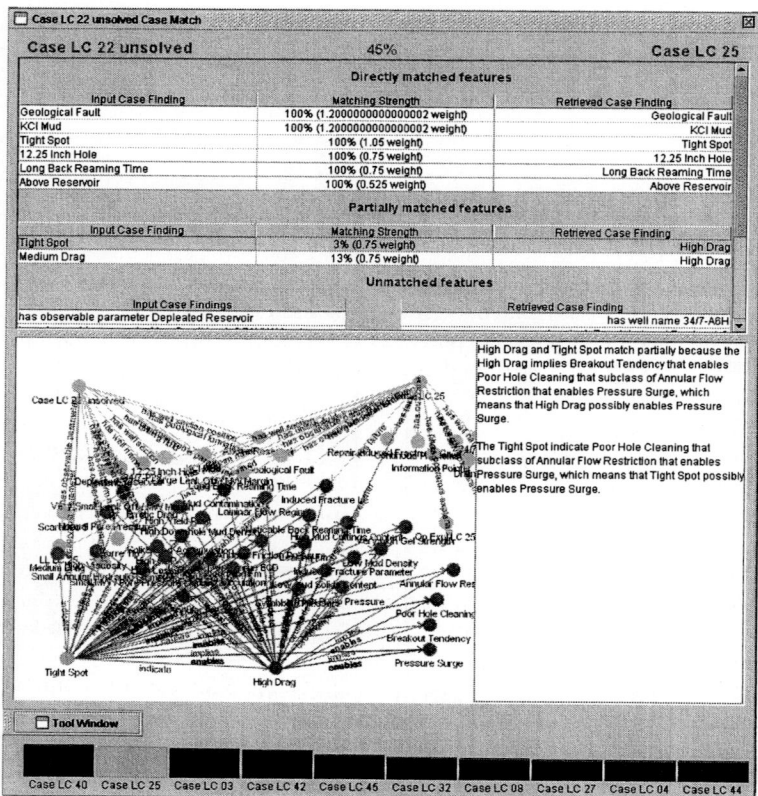

Fig. 9. Results of matching a new case (Case LC 22 unsolved) with the case base.

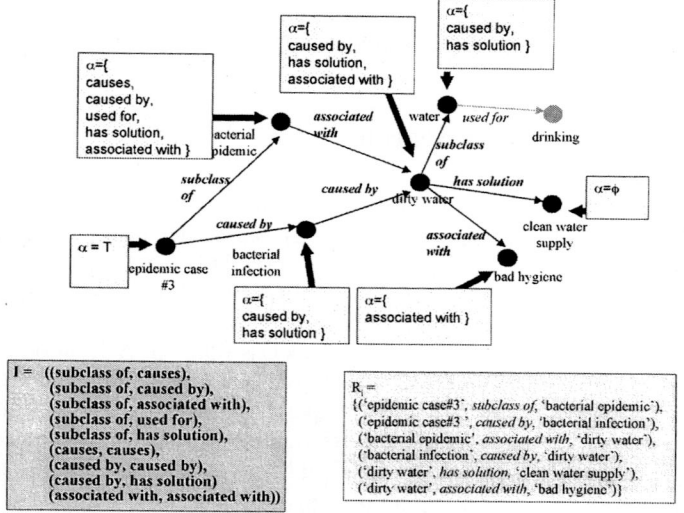

Fig. 10. Plausible inheritance example

Some current activities explore this method by designing systems were model-based reasoning play a strong part in itself, rather than only as part of the CBR process. Examples are two PhD projects where one is a method for generating and evaluating explanations for intelligent tutoring [17], and the other a method for generating explanations for gene–gene relationships and dependencies in order to understand the development of diseases at the level of functional genomics [18]. Our research into knowledge-intensive case-based explanation studies the combined use of case-specific and general domain knowledge from the perspective of user-targeted explanations (the two projects just mentioned), as well from the perspective of the system-internal explanation methods in CREEK. The transparency of the knowledge representation system in CREEK favours studies of mutual explanation mechanism, i.e. explanation methods serving both purposes. This is currently studied within a PhD project on conversational case-based reasoning for software component reuse [19], although the focus here is on internal explanations within a CCBR context. Quite another issue is studied in a PhD research done within the EU project Ambiesense [20], where an agent-based architecture is developed for CREEK, aimed to provide contextualized information to mobile users on business or tourist travels. Agent-based methods in are also explored by others, which should lead to a generic distributed architecture for CREEK. Cases are used to personalize the information provided. A thorough study of context modeling was done in an earlier research applied to the medical diagnosis area [21]. This work, as well as a study done in medical image understanding [22], also made significant contributions to the knowledge-level modeling approach within CREEK.

Additional methods for representing and reasoning with general domain knowledge are also being explored. In particular, the studies of Bayesian Networks within CREEK [23] has given additional insights to the knowledge modeling and representation issues, as well as triggered studies on data mining methods for learning of general domain knowledge. Examples of smaller project that have developed additional demonstrators as part of MSc works, include an ANN system integrated into CREEK [24], for face recognition, and a text mining system for extracting general domain relationships from text [25]. Sometimes, it is also useful to lean back and take a look at the more fundamental issues related to developing CBR systems and other AI systems, such as relating current practice to totally different development and modeling views, such as one suggested by an antipoetic analysis [26].

6 Conclusion

The paper has described the knowledge-intensive CBR approach that is at the core of the CREEK framework, architecture, and system. By starting out with the fundamental issues related to the nature of knowledge, and the modeling-perspective taken to the development of a CREEK knowledge base, the actual representation and reasoning methods – as exemplified by Retain – hopefully become clearer.

The current and future directions of research focus more strongly on experimental evaluation of the various methods of CREEK. Of special interest currently, are experimentations related to the combined explanatory power of general domain knowledge and cases. This includes more thorough studies of the representation and basic inferencing methods. In addition, multi-agent architectures, text mining of general and case-specific knowledge, and conversational CBR methods, are high up on the research agenda. Finally, continued tool development, in connection with development of real world applications, is a priority, for which we cooperate with the company Trollhetta AS.

References

1. Díaz-Agudo, B., González-Calero, P.A.: An Architecture for Knowledge Intensive CBR Systems. In Blanzieri, E., Portinale, L., (Eds.): Advances in Case-Based Reasoning (Procs. of the 5th European Workshop on Case-Based Reasoning, EWCBR 2000), Lecture Notes in Artificial Intelligence, 1898, Springer, 2000.
2. Aamodt A.: A Knowledge-Intensive Integrated Approach to Problem Solving and Sustained Learning. PhD. Dissertation. University of Trondheim, Department of Electrical Engineering and Computer Science, Trondheim (1991). [Downloadable from authors publications homepage].
3. Aamodt, A. 1994: Explanation-driven case-based reasoning. In *Topics in case-based reasoning*, edited by S. Wess et al., Springer Verlag, 274-288.
4. Jære, M.D., Aamodt, A., Skalle, P.: Representing temporal knowledge for case-based prediction. *Advances in case-based reasoning; 6th European Conference, ECCBR 2002*, Aberdeen, September 2002. Lecture Notes in Artificial Intelligence, LNAI 2416, Springer, pp. 174-188.
5. Skalle, P., Aamodt, A.: Knowledge-based decision support in oil well drilling; Combining general and case-specific knowledge for problem solving. To appear in *Proceedings of ICIIP-2004*, International Conference on Intelligent Information Processing, Beijing, October 2004.
6. Clancey, W.J.: The frame of reference problem in the design of intelligent machines, In K. VanLehn (ed.), *Architectures for Intelligence*. Lawrence Erlbaum, 1991, p. 357-423.
7. Agnar Aamodt, Mads Nygaard: Different roles and mutual dependencies of data, information, and knowledge - an AI perspective on their integration, *Data and Knowledge Engineering* 16 (1995), pp 191-222.
8. C.G. Hempel, *Aspects of scientific explanation.*, (Free Press, New York, 1965).
9. P. Thagard, *Computational Philosophy of Science*, (MIT Press/Bradford Books, 1988).
10. Clancey W.J.: Viewing knowldge bases as qualitative models. *IEEE Expert*, Vol.4, no.2. Summer 1989. pp. 9-23.
11. Newell, A.: The knowledge level, *Artificial Intelligence*, 18 (1982) 87-127.
12. Van de Velde, W.: Issues in knowledge level modelling, In J-M. David, J-P. Krivine, R. Simmons (eds.), *Second generation expert systems* (Spinger, 1993) 211-231.
13. Aamodt, A.: Modeling the knowledge contents of CBR systems. *Proceedings of the Workshop Program at the Fourth International Conference on Case-Based Reasoning*, Vancouver, 2001. Naval Research Laboratory Technical Note AIC-01-003, pp. 32-37.
14. Aamodt A.: A Knowledge Representation System for Integration of General and Case-Specific Knowledge. Proceedings from IEEE *TAI-94, International Conference on Tools with Artificial Intelligence* (1994). New Orleans, November 5-12.
15. Lippe, E.: Learning support by reasoning with structured cases. MSc Thesis, Norwegian University of Science and Technology (NTNU), Department of Computer and Information Science, 2001.
16. Sørmo F.: Plausible Inheritance; Semantic Network Inference for Case-Based Reasoning. MSc thesis, Norwegian University of Science and Technology (NTNU), Department of Computer and Information Science, 2000.
17. Frode Sørmo, Agnar Aamodt: Knowledge communication and CBR. 6th European Conference on Case-Based Reasoning, ECCBR 2002, Aberdeen, September 2002. Workshop proceedings. Robert Gordon University, pp. 47-59.

18. Waclaw Kusnierczyk, Agnar Aamodt and Astrid Lægreid: Towards Automated Explanation of Gene-Gene Relationships. RECOMB 2004, The Eighth International Conference on Computational Molecular Biology, Poster Presentations, E9, San Diego, March 2004.
19. Gu, M., Aamodt, A., Tong, X.: Component retrieval using conversational case-based reasoning. To appear in *Proceedings of ICIIP-2004*, International Conference on Intelligent Information Processing, Beijing, October 2004.
20. Anders Kofod-Petersen, Agnar Aamodt: Case-based situation assessment in a mobile context-aware system. Proceedings of AIMS2003, Workshop on Artificial Intgelligence for Mobil Systems, Seattle, October, 2003.
21. Pinar Ozturk, Agnar Aamodt: A context model for knowledge-intensive case-based reasoning. International Journal of Human Computer Studies. Vol. 48, 1998. Academic Press. pp 331-355.
22. Morten Grimnes, Agnar Aamodt: A two layercase-based reasoning architecture for medical image understanding. In Smith, I., Faltings, B. (eds). *Advances in case-based reasoning, (Proc. EWCBR-96)*, Springer Verlag, Lecture Notes in Artificial Intelligence 1168, 1996. pp 164-178.
23. Helge Langseth, Agnar Aamodt, Ole Martin Winnem: Learning retrieval knowledge from data. In Sixteenth International Joint Conference on Artificial Intelligence, Workshop ML-5: Automating the Construction of Case-Based Reasoners. Stockholm 1999. Sarabjot Singh Anand, Agnar Aamodt, David W. Aha (eds.). pp. 77-82.
24. Engelsli, S.E.: Intergration of Neural Networks in Knowledge - Intensive CBR. MSc thesis, Norwegian University of Science and Technology (NTNU), Department of Computer and Information Science, 2003.
25. Tomassen, S.L.: Semi-automatic generation of ontologies for knwoledge-intensive CBR. MSc thesis, Norwegian University of Science and Technology (NTNU), Department of Computer and Information Science, 2003.
26. Sverberg, P.: Steps towards an empirically responsible AI; A theoretical and methodological framework. MSc thesis, Norwegian University of Science and Technology (NTNU), Department of Computer and Information Science, 2004.

Designing Industrial Case-Based Reasoning Applications

Mehmet H. Göker

PricewaterhouseCoopers
Center for Advanced Research
Ten Almaden Boulevard, Suite 1600
San Jose, CA 95113
mehmet.goker@us.pwc.com

The development of knowledge management applications for business environments requires balancing the needs of various parties within the client's organization. While the end users desire to have a system that operates as effectively and efficiently as possible without changing their existing workflow, the business unit may be interested in capturing, verifying and endorsing corporate policies. The IT department of the client will be interested in applications that fit into their standard deployment environment and will certainly not appreciate the need for the business unit to modify some of the knowledge containers occasionally. Balancing these requirements without endangering the long term success of an application can become challenging.

The design decisions made during the development of Case-Based Knowledge Management systems impact the long term success of these applications drastically. The application has to be designed in such a way that it understand the user's query and delivers useful solutions to end users, accommodates the needs of users with different levels of knowledge and responsibility, operates within the existing knowledge creation and revision workflow of the company, makes use of existing knowledge sources without modifying their structure and the organization around them, supports authoring in a light-weight manner, facilitates long term maintenance by means of reporting facilities and maintenance operations, is easy to deploy and operate in a corporate environment, allows the business unit to make changes to application settings with immediate effect, can be deployed in a very short timeframe, is based on industry standards, requires no customizations and is very cheap. While this list of desired characteristics is only partial, it shows that some of the requirements can be rather contradictory.

Based on the framework of the INRECA methodology [1] and experience with various CBR projects, this talk will describe the tasks that have to be executed during the implementation and deployment of real-world CBR systems. We will contrast the issues to standard software engineering projects, highlight areas of potential problems and suggest solutions.

Reference

1. R. Bergmann, K.D. Althoff, S. Breen, M. Göker, M. Manago, R.Traphöner, S. Wess, *"Developing Industrial Case Based Reasoning Applications: The INRECA Methodology"*, 2nd Edition, Lecture Notes in Artificial Intelligence, LNAI 1612, Springer Verlag, Berlin, 2003

Maintaining Case-Based Reasoning Systems: A Machine Learning Approach

Niloofar Arshadi[1] and Igor Jurisica[1,2]

[1] Department of Computer Science, University of Toronto,
10 King's College Road, Toronto, Ontario M5S 3G4, Canada
`niloofar@cs.toronto.edu`
[2] Ontario Cancer Institute, Princess Margaret Hospital,
University Health Network, Division of Cancer Informatics
610 University Avenue, Toronto, Ontario M5G 2M9, Canada
`ij@uhnres.utoronto.ca`

Abstract. Over the years, many successful applications of case-based reasoning (CBR) systems have been developed in different areas. The performance of CBR systems depends on several factors, including case representation, similarity measure, and adaptation. Achieving good performance requires careful design, implementation, and continuous optimization of these factors. In this paper, we propose a maintenance technique that integrates an ensemble of CBR classifiers with spectral clustering and logistic regression to improve the classification accuracy of CBR classifiers on (ultra) high-dimensional biological data sets.

Our proposed method is applicable to any CBR system; however, in this paper, we demonstrate the improvement achieved by applying the method to a computational framework of a CBR system called *TA3*. We have evaluated the system on two publicly available microarray data sets that cover leukemia and lung cancer samples. Our maintenance method improves the classification accuracy of *TA3* by approximately 20% from 65% to 79% for the leukemia and from 60% to 70% for the lung cancer data set.

1 Introduction

Case-based reasoning (CBR) has been successfully applied to a wide range of applications, such as classification, diagnosis, planning, configuration, and decision-support [1]. CBR can produce good quality solutions in weak-theory domains, such as molecular biology, where the number and the complexity of the rules affecting the problem are very high, there is not enough knowledge for formal representation, and the domain understanding evolves over time [2]. In addition, similarly as other learning systems, CBR systems can suffer from the *utility problem*, which occurs when knowledge learned in an attempt to improve a system's performance degrades it instead [3].

These issues can be addressed by continuous *case-based reasoner maintenance* (CBRM) [4, 5], where the contents of one or more knowledge containers are revised in order to improve future reasoning for a particular set of performance objectives [6]. According to Richter's definition, there are four containers in which the knowledge could be stored in a CBR system: the vocabulary used, the similarity measure, the solution transformation, and the case-base [7]. During maintenance, the contents of each of the four knowledge containers may be revised in order to improve the performance objectives, e.g., improving the quality of the proposed solution.

Although several methods have been proposed for revising the case-base to reduce the number of stored cases [8–10], relatively little work has been carried out on revising the case-base to reduce the number of attributes[1] of stored cases. The problem, known as the "curse of dimensionality", occurs in (ultra) high-dimensional domains with tens of thousands of attributes and only a few hundred cases (samples). Such domains include microarray data sets, which measure the activity of tens of thousands of genes simultaneously. Microarrays are used in medical domains to produce molecular profiles of diseased and normal tissues, and thus increase the level of detail that can be stored about every patient. That is useful for understanding various diseases, and the resulting patient profiles support more accurate analogy-based diagnosis, prognosis, and treatment planning. Microarray data sets are represented by an $N \times M$ matrix, where M is the number of genes for the N samples, and they are labeled using clinical profiles (or phenotypes).

Clustering and *feature selection* techniques have been applied to many domains including microarrays [11–13]. Clustering groups samples (cases) into partitions, such that samples within a cluster are similar to one another and dissimilar to samples in other clusters. Clustering techniques can be categorized into *partitional* and *hierarchical* methods [14]. Partitional-based clustering techniques attempt to break a data set into k clusters, such that each cluster optimizes a given criterion, e.g., minimizes the sum of squared distance from the mean within each cluster. Hierarchical clustering proceeds successively by either merging smaller clusters into larger ones (agglomerative approach), or by splitting larger clusters (divisive approach).

The goal of feature selection is to identify "informative" features among thousands of available features, i.e., relevant features that improve CBR performance for a given reasoning task. In microarray data sets, "informative" features comprise genes with expression patterns that have meaningful biological relationships to the classification labels of samples (analogously, it could represent sample vectors that have meaningful biological relationship to the classification labels of genes). For microarray data sets, mining a subset of genes that distinguishes between cancer and normal samples can play an important role in disease pathology and drug discovery. Removing "non-informative" features helps overcome the "curse of dimensionality" and improves the prediction accuracy of classifiers.

---

[1] In this paper, we use attributes and features interchangeably, unless otherwise specified.

Feature selection techniques are classified into *filter* and *wrapper* methods [15]. The filter approach selects feature subsets that are independent of the induction algorithm, while the wrapper approach evaluates the subset of features using the inducer itself.

Our main challenge is to interpret the molecular biology data to find similar samples to eventually use them in case-based medicine, and to identify those genes whose expression patterns have meaningful relationships to their classification labels. Clustering and feature selection techniques have been successfully applied to CBR maintenance [16, 10]; however, in this paper, we show how those techniques can further improve the prediction accuracy of a CBR classifier when combined with mixture of experts to analyze microarray data sets.

Our CBR maintenance approach has three main components: ensemble of CBR systems, clustering, and feature selection. We use an ensemble of CBR systems, called *mixture of experts* (MOE) to predict the classification label of a given (input) case. A gating network calculates the weighted average of votes provided by each expert. The performance of each CBR expert is further improved by using clustering and feature selection techniques. We apply spectral clustering [17] to cluster the data set into k groups, and the logistic regression model [18] is used to select a subset of features in each cluster. Each cluster is considered as a case-base for the k CBR experts, and the gating network learns how to combine the responses provided by each expert.

Although the proposed method is applicable to any CBR system, we demonstrate the improvement achieved by applying it to a specific implementation of a CBR system, called *TA3* [19]. *TA3* is a computational framework for CBR based on a modified nearest-neighbor technique and employs a variable context, a similarity-based retrieval algorithm, and a flexible representation language.

The rest of the paper is organized as follows. Section 2 reviews case-based reasoner maintenance techniques. In Section 3, we present the MOE4CBR method that uses a mixture of experts of CBR to classify high-dimensional data sets. Also, we discuss the proposed maintenance method in terms of Leake and Wilson's case-base maintenance framework [20]. Section 4 introduces the *TA3* CBR system, which is used as a framework for evaluating MOE4CBR. In Section 5, we demonstrate experimental results of the proposed method on two publicly microarray data sets.

2 Related Work

In this section, we explain the algorithms employed to maintain the contents of the four knowledge containers – vocabulary used, the similarity measure, the solution transformation, and the case-based knowledge container – introduced by Richter [7].

Case-base maintenance (CBM) policies differ in the approach they use and the schedule they follow to perform maintenance. Leake and Wilson categorize maintenance policies in terms of how they gather data relevant to maintenance, how they decide when to trigger maintenance, the types of maintenance operations available, and how selected maintenance operations are executed [20].

Smyth and McKenna propose a method, that edits the case-base, such that the range of the problems that can be solved remains unchanged while the size of the case-base is minimized [8]. Their method is based on *condensed nearest neighbor* (CNN). This method builds up an edited set of training examples by incrementally adding examples to the set if they cannot be correctly classified by the current edited test [21].

In the CBM method proposed by Shiu and Yeung, a large case-base is transformed to a small case-base together with a group of adaptation rules that are generated by fuzzy decision trees [9]. These adaptation rules play the role of complementing the reduction of cases. Yang and Wu propose a method that does not remove cases from the case-base as they may be useful in the long run. Instead, the method reduces the size of case-base by creating small case-bases that are located on different sites [10].

DRAMA is an example of an interactive CBR system for *vocabulary maintenance* [22]. The cases in the system are conceptual aircraft designs, and the designers have freedom in defining new features to describe design cases. Each time before a new case is added to the case-base, the system examines the vocabulary container and suggests appropriate features that have been used previously. In this way, the vocabulary is built in parallel with the case-base.

Learning feature weights can be considered as an example of *similarity maintenance*. The system asks the user(s) to adjust feature weights for a set of cases, and applies the weights during case retrieval. Zhang and Yang propose a method for continually updating a feature-weighting scheme based on interactive user responses to the system's behavior [23].

Aha and Bankert discuss how using filter and wrapper techniques improve the classification accuracy of their case-based classifier on the cloud data set with 204 features and a few thousands data points [16]. Their results show that a wrapper FS method (called BEAM) applied to a nearest neighbor classifier IB1 improves its classification accuracy from 73% to 88%.

A system for disaster response planning called DIAL is an example of *solution transformation maintenance* [24]. The solution transformation container in DIAL comprises a set of adaptation cases and rules, which can be adjusted over time. In order to adapt a solution, the system checks for applicable adaptation case(s); if no adaptation cases apply, new adaptation cases can be learned by recording traces of rule-based or interactive manual adaptation.

Unlike speed-up learners that have first-principle problem solvers in addition to control rules, pure CBR systems do not usually have first-principle rules. Thus, without cases similar to a problem at hand, they cannot solve new problems. Therefore, in maintaining CBR systems, competence criteria (i.e., the range of target problems that a given CBR system can solve) should be considered, as well as efficiency criteria, which is the main focus of maintaining speed-up learners. However, based on which criterion had a higher optimization priority during maintenance, different CBR maintenance methods can be categorized into two groups [5]:

1. *Competence-directed* CBM methods attempt to maintain the case-base to provide the same (or better) quality solution to a broader range of problems.
2. *Efficiency-directed* methods consider the processing constraints, and modify knowledge containers to improve efficiency of storage or scalability of retrieval.

3 The MOE4CBR Method

The goal of our maintenance method is to improve the prediction accuracy of CBR classifiers, and at the same time reduce the size of the case-base knowledge container. According to Smyth's categorization [5], our maintenance method – Mixture Of Experts for CBR systems (MOE4CBR) – is both competence-directed, since the range of the problems the system can solve increases and efficiency-directed, since the size of case-base decreases.

The performance of each expert in MOE4CBR is improved by using clustering and feature selection techniques. Based on our initial analysis [25], we selected spectral clustering [17] for clustering the case-base, and the logistic regression model [18] as a filter feature selection for the *TA3* classifier. Given a labeled training data set, the system predicts labels for the unseen data (test set) following the process described below.

3.1 Clustering

Of the many clustering approaches that have been proposed, only some algorithms are suitable for domains with large number of features and a small number of samples. The two clustering approaches widely used in microarray data analysis [26, 27] are *k*-means clustering [14] and self-organizing maps (SOMs) [28]. Our earlier evaluation suggests that spectral clustering [17] outperforms *k*-means clustering and SOMs [25]. The comparison was based on two criteria:

1. **Dunn's index** [29], which does not require class labels and identifies how "compact and well separated" clusters are. It is defined as follows:

$$D = \min_{i=1,\ldots,k} \{ \min_{j=i+1,\ldots,k} (\frac{d(c_i, c_j)}{\max_{l=1,\ldots,k} diam(c_l)}) \},$$

where k denotes the number of clusters and $d(c_i, c_j)$ is the dissimilarity function between two clusters c_i and c_j defined as:

$$d(c_i, c_j) = \min_{x \in c_i, y \in c_j} d(x, y)$$

The diameter of a cluster c, represented by $diam(c)$, is considered as a measure of dispersion and is defined as follows:

$$diam(c) = \max_{x,y \in c} d(x, y)$$

2. **Precision** and **recall** [30] that compare the resulting clusters with pre-specified class labels [25]. Precision shows how many data points are classified (clustered) correctly, and recall shows how many data points the model accounts. They are defined as follows:

$$P_i = \frac{|c_i \cap g_i|}{|c_i|} \quad \text{and} \quad R_i = \frac{|c_i \cap g_i|}{|g_i|},$$

where c_i is the cluster output by a clustering algorithm for the ith data point, and g_i is the pre-specified classification label of that data point, and $1 \leq i \leq T$, where T is the number of data points. Precision and recall of clustering is defined as the weighted average of the precision and recall of each cluster. More precisely:

$$P = \sum_{i=1}^{k} \frac{|g_i|}{T} P_i \quad \text{and} \quad R = \sum_{i=1}^{k} \frac{|g_i|}{T} R_i$$

The classification error, E, is defined as:

$$E = \sum_{i=1}^{k} |g_i \cap \overline{f(g_i)}|,$$

where $|g_i \cap \overline{f(g_i)}|$ denotes the number of data points in class g_i which labeled wrong, k shows the number of clusters, and $f(g)$ is a one to one mapping from classes to clusters, such that each class g_i is mapped to the cluster $f(g_i)$.

Considering the results of our comparison, we apply spectral clustering, which has been successfully used in many applications including computer vision and VLSI [17]. In this approach, data points are mapped to a higher dimensional space prior to being clustered. More precisely, the k eigenvectors associated with the k largest eigenvalues of matrix X are clustered by k-means, where k represents the number of clusters and is set by the user. Matrix X is a transformation of the *affinity* matrix – the matrix holding the Euclidean distance between any two data points. In the next step, data point s_i is assigned to cluster j if and only if row i of the matrix X was assigned to cluster j, where $1 \leq i \leq N$, $1 \leq j \leq k$, and N is the number of data points.

3.2 Feature Selection

The goal of feature selection is to improve the quality of data by removing redundant and irrelevant features, i.e., those features whose values do not have meaningful relationships to their labels, and whose removal improves the prediction accuracy of the classifier. Feature selection techniques are classified into *filter* and *wrapper* methods [31]. The main difference is that the latter use the final classifier to evaluate the subset of features, while the former do not.

Fisher criterion and standard t-test are two statistical methods that have been successfully applied to feature selection problem in (ultra) high-dimensional data sets [32]. In order to select a suitable feature selection approach for CBM, we have evaluated performance of Fisher criterion, t-test, and the logistic regression model [18] when used in a CBR classifier [25]. Namely, we have applied the three feature selection techniques to the *TA3* classifier, and measured the improvement in *accuracy* and *classification error*. Accuracy measures the number of correctly classified data points, and classification error counts the number of misclassified data points. Based on our evaluation, logistic regression applied to feature selection outperforms Fisher and standard t-test techniques [25].

Assuming that classifier x is the logistic of a linear function of the feature vector, for two classes, the logistic regression model has the following form:

$$Pr(y=0|x,w) = \frac{1}{1+e^{-w^T x}}, \qquad (1)$$

where w is a $p+1$ column vector of weights, and p is the number of features [18]. Logistic regression has been successfully applied to classifying (ultra) high-dimensional microarrays [33]. However, we use logistic regression as a filter feature selection method. In order to select a subset of features (genes), the logistic regression classifier is trained on the training set using the above formula, and features corresponding to the highest ranking magnitude of weights are selected. The data sets are normalized, such that all features (regressor variables) have the same mean and the same variance. Since there are thousands of features in the microarray data sets, features are eliminated in chunks; however, better results might be obtained by removing one feature at a time, and training the classifier on the remaining features.

3.3 Mixture of Experts

The mixture of experts approach is based on the idea that each expert classifies samples separately, and individual responses are combined by the gating network to provide a final classification label [18]. A general idea of the mixture of experts approach is depicted in Fig. 1. In order to combine the responses of k experts, the following formulas are used [18]:

$$Pr(y=Y|x_i) = \sum_{j=1}^{k} Pr(C_j|x_i) \times Pr(y=Y|C_j, x_i), \qquad (2)$$

with the constraint that:

$$\sum_{j=1}^{N} Pr(C_j|x_i) = 1, \qquad (3)$$

where x_i represents the unseen data (test data), $\{C_1, ..., C_k\}$ denote the clusters, and Y is the class label. $Pr(C_j|x_i)$ is calculated as follows. Given a test data

x_i, the l similar cases are retrieved from the case-base, where l can be chosen by the user. Then $Pr(C_j|x_i)$ is calculated by dividing the number of retrieved cases belonging to C_j (represented by S) by the total number of the retrieved cases (which is l). $Pr(y = Y|C_j, x_i)$ is the number of retrieved cases with class label Y belonging to C_j divided by S.

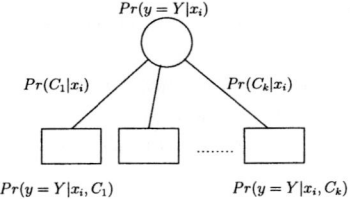

Fig. 1. Mixture of Experts: terminal nodes are experts, and the non-terminal node is the gating network. The gating network returns the probability that the input case x_i belongs to class Y.

As Fig. 2 depicts, the MOE4CBR maintenance method has two main steps: first, the case-base of each expert is formed by clustering the data set into k groups, then each case-base is maintained "locally" using feature selection techniques. Each of the k obtained sets will be considered as a case-base for our k CBR experts. We use formulas 2 and 3 to combine the responses of the k experts. Each expert applies the *TA3* model to decide on the class label, and the gating network uses *TA3* to assign weights to each classifier, i.e., to determine which class the input case most likely belongs to.

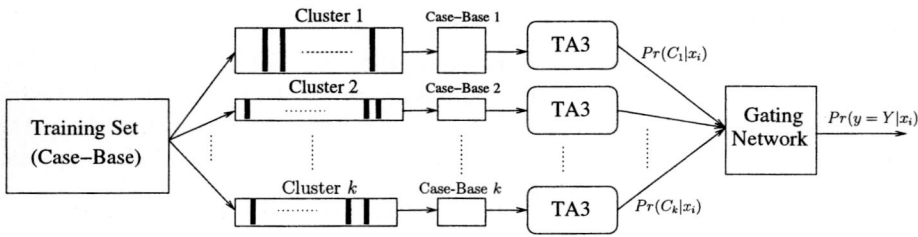

Fig. 2. Mixture of Experts for Case-Based Reasoning: training set is grouped into k clusters, and after selecting a subset of features for each group (shown with vertical bars), each group will be used as a case-base for the k experts of CBR. The gating network combines the responses provided by each *TA3* expert considering the weights of each expert (weights are shown on the arrows that connect *TA3* experts to the gating network).

Next, we describe the proposed maintenance method in terms of the maintenance framework introduced by Leake and Wilson [20]:

- **Type of data:** *none*. The method does not collect any particular data to decide when CBM is needed.
- **Timing:** *ad hoc, conditional*. The removal of "non-informative" attributes from case representation is performed at irregular intervals. To make the system more autonomous, we plan to make it conditional, i.e., whenever there is a change in the task, or whenever new cases are added to the case-base.
- **Integration:** *offline*. The maintenance is performed offline during a pause in reasoning.
- **Triggering:** *conditional*. Maintenance will be triggered whenever there is a change in the task, or new cases are added to the case-base.
- **Revision level:** *knowledge level*. Maintenance is mainly focused on removing "non-informative" features.
- **Execution:** *none*. The system makes no changes when the maintenance is needed, the maintenance method is invoked manually.
- **Scope of maintenance:** *broad*. The whole case-base is affected by the CBM operations.

It should be noted that unlike in other CBR application domains, where cases are usually added to the case-base one by one, cases are added in a batch mode in molecular biology domains. Thus, the maintenance can be performed offline. As a result, the complexity issues of the maintenance method are less important.

4 An Introduction to the TA3 Case-Based Reasoning System

We used the *TA3* CBR system as a framework to evaluate our method, although our maintenance method can be applied to any CBR system. The *TA3* system has been applied successfully to biology domains, such as *in vitro* fertilization (IVF) [34] and protein crystal growth [35]. We briefly describe the main features of the *TA3* CBR system.

4.1 Case Representation in *TA3*

A case C corresponds to a real world situation, represented as a finite set of attribute/value pairs [34]:

$$C = \{<a_0:V_0>, <a_1:V_1>, ..., <a_n:V_n>\}.$$

There are two types of cases: (1) an input case (target) that describes the problem and is represented as a case without a solution; and (2) a source case, which is a case stored in a case-base that contains both a problem description and a solution.

Using the information about the usefulness of individual attributes and information about their properties, attributes are grouped into two or more Telos-style categories [36]. This enhancement of case representations is used during the retrieval process to increase the accuracy of classification and flexibility of retrieval, and to improve system's performance. In classification tasks, each case has at least two categories: problem description and class. The problem description characterizes the problem and the class gives a solution to a given problem. Additional categories can be used to group attributes into separate equivalence partitions, and the system can treat each partition separately during case retrieval.

4.2 Case Retrieval in *TA3*

The retrieval component is based on a modified nearest-neighbor matching [37]. Its modification includes: (1) grouping attributes into categories of different priorities so that different preferences and constraints can be used for individual categories during query relaxation; (2) using an explicit context (i.e., set of attribute and attribute value constraints) during similarity assessment; (3) using an efficient query relaxation algorithm based on incremental context transformations [19].

Similarity in *TA3* is determined as a closeness of values for attributes defined in the *context*. Context can be seen as a view or an interpretation of a case, where only a subset of attributes are considered relevant. Formally, a context is defined as a finite set of attributes with associated constraints on their values:

$$\Omega = \{<a_0 : CV_0>, ..., <a_k : CV_k>\},$$

where a_i is an attribute name and the constraint CV_i specifies the set of "allowable" values for attribute a_i. By selecting only certain features for matching and imposing constraints on feature values, a context allows for controlling what can and what cannot be considered as a partial match: all (and only) cases that satisfy the specified constraints for the context are considered similar and are relevant with respect to the context. Machine learning and knowledge-mining techniques may be applied to determine an optimal context: selecting features which are most "relevant" for a given task and specifying characteristic values for them.

4.3 Case Adaptation in *TA3*

Considering the characteristics of microarray data sets, the current implementation uses only simple adaptation. Namely, for case-base classification, the average class label of the similar retrieved cases is considered as the class label for the input case.

5 Experimental Results

Here we demonstrate the results of applying the MOE4CBR method to the *TA3* classifier.

5.1 Data Sets

The experiments have been performed on the following microarray data sets:

1. **Leukemia:** The data set contains data of 72 leukemia patients, with 7,129 expression levels for each sample[2] [26]. 46 samples belong to type I Leukemia (called Acute Lymphoblastic Leukemia) and 25 samples belong to type II Leukemia (called Acute Myeloid Leukemia).
2. **Lung:** The data set taken from the *Ontario Cancer Institute*[3] contains 39 samples, with 18,117 expression levels for each sample. Samples are pre-classified into recurrence and non-recurrence. Missing values were imputed using KNNimputed software, which is based on the weighted k-nearest neighbor method [38].

5.2 MOE4CBR Results

Table 1 depicts the results of applying the MOE4CBR maintenance method to the leukemia and lung data sets. When there is a tie, the *TA3* classifier cannot decide on the label of data points; resulting cases are categorized as "undecided" in the table. As the table shows, before the maintenance method is applied, the classification accuracy of the $TA3_{Leukemia}$ [4] and $TA3_{Lung}$ is 65% and 60%, respectively. However, after our maintenance method selects a subset of 712 out of 7129 genes for leukemia and a subset of 1811 out of 18117 genes for the lung data sets, and combines *TA3* classifiers using mixture of experts, the accuracy improves to 79% and 70%, respectively. In our experiments, the number of clusters, k, was assigned to be the number of classification labels, i.e., k was set to be 2 for both the leukemia and lung data sets.

Table 1. Accuracy of *TA3* before and after maintenance.

Leukemia Data Set			
Method	Accuracy	Error	Undecided
No Maintenance	65%	35%	0%
MOE4CBR	79%	21%	0%

Lung Data Set			
Method	Accuracy	Error	Undecided
No Maintenance	60%	30%	10%
MOE4CBR	70%	30%	0%

We used the training and test data set suggested by the data set provider for the leukemia data set (38 samples in the training and 34 samples in the test

---
[2] http://www.broad.mit.edu/cgi-bin/cancer/publications/pub_menu.cgi
[3] http://www.cs.toronto.edu/juris/publications/data/CR02Data.txt
[4] $TA3_X$ denotes application of *TA3* into a domain X.

set). The leave-one-out cross-validation (LOOCV) method was used for the lung data set, and results are averaged over 20 trials.

The lung data set has also been analyzed by Jones et al. [39]. They developed a model-based clustering prior to using the SVM classifier. Their results show that the classification accuracy of SVM prior to applying the proposed model-based clustering is 72% using 10-fold cross-validation for evaluation. After the proposed method is applied, which selects 20 meta-genes, the classification accuracy drops to 67%. Considering that our method improves the classification accuracy of *TA3* on the lung data set from 60% to 70% after we reduce the size of the data-set by 90%, our results are encouraging.

6 Conclusions

Molecular biology domain is a natural application for CBR systems, since CBR systems can perform remarkably well on complex and poorly formalized domains. However, due to the large number of attributes in each case, CBR classifiers, similarly as other learning systems, suffer from the "curse of dimensionality". Maintaining CBR systems can improve the prediction accuracy of CBR classifiers by clustering similar cases, and removing "non-informative" features in each group.

In this paper, we introduced the *TA3* case-based reasoning system, a computational framework for CBR systems. We proposed the mixture of experts for case-based reasoning (MOE4CBR) method, where an ensemble of CBR systems is integrated with clustering and feature selection to improve the prediction accuracy of the *TA3* classifier. Spectral clustering groups samples, and each group is used as a case-base for each of the k experts of CBR. To improve the accuracy of each expert, logistic regression is applied to select a subset of features that can better predict class labels. We also demonstrated that our proposed method improves the prediction accuracy of the *TA3* case-based reasoning system on two public lung and leukemia microarray data sets.

Although we have used a specific implementation of a CBR system, our results are applicable in general. Generality of our solution is also not degraded by the application domains, since many other life sciences problem domains are characterized by (ultra) high-dimensionality and a low number of samples. Further investigation may take additional advantage of Telos-style categories in *TA3* for classification tasks, and perform more experiments on several other data sets. The system may also benefit from new clustering approaches, and new feature selection algorithms.

Acknowledgments

This work is supported by IBM CAS fellowship to NA, and the National Science and Engineering Research Council of Canada (NSERC Grant 203833-02) and IBM Faculty Partnership Award to IJ. The authors are grateful to Patrick Rogers, who implemented the current version of *TA3*.

References

1. Lenz, M., Bartsch-Sporl, B., Burkanrd, H., Wess, S., eds.: Case-based reasoning: experiences, lessons, and future directions. Springer (1998)
2. Jurisica, I., Glasgow, J.: Application of case-based reasoning in molecular biology. Artificial Intelligence Magazine, Special Issue on Bioinformatics **25(1)** (2004) 85–95
3. Francis, A.G., Ram, A.: The utility problem in case-based reasoning. In: Proceedings of the 1993 AAAI Workshop on Case-Based Reasoning, Washington, DC (1993)
4. Leake, D.B., Wilson, D.C.: Remembering why to remember: performance-guided case-base maintenance. In Blanzieri, E., Portinale, L., eds.: Advances in Case-Based Reasoning, Fivth European Workshop on Case-Based Reasoning, Trento, Italy, Springer (2000) 161–172
5. Smyth, B.: Case base maintenance. In Pobil, A.D., Mira, J., Ali, M., eds.: Eleventh International Conference on Industrial and Engineering Applications of Artificial Intelligence and Expert Systems. Volume 2., Castellon, Spain, Springer (1998) 507–516
6. Wilson, D., Leake, D.: Maintaining case-based reasoners: Dimensions and directions. Computational Intelligence **17** (2001) 196–212
7. Richter, M.M.: 1. In: Case-based reasoning: experiences, lessons, and future directions. Springer (1998) 1–15
8. Smyth, B., McKenna, E.: Building compact competent case-bases. In Althoff, K.D., Bergmann, R., Branting, K., eds.: Proceedings of the 3rd International Conference on Case-Based Reasoning Research and Development (ICCBR-99), Seeon Monastery, Germany, Springer (1999) 329–342
9. Shiu, S.C., Yeung, D.S.: Transferring case knowledge to adaptation knowledge: An approach for case-base maintenance. Computational Intelligence **17** (2001) 295–314
10. Yang, Q., Wu, J.: Keep it simple: a case-base maintenance policy based on clustering and information theory. In Hamilton, H., ed.: Advances in Artificial Intelligence, In Proceedings of the 13th Biennial Conference of the Canadian Society for Computational Studies of Intelligence, Montreal, Canada, Springer (2000) 102–114
11. Xing, E.P.: Feature selection in microarray analysis. In Berrar, D., Dubitzky, W., Granzow, M., eds.: A Practical Approach to Microarray Data Analysis. Kluwer Academic publishers (2003) 110–131
12. Quackenbush, J.: Computational analysis of microarray data. Nat Rev Genet **2** (2001) 418–427
13. Molla, M., Waddell, M., Page, D., Shavlik, J.: Using machine learning to design and interpret gene-expression microarrays. AI Magazine **25** (2004) 23–44
14. Han, J., Kamber, M.: Data Mining: Concepts and Techniques. Morgan Kauffmann Publishers (2000)
15. John, G., Kohavi, R., Pfleger, K.: Irrelevant features and the subset selection problem. In: Machine Learning: Proceedings of the Eleventh International Conference, Morgan Kauffmann (1994) 121–129
16. Aha, D.W., Bankert, R.: Feature selection for case-based classification of cloud types: an empirical comparison. In Aha, D.W., ed.: Proceedings of the AAAI-94 Workshop on Case-Based Reasoning, Menlo Park, CA: AAAI Press (1994) 106–112
17. Ng, A.Y., Jordan, M.I., Weiss, Y.: On spectral clustering: Analysis and an algorithm. In G. Dieterich, S. Becker, Z.G., ed.: Advances in Neural Information Processing Systems 14, MIT Press (2002)

18. Hastie, T., Tibshirani, R., Friedman, J.: The elements of statistical learning. Springer (2001)
19. Jurisica, I., Glasgow, J., Mylopoulos, J.: Incremental iterative retrieval and browsing for efficient conversational CBR systems. International Journal of Applied Intelligence **12(3)** (2000) 251–268
20. Leake, D., Wilson, D.: Categorizing case-base maintenance: dimensions and directions. In Smyth, B., Cunningham, P., eds.: Proceedings of the 4th European Workshop on Advances in Case-Based Reasoning (EWCBR-98), Dublin, Ireland, Springer (1998) 196–207
21. Hart, P.: The condensed nearest neighbor rule. IEEE on Information Theory **14** (1968) 515–516
22. Leake, D.B., Wilson, D.C.: Combining CBR with interactive knowledge acquisition, manipulation and reuse. In Althoff, K.D., Bergmann, R., Branting, K., eds.: Proceedings of the 3rd International Conference on Case-Based Reasoning Research and Development (ICCBR-99), Seeon Monastery, Germany, Springer (1999) 203–217
23. Zhang, Z., Yang, Q.: Dynamic refinement of feature weights using quantitative introspective learning. In: Proceedings of the fifteenth International Joint Conference on Artificial Intelligence (IJCAI 99), Quebec, Canada, Morgan Kauffmann (1999) 228–233
24. Leake, D.B., Kinley, A., Wilson, D.C.: Acquiring case adaptation knowledge: a hybrid approach. In: Proceedings of the Thirteenth National Conference on Artificial Intelligence and Eighth Innovative Applications of Artificial Intelligence Conference, AAAI 96, IAAI 96, Portland, Oregon, AAAI Press, Menlo Park (1996) 648–689
25. Arshadi, N., Jurisica, I.: Maintaining case-based reasoning in high-dimensional domains using mixture of experts. Technical Report CSRG-490, University of Toronto, Department of Computer Science (2004)
26. Golub, T., Slonim, D., Tamayo, P., Huard, C., Gassenbeek, M., Mesirov, J., Coller, H., Loh, M., Downing, J., Caligiuri, M., Bloomfield, C., Lander, E.: Molecular classification of cancer: class discovery and class prediction by gene expression monitoring. science **286** (1999) 531–537
27. Tamayo, P., Slonim, D., Mesirov, J., Zhu, Q., Dmitrovsky, E., Lander, E., Golub, T.: Interpreting patterns of gene expression with self-organizing maps: methods and application to hematopoietic differentiation. In: Proceedings of the National Academy of Science of the United States of America. Volume 96(6). (1999) 2907–2912
28. Kohonen, T.: Self-Organizing Maps. Springer (1995)
29. Dunn, J.: Well separated clusters and optimal fuzzy partitions. Journal of Cybernetics **4** (1974) 95–104
30. Baeza-Yates, R., Ribiero-Neto, B.: Modern information retrieval. Addison-Wesley (1999)
31. Kohavi, R., John, G.H.: Wrappers for feature subset selection. Artificial Intelligence **97** (1997) 273–324
32. Jaeger, J., Sengupta, B., Ruzzo, W.: Improved gene selection for classification of microarrays. In: Pacific Symposium on Biocomputing. (2003) 8:53–64
33. Xing, E.P., Jordan, M.L., Karp, R.M.: Feature selection for high-dimensional genomic microarray data. In Brodley, C.E., Danyluk, A.P., eds.: Proceedings of the Eighteenth International Conference on Machine Learning, Williamstown, MA, USA, Morgan Kauffmann (2001) 601–608

34. Jurisica, I., Mylopoulos, J., Glasgow, J., Shapiro, H., Casper, R.F.: Case-based reasoning in IVF: prediction and knowledge mining. Artificial Intelligence in Medicine **12** (1998) 1–24
35. Jurisica, I., Rogers, P., Glasgow, J., Fortier, S., Luft, J., Wolfley, J., Bianca, M., Weeks, D., DeTitta, G.: Intelligent decision support for protein crystal growth. IBM Systems Journal **40(2)** (2001) 394–409
36. Mylopoulos, J., Borgida, A., Jarke, M., Koubarakis, M.: Telos: Representing knowledge about information systems. ACM Transactions on Information Systems **8(4)** (1990) 325–362
37. Wettschereck, D., Dietterich, T.: An experimental comparison of the nearest neighbor and nearest hyperrectangle algorithms. Machine Learning **19(1)** (1995) 5–27
38. Troyanskaya, O., Cantor, M., Sherlock, G., Brown, P., Hastie, T., Tibshirani, R., Botstein, D., Altman, R.B.: Missing value estimation methods for DNA microarrays. Bioinformatics **17** (2001) 520–525
39. Jones, L., Ng, S.K., Ambroise, C., McLachlan, G.: Use of microarray data via model-based classification in the study and prediction of survival from lung cancer. In Johnson, K., Lin, S., eds.: Critical Assessment of Microarray Data Analysis. (2003) 38–42

JColibri: An Object-Oriented Framework for Building CBR Systems*

Juan José Bello-Tomás, Pedro A. González-Calero, and Belén Díaz-Agudo

Dep. Sistemas Informáticos y Programación
Universidad Complutense de Madrid, Spain
{juanjobt,pedro,belend}@sip.ucm.es

Abstract. We present an object-oriented framework in Java for building CBR systems that is an evolution of previous work on knowledge intensive CBR [8,9]. JColibri is a software artifact that promotes software reuse for building CBR systems, integrating the application of well proven Software Engineering techniques with a knowledge level description that separates the problem solving method, that defines the reasoning process, from the domain model, that describes the domain knowledge. Framework instantiation is supported by a graphical interface that guides the configuration of a particular CBR system, alleviating the steep learning curve typical for these type of systems.

1 Introduction

Developing a CBR system is a complex task where many decisions have to be taken. The system designer has to choose how the cases will be represented, the case organization structure, which methods will solve the CBR tasks and which knowledge (besides the specific cases) will be used by these methods. This process would greatly benefit from the reuse of previously developed CBR systems.

Software reuse is a goal that the Software Engineering community has pursued from its very beginning [16]. From this effort a number of technologies have appeared that directly or indirectly promotes software reuse: object-oriented frameworks, component technologies, design patterns, domain analysis, software architectures, software product lines, model driven architectures, to mention just a few. Most of these technologies have been applied in those software domains where mass production is required and where reuse is a must. Unfortunately AI systems have remained for too long in the prototype arena and, in general, AI researchers do not worry too much about software engineering concerns. The most significant and long term effort within the AI community to attain effective software reuse is the KADS methodology [21] and its descendants: CommonKADS[4] and UPML[10]. The KADS approach for building knowledge based systems proposes the reuse of abstract models consisting of reusable components, containing artificial problem solving methods, and ontologies of domain models.

---

* Supported by the Spanish Committee of Science & Technology (TIC2002-01961)

Nevertheless, the main emphasis in KADS is the definition of formal specification languages for the components, a formal approach to Software Engineering that departs from the mainstream results in this area.

In this paper we present JColibri, a framework for developing CBR systems. JColibri is a software artifact that promotes software reuse for building CBR systems, and tries to integrate the best of both worlds: the application of well proven Software Engineering techniques with the KADS key idea of separating the problem solving method, that defines the reasoning process, from the domain model, that describes the domain knowledge. JColibri is an evolution of the COLIBRI architecture [8], that consisted of a library of problem solving methods (PSMs) for solving the tasks of a knowledge-intensive CBR system along with an ontology, CBROnto [9], with common CBR terminology. COLIBRI was prototyped in LISP using LOOM as knowledge representation technology. This prototype served as proof of concept but was far from being usable outside of our own research group. JColibri is a technological evolution of COLIBRI that incorporates in a distributed architecture a description logics (DLs) engine, GUI clients for assembling a CBR system from reusable components and an object-oriented framework in Java.

The rest of this paper runs as follows. The next section describes the high-level organization of JColibri around tasks, methods and CBR terms. Section 3 describes the framework design, and Section 4 describes the framework instantiation process. Section 5 reviews related work and, finally, Section 6 concludes.

2 Knowledge Level Description

A useful way of describing problem solving behavior is in terms of the tasks to be solved, the goals to be achieved, the methods that will accomplish those tasks, and the domain knowledge that those methods need. A description along these lines is referred to as a *knowledge level description* [17].

JColibri is built around a task/method ontology that guides the framework design, determines possible extensions and supports the framework instantiation process. Task and methods are described in terms of domain-independent CBR terminology which is mapped into the classes of the framework.

2.1 CBR Ontology

Every CBR system makes use of CBR terminology, the type of entities that the CBR processes manage. A CBR ontology elaborates and organizes the terminology found in, ideally, any CBR system to provide a domain independent basis for new CBR systems. On this way, CBROnto [9] elaborates an extensive ontology over CBR terminology, the idea beyond this ontology is to have a common language to define the elements that compose a CBR system and to be able to build generic CBR methods independent of the knowledge domain.

In JColibri the CBR ontology is not represented as a separate resource in a knowledge representation formalism such as OWL or LOOM. The CBR concepts, such as Case, CaseBase, SimilarityFunction, GlobalSimilarityFunction, LocalSimilarityFunction, Query, Method, or Task, are mapped into abstract classes or interfaces of the framework. The is-a relations in the ontology are mapped into inheritance relations between classes and the part-of relations are mapped into composition of classes. This way, the classes representing concepts in the CBR ontology serve two purposes:

- they provide an abstract interface for the CBR methods and tasks that can be developed independently from the actual CBR building blocks (case structure, case base organization, similarity functions, etc.), and
- they serve as hooks where new types of CBR building blocks can be added.

The CBR ontology is already populated in the framework with a number of pre-packaged realizations of the CBR abstract entities that can be extended for particular applications.

2.2 Task/Method Ontology

Within a knowledge level description, problem solving methods (PSMs) capture and describe problem-solving behavior in an implementation and domain-independent manner. PSMs are used to accomplish tasks by applying domain knowledge. Although various authors have applied knowledge level analysis to CBR systems, the most relevant work is the CBR task structure developed in [1] influenced by the Components of Expertise Methodology [20]. At the highest level of generality, they describe the general CBR cycle in terms of four tasks: *Retrieve* the most similar case/s, *Reuse* its/their knowledge to solve the problem, *Revise* the proposed solution and *Retain* the experience. Each one of the four CBR tasks involves a number of more specific sub-tasks. There are methods to solve tasks either by decomposing a task in subtasks or by solving it directly. In our approach we use the notion of task structure proposed in [5]. The task structure identifies a number of alternative methods for a task, and each one of the methods sets up different subtasks in its turn. This kind of task-method-subtask analysis is carried on to a level of detail where the tasks are primitive with respect to the available knowledge (i.e. there are resolution methods).

Figure 1 depicts the task decomposition structure we use in our framework. Besides this task structure, our framework includes a library of PSMs to solve these tasks. It describes CBR PSMs by relating them within the CBR ontology concepts representing the tasks and domain characteristics.

PSMs in our library are organized around the tasks they resolve. We also need representing the method knowledge requirements (preconditions), and the input and output "types". These characteristics are described by using vocabulary (i.e. concepts) from the CBROnto ontology.

3 Framework Design

A framework is a reusable, "semi-complete" application that can be specialized to produce custom applications [14]. Application frameworks are targeted at a given application domain providing the design for a family of applications within that domain. The design of the JColibri framework comprises a hierarchy

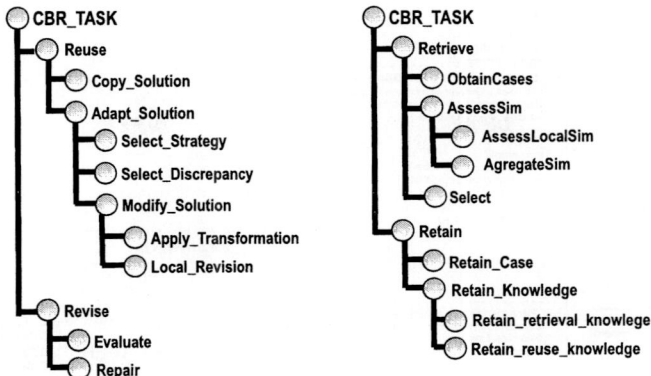

Fig. 1. CBROnto Task Structure

of Java classes plus a number of XML files. The framework is organized around the following elements:

Tasks and Methods. XML files describe the tasks supported by the framework along with the methods for solving those tasks.

Case Base. Different connectors are defined to support several types of case persistency, from the file system to a data base. Additionally, a number of possible in-memory Case Base organization are supported.

Cases. A number of interfaces and classes are included in the framework to provide an abstract representation of cases that support any type of actual case structure.

Problem Solving Methods. The actual code that supports the methods included in the framework.

3.1 Tasks and Methods

Tasks are the key element of the system since they drive the CBR process execution and represent the method goals. Tasks are just identified by its name and description included in an XML file like this:

```
<?xml version="1.0" encoding="UTF-8" standalone="yes"?>
<Tasks>
  <Task>
    <Name>CBR Task</Name>
    <Description>Main CBR task</Description>
  </Task>
  <Task>
    <Name>Retrieve Task</Name>
    <Description>CBR case retrieval</Description>
  </Task>
  ...
</Tasks>
```

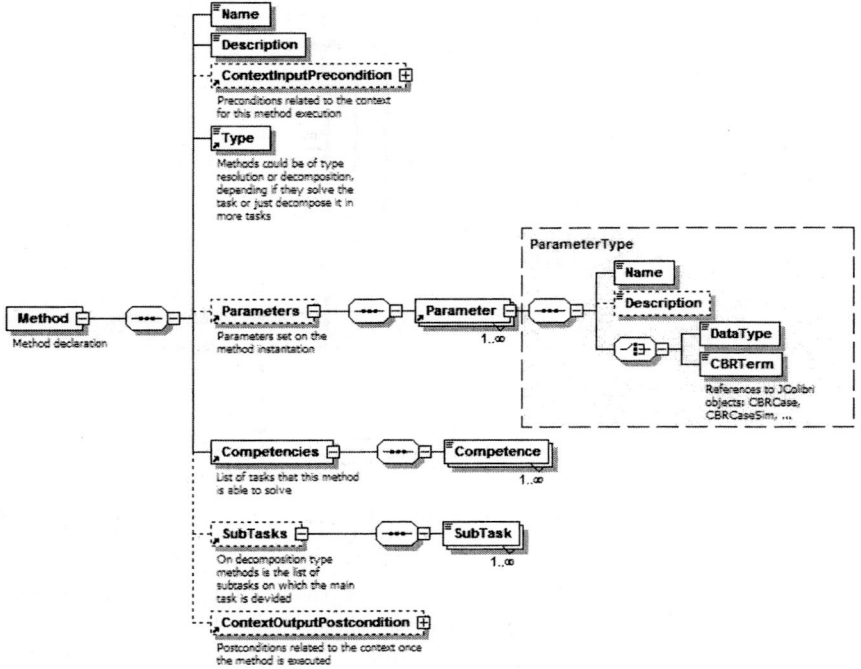

Fig. 2. Method declaration

Tasks can be added to the framework at any time, although including a new task is useless unless an associated method exists.

Method descriptions follow the XML schema shown in Figure 2. This elaborated description includes the following elements:

Name The fully qualified name of the class that implements the method. This class must implements the CBRMethod interface.
Description A textual description of the method.
ContextInputPrecondition A formal description of the applicability requirements for the method, including input requirements.
Type JColibri manages two types of methods: execution (or resolution) and decomposition. Execution methods are those that directly solve the task, for which has been assigned to, while decomposition ones divide the task into other tasks.
Parameters Method configuration parameters. These parameters are the variable hooks of the method implementation. For example, a retrieval method may be parameterized with the similarity function to apply. A parameter can be any object implementing CBRTerm, which is the root class for the CBROnto mapping.
Competencies The list of tasks this method is able to solve.

Subtasks In decomposition methods this element provides the list of tasks that result from dividing the original task.

ContextOutputPostcondition Output data information obtained from this method execution. The information will be used to check which method can take as input the output of this one.

As example we show here the description of the CBRMethod that implements the *CBR Task* by decomposing it in the 4 Rs processes. Notice how this description is coupled with task descriptions through the *Competence* and *SubTask* elements, and with the classes of the framework through the *Name* element, i.e., tasks with those names must have been included in the XML tasks file and a class with that name must exist in the framework.

```xml
<?xml version="1.0" encoding="UTF-8" standalone="yes"?>
<Methods>
  <Method>
      <Name>cbrarm.method.CBRMethod</Name>
      <Description>Main CBR method that will divide the CBR process
                   in the four typical tasks.</Description>
      <ContextInputPrecondition/>
      <Type>Decomposition</Type>
      <Parameters/>
      <Competences>
          <Competence>CBR Task</Competence>
      </Competencies>
      <SubTasks>
          <SubTask>Retrieve Task</SubTask>
          <SubTask>Reuse Task</SubTask>
          <SubTask>Revise Task</SubTask>
          <SubTask>Retain Task</SubTask>
      </SubTasks>
      <ContextOutputPostcondition/>
  </Method>
  ...
</Methods>
```

Building a CBR system with this framework (i.e., instantiating the framework) is a configuration process where the system developer selects the tasks the system must fulfill and for every task assigns the method that will do the job. The execution of the resulting CBR system can be seen as a sequence of method applications where a method takes as input the output of the previous one. Obviously, not every method applicable for a given task can be applied once the method that solve the previous task has been fixed. For example, it makes no sense to apply a voting mechanism to obtain the result in the reuse process if the retrieval one returns just one case.

Apart from input/output constraints, method applicability can be also determined by more general constraints such as the requirement of a particular organization for the Case Base or the availability of a given type of similarity

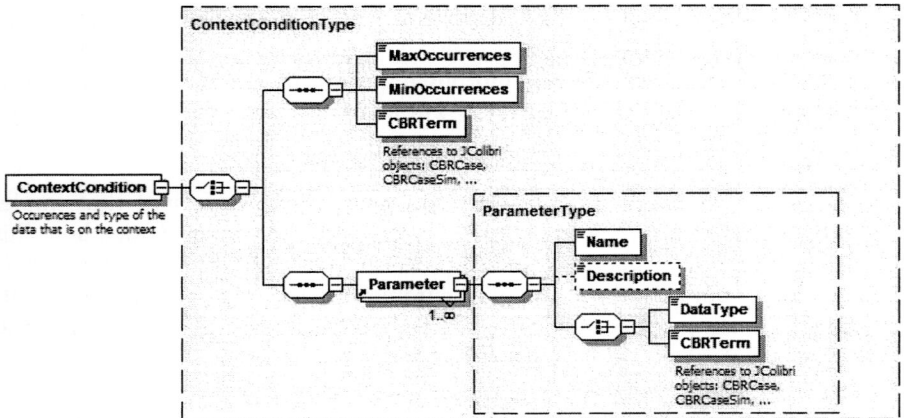

Fig. 3. Pre/Post condition specification

function defined on cases. These requirements are expressed as context conditions which specification language is shown in Figure 3. The element *ContextInputPrecondition* in a method description describes the requirements that the application of the method impose on the input context, while the element *ContextOutputPostcondition* describes how the context is affected by the execution of this method.

3.2 Case Base

CBR systems must access to the stored cases in an efficient way, a problem that becomes more relevant as the size of the Case Base grows. JColibri splits the problem of Case Base management in two separate although related concerns: persistency mechanism and in-memory organization.

Persistency is built around connectors. A connector represents the first layer of JColibri on top of the physical storage. Connectors are objects that know how to access and retrieve cases from the medium and return those cases to the CBR system in a uniform way. The use of connectors give JColibri flexibility against the physical storage so the system designer can choose the most appropriate one for the system at hand. Currently, JColibri implements three different connectors:

- File system connector to retrieve cases stored in XML files.
- JDBC connector that makes possible the use of JColibri with most of the DBs available in the market.
- RACER connector that allows the designer to use RACER [11], a Description Logics system, as source for cases.

The obvious interface for a connector must include methods to read the Case Base into memory and update it back into persistent media. An interface such that assumes that the whole Case Base can be read into memory for the CBR processes to work with it. However, in a real sized CBR application this approach may not be feasible. For that reason, connectors in JColibri implements a more sophisticated interface that allows to retrieve those cases that satisfy a query expressed in a subset of SQL. This way the designer can decide when and what part of the Case Base is loaded into memory.

The second layer of Case Base management is the data structure used to organize the cases once loaded into memory. The organization of the case base (linear, k-d trees, etc.) may have a big influence on the CBR processes, so the framework leaves open the election of the data structure that is going to be used. The Case Base is placed on top of the connector layer which serves to populate its storage structure.

In the same way connectors offer a common interface to the Case Base, the Case Base also implements a common interface for the CBR methods to access the cases. This way the organization and indexation chosen for the Case Base will not affect the implementation of the methods. The implementations of the *CaseBase* interface must provide at least the following functionality: construct or append a case base from persistent media through a query to a connector, make the case base persistent, learn a case, forget a case, and retrieve the K nearest neighbors to a given case. These methods are parameterized with, for example, the query to access the connector or the similarity function to apply for similarity assessment. Apart from the common interface, certain data structures may support additional operations on the Case Base that specific methods can exploit. For example, retrieval based on conceptual containment requires a hierarchy of is-a concepts on top of the cases. In that situation the given method will only be applicable if the supporting Case Base organization has been selected for the CBR system at hand.

The two-layers organization of the Case Base is a powerful approach that allows a number of different strategies for accessing the cases. A degenerate situation is one where all the operations are carried out through the connector, so that the Case Base is just a proxy for an external media. One of the key aspects of the COLIBRI approach to knowledge-intensive CBR was the use of already available ontologies to serve as indexes for the cases: cases are instances within a conceptual hierarchy that support sophisticated retrieval, adaptation and learning processes. Description Logics systems, such as RACER [11], are one of the leading technologies for ontology processing and reasoning, providing automatic classification and consistency checking. In JColibri, we support ontology-based CBR as a degenerate configuration of the two-layers approach: an external DLs system, RACER, is responsible for maintaining and giving access to the cases, while the Case Base in the CBR process memory is actually empty.

3.3 Cases

JColibri represents a case in a very general way. As shown in figure 4, a case is just an individual that can have any number of relationships with other individuals (the attributes of the case). The framework is populated with a number of

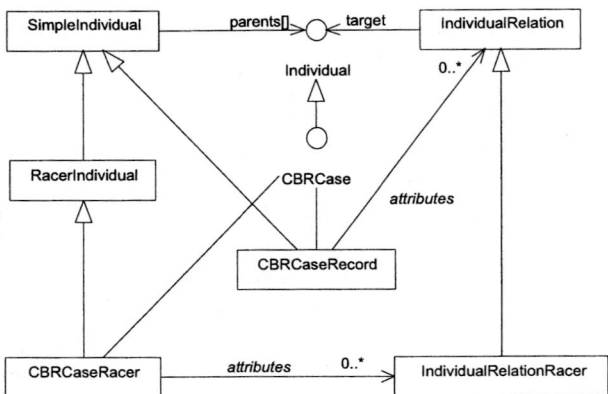

Fig. 4. CBR Case representation

predefined primitive data types that support the definition of any simple case. This abstract settlement, inspired on the Composite design pattern, allows for a uniform treatment of arbitrarily complex case structures as long as they conform to the *Individual* related through *IndividualRelation* to other *Individual*.

Figure 4 also shows a particular implementation of the *CBRCase* interface, namely *CBRCaseRacer*. This representation for cases is the one used when Case Base management is delegated to RACER, described in previous section, where cases are maintained externally and CBR processes must access them through a proxy that connects with the RACER engine.

3.4 Problem Solving Methods

It is out of the scope of this paper detailing the specific methods included in the framework, also considering that any list of implemented methods would be out of date as the framework keeps on growing. We are porting the methods previously included in COLIBRI, which are fully described in [7], and which have been published elsewhere. Apart from methods oriented to knowledge-intensive CBR in the line of our previous work, we are also including a growing list of standard CBR methods, needed to make JColibri an interesting framework for a bigger portion of the CBR community. The key features of the framework infrastructure for methods along the main CBR tasks:

Retrieve. Retrieval methods are organized around the tasks *ObtainCases, AssessSim* and *Select*. Since obtaining the cases is delegated to the Case Base, the methods in this category are mainly responsible for assessing similarity by parameterizing retrieval functionality. A number of similarity functions are provided both for local and aggregate similarity. Framework design imposes that similarity functions must be associated to specific individual types, the abstract constituents of cases. Similarity functions can be further parameterized through the context of a particular system configuration.

Reuse. It is well known how hard is to provide generic methods for CBR adaptation. JColibri provides an abstract design where slot-based and case-based adaptation methods can be hooked, along with a number of simple methods for adjusting primitive type values that populate this abstract design. The framework also provides the infrastructure to connect a CBR system with Jess[1], the Java version of CLIPS[2]. This way, a CBR system designer may define adaptation rules using the CLIPS formalism, and forget about the gory details of connecting to the Jess engine.

Revise. Revision is not supported by the framework.

Retain. Learning as the process of updating the Case Base is delegated to the concrete implementation of the Case Base. Adding and deleting cases is parameterized with retain and forget criteria specific to the given application.

Different types of parameters for the problem solving methods are organized around the classes which map the terms in CBROnto, whose interfaces must be conform to, when extending the framework.

4 Framework Instantiation: Building a CBR System

JColibri is designed to easily support the construction of CBR systems taking advantage of the task/method division paradigm described in previous sections. Building a CBR system is a configuration process where the system developer selects the tasks the system must fulfill and for every task assigns the method that will do the job. Different types of CBR systems can be built using JColibri, from retrieval only to full featured 4 Rs systems.

Ideally, the system designer would find every task and method needed for the system at hand, so that she would program just the representation for cases. However, in a more realistic situation a number of new methods may be needed and, less probably, some new task. Since JColibri is designed as an extensible framework, new elements will smoothly integrate with the available infrastructure as long as they follow the framework design.

One of the biggest problems with frameworks is learning how to use them. Since reusable systems are inherently more sophisticated, framework design tends to be more complex than the design of just one shoot system. A system developer needs to know the framework design to a certain extent, at least to determine what classes must be instantiated in order to obtain a given functionality. A deeper knowledge of the framework is needed when extending it.

In order to alleviate framework instantiation effort, JColibri features a semi-automatic configuration tool that guides the instantiation process through a graphical interface. This interface is dynamically built to reflect the actual contents of the task/method ontology, relying on the XML files describing task and method constraints and profiting from reflection facilities implemented in Java.

---

[1] http://herzberg.ca.sandia.gov/jess/
[2] http://www.ghg.net/clips/CLIPS.html

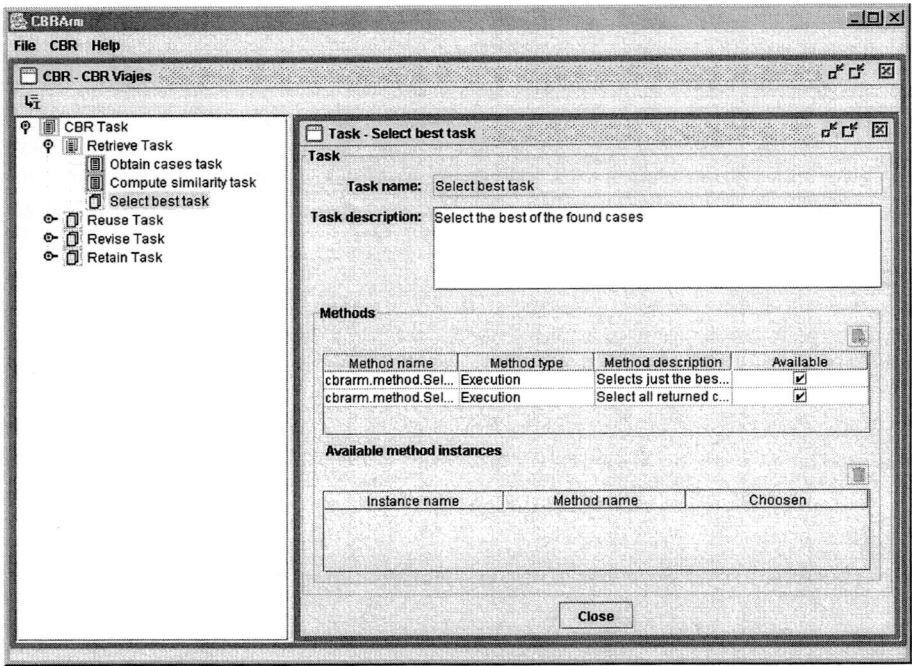

Fig. 5. JColibri configuration interface

Figure 5 shows the JColibri configuration interface. To the left is shown the task panel with the task tree. This tree shows the decomposition relations between tasks. To the right appears the task configuration panel where available methods for the given task in the given situation are provided. The configuration of a CBR system using this interface consists of the following processes:

- Defining the case structure, the source for cases and the case base organization.
- While the system is not complete, select one of the tasks without a method assigned, select and configure a method for that task. At startup the task tree has only one element, *CBRTask*, which is solved by a decomposition method that results in additional tasks. Task/method constraints are being tracked during the configuration process so that only applicable methods in the given context are offered to the system designer.
- Once the system is configured, the configuration code is generated so that a running CBR system is available. The configuration tool also provides a default interface for running the configured CBR system although in a real settlement an application specific interface should be developed.

The snapshot in Figure 5 corresponds to the configuration of a retrieval only system for the well known travel domain. In this example we are using RACER

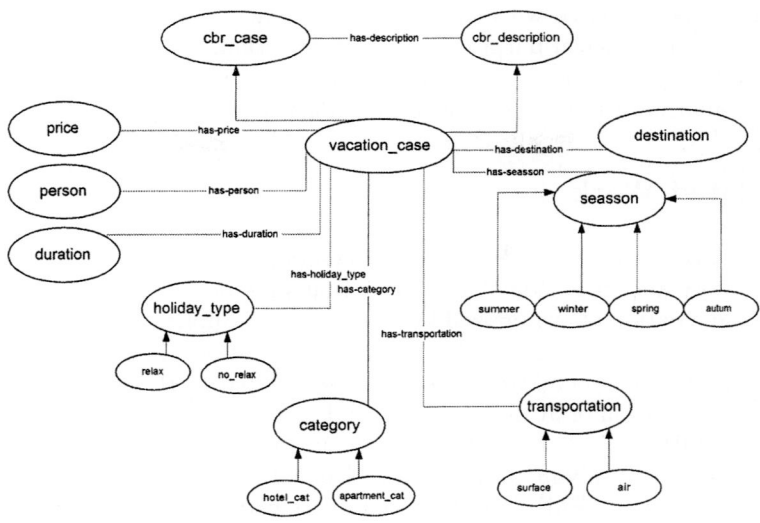

Fig. 6. Racer case definition

as case container, and the small ontology shown in Figure 6 defines the structure of the cases. Using this ontology we have a set of cases that are constructed with instances of the different concepts. Cases are retrieved through the RACER connector that returns instances of the *cbr_case* concept.

Once the Case Base and the structure of the cases have been set, the task-/method configuration has to be built. In this simple example, the resulting configuration would be:

- *CBRTask* solved by *CBRMethod* that decomposes it in Retrieve, Reuse, Revise and Retain. For a retrieval only system we just associate a method with *RetrieveTask*, leaving the other tasks unsolved.
  - *RetrieveTask* solved by *RetrieveComputationalMethod* that decomposes retrieval in the following tasks:
    * *ObtainCasesTask* solved by *ObtainCaseBaseMethod* that returns the whole Case Base.
    * *ComputeSimilarityTask* solved by *NumericSimComputationMethod* that computes similarity between the query and the cases obtained by the previous task.
    * *SelectBestTask* solved by *SelectBestCaseMethod* that selects the most similar case.

Additionally to task/method selection, a number of method parameters have to be set. This may require to program supporting code to parameterize the methods, or, as is the case in this simple example, to associate available *CBRTerms* (i.e., classes) with certain parts of the configured system. In the example, the *NumericSimComputationMethod* requires similarity functions to be associated with the cases so that, for instance:

- *duration* is compared with the *intervalSim* function,
- *season* with a special purpose *seasonSim* function,
- *destination* is compared through *equalSim*, and
- the similarity of the *cbr_case* is obtained through *averageSim*.

5 Related Work

Related to PSMs and ontologies we should mention the work on Protégé. Protégé is an ontology and knowledge-base editor that provides an extensible architecture for the creation of customized knowledge-based applications [6]. They have developed a methodology to construct knowledge systems that strongly relies on ontologies. The work here presented is closely related to this approach and we envision an evolution of JColibri that should integrate with Protégé.

The IBROW project intends to provide an Internet-based brokering service for reusing problem-solving methods. The Unified Problem-Solving Method Description Language (UPML) [10] has been developed to describe and implement such architectures and components to facilitate their semi-automatic reuse and adaptation. The main drawback of UPML is that it is a highly sophisticated formal language whose complexity is not justified by supporting reasoning tools.

In the Machine Learning community we can mention a number of efforts directed to building reusable libraries of ML methods. MLC++ [15], developed at Stanford University by Ronny Kohavi, provides a library of C++ classes to aid in the development of new ML algorithms, especially hybrid algorithms and multi-strategy algorithms, providing implementations for ID3, nearest-neighbor, naive Bayes, lazy decision trees, etc. David Mount, from the University of Maryland has developed ANN [3], a library written in C++, which supports data structures and algorithms for both exact and approximate nearest neighbor searching in arbitrarily high dimensions. The machine learning group of the University of Waikato, New Zealand, has developed Weka [22] a public domain class library in Java that incorporates several standard ML techniques. Weka contains implementations of a number of algorithms for classification and numeric prediction. Weka also includes a number of data filtering techniques, and two clustering algorithms. In order to exploit these efforts from the ML community we plan to incorporate in JColibri interfaces to some of the aforementioned resources.

In the CBR community, the work by Michel Jaczynski [12, 13] is closely related to the one presented here. CBR*Tools is an object-oriented framework, implemented in Java, designed to facilitate the development of CBR applications. They identify the following axes of variability: the delegation of reasoning steps, the separation of case storage and case indexing, the design of indexes as reusable components, and the design of adaptation patterns. The framework concentrates mainly on indexing, providing a large number of indexing alternatives. The key difference of JColibri with respect to CBR*Tools is the explicit model of task/method decomposition that imposes a high level architecture on top of the framework, facilitating framework use and evolution. However, in a certain sense, in CBR*Tools the knowledge level is also *explicit* as a part of its

UML-based model. Besides, JColibri incorporates a GUI for alleviating framework instantiation effort that is based on their task/method description (at the knowledge level).

The architecture of Orenge (the Open Retrieval engine from empolis.com) [19] also is related to JColibri. Orenge has been designed as a component based platform. Building an application includes the selection and composition of required components. Its pipeline/pipelet structure is very similar to the PSMs paradigm. In the same way that JColibri, Orenge also provides access to databases and XML files. JColibri enhances Orenge regarding two aspects. First, the incorporation of DLs connection. And second, regarding availability, Orenge is a commercial system and it is not available for free. JColibri will be (soon) available to the CBR community as an open source project.

Also closely related to JColibri, Plaza an Arcos [18] proposed a generic architecture for adaptation that has evolved into CAT-CBR [2], a component-based platform for developing CBR systems. CAT-CBR uses UPML for specifying CBR components and provides: a library of CBR components (currently for retrieval and for classification; reuse components are being developed); a language and a graphical editor to specify new components and a syntax to implement their operational code; a broker service allowing to specify the requirements of a target CBR application and the available models in a domain, and to search for a configuration of components that satisfy the requirements. CAT-CBR generates the "glue code" that binds together the operational code of the configured components into a stand alone application. The main difference between JColibri and CAT-CBR is a technological one. CAT-CBR is developed on top of the Noos framework, a monolithic Lisp system that can not compete with a Java based approach in terms of usability, extendibility and user acceptance.

6 Conclusions

We have presented an object-oriented framework in Java to build CBR systems. This framework is built around a task/method ontology that facilitates the understanding of an intrinsically sophisticated software artifact. A key aspect of this work is the availability of a semiautomatic configuration tool that facilitates the instantiation process.

The framework implementation is evolving as new methods are included. We are already porting previously developed CBR systems into the framework and, once tested, will make it publicly available to the CBR community. Our (ambitious) goal is to provide a reference framework for CBR development that would grow with contributions from the community. This reference would serve for pedagogical purposes and as bottom line implementation for prototyping CBR systems and comparing different CBR approaches to a given problem.

References

1. A. Aamodt and E. Plaza. Case-based reasoning: Foundational issues, methodological variations, and system approaches. *AI Communications*, 7(i), 1994.

2. C. Abásolo, E. Plaza, and J.-L. Arcos. Components for case-based reasoning systems. *Lecture Notes in Computer Science*, 2504, 2002.
3. ANN. http://www.cs.umd.edu/ mount/ANN/.
4. J. A. Breuker and W. Van de Velde. *CommonKADS Library for Expertise Modelling: Reusable Problem Solving Components*. 1994.
5. B. Chandrasekaran, T. Johnson, and J. Smith. Task structure analysis for knowledge modeling. *Communications of the ACM*, 33(8):124–136, September 1992.
6. M. Crubézy and M. A. Musen. Ontologies in support of problem solving. In S. Staab and R. Studer, editors, *Handbook on Ontologies*. Springer, 2004.
7. B. Díaz-Agudo. *Una aproximación ontológica al desarrollo de sistemas de razonamiento basado en casos*. PhD thesis, Universidad Complutense de Madrid, 2002.
8. B. Díaz-Agudo and P. A. González-Calero. An architecture for knowledge intensive CBR systems. In E. Blanzieri and L. Portinale, editors, *Advances in Case-Based Reasoning – (EWCBR'00)*. Springer-Verlag, Berlin Heidelberg New York, 2000.
9. B. Díaz-Agudo and P. A. González-Calero. CBROnto: a task/method ontology for CBR. In S. Haller and G. Simmons, editors, *Procs. of the 15th International FLAIRS'02 Conference (Special Track on CBR*, pages 101–106. AAAI Press, 2002.
10. D. Fensel, E. Motta, F. van Harmelen, V. R. Benjamins, M. Crubezy, S. Decker, M. Gaspari, R. Groenboom, W. Grosso, M. Musen, E. Plaza, G. Schreiber, R. Studer, and B. Wielinga. The unified problem-solving method development language upml. *Knowledge and Information Systems*, 5(1):83–131, February 2003.
11. V. Haarslev and R. Möller. Description of the racer system and its applications. In *Working Notes of the 2001 International Description Logics Workshop (DL-2001), Stanford, CA, USA, August 1-3, 2001*, 2001.
12. M. Jaczynski. *Modèle et plate-forme à objets pour l'indexation des cas par situations comportementales: application à l'assistance à la navigation sur le Web*. PhD thesis, L'Université de Nice-Sophia Antipolis, 1998. http://www-sop.inria.fr/axis/papers/thesemj/.
13. M. Jaczynski and B. Trousse. An object-oriented framework for the design and the implementation of case-based reasoners. In *Proceedings of the 6th German Workshop on Case-Based Reasoning*, 1998.
14. R. Johnson and B. Foote. Designing reusable classes. *J. Object-Oriented Programming*, 1(5):22–35, 1988.
15. R. Kohavi, D. Sommerfield, and J. Dougherty. Data mining using MLC++: A machine learning library in C++. In *Tools with Artificial Intelligence*, pages 234–245. IEEE Computer Society Press, 1996. Received the best paper award.
16. M. D. McIlroy. Mass produced software components. In *Proc. Nato Software Eng. Conf.*, pages 138–155, Garmisch, Germany, 1968.
17. A. Newel. The knowledge level. *Artificial Intelligence*, 18:87–127, 1982.
18. E. Plaza and J. L. Arcos. Towards a software architecture for case-based reasoning systems. In *Foundations of Intelligent Systems, 12th International Symposium, ISMIS 2000*, pages 265–276. Springer-Verlag LNCS 1932, 2000.
19. J. Schumacher. empolis orenge – an open platform for knowledge management applications. In M. Minor and S. Staab, editors, *1st German Workshop on Experience Management: Sharing Experiences About the Sharing of Experience, Berlin, March 7-8, 2002, Proceedings*, pages 61–62. Gesellschaft für Informatik GI, 2002.
20. L. Steels. Components of expertise. *AI Magazine*, 11(2):29–49, 1990.
21. B. Wielinga, A. Schreiber, and J. Breuker. Kads: A modelling approach to knowledge engineering. *Knowledge Acquisition*, 4(1), 1992.
22. I. Witten and E. Frank. *Data mining: Practical machine learning tools and techniques with Java implementations*. Morgan Kaufmann, San Francisco, 2000.

Mémoire: Case Based Reasoning Meets the Semantic Web in Biology and Medicine

Isabelle Bichindaritz

University of Washington
1900 Commerce Street
Tacoma, WA 98402, USA
ibichind@u.washington.edu
http://faculty.washington.edu/ibichind

Abstract. Mémoire is a framework for the sharing and distribution of case bases and case based reasoning in biology and medicine. Based on the fact that semantics account for the success of biomedical case based reasoning systems, this paper defends the suitability of a semantic approach similar to the semantic Web for sharing and distributing case bases and case based reasoning in biology and medicine. Mémoire will permit to bridge the gap between the multiple case based reasoning systems dedicated to a single domain, and make available to agents and Web services on the Web the case based competency of the CBR systems adopting its interchange language. This paper presents the components of Mémoire for the representation of cases, case structure, and case based ontologies in biology and medicine. The approach could be extended to other application domains of CBR.

1 Introduction

The semantic Web has been defined as "an extension of the current web in which information is given well-defined meaning, better enabling computers and people to work in cooperation." [1]. The semantic Web is typically described as a framework for spreading and distributing information/data, information/data structures, and information/data about articulation between ontologies. In this article, we hypothesize that the same approach would enable the distribution of cases, case structures, and information/data about articulation between the ontologies comprising these cases. As a matter of fact, the semantic Web is an endeavor to introduce semantics and semantic interpretation in Web documents and data. Taking as examples several case based reasoning (CBR) systems in biology and medicine, it becomes obvious that a semantic approach is required to understand and reuse cases well, and that in order to build shared, distributed case bases, the approach of the semantic Web is a good model to apply to the task of building large, shared case bases in medicine and biology. This paper introduces the Mémoire project, as a framework for the sharing of case bases and distributed case based reasoning in biology and medicine.

In the second section, we will introduce the reader to the semantic Web, then to the semantic Web current work in biology and medicine. The fourth section explains how biomedical case based reasoning makes use of semantics. The fifth section presents the Mémoire system, which is essentially a framework for sharing case bases in biology and medicine. It is followed by a discussion and the conclusion.

2 Semantic Web

The goal of the semantic Web spans beyond pure information retrieval purposes: "The Semantic Web is a vision: the idea of having data on the Web defined and linked in a way that it can be used by machines not just for display purposes, but for automation, integration and reuse of data across various applications" [6]. It is to reuse information and data available on the Web with all the word *reuse* can encompass. This implies reasoning from information and data on the Web, such as cases.

The semantic Web currently has three main components:

1. **Information/data in HTML or better XML format.** XML is a common language to represent Web content, and using it facilitates integration of We documents from different sources, in particular via XSLT transformation language. Nevertheless, the meaning of the different tags across applications is not provided in XML, so that another layer needs to provide that semantic mapping.
2. **Information/data structures in a semantic Web format such as RDF.** Resource Description Framework (RDF) [14] provides this mapping between different XML or database schemas. Information in RDF can be simply merged from different Web sources and queried as though they came from a single source. RDF permits to describe not only the data, but rules to interpret the data.
3. **Information/data about articulation between ontologies.** Extensions of RDF such as RDF-schema, or Web ontology language, such as DAML [7] and OWL [13], permit to represent ontologies of terms (thesauri) and concepts in hierarchies expressing how these terms relate to one another.

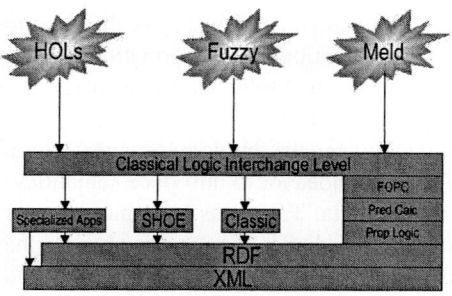

DAML and the "Semantic Web"

Fig. 1. DAML and the Semantic Web

Semantic Web framework enables so called Web services and agents to get information/data from different sources, interpret and integrate them seamlessly. Thus the goal is to foster the development of intelligent applications that can handle and reason from distributed data and information on the Web. A Web service is a server application available to users on the Web, often being other Web services, to accept a query in a semantic Web language, and to return results in the same language. Examples of Web services to integrate for company A might be: Purchasing parts from a vendor company B, Shipping from a large freight company C, and Providing space availability from the different plants in company A. Integrating these three Web services together will permit to answer a question such as a salesman in company A entering an order, and the orchestration of the other services providing the solution as the supply chain at work [11], and a complete delivery plan to the right plants of company A.

Ultimate ambition of the Semantic Web as a framework enabling software agents to interrogate, interoperate, and dynamically discover information and knowledge resources requires the explicit representation of the semantics associated to these resources. Examples of semantics are explanations about what this resource information/data/knowledge is *about*, and what it is *for* [9]. Specific languages and technologies have been developed for that purpose of representing and reasoning at a semantic level, such as first RDF [14], then DAML+OIL [7], and now OWL [13]. A Unique Resource Identifier (URI) identifies each concept/resource on the Web.

DAML (see Fig.1 and Table 1) and other XML/RDF-type systems such as a draft standard of the Joint Intelligence Virtual Architecture (JIVA) and topic maps promise to keep a record and capture semantic information better than is currently possible using Natural Language Processing (NLP) systems. DAML language has risen as a dominant ontology language for capturing distributed domain knowledge. DAML-OIL has been officially submitted to he World Wide Web Consortium (W3) in 2001, and accepted as a standard in 2002 under the name OWL, then as recommendation for Web Ontology Language on February 10th, 2004.

Table 1. Index of all DAML language elements

Cardinality	hasClass	Range
Class	hasValue	Restriction
ComplementOf	imports	sameClassAs
Datatype	intersectionOf	sameIndividualAs
DatatypeProperty	inverseOf	samePropertyAs
DatatypeRestriction	ObjectClass	subClassOf
Datatype value	ObjectProperty	subPropertyOf
DifferentIndividualFrom	ObjectRestriction	toClass
DisjointUnionOf	oneOf	TransitiveProperty
DisjointWith	onProperty	UnambigousProperty
Domain	Ontology	unionOf
EquivalentTo	Property	UniqueProperty

Many efforts in different communities, mostly in connection with artificial intelligence, have chosen DAML and OWL to represent their ontologies and semantic networks, for example in medicine in biology.

3 Semantic Web in Biology and Medicine

Since building semantic systems is a very ambitious task, we focus in this article on case bases and case based reasoning in biology and medicine, which is already a consequent domain. Another characteristic of this domain is that it is well studied and formalized, as is presented in this section, such that it is not acceptable in this domain to ignore past efforts in standardization, as is acceptable in most other application domains. Indeed biomedical informatics is now a well-established academic discipline, better equipped than most others to transition into the semantic Web.

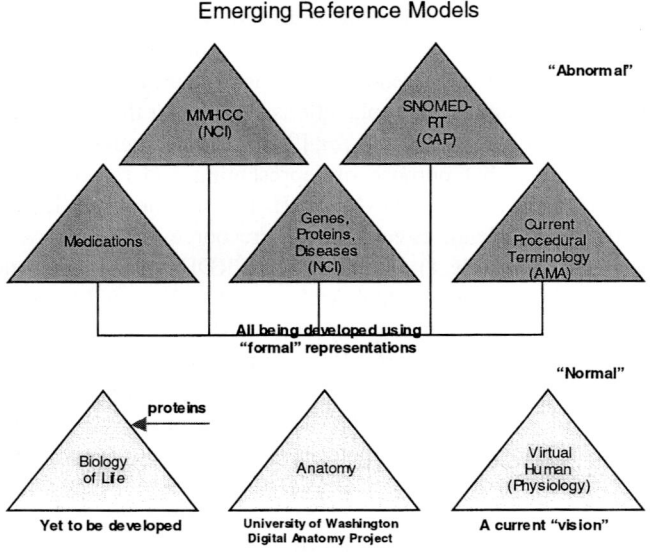

Fig. 2. Emerging Reference Terminologies in Biomedicine [16]

The advantage of biomedicine is that it has several standard terminologies to build on (see Fig. 2) [16]:

o Terminology servers, such as National Cancer Institute's Enterprise Vocabulary Server (EVS).
o GCPRMedications reference terminology defining for each drug its chemical structure class, mechanism of action, and therapeutic use.
o Mouse Models of Human Cancer Consortium (MMHCC) from the National Cancer Institute (NCI) describing detailed diagnostic terminologies for eight organ sites in mice, as a model for same sites in humans.
o Genes, proteins, diseases from NCI modeling 250 genes associated with cancer.
o Systematic Nomenclature of Medicine (SNOMED) from the College of American Pathologists (CAP), describing accepted terms of most diseases, symptoms, medications, and organisms.
o Current Procedural Terminology (CPT) 5 from the American Medical Association (AMA) for procedure codes.

A common characteristic of these projects is that they use a Description-Logic based representation [16]. Other reference terminologies are being developed for vertebrate anatomy, and human physiology.

Thus the effort of developing an ontology for biomedicine is well underway, and there are even efforts for the sharing of terminologies across subdomains. For example, HL7 [12] is a proposed standard for exchanging semantic messages in healthcare, and builds on the terminologies presented above. Another effort is the Unified Medical Language System (UMLS) [17] of the National Library of Medicine (NLM) that comprises a metathesaurus for bridging the gap between different terminologies, describing medical concepts with a unique identifier, similar to the semantic Web URI, their synonyms in different classifications and common usage, and a semantic network organizing these concepts through 54 relationships.

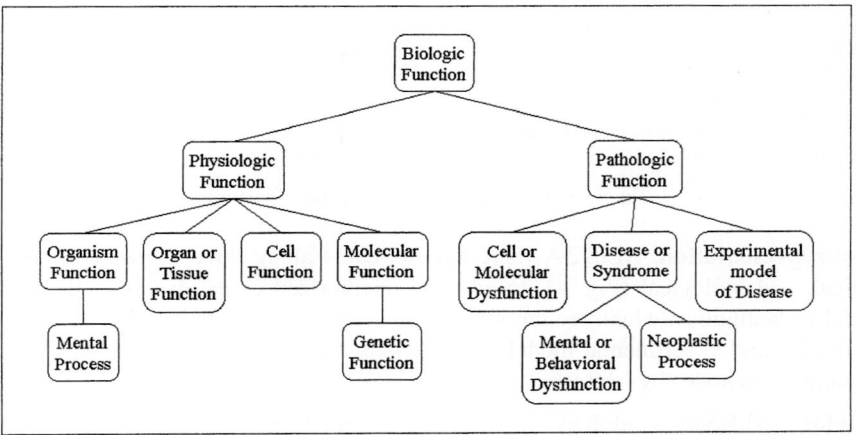

Fig. 3. A portion of the UMLS semantic network [17]

Nevertheless, the integration of these biomedical ontologies in the semantic Web is still to be performed, by adopting OWL as a representation language, or writing OWL mappings of UMLS, HL7, and others. [5] uses the semantic Web for querying multiple bioinformatics data sources, and [15] for connecting several distributed ontologies.

4 Semantics and Case Based Reasoning in Biology and Medicine

Case based reasoning systems in medicine generally do not comprise only patient cases. They resort to domain models at several steps of their reasoning process. These domain models are ontologies of a sub domain of medicine and/or biology. This section describes three such case based reasoning systems in biomedicine, focusing on their case representation, and ontologies. These systems have been successive implementations of the same concept of a case based reasoning system in biomedicine, and thus can be seen each as an improvement from the previous one.

4.1 ALEXIA

Presentation. ALEXIA[2] is case based problem solver. As usual case based systems, it uses an indexed memory of previously solved cases to propose a solving strategy for a new problem. However, since the application domain is the determination of a patient's hypertension etiology, the classical memory indexation architecture has been enriched with a meta-indexation level to estimate the most probable diagnosis by saturation of a causal physiopathological model. Moreover, the dependency relations expressed through the causal model provide a functional point of view that does objectivate the selection of the best analogous.

```
Mr. MARTIN :
     INTAKE            CLINICAL
length-AHT : 6              arterial-tension : (152 118)
gender : male               pulse : 80
resistance-AHT : present vascular-murmur : present
age : 50                            peripheral-pulse : present
observ-problem : absent     BIOLOGICAL
asthenia : present          creatininemia : 99
smoking : present           kaliemia : 2.8
anti-AHT-treatment: present natremia : 145
sport : absent              bicarbonatemia : 31.0
```

Fig. 4. ALEXIA's case representation (partial)

Case representation. ALEXIA represents its cases along three dimensions: intake, clinical, and biological (Fig. 4). In addition, memorized cases also store theoretical model instantiations, which are the values induced by the qualitative physiopathological model, and experimental model instantiations, which are the values measured for the same deep nodes by lab tests.

Ontology. ALEXIA's ontology is a set of classes and rules associated with the classes in frames. It comprises 20 nodes representing the main hormones regulating arterial tension (Fig. 5), 20 signs and symptoms, 111 observations, 31 complementary exams, and 26 edges.

Results. ALEXIA was tested on 18 new cases selected by the clinician as a good test sample because it contained both 'easy' cases, and 'difficult' ones. The 'difficult' cases were the ones that failed either a bayesian network, or an expert system, both tested on the same dataset. The original memory stored only 8 solved cases, equitably representing the three main etiologies: Conn adenoma, renal artery stenosis, and pheochromocytoma, as well as the etiology by default: essential AHT. ALEXIA solved satisfactorily all 18 cases, with a single iteration of its reasoning process, even for essential AHT. The exceptionally good results of the system were attributed to the combination of the knowledge-based approach of its physiopathological model, and the numeric approach of its case based reasoning.

4.2 MNOMIA

Presentation. MNAOMIA is a case based reasoning system providing assistance to clinical staff in psychiatry eating disorders for diagnosis, treatment, and research hypothesis recommendation [3]. Thus it is a system capable of adapting to different cognitive tasks, both analytical, such as diagnosis, and synthetic, such as research hypothesis recommendation. The memory model of the system comprises both an experimental and a theoretical memory, expressed in a unified knowledge representation language, and organization. The components of the memory are cases and concepts, in the experimental part, and prototypes and models, in the theoretical part. The reasoning supported by this memory model can be various, and takes advantage of all the components, whether experimental or theoretical. It is strongly constrained by some specialized models in theoretical memory, called the points of view.

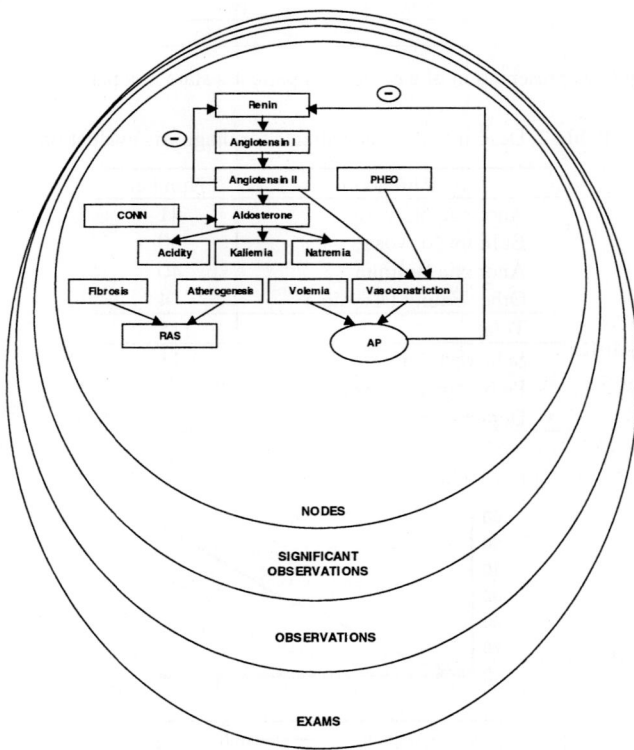

Fig. 5. ALEXIA's causal physiopathological model

Case representation. MNAOMIA represents its cases along several dimensions, namely general, behavioral, somatic, psychic, and biological (Fig. 6).

Ontology. MNAOMIA's ontology contains diagnostic category prototypes, as described in psychiatry nomenclature, normal subject prototypes, and average subject prototypes, a domain model about foods, and prototypical treatment plans. Other models are the points of view. Since the system can adapt to several cognitive tasks, its memories structures the information though several points of view, such as biological symptomatology point of view, or cognitive task point of view.

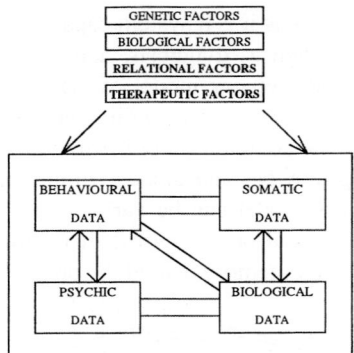

Fig. 6. Representation of a contextual patient's state in a patient's case

Table 2. Description of the patients for diagnosis evaluation

Patients	Number
Anorexia Nervosa	41
Bulimia Nervosa	30
Anorexia Bulimia	40
Other Eating Disorders	4
Total	115
Schizophrenia	13
Pathological Personality	43
Depression	3

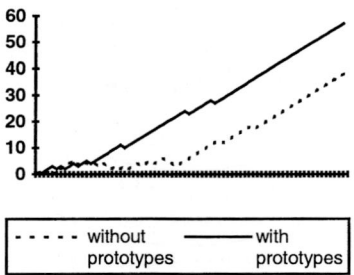

Fig. 7. Accuracy of diagnosis (each ascending line between two X-axis points is a diagnosis success, and each descending line a failure)

Results. MNAOMIA's performance was evaluated on diagnosis evaluation task. Results are given here for the diagnosis at patients' admission. The accuracy of the diagnosis has been compared with that of the clinical staff after several weeks of hospital care. Table 2 describes the patients' population, and Figure 7 shows the results for the first 60 cases processed. The diagnosis accuracy is about 80% for the first 30 cases, and about 95% from the 30th case to the 115th. It is compared with the results of the same diagnosis process performed only with the data of the food questionnaires of the patients, for which no prototype is available. The results after the 30th case are about the same (93% accuracy), but are very different for the first 30 cases. The advantage of the prototypes in theoretical memory is here obvious at least at the beginning of the reasoning process. These results show that in this domain also, although being much less formalization prone than hypertension, an ontology modeling the domain through prototypes and models, even partial, is indeed advantageous for case based reasoning.

4.3 CARE PARTNER

Presentation. CARE-PARTNER is a computerized decision-support system on the World-Wide Web (WWW) [4]. It is applied to the long-term follow-up (LTFU) of patients having undergone a stem-cell transplant (SCT) at the Fred Hutchinson Cancer Research Center (FHCRC) in Seattle, after their return in their home community. Home care providers use CARE-PARTNER to place contacts with LTFU on the Internet, and receive from the system decision-support advice in a timely manner for transplant patients follow-up. An essential characteristic of CARE-PARTNER is that it proposes to implement evidence-based medical practice by applying clinical guidelines developed by FHCRC for the care of their patients.

Case representation. CARE PARTNER cases are represented in an electronic medical patient record, along several dimensions, namely flowsheet, problems, contacts, demographics, pre transplant, day 80 workup, Graft Versus Host Disease (GVHD), medications, labs, reports, protocols, and risks.

Ontology. CARE-PARTNER resorts to a multimodal reasoning framework for the cooperation of case-based reasoning (CBR) and rule-based reasoning. The system's memory here also comprises both patient cases, and a theoretical memory, or ontology. The ontology of the system contains the description of 1109 diseases, 452 signs and symptoms, 1152 labs, 547 procedures, 2684 medications, and 460 sites expressed in SNOMED classification. Notable in this system are 91 prototypes, mainly associated with diagnostic categories, such as liver chronic GCHD (Fig. 8), and called clinical pathways.

Results. A sample evaluation of CARE-PARTNER decision-support performance has been performed by team statisticians, and is provided in Table 3. On 163 different clinical situations or cases, corresponding to contacts between the system and a clinician about three patients, the system was rated 82.2% as *Meets all standards*, and 12.3% as *Adequate*, for a total of 94.5% of results judged clinically acceptable by the medical experts. Table 1 also shows that the advice provided by the system covers most of the clinicians' tasks: labs and procedure results interpretation, diagnosis assessment plan, treatment plan, and pathways information retrieval. Pathways represent prototypical cases retrieved by the system, and correspond to diagnostic categories (see Fig. 8 for an example). Important in this system is the evolution of the competency of the system over time, reaching 98.6% *Meets all standards/Adequate* for patient 3 for all his 54 contacts.

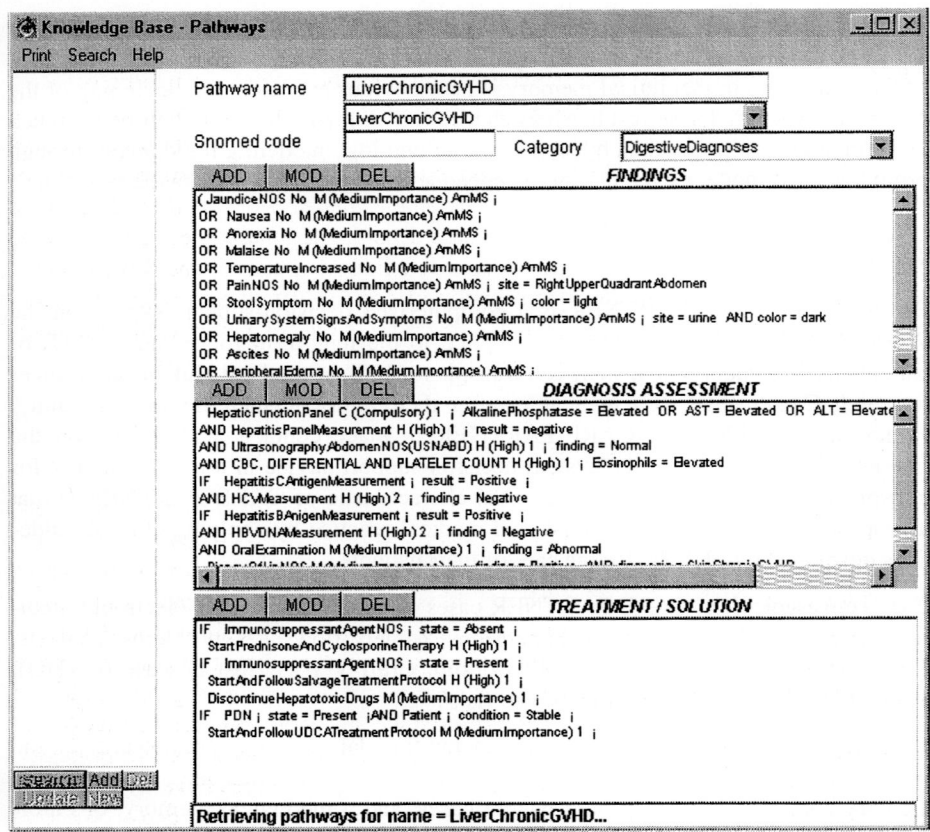

Fig. 8. Example of a LiverChronicGVHD clinical pathway

Table 3. CARE-PARTNER evaluation Form Inter-Rater Agreement and Summary Ratings for Two Raters over Three Patients

	Applicable Cases			Concordant Cases			
	Number	Percent Agreement Rating	Kappa coefficient of agreement	Number	Fails to meet standards	Adequate	Meets all standards
Labs	57	94.7	.71	54	3.7%	3.7%	92.6%
Procedures	70	95.7	.83	67	8.9%	3.0%	88.1%
Diagnosis	79	86.1	.74	68	16.2%	13.2%	70.6%
Treatment	77	92.2	.81	71	9.9%	11.3%	78.8%
Pathways	53	88.6	.71	47	8.5%	8.5%	83.0%
Overall Appreciation	178	91.6	.77	163	5.5%	12.3%	82.2%

4.4 Semantics in Biomedical CBR

All these systems show the importance of biomedical ontologies for interpretation of the data, thus proving the importance of a semantic approach in biomedical CBR applications. They also demonstrate the variety of knowledge to represent, mainly models, such as qualitative models, and prototypes to represent typical signs and symptoms, diagnostic evaluation plans, and treatment plans, associated with domain dependent diagnostic categories. Without these deep domain ontologies, these systems would not have been able to perform acceptable clinical assistance, and this finding is coherent with the improvement in the quality of care measured as a result of better, evidence-based formalization of medicine, fostering the development of the biomedical ontologies listed in the previous section.

5 Mémoire Framework

Case based reasoning systems in medicine have so far been developed as standalone systems. With that regard, they have kept away from the efforts to share and connect biomedical information and knowledge bases. One of the main reasons is that cases are patient identifiable data. Legislation about patient data requires institutional agreement to access, use, and transmit such data, making it difficult to consider transmitting these case bases between institutions, except in the context of consortiums of institutions, of which many examples exist such as the VA, or for large-scale clinical trials. Non patient identifiable data are restricted just the same, because institution are protective of their data as their assets for research and funding purposes. Nevertheless, single institutions may want to connect distributed CBR systems developed in their institution, for example connecting the three CBR systems presented above, where a patient may combine diseases from hypertension domain, eating disorders, and require stem cell transplantation, and a biomedical literature retrieval system through a terminology server. Also, it will be advantageous to develop CBR systems as Web services in the future, to receive patient input data from the Internet, securely, to process them against several CBR systems, combine with non-CBR systems, and give back a consolidated result from several sources. In this scenario, patients data would not have to be shared among institution, but only the system recommendations would be shared. Patients may want to query themselves these services, for alternate recommendations. Another reason would be to exchange CBR systems ontologies, as models and prototypes. Since prototypes are often processed as regular cases, then the problem of exchanging them will have to be solved in the same way as for real patient cases. In addition, advance in information assurance, such as trust agents, will even enable secure sharing of patient specific data [8, 16].

For all these reasons, the Mémoire project proposes a framework for the exchange of biomedical cases and related ontologies in the semantic Web, based on OWL ontology language. The choice of OWL, since it has been adopted as a recommendation by w3c, will provide a language format allowing for easy WWW integration, and is integrated in a common framework for connected applications on the WWW. Mémoire framework should also satisfy the following requirements [10]:

(1) The language should allow for easy extensibility since knowledge can be added iteratively.
(2) The language should be applicable to several biomedical domains.
(3) The language should support distributed, physically remote, maintenance of ontologies and cases.
(4) The language should allow for the representation of complex, non-hierarchical knowledge structures.
(5) The language should allow to distinguish between generic (IS-A) and partitive (PART-OF) relations.

OWL is a language providing a syntax and formal semantics that extend RDF, thus one way of writing an ontology in OWL is to code it in RDF/RDFS framework, which is what Mémoire has chosen to do because it is a generic representation language taking the intrinsic structuring capabilities of XML. In addition, OWL provides for three levels of semantic representation: OWL Lite, OWL DL, and OWL Full. OWL DL is both more expressive than Lite, and more strict than Full, such that it can be interpreted non-ambiguously.

OWL syntax defines the following elements:

- **Namespaces** indicate the vocabularies used, with their URIs, for example mem in Fig. 9 is defined inside in an opening rdf:RDF tag.
- **Ontologies** in owl:Ontology tags support the *annotations* associated with ontologies, such as comments, version control, and inclusion of other ontologies.
- **Data aggregation and privacy** is enabled by the presence of relationships such as owl:sameAs that permit to automatically infer properties from one element as they relate to another one, or to extend a previously defined element, thus satisfying our criteria (1) and (3).
- **Classes, properties, instances of classes, relationships between classes and instances** permit to define such classes as Case, Prototype for our prototypical cases, and Model and Concept for our CBR in Biology and Medicine domain. These classes are subclasses of owl:Class, but some domain specific classes, such as mem:Food are already defined in owl as an ontology of foods has already been defined, so that many domain specific objects have been defined, such as owl:Pasta, owl:Dessert, and so forth. Still, Mémoire has defined most of the classes from the ontologies of ALEXIA, MNAOMIA, and CARE PARTNER defined above. Cases are represented as instances of owl:Case. We can specialize this class in the future to accommodate different case representations, although we have defined a case structure, using the part-of relationship for different domains (<owl:inverseOf rdf:resource="#isPartOf"/>). OWL has been found suitable to answer the requirements (2), (4), and (5) listed above.

One limitation found so far in both OWL DL and OWL Full is that they do not support rules explicitly. DAML has RuleML to representation propositional logic rules, and since OWL builds from DAML, it can certainly reuse this representation. This is why we have coded rules with RuleML in Mémoire. Several proposals have been set forth for OWL first order logic rules, and we will adapt our chosen representation to these once one becomes a standard. Mémoire can reuse OWL ontologies already de-

```xml
<?xml version="1.0"?>
<rdf:RDF
xmlns:owl = "http://www.w3.org/2002/07/owl#"
xmlns:rdf = "http://www.w3.org/1999/02/22-rdf-syntax-ns#"
xmlns:rdfs= "http://www.w3.org/2000/01/rdf-schema#">
xmlns:mem=
"http://semantic.insttech.washington.edu/memoire/owl#">
<owl:Ontology rdf:about="">
<rdfs:comment>
Case Based Reasoning in Biology and Medicine ontology
</rdfs:comment>
</owl:Ontology>
<owl:Class rdf:ID="Prototype"
<rdf:subClassOf rdf:resource="#Class" />
</owl:Class>
<owl:Class rdf:ID="Case">
<owl:subClassOf mem:resource="#Prototype" />
<owl:disjointWith rdf:resource="#Concept" />
</owl:Class>
<owl:Class rdf:ID="Model">
<rdfs:subClassOf rdf:resource="#Class" />
</owl:Class>
<owl:Class rdf:ID="Concept">
<rdfs:subClassOf mem:resource="#Model" />
<owl:disjointWith rdf:resource="#Case" />
</owl:Class>
```

Fig. 9. Directed Labeled Graph representation of biomedical CBR domain

fined in biology and medicine, in particular an ontology of change [16], since medical and biological classifications change constantly, or easily translate those that were defined in DAML.

OWL semantics defines in addition:

- **Axioms** are used to associate class and property identifiers with specifications being either partial or complete, or additional specifications such as restrictions. For instance, it is possible to define a class as a set of instances, which is interesting for CBR. These additional specifications are particularly pertinent in biomedical domains where ontologies provide standards about classes and their properties. Examples of property axioms are: Symmetric, Transitive, Functional, InverseFunctional, which were added for a biomedical application before OWL [10].
- **Facts** are used to represent instanciations of class, for instance real patient cases from the mem:Case class.

6 Discussion

Although the evaluation of the framework has been so far limited to ALEXIA, MANOMIA, and CARE-PARTNER, a next step in this research will be to refine Mémoire framework to represent cases and case bases from other CBR systems in biology and medicine. The success of this work will permit to leverage the development of CBR systems in biology and medicine. First of all, by the definition of a common representation language for CBR cases, it will become possible to develop Web services and agents to federate the CBR process across several domains of medicine, patients often presenting mixed sets of symptoms. This work will permit the reuse of CBR systems outside of their domain of development, and to give them the formalization required for interacting with non-CBR systems, so that the whole is more than the parts. It will also provide the basis for developing a CBR shell for rapid development of CBR systems in biology and medicine. Another advantage of having this formalized interchange format is to enable to seamlessly integrate case based reasoning and information retrieval in biology and medicine.

7 Conclusion

The ability to exchange case bases and their ontologies will permit to link not only biomedical CBR systems with one another, but with other intelligent and information retrieval systems. The perspective of unlimited cooperation between these systems is extremely promising for the improvement of healthcare and biomedical research, as the whole is more than the concatenation of the parts: "Human endeavor is caught in an eternal tension between the effectiveness of small groups acting independently and the need to mesh with the wider community... The Semantic Web, in naming every concept simply by a URI, lets anyone express new concepts that they invent with minimal effort. Its unifying logical language will enable these concepts to be progressively linked into a universal Web. This structure will open up the knowledge and workings of humankind to meaningful analysis by software agents, providing a new class of tools by which we can live, work and learn together" [1].

References

1. Berners-Lee, T., Hendler, J., Lassila, D.: The Semantic Web. Scientific American. May (2001)
2. Bichindaritz, I., Séroussi, B.: Contraindre l'Analogie par la Causalité. Technique et Sciences Informatiques. Vol. **11**, N. **4** (1992) 69-98
3. Bichindaritz, I.: Case-Based Reasoning adaptive to several cognitive tasks. In: Aamodt A., Veloso M. (eds): International Conference on Case-Based Reasoning. Lecture Notes in Artificial Intelligence, Vol. 1010. Springer-Verlag, Berlin Heidelberg, New York (1995) 391-400
4. Bichindaritz, I., Kansu E., Sullivan K.M.: Case-Based Reasoning in CARE-PARTNER: Gathering Evidence for Evidence-Based Medical Practice. In: European Workshop on Case-Based Reasoning. Lectures Notes in Artificial Intelligence. Vol. 1488. Springer-Verlag, Berlin Heidelberg, New York (1998) 334-345
5. Buttler, D., Coleman, M., Critchlow, T., Fileto, R., Han, W., Liu, L., Pu, C., Rocco, D., Xiong, L.: Querying Multiple Bioinformatics Information Sources: Can Semantic Web Research Help? In: Meersman, R., Sheth, A. (eds.): Special Issue on Semantic Web and Data Management. SIGMOD Record. Vol. 31, **4** (2002) 59-64

6. Cruz, I.F., Decker, S., Euzenat, J., McGuinness, D.: Foreword. In: Cruz, I.F., Secker, S., Euzenat, J., McGuinness, D. (eds.): First Semantic Web Working Symposium. Stanford (2001) 1
7. Darpa Agent Markup Language (DAML). http://www.daml.org
8. Finin, T., Joshi, A.: Agents, Trust, and Information Access on the Semantic Web. In: Meersman, R., Sheth, A. (eds.): Special Issue on Semantic Web and Data Management. SIGMOD Record. Vol. **31**, Issue **4** (2002) 34-38
9. Goble, C., De Roure, D. The Grid: An Application of the Semantic Web. In: Meersman, R., Sheth, A. (eds.): Special Issue on Semantic Web and Data Management. SIGMOD Record. Vol. **31**, Issue **4** (2002) 65-70
10. Grütter, R., Eikemeier, C.: Development of a Simple Ontology Definition Language (SontoDL) and Its Application to a Medical Information Service on the World Wide Web. In: Cruz, I.F., Secker, S., Euzenat, J., McGuinness, D. (eds.): First Semantic Web Working Symposium. (2001) 587-597
11. Hendler, J., Berners-Lee, T., Miller, E.: Integrating Applications on the Semantic Web. Journal of the Institute of Electrical Engineers of Japan. Vol **122**(10) (2002) 676-680
12. HL7: http://www.hl7.org
13. OWL Web Ontology Language: http://www.w3.org/OWL
14. Resource Description Framework (RDF): http://www.w3.org/RDF
15. Staab, S.: The Semantic Web – New Ways to Present and Integrate Information. Comparative and Functional Genomics. 4(1), Jan/Feb (2003) 98-103
16. Tuttle, M.S., Brown, S.H., Campbell, K.E., Carter, J.S., Keck, K.D., Lincoln, M., Nelson, S.J., Stonebraker, M.: The Semantic Web as "Perfection Seeking:" A View from Drug Terminology. In: Cruz, I.F., Secker, S., Euzenat, J., McGuinness, D. (eds.): First Semantic Web Working Symposium. Stanford (2001) 5-16
17. Unified Medical Language System (UMLS): http://www.nlm.nih.gov/research/umls

Facilitating CBR for Incompletely-Described Cases: Distance Metrics for Partial Problem Descriptions*

Steven Bogaerts and David Leake

Computer Science Department, Indiana University, Lindley Hall 215
150 S. Woodlawn Avenue, Bloomington, IN 47405, USA
{sbogaert,leake}@cs.indiana.edu

Abstract. A fundamental problem for case-based reasoning systems is how to select relevant prior cases. Numerous strategies have been developed for determining the similarity of prior cases, given full descriptions of the problem at hand, and situation assessment methods have been developed for formulating appropriate initial case descriptions. However, in real-world applications, attempting to determine all relevant features of a new problem before retrieval may be impractical or impossible. Consequently, how to guide retrieval based on partial problem descriptions is an important question for CBR. This paper examines the problem of assessing similarity in partially-described cases. It proposes a set of similarity assessment strategies for handling missing information, evaluates their performance and efficiency on sample data sets, and discusses their tradeoffs.

1 Introduction

Case-based reasoning (CBR) systems solve new problems by retrieving cases capturing the solutions of similar prior problems, and adapting their solutions to fit new needs. Determining the most relevant prior cases is a fundamental issue for CBR systems, and may require special methods when a full case description is not immediately available. For example, in a common applied CBR approach, *conversational CBR* (CCBR) (Aha & Breslow 1997), users build up a problem description by successively answering questions, as the system incrementally ranks candidate cases and questions based on the partial information available. The more accurate the distance measure used in this process, the more quickly the system will be able to point the user to the most applicable cases. Likewise, the ability to rank cases based on partial information may be essential when feature values are costly to determine or simply unavailable. Thus an important issue for CBR is how to assess the similarity of *partial problem descriptions* – problems with incomplete feature descriptions.

Considerable attention has been devoted to the process of refining initial problem descriptions through situation assessment (Kolodner 1993), and handling incomplete problem descriptions is a fundamental problem for CCBR. In diagnostic tasks, for example, only a partial set of features may initially be available. Consequently, every CCBR system includes methods for handling incrementally-built case descriptions,

---

* This material is based upon work supported by NASA under award No NCC 2-1216 and by the U.S. Department of the Navy, NSWC Crane Division, under contracts N00164-04-C-6514 and N00164-04-C-6515.

and research has addressed the problem of deciding which features to request when elaborating a partially-described case during CCBR (e.g., (Carrick *et al.* 1999)). However, comparatively little attention has been given to examining alternative similarity assessment methods for cases with missing features. A better understanding of the performance of alternative strategies, their tradeoffs, and their applicability, could enable more effective retrieval of partially-described cases and could also provide useful information for guiding the CCBR process. Because cases in the case base may themselves have partial descriptions, understanding how to handle partial descriptions could also be valuable for case base maintenance (Leake *et al.* 2001), to determine when and how to augment partial descriptions of stored cases.

This paper first discusses general issues affecting similarity judgments for partially-described cases. It then examines a set of similarity assessment strategies, including two simple baseline strategies and two more complex strategies designed to take advantage of information offered by the case base to predict feature values. The strategies apply to feature-vector representations for any ordinal features, i.e., features whose values belong to an ordered set; these may be numeric, or may belong to other categories provided that notions of distance and average can be defined (e.g., for a finite set, the "average" might be determined by a vote). The first method, *Default Difference*, is a baseline method which simply assigns a fixed default distance whenever the values of one or both features are missing (e.g., if this distance is 0, missing features are assumed to match perfectly). The remaining methods use additional information extracted from the case base as a whole: *Full Mean*, another baseline, treats each missing value as if it were the mean feature value. *NN Mean* takes a similar approach, but relies on local information, using the mean values of "near-by" cases. A drawback of *NN Mean* is its increased expense to compute the predicted feature value, which can be extreme when many cases must be compared to the current situation. *Region Mean* addresses this problem by generating a case base of prototypical cases, providing a local approximation to use to predict missing features without additional computation. Finally, we consider the use of composite methods involving combinations of these strategies. An experimental evaluation compares (1) the ability of each method to select the most similar cases, for differing levels of partial information – which reflects the number of questions that must be answered for a CCBR system to achieve a desired level of accuracy, (2) their efficiency at providing their information, and (3) the potential benefit of combined strategies. After comparing these performance issues, we develop general hypotheses for the applicability of the methods and their tradeoffs.

1.1 Handling Unknown Features

A simple example illustrates the subtlety of handling unknown features. Consider a domain in which cases are described by a feature vector of four features, $[f_1, f_2, f_3, f_4]$, and for which the system must solve a problem p, for which only the values of the first three are known: $[5.0, 6.0, 7.0, -]$. Let $distance(p_1, p_2)$ denote the distance between two problems p_1 and p_2. Suppose that the case base contains two cases, c_1, described by $[5.1, 6.0, -, -]$ and c_2, described by $[5.0, -, -, -]$. Note that in the following, we will use the name of the case as a shorthand for referring to the problem it solves.

In order to select the right case, the system must predict whether $distance(p, c_1)$ or $distance(p, c_2)$ is smaller. More features of c_1 are known than c_2; this guarantees that $c_1[1]$ has no difference from $p[1]$, and $c_1[0]$ has an apparently small difference from $p[0]$. However, c_2 might be more promising. Because $c_2[0]$ has no difference from $p[0]$, the potential minimum difference between c_2 and p is smaller, even though selecting c_2 entails more risk, due to possible differences in the unknown features. Likewise, a difference of 0.1 between $p[0]$ and $c_1[0]$ *could* be important, and perhaps even so significant that the exact match on feature 1 is inconsequential. Thus determining how to treat missing features depends on both (1) the importance of known differences and (2) the potential importance of unknown features, given their likely values and the user's tolerance for the level of uncertainty that they entail for the quality of results.

Even the selection of quality measure may involve subtle considerations. For example, possible quality measures could include *rank quality*, which measures how close the top-ranked cases are to the actual best match, or – if the specific values of the predicted distances are important – the *error* in the distance prediction. For example, error might be important in medical domains, if a differential diagnosis accepts a diagnosis when it appears sufficiently superior to its competitors. Error may also be important when the system provides the user with distance estimates to help guide the choice of cases to examine.

2 Strategies for Handling Unspecified Features

For any particular domain, domain knowledge may suggest specific assumptions or strategies for handling partially-described problems. Here we examine simple domain-independent strategies for assigning distances between pairs of corresponding features, within the framework of the standard distance function:

$$distance(r_1, r_2) = \sqrt{\sum_i w_i [d(r_1[i], r_2[i])]^2}$$

If F_i represents the set of possible feature values for the ith feature, including a value used to designate unknown features, these are functions $d_i : F_i \times F_i \to [0, \infty)$.

2.1 Default Difference(x)

A simple baseline strategy is to treat the distances between unknown features as zero. This corresponds to a typical strategy of considering only differences in known features. This approach can be generalized to assign a fixed default difference, x, whenever either feature is unknown. *Default Difference(x)*, the corresponding similarity assessment strategy, is defined as:

$$d_i(r_1[i], r_2[i]) = \begin{cases} x & r_1[i] \text{ and/or } r_2[i] \text{ unknown} \\ |r_1[i] - r_2[i]| & \text{otherwise} \end{cases}$$

Default Difference with x equal to 0 can be seen as an "optimistic" measure. When x equals 0, a completely unknown problem has distance 0 from all cases; this might be considered appropriate because every case is potentially a perfect match. Alternatively, if the maximum possible feature distances are bounded and equal across all features, setting x to the maximal possible difference corresponds to a "pessimistic" measure.

This simple metric illustrates an interesting asymmetry between handling partially-specified *input problems* and handling *stored cases* whose problem descriptions are partially-specified. When stored cases include complete problem descriptions, different values of x may change the magnitude of computed difference values and the spacing between cases ranked by similarity, but will not affect the cases' *ranking* by difference values. However, if features may be missing from problem descriptions in stored cases as well as input cases, increases in x may change the ranking, causing the metric to favor stored cases for which more features are known.

Default Difference assumes a fixed difference for a pair of features whenever they are missing from *either* the input case or a stored case. A problem with this simple approach is that it may neglect useful information: if a problem feature in either the input or stored case has an atypical value, it is reasonable to consider the missing feature's value less likely to be similar. This should affect the prediction of a good match between the cases, but *Default Difference* does not take this into account. The next method, *Full Mean*, addresses this deficiency.

2.2 Full Mean

Full Mean exploits global feature information to estimate missing values, by replacing missing feature values with the mean values for those features when calculating similarity. If the feature is not known in any of the stored cases, it assigns a default difference value x. More formally, let

$$CasesKnowingFeature(i, CB) = \{c \in CB | f_i \text{ known in } c\}$$

and let $\mu(i, CB, x)$, the average of known value of feature i in the case base, with default x for completely unknown features, be defined by:

$$\mu(i, CB, x) = \begin{cases} \frac{\sum_{CasesKnowingFeature(i,CB)} c[i]}{|CasesKnowingFeature(i,CB)|} & CasesKnowingFeature(i, CB) \neq \phi \\ x & \text{otherwise} \end{cases}$$

Then with *Full Mean*,

$$d(r_1[i], r_2[i]) = |EstimatedValue(r_1, i, x) - EstimatedValue(r_2, i, x)|$$

where

$$EstimatedValue(r, i, x) = \begin{cases} r[i] & r[i] \text{ is known} \\ \mu(i, CB, x) & \text{otherwise} \end{cases}$$

Because the means for each feature in the case base can be precomputed offline and updated cheaply online as cases are added or removed, this is a low-cost strategy.

Although *Full Mean* makes better use of global feature information than *Default Difference*, it has potential drawbacks. First, like all average-based approaches in this paper, it considers only the average feature value, independent of the feature's distribution (which might be better captured, e.g., by the mean or mode). Second, it ignores possible dependencies between features, although the expected value of a feature may change dramatically based on the value of other features. For example, even if the average age of passenger cars is 8 years, predicting 8 years of age for a car would be misleading if it were also known that the car had only been driven 100 kilometers. The next strategy, *NN Mean*, attempts to better reflect local dependencies by taking a more case-based approach, using similar cases to predict feature values.

2.3 NN Mean

Nearest Neighbor Mean, or *NN Mean*, responds to *Full Mean*'s problems with a more case-based approach, predicting feature values based on the values of similar cases. Its premise is that nearby cases will be good predictors of feature values. Intuitively, if $r[i]$ is unknown and $Near_{r,i}$ is the set of all cases near r that know feature i, then a good predictor is the average feature value over $Near_{r,i}$. Unfortunately, there is one catch to this approach: Defining "nearby" cases requires predicting inter-case distances, which is the very problem that *NN Mean* is intended to address.

In *NN Mean*, we address this problem by recursively drawing on the distance metrics from this paper for the "internal" similarity computation. For example, *Default Difference*(x) can be used as an internal strategy to estimate distances for finding nearby cases, and then the k closest cases, or all cases within a distance threshold, can be used to obtain a mean according to *NN Mean*. We will denote the "internal" strategy as an argument to *NN Mean*, as in *NN Mean(Default Difference*(x)). If feature dependence information is available (though this often is not the case), an additional variant on the *NN Mean* strategy is to use only the dependent features in the search for nearby cases. We call this approach *NN Mean Dep*.

NN Mean is an expensive strategy. Unlike *Full Mean*, the average values for a feature cannot be precomputed, because they depend on r. No matter what internal strategy is used, at a minimum a new retrieval is required for each unknown feature.

2.4 Region Mean

Region Mean attempts to avoid the expense of *NN Mean* yet maintain its advantages over *Full Mean* by precomputing near means at various points in the case space, and predicting means based on the nearest precomputed cases to the input problem. In the offline process, the precomputation algorithm is:

- Cluster the case base and find a prototype for each class. We apply k-medoid clustering[1].
- For each prototype p_j
  - For each feature i
    * Let $Class_{p_j,i}$ be the set of cases in the equivalence class with prototype p_j that know feature i. Determine $\mu(i, Class_{p_j,i}, x)$, the mean value of feature i over $Class_{p_j,i}$, as follows:

---

[1] k-medoid clustering is robust to outliers and independent of the order in which objects are considered. For a comparison with other clustering methods, see (Kaufman & Rousseeuw 1990).

$$\mu(i, Class_{p_j,i}, x) = \begin{cases} \frac{\sum_{c \in Class_{p_j,i}} c[i]}{|Class_{p_j,i}|} & Class_{p_j,i} \neq \phi \\ x & \text{otherwise} \end{cases}$$

The online computation for *Region Mean* is analogous to *Full Mean*. The key difference is that $EstimatedValue(r, i, x)$ retrieves the p_j closest to r, and uses $\mu(i, Class_{p_j,i}, x)$, instead of *Full Mean*'s $\mu(i, CB, x)$.

As for *NN Mean*, an internal difference metric is required, this time to determine the nearest prototype p_j to r, as well as to measure the difference between problems in clustering. Again this can be found by recursively using any method described in this paper, provided the final method is defined. For example, *Default Difference*(x) could be used for finding the nearest prototype and for clustering. We would denote this strategy as *Region Mean(Default Difference*(x)).

2.5 Composite Strategies Exploiting Dependency Information

If information can be obtained about feature dependencies – which may itself be a significant challenge – it may be beneficial to apply a composite strategy, using one strategy for independent features and another for dependent features.

If a feature is independent, then, by definition, the values of other features are not helpful in predicting its value. Thus the best that can be hoped for is to simply use global information such as the average value across the entire case base; that is, to use *Full Mean*. Because *Full Mean* is inexpensive to compute, it is an obvious choice given a priori knowledge that a feature is independent. Only when handling dependent features are other strategies much more likely to be successful.

Because composite strategies use one strategy for independent features and another for dependent features, we write them in the form *independent-strategy/dependent-strategy*. For example, a composite strategy using *Full Mean* for independent features and *Region Mean(Default Difference*(0)) for dependent features is written *Full Mean/Region Mean(Default Difference*(0)).

3 Experiments

The previous discussion raises a number of general questions for comparing similarity assessment strategies for partial problem descriptions:

1. Their efficiency
2. Their accuracy for ranking candidate cases
3. Their accuracy for estimating difference levels between candidate cases
4. Their accuracy when different levels of information are available

It also raises some strategy-specific questions, on how performance is affected by:

1. Choice of internal strategy for *NN Mean*
2. Cluster count during initial clustering for *Region Mean*
3. Internal strategy for *Region Mean*
4. Composite strategies with different methods for independent/dependent features

To answer these questions, we tested the previous strategies for a number of domains. Our experiments focused on the ability of the methods to identify similar cases when some input features were missing, primarily for case bases in which all cases had complete problem descriptions.

3.1 Performance Measures

Three performance measures were used in the experiments:

- **Time:** The efficiency of the approaches is compared by measuring the CPU time required for the strategies to calculate distance values between the target and all the cases in the case base.
- **Normalized Absolute Error:** Given a strategy s, a partially-described target problem $\hat{t}$ generated by removing feature values from a completely-described problem t, and a case c in the case base, we define the absolute error as the difference between the actual distances between t and c, and the distance predicted when only $\hat{t}$ is known: $error_s(\hat{t}, p) = |distance(t, c) - distance_s(\hat{t}, c)|$.

  This metric is useful within a domain, to indicate of how misleading a predicted distance value may be. However, it may be less useful for comparing performance across domains, because it is sensitive to factors such as scaling of distance values. In order to facilitate comparison of errors across domains, we normalize absolute errors onto [0, 1], by dividing the absolute distance by the maximum observed distance in that case base (the distance between the two maximally distant cases in the case base). Our results report the percent of maximum observed distance between cases.
- **Rank Quality:** The rank quality measure reflects the ability of a distance metric to generate a ranking in which the quality of the top suggested cases is similar to the quality of the top cases which would be suggested if all features were known. Given a strategy s and a partial problem $\hat{t}$, rq_s measures the percent increase in distance between the input problem and the top suggested cases, compared to the true top cases. Thus it measures how much worse the top suggested cases are when only $\hat{t}$, rather than t, is known. To reflect that users in a CCBR system may be most likely to focus on the top-ranked cases, our metric weights suggestions by their order in the ranking: having a top-ranked case closest to the real top-ranked case is considered most important, with lower-ranked suggestions less important. More precisely, let $ClosestProb$ be the problem of the case that is nearest to t (when all features are known). The rank quality ratio is defined as:

$$rq_s = \frac{\sum_p w(p) * ratio(p)}{\sum_p w(p)}, \text{ where } ratio(p) = \frac{distance(t,p)}{distance(t, ClosestProb)}$$

and $w(p)$ is a function that assigns a weight to $ratio(p)$ that favors higher-ranked cases. Let $rank_s(p)$ be the 0-based rank of problem p according to strategy s. In our experiments, we set $w(p) = max(5 - rank_s(p), 0)$. Thus, only the top 5 cases had a non-zero weight.

Note that normalized absolute error and rank quality both measure the ability of the strategies to predict real inter-case distances, according to a given distance measure.

They do not directly compare solution accuracies, which would depend on the quality of the given distance measure.

3.2 Experimental Domains

The experiments were conducted in four domains, three from the University of California, Irvine, Machine Learning Repository (Blake & Merz 1998), and one artificial domain to observe performance for strongly-correlated problem description features:

1. Ecoli: 336 cases, 7 numerical features, predicting one of 8 protein localization sites.
2. Pima: 768 cases, 8 numerical features, predicting positive or negative diabetes test results in members of the Pima Native American population.
3. Liver: 345 cases, 6 numerical features, predicting the presence or absence of a liver disorder.
4. Dep7: Artificial domain, 300 cases, 7 numerical features, predicting a single numerical value. There are strong dependencies between the features: $f_0 \sim N(0, 10)$, $f_1 \sim N(f_0, 2)$, $f_2 \sim N(f_1^2 - f_0, 10)$, $f_3 \sim N(0, \pi)$, $f_4 \sim N(sin(f_3), 10)$, $f_5 \sim N(10, 20)$, $f_6 \sim N(-20, 10)$.

For all experiments, the underlying similarity metric was the Euclidean distance function of section 2, with all features given a weight of 1.

3.3 General Procedure

All implementations and experiments were done using the Indiana University Case-Based Reasoning Framework (IUCBRF) (Bogaerts & Leake 2004). IUCBRF is a Java framework, freely-available for research, designed to facilitate rapid and modular CBR system development. The general experimental procedure was as follows. Let t be the fully known target problem, $\hat{t}$ a partial target problem generated by removing features of t, p a problem (fully known) from a case in the case base, and s a similarity assessment strategy. All experiments were done for each feature prediction strategy, and were repeated 300 times per strategy (except as stated otherwise), with results averaged. For each feature prediction strategy s, steps were:

- Perform any required initialization (e.g., any strategy involving *Region Mean* builds a partition of the case base)
  - Perform leave-one-out testing. For each case c in the case base,
    * Hide c, and use c as the basis for generating a partial target $\hat{t}$. Initially, no features of $\hat{t}$ are revealed.
    * For each case c in CB - $\{t\}$, measure $distance_s(c, \hat{t})$ according to strategy s, and sort the case base by these distances.
    * Obtain performance measurements as described above
  - If $\hat{t} = t$, exit loop.
  - Else randomly choose a feature to "reveal" in $\hat{t}$ (obtained from t), and loop. The random choice simulates a user presenting a feature to the system, outside the system's control.

Thus for each t, data is collected for each strategy's calculated distances between the target problem and the remainder of the case base, from 0 features of the target problem revealed, through all its features revealed.

3.4 Classes of Tests

There were three classes of experiments, with different independent variables:

1. Cross-Domain Comparison: We compared performance for 12 strategies and variants, for four case bases of 300 cases, with *Region Mean* based on partitions created from 20 clusters.
2. Cluster Count Comparison: Performance of the 12 strategies was compared to three versions of *Region Mean*, respectively using 50, 20, and 6 clusters, each for the full ecoli case base of 336 cases.
3. Comparison for Unknown Features in the Case Base: Instead of using a fully-known case base, as is done in the other experiment classes, this experiment assessed performance with partially-described cases in the case base, for 100%, 75%, 50%, and 25% chance that a feature in the case base is known. This used the Pima case base of 768 cases, with *Region Mean* using 10 clusters.

4 Results

The comparative results in each of the UCI domains were remarkably similar. Figure 1 illustrates them with examples from the Pima domain. Figure 1 (a) lists the range of strategies considered in the experiments. However, because some strategies had almost identical performance, only a subset of lines is included in each figure, with similarities described in the text.

4.1 Cross-Domain Comparison

Figure 1 (b) shows the normalized absolute error as a function of the number of features known, for selected strategies in the pima domain. Note that *Default Difference*(0) is the worst strategy, with *Full Mean* in next to last place when 4 or more features are known. *Full Mean/Region Mean(Default Difference*(0)) initially performs worse, but becomes comparable to *NN Mean(Default Difference*(0)) when 4 or more features are known. The competetive performance of *Full Mean* is interesting in light of its much lower cost than *NN Mean(Default Difference*(0)), as shown in Figure 1 (c).

Figure 1 (c) compares the strategies' efficiency. *NN Mean(Full Mean)* is slowest, followed by *NN Mean(Default Difference*(0)), *NN Mean(Default Difference*(0)) *Dep*, and *Full Mean/NN Mean(Default Difference*(0)). The remaining strategies, essentially all those not involving *NN Mean* except as a prototype finder of *Region Mean*, were fast, requiring 5-12 ms on a Sun Blade 1000 (750Mz) to rank all cases in the pima domain.

Figure 1 (d) shows the rank quality for selected strategies in the pima domain. Note that this graph can also be used to determine the number of questions, on average, that a CCBR system would require to achieve a particular rank quality. Here *Full Mean* generally has the worst performance, followed by *Default Difference*(0). *Region Mean(Default Difference*(0)) and *Full Mean/Region Mean(Default Difference*(0)) start comparatively poorly, but catch up quickly to *NN Mean(Default Difference*(0)) and *Full Mean(NN Mean(Default Difference*(0))) *Dep*. Table 1 summarizes performance for all the strategies tested, for 4 and 6 features known.

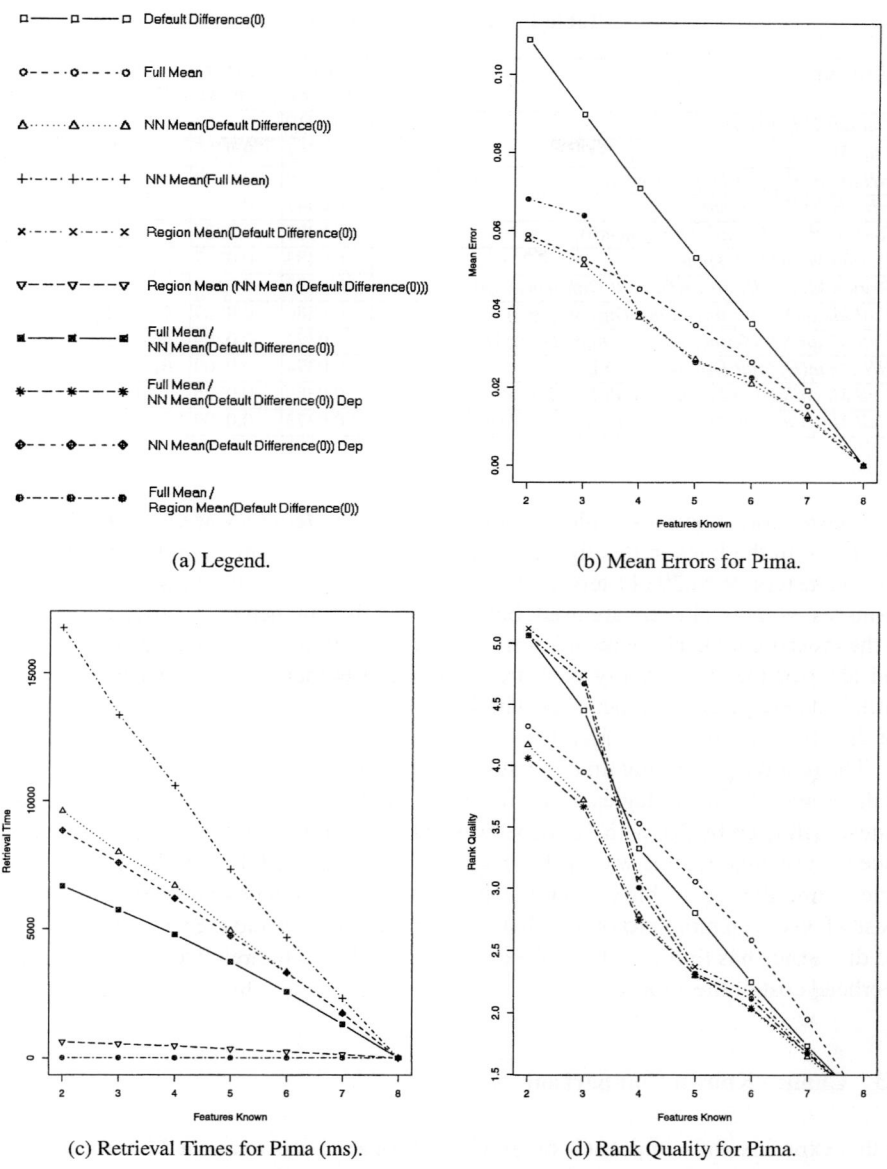

Fig. 1. a. Legend for (b), (c), and (d). b. Error versus number of features known, for selected strategies. c. Time in ms to select top-ranked case versus number of features known, for selected strategies. d. Rank quality ratios versus number of features known, for selected strategies.

4.2 Cluster Count Comparison

In this experimental setup, the *Region Mean* strategies were run for 6, 20, and 50 clusters, in the ecoli domain with a case base of 336 cases. Note that these cluster counts correspond to approximately 2%, 6%, and 15% of the number of cases.

Table 1. Mean Errors for Pima.

Strategy	Error, 4 Known	Error, 6 Known	Time, 4 Known	Time, 6 Known
Default Difference(0)	0.0710	0.0363	5.70	6.03
Full Mean	0.0451	0.0265	8.77	8.10
NN Mean(Default Difference(0))	0.0379	0.0209	6671.06	3332.70
NN Mean(Full Mean)	0.0447	0.0260	10583.25	4663.49
Region Mean(Default Difference(0))	0.0392	0.0226	9.88	8.75
Region Mean(Full Mean)	0.0433	0.0247	10.23	8.96
Region Mean(NN Mean(Default Difference(0)))	0.0373	0.0209	476.92	243.49
Full Mean/NN Mean(Default Difference(0))	0.0380	0.0209	4776.45	2566.61
Full Mean/NN Mean(Default Difference(0)) Dep	0.0374	0.0209	4648.30	2552.25
NN Mean(Default Difference(0)) Dep	0.0374	0.0209	6175.21	3305.66
Full Mean/Region Mean(Default Difference(0))	0.0389	0.0225	10.48	9.07
Full Mean/Region Mean(NN Mean(Default Difference(0)))	0.0373	0.0209	10.51	9.07

Figure 2 (a) shows a sample of results, for *Region Mean(NN Mean(Default Difference(0)))*. In the lines in this figure, points marked with □ correspond to performance for 50 clusters, × to 20 clusters, and △ to 6 clusters. The results show small improvements when more clusters are used, but also show that the behavior is generally robust to the cluster count. These results were typical for each of the *Region Mean* strategies, and also for the rank quality measure. This suggests that low cluster counts may be sufficient. Because speed increases with lower cluster counts, this result is encouraging for the efficiency of *Region Mean*.

The relative processing times versus cluster counts were also consistent across each of the *Region Mean* strategies. Experiments showed that strategies with 6 clusters were fastest, followed by 20, with 50 the slowest, although for each cluster count the difference in computation time was fairly small. This is as expected: Fewer clusters decreases time to find the applicable cluster, but even for a large number of clusters, there are at most a few dozen more prototypes that must be examined to find the nearest cluster, and the difference has limited effect on execution time due to the relatively larger constant overhead cost of the strategy.

4.3 Chance Known Comparison

In this experimental setup, each strategy's performance was examined for varying levels of missing information in the case base, in the pima domain, with 768 cases. As discussed above, previous experiments used a fully-known case base (a 100% chance that a case in the case base knows any given feature). This setup, however, examines not only a 100% chance known, but also 75%, 50%, and 25%. Runs were repeated a minimum of 186–270 times, with results averaged.

Figure 2 (b) shows the error using Full Mean / Region Mean(Default Difference(0)) for a chance known of 100% (+), 75% (△), 50% (○), and 25% (□). Note that, as expected, error increases as the chance that a feature in the case base is unknown increases. Results were very similar for the other strategies.

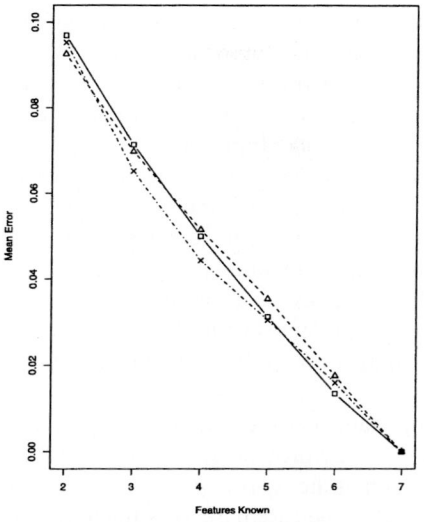 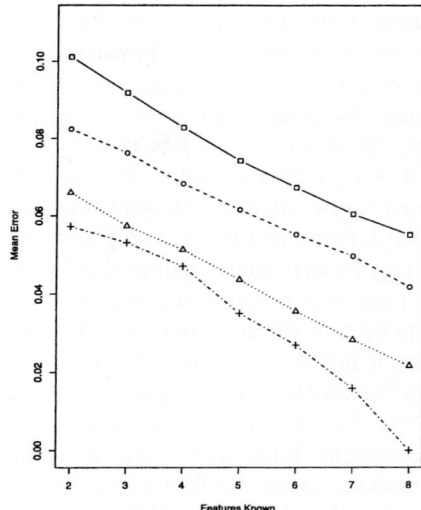

(a) Effect of Cluster Count on Errors for *Region Mean* Strategies.

(b) Effect of Chance Known on Errors for Composite Strategy.

Fig. 2. (a). The error for *Region Mean(NN Mean(Default Difference(0)))* for 50, 20, and 6 clusters. □ is for 50 clusters, × is for 20, and △ is for 6. (b) Error in Full Mean / Region Mean(Default Difference(0)) for a chance known of 100% (+), 75% (△), 50% (○), and 25% (□).

5 Discussion

The experiments illustrate a number of interesting properties. First, we note that the commonly-used trivial strategies, *Default Difference*(0) and *Full Mean*, consistently produce comparatively poor results, as shown in the error and rank quality measures. Thus we would expect a considerable boost to the prediction accuracy of a CBR system faced with partial problems (or a conversational CBR system in which not all questions have been answered for a given session) when any of the more advanced strategies are used.

The results also provide information to help in selecting a more advanced strategy. As hypothesized and experimentally verified, strategies involving *NN Mean* are prohibitively slow, requiring on the order of several seconds to sort a fully-known case base of a few hundred cases against a single partial problem. However, the *Region Mean* strategies were developed to address this are fairly fast and provide comparable accurate to *NN Mean* strategies.

It is interesting to note that in limited circumstances, *NN Mean* may still be appropriate. Specifically, experiments show that *Region Mean(NN Mean(Default Difference*(0))) (and the related composite method) is not slowed down dramatically by the use of a *NN Mean* strategy as its prototype finder. This can be explained because, when the case base is fully-known, there is only one partial problem, the target, for which the nearest cluster must be found. Thus, *NN Mean* must be used only once to determine the nearest cluster. Once the nearest cluster is determined, the mean values associated with that cluster can be used for the partial problem in comparing it with the entire case base. In fact, for a partial case base, once the partition is created off-line, the nearest cluster of any case is already known and need not be recomputed. So even for a partial case base, *NN Mean* must only be computed once for a target partial problem.

If information regarding the dependence between features is available (either as domain knowledge, or calculated via statistical analysis) then a composite method can be used. As argued above, *Full Mean* is the suitable when a feature is independent, and strategy for dependent features should use *Region Mean*. Assuming that the dependence information is accurate, a composite method should be just as accurate, or even more accurate, than the dependent part alone applied to all features. In addition, because *Full Mean* is fast, a composite method of the form *Full Mean/Region Mean* would be faster than *Region Mean* alone, applied to all features.

We note that none of the approaches exploit statistical information about feature distributions. When that information is available, it may provide even more useful information. An area for future study is the application of the *representativeness assumption* (Smyth & McKenna 1999) to use existing cases in the case base to estimate feature value distributions.

6 Related Work

Distance metrics have been the subject of extensive study in CBR (e.g., (Wettschereck, Aha, & Mohri 1997; Bergmann 2002)). CCBR systems must always include methods for handling partially described problems, and a number of methods have been applied. One common approach in CBR and instance-based learning is to assume a maximal difference between missing features (Witten & Frank 2000, p. 115), which is similar to *Default Difference*(x) for a large value of x.

To our knowledge, how to handle missing features in distance metrics and the tradeoffs between alternative strategies have received only limited study in the CBR community. However, missing features have been considered in a number of studies in machine learning. For example, in decision tree induction, Mingers (1989) uses a strategy similar to *Full Mean* as well as a strategy that assigns the most common feature value among training instances with the same classification, and Quinlan (1993) uses probability information on feature values while descending multiple paths of the tree. Other work has examined the theoretical learnability of a target function when features are missing (Decatur & Gennaro 1995; Goldman, Kwek, & Scott 1997).

CBR research has examined how to select the next question to ask in a dialogue (Aha, Breslow, & Munoz-Avila 2001; Kohlmaier, Schmitt, & Bergmann 2001), and how to select useful sets of cases to present in light of similarity and diversity concerns (Smyth & McGinty 2003). McSherry (2003) studies a related problem, the determination of when recommendation dialogues can be terminated without loss of solution quality, and compares the efficiency of alternative attribution-selection strategies, given a similarity metric in the spirit of *Default Difference*(0). However, these approaches assume a pre-existing method for assessing similarity based on partial descriptions; they do not examine which similarity metrics to use. Increased understanding of how to assess similarity for partial descriptions could have substantial benefits both for CCBR and for case-based recommender systems.

7 Conclusion

Being able to retrieve appropriate cases, based on partial information, is a fundamental problem for CCBR systems. This paper examines alternative strategies for addressing this problem. It compares a set of difference measures, evaluates their performance and efficiency on sample data sets, and discusses their tradeoffs as suggested by the experiments. It identifies difficulties in handling partial problem descriptions that may not be initially apparent, illustrates high-cost, high-accuracy strategies based on CBR, and shows that they may be effectively approximated by more efficient methods. This work provides a set of tools for building distance metrics for incompletely-described cases, and provides an initial foundation for further study of this area.

References

Aha, D., and Breslow, L. 1997. Refining conversational case libraries. In *Proceedings of the Second International Conference on Case-Based Reasoning*, 267–278. Berlin: Springer Verlag.

Aha, D.; Breslow, L.; and Munoz-Avila, H. 2001. Conversational case-based reasoning. *Applied Intelligence* 14:9–32.

Bergmann, R. 2002. *Experience Management: Foundations, Development Methodology, and Internet-Based Applications*. Berlin: Springer.

Blake, C., and Merz, C. 1998. UCI repository of machine learning databases. http://www.ics.uci.edu/~mlearn/MLRepository.html.

Bogaerts, S., and Leake, D. 2004. IUCBRF: A framework for rapid and modular CBR system development. In preparation.

Carrick, C.; Yang, Q.; Abi-Zeid, I.; and Lamontagne, L. 1999. Activating CBR systems through autonomous information gathering. In *Proceedings of the Third International Conference on Case-Based Reasoning*, 74–88. Berlin: Springer Verlag.

Decatur, S., and Gennaro, R. 1995. On learning from noisy and incomplete examples. In *Proceedings of the Eighth Annual ACM Conference On Computational Learning Theory*. ACM Press.

Goldman, S.; Kwek, S.; and Scott, S. 1997. Learning from examples with unspecified attribute values. In *Computational Learing Theory*, 231–242.

Kaufman, L., and Rousseeuw, P. 1990. *Finding Groups in Data: an Introduction to Cluster Analysis*. Wiley.

Kohlmaier, A.; Schmitt, S.; and Bergmann, R. 2001. A similarity-based approach to attribute selection in user-adaptive sales dialogues. In *Case-Based Reasoning Research and Development: Proceedings of the Fourth International Conference on Case-Based Reasoning*, 306–320. Berlin: Springer Verlag.

Kolodner, J. 1993. *Case-Based Reasoning*. San Mateo, CA: Morgan Kaufmann.

Leake, D.; Smyth, B.; Wilson, D.; and Yang, Q., eds. 2001. *Maintaining Case-Based Reasoning Systems*. Blackwell. Special issue of *Computational Intelligence*, 17(2), 2001.

McSherry, D. 2003. Increasing dialogue efficiency in case-based reasoning without loss of solution quality. In *Proceedings of the eighteenth International Joint Conference on Artificial Intelligence (IJCAI-03)*, 121–126. San Mateo: Morgan Kaufmann.

Mingers, J. 1989. An empirical comparison of selection measures for decision-tree induction. *Machine Learning* 3(4):319–342.

Quinlan, J. R. 1993. *C4.5: Programs for Machine Learning*. San Mateo, CA: Morgan Kaufmann.

Smyth, B., and McGinty, L. 2003. The power of suggestion. In *Proceedings of the eighteenth International Joint Conference on Artificial Intelligence (IJCAI-03)*, 127–132. San Mateo: Morgan Kaufmann.

Smyth, B., and McKenna, E. 1999. Building compact competent case-bases. In *Proceedings of the Third International Conference on Case-Based Reasoning*, 329–342. Berlin: Springer Verlag.

Wettschereck, D.; Aha, D.; and Mohri, T. 1997. A review and empirical evaluation of feature-weighting methods for a class of lazy learning algorithms. *Artificial Intelligence Review* 11(1-5):273–314.

Witten, I., and Frank, E. 2000. *Data Mining: Practical Machine Learning Tools and Techniques with Java Implementations*. San Francisco: Morgan Kaufmann.

Dialogue Management for Conversational Case-Based Reasoning

Karl Branting, James Lester, and Bradford Mott

LiveWire Logic, Inc.
2700 Gateway Centre Blvd., Suite 900
Morrisville, NC 27560
{branting,lester,mott}@livewirelogic.com

Abstract. Two key objectives of conversational case-based reasoning (CCBR) systems are (1) eliciting case facts in a manner that minimizes the user's burden in terms of resources such as time, information cost, and cognitive load, and (2) integrating CBR with other problem solving modalities. This paper proposes an architecture that addresses both these goals by integrating CBR with a discourse-oriented dialogue engine. The dialogue engine determines when CBR or other problem-solving techniques are needed to achieve pending discourse goals. Conversely, the CBR component has the full resources of a dialogue engine to handle topic changes, interruptions, clarification questions by either the user or the system, and other speech acts that arise in problem-solving dialogues.

1 Introduction

Conversational case-based reasoning (CCBR) is intended to improve the interaction between users and CBR systems by eliciting case facts in a manner that minimizes the user's burden in terms of resources such as time, information cost, and cognitive load. The goal of improving the interaction between users and CBR systems gives rise to a number of distinct issues:

1. Minimizing the number or cost of questions by determining the most informative question to ask at each stage of an interaction.
2. Giving users control over the degree to which initiative is held by the system or user.
3. Enabling the system to explain both why a question was asked and how the system's answer was reached.
4. Handling interruptions (temporary topic shifts) and subgoals (providing information the user needs to answer a system question, or eliciting information needed to answer a question the user is unable to answer).
5. Permitting users to ask clarifying questions.
6. Enabling the system to ask users clarifying questions when necessary.
7. Integrating CBR with other problem-solving modalities that can answer questions that would otherwise have to be posed to the user.

Most previous work in CCBR has focused on the first of these issues, minimizing the number of questions asked by the system. Approaches to minimizing questions that have been explored include inferring answers to redundant questions [Aha et al., 1998], recognizing the earliest point in the dialogue at which no more questions are required [McSherry, 2003], and ordering questions by information gain [Doyle and Cunningham, 2000,McSherry, 2001] or similarity variance [Kohlmaier et al., 2001].

Recent research has focused on CCBR as a dialogue amenable to the standard tools of discourse analysis. For example, [Göker and Thompson, 2000] identified a set of dialogue operators applicable to CCBR, and [Bridge, 2002] modeled the interactions in CCBR through a dialogue grammar. As CBR becomes increasingly embedded in general problem-solving agent architectures, rather than in stand-alone applications, these issues will become increasingly important.

This paper presents a general architecture for CCBR called the *Discourse Goal Stack Model* (DGSM). The next section briefly summarizes the key issues in dialogue management. Section 3 outlines the DGSM architecture. Section 4 describes an implementation of this architecture in RealDialog, a conversational agent for customer relationship management.

2 Dialogue Management

A long-term goal of the computational linguistics community has been to devise a conversational agent capable of interacting with humans in two-way natural language dialogue. Although a general natural language understanding facility is not in sight, with ever increasing compute cycles at their disposal, designers of conversational agents are approaching their goal at an accelerating pace. In addition to pursuing the fundamental research goals of creating a domain-independent architecture that can provide the language functionalities required by a conversational agent, computational linguists are motivated by the promise of creating conversational interfaces that can serve as the front-end to other, often complex, automated reasoning systems. By augmenting automated reasoning systems with dialogue functionalities, conversational interfaces can facilitate collaborative, mixed-initiative interactions in which problem-solving responsibilities are shared by the user and the application. We believe that a conversational CBR architecture that provides tightly integrated dialogue capabilities can take advantage of the communicative functionalities of conversational agents.

In the broadest formulation of the problem, conversational agents engage in spoken dialogues that are mixed-initiative, i.e., either the human or the agent can have control of the dialogue at a particular "turn" [Seneff, 2002]. These dialogues are characterized by all of the complexities that typify human-human conversations. For example, human-human dialogues frequently exploit the discourse context to effectively communicate using *anaphora* (using context-based referring expressions such as pronouns) and *ellipsis* (employing phrases that omit key syntactic components that are implicit).

Creating an end-to-end spoken dialogue system requires solving two families of problems: speech processing and natural language processing. In the classic architecture, speech recognition and speech synthesis modules bracket the natural language pipeline. The natural language pipeline itself proceeds from natural language understanding through dialogue management and closes the loop with natural language generation. Dialogue management lies at the heart of conversational agent architectures. Dialogue managers are assigned responsibility for two key problems: (1) ensuring that conversations are coherent across multiple interactions, and (2) supporting mixed-initiative interactions that achieve both the user's and the system's goals [Rudnicky and Xu, 1999]. In this work, we draw exclusively from the natural language work on conversational agents.

One can distinguish three fundamental architectures for performing dialogue management [Allen et al., 2000,Rudnicky and Xu, 1999]. First, *graph-based* architectures (sometimes referred to as "call-flow based systems") employ finite state machines to guide all interactions. Graph-based approaches offer the advantage of well-structured dialogues whose give-and-take can be clearly anticipated in advance. If a designer can lay out questions and expected alternate possible responses in a tree, e.g., making an operator-assisted long distance call, then at runtime the conversational agent can respond effectively to each of the possible "moves" that the user can make. However, graph-based approaches suffer from a rigidity that prohibits them from dealing well with unexpected conversational moves. Unless the designer can know in advance with high confidence what possible structure the dialogues will have, graph-based dialogue managers will encounter unexpected statements, questions, and imperatives of users and will fail to react in a manner that is helpful. This limitation is particularly problematic when dialogues are to be mixed-initiative and user-initiated topic shifts are the norm rather than the exception.

Second, *slot-filling* architectures (sometimes referred to as "frame-based" architectures) employ a feature vector with values to be determined during the course of the conversation. Slot-filling dialogue managers permit a broader range of conversations and do not impose the same topic ordering restrictions that graph-based systems do. For example, a simple travel reservation system could use a slot-filling architecture to determine the time of departure and arrival, travel dates, and seating preferences that a prospective passenger might request. Slot-filling architectures work well for conversational agents designed to identify values for a relatively small set of slots. However, they are ineffective for more complicated tasks that require the user and the agent to collaboratively create complex artifacts, e.g., forming a mission plan, creating a multi-faceted travel itinerary, or synthesizing a design [Allen et al., 2001] and where issues such as intent recognition and plan recognition are central.

Third, *plan-based* architectures offer the most general dialogue management capabilities [Allen et al., 2001]. The field has not yet converged on a single plan-based architecture, but many efforts have yielded dialogue managers with one or more of the following features. They may employ a planner to create domain-specific plans, the execution of which will solve the user's problem[1], they may use

---

[1] Similar techniques are used in non-natural-language-based approaches to mixed-initiative interaction, e.g., [Rich and Sidner, 1998].

an agenda to adaptively drive all conversations, or they may incorporate an array of domain-specific goal-handlers to perform arbitrary computations required to expand particular components of a plan or script that represents the evolving solution. In our work we draw on each of these approaches.

3 The Discourse Goal Stack Model

The Discourse Goal Stack Model (DGSM) is based on a view of CCBR as a specialized form of goal-oriented dialogue. The central tasks of CCBR – selecting appropriate cases, eliciting case descriptions, and responding to requests for clarification or topic changes – can all be viewed as handling specific types of discourse goals. We address these goals through a goal stack that (1) permits all dialogue goals to be handled in a uniform fashion and (2) handles interruptions and subgoals, even when interleaved or nested to arbitrary depth.

DGSM builds on the observation that there is a symmetry between the discourse goals that trigger CBR and the discourse goals that arise in CBR when the facts of a problem description are being elicited. When a system is engaged in a dialogue with a user, the user may make direct or indirect requests for information that can only be answered if the system elicits additional information from the user. For example, if the user requests information that can be provided through CBR, such as diagnostic or product selection information, the system generally must elicit facts specific to the user's request, such as symptoms or product requirements. Invoking CBR is thus one way among many of satisfying the discourse goal of providing information to a customer.

Similarly, during CBR a user may fail to understand a question, be unable or unwilling to find out the answer, or temporarily change the subject. Each of these events gives rise to new system discourse goals, such as answering the user's request for clarification or satisfying the system's need to clarify a question.

DGSM consists of a goal stack, a collection of discourse goal types, a forest of augmented transition networks (ATNs) in which nodes are discourse goals and arcs are speech acts by the user or the system, and a goal handler responsible for determining the appropriate action to take in response to the goal at the top of the stack. The goal handler selects from among the following actions, based on the value of the current top-of-stack and the most recent speech act by the user:

1. If the current goal corresponds to a node in an ATN and the user's utterance is recognized as a speech act matching a transition from that node, the goal handler pops the stack and pushes the node at the end of the transition.
2. If the current goal corresponds to a node in an ATN but the transition contains a speech act by the system, the speech act is generated, the stack is popped, and the top of stack is replaced by the node at the end of the transition.
3. If the user's utterance doesn't correspond to a transition from the state at the top-of-stack but matches an initial transition in another ATN, the utterance is interpreted as a change of topic. The state at the end of the transition is therefore pushed onto the stack.

4. If the state at the top-of-stack is the end state of an ATN, it is popped.
5. If the top-of-stack is a goal that can only be achieved by an external module, such as the case-based reasoner, a constraint-satisfaction problem solver, or an inference engine, the module is invoked. External modules may themselves generate discourse goals.

The algorithm for DGSM's goal handler is depicted in Figure 1.

4 Case-Based Reasoning in DGSM

In DGSM, CBR is invoked when the goal handler encounters a *selection goal*, that is, a goal that requires selecting one element from a set of entities, such as diagnoses or inventory items, based at least in part on information provided by, or specific to, the user. DGSM is consistent with the standard CCBR model [Aha et al., 1998] in assuming that each case is specified by a unique set of attribute/value pairs. Associated with each attribute is question text and type information specifying acceptable answers (described in more detail below in Section 4.1).

When a selection goal is encountered, the selection handler instantiates a *caseCollection* object with a collection of initial hypotheses corresponding to the selection goal. For example, if the system interpreted a statement by the user as a request to troubleshoot a printer[2] and the system had a collection of cases corresponding to the goal of selecting a printer diagnostic state, a caseCollection would be instantiated and the CBR module invoked by pushing its start state onto the stack.

Initially, all cases associated with the specific selection goal are candidates. The CBR module iteratively selects the question that discriminates best among the current candidate cases and poses it to the user until a unique case remains or there are no more questions that can discriminate among the remaining candidates. If there is a unique case, it is reported to the user; otherwise, the system reports a failure.

Figure 2 depicts the CBR module. Circles represent discourse goals, squares and diamonds represent procedures and branches, respectively, unitalicized arc labels represent the propositional content of speech acts, and the arc labeled "Call *Directed Elicitation(Q)*" causes the Directed Elicitation ATN (shown in Figure 3) to be invoked by pushing its start state onto the goal stack.

Because there is a unique set of hypotheses for each selection goal, DGSM is not limited to CBR in a single domain, but can handle an arbitrary number of distinct selection goals.

4.1 Directed Elicitation

Directed elicitation is a general mechanism for leading the user to provide information specific to a selection goal while permitting interruptions and clarification

---

[2] The techniques for interpreting statements by users used in RealDialog are set forth below in Section 5.

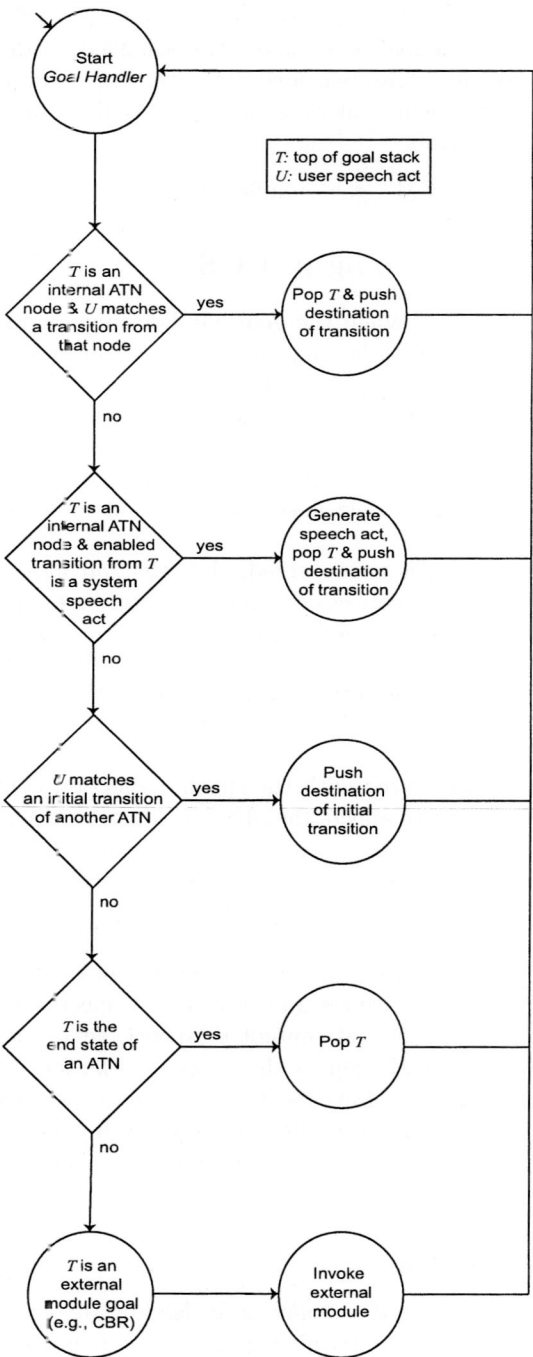

Fig. 1. The DGSM goal handler.

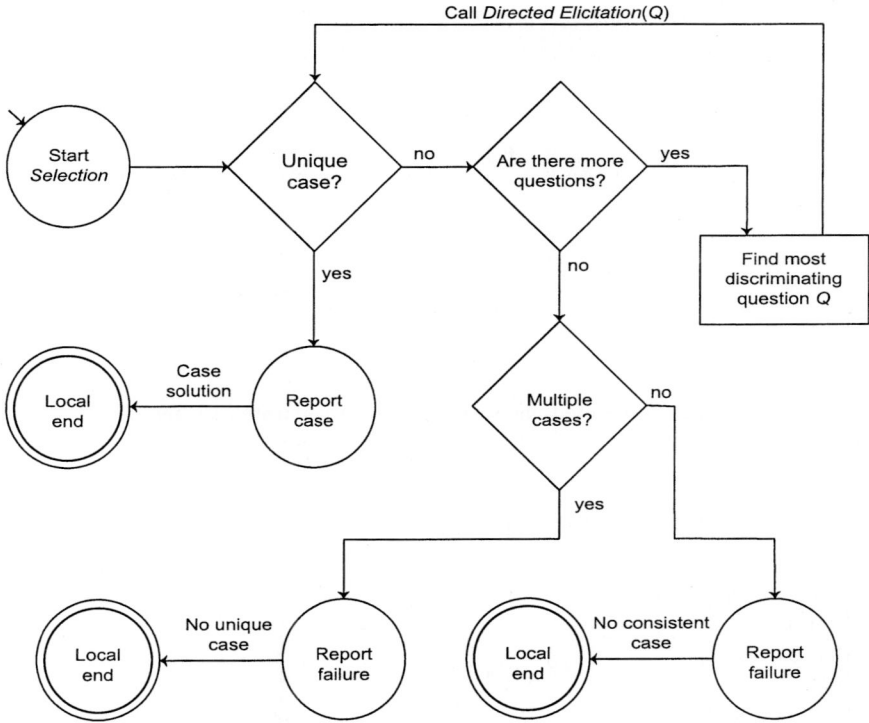

Fig. 2. The DGSM CBR module.

questions by either the system or the user. As mentioned above, each case attribute is associated with a question text and a specification of the acceptable answer type. After the CBR module has selected the attribute that discriminates best among the current hypotheses, it poses the question corresponding to the attribute and invokes directed elicitation with the required answer type.

Figure 3 illustrates the structure of directed-elicitation ATNs. A directed-elicitation ATN is invoked by pushing its start state onto the goal stack. The goal handler asks the question corresponding to the transition from this start state, then compares the user's utterance with the transition that is expected from the *get answer* state. If the utterance expresses a value of the expected type found, the value is recorded in a *conversation variable*, a global variable representing information specific to the current dialogue. If the utterance doesn't match the expected transition, then the goal handler searches for alternative ATNs with initial transitions that match the utterance. If one is found, the utterance is interpreted as an interruption, and the start state of the ATN with the matching initial transition is pushed onto the stack. When the local end state of this ATN is reached, it is popped and the dialogue context in which the interruption occurred is restored.

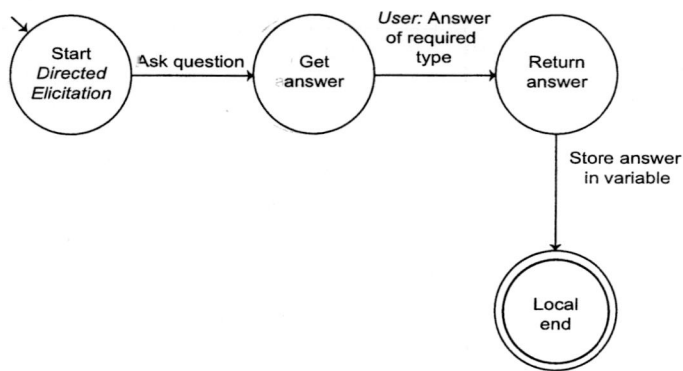

Fig. 3. The structure of directed-elicitation ATNs. A separate directed elicitation ATN exists for each question type.

Typical directed-elicitation ATN types include the following:
- Yes/no
- Selection from list
- Free text
- Integer
- Real
- Integer range
- Date
- Date range
- Date list

In addition to a directed-elicitation ATN, it is desirable to have a termination ATN, as shown in Figure 4, to permit the user to end the CBR episode without ending the dialogue with the system.

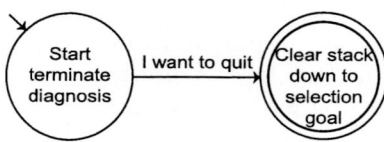

Fig. 4. An ATN to permit a CBR episode to be terminated without ending the user's dialogue with the system.

4.2 Example

The following highly simplified example illustrates how the DGSM model permits interruptions to be handled during a CBR interaction. Suppose that there is a diagnostic case library containing the following cases:

1. influenza
    - fever: true
    - rash: false
2. measles
    - fever: true
    - rash: true
3. dermatitis
    - fever: false
    - rash: true
4. food poisoning
    - fever: false
    - nausea: true

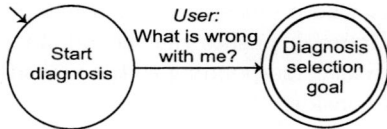

Fig. 5. An ATN to identify when a request for diagnosis has been made and to trigger a diagnosis selection.

Suppose that the dialogue system includes the ATN shown in Figure 5, which is intended to recognize when a request for diagnosis has been made and to trigger a diagnosis selection.

Consider the following dialogue between a user and a system:

```
...
User: What is wrong with me?
Agent: Do you have a fever?
User: How do I tell if I have a fever?
Agent: Measure your temperature with a thermometer.
User: How high of a temperature is a fever?
Agent: A temperature above 37 is considered a fever.
User: Then I don't have a fever.
Agent: Do you have a rash?
...
```

In order for CBR to be triggered, the system must recognize that the user's first utterance matches the transition shown in Figure 5. When the goal handler recognizes the utterance matching the initial (and only) transition of the Figure 5 ATN, it pushes the "Diagnosis selection goal" state onto the stack. The goal handler instantiates a caseCollection object with the cases corresponding to this diagnosis goal, i.e., the four cases shown above, pops the goal, and pushes the first state of the CBR module onto the stack.

Since there is not a unique case and there are multiple remaining questions, the CBR module finds the most discriminating attribute, in this case *fever*, poses the question text to the user ("Do you have a fever?"), and pushes the start state of the directed elicitation ATN for *Yes/No* onto the stack.

The user's answer, "How do I tell if I have a fever?", is not of the expected type (it is neither an affirmative nor a negative). If the system contains the ATN shown in Figure 6, the goal handler (following the third branch in the diagram shown in Figure 1) will push the second state of the top ATN in Figure 6 onto the stack, produce the text corresponding to the transition from that state, "Measure your temperature with a thermometer," and pop the local end state, returning the stack to a state in which the top-of-stack is the second state in the directed elicitation ATN.

The user's statement, "How high of a temperature is a fever?", once again does not match the transition from the state at the top of the goal stack, so again the system finds an ATN whose initial transition matches the user's utterance, i.e., the lower ATN in Figure 6, pushes the second state in this ATN onto the stack, and produces the text corresponding to the transition from that state, "A temperature above 37 is considered a fever."

The user's statement, "Then I don't have a fever," matches the transition in the directed-elicitation ATN corresponding because it is a negative. The negative response is recorded in a conversation variable, the local end state of the directed-elicitation ATN is popped, and the "Call directed elicitation" transition in Figure 2 is completed, returning the CBR module to a state in which it tests for a unique hypothesis. Since there is still no unique hypothesis and there is at least one remaining question, directed elicitation is invoked again, this time with the *rash* attribute, giving rise to the system statement "Do you have a rash?"

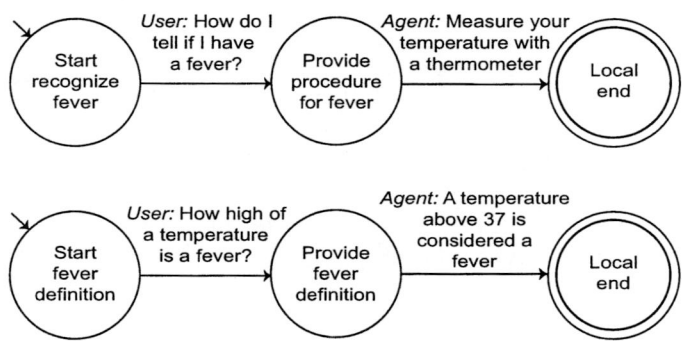

Fig. 6. ATNs providing the procedure to recognize a fever and the temperature threshold for a fever.

This example illustrates how topic shifts introduced by the user's need for additional information to help answer the system's question are handled in a simple and general fashion in a goal-stack architecture.

5 The Implementation of DGSM

Any implementation of DGSM must specify the modality in which users and agents interact and the manner in which user utterances are interpreted. DGSM is implemented in RealDialog, a web-based conversational agent for customer relationship management. While RealDialog is an enterprise software system in use at a number of companies, the implementation of DGSM in RealDialog is an experimental component that is currently in the prototype phase and has not yet been used in commercial installations. RealDialog's interface is shown in Figure 7. Users type queries into a text field, and answers are displayed in a conversation area. Optionally, additional information can be displayed in a web-display panel.

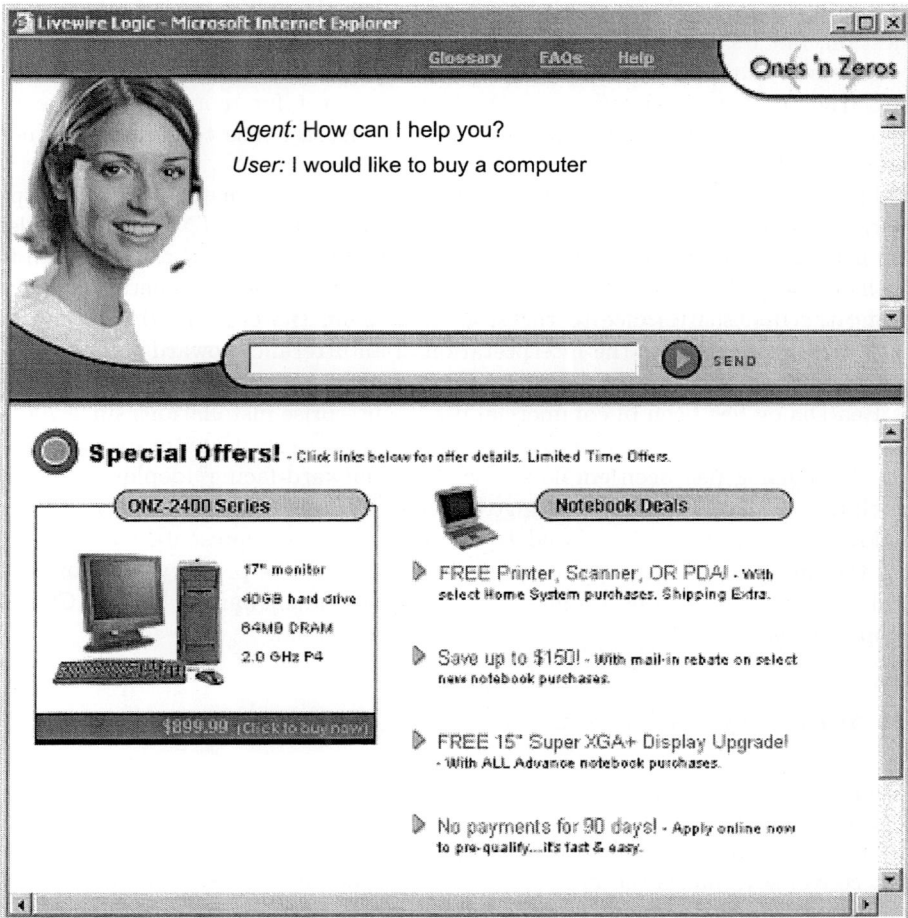

Fig. 7. The RealDialog interface.

The full details of the interpretation of utterances are beyond the scope of this paper (see [Lester et al., 2004] for a general discussion of utterance interpretation in conversational agent architectures). However, the basic steps are as follows. The first step is tokenization of the user's statement, that is, division of the input in a series of distinct lexical entities. Tokenization includes spell-correction and interpretation of apostrophes. The second step is syntactic analysis. In RealDialog, this consists of part-of-speech tagging and parsing. The result of the tokenization, tagging, and parsing is a parse tree.

Parse trees often require *reference resolution*, interpretation of referring expressions, such as the "it" in, "I would like to buy it now." A related problem is interpretation of *ellipsis*, that is, material omitted from a statement but implicit in the conversational context.

In general, a dialogue system must perform some form of pragmatic analysis, that is, determining the speech or communication act [Searle, 1969] that the utterance performs. For example, "Can you reach the salt?" is in the form of a question, but its pragmatic effect is a request for the salt. "I would like to buy it now" is in the form of a declaration, but its pragmatic effect is also a request. Similarly, the pragmatic effect of "Yes" is a request for more in response to "Would you like some more" but the opposite in response to "Have you had enough?"

In a stack-based dialogue architecture like DGSM, pragmatic analysis is typically performed implicitly as a side-effect of the locality of ATNs. For example, the meaning of a Yes/No answer obtained through directed elicitation depends on the question to which the user's utterance is a response. In general, by comparing the user's utterance to the transitions from the current top-of-state, a stack architecture biases the interpretation of an utterance toward the meaning that is most appropriate in the current context.

RealDialog has been in commercial use in enterprise installations since 2002. The primary customers are large commercial enterprises with extensive call centers. RealDialog has been employed both in "outward-facing" deployments, in which it is available to users visiting the business's web site, and "inward-facing deployments" in which it is used by customer service representatives to help find the answers to users' questions more efficiently. The primary functionality used by these applications is simply one-step question answering, but the CCBR component is an implemented component of the system.

6 Summary and Future Work

This paper has described an architecture that integrates CBR with a discourse-oriented dialogue engine. This architecture permits CBR or other problem-solving techniques to be selected when needed to achieve pending discourse goals and, conversely, makes the full resources of a dialogue engine available to CBR component to handle topic changes, interruptions, clarification questions by either the user or the system, and other speech acts that arise in problem-solving dialogues.

The DGSM described in this paper is a first step in the integration of CBR with discourse-oriented dialogue engines. In the enumeration of CCBR issues in the introduction, DGSM addresses Issue 2 – giving users control over the degree to which the initiative is held by the system or the user – by (1) taking the initiative from the user in response to discourse goals that require questions to be answered by the user but (2) permitting the user to seize the initiative at any point. Issues 4 and 5 are addressed by handling clarifying questions and other interruptions. Issue 7 – integrating CBR with other problem-solving modalities– is addressed by embedding the CBR module in a dialogue system that treats all goals in a uniform fashion. Under this approach, a single goal handler can invoke whatever problem-solving modules have been implemented in a given system.

However, several issues are not addressed by DGSM. DGSM does not in itself help with Issue 3, enabling the system to explain either why a question was asked and how the system's answer was reached, and it is completely independent of Issue 1, minimizing questions. Issue 6, enabling the system to ask users clarifying questions, can be addressed in the DGSM framework. However, it is a complex problem of interpretation to recognize when an utterance is relevant but ambiguous, equivocal, or vague (and therefore in need of clarification), as opposed to simply incoherent or irrelevant (and therefore a deviation from the topic).

As noted above, the implementation of DGSM in RealDialog is an experimental component that has not been used in commercial installations. It does not include constraint relaxing dialogues as proposed in [Göker and Thompson, 2000] to recover from situations in which no cases are consistent with the attribute/value pairs specified by the user. RealDialog's tool suite does not currently include an adequate case editor, and the criteria for selecting the most discriminating case attribute is not customizable. However, RealDialog illustrates how CBR can be integrated into a goal-stack architecture and how the resulting integration can significantly improve the flexibility and robustness of conversational case-based reasoning.

References

[Aha et al., 1998] Aha, D. W., Maney, T., and Breslow, L. A. (1998). Supporting dialogue inferencing in conversational case-based reasoning. *Proceedings of the Fourth European Workshop on Case-Based Reasoning, Lecture Notes in Computer Science*, 1488:262–270.

[Allen et al., 2000] Allen, J., Byron, D., Dzikovska, M., Ferguson, G., Galescu, L., and Stent, A. (2000). An architecture for a generic dialogue shell. *NLENG: Natural Language Engineering, Cambridge University Press*, 6.

[Allen et al., 2001] Allen, J. F., Ferguson, G., and Stent, A. (2001). An architecture for more realistic conversational systems. In *Proceedings of the International Conference on Intelligent User Interfaces*, pages 1–8.

[Bridge, 2002] Bridge, D. (2002). Towards conversational recommender systems: A dialogue grammar approach. In Aha, D., editor, *Proceedings of the Workshop in Mixed-Initiative Case-Based Reasoning, Workshop Programme at the Sixth European Conference in Case-Based Reasoning*, pages 9–22.

[Doyle and Cunningham, 2000] Doyle, M. and Cunningham, P. (2000). A dynamic approach to reducing dialog in on-line decision guides. In *European Workshop on Case-Based Reasoning (EWCBR)*, pages 49–60.

[Göker and Thompson, 2000] Göker, M. and Thompson, C. (2000). Personalized conversational case-based recommendation. In *Proceedings of the 5th European Workshop on Case-Based Reasoning*, Trento, Italy. Springer.

[Kohlmaier et al., 2001] Kohlmaier, A., Schmitt, S., and Bergmann, R. (2001). A similiarity-based approach to attribute selection in user-adaptive sales dialogs. In Aha, D. and Watson, I., editors, *Fourth International Conference on Case-Based Reasoning, ICCBR 2001, Lecture Notes in Artificial Intelligence 2080*, pages 306–320, Vancouver, BC, Canada. Springer.

[Lester et al., 2004] Lester, J., Branting, K., and Mott, B. (2004). Conversational agents. In Singh, M., editor, *Practical Handbook of Internet Computing*. CRC Press.

[McSherry, 2001] McSherry, D. (2001). Minimizing dialog length in interactive case-based reasoning. In *Proceedings of the Seventeenth International Joint Conference on Artificial Intelligence*, pages 993–998, Seattle, Washington, USA.

[McSherry, 2003] McSherry, D. (2003). Increasing dialogue efficiency in case-based reasoning without loss of solution quality. In *Proceedings of the Eighteenth International Joint Conference on Artificial Intelligence (IJCAI)*, pages 121–126, Acapulco, Mexico.

[Rich and Sidner, 1998] Rich, C. and Sidner, C. L. (1998). COLLAGEN: A collaboration manager for software interface agents. *User Modeling and User-Adapted Interaction*, 8(3-4):315–350.

[Rudnicky and Xu, 1999] Rudnicky, A. and Xu, W. (1999). An agenda-based dialog management architecture for spoken language systems. In *Proceedings of Workshop on Automatic Speech Recognition and Understanding*, Keystone, CO.

[Searle, 1969] Searle, J. (1969). *Speech Acts: An Essay in the Philosophy of Language*. Cambridge University Press, Cambridge.

[Seneff, 2002] Seneff, S. (2002). Response planning and generation in the Mercury flight reservation system. *Computer speech and language*, pages 283–312.

Hybrid Recommender Systems with Case-Based Components

Robin Burke

School of Computer Science, Telecommunications and Information Systems
DePaul University
Chicago, IL
rburke@cs.depaul.edu

Abstract. Hybrid recommender systems combine recommendation components of different types to achieve improved performance. Many such hybrids have been built but recent studies show that hybrids using case-based recommendation are rare. This paper shows how a range of different hybrids can be constructed using a case-based recommender as one component, and describes a series of experiments in which 20 different hybrids are built and evaluated. Cascade and feature augmentation hybrids are shown to have the highest accuracy over a range of different profile sizes.

1 Introduction

Recommender systems provide automated suggestions for users in e-commerce catalogs and other large multi-dimensional information spaces (Resnick & Varian, 1997). They have become a standard technology in electronic commerce (Schafer, et al., 1999). The most common implementations of this idea are collaborative (cross-user comparison) (for example, Hill, et al. 1995; Resnick, et al. 1994; Shardanand & Maes, 1995) and content-based (classification) (for example, Pazzani & Billsus, 1997). However, case-base reasoning technology has also been widely deployed to create knowledge-based recommender systems (Burke, 1999; Schmitt & Bergmann, 1999; Shimazu, 2001; Smyth & Cotter, 2000).

Every recommendation technique has inherent limitations, and for this reason, researchers have sought to build hybrid systems that combine techniques of different types. A recent survey (Burke, 2002) laid out a taxonomy of recommendation hybrids, finding that only a minority of the possible system designs had been explored in the research literature. In particular, very few knowledge-based hybrids were extant.

We have recently undertaken a large comparative study of 28 of these hybrid designs, slightly more than half of the design space (Burke, in preparation). This paper examines some of the results of that study, focusing on hybrid recommender systems in which a knowledge-based / case-based recommender is one component. From this study, this paper attempts to extract answers to the following questions: (1) How can a recommender system, particularly a case-based one, designed as a standalone entity, be adapted to serve as a recommendation component in different hybrid architectures? (2) Does hybridization deliver improved recommendation quality? (3) What hybridization techniques are the most promising for embedding a case-based recommendation component?

2 Recommendation Algorithms

Recommendation techniques can be distinguished on the basis of their knowledge sources: where does the knowledge needed to make recommendations come from? Three different classes of recommendation techniques are examined in this study[1].

Collaborative recommendation: In collaborative recommendation, the system generates recommendations using only users' rating profiles. When generating a recommendation for the current user U, a collaborative system uses data about what other users have preferred and extrapolates from the ratings of similar users to the preferences of U. This study uses two collaborative algorithms: a standard correlation-based technique, in which user profiles are correlated with the current user, and the predictions of the most highly-correlated neighbors are averaged to produce predictions for the current user (Herlocker, et al. 1999). This algorithm is labeled *CFP* in the figures below. A second technique, introduced in (Burke, 2000a), is a heuristic one. It depends on the peculiarities of the Entree dataset used in these experiments and is explained below. It is labeled *CFH*, and is included because early results demonstrated improved performance for this algorithm over CFP.

Content-based recommendation: A content-based recommender uses product features together with user ratings to learn a classifier that distinguishes between the "liked" and "disliked" categories for a given user. The implementation of this idea used in these experiments is the naive Bayes classifier, which has been shown to have good performance in many recommendation domains (Friedman, et al. 1997). The content-based algorithm is labeled *CN*.

Knowledge-based recommendation: As discussed above, a knowledge-based recommender attempts to suggest objects based on inferences about a user's needs and preferences. This knowledge will often contain explicit functional knowledge about how certain product features meet certain user needs. The knowledge-based recommender in these experiments is the Entree restaurant recommender (Burke, et al. 1997), labeled *KB*.

3 Hybrid Recommenders

We take the definition of a recommendation hybrid to be any recommender system that combines multiple recommender systems together to produce its output. These experiments examine four different types of hybrids:

- Weighted: The score of different recommendation techniques are combined numerically.
- Switching: The system chooses among recommendation techniques and applies the selected one.
- Cascade: Recommenders are given strict priority, with the lower priority ones breaking ties in the scoring of the higher ones.
- Feature Augmentation: One recommendation technique is used to compute a feature or set of features, which is then part of the input to the next technique.

---

[1] The fourth type described in (Burke, 2002), demographic recommendation, depends on the availability of demographic data, which was not available in the data set used in these experiments.

There are three hybrid types are not covered:
- Mixed: Recommendations from different recommenders are presented together, either side-by-side. This type cannot be evaluated using historical data in which options were not presented in this way.
- Feature Combination: Features derived from different knowledge sources are combined together and given to a single recommendation algorithm. The features that the knowledge-based recommender uses are the same as those used by the content-based recommender; they are just used in a different way, so a KB/CN feature combination is not truly a hybrid. A knowledge-based hybrid with a collaborative contributing recommender would be theoretically possible, but practically infeasible, and would run counter to the desire in this study to preserve the core recommendation logic of each component as much as possible.
- Meta-level: In a meta-level hybrid, one recommendation technique is applied and produces some sort of model, which is then the input used by the next technique. The meta-level hybrids were found to have inferior performances to other hybrid types and were omitted for reasons of space. See (Burke, in preparation) for these results.

Table 1 shows the design space explored in this paper. There are 20 two-component hybrids with 14 different designs (since the CFP and CFH hybrids differ in algorithmic details, not in design)[2]. The full design space for two-component hybrids has 25 designs: see (Burke, 2002). Note that the weighted recommender is symmetrical: there is no difference between a KB/CN and a CN/KB weighted hybrid. The CFH/KB feature augmentation recommender was precluded by efficiency considerations, as discussed below.

4 Methodology

The experiments described here use the Entree data set of restaurant ratings (Burke, 1999a; Burke, 2000b)[3]. It was implemented to serve as a guide to attendees of the 1996 Democratic National Convention in Chicago and operated as a web utility for approximately three years. The system is interactive, using a critiquing dialog (Burke et al. 1997; Shimazu, 2001) in which users' preferences are elicited through their reactions to examples that they are shown.

Figure 1 shows a user's interaction with the system. An initial query based on a favorite restaurant yields a similar Chicago establishment. The screen includes the critiquing buttons "Less $$", "Nicer", etc. by which the user navigates to other restaurants.

There are approximately 50,000 user sessions in the Entree data set, each of which consists of a starting point, which may be a restaurant or a query, a series of critiques, and finally an end point. This data set has some substantial differences from the standard collaborative-filtering data sets frequently used in the recommendation literature.

---

[2] There are other hybrid designs not considered. In particular, three-component designs and designs in which two components of similar design are used together. For example, News-Dude (Billsus & Pazzani, 2000) is a three component switching hybrid which uses two different kinds of content-based recommendation.

[3] The Entree data set is available from the UC Irvine KDD archive at http://kdd.ics.uci.edu/databases/entree/entree.html

Table 1. Hybrids described in the paper. (✓ indicates hybrids used in experiments, R indicates redundant designs, N hybrids that were not used)

	Weighted	Switching	Cascade	Feature Augmentation
KB/CN	✓	✓	✓	✓
CN/KB	R	✓	✓	✓
KB/CFP	✓	✓	✓	✓
CFP/KB	R	✓	✓	✓
KB/CFH	✓	✓	✓	✓
CFH/KB	R	✓	✓	N

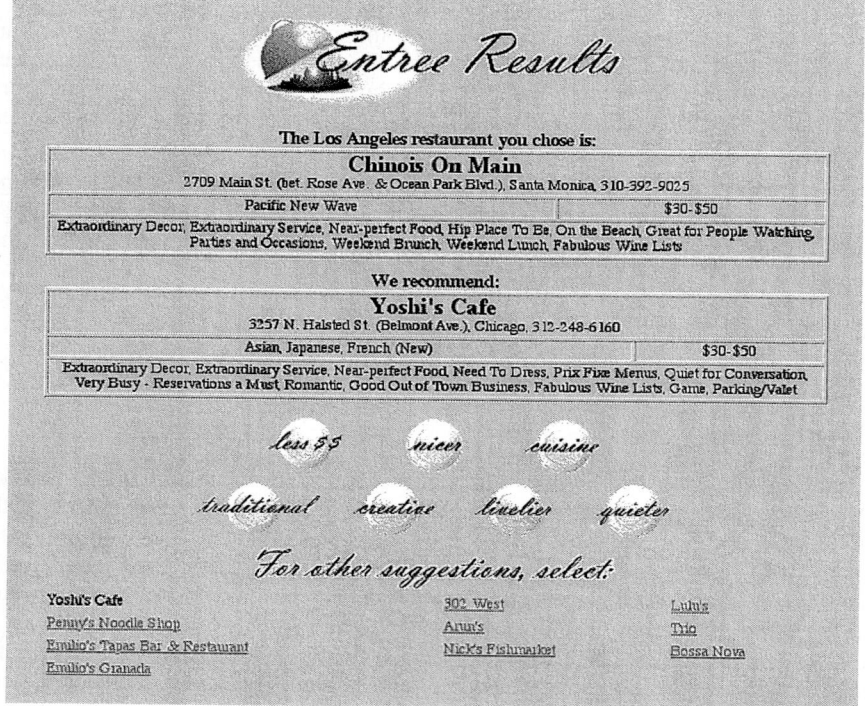

Fig. 1. Results of a query to the Entree restaurant recommender

The sessions are short, with only a small percentage containing more than a dozen interactions. User tracking technology was not employed when the system was deployed, but it is possible to heuristically join sessions into long-term user profiles of somewhat larger size. However, the task constraints of the restaurant search problem is such that long-term profiles are less likely to be valuable – an intuition borne out by experiment. With such short sessions, we cannot expect to get a large amount of information about a user, and this limits how well a recommender can be expected to perform.

Explicit rating data and standard web mining data such as dwell time are not available. However, we do have the evidence of the user's critiques. The critiques can be interpreted as negative ratings; they result in the user moving away from the suggestion that is shown. There are few actions that can be interpreted as positive ratings. The system allows a user to input a favorite restaurant as a starting point for recommendation, which can definitely be considered positive. However, this only occurs in about 10% of the sessions. End points may constitute either successful recommendations (which should be positive ratings) or abandoned sessions (noise). To determine the effects of this noise, we experimented using only the definite positive (starting point) ratings in the subset of the data in which these ratings are available. All of recommenders did better on this subset, but the pattern across recommenders was the same, exact what one would expect a less noisy rating signal. In the experiments described here, both start and end points are used as positive ratings, with the understanding that there is some noise in the positive rating data.

In the CFH algorithm, the profiles are not simplified by turning critiques into numeric ratings. Instead profile-to-profile comparison is performed using a similarity metric that takes the semantics of the critiques into account. Users who critique the same restaurant, but do so for different reasons ("Cheaper" vs "Nicer", for example) are considered different rather than similar.

In addition to single-visit profiles, we can examine multi-visit profiles. There are approximately 20,000 such profiles, collated using IP address. While there is some additional noise associated with these profiles (Mobasher, et al. 1999), they are included as an additional challenge that recommender systems are frequently called upon to meet.

The evaluation examines six different session sizes: three from single visits and three from multi-visit profiles: 5, 10 and 15 rating sessions from single visits; and 10, 20 and 30 rating sessions from multi-visit profiles. In figures, the single-visit profiles are marked with a capital "S" and the multi-visit profiles with a capital "M". In the case of 5-rating sessions, a 50% sample of the data is used for testing due to the large number of profiles of this size.

4.1 Evaluation

(Herlocker, et al. 2004) compares a variety of evaluation techniques for collaborative filtering systems. Herlocker and colleagues identify three basic classes of evaluation measures: discriminability measures (such as ROC-derived measures), precision measures (such as mean absolute error) and holistic measures (ones that work best when all user ratings and system predictions are pooled and evaluated as a group). In each of these groups, a wide variety of different metrics were found to be highly correlated, effectively measuring the same property. For the restaurant recommendation task, we are interested in a precision-type measure, and Herlocker's results tell us that we need not be extremely picky about how such a measure is calculated.

With short sessions and a dearth of positive ratings, there are some obvious constraints on how the Entree sessions can be employed and recommendation evaluated. An evaluation technique that requires making many predictions for a given user will not applicable, because there would not be enough of a profile left on which a collaborative system could base its prediction. This rules out such standard metrics as precision/recall and mean absolute error. Ultimately, in order to find good recommendations, the system must be able to prefer an item that the user rated highly. How well the system can do this is a good indicator of its success in prediction, so our evaluation will concentrate on the interactions interpreted as positive ratings. What we do is to record the rank of the positively-rated test item in the recommendation set returned by a given recommender. Averaging over many trials we can compute the "average rank of the correct recommendation" or ARC. The ARC measure provides a single value for comparing the performance of the hybrids, focusing on how well each can discriminate the item liked by the user from the others.

The evaluation of the recommenders proceeds as follows. The set of sessions is divided randomly into training and test parts of approximately equal size. This partition was performed five times and results from each test/training split averaged. Each algorithm is given the training part of the data as its input, each handling this data in its own way, and in some cases, such as with the knowledge-based recommender, it is ignored. Evaluation is performed on each session of the test data, simulating the interaction of the system with a single user. From the session, a single item with a positive rating is chosen at random, either the start or end point[4]. This item will be the test item on which the recommender's performance will be evaluated. All of the other ratings are considered part of the user profile.

The recommendation algorithm is then given the user profile without the positively-rated test item, and must make its recommendations. The result of the recommendation process is a ranked subset of the product database containing those items possibly of interest to the user. From this set, we record the rank of the positively-rated test item. Averaging over many trials we can compute the "average rank of the correct recommendation" or ARC. A perfect recommender would always rank the correct item in the top spot, so lower ARC scores are better. The ARC measure provides a single value for comparing the performance of the hybrids, capturing the recommender's performance from a user's perspective.

The content-based and collaborative components fit well into this evaluation paradigm. They are designed to accept a profile as input and produce a recommendation. A knowledge-based component is different. The Entree recommender needs a query in order to produce output, and in order to use such a component we must decide where its queries will come from. One possibility would be to use the features of all of the restaurants that appear in the profile and derive a composite representation that would serve as a query. This did not work well in practice, no doubt because the Entree interface encourages users to explore, and cumulative profiles contain many digressions. A better alternative is to pick the last item in the profile and use it as the query. It is temporally closest to the final entry and likely to be closest in terms of features as well.

5 Results

To provide a starting point for analysis of the hybrids, consider the results for the four basic algorithms, including the performance of the "average" recommender, which recommends restaurants based on their average rating from all users, and does not take the user profile into account.

Figure 2 shows the average rank of the correct recommendation (ARC) for each of the basic algorithms over the six different session size conditions. We should note that

---

[4] If there are no positive ratings, the session is discarded. We cannot evaluate the quality of recommendation if we have no information about what the user prefers.

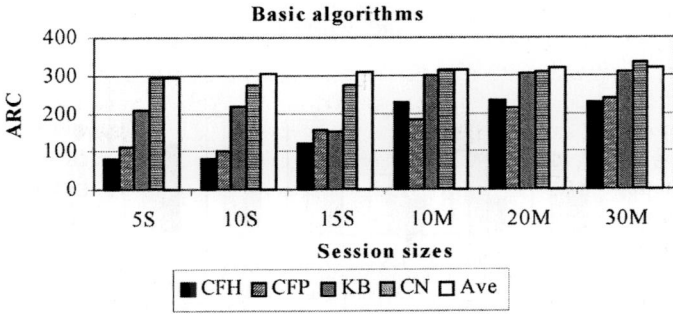

Fig. 2. Average rank results for the basic recommenders.

this recommendation task is shown to be quite difficult, especially for the multi-session profiles. The best any of these basic algorithms can manage is average rank of 80 for the correct answer, not inspiring in an e-commerce context where the user might be expected only to look at the first dozen results or so. This result is not unexpected: keep in mind the limited amount of data available on any given user an d the noise in the ratings data. The techniques vary widely in their performance on the Entree data. CFH is the best recommender for shorter single-visit profiles; CFP for multiple visit profiles. On the multi-visit profiles, all of the algorithms do worse, with the knowledge-based technique in particular falling back considerably from its single-session performance.

5.1 Weighted

Perhaps the simplest design for a hybrid system is a weighted one. Each component of the hybrid scores a given item and the scores are combined using a linear formula (Claypool, et al. 1999).

In a hybrid system, it is useful to separate the steps of candidate generation (the selection of possible recommendations) and scoring / ranking (the determination of the best recommendations). When a component operates alone, these steps naturally flow one to the other, but in a hybrid, their relationship may be more complex. A weighted hybrid in particular must handle items that are recommended by one component but not rated by the other. In my implementation, each recommender produces a set of candidates for recommendation, which are unioned together, then both recommenders score the candidate set and the candidates are ranked as recommendations. Entree returns integer scores[5], which are normalized to the range 0..1. To derive the optimum weighting, we examine all possible weightings (in discrete increments) and determine which weighting, over the training data, would yield the best ARC value.

Three combinations of the algorithms were used: KB/CFP, KB/CFH, and KB/CN. The results for this hybrid were rather surprising. Figure 3 shows the average rank results. In all but 3 of the 18 conditions, the performance of the combined recommenders was worse than the stronger recommender alone. In 8 of the conditions, the weighted hybrid was either the same or worse than the weakest recommender of the

---

[5] A peculiarity dictated by the system's similarity metrics (Burke, 2001).

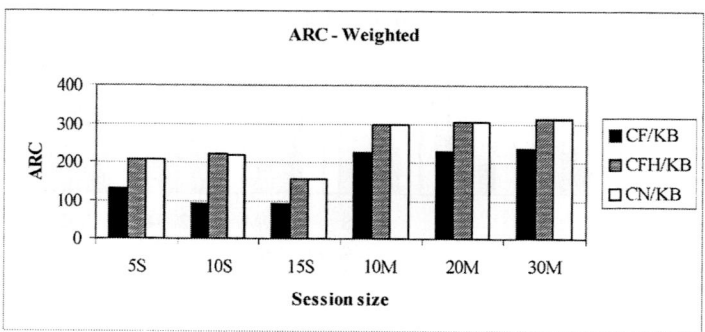

Fig. 3. Average rank results for weighted hybrids.

hybrid pair, with the remaining conditions showing performance in between the two components.

At first acquaintance, these are curious results, given that the recommender is merely using a weighted sum of the recommenders' scores. The reason has to do with the candidate selection step of the algorithm. Collaborative algorithms select items that have been rated by similar users, typically a small subset of the recommendation space. Knowledge-based recommenders are even more selective in their retrieval of only those items considered good recommendations. A content-based recommender, in our case, returns items containing positively-rated features, a larger and less discriminating candidate set. However, because the candidate sets do not overlap completely, a recommender will sometimes be required to rate products without a solid basis. In this way, a weighted hybrid that involves recommenders of differing degrees of selectivity always forces the more selective algorithms to compute ratings for items with essentially unknown relevance. Weighted recommendation should therefore be applied cautiously and with special attention to the problem of differing selectivity.

5.2 Switching

A switching hybrid is one that chooses a single recommender from among its constituents in each recommendation situation. In order to implement such a hybrid, there must be some criterion available to enable the switching decision. We can think of this value as a "confidence" value.

Ideally, we would survey the confidence values computed by each algorithm and choose the most confident. However, this would assume comparability between confidence values computed in different ways, and experiments showed this was not a valid assumption. An alternative is to select one component of the hybrid as the primary recommender and let it determine the confidence in its own prediction. If the primary recommender has confidence above some threshold, its recommendation will be used; otherwise, the secondary recommender takes over[6]. This distinction between

---

[6] There are other possibilities for implementing a switching hybrid. The system might look at the difference between confidence values or their ratio, for example. An alternative is to have a third metric outside of the hybrids as the switching criterion. Mobasher and Nakagawa (2003) describe a system in which a metric of site connectivity is used to determine which of two usage mining techniques to employ.

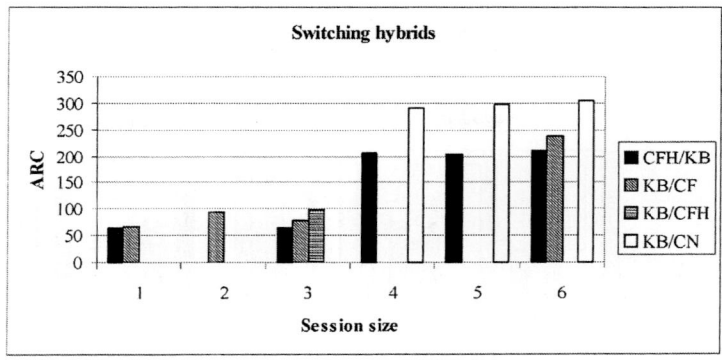

Fig. 4. Average rank results for switching hybrids

primary and secondary recommenders makes the switching hybrid an order-sensitive system. Like the weighted hybrid, all possible switching thresholds are tried and the threshold that maximizes ARC performance on the training set is used.

Each of the recommenders in the experimental set required a different confidence calculation. For the collaborative algorithms, the confidence value is computed using the inverse of the average distance between these peers and the user, since the closer the peers to the user, the more likely it should be that they are good predictors. For the naive Bayes algorithm, the choice of confidence metric is fairly straightforward – the value returned by the naive Bayes classifier is supposed to represent the probability that the classified object is a member of the given class. For the knowledge-based algorithm, the confidence is computed by finding the overlap in features between the top recommendation and the query. The intuition here is that if the knowledge-based system did not have to go far afield (and thereby making many inferences) to make its retrieval, then the results returned will be more confident.

To be a good primary recommender in this switching paradigm, the algorithm must have an accurate assessment of its own accuracy. Otherwise, it will turn over control to the secondary recommender when its own results might be more correct and make recommendations when the secondary one might be better. In some cases, the system determined that a threshold of 1.0 was the optimal confidence required for the primary algorithm, meaning that the recommender would have to compute a confidence > 1 in order for its recommendations to be used. This is an impossibility, and in such a case, the recommender falls back to being a non-hybrid made up only of the secondary component.

Figure 4 and the rest of the hybrid evaluation charts only show those hybrids that achieve synergy: that is, the hybrid together performs better than either of its components so the full range of results is not shown. Also, for switching hybrids, the degenerate (threshold = 1.0) cases have been omitted, so this chart shows only a subset of the systems tested. We find that the knowledge-based recommender seems to be a good primary component, perhaps having a more reliable confidence measure. In some conditions, strong synergy is achieved. The CFH algorithm alone achieved an ARC of 124 in the 15S condition, but the CFH/KB hybrid is close to half that value (65) in the same condition.

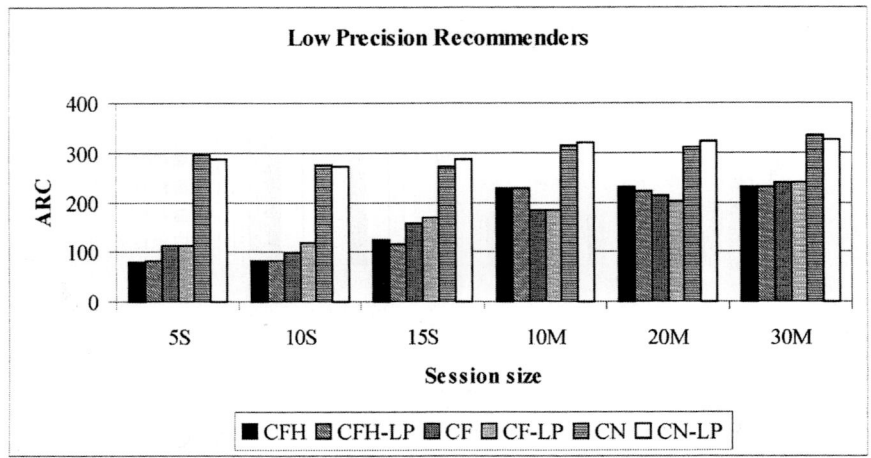

Fig. 5. Comparison of normal and reduced precision recommenders.

5.3 Cascade Hybrids

The idea of a cascade hybrid is to create a strictly hierarchical hybrid, one in which a weak recommender cannot overturn decisions made by a stronger one, but can merely refine them. A cascade recommender uses a secondary recommender only to break ties in the scoring of the primary one.

Many recommendation techniques have real-valued outputs and so the probability of identical scores is small. This would give the secondary recommender in a cascade little to do. In fact, the literature did not reveal any other instances of the cascade type at the time that the original hybrid recommendation survey was completed. However, the cascade hybrid raises the issue of the appropriate confidence interval for the score returned by recommendation algorithms, presumably much less precise than the full 32 bits in the computational representation. And, if the scoring of our algorithms is somewhat less precise, then there may be space in which a cascade can operate. Figure 5 shows the ARC graph comparing the CFP, CFH, and CN recommenders with full 32-bit precision against the same algorithms truncated to two decimal digits of precision (the LP versions). We see that overall the differences are very small and not always in the favor of the higher-precision algorithm. Our cascade hybrids therefore use these low-precision versions of the algorithms, generating ties that a secondary recommender can break.

With this result in mind, we can turn to the 6 available cascade recommenders. Figure 6 shows the ARC results for these hybrids. Again, only those recommenders demonstrating synergy are shown. The results are disappointing for the KB primary hybrids, the original systems explored in (Burke, 2002). However, the collaborative primary recommender, especially CFP/KB shows good accuracy. Most significant is the behavior on the multi-profile sessions, for which most systems examined so far have been inadequate.

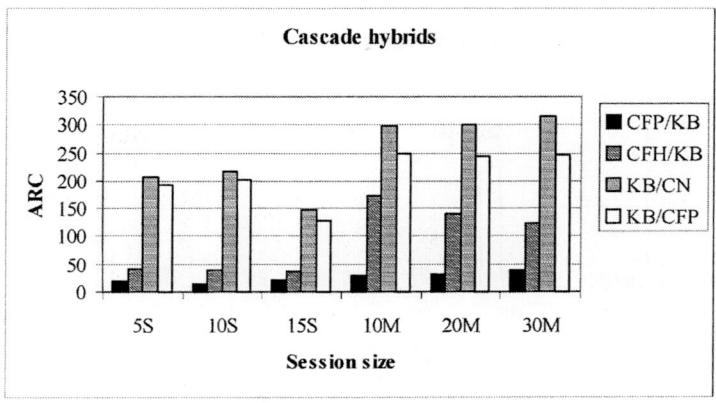

Fig. 6. Average rank results for cascade hybrids.

5.4 Feature Augmentation Hybrids

Feature augmentation is a strategy for hybrid recommendation in which a contributing recommender generates a new feature for each item, augmenting the data for the primary recommender with its own contribution. The augmentation can usually be done off-line, making this approach attractive when trying to strengthen an existing recommendation algorithm by adjusting its input.

The integration of components in a feature augmentation arrangement is somewhat trickier than in the hybrids seen so far. The contributing recommender must actually modify the input of the primary recommender and this is different than merely producing a score. So, the KB component must produce features associated with items that the other components can use, in order to be a contributing component, and it must reason with the features produced by the other components in order to be a primary recommender.

The feature generation technique used in these experiments is clustering. For example, to make CFP a contributing component, we cluster all of the restaurants using the user / ratings matrix. Each restaurant is then assigned a cluster id. This id becomes part of the input to the CN component, which is expecting input consisting of restaurants and their features.

When the KB component is the primary recommender, we use these ids in a very simple manner: an additional similarity metric is added to the recommender that prefers restaurants in the same cluster. This does require modification of the recommender, but it is the minimal amount required to make use of the new features.

When the KB component is the contributing recommender, there is no underlying data that can be used as features for this type of hybrid. When the CN component is primary, a similarity-based query is performed for each restaurant. The result set is then treated like a user profile and clustering is performed. Similar restaurants are those who get similar results when used as a query. The KB/CN feature augmentation hybrid uses these cluster ids as restaurant features.

The KB/CF feature augmentation hybrid is slightly different. The features that the CF component "understands" are profiles, lists of restaurants/rating pairs. A KB/CF hybrid can be achieved through "pseudo-users" (Sarwar, et al. 1998): computational-

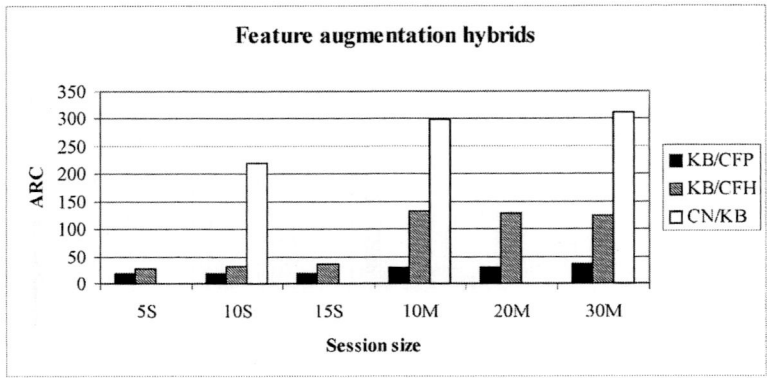

Fig. 7. Average rank results for feature augmentation hybrids

ly-generated "user" profiles. For a KB/CF hybrid, we create pseudo-users through retrieval. We perform retrieval based on the user profile and then create a pseudo-user, who gives positive ratings to all the restaurants returned by the query and negative ratings to the others.

No CFH/KB feature augmentation hybrid is considered here. That is not because the technique is inapplicable. However, because the data used by this version of the algorithm retains the semantics of the user's critiques, not just their valences. There are 10 possible values that may be associated with each restaurant in a profile. This increases the size and sparsity of the ratings matrix by a factor of 10 making the clustering operation computationally infeasible.

The results for these recommenders shown in Figure 7 are impressive for the cases where the knowledge-based component is contributing to the collaborative component. Here we see very strong performance, especially the KB/CFP recommender which has an ARC below 50 throughout all of the profile types. This follows the pattern seen in the cascade results, where a combination of a collaborative and a knowledge-based component produced the best results.

6 Discussion

These experiments have evaluated 20 different hybrid systems, and demonstrate that hybridization is worthwhile. Figure 8 shows average rank results for the best hybrids and for the best basic algorithms, and shows the dominance of the hybrids. Nowhere was this effect more striking than in the noisy multi-session profiles, which proved so much more difficult for even the stronger basic algorithms. Where the best result obtained on the 30-rating sessions by a basic algorithm was only an ARC of 227, the top two hybrids feature have ARC scores under 40. These top hybrids, which dominate in all conditions, are the feature augmentation and cascade hybrids in which CFP is the primary component and KB the secondary.

In retrospect, given the performance of the basic algorithms, the performance of the cascade recommenders is fairly predictable. The KB component as used here is

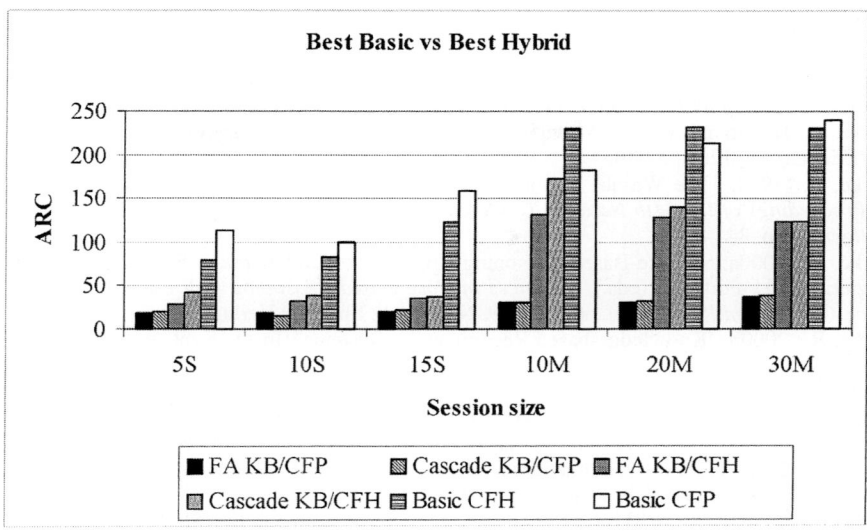

Fig. 8. Average rank results for best hybrids and best basic recommenders

relatively weak, but does take into account different data sources than the collaborative algorithms. A cascade design allows the KB recommender to have a positive impact on the recommendation process with no risk of negative impact – since it is only fine-tuning the judgments made by a stronger recommender. This performance was achieved by explicitly sacrificing numeric precision in the scoring of the primary recommender. In the feature augmentation designs also, we see a contributing recommender making a modest positive impact without the danger of interfering with the performance of the better algorithm.

Another consideration in the choice of hybridization techniques for recommendation is efficiency, particularly run-time efficiency, because recommendations are typically made on the fly to users expecting a quick interactive response. Of the hybrid designs, the weighted approach is the least efficient, requiring both recommenders to process every request. Among the strong performers in this study, the cascade hybrid also requires computation from both recommenders, but since the secondary recommender is only breaking ties, it is not required to retrieve any candidates and need only rate those items that need to be further discriminated. This can be done on demand as the user requests portions of the retrieval set. On the other hand, in the other top performing hybrid, the feature augmentation hybrid, the contributing recommender operates by adding features to the underlying representation. This step can be performed entirely off-line. So, the feature augmentation hybrid offers accuracy on par with the cascade hybrid with virtually no additional on-line computation.

These results are of course obtained in the domain of restaurant recommendation and with the Entree data set, so it is impossible to form any confident generalizations. These experiments do show that a case-based recommendation component can contribute to recommenders of varying configurations. These results should encourage implementers to experiment with a variety of hybrid designs.

References

Billsus, D. and Pazzani, M.: 2000. 'User Modeling for Adaptive News Access'. *User-Modeling and User-Adapted Interaction* 10(2-3), 147-180.

Burke, R., Hammond, K., and Young, B.: 1997, 'The FindMe Approach to Assisted Browsing'. *IEEE Expert*, 12(4), 32-40.

Burke, R.: 1999, 'The Wasabi Personal Shopper: A Case-Based Recommender System'. In: *Proceedings of the 11th National Conference on Innovative Applications of Artificial Intelligence*, pp. 844-849.

Burke, R.: 2000a, 'A Case-Based Reasoning Approach to Collaborative Filtering'. In E. Blanzieri and L. Portinale (eds.), *Advances in Case-Based Reasoning (5th European Workshop on Case-Based Reasoning)*, pp 370-379. New York: Springer Verlag.

Burke, R.: 2000b, 'Knowledge-based Recommender Systems'. In: A. Kent (ed.): *Encyclopedia of Library and Information Systems*. Vol. 69, Supplement 32.

Burke, R.: 2001, 'Ranking Algorithms for Costly Similarity Metrics'. In D. Aha, I. Watson and Q. Yang (eds.), *Case-Based Reasoning Research and Development (4th International Conference on Case-Based Reasoning)*, pages 105-117. New York: Springer Verla.

Burke, R.: 2002, 'Hybrid Recommender Systems: Survey and Experiments'. *User Modeling and User Adapted Interaction*, 12 (4), 331-370.

Burke, R.: in preparation, 'Hybrid Recommender Systems: Comparative Studies'.

Claypool, M., Gokhale, A., Miranda, T., Murnikov, P., Netes, D. and Sartin, M.: 1999, 'Combining Content-Based and Collaborative Filters in an Online Newspaper'. *SIGIR '99 Workshop on Recommender Systems: Algorithms and Evaluation*. Berkeley, CA.

Friedman, N., Gieger, M., and Goldszmidt, M.: 1997, 'Bayesian Network Classifiers'. *Machine Learning*, 29, 131-163.

Herlocker, J. L., Konstan, J. A., Borchers, A., and Riedl, J. T.: 1999, 'An Algorithmic Framework for Performing Collaborative Filtering'. In *ACM SIGIR 1999*, pp. 230-237.

Herlocker, J. L., Konstan, J. A., Terveen, L. G., and Riedl, J. T.: 2004, 'Evaluating Collaborative Filtering Recommender Systems'. *ACM Transactions on Information systems*. 22 (1).

Hill, W., Stead, L., Rosenstein, M. and Furnas, G.: 1995, 'Recommending and evaluating choices in a virtual community of use'. In: *CHI '95: Conference Proceedings on Human Factors in Computing Systems*, Denver, CO, pp. 194-201.

Mobasher, B. and Nakagawa, M.: 2003, 'A Hybrid Web Personalization Model Based on Site Connectivity'. In *Proceedings of the WebKDD Workshop at the ACM SIGKKDD International Conference on Knowledge Discovery and Data Mining*, Washington, DC, August 2003.

Mooney, R. J. and Roy, L.: 1999, 'Content-Based Book Recommending Using Learning for Text Categorization'. *SIGIR '99 Workshop on Recommender Systems: Algorithms and Evaluation*. Berkeley, CA.

Pazzani, M., Billsus, D.: 1997, 'Learning and Revising User Profiles: The Identification of Interesting Web Sites', *Machine Learning* 27, Kluwer Academic Publishers, pp. 313-331.

Resnick, P., Iacovou, N., Suchak, M., Bergstrom, P. and Riedl, J.: 1994, 'GroupLens: An Open Architecture for Collaborative Filtering of Netnews'. In: *Proceedings of the Conference on Computer Supported Cooperative Work*, Chapel Hill, NC, pp. 175-186.

Resnick, P. and Varian, H. R.: 1997, 'Recommender Systems'. *Communications of the ACM*, 40 (3), 56-58.

Sarwar, B. M., Konstan, J. A., Borchers, A., Herlocker, J. Miller, B. and Riedl, J.: 1998, 'Using Filtering Agents to Improve Prediction Quality in the GroupLens Research Collaborative Filtering System'. In: *Proceedings of the ACM 1998 Conference on Computer Supported Cooperative Work*, Seattle, WA, pp. 345-354.

Schafer, J. B., Konstan, J. and Riedl, J.: 1999, 'Recommender Systems in E-Commerce'. In: *EC '99: Proceedings of the First ACM Conference on Electronic Commerce*, Denver, CO, pp. 158-166.

Schmitt, S. and Bergmann, R.: 1999, 'Applying case-based reasoning technology for product selection and customization in electronic commerce environments.' *12th Bled Electronic Commerce Conference.* Bled, Slovenia, June 7-9, 1999.

Shardanand, U. and Maes, P.: 1995, 'Social Information Filtering: Algorithms for Automating "Word of Mouth"'. In: *CHI '95: Conference Proceedings on Human Factors in Computing Systems*, Denver, CO, pp. 210-217.

Shimazu, H.: 2001, 'ExpertClerk: Navigating Shoppers' Buying Process with the Combination of Asking and Proposing'. In B. Nebel, (ed.) *Proceedings of the Seventeenth International Joint Conference on Artification Intelligence*, pp. 1443-1448.

Smyth, B. and Cotter, P.: 2000, 'A Personalized TV Listings Service for the Digital TV Age'. *Knowledge-Based* Systems **13**: 53-59.

Measures of Solution Accuracy
in Case-Based Reasoning Systems

William Cheetham and Joseph Price

General Electric Company,
1 Research Circle, Niskayuna, NY 12309
{cheetham,pricejo}@research.ge.com

Abstract. The case-based reasoning (CBR) methodology can be augmented with the ability to determine the confidence in the correctness of individual solutions. A confidence calculation can be added to the REUSE portion of the CBR methodology. The confidence calculation takes confidence indicators, like "number of cases retrieved with best solution" and "average similarity of cases which suggest an alternative solution," and generates a confidence value. The information gain algorithm C4.5 can be used to select the best confidence indicators by evaluating their usefulness in historical cases. A genetic algorithm can be used to optimize and maintain the confidence calculation.

1 Introduction

Mark Twain is quoted as saying, "I was gratified to be able to answer promptly, and I did. I said I didn't know." If a person is asked a question and they do not know the answer, they are usually able to say that they are not confident in their ability to give a correct answer. When a person does not have confidence, they may not be able to answer at all (by saying "I don't know") or they may supply multiple guesses at what the answer could be. The ability to know the limits of one's knowledge is valuable in an intelligent system. This paper describes how a Case-Based Reasoning (CBR) [1, 9] system can be constructed to provide a measure of its solution accuracy that says when it is confident in its answer, when it is not able to answer the question, or when there are multiple possible answers.

Our primary motivation for creating an intelligent system that can determine its confidence in each solution it produces is to improve efficiency of business processes by automating actions when a CBR system has high confidence in its solution. Knowledge-based decision tasks that can benefit from automation include financial tasks such as granting or rejecting applications for insurance or credit and service tasks such as diagnosing or predicting failures with machinery. All of these tasks are currently performed by experts and are difficult to automate because some instances of each task can be quite complicated. An intelligent system that knows when it should and should not be used to automate a task can be very valuable because it can have a low error rate on the tasks that it does automate and pass the tasks where it is more likely to be incorrect on to the person who had been performing that task. This would free the person from the burden of dealing with routine instances of a task and allow them to focus on the unique and difficult to automate instances.

If there were always a person evaluating the output of a CBR system and deciding what action to perform, then similarity values, which most CBR systems output, would probably be sufficient for the person to make their decision. However, when the person is removed from the loop, more certainty that a specific action should be performed then is available from just the similarity values is often required. Having the CBR system determine the predicted accuracy of its solution is one way to provide the certainty that is needed to automate the task. There can be large financial benefits from automating even a percentage of the occurrences of expensive decision tasks. Other benefits of the automated process include speed, consistency, and the ability to monitor and optimize the process. These benefits, financial and otherwise, have driven General Electric to automate multiple decision tasks by using a CBR system with an integrated confidence calculation. Some example applications are described in section 5.

There are many other reasons that it would be beneficial to have intelligent systems that can give "I don't know" as a possible answer. First, if a system is presented with a problem that it was not designed to solve and is forced to give an answer it would probably give an inaccurate one. Second, the domain for which the system was created might change over time. If the system was forced to give an answer after the domain changed, there could be a situation when the system would not be able to give an informed answer, but will still give an answer. Third, if there is an alternative method of determining an answer, such as using a different system or having a person create it manually, then it would be good to know when these alternatives should be used instead of the usual system.

Before determining how a CBR system can produce a measure of confidence in its output, we should first observe how humans determine confidence in their decisions. Specifically, since we are determining confidence for CBR systems, we should analyze how humans determine confidence using experience. If a person has no experience relating to a decision they would have low confidence in any guess at a solution. If they had many previous experiences with similar problems, and if all of these experiences indicated the same solution could be applied to this problem, then they would have high confidence in that solution. If a person has conflicting evidence regarding the solution to a problem then their confidence level would be reduced to some 'medium' level. One method they might use to determine confidence is to list the evidence supporting the solution and the evidence against the solution, then determine if the supporting evidence outweighs the contrary evidence. There is also the possibility of giving multiple answers when there is no clear winner and there are multiple potential solutions. It is bad for people to have either too little of too much confidence in the decisions. Someone who has too little confidence can be thought of as timid or unsure of himself. Someone who has too much confidence can be thought of as arrogant or conceited.

Different problems could require different levels of certainty in order to have high confidence. If there is little harm done by giving an incorrect answer then a low level of certainty would be needed to provide an answer. An example of this type of CBR system would be one that presents possible solutions for review by a user. If an incorrect answer produces a large problem, then a high level of certainty would be needed. An example of this type of CBR system would be one that automatically takes an action based on the solution.

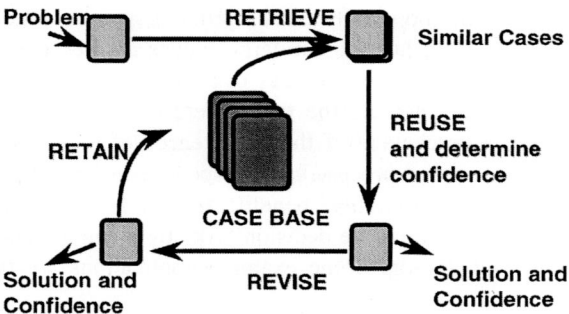

Fig. 1. Confidence Calculation in CBR Cycle

The computation of the confidence measure is added to the traditional CBR process [1] as is shown in Figure 1. The confidence calculation, which determines the confidence measure, is added to the REUSE phase and a confidence value is output along with the solution. The confidence calculation is calibrated off-line using information from the case base and executed at run-time using values that are calculated as part of the CBR process. A variety of values from the RETRIEVE and REUSE phases can be used by the confidence calculation. The values from the RETRIEVE phase can include the number of cases retrieved (cardinality), similarity of each retrieved case, span of solutions suggested by the set of all retrieved cases, and standard deviation in the set of solutions in the retrieved cases if the solutions are numeric. The values from the REUSE phase include the gross and net amount of adaptation done to the retrieved cases. The exact values used are determined in the off-line calibration. The confidence calculation uses these values to calculate a confidence measure. The confidence measure is used as input to the REVISE phase and as part of the output of the CBR system.

This paper will describe what output should be produced by the confidence calculation in section 2. The off-line calibration process for designing and tuning the confidence calculation will be described in section 3. Section 4 will describe the maintenance and optimization of the confidence calculation.

2 Output of a CBR System with Confidence

The output of a CBR system can include a number (e.g., a price or time), a discrete item (e.g., a recommendation, document, or plan), or a set of items. The confidence calculation will change slightly for different output types. The confidence calculation also depends on what will be done with that output. If a person will use the result to determine an appropriate action from a set of possible actions, then a discrete term should be used as the confidence (e.g., High or Low), with a different term for each possible action. For example, if the result will determine if a person's application for insurance should be accepted or not [3] then the confidence calculation should produce two values, High and Low. High indicates that the CBR system should be used for determining the acceptance and Low indicates that another method should be used (e.g., a detailed review by a human). However, if there is a third option (e.g., a human quickly reviewing issues highlighted by the CBR system) then three levels of confidence can be used (High, Medium, Low) with Medium corresponding to the quick review action.

If the result of the CBR system will be processed in some way before a crisp decision is needed (e.g., reviewed by a human or combined with the result of another decision support system) then a numeric value would be appropriate. The meaning of various values of the number should have specific meanings. For example, the number could be the predicted percentage that the solution is correct. Another example would be having the number be from [0,1] where 1 means predicted 90% correct, 0.75 means 80% correct, 0.50 means 70% correct, 0.25 means 60% correct, and 0 means 50% correct (random guess if there are only two options).

3 Creating a Confidence Calculation

This section presents a process for the off-line creation of the confidence calculation. The process includes

- Identifying potential indicators that could be used to determine confidence.
- Using statistics about the case base to determine which indicators work best and how those indicators correspond to confidence.
- Creating a simple formula that takes the indicators selected and produces a confidence value.

There are a few assumptions that need to hold in order to use a confidence calculation

- An evaluation method needs to exist for rating the performance of the system
- The case base needs to be a representative sample of the problems that the CBR system is to solve.
- The case base needs to be large enough to produce the desired confidence. Typical sizes are over 500 cases.

3.1 Identifying Confidence Indicators

A confidence indicator is any piece of information that can be used to determine if there should or should not be confidence in the result of the CBR system. A simple indicator of confidence is the similarity of an item retrieved to the problem the system is trying to solve. The reasoning for this is: the more similar the problem is to the retrieved case, the more applicable the solution suggested by that case should be to the problem, and thus the higher the confidence.

If the CBR system is based on k-nearest neighbor (kNN) retrieval and the final solution from the CBR system (when all nearest neighbors are combined into one solution) is a discrete item called the best solution, then the following indicators could be useful in determining confidence:

1. Sum of similarities for retrieved cases with best solution
2. Similarity of the single most similar case with best solution
3. Number of cases retrieved with best solution
4. Number of cases retrieved with second best solution
5. Percent of cases retrieved with best solution
6. Sum of similarities for second best solution
7. Sum of similarities for all other solutions (not best)
8. Average similarity of cases with best solution
9. Average similarity of cases with second best solution
10. Average similarity of cases not having best solution
11. Similarity of most similar case
12. A Boolean value that is one if the most similar case has the best solution and zero otherwise

Higher values of indicators 1, 2, 3, 5, 8, and 12 would give you higher confidence in the solution suggested, indicator 11 can give higher or lower confidence, and the other indicators would give you lower confidence. Both positive and negative indicators should be included in a confidence calculation.

If the solution of the CBR system is a numeric value the following indicators could be used, in addition to the ones above.

1. Standard deviation in the solution values of the k most similar cases
2. Range of solutions (Max solution value – Min solution value) in the k most similar cases

3.2 Determining Which Indicators Are Best

After the possible indicators are identified, an analysis of how historical cases were evaluated using the case-based reasoning process can show which indicators are best for determining confidence. The analysis involves using leave-one-out testing, which runs the CBR process to determine a solution for each case in the case base as if that case was a new problem not in the case base. The value of each indicator is stored for each case evaluated using leave-one-out testing. Table 1 shows some of these values for an equipment diagnostic system where k of kNN is 8 and the value "match" which is 1 if the suggested solution was correct and zero otherwise.

The algorithm C4.5 [12] can be used on the table to identify indicators that are best at determining confidence. C4.5 is an information gain algorithm for inducing decision trees and rules from data. In this case, the trees show the indicators which are best at determining if a solution produced by the case-based reasoner will be correct or not (i.e., if "match" is one or zero). The more likely the solution is to be correct the higher our confidence should be. An example of the output of C4.5 is given in Figure 2. The figure can be read as a tree where each line is a branch in the tree. That branch should be followed if the condition at the beginning of the line is true. Each branch that leads to a leaf of the tree has its condition followed by a colon, number, and either one or

Table 1. Confidence Indicators

Sum of Sim for Best	Max Sim for Best	Neighbor Count for Best	Total Neighbor Count	Sum of Sim for non-Best	Sum of Sim for 2nd solution	Suggested Solution (Best)	Real Solution	Match
16.923	2.21	8	8	0	0	Other	Other	1
20.286	2.83	8	8	0	0	Fault 1	Fault 1	1
19.511	2.63	8	8	0	0	Other	Fault 2	0
16.646	2.48	7	8	2.31	2.31	Other	Fault 3	0
20.695	2.85	8	8	0	0	Other	Other	1
12.783	2.23	6	8	4.21	4.21	Other	Other	1
14.384	2.53	6	8	4.64	2.32	Fault 4	Other	0
16.704	2.58	7	8	2.26	2.26	Other	Other	1
19.085	2.6	8	8	0	0	Other	Other	1

```
Sum_of_Sim_for_non-Best<= 15.1: 1 (377.0/34.0)
Sum_of_Sim_for_non-Best> 15.1
| 2nd_solution = Other
| | suggested_solution = Other: 1 (0.0)
| | suggested_solution = Fault 1
| | | case_count_for_SS <= 5: 1 (4.0)
| | | case_count_for_SS > 5: 0 (2.0)
| | suggested_solution = Fault 4: 1 (7.0/1.0)
| | suggested_solution = Fault 2: 0 (1.0)
| | suggested_solution = Fault 3: 1 (11.0)
| 2nd_solution = Fault 1
| | case_count_for_Best <= 4: 0 (10.0)
| | case_count_for_Best > 4
| | | Max_Confidence <= 27.86: 0 (2.0)
| | | Max_Confidence > 27.86: 1 (4.0/1.0)
| 2nd_solution = Fault 4: 1 (1.0)
| 2nd_solution = Fault 2
| | Max_Similarity_for_Best <= 8.94: 0 (7.0/1.0)
| | Max_Similarity_for_Best > 8.94: 1 (12.0)
| 2nd_solution = Fault 3: 0 (6.0/2.0)
| 2nd_solution = N/A: 1 (0.0)
```

Fig. 2. C4.5 Results

two numbers in parenthesis. The set of braches from the leaf branch to the root can be thought of as a rule. The fist number in the leaf branch is one if that rule classifies "match" as true, and zero if "match" is classified as false. The first number in parenthesis is the count of historical cases where this rule applied. If there is no second number in parenthesis then every historical case using this rule was classified correctly. If there is a number it is a count of cases that were classified incorrectly by this rule. For example, the first line of Figure 2 is a one branch rule that says if the sum of similarities for the cases which did not suggest the solution is less than 15.1 then the suggested solution was correct all but 34 times out of 377 historical cases where this condition existed. So, 343 out of 377 cases, or 91%, were correct. Since we assumed the case base is a representative sample of problems expected in the future, we can expect that 91% of the time this rule holds in the future the solution will be correct.

3.3 Confidence Formula

The confidence formula can be created to output a term (e.g., High or Low) or a number (e.g., real numbers from zero to one). Each of these options will be discussed in the following sections.

3.3.1 Confidence as a Term

If a term is produced by the confidence formula then the formula can simply implement a modified version of the C4.5 decision tree. In the case where only High and Low confidence values are generated, the formula would determine when the system should have High confidence. First users should specify what the meanings are for each term, such as

- High: the historical error rate should be 10% or less
- Low: the historical error rate can not be shown to be less than 10%

The tree is modified by combining, also called pruning [14], branches where all siblings have a historical correctness less than needed for High confidence (more than 10% incorrect) or too few historical cases (less than 10). Similarly, sibling branches can be combined when all siblings have a historical correctness greater than or equal to what is needed for high confidence. The modified tree is shown in Figure 3. This tree has two leaf nodes with error rate less than 10% and 10 or more cases. The tree can be implemented to give High confidence in these two situations and low confidence in all others. An alternative method of pruning is to modify the confidence parameter, c, of C4.5. The default confidence parameter is 25. Higher values give larger trees and smaller values give smaller trees. Using a lower value would be *prepruning* the tree as opposed to the *postpruning* described above. Witten and Frank [14] believe that most decision tree builders postprune and we agree with this.

```
Sum_of_Sim_for_non-Best<= 15.1: 1 (377.0/34.0)
Sum_of_Sim_for_non-Best> 15.1
| 2nd_solution = Other: 1 (25.0 / 4.0)
| 2nd_solution = Fault 1: 0 (16.0 / 3.0)
| 2nd_solution = Fault 4: 1 (1.0)
| 2nd_solution = Fault 2
| | Max_Similarity_for_Best <= 8.94: 0 (7.0/1.0)
| | Max_Similarity_for_Best > 8.94: 1 (12.0)
| 2nd_solution = Fault 3: 0 (6.0/2.0)
| 2nd_solution = N/A: 1 (0.0)
```

Fig. 3. Modified C4.5 Results (high confidence leafs in bold)

Different values of acceptable error rate (i.e., different definitions of High confidence) can produce different trees. If the error rate desired was 20% or less, then the modified tree would be the same, but three leaf nodes would indicate High confidence (the 2nd_solution = Other:1 (25.0/4.0) branch would now indicate High confidence).

Different error rates can be plotted in a graph that shows the relationship between precision and recall. Figure 4 is a plot that shows the precision (1 − error rate) and recall (percentage of historical cases in subtrees with High confidence) for three trees [14]. The three points are for differing error rates for High confidence; one where the historical error rate of a subtree needs to be 10% for it to have High confidence, a second where the historical error rate needs to be 20%, and a third where all historical items have High confidence. Obviously, high recall and high precision is desirable. However, if a tradeoff is forced, high precision is usually chosen in real world applications where an action is taken automatically. The high precision is desirable because the cost of an incorrect solution is higher than the cost of not giving a solution.

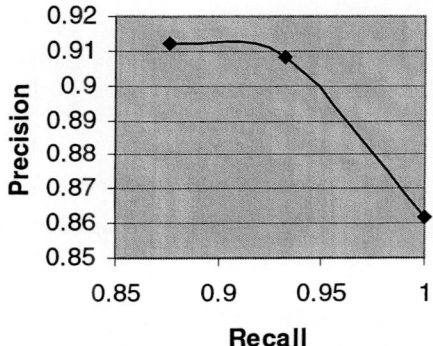

Fig. 4. Precision Recall Graph

A confidence algorithm can be constructed from the selected tree. The algorithm includes one conditional for each subtree that terminates in a High confidence leaf. If a new case being evaluated would have been classified by that subtree, then it is given High confidence. Otherwise, it is given Low confidence. For the example above with error rate equal to 10% the algorithm is shown Equation 1.

If Sum_of_Sim_for_non-Best <= 15.1 or
    (2nd_solution = Fault 2 and Max_Similarity_for_Best > 8.94)   (1)
then confidence is High
else confidence is Low

As the case base changes, the parameters 15.1 and 8.94 can be tuned to optimize the confidence calculation. This tuning process will be described in section 4.

3.3.2 Confidence as a Number

A different method for creating the confidence formula can be used if a numeric value is needed for confidence. This number should range from zero to one with zero indicating no confidence and one meaning maximum confidence. The process is to construct an algorithm that converts the quantitative confidence indicators into a normalized numeric indicator. The numeric indicators are then combined into one confidence value for the solution. A confidence indicator can be converted into a numeric indicator using a fuzzy membership function [7]. Figure 5 shows a fuzzy membership function that transforms the confidence indicator "Sum of Similarities for Best" into a normalized confidence value. The normalized confidence would be 0 for Sum of Similarity values less than 11 and 1 for values greater than 12. For values in between 11 and 12, the normalized confidence would equal (value − 11). Figure 6 shows the membership function for "Number of Neighbors with Best". A weighted sum of the normalized indicators will produce the confidence value in the solution. For more details on creating a numeric confidence value see [5].

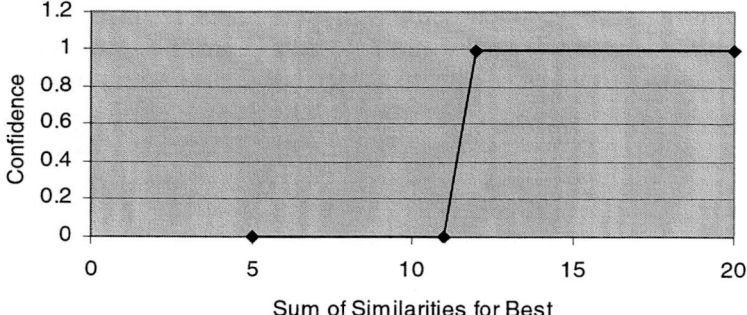

Fig. 5. Sum of Similarity Membership Function

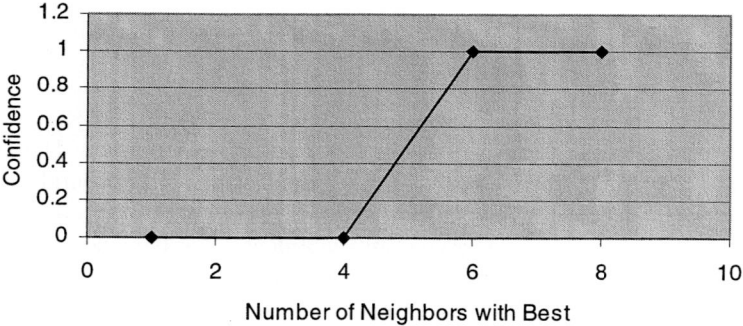

Fig. 6. Number of Neighbors Membership Function

4 Optimizing the Confidence Formula

The confidence formula may need to change over time as cases are added or removed from the case base. This section describes how to maintain the confidence calculation. The maintenance process can also be used to optimize the calculation when it is initially created. The optimization finds the best numerical parameters for the confidence calculations. One reasonable solution is to use a genetic algorithm to perform the optimization [2]. The major effort in using a genetic algorithm to optimize the confidence parameters lies in creating the evaluation function.

4.1 Evaluation Function

Creating the evaluation function is non-trivial once confidence enters the picture, and it becomes much more difficult if multiple guesses with different confidence levels are allowed as the output of the decision for one case. One way of evaluating a CBR system is with a single number created by the product of a confusion matrix, which summarizes the results of leave-one-out testing, and a reward matrix, which assigns a reward to each cell of the confusion matrix [11]. The confusion matrix contains one cell for every possible output of each input. As an example confusion matrix, we will assume the engine is classifying a machine into one of two classes, Broken (B) or Normal (N). The confusion matrix would then be as shown in Figure 7.

		Classified As		
		Broken	Normal	Totals
Reality	Broken	True Broken (TB)	False Normal (FN)	Real Broken (RB)
	Normal	False Broken (FB)	True Normal (TN)	Real Normal (RN)
	Totals	Classified Broken (CB)	Classified Normal (CN)	All Cases (AC)

Fig. 7. Confusion Matrix

To compute the score, simply multiply each cell of the confusion matrix by its corresponding cell in the reward matrix and sum the products. For this evaluation process, a higher sum indicates a better result.

For the example in Figure 8, the total score would be 4320+0-740+1895 or 5475. This provides a convenient way of comparing two confusion matrices (generated by two tests).

Confusion Matrix		
	Broken	Normal
Broken	432	25
Normal	37	379

Reward Matrix		
	Broken	Normal
Broken	10	0
Normal	-20	5

Products		
	Broken	Normal
Broken	4320	0
Normal	-740	1895

Fig. 8. Reward Matrix Example

If multiple guesses with different confidences are allowed, then the reward matrix can still be used for evaluation. The challenge comes in populating the confusion matrix. There are many different ways of doing this, and the authors currently favor one they created called "Insertion Halt". For each case, this method first sorts the different guesses in order of decreasing confidence (it is assumed that the confidences add up to 1 for each case). It then inserts the guesses into the confusion matrix, but instead of inserting a 1, the confidence value is inserted. When the correct answer is found, no guesses of lower confidence are placed in the confusion matrix. This attempts to mimic the fact that once the user finds the correct answer, he or she will not take the time to reject the remaining unverified guesses. This has the effect of increasing the score for sets that contain a correct guess by eliminating all penalties for guesses with lower confidence than the correct guess.

4.2 Optimizing Confidence as a Term

The parameters to be optimized when confidence is expressed as a term are the cutoffs or boundaries of the confidence rules. The two parameters from the confidence algorithm in Formula 1 are 15.1 and 8.94. The chromosome for the GA would include two real values, one for each of these parameters.

4.3 Optimizing Confidence as a Number

For confidence expressed as a number, the parameters to be optimized are the two inputs to each membership function (we will call them A & B), and the weights for each normalized indicator. For a given indicator, A is the least value where the normalized confidence is greater than zero. B is the least value where the normalized confidence equals one. For figure 6, A is four and B is six. Each chromosome would include three values for every confidence indicator – A, B, and its weight. Changes in the case base, the evaluation function, or the domain would trigger re-optimization.

4.4 Maintaining the Calculation

The problems solved by a CBR tool can change over time and the confidence calculation should also be able to change to reflect this. Some of the potential changes in a CBR tool are the addition of new cases to the case base, the changing importance of attributes, or changes in the problem domain. The changes to the CBR system could be minor or major. When minor changes take place, like attribute weights being changed or slight algorithm changes, then maintenance should optimize the parameters in the confidence calculation. When major algorithm changes are made or many new cases are added, then a thorough CBR maintenance process should be performed. This includes repeating the entire process for determining confidence (including identifying new attributes and re-optimizing those parameters).

The knowledge contained in a CBR application can be contained in the cases or the various compiled algorithms for retrieving, reusing, revising, and retaining the cases [13]. Both types of knowledge, cases and compiled algorithms, need to be maintained. This paper described the compiled knowledge in a new type of knowledge container called a confidence calculation.

The maintenance of the compiled knowledge will be simplified if these algorithms have tunable parameters that control the execution of the algorithm. Retuning the parameters would be easier than changing the source code of the algorithms. The genetic algorithm, described in section 3.4, can be used to maintain the parameters.

5 Applications

The methodology described here, or an earlier version, has been used by the authors during the development of the following applications:
- A system to estimate the value of residential real estate, called PROFIT. [4]
- A medical equipment diagnostic system, called ELSI. [8]
- A tool for selecting pigments that produce a given color when added to plastic, called FormTool. [6]
- A large gas turbine diagnostic system.

The PROFIT tool has been tested extensively. The ELSI and FormTool systems have been in use for at least five years. The fourth system is still under development. PROFIT resulted in a much lower average error for the real estate estimates when the system had high confidence. 63% of the test subjects were had high confidence. The set with high confidence had a median error or 5.4% and the set with low confidence had a median error of 9.3%. ELSI had high confidence 76% of the time. The set with high confidence was correct 91% of the time. The set with low confidence was correct under 50% of the time. FormTool was designed to automatically pass the task to a heuristic-based expert system when confidence was low. McLaren and Ashley have used a similar approach for providing advice on engineering ethics cases [10].

For industrial applications like these, the more an application can automate a task the more valuable it will be. An application that performs a portion of a process has some value, but an application that can automate the entire process, including taking any action that is required, would have greater value. A confidence value can specify when an action should be taken automatically or could guide a user in what action to take. This is valuable in many situations, but is specifically valuable when the CBR system will assist a human in performing some task that previously was done only by the human. In this common situation, a CBR tool that includes a confidence calculation can automate the repetitive tasks when confidence is high and assist the user with the unique or complicated tasks.

6 Conclusion

Many artificial intelligence techniques can be used to solve knowledge-based problems. However, many real world problems require their solution to have high accuracy. One of the great failings of AI is that few systems are always correct and it is often difficult to determine if a specific solution is likely to be correct or not. This causes even a small error rate to be a problem. But there is hope; we can increase the accuracy of the system by not forcing it to give a solution to every problem. Some of the time it can say, "I don't know." The knowledge in a case base for a CBR system is specifically useful in determining when the CBR system should say, "I don't know." This paper showed how the standard CBR methodology could be enhanced to include a determination of the confidence in the solution. The confidence value can be useful in determining what to do with the solution that was generated. The confidence enhanced CBR methodology allows CBR to be used in the frequent real world situation where large amounts of data exist, high accuracy is needed, and the system can say "I don't know" when the confidence of the best possible solution is low.

References

1. Aamodt, A., Plaza, E.: Case-Based Reasoning: Foundational Issues, Methodological Variations, and System Approaches, AICOM, Vol. 7, No. 1 (1994)
2. Aggour, K., Pavese, M., Bonissone, P., Cheetham, W.: SOFT-CBR: A Self-Optimizing Fuzzy Tool for Case-Based Reasoning, The 5th International Conference on Case-Based Reasoning, Trondheim, Norway, June 23 -26 (2003)
3. Bonissone, P., Cheetham, W.: Fuzzy Case-Based Reasoning for Decision Making. Proceedings of the IEEE International Conference on Fuzzy Systems. Melbourne, Australia (2001)
4. Bonissone, P., Cheetham, W.: Financial Applications of Fuzzy Case-Based Reasoning to Residential Property Valuation, Proc 6th IEEE Conf. on Fuzzy Systems, Barcelona, Spain (1997)
5. Cheetham, W.: Case-Based Reasoning with Confidence. Fifth European Workshop on Case-Based Reasoning. Trento, Italy, September (2000)
6. Cheetham, W.: Case-Based Reasoning for Color Matching, Second Int. Conf. Case-Based Reasoning, Providence, RI (1997)
7. Cheetham, W.: Case-Based Reasoning with Confidence, Ph.D. Thesis, Rensselaer Polytechnic Institute, August (1996)
8. Cuddihy, P., Cheetham, W.: ELSI: A Medical Equipment Diagnostic System. Third Int. Conf. Case-Based Reasoning. Seeon Monastery, Germany, July (1999).
9. Kolodner, J.: Case-Based Reasoning, Morgan Kaufmann Publishers Inc (1993)
10. McLaren, B., Ashley, K.: Helping a CBR Program Know What It Knows, International Conference on Case-Based Reasoning, Vancouver, British Columbia, Canada (2001)
11. D. Michie, D. J. Spiegelhalter & C. C. Taylor, eds.:. "Machine Learning, Neural and Statistical Classification", Ellis Horwood 1994
12. Quinlan, R.: C4.5: Programs for Machine Learning, Morgan Kaufmann (1993)
13. Richter, M.: The Knowledge Contained in Similarity Measures, Invited talk given at ICCBR'95, http://www.cbr-web.org/documents/Richtericcbr95remarks.html (1995)
14. Witten, I., Frank, E.: Data Mining: Practical Machine Learning Tools and Techniques with JAVA Implementations, Chapter 6, Morgan Kaufmann (2000)

Representing Similarity for CBR in XML

Lorcan Coyle, Dónal Doyle, and Pádraig Cunningham

Department of Computer Science
Trinity College Dublin
{Lorcan.Coyle,Donal.Doyle,Padraig.Cunningham}@cs.tcd.ie

Abstract. As Case-Based Reasoning has matured as a discipline; the need for a standard means of representing case-based knowledge has come to the fore. While proposals exist for representing the vocabulary and the case-base knowledge containers, there are still no proposed standards for representing similarity or adaptation knowledge. In this paper we present extensions for representing similarity knowledge to CBML, an XML-based CBR language.

1 Introduction

Kitano and Shimazu have proposed that CBR applications have been too narrowly focused on domain specific problems [12]. They suggested that a CBR system should be viewed as a *medium* to be used in conjunction with the mainstream corporate information system. We share this perspective and anticipate that a standard way of marking up cases will facilitate this. The standard proposed for marking up structured, knowledge-rich data is XML. Our earlier work [3, 9, 10] described an XML-based case representation language called CBML (Case-Based Markup Language). Several other XML-based CBR systems have appeared over the past few years, e.g. [8, 15]. However, as Wilson has pointed out, the benefits that accrue to XML in general will not be fully passed on to the CBR community until a *standard* means of representing case data in XML is developed [18]. We propose that CBML has the capabilities to become such a standard.

Richter has identified four different ways in which knowledge can be represented in a Case-Based Reasoning (CBR) system [14]. He has named these *knowledge containers* and they have met wide acceptance as a natural organisation of knowledge in CBR. Richter's knowledge containers are:

- The vocabulary used,
- The similarity measure,
- The casebase,
- The solution transformation

Given the wide acceptance of this organisation of knowledge in CBR, it is perhaps surprising that attempts to create a representation language for CBR have concentrated for the most part on the vocabulary and casebase containers, e.g. [8, 11]. Our earlier work also focused on the vocabulary and casebase containers. This paper describes our more recent work on the representation of the similarity measure container. This representation is an extension of the CBML standard and allows the CBR developer to make the definition of similarity completely independent from the application code. Section 2 outlines the requirements for such a representation and describes our approach. Section 3 describes some advantages that we have observed in the fields of personalization, distributed CBR, explanation-based CBR and collaborative CBR.

2 Representation of Similarity

This section outlines the representation of similarity in CBML. It begins with a brief description of the feature types, documents the requirements for representing the traditional similarity function, and finishes with a description of how this is achieved in CBML. A number of example CBML fragments are used to illustrate the representation.

2.1 CBML – Cases and Case Structures

CBML was originally developed to facilitate distributed CBR and modular CBR objects. There were two CBR objects in CBML; the case content object and the case structure object. The case structure object defines the hierarchy and cardinality of the features that can appear in a case. Within the case structure, there are a number of feature structures that define the features that can appear in a case. These feature structures defines the feature's type, its value restrictions, and other attributes. The following are a list of the possible feature types and the restrictions that can be imposed on them:

- Symbolic – the feature value must be one of an enumerated list of possible values
- Numeric – can be integer or double type (ranges can be set)
- Boolean – the value can be either true or false
- String – the value can be any string
- Taxonomy – similar to symbolic type except that the possible values are represented with a tree structure

The case content document contains the casebase information in XML format. It must conform to the specifications laid out in the case structure document both in structure and content to be considered valid.

2.2 Similarity Measures

Traditionally, the similarity between a query, Q and a case, C is defined as the sum of the similarities of its constituent features multiplied by their relevance weights:

$$Sim(Q,C) = \sum_{f \in F} w_f \times \sigma_f(q_f, c_f) \tag{1}$$

Where w_f is the feature relevance weight and σ_f is the local similarity measure (i.e. feature specific similarity measure). In order to provide a representation of the similarity measure it is therefore necessary to represent both a relevance weight and a description of the local similarity measure for every feature. Weights are just attributes of features but local similarity measures are more complex. We have defined three types of local similarity measures:

- Exact similarity measures - similarity is 1 if the feature values are equal, otherwise it is 0.
- Difference based similarity measures – Similarity is directly related to the difference, δ between feature values. This measure is only suitable where a difference can be defined between feature values, e.g. with numeric features the difference is the mathematical difference.
- Complex Similarity Measures – Any similarity measure that is different to the above representations falls under this category. It is impossible to provide for a representation scheme that could cover every possible type of complex similarity measure. However, if the number of possible values is finite, it is possible to calculate and store similarity values for every combination of feature value in advance.

In order for a good representation scheme to work we need to define the above similarity measures formally. The exact similarity function is trivial; it depends on value matching. The complex similarity measure is impossible to define completely due to the infinity of possible measures. It is impossible to define a single difference function for string types, and trivial to define one for Boolean types so we will confine ourselves to the definition of numeric, symbolic and taxonomic differences.

Table 1. Table 1 shows the definitions for the difference functions for numeric (integer and double), symbolic and taxonomic feature types.

Feature Type	Difference (δ) definition between Value1 and Value2
Numeric	Value1 – Value2
Symbolic	Relative difference in the positions of Value1 and Value2 in the list of possible values.
Taxonomy	Number of branches between the Value1 and Value2's nodes in the taxonomy

With a definition of difference in place it remains to come up with an adequate definition of the relationship between difference and similarity. In the next section we show how a graph may be defined relating them.

2.3 Representation of Similarity in CBML

All CBML is represented using the XML language. A discussion of CBML case content and structure definitions is beyond the scope of this paper; it is documented more fully on the CBML website[1]. The CBML Schema is tightly defined by an XML-

---

[1] http://www.cs.tcd.ie/research_groups/mlg/CBML/

Schema document. We have developed a number of parsers that will read valid CBML and convert them into Java objects. Only similarity documents that conform to the CBML Schema will be considered valid CBML.

```
<feature name="Gender" weight="0.25">
  <exact/>
</feature>
```

Fig. 1. *Gender* is a symbolic feature used in the breathalyzer domain [4]. This figure shows the CBML definition of *Gender*'s similarity measure. It defines it as having a relevance weight of 0.25, and that it uses an exact similarity function.

The CBML representation of a similarity measure is a composite of feature specific similarity definitions. These feature similarity definitions have mandatory attributes defining the feature name (*name*) and relevance weight (*weight*). The relevance weight is simply an attribute called weight that can have any normalized double value. The remainder of this section describes each of the similarity types and illustrates each one with a CBML example. Fig 1 shows the representation of a feature that uses an exact similarity measure.

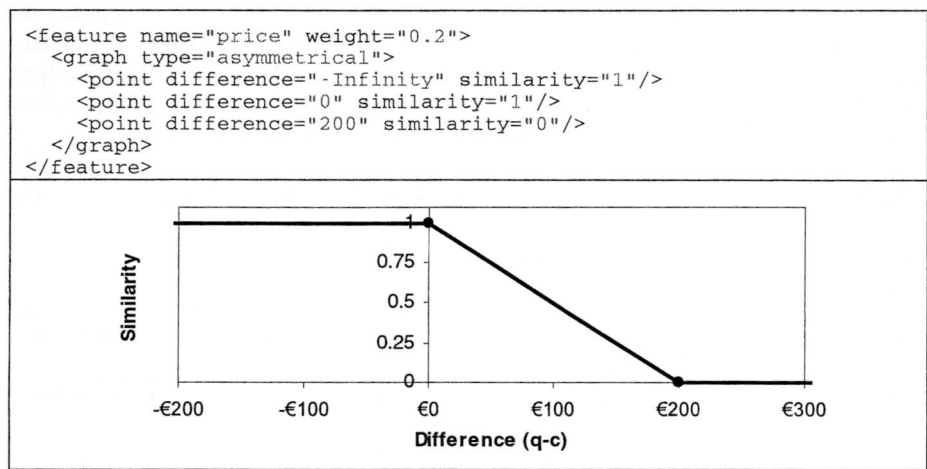

Fig. 2. *Price* is a numeric (double) feature used in the Personal Travel Assistant domain [1]. This figure shows the CBML definition of *Price*'s similarity measure. It defines it as having a relevance weight of 0.2. It then defines an asymmetrical graph of similarity versus difference by defining a number of points. For demonstrative purposes, this graph is also plotted. From the graph, the calculated similarity between two prices with a difference of €100 is 0.5.

Fig 2 shows the representation of a difference function similarity measure. The parser looks at the feature type from the case structure to determine which type of difference function to use, i.e. numeric, symbolic or taxonomic. The similarity graph is defined here too. This graph may be symmetrical (the default) or asymmetrical. A symmetrical graph only deals with absolute difference values. By adding more points to the graph any piece-wise linear relationship between similarity and difference can be represented.

Fig. 3 shows the representation of a complex similarity measure. This is used when neither of the above representations is appropriate. It is used for similarity measures that cannot be represented easily in XML. Our parser uses this attribute to refer to a predefined Java class for the similarity measure definition, but other parsers could use it to refer to something else, e.g. a MathML [19] document. We have implemented an interface that all similarity measures must implement (this contains one function that takes in two features and returns the similarity value). This ensures a level of interoperability, but since these objects are not as portable as XML documents the use of this similarity definition is discouraged.

```
<feature name="sepal-length" weight="0.25">
    <measure name="iris.similarity.SepalLength"/>
</feature>
```

Fig. 3. *Sepal Length* is a numeric (double) feature used in Fisher's iris domain [7]. This code is the CBML definition of *Sepal Length*'s similarity measure. It defines it as having a relevance weight of 0.25. It also tells the CBML parser to use the class *iris.similarity.SepalLength* to calculate similarity.

The array similarity measure is the final way to represent similarity in CBML. It is useful for features with a finite number of possible values, but requires the user to precalculate the similarities in advance. If a value cannot be found in the array of similarities the exact similarity measure is used. Fig 4 shows a representation for the array similarity measure.

3 Applications of CBML Similarity Measures

We have used CBML similarity measures in a number of research areas in the Machine Learning Group in Trinity College, most notably in our Personal Travel Assistant (PTA) application [1, 2] and in the explanation domain [4]. We have also developed a workbench that provides a set of utilities for CBR systems called Fionn[2] [5]. Fionn uses CBML as its internal representation format. This section describes some of the advantages we have observed from using CBML represented similarity measures in these applications.

The Personal Travel Assistant

The Personal Travel Assistant is an application that assists users in the booking and selection of flights. The main task for the PTA is the recommendation of suitable flights to the user using CBR. Fig 5 shows a diagram showing the flow of information through the PTA. The PTA recommendation engine uses Fionn components to make recommendations. The CBR functionality is all implemented as Fionn components, and because these components understand CBML we can switch them with ease.

---

[2] http://www.cs.tcd.ie/research_groups/mlg/Fionn

```xml
<feature name="meal" weight="0.05">
  <array>
    <primary name="none">
      <secondary name="snack" value="0.8"/>
      <secondary name="lunch" value="0.4"/>
    </primary>
    <primary name="snack">
      <secondary name="none" value="0.8"/>
      <secondary name="lunch" value="0.8"/>
      <secondary name="full" value="0.4"/>
    </primary>
    <primary name="lunch">
      <secondary name="none" value="0.4"/>
      <secondary name="lunch" value="0.8"/>
      <secondary name="full" value="0.8"/>
    </primary>
    <primary name="full">
      <secondary name="snack" value="0.4"/>
      <secondary name="lunch" value="0.8"/>
    </primary>
  </array>
</feature>
```

	none	*snack*	*lunch*	*full*
none	1	0.8	0.4	0
snack	0.8	1	0.8	0.4
lunch	0.4	0.8	1	0.8
full	0	0.4	0.8	1

Fig. 4. *Meal* is a symbolic feature used in the breathalyzer domain [4]. This code is the CBML definition of the similarity measure for *Meal*. It defines it as having a relevance weight of 0.05. It also contains an array of every possible feature value combination with a similarity value for each, e.g. the similarity between "none" and "snack" is 0.8. The array as defined is also shown.

To generate accurate recommendations we need to develop similarity measures that reflect the users travel preferences. Part of the personalization process involves updating these measures based on user feedback (this process is documented in more detail in [1]. By using CBML similarity measures we can do this easily and store personal similarity measures for each user (in the Personalisation Knowledge-base).

There are two ways in which we can learn a similarity measure. The first is by altering feature weights and the second by altering the local similarity measure in the manner proposed by Stahl [17]. By altering the feature weights, we adjust the relative importance of features for the user. We have experimented with altering the feature weights [1] and achieved positive results. We intend to assess the usefulness of altering the local measure for certain features in this domain over the coming months. In Fig. 2 we described the price similarity measure used in the PTA. By altering the position of the third point we can change this user's sensitivity to a difference in price, e.g. by changing the point from {200, 0} to {100, 0} we would focus the price similarity measure on offers with differences of less than €100.

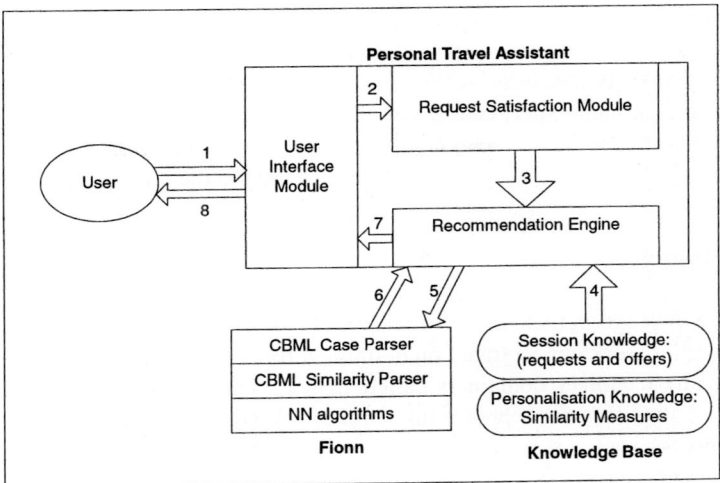

Fig. 5. Fig 5 shows a diagram of the architecture of the PTA application. The user makes a travel request (1) and this request is forwarded to the *Request Satisfaction Module* (2). This module sends the set of new offers to the Recommendation Engine (3). The recommendation engine gets the relevant user profile information from the knowledge base, i.e. the user's personal casebase and similarity measure. It then uses the Fionn module to generate a sub-set of recommended offers (5, 6) and sends these to the User (7, 8).

Each user of the PTA system has a personalized set of similarity measure and casebase describing their travel preferences. Much work has been done in the area of collaborative CBR [13] and we intend to implement some of these techniques to address bootstrapping problems and problems with case competence [16] in general. To address these we will need to be able to modularize the components we intend to share. CBML facilitates this modularization.

The original motivation for the PTA was as a distributed CBR application along the lines of Gardingen & Watson's HVAC system [8] where the user would access the PTA via a fat client browser. One advantage of using CBML similarity measures in this context is that the expensive personalization calculations on the similarity measure could be calculated and stored in a central server and the relatively cheap recommendation process could be done on the client side. With such a distributed CBR system we could implement different recommender systems depending on the target platform. As long as these heterogeneous CBR systems understand CBML there will not be any problems with transferring the CBR objects from server to client.

Explanation in CBR
Previous research has shown that case-based explanation is more convincing than other types of explanation in classification problems [4]. However it also showed that there is scope for improvement in the quality of our explanations. Our current research uses a two stage process to generate explanations; the first performs a standard CBR classification, and the second uses an explanation function specific to this classification to determine the best case for explanation [6].

As the structure and requirements for our explanation utility functions are the same as those for the similarity measure so it was logical to reuse the definitions and so we use CBML similarity measures as the basis for our explanation functions. Due to their modularity the domain expert can update the different explanation measures individually and without needing to write any code. For most features, our explanation functions are closely based on the similarity functions used in the classification task.

4 Conclusions

Richter's knowledge containers have received wide acceptance in the CBR community. Our earlier work concentrated on defining a formal representation schema for the casebase and vocabulary containers called CBML. This work is concerned with the definition of a schema for representing similarity knowledge. This paper outlines the requirements for such a schema and describes our implementation. We have incorporated this schema into CBML.

Before outlining a representation for similarity measures it is important to first review what is possible to represent. The most common similarity measures are based on exact matching or on numeric differences so our focus has been to develop a compact, intuitive way of representing these. We have also catered for more complex difference-based measures, i.e. taxonomic and symbolic difference functions. Finally we made it possible to define similarity arrays and to refer to user-defined similarity measures. Section 2.3 shows examples of representations of each of these similarity types.

Our experiences with CBML in the Machine Learning Group have been positive. There are currently six researchers in our group using CBML similarity measures in several applications. In Section 3 we outlined some of the advantages we have observed from using CBML similarity measures in personalization, distributed CBR, collaborative CBR and explanation-based CBR.

As the current implementation of CBML can represent three of the four knowledge containers, it is clear that our next step should be the creation of a representation for the fourth container – the solution transform.

References

1. Coyle, L., Cunningham, P (2004). Improving Recommendation Ranking by Learning Personal Feature Weights. To appear in the proceedings of the 7th European Conference on Case Based Reasoning, ECCBR 2004.
2. Coyle, L., Cunningham, P. & Hayes, C. (2002). A Case-Based Personal Travel Assistant for Elaborating User Requirements and Assessing Offers. Proceedings of the 6th European Conference, ECCBR 2002, Susan Craw, Alun Preece (eds.). LNAI Vol. 2416 pp. 505-518, Springer-Verlag
3. Coyle, L., Cunningham, P. & Hayes, C. (2002). Representing Cases for CBR in XML. Proceedings of 7th UKCBR Workshop, Peterhouse, Cambridge, UK.

4. Cunningham, P., Doyle, D., Loughrey, J., An Evaluation of the Usefulness of Case-Based Explanation, 5th International Conference on Case-Based Reasoning. K. D. Ashley & D. G. Bridge (Eds.). LNAI 2689, pp122-130, Springer Verlag, 2003.
5. Doyle, D., Loughrey, L., Nugent, C., Coyle, L., Cunningham, P., FIONN: A Framework for Developing CBR Systems. To appear in Expert Update 2004
6. Doyle, D., Cunningham, P, Bridge, D., Rahman, Y. (2004) Explanation Orientated Retrieval. To appear in the proceedings of the 7th European Conference on Case Based Reasoning, ECCBR 2004.
7. Fisher, R. A. (1936). "The Use of Multiple Measurements in Axonomic Problems," Annals of Eugenics 7, 179-188.
8. Gardigen D., Watson I. (1998). A Web based Case-Based Reasoning System for HVAC Sales Support. Proceedings of British Expert Systems conference 1998
9. Hayes, C. & Cunningham, P. (1999) Shaping a CBR View with XML. Proceedings of the Third International Conference on Case-Based Reasoning, ICCBR'99, Seeon Monastery, Germany. LNCS Vol. 1650. Althoff, K.-D., Bergmann, R., Branting, L.K. (Eds.) Springer-Verlag Berlin/Heidelberg 1999, pp.468-481
10. Hayes, C., Cunningham, P., & Doyle, M.. Distributed CBR using XML. In Proceedings of the KI-98 Workshop on Intelligent Systems and Electronic Commerce, number LSA-98-03E. University of Kaiserslauten Computer Science Department, 1998
11. INRECA consortium (1994). Casuel: A Common Case Representation Language, available at http://wwwagr.informatik.uni-kl.de/~bergmann/casuel/CASUEL_toc2.04.fm.html
12. Kitano, H. & Shimazu, H. (1996) The Experience Sharing Architecture: A Case Study in Corporate-Wide Case-Based Software Quality Control. In Case-Based Reasoning: Experiences, Lessons & Future Directions. Leake, D.B. (Ed.) pp235-268. AAAI Press/ The MIT Press Menlo Park, Ca, US
13. McGinty, L. & Smyth, B. (2001). Collaborative CBR for Real-World Route Planning. Proceedings of the 2001 International Conference on Artificial Intelligence (IC-AI'2001) Las Vegas, Nevada
14. Richter, M. (1998) Introduction – the basic concepts of CBR. In M. Bartsch-Sporl, H. D. B., and Wess, S., eds., Case-Based Reasoning Technology: From Foundations to Applications, LNAI Vol. 1400, Springer-Verlag
15. Shimazu, H. A Textual Case-Based Reasoning System Using XML on the World-Wide Web. Proceedings 4th European Workshop, EWCBR-98. Barry Smyth, Pádraig Cunningham (Eds.) LNCS 1488 pp274-285, Springer 1998
16. B. Smyth and E. McKenna. Modelling the competence of case-bases. In B. Smyth and P. Cunningham, editors, Advances in Case-Based Reasoning:Proceedings of the Fourth European Workshop on Case-Based Reasoning, pages 196--207. Springer-Verlag, Berlin, Germany, Sept. 1998.
17. Stahl, A., Gabel, T. (2003). Using Evolution Programs to Learn Local Similarity Measures. Proceedings of the 5th International Conference on Case-Based Reasoning, ICCBR 2003, Trondheim, Norway, June 2003. LNCS Vol. 2689, pp 537-551, Springer 2003.
18. Wilson, D. (2001) Case-Base Maintenance: The Husbandry of Experience. PhD dissertation, Indiana University, 2001
19. Mathematical Markup Language (MathML™) 1.01 Specification. Available online at http://www.w3.org/TR/REC-MathML/

An Analysis of Case-Base Editing in a Spam Filtering System*

Sarah Jane Delany[1] and Pádraig Cunningham[2]

[1] Dublin Institute of Technology, Kevin Street, Dublin 8
sarahjane.delany@comp.dit.ie
[2] Trinity College Dublin, Dublin 2
Padraig.Cunningham@cs.tcd.ie

Abstract. Because of the volume of spam email and its evolving nature, any deployed Machine Learning-based spam filtering system will need to have procedures for case-base maintenance. Key to this will be procedures to edit the case-base to remove noise and eliminate redundancy. In this paper we present a two stage process to do this. We present a new noise reduction algorithm called Blame-Based Noise Reduction that removes cases that are observed to cause misclassification. We also present an algorithm called Conservative Redundancy Reduction that is much less aggressive than the state-of-the-art alternatives and has significantly better generalisation performance in this domain. These new techniques are evaluated against the alternatives in the literature on four datasets of 1000 emails each (50% spam and 50% non spam).

1 Introduction

This paper presents an analysis of case-base editing techniques in a case-based reasoning (CBR) system for filtering spam email. The contributions of this work are twofold. First the analysis exercises the best case-base maintenance techniques currently available on a challenging problem with exacting accuracy requirements, namely spam filtering. Second, we present two new techniques for case-base maintenance, one for noise reduction and the other for redundancy reduction that significantly enhance the competence of the case-base.

While a case-based approach to spam filtering has great promise [1-3], a requirement for a deployed system is a process for maintaining the case-base. This is due to the issue of concept drift and the volume of messages that may be involved. A user may receive over a hundred legitimate emails a week and a multiple of that in spam. Our analysis suggests that between 600 and 1000 cases will provide good coverage for a spam filtering system. So there is an ongoing need to discard cases that are not contributing to competence.

The noise reduction technique we present, which we call Blame-Based Noise Reduction (BBNR), extends the competence based modelling ideas of Smyth and colleagues [4,5]. Their case coverage measure, used in case selection, indicates how well a case contributes to correctly classifying other cases in the case-base. We extend this

---

* This research was supported by funding from Enterprise Ireland under grant no. CFTD/03/219 and funding from Science Foundation Ireland under grant no. SFI-02IN.1I111.

model to include the notion of blame or *liability*. We introduce a measure for a case of how often it is the cause of, or contributes to, other cases being incorrectly classified. Traditional noise reduction mechanisms tend to focus on removing the actual cases that are misclassified. However, a misclassified case could have been classified incorrectly due to the retrieved cases that contributed to its classification. In contrast to traditional approaches we attempt to identify those cases *causing* the misclassifications and use this liability information coupled with coverage information to identify training cases we would be better off without. Our evaluation shows that, in the domain of spam-filtering, this is a better way of identifying noisy cases.

Some analysis of case-base editing techniques in the past has presented algorithms that aggressively prune the case-base at the cost of some classification accuracy [6,7]. This is not acceptable in spam filtering and our technique for redundancy reduction, which we call Conservative Redundancy Removal (CRR), focuses on a more conservative reduction of the case-base. It uses the competence characteristics of the case-base to identify and retain border cases.

This paper begins with a review of existing research on case-base editing techniques in Section 2. The enhanced competence model and our new case editing techniques are presented in Section 3. A comprehensive evaluation of these techniques on four email datasets is presented in Section 4. Some conclusions and directions for future work are presented in Section 5.

2 Review of Existing Case Editing Algorithms

Case base editing techniques involve reducing a case-base or training set to a smaller number of cases while endeavouring to maintain or even improve the generalization accuracy. There is significant research in this area, described in this section.

2.1 Early Techniques

Case editing techniques have been categorised by [8] as *competence preservation* or *competence enhancement* techniques. Competence preservation corresponds to redundancy reduction, removing superfluous cases that do not contribute to classification competence. Competence enhancement is effectively noise reduction, removing noisy or corrupt cases from the training set. Editing strategies normally operate in one of two ways; *incremental* which involves adding selected cases from the training set to an initially empty edited set, and *decremental* which involves contracting the training set by removing selected cases.

An early competence preservation technique is Hart's Condensed Nearest Neighbour (CNN) [9]. CNN is an incremental technique which adds to an initially empty edited set any case from the training set that cannot be classified correctly by the edited set. This technique is very sensitive to noise and to the order of presentation of the training set cases. Ritter [10] reported improvements on the CNN with his Selective Nearest Neighbour (SNN) which imposes the rule that every case in the training set must be closer to a case of the same class in the edited set than to any other training case of a different class. Gates [11] introduced a decremental technique which starts with the edited set equal to the training set and removes a case from the edited set where its removal does not cause any other training case to be misclassified. This technique will allow for the removal of noisy cases but is sensitive to the order of presentation of cases.

Competence enhancement or noise reduction techniques start with Wilson's Edited Nearest Neighbour (ENN) algorithm [12], a decremental strategy, which removes cases from the training set which do not agree with their k nearest neighbours. These cases are considered to be noise and appear as exceptional cases in a group of cases of the same class. Tomek [13] extended this with his repeated ENN (RENN) and his "all k-NN" algorithms. Both make multiple passes over the training set, the former repeating the ENN algorithm until no further eliminations can be made from the training set and the latter using incrementing values of k. These techniques focus on noisy or exceptional cases and do not result in the same storage reduction gains as the competence preservation approaches.

Competence preservation techniques aim to remove internal cases in a cluster of cases of the same class and can predispose towards preserving noisy cases as exceptions or border cases. Noise reduction on the other hand aims to remove noisy or corrupt cases but can remove exceptional or border cases which may not be distinguishable from true noise, so a balance of both can be useful. Later editing techniques can be classified as hybrid techniques incorporating both competence preservation and competence enhancement stages. Aha et al. [14] presented a series of instance based learning algorithms to reduce storage requirements and tolerate noisy instances. IB2 is similar to CNN adding only cases that cannot be classified correctly by the reduced training set. IB2's susceptibility to noise is handled by IB3 which records how well cases are classifying and only keeps those that classify correctly to a statistically significant degree. Other researchers have provided variations on the IBn algorithms [15,16,17].

2.2 Competence-Based Editing

More recent approaches to case editing build a competence model of the training data and use the competence properties of the cases to determine which cases to include in the edited set. Measuring and using case competence to guide case-base maintenance was first introduced by Smyth and Keane [5] and developed by Zhu and Yang [18]. Smyth and McKenna [3] introduce two important competence properties, the coverage and reachability sets for a case in a case-base. These are discussed in Section 3. The coverage and reachability sets represent the local competence characteristics of a case and are used as the basis of a number of editing techniques.

McKenna & Smyth [6] presented a family of competence-guided editing methods for case-bases which combine both incremental and decremental strategies. The family of algorithms is based on four features; (1) an ordering policy for the presentation of the cases that is based on the competence characteristics of the cases; (2) an addition rule to determine the cases to be added to the edited set, (3) a deletion rule to determine the cases to be removed from the training set and (4) an update policy which indicates whether the competence model is updated after each editing step. The different combinations of ordering policy, addition rule, deletion rule and update policy produce the family of algorithms.

Brighton and Mellish [8] also use the coverage and reachability properties of cases in their Iterative Case Filtering (ICF) algorithm. The ICF is a decremental strategy contracting the training set by removing those cases c, where the number of other cases that can correctly classify c is higher that the number of cases that c can correctly classify. This strategy focuses on removing cases far from class borders. After each pass over the training set, the competence model is updated and the process repeated until no more cases can be removed. ICF includes a pre-processing noise reduction stage, effectively RENN, to remove noisy cases.

McKenna and Smyth compared their family of algorithms to ICF and concluded that the overall best algorithm of the family delivered improved accuracy (albeit marginal, 0.22%) with less than 50% of the cases needed by the ICF edited set [6].

Wilson & Martinez [7] present a series of Reduction Technique (RT) algorithms, RT1, RT2 and RT3 which, although published before the definitions of coverage and reachability, could also be considered to use a competence model. They define the set of *associates* of a case c which is comparable to the coverage set of McKenna & Smyth except that the associates set will include cases of a different class from case c whereas the coverage set will only include cases of the same class as c. The RTn algorithms use a decremental strategy. RT1, the basic algorithm, removes a case c if at least as many of its associates would be classified correctly without c. This algorithm focuses on removing noisy cases and cases at the centre of clusters of cases of the same class as their associates will most probably still be classified correctly without them. RT2 fixes the order of presentation of cases as those furthest from their nearest unlike neighbour (i.e. nearest case of a different class) to remove cases furthest from the class borders first. RT2 also uses the original set of associates when making the deletion decision, which effectively means that the associate competence model is not rebuilt after each editing step which RT1 does. RT3 adds a noise reduction pre-processing pass based on Wilson's noise reduction algorithm.

Wilson & Martinez concluded from their evaluation of the RTn algorithms against IB3 that RT3 had a higher average generalization accuracy and lower storage requirements overall but that certain datasets seem well suited to the techniques while others were unsuited. Brighton & Mellish evaluated their ICF against RT3 and found that neither algorithm consistently out performed the other and both represented the "cutting edge in instance set reduction techniques".

3 Editing Using an Enhanced Competence Model

Smyth and McKenna's competence model defines how well a case performs when classifying other cases in the case-base. We have extended this competence model to include how badly a case performs when classifying other cases. This section firstly discusses our extensions to the competence model and then shows how they can be used in an alternative noise reduction algorithm BBNR that focuses on apportioning blame for misclassifications. We also present our competence-based redundancy reduction algorithm CRR which aims to maintain (and even improve) the generalisation accuracy of the case-base by focussing on less aggressive pruning of cases compared to that performed by many of the existing editing techniques.

3.1 The Enhanced Competence Model

Smyth and McKenna's case-base competence modelling approach proposes two sets which model the local competence properties of a case within a casebase; the *reachability set* of a target case t is the set of all cases that can successfully classify t, and the *coverage set* of a target case t is the set of all cases that t can successfully classify. Using the case-base itself as a representative of the target problem space, these sets can be estimated as shown in definitions 1 and 2.

$$\text{Coverage Set}(t \in C) = \{c \in C : \text{Classifies}(c,t)\} \quad (1)$$

$$\text{Reachability Set}(t \in C) = \{c \in C : \text{Classifies}(t,c)\} \quad (2)$$

where *Classifies(a,b)* means that case b contributes to the correct classification of target case a. This means that target case a is successfully classified and case b is returned as a nearest neighbour of case a and has the same classification as case a.

We propose to extend the model to include an additional property; the *liability set* of a case t which is defined as the set of all cases that t causes to be misclassified or contributes to being misclassified, see definition 3.

$$\text{LiabilitySet}(t \in C) = \{c \in C : \text{Misclassifies}(c,t)\} \quad (3)$$

where *Misclassifies(a,b)* means that case b contributes in some way to the incorrect classification of target case a. In effect this means that when target case a is misclassified by the case-base, case b is returned as a neighbour of a but has a different classification to case a. For k-NN with $k=1$, case b causes the misclassification but for $k>1$ case b contributes to the misclassification. Case a is therefore a member of the liability set of case b.

3.2 Blame Based Noise Reduction (BBNR)

Although a number of the competence-based editing techniques described in section 2 are designed to focus on removing redundant cases, all of them include both noise reduction and redundancy reduction stages. The noise reduction stage used by all the techniques is based on Wilson's noise reduction.

Noisy cases can be considered as training cases that are incorrectly labelled. Wilson's noise reduction technique removes from the case-base cases that would be misclassified by the other cases, implying that these are incorrectly labelled and are therefore noisy cases. However, a misclassified case may not necessarily be a noisy case but could be classified incorrectly due to the retrieved cases which contribute to its classification. Mislabelled cases which are retrieved as nearest neighbours of a target case can affect the classification of the target case. Therefore just because a case is misclassified does not imply that it is noise and should be removed.

Our BBNR approach emphasises the cases that *cause* misclassifications rather than the cases that *are* misclassified. In effect we are not just accepting the presumption that if a case is misclassified it must be mislabelled but try to analyse the cause of the misclassification. In our policy on noise reduction we attempt to remove mislabelled cases; we also remove "unhelpful" cases that cause misclassification. For example, a case that represents an actual spam email but looks just like a legitimate email.

The liability set captures this information. The greater the size of the liability set of a case, the more impact it has had on misclassifying other cases within the case-base. It is however important to consider this in light of how well cases are performing, how often they actually contribute to correct classifications. The coverage set captures this information. Our BBNR technique looks at all cases in the case-base that have contributed to misclassifications (i.e. have liability sets with at least one element). For each case c with a liability set of at least one element, if the cases in c's coverage set can still be classified correctly without c then c can be deleted. The BBNR algorithm is described in Figure 1.

```
Blame-based Noise Reduction (BBNR) Algorithm

T, Training Set
/* Build case-base competence model */
For each c in T
    CSet(c) ← Coverage Set of c
    LSet(c) ← Liability Set of c
End-For
/* Remove noisy cases from case-base */
TSet ← T sorted in descending order of LSet(c) size
c ← first case in TSet
While |LSet(c)| >0
    TSet ← TSet - {c}
    misClassifiedFlag ← false
    For each x in CSet(c)
        If x cannot be correctly classified by TSet
            misClassifiedFlag ← true
            break
        End-If
    End-For
    If misClassifiedFlag = true
        TSet ← TSet + {c}
    End-If
    c ← next case in TSet
End-While
```

Fig. 1. Blame-Based Noise Reduction Algorithm

This principle of identifying damaging cases is also there in IB3. Aha's IB3 algorithm is an algorithm more applicable for data streams and online learning in that the training set does not exist as a collection of cases before editing can be performed. The decision as to whether cases are kept in the case-base or not is made as the cases are presented.

There are a number of differences between IB3 and BBNR. First, IB3 maintains the classification records during the editing process rather than using the competence of the full training set as BBNR does through use of the competence model. Secondly, the classification record maintained by BBNR is based on actual classifications, whereas that maintained by IB3 is based on possible or potential classifications. IB3 updates the classification record of all cases that could potentially be neighbours whereas BBNR only uses the k retrieved neighbours to build its competence model. However, the most significant difference between the two algorithms is how they use case liability information. Although IB3 does collect information on the likely damage that certain cases may cause, it is not used actively to determine whether these potentially damaging cases should be removed or not. IB3 uses the classification accuracy, rather than classification error, to indicate how well a case is performing and waits for a case not to classify correctly at a satisfactory level before removing it. BBNR, on the other hand, uses the liability information available from the competence model of the case-base to decide whether these potentially damaging cases have any merit in being kept in the case-base.

3.3 Conservative Redundancy Reduction

The second stage in our competence-based editing technique is to remove redundant cases. Our proposed algorithm for removing redundant cases is based on identifying cases that are near class borders. The coverage set of a case captures this information. A large coverage set indicates that a case is situated in a cluster of cases of the same classification whereas a small coverage set indicates a case with few neighbours of the same classification. Cases near the class border will have small coverage sets. Cases with small coverage sets are presented first to be added to the edited set. For each case added to the edited set, the cases that this case can be used to classify (that is the cases that this case covers) are removed from the training set. This is the same as McKenna & Smyth's *coverage deletion rule* [6]. The CRR algorithm is presented in Figure 2.

```
Conservative Redundancy Removal(CRR) Algorithm

T, Training Set
/* Build case-base competence model */
For each c in T
    CSet(c) ← Coverage Set of c
End-For
/* Remove redundant cases from case-base */
ESet ← {}, (Edited Set)
TSet ← T sorted in ascending order of CSet(c) size
c ← first case in TSet
While TSet ≠ {}
    ESet ← ESet + {c}
    TSet ← TSet - CSet(c)
    c ← next case in TSet
End-While
```

Fig. 2. Conservative Redundancy Removal Algorithm

Existing editing techniques are very aggressive in their pruning of cases. Various cross validation experiments using existing techniques (ICF, RT*n* and a number of McKenna & Smyth's algorithmic variations) over our four datasets produced edited case-base sizes ranging from 3.5% to 46.4% of original case-base size with the average edited size of 22%. Such aggressive reductions in case-base size can have a detrimental effect on generalisation accuracy. By adding the cases near class borders to the edited set first, rather than working in the reverse order (that is with cases that are in the centre of a large cluster of cases of the same classification), our coverage deletion rule results in a more conservative reduction of the case-base. This, as shown in Section 4.4, results in larger edited case-bases and improved generalisation accuracy.

4 Evaluation

This section presents our results at two levels; firstly, an evaluation of the performance of our competence-based BBNR algorithm against Wilson's noise reduction as used by a majority of existing case editing techniques and secondly, an evaluation of the performance, in the domain of spam filtering, of existing case-based editing techniques compared with our new two-phased Competence-Based Editing technique incorporating BBNR and CRR.

4.1 Experimental Setup

The objective is to find a suitable case-base editing technique to reduce a case-base of spam and non-spam cases while maintaining case-base accuracy. Four datasets were used. The datasets were derived from two corpora of email collected by two individuals over a period of one year. Two datasets of one thousand cases were extracted from each corpus. Each included five hundred spam emails and five hundred non-spam or legitimate emails. Datasets 1.1 and 2.1 consisted of emails received up to and including February 2003 while datasets 1.2 and 2.2 consisted of emails received between February 2003 and November 2003. Given the evolving nature of spam it was felt that these datasets gave a representative collection of spam.

The emails were not altered to remove HTML tags and no stop word removal, stemming or lemmatising was performed. Since the datasets were personal it was felt that certain headers may contain useful information, so a subset of the header information was included. Each email, e_i was reduced to a vector of features $e_i = \langle x_1, x_2, ..., x_n \rangle$ where each feature is binary. If the feature exists in the email, $x_i = 1$, otherwise $x_i = 0$. It is more normal in text classification for lexical features to convey frequency information but our evaluation showed that a binary representation works better in this domain. We expect that this is due to the fact that most email messages are short. Features were identified using a variety of generic lexical features, primarily by tokenising the email into words. No domain specific feature identification was performed at this stage although previous work has indicated that the efficiency of filters will be enhanced by their inclusion [19].

Feature selection was performed to reduce the dimensionality of the feature space. Yang and Petersen's evaluation of dimensionality reduction in text categorisation found that Information Gain (IG) [20] was one of the top two most effective techniques in aggressive feature removal without losing classification accuracy [21]. Using IG with a k-nearest neighbour classifier, 98% removal of unique terms yielded an improved classification accuracy. The IG of each feature was calculated and the top 700 features were selected. Cross validation experiments, varying between 100 and 1000 features across the 4 datasets, indicated best performance at 700 features.

The classifier used was k-nearest neighbour with $k=3$. Due to the fact that false positives are significantly more serious than false negatives the classifier used unanimous voting to determine whether the target case was spam or not. All neighbours returned had to have a classification of spam in order for the target case to be classified as spam.

4.2 Evaluation Metrics

Previous studies into case editing techniques have compared performance on two measures; the accuracy of the edited casebase and the resulting size of the edited casebase. In the domain of spam filtering size and accuracy are not adequate measures of performance. A False Positive (FP), a legitimate email classified incorrectly as spam, is significantly more serious than a False Negative (a spam email incorrectly classified as a legitimate email). The occurrence of FPs needs to be minimised, if not totally eliminated. Accuracy (or error) as a measure, does not give full transparency with regard to the numbers of FPs and FNs occurring. Two filters with similar accuracy may have very different FP and FN rates.

Previous work on spam filtering use a variety of measures to report performance. The most common performance metrics are precision and recall [8]. Sakkis *et al.* [3] introduces a weighted accuracy measure which incorporates a measure of how much more costly a FP is than a FN. Although these measures are useful for comparison purposes, the FP and FN rate are not clear so the base effectiveness of the classifier is not evident. For these reasons we will report the error rate, the rates of FPs and the rate of FNs. For information purposes we will also indicate the resulting sizes of the edited case-bases.

A final justification for reporting this set of metrics is the fact that it reflects how commercial spam filtering systems are evaluated on the web and in the technical press.

4.3 Evaluation Methods

For each dataset we used 20 fold cross-validation, dividing the dataset into 20 stratified divisions or folds. Each fold in turn is considered as a test set with the remaining 19 folds acting as the training set. For each test fold and training set combination we calculated the performance measures for the full training set without editing and the performance measures for the training set edited with each selected editing technique. Where one case-base editing technique appeared to out perform another, confidence levels were calculated using a *t*-test on the paired fold-level results.

The case editing techniques that we evaluated include ICF, RT2, RT3 and a selection of the McKenna & Smyth's family of case editing techniques described in Section 2. The McKenna & Smyth algorithms can be identified as "*adc_o*"; where *a* indicates whether the addition rule is used (True/False), *d* indicates whether the deletion rule is used (T/F), *c* indicates whether the competence model is updated (T/F) and *o* indicates the order of presentation of cases. Their top two performing algorithms are FTF_*o* and FTT_*o*, where the addition rule is not used (*a*=F) and the deletion rule is used (*d*=T) irrespective of whether the competence model was rebuilt or not. The top two ordering sequences are order by relative coverage (RC) and reach for cover (RFC) [6]. Preliminary tests indicated those algorithms which require the competence model to be rebuilt after each editing step (i.e. FTT_RC and FTT_RFC) were not significantly different in accuracy but were prohibitively computationally expensive and were discarded.

4.4 Results

Figure 3 shows the results of comparing BBNR with RENN across the 4 datasets and the overall average results across all datasets. The graphs show percentage values for error, FP and FN rates. The average size across all 20 folds of the edited casebase is indicated (on the x-axis) as a percentage of the unedited training case-base size for the individual datasets.

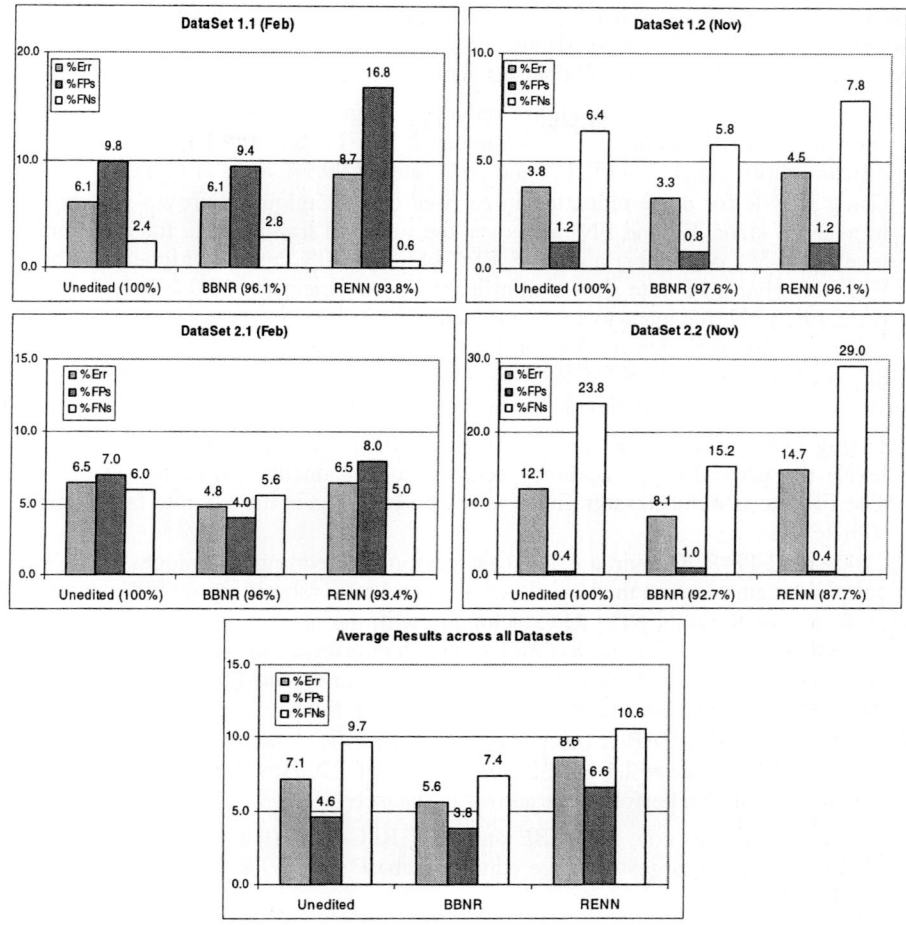

Fig. 3. Results of BBNR versus RENN

The results can be summarised as follows:

- BBNR performs very well and has a lower error rate than RENN (significant at confidence level 99.9% across all datasets). There are also significant improvements in FP rate and FN rate (at 99.9% level).
- The individual training sets reduced with BBNR have error rates that are at least as good as or better than the unedited training sets with the overall average showing significant improvement in FN rate and error rate at 99.9% level and FP rate at 99% level.

As BBNR shows better performance than Wilson noise reduction in the spam domain, we also evaluated replacing the noise reduction stage of those competence based case editing techniques with BBNR. Figure 4 displays these results for ICF, FTF_RC and FTF_RFC. Technique X with the Wilson based noise reduction phase replaced by BBNR is labelled as X-*bbnr* in Figure 4. Although RT2 and RT3 could be considered competence-based editing techniques, they use a different competence model without a liability set so BBNR was not applied to these. Figure 4 also includes overall average results across all datasets. The results can be summarised as follows:

- Using BBNR to perform the noise reduction stage improves the overall performance across all the datasets for techniques ICF, FTF_RC and FTF_FRC with significant improvements in FP, FN and error rates at 99.9% level or higher.
- Using BBNR for noise reduction in each editing technique improves performance in average error, FP and FN rates over the unedited training sets for ICF-bbnr (at levels of 95% or higher) and FTF_RFC-bbnr (at 90% level or higher). Although FTF_RC-bbnr's FP rate shows significant improvement (at 99.9% level) its deterioration in FN rate leads to an overall deterioration in error rate.

Figure 4 also includes results for RT2 and our new Competence-Based Editing (CBE) technique (i.e. BBNR+CRR). Results for RT3 were not included as RT2 outperformed RT3 for these datasets. The results for CBE can be summarised as follows:

- Taking average results across all datasets, CBE significantly improves (at 99.9% level) the generalisation accuracy achieved on an unedited training set of cases. The FP rate is reduced (significant at 99.9% level) as is the FN rate (significant at 97% level).
- CBE and FTF-RFC-bbnr are the best performing editing techniques on average across all datasets with the lowest average error rates (significant at 90% level).
- McKenna & Smyth's FTF_RFC technique with the noise reduction stage replaced by BBNR is a close second to CBE. It also demonstrates improved accuracy in average error, FP and FN rates when compared with an unedited training set, however, the improvements are at a lower level of significance.
- It may appear that CBE is out performed in specific datasets by other techniques, e.g. by RT2 in dataset 2.1 or ICF-bbnr in dataset 1.2. However CBE demonstrates the most consistent performance across all datasets.

It is interesting to note that CBE and FTF_RFC-bbnr (the top two editing techniques) result in the largest average edited casebase size (69% for CBE and 43% for FTF_RFC-bbnr).

5 Conclusions and Further Work

We have argued that a key component in any operational Machine Learning based spam filtering system will be procedures for managing the training data. Because of the volume of the training data a case-base editing process will be required. We have presented a novel competence-based procedure which we call CBE for this. CBE has two stages, a noise reduction phase called BBNR and a redundancy elimination phase called CRR.

BBNR focuses on the damage that certain cases are causing in classifications. Comparative evaluations of this algorithm with the standard Wilson's noise reduction technique in the domain of spam filtering have shown an improved performance across all four datasets. Experiments incorporating BBNR into existing competence-based case-base editing techniques have shown that BBNR improves all these techniques over the four datasets on which it was evaluated.

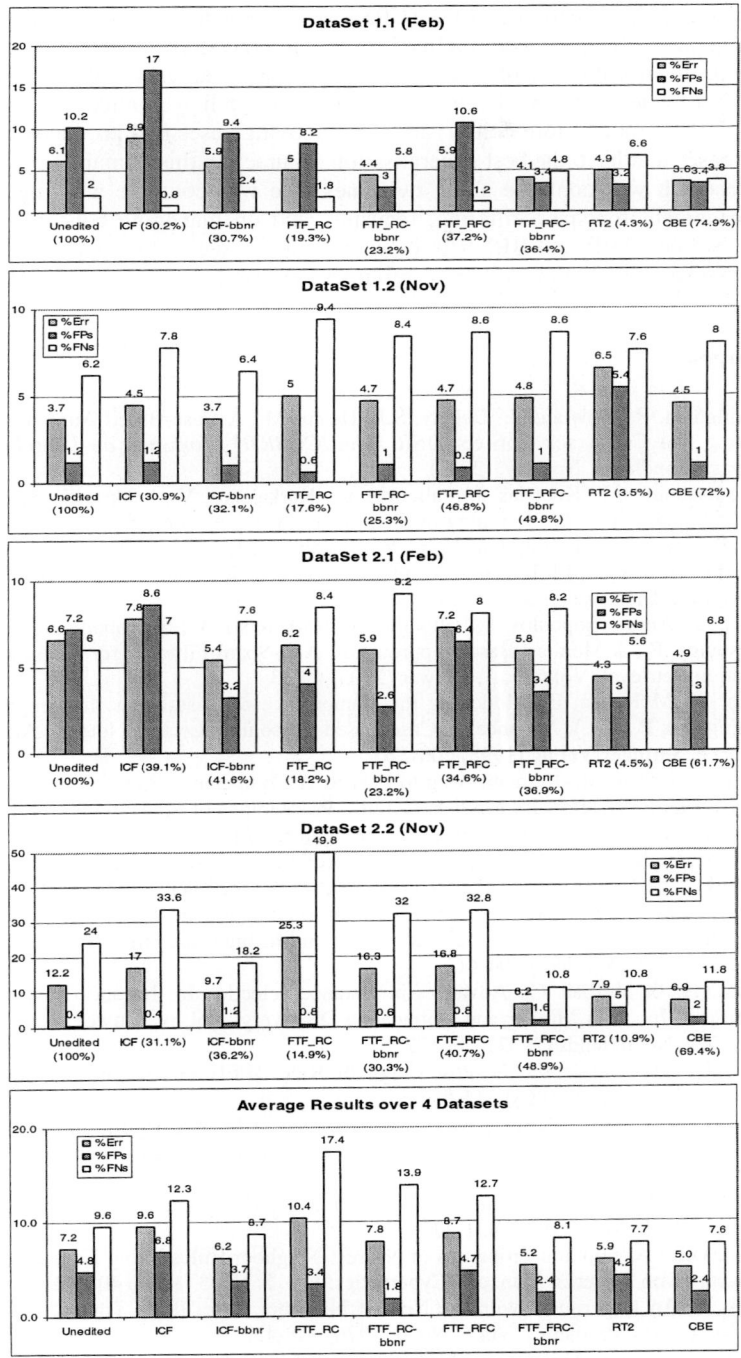

Fig. 4. Results of various case editing techniques

Our redundancy reduction process (CRR) was motivated by the observation that state-of-the-art techniques were inclined to be too aggressive in removing cases and tended to result in some loss of generalisation accuracy – at least in this domain. This is in effect a tendency to overfit the training data by finding minimal sets that cover the data. CRR is much more conservative in removing cases and produces larger edited case-bases that have the best generalisation accuracy in this domain.

This research will continue along two lines. We will continue working on case-base management for spam filtering, focusing next on managing concept drift. We will also evaluate CRR and BBNR in other domains to see if the good generalisation performance we have found on spam is replicated elsewhere.

References

1. Cunningham, P., Nowlan, N., Delany, S.J., Haahr, M., A Case-Based Approach to Spam Filtering that Can Track Concept Drift, *The ICCBR'03 Workshop on Long-Lived CBR Systems*, Trondheim, Norway, (2003).
2. Androutsopoulos, I., Koutsias, J., Paliouras, G., Karkaletsis, V., Sakkis, G., Spyropoulos, C., & Stamatopoulos, P..: Learning to filter spam e-mail: A comparison of a naive Bayesian and a memory-based approach. In: Workshop on Machine Learning and Textual Information Access, at 4th European Conference on Principles and Practice of Knowledge Discovery in Databases (PKDD) (2000)
3. Sakkis, G., Androutsopoulos, I., Paliouras, G., Karkaletsis, V., Spyropoulos C.D., &. Stamatopoulos, P., A Memory-Based Approach to Anti-Spam Filtering for Mailing Lists Information Retrieval, Vol 6 No 1, Kluwer (2003) 49-73
4. Smyth, B., McKenna, E.: Modelling the Competence of Case-Bases. In: Smyth, B. and Cunningham, P. (eds.): Advances in Case-Based Reasoning. Lecture Notes in Artificial Intelligence, Springer-Verlag (1998) 208-220
5. Smyth, B., Keane, M.: Remembering to Forget: A Competence Preserving Case Deletion Policy for CBR Systems. In: Mellish, C. (ed.): Proceedings of the Fourteenth International Joint Conference on Artificial Intelligence, Morgan Kaufmann (1995) 337-382
6. McKenna, E., Smyth, B.: Competence-guided Editing Methods for Lazy Learning. In Proceedings of the 14th European Conference on Artificial Intelligence, Berlin (2000)
7. Wilson, D.R., Martinez, T.R.: Instance Pruning Techniques. In: Fisher, D. (ed.) Proceedings of the Fourteenth International Conference on Machine Learning, Morgan Kaufmann, San Francisco, C.A. (1997) 404-411
8. Brighton.H., & Mellish. C.: Advances in Instance Selection for Instance-Based Learning Algorithms. In: Data Mining and Knowledge Discovery, Vol. 6. Kluwer Academic Publishers, The Netherlands (2002) 153-172
9. Hart, P.E.: The Condensed Nearest Neighbor Rule. IEEE Transactions on Information Theory. Vol. 14, No. 3 (1968) 515-516
10. Ritter, G.L., Woodruff, H.B., Lowry, S.R., Isenhour, T.L.: An Algorithm for a Selective Nearest Neighbor Decision Rule. IEEE Transactions on Information Theory, Vol. 21, No. 6 (1975) 665-669
11. Gates, G.W. : The Reduced Nearest Neighbor Rule. IEEE Transactions on Information Theory, Vol. 18, No. 3 (1972) 431-433
12. Wilson, D.L.: Asymptotic Properties of Nearest Neighbor Rules Using Edited Data. IEEE Transactions on Systems. Man, and Cybernetics, Vol. 2, No. 3 (1972) 408-421
13. Tomek, I.: An Experiment with the Nearest Neighbor Rule. IEEE Transactions on Systems, Man, and Cybernetics, Vol 6. No. 6 (1976) 448-452
14. Aha, D.W., Kibler, D., Albert, M.K.: Instance-Based Learning Algorithms. Machine Learning, Vol. 6 (1991) 37-66

15. Zhang, J.: Selecting Typical Instances in Instance-Based Learning. In: Proceedings of the Ninth International Conference on Machine Learning (1992) 470-479
16. Cameron-Jones, R.M.: Minimum Description Length Instance-Based Learning. In: Proceedings of the Fifth Australian Joint Conference on Artificial Intelligence (1992) 368-373
17. Brodley, C.: Addressing the Selective Superiority Problem: Automatic Algorithm/Mode Class Selection. In: Proceedings of the Tenth International Machine Learning Conference (1993) 17-24
18. Zhu, J., Yang, Q.: Remembering to Add: Competence Preserving Case-Addition Policies for Case-Base Maintenance. In: Proceedings of the Sixteenth International Joint Conference on Artificial Intelligence, Morgan Kaufmann (1997) 234-239
19. Sahami, M., Dumais, S., Heckerman, D., & Horvitz, E., A Bayesian Approach to Filtering Junk Email, In: AAAI-98 Workshop on Learning for Text Categorization pp. 55-62, Madison ,Wisconsin. AAAI Technical Report WS-98-05, (1998).
20. Quinlan, J. Ross: C4.5 Programs for Machine Learning, Morgan Kaufmann Publishers, San Mateo, CA. (1993).
21. Yang Y., Pedersen J.O.: A comparative study on feature selection in text categorization. In: Proceedings of ICML-97, 14th International Conference on Machine Learning, Nashville, US, (1997) 412–420.

A Case Based Reasoning Approach to Story Plot Generation*

Belén Díaz-Agudo, Pablo Gervás, and Federico Peinado

Dep. Sistemas Informáticos y Programación
Universidad Complutense de Madrid, Spain
{belend,pgervas}@sip.ucm.es, fpeinado@fdi.ucm.es
http://gaia.sip.ucm.es

Abstract. Automatic construction of story plots has always been a longed-for utopian dream in the entertainment industry, especially in the more commercial genres that are fuelled by a large number of story plots with only a medium threshold on plot quality, such as TV series or video games. We propose a Knowledge Intensive CBR (KI-CBR) approach to the problem of generating story plots from a case base of existing stories analyzed in terms of Propp functions. A CBR process is defined to generate plots from a user query specifying an initial setting for the story, using an ontology to measure the semantical distance between words and structures taking part in the texts.

1 Introduction

The explosion of the information society and the various communication technologies have progressively shifted the bottleneck for the entertainment industry from technological issues to content production. Whether in the web site industry, the game industry, or the animation industry, companies employ larger numbers of screen writers and content providers than actual technicians or programmers (or devote higher portions of their budgets to buying ready made content elsewhere). Automatic construction of story plots has always been a longed-for utopian dream in the entertainment industry, specially in the more commercial genres that are fuelled by a large number of story plots with only a medium threshold on plot quality, such as TV series or video games. Although few professionals would contemplate full automation of the creative processes involved in plot writing, many would certainly welcome a fast prototyping tool that could produce a large number of acceptable plots involving a given set of initial circumstances or restrictions on the kind of characters that should be involved. Such a collection of plots might provide inspiration, initiate new ideas, or possibly even include a few plot sketches worthy of revision. Subsequent selection and revision of these plot sketches by professional screen writers could produce revised, fully human-authored valid plots. By making such a collection

---

* Supported by the Spanish Committee of Science & Technology (TIC2002-01961)

of tentative plots available to company screen writers, a smaller number of writers might be able to provide the material needed to keep the technical teams in work.

In order for an automated plot generation tool to meet the requirements described above, its results would have to exhibit a degree of unpredictability. In his work on story generation, Turner [23] advocates the use of CBR in plot generation to provide a level of automated "creativity" to systems of this kind. We propose a Knowledge Intensive CBR (KI-CBR) approach to the problem of generating story plots from a case base of Propp functions. A CBR process is defined to generate plots from a user query specifying an initial setting for the story, using an ontology to measure the semantical distance between words and structures taking part in the texts. This constitutes an improvement on previous work [10, 3] similar solutions had been applied to generate poetic texts using CBR but employing only syntactic information during adaptation.

2 Previous Work

In this section, we outline here previous relevant work on story generation, and issues concerning natural language generation (NLG) that are relevant to our method of rendering plots for ease of comprehension.

2.1 Story Generation

In his Morphology of the Fairy Tale [21], Propp derives a morphological method of classifying tales about magic, based on the arrangements of "functions". This provides a description of the folk tales according to their constituent parts, the relationships between those parts, and the relations of those parts with the whole. Propp's work has been used as a basis for a good number of attempts to model computationally the construction of stories.

The main idea is that folk tales are made up of ingredients that change from one tale to another, and ingredients that do not change. According to Propp, what changes are the names - and certain attributes - of the characters, whereas their actions remain the same. These actions that act as constants in the morphology of folk tales he defines as *functions*.

For example, some Propp functions are: Villainy, Departure, Interdiction, Interdiction Violated, Acquisition of a Magical Agent, Guidance, Testing of the hero, etc. There are some restrictions on the choice of functions that one can use in a given folk tale, given by implicit dependencies between functions: for instance, to be able to apply the *Interdiction Violated* function, the hero must have received an order (*Interdiction* function).

PftML, a Proppian fairy tale Markup Language[18]utilizes a Document Type Definition (DTD) to create a formal model of the structure of narrative and to standardize the tags throughout a corpus – a subset of the corpus Propp used – when analyzing it. This allows for an empirical test of the conclusions of Propp's initial analysis against the original data. We have used Propp's original work and PftML as the basic sources for building the ontology that underlies our system.

The Proppian Fairy Tale Generator [18][1], works by randomly choosing a possible interpretation of a function – as a previously written piece of text, a fragment of a folk tale – and stringing them together to create a story. In the resulting stories characters appear and disappear from one passage to the next, resolutions occur for conflicts never mentioned, and events have to be extrapolate between passages to make sense of the plot. This suggests that it is not enough to find combinations of Propp's functions to create viable stories. From a CBR point of view, this implies that no simple retrieval process will address the issue, and specific adaptation processes must be devised to obtain a useful solution.

There have been various attempts in the literature to obtain a computational model of story generation. Important efforts along these lines are presented in [22, 13]. Minstrel [23] includes a CBR solution for generating stories about Arthurian characters. A moral for the story is used a a seed, and it attempts to model the way human bards compose their stories. It uses a semantic network as knowledge representation. Universe [14] defines characters in terms of frames, with a richer representation of their goals and restrictions. Particularly oriented towards generating plots in an ongoing serial.

Some options consider the role of planning in story generation. Tale-Spin [20] was the first approximation to story generation based on the transformational paradigm. The system has predefined rules that simulate a small environment that evolves while characters in it – based on Aesop's fables – try to achieve certain goals. The underlying mechanism is based on a planning engine that works on character goals. Resulting stories are not necessarily very interesting. IDA (I-Drama Architecture) [17] is an architecture incorporates both agents as actors that can be directed – but have a certain degree of autonomy – and a story director. It uses first order logic to represent the story and classic AI planning algorithms for reasoning. Fairclough and Cunningham [8] implement an interactive multiplayer story engine that operates over a way of describing stories based on Propp's work, and applies case-based planning and constraint satisfaction to control the characters and make them follow a coherent plot. A story director agent manages the plot using case-based planning. A plot is a series of character functions and a series of complication-resolution event pairs, where a complication occurs whenever a character performs a function that alters the situation of the hero. Stories are controlled by a story director agent who selects which functions should take place by applying a case based planning system. They use 80 cases extracted from 44 story scripts given by Propp, defined as lists of character functions. Stories are composed of various moves, but a given story can only be resolved with its own particular choice of moves. Retrieval is done by means of a k-nearest neighbour algorithm that takes into account the functions performed so far and the character and object resources needed to execute a story script.

Others explore the role of interactivity. Teatrix [16] is a software application that helps children to develop narrative abilities. It offers a 3D environment where stories – actually small school plays – can be created cooperatively, in-

---

[1] $http://www.brown.edu/Courses/FR0133/Fairytale\_Generator/theory.html$

tended for young children. The GEIST project [11] presents a story engine that generates digital interactive narrative in a mixed reality environment. It creates historic characters as ghostly apparitions that are combined with the users perception of reality. Automatic generation of stories is considered too complex, and the computer only takes part in the high level management of the story. They use a simplified version of Propp's morphology.

2.2 Natural Language Generation

The most natural format for presenting a plot to users is narrate it in natural language. Obtaining a high quality natural language text for a story is itself a subject of research even if the plot is taken as given [2]. This paper is concerned strictly with the process of generating valid plots, and only the simplest sketch of a natural language rendition is attempted as means of comfortably presenting the results. This is done by means of NLG based on templates, currently the most popular text-planning approach in applied NLG. Texts follow conventionalized patterns which can be encapsulated in *schemas* [19], template programs which produce text plans. Schemas are derived from a target text corpus by breaking them up into messages, organising the messages into a taxonomy, and identifying how each type of message is computed from the input data. The schema-based approach to NLG has striking parallelism to CBR approaches to problem solving, in that existing previous solutions, such as those obtained from a corpus of target texts, are extracted and prepared so they can be reused to solve future problems, much in the same way as cases in a case-base are prepared from previous problem solutions.

This has lead to attempts to apply explicitly CBR solutions to the task of text generation. In [3] poetry generation is chosen as an example of the use of the COLIBRI (*Cases and Ontology Libraries Integration for Building Reasoning Infrastructures*) system. COLIBRI assists during the design of KI-CBR systems that combine cases with various knowledge types and reasoning methods. It is based on CBROnto [4–6], an ontology that incorporates reusable CBR knowledge, including terminology plus a library of reusable Problem Solving Methods (PSMs). The transformation of a given prose text into a poem can be represented as a CBR process [10], where each case contains a sample – a sentence – of the source text as case description and a sample of the object poem as case solution.

3 Knowledge Representation for Plot Generation

Knowledge representation in our system is based on a basic ontology which holds the various concepts that are relevant to story generation. This initial ontology is subject to later extensions, and no claim is made with respect to its ability to cover all the concepts that may be necessary for our endeavour.

3.1 The Ontology

The ontology has been designed to include various concepts that are relevant to story generation. Propp's character functions are used as basic recurrent units of a plot. In order to be able to use them computationally, they have been translated into an ontology that gives semantic coherence and structure to our cases.

We have implemented this ontology using the last release of the Protégé ontology editor that was developed at Stanford University [9]. It can manage ontologies in OWL [1], a new standard that has recently reached a high relevance. The choice of OWL as a representation language provides the additional advantage, that it is designed to work with inference engines like RACER [12].

Although the functions of the *dramatis personae* are the basic components, we also have other elements. For instance, conjunctive elements, motivations, forms of appearance of the dramatis personae (the flying arrival of a dragon, the meeting with a witch), and the attributive elements or accessories (a witch's hat or her clay leg) [21]. An additional ontology provides the background knowledge required by the system, as well as the respective information about characters, places and objects of our world. This is used to measure the semantical distance between similar cases or situations, and maintaining an independent story structure from the simulated world. The domain knowledge of our application is the classic fairy tale world with magicians, witches, princesses, etc. The current version of the ontology contains a number of basic subconcepts to cover this additional domain knowledge that needs to be referred from within the represented function.

Propp Functions. In our approach, Propp's character functions act as high level elements that coordinate the structure of discourse. Each function has constraints that a character that is to perform it must satisfy. A view of the top of the function hierarchy is given in Figure 1 (left).

The contents of a function are the answers to the Wh-questions: what (the symbolic object), when, where (the place), who (who are the characters of the function) and why.

Moves. Morphologically, a tale is a whole that may be composed of *moves*. A move is a type of development proceeding from villainy or a lack, through intermediary functions to marriage, or to other functions employed as a *denouement* (ending or resolution). Terminal functions are at times a reward, a gain or in general the liquidation of a misfortune, an escape from pursuit, etc. [21].

One tale may be composed of several moves that are related between them. One move may directly follow another, but they may also interweave; a development which has begun pauses, and a new move is inserted.

We represent tales and their composing moves using structured descriptions. A tale is related with an ordered sequence of complete moves. We represent the temporal sequence between these moves using the CBROnto temporal relations. These representation issues are described in Section 3.2.

Character. The roles in the story must be filled by characters. Each character is defined by a set of relationships with other characters, objects in his possession, location... These characters are one of the elements that the user can choose to customize a story.

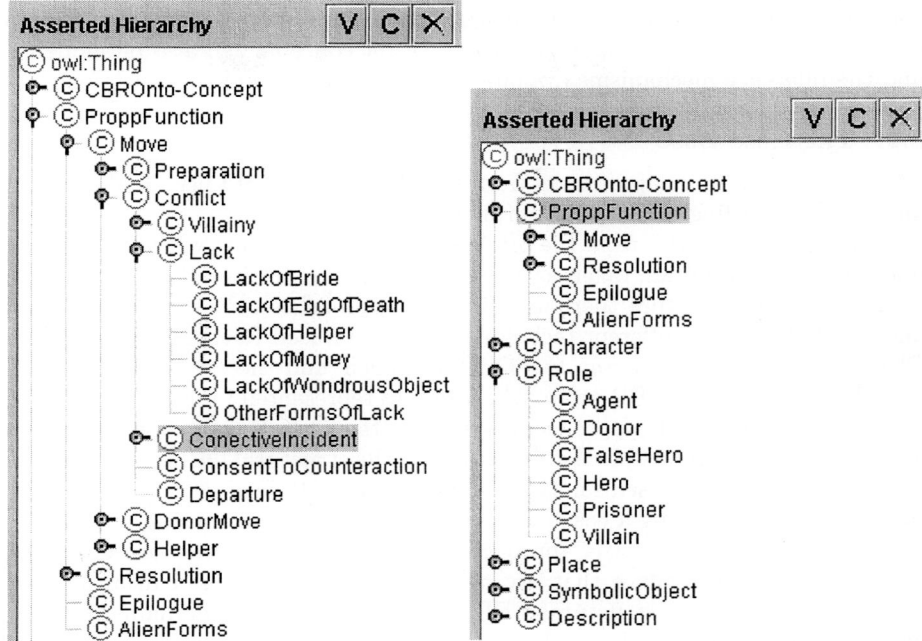

Fig. 1. Function and role sub-hierarchies in the ontology as modelled in Protégé

Properties of the Characters. By properties or attributes of the characters, we mean the totality of all the external qualities of the characters: their age, sex, status, external appearance, peculiarities of this appearance... These attributes provide the tale with its brilliance, charm and beauty. However, one character in a tale is easily replaced by another (permutability law) [21].

In our ontology we represent a character's attributes using three basic headings: external appearance (and nomenclature), particularities of introduction into the narrative, and dwelling (described by a relation with a place). Also there are other auxiliary elements.

Roles. Propp describes a number of 'spheres of action' that act as roles that certain characters have to fulfill in the story. The role sub-hierarchy of our ontology is given in Figure 1 (right).

Places and Objects. Certain locations (outdoors, indoors, countries, cities...) and symbolic objects (towels, rings, coins...) can be significant to the way a story develops, and any sort of substitution during adaptation must take this into account. Our ontology must have the ability to classify such locations and objects.

Descriptions. Since our system generates text by filling in templates with selected descriptions that correspond to instances of particular concepts, it was considered convenient to have these descriptions represented in the ontology in such a way that their relations with the relevant concepts can also be modelled and the inference mechanisms available can be employed in their selection.

3.2 The Case Base

The case base is built up of texts from the domain of fairy tales, analyzed and annotated according to Propp's morphology.

A selection of stories from the original set of the Afanasiev compilation originally used by Propp are taken as sources to generate our initial case base.

In the CBR literature there are different approaches to case representation and, related to that, different techniques for Case Based Reasoning: the *textual* CBR approach, the *conversational* CBR approach, and the *structural* CBR approach. In the textual CBR approach, cases are represented in free-text form. In the conversational CBR approach, cases are lists of questions and answers. For every case, there can be different questions. In the structural CBR approach, the developer of the case-based solution decides ahead of time what features will be relevant when describing a case and then stores the cases according to these.

We use a structural CBR approach that relies on cases that are described with attributes and values that are pre-defined, and structured in an object-oriented manner. This structural CBR approach is useful in domains (like the one we are considering) where additional knowledge, beside cases, must be used in order to produce good results. The domain ontology assures the quality of new cases (regarding the ontology commitments) and the low effort in maintenance.

Within the defined case structures we represent the plots of the fairy tales. Besides this structural representation of the cases we also associate a textual representation to each case that can be used to generate texts from the plot descriptions (see Section 4.2).

We facilitate the case structure authoring tasks by proposing a framework to represent cases that is based on the Description Logics (DLs) instance definition language and the CBROnto terminology. Besides, we define a reasoning system (based on generic CBR PSMs) that works with such representations [6].

Cases are built based on CBROnto case representation structure [4-6] using the vocabulary from the domain ontology described in Section 3.1. The semantic constraints between scene transitions are loosely based on the ordering and co-occurrence constraints established between Proppian functions. Because the case base is made using cases proposed by Propp, we know that the system makes correct versions of folk tales.

CBROnto provides a *primitive* concept CASE. Subconcepts of CASE are referred to as *case-type* concepts. Cases of different types are represented as instances of different CASE subconcepts, so they will not have, in general, the same structure. The designer will define case-type concepts to represent the new types of cases.

Each case-type concept (more exactly its set of instances) defines a case base where CBR processes can be applied. This mechanism allows having different level of abstraction where there are cases that are part of other cases (see Figure 2).

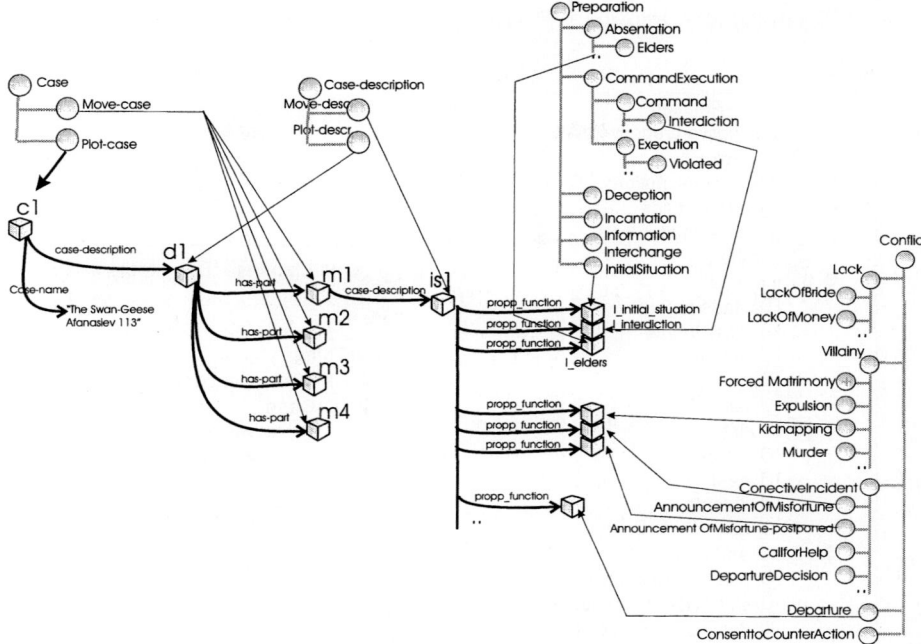

Fig. 2. Case Structure

In our application each case represents a complete tale that is typically composed of one or more interrelated moves (that are also cases). For representational purposes, relations between moves are basically of two types: *temporal* relations (before, after, during, starts-before, ends-before, ...) or *dependencies* (meaning that a change in one of them strongly affects the other) like *place-dependency*, *character-dependency* and *description-dependency* [5].

DLs allows representing hierarchies between relations (see Figure 3) what eases defining reasoning methods (using the top level relation) that are applicable (and reusable) with all the sub-relations.

As an example of the type of stories that are being considered, the following outline of one of the tales that Propp analyses is given below[2]. The main events of the plot are described in terms of character functions (in bold):

The Swan Geese (113 of Afanasiev Collection). **Initial situation** (a girl and her small brother). **Interdiction** (not to go outside), **interdiction violated, kidnapping** (swan geese take the boy to Babayaga's lair), **Competition** (girl faces Babayaga), **Victory, Release from captivity, Test of hero** (swan geese pursue the children), **Sustained ordeal** (children evade swan geese), **Return**.

---
[2] Complete text in $http://gaia.sip.ucm.es/people/fpeinado/swan-geese.html$

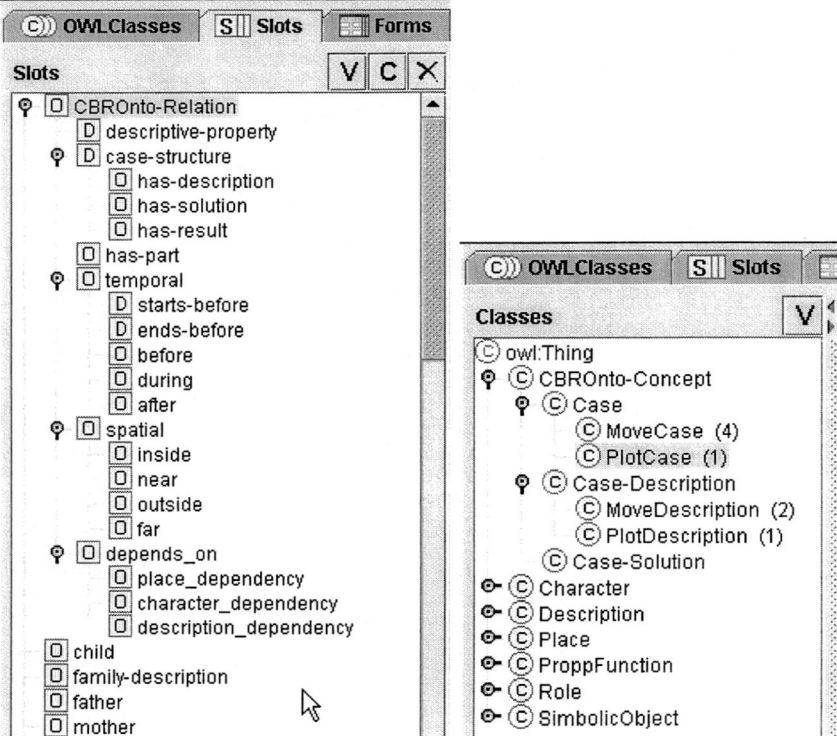

Fig. 3. CBROnto relation (left) and concept (right) hierarchies in Protege

4 How the System Works

We propose a Knowledge Intensive CBR approach to the problem of generating story plots from a set of cases consisting of analyzed and annotated fairy tales. Our system operates in two phases: an initial one that applies CBR to obtain a plot plan from the conceptual description of the desired story provided by the user, and a final phase that transforms the resulting plot plan into a textual rendition by means of template based NLG.

4.1 The First Stage: Description to Plot Plan

We use the descriptive representation of the tale plots with a CBR system, that retrieves and adapts these plots in several steps and using the restrictions given in the query.

Query Specification, Similarity Assessment and Case Retrieval. A query determines the components of the tale we want to build. For example, its characters, descriptive attributes, roles, places, and the Propp functions describing the actions involved in the tale. Although there are roles whose existence (a character that plays that role) is mandatory in every plot, like the hero and the villain, they are not required in the query as they can be reused from other plots (cases).

Query description is an iterative and interactive process. The user first describes: the characters in the tale , their roles and attributes, the places where the story occurs, and so on. The user can do this, either by selecting individuals (predefined instances) from the ontology or creating new ones (new instances of the ontology concepts). Afterwards, the user determines the set of character functions that are going to be involved in the story. The user selects these functions from the given set of Propp functions represented in our ontology (see Figure 1 (left)). Optionally the user indicates which characters take part in each function. The knowledge in the ontology (and the associated reasoning processes) helps the user to fill the attributes of each function while maintaining the corresponding restrictions between the concepts and individuals.

If the function set is incompatible the system guides the user toward an appropriate query definition. For Propp the plot is a causal closed system where adequate characters, places, etc. are selected.

We propose an interactive case retrieval process taking into account progressive user inputs. The system retrieves the more similar case with the restriction of Propp morphology and characters available. As CBROnto provides with a general test-bed of CBR methods we have made different tests with different similarity measures between the complex descriptions that represents the plots([5]).

Each retrieved case constitutes a plot-unit template. The retrieved case components are *hot-spots* (or flex points) that will be substituted with additional information obtained from the context, i.e. the query, the ontology and other cases, during the adaptation process. Similarity measures should guarantee that (when possible) all the query elements are valid elements to be allocated in the retrieved cases.

For instance, let us say we want a story about a *princess*, where **murder** occurs, where an **interdiction** is given and **violated**, there is a **competition**, and a **test of the hero**. We can use that information to shape our query. The system retrieves the case story number 113, Swan-Geese (whose analysis has been given in the previous section).

Retrieval has occurred using structural similarity over the ontology (described in [5]) because the structure of this story satisfies straight away part of the conditions (interdiction, competition, test of hero) imposed by the query. No murder appears, but there is a *similar* element: a kidnapping. **Kidnapping** and **murder** are similar because they are different types of villainies; so, they are represented as children of the same concept **Villainy** in the ontology.

Adaptation. The retrieval process provides with the plot skeleton where the system makes certain substitutions. A basic and simple initial adaptation step is to substitute the characters given in the query into the template provided by the retrieved case. The retrieval process described above together with this simple adaptation mechanism provides a starting point for the plot generation, but it will not produce original results.

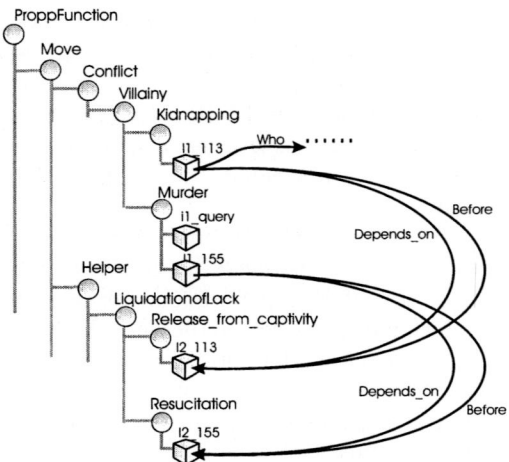

Fig. 4. Substitution example

We also propose an adaptation method based on substitutions, but more creative results may be achieved by generating a solution as a mixture of the ingredients from various cases. During the adaptation of our *plot case*, we use additional retrieval steps (defining adequate queries) over the case base of *move cases* (that are part of the plot cases, see Figure 2) to find appropriate substitutes maintaining the dependencies and temporal relations.

In our example, the system should suggest an adaptation where **murder** is substituted for the **kidnapping**. However, the **kidnapping** in the retrieved case has *dependencies* with the **release from captivity** that appears later on (which is a **liquidation of lack** according to the ontology) (see Figure 4). To carry out a valid adaptation, the adaptation process is forced to define a query and retrieve cases in which **murder** appears with a *similar* dependency (i.e. dependency with another **liquidation of lack**).

The following case is retrieved (only a part of which is relevant to the issue):

(*155 of Afanasiev Collection*). (...) **Absentation** of the hero (brother goes hunting), **Deception** of the villain (beautiful girl entices him), **Murder** (girl turns into lioness and devours him), (...) **Consent to counteraction** (other brother sets out), **Competition** (faces beautiful girl), **Victory** (kills lioness), **Resurrection** (revives brother), **Return**.

In this case there is a dependency between the **murder** and the **resuscitation**. The adaptation system can therefore substitute the kidnapping-release pair in the first retrieved case with the murder-resuscitation pair in the second, obtaining a better solution for the given query. Additional adaptations can be carried out to substitute the hero of the first case (the girl) or the prisoner (the boy) for the princess specified in the query. Besides, the swan-geese character in the retrieved case can be substituted for a similar element (for instance, another animal like the lioness that appears in the second retrieved case).

Additionally, those character functions that appear in the retrieved case but not in the query and that are not relevant for the story as developed so far can be filtered out during adaptation. This involves taking into account the explicit representation of dependencies between functions represented in the cases.

The resulting plot, showing how the two cases are combined, could be a story like this:

> *The Lioness (new fairy tale).* **Initial situation** (a knight and his beloved princess), **Interdiction** (not to go outside), **Interdiction violated**, **Murder** (a lioness devours her), **Competition** (knight faces the lioness), **Victory** (kills lioness), **Resurrection** (revives the princess), **Return**.

4.2 The Second Stage: Plot Plan to Textual Sketch

This corresponds to the natural language generation basics to be applied to the plot plan in order to obtain a readable rendition of it. The current version is not focused on these issues, so this stage is currently covered by a skeleton solution to the problem. The NLG is simple, it uses templates without a grammar. If the CBR process of the first stage has taken place successfully, the second stage will accept as input a data structure satisfying the following constraints:

- The case that has been selected during retrieval, has been pruned or combined with other cases retrieved during adaptation and strung into a case sequence that makes up a plot skeleton.
- The character functions, acting as templates for the basic units of the plot, have been filled in during adaptation with identifiers for the characters described in the query.

This result corresponds to the sort of structure that in NLG is termed a text plan, and we will refer to it as a *plot plan*. Various operations of increasing degree of difficulty are possible from this stage.

First Approximation: Direct Surface Realization of the Plot Plan. A one-to-one correspondence can be established between character functions in the plot plan and sentences to be expected in the output. In this case, a simple stage of surface realization can be applied to the plot plan. Such a stage converts the templates into strings formatted in accordance to the orthographic rules of English - sentence initial letters are capitalized, and sentences are ended with a colon.

This approach is very similar to the process of syntax-based substitution applied in [3], with a number of interesting improvements. Having access to the sort of relations embodied in an ontology provides the means for finding the most suitable substitutions during adaptation. To avoid ambiguity problems during this process, each instance of a concept in the ontology must have a unique identifier. Semantic correctness of the output text is enforced by the substitution process.

The fact that we are using an ontology to represent concepts, and not a set of axioms encoding their meaning somehow restricts the degree of correctness that can be guaranteed by the substitution process. Any checking algorithm can only test for structural equivalence within the ontological taxonomy, and it cannot carry out proper inference over the meanings of concepts.

Nevertheless, in order to solve the problem of syntactical coherence of the texts, issues like number and gender agreement, some sort of syntactic information must be available in the system. Templates partly solve the need for having an explicit grammar, but some of these questions must be taken into account and therefore must be explicitly represented in the system.

In view of the various arguments outlined so far, it is perceived that the system would greatly benefit from incorporating semantic information in the form of a knowledge rich ontology. This addition must be done in some way that allows the new information to play a role easily in the various processes carried out by the system.

A More Elaborate Approximation: Micro-plan the Sentences of the Plot Plan. Additional stages of *micro-planning* (or *sentence planning*) are performed on the elements that constitute the plot plan. This involves operations like joining sentences together wherever this gives more fluency to the text, substituting character identifiers for pronouns or definite descriptions wherever appropriate, or selecting specific words to use in realizing templates whenever options are available.

Due to the inherent heuristic nature of their application in the present context, these operations are better carried out by applying rule-based solutions.

An alternative is to employ a CBR solution. This would imply associating a textual representation to each case, with adequate links established explicitly between the ingredients that play particular roles in the case - characters, locations or objects - and their textual representations. These links would have to be used during adaptation to ensure that the textual descriptions corresponding to the character identifiers that have been introduced in the case during the adaptation of the first stage are substituted in the relevant textual templates.

CBR might be applied to the process of selecting an appropriate description for a given identifier when it has to be mentioned in a specific context of the discourse. If each character - represented in our ontology - has a set of possible descriptions - also represented in our ontology - associated with it, the system could resort to such annotated cases as described above to find which of the possible descriptions might be better used in the context. For this operation to be successful, the cases employed - discourse configuration cases - would probably have to represent a larger window of the previous context than was necessary for the CBR process of the first stage, which focused on cases as basic plot-units.

5 Conclusions

Although the system is not fully-implemented yet, the progress so far points to a reasonable solution for Story Generation. Our approach follows the lines of structuralist story generation, which distinguishes it from more transformational work [20, 17]. It constitutes an evolution on Minstrel [23] in as far as the ontology used for representation is a formal evolution of the semantic networks it used. It improves on [11] in terms of a full implementation of Propp's morphology and actual involvement of the computer in story generation. Unlike the uses of Proppian functions described for other systems [18, 8], our approach represents character functions with more granularity. This allows the establishment of relations between characters and attributes and the functions in which they appear. Using this facility, a coherent character set can be guaranteed throughout the story. Additionally, dependencies between character functions are modelled explicitly, so they can be checked and enforced during the process of plot generation without forcing the generated plots to be structurally equivalent to the retrieved cases.

The system architecture is general in as much as one accepts Propp's set of character functions as complete. In the face of disagreement, the ontology is easy to extend, and, as mentioned before, it is not intended to be complete as it is. Under these conditions, the approach described in this paper may be extend to work in other domains.

In future work we intend to address the specific problems of the second stage, involving the transition from plot plan to textual sketch, and to explore the possible interactions between the two stages. Once these issues have been solved, the integration of the generator with software applications for script writing – along the lines of classics [24, 7] – can be contemplated.

Given the facilities that COLIBRI provides for reusing knowledge that exists in the form of ontologies, we contemplate using Mikrokosmos [15] as an additional resource to support richer implementations of the NLG tasks involved in the second stage. An effort to port Mikrokosmos from its frame-based format to a DL format like OWL is under way.

References

1. S. Bechhofer, F. van Harmelen, J. Hendler, I. Horrocks, D. L. McGuinness, P. F. Patel-Schneider, and A. Stein. OWL web ontology language reference. W3C http://www.w3.org/TR/2004/REC-owl-ref-20040210/, February 2004.
2. C. B. Callaway and J. C. Lester. Narrative prose generation. *Artificial Intelligence*, 139(2):213–252, 2002.
3. B. Díaz-Agudo, P. Gervás, and P. González-Calero. Poetry generation in COLIBRI. In S. Craw and A. Preece, editors, *ECCBR 2002, Advances in Case Based Reasoning*. Springer, 2002. Lecture Notes in Artificial Intelligence.
4. B. Díaz-Agudo and P. A. González-Calero. An architecture for knowledge intensive CBR systems. In *Advances in Case-Based Reasoning – (EWCBR 2000)*. Springer-Verlag, 2000.
5. B. Díaz-Agudo and P. A. González-Calero. A declarative similarity framework for knowledge intensive CBR. In *Procs. of the (ICCBR 2001)*. Springer-Verlag, 2001.
6. B. Díaz-Agudo and P. A. González-Calero. Knowledge Intensive CBR through Ontologies. *Expert Update*, 2003.
7. Dramatica. Pro 4.0, 2004. http://www.screenplay.com/products/dpro/index.html.

8. C. Fairclough and P. Cunningham. A multiplayer case based story engine. In *4th International Conference on Intelligent Games and Simulation*, pages 41–46. EUROSIS, 2003.
9. J. Gennari, M. A. Musen, R. W. Fergerson, W. E. Grosso, M. Crubézy, H. Eriksson, N. F. Noy, and S. W. Tu. The evolution of Protégé: An environment for knowledge-based systems development. Technical report, Stanford University, 2002.
10. P. Gervás. An expert system for the composition of formal Spanish poetry. *Journal of Knowledge-Based Systems*, 14(3–4):181–188, 2001.
11. D. Grasbon and N. Braun. A morphological approach to interactive storytelling. In M. Fleischmann and W. Strauss, editors, *Artificial Intelligence and Interactive Entertainment, Living in Mixed Realities*, Sankt Augustin, Germany, 2001.
12. V. Haarslev and R. Moller. *RACER User s Guide and Reference Manual Version 1.7.7*. Concordia University and Univ. of Appl. Sciences in Wedel, November 2003.
13. R. R. Lang. *A Formal Model for Simple Narratives*. PhD thesis, Tulane University, 1997.
14. M. Lebowitz. Storytelling and generalization. In *Seventh Annual Conference of the Cognitive Science Society*, pages 100–109, Berkeley, California, 1987.
15. E. Lonergan. Lexical knowledge engineering: Mikrokosmos revisited. In *PACLING2001 - Pacific Association for Computational Linguistics 2001*, Kitakyushu, Japan, 2001.
16. I. Machado, R. Prada, and A. Paiva. Bringing drama into a virtual stage. In *Proceedings of CVE 2000*. ACM Press, 2000.
17. B. Magerko. A proposal for an interactive drama architecture. In *AAAI Spring Symposium on Artificial Intelligence and Interactive Entertainment*, Stanford, CA, 2002. AAAI Press.
18. S. A. Malec. Proppian structural analysis and XML modeling. http://clover.slavic.pitt.edu/~sam/propp/theory/propp.html, February 2004.
19. K. R. McKeown. The text system for natural language generation: An overview. In *20th Annual Meeting of the ACL*, pages 261–265, Canada, 1982.
20. J. R. Meehan. Tale-spin and micro tale-spin. In R. C. Schank and C. K. Riesbeck, editors, *Inside computer understanding*. Erlbaum Lawrence Erlbaum Associates, Hillsdale, NJ, 1981.
21. V. Propp. *Morphology of the Folktale*. University of Texas Press, Austin, 1968.
22. D. E. Rumelhart. Notes on a schema for stories. In D. G. Bobrow and A. Collins, editors, *Representation and Understanding: Studies in Cognitive Science*, pages 211–236. Academic Press, Inc., New York, 1975.
23. S. R. Turner. Minstrel: A computer model of creativity and storytelling. Technical Report UCLA-AI-92-04, Computer Science Department, 1992.
24. WritePro. Fictionmaster, 2004. http://www.writepro.com/.

Explanation Oriented Retrieval

Dónal Doyle[1], Pádraig Cunningham[1], Derek Bridge[2], and Yusof Rahman[1]

[1] Computer Science, Trinity College, Dublin 2, Ireland
{Donal.Doyle,Padraig.Cunningham,Yusof.Rahman}@cs.tcd.ie
[2] Computer Science, University College Cork, Cork, Ireland
d.bridge@cs.ucc.ie

Abstract. This paper is based on the observation that the nearest neighbour in a case-based prediction system may not be the best case to explain a prediction. This observation is based on the notion of a *decision surface* (i.e. class boundary) and the idea that cases located between the target case and the decision surface are more convincing as support for explanation. This motivates the idea of *explanation utility*, a metric that may be different to the similarity metric used for nearest neighbour retrieval. In this paper we present an explanation utility framework and present detailed examples of how it is used in two medical decision-support tasks. These examples show how this notion of explanation utility sometimes select cases other than the nearest neighbour for use in explanation and how these cases are more convincing as explanations.

1 Introduction

This paper presents a framework for retrieving cases that will be effective for use in explanation. It is important to distinguish the type of explanation we have in mind from *knowledge intensive* explanation where the cases contain explanation structures [9,10]. Instead, this framework is concerned with *knowledge light* explanation where case descriptions are used in much the same way that examples are invoked for comparison in argument [6,8,10,11]. In this situation the most compelling example is not necessarily the most similar. For instance, if a decision is being made on whether to keep a sick 12 week old baby in hospital for observation, a similar example with a 14 week old baby that was kept in is more compelling than one with an 11 week old baby (based on the notion that younger babies are more likely to be kept in)[1].

The situation where the nearest neighbour might not be the best case to support an explanation arises when the nearest neighbour is further from the decision boundary than the target case. A case that lies between the target case and the decision boundary will be more useful for explanation. Several examples of this are presented in Section 4. In this paper we present a framework for case retrieval that captures this idea of explanation utility. We describe how this framework works and show several examples of how it can return better explanation cases than the similarity metric.

An obvious question to ask is, why not use this explanation utility metric for classification as well as explanation? An investigation of this issue, presented in Section 5,

---

[1] This is sometimes referred to as an *a fortiori* argument with which all parents will be familiar: the classic example is "How come Joe can stay up later than me when I am older than him?".

shows that classification based on similarity is more accurate than classification based on our explanation utility metric. This supports our core hypothesis that the requirements for a framework for explanation are different to those for classification.

The next section provides a brief overview of explanation in CBR before the details of the proposed explanation utility framework are described in section 3. Some examples of the explanation utility framework in action are presented in section 4 and the evaluation of the framework as a mechanism for classification (compared with classification based on similarity) is presented in section 5.

2 Explanation in Case Based Reasoning

It has already been argued in [6] that the defining characteristic of Case-Based Explanation (CBE) is its concreteness. CBE is explanation based on specific examples. Cunningham et al. have provided empirical evidence to support the hypothesis that CBE is more useful for users than the rule-based alternative [6].

In the same way that CBR can be knowledge intensive or knowledge light, these distinct perspectives are also evident in CBE. Examples of knowledge intensive CBE are explanation patterns as described by Kass and Leake [9], CATO [2], TRUTH-TELLER [3] or the work of Armengol et al. [1]. Characteristic of the knowledge light approach to CBE is the work of Ong et al. [15], that of Evans-Romaine and Marling [8] or that of McSherry [12,13].

There has been some recent work to improve the quality of explanations in knowledge light CBR systems. One example is First Case [12] a system that explains why cases are recommended in terms of the compromises they involve. These compromises are attributes that fail to satisfy the preferences of the user.

> *Case 38 differs from your query only in speed and monitor size. It is better than Case 50 in terms of memory and price.*

The above example from First Case shows how it can also explain why one case is more highly recommended than another by highlighting the benefits it offers.

Another recent system for improving the quality of explanations is ProCon [13]. This system highlights both supporting and opposing features in the target case. The system works by constructing lists of features in the target problem that support and oppose the conclusion. The user is then shown output which contains:

- Features in the target problem that support the conclusion.
- Features in the target problem, if any, that oppose the conclusion.
- Features in the most similar case, if any that oppose the conclusion.

Including the opposing features in the explanation and highlighting them aims to improve the user's confidence in the system.

Whereas First Case and ProCon are concerned with highlighting features that support or oppose a prediction, the emphasis in this paper is on selecting the best cases to explain a prediction.

3 Explanation Utility Framework

Because the most similar case to a target case may not be the most convincing case to explain a classification, we have developed a framework for presenting more convincing cases during the retrieval process. This framework is based on the principle that a case lying between the target case and a decision boundary is more convincing than a case that lies on the opposite side of the target case. For example, consider the two feature problem in Fig. 1 and the justification for the classification of query case Q. There must be a decision boundary in the solution space, however the exact location of this boundary is not known. The boundary must lie between the nearest neighbour NN and the nearest unlike neighbour NUN. Typically users will have some intuition about the decision boundary and will be less comfortable with NN as a justification for the classification of Q if Q is considered to be closer to the decision boundary than NN. The case EC would be a more convincing example because it is more *marginal*.

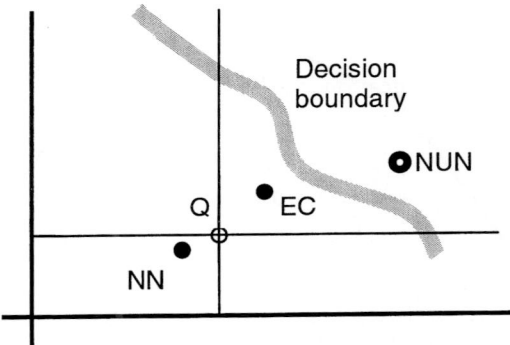

Fig. 1. A nearest neighbour example where case EC would be a better explanation for the decision on query case Q than the nearest neighbour NN; case NUN is the nearest unlike neighbour

For example, we have done some work in the area of predicting blood alcohol levels relative to drink driving limits [6]. In this domain an important feature is the units of alcohol consumed. If trying to explain that a query case who has consumed 6 units is over the drink-driving limit, other things being equal, a case that is over the limit and has consumed 4 units is a more convincing explanation case than one who is over the limit and has consumed 7 units.

3.1 Similarity

The explanation utility framework was implemented using FIONN [7], a Java based workbench based on CBML [5]. The framework uses a standard nearest neighbour algorithm implemented using a Case-Retrieval Net to perform a classification [11]. In this framework, the similarity between a target case q and x, a case in the case base, is given in (1).

$$Sim(q, x) = \sum_{f \in F} w_f \, \sigma(q_f, x_f) \tag{1}$$

where f is an individual feature in the set of features F, w_f is the weight of the feature f and $\sigma()$ is a measure of the contribution to the similarity from feature f.

The similarity measure includes standard metrics such as those for binary and normalised numeric features shown in (2).

$$\sigma(q_f, x_f) = \begin{cases} 1 & f \text{ discrete and } q_f = x_f \\ 0 & f \text{ discrete and } q_f \neq x_f \\ 1 - |q_f - x_f| & f \text{ continuous} \end{cases} \quad (2)$$

We also use similarity graphs to refine some of the numeric and symbolic similarity measures (see [17,18]). These graphs provide a look-up for the actual similarity between a feature/value pair when the difference between the values has been calculated. For example, a similarity graph for the feature Units Consumed in the blood alcohol domain is shown in Fig. 2.

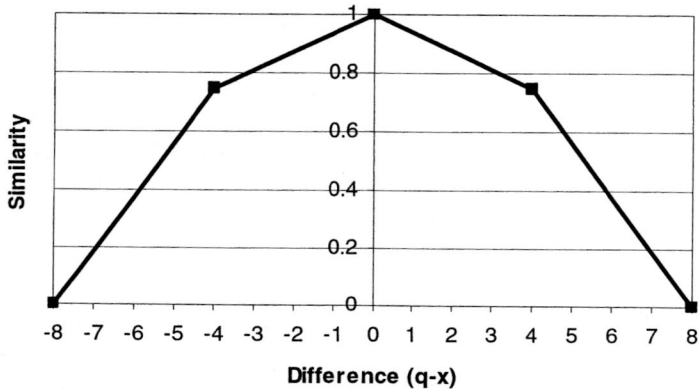

Fig. 2. Similarity graph for the feature Units Consumed

In this scenario consider a query case, q, with Units Consumed equal to 6 and a retrieved case, x, with units consumed equal to 9. The difference between these two values $(q-x)$ is -3. By looking up the graph it can be seen that a difference of -3 returns a similarity of 0.8.

The similarity between ordered symbolic feature values can be determined in a similar manner. Again taking an example from the blood alcohol domain, the feature Meal has an impact on the blood alcohol level. The more a person has eaten the slower the rate of absorption of alcohol in the blood. Therefore, all other factors being equal, the more a person has eaten the lower the maximum blood alcohol level will be for that person.

In the blood alcohol domain we are using, None, Snack, Lunch and Full are the possible values for Meal. These possible values are ordered, i.e. Lunch is more similar to Full, than None is. In this situation similarities can again be read from a graph. This time instead of the difference between two values being calculated as a mathematical subtraction, the difference is calculated in terms of the number of possible values between the two supplied values [14]. For example the difference between the values Lunch and Full would be 1, but the difference between Snack and Full would be 2. Using this value for difference and the graph in Fig. 3, it can be seen that the similarity between Lunch and Full is 0.8 while the similarity between Snack and Full would be 0.4.

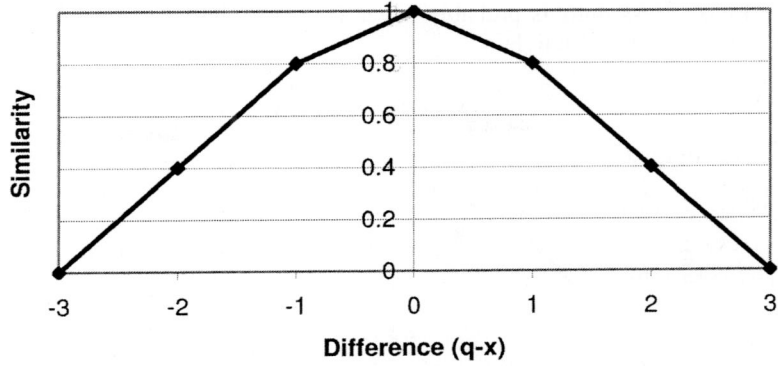

Fig. 3. Similarity graph for the feature Meal

Representing similarity measures as a graph has a number of advantages. One advantage is the ease of changing the graph. Since the graph is stored as points in an XML file, no coding is needed to change the details. In our situation the main benefit of using similarity graphs is that they provide a basis for creating our explanation utility measures.

3.2 Explanation Utility

Once a classification is performed, the top ranking neighbours are re-ranked to explain the classification. This ranking is performed using a utility measure shown in (3).

$$Util(q,x,c) = \sum_{f \in F} w_f \xi(q_f, x_f, c) \qquad (3)$$

where $\xi()$ measures the contribution to explanation utility from feature f. The utility measure closely resembles the similarity measure used for performing the initial nearest neighbour classification except that the $\xi()$ functions will be asymmetric compared with the corresponding $\sigma()$ functions and will depend on the class label c.

If we consider the graph used as the similarity measure for Units (Fig, 2): this graph can be used as a basis for developing the explanation utility measure for Units. Suppose the classification for the target case is over the limit. Other things being equal, a case describing a person who has drunk less than the target case (so the difference between q and x will be positive) and is over the limit is a more convincing explanation than one who has drunk more and is over the limit. The explanation utility of cases with larger values for Units than the target case diminishes as the difference gets greater, whereas cases with smaller values have more explanation utility (provided they are over the limit). The utility graph that captures this is shown in Fig. 4; the utility graph to support Under the Limit predictions is shown as well.

This method of creating utility measures leaves us with one problem. In the case of Over the Limit, all examples with a positive or zero difference have a utility of 1 in this dimension. This implies that the utility measure is *indifferent* over a large range of difference values. This results in the order of the cases stored in the case base having an impact on the cases returned for explanation. It also ignores the fact that a case that has drunk 2 less units is probably better for explaining Over the Limit than a case that has only drunk 1 unit less.

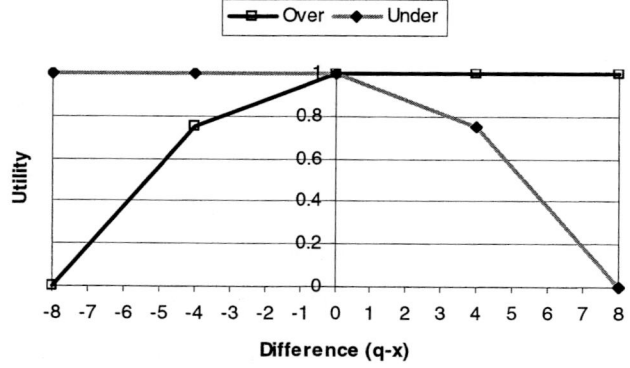

Fig. 4. Utility measures for the feature Units Consumed

To address both of these problems the utility measure is adjusted so that maximum utility is not returned at equality. An alternative utility graph is shown in Fig. 5. It is difficult to determine the details of the best shape for this graph; the shape shown in Fig. 5. captures our understanding after informal evaluation.

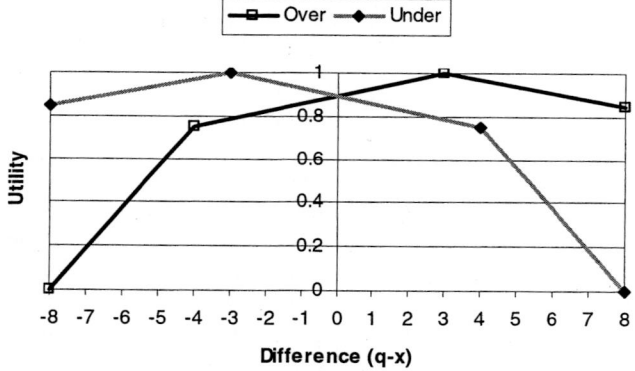

Fig. 5. Adjusted measures for the feature Units Consumed

4 Evaluation

In this section we examine some examples from two domains where we have evaluated our explanation utility framework. One domain is the blood alcohol domain we have mentioned earlier; this domain has 73 cases. The other is a decision support system for assessing suitability for participation in a diabetes e-Clinic. Patients with stable diabetes can participate in the e-Clinic whereas other patients need closer monitoring. The decision support system acts as a triage process that assesses whether the patient is stable or not. In this domain we have 300 cases collected in St. James' Hospital in Dublin by Dr. Yusof Rahman [16].

In case-based explanation it is reasonable to assume that explanation will be based on the top cases retrieved. Our evaluation involved performing a leave-one-out cross validation on these data sets to see how often cases selected by the explanation utility measure were not among the nearest neighbours (The top three were considered). In both the blood-alcohol domain and the e-clinic domain, the evaluation showed that the case with the highest utility score was found outside the three nearest neighbours slightly over 50% of the time. Thus, useful explanation cases – according to this framework – are not necessarily nearest neighbours. The following subsections show examples of some of these.

4.1 Blood Alcohol Content

The first example from the blood-alcohol domain is a case that is predicted (correctly) to be under the limit, see example Q_1 in Table 1. When Q_1 was presented to a nearest neighbour algorithm the most similar retrieved case was found to be NN_1. If this case were presented as an argument that Q_1 is under the limit, the fact that Q_1 has drunk more units than NN_1 makes this case unconvincing, as the more units a person drinks the more likely they are to be over the limit (see also Fig 6). The utility measures were then used to re-rank the 10 nearest neighbours retrieved. This gave us EC_1 as the most convincing case to explain why Q_1 is over the limit. EC_1 has consumed more units and is lighter than Q_1. Since all other feature values are the same, if EC_1 is under the limit then so should Q_1. On investigation it was found that EC_1 was in fact the 9th nearest neighbour in the original retrieval. Without using the utility measures this case would never be presented to a user.

Table 1. Example case from the blood alcohol domain where the prediction is 'under the limit'

	Target Case (Q_1)	Nearest Neighbour (NN_1)	Explanation Case (EC_1)
Weight (Kgs)	82	82	73
Duration (mins)	60	60	60
Gender	Male	Male	Male
Meal	Full	Full	Full
Units Consumed	2.9	2.6	5.2
BAC	Under	Under	Under

Another example supporting an over the limit prediction is shown in Table 2. In this situation the nearest neighbour NN_2 to a query case Q_2 has consumed more units than the query case. This situation is not as straightforward as the earlier example. NN_2 is in the right direction in the **Weight** dimension but in the wrong direction in the **Units** dimension. Once again the case (EC_2) retrieved using the utility measure is a more convincing case to explain why Q_2 is over the limit. This time EC_2 was the 7th nearest neighbour in the original nearest neighbour retrieval.

Table 2. Example case from the blood alcohol domain where the prediction is 'over the limit'

	Target Case (Q_2)	Nearest Neighbour (NN_2)	Explanation Case (EC_2)
Weight (Kgs)	73	76	79
Duration (mins)	240	240	240
Gender	Male	Male	Male
Meal	Full	Full	Full
Units Consumed	12.0	12.4	9.6
BAC	Over	Over	Over

As these two examples only differ in two dimensions (**Weight** and **Units**), they can be represented graphically as shown in Fig. 6 and Fig. 7. If we look at these in more detail, the shaded quadrant in both figures shows the region for a case to be a convincing explanation. This region is where a case lies between the query case and the decision surface for both features. In these examples both EC_1 and EC_2 lie inside the shaded region, while the nearest neighbours NN_1 and NN_2 lie outside the region. It should be noted that in these particular examples only two features are shown, however the principle generalises to higher dimensions in much the same way that the similarity calculation does.

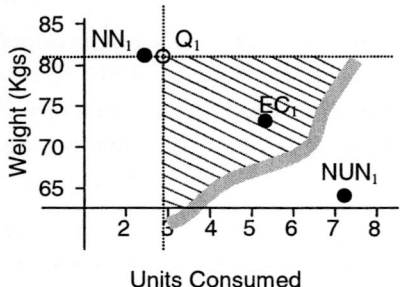

Fig. 6. Utility ranking for an Under the Limit example

Fig. 7. Utility ranking for an Over the Limit example

4.2 e-Clinic

Some of the factors for deciding if a patient is stable and suitable for the e-clinic include: the type of diabetes they have, the treatment they are on, if they have any complications and their HbA1c level (see below for details). For example, if a patient has any complications, if they have type II diabetes or are treated by injecting insulin instead of being treated by oral hypoglycaemic agents (OHA) they would not be considered suitable for the e-Clinic. The HbA1c feature is a test that can provide an average rating for blood sugar levels over the three month period prior to testing. The lower the value for HbA1c the more likely a patient is to be stable enough to remain in the e-clinic. However if the value for HbA1c is greater than 7- 7.5 % the patient is unlikely to be suitable for the e-clinic.

First we consider a situation in which the patient is predicted to be stable enough to stay in the e-clinic system, see Table 3.

Table 3. A diabetes e-clinic example where the patient is considered to be stable

	Target Case (Q_3)	Nearest Neighbour (NN_3)	Explanation Case (EC_3)
HbA1c (%)	5.6	5.5	6
Type of Diabetes	II	II	II
Treatment	Diet	Diet	Diet
Complication	No	No	No
Stable	Yes	Yes	Yes

In this situation we see once again that the retrieved nearest neighbour is on the wrong side of the query case relative to the decision boundary (albeit marginally). Again, the utility measure retrieves an explanation case (EC_3) that lies between the query case and the decision boundary. In this situation EC_3 was the seventh nearest neighbour in the original nearest neighbour process.

In order to support the assertion that these cases are in fact better explanations, we asked an expert in the diabetes domain to evaluate some of the results. The expert was presented with nine target cases and associated nearest neighbour and explanation cases – labelled as Explanation 1 and Explanation 2. In eight of nine cases the domain expert indicated that the case selected by the utility measure was more convincing than the nearest neighbour. The one situation where the expert felt the nearest neighbour was better is shown in Table 4.

The situation in Table 4 is unusual in that the nearest neighbour, NN_4, has exactly the same values as the target case Q_4. The Explanation case is EC_4, originally the eighth nearest neighbour. Presumably, the expert is more impressed with the nearest neighbour in this case because it is an exact match.

Table 4. A diabetes e-clinic example where the patient is considered to be not stable

	Target Case (Q_4)	Nearest Neighbour (NN_4)	Explanation Case (EC_4)
HbA1c (%)	8.9	8.9	8.7
Type of Diabetes	II	II	II
Treatment	OHA	OHA	OHA
Complication	No	No	No
Stable	No	No	No

5 Explanation Utility as a Classification Mechanism

We have received a few suggestions that the explanation utility framework could be considered as a classification mechanism and should be used to perform the classification as well. So we have investigated the possibility of using the utility measure for performing the entire retrieval process, instead of using it simply to re-rank the highest neighbours based on the classification. This is not completely straightforward as the utility metric is class dependent as shown in equation (3). This can be addressed by using the utility metric to rank the entire case-base twice, once for each outcome class. The utility score for the k nearest neighbours for each class is summed and the class with the highest score is returned as the prediction.

In order to test the effectiveness of this approach to classification, a leave-one-out cross-validation was performed comparing this utility based classification with the standard similarity based process. The results of this comparison are shown in Fig. 8. The explanation oriented retrieval has an accuracy of 74% in the alcohol domain compared with 77% for nearest neighbour classification. In the e-clinic database it has an accuracy of 83% compared to a normal accuracy of 96%.

This shows that the requirements for classification accuracy and explanation are different and supports the idea of having an explanation utility framework that is separate from the similarity mechanism used for classification.

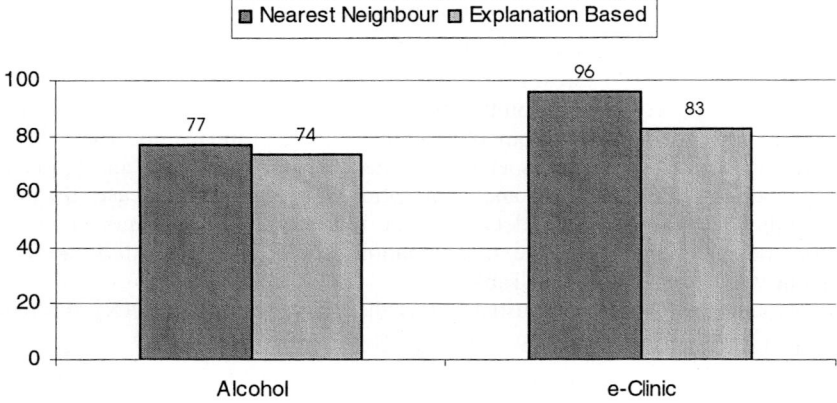

Fig. 8. A comparison of the classification accuracy of the Explanation Oriented Retrieval compared with standard Nearest Neighbour

6 Conclusions

This research is based on the idea that, in case-based explanation, the nearest neighbours may not be the best cases to explain predictions. In classification problems there will normally be a notion of a decision surface and cases that are closer to the decision surface should be more compelling as explanations. We introduce an explanation utility framework that formalises this idea and show how it can be used to select explanation cases in two problem domains.

The preliminary evaluation that we present shows that the utility framework will frequently (about 50% of the time) choose different cases to the nearest neighbours and, on inspection, these look like better explanations. An assessment by a domain expert on nine explanation scenarios supported this view.

The next stage in this research is to comprehensively evaluate the usefulness of the cases selected by the utility framework against the nearest neighbours in user studies. The determination of the number of nearest neighbours to be re-ranked for explanation requires some work. In our research to date we have produced explanation by using the 10 nearest neighbours during retrieval. We are currently researching the possibility of using the NUN to define the set that gets re-ranked. Some research on the best shape for utility curves is also needed. Once the effectiveness of the utility framework is established it can be combined with the techniques for highlighting features in explanation as proposed by McSherry [12,13]; this will further increase the impact of the explanation.

In the future we would like to look at the role that the nearest *unlike* neighbour can play in explanation. The nearest unlike neighbour is interesting in the context of the framework presented here as it is just on the *other* side of the decision surface.

References

1. Armengol, E., Palaudàries, A., Plaza, E., (2001) Individual Prognosis of Diabetes Long-term Risks: A CBR Approach. Methods of Information in Medicine. Special issue on prognostic models in Medicine. vol. 40, pp. 46-51
2. Aleven, V., Ashley, K.D. (1992). Automated Generation of Examples for a Tutorial in Case-Based Argumentation. In C. Frasson, G. Gauthier, & G. I. McCalla (Eds.), Proceedings of the Second International Conference on Intelligent Tutoring Systems, ITS 1992, pp. 575-584. Berlin: Springer-Verlag.
3. Ashley, K. D., McLaren, B. 1995. Reasoning with reasons in case-based comparisons. Proceedings of the First International Conference on Cased-Based Reasoning (ICCBR-95), pp. 133-144. Berlin: Springer.
4. Brüninghaus, S., Ashley, K.D., (2003) Combining Model-Based and Case-Based Reasoning for Predicting the Outcomes of Legal Cases. , *5th International Conference on Case-Based Reasoning*. K. D. Ashley & D. G. Bridge (Eds.). LNAI 2689, pp65-79, Springer Verlag, 2003
5. Coyle, L., Doyle, D., Cunningham, P., (2004) Representing Similarity for CBR in XML, *to appear in 7th European Conference in Case-Based Reasoning.*
6. Cunningham, P., Doyle, D., Loughrey, J., An Evaluation of the Usefulness of Case-Based Explanation, *5th International Conference on Case-Based Reasoning*. K. D. Ashley & D. G. Bridge (Eds.). LNAI 2689, pp122-130, Springer Verlag, 2003
7. Doyle, D., Loughrey, J.,Nugent, C., Coyle, L., Cunningham, P., FIONN: A Framework for Developing CBR Systems, *to appear in Expert Update*
8. Evans-Romaine, K., Marling, C., Prescribing Exercise Regimens for Cardiac and Pulmonary Disease Patients with CBR, in *Workshop on CBR in the Health Sciences at 5th International Conference on Case-Based Reasoning (ICCBR-03)*Trondheim, Norway, June 24, 2003, pp 45-62
9. Kass, A.M., Leake, D.B., (1988) Case-Based Reasoning Applied to Constructing Explanations, in Proceedings of 1988 Workshop on Case-Based Reasoning, ed. J. Kolodner, pp190-208, Morgan Kaufmann. San Mateo, Ca
10. Leake, D., B., (1996) CBR in Context: The Present and Future, in Leake, D.B. (ed) Case-Based Reasoning: Experiences, Lessons and Future Directions, pp3-30, MIT Press
11. Lenz, M., Burkhard, H.-D. (1996) Case Retrieval Nets: Basic ideas and extensions, in: Gorz, G., Holldobler, S. (Eds.), KI-96: Advances in Artificial Intelligence, Lecture Notes in Artificial Intelligence 1137, Springer Verlag, pp. 227–239
12. McSherry, D., (2003) Similarity and Compromise, *5th International Conference on Case-Based Reasoning*. K. D. Ashley & D. G. Bridge (Eds.) LNAI 2689, pp122-130, Springer Verlag, 2003
13. McSherry, D., (2003) Explanation in Case-Based Reasoning: an Evidential Approach, in Procceedings 8th UK Workshop on Case-Based Reasoning, pp 47-55

14. Osborne, H.R., Bridge, D.G., (1996) A Case Base Similarity Framework, 3rd European Workshop on Case-Based Reasoning, I. Smith & B. Faltings (Eds), LNAI 1168, pp. 309-323, Springer, 1996
15. Ong, L.S., Shepherd, B., Tong, L.C., Seow-Choen, F., Ho, Y.H., Tang, L.C., Ho Y.S, Tan, K. (1997) The Colorectal Cancer Recurrence Support (CARES) System. Artificial Intelligence in Medicine 11(3): 175-188
16. Rahman, Y., Knape, T., Gargan, M., Power, G., Hederman, L., Wade, V., Nolan, JJ., Grimson, J., e-Clinic: An electronic triage system in Diabetes Management through leveraging Information and Communication Technologies, accepted for MedInfo 2004
17. Stahl, A., Gabel., T (2003) Using Evolution Programs to Learn Local Similarity Measures, *5th International Conference on Case-Based Reasoning*. K. D. Ashley & D. G. Bridge (Eds.). LNAI 2689, pp537-551, Springer Verlag, 2003
18. Stahl, A., (2002) Defining Similarity Measures: Top-Down vs. Bottom-Up, *6th European Conference on Case-Based Reasoning*. S. Craw & A. Preece (Eds.).LNAI 2416, pp406-420, Springer Verlag, 2002

Exploiting Background Knowledge when Learning Similarity Measures

Thomas Gabel[1] and Armin Stahl[2]

[1] University of Karlsruhe, Institute AIFB
thomas.gabel@aifb.uni-karlsruhe.de
[2] German Research Center for Artificial Intelligence DFKI GmbH
Research Group Image Understanding and Pattern Recognition (IUPR)
stahl@informatik.uni-kl.de

Abstract. The definition of similarity measures – one core component of every CBR application – leads to a serious knowledge acquisition problem if domain and application specific requirements have to be considered. To reduce the knowledge acquisition effort, different machine learning techniques have been developed in the past. In this paper, enhancements of our framework for learning knowledge-intensive similarity measures are presented. The described techniques aim to restrict the search space to be considered by the learning algorithm by exploiting available background knowledge. This helps to avoid typical problems of machine learning, such as overfitting the training data.

1 Introduction

Similarity measures are certainly one of the most import aspects of Case-Based Reasoning. Since they are required for the first step of the CBR cycle [1], namely the retrieval of useful cases [3], the quality of the employed similarity measure strongly influences the entire problem solving process. For example, if suboptimal cases are retrieved, the subsequent adaptation process will be more expensive, might result in suboptimal solutions, or might even fail completely. In most commercial CBR systems applied nowadays (typically classification, diagnosis or help-desk systems), the situation is even harder. Here, usually no case adaptation functionality is provided at all. Hence, the quality of the final output of the CBR system completely depends on the quality of the case data provided and the system's ability to retrieve the best cases available.

When employing quite simple distance metrics (e.g. the Hamming or the Euclidean distance), retrieval results are often unsatisfactory. While these *knowledge-poor similarity measures (kpSM)* can be defined with little effort, the drawback of them is, that they are 'blind' regarding the application and domain specific requirements. Hence, in many applications more sophisticated and domain specific heuristics to select accurate cases have been used. However, when employing such *knowledge-intensive similarity measures (kiSM)*, one is confronted again with a serious knowledge acquisition problem. Domain experts able to provide the mandatory domain knowledge and experienced knowledge engineers able to model this knowledge by using formal similarity measures are required. If such experts are available at all, this results in significantly increased development costs for the CBR application.

In order to avoid this drawback of kiSM, we have proposed to support their definition by applying machine learning techniques [9–12]. The basic idea of this approach is to acquire feedback about the quality of retrieval results from which learning algorithms can infer proper similarity measures automatically. Although experimental evaluations have shown that our framework allows to facilitate the definition of kiSM significantly, under certain circumstances some open problems might prevent its application in daily practice.

This paper presents some techniques leading to a broader and improved applicability of our framework. The major idea is to incorporate easily available background knowledge into the learning process in order to avoid typical problems of machine learning, such as overfitting. Section 2 provides some basics of our learning framework and points out the objectives of the extensions presented in this paper. However, since these extensions described in Section 3 and 4 directly build on our previous work, for more details about our learning approach the reader is referred to [12]. Section 5 presents the results of an experimental evaluation demonstrating the power of the described techniques. Finally, Section 6 concludes with some remarks on related work and further research issues.

2 Learning Similarity Measures

In principle, learning similarity measures from some kind of training data is not a novel issue. A lot of work in this direction has been done, for example, in the area of nearest-neighbour classification [13]. Here, one tries to adjust feature weights – which can also be seen as a simple form of a kiSM – by examining pre-classified training data. However, our learning framework [9–12] particularly addressed two novel issues:

Applicability Beyond Classification Domains. In recent years CBR has become very popular in quite different areas, such as e-Commerce or Knowledge Management. Here, traditional learning approaches originally developed for classification tasks are usually not applicable due to the absence of pre-classified data required for learning. One of our objectives was the development of a learning framework suited for a broader range of CBR applications. This framework is based on a particular kind of training data, called *utility feedback*, where the cases' utility has to be estimated by some *similarity teacher*. This similarity teacher might be, for example, a human domain expert, the users of the system, or some software agent [9].

Learning of Local Similarity Measures. Besides the definition of attribute weights, successful CBR tools applied nowadays also allow the specification of so-called *local similarity measures*. These measures are responsible for the similarity calculation regarding one single aspect of the case representation[1],

---

[1] We assume the commonly used attribute-value based representation.

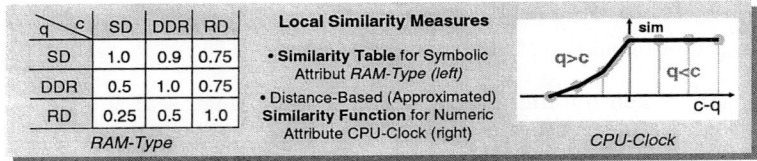

Fig. 1. Modelling Local Similarity Measures

i.e. the local similarity between the query and the case value of a particular attribute. Depending on the data type of the attribute, quite different representation formalisms are used for modelling local measures (see Figure 1). These measures can be used to encode a lot of knowledge about the underlying domain making their definition difficult and time-consuming. One novelty of our learning framework is that it embraces also learning of local similarity measures.

While the first issue concerns the availability of training data mandatory for applying learning techniques, the second issue concerns the learning algorithms to be applied. In this paper we focus on techniques to improve these learning algorithms particularly when being used to learn local similarity measures.

2.1 Usage of Evolutionary Algorithms

When considering attribute weights only, the learning process can efficiently be realised using gradient descent algorithms [13, 9]. However, when extending the learning functionality to local similarity measures, the more complex and heterogeneous representations demand alternative, more flexible learning algorithms.

We have employed evolutionary algorithms (EAs) which are well-known for their capability to perform well in such environments. The idea is to encode local similarity measures as vectors of real numbers on which the EA's specialised crossover and mutation operators operate upon, where the fitness of generated measures is determined by the resulting retrieval accuracy with respect to the given utility feedback [12, 11]. Experimental results have shown that the combination of utility feedback and evolutionary algorithms represents a powerful approach for supporting the modelling of kiSM in different application scenarios. However, some open questions and interesting research issues motivate an enhancement of our framework to be presented in this paper.

2.2 Motivation for an Enhancement

Extending learning on local similarity measures leads to a serious problem: the algorithm has a huge search or hypothesis space. In particular the representations (see Figure 1) that we have chosen for representing typical local similarity measures [12], namely similarity tables (for unordered data types) and difference-based similarity functions (for ordered data types), consist of numerous parameters enabling the learning algorithm to generate very specific measures. The following reasons motivate an enhancement of the learning algorithms in order to ensure a more goal-directed learning process:

- Especially when obtaining little training data, huge search spaces increase the risk that the learner creates models (here, similarity measures) that fit 'too' well to the training data, while showing poor performance and little ability in generalising on some independent test data set. This behaviour is known as overfitting in many machine learning approaches.
- Due to the chosen representation, the huge search space is populated with plenty of (local) similarity measures whose usage in practice is highly improbable. Hence, the evolutionary algorithm wastes time searching regions of the search space which do not correspond to 'realistic' measures. Since evolutionary algorithms are well-known to be very demanding regarding computational resources, a speeding up of the learning process will increase the applicability of our framework in commercial practice.
- Completely manual definition and fully automated learning of knowledge-intensive similarity measures are two extremes of a wide spectrum of modelling possibilities [10]. Both approaches are coupled with certain advantages and disadvantages. For example, learning might result in suboptimal measures (e.g. caused by overfitting) while a manual definition might lead to unacceptable development costs. In order to benefit from the advantages of both approaches, it seems promising to apply a hybrid approach. This means, one should consider easily available knowledge by defining it directly, while learning unknown or uncertain knowledge by applying our framework.

The three mentioned issues are the foundation of the extensions presented in the following. Here, the basic idea is to exploit easily available background knowledge in order to restrict the hypothesis space to be considered by the evolutionary algorithm. Therefore, we identified two main sources of background knowledge that can be exploited easily and utilised to improve the process of learning similarity measures.

3 Determination of Knowledge Sources

The knowledge sources we employ to enhance the learning can be divided into two groups: Firstly, our representation of local similarity measures allows us to define several forms of *meta knowledge* representing general demands on the appearance of learnt measures. Secondly, the aid of a knowledge engineer and the incorporation of his/her *expert knowledge* into the learning process may be worthwhile (see Section 3.2).

3.1 Similarity Meta-knowledge

Experience in the practical usage of CBR systems has shown that most of the similarity measures that are applied feature certain characteristics. We refer to that kind of experience as similarity meta knowledge.

3.1.1 Heuristic Constraints

There are awkward definitions for similarity measures (e.g. non-reflexive) which actually contradict the CBR paradigm, according to which similar problems have similar solutions, and which thus are very improbable to be used in practice. Nevertheless, those peculiar measures are part of the search space and, accordingly, have the chance of getting involved in the learning process. By defining a set of basic heuristic constraints, that should be fulfilled by local similarity measures, we intend to exclude unusual, highly improbable metrics from the search and thus to restrict the search space.

Reflexivity Constraint. Most similarity measures employed in practice are supposed to be reflexive, as any entity can be characterised as being maximally similar to itself. Hence, if there is no justified reason to make use of non-reflexive similarity measures, the constraint for reflexivity of a local similarity measure sim_A for attribute A with domain D_A seems to be advantageous:
$$c_{refl} = \ll sim_A(x,x) = 1 \ \forall x \in D_A \gg$$

Symmetry Constraint. The idea of introducing a symmetry constraint is inviting, since its application would approximately halve the search space. In the case of a symbolic attribute A_s with $|D_{A_s}| = n$, for example, the number of alterable entries in the respective similarity measure (individual) sinks from n^2 to $\frac{n^2+n}{2}$. The symmetry constraint is denoted as follows:
$$c_{symm} = \ll sim_A(x,y) = sim_A(y,x) \ \forall x,y \in D_A \gg$$
Of course, in many application scenarios, asymmetric local similarity measures are indispensable (e.g. in product recommendation systems), in which case we would not impose that constraint.

Monotony Constraint. According to common understanding, larger distances between the query's and case's value of an attribute make them more dissimilar, while smaller ones let them appear rather similar. Based on that foundation, we now define a constraint for monotony (only applicable to distance-based similarity functions, i.e. for ordered data types):
$$c_{mon} = \ll sim_A(x,y_2) - sim_A(x,y_1) \leq 0 \ \forall x, y_1, y_2 \in D_A$$
$$\text{with } 0 \leq y_1 - x \leq y_2 - x \text{ or } x - y_2 \leq x - y_1 \leq 0 \gg$$

3.1.2 Mining Knowledge from the Case Base

Considering a single local similarity measure sim, one can say that the similarity knowledge that is included in sim is distributed over several elements: for similarity tables over its n^2 entries; and for similarity functions over a few parameters or sampling points describing that function.

Without any doubt, some of the measure's elements can be characterised as carrying 'more valuable knowledge' insofar as they are consulted more frequently. That means they are more frequently used to determine a query's and a case's similarity regarding the respective attribute. Therefore, we ought to aim that those parts of the measure are most correct, as an erroneous similarity definition in these regions would have a higher negative impact on the CBR system's average percentage accuracy in solving new cases. For a learning algorithm this implies that it should focus more on such 'high-importance regions', searching more thoroughly there, while it should be permitted to spend less effort in other 'low-importance regions'.

But, which regions are of high importance? We intend to answer that question in the following by means of a statistical case base analysis. In so doing, we want to find out which entries within a similarity table and which regions of a similarity function's domain are more frequently consulted and which can thus be considered to be of higher importance. We need to stress in advance, that all considerations we are doing here presume a sufficiently substantial case base which is representative (in its attribute-value distributions for all attributes) of typical queries.

Illustrating our idea of obtaining knowledge from analysing case data, we present a little example regarding a local similarity measure for a symbolic attribute $A_{optDrive}$, which describes optical disc drives and which might be used in an application scenario where personal computers are described.

We assume a case base CB of 160 cases whose attribute values for $A_{optDrive}$ (with $D_{A_{optDrive}} = \{CD\text{-}R, CD\text{-}RW, DVD\text{-}R, Combo, DVD\text{-}RW\}$) are distributed according to Figure 2. We call that distribution attribute-specific value frequency $h_{A_{optDrive}}$ and we proceed on the assumption that it is representative and reflects the frequency with which certain values from $D_{A_{optDrive}}$ occur in practice.

$D_{optDrive}$	$h_{A_{optDrive}}$
CD-R	15
CD-RW	40
DVD-R	30
Combo	50
DVD-RW	25

Consultation Frequencies $c_s(x,y)$

q \ c	CD-R	CD-RW	DVD-R	Combo	DVD-RW
CD-R	210	600	450	750	375
CD-RW	600	1560	1200	2000	1000
DVD-R	450	1200	870	1500	750
Combo	750	2000	1500	2450	1250
DVD-RW	375	1000	750	1250	600

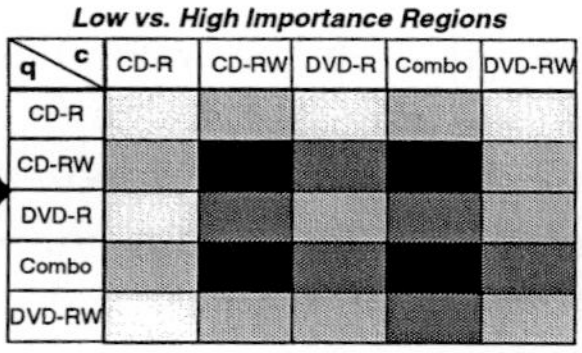

Fig. 2. Example for Low and High Importance Regions in a Similarity Table

To find out which combinations of certain case values and query values are used how often (and thus to find out which elements of the respective similarity table are supposed to be consulted how frequently), we introduce the concept of *consultation frequency* $c_{s/n}$ of a local similarity measure's domain. Here, the main idea is to regard the cases from CB as queries occurring in practice. So, the consultation frequency function (called $c_s : D_A \times D_A \rightarrow \mathbb{N}$ for symbolic attributes) basically counts and sums up over all $c \in CB$ how many table look-ups (separately for each table element) would have to be performed if an entire retrieval with c as query would be carried out, i.e. when determining the similarity between c and all other cases in CB. So, for example, it holds $c_s(CD\text{-}R, Combo) = 750$ since $sim_{A_{optDrive}}$'s similarity table's entry for $sim(CD\text{-}R, Combo)$ would be consulted 15×50 times, if for each case c with $c.A_{optDrive} = CD\text{-}R$ a retrieval would be made and in so doing the similarity to all cases with $c.A_{optDrive} = Combo$ would be looked up.

Figure 2 summarises the consultation frequencies for the given example and highlights high vs. low importance regions of $sim_{optDrive}$'s similarity table with different shades of gray (darker gray indicates higher importance).

Although our example was designed for a symbolic attribute we want to emphasise that the analysis of consultation frequencies of certain case-query attribute values can be applied to numeric attributes as well. Then, however, the determined frequencies (via corresponding function $c_n : D_A \to \mathbb{N}$) refer to specific case-query distances, i.e. parts along the similarity function's x-axis instead of single elements within a similarity table.

3.1.3 Exploitation of the Knowledge

The crucial issue, after having defined heuristic constraints and/or conducted a case base analysis, concerns the employment of the knowledge obtained. In the former case a straightforward application of the constraints is possible: Local measures not conforming to those heuristics are disregarded and excluded from the search. For knowledge about high/low importance regions we have defined two approaches by means of which the knowledge about consultation frequencies c_n or c_s can be incorporated into the optimisation process.

a) Granularity Restriction

Each entry v in a similarity table or each similarity value v for a function's sampling points can be chosen from $[0;1] \subset \mathbb{R}$. Accordingly, a self-evident strategy to efficiently restrict the search space is to introduce a grid for the respective similarity value v forcing it to be an element of $\{0, \frac{1}{g}, \ldots, \frac{g-1}{g}, 1\}$, where $g \in \mathbb{N}^+$ determines the allowed degree of granularity.

The results from a statistical case base analysis may be perfectly used to determine appropriate granularities. On the one hand, the consultation frequency $c_s(x, y)$ of a specific entry in a similarity table may be very high. So, this entry is supposed to be consulted very frequently and therefore should be adjusted to be as accurate as possible. Moreover, this reveals that the case base contains a lot of information about the combination 'x as query value and y as case value'. Then, one may conclude that learning of $sim_A(x, y)$ is less vulnerable to overfitting and that its value may be chosen on the basis of a finer granularity.

On the other hand, $c_s(x, y)$ may be rather low. Then, a fine-grained definition for $sim_A(x, y)$ is, generally speaking, not necessary or, at least, not very important (regarding the CBR system's overall performance). Furthermore, the low value of $c_s(x, y)$ suggests that CB features little information about that case-query combination for attribute A only. Hence, learning $sim_A(x, y)$ suffers from a high risk of overfitting, so that the restriction of $sim_A(x, y)$ to a comparatively low number of possible values seems promising. The following definition introduces our approach to restrict the search space via granularity levels.

Definition 1 (Granularity Values from Consultation Frequencies). *Let A be an attribute with domain D_A, CB a case base of m cases and sim_A the local similarity measure under consideration*

- where $sim_A(x,y) \in [0;1]$ with $x,y \in D_A$, if A is symbolic
- with sampling points $s_k \in [A_{min} - A_{max}, A_{max} - A_{min}]$ ($k \in \{1,\ldots,s\}$) and having similarity values $sim_{s_k} = sim(x,y)$ with $x - y = s_k$, if A is numeric.

Then, it holds for the **granularity value** g:

- if A is symbolic: $g = 1 + \left\lceil \frac{c_s(x,y)}{m^\gamma} \right\rceil$
- if A is numeric: $g = 1 + \left\lceil \frac{\int_{s_k-\delta}^{s_k+\delta} w(x,s_k) \cdot c_n(x) dx}{m^\gamma} \right\rceil$ with $\delta = \frac{2 \cdot (A_{max} - A_{min})}{s-1}$

and $w(x,y) = 1 - \frac{|x-y|}{\delta}$

where γ is a parameter to scale the entire granularity assessment.

In the case of dealing with a symbolic attribute, the consultation frequencies can be employed directly to determine appropriate granularity values. As A's domain is continuous, if it is a numeric attribute, the computation of integrals is necessary. However, because the amount of available case data is finite, that calculation can be done by computing according finite sums instead of integrals. In practical tests we found that setting $\gamma = 1$ produces convincing results. While this granularity approach may be employed for all kinds of local measures, the following strategy works for numeric attributes only.

b) Modified Sampling Point Distribution
In [12] we have presumed that the sampling points, that are used to represent a distance-based similarity function sim_A, are distributed uniformly over $D_A = [A_{min}-A_{max}, A_{max}-A_{min}]$ of sim_A. As mentioned above some regions of D_A may be of less importance than other ones – namely those regions with a rather low consultation frequency c_n. Consequently, in those regions we actually need not to interpolate sim_A as elaborately as in other, high-importance regions. So, less sampling points ought to be placed in the former, while a higher sampling rate and thus a better approximation of sim_A seems suitable for the latter regions. In short, an equidistant distribution of sampling points does not correspond to nuances in consultation frequency. Due to space limitations the reader is referred to [7] for more details on our algorithm to distribute the sampling points with respect to computed consultation frequencies.

3.2 Expert Knowledge

Without learning functionality, a similarity measure's competence relies exclusively on the expert modelling it. Contrarily, if the knowledge engineer lacks sufficient domain knowledge, the only way to obtain adequate retrieval knowledge is via machine learning (provided that training data is available). Thus, as proclaimed in Section 2.2 a combination of these two converse ways to define similarity measures permits several advantages:

- The knowledge acquisition effort is decreased. The expert first issues his/her (partial) knowledge about the respective measure, and the remaining parts of the similarity measure are learnt automatically.

- Since the expert is not urged to specify the similarity measure completely, he/she is not forced to make educated 'guesses' about elements of the measure he/she actually does not know much about.
- Due to the additional partial knowledge given by the expert, the learner might be less likely to overfit its learning results to the training data.

In the following we examine three strategies to incorporate a knowledge engineer's partial knowledge into the learning process.

3.2.1 Attribute and Weight Preferences

Feature weights have a crucial influence on the entire similarity calculation [9]: A wrong choice of weights can distort the entire similarity assessment, even if a lot of effort has been put into tuning local measures. Experts usually do not care or cannot say, whether A_1 is two or three times as important as A_2. We argue that it is much easier for an expert to formulate a number of preference relations by which he/she can determine a partial order of weights, ordered with respect to the relevance of the corresponding attributes. The task of assigning concrete numerical values to the weights can then be left to a learning algorithm.

An expert may, for example, utter that he/she considers A_1 to be less important than A_3, A_2 to be more important than A_3, while having no idea about A_4's importance. The number of allowed weight values for $w_1, \ldots, w_4$ – and thus the number of corresponding individuals that may be created in the scope of an evolutionary algorithm – is reduced when those relational constraints are taken into consideration. Of course, the degree of restriction depends on the number of preference relations the expert is able to provide.

3.2.2 Expert Estimations

The situation for local similarity measures, is even worse, because here a large number of concrete parameter or similarity values has to be devised for each attribute. As a consequence, many of the values that have to be determined during a manual definition of a similarity measure are left to the expert's intuition and thus mostly represent estimations of the correct value only. Nevertheless, even estimated values may help to support and bias the learning process:

Bounds Approach. An obvious possibility enabling an expert to directly cut off parts of the search space is by allowing him/her to define lower and upper bounds for specific similarity values. For instance, he/she may decide that for a symbolic attribute's values d_1 and d_2 it holds: $sim(d_1, d_2) \in [0.6; 0.8]$. Consequently, the learning algorithm does not have to take the whole interval $[0; 1]$ into consideration for $sim(d_1, d_2)$, but only that subinterval. In fact, our realisation of this approach also permits the interpretation of the bounds in a relaxed way by using a probability distribution that favours the bounded range.

Confidence-Based Approach. In response to the increased specification effort of the bounds approach (e.g. $2n^2$ bound values for a similarity table) we also introduce a more human-centred, confidence-based approach. Here, the expert may (eventually only partially) define the similarity measure in the usual manner, but is allowed to add an assertion about his/her level of confidence $c \in C = \{uncertain, low, average, high, certain\}$ regarding his/her specification. For example, he/she may state $sim(d_1, d_2) = 0.7$ and $c_{sim(d_1,d_2)} = high$ to express that it holds $sim(d_1, d_2) \approx 0.7$.

The specificational effort is less for the second approach as confidence levels may be defined for an entire measure as a whole or a part of it (e.g. for a number of rows in a table). The semantic of levels from C may be interpreted differently by the learner, e.g. depending on the application domain or on the knowledge engineer's experience. Therefore, the search space restriction induced by confidence levels is not as strict and inflexible as the one induced by bound specifications.

3.2.3 Exploitation of Structured Data Types

The knowledge engineer is fully responsible for the definition of the CBR system's vocabulary knowledge as well. That task comprises not only the definition of an appropriate case representation, but also the determination of attributes and their data types. Knowledge about the vocabulary, in particular about structured data types, can be employed a-priori to restrict the search space. With the term 'structured data types' we here refer to symbolic data types, namely taxonomic and ordered symbolic data types, whose values $D = \{d_1, \ldots, d_n\}$ can be arranged in a tree structure or total order, respectively. Of course, that taxonomic/total ordering affects the local similarity measures and the way the similarity between a query and a case value is computed [2].

Our approach to exploit that kind of vocabulary knowledge is primarily based upon employing a more compact representation of local measures as an evolutionary algorithm's individuals (compared to a similarity table with n^2 entries). For instance, for taxonomic symbolic attributes we defined similarity tree individuals (consisting maximally of $2n-1$ entries), devised appropriate specialised genetic operators for those individuals and thus enabled the EA to directly operate on tree structures. The actual search space restriction is reached not only by that more compact representation of local measures, but also via implicit constraints (e.g. restrictions of the similarity values to be associated with single tree nodes) that hold for parts of taxonomic/ordered symbolic individuals. A more detailed description of that approach can be found in [7].

4 Incorporation of Background Knowledge

As mentioned in the previous section it is one of our aims to restrict the search space by exerting a bias on the respective learning algorithm so that it prefers certain regions of that space to other ones or completely avoids searching some subspaces of the entire search space.

4.1 Knowledge-Based Optimisation Filters

In order to realise the restriction of the search space we introduce the concept of *knowledge-based optimisation filters (kbOF)* restricting the search space. With that term we refer to entities that, on the one hand, hold the gathered knowledge concerning the learning of similarity measures. On the other hand, they are meant to play an active role to explicitly direct the search. As similarity measures are composed of several elements (e.g. a local measure for each attribute of the chosen case representation), we should avoid using a single filter for the entire measure. Instead, the definition of a special kbOF for each attribute (i.e. each local measure) as well as one additional filter for the feature weights is necessary. Hence, for a case representation consisting of n attributes we need $n + 1$ filters.

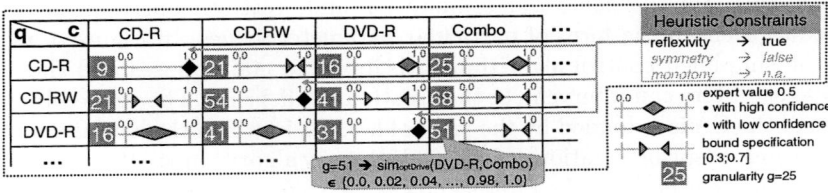

Fig. 3. Example of a Knowledge-Based Optimisation Filter for $A_{optDrive}$

In particular, each kbOF for a local similarity measure (we disregard feature weights here) may include the following pieces of knowledge:

- set of heuristic constraints (e.g. constraint for symmetry)
- set of granularity values g
- list of non-equidistantly distributed sampling points for numeric attributes
- set of bound specifications (subintervals of $[0; 1]$)
- set of expert-estimated similarity values with corresponding confidence levels
- characteristic information on how to exploit structured data types, only for (taxonomic and ordered) symbolic attributes

In Figure 3 we give a visualisation of a possible kbOF for the example of attribute $A_{optDrive}$ introduced in Section 3.1.2.

4.2 Intervening in the Learning Process

An important question is how a kbOF interferes with the search process in order to exert a bias towards certain types of similarity measures. Our approach considers the filter's background knowledge already during the creation of new hypotheses, i.e. during the creation of new candidate similarity measures. Here, the kbOFs' task is to supervise and control the generation of new candidates in such a way that no (or as few as possible) contradictions to its prior knowledge occur, i.e. hard constraints must always and soft ones should mostly be met.

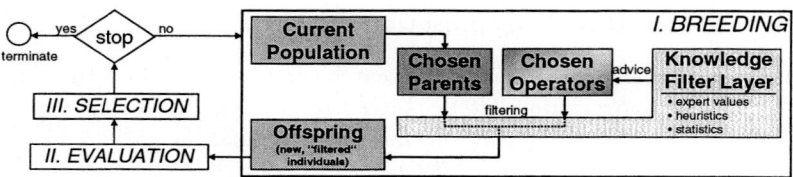

Fig. 4. Intervention of Knowledge-Based Optimisation Filters

In the context of an EA this bias is supposed to be done during the generation of new individuals in the breeding stage of the evolutionary loop. At this, the kbOFs exert their influence at the level of chromosomes: Based on the information they carry, these filters may make some values for the genes of a new individual more probable or forbid other values, for instance. They are also allowed to adapt the behaviour of mutation and crossover operators by giving advice to them in the form of particular parameter values. In Figure 4 we outline the simplified control algorithm with its three main phases and show how knowledge filters can intervene in the creation of offspring. The refined breeding phase of the EA is extended by the layer of kbOFs, in which the actual intentions (concerning offspring creation) of the evolutionary algorithm are 'filtered' so that they are in accordance to the filter's knowledge. Hence, a kbOF uses its heuristic, expert and statistical knowledge to manipulate the creation of descendants.

5 Evaluation

The main focus of our experiments is based upon a comparison of filterless and kbOF-enhanced learning of similarity measures. We have chosen a set of classification and regression application domains from the UCI Machine Learning Repository[2] and used our learning framework to learn the similarity measures in such a way that the CBR system's prediction accuracy is maximised. The CBR system's predictions (classification and regression) are based on a k-nearest neighbour approach.

5.1 Experimental Settings

The number of presented techniques to improve the learning of similarity measures is numerous and, accordingly, the number of definable kbOF is extremely high as well. Hence, to structure our experiments we have identified a number of *classes* of kbOF we compare against one another:

m-Filters contain similarity meta knowledge only (cf. Section 3.1). This means, they may make use of the reflexivity, symmetry or monotony constraint, or of an arbitrary combination of them. Moreover, they are allowed to employ the knowledge mined from the case base, e.g. by introducing a grid all similarity values have to fit in. It should be noted that m-Filters are of special interest since the knowledge acquisition effort to define them is only marginal.

---

[2] http://www.ics.uci.edu/~mlearn/MLRepository.html

e-Filters are enhanced via specific expert knowledge. Hence, those filters can include bound specifications, expert estimations, confidence levels etc. The expert knowledge we incorporated represented a compilation of common sense and (partially) available domain theories. Although e-Filters are also permitted to exploit the advantages of structured (taxonomic and ordered symbolic) attributes, none of our experiments covers these opportunities.

me-Filters represent the combination of the former ones, incorporating both kinds of additional knowledge to guide the optimisation process.

Apart from comparing the effect of utilising several filter types we also distinguished between different amounts of training examples used for learning. In each experiment (consisting of 10 repetitions for each domain) we have split the set of available cases into a training and test data set, CB_{train} and CB_{test}. Then, we started the learning of similarity measures for incrementally increasing subsets (15, 25, 50, ... cases) of CB_{train} and calculated average classification and regression (i.e. numeric difference between correct and predicted value of the solution attribute) accuracies, respectively, on CB_{test}.

5.2 Results

All in all, the employment of knowledge-based optimisation filters led to improved learning results. However, the magnitudes of achieved improvements differed enormously over the various application domains. In most cases, the me-Filter produced the highest learning improvements, which is plausible as those kbOFs had been enriched by the maximal amount of available background knowledge. Furthermore, it became obvious that the incorporation of expert knowledge in general generates higher gains than the usage of similarity meta knowledge only. This is not too surprising insofar as expert knowledge can be described as more exhaustive and substantial than similarity meta knowledge. That kind of outperforming, however, must be paid with the higher knowledge acquisition effort that has to be invested when employing expert knowledge.

In Figure 5 we summarise the achieved error reductions (for two of the application domains we have chosen) for increasing training data sizes (x-axis). The baseline similarity measure represents, on the one hand, a knowledge-poor (default) similarity measure, into whose construction no further knowledge engineering effort has been put, i.e. the similarity assessment here is based on an uninformed syntactic match. On the other hand, we illustrate the accuracies that resulted from a similarity measure that was obtained from filterless learning.

The charts' subsequent data rows sketch the increased accuracies that could be gained due to the incorporation of explicit background knowledge through the three types of kbOFs mentioned. So, for example, in the *hayesroth* domain (left chart) the additional knowledge yields the creation of high-quality similarity measures and thus of a k-nearest neighbour CBR classifier which produces a 7% − 17% smaller classification error. In the *housing* scenario (prediction of real-estate prices) the resulting CBR system's prediction accuracy is increased clearly (regression error reduction down to a level of between 65% and 85% compared to

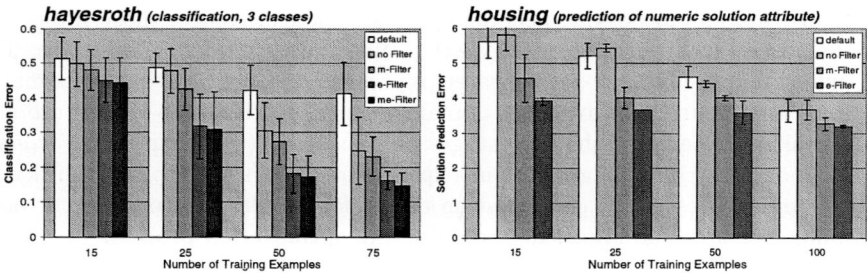

Fig. 5. Achieved Results for two Exemplary Domains

filterless learning), especially for small training data sizes which means that the system's susceptibility to overfitting is reduced. Similar results could be achieved for the remaining application domains as well [7]. Interestingly, convergence of learning results could be observed for increasing training data sizes. This leads to the assumption that no additional domain knowledge may be needed if a sufficient amount of training examples is available.

Although the additional learning improvements that could be obtained due to the utilisation of kbOFs compared to filterless learning varied with respect to application domain and training data sizes used, in Table 1 we summarise the average 'kbOF gains' in percent ($100\% \cdot \frac{error_{filtered}}{error_{unfiltered}}$).

Table 1. Relative Reductions of Classification/Regression Errors due to kbOFs (averaged over 6 application domains)

$|S_{train}|$	15	25	50	100	200
no kbOF	100.0%	100.0%	100.0%	100.0%	100.0%
m-Filter	93.6%	86.9%	90.1%	92.8%	93.6%
e-Filter	83.2%	78.4%	80.9%	87.6%	94.5%
me-Filter	83.2%	73.4%	80.2%	85.8%	91.9%

6 Related Work and Conclusion

Besides the classic work in feature weight learning (for an overview see [13]), in the last years also learning of user preferences has come into focus of research [5, 6]. Concerning the exploitation of re-ranking feedback some work can be found in [6, 14]. While these approaches usually apply gradient descent algorithms, Jarmulak et al. presented an approach based on a genetic algorithm [8]. However, all these learning approaches are restricted to learning weights only and do not incorporate local similarity measures.

In this paper we have presented further improvements of our learning framework [9–12] which particularly addresses two novel issues: learning of local similarity measures and a broad applicability beyond classification tasks. The core idea of these improvements is a restriction of the search space to be considered during learning by exploiting different sources of background knowledge. While we have shown the power of our learning techniques in several test domains, an application in commercial practice is still outstanding. Moreover, an interesting issue for further research may be an extension of our framework to more sophisticated similarity measures, e.g. like those required for object-oriented case representations [4].

References

1. A. Aamodt and E. Plaza. Case-based reasoning: Foundational Issues, Methodological Variations, and System Approaches. *AI Communications*, 7(1):39–59, 1994.
2. R. Bergmann. On the Use of Taxonomies for Representing Case Features and Local Similarity Measures. In *Proceedings of the 6th German Workshop on Case-Based Reasoning*, 1998.
3. R. Bergmann, M. Michael Richter, S. Schmitt, A. Stahl, and I. Vollrath. Utility-Oriented Matching: A New Research Direction for Case-Based Reasoning. In *Professionelles Wissensmanagement: Erfahrungen und Visionen. Proceedings of the 1st Conference on Professional Knowledge Management*. Shaker, 2001.
4. R. Bergmann and A. Stahl. Similarity Measures for Object-Oriented Case Representations. In *Proceedings of the 4th European Workshop on Case-Based Reasoning*. Springer, 1998.
5. K. Branting. Acquiring Customer Preferences from Return-Set Selections. In *Proceedings of the 4th International Conference on Case-Based Reasoning*. Springer, 2001.
6. L. Coyle and P. Cunningham. Exploiting Re-ranking Information in a Case-Based Personal Travel Assistent. In *Workshop on Mixed-Initiative Case-Based Reasoning at the 5th International Conference on Case-Based Reasoning*. Springer, 2003.
7. T. Gabel. Learning Similarity Measures: Strategies to Enhance the Optimisation Process. Master thesis, Kaiserslautern University of Technology, 2003. http://www.iupr.org/~stahl/Papers/GabelDA.ps.
8. J. Jarmulak, S. Craw, and R. Rowe. Genetic Algorithms to Optimise CBR Retrieval. In *Proceedings of the 5th European Workshop on Case-Based Reasoning*. Springer, 2000.
9. A. Stahl. Learning Feature Weights from Case Order Feedback. In *Proceedings of the 4th International Conference on Case-Based Reasoning*. Springer, 2001.
10. A. Stahl. Defining Similarity Measures: Top-Down vs. Bottom-Up. In *Proceedings of the 6th European Conference on Case-Based Reasoning*. Springer, 2002.
11. A. Stahl. *Learning of Knowledge-Intensive Similarity Measures in Case-Based Reasoning*. Ph.D. thesis, Technical University of Kaiserslautern, 2003.
12. A. Stahl and T. Gabel. Using Evolution Programs to Learn Local Similarity Measures. In *Proceedings of the 5th International Conference on Case-Based Reasoning*. Springer, 2003.
13. D. Wettschereck and David W. Aha. Weighting Features. In *Proceeding of the 1st International Conference on Case-Based Reasoning*. Springer, 1995.
14. Z. Zhang and Q. Yang. Dynamic Refinement of Feature Weights Using Quantitative Introspective Learning. In *Proceedings of the 16th International Joint Conference on Artificial Intelligence*, 1999.

Software Design Retrieval Using Bayesian Networks and WordNet

Paulo Gomes

CISUC – Centro de Informática e Sistemas da Universidade de Coimbra,
Departamento de Engenharia Informática, Universidade de Coimbra,
3030 Coimbra, Portugal
pgomes@dei.uc.pt

Abstract. The complexity of software systems makes design reuse a necessary task in the software development process. CASE tools can provide cognitive assistance in this task, helping the software engineers to select designs to be reused. In this paper, we propose an approach for case indexing and retrieval based on Bayesian Networks, Case-Based Reasoning and WordNet. This approach is integrated in a CASE tool that reuses UML class diagrams, providing cognitive help for the software design phase.

1 Motivations

Software design [1] is a complex task involving the modelization of software systems representing the world around us. Despite the design guidelines described in software engineering methodologies, designers still rely on experience to build the system model. The experience level often distinguishes good designers from average ones.

A possible solution to overcome the lack of experience is to reuse software [2, 3]. Reuse enables more efficient development of software systems, because the development costs and the number of software errors decrease. But, due to the abstract level of software design, reuse of designs is not a simple task.

In our work, we are interested in developing CASE (Computer Aided Software Engineering) tools capable of assisting the software designer in the reuse of designs. Common CASE tools do not provide help in this field, they are just complex diagram editors, some with syntax verification functionalities. Our goal is to go a step further and to enable the CASE tools to provide semantic and structural retrieval functionalities.

One mechanism that has provided good results in case indexing and retrieval is Bayesian Networks (BNs, [4]). BNs can provide an efficient retrieval mechanism based on probabilistic knowledge. One of our goals is to integrate this reasoning mechanism in a CASE tool, in order to provide retrieval functionalities for the software designer. An interesting challenge that we encountered was how to consider structural and semantic similarity in the BN. We have developed an approach that deals with both similarity aspects.

2 Our Approach

Case-Based Reasoning (CBR) [5, 6] is an Artificial Intelligence [7] field, based on reuse of experience. The reasoning framework is based on the storage of experience episodes in the form of cases. Each case represents a specific situation or entity, and is stored in a case library ready for reuse in new situations. Cases can be retrieved from the case library through a query defined by the designer. This query describes the current situation which needs to be solved or completed. The retrieval output is a list of cases ranked by similarity to the query. A CBR system can go further and adapt one or more retrieved cases to generate a new solution for the query. This new solution can then be stored in the library as a new case closing the reasoning cycle [8] and enabling the CBR system to learn and evolve in time.

In our previous work, we have developed REBUILDER [9, 10], a CASE tool based on CBR and WordNet [11]. In REBUILDER, cases are UML class diagrams and they are stored in a central repository, making them available for reuse within the development team or company. This tool also provides several cognitive functionalities for aiding the software design task.

One important functionality of REBUILDER is the capacity of understanding natural language. This capability is possible due to WordNet, which is used as an ontology, enabling the association of senses to words and other natural language processing tasks.

As seen before, CBR and WordNet are central issues in our system, constraining the integration of BNs in REBUILDER. In this paper, we present this integration and how issues such as semantic and structural similarity of class diagrams are addressed. The next session provides some background knowledge about BNs and WordNet. Section 4 describes REBUILDER architecture briefly. Section 5 describes our approach to retrieval using BNs within REBUILDER. Section 6 compares our approach with several research works on CBR and BNs. Finally section 7 concludes this paper with some final remarks and future work.

3 Background Knowledge

This section presents some background knowledge about Bayesian networks and WordNet, so that our approach becomes clearer to the reader.

3.1 Bayesian Networks

A Bayesian Network[4] is an acyclic directed graph that represents dependencies between variables and their associated probabilities. It can be used for diagnostic tasks, causal inferences, explanation inferences or mixed inferences. Nodes represent variables and directed links represent influences between variables. The semantics of a link can be described in the following way: there is a link from X to Y, if X has a direct influence on Y. Each node has a conditional probability table (CPT) associated that quantifies the effects that the parents have on the node.

An example of a simple Bayesian network (BN) is given in figure 1 (tables represent CPT for nodes). In this example, there is a burglar alarm that can be fired by a burglar or by mistake due to an earthquake. The probability of happening a burglary (P(B)) is 0.001, and the probability of happening an earthquake (P(E)) is 0.002. The probability of the alarm going off depends on the nodes *Burglary* and *Earthquake*, which is depicted in the table near the alarm node. Supposing that there are two persons that can call when the alarm goes off, John and Mary, the probability of any of them calling because the alarm went off is also represented in the tables for nodes *John Calls* and *Mary Calls*.

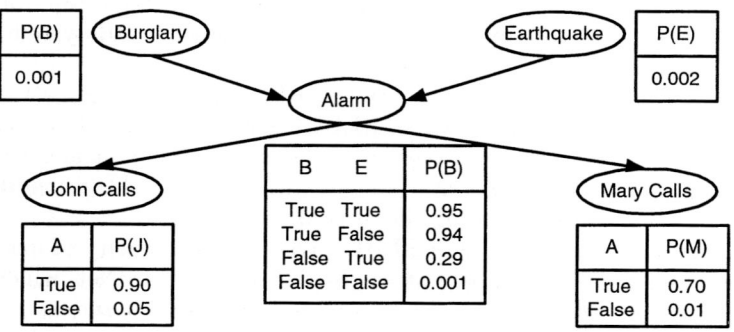

Fig. 1. An example of a Bayesian network taken from [7].

Inference in a BN is the computation of the posterior probability distribution for the set of query variables. Given a set of evidence variables for which the exact value is known, an inference algorithm is used to propagate these values through the BN, according to Bayes rule. There are several inference algorithms, but basically they fall in two categories: exact inference and approximate inference. Exact inference algorithms perform the exact computation of the probability distributions. Belief propagation in trees is linear, while belief propagation in multiply connected graphs has been shown to be NP-hard [12]. Approximate inference algorithms try to deal with this difficulty in a more tractable way, trying to provide an approximation to the probability distribution for query variables.

3.2 WordNet

WordNet [11] is used in REBUILDER as a common sense ontology. It uses a differential theory where concept meanings are represented by symbols that enable a theorist to distinguish among them. Symbols are words, and concept meanings are called synsets. A synset is a concept represented by one or more words. Words that can be used to represent a synset are called synonyms. A word with more than one meaning is called a polysemous word. For instance, the word mouse has two meanings, it can denote a rat, or it can express a computer mouse.

WordNet is built around the concept of synset. Basically a synset comprises a list of words and a list of semantic relations between other synsets. The first part is a list of words, each one with a list of synsets that the word represents. The second part, is a set of semantic relations between synsets, like *is-a* relations, *part-of* relations, and other relations. REBUILDER uses the word synset list and four semantic relations: *is-a, part-of, substance-of,* and *member-of.* Synsets are classified in four different types: nouns, verbs, adjectives, and adverbs.

Synsets are used in REBUILDER for categorization of software objects. Each object has a context synset which represents the object meaning. In order to find the correct synset, REBUILDER uses the object name, and the names of the objects related with it, which define the object context. The object's context synset can then be used for computing object similarity (using the WordNet semantic relations), or it can be used as a case index, allowing rapid access to objects with the same classification. WordNet is used to compute the semantic distance between two context synsets. This distance is the length of the shortest path between the two synsets. Any of the four relation types can be used to establish the path between the synsets. This distance is used in REBUILDER to assess the type similarity between objects, and to select the correct synset when the object name has more than one synset. This process is called name disambiguation [13] and is a crucial task in REBUILDER. If a diagram object has a name with several synsets, then more information about this object has to be used to find which synset is the correct one. The extra information are the diagram objects that directly or indirectly are associated with it. In case of the object being a class, its attributes can also be used in the disambiguation process. This process is used when a case is inserted in the case library or when the designer calls the retrieval module.

4 REBUILDER

REBUILDER creates and manages a repository of software designs, providing the software designer with a set of functionalities that promote the reuse of previous design experiences. This section gives an overview on REBUILDER describing it's architecture and modules.

Figure 2 illustrates the architecture of REBUILDER. It comprises four main modules: the UML editor, the knowledge base manager, the knowledge base (KB), and the CBR engine. It also depicts the two different user types: software designers and KB administrators. Software designers use REBUILDER as a CASE tool and subsequently reuse the software design knowledge previously stored. The KB administrator keeps the KB updated and consistent. The UML editor serves as the intermediary between REBUILDER and the software designer while the KB manager is the interface between the KB administrator and the system (see [9] for a more detailed description of REBUILDER).

The CBR engine performs all the inference work in REBUILDER. It comprises six sub modules: retrieval, analogy, composition, design patterns, verification, and learning. The retrieval module searches the case library for designs or design objects similar to the query. The most similar ones are presented to the

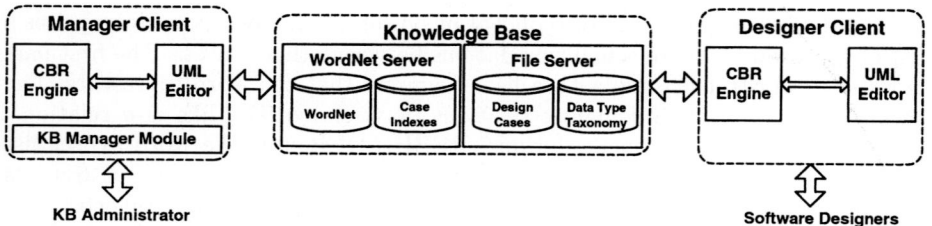

Fig. 2. REBUILDER's Architecture.

Fig. 3. REBUILDER solution generation cycle.

user, allowing the designer to reuse these designs or part of them. The analogy module maps designs from the case library, to the query design. The resulting mapping establishes the knowledge transfer from the old design to the query design. The composition module can be used to adapt a past design (or part of it) to the query using design composition. The design patterns module uses a CBR approach to the application of software design patterns [14]. This module is able to generate new diagrams through the automatic application of design patterns. The verification module checks the current design for inconsistencies. The learning module acquires new knowledge from the user interaction, or from the system reasoning.

Figure 3 describes how a new UML diagram can be generated in REBUILDER. Note that adaptation stands for analogy, composition or design patterns. These are adaptation strategies, and can be used to generate a new UML diagram using one or more cases.

5   Retrieval Using Bayesian Networks and WordNet

This section presents our approach to the retrieval of software designs using BNs and WordNet. We start by describing how the BNs are built and then we explain the retrieval process.

5.1   Building the Bayesian Network

REBUILDER uses BNs to index cases, to retrieve cases and to rank cases. The network construction is possible using WordNet synsets and *is-a* arcs.

Network nodes represent three types of entities: cases, synsets and relations. For each case in the library a node is created, with the synsets associated to the case objects as parent nodes. All the parents of each synset are recursively added to the network, until the top nodes are reached, using the *is-a* arcs of WordNet.

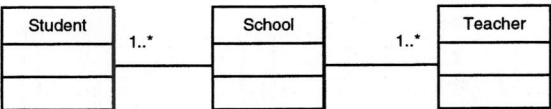

Fig. 4. *Case1* diagram.

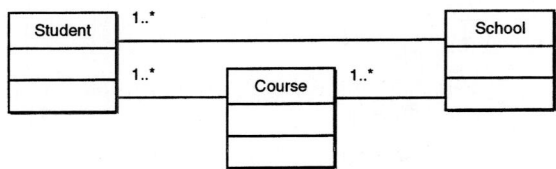

Fig. 5. *Case2* diagram.

Relations in the library cases are also represented as nodes in the network, with a node for each relation. The synsets involved in the relation are parent nodes of the relation node, and the case node having this relation is a child of the relation node.

As an example, consider cases *Case1* and *Case2* in figures 4 and 5 (attributes and methods are not considered for the sake of simplicity). Figure 6 represents the BN built from these two cases. Each case is represented by a node with the respective objects added, for instance *Case1* related with *Student*, *School* and *Teacher*. Then each of the synsets associated with a case adds it's parents recursively to the network until it reaches a top synset, synset *Student* parents go from *Enrollee* to *Entity*. The relation nodes are also represented, for example the relation *Student-School* has *Student* and *School* as parents and *Case1* as a child.

Conditional probability tables for each node are defined accordingly to each node type. The node types are: top nodes, synset nodes with only one parent, synset nodes with several parents, case nodes and relation nodes.

Top nodes correspond to WordNet top nodes, and their probability is given by:

$$P(TopNode) = \frac{1}{TopNodes(BN)} \qquad (1)$$

where $TopNodes(BN)$ returns the number of top nodes in the BN.

The CPT of synset nodes with only one parent, which corresponds to the majority of synsets, are computed using table 1.

Table 1. The CPT for a single parent synset node.

Parent	P(Synset)	P(¬Synset)
True	α	$1 - \alpha$
False	0	1

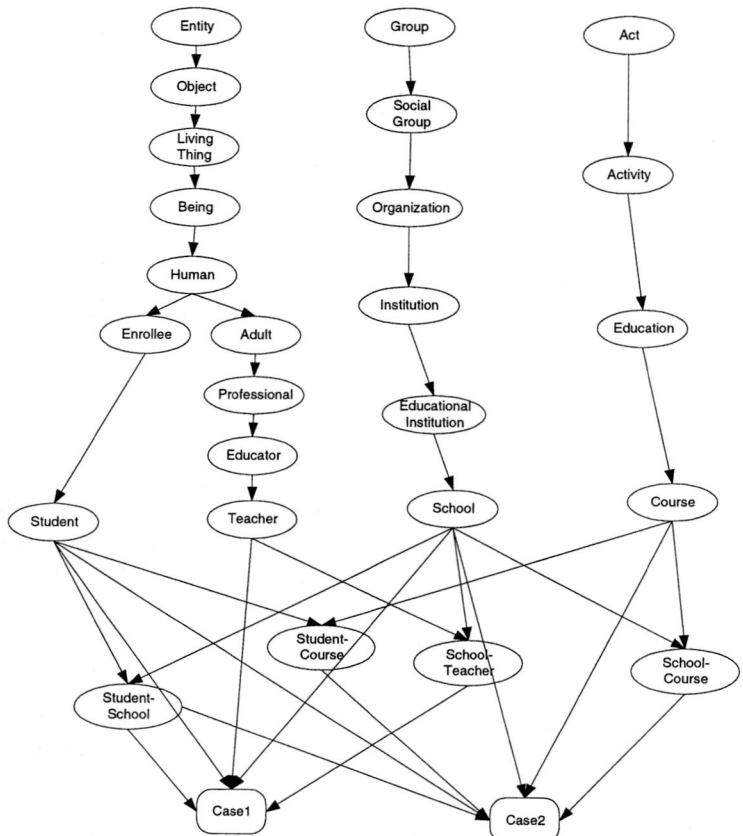

Fig. 6. The Bayesian Network resulting from cases $Case1$ and $Case2$.

Where α is given by:

$$\alpha = \frac{1}{Children(Parent)} \quad (2)$$

and $Children(Parent)$ returns the number of children for node $Parent$.

In the computation of the CPT for nodes with more than one parent, we consider that each cause has an independent chance of causing the effect according to the noisy-OR model [15]. In the case of synset nodes, the probability for a synset S is given by:

$$P(S|Parents(S)) = 1 - P(\neg S|Parents(S)) \quad (3)$$

$$P(\neg S|Parents(S)) = \prod_{(p_i \in Parents(S)) \wedge (p_i = True)} (1 - P(S|p_i)) \quad (4)$$

where $Parents(S)$ represents the parent nodes of S and p_i one of these nodes. $P(S|p_i)$ is given by:

$$P(S|p_i) = \frac{1}{Children(p_i)} \qquad (5)$$

where $Children(p_i)$ returns the number of children nodes of p_i.

The computation of the CPT for a case node C is given using:

$$P(C|Parents(C)) = 1 - P(\neg C|Parents(C)) \qquad (6)$$

$$P(\neg C|Parents(C)) = \prod_{(p_i \in Parents(C)) \wedge (p_i = True)} (1 - P(C|p_i)) \qquad (7)$$

where $Parents(C)$ represents the parent nodes of C and p_i one of these nodes. Node p_i can be a synset or a relation node, and $P(C|p_i)$ is given by:

$$P(C|p_i) = \frac{1}{Occurrences(p_i)} \qquad (8)$$

where $Occurrences(p_i)$ returns the number of occurrences of p_i in library cases.

Relation nodes have exactly two parent nodes, the synsets participating in the relation. Considering a relation node R having two parents S_1 and S_2, the CPT for R is defined in table 2.

Table 2. The CPT for a relation node.

S_1	S_2	P(R)	P(¬R)
False	False	0	1
False	True	0	1
True	False	0	1
True	True	$P(R|S_1, S_2)$	$1 - P(R|S_1, S_2)$

The probability $P(R|S_1, S_2)$ is given by:

$$P(R|S_1, S_2) = \frac{Relations(S_1, S_2)}{Relations(S_1) + Relations(S_2)} \qquad (9)$$

where $Relations(S_1, S_2)$ returns the number of relations in the case library with both S_1 and S_2, and $Relations(S_1)$ returns the number of relations in the library with S_1.

Using the BN example of figure 6, the CPT for node *Entity* is 0.33, since there are three top nodes in the network. As an example of a CPT for a synset node, table 3 shows the CPT for node *Adult*, notice that α is 0.5 since there are two children nodes for *Human*.

The CPT for node *Case*1 is computed based on the conditional probabilities for each of the node's parents, which are given by:

$$P(Case1|Student = True) = \frac{1}{2} = 0.5$$

$$P(Case1|School = True) = \frac{1}{2} = 0.5$$

Table 3. The CPT for the *Adult* node.

Human	P(Adult)	P(¬Adult)
True	0.5	0.5
False	0	1

$$P(Case1|Teacher = True) = \frac{1}{1} = 1$$
$$P(Case1|StudentSchool = True) = \frac{1}{2} = 0.5$$
$$P(Case1|SchoolTeacher = True) = \frac{1}{1} = 1$$

Just to illustrate the computation of the CPT, the probability of the node *Case1* having *Student* and *School* as true is:

$$P(\neg Case1|Student = True, School = True) = (1 - 0.5) \cdot (1 - 0.5) = 0.25$$
$$P(Case1|Student = True, School = True) = 1 - 0.25 = 0.75$$
$$P(\neg Case1|Student = True, School = True, StudentSchool = True) =$$
$$(1 - 0.5) \cdot (1 - 0.5) \cdot (1 - 0.5) = 0.125$$
$$P(Case1|Student = True, School = True, StudentSchool = True) =$$
$$1 - 0.125 = 0.875$$

Table 4 presents the CPT for relation node *StudentSchool*. Notice that the $P(StudentSchool|Student = True, School = True)$ is:

$$P(StudentSchool|Student = True, School = True) = \frac{2}{3+4} = 0.29$$

Table 4. The CPT for the *StudentSchool* node.

Student	School	P(StudentSchool)	P(¬StudentSchool)
False	False	0	1
False	True	0	1
True	False	0	1
True	True	0.29	0.71

If a new case is added to the case library, the BN must be rebuilt, adding all the cases and updating the CPTs.

5.2 Retrieval Process

The retrieval process starts with a query, which is a class diagram (query diagram). Then the BN nodes corresponding to the synsets of the query diagram objects, are set to true. The same happens with the nodes corresponding to query diagram relations. If there isn't a corresponding node in the network for an object or relation, then a node representing the missing object/relation is added to the BN, along with edges and parent nodes.

After the evidence nodes are set to true, the goal of the retrieval process is to assess the probability of the case nodes. These probabilities are used to retrieve and to rank the corresponding cases. In REBUILDER, we use the Bayesian Network tools in Java (BNJ[1]), which is an open-source implementation of BNs inference algorithms for research and development. This package provides several reasoning algorithms, both for exact inference and for approximate inference. These algorithms are used for assessing the case node's probabilities.

Using the example from the previous subsections, suppose that the user query comprises the software objects *School* and *Teacher*, and a relation between the two objects. Using the clustering algorithm developed by Lauritzen and Spiegelhalter [16], the probability for *Case1* is 1, and for Case2 is 0.503289. This makes sense, since *Case1* comprises the query, and *Case2* only comprises the object *School*. These probability values are used for ranking retrieved cases. Other examples of queries and the respective node probabilities (for *Case1* and *Case2*) are presented in table 5.

Table 5. Table with the probabilities associated with case nodes for several retrieval examples (queries comprise objects and relations between objects).

Query	Probability for *Case1*	Probability for *Case2*
Student, School, Student-School	0.875	0.875107
Student, School	0.78625	0.786433
School, Course, School-Course	0.5	1
School, Teacher, School-Teacher	1	0.503289
Course, Teacher	1	1
Course, Teacher, School	1	1
Educator, Course	0.0448002	1
Human, Institution	0.0159545	0.0167973

6 Related Work

There are several research works combining CBR and BNs, with different purposes and ways of integration. This section compares these works to our approach, focusing in the relevant differences and similarities.

Aamodt and Langseth [17] describe an approach for integration of BNs with CBR. The BN is used for indexing cases using binary features, with this network built from a semantic network. Retrieval is a two step process: first the BN is used for retrieving a relevant set of cases and then the BN is used for selecting what observable nodes (evidence nodes) are best for discriminating between plausible cases. This approach implies that nodes are classified as observable or not, which in our approach would correspond to any synset or relation node. Despite the

---

[1] http://bndev.sourceforge.net/

similarities with our approach in the network construction, the retrieval process is rather different, with our approach having only one pass, yielding a ranked set of cases.

Another approach to the integration of CBR and BNs is presented by Rodríguez et. al. [18], in which two BNs are used: one for indexing and another for retrieval. They also use cases for building both networks, updating them each time a new case is added to the case library. The indexing network ranks the order in which categories can be searched for similar exemplars. Then each category, in the retrieval network, is searched to find cases that are similar to the target case. As in our approach, similarity is interpreted as the probability associated with a case. Both the network structure and retrieval process are different from our approach, having the limitation of depending on an initial case base to reason.

The approach presented by Dingsoyr [19] uses a BN for computing similarity metrics. This approach uses the case base to build a BN, which will then be used for assessing the similarity between the query and the cases. As in other described approaches, this approach has the limitation of depending of an initial case base. There is an important difference with our approach, the level of abstraction in the representation is shallow, since it only uses the case features for indexing, while the BNs in REBUILDER allow deeper inferences using *is-a* arcs.

Tirri et. al. [20] present a Bayesian framework for CBR in data-intensive domains. In their approach, cases are used to provide the approximate model for the underlying joint probability distribution of attributes, allowing two major operations: retrieval and adaptation. Comparing with our approach, we only use the BN for indexing and retrieval, though adaptation based on the BN is possible, but is a future issue in our approach. One limitation of their approach is the need of a good representative initial case base that can be used to generate the BN. This can be a problem in some application domains, due to the lack of experience in the form of cases.

Lazkano and Sierra [21] describe an approach that combines Nearest Neighbour algorithm with a BN for case classification. The main idea of this work can be presented in two steps: given a query case, first retrieve the most similar case using the Nearest Neighbour algorithm; and then use a BN to identify the case's classification. This approach has a different purpose from our's combining CBR and BNs in a different way.

Aha and Chang [22] describe an approach for multiagent planning using BNs and CBR. BNs are used to provide contextual information to the case-based reasoner, assisting in the feature selection. Then the case-based reasoner is used to determine how to implement the agent's actions. Their approach is rather different from ours, with one BN for each possible agent action. The agent will select the action corresponding to the BN with highest probability. As in our approach, an agent learns new knowledge in the form of BN update when new experience is acquired.

Breese and Heckerman [23] present an approach for diagnostic and troubleshooting applications using BNs and CBR. In a diagnosis session, a subnetwork is extracted from a BN database describing a large number of diagnostic interactions and cases. This network is used to make suggestions of possible repairs and additional observations. The network structure comprises three layers representing: causes, issues and symptoms. Though this approach has some similarities with our approach, the reasoning model and main goal is different from our approach.

Schiaffino and Amandi [24] present an approach for learning user profiles using CBR and BNs. As in our approach, cases are used for the network construction. User profiles have two parts: one built from CBR using the classification of queries by similarity and the other part by using the BN to infer attribute values. In the end of this parallel reasoning process, a set of suggested queries is shown to the user. This is another way of integration of CBR and BNs, in which cases constitute the probabilistic model used for network construction. In our approach, we also use cases as part of the probabilistic model, but the retrieval process is different.

Wiebe et. al. [25] presented an approach for the construction of BNs using WordNet for word-sense disambiguation. Their use of WordNet for network construction is similar to our approach, presenting two alternative ways of mapping nodes. One where a node represents a synset and another where a node represents a word. In our approach, we use the first alternative with the difference that we also have two other types of nodes, representing cases and diagram relations. As in our approach, they also use the WordNet *is-a* arcs to build the network. Besides the difference of using the BN for word-sense disambiguation, in our approach the CPTs are defined in a different way, they are built from data in cases and in Wiebe's approach they are built from tagged training data.

There are several research works that explore case retrieval and similarity mechanisms for software design. González et. al. [26] presented a CBR approach to software reuse and design at the code level. The work developed is based on the reuse and design of object-oriented code. Using the object description they use two retrieval algorithms, a lexical retrieval using a natural language query, and a conceptual retrieval using an entity and slot similarity measures. Djà vu [27] is a CBR system for code reuse and generation using hierarchical CBR. Like the case representation of González, Djà Vu uses a hierarchical case representation, indexing cases using functional features. Althoff and Tautz [28] have a different approach to software reuse and design. Instead of reusing code, they reuse system requirements and associated software development knowledge.

7 Conclusions and Future Work

This paper presents an approach to the retrieval of class diagrams integrating BN, CBR and WordNet. We describe how the BN is built from WordNet and from the case library, and a detailed example of network retrieval is given.

One advantage of our approach, is the capability of assessing not only the similarity between diagram objects, but also the structure similarity of diagrams, through the use of network nodes representing diagram relations. This enables the BN to compute structural similarity, which is important for assessing diagram similarity. Another advantage is the leaning of new cases through the network updating. In relation, to other systems using BN for retrieval, our approach has the advantage of not depending entirely on cases for building the BN. An initial BN can be built using only WordNet and the query, which will then be updated with new cases.

One of the limitations of our approach is the updating algorithm (used to rebuild the BNs when a new case is added to the case base), which implies the rebuilding of the entire BN. Although the network construction is fast, it is not the most efficient. We are looking into ways of making it more efficient. Synset CPTs are only defined based on the WordNet structure. This is not the most accurate way to compute the associated probabilities, because a synset may depend in different degrees from their parents. One way to deal with this issue is to use text corpus to compute the CPTs, as in Wiebe's approach.

There are several issues that we intend to address, namely the representation of attributes and methods in the BN. This is not an easy issue, because the network complexity will affect the retrieval performance. Other future issues are related with the integration of user preferences in the BN, so that retrieval would take into account user preferences. This topic follows the development guidelines of REBUILDER, trying to adapt the system to the user and not the opposite.

References

1. Boehm, B.: A Spiral Model of Software Development and Enhancement. IEEE Press (1988)
2. Prieto-Diaz, R., Jones, G.: Breathing new life into old software. In Tracz, W., ed.: Software Reuse: Emerging Technology, Washigton, USA, Computer Society Press (1988)
3. Coulange, B.: Software Reuse. Springer Verlag, London (1997)
4. Pearl, J.: Probabilistic Reasoning in Intelligent Systems. Morgan-Kaufman (1988)
5. Kolodner, J.: Case-Based Reasoning. Morgan Kaufman (1993)
6. Maher, M.L., Balachandran, M., Zhang, D.: Case-Based Reasoning in Design. Lawrence Erlbaum Associates (1995)
7. Russel, S., Norvig, P.: Artificial Intelligence: A Modern Approach. Prentice Hall, New Jersey (1995)
8. Aamodt, A., Plaza, E.: Case–based reasoning: Foundational issues, methodological variations, and system approaches. AI Communications **7** (1994) 39–59
9. Gomes, P., Pereira, F.C., Paiva, P., Seco, N., Carreiro, P., Ferreira, J.L., Bento, C.: Case retrieval of software designs using wordnet. In Harmelen, F.v., ed.: European Conference on Artificial Intelligence (ECAI'02), Lyon, France, IOS Press, Amsterdam (2002)
10. Gomes, P., Pereira, F.C., Paiva, P., Seco, N., Carreiro, P., Ferreira, J.L., Bento, C.: Solution verification in software design: A CBR approach. In Bridge, D., Ashley, K., eds.: Fifth International Conference on Case-Based Reasoning (ICCBR'03), Trondheim, Norway, Springer (2003)
11. Miller, G., Beckwith, R., Fellbaum, C., Gross, D., Miller, K.J.: Introduction to wordnet: an on-line lexical database. International Journal of Lexicography **3** (1990) 235 – 244

12. Cooper, G.F.: The computational complexity of probabilistic inference using Bayesian belief networks. Artificial Intelligence **42** (1990) 393–405
13. Ide, N., Veronis, J.: Introduction to the special issue on word sense disambiguation: The state of the art. Computational Linguistics **24** (1998) 1–40
14. Gamma, E., Helm, R., Johnson, R., Vlissides, J.: Design Patterns: Elements of Reusable Object-Oriented Software. Addison-Wesley, Reading (1995)
15. Díez, F.J.: Parameter adjustment in bayes networks. the generalized noisy ORgate. In Heckerman, D., Mamdani, A., eds.: Proceedings of the 9th Conference on Uncertainty in Artificial Intelligence, San Mateo, CA, USA, Morgan Kaufmann Publishers (1993) 99–105
16. Lauritzen, S.L., Spiegelhalter, D.J.: Local computations with probabilities on graphical structures and their applications to expert systems. The Journal of the Royal Statistical Society **50** (1988) 157–224
17. Aamodt, A., Langseth, H.: Integrating bayesian networks into knowledge-intensive cbr. In: AAAI Workshop on Case-Based Reasoning Integrations. (1998)
18. Rodríguez, A.F., Vadera, S., Sucar, L.E.: A probabilistic model for case-based reasoning. In Leake, D.B., Plaza, E., eds.: Proceedings of the 2nd International Conference on Case-Based Reasoning (ICCBR-97). Volume 1266 of LNAI., Berlin, Springer (1997) 623–632
19. Dingsoyr, T.: Retrieval of cases by using a bayesian network. In: AAAI Workshop on Case-Based Reasoning Integrations. (1998)
20. Tirri, H., Kontkanen, P., Myllymäki, P.: A bayesian framework for case-based reasoning. In Smith, I., Faltings, B., eds.: Proceedings of the Third European Workshop on Case-Based Reasoning. Volume 1168 of LNAI., Berlin, Springer (1996) 413–427
21. Lazkano, E., Sierra, B.: BAYES–NEAREST: A new hybrid classifier combining bayesian network and distance based algorithms. In: Progress in Artificial Intelligence (EPIA–03). Volume 2902 of LNCS., Berlin, Springer (2003) 171–183
22. Aha, D., Chang, L.: Cooperative bayesian and case-based reasoning for solving multiagent planning tasks. Technical Report AIC-96-005, Navy Center for Applied Research in Artificial Intelligence (1996)
23. Breese, J., Heckerman, D.: Decision-theoretic case-based reasoning. Technical Report MSR-TR-95-03, Microsoft Research (1995)
24. Schiaffino, S., Amandi, A.: User profiling with case-based reasoning and bayesian networks. In: Open Discussion Track - International Joint Conference IBERAMIA-SBIA 2000. (2000) 12–21
25. Wiebe, J., O'Hara, T., Bruce, R.: Constructing Bayesian networks from WordNet for word-sense disambiguation: Representational and processing issues. In Harabagiu, S., ed.: Use of WordNet in Natural Language Processing Systems: Proceedings of the Conference, Somerset, New Jersey, Association for Computational Linguistics (1998) 23–30
26. González, P.A., Fernández, C.: A knowledge-based approach to support software reuse in object-oriented libraries. In: 9th International Conference on Software Engineering and Knowledge Engineering, SEKE'97, Madrid, Spain, Knowledge Systems Institute, Illinois (1997) 520–527
27. Smyth, B., Cunningham, P.: Deja vu: A hierarchical case-based reasoning system for software design. In Neumann, B., ed.: 10th European Conference on Artificial Intelligence (ECAI'92), Vienna, Austria, John Wiley and Sons (1992)
28. Tautz, C., Althoff, K.D.: Using case-based reasoning for reusing software knowledge. In Leake, D., Plaza, E., eds.: International Conference on Case-Based Reasoning (ICCBR'97), Providence, RI, USA, Springer-Verlag (1997) 156–165

Case-Base Injection Schemes to Case Adaptation Using Genetic Algorithms

Alicia Grech and Julie Main

La Trobe University, Bundoora 3086, Australia
ajgrech@cs.latrobe.edu.au

Abstract. Case adaptation has always been a difficult process to engineer within the case-based reasoning (CBR) cycle. To combat the difficulties of CBR adaptation, such as its domain dependency, computational cost and the inability to produce novel cases to solve new problems, genetic algorithms (GAs) have been applied to CBR adaptation. As the quality of cases stored in a case library has a significant effect on the solutions produced by a case-based reasoner, it is important to investigate the impact of the quality and quantity of cases injected into a GA initial population for adapting fitter solutions to new problems. This work explores a method applying a GA to CBR adaptation, where a learning mechanism is applied to feed knowledge back from the CBR revision stage into the reuse stage, allowing the GA to learn which mutations result in invalid solutions. In collaboration with this learning mechanism, the number of cases to be injected, and the fitness of cases to be injected from retrieval into reuse is explored. The fitness of adapted cases and their response to our developed learning feedback is also trialled through varying the size and quality of the GA initial population.

1 Introduction

The use of past experience to understand and solve new problems by learning is a critical advantage of case-based reasoning (CBR). However, CBR has also been known to exhibit some disadvantages, such as poor, slow retrieval techniques; a case memory that can overflow with redundant, repetitive cases; and poor attempts to adapt solutions to the needs of a current problem [1]. In an effort to reduce the effects of these disadvantages, hybrid approaches have been taken when developing CBR systems. Genetic algorithms (GAs) are search algorithms reflecting the natural processes of evolution and can be used to combat CBR disadvantages. Genetic algorithms have been successfully applied to optimise case retrieval, to create novel and unique cases for new problems and, by using a fitness measure, to clean up the case memory leaving only better cases to be used. Adaptation is often considered as the most difficult component of a CBR system [2]. It has been argued that adaptation may be the most important step of case-based reasoning as it adds intelligence to what would otherwise be a simple pattern matcher [3]. The application of genetic algorithm methods for case adaptation has been an attempt to combat the difficulty of the adaptation task, as well as to promote intelligence through adaptation. Applying GAs in the CBR adaptation stage has been applied across varied problem domains. This is a successful innovation over traditional CBR adaptation techniques, as CBR adaptation tends to be domain specific [4].

The work presented follows the general four-step CBR cycle defined by Aamodt and Plaza [5], identify the current problem; *retrieve* by finding a past case similar to the new case; *reuse* the past case to suggest a solution to the current problem; evaluate the proposed solution in *revise*; *retain* the solution and update the system by learning from experience. A GA is used for the *reuse* (adaptation) stage of the CBR cycle, and then a proposed learning feedback method is applied to feed knowledge learnt in the *revise* stage of the CBR cycle back into the *reuse* stage. The main aim of this learning feedback is to teach GA adaptation which mutations are better to apply when adapting cases. Along with this learning feedback, we investigate an ideal type of case population to initialise the GA adaptation method. This includes finding an ideal size of the initial population and the best spread of fitness to feed into the GA adaptation method from CBR retrieval. These tests have been conducted with a prototype case-based reasoner, known as CBR-GAALTA (CBR-GA Adaptive Learning Timetabling Application). This prototype is applied to the domain of automated timetabling.

1.1 Previous Adaptation and Learning Methods

Case adaptability has been modelled in many ways. Previous approaches to case adaptation include *adaptation by substitution*, where one or more pieces of a solution that does not fit the current situation requirements has the invalid pieces replaced by new pieces [2], and *parameterised adaptation*, where a formula for deriving a solution in a retrieved case is used to find a solution to an input case. Similar to parameterised adaptation is *procedural adaptation*, where a procedure for deriving a solution from a retrieved case is used to find a solution for an input case [6]. Khan and Hoffman applied *critic based adaptation* to their system, MIKAS, where a user (critic) manually adapts a retrieved solution to fit an input case [7]. Smythe and Keane used *Adaptation Guided Retrieval* (AGR) in Déjà Vu, where specially formulated adaptation knowledge is used during retrieval to measure a candidate case's adaptation requirements [8,9]. Similar to AGR, Tonindandel and Rillo developed *Action Distance-Guided* (ADG), which estimates the amount of effort needed to adapt each case [10]. For the COMPOSER system, developed by Purvis and Pu, the constraint satisfaction problem (CSP) structure is imposed on the adaptation process. A formal CSP algorithm called the *minimum conflicts algorithm* is applied, as it provides a common case representation, allowing easy integration into a new solution [2]. *Derivational Analogy* is an adaptation technique that computes a new solution using the steps taken to compute the old solution [2]. Derivational Analogy has been applied in many CBR applications, including POPART, VEXED, BOGART REDESIGN and ARGO [11]. The main focus of these adaptation methods is to lift the burden of the adaptation problem rather then fix adaptation's problematic aspects. Applying a GA to case adaptation has been seen across various domains.

Previous work has been devoted to the fields of CBR and GAs, and to combining the techniques, producing hybrid CBR-GA systems. GAs have been successfully applied in the retrieve and reuse phases of the CBR cycle, used for retrieval optimisation or adaptation consistency respectively. Applying GAs in the CBR adaptation stage across varied domains is a successful innovation over traditional CBR adaptation techniques, as CBR adaptation tends to be very domain specific [4]. The work of Oppacher and Duego revealed that using a GA for case adaptation can produce strong cases in a smaller case library [4], where De Silva Garza et al. and Louis and Xu found that GA adaptation produces novel solutions to new problems [4, 12]. Domains covered using a GA for CBR adaptation include: tablet formulation [13, 14]; modelling a Checkers game [1]; Open Shop Scheduling and Rescheduling [12]; developing lay out design of residences so they conform to the principles of feng shui [4]; reducing database size in applications [15]; and estimating the flow rates in Estuaries [16].

2 Genetic Algorithms for Case Adaptation

Genetic algorithms operate well under conditions where little domain knowledge is known or the search space is increasingly difficult. This fits well in CBR and the adaptation task, as CBR is often used for systems where there is little domain knowledge known. GAs for case adaptation has been applied across varied CBR implementation domains, proving to be a versatile adaptation method for a case-based reasoner. However, certain aspects of a GA must be customised to the domain to which the reasoner is applied, requiring the GA to be engineered to the specifications of the reasoner and its domain.

Certain constants exist in the implementation of a *simple GA* (see Figure 1), for a GA applied to any domain. These include an initial *population* of individuals (*chromosomes*) which is operated upon, and assigning a *fitness* score which assesses how good a solution the chromosome is to the problem. Highly fit chromosomes are given opportunities to *reproduce* themselves by *cross breeding* with other individuals in the population. New individuals are produced from this cross breeding, known as *offspring*. To produce offspring, GAs apply the genetic operators *crossover* and *mutation*. Crossover is an operator allowing new points in the search space to be tested, where mutation maintains that no point in the search space has zero probability of being explored [17]. Offspring share features taken from each parent. Less fit members of the population are less likely to be selected for reproduction, and hence die out of the population due to survival of the fittest [18]. A GA must also have an applied selection scheme (to select chromosomes for reproduction), as well as values for probability of crossover (P_c) and probability of mutation (P_m). The general process for a simple GA is shown in Figure 1.

This natural selection approach to case reuse must be merged into the CBR cycle. When applying GA adaptation to the CBR cycle, schemes need to be

1. **[Start]:** Generate random population of n chromosomes (suitable solutions for the problem)
2. **[Fitness]:** Evaluate the fitness $f(x)$ of each chromosome x in the population
3. **[New Population]:** Create a new population by repeating the following steps until the new population is complete
   (a) **[Selection]:** Select two parent chromosomes from a population according to their fitness (the better fitness, the greater chance to be selected)
   (b) **[Crossover]:** With a crossover probability, P_c, cross over the parents to form new offspring (children). If no crossover was performed, offspring is the exact copy of the parents
   (c) **[Mutation]:** With a mutation probability, P_m, mutate new offspring at each locus (position in the chromosome)
   (d) **[Accepting]:** Place new offspring in the new population
4. **[Replace]:** Use a new generated population for further run of the algorithm.
5. **[Test]:** If the end condition is satisfied, **stop**, and return the best solution in current population.
6. **[Loop]:** Go to step **2**

Fig. 1. Simple GA Cycle [19]

developed to resolve problematic areas between the CBR and GA cycles. These major problems between the CBR cycle and GA cycles that must be addressed are:

- Mapping a CBR case to a GA chromosome.
- Evaluating a fitness function to calculate the viability of a chromosome that maps back to CBR relevance.
- Construction of a feedback mechanism from CBR revise to reuse.
- Evaluating which cases from the CBR retrieve phase should initialise the GA population.

3 Applying a Genetic Algorithm to Case Adaptation for the Timetabling Domain

CBR-GAALTA produces generic timetable solutions to a new case containing requirements for a new timetable problem. Central tasks in the CBR process must be tailored to the timetabling domain, as well as engineering GA entities and processes so that it fits within the CBR cycle. The problem of creating a valid educational timetable involves scheduling lessons, teachers and rooms into a fixed number of periods, in such a way that no *teacher*, *class* or *room* is used more than once per time period [20].

3.1 Case-Representation

The success of a case-based reasoner bears a strong correlation to the content and structure of the central part of the reasoning system - cases. The reasoning process is heavily dependent on the structure and content of the collection of cases stored [5, 21]. For CBR-GAALTA, a case's representation and content is dependent on information needed to best describe a timetable. Cases are represented as objects, as the CBR-GAALTA is implemented in the Object Oriented Paradigm (OO). Storing the case as an object while working in the OO domain makes the creation and manipulation of cases, and their GA chromosome structuring, fairly straightforward. Storing the case as an object also allows a new case description to be described in an object format, ensuring that the past case and a new case can be compared in a manner that ensures the most appropriate case is retrieved in each new case situation. The content of a case is an entire solution to a timetable, for all subjects on all days of the week. Figure 2 is a UML representation of a case, displaying all objects and attributes stored within a timetable.

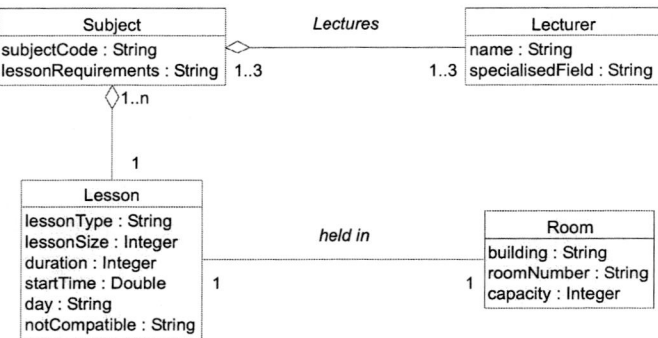

Fig. 2. Object Oriented Case Format

The new case must be described in a manner allowing it to be compared with the description of past cases in the case memory. As all elements in a timetable are stored in an object, the new case constraints are also stored in an object. A new case is stored in an object whose elements can be compared with elements of past timetables.

A flat case-base is implemented to store cases within CBR-GAALTA. CBR-GAALTA originates with a relatively small case-base, and retrieval time is already minimal. For larger case-bases where retrieval time is impacted upon by the case-base size, alternative ways to structure the case-base can be applied. Hierarchical structuring for larger case-bases is an option, where the search space of solutions is reduced by the organisation of the case-base.

3.2 Mapping a CBR Case to a GA Chromosome

The structure of a case within the CBR mechanism is a timetable object. For GAs, chromosomes in the population are represented as a string encoded with genetic information relevant to the individual's makeup. The chromosome is divided into genes and alleles, where genes are functional blocks, each encoding a particular trait of a timetable. Alleles are the individual 'settings' for a trait. A CBR case must be mapped to a GA chromosome, allowing adaptation to be executed. Genes encode a trait, the trait of the Timetable being a particular subject lesson within the timetable. The different possible settings for a particular subject lesson are classified as the attributes of the genes, such as the day, time, class size, and so forth.

Within CBR-GAALTA, a chromosome is encoded as a Vector object containing subject lesson genes, where genes are encoded as a consecutive block of 13 adjacent vector spaces. The sequence of genes continues until all subject lessons within a timetable case are encoded into the chromosome. Genes and allele values mapped to case attributes are presented in Figure 3.

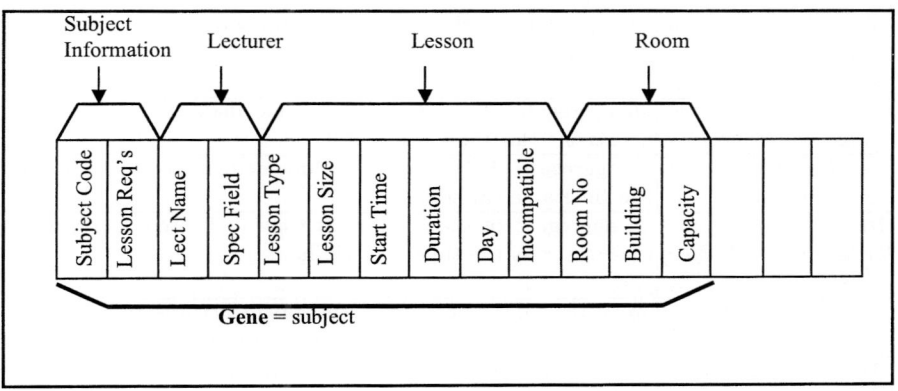

Fig. 3. Genes and Alleles of a CBR Case Mapped to a GA Chromosome

3.3 CBR Retrieval and GA Fitness Function

CBR retrieval begins with a partial problem description, in the form of a 'new case'. It ends when a past case has been found that best matches the new case. Each case in the case memory is tested for a relevance factor with respect to the new input problem. A new case is introduced to the system via a partial problem description, or a set of elements that describe factors of a new problem. Within the timetabling domain, a partial problem description is read in from a flat file, containing information relevant to the classes in the new problem and the rooms available when solving the new problem. The relevance factor is determined by comparing important factors within the past case timetable and awarding points depending on the closeness of the values to the new case. In CBR-GAALTA, Ten relevance metrics are calculated across the new case, **y**, and for the comparison past case, **x**. These relevance metrics are related to information based on:

- The lesson type and duration of the lesson type across the whole timetable
- The size of classes for each lesson type

The proposed CBR retrieval scheme operates on a point-awarding scheme, where a certain amount of points is awarded for each stored metric, depending on closeness in values between the new case and the past case. Table 1 lists and describes the 10 relevance metrics for CBR-GAALTA retrieval.

Table 1. Ten Relevance Metrics and Descriptions

Relevance Metric Name	Description
Number of Lectures in the Timetable	an aggregate of the number of lecture classes across the entire timetable
Number of Labs in the Timetable	an aggregate of the number of lab classes across the entire timetable
Number of Problem Classes in the Timetable	an aggregate of the number of problem classes across the entire timetable
Number of hours dedicated to Lectures	an aggregate of the total class time dedicated to lectures across the timetable (in hours)
Number of hours dedicated to Labs	an aggregate of the total class time dedicated to labs across the timetable (in hours)
Number of hours dedicated to Problem Classes	an aggregate of the total class time dedicated to problem classes across the timetable (in hours)
Average Number of Students per Lecture	an average of the number of students in lectures, taken across all lectures in the timetable (rounded to the nearest whole)
Average Number of Students per Lab	an average of the number of students in labs, taken across all labs in the timetable (rounded to the nearest whole)
Average Number of Students per Lab	an average of the number of students in problem classes, taken across all problem classes in the timetable (rounded to the nearest whole)
Number of Classes in the Timetable	a sum of the number of different subject codes across the timetable

The number of points awarded for each relevance metric is summed to give the final relevance factor. The relevance factor can be mathematically explained as:

$$Relevance = \sum_{p=1}^{10} PM_p$$

Where PM is the amount of points awarded for relevance metric, p. A GA requires a fitness function that assigns a score (fitness) to each chromosome in the current population, the fitness depending on how well that chromosome solves the problem at hand. Fitness functions are customised for each problem domain, as the requirements of a given domain determine the viability of a solution. For the timetabling domain, it is fair to say that the 'fitter' a timetable chromosome solution is, the higher 'relevance' it should have to an original input case, similar to the CBR retrieval. Therefore chromosome fitness is mapped to the CBR relevance factor, also ensuring that relevance is maintained if a solution chromosome is accepted at CBR *retain* phase. The highest possible relevance/fitness score that can be evaluated for a solution in CBR-GAALTA is 50.

3.4 Setting GA Adaptation Parameters and Reproduction Schemes

When implementing a GA, there are main parameters which must be applied for the algorithm to operate. For CBR-GAALTA, the vital parameters and their assigned values are set to the values listed in Table 2. The crossover probability is set to a standard value for a GA [19], though the mutation probability is set at a higher value than usual, as 0.001 is a standard probability of mutation. This probability has been set higher to allow the application to exploit the potential for mutations to examine the search space thoroughly. With a greater chance of mutation, the opportunity to learn through mutations is increased allowing learning to be fed back into case reuse.

Table 2. GA Main Parameters

GA Parameter	Assigned Value
Size of Population	75
Number of Generations	100
Crossover Probability (P_c)	0.7
Mutation Probability (P_m)	0.01

Along with setting the GA parameters, a selection scheme must be applied to determine how to choose individuals in the population that will create offspring for the next generation. A tournament selection algorithm is applied for GA adaptation in CBR-GAALTA, due to the fact that it is the least computationally expensive selection method. Adaptation can be a costly operation in terms of computation; therefore a selection method was employed to remove some of the expense from the adaptation task. The Tournament Selection scheme employed follows the general algorithm in Figure 4, adapted from Mitchell [19]:

1. Select two chromosomes at random from the population
2. Generate a random number, **r**, between 0 and 1
3. Set a parameter, **k**, between 0 and 1, as the probability that the fittest of the two individuals will be selected for crossover
4. If **r** < **k**, then the fitter of the two individuals is selected to be parent. Otherwise, the less fit chromosome is selected as a parent.

Fig. 4. GA Tournament Selection Algorithm [19]

4 Applying Learning Feedback from Revise to Reuse

The aim of this research is to implement a new method of learning that filters information learnt in revise stage of the CBR cycle back into reuse stage. The purpose of the feed back mechanism is to aid in learning what values are better to use for mutations. Within the structure of genes, there are certain values within the timetabling domain that will not produce viable solutions if they are mutated to illegal values. Take for example, the duration of a lesson. Generally, a lesson will range from one to four hours in duration, depending on the lesson type. If a lesson duration is mutated to a value that is not valid and out of range, such as 24 hours, this causes the solution to be invalid in the application domain. Not only is the solution invalid, but when reintroduced into the GA population the badly mutated gene can spread throughout the population if the opportunity for reproduction arises. The main motivation for feeding the knowledge between adaptation and learning is to limit the chances of illegal values spreading throughout the GA population. In order for initial learning to arise, rules are input to the system explaining illegal values and circumstances within a timetable. Domain input rules are provided and input by system users, and are accessible by the system at the reuse and revise stage. These rules can also be modified and added based on user input. The rules are stored in a Vector format as shown in Table 3, where each index of the vector is stored as a column value of Table 3.

Table 3. Storage Of a Learning Rule for CBR Revision and Reuse

Index x	Operator	Index y	yIndexOrVal	Rule Name
12	1	5	1	class size < room size
7	1	8	0	start time < 8
6	5	0	0	Duration != 0
5	5	0	0	lessonSize != 0

A description of each element in a rule is listed below.

Index x - A value of which allele within the gene the rule will affect

Operator - The operator to be applied to the Index x and Index y. The operator can be any of the following values:
1. *Less than*
2. *Less than or equal to*
3. *Greater than*
4. *Greater than or equal to*
5. *Not equal*

Index y - A value either of an allele or a numerical value, which the operator is compared with

yIndexOrVal - Determines whether index y should be taken as an index, or as a numerical value (1 indicates and index, 0 indicates a value)

Rule Name - A name that can be given to the rule, used for referencing and explanatory purposes

These rules are applied during revision, ensuring all genes within the chromosomes comply. The user is warned of any possible errors remaining in the chromosome prior to cross checking the solution in preparation for solution acceptance. These domain rules are also used to check that core subjects are not running at the same time in a timetable, and that any requirements within the incompatible list are considered before allowing experts to assess the timetable.

If errors according to the domain rules are present, it can be assumed that errors have arisen due to bad mutations, as all stored cases are validated. In order to use these revision rules to prevent problems from arising at revision, the rules are fed back into the application at an adaptation level, allowing the system to learn which mutations are not favourable to use. This domain knowledge is used solely to aid mutations in covering more valid, applicable values. As repair is applied, the user of the system is alerted to problems remaining within the chromosomes structure, as well as warning of any incompatibilities in the placement of lessons. At this point, it is up to the user to evaluate and trial the solution in the real world domain. Dependent on the application of the solution, the user will choose to retain the solution or not.

5 Case-Base Injection for the Genetic Algorithm Initial Population

Based on Aamodt and Plaza's four step CBR cycle [5], cases retrieved by the case-based reasoner are modified, if required, to more closely fit a new problem description at the reuse stage. Using a GA for reuse implies that the cases returned by case retrieval can be used as input to the GA initial population for adaptation. The decision of which cases to feed into the GA initial population, and how many cases to feed may make a difference to the performance of GA adaptation. Many strategies can be applied to the initialisation of the GA population at reuse, and this initialisation process may have a significant effect on the performance of the GA in terms of producing new, fitter solutions to a new input problem. If the GA population is initially injected with a small population of high fitness individuals, the diversity needed to find an optimal solution to the problem may not be reached. To cover all spectrums of diversity input to a GA, three separate case bases were developed, with low, medium, and high averages of fitness. These three type of case base are then created with three different case base sizes, initialised with 4, 8 and 16 cases. These initial case bases vary the size and fitness of the initial GA population when entering the GA adaptation cycle. The low fitness case base has an average fitness of around 10, where as the average case base fitness was set at around 18, just under the expected average of 25. The high fitness solutions average was 25, the mean expected average for a population. In order to fully test the GAs adaptability and the effect of our learning feedback mechanism on case size and population, the highest average fitness does not exceed the expected average fitness of the case base (25).

6 Results and Discussion

The results presented are the output from running tests on each type of case base with each size of case base. The case base sizes were tested with our learning feedback mechanism activated and deactivated. The GA is run 10 times for each case base population size, and the average of the 10 runs is presented as the result. The new input case and GA parameters remain constant throughout all tests. Table 4 shows the average fitness's for each case base and then each population size, with our learning mechanism activated and also deactivated.

Table 4. Results of GA adaptation using three separate case bases and population sizes

Case Base Type	Low Relevance Case Base	Medium Relevance Case Base	High Relevance Case Base
Initial GA Population of 4 Cases			
Average fitness with learning	27.85	30.35	31.70
Average fitness without learning	26.95	29.40	29.25
Initial GA Population of 8 Cases			
Average fitness with learning	27.45	32.30	33.35
Average fitness without learning	26.70	31.40	32.80
Initial GA Population of 16 Cases			
Average fitness with learning	28.05	33.55	35.85
Average fitness without learning	28.30	32.50	34.65

The results presented show that GA adaptation can greatly increase the relevance of solutions retrieved by a case-based reasoner. Considering that the initial average fitness of the low relevance case base is 10, and this is increased to a solution yielding fitness of 28, it is obvious that the GA adaptation cycle has a significant impact on improving solutions to a new input problem. Not only are solutions higher in fitness when the GA is applied, but with the activation of our learning feedback mechanism the fitness of solutions is also improved. This improvement in fitness would be due to the adaptation process avoiding the introduction of invalid mutations to the population.

It is also evident that feeding in a higher fitness of cases to the GA initial population yields results with higher fitness. The average fitness of solutions produced by a GA cycle fed with a high relevance case base compared to the low relevance case base for a given case base size is significant, when learning is activated and deactivated. This demonstrates that when the opportunity arises to feed higher fitness cases into a GA adaptation cycle, fitter solutions can be produced. Another significant result arises from the variation of case base size. When the GA initial population size is increased, the adapted solutions produced are higher in fitness for a given case base relevance. This is again consistent for learning activated and deactivated, though learning activated once again maintains that solutions produced are a closer match to the original input case.

The fact that higher fitness solutions are produced when initial case base size is increased is significant, as for all implementations of the GA, population size is maintained at a maximum population size of 75 with a degree of elitism applied. This implies that even though the GA operates on a constant population size and discards unfit solutions from the population, the injection of fitter cases to the GA adaptation cycle acts as a catalyst for fit initial crossbreeding within the population.

7 Conclusions and Future Work

When entering a GA adaptation cycle from CBR retrieval, the relevance of cases injected into the GA population can make a significant impact on the production of fit solutions to a new input problem. Not only does the relevance of cases impact on fitness of solutions, but the number of fit solutions fed into the GA adaptation cycle can produce fitter solutions to a new input problem. These factors should be taken into consideration when selecting which cases should initialise a GA adaptation cycle. When the opportunity arises for GA adaptation, the solutions from the case base which are closer in relevance to the new input problem should be injected into the GA initial population. The success of a GA adaptation cycle can also be improved by injecting a greater number of fit solutions into the initial GA population. The application of a learning feedback mechanism from revise into reuse also aids in producing fitter solutions in adaptation. Our learning feedback allowed adaptation to avoid illegal and invalid mutations, demonstrating that when applying a strong initial population to the GA adaptation cycle and activating the learning mechanism, adaptation can produce fitter solutions to a new input case. Future work that can add to the success of the proposed schemes for this research are:

- The expansion of the timetabling problem domain. As the problem domain was reduced for the implementation of this project, it is possible to expand this domain and have the reasoner operating on a much larger schedule.
- Tracking more adaptable solutions to feed into the GA adaptation. This can involve finding sets of solutions that are not necessarily the highest relevance value solutions, but are a range of solutions that are more adaptable and are able to directly map parts of one solution to another solution in respect to solving the problem case.

References

1. Oppacher, F., Deugo, D.: Integrating case-based reasoning with genetic algorithms. In Cercone, N., Gardin, F., eds.: Computational Intelligence III, Elsevier Science Publishers B.V (1991) 103–114
2. Purvis, L., Pu, P.: Composer: A case-based reasoning system for engineering design. In: Robotica. (1998) 285–295
3. Adalier, M., Tsatsoulis, C.: Redesigning for manufacturability using REINRED. Applied Artificial Intelligence **6** (1992) 285–302

4. de Silva Garza, A.G., Maher, M.L.: An evolutionary approach to case adaptation. In: Proceedings of Third International Conference on Case-Based Reasoning. (1999) 162–172
5. Aamodt, A.: Case-based reasoning: Foundational issues, methodological variations, and system approaches. In: AICOM. (1994) 39–58
6. Lewis, L.: A case-based reasoning approach to the management of faults in communications networks. In: INFOCOMM. (1993) 1422–1429
7. Khan, A., Hoffman, A.: A new approach for the incremental development of adaptation function for cbr. In: EWCBR 2000, Springer (2000)
8. Smyth, B., Keane, M.: Retrieving adaptable cases. the role of adaptation knowledge in case retrieval. In: EWCBR 1993, Springer-Verlag (1993)
9. Smyth, B., Keane, M.: Adaptation-guided retrieval: Questioning the similarity assumption in reasoning. In: Artificial Intelligence Review. (1998) 249–293
10. Tonidandel, F., Rillo, M.: An accurate adaptation-guided similarity metric for case-based planning. In: ICCBR 2001, Springer (2001)
11. Mostow, J.: Design by derivational analogy: Issues in the automated replay of design plans. In: Artificial Intelligence. (1989) 119–184
12. Louis, S., Xu, Z.: Genetic algorithms for open shop scheduling and re-scheduling. In Cohen, M., Hudson, D., eds.: 11th International Conference on Computers and their Applications. (1996)
13. Jarmulak, J., Craw, S., Rowe, R.: Self-optimising cbr retrieval. In: Proceedings 12th IEEE International Conference on Tools with Artificial Intelligence. (2000) 376–383
14. Jarmulak, J., Craw, S., Rowe, R.: Genetic algorithms to optimise cbr retrieval. In Blanzieri, E., Portinale, L., eds.: EWCBR. Volume 1898 of LNAI., Springer-Verlag Berling Heidelberg (2000) 136–147
15. Babka, O., Lei, C.: Reducing case library. In: Proceedings of the International ICSC Congress on Computational Intelligence Methods and Applications. (1999) 321–327
16. Passone, S., Chung, P.W., Nassehi, V.: Case-based reasoning for estuarine model design. In Craw, S., Preece, A., eds.: ECCBR. Volume 2416 of LNAI. (2002) 590–603
17. Koza, J.: Genetic Programming On the Programming of Computers by Means of Natural Selection. MIT Press (1992)
18. Beasley, D., Bull, D., Martin, R.: An overview of genetic algorithms: Part 1, fundamentals. University Computing (1993) 58–69
19. Mitchell, M.: An Introduction to Genetic Algorithms. MIT Press (1996)
20. Abramson, D., Abela, J.: A parallel genetic algorithm for solving the school timetabling problem. In: Division of Information Technology, Melbourne (1992)
21. Main, J., Dillon, T.S., Shiu, S.C.: A tutorial on case based reasoning. Soft Computing in Case Based Reasoning (1999) 1–28

Learning Feature Taxonomies for Case Indexing

Kalyan Moy Gupta[1], David W. Aha[2], and Philip Moore[1]

[1] ITT Industries, AES Division, Alexandria, VA 22303
[2] Navy Center for Applied Research in Artificial Intelligence,
Naval Research Laboratory (Code 5515), Washington, DC 20375
surname@aic.nrl.navy.mil

Abstract. Taxonomic case retrieval systems significantly outperform standard conversational case retrieval systems. However, their feature taxonomies, which are the principal reason for their superior performance, must be manually developed. This is a laborious and error prone process. In an earlier paper, we proposed a framework for automatically *acquiring* features and *organizing* them into taxonomies to reduce the taxonomy acquisition effort. In this paper, we focus on the second part of this framework: automated feature organization. We introduce TAXIND, an algorithm for inducing taxonomies from a given set of features; it implements a step in our FACIT framework for knowledge extraction. TAXIND builds taxonomies using a novel bottom up procedure that operates on a matrix of asymmetric similarity values. We introduce measures for evaluating taxonomy induction performance and use them to evaluate TAXIND's learning performance on two case bases. We investigate both a knowledge poor and a knowledge rich variant of TAXIND. While both outperform a baseline approach that does not induce taxonomies, there is no significant performance difference between the TAXIND variants. Finally, we discuss how a more comprehensive representation for features should improve measures on TAXIND's learning and performance tasks.

1 Introduction

Retrieval of text documents can be significantly improved by semantically indexing them with their concepts and relations rather than using the keyword and term indexing technique that is standard in information retrieval systems. Semantic indices can be used to guide the user during query formulation and to effectively retrieve documents at a conceptual level, which should increase user satisfaction.

Conversational case-based reasoning (CCBR) (Aha *et al.*, 2001) is a suitable methodology for conceptual retrieval of text documents. CCBR is a case-based reasoning (CBR) methodology (Aamodt & Plaza, 1994; Watson, 1999) in which a user engages in a question answer dialog (i.e., a *conversation*) with the system to incrementally specify a query. In response, the system displays ranked solutions with increasing precision. The CCBR methodology has been used to develop hundreds of customer support and equipment troubleshooting applications (Watson, 1997). In these diagnosis tasks the CCBR system identifies and retrieves information that could be used to solve the problem described by the user's query. This retrieved information could be in the form of text documents. Thus, indices must be assigned to these documents so that users can efficiently retrieve them through an incremental querying process.

Creating semantic indices for text documents can be a laborious and time-consuming task. For example, this is true for the Taxonomic CCBR methodology, which outperforms other CCBR approaches (Gupta *et al.*, 2002). The taxonomic method requires constructing a set of feature taxonomies for indexing the documents. Although this distributed indexing approach imposes strict constraints for guiding taxonomy development (e.g., each feature in a taxonomy must be a semantic refinement of its parent, and there can be at most one leaf in a taxonomy per document), constructing the taxonomies is difficult because there is a large space of possible taxonomy sets to choose from. Currently, constructing taxonomies is a manual process; a knowledge engineer must create a set and validate that it yields good retrieval performance. Clearly, the process of taxonomy generation could be accelerated and improved by automating it.

We introduce and describe an initial empirical analysis for TAXIND (TAXonomy INDuction), an automated approach for organizing extracted features into a set of taxonomies. This builds on our earlier research (Gupta & Aha, 2004), in which we introduced a semi-automated framework (named FACIT) to ease the task of constructing taxonomies for Taxonomic CCBR applications. TAXIND focuses on FACIT's feature organization subtask. We report results showing that, for a pair of case bases, TAXIND outperforms a baseline strategy on the learning task (i.e., taxonomy induction), but variants of TAXIND that exploit semantic knowledge do not significantly enhance its performance. This motivates our future investigation of a semantically richer approach for feature organization.

The rest of this paper focuses on TAXIND's learning task. Section 2 describes the context for this problem, explaining how it differs from previous research. Sections 3 and 4 introduce TAXIND and present its empirical evaluation. Finally, we discuss the results and our future plans for FACIT in Section 5.

2 Problem and Related Work

2.1 Taxonomic CCBR and the Feature Organization Task

We address the problem of organizing features to index documents for a Taxonomic CCBR methodology (Figure 1), which implements a mixed-initiative case retrieval process (Gupta, 2001). Table 1 summarizes our notation. In this methodology, users incrementally provide a *query* Q. We assume that Q is composed of a set of features, each of which is a <question,answer> pair qa_i, although there is no theoretical constraint on the representation of CCBR queries and a structural representation could instead be used (Bergmann, 2002). As shown in step 1, the user describes an initial problem to the system by pro-

Table 1. Notation used in Section 2.1.

Notation	Meaning
c	Case
c_p and c_s	Problem and solution components of case c
L	Case library
Q	Query
QA	Set of features (question-answer pairs)
qa_i	i^{th} feature (question-answer pair string) in QA
T	Set of induced taxonomies
T_k	k^{th} taxonomy in T
t_i	Node i in a taxonomy

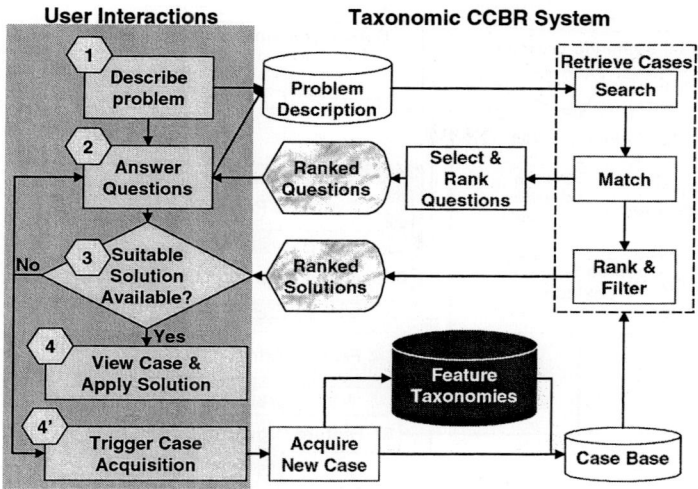

Fig. 1. The Taxonomic CCBR methodology.

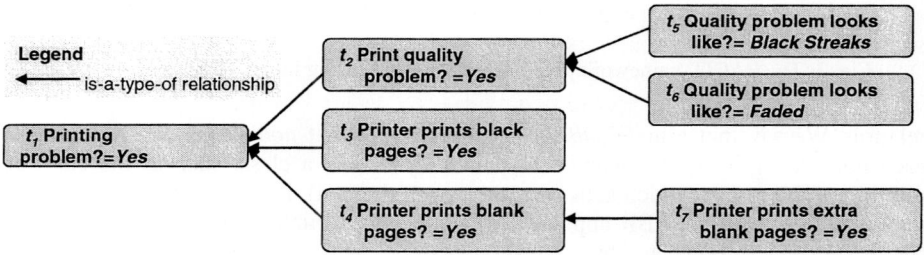

Fig. 2. Subset of a feature taxonomy for a printer troubleshooting application (Gupta, 2001).

viding text that the system can convert to a set of feature(s). The system then compares Q with the problem component c_p of each case c in a library L, where we assume a simple <problem, solution> representation for cases (i.e., $c=<c_p,c_s>$). For simplicity, we assume problems are also represented as a set of features and that solutions are text documents. Using a matching function, the system ranks each case c using $sim(Q,c_p)$, the similarity of its problem to Q. It then displays the solution c_s for each retrieved case, along with questions in their problems that are not answered in Q. In step 2, the user may select and answer a proffered question, which adds a <question,answer> pair to Q, or otherwise modifies Q. The system then cycles with the modified query. Alternatively, the user could decide (step 3) to select and view a displayed solution (step 4). However, if none are acceptable and the user has completed the query, they may decide to trigger case acquisition (step 4').

The primary distinguishing characteristic of Taxonomic CCBR is its reliance on a set of feature subsumption taxonomies T. Each taxonomy $T_k \in T$ is an acyclic directed graph whose nodes t_i are features drawn from the features of L's cases. All nodes in T except the root are related to their parent node by either an *is-a-type-of* or *is-a-part-of*

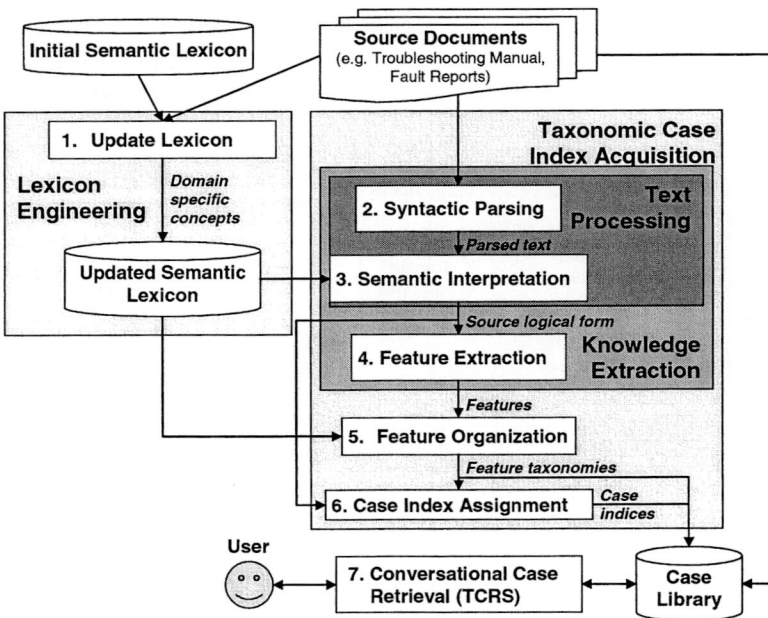

Fig. 3. The FACIT framework processes and steps, feeding into a TCRS application.

relation. We say that a node *subsumes* all its descendent nodes (i.e., while we label each node using a <question,answer> pair, they denote a class, such as the class of printing problems, on which subsumption is well defined). Figure 2 shows a subset of the taxonomy from a CCBR application for a printer troubleshooting domain. In this figure, node t_2 represents the <question,answer> pair <"Print quality problem?", "Yes">, has one parent node (t_1) and two children nodes (t_5 and t_6).

In this paper we address the problem of how to organize a given set of features into a set of subsumption taxonomies. Figure 3 shows this as the feature organization task (step 5) of FACIT (Feature Acquisition and Case Indexing from Text), the knowledge extraction framework we introduced in (Gupta & Aha, 2004). FACIT requires an initial semantic lexicon and a set of source documents as input. We argued that this lexicon should be generative rather than enumerative in its behavior, and should exploit a representation that extends Generative Lexicon theory (Gupta & Aha, 2003). We also argued for extracting a *source logical form* for each concept in the documents; it uses predicate argument structures to represent the meaning of sentences contained in the text as propositions. This representation eliminates the syntactic variances in text because sentences with different grammatical structure but the same meaning will have, or be reducible to, the same logical form. Also, we can apply predicate calculus operations to logical forms, such as those we will use to select and organize features into taxonomies.

To date, we have only partially implemented FACIT. We have developed a suite of tools for lexicon engineering and syntactic parsing, along with a preliminary implementation for semantic interpretation. Also, we have developed TCRS, an implementation of Taxonomic case retrieval (Gupta *et al.*, 2002). However, we have not previously developed tools for feature extraction, feature organization, and case indexing. TAXIND is FACIT's initial feature organization component (step 5 in Figure 3). Our objective for introducing and evaluating it is to gain further understanding on the feature organization process. Because the source logical forms for the extracted features do not yet exist, we will use the <question,answer> representation for them, where both of its components are represented by text strings. We also have a lexicon that can help identify subsumption relations for these features, although together they do not support the more powerful logical subsumption approach that we will use when FACIT is fully implemented. We discuss this further in Section 5.

The learning task we address here is the induction of a set of feature-subsumption taxonomies from a set of cases whose problems are defined by a set of features. The taxonomies are constrained; a feature can appear in only one taxonomy, and only once in that taxonomy. Also, among the features at the leaves of a hierarchy, at most one can appear in a case. See (Gupta, 2001) for more details on these constraints. The performance task that we address concerns TCRS's retrieval performance.

2.2 Related Work

TAXIND's learning task is unusual because it must induce one or more subsumption taxonomies from a given set of features, and the taxonomies have certain constraints. This is an unsupervised task: no labels are provided with these features (e.g., an associated class label). Yang and Wu (2001) investigated the induction of a set of taxonomies (i.e., "decision forest") for their CaseAdvisor CCBR system. However, nodes in their trees are attributes rather than features, they do not discover nor use feature subsumption to organize their trees, and their case indices do not have a distributed representation. Aha et al.'s (2001) CLIRE also induces a tree for a CCBR system, but it induces only a single tree, and uses attributes rather than features at nodes. Neither approach used the semantics of features to guide taxonomy induction.

In the greater CBR and related literatures (e.g., machine learning), we again find several algorithms exist that induce case-indexing hierarchies (e.g., Daelemans *et al.*, 1997). However, unlike TAXIND, these algorithms typically do not consider the semantics of the features, nor induce trees intended to guide a mixed-initiative querying process.

FACIT relates to Textual CBR (Lenz *et al.*, 1998) because it focuses on textual cases. TAXIND induces a distributed indexing representation that is also a characteristic of case retrieval nets (CRNs), which Lenz and his colleagues used for several Textual CBR problems. However, TAXIND induces strict taxonomies rather than a more general semantic network, it does not use spreading activation for case retrieval, and we designed it specifically for the CCBR methodology.

Several researchers (e.g., Müller *et al.*, 1999; Kashyap *et al.*, 2004) have investigated methods to learn taxonomies for information retrieval tasks. Their approaches have typically involved using clustering algorithms to create intermediate nodes. In contrast, TAXIND must select and relate leaf nodes to the intermediate nodes (i.e., features), which are already given.

FACIT is a knowledge extraction framework, which differs from information extraction frameworks that assume the existence of an initial set of features and focus on the simpler task of feature assignment (i.e., determining which among a given set of features to use as indices for a case). FACIT does not make this initial assumption. We discuss other issues concerning FACIT in (Gupta & Aha, 2004).

3 The TAXIND Approach for Learning Indexing Taxonomies

In this section we present TAXIND. It organizes a set of features QA, each of which is a <question,answer> pair, into a set of taxonomies T as follows:

(1) *Feature pre-processing*: This step prepares each $qa_i \in QA$ for similarity computations using either a bag-of-words or a phrasal tokenization process.
(2) *Similarity matrix computation*: This step computes the similarity of a feature qa_i to all other features $qa_j \in QA$ (i≠j) and generates a feature similarity matrix. When the features have been phrasally processed, this step can use application-specific ontologies to improve similarity computation.
(3) *Taxonomy induction*: This step identifies potential subsumption relations among features in QA using the feature similarity matrix and a two step regularization subprocess that induces a strict taxonomy, which we present below using a standard printer troubleshooting application.

3.1 Feature Pre-processing

This step converts each feature into its signature, S, which includes a list of signature elements for use in computing similarity between any two features. Each signature element consists of a token t, the frequency f with which the token occurs in the feature, and its weight w (see Section 3.2). TAXIND creates signature element tokens via either *bag-of-words processing*, which creates signature elements for each word in a feature, or *phrasal processing*, which parses each feature into a signature of elements containing part-of-speech tagged phrases as tokens. With the assistance of an application-specific ontology, phrasal tokens can be used to compute the similarity between two terms that cannot be otherwise related. For example, it would allow us to compute the similarity between two distinct phrases "jam[n]" and "problem [n]". The following paragraphs provide additional detail on these two processing methods.

Bag-of-words processing: This approach converts a feature into its signature with words as tokens. No stemming is performed. A list of predefined stopwords is used to eliminate words deemed useless for similarity assessment. For example, assuming the stopwords *are*, *you*, and *?*, then the feature <"Are you having print quality problems?","Yes"> would have five signature elements with word-tokens *having*, *print*, *quality*, *problems*, and *Yes*, each with a frequency of one. Their weights are assessed during similarity matrix computation.

Phrasal processing: This approach tags each word in a given feature with its part of speech and creates phrases to enable syntactic phrasal subsumption detection and similarity computation with an application-specific ontology (see Section 3.2). It then removes pronouns, prepositions, and linking verbs, which has an effect similar to using the stopwords in the bag-of-words approach. Unlike the stopwords approach, this procedure does not require any additional knowledge engineering effort. Simple inflexional morphological processing is also performed. For example, verb forms are reduced to their base forms (e.g., "having [v]" is transformed to "have [v]") and plural nouns are reduced to their singular forms (e.g., "problems [n]" is transformed to problem [n]"). Table 2 shows the three signature elements with phrasal tokens generated by processing the example feature.

Table 2. Phrase-processed signature for the feature
<"Are you having print quality problems?","Yes" >.

Token (t)- Phrase	Frequency (f)	Weight (w)
have [v] *	1	undefined
print [n]	1	undefined
quality[n]	1	undefined
print quality problem [n] **	1	undefined
Yes [d]	1	undefined

* *having* was stemmed to *have*
** noun phrase generated and *problems* stemmed to *problem*
[] part-of-speech tags: [v]-verb, [n]-noun, [d]-adverb

3.2 Feature Similarity Matrix

To organize question-answer features into taxonomies we need to identify subsumption (*is-a-type-of*) relations between them. Subsumption is a directed relation: for any two distinct features qa_1 & qa_2, at most one subsumes the other (i.e., *subsumes*(qa_1,qa_2), *subsumes*(qa_2,qa_1), or neither is true) and, by definition, if either feature subsumes the other then the truth values of *subsumes*(qa_1,qa_2) and *subsumes*(qa_2,qa_1) must differ. By defining similarity as subsumption (i.e., yielding "1" for an ordered pair of features, and "0" otherwise), then if $sim(qa_1,qa_2)$ denotes the similarity of qa_1 with respect to qa_2, $sim(qa_1, qa_2) \neq sim(qa_2, qa_1)$ when either similarity value is non-zero. Thus, $sim()$ is an asymmetric similarity function. Also, we compute it using the features' signatures, and define it to yield values in [-1,1].

Signature Similarity Computation: We define the similarity of two signatures $sim(S_1,S_2)$ as a weighted sum of their token similarities, as shown in Equation 1:

$$sim(S_i, S_j) = \frac{\sum_{\forall t \in S_i} sim_t(t_i, t \in S_j) * w_t}{\sum_{\forall t \in S_j} w_t} \quad (1)$$

where S_i and S_j are the signatures of features qa_i and qa_j, respectively, $sim_t()$ defines the similarity among a token and a signature (see below), and w_t is the weight associated with token t. Token weights are computed using an adaptation of the term frequency (*tf*) and inverse document frequency (*idf*) weight computation procedure used in information retrieval systems, as shown in Equation 2:

$$w_t = tf * \log(N / df) \quad (2)$$

where N is the number of features used in a given case library, *tf* is the frequency of token t among them, and *df* is the number of the cases that contain t.

Token Similarity Computation. The token similarity function $sim_t()$ (Equation 3) compares a token from one signature to all the tokens in the other feature's signature and returns the first non-zero similarity value found.

$$sim_t(t_k, t_l) = \begin{cases} if\ String\ (t_k) = String\ (t_l)\ then\ 1.0 \\ else\ if\ phrasalSim\ (t_k, t_l) > 0\ then\ phrasalSim\ (t_k, t_l) \\ else\ if\ ontoSim\ (t_k, t_l) \neq 0\ then\ ontoSim\ (t_k, t_l) \\ else\ 0 \end{cases} \quad (3)$$

$sim_t()$ returns values in [-1,1]. If defined using only the first and final lines of this equation, then $sim_t()$ would define a string-comparison function that yields 1 for identical strings and 0 otherwise. However, this string-comparison function would be inadequate for tokens that do not share any words in common, but are semantically related. Therefore, we introduce two additional types of similarity computations:

(a) *Syntactic phrasal similarity*: *phrasalSim()* computes the similarity between multi-word phrases that have the same last word. For example, "problem" is the last word in "print quality problem". This computation can be used to identify subsumption relations between phrases. It computes the similarity of a phrase-token with respect to another as the ratio of the number of words they have in common and the number of words in the other phrase:

$$phrasalSim(t_i, t_j) = \frac{\sum_{w \in t_i \cap t_j} f(w, t_j)}{\sum_{w \in t_j} f(w, t_j)} \quad (4)$$

where $f(w, t_j)$ is the number of times word w occurs in token t_j. This asymmetric function can be applied only when phrasal pre-processing has been performed. For example, *phrasalSim*("Problem [n]", "Print quality problem [n]")=1/3=0.33 and *phrasalSim*("Print quality problem [n]" ,"Problem [n]",)=1/1=1.0. Clearly, "Print quality problem" *is-a-type-of* problem. Section 3.3 describes how we use similarity values to detect subsumption relations. While *phrasalSim()* can help detect subsumption relations between phrases, it is still inadequate for semantically related phrases that do not share tokens. To compute similarity between semantically related phrases, we rely on predefined application specific ontologies, which might specify these relations between terms (see (b) below).

(b) *Ontological similarity*: Similarity computations can be extended by using an application-specific ontology. We assume the existence of simple ontologies that organize terms with *is-a-type-of*, *is-a-part-of*, and *is-opposite-of* relations. Linguistic ontologies (i.e., *semantic lexicons*) like WordNet (Felbaum, 1998) and more sophisticated generative ontologies (Gupta & Aha, 2003) include these relations.

As seen in Figure 4, we represent the relationship between "error" and "problem" using an *is-a-type-of* relation. Likewise, "printing" has "quality" or "quality" *is-a-part-of* "printing" for this printer troubleshooting application. The similarity between two terms in the ontology is computed as shown in Equation 5.

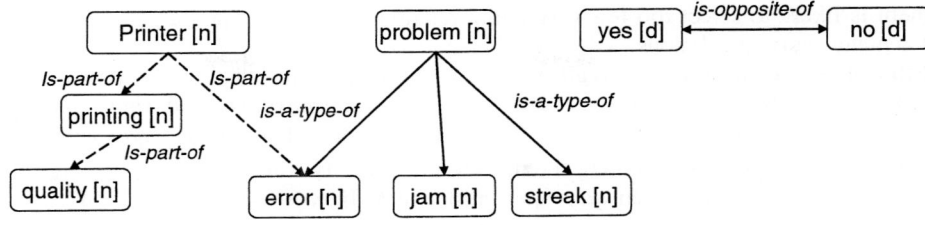

Fig. 4. A fragment from the Printer troubleshooting ontology.

$$ontoSim(t_i,t_j) = \begin{cases} 1/(1+ path\_length(t_i,t_j)) \\ \quad if \ (t_j \ is-a-type-of(t_i) \vee \\ \quad t_j \ is-a-part-of(t_i)) \\ 1.0 \ if \ t_i \ is-a-type-of(t_j) \\ 0.8 \ if \ t_i \ is-a-part-of(t_j) \\ -1 \ if \ t_i \ is-opposite-of(t_j) \\ 0 \ otherwise \end{cases} \quad (5)$$

The path length from a node n to one of its descendants d is the number of links from n to d. Therefore, using the ontology fragment shown in Figure 5 *ontoSim*("printing [n]", "quality [n]")= 1/(1+1) = 0.5 and *ontoSim*("quality [n]", "printing [n]") = 1.0. Likewise *ontoSim*("yes [d]", "no [d]") = -1.0.

3.3 Taxonomy Induction

Identifying Taxonomic Relations. We denote a taxonomic relation between two features, qa_i and qa_j (i ≠j), by $qa_i \rightarrow qa_j$, implying that qa_j *is-a-subtype-of* qa_i. We identify potential taxonomic relations between features by reference to the feature similarity matrix. The following rule for selecting taxonomic relations is used:

> IF ($sim(S_i, S_j) > \Pi$) & ($sim(S_j, S_i) > \Pi$) THEN
>   IF ($sim(S_i, S_j) > sim(S_j, S_i)$)
>   THEN $qa_i \rightarrow qa_j$
>   ELSE $qa_j \rightarrow qa_i$
>   ELSE IF ($sim(S_i, S_j) > \Pi$) & ($sim(S_j, S_i) > \Psi$) THEN
> $qa_i \rightarrow qa_j$
>   ELSE IF ($sim(S_j, S_i) > \Pi$) & ($sim(S_i, S_j) > \Psi$) THEN
> $qa_j \rightarrow qa_i$
>   ELSE No relation

where Π is a user-specified parent selection threshold, typically set to a value representing a high degree of similarity (e.g., 0.5), and Ψ is the user-specified child selection threshold ($\Psi<\Pi$). It is typically set to a value representing a reasonable degree of similarity between a child and its parent (e.g., 0.15). Suitable values of Ψ and Π must be empirically determined for a particular set of features *QA*. Too large a gap between them is likely to select too few taxonomic relations while too small a gap will yield too many spurious relations.

Enforcing Taxonomic Constraints. Gupta (2001) explains that the relations in a Taxonomic CBR taxonomy must satisfy the *relation transitivity* and *single parent* constraints. The former implies that, for any three distinct features qa_1, qa_2, and qa_3, with taxonomic relations among them, they must satisfy transitivity criteria (e.g., if $qa_1 \rightarrow qa_2$ and $qa_2 \rightarrow qa_3$ then $qa_1 \rightarrow qa_3$ must exist). If $qa_1 \rightarrow qa_3$ is found, TAXIND regularizes the set of taxonomic relations by marking $qa_1 \rightarrow qa_3$ for deletion because it can be derived by a transitive operation. If $qa_1 \rightarrow qa_3$ is not found, then TAXIND marks for deletion the taxonomic relation at the higher level (i.e., $qa_1 \rightarrow qa_2$).

In Taxonomic CBR, each feature can appear in only one taxonomy, and nodes with multiple parents are not permitted. For example, for any three distinct features qa_1, qa_2, and qa_3, if there exist taxonomic relations $qa_1 \rightarrow qa_3$ and $qa_2 \rightarrow qa_3$, the single parent constraint is violated (i.e., qa_3 has two parents). TAXIND enforces this constraint via a bottom-up approach; it retains only the taxonomic relation between the child and the strongest parent and marks for deletion the other relation. For example, if $sim(qa_3, qa_1) > sim(qa_3, qa_2)$, then it retains $qa_1 \rightarrow qa_3$ and marks $qa_2 \rightarrow qa_3$ for deletion. The relations marked for deletion are removed at the end of this step and the remaining taxonomic relations are transformed into taxonomies.

4 Evaluation

4.1 Methodology

Performance Measures: We define TAXIND's learning performance as its ability to accurately induce (i.e., generate) taxonomic relations from a space of possible relations. The relations in a taxonomy are the those between its nodes and their descendants (see Figure 5). For single-node taxonomies, a null relation is counted.

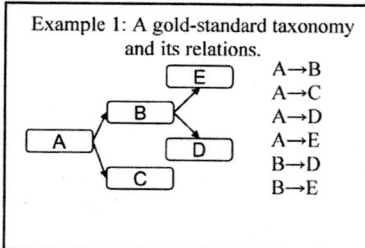
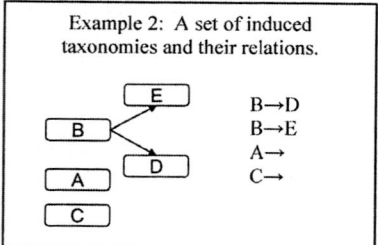

Fig. 5. Example taxonomies and their relations.

For this evaluation, we assume the availability of a "gold-standard" (i.e., ideal) set of taxonomic relations that can be compared with the relations induced by TAXIND. In our evaluation we used a printer troubleshooting and a consumer electronics taxonomic case base. In our previous work, we manually prepared taxonomies for these databases that employ the gold-standard relations we need for this evaluation.

Like the Recall, Precision, and F-Measure equations used to evaluate information retrieval performance, we propose the following three measures:

$$Taxonomic\ Relations\ Recall\ (TRR) = \frac{\#Gold-Standard\ Relations\ Retrieved}{\#Gold-Standard\ Relations} \quad (6)$$

$$Taxonomic\ Relations\ Precision\ (TRP) = \frac{\#Gold-Standard\ Relations\ Retrieved}{\#Total\ Relations\ Retrieved} \quad (7)$$

$$Taxonomic\ F-Measure\ (TF-Measure) = \frac{2*TRR*TRP}{(TRR+TRP)} \quad (8)$$

For example, using the gold-standard and the relations shown in example 2 of Figure 5 yields: TRR=2/6=0.33, TRP=2/4=0.5, and TF-Measure=0.4.

An alternative to inducing taxonomies is a degenerate approach that generates only single-node taxonomies. That is, it creates one taxonomy for each feature $qa_i \in QA$. In the absence of alternative taxonomy generation methodologies, we will use this approach as a baseline for assessing TAXIND's performance. For example, the learning performance values for the baseline approach for example 1 in Figure 5 are: TRR=0/6=0, TRP= 0/4=0, and TF-Measure=0.

Test Data: We selected two taxonomic case bases (Gupta et al., 2002) pertaining to printer troubleshooting ("Printer") and consumer electronics troubleshooting ("Electronics") as our test data sets. Their existing taxonomies were used as gold standards for our empirical evaluation of TAXIND. Printer's cases refer to 54 distinct features, while Electronics' cases refer to 121.

Test Procedure and Hypotheses: In addition to varying the dataset, we also varied the version of TAXIND that we applied. In particular, we used two versions:

1. *Knowledge poor*: This used bag-of-words processing with the string similarity computation option.
2. *Knowledge rich*: This used phrasal processing with string similarity, phrasal similarity, and ontological similarity.

We ran both versions of TAXIND for each application using a range of thresholds for Π and Ψ, report only the best results in Section 4.2, and evaluated two hypotheses:

(1) Both versions of TAXIND will outperform the baseline approach.
(2) The knowledge rich approach will outperform the knowledge poor approach.

TAXIND Implementation: We implemented TAXIND and used our Java implementation of Brill's (1992) Tagger for phrasal processing. We compiled a list of stopwords and domain-specific ontologies for Printer and Electronics. We also developed ontologies using our Generative Sublanguage Ontology Editor. Only *is-a-type-of*, *is-a-part-of*, and *is-opposite-of* were used from among the many possible types of relations available.

4.2 Analysis of the Learning and Performance Tasks

The learning task being addressed is TAXIND's ability to induce good taxonomies, as assessed by the measures described in Section 4.1. After discussing its learning results, we will then briefly summarize its results for our intended performance task: retrieval performance when using the resulting taxonomic cases in TCRS.

```
What is the general nature of the video problem? TV
  What is the general nature of the TV problem? Power
    What is the general nature of the VCR problem? No power to unit/Unit shuts itself off
  What is the general nature of the TV problem? Channel Tuning
  What is the general nature of the TV problem? Channel Labelling
  What is the general nature of the TV problem? Picture Quality
    What is the general nature of the TV picture quality problem? Picture quality problem
    What is the general nature of the TV picture quality problem? Color contrast adjustment
    What is the general nature of the TV picture quality problem? Localized distortion ...
    What is the general nature of the TV picture quality problem? Black screen/ Black block
    What is the general nature of the TV picture quality problem? Too red/too bright/too...
    What is the general nature of the TV picture quality problem? Other
      Is the picture the same poor quality on the other tv(s)? Yes
      Is the picture the same poor quality on the other tv(s)? No
```

Fig. 6. A taxonomy for Electronics learned by the knowledge poor version of TAXIND.

To illustrate TAXIND's capabilities, we display one of the taxonomies that the knowledge poor approach learned for Electronics in Figure 6. It has three features that do not belong to it by reference to its gold standard. Still, the knowledge poor approach is effective when the cases have been prepared using consistent terminology and phrasing by experienced case base developers, as was done for both data sets.

Tables 3 and 4 display the results of the baseline and TAXIND variants for the two case bases. The knowledge poor and the knowledge rich approaches did indeed outperform the baseline approach for both datasets. For example, this is clear from the results of the TF-Measures in these tables. Therefore, our first hypothesis has some support. TAXIND performs comparatively better on Electronics than on Printer because the expected taxonomies for Electronics are deeper and more complex.

Table 3. Baseline and TAXIND's performances for the Printer case base.

Option	Generated Taxonomies				TRR	TRP	TF
	No.	Avg. Depth	Max. Depth	Single Nodes			
Baseline	54	0.0	0	54	0.50	0.50	0.50
Knowledge poor[1]	43	0.20	1	40	0.50	0.57	0.53
Knowledge rich[2]	36	0.33	1	27	0.48	0.58	0.53

1: Π=0.30, Ψ=0.08; 2: Π=0.45, Ψ=0.18

Table 4. Baseline and TAXIND's performances for the Electronics case base.

Option	Generated Taxonomies				TRR	TRP	TF
	No.	Avg. Depth	Max. Depth	Single Nodes			
Baseline	121	0.0	0	121	0.43	0.59	0.50
Knowledge poor[1]	73	0.52	3	62	0.51	0.69	0.58
Knowledge rich[2]	96	0.29	3	91	0.52	0.70	0.60

1: Π=0.63, Ψ=0.15; 2: Π=0.65, Ψ=0.23

There was little learning performance difference between the knowledge poor and knowledge rich versions of TAXIND on both the sets. The knowledge rich version does marginally better in TRP (0.58 vs. 0.57 on Printer and 0.70 vs 0.69 on Electronics). This small improvement in TRP is offset by a decrease in TRR as in the case of Printer (0.48 vs. 0.50). This result leads to us to reject our second hypothesis that the knowledge rich approach will outperform the knowledge poor approach on the measures we are using. Adding background knowledge at a phrasal level and performing linguistic (i.e., phrasal and morphological) processing did not noticeably improve TAXIND's performance. In particular, the improvement in computation of token level similarities did not appear to have a significant impact on the overall similarity computations due to their aggregation, and this marginal improvement did not have a large positive effect on TAXIND's overall performance.

We reviewed the taxonomic relations in the gold standard taxonomies with reference to the relations in the background ontologies. Because the Taxonomic CCBR methodology uses *strict* taxonomies (i.e., a feature can only have one parent), ambiguities can arise when assigning features to taxonomies. The knowledge engineer must often make an assessment based on cases at hand to resolve these ambiguities and organize the features. For example in the printer gold standard the feature <"What is the display message?","13 Paper Jam"> is taxonomically related to <"What are you having a problem with?","Paper"> instead of <"What are you having a problem with?","Error Message"> because "13 Paper Jam" is a type of "Error Message". In other cases, complex negations, which are difficult to detect using only phrasal processing, were missed. For example, <"Is power outlet working?","No"> is a subtype of <"Do you have a power source problem?","Yes">.

In addition to assessing TAXIND's comparative abilities on the learning task (i.e., taxonomy induction), we also briefly examined its capabilities on the performance task (i.e., retrieval using TCRS). In our previous work (Gupta *et al.*, 2002), we used the *leave-one-in* evaluation methodology, which was designed for data sets in which each case's solution was unique (Aha *et al.*, 2001). For each "target" case, the simulated user submitted, for each of its conditions, one query for its node and for each of that condition's ancestor nodes in the same taxonomy. For each query, a simulated TCRS conversation iterated until the target case attained a similarity value of 100% and all its questions were answered. The simulated user answered exactly one question per iteration by selecting the highest-ranking question that is answered in the target case. For each iteration, we recorded the rank of the target case, number of retrieved cases, rank of the answered question, and the total number of questions presented. TCRS retrieved all cases with similarities greater than zero and presented all eligible questions selected by the methodologies.

Table 5 shows the results obtained from running three of the four approaches tested on the Printer case base. That is, we report results for the baseline (i.e., degenerate), gold-standard, and TAXIND's knowledge poor approach. Although we already have the results for the baseline and gold-standard taxonomies, this required creating a taxonomic case base of the printer application using the taxonomies induced by the knowledge poor approach. Therefore, we re-indexed the original set of standard CCBR printer cases on TAXIND's induced taxonomy. The induced taxonomy contained some errors, including incorrect and missing taxonomic relations. Therefore, some of the cases could not be fully indexed. Nonetheless, we expected the end-user performance of this partially correct case base to be better than the baseline CCBR and poorer than the gold-standard taxonomies.

Table 5. Comparison of Expert End user TCRS performance on Printer with taxonomies induced by TAXIND's knowledge poor approach.

Measures	Expert End User Performance		
	Baseline (Degenerate)	Gold-standard Taxonomic	Knowledge Poor Taxonomic
Rank of Retrieved Case	2.03	1.59	1.38
No of Retrieved Cases	6.02	2.85	3.45
Length of Conversation	5.20	2.67	3.22
Rank of Ans. Question	1.10	1.00	1.10
No. of Ques. Displayed	7.30	3.62	2.82

The results shown in Table 5 confirm our expectation. For example, the number of retrieved cases of Baseline, Gold-Standard Taxonomic, and Knowledge Poor Taxonomic are 6.02, 2.85, and 3.45 respectively. Thus, TAXIND retrieved fewer cases on average than did the baseline approach, but didn't perform quite as well as when TCRS used the gold-standard taxonomies. Likewise, the results for conversation length and rank of answered questions were expected. However, the average rank of the retrieved case and the number of questions presented suggested that TAXIND's taxonomies outperformed the gold standard. These are anomalous results; they are more positive for TAXIND then expected due to the errors we described above concerning case indexing. In future comparisons, a human many be required to be in the loop to fix the errors in the set of induced taxonomies prior to their evaluation with TCRS.

5 Discussion

Creating case bases and gold standard taxonomies for the types of analysis we described is a manpower-intensive effort. This limited the extent of experimentation discussed here. We plan to create gold-standard taxonomies for additional case bases in our future work, thus permitting a more comprehensive evaluation of TAXIND.

TAXIND induces taxonomies that must adhere to the constraints imposed by the Taxonomic CCBR methodology. For example, these are feature subsumption taxonomies rather than decision trees, a feature can be in only one taxonomy, and there can be at most one leaf per case in each taxonomy. Thus, it is difficult to compare TAXIND's learning approach with existing approaches that induce taxonomies that do not abide by these constraints.

The logical form representation that we intend to use to represent features will be derived using a generative ontology approach that we described in (Gupta & Aha, 2003). This representation captures the meaning of features more accurately, and is able to support negations and more complex semantic equivalences that are not recognized by TAXIND's representation for features as described in this paper. Using this more powerful representation should yield a taxonomy induction algorithm for FACIT with dramatically improved performance.

Finally, we will analyze TAXIND's computational complexity, and will empirically compare its performance vs. the logical form approach described above.

6 Conclusion

Manually generating taxonomies for conversational CBR applications is laborious. We described TAXIND (TAXonomy INDuction), a machine learning approach, for inducing these taxonomies. We evaluated two versions of TAXIND on two case bases versus a baseline strategy that did not induce any taxonomies. To do this, we compared their abilities to induce the taxonomic relations found in the gold-standard set of taxonomies that we had previously developed manually for both case bases. We found that TAXIND outperformed the baseline strategy on both our learning (i.e., taxonomy induction) and performance (i.e., case retrieval) tasks. In our future work, we intend to conduct a more thorough evaluation of TAXIND and investigate an alternative approach that exploits a logical form representation for features.

Acknowledgements

This research was supported by the Naval Research Laboratory. Thanks to Kurt Fenstermacher and our reviewers for comments on an earlier version of this paper.

References

Aamodt, A., & Plaza, E. (1994). Case-based reasoning: Foundational issues, methodological variations, and system approaches. *AI Communications, 7*, 39-59.

Aha, D.W., Breslow, L.A., & Munoz-Avila, H. (2001). Conversational case-based reasoning. *Applied Intelligence, 14*(1), 9-32.

Bergmann, R. (2002). *Experience management: Foundations, development methodology, and Internet-based applications*. Berlin: Springer.

Brill, E. (1992). A simple, rule-based part-of-speech tagger. *Proceedings of the Third Conference on Applied Natural Language Processing*. Trento, Italy: ACL.

Daelemans, W., van den Bosch, A., & Weijters, T. (1997). IGTree: Using trees for compression and classification in lazy learning algorithms. *Artificial Intelligence Review, 11*, 407-423.

Felbaum, C. (Ed.) (1998). *WordNet: An electronic lexical database*. Cambridge, MA: MIT Press.

Gupta K.M. (2001). Taxonomic case-based reasoning. *Proceedings of the Fourth International Conference on CBR* (pp. 219-233). Vancouver, Canada: Springer.

Gupta, K.,M., & Aha, D.W. (2003). Nominal concept representation in sublanguage ontologies. *Proceedings of the Second International Workshop on Generative Approaches to the Lexicon* (pp. 53-62). Geneva, Switzerland: Univ. of Geneva.

Gupta, K.M., & Aha, D.W. (2004). Acquiring case indexing taxonomies from text. In *Proceedings of the Sixteenth International Conference of the Florida Artificial Intelligence Research Society*. Miami Beach, FL: AAAI Press.

Gupta, K.M., Aha, D.W., & Sandhu, N. (2002). Exploiting taxonomic and causal relations in conversational case retrieval. *Proceedings of the Sixth European Conference on CBR* (pp. 133-147). Aberdeen, Scotland: Springer.

Kashyap, V., Ramakrishnan, C., Thomas, C., Bassu, D., Rindflesch, T.C., & Sheth, A. (2004). TaxaMiner: An experimentation framework for automated taxonomy bootstrapping. Unpublished manuscript.

Lenz, M., Hubner, A., & Kunze, M. (1998). Textual CBR. In M. Lenz, B. Bartsch-Sporl, H.-D. Burkhard, & S. Wess (Eds.) *Case-based reasoning technology: From foundations to applications*. Berlin: Springer.

Müller, A., Dörre, J., Gerstl, P., & Seiffert, R. (1999). The TaxGen framework: Automating the generation of a taxonomy for a large document collection. *Proceedings of the 32nd Hawaii International Conference on System Sciences* (pp. 20-34). Maui, Hawaii: IEEE Press.

Watson, I. (1997). *Applying case-based reasoning: Techniques for enterprise systems.* San Francisco, CA: Morgan Kaufmann.

Watson, I., (1999). CBR is a methodology not a technology. *Knowledge Based Systems Journal, 12*(5-6), 303-308.

Yang, Q., & Wu, J. (2001). Enhancing the effectiveness of interactive case-based reasoning with clustering and decision forests. *Applied Intelligence, 14*(1), 49-64.

Maintenance Memories: Beyond Concepts and Techniques for Case Base Maintenance

Ioannis Iglezakis[1], Thomas Reinartz[1], and Thomas R. Roth-Berghofer[2]

[1] DaimlerChrysler AG, Research and Technology, RIC/AM,
P.O. Box 2360, 89013 Ulm, Germany
{ioannis.iglezakis,thomas.reinartz}@daimlerchrysler.com
[2] German Research Center for Artificial Intelligence DFKI GmbH,
Erwin-Schrödinger-Straße 57, 67655 Kaiserslautern, Germany
thomas.roth-berghofer@dfki.uni-kl.de

Abstract. Maintenance of Case-Based Reasoning (CBR) systems became an important area since applications of CBR technologies were established in different real-world domains. Maintenance issues cover all aspects that help to keep a running CBR system in a usable state of high quality. Concepts and techniques that were developed for maintenance of CBR systems range from methodologies and frameworks that particularly define phases, steps, and tasks necessary to integrate maintenance into the CBR process up to specific programs that enable CBR engineers to carry out the maintenance activities. In this paper, we exemplify this range of research on maintenance of CBR systems by brief characterizations of the SIAM methodology, the MAMA maintenance manual, and the MASH maintenance shell. The overall goal of this paper is then to conclude areas for further research in maintenance for CBR systems from the experience of the work on SIAM, MAMA, MASH, and related approaches.

1 Introduction

Case-Based Reasoning (CBR) has become well-known as a viable technology for problem solving, finding similar objects, or classifying items with unknown class labels. CBR became an accepted technology, which is now applied in many different application domains. However, most research covered only aspects of defining vocabularies for knowledge representation, building up cases and case bases, developing sophisticated organizational structures of case bases, and implementing intelligent similarity measures and retrieval mechanisms. Most of these efforts were about usage of CBR, but did not deal with methods for keeping a CBR system up and running over longer periods of time.

Driven by practical applications of CBR in real-world domains such aspects of *maintenance* arose at the end of the last century. The CBR community and system providers became aware of issues such as dealing with changes in the environment of the application domain, handling quality issues of the CBR system, optimizing retrieval performance over time, or reacting on new customer requirements.

Since this awareness, a rather small number of people in the CBR community started to think about maintenance issues, and to come up with solution approaches for different maintenance purposes. Work in the area of maintenance for CBR systems covered both the development of methodologies and maintenance task models as well as the specification of guidelines for how to perform maintenance and concrete algorithms and systems to execute programs that deal with maintenance tasks.

The overall goal of this paper is to recapitulate research on CBR maintenance and to draw conclusions that point to limitations of existing approaches and propose directions for future work that go beyond the current state of maintenance research. In particular, we exemplify the discussion on different work on case base maintenance by remembering research on the SIAM methodology, the MAMA maintenance manual, and the MASH maintenance shell.

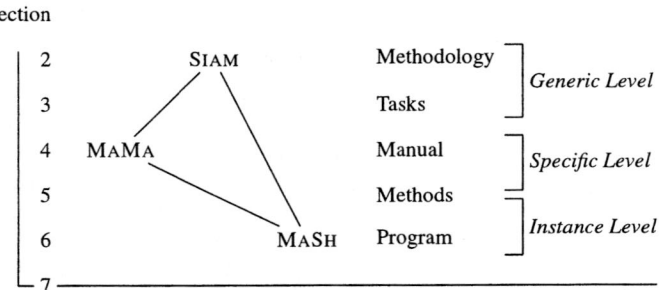

Fig. 1. Maintenance Research at Different Levels of Abstraction

Figure 1 shows an overview of the structure of this paper along the different levels of abstraction of research on maintenance for CBR systems and their relation to each other. In the following section, we describe SIAM, a methodology that covers all phases of CBR starting with the setup and initialization of a CBR system up to its application and maintenance. SIAM is at the most generic level of abstraction and is general enough to hold for any CBR application.

The third section is devoted to a more specific description of maintenance tasks that define which generic activities belong to the different phases of the SIAM methodology. In this paper, we focus on task descriptions for the maintenance phase of SIAM. Within the fourth section, we exemplify contents of the maintenance manual MAMA. This manual is at the first specific level of abstraction and includes more concrete guidelines how to perform maintenance in detailed situations. Hence, MAMA is a specialization of (the maintenance phase of) the SIAM methodology.

The most specific part of this paper at the instance level of abstraction elaborates methods and programs that enable maintenance engineers to actually run executable code to perform the maintenance tasks. The fifth section describes methods of case properties and performance measures that define quality measures for case base maintenance as well as operators that modify cases to perform case base maintenance on concrete case bases. Thereafter, the sixth section is on the maintenance shell MASH, which implements the described methods, and its evaluation within a few example domains. MASH achieves both, it specializes the methodology SIAM as well as implements techniques for the maintenance manual MAMA.

The seventh section summarizes lessons learned from the work on SIAM, MAMA, and MASH. Thereby, we discuss several limitations at all three levels of abstraction and suggest issues for future work that go beyond current efforts in the area of maintenance for CBR systems.

2 Maintenance Methodologies

Methodologies, at the top most level of abstraction, define frameworks that categorize different aspects of a discipline in order to structure issues related to this discipline. Moreover, methodologies often cover process models that describe the general workflow and the various tasks for some field. For maintenance of CBR systems, the following subsections describe such categorizations as well as SIAM as an example for a well-structured process model for CBR in general and maintenance of CBR systems in particular.

2.1 Types of Maintenance

Knowledge maintenance of CBR systems [17] partly builds upon principles of software maintenance, which aims at eliminating errors and adapting software to changes of user requirements regarding functionality and performance. Swanson [21] distinguished *corrective*, *adaptive*, and *perfective* maintenance.

Corrective maintenance deals with processing failure, which is due to incorrect computations. Other failures are performance failures (i.e., performance criteria are not met) and implementation failures.

Adaptive maintenance is needed whenever the environment of a program changes, typically leading to corrective maintenance. Anticipating environment changes to avoid such failures leads to adaptive maintenance.

Perfective maintenance is performed to eliminate processing inefficiencies, to enhance performance, or to improve maintainability. This type of maintenance is directed to keep a program up and running at less expense, or to better serve the needs of its users.

These three types of maintenance can be grouped as *function preserving maintenance* in contrast to *function enhancing* and *supporting maintenance* [10]. *Function enhancing maintenance* aims at the implementation of further functionality into the system. User training, help in using the system, and planning of maintenance activities are examples of *supporting maintenance*. Our own work concentrated on function preserving maintenance. Function enhancement is, in our view, similar to development tasks. For this and supporting maintenance we refer to the INRECA methodology [2].

2.2 The SIAM Methodology

After considering the different types of knowledge maintenance, we looked at CBR process models as the starting point for the development of a maintenance methodology. Early on, CBR has been decomposed into sub processes. Riesbeck and Bain [15] illustrated the basic process of CBR in a flowchart, and Kolodner [8] described CBR as a process of remember and adapt or remember and compare. The most influential model of CBR is the 4RE process according to Aamodt and Plaza [1] with its four steps *retrieve*, *reuse*, *revise*, and *retain*. This four step process was the foundation for the formulation of the SIAM methodology [16].

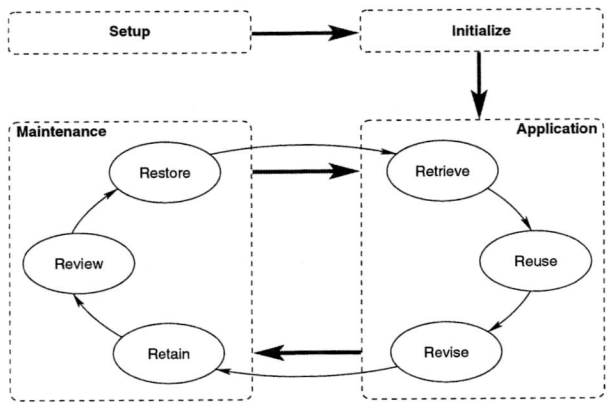

Fig. 2. The SIAM methodology and the six steps process model

SIAM, described as an extension or completion of the INRECA framework [2], is a methodology for developing and maintaining CBR solutions. Figure 2 shows an overview of the SIAM process model comprising the four phases *setup*, *initialization*, *application*, and *maintenance*.

Setup addresses all issues that a CBR project has to deal with in its early stages such as setting up the project's goals and designing the CBR system, always staying focused on the customer's aims. In the initialization phase, the knowledge containers are filled as soon as the CBR system has been implemented or configured. Then, the CBR system is ready for use and enters the phases application and maintenance in turn.

The application phase comprises the three steps *retrieve*, *reuse*, and *revise* of the original four steps process model [1]. Those three steps do not change the knowledge of the CBR system. As soon as knowledge is to be learned, e.g., by storing revised cases in the *retain* step, the maintenance phase begins. This maintenance phase contains the steps *retain*, *review*, and *restore*. All in all, we thus proposed a six steps process model for handling application and maintenance of CBR systems [13].

3 Maintenance Tasks

The steps *review* and *restore* were introduced to handle the maintenance control loop [17]. They are further divided into tasks at the next lower level of abstraction. In terms of the control loop metaphor, the review step observes the current state of a given CBR system, measures its quality, and invokes the restore step if necessary. In the review step, we distinguish the tasks *measure* and *monitor*. The restore step, responsible for bringing the CBR system back to a desired quality level, actually changes the CBR system. Its tasks *suggest*, *select*, and *modify* are executed as soon as the review step indicates the necessity. In the following, we describe the five tasks at a generic level.

Measure. Before any repair can take place one has to determine what to repair, i.e., some kind of quality assessment has to take place. In our framework, the measure task computes an analysis of the current quality level with respect to the knowledge of the case-based reasoner, thus providing a measurement of the current quality level as an input to the monitor task.

Monitor. The outcomes of the measure task are fed into the monitor task for further evaluation. In interactive scenarios, the measurements can be visualized for discussion among the maintenance engineers and domain experts. In automated scenarios, measurements are analyzed and compared to past quality measurements as well as to specifications of the setup and initialization phases. The main goal of the monitor task is to decide *if* there is a decline in quality and if it is necessary to react to such a decline. If the respective maintenance engineer or program comes to the conclusion that maintenance is imminent, a notification must be issued.

Suggest. The suggest task compiles a list of alternative possible repair operations on the basis of the measurements, taken during execution of the measure task, and on the basis of the monitor task's outcomes. Each of the repair operations should be accompanied by its (estimated) execution costs.

Select. From the list of applicable repair operations, the select task chooses the appropriate ones. Therefore, the operations are ranked by, e.g., estimated execution costs or the number of side effects of each operation. In knowledge intensive scenarios, where actually changing the CBR system would be too costly, it may be even appropriate to simulate the execution of different promising sets of proposed operations and then to check the quality level of the different generated CBR systems, in order to select the best set of repair operations. The main goal of the select task is to decide *what* to do.

Modify. Finally, the selected repair operations are executed in the modify task, thus updating the knowledge containers accordingly. The outcome of the operations should be checked again by returning to the measure task. An inner maintenance loop of review and restore could be used to increase the level of quality until a desired threshold is reached.

4 Maintenance Manuals

The maintenance manual MAMA is located at the specific level. At this level of description, the context for such a maintenance manual is fixed with respect to the type of CBR, type of CBR application, type of CBR tool, and affected knowledge containers. The user of such a manual is guided from setting up maintenance and initializing all necessary parameters up to performing appropriate activities in certain situations.

Each maintenance task within the maintenance manual is an atomic unit of description of our process model and consists of several components: *inputs*, *activities*, *methods*, *resources*, and *outputs* [16].

The *inputs* describe whatever is necessary before the respective task can be carried out, e.g., outputs from a previously executed task or required data in form of reports, evaluations, or management decisions. A series of *activities* describes how the task could be accomplished using the task's *methods*. Such methods need not only be technical ones but could also be managerial or organizational techniques. Another component states which *resources* are required to perform the task. We distinguish between two types of resources, namely human resources and (software) tools. Finally, the *outputs* element of a task specifies the expected results of carrying out this task.

The maintenance manual addresses the maintenance engineer and the CBR system administrator, not the CBR system user [17]. The manual users are mostly interested in *when* to maintain the respective CBR system and in *what* to do. Event-Condition-Action (ECA) rules [14] are used to structure the maintenance manual. Events from organizational processes (e.g., timer-based events) trigger the review step which, in turn, activates restore operations. An example maintenance manual for EMPOLIS ORENGE used in case-based decision support can be found in [17].

5 Maintenance Methods

Now, we turn to the next lower level of abstraction in the hierarchy of concepts and techniques for case base maintenance. This section on maintenance methods describes specific techniques to carry out the various activities defined in MAMA, and to work on the tasks specified within the SIAM methodology, respectively.

5.1 Performance Measures

First, we describe concrete performance measures that implement quality measures for case base maintenance and correspond to typical customer requirements that use a CBR system in practice [7, 6]. Since customer requirements vary for different types of applications, we restrict our view on customer requirements in classification domains.

Coverage. The first customer requirement denotes that customers want an answer to their problems. The corresponding performance measure is coverage P_V. We assume, a case base *covers* a customer's query if there exists a case within the case base that is at least as similar to the query as a pre-defined similarity threshold τ. The overall *coverage* of a case base in relation to a set of queries is the total number of covered queries divided by the total number of queries in the query set.

Positive Coverage. An extension of coverage is positive coverage P_V^+, which additionally considers the correctness of the retrieved answer. A case base *correctly covers* a query if there exists a case within the case base that covers the query and the solution of this case solves the problem of this query. The overall *positive coverage* of a case base in relation to a set of queries is the total number of correctly covered queries divided by the total number of queries in the query set.

Accuracy. The third performance measure, accuracy P_A^+, also considers correctness of answers to customer's queries. But rather than requiring a minimum similarity τ as positive coverage, accuracy takes into account the correctness of the actual solution of the retrieved most similar case given a query. We say, a case within the case base *classifies* a query, if the problem description of this case is most similar to the query. Similarly, a case *correctly classifies* a query, if the case classifies the query and the solution of the case actually solves the query. The *accuracy* of a case base in relation to a set of queries is the number of correctly classified queries divided by the total number of queries in the query set.

Confidence. The next performance measure is *confidence* P_C, which is the average similarity of all classified queries by a case base in relation to a set of queries. Confidence is a measure that corresponds to the customer requirement that expects for each received solution to a query a high probability of correctness.

Positive Confidence. As for coverage and positive coverage, we also extend confidence to positive confidence P_C^+, which is the average similarity of all correctly classified queries by a case base in relation to a set of queries.

Storage Space. Finally, the last performance measure takes into account that retrieval speed is related to costs and hence, customers want quick answers to their problems. In turn, retrieval time is related to storage space. Hence, we define the performance measure for *storage space* P_T, which is the total number of cases in the case base.

Although the performance measures reflect the customer requirements well, there are two fundamental drawbacks. First, the performance measures provide no information how to maintain a CBR system. Thus, we cannot infer the maintenance operations necessary to restore the quality of a CBR system from values of performance measures. Second, we must apply a CBR system before we can compute the performance measures. For both reasons, we have to find a way to measure some criteria that reflect these performance measures and that are computable before really using the system in practice. In addition, such criteria should provide hints for specific maintenance operations to restore a CBR system if desired.

5.2 Case Properties

We define the respective criteria to overcome the previously mentioned drawbacks with the use of case properties, which indicate conflicts between cases before the CBR system is in real use. Later on in the next subsection, we also define modify operators to eliminate the indicated conflicts. Hence, the case properties and their relation to the modify operators allow direct clues for concrete maintenance operations.

In this paper, we shortly recapitulate four basic case properties (see also [13] and [6] for formal definitions):

Consistent. A case $c = (p,s)$ with problem description p and solution s is *consistent*, if there does not exist any other case $c' = (p',s')$ for which the problem description p' is the same or more general as p and the solution s' is different to s.

Unique. A case $c = (p,s)$ with problem description p and solution s is *unique*, if there does not exist any other case $c' = (p',s')$ for which the problem description p' is the same as p and the solution s' is the same as s.

Minimal. A case $c = (p,s)$ with problem description p and solution s is *minimal*, if there does not exist any other case $c' = (p',s')$ for which the problem description p' is the same or more general as p and the solution s' is the same as s.

Incoherent$_\Delta$. A case $c = (p,s)$ with problem description p and solution s is *incoherent$_\Delta$*, if there does not exist any other case $c' = (p',s')$ for which the attribute values of problem description p' overlap with the attribute values of problem description p except for a small specific number (Δ) of attribute values and the solution s' is the same as s.

5.3 Modify Operators

As mentioned previously, modify operators allow to restore the quality of the case base. Here, we shortly describe five modify operators that work on single cases and two modify operators that work on two cases. Again, we refer to [13] and [6] for complete formal definitions:

The *Remove Case* modify operator deletes a specific case from the case base C.
The *Specialize Case* modify operator adds an attribute value to a specific case.
The *Generalize Case* modify operator deletes an attribute value of a specific case.
The *Adjust Case* modify operator changes an attribute value of a specific case.
The *Alter Case* modify operator deletes an attribute value of a specific case and subsequently adds a different attribute and its value to this case.
The *Cross Cases* modify operator reduces two cases into one case by building the intersection of the two problem components. The two cases must be either not incoherent$_\Delta$ or the one case is not minimal in comparison to the other case.
The *Join Cases* modify operator reduces two cases into one case by building the union of the two problem components. The two cases must be either not incoherent$_\Delta$ in a way that the differences do not share an attribute or the one case is not minimal in comparison to the other case.

6 Maintenance Programs

At the most specific level of maintenance, we have concrete programs that enable the maintenance personnel to accomplish the activities described in the maintenance manual MAMA, or to perform the maintenance tasks defined in the methodology SIAM.

By now, several programs for maintenance of CBR systems have been proposed. For example, Smyth and McKenna [19] developed a tool for competence-guided authoring and visualization of cases. Another system helps to maintain the case base through continuous support for case authoring and design consistency in the domain of aerospace design [22]. McSherry [12] described CaseMaker-2, which also supports authoring of cases by indicating uncovered spaces in the case base that show potentials for adding new cases interactively by the maintenance personnel. Other work on maintenance programs includes the maintenance management system Dr. orenge [11] that implements the review step of the SIAM methodology and supports different types of measures such as case properties that are monitored for interactive maintenance as well as the BASTIAN (case BAsed SysTem In clAssificatioN) platform, which implements an additional component for automatic maintenance using rough sets [18].

6.1 MASH – The Maintenance Shell

In this paper, we focus on a more detailed description and evaluation of the maintenance shell MASH, which is a complete implementation of the maintenance phase of SIAM at the instance level. MASH implements the review and restore steps and their corresponding tasks measure, monitor, suggest, select, and modify. MASH supports automatic as well as interactive execution of these tasks.

The complete maintenance shell realizes the tasks as components with an additional preceding component that reads a data stream and with a following component that implements a simple CBR algorithm for simulation purposes. The current implementation of MASH works on the case base, requires no domain knowledge, and focuses on classification domains with no adaptation. The different components of the implementation use the *factory*, *flyweight*, and *singleton* design patterns as described by Gamma et al. [4]. Thereby, we can easily extend the actual implementation. For example, the factory pattern allows exchanging different component objects without changing the underlying code structure.

6.2 Evaluation of MASH

To exemplify that maintenance applications like MASH actually work in practice, we present the results of an evaluation. The first purpose of this evaluation is to show effects on the performance measures when modify operators are applied in a 10-fold cross validation to a case base with the help of the case properties. The second purpose is to show the robustness of the case properties and modify operators in comparison to the corresponding unchanged case base when the size of the case base varies, but the test case base remains the same.

Experimental Design. The evaluation uses the crx case base for credit approval from the UCI machine learning repository [3]. This case base has 690 cases that consist of 15 attributes (9 nominal and 6 numeric) with missing values and two classes. We performed a 10-fold cross validation with a simple 1-nearest-neighbor algorithm with 5%, 10%, 15%, ..., 100% of the original training set as varying training case bases. The used case properties consistency, minimality, uniqueness, incoherence$_1$, and incoherence$_2$ detected conflicts that we maintained with a modify operator to record the performance measures and to compare these values with the results of the performance measures for the corresponding unchanged case base.

Evaluation Results. Table 1 shows the results of the different modify operators and the performance measures in comparison to the corresponding unchanged case base when 100% of the original training set is used as the training case base.

The overall best results for the performance measures coverage P_V, positive coverage P_V^+, accuracy P_A^+, confidence P_C, and positive confidence P_C^+ shows the modify operator generalize case, followed by specialize case. In contrast, the overall poorest results for these performance measures shows the remove case modify operator. For the performance measure storage space P_T, the remove case modify operator shows the best result.

Table 2 displays in a qualitative way the results for the performance measures over different training case base sizes. This robustness tells us something about the effects on

Table 1. Results on the whole crx case base for the performance measures and the modify operators using the case properties consistency, minimality, uniqueness, incoherence$_1$, and incoherence$_2$.

	P_V	P_V^+	P_A^+	P_C	P_C^+	P_T
None	95.07	92.46	89.13	86.82	77.18	621.0
Adjust Case	94.64	91.74	88.84	86.68	76.88	621.0
Alter Case	95.07	92.46	89.42	86.80	77.44	621.0
Cross Cases	95.94	93.77	87.68	87.35	76.34	605.8
Remove Case	93.62	90.14	88.12	85.09	74.77	409.9
Generalize Case	95.51	93.62	90.58	87.44	79.00	621.0
Join Cases	95.07	92.32	88.99	86.81	77.05	620.2
Specialize Case	95.07	92.46	89.57	86.78	77.57	621.0

Table 2. Qualitative results on $\{5\%, 10\%, 15\%, \ldots, 100\%\}$ of the crx case base for the subtracted performance measures and the modify operators using the case properties consistency, minimality, uniqueness, incoherence$_1$, and incoherence$_2$.

the performance measures applying a modify operator on different sizes of training case bases. Each of the ticks represents the value of a performance measure in a modified case base minus the corresponding value of the unchanged case base. Every first tick is computed on 5% of the training case base, while the last tick is computed on 100% of the training case base. Hence, the values of the last ticks correspond to the values of table 1. For example, the coverage for the case base that is changed with the adjust case modify operator is 94.64% and the corresponding coverage for the unchanged case base is 95.07%. The difference is -0.43%, which is the amplitude of the last tick in the corresponding diagram of table 2.

For the performance measures coverage, positive coverage, accuracy, and confidence, the results of the modify operators cross cases, generalize case, and remove case are robust over the changing training case base size. For positive confidence, the results of the modify operators generalize case and remove case are robust over the changing training case base size. Finally, for storage space, the results of cross cases and remove cases are robust. These results for robustness help us to decide which modify operator we can use to improve the quality of the resulting case base. Hence, for maintenance of case bases like crx we advice to use the generalize modify operator.

7 Further Maintenance Research Issues

In this paper, we described various example research contributions to maintenance for CBR systems at different levels of abstraction. At the generic level, we briefly summarized the SIAM methodology and its maintenance task descriptions. At the specific level, we outlined the maintenance manual MAMA and exemplified maintenance methods based on case properties and modify operators. And finally, at the instance level, we introduced several maintenance programs, especially the maintenance shell MASH. The evaluation of MASH showed that our well-structured approach along all levels of abstraction yields satisfying results for maintenance in practice.

In this section, we put together conclusions from lessons learned in about five years maintenance research and some initial practical experience that we made in applying the methodology and techniques briefly presented in this paper. These conclusions result in several open issues and in suggestions for future research in case base maintenance and beyond. These topics can form the basis for further research in the area of maintenance for CBR systems.

7.1 Beyond Current Limitations

The first subsection of future work covers concrete aspects that aim to overcome specific limitations of the presented approaches.

More Experiments in Real Real-World Settings. We mostly tested our approaches in domains of the UCI machine learning repository. Furthermore, we used MASH within one industrial project on case-based help-desk support. Although results in this project were very promising, we encourage more experiments in more industrial settings to get more experience in "real" practical applications.

Meta Information. In several publications, we mentioned an additional case component, called the meta information q. For example, this meta information includes counters on usage patterns of cases. The basic idea for meta information q that we proposed within the framework of SIAM, MAMA, and MASH still needs more work to specifically define the concrete measures with use of this type of meta information and their applications for maintenance.

Alternative Quality and Performance Measures. In a similar vein, we proposed several quality and performance measures for case base maintenance. Again, we can think of alternative measures that take into account completely novel aspects such as the meta information q. Similarly, there is still potential for the development of more techniques to control the quality of a CBR system and to monitor when a CBR system needs maintenance. For example, time series prediction techniques may take series of quality measure's values and predict future values. Thereby, maintenance becomes possible in a preventive manner, even before the CBR system does not fulfill any quality criteria any longer.

Maintenance Advice. Another potential of improvement in case base maintenance is the definition of heuristics that suggest in which specific situations which concrete maintenance operators are best for applications. Initial work along such heuristics showed that proposals at the instance level often depend on the characteristics of the application domain and that it is hard to explicitly identify which characteristic is responsible for which effect. Consequently, we believe that more work is necessary here.

Case-Base Versioning. Another idea in the area of case base maintenance is the concept of keeping a trace of case base versions. One possibility of this kind of case base versioning is to keep copies of different states of the case base. An alternative way is to store only protocols of changes between different versions of the case base. In any case, versioning allows to trigger maintenance by reasoning on differences between complete case bases rather than only considering single cases or pairs of cases. Again, we believe that this aspect of diachronic approaches [9] possibly opens new opportunities for case base maintenance.

Beyond Function Preserving Maintenance. Finally, we conclude that most of the research on case base maintenance is only function preserving and does not yet deal with function enhancing maintenance.

7.2   Outside Case-Base Maintenance

This subsection on issues for future maintenance research emphasizes that current research mostly deals with maintenance of the case base, mainly neglecting the three other containers vocabulary, similarity measures, and adaptation knowledge.

Vocabulary Maintenance. Maintenance that takes into account the vocabulary container relates to representation issues in CBR. For example, vocabulary maintenance should detect missing attributes, redundant or unnecessary attributes, or potentials for generalizations of different attributes. Vocabulary maintenance must be able to perceive and handle problems with values of attributes' domains [5]. Changes of the vocabulary often result in the necessity for changes of all the other containers.

Similarity Measures Maintenance. Maintenance on similarity measures is most likely to analyze the retrieval behavior of a CBR system. Automatic learning of attribute weights is an example of such maintenance, and most existing research on maintenance related to similarity measures is within this area (e.g., [20]). A potential drawback of this type of maintenance is the sort of locality that changes of similarities possibly mean. If for some cases an adapted similarity measure sorts retrieval results in a more meaningful sense, for other cases the same adaptation might result in the contrary.

Adaptation Knowledge Maintenance. Maintenance on adaptation knowledge is the most difficult issue from our perspective. Although initial work towards maintenance of adaptation knowledge exists, this type of maintenance is probably highly application dependent as the usage of adaptation knowledge itself is. Hence, we expect that solutions for adaptation knowledge maintenance are not generally applicable, and that results in this area will only be at the specific or instance level of abstraction.

Relations Between Knowledge Container Maintenance. Another idea for future work is the analysis of relations between the different knowledge containers and maintenance operations on them. For example, if we maintain the case base, it is not explicitly necessary to change one of the other knowledge containers since there is no explicit relation between the case base and vocabulary, similarity measures, and adaptation knowledge. However, changing the case base might lead to a different retrieval behavior of a CBR system, and hence it also might then make sense to think about maintenance of the similarity measures container as well.

7.3 Towards New Maintenance-Related Areas

The third list of topics for future work is more on maintenance-related issues that generally deal with tasks that enable or improve maintenance but that do not directly contribute to specific maintenance solutions.

Environment Changes. As mentioned before, changes in the environment of an application outside the CBR system in use often result in the need for maintenance. However, it is an open question how to recognize changes of the environment and which type of changes are possible at all. Whereas the automatic detection of such changes is perhaps not possible, it is reasonable to think about strategies that guide maintenance for specific types of changes. ECA rules as mentioned in section 4 are possibly one potential mechanism to handle environmental changes.

Domain Knowledge. Up to now, maintenance research does not utilize domain knowledge, except for the knowledge represented in one of the knowledge containers of the CBR system. If we think of domain dependent rules, that describe relationships between attribute values across different attributes, for example, we can also imagine using these rules not only for query completion but also for maintenance operations.

Maintenance Explanations. For all changes that maintenance performs on a CBR system, there is a specific reason. Hence, it is helpful for the maintenance personnel, to understand why a maintenance program such as MASH proposes some maintenance operations for execution. Consequently, an explanation component of a maintenance system is a reasonable extension of current maintenance capabilities to increase acceptance of automatic and computer-assisted maintenance for CBR systems.

Maintenance Tutoring System. When a component for maintenance is available, it is possibly not straight-forward when and how to use it. A maintenance tutoring system, along with maintenance examples or e-learning modules, is consequently again a helpful extension for a maintenance system that aids maintenance personnel in their daily job. Such tutoring also leads to consistent maintenance behavior among the different maintenance engineers, and can be classified as supporting maintenance.

Maintenance Support by Maintenance Programs. A similar idea proposes to utilize maintenance programs only to support maintenance personnel that performs maintenance manually. For example, if a maintenance engineer decides to remove a case since it is in conflict with another case, MASH possibly evaluates this specific change in advance and suggests an alternative operation that does not only resolve this conflict by removing this case but eliminates more conflicts by modifying a different case.

Manual vs. Automatic Maintenance. The last idea to use maintenance programs to support manual maintenance opens the discussion on the relation between human-centered and automatic maintenance. It is interesting to analyze the limitations of both approaches and to develop processes that enable best mutual benefits from both approaches. In this paper, MAMA is an example for the human-centered approach whereas MASH is an automatic instrument.

Meta Maintenance. Finally, while seeking the memories of maintenance research, we recalled the idea of meta maintenance (e.g., [9]). This meta maintenance means that it is also important to keep track of maintenance operations, of the resulting changing quality of the CBR system, and whether automatic maintenance operations are accepted by the maintenance personnel. These considerations lead to an analysis of the maintenance itself. If we detect that maintenance does not lead to high quality CBR over time or that maintenance operations suggested by the maintenance system are seldomly accepted by the personnel, it is necessary to maintain the maintenance program itself.

References

1. Agnar Aamodt and Enric Plaza. Case-based reasoning: Foundational issues, methodological variations, and system approaches. *AI Communications*, 7(1):39–59, 1994.
2. Ralph Bergmann, Sean Breen, Mehmet Göker, Michel Manago, and Stefan Wess. *Developing Industrial Case-Based Resoning Applications: The INRECA Methodology*. Lecture Notes in Artificial Intelligence, State-of-the-Art-Survey, LNAI 1612. Springer-Verlag, Berlin, 1999.
3. Catherine L. Blake and Christopher J. Merz. UCI repository of machine learning databases, 1998.
4. Erich Gamma, Richard Helm, Ralph Johnson, and John Vlissides. *Design Patterns: Elements of Reusable Object-Oriented Software*. Addison-Wesley, 1997.
5. Frank Heister and Wolfgang Wilke. An Architecture for Maintaining Case-Based Reasoning Systems. In Barry Smyth and Pádraigh Cunningham, editors, *Proceedings of the Fourth European Workshop on Case-Based Reasoning, EWCBR 98, Dublin, Ireland*, pages 221–232, Berlin, 1998. Springer-Verlag.
6. Ioannis Iglezakis. *Case-Base Maintenance of Case-Based Reasoning Systems in Classification Domains: Methods, Implementation, and Evaluation*. submitted PhD thesis, University of Würzburg, 2004.
7. Ioannis Iglezakis and Thomas Reinartz. Relations between customer requirements, performance measures, and general case properties for case base maintenance. In Susan Craw and Alun Preece, editors, *Proceedings of the 6th European Conference on Case-Based Reasoning (ECCBR)*, pages 159–173. Springer-Verlag, 2002.
8. Janet Kolodner. *Case-Based Reasoning*. Morgan Kaufmann Publishers, Inc., 1993.

9. David B. Leake and David C. Wilson. Categorizing Case-Base Maintenance: Dimensions and Directions. In *Proceedings of the 4th European Workshop on Case-Based Reasoning, EWCBR98*, pages 196–207, Berlin, 1998. Springer-Verlag.
10. Franz Lehner. Ergebnisse einer Untersuchung zur Wartung von wissensbasierten Systemen. *Information Management*, 2:38–47, 1994.
11. Rainer Maximini. Basesystem for maintenance of a case-based reasoning system. Diploma thesis, University of Kaiserslautern, 2001.
12. David McSherry. Intelligent case-authoring support in casemaker-2. *Computational Intelligence: special issue on maintaining CBR systems*, 17(2):331–345, 2001.
13. Thomas Reinartz, Ioannis Iglezakis, and Thomas Roth-Berghofer. Review and restore for case base maintenance. *Computational Intelligence: Special Issue on Maintaining Case-Based Reasoning Systems*, 17(2):214–234, 2001.
14. Joachim Reinert and Norbert Ritter. Applying ECA-rules in DB-based design environments. In *Tagungsband CAD'98 "Tele-CAD – Produktentwicklung in Netzen"*, pages 188–201. Informatik Xpress 9, 1998.
15. C. Riesbeck and W. Bain. A methodology for implementing case-based reasoning systems. Technical report, Lockheed, 1987.
16. Thomas Roth-Berghofer and Thomas Reinartz. MaMa: A maintenance manual for case-based reasoning systems. In David W. Aha and Ian Watson, editors, *Proceedings of the Fourth International Conference on Case-Based Reasoning, ICCBR 2001, Vancouver, Canada*, pages 452–466, Berlin, 2001. Springer-Verlag.
17. Thomas R. Roth-Berghofer. *Knowledge Maintenance of Case-Based Reasoning Systems – The SIAM Methodology*, volume 262 of *Dissertationen zur Künstlichen Intelligenz*. Akademische Verlagsgesellschaft Aka GmbH / IOS Press, Berlin, Germany, 2003.
18. Maria Salamó, Elisabet Golobardes, David Vernet, and Mireya Nieto. Weighting methods for a case-based classifier system. In *Proceedings of the IEEE Learning'00*, 2000.
19. Barry Smyth and Elizabeth McKenna. Competence models and the maintenance problem. *Computational Intelligence: special issue on maintaining CBR systems*, 17(2):235–249, 2001.
20. Armin Stahl. *Learning of Knowledge-Intensive Similarity Measures in Case-Based Reasoning*. PhD thesis, University of Kaiserslautern, 2003.
21. E. Burton Swanson. The dimensions of maintenance. In *Proceedings of the 2nd International Conference on Software Engineering*, pages 492–497, 1976.
22. David C. Wilson. *Case-Base Maintenance: The Husbandry of Experience*. PhD thesis, Indiana University, 2001.

Textual Reuse for Email Response

Luc Lamontagne[1,2] and Guy Lapalme[2]

[1] Département d'informatique et génie logiciel,
Université Laval, Québec, QC, Canada
luc.lamontagne@ift.ulaval.ca
[2] Département d'informatique et recherche opérationnelle,
Université de Montréal, Montréal, QC, Canada
lapalme@iro.umontreal.ca

Abstract. The case-based reasoning approach to email response consists of reusing past messages to synthesize new responses to incoming requests. This task presents various challenges due to the nature of the messages: Textual descriptions, multiple topics, heterogeneous content, variable text length and varying recurrence of the statements. In this paper, we address the problem of determining which portions of past cases are reusable. Our scheme consists of identifying parts of a past message and declaring them variable, optional or reusable. This formulation of case reuse corresponds, from an application point of view, to the dynamic creation of a response template from antecedent messages. We describe and compare two strategies for selecting the messages portions to be reused: Case grouping and condensation models. Our results indicate that the case grouping strategy is a better choice. We also describe some of our experiments for identifying variable parts, based on named entity extraction techniques.

1 Introduction

Contrary to structural case-based reasoning (CBR) approaches that offer numerous strategies for adapting structured cases, the reuse of textual solutions remains mainly an unexplored research topic in CBR. This situation can be explained by the nature of the work in textual CBR mostly dedicated to retrieval tasks [1], [2], and to its applications to tasks such as legal jurisprudence [3], [4], a domain that does not require the modification of solutions descriptions.

Nonetheless, many tasks requiring that new descriptions be written could benefit from a capacity to adapt the textual solutions content. An example of such a task is the response to email exchanges. Many organizations face the problem of managing the response to a large volume of incoming requests. Tools to support the writing of recurrent responses offer many advantages and could be easily integrated into current email client software. A response is defined as a sequence of statements satisfying the content of a given request. To be reused in a different context, a response requires some personalization and the adjustment of specific information.

In this paper, we study and evaluate an approach to reuse past solutions when the content is textual. The reuse process consists of two parts: Determining the portions from past responses that could be reused and identifying how to adapt these portions. Most of the reuse approaches in structural CBR consist of modifying the feature values of well-structured solutions. Furthermore, these features are determined in advance. In a textual setting such as email response, this scheme is difficult to implement because the solutions are unstructured and because the portions of the response to be modified cannot be determined a priori since they will differ depending on the new incoming request. Hence, a first step is to determine the basic units of text to process, their pertinence and their specificity.

In our application, the cases consisting of requests (problems) and responses (solutions) messages are short separate textual descriptions. Email messages present some particular characteristics that make them difficult to reuse. First, they are usually heterogeneous and contain multiple topics. Their writing and grammatical style can present some weaknesses, which makes syntactic approaches difficult to use. Contrary to texts written for official usage (e.g. news reports, legal documents), their content does not present any specific structure or rhetorical forms.

This paper is organized as follows: In section 2, we give a brief overview of our CBR approach to email response. We describe in section 3 the reuse approach methodology that we have developed. In sections 4 and 5 we present two strategies based on case grouping and case condensation. Section 6 contains some experimental results indicating that the case grouping strategy is superior to the condensation strategy. We propose some ideas for future work in section 7 and conclude in section 8.

2 Overview of the LUG Approach to Email Response

Our work was conducted as part of a project to study the applicability of natural language processing techniques to email response [5]. Various potential approaches were identified from current commercial systems and from the current NLP literature:

- *Static text*: Systems, such as autoresponders, send pre-written messages to respond to new requests. The system associates these messages to the presence of an email address in the header or keywords in the body of a message. Each message received by the response system can trigger rules to select and send predefined and completely specified responses. This approach offers little flexibility and requires that most situations be anticipated in advance.
- *Structured requests*: Another approach is the mandatory use of forms accessible from a web server in order to constrain the content of the requests. The different sections of the form bring the user to better describe the purpose of his/her request. The requests generated by these web sites consist of a mixture of keywords, attribute-value pairs and some predefined textual formulations. This structuring facilitates the processing of the requests but does not propose a way to formulate new responses.
- *Response templates:* Templates are patterns made available to the writer to help in the formulation of a new response. A template is a form that dictates the structure of the response message. Some systems only insert a header to new messages. Others propose pre-specified responses with sections that can be modified or removed by the user. While they are inexpensive and rapid to deploy, these systems present some limitations since the number of possible situations must be determined in advance. Templates must be written for each of these situations which might not be feasible for evolving and complex domains. They require therefore constant human intervention for the creation or modification of the patterns.

- *Free-text generation*: One may consider using text generation approaches combined with techniques for the understanding of incoming requests. Unfortunately, such systems would be far too complex since they must rely on the linguistic generation of the messages and make use of NLP techniques to manage communicational, semantic, syntactic and lexical aspects. Considerable effort would be required for the construction of grammars. At the present time, few resources are available to implement such systems and the efficiency of these approaches would depend on a good understanding of the incoming requests, another difficult problem to tackle.

Our CBR approach to email response consists mainly of two steps [6]:

- A past case is selected from the case base as a basis to build a new response (i.e. the retrieval phase). The case base contains {request, response} pairs corresponding to the problems and solutions of our application.
- Modifications to the solution part of the case (the response) are proposed as a function of the new incoming request, to help adjust the content (the reuse phase).

In order to support the retrieval phase, we exploit word associations between the requests and their responses. This scheme takes advantage of the homogeneity of responses and helps improve the precision of the system. We refer the reader to [7] for additional details on the use of word co-occurrences and translation models to implement this approach.

After selecting a case, our CBR module proposes to the user a response description annotated as follows:

- some regions indicate the portions of text deemed optional that could be pruned by the writer.
- some regions indicate that some specific information may be modified by the user to take into account the context of the new request.

An example of how a response is annotated is presented in Figure 1. The final decision regarding the modification or the withdrawal of the textual passages is the writer's responsibility. Hence, the purpose of this scheme is not to automatically reshape a structured text but rather to guide the user in identifying the portions that should be modified. From a CBR point of view, the system is responsible for the reuse phase and leaves the case revision up to the user.

By producing a text containing reuse annotations, we borrow from the approaches based on response templates. However, our approach has the following important features that make it more attractive. The positions of the gaps to be filled out, i.e., the response annotations, are chosen dynamically and depend on the reuse potential of the text with respect to the request. Hence, each new response created by the writer can become a new template to be reused for the processing of subsequent requests. This means that the patterns do not have to be created manually. Furthermore, their integration in the case base increases the number of future situations that can be addressed while avoiding substantial modifications of the system.

The insertion of « *optional* » and ?*variable* annotations corresponds to a text generalization. As illustrated in part (a) of Fig. 2, a light generalization will present a smaller subset of the passages to be modified, hence making the selection of the passages clearer to the writer. On the other hand, a generalization of the courtesy sentences makes it more difficult to select the reusable portions of the text (Fig 2(b)).

This example illustrates the need to avoid aggressive strategies for annotating the text passages.

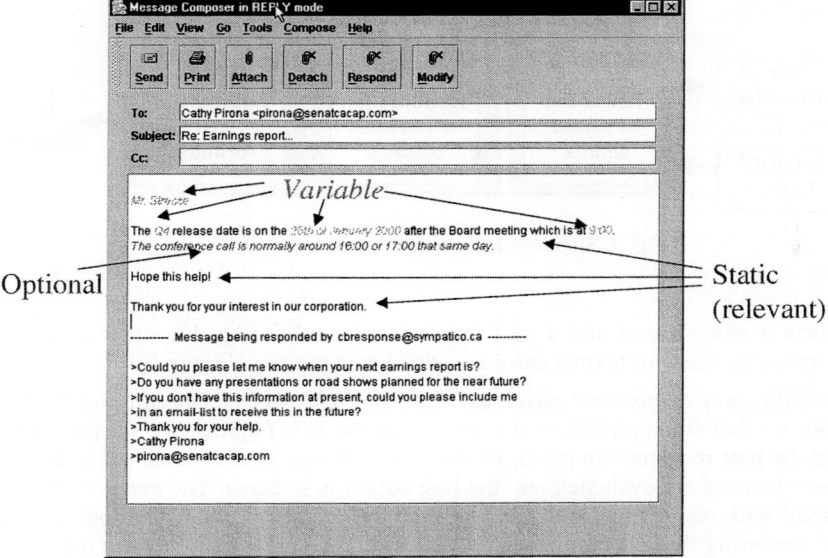

Fig. 1. Recommendations on the reuse of a past response

Dear *?PERSON_NAME*
« *The year ended on ?DATE* »
The release date for the next earnings report is on *?DATE*.
Please, do not hesitate to contact us for any other questions.
Sincerely...
(a)

« Dear *?PERSON_NAME* »
« *The year ended on ?DATE* »
The release date for the next earnings report is on *?DATE*.
« *Please, do not hesitate to contact us for any other questions.* »
« *Sincerely...* »
(b)

Fig. 2. Generalization of a past response: (a) generalization of some passages, and (b) generalization of courtesy sentences

3 The Reuse Scheme

The sequence of statements in a solution (a response) is meant to satisfy the sequence of statements of a problem (a request). When the context of the problem is modified, some of the statements become irrelevant while some others become erroneous. While a complete restructuring of the solutions can not be considered with current NLP techniques, some approaches can help to:

- Preserve the relevance of cases with respect to the context of a new problem;
- Ensure that the descriptions are adequately specified.

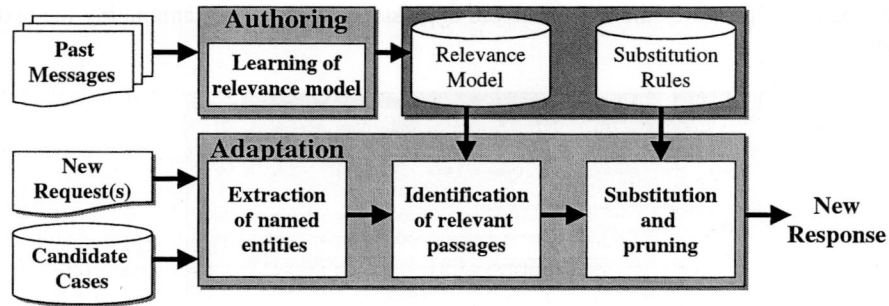

Fig. 3. Steps of the reuse process of textual solutions

Given a new request and a past response selected during the retrieval phase, we implement the reuse of textual cases as a three step process (Figure 3):

1. *Identification of optional passages:* This step consists of determining the textual portions that are applicable to the context of the new request. We start by segmenting the past responses in passages, more specifically in individual sentences. Then, the sentences are evaluated and the best subset is selected. The pertinence is established with respect to the content of the new request. This evaluation is the basis for rendering the relevant passages static (i.e. recommending them to the user) and making the rest of the solution description optional (i.e. inviting the user to review these passages). The description of this approach is presented in Section 4 of this paper.
2. *Modification of the specific content:* Among the relevant sentences, the next step is to identify which portions of text are subject to being modified. At this point of the reuse scheme, we identify the different portions that might present discrepancies with the context of the request. These portions usually refer to information such as individuals, locations, and addresses that will vary according to the context or temporal references. This information often takes the form of named entities and their pertinence is established as a function of the new request. The usage of information extraction techniques [8] for this step is presented in Section 5.
3. *Pruning and substitution:* The withdrawal of irrelevant portions and the substitution of portions to be specified are made in this step. Although mainly manual, we discuss some of these aspects in Sections 4 and 5.

The process presented above has many advantages. By reusing valid responses, no syntactic processing is required and we are able to control text uniformity, quality and fluency. By inheriting the content of past messages, we avoid the efforts devoted to content planning. By limiting the variable portions to factual information contained in named entities, we avoid surface generation problems (morphology, punctuation, genre, and agreement...). Although past responses usually contain few sentences (usually less than 10), it is still faster to find them automatically (a few milliseconds) than asking the user to select them manually and to cut and paste them in the new response message.

4 Identification of Optional Portions

The identification of optional portions makes it possible to reorganize the content of an antecedent response by presenting the superfluous parts. By declaring sentences to be optional (or static), we ensure that the response content will adequately cover the content of the new request.

Passage granularity in terms of individual terms, syntactic groups, sub-sequences of words, etc., will vary according to the application domain. In our application, the relevance of the statements in a solution relies on the sentence as the basic unit. This favours the coherence and the intelligibility of the subset resulting from the pruning process. We assume that a statement corresponds to a sentence and that this statement pertains to a single theme. Nevertheless, this choice is not a critical issue for the application of the techniques we propose.

In order to find the sentences of the response that best cover the new request, we execute the three following tasks:

- Segmentation: We break the past responses into individual sentences. The software we used in our experimentation (*lmtag*) provides a tagging of the beginning of the sentences and paragraphs;
- Evaluation of relevance: We estimate the relevance of each individual sentence with respect to the content of the request;
- Selection: We choose the sentences that seem the most promising and present them to the user as static (i.e. no highlighting). The others are presented as optional (highlighted using various colors).

To identify the static/optional sentences, we must first establish a correspondence between the statements found in the solutions and problems. Relationships between words can contribute to establish some correspondence between a request and a response. However, relationships are weak or absent from *accessory* sentences such as greetings, courtesy forms and general information. While these sentences are not essential, they play an important role in the narrative form of the solution and they should ideally be preserved when the do not contradict the context of the request.

We study and compare two strategies for the evaluation and selection phases:

- We evaluate each sentence individually and we select those that obtain a satisfactory support from the content of the request. To evaluate a sentence coming from a past solution, we identify the cases that confirm or reject the correspondence between a target sentence and a request. The similarity between the various cases in the case base indicates whether the sentence should be selected or not. We present this approach in Section 4.1.
- The second strategy is to select a subset of the sentences that best covers the content of the request. This processing of the relevance at the sentences group level corresponds to a reduction of the text. This type of summary is frequently referred to as *query-biased* [9]. We present this strategy in Section 4.2.

Our goal is to preserve the sentences of the response that obtain a sufficient support from the request. To determine this support, the case base is used to model the knowledge necessary to apply both strategies. The base contains different examples that establish a correspondence between problem and solution descriptions.

4.1 Case Grouping Strategy

Our first strategy is to determine whether each individual sentence should be kept in the solution proposed to the user. For each sentence $sent_j$ of an antecedent solution we are reusing, we identify from the case base of the CBR module the cases $Cases_{support}$ that comprise one or more statements similar to $sent_j$ and the cases $Cases_{reject}$ which do not contain it. This corresponds to determining, given a new problem P (a request) and some pairs <*problem, solution*> from the case base, whether the solution recommended to the user should contain the target sentence $sent_j$ (Figure 4).

```
Case_Grouping_Select(sent_j, P, CB)
       cases_support := Supporting_Cases(sent_j, CB)
       cases_reject := CB - cases_support
       R ← Similarity( Centroid(cases_support), P ) >
          Similarity( Centroid(cases_reject), P )
       return R

Supporting_Cases(sent_j, CB)
       R := {}
       for each case c of CB
              s := solution(c);
              if Contains(sol, sent_j)
                     R := R + problem(c);
       return R

where Contains is implemented as an Overlap metric, Similarity
is a cosine function, and Centroid as a weighted sum of term
vectors.
```

Fig. 4. Recommendation algorithm for including a sentence in the reused solution using a case grouping strategy

As illustrated in Figure 5, we partition our case base into two groups used to determine the content of the problems supporting the usage of a specific sentence in the response. We then create a distribution of the requests that characterizes the sets $Cases_{support}$ and $Cases_{reject}$. By interpolating between these distributions and the new request, we determine the membership of the target sentence to the solution.

The membership of a target sentence to a solution (i.e., the predicate *Contains*) is estimated according to the similarity between the target sentence and each of the sentences of a solution. In our work, we evaluate the similarity between sentences of solutions by an *Overlap* metric, i.e.

$$Contains_{Overlap}(sent_{target}, solution) = \max_{sent_i \in solution} \left(\frac{|sent_{target} \cap sent_i|}{\min(|sent_{target}|, |sent_i|)} \right)$$

This metric estimates the proportion of words that the sentences have in common. A statistical similarity metric gives good results for our domain solutions since these are highly homogeneous. We have observed in our corpus that the users tend to cut and paste portions of past responses, resulting in few variations among similar statements. Other metrics based either on domain or linguistic resources could be useful for messages from application domains presenting less uniformity in the statements.

All the cases with a value $Contains_{Overlap}$ superior to a given threshold are associated to the set $Cases_{support}$ while others are associated to the group $Cases_{reject}$. Some experiments helped in choosing empirically a threshold value for the similarity between sentences. Since they do not depend on the content of the new request, these sets can be authored during the construction of the CBR module.

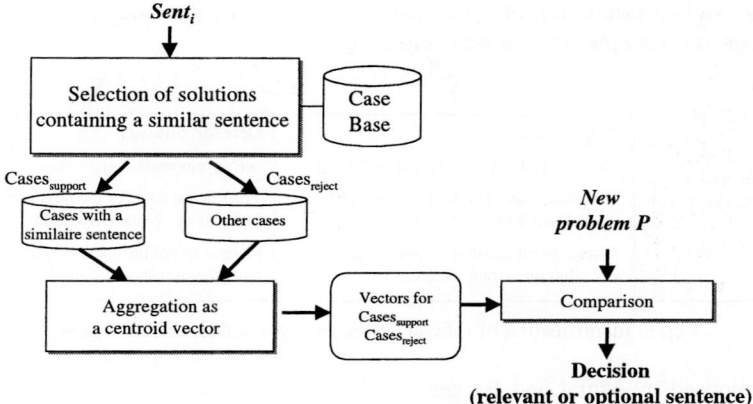

Fig. 5. Partitioning of the case base and similarity of a new problem with the partitions

The two groups obtained by the partitioning of the case base characterize the problems that favour or reject the usage of a sentence similar to $sent_{target}$. By estimating the proximity of the new problem P with the cases of the two groups, we can interpolate the correspondence between P and $sent_{target}$. To estimate their proximity, we represent each of the groups by a structure that merges the vectorial representations of the problem descriptions after the problems terms have been lemmatized and filtered according to the vocabulary of the CBR module. We compute the centroid of each group from the term frequency vectors of the requests. The similarity between the request P and the centroid of each group is determined by a cosine of the two vectors. We select the sentence (i.e. make it static) if the similarity of the request with $Cases_{support}$ is the greatest, i.e.

$$similarity(new\_request, Cases_{support}) > similarity(new\_request, Cases_{reject})$$

If this inequality is not verified or if the case base does not contain a solution with a similar statement, then the sentence is deemed optional.

4.2 Condensation Strategy

The second strategy that we study is not based on the evaluation of each individual sentence but on the global quality of a subset of sentences selected from a reused solution. The presence of irrelevant passages is mostly due to the occurrence of multiple themes in the requests and solutions. The identification of these passages corresponds to the production of a subset of antecedent responses that covers most of the context of the new request. In natural language processing, this is often referred to as a *query-biased* or *user-centered* summarization process. More specifically, it corresponds to the production of a condensed text based on the terms of the request. In this variation, a request indicates the focus of the user (what is being looked for) and the portions of text that are found in the summary should be in agreement with the statements of the request.

As illustrated in Figure 6, the resulting solution S_c can be produced by the deletion, from the original solution S, of sentences (or text portions like noun phrases) that can be associated (or *aligned*) to the new request Q.

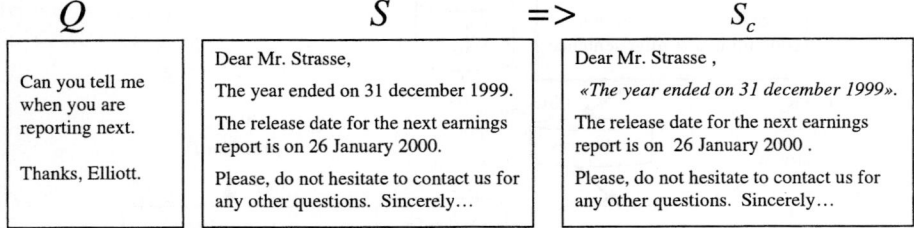

Fig. 6. Identification of relevant passages by a condensation process

As proposed by Mittal and Berger [9], this matching process tries to determine a subset S_c that covers most of the request Q. In terms of probability, we are trying to find a condensed response S' that maximize the following probability estimate:

$$S_c = f(Q,S) = \arg\max_{S'} P(S'|S,Q)$$

Using Bayes rule, this expression can be approximated as follows:

$$\begin{aligned} S_c &= \arg\max_{S'} P(S'|S,Q) \\ &= \arg\max_{S'} P(Q|S',S)P(S'|S) \\ &\sim \arg\max_{S'} P(Q|S')P(S'|S) \end{aligned}$$

Hence, this formulation suggests that the text being recommended to the user (i.e. the static text) is a compromise between the integrity of the past response and a subset of the response that best fits the new request.

The expression $P(S'|S)$ can be modeled as a random withdrawal of terms from the original request Q. Some probability distributions (for instance multinomial or hypergeometric) allow the evaluation of the resulting condensate. In our work, we model the distribution $P(S'|S)$ by a multinomial distribution.

$$P(S'|S) = \frac{\prod_{i \in S} tf_i! \times \left(tf_i/N\right)^{c(i \in S')}}{N!}$$

where tf_i is the frequency of the term i in response, c is the number of occurrences of term i in the condensate S', and N is the number of terms in the response. Since the responses are relatively short and since most of the terms appear only once in each description, we can approximate this distribution by:

$$P(S'|S) = \frac{1}{|S|! \times |S|^{|S'|}}$$

Therefore a severe reduction will diminish the fidelity of the recommended solution. This indirectly quantifies the textual support provided to the user.

The expression $P(Q|S')$ corresponds to the probability that a new request Q is at the origin of a response S'. We modeled this distribution as an IBM1 model [10] obtained during our work on the retrieval phase. We exploit the case base of the CBR module to learn the distribution of the model. Some parameters of the model are obtained during the training. To assign a probability to missing values (or values deemed insignificant by the learning process), we smooth the distribution using a backoff formulation, i.e.

$$p(q_i | s_j) = \begin{cases} t(q_i | s_j) & \text{the value of the transfer probability} \\ \alpha p_{CB}(q_i) & \text{otherwise} \end{cases}$$

where t is the transfer model obtained during the training and p_{CB} is the distribution of terms in the case base (i.e. in our corpus of email messages).

5 Identification of the Variable Portions

For our application, we have observed that most modifications necessary to reuse antecedent messages rely on specific information like phone numbers, company names, dates, and so on. These information items refer to named entities and can be obtained using information extraction techniques. Hence, an adequate extraction of these entities combined with a modeling of their role will capture most of the substitution information. This part of our application is domain dependent and was constructed manually based on an analysis of our corpus.

The three steps to process the variable portions are the extraction of named entities, the assignment of roles and the substitution decisions.

a) Named entity extraction: we have identified the following domain entities that offer a potential for reuse:

- Dates: Specific dates (e.g. *Jan/01, Tuesday May 12, tomorrow, coming year*), time periods (e.g. *last ten years, past 6 months, first quarter*) and temporal references (e.g. 16h00, 9:00AM, 2:00EST).
- Persons: Combinations of names, initials and titles (e.g. *Mr. P. J. Smith*).
- Organizations: Proper names not designating individuals. Many messages contain keywords such as *Capital, Corporation, Associates, Bank, Trust, Inc, Department,*
- Addresses: Some URLs, email addresses and civic numbers.
- Locations: Names & acronyms of countries, states, regions and cities (e.g. *Canada, Boston, Thames Valley, USA, UK, NY*).
- Quantities: *Currency*, real, integers, fractions, percentages.
- Phone numbers: Most of these are in North American format.

Most of these entities were obtained using Gate [11], an information extraction system with predefined rules for extracting named entities. We also used regular expressions to capture some information specific to our domain. We are therefore able to obtain solutions annotated according to the preceding categories.

b) Role assignment: The entity categories give an estimation of the portions with potential for substitution. However, their role in the application domain (in our case, investor relations) must first be defined prior to taking a decision on their reuse value. To define the role of an entity, we take into account its category, its type (e.g. a date of type *time*), the character strings it might contains, and the context defined by the words either preceding or following it. For instance, the role *"conference_time"* is defined as a date of type *time* preceded either by the words *conference* or *call*.

c) Entities substitution: The investor relations domain presents low predictability on how to recommend substitution values for the named entities. We considered three substitution cases:

- A role is never modified: Some roles are invariant for the domain (e.g. the name of the main corporation) and some others can not be determined based on the context of the problem (names of locations). Also, some roles occur only in the problem descriptions (e.g. names of newspapers, personal URLs, employers names).
- The value of a role can be extracted from the request: The substitution value can be obtained from entities present in the content of the problem. For instance, the name of the investor that submitted the request or the fiscal year pertaining to the discussion could follow this substitution pattern.
- The value of the role can be modified if declared in the CBR module: For these roles, a value can not be located or inferred from the context of the problem. This role remains invariant for a given period of time and a recommendation could be made if its value is declared in a lookup table or by some other persistent means. Most of the entities of our application domain are of this type (e.g. financial factors, dates, temporal references, names of documents, web site addresses...).

By restricting the selection of substitution values with respect to the role of the entities, the efficiency of our approach relies mostly on the capacity of the CBR module to extract the named entities and to assign an adequate role to them. We evaluate these two capacities in the following section.

6 Some Experimental Results

For this experimentation, we used a corpus pertaining to the Investor Relations domain (i.e. the assistance provided by enterprises to their individual and corporate investors). The messages cover a variety of topics such as requests for documents, financial results, stock market behaviour and corporate events. We worked with 102 messages after having removed the headers and signatures. The length of the textual body parts of these messages varies from a few to over 200 words with an average of 87 words. The courtesy and accessory sentences were kept in order to evaluate their influence on the reuse process.

a) Results for the selection of optional portions: Our first experimentation was to evaluate, with the two strategies proposed in Section 4, the pertinence of each response of our corpus with respect to their corresponding requests. We performed a leave-one-in evaluation (i.e. we left the target problem in the case base) and estimated the accuracy by the proportion of sentences declared relevant by the algorithm. We obtained an accuracy of 89% for the case grouping strategy and 77% for the condensation strategy. These results are superior to a random strategy (i.e. an average accuracy of 50%). Since the target cases were present in the case base, we assume that these results are upper bounds for system performance. At this point, we note a major difference between the two strategies. The condensation strategy tends to drop most of the accessory sentences while case grouping tends to preserve them. The condensation approach is hence more conservative.

To obtain a more representative estimation of the performance of the reuse module, we selected a sample of 50 pairs of <request, response> messages obtained through our retrieval module. For these pairs, we manually determined the subset of sentences that should be selected by the CBR system. This was made possible since we have responses provided by financial analysts for each of the requests. However, we found it difficult to determine whether accessory sentences (for instance, the courtesy sentences) should be included or not in the reused message. In order to take this into account, we produced two sets of results where these sentences are either required or not. The results are presented in Tables 1 and 2.

Table 1. Selection of relevant portions with accessory sentences

Strategy	Precision	Recall	Accuracy
Case grouping	84.1%	68.0%	70.8%
Condensation	78.4%	39.6%	50.2%

Table 2. Selection of relevant portions without accessory sentences

Strategy	Precision	Recall	Accuracy
Case grouping	77.7%	76.0%	71.8%
Condensation	78.5%	53.1%	62.2%

The case grouping strategy selects most of the sentences pertaining to the request. The results in both tables indicate that it preserves most of the accessory sentences. Some sentences are rejected because they are too widely spread in the case base which makes it difficult to decide whether their usage is appropriate.

The condensation approach presents a totally different behaviour. Many words contained in the sentences are infrequent and can not be associated with some other words of the requests. Moreover, almost all of the accessory sentences are rejected, since they have no statistical associations with request words. This explains why recall figures increase when accessory sentences are not taken into account (Table 2).

b) Results for the selection of the variable portions: We retained 130 sentences from our corpus of responses that contains over 250 named entities. We conducted the entity extraction and role assignment on these sentences. The results we obtained are presented in the Table 3.

We note that the extraction of most of the categories give good results (precision and recall columns of the table). For instance, the few errors for dates are references to financial quarters (e.g. *Q4, 4th quarter*). Also some company names like *Bell Canada* are annotated by Gate as a combination of a name and a location. Such errors can easily be removed by augmenting the lexicon and extraction patterns of the system.

We manually constructed a rule base for the subset of our original corpus and we assigned roles to the entities of the 130 sentences of our test corpus. The entities were initially assigned to their true category. The results indicate that the global accuracy of the role assignment is approximately 76.7%. We estimate that such a result is satisfying given the simplicity of the rules that we constructed. For some entities, it is sometimes difficult to establish their role based on a single sentence. Other times, coreference limits sentence interpretation. For instance, various meanings can be assigned to the temporal reference "It will be at 17:00". However, most of the errors were due to role descriptions that we had not anticipated while constructing our rule base.

Table 3. Results for the extraction of entities and the assignment of roles

Entity	Entity extraction		Role Assignment
	Precision	Recall	Accuracy
Date	91.7%	85.6%	82.9%
Time	100%	100%	61.1%
Location	71.4%	93.5%	66.6%
Person	100.0%	80.0%	81.8%
Quantity	92.2%	95.6%	68.7%
Organization[a]	97.2%	83.3%	94.4%
Phone number	95.4	90.9%	81.8%

[a] The term "BCE" account for more than half of the organization entities occuring in our test corpus. If we remove these, we obtain a precision of 95.5% and a recall of 68.3%.

7 Related Work

In order to position our work with respect to adaptation techniques used in structural CBR, we remark that our scheme offers both substitutional and transformational components for the reuse of antecedent solutions. Recommending which specific passages should be modified corresponds to parametric variations found in substitutional approaches. Moreover, the identification of optional passages leads to the pruning of some statements, which corresponds to a transformation of the response structure. Since our reuse scheme relies on a single message, our approach is not compositional nor do we consider a complete reformulation of the solutions as performed by generative approaches. Because the user of the response system supervises pruning and substitution of the passages, our approach addresses the problem of case reuse and leaves the revision of solutions to the user.

Some substitutional methods to acquire knowledge for the adaptation of structured cases were proposed [12], [13], [14]. Our approach differs from these methods since it is a transformational algorithm that learn term distributions and translations models instead of rules or cases. Furthermore, our adaptation process is driven by the solutions to be reused (i.e. the pertinence of their sentences and their named entities) while other approaches rely on a comparison of the features of problems descriptions.

8 Conclusion

In this paper, we presented a CBR approach to reuse antecedent responses to respond to new requests. We proposed two strategies to select relevant portions of antecedent messages. We observed that case condensation is a conservative selection strategy. We recommend using a case grouping strategy that offers better performance in terms of precision and recall. Case condensation could also be a useful alternative for applications built from a large case base. We also explored the use of techniques for named entity extraction in order to determine the variable parts of a response. The efficiency of this step relies mainly on the availability of tools to locate the entities. The results we obtained indicate that the identification of roles, once the entities are extracted, is rather simple to implement with rules based on regular expressions.

To our knowledge, our work represents a first attempt for textual case adaptation and it brings up numerous directions in which this research could be pursued. We believe that the idea of dynamically created templates is a metaphor sufficiently generic to be applied to other contexts than email response. It preserves the narrative form of the solutions and overcomes the limitations of the generative approaches that, in a textual setting, are difficult to achieve. We have chosen, for this work, to concentrate our efforts on the reuse of a single case. However, a compositional approach, which takes into account multiple cases, would offer a better covering of the various themes occurring in a request. The reuse of multiple cases could be based on voting schemes to select messages portions. Another issue related to the multi-case reuse is the identification of variable passages that could be conducted by comparing the statements of the solutions and lead to the selection of passages based on syntactic and/or semantic features. This would overcome the main limitations of our work where the roles of the domain entities are manually defined. Finally, the case grouping strategy could be extended so that the two case groups providing positive or negative support may be used to learn categorization rules.

References

1. Lamontagne L., Lapalme G., 2002. Raisonnement à base de cas textuels – état de l'art et perspectives, *Revue d'Intelligence Artificielle*, Hermes, Paris, vol. 16, no. 3, pp. 339-366.
2. Lenz M., 1998; Textual CBR, in Lenz M., Bartsch-Spörl B., Burkhard H.-D., Wess S. (Eds.), *Case-Based Reasoning Technology - From Foundations to Applications*, Lecture Notes in Artificial Intelligence 1400, Springer Verlag.
3. Weber R., Martins A., Barcia R, 1998. On legal texts and cases, *Textual Case-Based Reasoning: Papers from the AAAI-98 Workshop*, Rapport technique WS-98-12, AAAI Press, pp. 40-50.
4. Brüninghaus S., Ashley K. D., 1999. Bootstrapping Case Base Development with Annotated Case Summaries, *Proceedings of the Third International Conference on Case-Based Reasoning (ICCBR-99)*, Lecture Note in Computer Science 1650, Springer Verlag, pp. 59-73.
5. Lapalme G., Kosseim L., 2003. Mercure: Toward an automatic e-mail follow-up system, *IEEE Computational Intelligence Bulletin*, vol. 2, no. 1, p. 14-18.
6. Lamontagne, L.; Lapalme, G.; 2003 "Applying Case-Based Reasoning to Email Response", Proceedings of ICEIS-03, Angers, France, pp. 115-123.
7. Lamontagne L., Langlais, P., Lapalme, G., 2003, Using Statistical Models for the Retrieval of Fully-Textual Cases, in Russell. I, Haller, S. (Editors), Proceedings of FLAIRS-2003, AAAI Press, Ste-Augustine, Florida, pp.124-128.
8. Cowie, J., Lehnert, W., 1996. Information Extraction, Communications of the ACM, vol. 39 (1), pp. 80-91.
9. Mittal, V., Berger, A., 2000. Query-relevant summarization using FAQs,. In Proceedings of the 38th Annual Meeting of the Association for Computational Linguistics (ACL). Hong Kong.

10. Brown, P. F.; Della Pietra, S. A.; Della Pietra, V. J.; and Mercer, R. L. 1993. The mathematics of statistical machine translation: Parameter estimation, Computational Linguistics, vol. 19, no. 2, pp. 263-311.
11. Cunningham H., Maynard D., Bontcheva K., Tablan V., 2002. GATE: A Framework and Graphical Development Environment for Robust NLP Tools and Applications, *Proceedings of the 40th Anniversary Meeting of the Association for Computational Linguistics (ACL'02)*, pp. 168-175.
12. Hanney K., Keane M., 1997. The Adaption Knowledge Bottleneck: How to Ease it by Learning from Cases, *Proceedings of the Second International Conference on Case-Based Reasonining (ICCBR-97)*, Springer Verlag, pp. 359-370.
13. Jarmulak J., Craw S., Rowe R., 2001. Using Case-Base Data to Learn Adaptation Knowledge for Design, *Proceedings of the 17th International Joint Conference on Artificial Intelligence (IJCAI-01)*, Morgan Kaufmann, pp. 1011-1016.
14. Leake D. B., Kinley, A., and Wilson D., 1996. Acquiring Case Adaptation Knowledge: A Hybrid Approach, *Proceedings of the Thirteenth National Conference on Artificial Intelligence (AAAI-96)*, AAAI Press, Menlo Park, CA, pp. 684-689.

Case-Based, Decision-Theoretic, HTN Planning

Luís Macedo[1,2] and Amílcar Cardoso[2]

[1] Department of Informatics and Systems Engineering, Engineering Institute,
Coimbra Polytechnic Institute,
3030-199 Coimbra, Portugal
lmacedo@isec.pt
http://www2.isec.pt/~lmacedo
[2] Centre for Informatics and Systems of the University of Coimbra,
Department of Informatics, Polo II,
3030 Coimbra, Portugal
{lmacedo,amilcar}@dei.uc.pt

Abstract. This paper describes ProCHiP, a planner that combines CBR with the techniques of decision-theoretic planning and HTN planning in order to deal with uncertain, dynamic large-scale real-world domains. We explain how plans are represented, generated and executed. Unlike in regular HTN planning, ProCHiP can generate plans in domains where there is no complete domain theory by using cases instead of methods for task decomposition. ProCHiP generates a variant of a HTN - a kind of AND/OR tree of probabilistic conditional tasks - that expresses all the possible ways to decompose an initial task network. As in Decision-Theoretic planning, the expected utility of alternative plans is computed, although in ProCHiP this happens beforehand at the time of building the HTN. ProCHiP is used by agents inhabiting multi-agent environments. We present an experiment carried out to evaluate the role of the size of the case-base on the performance of the planner. We verified that the CPU time increases monotonically with the case-base size while effectiveness is improved only up to a certain case-base size.

1 Introduction

Hierarchical Task Network (HTN) planning [4] is a planning methology that is more expressive than STRIPS-style planning. Given a set of tasks that need to be performed (the planning problem), the planning process decomposes them into simpler subtasks until *primitive tasks* or actions that can be directly executed are reached. *Methods* provided by the domain theory indicate how tasks are decomposed into subtasks. However, for many real-world domains, sometimes it is hard to collect methods to completely model the generation of plans. For this reason an alternative approach that is based on cases of methods has been taken in combination with methods [14].

Real-world domains are usually dynamic and uncertain. In these domains actions may have several outcomes, some of which may be more valuable than others. Planning in these domains require special techniques for dealing with uncertainty. Actually, this has been one of the main concerns of planning research in recent years, and several decision-theoretic planning approaches have been proposed and used successfully, some based on the extension of classical planning and others on Markov-Decision Processes (see [3, 9] for a survey). In these decision-theoretic planning frameworks actions are usually probabilistic conditional actions, preferences over the outcomes of the actions is expressed in terms of an utility function, and plans are evaluated in terms of their Expected Utility (EU). The main goal is to find the plan or set of plans that maximizes an EU function [17], i.e., to find the optimal plan. However, this might be a computationally complex task.

In this paper we present ProCHiP (Probabilistic, Case-based, Hierarchical-task network Planning), a planner that combines CBR with the techniques of decision-theoretic planning and HTN planning in order to deal with uncertain, dynamic large-scale real-world domains. Unlike in regular HTN planning, we don't use methods for task decomposition, but instead cases of plans. ProCHiP generates a variant of a HTN - a kind of AND/OR tree of probabilistic conditional tasks - that expresses all the possible ways to decompose an initial task network. The EU of tasks and of the alternative plans is computed beforehand at the time of building the HTN. ProCHiP is implemented in artificial cognitive agents inhabiting multi-agent environments.

The next section describes the features of ProCHiP related with plan representation, generation and execution. Subsequently, we present an experiment in which we evaluate the influence of the case-base size on the performance of ProCHiP. Finally, we present related work, discuss our findings and present conclusions.

2 Case-Based, Decision-Theoretic, HTN Planning

2.1 Representation

Within our approach we may distinguish two main kinds of plans: concrete plans, i.e., cases of plans, and abstract plans (for more details about abstraction in CBR see for instance [2]). Concrete plans and abstract plans are interrelated since concrete plans are instances of abstract plans and these are built from concrete plans. Since the concept of abstract plan subsumes the concept of concrete plan, let us first describe the representation issues related with abstract plans and then present the main differences between concrete plans and abstract plans.

We represent abstract plans as a hierarchy of tasks (a variant of HTNs [4, 15]) (Fig. 1). Formally, an abstract plan is a tuple $AP = <T, L>$, where T is the set of tasks and L is the set of links. More precisely, we represent an abstract plan by a hierarchical graph-structured representation comprising tasks (represented by the nodes) and links (represented by the edges). We adopted the adjacency matrix approach to represent these graphs [11]. The links may be of hierarchical (abstraction or decomposition), temporal, utility-ranking or adaptation kind. This structure has the form of a planning tree [10], i.e., it is a kind of AND/OR tree that expresses all the possible ways to decompose an initial task network. Like in regular HTNs, this hierarchical structure of a plan comprises primitive tasks or actions (non-decomposable tasks) and non-primitive tasks (decomposable or compound tasks). Primitive tasks correspond to the leaves of the tree and are directly executed by the agent, while compound tasks denote desired changes that involve several subtasks to accomplish it (e.g., the leaf node *driveTruck* of Fig. 1 is a primitive task, while *inCityDel* is a compound task). The decomposition of a compound task into a sequence of subtasks is represented by linking the compound task to each subtask by a hierarchical link of type decomposition (denoted by *dcmp*). This corresponds to an AND structure. In addition, a hierarchical plan may also include special tasks in order to express situations when a decomposable task has at least two alternative decompositions. Thus, these special tasks are tasks whose subtasks are heads of those alternative decompositions. We called abstract tasks (e,g., the root task *transport* of Fig. 1) to those special decomposable tasks because they may be instantiated by one of their alternative subtasks. Thus, they are a kind of abstractions of their alternative instances. The subtasks of an abstract task may themselves be abstract tasks. The decomposition of abstract tasks into several alternative instances is expressed by linking the abstract task to each subtask by a hierarchical link of type abstract (denoted by *abst*). This corresponds to an OR structure.

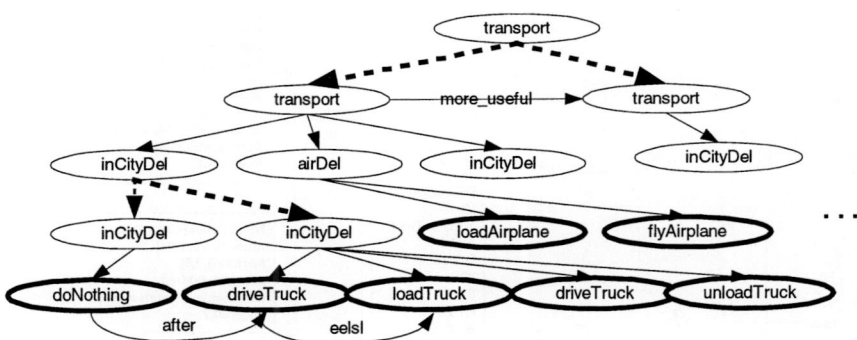

Fig. 1. Example of an abstract plan. Primitive tasks are represented by thick ellipses while non-primitive tasks are represented by thin ellipses. Dashed arrows represent *abst* links, while thin arrows represent *dcmp* links

As we said, in addition to hierarchical links that express AND or OR decomposition (*dcmp* and *abst*), there are also temporal, utility-ranking and adaptation links between tasks. Temporal links are just like in regular HTNs. We followed the temporal model introduced by [1]. Thus, links such as *after, before, during, overlap*, etc., may be found between tasks of an abstract plan. Utility-ranking links (denoted by *more_useful*) are used between subtasks of abstract tasks in order to express a relation of order with respect to their EU, i.e., the head tasks of the alternative decompositions of a given abstract task are ranked according to the EU of their decompositions. Adaptation links [8] are useful to generate an abstract plan from several cases of plans. They explain how tasks and their components are related in a plan and therefore they explain how to adapt portions of cases of plans when they are reused to construct an abstract plan. For instance, the link *eelsl* (*end location equal to start location*) means that the start location of the truck when *loadTruck* takes place is equal to the end location of the truck when *driveTruck* is executed.

A task T is both conditional and probabilistic (e.g., [3, 6, 24]). This means each primitive task has a set of conditions C=$\{c_1, c_2, ..., c_m\}$ and for each one of these mutually exclusive and exhaustive conditions, c_i, there is a set of alternative effects $\mathcal{E}^i = \{<p_1^i, E_1^i>, <p_2^i, E_2^i>, ..., <p_{n_i}^i, E_{n_i}^i>\}$, where E_j^i is the jth effect triggered with probability $p_j^i \in [0,1]$ by condition c_i (i.e., $P(E_j^i | c_i) = p_j^i$), and such that $\sum_{j=1}^{n_i} p_j^i = 1$. Fig. 2 presents the structure of a task. The probabilities of conditions are represented in that structure although we assume that conditions are independent of tasks. Thus, $P(c_i|T) = P(c_i)$. The main reason for this is to emphasize that the EU of a task, in addition to the probability of effects, depends on the probability of conditions too. In addition to conditions and effects, a task has other information components. Formally, a task (primitive or not) may be defined as follows.

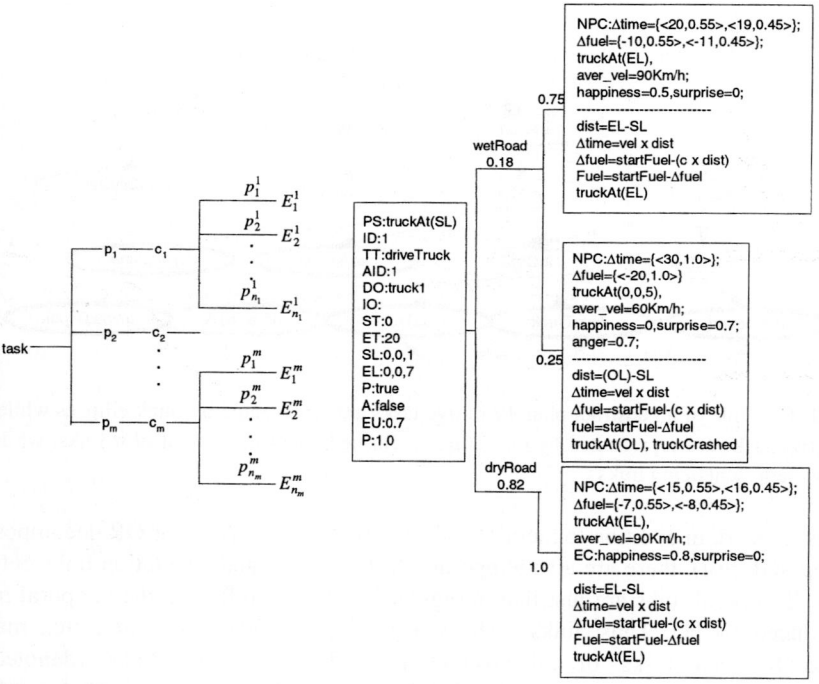

Fig. 2. Schematic representation of a task in an abstract plan: general form and example. Horizontal, dashed lines inside the boxes describing the effects separate non-procedural from procedural components

Definition 1. A *task* is a tuple <PS, ID, TT, AID, DO, IO, ST, ET, SL, EL, PR, A, EP, EU, P>, where: PS is the set of preconditions that should be satisfied so that the task can be executed; ID is the task's identifier, i.e., an integer that uniquely identifies the task in a plan; TT is the task category (e.g., *driveTruck*, *transport*); AID is the identifier of the agent that is responsible for the execution of the task[1]; *DO* is the direct object of the task, i.e., the identifier of the entity that was subjected to the task directly (e.g., for a task of type *driveTruck*, the direct object is the object - its identifier - to be driven; for a task of type *transport*, the direct object is the entity that is transported – for instance, a package); *IO* is the indirect object of the task, i.e., the answer to the question "To whom?" (e.g., for a task of type *give*, the indirect object is the entity that receives the entity (the direct object) that is given – for instance, the person who receives money); *ST* is the scheduled start time of the task; *ET* is the scheduled end time of the task, *SL* is the start location of the agent that is responsible for executing the task; *EL* is the end location of the agent that is responsible for the execution of the task; *PR* is a boolean value that is true when the task is primitive; *A* is a boolean value that is true when the task is abstract (for primitive tasks it is always false); *EP* is the set of alternative probabilistic conditional effects of the task, i.e., $EP = \{<c_i, e^i>: 1 =< i <= m\}$; *EU* is the EU of the task; *P* is the probability of the task (this is always 1.0 for every task except the heads of alternative decompositions of an abstract task as we'll explain below).

Although non-primitive tasks are not directly executed by an agent, they are represented like primitive tasks. Some of the components are meaningful only for primitive tasks. However, others such as the set of alternative probabilistic conditional effects are essential for the ranking of the alternative decompositions of the abstract tasks in terms of the EU. That is why the set of conditional probabilistic effects and other meaningful properties are propagated upward through the hierarchy from the primitive tasks to the non-primitive tasks (this propagation will be explained below).

Each effect (see Fig. 2) is composed of a few components of several kinds such as temporal, emotional (notice that in our work, agents are of cognitive kind with a module of emotions and other motivations included in their architecture [12]), etc. These components may be of two kinds: non-procedural and procedural. The non-procedural component refers to the data collected from previous occurrences of the effect (contains the duration of the task, the emotions and respective intensities felt by the agent, the fuel consumed, etc., in previous executions of the task as stored in cases of plans). The procedural component refers to the process through which the temporal, emotional and other kinds of data may be computed (contains descriptions or rules of how to compute the components).

Formally, an effect may be defined as follows.

Definition 2. An *effect* is a tuple <*ID, EC, EU, P, NPC, PC*>, where: *ID* is the identifier of the effect, i.e., an integer value that uniquely identifies the effect in the list of effects of the task; *EC* is the effect category to which it belongs (like tasks, effects are classified into categories); *EU* is the utility value (EU value for the case of tasks in abstract plans) of the effect; *P* is the probability value of the effect, i.e., the relative frequency of the effect (this gives us the number of times the effect occurred given that the task and the condition that triggers it occurred); *NPC* is the non-procedural component; *PC* is the procedural component.

---

[1] The planner is used by agents inhabiting multi-agent environments.

Cases of plans share most of the features of abstract plans because they are also represented hierarchically. The major differences are: unlike abstract plans, cases of plans don't have OR structures and consequently don't have abstract tasks; the primitive tasks have a probability of 1.0 (otherwise they won't belong to the case) and can only have a conditional effect since the conditions are mutually exclusive and exhaustive. Notice that, although a non-primitive task of a case of a plan may exhibit an effect, this is not relevant, since in the real world only the primitive tasks are executed. However, the way a non-primitive task was decomposed is of primary importance for the generation of abstract plans, as we will explain in the following section. Fig. 3 shows an example of two cases of plans, which are instances of the abstract plan presented in Fig. 1.

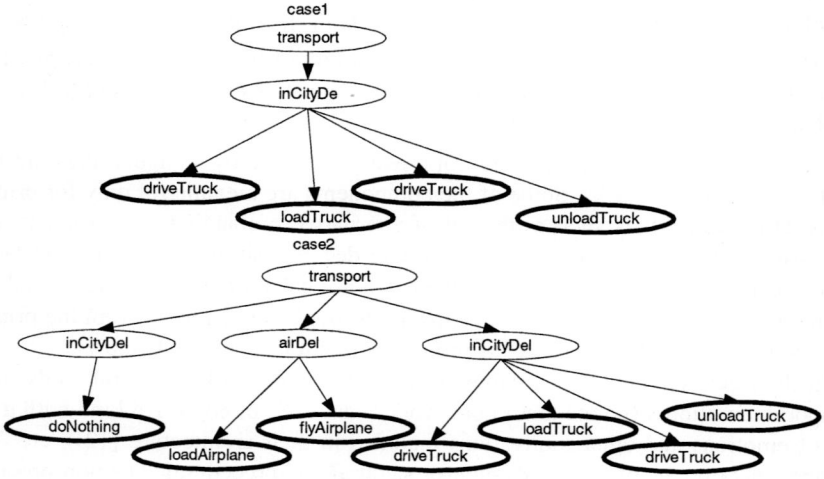

Fig. 3. Example of a case-base with two concrete plans (instances of the abstract plan of Fig. 1)

2.2 Plan Generation

Since the planner is used by an agent that is part of a multi-agent environment, in order to solve a planning problem, the agent should have in memory the information of the initial state of the environment. This comprises a three-dimensional metric map of the environment [21] in which inanimate and other animate agents are spatially represented. Fig. 4 presents an example of a metric map that represents an initial state of the world.

A problem is an initial and incomplete HTN, i.e., a set of goal tasks. Planning is a process by which that initial HTN is completed resulting in an abstract plan ready to be executed and incorporating alternative courses of action, i.e., it includes replanning procedures. Roughly speaking, this involves the following steps (the respective algorithms are presented in later figures): first, the structure of the abstract plan (HTN) is built based on cases of past plans (this is closely related to the regular HTN planning procedure); then the conditional effects, probabilities as well as the EU are computed for the primitive tasks of this abstract plan based on the primitive tasks of cases of past plans; finally, these properties (conditional effects and respective probabilities, and EU) are propagated upward in the HTN, from the primitive tasks to the main task of the HTN. Fig. 5 presents this algorithm.

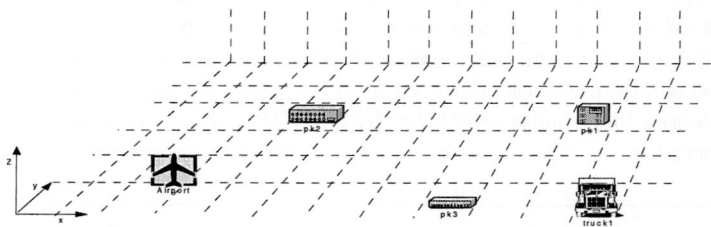

Fig. 4. Example of the metric map of an initial state of the environment in the logistics domain. It comprises: one truck (*truck1*) located at coordinates (11,0,0); three packages, *pk1*, *pk2* and *pk3*, located at, respectively, (10,3,0), (4,3,0), and (8,0,0); and one plane located at the airport with coordinates (2,1,0)

```
Algorithm CONSTRUCT-ABSTRACT-PLAN(abstPlan)
    abstPlan ← BUILD-STRUCTURE(abstPlan)
    primTasks ← GET-PRIMTASKS(abstPlan)
    primTasksAllPlanCases← GET-PRIMTASKS-ALL-PLAN-CASES()
    COMPUT-PRIMTASKS-PROPS(primTasks,primTasksAllPlanCases)
    abstPlan←PROPAGAT-PROPS-UPWARD(primTasks,abstPlan)
    return abstPlan
end
```

Fig. 5. Algorithm for the construction of an abstract plan

Much like regular HTN planning, building the structure of the abstract plan (algorithm of Fig. 7) is a process by which the initial HTN is completed by recursively decomposing its compound tasks. Unlike regular HTN planning, within our approach the domain theory (methods and operators in regular HTN planning) is confined to a finite set of actions/operators. Thus there are no explicit methods to describe how to decompose a task into a set of subtasks. Actually, methods are implicitly present in cases of past plans (see [14] for a similar approach). This is particularly useful in domains where there is no theory available. Therefore, the process of decomposing a task into subtasks is case-based and is performed as follows. Given a task, the possible alternative decompositions (task and its subtasks, as well as the links between them) are retrieved from cases of past plans. Two situations might happen. If there are more than one alternative decomposition, the given task is set as abstract and the set of decompositions are added to the HTN, linking each head task to the abstract task through a hierarchical link of type *abst*. Thus, these head tasks are now the subtasks of the abstract task (see Fig. 6 for an illustration of this process). The result is a decomposition with an OR structure. On the other hand, if only one decomposition is retrieved, its subtasks are added as subtasks of the given task, linked by a hierarchical link of type *dcmp* (see Fig. 6 for an illustration of this process). This corresponds to an AND structure. Whether a single decomposition or multiple decompositions are retrieved, the addition of it/them comprises an adaptation process [8], i.e., the retrieved decomposition(s) is/are changed if necessary so that it/they is/are consistent with the rest of the HTN. Each adaptation link triggers a process. Thus, for instance, the adaptation link *ea* (*equal AID*) in Fig. 6 indicates that the tasks *transport* and *inCityDel* have the same component *AID*, i.e., they are executed by the same agent. This means that the *AID* component of those tasks retrieved from past plans are changed so that it refers to the agent whose identifier is referred to by the *AID* of *transport* belonging to the current abstract plan.

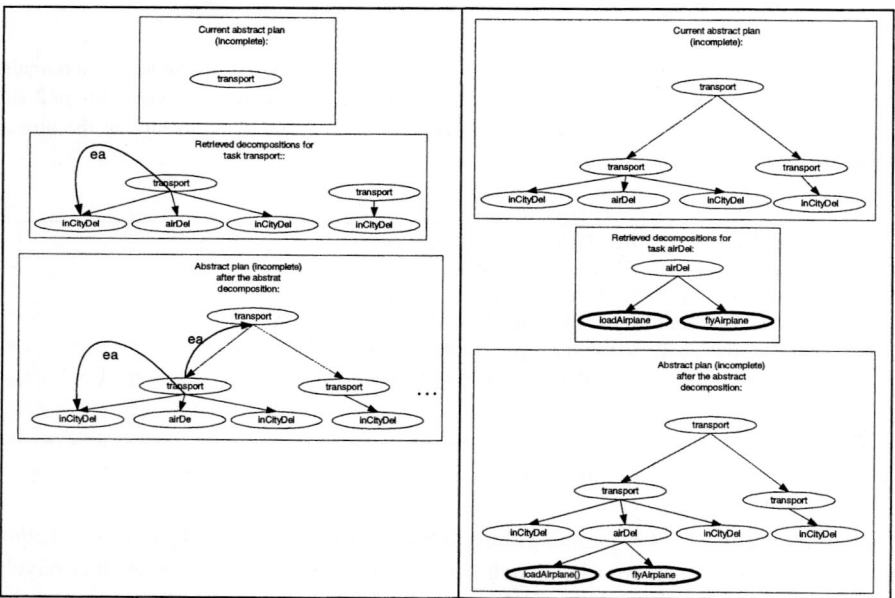

Fig. 6. Illustrative example of: an OR-decomposition of an abstract task (on the left); an AND-decomposition of a regular compound task (on the right)

The process of building the HTN ends when there are no more compound tasks to decompose, i.e., when the leaves of the tree are primitive tasks, or when there are no available decompositions in the case-base for at least one compound task.

Within our approach, a task belonging to an HTN has a probability value associated to it. This value expresses the probability of being executed given that its ancestor is executed. Thus, this probability is actually a conditional probability. Obviously, the probability of a task belonging to a case of a past plan is always 1.0 because it was executed (otherwise it won't belong to the case). The probability of the tasks belonging to an abstract plan is computed during the process of building the HTN as follows. Given the ith subtask, ST_i, of a task T both belonging to an abstract plan, the probability of ST_i be executed given that T is executed is given by the conditional probability formula $P(ST_i/T) = \frac{P(ST_i \cap T)}{P(T)}$. According to frequency interpretation of probability, this is estimated by: $P(ST_i/T) = \frac{P(ST_i \cap T)}{P(T)} = \frac{S_r(ST_i \cap T)}{S_r(T)}$, which expresses the number of times ST_i and T occurred together in the total amount of times T occurred, or in the context of HTN planning, this expresses the number of times ST_i was subtask of T in the total amount of times T was the task decomposed in past HTN plans in r decompositions. When ST_i is not a head of an alternative decomposition in the new plan (i.e., when T is not an abstract task), it means that T was always decomposed in the same way in past plans, i.e., into the same subtasks, which means ST_i occurred always when T occurred, otherwise ST_i won't be subtask of T. Thus, in this situation, the numerator and denominator of the above equation are equal and therefore $P(ST_i/T)=1.0$. However, when ST_i is a head of an alternative decomposition, it means there were more than one way to decompose T in past plans, the decomposition headed by ST_i being one of them. Thus, counting the number of times the decomposition headed by ST_i was taken to decompose T, i.e., the number of times ST_i instantiated T, $S_r(ST_i \cap T)$, in all past plans and dividing this number by the number of times T was decomposed, i.e., $S_r(T)$, yields the value for $P(ST_i/T)$ for this situation.

After the abstract HTN is built, the conditional effects (and respective probabilities) and the EU are computed for the primitive tasks based on the past occurrences of those primitive tasks (notice that the probability of the tasks has already been computed during the process of building the HTN as described above). Remember that tasks (either primitive or not) have a list of possible effects each one associated with a probability value (see Fig. 2). Thus, this is once more a case-based process that is carried out as described by the algorithm of Fig. 8.

After the primitive tasks have their properties computed based on cases of past plans, these properties are propagated bottom-up (from primitive to non-primitive tasks), from the subtasks to the task of a decomposition and from the subtasks (heads of alternative decompositions) to the abstract task of an abstract decomposition. The goal of this propagation is twofold: to complete the non-primitive tasks so that they can be ranked according to their EU when they are heads of alternative decompositions, and to know the overall EU of the abstract plan which is given by the EU of the main task of the plan. Fig. 9 presents the algorithm for the propagation of properties. Function PROPAGAT-PROPS-ABST and PROPAGAT-PROPS-DCMP relies heavily on the notions of inter-action abstraction described in [6].

2.3 Plan Execution and Replanning

Finding the optimal plan in ProCHiP consists simply of traversing the abstract plan, selecting the most EU subtask of an abstract task. Backtracking occurs when an alternative decomposition fails execution. In this case, the next alternative decomposition that follows the previous in the EU ranking is selected for execution.

```
Algorithm BUILD-STRUCTURE(abstPlan,CB)
    goalTasks ← getLeafTasks(AbstPlan)
    taskQueue ← goalTasks
    while taskQueue ≠ ∅
        task ← popFrontTask(taskQueue)
        listAlternDcmps ← getListAlternDcmps(task, CB)
        if size(listAlternDcmps) > 1
            task type ← "abstract"
            for each decomposition in listAlternDcmps do
                headTask ← getHeadTask(decomposition)
```
$$P(headTask \mid task) \leftarrow \frac{S_r(headTask \cap task)}{S_r(task)}$$
```
                adapt(headTask, task, "abst")
                insert headTask in AbstPlan; link it to task by "abst" link
                subtasksDcmp ← getSubTasks(decomposition)
                for each subtask (with adaptationLinks from headTask) in subtasksDcmp do
                    adapt(subtask, headTask, adaptionLinks)
                    for each othertask with adaptationLinks to subtask do
                        adapt(subtask, othertask, adaptionLinks)
                    end for each
                    if notPrimitive(subtask) then
                        insertTask(subtask, taskQueue)
```
$$P(subtask \mid headTask) \leftarrow \frac{S_r(subtask \cap headTask)}{S_r(headTask)} = 1.0$$
```
                    insertTask(subtask, AbstPlanStructure)
                end for each
                copy all links from decomposition to AbstPlan
            end for each
        else
            subtasksDcmp ← getSubTasks(decomposition)
            for each subtask (with adaptationLinks from subTask) in subtasksDcmp do
                adapt(subtask, task, adaptionLinks)
                for each othertask with adaptationLinks to subtask do
                    adapt(subtask, othertask, adaptionLinks)
                end for each
                if notPrimitive(subtask) then insertTask(subtask, taskQueue)
```
$$P(subtask \mid task) \leftarrow \frac{S_r(subtask \cap task)}{S_r(task)} = 1.0$$
```
                insertTask(subtask, AbstPlan)
            end for each
            copy all links from decomposition to abstPlan
        endif
    endwhile
    return abstPlan
end
```

Fig. 7. Algorithm for constructing the structure of an HTN

```
Algorithm COMPUT-PRIMTASKS-PROPS(primTasks, primTasksAllPlanCases)
  for each primTask in primTasks do
    taskList ← {i: i ∈ primTasks and i is of the same type of primTask}
    condEffectList ← ∅
    for each task in taskList do
      condEffectListTask ← ⋃_{i=1}^{m} ⟨c_i, E_i⟩ , m is the number of conditional effects of task,
      Ei={ E^i_{a_{task}} }
      condEffectList ← condEffectList ∪ condEffectListTask
    end for each
    genCondEffectList ← GENERALIZE-COND-EFFECT-LIST(condEffectList )
    set the conditional effects of primTask with genCondEffectList
    EU(primTask)← ∑_i P(⟨c_i,ε'⟩)×EU(⟨c_i,ε'⟩) = ∑_i P(c_i)×EU(ε')
  end for each
  return primTasks
end
```

Fig. 8. Algorithm for computing the conditional effects (and respective probabilities) and the EU of primitive tasks

```
Algorithm PROPAGAT-PROPS-UPWARD(primTasks, mainTask, abstPlan)
  if primitive(mainTask) nothing to do
  else
    subTasks ← getSubTasks(mainTask)
    for each subTask in subTasks do
      PROPAGAT-PROPS-UPWARD(primTasks, subTask, abstPlan)
    end for each
    if abstract(mainTask) then
      PROPAGAT-PROPS-ABST(subTasks, mainTask, mainTask1)
      replace mainTask by mainTask1 in abstPlan
    else
      PROPAGAT-PROPS-DCMP(subTasks, mainTask, mainTask1)
      replace mainTask by mainTask1 in abstPlan
    endif
  endif
end
```

Fig. 9. Recursive algorithm for propagating properties upward, from primitive tasks to all non-primitive tasks

2.4 Retaining Plans

As mentioned in section 2.3, executing a plan corresponds to an instantiation of an abstract plan. After a plan is executed, the instantiation that was actually executed is stored in memory for future reuse. In addition, the abstract plan is also stored in memory. This way, it might be useful in the future since it might avoid an unnecessary process of generating it again.

3 Experiment

We conducted an experiment in order to evaluate the role played by the case-base size on the performance of ProCHiP. Given a kind of goal task such as *transport*, we constructed 5 case-bases, ranging in size from 1 to 5 cases of plans, each case describing a different way of achieving the specified goal task. For each one of these case-bases, we ran ProCHiP with 10 different goal tasks of type *transport*. The CPU time taken by the planner to build an abstract plan for the specified goal task was measured. In addition, the number of those 10 goal tasks solved successfully was computed, as well as the number of tasks in those abstract plans. The results are plotted in Fig. 10.

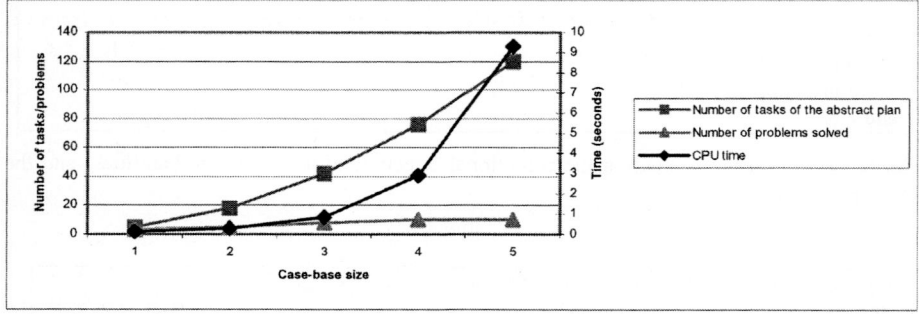

Fig. 10. Performance of ProCHiP with case-bases varying in size

The CPU time taken by the planner to build the abstract plan increases monotonically with the size of the case-base. The same happens with the number of tasks in the abstract plan. An interesting result is noticed with the number of problems successfully solved. With 3 cases, the planner is able to find a correct solution for 80% of the goal tasks, and with 4 or more cases the effectiveness is 100%, which means the addition to the case-base of more cases for solving problems of this kind (*transport*) seems to decrease the efficiency of the planner, because the effectiveness is not and could not be increased (100%). This issue is related to the utility problem (e.g., [5, 13, 19]) and case-base maintenance (e.g., [18, 20]).

4 Related Work

Our work is closely related to HTN planning. This methology has been extensively used in planning systems such as UMCP [4], SHOP and SHOP2 [16]. Unlike these planners, ProCHiP don't use methods as part of the domain theory for task decomposition, but instead methods that are implicitly included in cases that describe previous planning problem solving experiences. SiN [14] also uses a case-based HTN planning algorithm, in which cases are instances of methods.

Learning hierarchical plans or HTNs is still rarely addressed by the machine learning community, although there are a few exceptions. Garland, Ryall and Rich [Garland, 2001 #161 infer task models from annotated examples, i.e., through demonstration by a domain expert. [7]. van Lent and Laird [22] used a learning-by-observation technique which involves extracting knowledge from observations of an expert performing a task and generalizes this knowledge to a hierarchy of rules. Xu and Muñoz [23] use an algorithm that gather and generalize information on how domain experts solve HTN planning problems.

Among decision-theoretic planners, DRIPS [6] is probably the most closely related to ProCHiP. Actually, DRIPS shares a similar representation approach for abstract plans (an abstraction/decomposition hierarchy) and for actions. Besides, it also returns the optimal plan according to a given utility function. However, in contrast to DRIPS, in ProCHiP the variant of a HTN that represents abstract plans is automatically built from cases and not given as input for the planning problem. Besides, it includes temporal, utility ranking and adaptation links in addition to decomposition links. Another major difference is that, in ProCHiP, the EU of tasks and of alternative plans is computed when the abstract plan is built, while in DRIPS this occurs when the optimal plan is searched. In ProCHiP, there is the possibility of computing the EU of tasks based on the non-procedural component of their effects, which avoids some additional computations at the cost of being less accurate. Moreover, finding the optimal plan in ProCHiP consists simply of traversing the HTN with backtracking (or replanning) points located at the subtasks of an abstract task. In ProCHiP the propagation of properties upward in the hierarchy is closely related with the approach taken in DRIPS for abstracting actions [6]. A propagation of properties in the planning tree, bottom-up and left-to-right, is also used in GraphHTN [10] in order to improve the search algorithm.

5 Conclusions

We presented ProCHiP, a planner that combines CBR with the techniques of decision-theoretic planning and HTN planning in order to deal with uncertain, dynamic large-scale real-world domains. We conducted an experiment in order to evaluate the dependence of the time taken by ProCHip to build abstract plans on the size of a case-base containing cases representing implicit methods. We concluded that the CPU time increases monotonically with the case-base size. However, we also concluded that the case-base size improves the effectiveness of ProCHiP only up to a certain size. After that size the performance of ProCHiP corresponds to a low efficiency while the effectiveness is almost unaltered.

Acknowledgments

The PhD of Luís Macedo is financially supported by PRODEP III.

References

1. J. Allen, "Maintaining knowledge about temporal intervals," *Communications of the ACM*, vol. 26, pp. 832-- 843, 1983.
2. R. Bergmann and W. Wilke, "On the Role of Abstraction in Case-Based Reasoning," in *Advances in Case-Based Reasoning - Proceedings of the Third European Workshop on Case-Based Reasoning*, vol. 1168, *Lecture Notes in Artificial Intelligence*, I. Smith and B. Faltings, Eds. Berlin: Springer Verlag, 1996, pp. 28-43.
3. J. Blythe, "Decision-Theoretic Planning," *AI Magazine, Summer 1999*, 1999.
4. K. Erol, J. Hendler, and D. Nau, "UMCP: A sound and complete procedure for hierarchical task-network planning," in *Proceedings of the International Conference on AI Planning Systems*, 1994, pp. 249-254.
5. A. Francis and A. Ram, "The utility problem in case-based reasoning," in *Proceedings of the AAAI-93 Case-based Reasoning Workshop*, 1993.
6. P. Haddawy and A. Doan, "Abstracting probabilistic actions," in *Proceedings of the Tenth Conference on Uncertainty in Artificial Intelligence*. San Mateo, CA: Morgan Kaufmann, 1994, pp. 270-277.
7. O. Ilghami, D. Nau, H. Muñoz-Avila, and D. Aha, "CaMeL: Learning methods for HTN planning," in *AIPS-2002*, 2002.
8. J. Kolodner, *Case-Based Reasoning*. San Mateo, CA: Morgan-Kaufmann, 1993.
9. M. Littman and S. Majercik, "Large-Scale Planning Under Uncertainty: A Survey," in *Workshop on Planning and Scheduling for Space*, 1997, pp. 27:1--8.
10. A. Lotem and D. Nau, "New advances in GraphHTN: Identifying independent subproblems in large HTN domains," in *Proceedings of the International Conference on AI Planning Systems*, 2000, pp. 206-215.
11. L. Macedo and A. Cardoso, "Nested-Graph structured representations for cases," in *Advances in Case-Based Reasoning - Proceedings of the 4th European Workshop on Case-Based Reasoning*, vol. 1488, *Lecture Notes in Artificial Intelligence*, B. Smyth and P. Cunningham, Eds. Berlin: Springer-Verlag, 1998, pp. 1-12.
12. L. Macedo and A. Cardoso, "SC-EUNE - Surprise/Curiosity-based Exploration of Uncertain and Unknown Environments," in *Proceedings of the AISB'01 Symposium on Emotion, Cognition and Affective Computing*. York, UK: University of York, 2001, pp. 73-81.
13. S. Minton, "Qualitative results concerning the utility of explanation-based learning," *Artificial Intelligence*, vol. 42, pp. 363-391, 1990.
14. H. Muñoz-Avila, D. Aha, D. Nau, L. Breslow, R. Weber, and F. Yamal, "SiN: Integrating Case-based Reasoning with Task Decomposition," in *Proceedings of the Seventeenth International Joint Conference on Artificial Intelligence (IJCAI-2001)*. Seattle, WA: Morgan Kaufmann, 2001.
15. D. Nau, H. Muñoz-Avila, Y. Cao, A. Lotem, and S. Mitchell, "Total-order planning with partially ordered subtasks," in *Proceedings of the Seventeenth International Joint Conference on Artificial Intelligence*. Seattle, WA: Morgan Kaufmann, 2001.
16. D. Nau, T. Au, O. Ilghami, U. Kuter, W. Murdock, D. Wu, and F. Yaman, "SHOP2: An HTN planning system," *Journal of Artificial Intelligence Research*, vol. 20, pp. 379-404, 2003.
17. S. Russel and P. Norvig, *Artificial Intelligence - A Modern Approach*. Englewood Cliffs, NJ: Prentice Hall, 1995.

18. B. Smyth and M. Keane, "Remembering to forget: a competence preserving case deletion policy for CBR systems," in *Proceedings of the 14th International Joint Conference on Artificial Intelligence*. San Mateo, CA: Morgan Kaufmann, 1995, pp. 377-383.
19. B. Smyth and P. Cunningham, "The utility problem analysed," in *Advances in Case-Based Reasoning - Proceedings of the Third European Workshop on Case-Based Reasoning*, vol. 1168, *Lecture Notes in Artificial Intelligence*, I. Smith and B. Faltings, Eds. Berlin: Springer Verlag, 1996, pp. 392-399.
20. B. Smyth and E. McKenna, "Building compact competent case bases," in *Proceedings of the Third International Conference on Case-Based Reasoning*. Berlin: Springer Verlag, 1999, pp. 329-342.
21. S. Thrun, "Robotic mapping: A survey," in *Exploring Artificial Intelligence in the New Millenium*, G. Lakemeyer and B. Nebel, Eds. San Mateo, CA: Morgan Kaufmann, 2002.
22. M. van Lent and J. Laird, "Learning Hierarchical Performance Knowledge by Observation," in *Proceedings of the International Conference on Machine Learning*, 1999.
23. K. Xu and H. Munõz-Avila, "CBM-Gen+: An algorithm for reducing case base inconsistencies in hierarchical and incomplete domains," in *Proceedings of the International Conference on Case-Based Reasoning*. Berlin: Springer, 2003.
24. H. Younes, "Extending PDDL to model stochastic decision processes," in *Proceedings of the ICAPS-02 Workshop on PDDL*, 2003.

Using CBR in the Exploration of Unknown Environments with an Autonomous Agent

Luís Macedo[1,2] and Amílcar Cardoso[2]

[1] Department of Informatics and Systems Engineering, Engineering Institute,
Coimbra Polytechnic Institute,
3030-199 Coimbra, Portugal
lmacedo@isec.pt
http://www2.isec.pt/~lmacedo
[2] Centre for Informatics and Systems of the University of Coimbra,
Department of Informatics, Polo II,
3030 Coimbra, Portugal
{lmacedo,amilcar}@dei.uc.pt

Abstract. Exploration involves selecting and executing sequences of actions so that the knowledge of the environments is acquired. In this paper we address the problem of exploring unknown, dynamic environments populated with both static and non-static entities (objects and agents) by an autonomous agent. The agent has a case-base of entities and another of plans. This case-base of plans is used for a case-based generation of goals and plans for visiting the unknown entities or regions of the environment. The case-base of entities is used for a case-based generation of expectations for missing information in the agent's perception. Both case-bases are continuously updated: the case-base of entities is updated as new entities are perceived or visited, while the case-base of plans is updated as new sequences of actions for visiting entities/regions are executed successfully. We present and discuss the results of an experiment conducted in a simulated environment in order to evaluate the role of the size of the case-base of entities on the performance of exploration.

1 Introduction

Exploration may be defined as the process of selecting and executing actions so that the maximal knowledge of the environment is acquired at the minimum cost (e.g.: minimum time and/or power) [38]. The result is the acquisition of models of the physical environment. There are several applications like planetary exploration [4, 16], rescue, mowing [18], cleaning [12, 36], etc. Strategies that minimize the cost and maximize knowledge acquisition have been pursued (e.g., [2, 3, 10, 22, 25, 35, 38-41]). These strategies have been grouped into two main categories: undirected and directed exploration [38]. Strategies belonging to the former group (e.g., random walk exploration, Boltzman distributed exploration) use no exploration-specific knowledge and ensure exploration by merging randomness into action selection. On the other hand, strategies belonging to the latter group rely heavily on exploration specific-knowledge for guiding the learning process. Most of these directed strategies rely on the maximization of knowledge gain (e.g., [35]). This technique agrees with some psychological studies that have shown that novelty and new stimuli incite exploration in humans (e.g., [6]). Curiosity is the psychological construct that has been closely related with this kind of behavior. However, as argued by Berlyne [6], in addition to novelty, other variables such as change, surprisingness, complexity, uncertainty, incongruity and conflict also determine this kind of behaviour related to exploration and investigation activities. Therefore, in addition to curiosity (or novelty) other motivations such as surprise and hunger seem to influence the exploratory behaviour of humans [19].

Most of these approaches assume that the environment is static. Exceptions are, for instance, the works of [3] and [7]. These works address the problem of acquiring models of the environment where objects change their location frequently.

Most of the environments in which exploration occurs lack a domain theory and are characterized by unpredictability or uncertainty. Therefore, the agent may take advantage of using CBR for dealing with autonomous generation and management of goals as well as plans to accomplish these goals. Besides, together with a Bayesian approach, CBR may be used to deal with uncertainty.

In this paper we describe an approach for the exploration of unknown, dynamic environments populated with static and non-static entities by an agent whose decision-making/reasoning process relies heavily on CBR. The agent is continuously moving in the environment from location to location, visiting unknown entities that inhabit the environment as well as unknown regions. At each time, the agent generates goals that express the intention to visit regions or entities. For each goal a Hierarchical Task Network (HTN) plan [13] is generated. Both the generation of goals and plans is the result of CBR since they are generated from past cases of successful plans. Every time a plan is finished, the case-base of plans is updated with it. Likewise, as exploration is performed, the agent continuously updates its map of the environment with the geometric locations of the entities perceived and updates its episodic memory with those cases of entities built from the entities visited or perceived.

The next section describes how an agent represents entities internally, their geometric locations in the environment (maps) and courses of action (plans). Then, we present the strategy adopted for the exploration of unknown, dynamic environments. The components in which CBR plays a central role, such as the generation of expectations/assumptions and generation of goals and plans, are described. Then, we present and discuss an experiment carried out to evaluate the role of the case-base size in the performance of exploration. Finally, we present conclusions.

2 Agent's Memory

The memory of an agent stores information about the world. This information comprises the configuration of the surrounding world such as the position of the entities (objects and other animated agents) that inhabit it, the description of these entities themselves, descriptions of the sequences of actions (plans) executed by those entities and resulting from their interaction, and, generally, beliefs about the world. This information is stored in several memory components. Thus, there is a metric (grid-based) map [40] to spatially model the surrounding physical environment of the agent. Descriptions of entities (physical structure and function) and plans are stored both in the episodic memory and in the semantic memory [1, 14]. We will now describe in more detail each one of these distinct components.

2.1 Metric Map

In our approach, a (grid-based) metric map (Fig. 1) of the world is a three-dimensional grid in which a cell contains the information of the set of entities that may alternatively occupy the cell and the probability of this occupancy. Thus, each cell $<x,y,z>$ of the metric map of an agent i is set to a set of pairs $\phi^i_{x,y,z} = \{<p^i_1, E^i_1>, <p^i_2, E^i_2>, ..., <p^i_{n_i}, E^i_{n_i}>, <p^i_{n_{i+1}}, 0>\}$, where E^i_j is the identifier of the jth entity that may occupy the cell $<x,y,z>$ of the metric map of agent i with probability $p^i_j \in [0,1]$, and such that $\sum_{j=1}^{n_{i+1}} p^i_j = 1$. Note that the pair $<p^i_{n_{i+1}}, 0>$ is included in order to express the probability of the cell being empty. Cells that are completely unknown, i.e., for which there are not yet any assumptions/expectations about their occupancy, are set with an empty set of pairs $\phi^i_{x,y} = \{\}$. Note also that each entity may occupy more than a single cell, i.e., there might be several adjacent cells with the same E^i_j.

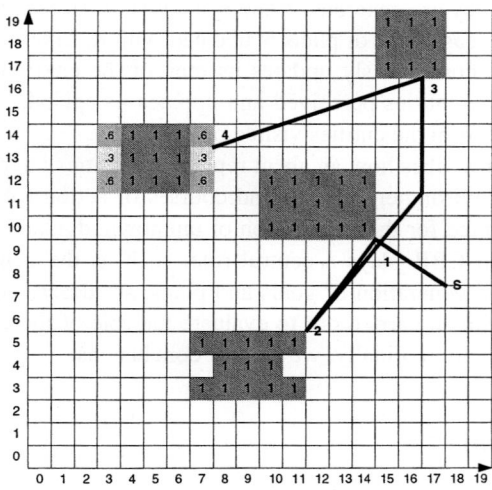

Fig. 1. An example of a metric map. Although metric maps are of three-dimensional kind, for the sake of simplicity, it is represented here only in two dimensions. For the same reason the identifier of the entities are not represented. The path followed by the agent to explore this environment (comprising buildings) is also depicted

2.2 Memory for Entities

The set of descriptions of entities perceived from the environment are stored in the *episodic memory of entities*. Each one of these descriptions is a case of the form <*ID,PS,F*>, where *ID* is a number that uniquely identifies the entity in the environment, *PS* is the physical structure, and *F* is the function of the entity [15]. The sensors may provide incomplete information about an entity (for instance, only part of the physical structure may be seen or the function of the entity may be undetermined). In this case the missing information is filled in by making use of Bayes' rule [34], i.e., the missing information is estimated taking into account the available information and cases of other entities previously perceived and already stored in the *episodic memory of entities*. This means some of the descriptions of entities stored in memory are uncertain or not completely known (e.g., element 4 of Fig. 2).

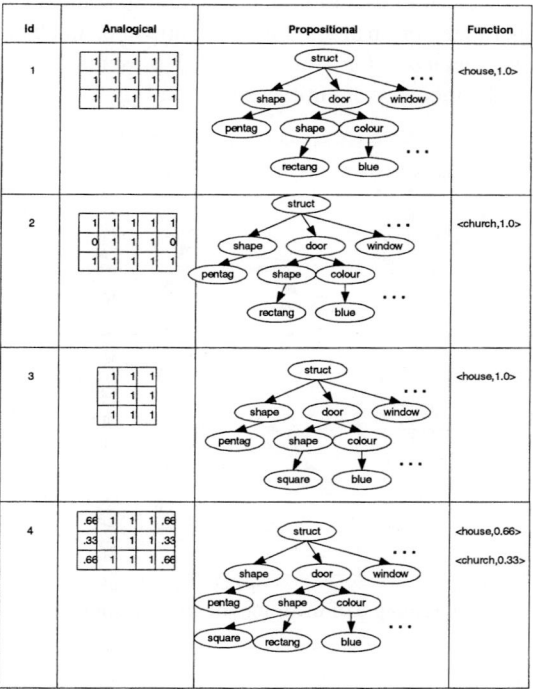

Fig. 2. Example of the episodic memory of entities in the domain of buildings. Although the matrix of the analogical description is of three-dimensional kind, for the sake of simplicity, it is represented here as a two-dimensional matrix corresponding to the upper view of the entity

The physical structure of an entity may be described analogically or propositionally [1, 14]. The analogical representation reflects directly the real physical structure while the propositional representation is a higher level description (using propositions) of that real structure.

The analogical description of the physical structure of an entity comprises a three-dimensional matrix and the coordinates of the centre-of-mass relative to the entity and to the environment spaces. Notice that the three-dimensional matrix of the entity is a submatrix of the matrix that represents the metric map.

The propositional description of the physical structure of an entity relies on the representation through semantic features or attributes much like in semantic networks or schemas [1]. According to this representation approach, entities are described by a set of attribute-value pairs that can be represented in graph-based way [24].

The function is simply a description of the role or category of the entity in the environment. For instance, a house, a car, a tree, etc. Like the description of the physical structure, this may be probabilistic because of the incompleteness of perception. This means, this is a set $F = \{<function_i, prob_i>: i=1,2, ..., n$, where n is the number of possible functions and $P("function" = function_i) = prob_i\}$.

Concrete entities (i.e., entities represented in the episodic memory) with similar features may be generalized or abstracted into a single one, an abstract entity, which is stored in the *semantic memory for entities*. Fig. 3 presents a semantic memory obtained from the episodic memory of entities shown in Fig. 2.

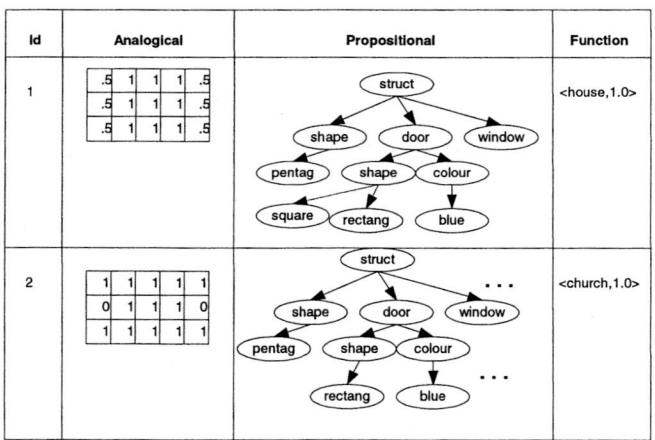

Fig. 3. Example of the semantic memory of entities

2.3 Memory for Plans

Like entities, we may distinguish two main kinds of plans: concrete plans, i.e., cases of plans, and abstract plans (e.g., [5]). Concrete plans and abstract plans are interrelated since concrete plans are instances of abstract plans and these are built from concrete plans.

We represent plans as a hierarchy of tasks (a variant of HTNs (e.g., [13]) (see Fig. 4). Formally, a plan is a tuple $AP = <T, L>$, where T is the set of tasks and L is the set of links. This structure has the form of a planning tree [23], i.e., it is a kind of AND/OR tree that expresses all the possible ways to decompose an initial task network. Like in regular HTNs, this hierarchical structure of a plan comprises primitive tasks or actions (non-decomposable tasks) and non-primitive tasks (decomposable or compound tasks). Primitive tasks correspond to the leaves of the tree and are directly executed by the agent, while compound tasks denote desired changes that involve several subtasks to accomplish it. For instance, the leaf node *PTRANS* of Fig. 4 is a primitive task, while *visitEntity* is a compound task. A task *t* is both conditional and probabilistic (e.g., [8]). This means each task has a set of conditions C={ $c_1, c_2, ..., c_m$} and for each one of these mutually exclusive and exhaustive conditions, c_i, there is a set of alternative effects $\mathcal{E}^i=\{<p_1^i, E_1^i>, <p_2^i, E_2^i>, ..., <p_{n_i}^i, E_{n_i}^i>\}$, where E_j^i is the jth effect triggered with probability $p_j^i \in [0,1]$ by condition c_i (i.e., $P(E_j^i | c_i) = p_j^i$), and such that $\sum_{j=1}^{n_i} p_j^i = 1$. Each effect contains information about changes produced in the world by achieving the goal task. Thus, an effect may give information about the amount of power consumed, the new location of the agent, the emotions felt, etc.

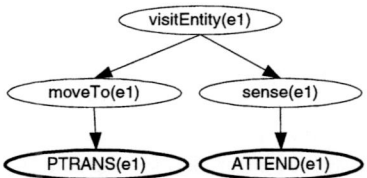

Fig. 4. Example of simple plan. Primitive tasks are represented by thick ellipses while non-primitive tasks are represented by thin ellipses

3 Exploration Using CBR

Each agent is continuously performing the following deliberative reasoning/decision-making algorithm. Each agent at a given time senses the environment to look for entities and compute the current world state (location, structure and function of those entities) based on the sensorial information and on the generation of expectations for the missing information. The result is a set of cases of entities, each one describing an entity that was perceived. Then, the episodic memory and metric map are updated based on these episodic entities. New intentions/goals of kind *visitEntity* are generated for each unvisited entity within the visual range based on the goal tasks of cases of past plans. In addition, a goal of the kind *visitLoc* is generated for some frontier cells [41] (another possible kind of goal is *rechargeBattery*). These goals are then ranked according to their Expected Utility (EU) [33], which is computed based on the estimated intensities for the motivations that they may elicit as explained below [27]. The first one in the ranking, i.e., the goal with the highest EU is taken and a HTN plan is generated based on cases of past plans. Then, the agent executes this plan.

We will now describe in more detail the steps related with the generation of assumptions/expectations and generation of agent's goals and respective plans.

3.1 Case-Based Generation of Assumptions/Expectations

As we said before, it is very difficult for an agent to get all the information about the surrounding environment. One reason is that the perceptual information is incomplete. However, taking as evidence the available information it is possible to generate expectations/assumptions for the missing information using a Bayesian approach [34]. Actually, Bayes' rule, represented as follows, may be used:

$$P(H_i | E_1, E_2, ..., E_m) = \frac{P(E_1|H_i) \times P(E_2|H_i) \times ... \times P(E_m|H_i) \times P(H_i)}{\sum_{l=1}^{n} P(E_1|H_l) \times P(E_2|H_l) \times ... \times P(E_m|H_l) \times P(H_l)} \quad (1)$$

where E_1, E_2, ..., E_m are pieces of evidence, i.e., the available information, and H_i, $i=1,2,...,n$, are mutually exclusive and collectively exhaustive hypotheses (retrieved from past cases of entities) for a specific piece of the missing information. Each conditional probability $P(E|H)$ is given by the number of times E and H appeared together in the cases of entities stored in memory divided by the number of times H appeared in those case of entities (when E and H have never appeared together $P(E|H) = P(E)$). In our work the evidence is the description (propositional) of the physical structure of the entities such as their shape (rectangular, squared, etc.), shape of their constituent parts (in case there are any), color, etc. The hypotheses could be not only for parts of the descriptions of the physical structure but also for the function or category of the entity. In this case, the result is a probability distribution for the function of the entity (e.g., $P(Function=house)=0.666$; $P(Function=church)=0.333$). Based on this distribution, the analogical description of the entity may be now estimated taking into account the analogical descriptions of the entities with these functions. This means that we are considering the reference class as comprising the entities with the same function. Notice that this resulting analogical description is probabilistic. Thus, for instance, considering the semantic memory presented in Fig. 3 and the probability distribution for the function of an entity [$P(Function=house)=0.66$, $P(Function=church)=0.33$], the resulting analogical description is similar to that of entity 4 of the episodic memory depicted in Fig. 2. This is computed as follows. For all function X: (i) take the analogical description of each possible entity with function X and multiply the occupancy value of each cell by $P(Function=X)$; (ii) superimpose the analogical descriptions obtained in the previous step summing the occupancy values of the superimposed cells.

3.2 Case-Based Generation of Goals and Plans

The algorithm for the generation and ranking of goals/intentions (Fig. 5) is as follows. First, the set of different goal tasks present in the memory of plans are retrieved and, for each kind, a set of new goals is generated using the following procedure: given a goal task retrieved from a plan in the memory of plans, the memory and the perception of the agent, similar goals are generated by adapting the past goal to situations of the present state of the world. The adaptation strategies used are mainly substitutions [20].

Thus, for instance, suppose the goal task *visitEntity(e7)* is present in the memory of the agent. Suppose also that the agent has just perceived three entities present in the environment, *e1*, *e2* and *e3*. The entity to which *visitEntity* is applied (*e7*) may be substituted by *e1*, *e2* or *e3*, resulting in three new goals: *visitEntity(e1)*, *visitEntity(e2)*, *visitEntity(e3)*. Then, the EU of each goal task is computed. As said above, a task *T* is both conditional and probabilistic (e.g.: [8]). Thus, the execution of a goal task under a given condition may be seen according to Utility Theory as a lottery [33]:

$$Lottery(T) = \left[p^1 \times p_1^1, E_1^1; p^1 \times p_2^1, E_2^1; ...; p^m \times p_{n_m}^m, E_{n_m}^m \right], \quad (2)$$

where p^i is the probability of the condition c_i, p_j^i is the probability of the jth effect, E_j^i, of condition c_i.

The EU of *T* may be then computed as follows:

$$EU(T) = \sum_{k,j} p^k \times p_j^k \times EU(E_j^k) \quad (3)$$

The computation of $EU(E_j^k)$ is performed predicting the motivations that could be elicited by achieving/executing the goal task [11, 32]. We confined the set of motivations to those that are more related with exploratory behaviour in humans [6]. Thus, the intensities of surprise, curiosity and hunger felt by the agent when the effect takes place are estimated based on the information available in the effect about the changes produced in the world or based on the intensities of emotions and other motivations felt in past occurrences of the effect of the task.

Surprise is given by [26]:

$$SURPRISE(Agt, Obj_k) = UNEXPECTEDNESS(Obj_k, Agt(Mem)) = 1 - P(Obj_k), \quad (4)$$

where Obj_k is the direct object of task *T* when E_j^k takes place, i.e., the entity that is visited.

Curiosity is computed as follows:

$$CURIOSITY(Agt, Obj_k) = DIFFERENCE(Obj_k, Agt(Mem)) \quad (5)$$

The measure of difference relies heavily on error correcting code theory [17]: the function computes the distance between two entities represented by graphs, counting the minimal number of changes (insertions and deletions of nodes and edges) required to transform one graph into another (for a similar approach see [31]).

The hunger drive is defined as the need of a source of energy. Given the capacity *C* of the storage of that source, and *L* the amount of energy left ($L \leq C$), the hunger elicited in an agent is computed as follows:

$$HUNGER(Agt) = C - L \quad (6)$$

The following function is used to compute $EU(E_j^k)$:

$$EU(E_j^k) = \frac{\alpha_1 \times U_{surprise}(E_j^k) + \alpha_2 \times U_{curiosity}(E_j^k) + \alpha_3 \times U_{hunger}(E_j^k)}{\sum_i \alpha_i} = \qquad (7)$$

$$= \frac{\alpha_1 \times Surprise(E_j^k) + \alpha_2 \times Curiosity(E_j^k) + \alpha_3 \times Hunger(E_j^k)}{\sum_i \alpha_i},$$

where, $\alpha_3 = -1$ and α_i ($i \neq 3$) may be defined as follows:

$$\alpha_i = \begin{cases} 1 \Leftarrow C - HUNGER(Agt) - D > 0 \\ 0 \Leftarrow otherwise \end{cases}, \qquad (8)$$

where D is the amount of energy necessary to go from the end location of goal task T to the closer place where energy could be recharged, and C is the maximum amount of energy that could be stored by the agent. The functions $Surprise(E_j^k)$, $Curiosity(E_j^k)$ and $Hunger(E_j^k)$ are replaced by the functions of curiosity, surprise and hunger defined above and applied for the entities perceived when the effect E_j^k takes place.

The surprise and curiosity of an effect of a task are elicited by the entities that the agent perceives.

Algorithm generateRankGoals(*newRankedGoals*)
Output: *newRankedGoals* – the set of ranked goals
newGoals ← ∅
setPastGoals ← {*x*: *x* is a goal task belonging to some plan in memory}
for each *goal* in *setPastGoals* **do**
  adaptationGoal←adaptGoal(*goal,agtMemory,agtPercepts*)
  newGoals ← *newGoals* ∪ *adaptationGoals*
end for each
for each *goal* in *newGoals* **do**
  $EU(T) = \sum_{k,j} p^k \times p_j^k \times EU(E_j^k)$
end for each
insert(*goal,newRankedGoals*)
return *newRankedGoals*
end

Fig. 5. Algorithm for the case-based generation of goals

This dependence of the parameters α_i ($i \neq 3$) on the hunger of the agent partially models the results of Berlyne's experiments (e.g., [6]) that have shown that in the absence of (or despite) known drives, humans tend to explore and investigate their environment as well as seek stimulation. Actually, surprise and curiosity are taken into account to compute the EU of a task only when there is enough energy to go from the end location of goal task T to the closest place where an energy source could be found.

Otherwise, only hunger is taken into account for the EU of tasks and further ranking. This means that in this situation (when hunger is above a specific threshold), only the goal of *rechargeBattery* has an EU > 0. In the other situations (hunger below a specific threshold), hunger plays the role of a negative reward decreasing the utility of a task by the percentage of energy needed after the task is completed. Thus, the more the distance to the location after the execution of a task the more the energy required and the less the utility of that task.

However, the environment is not confined to entities. It might have regions that are not yet explored. Therefore, goals of kind *visitLoc* are also retrieved from past plans and adapted for the current frontier cells. Not all the cells are considered. We followed an approach similar to [9], i.e., different target cells are assigned to each agent so that the overlapped area of the visual fields of the agents in those cells is minimized. The EU of a goal task of this kind is also computed with the above equation 3, although in this case curiosity is computed based on the estimation of the amount of unknown cells inside the visual field if the agent is at the destination location. Surprise is assumed to be 0.

A HTN plan is generated for the first goal in the ranking as follows. A problem is an initial and incomplete HTN, i.e., a set of goal tasks. Planning is a process by which that initial HTN is completed resulting in an abstract plan ready to be executed and incorporating alternative courses of action, i.e., it includes replanning procedures. Roughly speaking, this involves the following steps: first, the structure of the abstract plan (HTN) is built based on cases of past plans (this is closely related to the regular HTN planning procedure); then the conditional effects, probabilities as well as the EU are computed for the primitive tasks of this abstract plan based on the primitive tasks of cases of past plans; finally, these properties (conditional effects and respective probabilities, and EU) are propagated upward in the HTN, from the primitive tasks to the main task of the HTN. Fig. 6 presents this algorithm and Fig. 7 illustrates the process of building the structure of a plan using an AND/OR decomposition approach. For more details about the algorithm for constructing an abstract plan see [29].

```
Algorithm CONSTRUCT-ABSTRACT-PLAN(abstPlan)
    abstPlan ← BUILD-STRUCTURE(abstPlan)
    primTasks ← GET-PRIM-TASKS(abstPlan)
    primTasksAllPlanCases← GET-PRIMTASKS-ALL-PLAN-CASES()
    COMPUT-PRIMTASKS-PROPS(primTasks,primTasksAllPlanCases)
    abstPlan←PROPAGAT-PROPS-UPWARD(primTasks,abstPlan)
    return abstPlan
end
```

Fig. 6. Algorithm for constructing an abstract plan

4 Experiment

We conducted an experiment in a simulated environment comprising buildings in order to evaluate the role of the size of the case-base of entities on the exploration performance of an agent. To do so, we ran an agent in the same environment (see

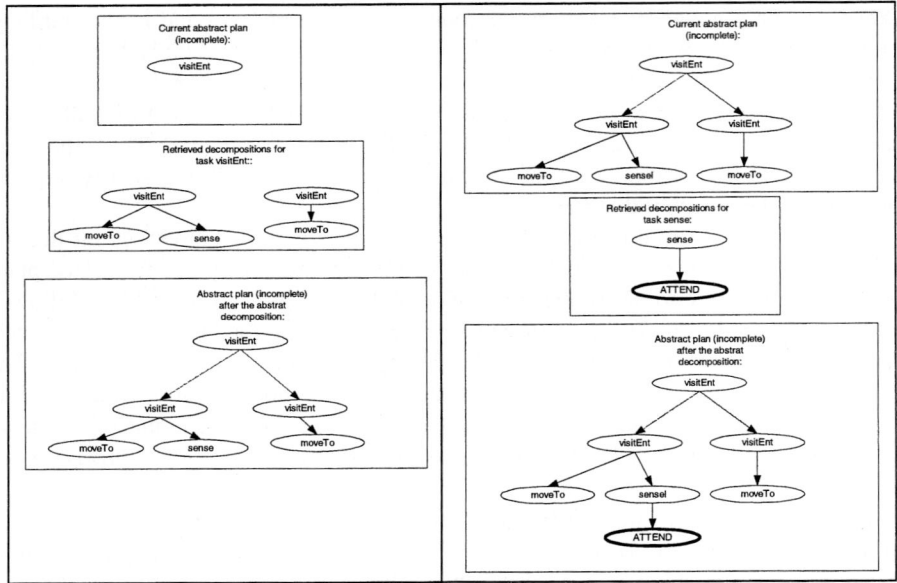

Fig. 7. Two illustrative examples of the process of building the structure of a plan using an AND/OR decomposition approach

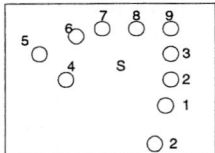

Fig. 8. Environment with 10 entities (two of them, entities with identifier 2, are identical). Entities 1, 2 and 3 are those described in the episodic memory of Fig. 2

Fig. 8) with different starting case-bases of entities. These memories ranged from 1 to 5 cases. All of these cases were built from 5 entities, selected randomly among the 10 entities that populate the environment. For instance, the case-base of size 3 comprised the cases 1, 2 and 3 described in Fig. 2, while the case-base of size 1 comprised only case 1, and the case-base of size 2 was formed with cases 1 and 2. The other larger case-bases of size 4 and 5 comprised in addition cases of entities 4 and 5, respectively. We then let the agent explore the environment during a limited time so that it can't explore exhaustively the whole environment. Actually, this time limit was defined so that it can't even visit any entity (stopped at position S). Therefore, the agent had to build the map of the environment by generating assumptions/expectations for the unvisited entities as described in section 3.1. Finally, we compared these maps built by the agent with the real map (the map that should had been built by an ideal agent). The difference or inconsistency between two maps was measured summing the difference between the occupancy values of any two correspondent cells (cells with similar coordinates) of the two maps. Fig. 9 presents the results of the experiment. As it can be seen the map inconsistency decreases monotonically with the increasing size of the case-base. This can be explained as follows. The entities are only perceived at a certain distance. For these entities, the cases generated are probabilistic (especially their analogical physical description). With larger case-bases the agent is able to generate more accurate probabilistic analogical descriptions for the entities, i.e., the expectations are closer to the reality. However, this higher accuracy is achieved by a slower reasoning process because the agent has to take into account more cases. This is related with the Utility Problem [37] since it is expected that the increase of the size of the case-base is of significant benefit only up to a certain size. Case-bases larger than that point are expected to include redundant cases. Case base maintenance techniques (e.g., [21]) might be applied in order to avoid this.

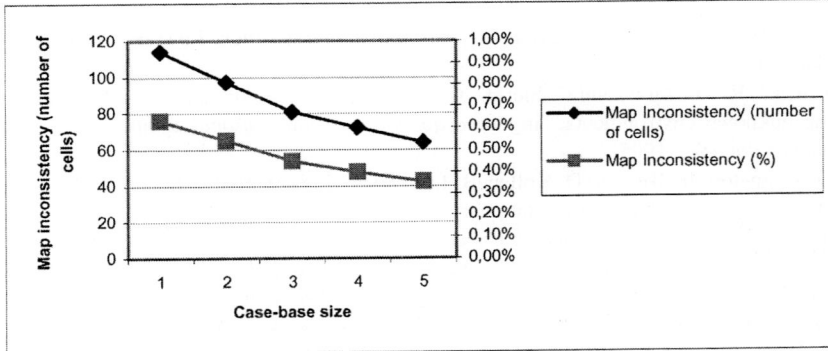

Fig. 9. Inconsistency between real and built maps represented from two points of view: number of inconsistent cells; percentage of inconsistency (computed dividing the number of inconsistent cells by the total amount of cells in the three-dimensional environment – in this case this was 18000 cells).

5 Discussion and Conclusions

We presented a case-based approach for the exploration of unknown environments. The experiment conducted allow us to conclude that the exploration performance may be improved by previously training the agent in similar environments so that case-bases of entities and plans are acquired. The main advantage is that agents are able to build more accurate maps of the world when using larger case-bases especially when they can't explore exhaustively the whole environment. Actually, the agent does not have to explore all the regions of the environment, such as the invisible side of the entities, since it is able to predict that inaccessible information. However, too much larger case-bases do not improve significantly the exploration performance relative to medium size case-bases because they imply higher computation times and therefore the exploration task is delayed because fewer entities are visited or perceived. The disadvantage of this approach is that the built maps may be more inconsistent than those acquired from an exhaustive exploration of the environment. However, this inconsistency is almost insignificant since, for instance, for a case-base with a single case, in the three-dimensional environment of the experiment with 18000 cells, the inconsistency was 114 cells, i.e., 0.63% of the environment. However, this depends on the kind of cases stored in the case-base as well as on the complexity of the environment (for a similar experience with different environments see [30]; for another experiment about the trade-off between exploration and exploitation see [28]).

Acknowledgments

The PhD of Luís Macedo is financially supported by PRODEP III.

References

1. Aitkenhead and J. Slack, *Issues in cognitive modelling*. London: Lawrence Erlbaum Associates, 1987.
2. J. Amat, R. Màntaras, and C. Sierra, "Cooperative autonomous low-cost robots for exploring unknown environments," in *Proccedings of the International Symposium on Experimental Robotics*, 1995.
3. D. Anguelov, R. Biswas, D. Koller, B. Limketkai, S. Sanner, and S. Thrun, "Learning hierarchical object maps of non-stationary environments with mobile robots," in *Proceedings of the 17th Annual Conference on Uncertainty in AI*, 2002.
4. D. Apostolopoulos, L. Pedersen, B. Shamah, K. Shillcutt, M. Wagner, and W. Whittaker, "Robotic antarctic meteorite search: outcomes," in *Proceedings of the IEEE International Conference on Robotics & Automation (ICRA)*, 2001, pp. 4171-4179.
5. R. Bergmann and W. Wilke, "On the Role of Abstraction in Case-Based Reasoning," in *Advances in Case-Based Reasoning - Proceedings of the Third European Workshop on Case-Based Reasoning*, vol. 1168, *Lecture Notes in Artificial Intelligence*, I. Smith and B. Faltings, Eds. Berlin: Springer Verlag, 1996, pp. 28-43.
6. D. Berlyne, "Novelty and curiosity as determinants of exploratory behavior," *British Journal of Psychology*, vol. 41, pp. 68-80, 1950.
7. R. Biswas, B. Limketkai, S. Sanner, and S. Thrun, "Towards object mapping in non-stationary environments with mobile robots," in *Proceedings of the Conference on Intelligent Robots and Systems*, 2002.
8. J. Blythe, "Decision-Theoretic Planning," *AI Magazine, Summer 1999*, 1999.
9. W. Burgard, D. Fox, M. Moors, R. Simmons, and S. Thrun, "Collaborative Multi-Robot Exploration," in *Proceedings of the IEEE International Conference on Robotics and Automation*: IEEE, 2000.
10. W. Burgard, M. Moors, and F. Schneider, "Collaborative exploration of unknown environments with teams of mobile robots," in *Advances in plan-based control of robotic agents*, vol. 4266, *Lectures Notes in Computer Science*, M. Beetz, J. Hertzberg, M. Ghallab, and M. Pollack, Eds. Berlin: Springer Verlag, 2002.
11. Castelfranchi, R. Conte, M. Miceli, and I. Poggi, "Emotions and goals," in *Perspectives on Cognitive Science*, B. Kokinov, Ed. Sofia: New Bulgarian University, 1996, pp. 131-145.
12. H. Endres, W. Feiten, and G. Lawitzky, "Field test of a navigation system: autonomous cleaning in supermarkets," in *Proceedings of the IEEE International Conference on Robotics & Automation (ICRA)*, 1998.

13. K. Erol, J. Hendler, and D. Nau, "UMCP: A sound and complete procedure for hierarchical task-network planning," in *Proceedings of the International Conference on AI Planning Systems*, 1994, pp. 249-254.
14. M. Eysenck and M. Keane, *Cognitive psychology*. London: Lawrence Erlbaum Associates, 1991.
15. A. Goel, "Representation of Design Functions in Experience-Based Design," in *Intelligent Computer Aided Design*, D. Brown, M. Walderon, and H. Yosnikawa, Eds.: Elsevier Science, 1992.
16. V. Goldberg, V. Cicirello, M. Dias, R. Simmons, S. Smith, T. Smith, and A. Stentz, "A Distributed Layered Architecture for Mobile Robot Coordination: Application to Space Exploration," in *3rd International NASA Workshop on Planning and Scheduling for Space*. Houston, 2002.
17. R. Hamming, "Error Detecting and Error Correcting Codes," *The Bell System Technical Journal*, vol. 26, pp. 147-60, 1950.
18. Y. Huang, Z. Cao, S. Oh, E. Kattan, and E. Hall, "Automatic operation for a robot lawn mower," in *SPIE Conference on Mobile Robots*, vol. 727, 1986, pp. 344-354.
19. Izard, *The Psychology of Emotions*. NY: Plenum Press, 1991.
20. J. Kolodner, *Case-Based Reasoning*. San Mateo, CA: Morgan-Kaufmann, 1993.
21. Leake, Wilson, D., "Categorizing case-base maintenance: dimensions and directions," in *Proceedings of the 4th European Workshop on Case-Based Reasoning*. Berlin: Springer-Verlag, 1998.
22. D. Lee and M. Recce, "Quantitative evaluation of the exploration strategies of a mobile robot," *AAAI-94*, 1994.
23. A. Lotem and D. Nau, "New advances in GraphHTN: Identifying independent subproblems in large HTN domains," in *Proceedings of the International Conference on AI Planning Systems*, 2000, pp. 206-215.
24. L. Macedo and A. Cardoso, "Nested-Graph structured representations for cases," in *Advances in Case-Based Reasoning - Proceedings of the 4th European Workshop on Case-Based Reasoning*, vol. 1488, *Lecture Notes in Artificial Intelligence*, B. Smyth and P. Cunningham, Eds. Berlin: Springer-Verlag, 1998, pp. 1-12.
25. L. Macedo and A. Cardoso, "SC-EUNE - Surprise/Curiosity-based Exploration of Uncertain and Unknown Environments," in *Proceedings of the AISB'01 Symposium on Emotion, Cognition and Affective Computing*. York, UK: University of York, 2001, pp. 73-81.
26. L. Macedo and A. Cardoso, "Modelling Forms of Surprise in an Artificial Agent," in *Proceedings of the 23rd Annual Conference of the Cognitive Science Society*, J. Moore and K. Stenning, Eds. Mahwah, NJ: Erlbaum, 2001, pp. 588-593.
27. L. Macedo and A. Cardoso, "A Motivation-based Approach for Autonomous Generation and Ranking of Goals in Artificial Agents," in *Proceedings of the AISB'04 Fourth Symposium on Adaptive Agents and Multi-Agent Systems*, D. Kudenko, Ed. Leeds: SSAISB, 2004.
28. L. Macedo and A. Cardoso, "Exploration of Unknown Environments with Motivational Agents," in *Proceedings of the Inhird International Joint Conference on Autonomous Agents and Multiagent Systems*, N. Jennings and M. Tambe, Eds.: ACM Press, 2004.
29. L. Macedo and A. Cardoso, "Case-Based, Decision-Theoretic, HTN Planning," in *Proceedings of the 7th European Conference on Case-Based Reasoning*, P. Calero and P. Funk, Eds. Berlin: Springer, 2004.

30. L. Macedo and A. Cardoso, "Building maps from incomplete environment information: a cognitive approach based on the generation of expectations," in *Proceedings of 5th IFAC Symposium on Intelligent Autonomous Vehicles*, M. Ribeiro, Ed. Oxford, UK: Elsevier Science, 2004.
31. B. Messmer and H. Bunke, "A new algorithm for error-tolerant subgraph isomorphism detection," *IEEE Transactions on Pattern Analysis and Machine Intelligence*, vol. 20, 1998.
32. R. Reisenzein, "Emotional Action Generation," in *Processes of the molar regulation of behavior*, W. Battmann and S. Dutke, Eds. Lengerich: Pabst Science Publishers, 1996.
33. S. Russel and P. Norvig, *Artificial Intelligence - A Modern Approach*. Englewood Cliffs, NJ: Prentice Hall, 1995.
34. Shafer and J. Pearl, "Readings in Uncertain Reasoning". Palo Alto, CA: Morgan Kaufmann, 1990.
35. R. Simmons, D. Apfelbaum, W. Burgard, D. Fox, M. Moors, S. Thrun, and H. Younes, "Coordination for Multi-Robot Exploration and Mapping," in *Proceedings of the AAAI-2000*, 2000.
36. M. Simoncelli, G. Zunino, H. Christensen, and K. Lange, "Autonomous pool cleaning: self localization and autonomous navigation for cleaning," *Journal of Autonomous Robots*, vol. 9, pp. 261-270, 2000.
37. B. Smyth and P. Cunningham, "The utility problem analysed," in *Advances in Case-Based Reasoning - Proceedings of the Third European Workshop on Case-Based Reasoning*, vol. 1168, *Lecture Notes in Artificial Intelligence*, I. Smith and B. Faltings, Eds. Berlin: Springer Verlag, 1996, pp. 392-399.
38. S. Thrun, "Efficient exploration in reinforcement learning," Carnegie Mellon University, Computer Science Department, Pittsburgh, PA CMU-CS-92-102, 1992.
39. S. Thrun, "Exploration in active learning," in *Handbook of Brain Science and Neural Networks*, M. Arbib, Ed., 1995.
40. S. Thrun, "Robotic mapping: A survey," in *Exploring Artificial Intelligence in the New Millenium*, G. Lakemeyer and B. Nebel, Eds. San Mateo, CA: Morgan Kaufmann, 2002.
41. B. Yamauchi, "Frontier-based exploration using multiple robots," in *Proceedings of the Second Iinnternational Conference on Autonomous Agents*. Minneapolis, MN, 1998.

Ceaseless Case-Based Reasoning

Francisco J. Martin[1] and Enric Plaza[2]

[1] School of Electrical Engineering and Computer Science
Oregon State University
Corvallis, 97331 OR, USA
fmartin@cs.orst.edu

[2] IIIA – Artificial Intelligence Research Institute
CSIC – Spanish Council for Scientific Research
Campus UAB, 08193 Bellaterra, Catalonia, Spain
enric@iiia.csic.es

Abstract. Most CBR systems try to solve problems in one shot neglecting the sequential behavior of most real world domains and the simultaneous occurrence of interleaved problems proper to multi-agent settings. This article provides a first answer to the following question: how can the CBR paradigm be enriched to support the analysis of unsegmented sequences of observational data stemming from multiple coincidental sources? We propose Ceaseless CBR, a new model that considers the CBR task as on-going rather than one-shot and aims at finding the best explanation of an unsegmented sequence of alerts with the purpose of pinpointing whether undesired situations have occurred or not and, if so, indicating the multiple responsible sources or at least which ones are the most plausible.

1 Introduction

In an ever-increasing diversity of domains such as intrusion detection, forecasting conflicts in international event analysis, fraud detection in cellular telephones, etc, automated sensors (in addition to being noisy and imperfect) lack the intelligence to disambiguate (differentiate and synthesize) the parts corresponding to distinct problems so they resort to piecing all the sensed parts together into only one sequence. That is, several problem descriptions corresponding to problems occurring in parallel are serialized into a unique sequence without comprehensible criteria for its further understanding. Most CBR systems commonly presuppose individualized problem descriptions with well-specified boundaries that encompass all the information needed to solve the current problem in only "one shot". This assumption makes impracticable their direct deployment in the above domains. The fact of the matter is that most CBR systems, built on the dominant mainstream CBR model, are devised bearing in mind the following three interrelated assumptions: (i) *non-coincidental sources*: there is only a problem occurring at a time. Said differently, problems are solved successively one after another without considering problems that concur and whose origin could be related and could require a joint solution; (ii) *full-fledged problem descriptions*: a problem description is provided in only one shot (instantaneous situations) with well-defined and clear limits – i.e., the boundaries of each case are perfectly delimited; and (iii) *individual cases independency*: cases are manipulated (retrieved, reused, revised or retained) in isolation without contemplating their sequential (spatial or temporal) structure or (serial or parallel) relationship with other cases in the past. That is, they assume (snapshot) cases that are independent of each other, and therefore relations among cases (e.g., sequential relationships) are not taken into account.

These assumptions make CBR unsuitable for a number of challenging problems – mainly those that involve temporally-evolving sequences of observational data. Thus our interest in investigating new techniques that allow one to alleviate such constraints and applying CBR in a variety of much more complex domains. In this article we give a first answer to the following question: how can the CBR paradigm be enriched to support the analysis of unsegmented sequences of observational data stemming from multiple coincidental sources? We propose Ceaseless CBR a new CBR model that aims at finding the best explanation of an unsegmented sequence of alerts with the purpose of pinpointing whether undesired situations (an attack, fault, etc) have occurred or not and, if so, indicating the multiple responsible sources (if more than one intervened) or at least which ones are the most plausible. Moreover, Ceaseless CBR prioritizes each individual alert according to the proposed explanations.

This article proceeds as follows. We initially describe the concrete application domain where we have evaluated Ceaseless CBR in Sec. 2. Sec. 3 puts the work covered in perspective. We see Ceaseless CBR as a constructive situation awareness process governed ceaselessly by *observational data*, *sequential cases*, and *case activations*. We discuss each of these concepts in detail in Sec. 4, Sec. 5, and Sec. 6 respectively. The description of Ceaseless Retrieve and Ceaseless Reuse in Sec. 7 and Sec. 8 constitute the bulk of this article. Finally, Sec. 9 concludes the article with a succinct discussion about Ceaseless CBR.

2 Application Domain

We have conducted an exploratory analysis of Ceaseless CBR in *intrusion detection*, concretely in *alert triage* – the rapid and approximate prioritization for subsequent action of an Intrusion Detection System (IDS) alert stream [1]. The fact of the matter is that current IDSes generate an unmanageable number of false positive alerts[1] which in turn increases the difficulties for the proper identification of real and malicious attacks. Security managers are so overwhelmed that they frequently disable the alert device due to the consistent assumption that nothing is wrong reinforced by the fact that the alert device "cried wolf" too often. There are those who even postulate that current IDSes not only have failed to provide an additional layer of security but have also added complexity to the security management task. Therefore, there is a compelling need for developing a new generation of tools that help to automate security management

---

[1] Alerts signaled when there is a manifest absence of intrusive behavior.

tasks such as alert triage. Generally speaking, two kinds of components can be distinguished in the current state of the art IDSes [2]: *probes* and and *aggregation and correlation components* (ACCs). Probes compile information using host-based sensors as well as network-based sensors and evoke an alert whenever suspicious activity is detected. Probes can be considered low-level sensors such as firewalls or integrity checkers. Snort is a representative example of a signature-based sensor that we have used for our experiments. Snort performs lightweight real-time traffic analysis and packet logging on IP networks [3]. An ACC takes as input alerts from probes and after analyzing and correlating received alerts decides whether to send such alerts to the network manager or not [2]. Ceaseless CBR aims at increasing the performance of such decisions. The different techniques devised throughout this work have been embodied within a research prototype – called Alba (Alert Barrage) – that could be cataloged as a striking example of these components [1].

We have constructed three data sets for measuring the performance of our techniques using *honeypots* to compile alerts in three different real-world scenarios. The Rustoord data set consists of 31483 alerts with an average frequency of 1968 alerts/week. The Naxpot data set contains 204977 alerts with an average frequency of 5856 alerts/week. The Huckleberry data set is composed of 219886 alerts with an average frequency of 13743 alerts/week. We have used the ROC^2 evaluation framework described elsewhere to analyze the performance of Ceaseless CBR in the above data sets [1]. Our results showed a significant increase in performance, as measured by ROC AUC (Area Under the Curve) [1]. Ceaseless CBR was able to keep the true positive rate over and above 99% and the false positive rate under and below 1%. We have achieved significant reductions in the weekly alert load. We got reductions up to a 95.90% in Rustoord data set, to 80.89% in Naxpot, and to 93.02% in Huckleberry. Our evaluations demonstrated how a Ceaseless CBR-enhaced IDS system is not only able to significantly reduce the weekly alert load but also to keep the number of false negatives very low and an admissible rate of false positives. This level of performance demonstrates that Ceaseless CBR can perform sufficiently for real world deployment.

3 Related Work

Four of the unusual CBR issues that we deal with in this work were partially opened, most of them early in the 90s, by separate seminal works [5–9]. Shavlik was the first to notice that most CBR systems usually presuppose *well-defined current situations* – situations where the boundaries of the current case are cleanly defined [6]. Ram and Santamaría observed with much truth that CBR is mostly deployed as a high-level problem solving paradigm where situations are represented using discrete and static symbolic representations [8]. Ceaseless CBR

---

[2] The term ROC (Receiver Operating Characteristic) refers to the performance (the operating characteristic) of a human or mechanical observer (the receiver) that has to discriminate between radio signals contaminated by noise (such as radar images) and noise alone [4].

is closely-related to Continuous CBR. Both methods need to provide a timely response to a time-varying situation (i.e., continuous on-line performance). While Continuous CBR practically operates in real-time Ceaseless CBR only aspires to work on a quasi-real time basis. This is due to the fact that we have to evaluate time-evolving sequences of complex objects as opposed to only vectors of analog values as Continuous CBR does. The input of Ceaseless CBR are unsegmented sequences of events dispersed over time and the task is to segment the sequence to provide the best explanation of the current situation and suggest an action. In Continuous CBR the current situation is given by a series of equally time-spaced real values and the task is to directly execute the actions. A drawback of Continuous CBR is that continuous cases are neither easily-interpretable by a human nor easy-to-integrate with higher-level reasoning and learning methods. Jacynski observed that most CBR approaches only cope with *instantaneous situations* (aka snapshot cases [10]) [9] and only few CBR systems deal with *time-extended situations* (aka time-dependent situations [10]). An instantaneous situation is a finite set of data that represents the state of the world at a particular point in time whereas a time-extend situation reflects the evolution of the world either through a continuum of instantaneous situations along a specific time line or through a sequence of events like Ceaseless CBR. Only a few additional CBR works have dealt with time-extended situations, the most noticeable being the work due to Jaere et al [10] who introduced *temporal cases* as a method for representing time-dependent situations within a knowledge-intensive CBR framework. Relatively little attention has been spent on CBR systems that are able to combine relevant pieces of several past cases when solving a new problem. The pioneering works in this aspect are Barletta et al [5] and Redmond [7].

The Ceaseless CBR inference process can be considered as an instantiation model of the inference process of parsimonious covering theory. In a nutshell, parsimonious covering theory is able to formalize many imprecise and intuitive aspects of abduction providing a good theoretical foundation for automated diagnostic problem-solving [11]. Traditional knowledge-based troubleshooting techniques such those used by rule-based systems or model-based systems cannot precisely capture the dynamic complexity of large systems, and thus CBR emerges as a suitable paradigm to do so [12, 13]. Lewis extended a Ticket Troubleshooting System (TTS) system with CBR methods that aided in computer network alarm management [12]. Gupta introduced SPOTLIGHT, a CBR tool for complex equipment troubleshooting [13]. Breese and Heckerman defined a decision-theoretic methodology for developing diagnosis and troubleshooting applications based on CBR [14]. They represented diagnostic cases by means of a specific belief network structure where nodes represented *issues*, *causes* and *symptoms*. This approach is similar in essence to Ceaseless CBR. However, in our approach a sequential case only stores part of the complete model for problem determination that helps to determine its plausibility given a collection of alerts. Since we store sequential cases individually, we avoid on-the-fly construction for each new problem. Moreover, we consider a number of distinct problems (attacks) occurring coincidentally whereas they solved problems sequentially (one-by-one) supposing the occurrence of only one problem at a time. Their input is provided by an user and they used a myopic approximation (i.e., they presupposed that the user made just one observation at a time) whereas we receive the input from an automated process and deal with a sequence of interlaced observations corresponding to simultaneous problems. Conversational CBR also assumes partial rather than complete problem descriptions. However, when only a partial problem description is provided, an interactive dialog is engaged with the user to better delimit and clarify the descriptions provided [15]. Through this conversation with the user, a complete and individual description is obtained in the end. Cunningham and Smith [16] proposed an incremental case retrieval technique based on a simple information theoretic metric to find the feature that best discriminates between the current set of retrieved cases and produce focused questions in electronic fault diagnosis.

To the best of our knowledge, only a few case-based approaches to intrusion detection have been published [17,18]. Esmaili et al proposed a Case-Based Intrusion Detection System (CBIDS) whose input was the audit trail produced by an operating system and whose output was a collection of countermeasure actions that the system performed based on the severity of the intrusion detected so far [17]. Recently Schwartz et al proposed to improve the capabilities of Snort IDS [3] using a case-based approach [18]. They proposed a similarity measure based on a collection of distinct comparators for each feature (Snort rule properties) rather than using a complete match on all features as Snort. There are two main differences to our approach. First, we work at higher-level of abstraction using alerts provided by Snort as input and providing a priority as output whereas they used directly suspect network packets as input and provided alerts as output. Second, their approach was stateless since they assessed the danger of each suspect network packet (case) individually whereas our approach can be considered stateful since we consider a whole sequence of alerts before determining the priority of individual alerts.

4 Observational Data

We suppose alerts that are triggered by automated real-time systems that collect and interpret sensor data in real-time. Alerts are complex objects made up of a set $\mathcal{F}$ of numeric, qualitative and structured features. We model alerts using *feature terms* that organize concepts into a hierarchy of *sorts*, and represent *terms* or *individuals* as collections of *features* (functional relations). For further details and examples see [1]. We assume that at a given point in time t there is a sequence of n alerts (alert stream) in the system. We denote by $\boldsymbol{S}^{(t)}$ the sequence of alerts received so far. Each alert ψ_i in $\boldsymbol{S}^{(t)}$ belongs to a pre-specified alert signature Σ. An alert signature $\Sigma = \langle \mathcal{S}, \bot, \mathcal{F}, \preceq \rangle$ is a four-tuple where $\mathcal{S}$ is a set of sort symbols; $\mathcal{F}$ is a set of feature symbols; and $\preceq$ is a decidable partial order on $\mathcal{S}$ such that $\bot$ is the least element. Based on that order among sorts, intuitively, we say of two alerts ψ, ψ' that ψ subsumes ψ' ($\psi \sqsubseteq \psi'$) when all that is true for ψ is also true for ψ'. Let $\boldsymbol{X}$ and $\boldsymbol{Y}$ be two sequences of alerts such that $\boldsymbol{X} = [\psi_1, \cdots, \psi_n]$ and $\boldsymbol{Y} = [\psi'_1, \cdots, \psi'_m]$, $|\boldsymbol{X}| = n$, $|\boldsymbol{Y}| = m$, and $n \geqslant m$. We say that $\boldsymbol{Y}$ subsumes $\boldsymbol{X}$ if there exists a sequence of indices $1 \leq i_1 < \cdots < i_m \leq n$

such that: $\psi'_1 \sqsubseteq \psi_{i_1}, \cdots, \psi'_m \sqsubseteq \psi_{i_m}$. We also define the function $sort(\psi)$ that returns the sort of alert ψ. A *path* $\rho(X, f_i)$ is defined as a sequence of features going from the variable X to the feature f_i. There is a *path equality* when two paths $\rho(X, f_i)$ and $\rho(Y, f_j)$ point to the same value (i.e., $\rho(X, f_i) = \rho(Y, f_j)$).

In an ever-changing environment, recalling the history of the system can be the only way to reduce uncertainty. Our model considers that as the analysis of the alert stream proceeds, it produces a probability distribution over the set of all received alerts. This probability distribution constitutes the foundation of our similarity between sequences as well as the basis that allow us to go from observations to hypotheses and from hypotheses to explanations. For each sort i in $\mathcal{S}$ we denote by $q_i^{(t)}$ the relative frequency of sort i at time t. We use the relative frequency of a sort to estimate its a priori probability $P^{(t)}(i) = q_i^{(t)}$. When there is no risk of confusion with the instant of time that we are referring to we simply use $P(i)$ and q_i. We say that the probability of occurrence of an alert ψ_j whose sort is $i = sort(\psi_j)$ is $P(\psi_j) = q_{sort(\psi_j)} = q_i$. Notice that given two sorts $i, j \in \mathcal{S}$ such that $i \preceq j$ then $P(i) \geqslant P(j)$ and that $P(\bot) = 1$.

We consider that our model is unable to capture all possible alerts (observable symptoms events) that affect the system under supervision. Alerts may be not evoked due to a number of causes. For example, because the corresponding network sensors cannot detect an attacker's action that corresponds to a new and unknown vulnerability. Alerts could also be lost before reaching the ACC because they are transmitted through unreliable or corrupted communication channels. We define the alert loss ratio as the probability that an alert of a given sort is lost and denote it by $L(i)$. This value is adjusted based on the gathered experience about the system under supervision. For example, using the packet loss rate in the communication channel or other parameters that allow us to derive the reliability of the different components that underpin the CBR component [19].

5 Sequential Cases

A compositional (or composite) case is an assemblage of several cases that lies in a hierarchical structure. The cases on the upper levels are made up of small cases that in turn are compositional. The lowest level is made of indivisible cases. The highest level is made up of only one case that refers to the whole compositional hierarchy. Intermediate compositional cases (the cases that lie between the highest level and the lowest level) are considered as part of a larger ensemble solution rather than as individual solutions to the case at hand. We say that a case C_i is a *direct part* of a case C_j, denoted by $C_i \triangleleft C_j$, iff $C_i \subset C_j \wedge \nexists C_k \neq C_i : C_i \triangleleft C_k \wedge C_k \triangleleft C_j$ (i.e., they are a step away). We say that case C_i is a *part* of case C_j, denoted by $C_i \triangleleft^* C_j$, iff there exist $n \geq 0$ cases $C_{k+1}, \cdots, C_{k+n}$ such that $C_i \triangleleft C_{k+1} \triangleleft \cdots \triangleleft C_{k+n} \triangleleft C_j$.

A sequential case is a compositional case where a temporal order is established among all the parts that comprise it. If all the sub-cases that make up a sequential case are totally-ordered then we say that the sequential case is serial.

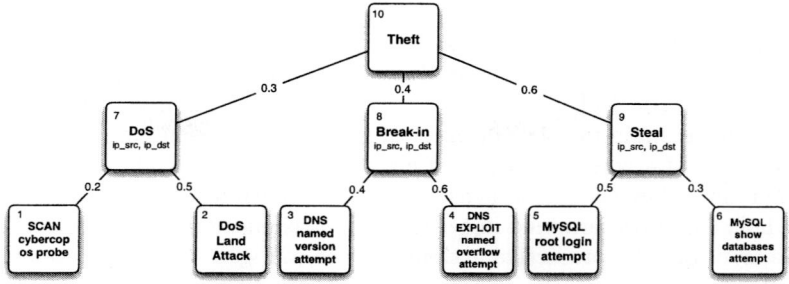

Fig. 1. An actionable tree of a Theft attack. An attacker launches a DoS against a machine running an IDS, subsequently breaks in to a DNS server, spawns a remote shell, and steals some information from a MySQL database.

If the order of all the sub-cases are interchangeable then we say that the sequential case is parallel. Otherwise, if they are partially-ordered we say that the sequential case is arbitrary (i.e., a sequential case made up of serial and parallel subcases). Sequential cases are represented by means of *actionable trees*.

An actionable tree is a predictive compositional hierarchy modeled using a Multi-Rooted Acyclic Graph (see Fig. 1) with the semantics that a single distinguished node is designated as the *crown* (node 10), a number of (evidence) nodes are designated as the *roots* (nodes 1 to 6), the intermediate nodes in the path between the crown and a root node are designated as the *trunk* (nodes 7 to 9), and the arcs represent part-whole relationships. Roots represent observable symptom events and allow one to specify sorts to which each alert belongs. Inference is engaged upon their individual observation thus we call them roots. Nodes in the trunk represent composite (serial or parallel) cases and specify constraints (e.g. ip_src and ip_dst) among the direct parts of a sequential case. The crown represents a sequential case made up of a combination of all the events in the roots ordered according to the constraints expressed by the trunk.

A *predictive actionable tree* embodies an actionable tree in a representation that allows predictive inference. Formally, given an alert signature Σ, a predictive actionable tree is defined as a 7-tuple $\langle G, \mu, \tau, \kappa, \phi, \triangleleft, L \rangle$ where: G is a multi-rooted acyclic graph $G = \langle V, E \rangle$ where V is partitioned in three mutually exclusive sets: R (the set of roots), T (the set of trunk nodes), and C (the singleton set containing the crown); E defines part-of relationships $\triangleleft$ among the subsets of R; $\mu : R \rightarrow \Sigma.\mathcal{S}$ is a mapping that associates each root node with a sort in $\Sigma.\mathcal{S}$; $\tau : T \cup \{C\} \rightarrow \{\textbf{serial}, \textbf{parallel}\}$ is a mapping that associates each non-root node with an order type; $\kappa : T \cup C \rightarrow 2^{\Sigma.\mathcal{F}}$ is a mapping that associates each non-root node with a subset of features (constraints) in $\Sigma.\mathcal{F}$; $\phi : E \rightarrow L$ is a mapping that labels each arc $e \in E$ to a casual strength in L; and L is a likelihood model that assigns a measure of strength to the part-whole relation. L provides a probabilistic model based on the following semi-ring: $P = \langle [0,1], \cdot, 1 - \prod_{i=1}^{k}(1-l_i), 0, 1 \rangle$ where the multiplicative operation is the product ($\cdot$) of probabilities and the additive operation is defined as: $l_1 + \cdots + l_k = 1 - \prod_{i=1}^{k}(1-l_i)$. Therefore, the probability of the crown C given a root node $r \in R$ is: $P(C|r) = \prod_{e \in path(r,C)} \phi(e)$ and the probability of the crown C given a sequence of root nodes $r_1, \cdots, r_n \in R$ is: $P(C|r_1, \cdots, r_n) = 1 - \prod_{i=1}^{n}(1 - \prod_{e \in path(r_i,C)} \phi(e))$. Actionable trees have been devised with the main purpose in mind of providing a measure of confidence on the occurrence of a whole sequence of alerts given a number of observed alerts. Said differently, they provide a measure of the strength with which the existence of the whole can be determined in terms of the existence of some of its parts. For example, consider the predictive actionable tree of Fig. 1. If we observe an alert of sort SCAN cybercop os probe then the probability of observing a Theft attack is $0.06 = 0.2 \cdot 0.3$. If we additionally observe an alert of sort DNS named version attempt then the probability of Theft is $0.2104 = 1 - ((1 - 0.06)(1 - 0.16))$.

Additionally, we consider *sequential abstract cases*. Given an alert signature Σ, a sequential abstract case is constructed based on the informational order provided by the taxonomic hierarchy (i.e., $\Sigma.\mathcal{S}$) used to represent the alerts at the roots of the actionable tree. Sequential abstract cases allow Ceaseless CBR to find explanations for those alerts corresponding to attacks that have never occurred in the system before. That is, they are used as a back-up for the explanation of unknown situations. We use the predicate **abst?**(C_i) to determine whether a case C_i is abstract or not.

6 Case Activations

We deal with new cases that are not assembled but broken up into pieces that arrive over time without fixed boundaries and mixed in with other cases' pieces that correspond to problems that occur coincidentally. Therefore, an incremental case acquisition process is required. This process entails piecing together different parts that resemble a past case. While this happens our model needs to keep a number of plausible hypotheses that continuously best match the different partial descriptions received during a specified time span. These hypotheses, that we have called *case activations*, are generated by retrieving similar cases from the case base and are constantly updated as soon as new evidence is gathered. A case activation is a hypothesis on the occurrence of a similar past case and is represented formally as a 6-tuple $h = \langle C, \hat{a}, \check{a}, \varrho, \tilde{e}, t \rangle$ where: C is a reference to the sequential case being activated; $\hat{a}$ represents a partial binding between the sequence of alerts that occurred and are subsumed by C; $\check{a}$ represents those alerts in C that have not been observed yet and that were abduced in the dynamic sequence similarity computation; ϱ represents the rareness of the observed alerts. We compute it as the sequence similarity between C and ϱ, i.e., $\varrho = C \sim_s \hat{a}$; $\tilde{e}$ measures the level of confidence (evidence) we have in the occurrence of a complete similar sequence of alerts to those that the sequential case C represents. We compute it as the normalized sequence similarity between C and $\hat{a}$, i.e., $\tilde{e} = \|C \sim_s \hat{a}\|$; and t is the time at which the last alert on $\hat{a}$ occurred.

We define an *equality path checking* process that ensures when two case activations are compounded together the constraints established by the corresponding sequential case are followed. We say that a sequence of alerts $\boldsymbol{S}$ is constrainable given a set of constraints $\mathcal{C} = \{f_1, \cdots, f_m\} : f_i \in \Sigma.\mathcal{F}$ when path equality is kept for all features in $\mathcal{C}$ and for all alerts in $\mathcal{S}$. This process guarantees that all the alerts in a given sequence share a number of common features. For example, the same source and destination IP address. This process is part of the *fusion* of case activations. The fusion of two case activations $h_i = \langle C_i, \hat{a}_i, \check{a}_i, \varrho_i, \tilde{e}_i, t_i \rangle$ and $h_j = \langle C_j, \hat{a}_j, \check{a}_j, \varrho_j, \tilde{e}_j, t_j \rangle$, denoted by $h_i \uplus h_j$, is defined as $\langle C_i, \hat{a}_i \cup \hat{a}_j, \check{a}_i - \hat{a}_j, C_i \sim_s (\hat{a}_i \cup \hat{a}_j), \|C_i \sim_s (\hat{a}_i \cup \hat{a}_j)\|, \max(t_i, t_j)\rangle$ if h_i and h_j are *compoundable* and as $\{\langle C_i, \hat{a}_i, \check{a}_i, \varrho_i, \tilde{e}_i, t_i\rangle, \langle C_j, \hat{a}_j, \check{a}_j, \varrho_j, \tilde{e}_j, t_j\rangle\}$ otherwise. We say that two case activations $h_i = \langle C_i, \hat{a}_i, \check{a}_i, \varrho_i, \tilde{e}_i, t_i\rangle$ and $h_j = \langle C_j, \hat{a}_j, \check{a}_j, \varrho_j, \tilde{e}_j, t_j\rangle$ are compoundable when: (i) the corresponding sequential cases do not subsume repeated alerts. That is, the observed alerts in both case activations do not intersect (i.e., $\hat{a}_i \cap \hat{a}_j = \emptyset$); (ii) the observed alerts are constrainable according to the constraints expressed by the corresponding sequential case; and either (iii.a) both case activations correspond to the same sequential case, i.e., $C_i = C_j$; (iii.b) or one of the case activations corresponds to a new abstract case, i.e., $(\mathbf{abst?}(C_i) \wedge \neg\mathbf{abst?}(C_j)) \vee (\neg\mathbf{abst?}(C_i) \wedge \mathbf{abst?}(C_j))$; or both case activations correspond to a new abstract case and there exists a sequential case that can be abstracted to subsume the corresponding composition, i.e., $\mathbf{abst?}(C_i) \wedge \mathbf{abst?}(C_j) \wedge \exists C_k \in C^{(t)} : C_k \sqsubseteq \hat{a}_i \cup \hat{a}_j$. The above definition can be easily extended to the union of n case activations [1].

7 Ceaseless Retrieve

Ceaseless Retrieve continuously compares the sequence of alerts at hand with sequential cases in the case base and keeps updated a collection of case activations that represent the current *situation*. Ceaseless Retrieve proceeds as sketched by Algorithm 1. We assume a case base initially composed of $n \geqslant 0$ sequential cases $\mathbf{C}^{(0)} = \{C_1, \cdots, C_n\}$. We use $\boldsymbol{W}_{wm}^{(t)}$ to represent the most recently received alerts according to a specific window model wm. A window model determines how much context is considered each time that inference is invoked upon the arrival of new events. Time-based or space-based sliding windows are common window models. $\mathbf{H}^{(t)}$ denotes the set of current case activations. Initially $\mathbf{H}^{(0)} = \emptyset$. $\mathbf{A}^{(t)}$ denotes the set of all new case activations at iteration t. It is set to $\emptyset$ at the beginning of each iteration (line: 3). Ceaseless Retrieve establishes a case retrieval policy based on the frequency of occurrence of alerts. This policy promotes rareness. Those cases that subsume alerts that are very common receive a low score whereas those cases that subsume rare alerts receive a high score. Namely, the rarer the alerts that comprise an attack the higher the score. This helps our system to notice those situations that apparently convey more peril since the system is less used to dealing with them. The match is carried out using the dynamic sequence similarity measure that we introduced elsewhere and behaves according to such policy [1]. We denote by $\mathbf{R}^{(t)}$ the set of sequential cases retrieved at iteration t (line: 4). Using the sequence of sorts returned by $sort(\boldsymbol{W}_{wm}^{(t)}(S^{(t)}))$ and our dynamic similarity measure $\sim_s$, those cases that are similar to the sequence above a user-defined threshold $0 < \theta \leqslant 1$ are retrieved. A case activation $\mathbf{h}_i$ is created for each retrieved case and fused toghether with previous case activations generated during the same iteration (lines: 5–8).

Algorithm 1 Ceaseless Retrieve

Require: $\mathbf{C}^{(0)}, S^{(0)}, \theta, \tau, wm$;
Local: $\mathbf{H}, \mathbf{R}, \mathbf{A}, C_i, \mathbf{h}_i$
1: $\mathbf{H}^{(0)} = \emptyset$;
2: **while** true **do**
3:    $\mathbf{A}^{(t)} = \emptyset$;
4:    $\mathbf{R}^{(t)} = \text{retrieve}(sort(\boldsymbol{W}_{wm}^{(t)}(S^{(t)})), \mathbf{C}^{(t-1)}, \theta)$;
5:    **for** each $C_i \in \mathbf{R}^{(t)}$ **do**
6:       $\mathbf{h}_i = \langle C_i, \hat{a}_i, \check{a}_i, \varrho_i, \bar{e}_i, t \rangle$;
7:       $\mathbf{A}^{(t)} = \mathbf{A}^{(t)} \uplus \{\mathbf{h}_i\}$;
8:    **end for**
9:    **for** each $\psi_i \in \boldsymbol{W}_{wm}^{(t)} : \mathbf{D}^{(t)}(\psi_i) = \emptyset$ **do**
10:       $\mathbf{h}_i = \langle \bot, \psi_i, \emptyset, \varrho^*, 1, t \rangle$;
11:       $\mathbf{A}^{(t)} = \mathbf{A}^{(t)} \uplus \{\mathbf{h}_i\}$;
12:    **end for**
13:    $\mathbf{H}^{(t)} = \mathbf{H}^{(t-1)} \uplus \mathbf{A}^{(t)}$;
14:    **for** each $\mathbf{h}_i \in \mathbf{H}^{(t)}$ **do**
15:       **if** $\mathbf{h}_i.t - t \geq \tau$ **then**
16:          $\mathbf{H}^{(t)} = \mathbf{H}^{(t)} - \{\mathbf{h}_i\}$;
17:       **end if**
18:    **end for**
19:    send($\mathbf{H}^{(t)}$, _CEASELESSREUSE); /* non-blocking call */
20:    $[\mathbf{H}^{(t)}, \boldsymbol{P}^{(t)}] = \text{recv}(\_\text{CEASELESSREUSE})$;
21: **end while**

We denote the domain of an alert ψ_i over time by $\mathbf{D}^{(t)}(\psi_i) = \{C_j \in \mathbf{C}^{(t-1)} : sort(\psi_i) \triangleleft^* C_j\}$. We say that an alert is *uncovered* when its domain is $\emptyset$. For each uncovered alert in $\boldsymbol{W}_{wm}^{(t)}$, a new case activation $\mathbf{h}_i$ is created using a simple actionable tree composed uniquely of the observed alert and fused with case activations created in previous iterations (lines: 9–12). The evidence of this kind of case activation is originally set to 1 and their rareness to a maximal value (i.e., $\varrho^* = \max \varrho_i, \forall \mathbf{h}_i$) so that they could promptly be prioritized.

Those case activations that have not been altered during a certain period of time (given by the parameter τ) are filtered out from consideration (lines: 14–17). We denote by $\boldsymbol{P}^{(t)}$ the sequence of pending alerts at time t. That is, alerts that have not yet been prioritized either because they have just arrived or they were not prioritized in a previous iteration because they had a low *urgency*. We discuss this issue later on in Sec. 8. Therefore, we say that $\mathbf{H}^{(t)}$ always keeps a number of up-to-date case activations for each pending alert. We also say that, $\mathbf{H}^{(t)}$ defines the current situation that is then sent to the Ceaseless Reuse (line: 19). Ceaseless Reuse decides on which alerts to explain/prioritize first and returns those case activations and associated alerts for which it estimates that more evidence is needed before the corresponding alerts can be prioritized conveniently (line: 20).

8 Ceaseless Reuse

Ceaseless Reuse constantly searches the combination of case activations that best explains the sequence of alerts most recently received and those that did not find an explanation in previous iterations (pending alerts). Ceaseless Reuse uses a belief function to determine which case activations are susceptible of being used to prioritize the corresponding alerts. However, if this process prioritizes alerts too soon, that is, without being completely sure of the presence of a (possible) exceptional situation the number of false positives will be high and the ultimate objective (to triage the alert stream) will not be achieved. On the contrary, if it prioritizes too late and an exceptional situation is really occurring then the time to enable a prompt response is reduced. Thus we take a decision-theoretic approach that maximizes the overall utility of each complete explanation and define a measure of urgency that guides the decisions of this process over time. Algorithm 2 sketches the tasks performed by Ceaseless Reuse.

Algorithm 2 Ceaseless Reuse

Local: H, h_i, b, B, E, e, e^*, U,
1: **while** true **do**
2: $\quad \mathbf{H}^{(t)} = \text{recv}(\_\text{CEASELESSRETRIEVE})$;
3: $\quad$ **for** each $h_i^{(t)} \in \mathbf{H}^{(t)}$ **do**
4: $\quad\quad \mathbf{b}^{(t)+}(\mathbf{h}_i) = 1$;
5: $\quad\quad$ **for** each $\psi_j \in \mathbf{h}_i.\tilde{a}$ **do**
6: $\quad\quad\quad \mathbf{b}^{(t)+}(\mathbf{h}_i) = \mathbf{b}^{(t)+}(\mathbf{h}_i) \times (L(\psi_j) + ((1 - L(\psi_j)) \times (1 - P(\psi_j|\mathbf{h}_i))))$;
7: $\quad\quad$ **end for**
8: $\quad\quad \mathbf{b}^{(t)-}(\mathbf{h}_i) = P(\mathbf{h}_i)P(\boldsymbol{P}^{(t)}|\mathbf{h}_i)$;
9: $\quad\quad \mathbf{b}^{(t)}(\mathbf{h}_i) = \mathbf{b}^{(t)+}(\mathbf{h}_i) \times \mathbf{b}^{(t)-}(\mathbf{h}_i)$;
10: $\quad$ **end for**
11: $\quad [\mathbf{H}^{(t)}, \mathbf{H}_U^{(t)}, \boldsymbol{P}^{(t)}, \boldsymbol{U}^{(t)}] = \text{rank}(\mathbf{H}^{(t)}, \mathbf{b}^{(t)})$;
12: $\quad \text{send}([\mathbf{H}^{(t)}, \boldsymbol{P}^{(t)}], \_\text{CEASELESSRETRIEVE})$; % non-blocking call
13: $\quad \mathbf{E}^{(t)} = \{\mathbf{e}_i \subseteq \mathbf{H}_U^{(t)} : \forall_{\psi_i \in U^{(t)}} \exists \mathbf{h}_i \in \mathbf{e}_i : \mathbf{h}_i.C_i \sqsubseteq \psi_i \wedge \nexists \mathbf{e}'' : |\mathbf{e}''| < |\mathbf{e}'| \wedge (\mathbf{e}' \cap \mathbf{e}'') \neq \emptyset\}$;
14: $\quad$ **for** each $\mathbf{e}_i \in \mathbf{E}^{(t)}$ **do**
15: $\quad\quad \mathbf{B}^{(t)+}(\mathbf{e}_i) = 1$;
16: $\quad\quad$ **for** $\mathbf{h}_j \in \mathbf{e}_i$ **do**
17: $\quad\quad\quad \mathbf{B}^{(t)+}(\mathbf{e}_i) = \mathbf{B}^{(t)+}(\mathbf{e}_i) \times \mathbf{b}^{(t)+}(\mathbf{h}_j)$;
18: $\quad\quad$ **end for**
19: $\quad\quad \mathbf{B}^{(t)-}(\mathbf{e}_i) = P(\mathbf{e}_i)P(\boldsymbol{U}^{(t)}|\mathbf{e}_i)$;
20: $\quad\quad \mathbf{B}^{(t)}(\mathbf{e}_i) = \mathbf{B}^{(t)+}(\mathbf{e}_i) \times \mathbf{B}^{(t)-}(\mathbf{e}_i)$;
21: $\quad$ **end for**
22: $\quad \mathbf{e}^{*(t)} = \mathbf{e}_i \in \mathbf{E}^{(t)} : \mathbf{B}^{(t)}(\mathbf{e}_i)$ is maximal;
23: $\quad \text{send}([\mathbf{e}^{*(t)}, \boldsymbol{U}^{(t)}], \_\text{CEASELESSREVISE})$; % non-blocking call
24: **end while**

At each iteration Ceaseless Reuse receives a number of competing hypotheses expressed in terms of case activations that explain the current situation (line: 2). We say that a case activation $\mathbf{h}_j$ explains an alert ψ_k if the corresponding sequential case $\mathbf{h}_j.C$ subsumes ψ_k (i.e., $\mathbf{h}_j.C_j \sqsubseteq \psi_k$). For each case activation Ceaseless Reuse computes a belief function as the product of two other belief components (lines: 3–10): a negative component (that takes into account observed alerts) and a positive component (that takes into account those alerts that have not been observed yet): $\mathbf{b}^{(t)}(\mathbf{h}_i) = \mathbf{b}^{(t)+}(\mathbf{h}_i)\mathbf{b}^{(t)-}(\mathbf{h}_i)$.

On the one hand, the positive component is computed in terms of the alerts that have been abduced during the sequence similarity computation as follows: $\mathbf{b}^{(t)+}(\mathbf{h}_i) = \prod_{\psi_j \in \mathbf{h}_i.\tilde{a}} \left(L(\psi_j) + ((1 - L(\psi_j))(1 - P(\psi_j|\mathbf{h}_i)))\right)$. For each abduced alert we consider every possible alternative. Namely, we consider the probability that the alert is lost $L(\psi_j)$ and the probability that the alert is not lost $(1 - L(\psi_j))$ but it was not observed given the sequential case corresponding to the case activation at hand $(1 - P(\psi_j|\mathbf{h}_i))$. Later we will show through Eq. 2 how to compute $P(\psi_j|\mathbf{h}_i)$, the probability that the alert was in fact observed given such case activation. On the other hand, the negative belief on a case activation $\mathbf{h}_i$ is computed as the posterior probability of the case activation given the current sequence of pending alerts: $\mathbf{b}^{(t)-}(\mathbf{h}_i) = P(\mathbf{h}_i|\boldsymbol{P}^{(t)})$. Using Bayes' theorem the posterior probability can be computed as follows: $P(\mathbf{h}_i|\boldsymbol{P}^{(t)}) = \frac{P(\mathbf{h}_i)P(\boldsymbol{P}^{(t)}|\mathbf{h}_i)}{P(\boldsymbol{P}^{(t)})}$. Notice that the denominator, the probability of the sequence of pending alerts, is a constant for all case activations at the current iteration. Therefore the relative rank produced is the same if we only use the numerator. Thus, the computation of $\mathbf{b}^{(t)-}(\mathbf{h}_i)$ can be approximated as follows: $P(\mathbf{h}_i|\boldsymbol{P}^{(t)}) \propto P(\mathbf{h}_i)P(\boldsymbol{P}^{(t)}|\mathbf{h}_i)$. The probability of a case activation $P(\mathbf{h}_i)$ represents the probability of occurrence of the associated sequential case that in turn represents the probability of occurrence of the corresponding undesired situation. This probability is computed using the inference mechanism provided by predictive actionable trees that we saw in Sec. 5 as follows:

$$P(\mathbf{h}_i) = 1 - \prod_{\psi_j \in \mathbf{h}_i.\hat{a}} \left(1 - \prod_{e \in path(\psi_j, \mathbf{h}_i.C_i)} \phi(e)\right) \qquad (1)$$

The probability that we observe the sequence of alerts $\boldsymbol{P}^{(t)}$ given the occurrence of a sequential case is computed as follows: $P(\boldsymbol{P}^{(t)}|\mathbf{h}_i) = \prod_{\psi_i \in \boldsymbol{P}^{(t)}} (1 - P(\psi_i|\mathbf{h}_i))$. Using Bayes' theorem $P(\psi_i|\mathbf{h}_i) = \frac{P(\psi_i)P(\mathbf{h}_i|\psi_i)}{P(\mathbf{h}_i)}$. By actionable trees the probability of occurrence of a sequential case given an alert is $P(\mathbf{h}_i|\psi_i) = \prod_{e \in path(\psi_j, \mathbf{h}_i.C_i)} \phi(e)$. Therefore substituting we get:

$$P(\psi_i|\mathbf{h}_i) = \frac{P(\psi_i) \prod_{e \in path(\psi_j, \mathbf{h}_i.C_i)} \phi(e)}{1 - \prod_{\psi_j \in \mathbf{h}_i.\hat{a}} \left(1 - \prod_{e \in path(\psi_j, \mathbf{h}_i.C_i)} \phi(e)\right)} \qquad (2)$$

Therefore $\mathbf{b}^{(t)-}(\mathbf{h}_i)$ can be approximated using Eq. 1 and Eq. 2. Notice that a belief on a case activation does not need to be computed again and again at each new iteration. We only need to recompute them when their evidence varies at the current iteration (i.e., when $\mathbf{h}_i.t$ is equal to t). Once we have computed the belief on each case activation we rank them and select a number of alerts to build an overall explanation (line: 11). The motivation for not considering all the alerts at each iteration is twofold. First, to reduce the combinatorial explosion in successive steps. The larger the number of alerts considered, the longer it will take to build an overall explanation. Second, it does not make sense to consider alerts for which our belief is too low, since it increases the probability of making a wrong judgment and therefore decreasing the expected utility. Different criteria could be applied to select which alerts should be explained first. We propose to use a measure of *urgency* in the same way that it is applied to health care patient monitoring and to mass casualty incidents [20].

We define urgency as the degree to which an immediate prioritization is required [20]. We compute the urgency of each alert in terms of the expected utility of prioritizing it right now, using our current belief on the hypotheses that explain it, versus the expected utility of waiting to do it after more evidence has been gathered. We say that urgency allows us to trade off in prioritizing an alert versus continuing computation as well as choosing among competing case activations (see [1] for further details). Thus, given a set of case activations $\mathbf{H}^{(t)}$ and their current beliefs $\mathbf{b}^{(t)}$ the function **rank** (line: 11) partitions alerts and their corresponding case activations into those that are urgent and and those that will remain will remain waiting for further evidence. We denote by $\boldsymbol{U}^{(t)}$ the alerts that are urgent and need to be explained at the current iteration. Likewise, $\mathbf{H}_U^{(t)}$ denotes the set of case activations that explain urgent alerts and that is used at the current iteration to compound explanations whereas $\mathbf{H}^{(t)}$ denotes the set of case activations that remains for further iterations. Both case activations that remains for further iterations and pending alerts are sent back to Ceaseless Retrieve (line: 12). Then, Ceaseless Reuse creates explanations using only case activations that explain urgent alerts $\mathbf{H}_U^{(t)}$ and select the explanation whose belief is maximal to propose it to the user as the most plausible explanation.

An explanation $\mathbf{e}_i$ is a subset of $\mathbf{H}_U^{(t)}$ that explains all alerts in $\boldsymbol{U}^{(t)}$. An explanation $\mathbf{e}_i$ is said to explain an alert ψ_k if it contains at least a case activation $\mathbf{h}_j$ that explains ψ_k. $\mathbf{E}^{(t)}$ represents the set of all explanations. $\mathbf{E}^{(t)}$ is computed following a parsimonious principle [11]. Based on the observation that the probability of multiple coincidental sources is low we induce the following heuristic: $\mathbf{e}'$ is not included in $\mathbf{E}^{(t)}$ if it contains a case activation that is already contained by $\mathbf{e}'' \in \mathbf{E}^{(t)}$ such that its size is smaller. Thus those explanations that contain case activations that appear in other explanations that are already in $\mathbf{E}^{(t)}$ and whose size is smaller are not contemplated (line: 13). The next step is to compute an estimation of the goodness for each explanation in $\mathbf{E}^{(t)}$ (lines: 14–21). We define $\mathbf{B}^{(t)}(\mathbf{e}_i)$ as a belief function that represents the likelihood that all cases in $\mathbf{e}_i$ have occurred and $\mathbf{e}_i$ explains all alerts in $\boldsymbol{U}^{(t)}$. $\mathbf{B}^{(t)}$ is computed using the beliefs $\mathbf{b}^{(t)}$ previously computed for each case activation $\mathbf{h}_i$. $\mathbf{B}^{(t)+}$ is based on a double component: $\mathbf{B}^{(t)}(\mathbf{e}_i) = \mathbf{B}^{(t)+}(\mathbf{e}_i)\mathbf{B}^{(t)-}(\mathbf{e}_i)$.

The belief based on positive symptoms gives a degree of suitability for each explanation. The intuition is that when some of the expected alerts have not yet occurred this is considered a positive symptom; therefore we can decrease our belief on the hypotheses at hand: $\mathbf{B}^{(t)+}(\mathbf{e}_i) = \prod_{\mathbf{h}_i \in \mathbf{e}_i} \prod_{\psi_j \in \mathbf{h}_i.\tilde{a}} \mathbf{b}^{(t)}(\mathbf{h}_i)$. The belief component based on negative symptoms determines the relative likelihoods of multiple case activations according to their posterior probabilities: $\mathbf{B}^{(t)-}(\mathbf{e}_i) = P(\mathbf{e}_i|\boldsymbol{U}^{(t)})$. By Bayes' theorem $P(\mathbf{e}_i|\boldsymbol{U}^{(t)}) = \frac{P(\mathbf{e}_i)P(\boldsymbol{U}^{(t)}|\mathbf{e}_i)}{P(\boldsymbol{U}^{(t)})}$. To rank posterior probabilities it is only necessary to compare the joint probabilities since the normalization factor $P(\boldsymbol{U}^{(t)})$ is a constant for all competing explanations at iteration t. Therefore: $P(\mathbf{e}_i|\boldsymbol{U}^{(t)}) \propto P(\mathbf{e}_i)P(\boldsymbol{U}^{(t)}|\mathbf{e}_i)$. The a priori probability of a explanation $\mathbf{e}_i$ is given by: $P(\mathbf{e}_i) = \prod_{\mathbf{h}_i \in \mathbf{e}_i^{(t)}} P(\mathbf{h}_i)$ that can be estimated using Eq. 1 as follows:

$$P(\mathbf{e}_i) = \prod_{\mathbf{h}_i \in \mathbf{e}_i} \left(1 - \prod_{\psi_j \in \mathbf{h}_i.\hat{a}} \left(1 - \prod_{e \in path(\psi_j, \mathbf{h}_i.C_i)} \phi(e)\right)\right) \qquad (3)$$

The conditional probability of $U^{(t)}$ given $\mathbf{e}_i$ is computed as follows: $P(U^{(t)}|\mathbf{e}_i) = \prod_{\psi_i \in U^{(t)}}(1 - \prod_{\mathbf{h}_i \in \mathbf{e}_i}(1 - P(\psi_i|\mathbf{h}_i)))$. Then, by Eq. 2, $P(U^{(t)}|\mathbf{e}_i) =$

$$\prod_{\psi_i \in U^{(t)}} \left(1 - \prod_{\mathbf{h}_i \in \mathbf{e}_i} \left(1 - \frac{P(\psi_i) \prod_{e \in path(\psi_j, \mathbf{h}_i.C_i)} \phi(e)}{1 - \prod_{\psi_j \in \mathbf{h}_i.\hat{a}} \left(1 - \prod_{e \in path(\psi_j, \mathbf{h}_i.C_i)} \phi(e)\right)}\right)\right) \quad (4)$$

$\mathbf{B}^{(t)-}$ can be approximated from Eq. 3 and Eq. 4. All explanations $\mathbf{e}_i$ in $\mathbf{E}^{(t)}$ are ranked according to $\mathbf{B}^{(t)}$. The best explanation $\mathbf{e}^{*(t)}$, the one that is maximal, among all competing explanations, is chosen as the problem solution and sent to Ceaseless Revise for operator's revision (line: 23). Ceaseless Revise continuously provides an operator with the most likely explanations given the alerts received so far. The operator's feedback produces a set of revised solutions that are used to produce the prioritization of the corresponding alerts. Then, Ceaseless Revise sends revised solutions and prioritized alerts to Ceaseless Retain. Finally, Ceaseless Retain constantly updates the case base $\mathbf{C}^{(t)}$ with the revised solutions and the likelihood of occurrence of each sequential case as well as the likelihood of occurrence of each alert in each sequential case. For further details see [1].

9 Conclusions

CBR practitioners are sometimes oblivious that there often situations in the real world where problems occur simultaneously and whose descriptions come interleaved or in continuous form – i.e., without well-defined boundaries between adjacent problem descriptions – and additionally require continuous response to changing circumstances – i.e., a timely action once a proper solution has been identified. We have proposed to enhance the CBR paradigm to support the analysis of unsegmented sequences of observational data stemming from multiple coincidental sources. We aimed at establishing a first CBR model, that we have called Ceaseless CBR, to solve situations that are expressed by means of unsegmented, noisy sequences of complex events that arrive continuously over time. We provided a model that considers the CBR task as on-going rather than one-shot and enables reasoning in terms of problem descriptions that are broken up into small pieces that are mixed with other problems' pieces and the possibility of combining a number of cases that best match the sequential structure of the problem at hand. To put the whole matter in a nutshell, we coped here with problems that include an additional challenge compared to most of those solved by CBR practitioners before, given that each problem description is composed of an undetermined number of parts that arrive continuously over time and are blurred together with other problems' parts into a single on-line stream.

Acknowledgments

We wish to acknowledge anonymous reviewers for useful suggestions and valuable corrections.

References

1. Martin, F.J.: Case-Based Sequence Analysis in Dynamic, Imprecise, and Adversarial Domains. PhD thesis, Technical University of Catalonia (2004)
2. Debar, H., Wespi, A.: Aggregation and correlation of intrusion detection alerts. In: Proceedings of the 4th Symposium on RAID. (2001)
3. Roesch, M.: Snort - lightweight intrusion detection for networks. In: Proceedings of 13th Systems Administration Conference. (1999)
4. Swets, J.A.: Signal Detection Theory and ROC Analysis in Psychology and Diagnostics. Collected Papers. Lawrence Erlbaum Associates (1996)
5. Barletta, R., Mark, W.: Breaking cases into pieces. In: AAAI-88 Case-Based Reasoning Workshop. (1988) 12–16
6. Shavlik, J.W.: Case-based reasoning with noisy case boundaries: An application in molecular biology. Technical Report 988, University of Wisconsin (1990)
7. Redmond, M.: Distributed cases for case-based reasoning; facilitating use of multiple cases. In: Proceedings of AAAI-90, AAAI Press/MIT Press (1990)
8. Ram, A., Santamaría, J.C.: Continuous case-based reasoning. In: Proceedings of the AAAI-93 Workshop on Case-Based Reasoning. (1993) 86–93
9. Jacynski, M.: A framewok for the management of past experiences with time-extended situations. In: 6th ACM CIKM. (1997)
10. Jaere, M.D., Aamodt, A., Skaalle, P.: Representing temporal knowledge for case-based prediction. In: 6th European Conference in Case-Based Reasoning. Lecture Notes in Artificial Intelligence, LNAI 2416. Springer (2002) 174–188
11. Peng, Y., Reggia, J.A.: Abductive Inference Models for Diagnostic Problem-Solving. Springer-Verlag (1990)
12. Lewis, L.: Managing Computer Networks. A Case-Based Reasoning Approach. Artech House Publishers (1995)
13. Gupta, K.M.: Knowledge-based system for troubleshooting complex equipment. International Journal of Information and Computing Science 1 (1998) 29–41
14. Breese, J.S., Heckerman, D.: Decision theoretic case-based reasoning. Technical Report MSR-TR-95-03, Microsoft Research, Advanced Technology Division (1995)
15. Aha, D.W., Maney, T., Breslow, L.A.: Supporting dialogue inferencing in conversational case-based reasoning. LNCS **1488** (1998) 262–266
16. Cunningham, P., Smyth, B.: A comparison of model-based and incremental case-based approaches to electronic fault diagnosis. In: Proceedings of the Case-Based Reasoning Workshop, AAAI-1994. (1994)
17. Emaili, M., Safavi-Naini, R., Balachandran, B., Pierprzyk, J.: Case-based reasoning for intrusion detection. In: 12th Annual Computer Security Applications Conference. (1996)
18. Schwartz, D., Stoecklin, S., Yilmaz, E.: A case-based approach to network intrusion detection. In: 5th International Conference on Information Fusion, IF'02, Annapolis, MD, July 7-11. (2002) 1084–1089
19. Steinder, M., Sethi, A.S.: Probabilistic event-driven fault diagnosis through incremental hypothesis updating. In: Proceedings of IFIP/IEEE Symposium on Integrated Network Management. (2003)
20. Huang, C., Schachter, R.: Alarms for monitoring: A decision-theoretic framework. Technical Report SMI-97-0664, Section on Medical Informatics, Stanford University School of Medicine (1997)

Explanation Service for Complex CBR Applications

Rainer Maximini[1], Andrea Freßmann[1], and Martin Schaaf[2]

[1] University of Trier
Department of Business Information Systems II
54286 Trier, Germany
{rainer.maximini,andrea.fressmann}@wi2.uni-trier.de
[2] University of Hildesheim
Institute for Mathematics and Applied Computer Science
Data and Knowledge Management Group
31113 Hildesheim, Germany
schaaf@dwm.uni-hildesheim.de

Abstract. Case-based Reasoning (CBR) is a mature technology for building knowledge-based systems that are capable to produce useful results even if no answer matches the query exactly. Often the result sets presented to users are ordered by means of similarity and utility. However, for complex applications with knowledge intensive domains we have discovered that results sets enriched by calculated similarity values for particular answers are not sufficient. Users have a demand for additional information and explanations making the proposed results more transparent. By presenting additional explanations to them, their confidence in the result set increases and possible deficiencies, e. g., in the weight model, can be revealed and corrected. This paper presents a realized explanation service that combines several existing and new explanation technologies into one system.

1 Introduction

CBR-based applications can become highly complex with regards to the knowledge stored in the various knowledge containers. In the scope of this paper, the complexity of CBR applications is denoted to the highly extensive vocabulary, user specific similarity measures, completion rules to refine the query, and the highly structured case base. The underlaying hierarchical model and domain knowledge are gained during a work intensive and difficult elicitation process, usually hidden from the user and compacted into a single similarity value used for ranking the retrieval results [1]. For highly knowledge intensive tasks executed by domain experts, a growing demand for additional explanations is observed that make the retrieval process and the proposed results more transparent. Within the IPQ project several requirements are encountered concerning the explanations: the suggested results should be understood according to the performed query, the retrieval process should be comprehended for increasing the users' confidence, and the results should be automatically analysed to support the user. Such explanations cannot only reveal the knowledge behind the CBR application, but also provide additional assistance in interpreting the result set. The reasons are manifold: Weights encoded in the similarity model may not reflect the user preferences or the underlying case base may not have been consolidated.

In this paper, a strategy is presented that combines different components for achieving an explanation support for highly complex domains. In the following section the IP Broker Tool Suite is briefly introduced that incorporates among other things a CBR-based retrieval service. Within the scope of this service, a demand for explanations occurred because of domain based requirements described in Section 2. After that, related works are summarised, which form the basis of the explanation strategy presented in Section 4, continued by a discussion in Section 5. Finally, this paper concludes with a short summary and an outlook of future work.

1.1 About the Context of This Work

The problems tackled in this paper occur within the context of the IPQ[1] Project (Intellectual Property Qualification) that aims at supporting developers of microelectronic circuits in their search for design components to be reused. For such components the term Intellectual Property (IP) [2] has been assigned within the Electronic Design Automation community. The application of CBR to the selection of IPs has been published for example in [3, 4]. Within the scope of this paper, it is sufficient to mention that IPs are characterised by a set of about 200 hierarchical ordered attributes, typically consisting of a value from a well-defined type and an associated metrics. Object-oriented techniques like inheritance are used for the data types as well as for the cases that have a maximum aggregation depth of three. The set of types includes, beside primitive types like real or integer values, sets, taxonomies, and intervals. For the retrieval of IPs the user specifies a query by providing a subset of attributes reflecting his/her current design situation and his/her weight preferences. The set of retrieved IPs is used as input for subsequent steps towards the final decision about the IP to be integrated into a microelectronic design.

The CBR application for IP retrieval is part of the IP Broker Tool Suite and based on the structural CBR approach [1] that makes use of a default similarity model containing local similarity measures for each IP attribute type of the characterisation as well as global similarity measures facilitated by aggregation functions for higher-level categories.

1.2 Architecture of the IP Broker Tool Suite

The IP Broker Tool Suite is a set of tools an IP provider can use for developing, deploying, and tailoring a retrieval service to his/her specific needs. The suite contains tools for specifying and maintaining IP assets and for capturing or maintaining IP domain knowledge. The core is the CBR-based Open Retrieval Engine orenge [5] due to its flexibility and its modular concept. The architecture of the suite is depicted in Figure 1.

The Consumer Suite is the web-based user front end[2] for IP retrieval. It includes three services: Retrieval, Explanation and Information Service.

---

[1] IPQ Project (12/2000-11/2003). Partners: AMD, Fraunhofer Institute for Integrated Circuits, FZI Karlsruhe, InfineonTechnologies, Siemens, sci-worx, Empolis, ThomsonMultiMedia, TU Chemnitz, University of Hildesheim, University of Kaiserslautern, and University of Paderborn. See http://www.ip-qualifikation.de/

[2] See http://demo.dwm.uni-hildesheim.de:8080/ipq2/demo

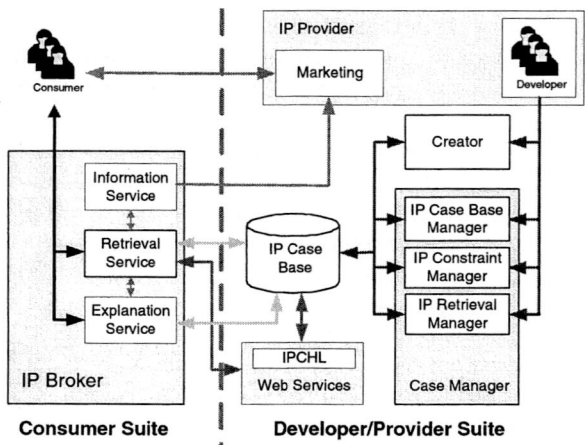

Fig. 1. Architecture of the IP Broker Tool Suite

The Retrieval Service enables the IP user to formulate queries, consisting of detailed technical requirements entered into a structural form. Further it allows to specify individual preferences on the level of the different application and quality criteria that enables users to impact on the similarity assessment. The queries are sent to the CBR retrieval kernel and the results are analysed and presented by the Explanation Service, detailly described in Section 4.

The Information Service can be seen as an interface between IP users and IP providers, because it informs the IP providers about users' needs. It captures the queries posed by the IP users and transmits them to the respective IP providers to enable the provider to better focus their future product development. Further, if the IP user has asked for a particular IP, the affected provider automatically gets a respective notification.

The Developer/Provider Suite contains the IP case base and several tools to manage the vocabulary and the similarity measures. For defining the object-oriented vocabulary, designers utilise the orenge Creator to define the domain model, which contains all relevant attributes. Furthermore, the orenge Creator can be used to define similarity measures via functions, tables, or taxonomies.

The Case Manager uses the vocabulary for capturing and managing the IP case base. Therefore, three tools are integrated: The IP Case Base Manager allows developers to capture case knowledge as well as to define constraints among IP attributes. Such defined generalised cases [6] can be converted into point cases by the IP Constraint Manager [7]. Finally, the IP Retrieval Manager is a front end for connecting local or remote case bases and for performing retrieval activities on the part of the developers.

2 Requirements for Explanations Within the IPQ Context

Within the context of the IPQ Project it is a great demand on giving users an understanding of the functionalities and the search process provided by the IP Broker. Therefore, a variety of goals are identified in cooperation with industrial partners and pursued during the implementation of the Explanation Service. Without going into details of the IP qualification process, three different aims are distinguished on the conceptual level.

Report Generation. Generating a report for each proposed IP with respect to the user query is a fundamental demand for explanation support. It includes the determination of the most relevant attributes leading to the proposed result by calculating the absolute relevance of each attribute. Furthermore, users can request for short text explanations in order to get more information about included design rationales of domain experts. While this kind of explanation support mostly operates on the IP characterisation and the similarity model, it also includes text patterns connected to concepts defined in the vocabulary of the CBR application.

Increasing User Confidence. The selection of IPs is a highly knowledge intensive task. Before an IP is considered as candidate for the subsequent entry check, a task that consumes significant time and money, the designer needs more confidence in the results proposed by the IP retrieval system. This is especially true if the coverage of attributes specified in the query and in the case is low. Explanations providing appropriate visualisations of the recommended IPs, e. g., by determining and graphically rendering the attributes with the highest impact on the assessment, aid the designer in getting a quick overview.

Determine Deficiencies. Another purpose of explanations is the identification of deficiencies in the result set. This can be either that a high number or that no perfect matching cases are retrieved. A high number of perfect matching cases is a deficiency is the query, because the query is defined too generally (under specification). By specialising the query with additional attributes the result can be improved. A result set without perfectly matching cases is a deficiency in the case base. The query is a demand for a case that does not exist. This deficiency must be handled in two ways. On the one side, the case provider must be informed that there exists a new demand, and on the other side, the user has to be supported to refine the query.

The distinction between the purpose of increasing the user's confidence and determining deficiencies of results is justified because it leads to contrasting strategies for the explanation support. Consequently, a part of this work was to identify criteria that enable the intelligent selection of analysis approaches that pursue the different strategies.

3 An Overview of Related Explanation Techniques

In knowledge-based systems explanations have been a main issue, focusing on helping users to understand the reasoning process and to decide whether to accept or reject a recommendation. Richards [8] describes two main approaches to explanation. The intension of the first approach is to present users explanations with respect to their needs concluded from the corresponding user model. The second approach focuses on interactive communication between humans and computers. Normally, users are able to question for reasons when the system asks for information and to question for the way how a conclusion is reached.

In the scope of systems based on structural CBR within a knowledge intensive domain, the first approach becomes vitally important for enabling users to interpret the proposed results according to the query. Particularly, the complex knowledge model that lies behind a structural CBR application has to be made more transparent to users. Furthermore, it is often difficult to make any assumptions about the quality of the case base itself. To cope with these claims, techniques are presented that are related to explanation services but that are not explicitly CBR specific.

Simple "Colored Explanations". A first step towards explanations is to give an overview, which attributes specified by the user have the highest impact on the similarity, and to separate them from the attributes with lower impact. A simple technique for CBR-based applications concerns the coloring of requested attributes within a query-result-comparison with respect to the corresponding local similarity. Hence, users get a quick overview about the attributes that have an impact on the similarity assessment. This kind of explanation support was implemented by the READee prototype [9], a predecessor of the CBR retrieval engine orenge that provides this simple technique and applies it within, e. g., its demos like Carsmart24 and SmartCooking[3].

Report Generation. In-depth approaches of natural language generation focus on deep analysis techniques to automatically understand every part of the input but for some application it is useful to identify only parts of interest for a particular application [10]. The latter technique is called shallow text generation. An example implementation is the multi-lingual text generator developed within the TEMSIS project[4]. Shallow generation is not inherently knowledge-based and theoretically motivated as in-depth techniques and are, therefore, predestinated for small applications in order to reduce the implementation effort.

Data Mining. A third alternative to generate explanations encompasses various techniques for either knowledge-based or statistical data analysis in order to detect interesting relationships or other regularities. For complex domains, these techniques are suitable for mining, describing, or explaining result sets. For revealing connections among result sets different cluster algorithms can be utilised.

First, the representatives of partitioning clustering algorithms calculate disjoint clusters among elements by typically considering distance measures like Euclidean distance or weighted Euclidean distance. Before utilising these kinds of cluster algorithm the number of clusters has to be preselected; the main representatives are the k-means and k-medoid cluster algorithm [11]. Second, density-based clustering algorithms discover arbitrary clusters densely occupied and distinguish them from other regions that have less density, e. g., the DBSCAN algorithm [12]. Third, conceptual clustering algorithms imply grouping the result sets with respect to their characteristics. The main goal is to

---

[3] http://www.empolis.de/
[4] http://www-temsis.dfki.uni-sb.de/

build a hierarchical cluster tree whose nodes are assigned to characteristic attributes. The COBWEB algorithm belongs to conceptual clustering algorithms and is based on probabilities for calculating clusters [13].

Visualisation of a Set of Cases. Approaches for visualising search results comprise techniques to both graphically representing result sets and case bases. In both cases, it is a crucial point how to render multi-dimensional data in a two-dimensional representation form without loosing information. To tackle this problem Mullins and Smyth [14] use a force-directed algorithm for calculating the two-dimensional distances among cases that also imply the similarity between these cases: similar cases are close together, and dissimilar cases are far apart. Another technique described by McArdle and Wilson [15] utilises the MDS[5]- Algorithm for transforming multi-dimensional data points in a two-dimensional space. For visualising, the generated distance between two points is derivated from the former n dimensions. The user obtains a better survey how similar the retrieved cases are to the query and to each other. This provides more insights into the similarity assessment than the usual single dimensioned similarity attribute value.

Determination of the Most Decisive Attributes. The determination of attributes with a high impact on the overall similarity assessment is also tackled by current research for conversational CBR methods [16]. Here, important attributes are determined step by step during a dialog process with the user depending on the customer's previous answers and the remaining potential cases of the case base.

Detection of Retrieval Mismatches. Within the scope of retrieval processes, situations occur in which no results can be retrieved that exactly meet the users' requirements. McSherry [17, 18] presents a technique that deals with subqueries of the user query for detecting retrieval mismatches. The first step is to build the power set of the set of all attributes specialised in the user query. Then, every element of this power set is performed as subquery. By revealing which subqueries have no exact matches, attributes or attribute combinations are detected causing the mismatches.

4 Explanation Service

To cope with the requirements for explanations in highly complex domains, the development of an explanation strategy has considered the evaluation of the pros and cons of the presented techniques for building a complex process pipeline. This pipeline takes advantage of each of the techniques and links them together as single explanation components shown in Figure 2. When developing the explanation strategy two different lines of action are pointed out. The first one concerns the analysis of the result set explained by the *Result Set Explainer*, and the second regards the generation of an explanation report realized by the *Result Case Explainer*.

After retrieval, the Result Set Explainer starts with branches depending on the number of exact matches. When the retrieval contains some exact matches, the result representation is displayed without any further explanations. When no result is received, an

---

[5] Multi-Dimensional Scaling

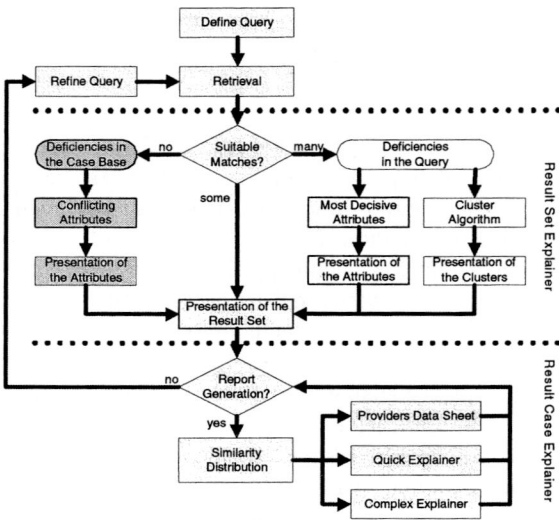

Fig. 2. Explanation Service Process Pipeline

analyser for conflicting attributes implies that there are deficiencies in the case base and detects the conflicting attributes for informing the user. The last branch concerns many suitable matches. In that case, deficiencies in the query are assumed that are differently handled for users' convenience. When just a few suitable hits are retrieved, an analyser of the most decisive attributes gives users support in differentiating among the results. For representing a large amount of hits, a cluster analyser prepares a hierarchical and conceptual arrangement for enabling users to navigate through.

Independent of the branching within the Result Set Explainer, the Result Case Explainer provides report generations about query-result-comparisons. Therefore, different report opportunities like an IP data sheet and a quick or complex explanation give support in further explanations. The components of the Result Set Explainer and the Result Case Explainer are described in more detail in the following sections.

4.1 Result Set Explainer

The retrieval result presentation is subdivided into two parts: The first part is presented at the top and is the explanation of the result set. It only occurs if a deficiency is detected; otherwise it is hidden because no explanation is necessary. The second part is always the usual list of retrieved cases with the possibility for further analyses by the Result Case Explainer. The user can decide him/herself if he/she is satisfied with the result set and can inspect the candidates in detail or can follow the explanation proposals to refine the query.

Conflicting Attributes. To refine the query it is important for the user to understand why there is no matching case. Especially for underlaying models with a high number of

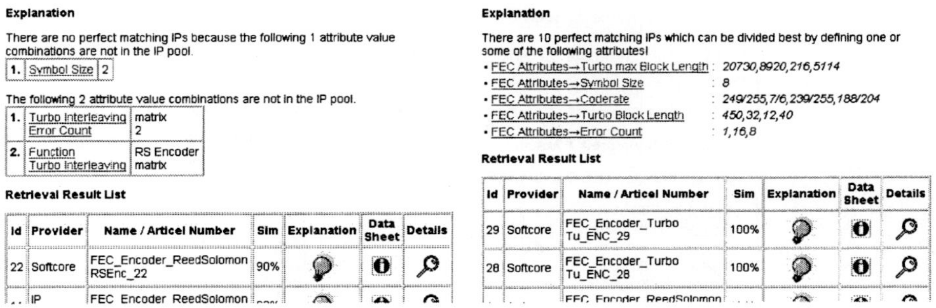

(a) Conflicting Attributes (b) Most Decisive Unspecified Attributes

Fig. 3. Result Set Explanations

attributes it can be difficult to find the correct reason for the insufficient results. For these situations McSherry [18] has presented an explanation technique that is used to analyse deficiencies in the query. The idea is quite simple but efficient: find the minimum of sub-queries that are not covered by the case base.

The list of the conflicting attributes and conflicting attribute combinations are presented to the user. In Figure 3a a typical explanation is shown: The database contains no case where the attribute "Symbol Size" has the value two and no case with the specified attribute combination. For refining the query the user has now the possibility to navigate to the corresponding attribute specification by selecting an attribute. All conflicting attributes are highlighted in the query form to show the user which attributes have caused the conflicts.

Tests have shown that conflicts with more than three attributes are of less interest because in general many of such conflicts occur. The reason is that the whole query seems to be over specified and full of inconsistencies. In this case, the explanation component advices the user to create a new query with less specified attributes.

Most Decisive Unspecified Attributes. In contrast to an over specified query an under specified query results into a result set with many perfectly matching cases. These deficiencies in the query can be explained by computing the most decisive unspecified attributes. By defining the proposed attributes the number of suitable candidates is further reduced. The decisive attributes together with some typical values are presented to the user, see Figure 3b. The Result Set Explainer contains no knowledge about the users' preferences why the best proposed attribute could be one the users do not want to specify. Therefore, beside the most decisive attribute also some minor decisive ones are presented. The user is capable to decide which attribute is to be set.

The downside of the algorithm, firstly proposed by Schmitt [16], is the poor performance that shrinks with the number of perfectly matching cases and the number of unspecified attributes. Especially for queries with only a few number of specified attributes the algorithm is not usable in a real time application. Therefore, if a deficiency in the query is detected, the decision for this algorithm or a cluster algorithm is made on the basis of the number of perfectly matching cases.

Clusters	IPs	Typical Attributes
1	31	Hardness
- 1.1	7	Symbol Size=8, Function=RS Decoder, Hardness=soft
+ 1.1.1	4	Provider=Softcore
- 1.1.2	2	Provider=IP Vendor
- 1.1.3	1	Coderate=249/255, Throughput [MBits/Sec]=85.0, Frequency=37.36, Gatecount=9300.0, Provider=IP Vendor
+ 1.2	24	Hardness, Function

Typical Attribute Value Combinations of most but not all IPs

- Symbol Size   8
- Function   RS Decoder
- Hardness   soft
- Provider   Softcore
- Provider   IP Vendor

IPs of this Cluster

ID	Provider	Name / Articel Number	Sim	Explanation	Data Sheet	Details
17	Softcore	FEC_Decoder_ReedSolomon RSdec17	100%			
18	Softcore	FEC_Decoder_ReedSolomon RSD_18	100%			

Fig. 4. Cluster Explanation; Cluster 1.1 is selected

Cluster Algorithm. Several kinds of cluster algorithm exists with different pros and cons. The main disadvantage of most algorithms is the lack of cluster descriptions that should help the user to select the clusters. One exception is COBWEB [13] that creates a cluster tree and returns reasons for each cluster.

The reasons are based on the predictability and the predictiveness for each cluster that are used by the algorithm to optimise the tree. For both probabilities statistics of the attribute value distribution are computed that are used by the explanation component to characterise the clusters. Each characterisation contains the cluster id, the number of included cases, and the typical attribute value combination.

For example, the cluster 1.1.1 of Figure 4 contains four cases and is characterised by the typical attribute value combination: Provider = Softcore, Symbol Size = 8, Function = RS Decoder, and Hardness = soft.

The navigation through the cluster tree is realised by selecting the cluster ids. The corresponding typical attribute value combinations are presented among and at the bottom is the list of the cluster's cases. The complete result set can be accessed at the root cluster, because each cluster contains all cases of its child clusters.

2D Visualisation. The 2D visualisation of the result set seems to be a very promising technique, but tests have shown that non CBR experts are not able to interpret the graphics. The reason is the dimension reduction that results in abstract axis without direct relations to the attributes, particularly, in domains with a high number of attributes. Therefore, such explanations are not included to the system.

4.2 Result Case Explainer

The Result Case Explainer comprises three explanation components for representing an IP with respect to the query: the IP Data Sheet, the Quick Case Explainer, and the Complex Case Explainer.

Providers Data Sheet. Mostly, the IP recommended by the Retrieval Service is also offered by its provider via internet. Hence, the explanation component incorporates the link to the providers IP description.

Quick Case Explainer. For giving a brief survey of a result IP, the Quick Case Explainer shows users all IP attributes while partly representing the similarity assessment. For example, the attributes, which are also defined in the query, are highlighted in terms of color depending on the local similarity. Moreover, by moving the mouse over the highlighted attributes, the absolute similarity values are displayed. Hence, users are supported in getting the local similarities of the requested attributes that give a better understanding in comparing single attributes. But there is still a lack of the over-all connection between the similarity assessment and the result IP.

Complex Case Explainer. In contrast to the Quick Case Explainer the Complex Case Explainer involves not only the local similarity, but the whole similarity assessment of the selected IP that is denoted as reasoning trace of the selected IP. The important information for users is figured out and presented and, thereby, the focus is laid on illustrating users the similarity assessment in a most understandable way. But for a better understanding the underlying model has to be aware that it is utilising an object-oriented vocabulary representation. Figure 5 illustrates an excerpt of the object-oriented

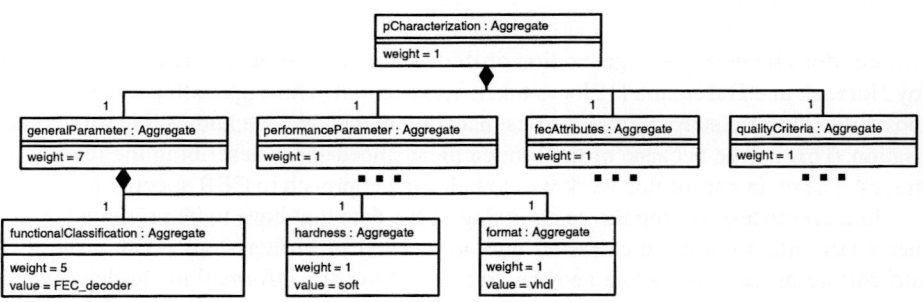

Fig. 5. Object-Oriented Representation of the User Query

representation that shows the user query in two levels. Here, the IP characterisation is constituted by four attribute groups on the first level: General Parameter, Performance Parameter, FEC Attributes, and Quality Criteria. On the second level the General Parameter comprises the Functional Classification, Hardness, Format, etc. Local weights are assigned to every object, but global weights depend on the entire weight model. According to this IP representation, the Complex Case Explainer automatically generates text and charts.

The text generator verbalises data and presents supporting information in order to give users an understanding of the rationales behind the CBR-based application. Hence, the text generator processes data like similarities, weights, query attributes, and completion rules that have been applied.

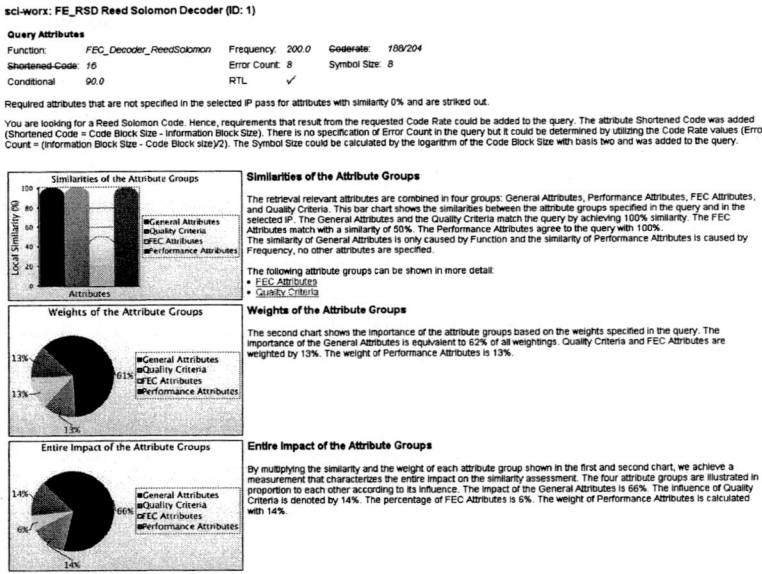

Fig. 6. Illustrations of the Similarity Assessment

For developing the text generation procedure the shallow text generation described by Horacek and Busemann [19] was taken into account. This approach provides a purposeful strategy to support applications that contain manageable knowledge for verbalisation. This is true because of the limited means needed for describing the reasoning traces. The main part of this work was to tailor the approach to CBR specific needs.

In a preprocessing step the categorising of the data that have to be presented, e. g., necessary information are extracted that are needed in further steps. Within the text structuring process the layout and the arrangement of the information are determined before the text is enriched by selecting suitable text patterns and phrases. After that, the selected text patterns or phrases are grammatically adapted and the verbalisation process is finished. At least, the formulated and generated text is integrated into the HTML pages for being presented to users.

Because reading the textual reports is very time-consuming, its content is also visualised by utilising appropriate chart forms. Visualisations of the IP result aid the designer in getting a quick overview as depicted in Figure 6. First, a bar chart makes obvious the local similarity values of the attribute groups. Second, the local weights of the corresponding groups are shown by a pie chart. Third, the impact of the attribute groups is illustrated by a pie chart. By multiplying the similarity and the weight of each group a measurement for characterising the entire impact on the similarity assessment is calculated. For example, the FEC attributes are weighted by 13%, but have the similarity of 50%. Hence, there is a low impact (6%) on the similarity assessment as shown by the last chart. When containing more than one requested attribute the attribute groups can be optionally shown on the second level in the similar illustration form. These charts help users to derivate the impact of attribute value modifications and to understand the consequences of refining queries if the result set is not sufficient.

On the second level, the Complex Case Explainer reveals the sophisticated rule system implemented in the complex CBR application. The rule system mainly contains completion rules that are derived for the sophisticated domain. These rules consist of a condition and a conclusion part for completing queries and cases. Getting to know the internal application of the rules and its consequences is an issue for users, because the rules may have a deep impact on the similarity assessment. Therefore, the explanation component uncovers the applied completion rules by describing the corresponding condition and conclusion parts with respect to the user query.

For example, a user is looking for a Reed Solomon Decoder and specialises the code rate for request. Then some other attributes can be calculated because of their dependence on the code rate, e. g., error count and symbol size. The automatic extension of the user query considers the completed attributes within the search process. Consequently, IPs can be found that would not have been found when the enhanced attributes would have been left out. Figure 6 shows an automatically verbalised text, that briefs users about applied completion rules.

5 Discussion

Swartout and Moore [20] propose five aspects of a good explanation. They are developed in the context of the second generation of expert systems and are also applicable on the presented CBR-based application for discussion. The five criteria are fidelity, understandability, sufficiency, low construction overhead, and efficiency. In the following, these explanation criteria are verified and discussed with respect to the Explanation Service described in Section 4.

Fidelity. Fidelity stands for accuracy of the explanation representation. The Explanation Service gives explanations for reasoning processes, for completion rules, and for received result sets. The explanations of reasoning processes base on the similarity assessment that are composed of local similarity measures, which are acquired by domain experts, and of weightings, which are modifiable by the user. For the Result Case Explainer the reasoning trace is reconstructed with respect to the selected IP and to the user query. Because of the unambiguity of the similarity measures and the weighting the reconstruction is also unambiguous. The explanations of the completion rules are automatically generated from the complex rule system, and also emphasise the explanation fidelity.

Understandability. The criterion understandability testifies whether the content and the context is understandable to users. Therefore, it is crucial to determine the user target group of the application. Here, it is assumed that the people using the IP Broker are domain experts about IPs, but are no experts in CBR-based applications. According to that, users have to be given rather an understanding of the reasoning process than an understanding of the domain knowledge.

Particularly, the understandability depends on terminology, the grammatical verbalisation, and the interdependency of different kinds of explanation. First, the terminology is adapted to a general style without using technical terms of CBR. Second, the text generations include techniques for considering grammatical rules and correct linguistic usage. This is emphasised by the utilisation of text patterns and phrases that only are grammatically modulated. Third, the Result Set Explainer and the Result Case Explainer complement each another in representing the results and partial results of the CBR-based retrieval. Additionally, the results of the Result Case Explainer provide an understanding of the reasoning process. Moreover, the explainers give comments that act as guidelines how to use the full capacity of the CBR technique. For example, the Explanation Service includes a call for modifying the user query in order to improve the result set.

Sufficiency. Sufficiency signifies the sufficient amount and quality of knowledge for providing explanations. But it is debatable how much knowledge should form the basis of an explanation service. Richards [8] details this knowledge in knowledge about the system's behavior, justification, user preferences, domain explanations, and terminology definitions. First, in the Explanation Service the system's behavior is covered by comments acting as guidelines that are represented to users. Second, justification in the actual sense is not included by the Explanation Service but transparency and understandability are parts of this notion and are aspired by explaining the reasoning process. Third, user preferences are partly integrated into the application by the users weight model but it would be an enrichment if the Explanation Service would support every single user according to his/her knowledge level. Fourth, the Explanation Service contains domain explanation because of representing, e. g., completion rules. But at least, the Explanation Service does not contain information about local similarity measures that will be a challenge for future work as well as the integration of terminology definitions. Furthermore, the search for conflicting attributes is sometimes cancelling because of the long computation time. This can result in a loss of explanation knowledge but it is still sufficient because the serious conflicts are presented in any case.

Low Construction Overhead. Construction overhead identifies the time consuming and the degree of difficulty to generate the explanations. Most of the explanations are generated automatically, which can be done without precalculations. Only the determination of the most decisive unspecified attributes includes a small preprocessing step and, therefore, causes some construction overhead.

Efficiency. Efficiency of the Explanation Service regards the response time in which explanations are presented. Again, the Result Case Explainer works efficient in generating explanations, but the Result Set Explainer utilises approaches that normally belong to problems whose costs exponentially grow when the input becomes more complex. Here, the approaches are simplified and partially canceled. The data, which has been extracted till then, are utilised for explaining, and an arguable and comfortable response time is achieved.

6 Summary and Outlook

For highly complex domains, such as electronic designs with more than 200 hierarchically ordered attributes and complex similarity functions, the presentation of an ordered list of retrieval results is not sufficient. Users have a demand for additional information and explanations making the proposed results more transparent.

The presented Explanation Service combines several techniques producing additional explanations that increase the confidence in the result set so that possible deficiencies can be revealed and corrected. If the coverage of attributes specified in the query and in the case is low, a deficiency in the case base is indicated, which is traced back to conflicting attributes posed in the query. For aiding the users to improve and refine the query, these attributes or attribute combinations are analysed and presented.

But also the query can have deficiencies, which is the case if a high number of suitable matching cases are retrieved. Here, appropriate analysis techniques determine the most decisive unspecified attributes in order to propose a refinement of the query. Alternatively, a modified COBWEB algorithm is used to cluster the result set hierarchically to facilitate the IP user's navigation through the set.

Generating a report for each proposed IP with respect to the user's query is a fundamental demand for explanation support. Graphical rendering of the attributes with highest impact on the assessment and textual explanations aid the user in getting a quick overview of the product.

A couple of open questions have already been raised in this paper. Additionally, the handling of generalised cases and the explanation of their constraints is still open. They are currently under investigation or will be investigated in the near future.

References

1. Bergmann, R.: Experience Management - Foundations, Development Methodology, and Internet-Based Applications. Lecture Notes in Artificial Intelligence 2432. Springer Berlin, Heidelberg, New York, Hong Kong, London, Milan, Paris, Tokyo (2002)
2. Lewis, J.: Intellectual property (IP) components. Artisan Components, Inc., [web page], http://www.artisan.com/ip.html (1997) [Accessed 28 Oct 1998].
3. Schaaf, M., Maximini, R., Bergmann, R., Tautz, C., Traphöner, R.: Supporting electronic design reuse by integrating quality-criteria into CBR-based IP selection. In: Proceedings of the European Conference on Case-Based Reasoning ECCBR-02, Springer (2002)
4. Schaaf, M., Visarius, M., Bergmann, R., Maximini, R., Spinelli, M., Lessmann, J., Hardt, W., Ihmor, S., Thronicke, W., Franz, J., Tautz, C., Traphöner, R.: IPCHL - a description language for semantic IP characterization. In: Forum on Specification & Design Languages. (2002)
5. empolis knowledge management GmbH: The orenge Framework - A Platform for Intelligent Industry Solutions Based on XML and Java. empolis knowledge management GmbH, Kaiserslautern. (2001)
6. Maximini, K., Maximini, R., Bergmann, R.: An investigation of generalized cases. [22] 261–275
7. Maximini, R., Tartakovski, A.: Approximative retrieval of attribute dependent generalized cases. In: FGWM 2003 Workshop Wissens- und Erfahrungsmanagement, http://km.aifb.uni-karlsruhe.de/ws/LLWA/fgwm, GI Workshop Woche LLWA (2003)
8. Richards, D.: Knowledge-based system explanation: The ripple-down rules alternative. In: Knowledge and Information Systems, London, Great Britain, Springer-Verlag (2003) 2–25
9. Oehler, P., Vollrath, I., Conradi, P., Bergmann, R., Wahlmann, T.: READee - decision support for IP selection using a knowledge-based approach. In: Proceedings of IP98 Europe, Miller Freeman (1998)

10. Busemann, S., Horacek, H.: A flexible shallow approach to text genertion. In: The 9th International Workshop on Natural Language Generation, Niagara-on-the-Lake, Canada (1998) 238–247
11. MacQueen, J.: Some methods for classification and analysis of multivariate observations. [21] 281–297
12. Ester, M., Kriegel, H.P., Sander, J., Xu, X.: A density-based algorithm for discovering clusters in large spatial databases with noise. [21] 226–231
13. Fisher, D.H.: Knowledge aquisition via incremental conceptual clustering. Machine Learning **2** (1987) 139–172
14. Mullins, M., Smyth, B.: Visualisation methods in case-based reasoning. In Weber, R., Gresse von Wangenheim, C., eds.: The 4th International Conference on Case-Based Reasoning, Vancouver, Canada (2001)
15. McArdle, G.P., Wilson, D.C.: Visualising case-base usage. [23] 105–124
16. Schmitt, S.: Dialog Tailoring for Similarity-Based Electronic Commerce Systems. PhD thesis, University of Kaiserslautern, Germany (2003)
17. McSherry, D.: Similarity and compromise. [22] 291–305
18. McSherry, D.: Explanation of retrieval mismatches in recommender system dialogues. [23] 191–199
19. Horacek, H., Busemann, S.: Towards a methodology for developing application-oriented report generation. In Herzog, O., ed.: The 22th German Conference on Artificial Intelligence, Bremen, Germany (1998) 189–200
20. Swartout, W., Moore, J.: Explanation in second generation expert systems. In David, J., Krivine, J.P., Simmons, R., eds.: Second Generation Expert Systems, Berlin, Springer-Verlag (1993) 543–585
21. Le Cam, L., Neyman, J., eds.: 5th Berkeley Symposium on Mathematics, Statistics and Probability. In Le Cam, L., Neyman, J., eds.: 5th Berkeley Symposium on Mathematics, Statistics and Probability. (1967)
22. Ashley, K.D., Bridge, D.G., eds.: 5th International Conference on Cased Base Reasoning (ICCBR 2003). In Ashley, K.D., Bridge, D.G., eds.: 5th International Conference on Cased Base Reasoning (ICCBR 2003). Lecture Notes in Artificial Intelligence 2689, Berlin Heidelberg New York, Springer-Verlag (2003)
23. McGinty, L., ed.: Workshop Proceedings. In McGinty, L., ed.: The 5th International Conference on Case-Based Reasoning, Norwegian, Norwegian University of Sience & Technology (NTNU), Department of Computer and Information Science (2003)

Explaining the Pros and Cons of Conclusions in CBR

David McSherry

School of Computing and Information Engineering,
University of Ulster, Coleraine BT52 1SA, Northern Ireland
dmg.mcsherry@ulster.ac.uk

Abstract. We begin by examining the limitations of *precedent-based* explanations of the predicted outcome in case-based reasoning (CBR) approaches to classification and diagnosis. By failing to distinguish between features that support and oppose the predicted outcome, we argue, such explanations are not only less informative than might be expected, but also potentially misleading. To address this issue, we present an *evidential* approach to explanation in which a key role is played by techniques for the discovery of features that support or oppose the predicted outcome. Often in assessing the evidence provided by a continuous attribute, the problem is where to "draw the line" between values that support and oppose the predicted outcome. Our approach to the selection of such an *evidence threshold* is based on the *weights of evidence* provided by values above and below the threshold. Examples used to illustrate our evidential approach to explanation include a prototype CBR system for predicting whether or not a person is over the legal blood alcohol limit for driving based on attributes such as units of alcohol consumed.

1 Introduction

It is widely recognised that users are more likely to accept intelligent systems if they can see for themselves the arguments or reasoning steps on which their conclusions are based. In many problem-solving situations, the solution is not clear-cut, and it is reasonable for users to expect an intelligent system to explain the *pros* and *cons* of a suggested course of action [1-3]. In domains such as fault diagnosis, it is also reasonable for users to expect the system to explain the relevance of test results they are asked to provide, for example in the case of tests that carry high risk or cost [4-6]. Explanation is also a topic of increasing importance in areas such as intelligent tutoring and product recommendation [7-8]. However, we confine our attention in this paper to explanation of conclusions in CBR systems for classification and diagnosis.

While rule-based approaches to explanation remain an important legacy from expert systems research, a view shared by many CBR researchers is that explanations based on previous experience may be more convincing than explanations based on rules [9-10]. Recent research by Cunningham *et al.* [9] provides empirical evidence to support this hypothesis. In experiments involving human subjects, simply showing the user the most similar case in a classification task was found to be a more convincing explanation of the predicted outcome than a rule-based explanation generated from a decision tree. But what does it *mean* for an explanation to be convincing? In the case of a decision that is not clear-cut, trying to convince the user that the predicted outcome is *correct* does not make sense. Instead, the challenge is to convince the user that the predicted outcome is *justified* in spite of the evidence that opposes it. However, we argue that failure to distinguish between positive and negative evidence limits the usefulness of precedent-based explanations as a basis for showing how a predicted outcome is justified by the available evidence.

We do not suggest that there is no value in showing the user the case on which the predicted outcome is based. An obvious advantage is that the user can assess for herself how closely it matches the problem description. But attempting to justify the predicted outcome simply by showing the user the most similar case ignores the possibility that some of the features it shares with the target problem may actually *oppose* rather than support the predicted outcome [2]. The result is that the explanation is not only less informative than might be expected, but also potentially misleading. In the absence of guidance to the contrary, any feature that the target problem shares with the most similar case may be interpreted by the user as evidence in favour of the predicted outcome even if it has the opposite effect.

Unfortunately, the chances of precedent-based explanations being open to misinterpretation in this way are far from remote. Given that similarity measures reward matching features whether or not they support the predicted outcome, it is not unlikely that one or more of the features that the most similar case has in common with the target problem actually provide evidence against the predicted outcome. It is worth noting that the problems we have identified are not specific to precedent-based explanations. In fact, rule-based explanations also fail to distinguish between positive and negative evidence, and as we show in Section 2, can also be misleading.

To address the need for more informative explanations, we present an *evidential* approach to explanation in which the user is shown the evidence, if any, that opposes the predicted outcome as well as the evidence that supports it. As in previous work [2], a key role in our approach is played by techniques for the discovery of features that support and oppose the predicted outcome. However, our initial approach was limited to assessing the evidence provided by nominal or discrete attributes. Here we present new techniques for explaining the pros and cons of a predicted outcome in terms of the evidence provided by continuous attributes, a requirement we consider essential to provide a realistic basis for explanation in CBR. Often in the case of a continuous attribute, the problem is where to "draw the line" between values that support and oppose the predicted outcome. Our approach to the selection of such an *evidence threshold*, which currently focuses on binary classification tasks, is based on the *weights of evidence* provided by values above and below the threshold.

In Section 2, we examine the limitations of approaches to explanation in which the user is simply shown the case or rule on which a conclusion is based. In Section 3, we describe the techniques for discovery of features that support and oppose a predicted outcome used in our evidential approach to explanation, and our approach to assessing the evidence provided by continuous attributes. In Section 4, an example case library based on Cunningham *et al.*'s [9] breathalyser dataset is used to illustrate our evidential approach to explanation as implemented in a prototype CBR system called *ProCon-2*. Related work is discussed in Section 5 and our conclusions are presented in Section 6.

2 Limitations of Existing Approaches

In this section, we examine more closely the limitations of precedent-based and rule-based explanations that motivate our evidential approach to explaining the pros and cons of the conclusions reached by a CBR system.

2.1 Rule-Based Explanations

In problem-solving based on decision trees, the standard approach to explaining how a conclusion was reached is to show the user all features on the path from the root node to the leaf node at which the conclusion was reached [5,9]. A similar approach is possible in CBR systems in which a decision tree is used to guide the retrieval process. Because any solution path in a decision tree can be regarded as a rule, the resulting explanation is often referred to as a *rule-based* explanation. In fact, explaining conclusions in this way is very similar to the standard expert systems technique of showing the user the rule on which the conclusion is based [6].

However, one of the problems associated with rule-based explanations is that some of the evidence that the user is shown may not support the conclusion [5]. Even worse, it is possible that some of the evidence presented actually *opposes* the conclusion. The example we use to illustrate this problem is based on Cendrowska's contact lenses dataset [11]. This well-known dataset is based on a simplified version of the optician's real-world problem of selecting a suitable type of contact lenses (none, soft, or hard) for an adult spectacle wearer.

Fig. 1 shows part of a decision tree induced from the contact lenses dataset with Quinlan's information gain measure [12] as the splitting criterion. The following explanation for a conclusion of no contact lenses was generated from the contact lenses decision tree.

> **if** tear production rate = normal
> **and** astigmatism = absent
> **and** age = presbyopic
> **and** spectacle prescription = myope
> **then** conclusion = no contact lenses

However, it is clear from the contact lenses decision tree that a normal tear production rate cannot be regarded as evidence in favour of no contact lenses, since a reduced tear production rate is enough evidence on its own to reach the same conclusion. So the first condition in the explanation that the user is shown is not only redundant but also potentially misleading.

Another problem associated with decision trees is that the user may be asked for the results of tests that are not strictly necessary to reach a conclusion [11]. In recent work, we presented a *mixed-initiative* approach to classification based on decision trees in which the system does not insist on asking the questions and is capable of eliminating redundant conditions from the explanations it generates [5]. However, even if a rule-based explanation contains no redundant or opposing conditions, it remains open to the criticism of presenting only positive evidence in favour of the conclusion. The user has no way of telling whether evidence that is not mentioned in the explanation has a positive or negative effect on the conclusion.

2.2 Precedent-Based Explanations

Typically in CBR approaches to classification and diagnosis, the predicted outcome is explained by showing the user the case that is most similar to the target problem [9,13,14]. The example we use to illustrate the limitations of precedent-based explanations is based on Cunningham *et al.*'s [9] breathalyser dataset for predicting whether or not a person is over the legal blood alcohol limit for driving in Ireland.

Attributes in the dataset are the weight and sex of the subject, duration of drinking in minutes, meal consumed, and units of alcohol consumed. The outcomes to be predicted in this binary classification task are over-limit and not-over-limit.

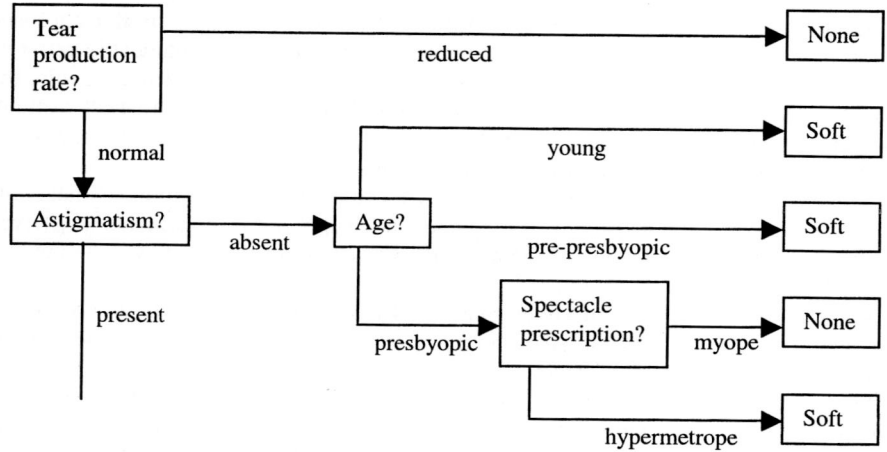

Fig. 1. Partial decision tree based on the contact lenses dataset

Target problem:	*Most similar case*:
weight = 79	weight = 79
duration = 90	duration = 240
sex = male	sex = male
meal = full	meal = full
units = 10.1	units = 9.6
predicted outcome: over-limit	outcome: over-limit

Fig. 2. A precedent-based explanation of the predicted outcome for a target problem in the breathalyser domain

A target problem and the outcome predicted by a CBR system based on the breathalyser dataset are shown in Fig. 2. The most similar case on which the predicted outcome is based in our system is also shown. The target problem and most similar case are the same as those used in [9] to illustrate a typical precedent-based explanation in the breathalyser domain.

Given that the most similar case exactly matches the target problem on three of its five features, it is not surprising that its similarity to the target problem is very high (0.97). But this is *not* the same as saying that there is strong evidence in favour of the predicted outcome. In fact, as we show in Section 3, none of the three features that the most similar case shares with the target problem supports the predicted outcome.

So how useful is showing the user the most similar case likely to be as an explanation of the predicted outcome in this example? One problem is that the user could be forgiven for thinking that the matching features sex = male, meal = full, and weight =

79 are evidence in favour of the subject being over the limit when in fact they *oppose* the predicted outcome. The explanation also fails to comment on the much shorter duration of drinking in the target problem or how this should affect our confidence in the predicted outcome.

An important message that the explanation fails to convey is that the predicted outcome, though perhaps justifiable on the basis of the number of units consumed, is far from being a clear-cut decision. As described in the following sections, showing the user the evidence that opposes the predicted outcome as well as the evidence that supports it is one of the ways in which we propose to provide more informative explanations in CBR approaches to classification and diagnosis.

3 The Pros and Cons of a Predicted Outcome

In classification and diagnosis, it is seldom the case that all the reported evidence supports the conclusion reached by an intelligent system, or indeed by a human expert. More typically in practice, some features of the target problem will provide evidence in favour of the conclusion while others provide evidence against it. In a CBR system, it is equally unlikely that all the features in the most similar case support the outcome recorded for that case. Our evidential approach to explanation in CBR aims to address the limitations of precedent-based explanations highlighted in Section 2 by showing the user the evidence, if any, that opposes the predicted outcome as well as the supporting evidence.

3.1 Criteria for Support and Opposition

An important point to be considered in assessing the evidence for and against a predicted outcome is that certain features (or test results) may sometimes increase and sometimes decrease the probability of a given outcome class, depending on the evidence provided by other features [15,16]. However, it has been shown to follow from the independence (or Naïve) version of Bayes' theorem that a given feature always increases the probability of an outcome class if it is more likely in that outcome class than in any competing outcome class [15]. We will refer to such a feature as a *supporter* of the outcome class. Conversely, a feature always decreases the probability of an outcome class if it is less likely in that outcome class than in any competing outcome class. We will refer to such a feature as an *opposer* of the outcome class. A feature that is neither a supporter nor an opposer of an outcome class may sometimes provide evidence in favour of the outcome class, and sometimes provide evidence against it.

Below we define the criteria for support and opposition of a given outcome class on which our evidential approach to explanation is based.

The Support Criterion. *A feature E is a supporter of an outcome class H_1 if there is at least one competing outcome class H_2 such that $p(E \mid H_1) > p(E \mid H_2)$ but no competing outcome class H_2 such that $p(E \mid H_1) < p(E \mid H_2)$.*

The Opposition Criterion. *A feature E is an opposer of an outcome class H_1 if there is at least one competing outcome class H_2 such that $p(E \mid H_1) < p(E \mid H_2)$ but no competing outcome class H_2 such that $p(E \mid H_1) > p(E \mid H_2)$.*

In our approach to explaining the pros and cons of a predicted outcome, a feature may be the observed value of an attribute, such as age = young in the contact lenses dataset, or a condition defined in terms of a continuous attribute, such as units ≥ 6 in the breathalyser dataset. In practice, though, the reliability of the evidence provided by a given feature is likely to depend on whether it occurs with sufficient frequency in the dataset for its conditional probability in each outcome class to be estimated with reasonable precision.

Our criteria for support and opposition of an outcome class can be expressed in simpler terms when applied to a binary classification task.

Proposition 1. *In a classification task with two possible outcomes H_1 and H_2, a given feature E is a supporter of H_1 if $p(E \mid H_1) > p(E \mid H_2)$ and an opposer of H_1 if $p(E \mid H_1) < p(E \mid H_2)$.*

It can also be seen from Proposition 1 that in a classification task with only two possible outcomes, a given feature must either support or oppose a given outcome class except in the unlikely event that its conditional probability is the same in both outcome classes. As we shall see, however, this is not the case in datasets in which there are more than two outcome classes.

3.2 Nominal and Discrete Attributes

Values of a nominal or discrete attribute that support and oppose the outcome classes in a given case library can easily be identified from the conditional probabilities of the attribute's values. Table 1 shows the conditional probabilities for two of the attributes, age and tear production rate, in the contact lenses dataset. For example, it can be seen that:

$$p(\text{age} = \text{young} \mid \text{none}) = 0.27$$
$$p(\text{age} = \text{young} \mid \text{soft}) = 0.40$$
$$p(\text{age} = \text{young} \mid \text{hard}) = 0.50$$

So according to our criteria for support and opposition, age = young is a *supporter* of hard contact lenses and an *opposer* of no contact lenses. On the other hand, age = young is neither a supporter nor an opposer of soft contact lenses.

Table 1. Conditional probabilities for two of the attributes in the contact lenses dataset

Type of contact lenses:	None	Soft	Hard
Age:			
young	0.27	0.40	0.50
pre-presbyopic	0.33	0.40	0.25
presbyopic	0.40	0.20	0.25
Tear production rate:			
normal	0.20	1.00	1.00
reduced	0.80	0.00	0.00

It can also be seen from Table 1 that tear production rate = normal is an *opposer* of no contact lenses, a finding that is consistent with our impression from the contact lenses decision tree in Fig. 1.

Table 2 shows the conditional probabilities for sex and meal consumed in the breathalyser dataset [9]. According to our criteria for support and opposition, sex = female is a supporter of over-limit as it is more likely in this outcome class than in the only competing outcome class. Interestingly, meal = full is a supporter of not-over-limit while meal = lunch is a supporter of over-limit. The estimated conditional probabilities for meal = snack and meal = none should perhaps be regarded more cautiously as neither of these values is well represented in the dataset.

Table 2. Conditional probabilities for two of the attributes in the breathalyser dataset

		over-limit	not-over-limit
Sex:	female	0.23	0.19
	male	0.77	0.81
Meal:	full	0.33	0.51
	lunch	0.43	0.19
	snack	0.10	0.14
	none	0.13	0.16

3.3 Explanation in ProCon

In previous work we presented a CBR system for classification and diagnosis called ProCon that can explain the pros and cons of a predicted outcome in terms of the evidence provided by nominal or discrete attributes [2]. As often in practice, the predicted outcome for a target problem in ProCon is the outcome associated with the most similar case. An example case library based on the contact lenses dataset was used in [2] to illustrate ProCon's ability to construct a structured explanation of a predicted outcome in which the user is shown any evidence that opposes the conclusion as well as the evidence that supports it. When explaining a predicted outcome of no contact lenses, for example, ProCon recognises a normal tear production rate, if reported by the user, as evidence *against* the predicted outcome.

In the case of a feature that is neither a supporter nor an opposer of the predicted outcome, ProCon *abstains* from commenting on the impact of this feature in its explanation of the predicted outcome. When explaining a predicted outcome of soft contact lenses, for example, ProCon would abstain from commenting on age = young while recognising age = pre-presbyopic as evidence in favour of the predicted outcome and age = presbyopic as evidence against it.

In Section 4 we present a new version of ProCon called ProCon-2 that can also explain the pros and cons of a predicted outcome in terms of the evidence provided by continuous attributes such as units of alcohol in the breathalyser dataset.

3.4 Continuous Attributes

Focusing now on classification tasks in which there are only two possible outcomes, we present the techniques used in ProCon-2 to explain the pros and cons of a predicted outcome in terms of the evidence provided by continuous attributes. Often in assessing the evidence provided by a continuous attribute, the problem is where to "draw the line" between values that support the predicted outcome and values that oppose it. Choosing a realistic evidence threshold for a continuous attribute can be more difficult than it might seem at first sight. In the case of units of alcohol in the breathalyser dataset, the problem is that for any value x of units apart from the minimum value in the dataset:

$$p(\text{units} \geq x \mid \text{over-limit}) > p(\text{units} \geq x \mid \text{not-over-limit})$$

Thus according to our criteria for opposition and support, units $\geq x$ is a supporter of over-limit for *any* value x of units apart from the minimum value in the dataset. If we choose a high value of units such as 15 as the evidence threshold, it is intuitive that values above the threshold will provide strong evidence in favour of over-limit. However, it is equally intuitive that values below the threshold will provide little evidence *against* over-limit. A system that attempts to justify a conclusion that the subject is not over the limit on the basis that units < 15 is unlikely to inspire user confidence in its explanation capabilities.

Similarly, if we choose a low value of units as the evidence threshold, then values below the threshold will provide strong evidence in favour of not-over-limit, whereas values above the threshold will provide only weak evidence in favour of over-limit. Our solution to this dilemma is based on the concept of weights of evidence [4,15,17].

Definition 1. *If H_1 and H_2 are the possible outcomes in a binary classification task, then for any feature E such that $0 < p(E \mid H_2) \leq p(E \mid H_1) \leq 1$, we define the weight of evidence of E in favour of H_1 to be*:

$$we(E, H_1) = \frac{p(E \mid H_1)}{p(E \mid H_2)}$$

For example, a weight of evidence of two in favour of H_1 means that E is twice as likely in H_1 as it is in H_2. The usefulness of weight of evidence as a measure of the impact of reported evidence on the probabilities of the competing outcome classes can be seen from the following proposition, which follows easily from the independence (or Naïve) form of Bayes' theorem [15].

Proposition 2. *If H_1 and H_2 are the possible outcomes in a binary classification task, then for any feature E such that $0 < p(E \mid H_2) \leq p(E \mid H_1) \leq 1$,*

$$\frac{p(H_1 \mid E)}{p(H_2 \mid E)} = we(E, H_1) \times \frac{p(H_1)}{p(H_2)}$$

Our intuitions regarding the trade-off associated with 15 as an evidence threshold for units consumed are borne out by the following calculations based on the breathalyser dataset [9].

$p(\text{units} \geq 15 \mid \text{over-limit}) = 0.33$ $p(\text{units} < 15 \mid \text{over-limit}) = 0.67$
$p(\text{units} \geq 15 \mid \text{not-over-limit}) = 0.07$ $p(\text{units} < 15 \mid \text{not-over-limit}) = 0.93$

$we(\text{units} \geq 15, \text{over-limit}) = \dfrac{0.33}{0.07} = 4.7$ $we(\text{units} < 15, \text{not-over-limit}) = \dfrac{0.93}{0.67} = 1.4$

As might be expected, $we(\text{units} \geq 15, \text{over-limit})$ is relatively high whereas $we(\text{units} < 15, \text{not-over-limit})$ is close to its minimum possible value.

In the case of units, our approach to the selection of a realistic evidence threshold is to select the threshold x that maximises the minimum of the weights of evidence that units $\geq x$ provides in favour of over-limit and units $< x$ provides in favour of not-over-limit. That is, we choose the value x of units that maximises:

$$\text{MIN}(we(\text{units} \geq x, \text{over-limit}), we(\text{units} < x, \text{not-over-limit}))$$

In general for a continuous attribute, the evidence threshold selected in our approach is the value that maximises the minimum of the weights of evidence provided by values above and below the threshold.

3.5 Experimental Results

Fig. 3 shows the results of an empirical evaluation of possible evidence thresholds for units consumed in the breathalyser dataset [9]. We confine our attention here to values x of units for which $we(\text{units} \geq x,$ over-limit) and $we(\text{units} < x,$ not-over-limit) are both defined. For example, we exclude units ≥ 17 because $p(\text{units} \geq 17 \mid \text{not-over-limit}) = 0$.

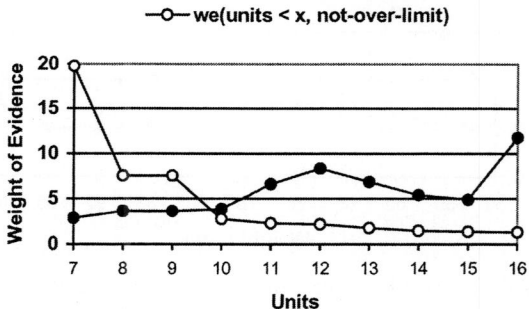

Fig. 3. Weights of evidence for units of alcohol consumed in the breathalyser dataset

Two of the possible thresholds, 8 and 9, can be seen to maximise the minimum of the weights of evidence in favour of over-limit and not-over-limit. For example, $we(\text{units} \geq 8,$ over-limit) = 3.6 and $we(\text{units} < 8,$ not-over-limit) = 7.5. The fact that the weights of evidence are the same for units = 8 and units = 9 can be explained by the fact that there are no cases in the dataset with values of units between 8 and 8.9. On this basis, a reasonable choice of evidence threshold would be 8 or 9 (though of course it is possible for a person who has consumed much less than 8 units to be over the limit). In practice, the selected evidence threshold is based in our approach on actual values that occur in the dataset rather than equally spaced values as in this analysis. The threshold selected by ProCon-2, based on a minimum weight of evidence of 4.0 in favour of over-limit, is 9.1.

Fig. 4 shows the results of a similar evaluation of evidence thresholds for duration of drinking in the breathalyser dataset. In this case the choice is more clear-cut. The evidence threshold that maximises the minimum weight of evidence is duration $\geq$ 150. The evidence threshold selected by ProCon-2 from the actual values that occur in the dataset is also duration $\geq$ 150.

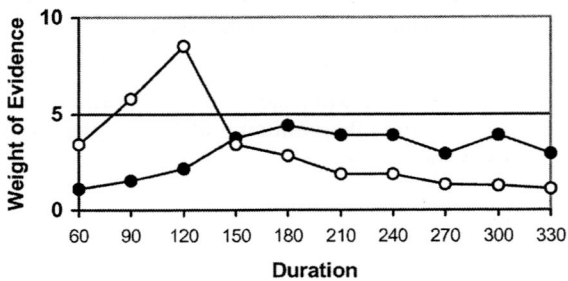

Fig. 4. Weights of evidence for duration of drinking in the breathalyser dataset

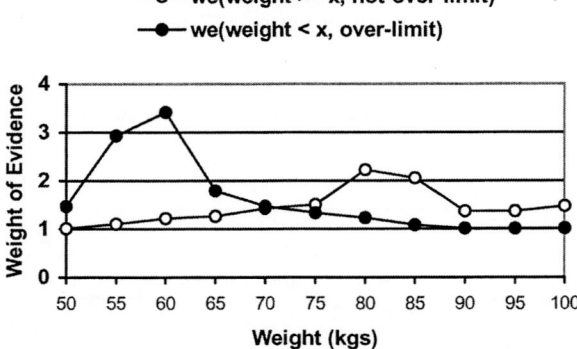

Fig. 5. Weights of evidence for weight in kgs in the breathalyser dataset

Finally, Fig. 5 shows the results of an evaluation of evidence thresholds for weight in the breathalyser dataset. This attribute differs from units and duration in that values *below* a given threshold tend to support the conclusion that the subject is over the limit. The evidence threshold that maximises the minimum weight of evidence in this case is weight ≥ 70. The threshold selected by ProCon-2 from the actual values that occur in the dataset is weight ≥ 73.

Table 3. Evidence thresholds in the breathalyser dataset selected by two different strategies and their minimum weights of evidence (WE)

	Units (WE)	Duration (WE)	Weight (WE)
Mid-Point	16.2 (1.3)	220 (1.9)	74 (1.3)
Max-Min	9.1 (4.0)	150 (3.4)	73 (1.5)

In Table 3 we summarise the results of an empirical comparison of our "Max-Min" strategy of maximising the minimum weight of evidence with an alternative "Mid-

Point" strategy of selecting the mid-point of the attribute's range of values in the dataset as the evidence threshold. For each continuous attribute in the breathalyser dataset, the evidence threshold selected in each strategy is shown together with the minimum of the weights of evidence provided by values above and below the threshold. While the evidence thresholds selected in the two strategies differ only slightly in the case of weight, there are marked differences in the evidence thresholds selected for units and duration. In the case of units, the evidence threshold selected by our Max-Min strategy can be seen to *treble* the minimum weight of evidence provided by the mid-point value. In the case of duration, the minimum weight of evidence is increased by nearly 80% from 1.9 to 3.4.

4 Explanation in ProCon-2

We now present an implementation of our evidential approach to explanation in ProCon-2, a CBR system for classification and diagnosis in which the predicted outcome is based on nearest-neighbour retrieval. Initially on entering the description of a target problem, the user is shown the *three* most similar cases and the predicted outcome from the most similar case. If the outcome for the three most similar cases is the same, this may help to increase the user's confidence in the predicted outcome. On requesting an explanation of the predicted outcome, the user is also shown:

- Features in the target problem that *support* and *oppose* the predicted outcome
- Features in the most similar case, if any, that *oppose* the predicted outcome

Showing the user features in the most similar case that oppose the predicted outcome may help to convince the user that the predicted outcome is *justified* if one or more of the opposing features are also present in the target problem. Thus the fact that the predicted outcome was the correct outcome for the most similar case, in spite of any opposing evidence it shares with the target problem, is used in our approach as additional justification of the predicted outcome.

The example dialogue in Fig. 6 is based on the breathalyser dataset [9]. Attributes in the case library and weights assigned to them in ProCon-2 are weight (3), duration (2), sex (2), meal (3) and units (4). The similarity of each case to the target problem is shown in brackets.

The example dialogue shows how ProCon-2 attempts to justify the predicted outcome in terms of the features that support and oppose the predicted outcome. When the user asks for an explanation, she is shown one feature in the target problem that supports the predicted outcome and three features that oppose the predicted outcome. ProCon-2 also shows the user the most similar case and points out that the outcome in that case was over-limit in spite of three opposing features that it shares with the target problem. However, it should be obvious to the user from the evidence presented that the decision is not clear-cut. The fact that the outcome in the second and third most similar cases differs from the predicted outcome may also help to convey this important point.

Discovery of the supporters and opposers of the predicted outcome is *demand driven* in ProCon-2. The selection of evidence thresholds for continuous attributes is also based on the available cases at problem-solving time. In the example dialogue, the user is not shown the evidence thresholds used by ProCon-2 to assess the evidence provided by continuous attributes. The possible benefit of providing this additional information is one of the issues to be addressed by further research.

ProCon-2: Please describe the target problem.

User: weight = 79, duration = 90, sex = male, meal = full, units =10.1

ProCon-2: The 3 most similar cases are:

   Case 13: 79, 240, male, full, 9.6, over-limit (0.97)
   Case 26: 73, 120, male, full, 9, not-over-limit (0.96)
   Case 56: 79, 120, male, full, 7.2, not-over-limit (0.96)

   The predicted outcome is: over-limit.

User: **why**

ProCon-2: Features of the target problem that SUPPORT the prediction:

   units = 10.1

   Features of the target problem that OPPOSE the prediction:

   weight = 79
   duration = 90
   sex = male
   meal = full

   The most similar case is:

   Case 13: 79, 240, male, full, 9.6, over-limit

   The outcome in this case was over-limit in spite of the opposing evidence that:

   weight = 79
   sex = male
   meal = full

Fig. 6. Example ProCon-2 dialogue based on the breathalyser dataset

5 Related Work

Existing approaches to explaining the pros and cons of a suggested action or hypothesis in CBR tend to be more knowledge intensive than our approach. Murdock *et al.* [3] describe an interpretive CBR approach to assisting intelligence analysts in the evaluation of hypothesised asymmetric threats such as an attempt by an organised crime group to take over a commercial industry. Given such an hypothesis, their system generates a structured summary of the arguments for and against the hypothesis by comparing the available evidence with the retrieved model that most closely matches the hypothesised activity. Currently, the decision as to whether or not the hypothesis is valid given the evidence presented is left to the user.

Brüninghaus and Ashley [1] describe an approach to predicting the outcome of legal cases in which the predicted outcome is accompanied by an annotated, *issue-based* analysis of factors that favour the defendant and factors that favour the plaintiff. Relying on a weak domain model to identify issues raised in a case, the system also uses cases to reason about conflicting evidence related to each issue.

An interesting example of an approach to explanation in which precedent-based and rule-based explanations play complementary roles is Evans-Romaine and Marling's [13] prototype system for teaching students in sports medicine to prescribe exercise regimes for patients with cardiac or pulmonary diseases. On entering the description of a patient in terms of attributes such as age, sex, weight and diagnosis, students are shown both a recommendation based on rules and a possibly conflicting solution based on CBR. The former solution is supported by a rule-based explanation, and the latter by showing the student the most similar case. In this way, it is argued, students learn not only to apply the standard rules but also how experienced prescribers look beyond the rules to the needs of individual patients.

6 Conclusions

Our evidential approach to explaining the pros and cons of conclusions in CBR aims to address the limitations of approaches to explanation in which the user is simply shown the case (or rule) on which a predicted outcome is based. An important role in our approach is played by techniques for the discovery of features that support or oppose the outcome predicted by the system. We have also presented a principled approach to the selection of evidence thresholds for assessing the evidence provided by continuous attributes. Initial results suggest that our strategy of maximising the minimum of the weights of evidence provided by values above and below the threshold produces more realistic evidence thresholds than simply selecting the mid-point of the attribute's range of values in the dataset. Finally, we have presented an implementation of our evidential approach to explanation in a CBR system called ProCon-2 and demonstrated its ability to provide explanations that are more informative than is possible by simply showing the user the most similar case.

Currently our approach is best suited to binary classification tasks. One reason is that our techniques for assessing the evidence provided by continuous attributes are currently limited to binary classification tasks. Another is that in a dataset with several outcome classes, some of the features in the target problem may be neither supporters nor opposers of the predicted outcome according to our criteria for support and opposition. A possible approach to addressing both issues that we propose to investigate in future research is to treat the problem as a binary classification task for the purpose of explaining the predicted outcome.

An interesting question is whether it is possible to explain the pros and cons of the conclusions reached by a CBR system without relying on probabilistic criteria for support and opposition. We are currently investigating an approach to explanation that closely resembles our evidential approach but in which the criteria for support and opposition of an outcome class are defined in terms of the underlying similarity measure on which retrieval is based rather than in probabilistic terms.

Acknowledgements. The author would like to thank Pádraig Cunningham, Dónal Doyle and John Loughrey for providing the breathalyser dataset used here to illustrate our evidential approach to explanation in CBR.

References

1. Brüninghaus, S., Ashley, K.D.: Combining Case-Based and Model-Based Reasoning for Predicting the Outcome of Legal Cases. In: Ashley, K.D., Bridge, D.G. (eds.) Case-Based Reasoning Research and Development. LNAI, Vol. 2689. Springer-Verlag, Berlin Heidelberg New York (2003) 65-79
2. McSherry, D.: Explanation in Case-Based Reasoning: an Evidential Approach. In: Lees, B. (ed.) Proceedings of the 8th UK Workshop on Case-Based Reasoning (2003) 47-55
3. Murdock, J.W., Aha, D.W., Breslow, L.A.: Assessing Elaborated Hypotheses: An Interpretive Case-Based Reasoning Approach. In: Ashley, K.D., Bridge, D.G. (eds.) Case-Based Reasoning Research and Development. LNAI, Vol. 2689. Springer-Verlag, Berlin Heidelberg New York (2003) 332-346
4. McSherry, D.: Interactive Case-Based Reasoning in Sequential Diagnosis. Applied Intelligence **14** (2001) 65-76
5. McSherry, D.: Mixed-Initiative Intelligent Systems for Classification and Diagnosis. Proceedings of the 14th Irish Conference on Artificial Intelligence and Cognitive Science (2003) 146-151
6. Southwick, R.W.: Explaining Reasoning: an Overview of Explanation in Knowledge-Based Systems. Knowledge Engineering Review **6** (1991) 1-19
7. Sørmo, F., Aamodt, A.: Knowledge Communication and CBR. In: González-Calero, P. (ed.) Proceedings of the ECCBR-02 Workshop on Case-Based Reasoning for Education and Training (2002) 47-59
8. McSherry, D.: Similarity and Compromise. In: Ashley, K.D., Bridge, D.G. (eds.) Case-Based Reasoning Research and Development. LNAI, Vol. 2689. Springer-Verlag, Berlin Heidelberg New York (2003) 291-305
9. Cunningham, P., Doyle, D., Loughrey, J.: An Evaluation of the Usefulness of Case-Based Explanation. In: Ashley, K.D., Bridge, D.G. (eds.) Case-Based Reasoning Research and Development. LNAI, Vol. 2689. Springer-Verlag, Berlin Heidelberg New York (2003) 122-130
10. Leake, D.B.: CBR in Context: the Present and Future. In Leake, D.B. (ed.) Case-Based Reasoning: Experiences, Lessons & Future Directions. AAAI Press/MIT Press (1996) 3-30
11. Cendrowska, J.: PRISM: an Algorithm for Inducing Modular Rules. International Journal of Man-Machine Studies **27** (1987) 349-370
12. Quinlan, J.R.: Induction of Decision Trees. Machine Learning **1** (1986) 81-106
13. Evans-Romaine, K., Marling, C.: Prescribing Exercise Regimens for Cardiac and Pulmonary Disease Patients with CBR. In: Bichindaritz, I., Marling, C. (eds.) Proceedings of the ICCBR-03 Workshop on Case-Based Reasoning in the Health Sciences (2003) 45-52
14. Ong, L.S., Shepherd, B., Tong, L.C, Seow-Cheon, F., Ho, Y.H., Tang, C.L., Ho, Y.S., Tan, K.: The Colorectal Cancer Recurrence Support (CARES) System. Artificial Intelligence in Medicine **11** (1997) 175-188
15. McSherry, D.: Dynamic and Static Approaches to Clinical Data Mining. Artificial Intelligence in Medicine **16** (1999) 97-115
16. Szolovits, P., Pauker, S.G.: Categorical and Probabilistic Reasoning in Medical Diagnosis. Artificial Intelligence **11** (1978) 115-144
17. Spiegelhalter, D.J., Knill-Jones, R.P.: Statistical and Knowledge-Based Approaches to Clinical Decision-Support Systems with an Application in Gastroenterology. Journal of the Royal Statistical Society Series A **147** (1984) 35-77

Incremental Relaxation of Unsuccessful Queries

David McSherry

School of Computing and Information Engineering, University
of Ulster, Coleraine BT52 1SA, Northern Ireland
dmg.mcsherry@ulster.ac.uk

Abstract. Increasingly in case-based reasoning (CBR) approaches to product recommendation, some or all of the user's requirements are treated, at least initially, as constraints that the retrieved cases must satisfy. We present a mixed-initiative approach to recovery from the retrieval failures that occur when there is no case that satisfies all the user's requirements. The recovery process begins with an explanation of the retrieval failure in which the user's attention is drawn to combinations of constraints in her query for which there are no matching cases. The user is then guided in the selection of the most useful attribute, and associated constraint, to be eliminated from her query at each stage of an incremental relaxation process. If not prepared to compromise on the attribute suggested for elimination at any stage, the user can select another attribute to be eliminated. On successful completion of the recovery process, the retrieved cases involve only compromises that the user has chosen, in principle, to accept.

1 Introduction

Increasingly in CBR approaches to product recommendation, some or all of the user's requirements are treated, at least initially, as constraints that the retrieved cases must satisfy [1-3]. Typically these approaches rely on query relaxation to recover from the retrieval failures that occur when none of the available cases satisfies all the user's requirements. We focus here on approaches in which relaxing a query means *eliminating* one or more constraints from the query rather than requiring the user to revise individual constraints, for example as in Bridge's Sermo [1]. In Thompson *et al.*'s Adaptive Place Advisor [2], retrieval failures trigger a recovery process in which the selection of a constraint to be eliminated from the unsuccessful query is based on the system's current understanding of the user's personal priorities. In Ricci *et al.*'s Intelligent Travel Recommender [3] the user is told how many results she will get, if any, by eliminating each of the constraints in her query.

The assistance that the user is given in these approaches is a significant improvement on traditional database approaches that force the user to adopt a trial-and-error approach to revising her query when there is no product that satisfies all her requirements [4]. However, a limitation of existing techniques is that recovery may not be possible by eliminating a single constraint [5]. Of course if queries are incrementally elicited as in Adaptive Place Advisor, then recovery is always possible by eliminating the most recently elicited constraint. But often queries are not elicited incrementally, and even if recovery is possible by eliminating a single constraint, this may be a *com-*

promise that the user is not prepared to accept. In this paper, we present a mixed-initiative approach to recovery in which queries need not be incrementally elicited and there is no assumption that recovery is possible by eliminating a single constraint. The recovery process begins with an *explanation* of the retrieval failure in which the user's attention is drawn to combinations of constraints in her query for which there are no matching cases. As well as highlighting areas of the product space in which the case library may be lacking in coverage, the explanation provided may reveal *misconceptions* on the part of the user, such as the price she expects to pay for the product she is seeking.

The user is then guided in the selection of the most useful attribute to be eliminated from her query, with its associated constraint, at each stage of an incremental relaxation process. The aim of the attribute-selection strategy in our approach is to minimise the number of compromises required to recover from the retrieval failure. However, if not prepared to compromise on the attribute suggested for elimination at any stage, the user can select another attribute to be eliminated. In this respect, our approach resembles the test selection process in mixed-initiative CBR tools for fault diagnosis such as NaCoDAE [6]. On successful completion of the recovery process, the retrieved cases involve only compromises that the user has chosen, in principle, to accept.

In Sections 2 and 3, we describe our approaches to explanation of retrieval failure and recovery from retrieval failure. In Section 4, we present an implementation of the proposed techniques in a recommender system prototype called *ShowMe*. Our experimental results and conclusions are presented in Sections 5 and 6.

2 Explanation of Retrieval Failure

In previous work, we have argued that a natural approach to explanation of retrieval failure in product recommendation is to draw the user's attention to *sub-queries* of her query for which there are no matching cases [5]. Our approach is also influenced by research aimed at providing more "co-operative" responses to failing database queries [7-11]. For example, if a computer salesperson is asked for a laptop computer with a 19 inch screen made by Dell, she is likely to point out that there is no such thing as a laptop with a 19 inch screen. Implicitly, she is also telling the customer that there is no problem getting a Dell laptop, or a Dell computer with a 19 inch screen. While a CBR system that has no knowledge of what products are available elsewhere cannot say for certain that there is no such thing as a laptop with a 19 inch screen, it can tell the user that there is no such product in the case library.

We assume that the user's query Q, over a subset $atts(Q)$ of the case attributes, is represented as a set of constraints that the retrieved cases are required to satisfy. Depending on the attribute type, the constraint $c_a(Q)$ associated with a given attribute $a \in atts(Q)$ may be expressed, for example, in terms of a required value, a maximum or minimum value, or a range of acceptable values. We will refer to $|atts(Q)|$ as the *length* of the query.

Definition 1. *A given query Q_1 is a sub-query of another query Q_2 if $atts(Q_1) \subseteq atts(Q_2)$ and $c_a(Q_1) = c_a(Q_2)$ for all $a \in atts(Q_1)$. If $atts(Q_1) \subset atts(Q_2)$, we say that Q_1 is a proper sub-query of Q_2.*

Lemma 1. *If a given query Q_1 is a sub-query of another query Q_2, and Q_1 is an unsuccessful query, then Q_2 is also an unsuccessful query.*

Given a query for which a retrieval failure has occurred, our aim is to construct an explanation of the shortest possible length that will enable the user to avoid further retrieval failures that can be predicted from the current failure. To illustrate our approach, Fig. 1 shows all sub-queries of a query Q^{1234} involving attributes a_1, a_2, a_3, and a_4. We denote by Q^{134} the sub-query involving only a_1, a_3, and a_4, and by Q^{34} the sub-query involving only a_3 and a_4. We use a similar notation for each of the other sub-queries apart from the empty query $\emptyset$. We will assume in this example that all sub-queries of Q^{1234} are successful queries except those that are marked '×' in Fig. 1.

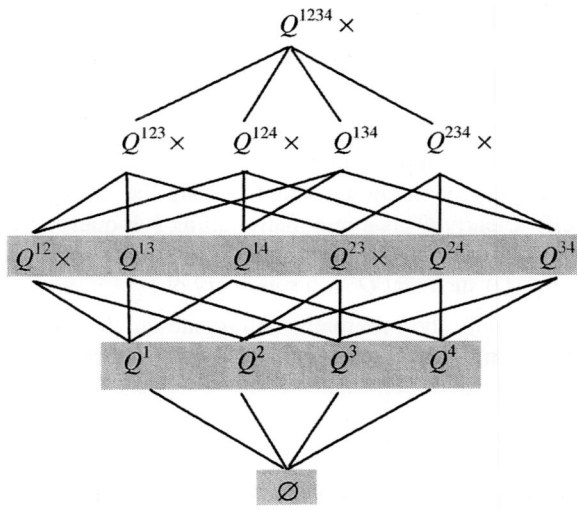

Fig. 1. Sub-queries of an example query involving four attributes

As any query is a sub-query of itself, Q^{1234} can be seen to have six failing sub-queries. An obvious candidate to be included in our explanation of retrieval failure is Q^{12} as its failure also accounts for the failure of three other sub-queries. If there is no matching case for Q^{12}, then by Lemma 1 there can be no matching cases for Q^{123}, Q^{124}, or Q^{1234}. The only remaining candidates among the failing sub-queries of Q^{1234} are Q^{23} and Q^{234}. If our explanation fails to mention at least one of these sub-queries, the user might be tempted to try Q^{234} as her next query, only to be faced with another retrieval failure. But provided the user is informed that there is no matching case for Q^{23}, there is no need to include Q^{234} in our explanation.

The failing sub-queries Q^{12} and Q^{23} that we have identified as being most useful for explaining why there is no matching case for the user's query are in fact the *minimally* failing sub-queries of Q^{1234} in the sense of the following definition.

Definition 2. *A failing sub-query Q^* of a given query Q is a minimally failing sub-query of Q if no proper sub-query of Q^* is a failing query.*

For example, Q^{123} is a failing sub-query of Q^{1234} but not a *minimally* failing sub-query since its proper sub-queries Q^{12} and Q^{23} are also failing queries.

Definition 3. *Given any query Q, we will denote by mfs(Q) the set of all minimally failing sub-queries of Q.*

For the example query in Fig. 1, $mfs(Q^{1234}) = \{Q^{12}, Q^{23}\}$. In general, a retrieval failure is explained in our approach by showing the user the minimally failing sub-queries of her unsuccessful query. As we show in the following theorem, whether or not a given sub-query of a failing query Q is successful can be inferred from the minimally failing sub-queries of Q. This is an important result as it confirms the *sufficiency* of minimally failing sub-queries as a basis for explanation of retrieval failure.

Lemma 2. *If Q_1, Q_2, and Q_3 are any queries such that Q_1 is a sub-query of Q_2 and Q_2 is a sub-query of Q_3, then Q_1 is a sub-query of Q_3.*

Theorem 1. *A sub-query Q^* of a failing query Q is also a failing query if and only if there exists $Q° \in mfs(Q)$ such that $Q°$ is a sub-query of Q^*.*

Proof. If there exists $Q° \in mfs(Q)$ such that $Q°$ is a sub-query of Q^*, then Q^* is a failing query by Lemma 1. Suppose now that Q^* is a failing sub-query of Q, and let $Q°$ be a failing sub-query of minimum length among the failing sub-queries of Q^* (including Q^* itself). Clearly $Q°$ is a minimally failing sub-query of Q^* and therefore a minimally failing sub-query of Q by Lemma 2. We have established as required the existence of $Q° \in mfs(Q)$ such that $Q°$ is a sub-query of Q^*.

For example, given only the minimally failing sub-queries Q^{12} and Q^{23} of Q^{1234}, we can infer that Q^{134} must be a successful query as neither Q^{12} nor Q^{23} is a sub-query of Q^{134}. In the domain of personal computers, suppose that Q^{1234} is the query:

price ≤ 700, type = laptop, screen size = 19, make = Dell

and that its failing sub-queries are as shown in Fig. 1. In this instance, the user would be informed that there are no matching cases for the following combinations of constraints in her query:

price ≤ 700, type = laptop	(Q^{12})
type = laptop, screen size = 19	(Q^{23})

By Theorem 1, the user would be entitled to infer that the following sub-query of her initial query is bound to succeed:

price ≤ 700, screen size = 19, make = Dell	(Q^{134})

Of course, this might not be a trivial step for users with little experience of query formulation. In Section 3, we present an approach to recovery from retrieval failure that does not rely on the user's ability to make such inferences.

Our algorithm for finding all minimally failing sub-queries of a given query, called *Explainer*, is shown in Fig. 2. *SubQueries* is a list of all sub-queries, in order of increasing query length, of a query Q for which a retrieval failure has occurred. For each sub-query Q_1 for which there is no matching case in the case library, *Explainer* adds Q_1 to the list of minimally failing sub-queries and deletes any sub-query Q_2 that includes Q_1 as a sub-query from the remaining list of candidate sub-queries.

```
algorithm Explainer(Q, SubQueries)
begin
    MFSubQueries ← φ
    while |SubQueries| > 0 do
    begin
        Q_1 ← first(SubQueries)
        Deletions ← {Q_1}
        if there is no matching case for Q_1
        then begin
            MFSubQueries ← MFSubQueries ∪ {Q_1}
            for all Q_2 ∈ rest(SubQueries) do
            begin
                if Q_1 is a sub-query of Q_2
                    then Deletions ← Deletions ∪ {Q_2}
            end
        end
        SubQueries ← SubQueries - Deletions
    end
    return MFSubQueries
end
```

Fig. 2. Algorithm for finding all minimally failing sub-queries of a given query

3 Recovery from Retrieval Failure

A major role in our mixed-initiative approach to recovery from retrieval failure is played by the minimally failing sub-queries that also provide the basis of our approach to explanation of retrieval failure. Following a brief discussion of how minimally failing sub-queries can inform the recovery process, we present the algorithm for incremental relaxation of an unsuccessful query on which our mixed-initiative approach to recovery is based. Finally, we describe how our algorithm for incremental relaxation has been adapted to support mixed-initiative interaction in *Show Me*, our recommender system prototype.

3.1 First Steps to Recovery

We have already seen that the success or failure of any sub-query of an unsuccessful query Q can be inferred from the minimally failing sub-queries of Q. As we now show, minimally failing sub-queries also provide other important clues that can help to guide the process of recovery from retrieval failure.

Theorem 2. *A sub-query Q^* of a failing query Q is a successful query if and only if for each $Q^\circ \in mfs(Q)$ there exists $a \in atts(Q^\circ)$ such that $a \notin atts(Q^*)$.*

Proof. Immediate from Theorem 1.

It follows from Theorem 2 that to recover from a retrieval failure by eliminating constraints, it is necessary (and sufficient) to eliminate one of the constraints in each of the minimally failing sub-queries of the unsuccessful query. However, as some of the minimally failing sub-queries may have constraints in common, the number of constraints that need to be eliminated is often less than the number of minimally failing sub-queries. In fact, it is often possible to recover from a retrieval failure by eliminating a single constraint. That is, one or more of the *immediate* sub-queries of a failing query, in the sense of the following definition, may be a successful query.

Definition 4. *For any query Q and $a \in atts(Q)$, we denote by $R_a(Q)$ the immediate sub-query of Q that results from the elimination of a and its associated constraint from Q.*

As we show in the following theorem, the minimally failing sub-queries of an immediate sub-query can be identified from those of the parent query.

Theorem 3. *For any unsuccessful query Q and $a \in atts(Q)$, $mfs(R_a(Q)) = \{Q^\circ \in mfs(Q) : a \notin atts(Q^\circ)\}$*

Proof. It is clear from Lemma 2 that any minimally failing sub-query Q° of $R_a(Q)$ is also a minimally failing sub-query of Q. By the definition of $R_a(Q)$, we also know that $a \notin atts(Q^\circ)$, and so $mfs(R_a(Q)) \subseteq \{Q^\circ \in mfs(Q) : a \notin atts(Q^\circ)\}$. It remains only to observe that any minimally failing sub-query Q° of Q such that $a \notin atts(Q^\circ)$ is also a minimally failing sub-query of $R_a(Q)$.

An important point to note is that any proper sub-query of an unsuccessful query can be reached via a sequence of sub-queries in which each sub-query (except the first) is an immediate sub-query of its predecessor. Thus by repeated application of Theorem 3, we can identify the minimally failing sub-queries of *any* sub-query of an unsuccessful query. Also, it can be seen from the following theorem that recovery from retrieval failure amounts to finding a sub-query of the unsuccessful query that has *no* minimally failing sub-queries.

Theorem 4. *A given query Q is successful if and only if $mfs(Q) = \emptyset$.*

Proof. If $mfs(Q) \neq \emptyset$ then Q has at least one failing sub-query and so Q cannot be successful by Lemma 1. Suppose now that Q is an unsuccessful query, and let Q^* be a sub-query of minimum length among the failing sub-queries of Q (including Q itself). Clearly Q^* is a minimally failing sub-query of Q and so $mfs(Q) \neq \emptyset$.

3.2 Recovery by Incremental Relaxation

Given an unsuccessful query Q, the aim of our algorithm for incremental relaxation is to find a sequence $Q_1, Q_2, ..., Q_r$ of sub-queries of Q such that:

- $Q_1 = Q$
- Q_{i+1} is an immediate sub-query of Q_i for $1 \leq i \leq r - 1$
- Q_r is a successful query

For the example query in Fig. 1, one such sequence of sub-queries is Q^{1234}, Q^{234}, Q^{23}, Q^3. A shorter sequence of sub-queries that also has the required properties is Q^{1234}, Q^{134}. The first sequence involves three compromises, whereas only a single compromise is needed to recover from the retrieval failure in the second sequence. Thus to minimise the number of compromises required to recover from retrieval failure, some method is needed to guide the selection of an attribute to be eliminated at each stage of the relaxation process. Below we examine a possible approach in which a key role is played by the concept of *coverage* that we now define.

Definition 5. *For any unsuccessful query Q and $a \in atts(Q)$, $coverage(a) = \{Q° \in mfs(Q) : a \in atts(Q°)\}$.*

The importance of coverage in this sense can be seen from Theorem 3. For any unsuccessful query Q and $a \in atts(Q)$ it follows from Theorem 3 that:

$$mfs(R_a(Q)) = mfs(Q) - coverage(a)$$

Thus by choosing the attribute $a \in atts(Q)$ for which $|coverage(a)|$ is maximum, we can minimise the number of minimally failing queries that survive following the elimination of a from Q.

Our algorithm for incremental relaxation, which we call *Recover*, is outlined in Fig. 3. *MFS* is the set of all minimally failing sub-queries of an unsuccessful query Q, for example as identified by our *Explainer* algorithm from Section 2. At each stage in the recovery process, *Recover* eliminates the most promising of the remaining attributes in the query on the basis of its coverage of the minimally failing sub-queries that survive the elimination of any previous attributes. The process continues until a successful sub-query of the original query is found. Only the final sub-query generated in the recovery process is returned by *Recover*.

```
algorithm Recover(Q, MFS)
begin
    a* ← first(atts(Q))
    coverage(a*) ← {Q° ∈ MFS : a* ∈ atts(Q°)}
    for all a ∈ rest(atts(Q)) do
    begin
        coverage(a) ← {Q° ∈ MFS : a ∈ atts(Q°)}
        if |coverage(a)| > |coverage(a*)|
            then a* ← a
    end
    Q* ← R_a*(Q)
    MFS* ← MFS - coverage(a*)
    if MFS* = ∅
        then return Q*
        else Recover(Q*, MFS*)
end
```

Fig. 3. Algorithm for incremental relaxation of an unsuccessful query

An important point to note is that *Recover* takes as input only the unsuccessful query and its minimally failing sub-queries. No further testing of sub-queries is required in the recovery process. Although *Recover* never fails to recognise when recovery is possible by eliminating a single constraint, its greedy approach to attribute selection is not guaranteed to find a successful sub-query that involves the fewest possible compromises. A more serious limitation of *Recover* is that elimination of the most promising constraints may involve compromises that the user is not prepared to accept. As we now show, however, *Recover* can easily be modified to support a *mixed-initiative* approach to recovery that does take account of the user's willingness, or otherwise, to compromise.

3.3 Recovery by Mixed-Initiative Relaxation

We are now in a position to describe our mixed-initiative approach to recovery from retrieval failure as implemented in *ShowMe*, our recommender system prototype. When a retrieval failure occurs in *ShowMe*, the user is shown one or more "combinations of constraints" in her query for which there are no matching cases and informed that she needs to "relax" (that is, eliminate) one of the constraints in each of the unmatched combinations. As described in Section 2, the combinations of constraints that the user is shown are the minimally failing sub-queries of her query. The mixed-initiative recovery process that follows in *ShowMe* is based on *Recover*, our algorithm for incremental relaxation, modified to support mixed-initiative interaction as described below.

- On each cycle of the recovery process, *ShowMe* shows the user the most promising attribute to be eliminated from her query. The user can either accept *ShowMe*'s suggestion or select another attribute to be eliminated.
- *ShowMe* keeps track of previous suggestions that the user has declined to avoid repeating the same suggestions in future cycles
- Following the elimination of the attribute that the user selects on each cycle, the user is shown any minimally failing sub-queries that remain to be addressed

As in *Recover*, the most promising attribute to be eliminated is selected in *ShowMe* on the basis of its coverage of minimally-failing sub-queries that remain after the elimination of any previous attributes. If two or more attributes are equally promising in terms of coverage, *ShowMe* uses the importance weights typically assigned to query attributes in a CBR system as a secondary selection criterion. That is, it selects the *least* important of the equally promising attributes. Also as in *Recover*, the incremental relaxation process continues until a successful sub-query is reached. For our example query in the domain of personal computers, the user would be informed as in Section 2 that there are no matches for the following combinations of constraints in her query:

$$\text{price} \leq 700, \text{type} = \text{laptop}$$
$$\text{type} = \text{laptop}, \text{screen size} = 19$$

Now she would also be informed that by relaxing her *type* constraint she can eliminate both of the unmatched combinations of constraints. If not prepared to compromise on type, the user might instead choose to compromise on screen size. In this case, she would be informed that she also needs to relax one of the constraints in the unmatched combination:

$$\text{price} \leq 700, \text{type} = \text{laptop}$$

If still not prepared to compromise on type, the user can see that her only option, apart from abandoning her query, is to compromise on price as well as screen size.

The approach to product recommendation on which *ShowMe* is based is described more fully in the following section.

4 Recommendation in ShowMe

Initially in *ShowMe*, the user's requirements are treated as constraints that the retrieved cases must satisfy. Recovery from retrieval failure is based on our mixed-initiative approach to identifying compromises, if any, that the user is prepared to accept. On successful completion of the recovery process, the cases retrieved by *ShowMe* involve only compromises that the user has chosen, in principle, to accept. The case recommended by *ShowMe* is the most similar of the retrieved cases with respect to *all* attributes in the user's initial query, including those on which she has chosen to compromise.

Of course, it cannot be guaranteed that the recommended case will be acceptable to the user. Though involving only compromises that the user has chosen to accept in principle, it may not be acceptable because of the *extent* of the compromises it involves. For example, it is unlikely that a user who chooses to compromise on price would be willing to pay double the amount she initially intended. However, the fact that the recommended case is also selected on the basis of its similarity to the user's initial query helps to reduce the likelihood of such extreme compromises. Ultimately, of course, *ShowMe*'s ability to balance the trade-offs involved depends on its similarity knowledge and the available cases.

4.1 Example Dialogue

The example dialogue in Fig. 4 is based on the *Travel* case library (www.ai-cbr.org), a standard benchmark containing the descriptions of over 1,000 holidays. Attributes in the case library and weights assigned to them in our experiments are price (8), month (7), region (6), persons (5), duration (4), type (3), accommodation (2), and transport (1). Minor editing of the example dialogue in the interest of clarity includes the format of the user's query.

Our example dialogue is based on a full-length query that fails for several reasons. Some of the "unmatched combinations of constraints" mentioned in *ShowMe*'s explanation of the retrieval failure may reflect *misconceptions* on the part of the user, for example about the availability of skiing holidays in Ireland. Others, such as the absence of a holiday for two in Ireland, can obviously be attributed to lack of coverage in the case library. However, our approach to recovery from retrieval failure is the same regardless of the etiology.

In the first cycle of the recovery process, the user agrees to relax her transport constraint as suggested by *ShowMe*. However, she is not prepared to compromise on holiday type as suggested by *ShowMe* in the second cycle and chooses instead to relax her region constraint. Although type is involved in both unmatched combinations of constraints that survive in the next cycle, *ShowMe* does not repeat a suggestion that the user has chosen not to accept in a previous cycle.

ShowMe:	Please enter your query:
User:	price ≤ 1000, month = august, region = ireland, persons = 2, duration = 14, type = skiing, accom = flat, transport = plane
ShowMe:	There are no matches for the following combinations of constraints in your query:

    price ≤ 1000, region = ireland
    month = august, type = skiing
    region = ireland, persons = 2
    region = ireland, type = skiing
    region = ireland, transport = plane
    type = skiing, transport = plane
    accom = flat, transport = plane
    price ≤ 1000, month = august, transport = plane
    price ≤ 1000, persons = 2, transport = plane
    price ≤ 1000, duration = 14, transport = plane
    price ≤ 1000, duration = 14, type = skiing, accom = flat

To solve this problem, you need to relax one of the constraints in each of the unmatched combinations

By relaxing *transport* you can eliminate 6 of the unmatched combinations

User:	**relax** transport
ShowMe:	There are no matches for the following combinations of constraints:

    price ≤ 1000, region = ireland
    month = august, type = skiing
    region = ireland, persons = 2
    region = ireland, type = skiing
    price = 1000, duration = 14, type = skiing, accom = flat

By relaxing *type* you can eliminate 3 of the unmatched combinations

User:	**relax** region
ShowMe:	There are no matches for the following combinations of constraints:

    month = august, type = skiing
    price ≤ 1000, duration = 14, type = skiing, accom = flat

User:	**relax** accom
ShowMe:	There is no match for the following combination of constraints:

    month = august, type = skiing

User:	**relax** month
ShowMe:	The following case is recommended:

    Case 930: 604, december, erzgerbirge, 2, 14, skiing, 3 star, car (0.55)

Fig. 4. Example recommendation dialogue in *ShowMe*

In the last two cycles of the recovery process, the user chooses to relax her accommodation and month constraints. Now that the recovery process has been successfully completed, *ShowMe* recommends the most similar case involving only compromises that the user has chosen, at least in principle, to accept. The similarity of the recommended case to the user's initial query is 0.55, with the change in timing of the holiday being perhaps the most extreme of the compromises that the user faces. A feature of *ShowMe* not shown in the example dialogue is that the user can ask to see other cases, if any, that also involve only compromises she has chosen to accept.

4.2 Discussion and Related Work

A distinctive feature of our approach to product recommendation in *ShowMe* is that a retrieval failure is not merely regarded as a problem to be solved, but as an opportunity to identify compromises that the user is prepared to accept. In future research, we propose to investigate the potential benefits of the approach in comparison with existing recommendation strategies. It is worth noting that the case ranked highest by similarity-based retrieval in response to our example query would be a *wandering* holiday. Given that she was unwilling to compromise on holiday type, it seems unlikely that this case would be acceptable to our hypothetical user. In fact, none of the 20 most similar cases offers *skiing* as the holiday type, and the most similar case that does satisfy this constraint fails to satisfy the price constraint.

A known weakness of similarity-based retrieval is that the most similar cases also tend to be very similar to each other, and not sufficiently representative of compromises that the user may be prepared to accept [12,13]. Compromise-driven retrieval [13] is a special case of coverage-optimised retrieval [14,15] that aims to address this issue by ensuring that all possible compromises are represented in the retrieval set. However, a trade-off in the approach is that the size of the retrieval set required to cover all possible compromises cannot be predicted in advance, which means that the user may be faced with a difficult choice between several cases that involve different compromises.

5 Experimental Results

Following an evaluation of our approach to explanation of retrieval failure in terms of cognitive load, we examine the performance of our approach to recovery from retrieval failure on the Travel case library.

5.1 Explanation Length

We will refer to the number of failing sub-queries that the user is shown in our approach to explanation of retrieval failure as the *length* of the explanation. While showing the user only the *minimally* failing sub-queries of her query helps to reduce cognitive load, explanation length can still be expected to increase as query length increases. Our experimental method is based on a *leave-one-out* approach in which we temporarily remove each case from the Travel case library, generate all possible queries of length from 1 to 8 from its description, and present each query to *ShowMe*, our recommender system prototype. For each unsuccessful query, we observe the length of the explanation generated by *ShowMe*. For queries ranging in length from 1 to 8, Fig. 5 shows the maximum, average and minimum length of *ShowMe*'s explanations of retrieval failure.

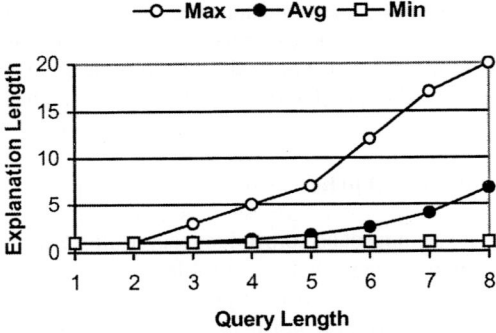

Fig. 5. Explanation lengths for queries of increasing length on the Travel case library

A detail not shown in Fig. 5 is that the likelihood of retrieval failure increases from less than 1% for queries involving only a single attribute to 97% for full-length queries. Though increasing as expected with query length, average explanation length remains below 2 until query length reaches 6. For full-queries involving all eight attributes in the case library, average explanation length is 6.7. Though reaching a maximum of 20 for two of the 996 full-length queries that were unsuccessful, explanation length is more than 10 in only 13% of full-length queries. Thus even for full-length queries involving all eight attributes in the case library, explanation lengths are within reasonable limits for the majority of unsuccessful queries.

5.2 Attribute-Selection Strategy

An important role in our mixed-initiative approach to recovery from retrieval failure is played by the strategy used to select the most useful attribute to be eliminated at each stage of the recovery process. As described in Section 3.3, *ShowMe* gives priority to the attribute that is most promising on the basis of its coverage of minimally failing sub-queries that remain after the elimination of any previous attributes. It also uses attribute importance as a secondary selection criterion in the event of a tie on the basis of coverage. Our evaluation of this strategy, which we will refer to here as *Most Coverage*, focuses on the number of compromises that the user faces when accepting the system's suggestions at each stage of the recovery process.

Two other approaches to attribute selection included in our evaluation are:

Least Important. Select the least important of the attributes that appear in the minimally failing sub-queries that remain following the elimination of any previous attributes.

Random. Randomly select one of the attributes that appear in the minimally failing sub-queries that remain following the elimination of any previous attributes.

We also include in our evaluation a non-incremental approach to recovery from retrieval failure called *Fewest Compromises*. Our *Explainer* algorithm from Section 2 can easily be modified to identify a successful sub-query of maximum length among the successful sub-queries it encounters in its search for minimally failing sub-queries. A successful sub-query identified in this way provides a benchmark for the performance of the three incremental strategies in our evaluation as it represents the smallest possible number of compromises required to recover from retrieval failure.

Once again, we temporarily remove each case from the Travel case library, now presenting its description as a full-length query to a recommender system using each of the four recovery strategies in our evaluation. For each unsuccessful query, we record the number of compromises required to recover from retrieval failure in each strategy. We also record the number of unsuccessful queries for which recovery is possible by eliminating a single constraint. The maximum, average, and minimum numbers of compromises in each strategy are shown in Fig. 6.

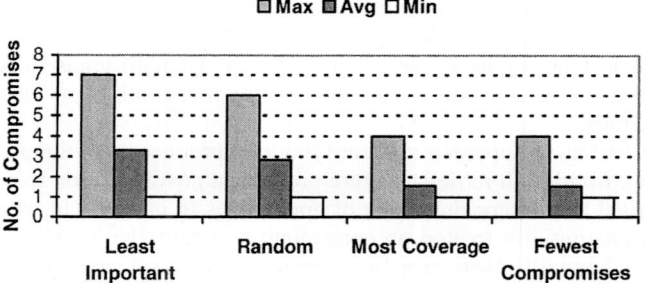

Fig. 6. Number of compromises required to recover from retrieval failure in four recovery strategies for full-length queries on the Travel case library

Apart from a very slight difference in the average number of compromises, the results for *Most Coverage* and *Fewest Compromises* are indistinguishable, suggesting that the performance of *Most Coverage* is close to optimal on the Travel case library.

As shown by the results for *Fewest Compromises*, the smallest number of compromises required for recovery may be as many as 4, though this was the case in only one of the 996 queries that were unsuccessful. Relative to *Fewest Compromises*, *Least Important* increases the average number of compromises required for recovery by more than 100% from 1.6 to 3.3. In *Least Important*, as many as 7 compromises may be required for recovery. The fact that *Random* appears to require fewer compromises on average than *Least Important* is perhaps unsurprising given that an attribute's usefulness, in terms of minimising the number of compromises, is unrelated to its importance.

A detail not shown in Fig. 6 is that recovery is possible by eliminating a single constraint in only 48% of unsuccessful queries.

6 Conclusions

We have presented a mixed-initiative approach to recovery from retrieval failure in which the user is guided in the selection of the most useful attribute (and constraint) to be eliminated from her query at each stage of an incremental relaxation process. Queries need not be elicited incrementally and there is no assumption that recovery is possible by eliminating a single constraint. An important role in our approach is played by the strategy used to select the most useful attribute to be eliminated at each stage of the recovery process. In terms of minimising the number of compromises required for recovery, our results suggest that its performance is close to optimal on the Travel case library.

However, if not prepared to compromise on the attribute suggested for elimination at any stage, the user can select another attribute to be eliminated, in which case the trade-off is likely to be an increase in the number of compromises required for recovery. An important benefit of our mixed-initiative approach is that the cases retrieved on successful completion of the recovery process involve only compromises that the user has chosen, in principle, to accept.

We have also presented an approach to explanation of retrieval failure in which the user's attention is drawn to sub-queries of her query for which there are no matching cases. Showing the user only the *minimally* failing sub-queries of her query, a technique we have adapted from database research [7-11], helps to reduce cognitive load in our approach. Our results suggest that explanation length tends to remain within reasonable limits even for full-length queries involving all eight attributes in the Travel case library.

Our mixed-initiative approach to identifying compromises that the user is prepared to accept when faced with retrieval failure provides a novel solution to a problem that is often regarded as a major drawback of approaches to retrieval in which the user's requirements are initially treated as constraints that must be satisfied [4,16,17]. In future research we will investigate the potential benefits of an approach to product recommendation in which identifying acceptable compromises is recognised as an essential part of the recommendation process.

References

1. Bridge, D.: Towards Conversational Recommender Systems: a Dialogue Grammar Approach. In: Aha, D.W. (ed.) Proceedings of the EWCBR-02 Workshop on Mixed-Initiative Case-Based Reasoning (2002) 9-22
2. Thompson, C.A., Göker, M.H., Langley, P.: A Personalized System for Conversational Recommendations. Journal of Artificial Intelligence Research **21** (2004) 393-428
3. Ricci, F., Arslan, B., Mirzadeh, N., Venturini, A.: ITR: A Case-Based Travel Advisory System. In: Craw, S., Preece, A. (eds.) Advances in Case-Based Reasoning. LNAI, Vol. 2416. Springer-Verlag, Berlin Heidelberg New York (2002) 613-627
4. Wilke, W., Lenz, M., Wess, S.: Intelligent Sales Support with CBR. In: Lenz, M., Bartsch-Spörl, B., Burkhard, H.-D., Wess, S. (eds.) Case-Based Reasoning Technology. Springer-Verlag, Berlin Heidelberg New York (1998) 91-113
5. McSherry, D.: Explanation of Retrieval Mismatches in Recommender System Dialogues. In: Aha, D.W. (ed.) Proceedings of the ICCBR-03 Workshop on Mixed-Initiative Case-Based Reasoning (2003) 191-199
6. Aha, D.W., Breslow, L.A., Muñoz-Avila, H.: Conversational Case-Based Reasoning. Applied Intelligence **14** (2001) 9-32
7. Corella, F., Kaplan, S.J., Wiederhold, G., Yesil, L.: Cooperative Responses to Boolean Queries. Proceedings of the First International Conference on Data Engineering (1984) 77-85
8. Godfrey, P.: Minimisation in Cooperative Response to Failing Database Queries. International Journal of Cooperative Information Systems, **6** (1997) 95-149
9. Janas, J.M.: How to Not Say Nil - Improving Answers to Failing Queries in Data Base Systems. Proceedings of the Sixth International Joint Conference on Artificial Intelligence (1979) 429-434

10. Janas, J.M.: On the Feasibility of Informative Responses. In: Gallaire, H., Minker, J., Nicolas, J.-M. (eds.) Advances in Database Theory, Vol. 1. Plenum Press, New York (1981) 397-414
11. Kaplan, S.J.: Cooperative Responses from a Portable Natural Language Query System. Artificial Intelligence, **19** (1982) 165-187
12. Smyth, B., McClave, P.: Similarity vs. Diversity. In: Aha, D.W., Watson, I. (eds.) Case-Based Reasoning Research and Development. LNAI, Vol. 2080. Springer-Verlag, Berlin Heidelberg New York (2001) 347-361
13. McSherry, D.: Similarity and Compromise. In: Ashley, K.D., Bridge, D.G. (eds.) Case-Based Reasoning Research and Development. LNAI, Vol. 2689. Springer-Verlag, Berlin Heidelberg New York (2003) 291-305
14. McSherry, D.: Coverage-Optimized Retrieval. Proceedings of the Eighteenth International Joint Conference on Artificial Intelligence (2003) 1349-1350
15. McSherry, D.: Balancing User Satisfaction and Cognitive Load in Coverage-Optimised Retrieval. In: Coenen, F., Preece, A., Macintosh, A. (eds.) Research and Development in Intelligent Systems XX. Springer-Verlag, London (2003) 381-394
16. Bridge, D., Ferguson, A.: An Expressive Query Language for Product Recommender Systems. Artificial Intelligence Review, **18** (2002) 269-307
17. Burke, R.: Interactive Critiquing for Catalog Navigation in E-Commerce. Artificial Intelligence Review, **18** (2002) 245-267

Justification-Based Case Retention

Santiago Ontañón and Enric Plaza

IIIA, Artificial Intelligence Research Institute
CSIC, Spanish Council for Scientific Research
Campus UAB, 08193 Bellaterra, Catalonia (Spain)
{santi,enric}@iiia.csic.es
http://www.iiia.csic.es

Abstract. A CBR system needs a good *case retention* strategy to decide which cases to incorporate into the case base in order to maximize the performance of the system. In this work we present a collaborative case retention strategy, designed for multiagent CBR systems, called the *Collaborative Case Bargaining* strategy. The CCB strategy is a bargaining mechanism in which each CBR agent tries to maximize the utility of the cases it retains. We will present a case utility measure called the *Justification-based Case Utility* (JCU) based upon the ability of the individual CBR agents to provide *justifications* of their own results. An empirical evaluation of the CCB strategy shows the benefits for CBR agents to use this strategy: individual and collective accuracy are increased while the size of the case bases is decreased.

1 Introduction

Obtaining a good case base is a main problem in Case Based Reasoning. The performance of any CBR system depends mainly in the contents of the case base. Therefore, maintaining compact and competent case base has become a main topic of CBR research. Empirical results have shown that storing every available case in the case base does not automatically improve the accuracy of a CBR system [7]. Therefore any CBR system needs a good *case retention* strategy to decide which cases to incorporate into the case base in order to maximize the performance of the system.

Our work focuses on *multiagent CBR systems* ($\mathcal{M}$AC) [6] where the agents are able to solve problems individually using CBR methods and where only local case bases are accessible to each individual agent. Problems to be solved by an agent can be sent by an external user or by another agent. The main issue is to find good collaboration strategies among CBR agents that can help improving classification accuracy both individually and collectively. In a previous work [4] we presented several strategies for collaborative case retention among groups of CBR agents that try to take advantage of being in a multiagent scenario. In this work we will present a new collaborative retention strategy called *Collaborative Case Bargaining* (CCB) and a case utility measure called *Justification-based Case Utility* (JCU).

The main difference between the new CCB strategy and the retention strategies in [4] is that we now present, a new measure for assessing the utility of retaining a case. A case has a high utility value for a CBR agent if it can prevent the agent in making errors in the future, and a case has a low utility value if it will not contribute in reducing the number of errors that the agent will make in the future. Moreover, we also present a new way in which the CBR agents negotiate among them: the CCB strategy is a bargaining mechanism in which each agent tries to maximize the utility of the individually retained cases.

The *Justification-based Case Utility* (JCU) is based upon the ability of the individual CBR agents to provide *justifications* of their own results, i.e. that CBR agents are able to explain why they have classified a problem in a specific solution class. If a CBR agent is able to provide a justification for an incorrectly solved problem, this justification can be examined and try to prevent that the same error is made in the future. The Justification-based Case Utility does exactly this, and uses justifications to detect which cases can prevent a CBR agent to repeat an error in the future and assigns them higher utility values.

The structure of the paper is as follows. Section 2 gives the basic notions of multiagent CBR systems. Then, Section 3 introduces the concept of justifications in CBR systems. Section 4 explains in detail the Collaborative Case Bargaining retention strategy, including an illustrative example and discussion. Finally, Section 5 presents an empirical evaluation of the CCB strategy compared against some other case retention strategies. The paper closes with the conclusions section.

2 Multiagent CBR Systems

Formally, a $\mathcal{MAC}$ system $\mathcal{M} = \{(A_i, C_i)\}_{i=1...n}$ is composed on n agents, where each agent A_i has a case base C_i. In this framework we restrict ourselves to analytical tasks, i.e. tasks (like classification) where the solution is achieved by selecting from an enumerated set of solutions $K = \{S_1 ... S_K\}$. A case base $C_i = \{(P_j, S_k)\}_{j=1...N}$ is a collection of problem/solution pairs. Each agent A_i is autonomous and has learning capabilities, i.e. each agent is able to collect autonomously new cases that can be incorporated to its local case base.

Moreover, since we focus on analytical tasks, there is no obvious decomposition of the problem in subtasks. When an agent A_i asks another agent A_j help to solve a problem the interaction protocol is as follows. First, A_i sends a problem description P to A_j. Second, after A_j has tried to solve P using its case base C_j, it sends back a message with a solution endorsement record.

Definition: A *solution endorsement record* (SER) is a record $\langle \{(S_k, E_k^j)\}, P, A_j \rangle$, where the collection of *endorsing pairs* (S_k, E_k^j) mean that the agent A_j has found E_k^j cases in case base C_j endorsing solution S_k—i.e. there are a number E_k^j of cases that are relevant (similar) for endorsing S_k as a solution for P. Each agent A_j is free to send one or more endorsing pairs in a SER record.

In our framework, collaboration among agents is done by using *collaboration strategies*. A collaboration strategy defines the way a group of agents can cooperate to jointly solve some task. In our framework, a collaboration strategy consist in an interaction protocol and a set of individual policies that the agents follow. The interaction protocol determines the set of possible actions an agent can take in each moment. Each agent uses his individual policies to autonomously choose which of the possible actions to take at each moment is the best according to its individual goals and preferences.

The next section presents the *Committee* collaboration strategy, that the agents use in order to solve problems.

2.1 Committee Collaboration Strategy

In this collaboration strategy the agent members of a $\mathcal{MAC}$ system $\mathcal{M}$ are viewed as a committee. An agent A_i that has to solve a problem P sends it to all the other agents in $\mathcal{M}$. Each agent A_j that has received P sends a solution endorsement record $\langle \{(S_k, E_k^j)\}, P, A_j \rangle$ to A_i. The initiating agent A_i uses a voting scheme above upon all SERs, i.e. its own SER and the SERs of all the other agents in the multiagent system. The problem's solution is the class with maximum number of votes.

Since all the agents in a $\mathcal{MAC}$ system are autonomous CBR agents, they will not have the same problem solving experience (in general, the cases in their case bases will not be the same). This makes it likely that the errors that each agent make in the solution of problems will not be very correlated, i.e. each agent will not err in the same problems. It is known in machine learning that the combination of the predictions made by several classifiers with uncorrelated errors improves over the individual accuracies of those classifiers [3] ("ensemble effect"). Thus, using the committee collaboration strategy an agent can increase its problem solving accuracy.

The principle behind the voting scheme is that the agents vote for solution classes depending on the number of cases they found endorsing those classes. However, we want to prevent an agent having an unbounded number of votes. Thus, we will define a normalization function so that each agent has one vote that can be for a unique solution class or fractionally assigned to a number of classes depending on the number of endorsing cases.

Formally, let $\mathcal{A}^t$ the set of agents that have submitted their SERs to the agent A_i for problem P. We will consider that $A_i \in \mathcal{A}^t$ and the result of A_i trying to solve P is also reified as a SER. The vote of an agent $A_j \in \mathcal{A}^t$ for class S_k is $Vote(S_k, A_j) = \frac{E_k^j}{c + \sum_{r=1...K} E_r^j}$ where c is a constant that on our experiments is set to 1. It is easy to see that an agent can cast a fractional vote that is always less than 1. Aggregating the votes from different agents for a class S_k we have ballot for S_k as $Ballot^t(S_k, \mathcal{A}^t) = \sum_{A_j \in \mathcal{A}^t} Vote(S_k, A_j)$ and therefore the winning solution class is the class with more votes in total.

3 Justifications in Multiagent Systems

Many expert systems and CBR applications have an explanation component [9]. The explanation component is in charge of justifying why the system has provided a specific answer to the user. The line of reasoning of the system can then be examined by a human expert, thus increasing the reliability of the system.

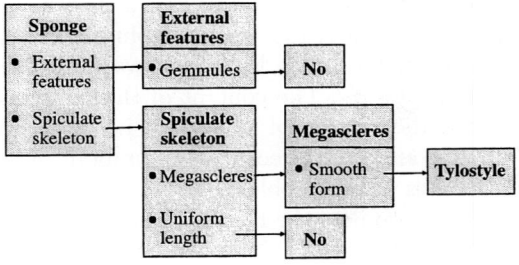

Fig. 1. Simbolic justification returned by LID.

All the existing work on explanation generation focuses on generating explanations to be provided to the user. However, in our approach we will use explanations (or justifications) as a tool for improving coordination among agents. Allowing the agents to give a justification of their individual results is crucial in multiagent systems since in an environment where one's conclusions may depend on knowledge provided by third parties, justifications of these conclusions become of prime importance [8]. In our work, we focus on individual agents that can provide justifications of their answers, and that can communicate those justifications to other agents. A CBR agent that receives a justification can then autonomously examine this justification in order to obtain information about the agent that created the justification. Moreover, we take benefit from the ability of some machine learning methods to provide more information than just the solution class, i.e. the ability to provide justifications.

Definition: A *justification* J built by a CBR method to solve a problem P that has been classified into a solution class S_k is a record that contains the relevant information that the problem P and the retrieved cases $C_1, ..., C_n$ (all belonging to class S_k have in common.

In our work, we use LID [2], a CBR method capable of building symbolic justifications. LID uses the feature term formalism to represent cases. *Feature Terms* (or ψ-terms) are a generalization of the first order terms. The main difference is that in first order terms (e.g. $person(barbara, john, dianne)$) the parameters of the terms are identified by position, while in a feature term the parameters (called *features*) are identified by name (e.g. $person[name \doteq barbara, father \doteq john, mother \doteq dianne]$). Another difference is that feature terms have a *sort*, for instance, the previous example belongs to the sort *person*. These sorts can have subsorts (e.g. *man* and *woman* are subsorts of *person*). Feature terms have an informational order relation ($\sqsubseteq$) among them called subsumption, where $\psi \sqsubseteq \psi'$ means all the information contained in ψ is also contained in ψ' (we say that ψ subsumes ψ'). When a feature term has no features (or all of its features are equal to $\bot$) it is called a *leaf*.

Figure 1 shows a symbolic justification returned by LID, represented as a feature term. Each box in the figure represents a node. On the top of a box the sort of the node is shown, and on the lower part, all the features with a known value are shown. The arrows mean that the feature on the left part of the arrow takes the node on the right as value. When LID returns this justification J for having classified a problem P in a specific solution class S_k, the meaning is that all the retrieved cases $C_1, ..., C_n$ by LID relevant for solving the problem P belong to the solution class S_k. The content of the justification J should be considered as a symbolic description of similarity, i.e. a description of what is common among $C_1, ..., C_n$ and P. Moreover, the symbolic similarity J contains the most relevant attributes of the problem P.

When an agent solves a problem the result is reified as a *justification endorsing record* (JER):

Definition: A *justified endorsing record* (JER) $\mathbf{J} = \langle P, S, J, A \rangle$ is a tuple containing the problem P, the solution class S found by the agent A for the problem P, and the justification J for that problem. (To refer to the elements of a JER, we will use the dot notation, i.e. we will use $\mathbf{J}.J$ to refer to the justification J contained in the JER $\mathbf{J}$).

Justifications can have many uses for CBR systems: in a previous work [5] we applied justifications in order to improve the classification accuracy of the committee collaboration strategy. In this paper, we are going to use justifications to compute the expected utility of individual cases in order to create case retention strategies.

4 Collaborative Case Bargaining Retention Strategy

When an agent has access to a new case, a Case Retention strategy is needed to decide whether to incorporate this new case into the agent's case base or not. In this section we are going to present a collaborative retention strategy called *Cooperative Case Bargaining* (CCB).

The CCB strategy is a collaborative case retention strategy that tries to maximize the utility of the cases retained in the individual agents' cases bases. The basic idea of the CCB strategy is the following: each agent has an individual case utility estimation policy with which the agent can estimate the utility of retaining a given case (i.e. how much the new case will contribute to the agent's performance if retained). Moreover, different agents may assign different utility values to to same case, and a case that has a low utility for an agent may have a high utility for another agent. Using the CCB strategy, agents that receive cases with low utility values can give them to other agents if the case has a higher utility for them (expecting to be reciprocated in the future).

As all the collaboration strategies in $\mathcal{MAC}$ systems, we will define the CCB strategy as an interaction protocol and a set of individual agent policies. In this section we will present the *Cooperative Case Bargaining* (CCB) protocol, and the *Justification-based Case Utility* (JCU) policy, an utility function based on justifications is used to estimate the utility of a given case for an agent.

4.1 Cooperative Case Bargaining Protocol

In this section, we are going to explain the Cooperative Case Bargaining (CCB) protocol, designed to perform case retention among a group of agents. The CCB protocol is based in four principles:

- Utility assessment: the individual agents are able to assess an utility value to estimate how much a new case will contribute to the agent's performance if retained in its individual case base.
- Delayed retention: when an agent A_i receives new cases, they are stored in a *pool of delayed retention cases* B_i instead of being retained directly into A_i's case base. These individual pools have a limited size m.
- Bargaining of cases: all the agents in the system compute the utility value for any case c_k in a pool of delayed retention cases, and then bargain for those cases with maximum utility for them.
- Small competent case bases: the protocol assumes that the goal of the agents is to achieve competent cases bases with a minimum number of cases necessary for a good performance to be maintained.

In the following we will first informally describe some aspects of the CCB protocol, and at the end of the section, the CCB protocol is formally presented.

When an agent A_i uses the CCB protocol all the new cases received go to B_i (the pool of A_i). When the pool B_i is full, A_i sends a message to the rest of agents stating that A_i wants to start the CCB protocol. The agent A_i that initiates the CCB protocol is called the *convener* agent. During the CCB protocol all the cases in the pools of the agents (including the cases in the pool of the convener agent A_i) will be bargained for by the agents.

Before the bargaining starts, every agent should notify the rest of agents about the contents of its local pool of delayed retention cases (so that every agent knows which are the cases that are going to be bargained). We will call $B = \bigcup_j B_j$ to the union of the pools of delayed retention cases.

The bargaining among the agents for the cases in B is performed in a series of rounds. At each round t an agent will retain a case. Therefore at each round t we can define the set $B^t \subseteq B$ as the set of cases that still haven't been retained by any agent. In the first round, $t = 0$ and $B^t = B$.

At each round t every agent A_j computes an *utility record* $\mathbf{U}$ for each case $c_k \in B^t$. An utility record $\mathbf{U} = \langle A, C, V \rangle$ is a record containing the utility value V computed by the agent A for the case C. For each case $c_k \in B^t$, an agent A_j will compute the utility record $\mathbf{U} = \langle A_j, c_k, u_j(c_k) \rangle$. We will note by $U_j = \{\langle A_j, c_k, u_j(c_k)\rangle | c_k \in B^t\}$ to the set of all the utility records computed by an agent A_j in a round t. When all the agents have computed these utility records, they are sent to the convener agent. In a second step, the convener agent examines all the utility records for each case in B^t, and selects the record $\mathbf{U}^t$ with the highest utility value. Finally, the agent $\mathbf{U}^t.A$ receives the case $\mathbf{U}^t.C$ and retains it. This finishes one round, and in the next round the agents will continue bargaining for the cases still not retained by any agent. The bargain ends when no agent is interested in any of the remaining cases (when an agent A_j sends an utility equal to zero for a case c_k, we say that A_j is not interested in the case c_k) or when there are no more cases to bargain (i.e. $B^t = \emptyset$). When the bargaining ends because no agent is interested in any of the remaining cases, the cases in B^t are discarded (of course, the agents cannot be sure that the discarded cases will not become interesting in the future, but they are discarded to save space in the pools of cases, expecting to receive more interesting cases in the future).

Notice that when an agent A_j retains a case $c_k \in B$ the individual utility values of A_j must be recomputed (since the case base C_j of A_j has changed). Moreover, in the case of a tie (i.e. more than one agent have given the same maximum utility for some case), the winner is chosen randomly (but any other more informed criterion can be used). Notice also that in order to use the CCB protocol, the agents should have agreed before in some parameters of the protocol (such as the size of the pools, etc.) in the following, we will assume that all the agents have previously agreed in such parameters.

Specifically, the CCB protocol for a set of agents $\mathcal{A}$ is defined as follows:

1. An agent $A_i \in \mathcal{A}$ decides to initiate the CCB protocol because its pool of delayed retention cases B_i is full, and sends an initiating message to the rest of agents in $\mathcal{A}$. A_i will be called the *convener* agent.
2. The other agents in $\mathcal{A}$ send an acknowledgment message to the convener agent A_i meaning that they are ready to start the CCB protocol.
3. A_i broadcasts the cases contained in its pool B_i to the rest of agents.
4. In response to A_i, the rest of agents also broadcast the cases in their pools to the other agents.
5. When an agent A_j receives all the cases from the pools of the rest of agents, an acknowledgment message is sent back to A_i.
6. When A_i has received the acknowledgments from the rest of agents, every agent can compute the set $B = \bigcup_j B_j$. The first round $t = 0$ starts with $B^t = B$, and A_i broadcasts a message requesting for the individual utility records.
7. Every agent A_j computes the set of utility records $U_j = \{\langle A_j, c_k, u_j(c_k)\rangle | c_k \in B^t\}$ (computed using its own utility function. In our experiments, using the JCU policy), and sends them to the convener agent.
8. When A_i has received the utility records U_j from every agent A_j (and has computed its own utility values U_i), the record with the highest utility $\mathbf{U}^t \in \bigcup_j U_j$ is selected.
   - If $\mathbf{U}^t.V > 0$, A_i sends the case $\mathbf{U}^t.C$ to $\mathbf{U}^t.A$, and also sends a message to the rest of agents telling the the agent $\mathbf{U}^t.A$ has received the case $\mathbf{U}^t.C$. The protocol moves to state 9.
   - Otherwise ($\mathbf{U}^t.V = 0$), A_i sends a message to the rest of agents telling that the protocol is over and the remaining cases are discarded. The protocol ends.
9. All the agents send a message to A_i acknowledging that the round is over.
10. A_i computes the set of remaining cases for the next round $B^{t+1} = B^t - \{\mathbf{U}^t.C\}$. If $B^{t+1} \neq \emptyset$, A_i sends a message to the rest of agents requesting their new utility records for the remaining cases in B^{t+1}. A new round $t+1$ starts and the protocol moves to state 7. Otherwise, A_i sends a message to the rest of agents telling that the protocol is over. The protocol ends.

Delayed retention allows the agents to have a pool of cases to compute the utility from (using the JCU policy), and bargaining cases ensures that a good distribution of cases among the agents is achieved. The next section explains the Justification-based Case Utility policy used to assess case utility.

4.2 Justification-Based Case Utility Policy

The *Justification-based Case Utility* (JCU) policy uses justifications in order to estimate the utility of adding a case c_k to the case base of an agent. The basic idea of the JCU policy is to determine if a case c_k will prevent a CBR agent to perform classification errors in the future. Therefore, the JCU policy favors cases that increase the classification accuracy of the system without taking into account the size of the case base.

Let agent A_j have access to a set of cases $B = \{(P_1, S_{P_1}), ..., (P_m, S_{P_m})\}$. None of cases in B is present in the agent's case base, therefore they are all candidates to be retained. However, before retaining any case, A_j wants to compute an utility function to decide which of them are worth retaining in the case base. For this purpose we define the set $E = \{P_j | (P_j, S_{P_j}) \in B\}$ as the set of all the problems contained in the cases in B.

To estimate the case utility values using the JCU policy, an agent A_j has to individually solve each one of the problems in E. After the agent has solved each problem in E, a *justified endorsing record* is build for each case. We will note $\mathbf{J}_E = \{\mathbf{J} | \mathbf{J}.P \in E\}$ as the set of JERs build by A_j for all the problems in the set E. Notice that the agent knows the correct solution for each of those problems, therefore the agent can test for each individual problem $P \in E$ whether P has been solved correctly or not. Thus, the agent can define $\mathbf{J}_E^- = \{\mathbf{J} | \mathbf{J} \in \mathbf{J}_E \land \mathbf{J}.S \neq S_{\mathbf{J}.P}\}$ as the set of JERs of the problems in E that A_j has solved incorrectly (where $S_{\mathbf{J}.P}$ is the correct solution class for the problem $\mathbf{J}.P$).

We can say that a case $c_k = (P_k, S_k)$ is a *counterexample* of an incorrect JER $\mathbf{J} \in \mathbf{J}_E^-$ if c_k is subsumed by the incorrect justification $\mathbf{J}$ and c_k belongs to a different solution class than the predicted one, i.e. $\mathbf{J}.J \sqsubseteq P_k$ and $S_k \neq \mathbf{J}.S$. Moreover, we can define also a *valid counterexample* of an incorrect justification as a counterexample c_k that belongs to the correct solution class of the problem P for which the justification $\mathbf{J}$ was created. i.e. a counterexample such that $S_k = S_{\mathbf{J}.P}$. Notice that the condition $S_k = S_{\mathbf{J}.P}$ implies that $S_k \neq \mathbf{J}.S$ if $\mathbf{J}$ is an incorrect JER. With the notion of valid counterexample, we can define the *refutation set*:

Definition: The *refutation set* $R_{\mathbf{J}}^B$ drawn from a pool of cases B for an incorrect JER $\mathbf{J}$ is defined as the set of cases from B that are valid counterexamples of that JER. Formally: $R_{\mathbf{J}}^B = \{(P_k, S_{P_k}) \in B | \mathbf{J}.J \sqsubseteq P_k \land S_{P_k} = S_{\mathbf{J}.P}\}$.

Notice that the cases in a refutation set $R_{\mathbf{J}}^B$ are the cases from B that can potentially prevent A_j from making the same error in the future (since they are valid counterexamples of the justification provided by A_j). We will call $\mathcal{R} = \{R_{\mathbf{J}}^B | \mathbf{J} \in \mathbf{J}_{B^p}^-\}$ the collection of all the refutation sets for all the incorrect justifications $\mathbf{J}_E^-$.

We can now define the *utility* $u_i(c_k)$ of a case c_k in terms of the number of errors that it will fix for an agent A_j. If a case $c_k \in B$ is not present in any refutation set in $\mathcal{R}$, that case cannot fix any of the errors made by A_j while solving the problems in E. However, if a case $c_k \in B$ is present in some of the refutation sets in $\mathcal{R}$, c_k can fix some of the errors made by the agent. We will use the number of refutation sets $R_\mathbf{J}^B$ where a case c_k is present as as utility measure, that will be called *Justification-based Case Utility* (JCU):

$$u_i(c_k) = \#(\{R_\mathbf{J}^B \in \mathcal{R} | c_k \in R_\mathbf{J}^B\})$$

Notice that the utility estimation for a case c_k depends on two factors: the case base C_i of the agent (the better the case base is, the less the errors made in the set E, and the less the utility of new cases will be), and of the set of cases B. The larger (and more representative) the set B is, the more accurate the utility values assessment will be. This is the reason for delayed retention in the CCB protocol: the larger the agents' pools, the larger the set of cases B will be and the more accurate the utility values assessment will be.

In JCU, justifications help to identify which cases can help avoiding errors in solving the problems in E. Notice also that an utility equal to 0 means that an agent is not interested in that case.

We can summarize the process of determining the utility of a set of cases B for an agent A_j as follows:

1. Let $E = \{P_j | (P_j, S_{P_j}) \in B\}$ be the set with the problems in B.
2. Let $\mathbf{J}_E = \{\mathbf{J} | \mathbf{J}.P \in E\}$ be the set of JERs for the problems in E.
3. Let $\mathbf{J}_E^- = \{\mathbf{J} | \mathbf{J} \in \mathbf{J}_E \wedge \mathbf{J}.S \neq S_P\}$ be the set of incorrect JERs.
4. Let $\mathcal{R} = \{R_\mathbf{J}^B | \mathbf{J} \in \mathbf{J}_{B^p}^-\}$ be the collection of refutation sets.
5. Compute $u_i(c_k) = \#(\{R_\mathbf{J}^B \in \mathcal{R} | c_k \in R_\mathbf{J}^B\})$ for each $c_k \in B$.

The JCU values could be normalized between 0 and 1 dividing by the size of the set B, but for simplicity no normalization is applied. Next section presents an example of the execution of the BCC protocol and of the JCU policy.

4.3 Example

Let us illustrate the behavior of the CCB protocol with an example. Consider a system composed of 3 agents $\{A_1, A_2 \text{ and } A_3\}$, that have individual pools of delayed retention cases B_1, B_2 and B_3 that can store 3 cases each. At a given time, the pools of the three agents contain the following cases: $B_1 = \{c_1, c_2, c_3\}$, $B_2 = \{c_4\}$ and $B_3 = \{c_5\}$, where $c_1 = (P_1, S_1)$, $c_2 = (P_2, S_2)$, etc.

When the pool B_1 of agent A_1 is full the agent A_1 initiates the CCB protocol. Both A_2 and A_3 broadcast the cases in their pools so that all the agents have access to the set of all delayed retention cases $B = \{c_1, c_2, c_3, c_4, c_5\}$.

When the first round $t = 0$ starts, all the agents apply the JCU policy to compute the utility records of the cases in $B^0 = B$. Let us focus on how agent A_1 uses the JCU policy: first, A_1 takes the set $E = \{P_1, ..., P_5\}$ and builds a JER for each problem in E. Assume that A_1 fails to correctly solve three problems, P_2, P_3 and P_5, and therefore the set $\mathbf{J}_E^- = \{\mathbf{J}_2, \mathbf{J}_3, \mathbf{J}_5\}$ has three JERs. A_1 builds then the refutation sets for those three JERs: $R_{\mathbf{J}_2}^B = \{c_2, c_3\}$, $R_{\mathbf{J}_3}^B = \{c_3\}$ and

Table 1. Evolution of the utility values, for 3 agents A_1, A_2 and A_3 and a set $B = \{c_1, c_2, c_3, c_4, c_5\}$ of 5 cases in the CCB protocol.

Round 1

a)

	c_1	c_2	c_3	c_4	c_5
A_1	0	2	3	0	1
A_2	2	0	2	0	0
A_3	0	0	0	1	2

Round 2

b)

	c_1	c_2	c_3	c_4	c_5
A_1	0	0	-	0	0
A_2	2	0	-	0	0
A_3	0	0	-	1	2

Round 3

c)

	c_1	c_2	c_3	c_4	c_5
A_2	-	0	-	0	0
A_1	-	0	-	0	0
A_3	-	0	-	1	2

Round 4

d)

	c_1	c_2	c_3	c_4	c_5
A_1	-	0	-	0	-
A_2	-	0	-	0	-
A_3	-	0	-	0	-

$R^B_{J_5} = \{c_2, c_3, c_5\}$. With these refutation sets $\mathcal{R} = \{R^B_{J_2}, R^B_{J_3}, R^B_{J_5}\}$ the JCU value of the 5 cases in B for the agent A_1 can now be computed:

$u^1(c_1) = \#(\emptyset) = 0$
$u^1(c_2) = \#(\{R^B_{J_2}, R^B_{J_5}\}) = 2$
$u^1(c_3) = \#(\{R^B_{J_2}, R^B_{J_3}, R^B_{J_5}\}) = 3$
$u^1(c_4) = \#(\emptyset) = 0$
$u^1(c_5) = \#(\{R^B_{J_5}\}) = 1$

In the same way, A_2 and A_3 compute their JCU values. All the agents send their utility records to A_1, that can now examine the utility records to determine the winner. Table 1.a shows the utility values for all the agents: the winner is the agent A_1, since the utility $u_1(c_3)$ is the highest. Therefore, A_1 retains the case c_3, the case is not available any more, and the rest of agents are notified.

When A_2 and A_3 answer with an acknowledgment to A_1, A_1 sends again a message to A_2 and A_3 requesting for the utility records of the remaining cases $B^1 = \{c_1, c_2, c_4, c_5\}$ for the second round of the protocol. A_1 has to recompute its own JCU values since has retained a new case, and the new JCU values are shown in Table 1.b. This time there is a tie between A_2 and A_3 that is resolved randomly: the winner is A_2, that receives the case c_1 to be retained.

The JCU values in the third round for the cases $B^2 = \{c_2, c_4, c_5\}$ can be seen in Table 1.c, where the winner is A_3 that receives the case c_5.

In the fourth round, no agent wants any case in $B^3 = \{c_2, c_4\}$, as shown in Table 1.d where all the JCU values are zero. A_1 sends a message to A_2 and A_3 telling that the CCB protocol is over, the cases c_2 and c_4 are discarded, and the pools of the three agents are cleared.

One may think that, if every agent has access to all the cases during the CCB protocol, why isn't it the best policy to allow each agent to retain every case? In fact, allowing each agent to retain every case is not the best policy (as we are going to show in the experiments section), since the resulting system would be equivalent to a single agent (since as each agent would have all the cases). In the experiments section we will show how a group of agents using the CCB protocol can outperform a single agent that has all the cases.

The CCB protocol may appear to be a complex way to distribute the cases among the agents. However, it is designed in this way since the order in which the cases are bargained does matter. A simpler protocol that would consider the cases one at a time could lead to suboptimal results.

5 Experimental Results

This section evaluates the performance of the CCB strategy and of the JCU policy. For that purpose, we are going to compare the performance of groups of agents using the CCB strategy against groups of agents using other retention strategies. The presented results will be related to classification accuracy and case base sizes of the agents.

We use the marine sponge classification problem as our test bed. We have designed an experimental suite with a case base of 280 marine sponges pertaining to three different orders of the *Demospongiae* class (*Astrophorida*, *Hadromerida* and *Axinellida*). The goal of the agents is to identify the correct biological order given the description of a new sponge. In each experimental run the whole collection of cases is divided in two sets, a training set (containing a 90% of the cases), and a test set (containing a 10% of the cases). The cases in the training set are sent to the agents incrementally, i.e. each problem in the training set arrives randomly to one agent in the $\mathcal{MAC}$. The agent receiving the case will apply a retention strategy to decide whether to retain the case or not. Each time that a 10% of the training set is sent to the agents, the test set is also sent to them to evaluate their classification accuracy at that moment in time. Thus, the test set is sent to the agents 11 times (one at the beginning, and 10 as each 10% of the training set is sent) to obtain the evolution of the classification accuracy of the agents as they retain cases from the training set. Both, the accuracy of the committee and the individual accuracy of the agents will be measured. The results presented in this section are the average of the accuracies obtained for the test sets in 5 10-fold cross validation runs. All the agents use the LID CBR method to solve problems.

These experiments evaluate the effectiveness of the collaborative learning policies, so it is important that the agents really have an incentive to collaborate. If every agent receives a representative (not biased) sample of the data, they will have a lower incentive to ask for cases to other agents since they already have a good sample. For this reason, for experimentation purposes, the agents do not receive the problems randomly. We force biased case bases in every agent by increasing the probability of each agent to receive cases of some classes and decreasing the probability to receive cases of some other classes. Therefore, each agent will have a biased view of the data. This will lead to a poor individual performance, as we will see when we present the individual accuracy results, and an incentive to collaborate. However, we will also give some experimental results on the non biased scenario.

We will compare the performance of 4 different retention strategies:

- Cooperative Case Bargaining (CCB) strategy: This is the strategy presented in this paper, where the agents store cases in their pools of delayed retention cases, and when the pools are full the CCB protocol is engaged.
- Always Retain (AR) strategy: In this strategy, an agent simply retains all the cases individually received.
- On Failure Retain (OFR) strategy: In this strategy, an agent tries to solve a case before retaining it. If the agent fails to solve the problem correctly, the case is retained (this strategy is essentially that of IB2 [1] for instance based learners).
- Individual Justification Case Utility (IJCU) strategy: In this strategy, the agents store cases in their pools, but when the pools are full, the agents simply apply the JCU policy to decide which cases to retain from their individual pool without sharing cases with other agents. The cases not wanted by the agents are discarded. Since this strategy avoids collaboration, it is a valid retention strategy for individual CBR systems as well.

Figure 2 shows the evolution of the classification accuracy for a 5 agents $\mathcal{MAC}$ where the agents use the committee collaboration strategy to solve problems. Four different lines are shown, one per each retention strategy tested. The horizontal axis shows the percentage of cases from the training set that the agents have received. Notice that each problem of the training set is only received by a single agent. Therefore, each agent receives only a fifth of the total training set (since there are 5 agents in our experiments).

Figure 2 shows that the agents using the CCB retention strategy obtain the highest accuracies, reaching an accuracy of 91.5%. Agents using the AR (retaining every case they receive) are behind the agents using CCB, reaching an accuracy of 88.14%. Finally, OFR and IJCU reach similar accuracies: 83.78% and 84.57% respectively, but with IJCU winning for a slight difference. Notice that the IJCU curve grows a little slower at the beginning than OFR (due to the delayed retention), but this effect is very soon compensated.

For comparison purposes, notice that the classification accuracy of a single agent owning *all* the cases in the training set (i.e. the accuracy of a centralized approach) is of 88.20% (lower than the accuracy of 91.5% obtained by the committee using the CCB strategy). Moreover, the accuracy obtained by the committee using a unbiased distribution of cases among the 5 agents (i.e. using AR without bias) is of 88.36%, still lower than the accuracy obtained by CCB. Therefore, we can conclude that CCB obtains a better distribution of cases than a random unbiased distribution or a centralized approach.

We can also compare the different retention strategies concerning the sizes of the case bases of the CBR agents at the end of the experiments shown in Table 2. The strategy that obtains larger case bases is the AR strategy (since the agents always retain every case they receive), with an average size of 50.4 cases. Agents using the CCB strategy retain only 27.6 cases in average, about a 55% of the cases retained by the AR strategy. The OFR strategy retains less

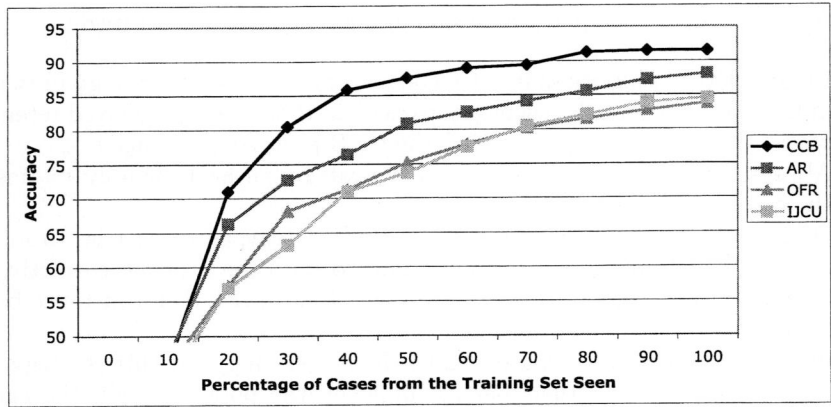

Fig. 2. Comparison of the evolution of classification accuracy for the committee using different retention strategies.

Table 2. Average case base sizes of the individual agents after having received all the cases o the training set.

CCB	AR	OFR	IJCU
27.6	50.4	19.0	16.6

cases, obtaining an average of 19.0 cases per agent. Finally, the strategy that obtains smaller case bases is the IJCU strategy (where the agents use the IJUC policy, but only with the cases in their local pools).

Taking into account both the results in classification accuracy and the case base size we can conclude that CCB is clearly better than AR, since retains less cases and achieves higher accuracies. IJCU is also clearly better than OFR, since IJCU achieves slightly higher accuracies and with smaller case bases. We can also see that CCB is clearly better than IJCU and OFR, since there is a large increase on accuracy of CCB with respect to IJCU and OFR. The cases that CCB retains (and OFR or IJCU do not) are the reason for the increased classification accuracy. Moreover, since CCB is equivalent to adding collaboration to IJCU, we can conclude that collaboration is beneficial for the CBR agents.

Finally, we also present results of individual classification accuracy. Figure 3 shows the evolution of classification accuracy for a 5 agents $\mathcal{MAC}$ where the agents solve problems individually. This time, the increment in classification accuracy of CCB with respect to the rest of strategies is increased: agents using CCB obtain a 82.88% of individual accuracy, agents using AR obtain a 73.11% of classification accuracy, agents using OFR a 66.34% and agents using IJCU a 66.88%. The increase in the committee accuracy obtained by CCB with respect to the other retention strategies is mostly due to the increase of accuracy of the individual CBR agents, from 73.11% to 82.88%. Moreover, the increase from the individual accuracy to the committee accuracy is due to the ensemble effect, from

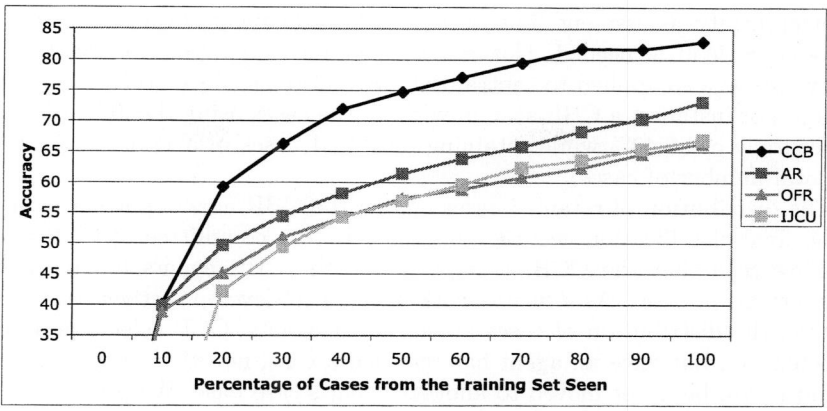

Fig. 3. Comparison of the evolution of agents' individual classification accuracy using different retention strategies.

82.88% to 91.5% with the CCB strategy. Notice that the ensemble effect requires that the errors made by the individual agents are not correlated. Therefore, we can conclude that the CCB strategy is able to keep the error correlation among the agents low so that they can still benefit from the ensemble effect.

6 Conclusions

This paper has presented the Collaborative Case Bargaining (CCB) strategy for case retention, in which individual agents collaborate in order to select which cases to retain. We have introduced the concept of justification. A justification contains information concerning why a CBR agent has classified a problem into a specific solution class. We have presented the Justification-based Case Utility (JCU) policy, that is able to compute an utility measure of the cases to be retained using justifications. Justifications allow JCU to determine which cases can avoid making errors in the future, and give higher utility values to those cases that can avoid the higher number of errors in the future. Therefore, justifications have proven to be a useful tool in CBR systems. We have also shown that using the CCB strategy in combination with the committee collaboration strategy, agents can obtain better results than a centralized approach (where a single case base would contain all the available cases).

Moreover, we have introduced the concept of delayed retention. By using delayed retention, a CBR agent does not decide whether to retain a case until a pool of delayed retention cases is full. This allows the CBR agents to better decide which are the cases to retain in the case base. Moreover, delayed retention requires a certain amount of cases to perform good estimation of the utility of the cases. In our experiments, the size of the individual agents' pools is 5. However, we plan to make experiments with different pool sizes. A larger pool size implies a better utility assessment, but at the cost of delaying the learning process, so some tradeoff is needed. Notice also that delayed retention and the JCU policy can be also applied to centralized CBR systems, since no collaboration is needed. For instance, a CBR system with all the cases using the JCU policy has an accuracy of 86.42% while retaining only 61.1 cases in average (a 24.24% of the total number of cases).

The distribution of retained cases among the CBR agents plays a main role in the final classification accuracy obtained by the committee of CBR agents. We have seen that the CCB strategy allows the CBR agents to obtain good distributions of cases. As a future work we plan to develop further strategies to improve the distribution of cases among CBR agents. CCB selects good cases for retention, but once an agent has retained a case, no other agent can retain it, and it will be never moved to another agent's case base. We plan to develop strategies for case redistribution among individual agents' case bases to improve the individual and collective performance.

Acknowledgements

The authors thank Eva Armengol and Josep-Lluís Arcos of the IIIA-CSIC for the development of the LID and of the Noos agent platform respectively. Support for this work came from CIRIT FI/FAP 2001 grant and project SAMAP (MCYT-FEDER) TIC2002-04146-C05-01.

References

1. David W. Aha, Dennis Kibler, and Marc K. Albert. Instance-based learning algorithms. *Machine Learning*, 6(1):37–66, 1991.
2. E. Armengol and E. Plaza. Lazy induction of descriptions for relational case-based learning. In Luc de Raedt and Peter Flach, editors, *EMCL 2001*, number 2167 in Lecture Notes in Artificial Intelligence, pages 13–24. Springer-Verlag, 2001.
3. L. K. Hansen and P. Salamon. Neural networks ensembles. *IEEE Transactions on Pattern Analysis and Machine Intelligence*, 12:993–1001, 1990.
4. S. Ontañón and E. Plaza. Cooperative case retention strategies for cbr agents. In Derek Bridge and Kevin Ashley, editors, *ICCBR-2003*. Springer-Verlag, 2003.
5. S. Ontañón and E. Plaza. Justification-based multiagent learning. In *Proc. 20th ICML*, pages 576–583. Morgan Kaufmann, 2003.
6. E. Plaza and S. Ontañón. Ensemble case-based reasoning: Collaboration policies for multiagent cooperative cbr. In I. Watson and Q. Yang, editors, *ICCBR-2001*, number 2080 in LNAI, pages 437–451. Springer-Verlag, 2001.
7. B. Smyth. The utility problem analysed: A case-based reasoning persepctive. In *EWCBR-96*, LNAI, pages 234–248. Springer Verlag, 1996.
8. Frank van Harmelen. How the semantic web will change KR. *The Knowledge Engineering Review*, 17(1):93–96, 2002.
9. Bruce A. Wooley. Explanation component of software systems. *ACM Crossroads*, 1998.

Case Retrieval Using Nonlinear Feature-Space Transformation

Rong Pan[1], Qiang Yang[2], and Lei Li[1]

[1] Software Engineering Institute
Zhngshan University
Guangzhou, China
gzpanrong@etang.com, lncsri07@cs.zsu.edu.cn
[2] Department of Computer Science
Hong Kong University of Science and Technology
Clearwater Bay, Kowloon Hong Kong, China
qyang@cs.ust.hk

Abstract. Good similarity functions are at the heart of effective case-based reasoning. However, the similarity functions that have been designed so far have been mostly linear, weighted-sum in nature. In this paper, we explore how to handle case retrieval when the case base is *nonlinear* in similarity measurement, in which situation the linear similarity functions will result in the wrong solutions. Our approach is to first transform the case base into a feature space using kernel computation. We perform correlation analysis with maximum correlation criterion(MCC) in the feature space to find the most important features through which we construct a feature-space case base. We then solve the new case in the feature space using the traditional similarity-based retrieval. We show that for nonlinear case bases, our method results in a performance gain by a large margin. We show the theoretical foundation and empirical evaluation to support our observations.

Keywords: Similarity, Case Base Transformation, Nonlinear Case Bases.
Paper type: Research.

1 Introduction

Case-based reasoning (CBR) is a problem-solving strategy that uses previous cases to solve new problems ([5], [6]). Over the years, CBR has enjoyed tremendous success as a technique for solving problems related to knowledge reuse. Several practical systems and applications [15] highlight the use of similarity based functions to find relevant cases from case bases. In building a case base, important descriptors of the case, which distinguish between the cases, are singled out and represented as features. The features are typically combined in some numerical computation for similarity. When a new problem is input, its features will be extracted to compute its similarity measure to other cases in the case base. The cases with the most similar measure will be retrieved for further analysis and adaptation ([5], [6]).

The quality of the retrieved case in a CBR system depends heavily on how to use the features to compute similarity measures. Various methods have been proposed to compute the similarity ([2], [1], [6], [12], [13], [14]), where most approaches rely on linear combination of features to perform this function. However, when the nature of the case base is *nonlinear*, where similar cases cannot be found by a linear combination of the features, such a method will fail to deliver the most relevant cases. In this paper, we present a solution to solving this problem.

As an example, suppose that in a problem domain there are N different features. If the similarity in the domain is based on a high-order polynomial function of the features' values, then the similarity of the features cannot be explained by a simple weighted sum of the input features alone. A real world example of this nature is when we define the similarity of two boxes by their weight. Suppose the input features given are the boxes' three dimensions x_1, x_2 and x_3 and the density d of the material that makes up the boxes. Then the computation of the boxes' weight which defines the similarity function is not a linear weighted sum of the three dimensions; instead, it involves the multiplication of the four features x_1, x_2, x_3 and d.

One can argue that in the above example, one can input the nonlinear features such as $x_1 * x_2 * x_3$ directly as part of an input feature, but we cannot expect the designer of case bases to have this insight for every domain that he encounters. We would rather have the system find out these nonlinear features directly using an automatic method. This issue is the focus of our paper.

In this paper, we present a kernel-based method by which we transform a case base from the original space to a feature space with the *kernel trick*. For a nonlinear target case base, we propose nonlinear feature-extraction methods with a Maximum Correlation Criterion(MCC). With this criterion, one can find in feature space those features that have the highest correlation to target solution. We call this method the Kernel Case Correlation Analysis (KCCA). Our empirical results show that for many nonlinear domains, our KCCA method outperforms the traditional linear similarity functions applied in the original case space.

2   Transformation of a Case Base to Feature Case Space

In this paper, we focus on a dot-product formulation of the similarity computation. Consider a given case base $D = \{(x_i, y_i), i = 1, \ldots, M, x_i \in \mathbb{R}^N, y_i \in \mathbb{R}\}$, where $\mathbb{R}$ is the real domain, x_i is a vector of input attributes (features), and y_i is the case-solution which corresponds to a target variable. For generality, we assume that the target variable is a continuous variable; discrete variables that are ordinal can also be converted to continuous ones. Then a popular method for computing the similarity between two cases is as follows: for an input problem $\vec{c}$, the similarity between a case $\vec{x}$ in the case base and the input case is computed as the $\mathbb{S}$ function:

$$S(\vec{c}, \vec{x}) = \frac{\vec{w} \cdot (\vec{c} - \vec{x})}{|\vec{w}|}$$

where $\vec{w}$ is a weight vector. Then, the cases with the largest value of the above similarity function are chosen as a candidate case. These cases are *adapted* to obtain a new solution. In this paper, we consider a simplified situation where we choose a highest ranked case by the similarity function and use the target value of that case as a recommended solution for the input case. This corresponds to using a 1-NN method for case retrieval. Our work can be easily extended to k-NN computations. In cases where the case solution is a compound structure, such as in the case of planning [3], our solution corresponds to predicting a solution index for the corresponding target case.

Given a case base $\mathbb{D}$, we now consider how to transform the cases to the *feature space*. Our intuition is illustrated by the following example.

Consider a problem domain where the target $z = x^2 + 2y^2$, where x, y are the attributes. In the original space ($\mathbb{R}^2$), we cannot find a direction which correlates well with z, where the correlation coefficient is defined in $[-1, 1]$. Thus, if we use an 1-NN in the original space, we are not going to get good result.

Now consider the case in a nonlinear space induced by a 2-degree polynomial kernel [10]. The corresponding nonlinear map of the kernel is:

$$\phi : ([x], [y]) \mapsto ([x]^2, [y]^2, [x][y], [y][x])$$

With this kernel function, there exists $u = [x]^2 + 2[y]^2$, which is a linear transformation in the nonlinear feature space. We can see that u completely correlates to the target z. We can now solve the nonlinear case-base retrieval problem better by considering the correlation in a nonlinear feature space.

We now consider the general case. Let $\phi(x)$ be the nonlinear function which maps the input data into feature space, $\mathcal{F}$. Then in $\mathcal{F}$, we can define a matrix, in terms of a dot product in that space i.e. $K(i, j) = \langle \phi(x_i), \phi(x_j) \rangle$. Typically we select the matrix K based on our knowledge of the properties of the matrix rather than any knowledge of the function $\phi()$. The kernel trick allows us to define every operation in feature space in terms of the kernel matrix rather than the nonlinear function, $\phi()$.

Much research has been done in machine learning on feature selection and feature transformation in nonlinear feature space; some examples are Principal Component Analysis(PCA), single value decomposition(SVD)([4]), Kernel PCA, Sparse Kernel Feature Analysis, Kernel Projection Pursuit ([9], [10], [11]). However, in case-based reasoning, it is important to relate between the input and target variables and these works do not address this issue directly. In order to draw this relationship, we turn to Kernel Fisher Discriminant Analysis (KFDA)([7], [8]) which takes the class label of target into consideration. However, KFDA restricts the target to be of discrete values. In this paper, we present a novel nonlinear feature transformation method, by which we consider the correlation of input features with *a continuous valued target variable* in the feature space. Our questions are: first, for a given case base, how do we tell if a transformation to a feature space will give better result? Second, how do we perform feature selection in the feature space to result in maximal retrieval accuracy?

3 Kernel Correlation Analysis in the Feature Space

3.1 Review of Correlation Coefficient

In multivariate statistics, the correlation coefficient is used to measure the linear dependency between two random variables. Suppose that Y_1 and Y_2 are random variables with means μ_1 and μ_2 and with standard deviations σ_1 and σ_2, the correlation coefficient between Y_1 and Y_2 is defined as

$$\rho = \frac{\sum_1^M (Y_1 - \mu_1)(Y_2 - \mu_2)}{\sigma_1 \sigma_2} \qquad (1)$$

It is easy to prove that the value of correlation coefficient ranges from -1 to 1. The larger the absolute value of ρ, the greater the linear dependence between Y_1 and Y_2. Positive values indicate that Y_1 increases with Y_2 ; negative values indicate that Y_1 decreases with Y_2. A zero value indicates that there is no linear dependency between Y_1 and Y_2. (see Fig.1.) If we normalize Y_1 and Y_2 as

$$Y_1' = \frac{Y_1 - \mu_1}{\sigma_1}$$

and

$$Y_2' = \frac{Y_2 - \mu_2}{\sigma_2}$$

and define two vectors as follows

$$\mathbf{x_1} = (Y_{11}', Y_{12}', \ldots, Y_{1M}') \qquad (2)$$

and

$$\mathbf{x_2} = (Y_{21}', Y_{22}', \ldots, Y_{2M}') \qquad (3)$$

then, $\mathbf{x_1}$, $\mathbf{x_2}$ are identity vectors (whose 2-norms are equal to one) and the correlation coefficient is the inner product of $\mathbf{x_1}$, $\mathbf{x_2}$

$$\rho = \langle \mathbf{x_1}, \mathbf{x_2} \rangle$$

(see the right one of fig.1) On the left of the figure are two sets of scatter points(circles

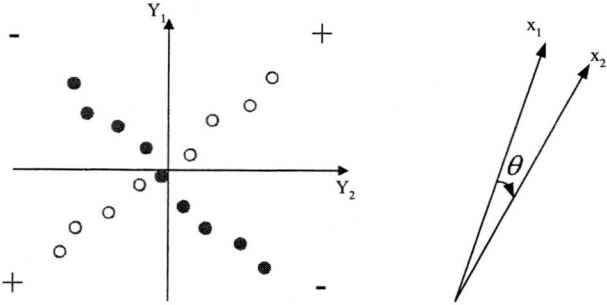

Fig. 1. Illustration of the correlation coefficient.

and dots) corresponding to Y_1 and Y_2 as they center around the mean point (μ_1, μ_2). If the scatter points mainly distribute in the 1-st and 3-rd quadrants(circle points), the correlation coefficient is positive; if the scatter points mainly distribute in the 2-nd and 4-th quadrants, the correlation coefficient is negative(dots). If the scatter points equally distribute in the four quadrants, the correlation coefficient trends to zero. On the right of the figure are two vectors x_1 and x_2 as defined in (2) and (3), where θ is their angle. The correlation coefficient equals $\cos\theta$, where $\theta = 0$ means that they positively correlate, $\theta = \pi$ means that they completely negatively correlate, and $\theta = \pi/2$ means that they do not correlate.

3.2 Correlation Analysis on Input Case Base

We now propose a new feature extraction method similar to Fisher Linear Discriminant Analysis (FDA), extended to handle continuous target values. First, we consider the case in the input case space. Given an original case base with M cases:

$$D = \{(x_i, y_i), i = 1, \ldots, M, x_i \in \mathbb{R}^N, y_i \in \mathbb{R}\}$$

We assume that the attributes are centered around the origin and y_i is also normalized (assuming continuous attributes):

$$\sum_{i=1}^{M} x_i = 0, \sum_{i=1}^{M} y_i = 0, \sum_{i=1}^{M} y_i^2 = 1 \quad (4)$$

The correlation coefficient between the j-th coordinate $x^{(j)}$ and y is defined as follows:

$$cor\left(x^{(j)}, y\right) = \frac{\sum_{i=1}^{M} x_i^{(j)} y_i}{\sqrt{\sum_{i=1}^{M} \left(x_i^{(j)}\right)^2} \sqrt{\sum_{i=1}^{M} y_i^2}} = \frac{\sum_{i=1}^{M} x_i^{(j)} y_i}{\sqrt{\sum_{i=1}^{M} \left(x_i^{(j)}\right)^2}}$$

We now consider how to find features that best describe the correlation between attributes and the target. For many problems, there does not exist an independent variable whose correlation coefficient with the target variable is either 1 or −1. In such cases, we wish to find a new direction $\mathbf{w}$ in which the correlation coefficient between the projection of all cases on this direction and the target variable is maximized (absolute value maximizing). This new direction will serve as a *new feature* in the feature space and be used for computing case similarities. Suppose that $z_\mathbf{w}$ is the coordinate on the new direction $\mathbf{w}$ when a case $\mathbf{x}$ is projected on $\mathbf{w}$,

$$z_\mathbf{w} = \langle \mathbf{w}, \mathbf{x} \rangle = \mathbf{w}^T \mathbf{x}$$

Then the correlation coefficient of z and the target variable y is:

$$cor(z_\mathbf{w}, y) = \frac{\sum_{i=1}^{M} \langle \mathbf{w}, \mathbf{x}_i \rangle y_i}{\sqrt{\sum_{i=1}^{M} \langle \mathbf{w}, \mathbf{x}_i \rangle^2} \sqrt{\sum_{i=1}^{M} y_i^2}} = \frac{\sum_{i=1}^{M} \langle \mathbf{w}, y_i \mathbf{x}_i \rangle}{\sqrt{\sum_{i=1}^{M} \langle \mathbf{w}, \mathbf{x}_i \rangle^2}}$$

To increase the correlation between z_w and y is equivalent to maximizing the absolute value of the correlation coefficient between z_w and y. We know the following:

$$\arg\max_\mathbf{w} |cor(z_\mathbf{w}, y)| = \arg\max_\mathbf{w} (cor(z_\mathbf{w}, y))^2$$

Thus, we can get

$$(cor(z_{\mathbf{w}}, y))^2 = \frac{\left(\sum_{i=1}^M \langle \mathbf{w}, \mathbf{x}_i \rangle y_i\right)^2}{\sum_{i=1}^M \langle \mathbf{w}, \mathbf{x}_i \rangle^2}$$

$$= \frac{\langle \mathbf{w}, \sum_{i=1}^M y_i \mathbf{x}_i \rangle^2}{\sum_{i=1}^M w^T \mathbf{x}_i \mathbf{x}_i^T \mathbf{w}}$$

$$= \frac{\mathbf{w}^T \left(\sum_{i=1}^M y_i \mathbf{x}_i\right) \left(\sum_{i=1}^M y_i \mathbf{x}_i\right)^T \mathbf{w}}{\mathbf{w}^T \left(\sum_{i=1}^M \mathbf{x}_i \mathbf{x}_i^T\right) \mathbf{w}}$$

If we define $\mu = \sum y_i \mathbf{x}_i$, $C = \sum \mathbf{x}_i \mathbf{x}_i^T$, we can get a new *Rayleigh coefficient*:

$$J(\mathbf{w}) = \frac{(\mathbf{w}^T \mu)^2}{\mathbf{w}^T C \mathbf{w}}$$

Finally, to obtain the important directions which mostly correlate with the target variable and be used as the new feature, we compute $\arg\max_{\mathbf{w}} J(\mathbf{w})$. We call this the *Maximum Correlation Criterion*(abr. MCC).

To provide some intuition on how Correlation Analysis generates new feature, we show an experiment with an artificial 3-d linear target-function case base in Fig. 2. In this example, the input variables' x, y-values are elliptically distributed as the righthand figure shows. The target z-values are generated from $\mathbf{z} = \mathbf{x} - \mathbf{2y} + \xi$, where ξ is the white noise with a standard deviation of 0.2. The lefthand figure shows the 3-d coordinate of the case base. The right hand figure is the projection on the $x - y$ plane and illustrates the Principle Component Analysis (PCA) and Correlation Analysis for this case base. PCA does not consider the target variable and simply returns the direction of statistical maximum variance as the first eigenvector. Correlation Analysis, on the other hand, returns a direction $(1, -2)$ that correlate to the continuous target variable the most.

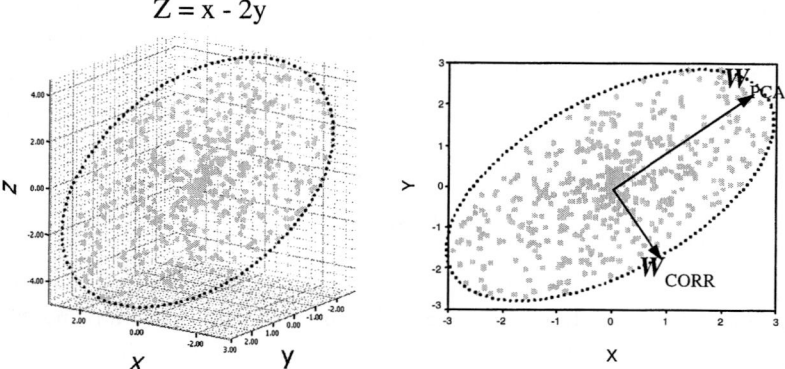

Fig. 2. 2-dimension input and 1-dimension target artificial example, with 500 cases generated.

3.3 Transformation of Case Base by KCCA

In a nonlinear target domain, it is often difficult to find one or several directions that correlates well with the target variable. With the "kernel trick", we now consider projecting a case base into a nonlinear feature space. Then, we attempt to transpose the linear correlation analysis to the nonlinear case base also with MCC. We call this method *Kernel Case Correlation Analysis* (abr. KCCA). In the next subsection, we give some examples of an artificial domain to demonstrate the merit of KCCA with 1-NN.

Given an original case base with M centered observations, the new case base can be obtained in a feature space FS by:

$$\Phi(D) = \{(\phi(x_i), y_i), i = 1, \ldots, M, x_i \in \mathbb{R}^N, y_i \in \mathbb{R}\}$$

where $\phi(x)$ and y_i are centered on the origin:

$$\sum_{i=1}^{M} \phi(x_i) = 0, \sum_{i=1}^{M} y_i = 0, \sum_{i=1}^{M} y_i^2 = 1$$

We project our input case in the new direction $\mathbf{w}$ in the feature space. Like the Kernel PCA [9], we assume that $z_\mathbf{w}$ is a new coordinate:

$$\mathbf{w} = \sum_i \alpha_i \phi(x_i) \quad \text{and} \quad z_\mathbf{w} = \langle \mathbf{w}, \phi(x) \rangle$$

Then the correlation coefficient of $z_\mathbf{w}$ and y is:

$$(cor(z_\mathbf{w}, y)) = \frac{\sum_i \langle \mathbf{w}, y_i \phi(x_i) \rangle}{\sqrt{\sum_i \langle \mathbf{w}, \phi(x_i) \rangle^2}} = \frac{\sum_i \sum_j \alpha_j \langle \phi(x_i), \phi(x_j) \rangle y_i}{\sqrt{\sum_i \left(\sum_j \alpha_j \langle \phi(x_j), \phi(x_i) \rangle \right)^2}}$$

$$= \frac{\alpha^\tau K y}{\sqrt{\sum_i (\alpha^\tau K_i)^2}} = \frac{\alpha^\tau K y}{\sqrt{\alpha^\tau \sum_i (K_i K_i^\tau) \alpha}} = \frac{\alpha^\tau K y}{\sqrt{\alpha^\tau K K^\tau \alpha}}$$

where K is the Kernel Matrix, and $\alpha = (\alpha_1, \ldots, \alpha_M)^\tau$.

Next, we consider the Rayleigh coefficient

$$J(\alpha) = (cor(z, y))^2 = \frac{(\alpha^\tau K y)^2}{\alpha^\tau K K^\tau \alpha}$$

where K is the kernel matrix and $y = (y_1, \ldots, y_M)^\tau$. Let $\mu = Ky$, $\mathbf{M} = \mu \mu^\tau$, and $N = KK^\tau$. Finally we obtain an expression for

$$J(\alpha) = \frac{(\alpha^\tau \mu)^2}{\alpha^\tau N \alpha} = \frac{\alpha^\tau \mathbf{M} \alpha}{\alpha^\tau N \alpha} \tag{5}$$

[10] presents several equivalent ways of the similar problems of maximizing Equation (5). One method is to solve the generalized eigenvalue problem and then selecting eigenvectors α with maximal eigenvalues λ, as follows:

$$\mathbf{M}\alpha = \lambda N \alpha \tag{6}$$

Like Kernel PCA, we can compute the projection on the eigenvectors $\mathbf{w}^k$ in the feature space as follows:

$$\left(\mathbf{w}^k, \phi(x)\right) = \sum \alpha_i^k \left(\phi(x_i), \phi(x)\right) = \sum \alpha_i^k K(x_i, x) \qquad (7)$$

Each eigenvector then corresponds to an attribute that we can select in the feature space for defining the cases. Let $< X_1, X_2, \ldots, X_n >$ be the selected attributes in the feature space, where the target value remains the same. We can then build a feature-space case base for case based reasoning. In particular, our feature-space case-based reasoning algorithm is shown as follows:

Algorithm	Kernel Case Correlation Analysis(KCCA)
Step1.	Transform the case base by solving the Eq.(6) and computing the selected attributes for the case base with Eq.(7).
Step2.	For an input case c, transform c to the feature space using the Eq.(7). The weight is determined by the correlation coefficient between the nonlinear feature and the target.
Step3.	Compute the weighted similarity between c and every case in the Case Base
Step4.	Select the case x_i with the largest similarity value.
Step5.	Return the target value y of x_i as the solution.

The KCCA algorithm is based on an 1-NN computation in the feature space. However, it would be straightforward for us to extend it to a k-NN algorithm.

3.4 An Example for KCCA

To give some intuition on how KCCA generates new case base and the merit of KCCA, we show in Fig. 3 an experiment on an artificial case base with two input dimensions and one target dimension using a polynomial kernel of degree two.

In this example, we have 500 data randomly generated cases in the following way: the input variable's (x,y) values are distributed in a circle, and the target z-values are generated from $z = 100x^2 + 200y^2 + \xi$, where ξ is the white noise with a standard deviation 0.2. The top left figure shows the 3-d coordinate of the case base. The top right one is the result of our KCCA on this case base. V_1, V_2 are the first two directions with which the linear regression plane (the hexagonal plane) is a good fit for the actual values. The table at the bottom shows the result of a segment with 6 cases in 500 cases before and after applying KCCA. The case numbers are also marked in the top figures. In this table, we can find that the overall MAE (Mean Absolute Error) of 1-NN with KCCA is about 40% lower than the overall MAE of 1-NN with original case base. Moreover, we can find that the nearest neighbors in the original case base of case no. 148 and case no. 348 are no. 204 and no. 149. The errors are respectively 108.03 and 50.289. In contrast, KCCA put these cases (symmetrical in original case base) together, so that the errors reduce to 7.139.

4 Experimental Analysis

We claim that KCCA benefits from superior efficiency and performance in terms of retrieval accuracy. We test our algorithms on a number of case bases. Our experiments

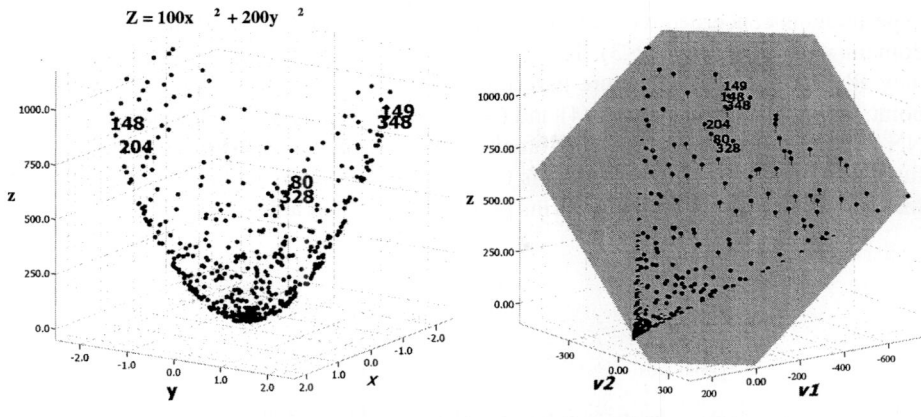

			Original Case Base				KCCA				
Case No.	x	y	Target Value	1-NN Case No.	1-NN Output	Absolute Error	V1	V2	1-NN Case No.	1-NN Output	Absolute Error
...											
80	1.246799	1.69054	723.6435	328	704.506	19.138	275.286	189.7407	328	704.506	19.138
148	1.339216	-1.92838	918.2133	204	810.183	108.03	341.6025	240.2621	348	911.074	*7.139*
149	-1.35932	1.975726	961.3629	348	911.074	50.289	365.5675	257.0333	148	918.213	43.15
204	1.225457	-1.81911	810.1831	148	918.213	108.03	261.0379	215.4208	80	723.644	86.539
328	1.274692	1.648425	704.506	80	723.644	19.138	274.8932	168.949	80	723.644	19.138
348	-1.35658	1.912332	911.0737	149	961.363	50.289	344.0176	230.023	148	918.213	*7.139*
...											
					MAE:	27.901				MAE:	16.75

Fig. 3. A 2-dimension input and 1-dimension target artificial example.

are performed on an artificial case base and several publicly available case bases; in this paper, the case bases are: *Wine Recognition, Boston House, bank, travel* and *comp-activ*[1]. For each application domain, we validate our KCCA with linear regression and 1-NN respectively.

We first used an artificial domain where there are three attributes and a numerical target value. This domain is designed to be a nonlinear one, and is aimed at showing the validity of our KCCA algorithm to show that for nonlinear domains where the linear regression technique cannot produce good results, our KCCA method can indeed make a dramatic improvement. For each system the retrieval similarity criterion is based on a cosine-similarity threshold; an input problem was successfully solved if the similarity between the problem and the retrieved case exceeded the threshold.

4.1 Testing KCCA

Artificial Domain Experiments. We now conduct experiments to test the effect of KCCA in several domains, to demonstrate how effective the new algorithm is. The first

---

[1] The Wine and Boston domains are available in
http://www.ics.uci.edu/~mlearn/MLSummary.html. The bank and comp-activ domains are available in http://www.cs.utoronto.ca/~delve/data/datasets.html. For the Travel domain, we thank Lorraine McGinty and Barry Smyth for the data.

experiment is concerned with evaluating the KCCA method in an artificially generated domain(same domain of fig.3). The common feature of these problem domains is that they all exhibit nonlinear nature in terms of feature descriptions. To demonstrate this point, we first show, in Figures (4) and (5), the result of linear regression, 1-NN and 1-NN with KCCA in these problem domains. "Actual" means the true value of the target function. Thus, the closer a method is to the actual value, the better the method is. As we can see, linear regression performs poorly in these domains.

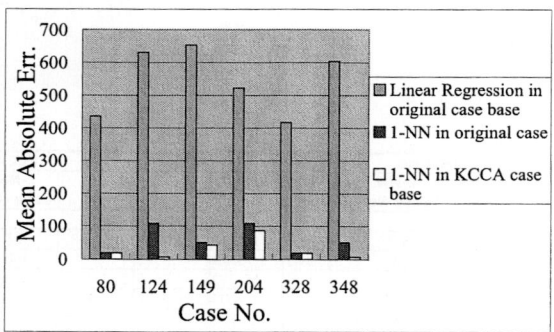

Fig. 4. Comparison of KCCA with linear regression and 1-NN in the original space.

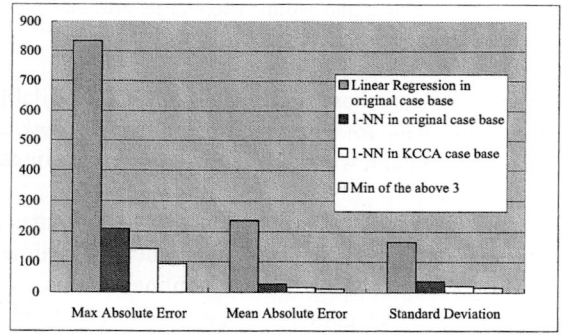

Fig. 5. The retrieval result of 6 cases from the artificial data set, when compared with Linear Regression and 1-NN in the original space and 1-NN with KCCA.

To test the efficiency of the KCCA method, we plotted the mean absolute error of KCCA as a function of the number of features. The result is shown in Figure (6). As we can see, the first several eigenvectors found by KCCA are in fact much better features than the rest in the feature space. This gives us confidence as to the use of KCCA in case-based reasoning.

Public Domain Experiments. We used the Bank domain, the com-activ domain and the Wine domain (available from the UCI Machine Learning Repository). The result is

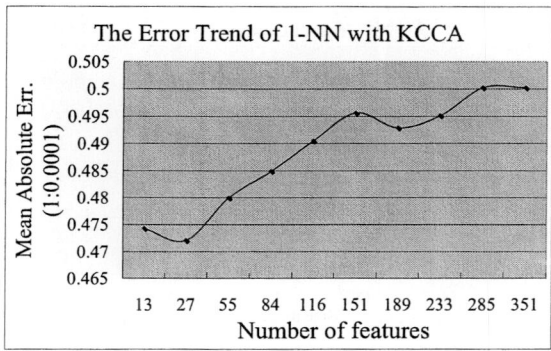

Fig. 6. The trend of average error as a function of different number of features computed by KCCA.

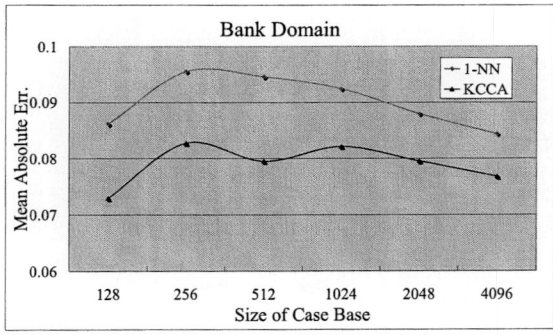

Fig. 7. Test KCCA on the Bank Base. The figure shows the average error as a function of different sizes of the case base.

shown in Figure (7), where we compare the mean absolute error KCCA and 1-NN in the original space as a function of different case-base size. As can be seen, using the KCCA uniformly outperforms 1-NN in terms of the MAE, and the difference in the error rate is the largest when the case base size reaches 512. Figure (8) shows the test result on the Travel database used often in case-based reasoning testing [14], where the objective is defined on the Price attribute, and Figure (9) shows the result of the com-activ base. As can be seen from both bases, the KCCA method outperforms 1-NN in the original space.

Table (1) shows a similar comparison with different kernels for the KCCA. As we can see, the MAE for the 1-NN method in the original space is as large as 172.944, whereas for the Gaussian kernel with the appropriately chosen parameters the MAE can be made smaller. One interesting fact is that the polynomial kernel in fact results in larger MAE error; this indicates to us that the Wine domain is in fact a linear domain, and thus 1-NN in the original space will perform just fine. It also indicated to us that the performance of the KCCA method is sometimes sensitive to the choice of kernel functions.

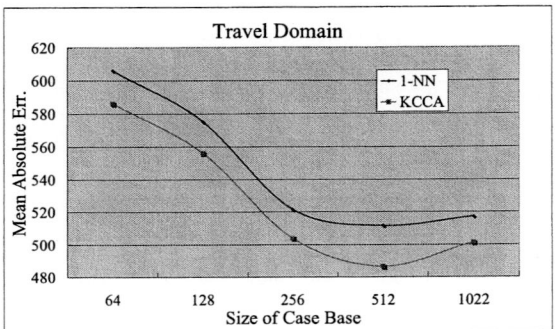

Fig. 8. Test KCCA on the Travel Database. The figure shows the average error as a function of different sizes of the case base.

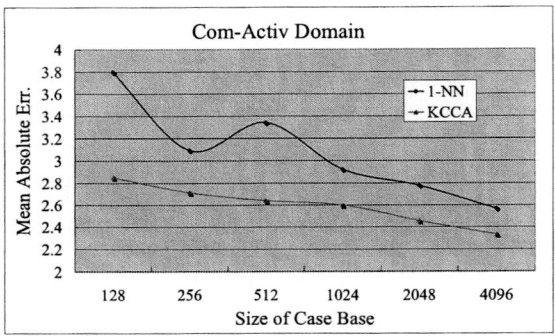

Fig. 9. Test KCCA on the Computer Database. The figure shows the average error as a function of different sizes of the case base.

We also noted that the time for the KCCA computation involves building the feature space case base and case correlation analysis. This is a one time cost. Once done, we can use the result to measure the similarity of each new case. This latter computation has the same time complexity as the original case based retrieval cost.

5   Conclusions and Future Work

In this paper we proposed a new solution to case base retrieval using a new nonlinear similarity function, when the nature of the problem domain is nonlinear. We used an FDA for finding the best attributes to compute a new case base in the feature space. We noted that the FDA cannot handle the continuous target case. We then proposed a new correlation analysis in the feature space, where we designed a new case based reasoning algorithm we call KCCA. Our approach is to first transform the case base into a feature space using kernel computation. We perform correlation analysis with maximum correlation criterion(MCC) in the feature space to find the most important features through which we construct a feature-space case base. We solve the new case in the feature space using the traditional similarity-based retrieval. We then empirically

Table 1. Test KCCA on the Wine data set. We compare the Mean Absolute Error with different kernels.

Original Space					
MAE	172.944				
KCCA with polynomial kernels of different parameters					
degree	2	3	4	5	6	7
MAE	217.96	165.6	217.9	179.8	267.5	191
KCCA with Gaussian kernels of different parameters					
Gamma	0.05	0.1	0.2	0.3	0.4	0.5
MAE	166.48	178.1	167.3	163.8	168.9	176

tested the KCCA for artificially generated data and for UCI data sets. Our result supports our initial claim that in nonlinear domains the KCCA will be more appropriate measure of similarity.

In the future we wish to extend this work to other methods for the construction of case bases. One important subject is to design kernel functions for the purpose of selecting cases from raw datasets, so that the CBR solution can be carried out. Another direction is to apply the kernel computation to more sophisticated kinds of target values, instead of just a single real value.

Acknowledgment

We thank Lorraine McGinty and Barry Smyth for the travel data. Rong Pan and Lei Li are supported by Zhong Shan University. Qiang Yang is supported by a Hong Kong RGC grant and an ITF grant, and a Chinese National 973 project.

References

1. A. Aamodt and E. Plaza. Case-based reasoning: Foundational issues, methodological variations, and system approaches. *AI Communications*, 7(1):39–52, 1994.
2. D. Aha, D. Kibler, and M. Albert. Instance-based learning algorithms. *Machine Learning*, 6(1):37–66, 1991.
3. K. Hammond. *Case-Based Planning: Viewing Planning as a Memory Task*. Academic Press, San Diego, 1989.
4. I. T. Jolliffe. *Principal Component Analysis*. Springer Verlag, New York, 2002.
5. J. Kolodner. *Case-Based Reasoning*. Morgan Kaufmann, San Mateo, CA, 1993.
6. D. Leake, A. Kinley, and D. Wilson. Case-based similarity assessment: Estimating adaptability from experience. In *Proceedings of the Fourteenth National Conference on Artificial Intelligence*. AAAI Press, 1997.
7. S. Mika, G. Rätsch, J. Weston, B. Schölkopf, and K.-R. Müller. Kernel fisher discriminant analysis. In *Neural Networks for Signal Processing 9 – Proceedings of the 1999 IEEE Workshop*, New York, 1999. IEEE.
8. V. Roth and V. Steinhage. Nonlinear discriminant analysis using kernel functions. In S.A. Solla, T.K. Leen, and K.-R. Müller, editors, *Advances in Neural Information Processing Systems*, volume 12, pages 568–574. MIT Press, 1999.
9. B. Schölkopf, A. Smola, and K.-R. Müller. Nonlinear component analysis as a kernel eigenvalue problem. *Neural Computation*, 10:1299–1319, 1998.

10. B. Schölkopf and A. J. Smola. *Learning with Kernels*. MIT Press, 2002.
11. A. Smola, O. Mangasarian, and B. Schölkopf. Sparse kernel feature analysis, 1999.
12. B. Smyth and M. Keane. Remembering to forget: A competence-preserving case deletion policy for case-based reasoning systems. In *Proceedings of the Thirteenth International Joint Conference on Artificial Intelligence*, pages 377–382, San Francisco, August 1995. Morgan Kaufmann.
13. B. Smyth and M. Keane. Adaptation-guided retrieval: Questioning the similarity assumption in reasoning. *Artificial Intelligence*, 102(2):249–293, 1998.
14. B. Smyth and E. McKenna. Footprint-based retrieval. In *Proceedings of the Third International Conference on Case-Based Reasoning*, pages 343–357, Berlin, 1999. Springer Verlag.
15. I. Watson. *Applying Case-Based Reasoning: Techniques for Enterprise Systems*. Morgan Kaufmann, San Mateo, CA, 1997.

Case-Based Object Recognition

Petra Perner and Angela Bühring

Institute of Computer Vision and applied Computer Sciences, IBaI,
Körnerstr. 10, 04107 Leipzig
ibaiperner@aol.com, www.ibai-institut.de

Abstract. Model-based object recognition is a well-known task in Computer Vision. Usually, one object that can be generalized by a model should be detected in an image based on this model. Biomedical applications have the special quality that one object can have a great variation in appearance. Therefore the appearance of this object cannot be generalized by one model. A set of cases of the appearance of this object (sometimes 50 cases or more) is necessary to detect this object in an image. The recognition method is rather a case-based object recognition than a model-based object recognition. Case-based object recognition is a challenging task. It puts special requirements to the similarity measure and needs a matching algorithm that can work fast on a large number of cases. In this paper we describe the chosen case representation, the similarity measure and the recent matching algorithm. Finally, we give results on the performance of the system.

1 Introduction

Case-based object recognition is used to detect objects of interest on a complex background where thresholding-based image segmentation methods fail. The basis for such a recognition method is a set of cases of the appearance of the object that should be recognized. A case is comprised of a set of contour points of an object and the object name. The recognition is done by retrieving similar cases from the case base and successively matching these cases against the images. Objects whose pixel points match the case points give a high recognition score and they are marked in the actual image.

In this respect case-based object recognition differs from model-based object recognition [1][2]. Model-based object recognition is a well-known task in Computer Vision. Usually, one object that can be generalized by a model should be detected in an image based on this model. Biomedical applications have the special quality that one object can have a great variation in appearance. Therefore the appearance of this object cannot be generalized by one model. A set of cases of the appearance of this object (sometimes 50 cases or more) is necessary to detect this object in an image.

Case-based object recognition is a challenging task. It puts special requirements to the similarity measure and needs a matching algorithm that can work fast on a large number of cases. In this paper we describe the basic architecture of a case-based object recognition system (Section 2). The chosen case and case representation are presented in Section 3. Similarity measures and our similarity measure are discussed in Section 4. The overview about the recent matching algorithm is given in Section 5. This matcher was tested on a set of images, see Section 6. Finally, we give results on the performance of the system in Section 7 and discuss implementation details. Conclusions and an outlook to further research is given in Section 8.

2 Case-Based Object Recognition

The heart of our case-based object recognition system is a case base of shapes. These shapes are represented as contour chains. Therefore a case is comprised of a set of contour points $S_c = \{s_c(x_o, y_o); 1 \leq c \leq n\}$ where each contour point has the grey value 1 and a class label for the shape. Based on this information we can transform the shape from the contour point list into a 2-D image matrix, further called case image. The case base is filled up for the actual application by shapes that we learnt based on our tool for information gathering, case acquisition and case mining $CACM$ [3]. An index over the case base should allow us to find the closest case among the numerous cases in short time. A case image is matched against the image by constructing an image pyramid from the actual image and the case image. This allows us to reduce the computation time while matching. Beginning with the highest level of the image pyramid the scores are calculated and the areas of interest are marked. The area of interest is the area where an object can be detected. This area is recursively used for further matching by going downward the levels of the image pyramid. Finally the closest match is given to the output. Depending on the actual value of the similarity measure the next level of the index structure is selected and the process repeats until a final node is reached.

The construction of this index is not part of this paper. It is left for further work. In this paper we want to describe the image representation, the image similarity and the implementation of the system as well as matching results. The architecture of our case-based object recognition system is shown in Fig. 1.

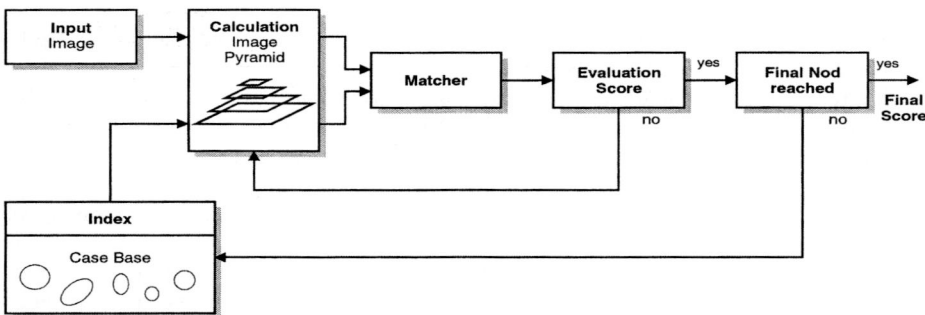

Fig. 1. Architecture of a Case-Based Object Recognition System

3 Data Representation

3.1 Image Representation

Images can be represented by their original 2-D grey level matrix. But in most applications this simple description of the image content is not expressive enough and therefore some low level features are calculated. One such low level feature can be the gradient of the pixels. The gradient represents the maximum grey value change between neighbouring pixels. Grey value changes are high where edges appear in the image. The boundary between an object and the background is usually an area of high grey level change. Therefore it is useful to highlight these features by representing the image by its gradients.

In order to determine the gradient, firstly the direction vector $\vec{z}_{(x,y)} = (\Delta x, \Delta y)^T$ of a pixel at the position (x, y) is calculated from the grey level matrix. The direction vector indicates the change of the grey value in vertical and horizontal direction respectively. The length of this vector is equal to the gradient and it is commonly determined from the direction vector through the following formula:

$$\|\vec{z}_{(x,y)}\| = \sqrt{(\Delta x)^2 + (\Delta y)^2} \tag{1}$$

Due to the discreteness of the grey level matrix which represents the grey value function only in some well-chosen points, the direction vectors cannot be calculated by the known analytic derivation formula. Therefore many operators were developed that allow us to determine the direction vectors from the grey level matrix, for example the Sobel operator. The corresponding edge image is obtained by applying such an operator to the grey level image. After that the pixels represent the gradient instead of the grey level value. Besides that the direction vectors for each pixel are stored.

The direction vectors along an ideal edge are perpendicular to the edge while the pixels inside a textured area have random directions. Therefore comparing two edges based on the direction vectors will give a good similarity value while two textured areas will have a low similarity value because of the randomness of the direction vectors.

3.2 Case Representation

In general, we can distinguish between three different case representations according to the pixels that are used for matching:

1. *Region of Interest (ROI)*: A region of interest ROI (see Fig. 2b) is obtained by taking a cut-out from the original image (see Fig. 2a). All pixels of the obtained image matrix are used as case pixels regardless if they are object or background pixels.
2. *Object case*: In the image matrix shown in Fig. 2b are only used those pixels as case points that lie inside and at the contour of the object (see Fig. 2c). In this case the shape and the inner structure of the object are taken into consideration.
3. *Contour case*: Only pixels that lie on the contour of an object are taken as case points (see Fig. 2d). Thus only the shape of the object of interest is matched.

The case that should be matched against the search image must have the same image representation as the image. Therefore the case is transformed into a gradient image (see Fig. 2e-2h).

Note that an object might appear in an image with different size and under a different rotation angle and on various locations in an image. But it is still the same object. It makes no sense to store all these identical but different sized and rotated objects in the case base. Rather there should be stored a unit object with the origin coordinates x_0 and y_0 that can be translated, resized and rotated during the matching process.

4 Similarity Measure

Remember, that model-based object recognition is used if the object can be generalized by one template and that case-based object recognition is applied if several tem-

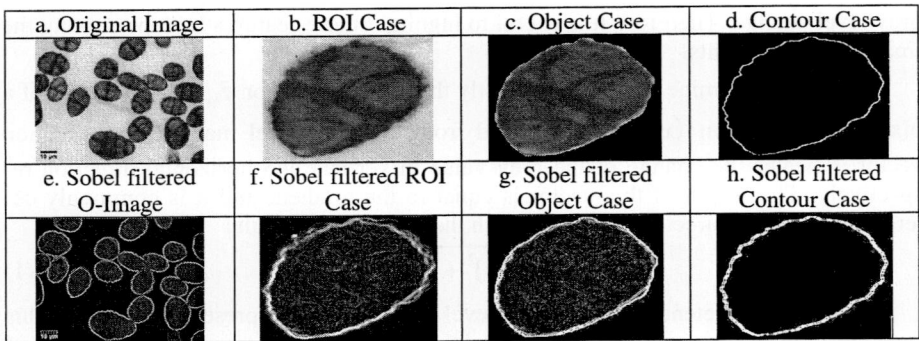

Fig. 2. Different Case Representations

plates describe the different appearances of the object. Due to the close relation of the model-based and the case-based approach the similarity measures which are known from model-based object recognition can also be applied to case-based object recognition. In this Section we want to review some known similarity measures and we present the similarity measure that we use in our case-based object recognition system.

4.1 Basics

Common similarity measures for model-based object recognition are the normalized sum of squared differences [4] (NSSD) and the normalized cross correlation [4] (NCC). The measure NSSD calculates the difference between each normalized point of the model and each normalized point in the image. Then the difference is squared and summed up. The measure NCC calculates the sum of the product between each point of the model and the corresponding point of the image and normalizes this value to the second order moment of the image and the model points.

The normalized cross correlation and the normalized sum of squared differences are invariant to linear brightness changes but they are very sensitive to non-linear brightness changes. But if the sum of squared differences is not normalized then it is also sensitive to linear brightness changes.

It can be shown that both measures behave similar. The realization of the SSD measure is simpler than the correlation measure which was of advantage in times where computers were not so powerful. In general the SSD measure is also more intuitive than the normalized cross correlation because the meaning of the difference of two values is easier to understand for a human than the meaning of the product.

Another commonly used measure is the Hausdorff distance [5]. It is a measure for comparing binary features. A binary feature in an image can be produced by thresholding. The image pixels that go over a given threshold are set to one otherwise they are set to zero. In our case the model points are given the value one and the background pixels are set to zero.

Let A be the set of the model pixels and let B be the set of the image pixels with the value of one. The directed Hausdorff $h(A,B)$ distance ranks each point in A based on its closeness to a point in B. It takes the value of the most mis-matched point of A. In general $h(A,B)$ is unequal to $h(B,A)$. The Hausdorff distance $H(A,B)$ of the model and the image is the maximum of the both directed Hausdorff distances. If the model and the image are identical then the score takes on the value of zero. The similarity of the model and the image decreases as much as the score increases; but there is no distinct value of inequality.

The disadvantage of the Hausdorff distance is its sensibility to occlusion and clutter: The score increases if some of the model pixels are missing in the image (this means occlusion) as well as if the image contains more pixels than the model (this means clutter). In order to overcome this weakness, in Huttenlocher et al. [5] is presented a modified Hausdorff distance which calculates the maximum of the k-th largest distance between the image and the model pixels and the maximum of the l-th largest distance between the model and the image pixels, respectively. If the number n of model pixels and the number m of image pixels are known then the modified Hausdorff distance is robust against $100k/n\%$ occlusion and $100l/m\%$ clutter.

Olson and Huttenlocher [6] extend the Hausdorff distance to oriented edge pixels. An oriented edge pixel is described by the three dimensional vector $p = (p_x, p_y, p_o)$. The Hausdorff distance is adapted to handle also oriented edge pixels. Olson and Huttenlocher point out that the recognition process is faster, if the orientation is considered.

However, another disadvantage of the Hausdorff distance is that we have to search for each pixel in the set A the closest pixel of the set B. This process may be very time-consuming. Olsen and Huttenlocher [6] improve the performance by restricting the set of image pixels so that the distance between any image pixel to the next model pixel is lower than a predefined value δ.

The similarity measure which is introduced in Latecki and Lakämper [7] is based on the contour of an object which is represented by a polygon. This polygon is subdivided into a set of consecutive line segments and the corresponding tangent function is determined. The similarity of a model and an object is defined as the distance of their tangent functions. Since this distance is normalized with the lengths of the line segments, the similarity measure is invariant against scale differences of the model and the object.

4.2 Similarity Measure Based on the Dot Product

As we have pointed out above the calculation of the Hausdorff distance is more costly than the calculation of the cross correlation. While we have to search for correspondences between model and image pixels in case of using the Hausdorff distance, we evaluate the image pixels that coincidence with the model pixels by using the cross correlation. On the other hand we are interested in matching oriented edge pixels which Olson and Huttenlocher [6] described for the Hausdorff distance. Therefore we propose a similarity measure based on the cross correlation and by using the direction vectors of an image. This approach requires the calculation of the dot product between each direction vector of the model $\vec{m}_k = (v_k, w_k)^T$ and the corresponding image vector $\vec{i}_k = (d_k, e_k)^T$:

$$s_1 = \frac{1}{n}\sum_{k=1}^{n} \vec{m}_k \cdot \vec{i}_k = \frac{1}{n}\sum_{k=1}^{n} \langle \vec{m}_k, \vec{i}_k \rangle = \frac{1}{n}\sum_{k=1}^{n} (v_k \cdot d_k + w_k \cdot e_k) \qquad (2)$$

We assume that the model consists of $k = 1, \ldots, n$ pixels.

The similarity measure of Equation (2) is influenced by the length of the vector. That means that s_1 is influenced by the contrast in the image and the model. In order to remove the contrast, the direction vectors are normalized to the length one by dividing them through their gradient:

$$s_2 = \frac{1}{n}\sum_{k=1}^{n}\frac{\vec{m}_k \cdot \vec{i}_k}{\|\vec{m}_k\| \cdot \|\vec{i}_k\|} = \frac{1}{n}\sum_{k=1}^{n}\frac{v_k \cdot d_k + w_k \cdot e_k}{\sqrt{v_k^2 + w_k^2} \cdot \sqrt{d_k^2 + e_k^2}} \quad (3)$$

In this respect the similarity measure differs from the normalized cross correlation (NCC). The NCC normalizes each pixel value by the expected mean of all values of the considered pixels. Therefore the normalized cross correlation is sensitive to nonlinear illumination changes while our method is not because it takes only into account the angle between two corresponding direction vectors.

4.3 Invariance Discussion

As described in Section 4.2 the similarity measure s_2 is invariant against illumination changes. The value of arccos s_2 indicates the mean angle between the model vectors and the image vectors.

a. Model	b. Object with identical Contrast	c. Object with globally inversed Contrast	d. Object with locally inversed Contrast
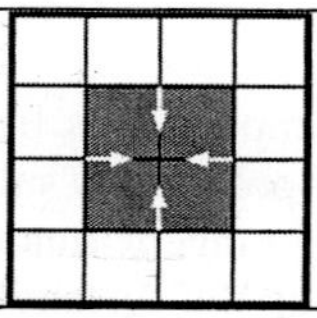	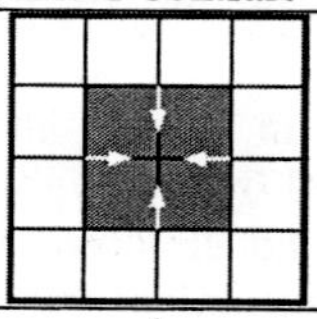	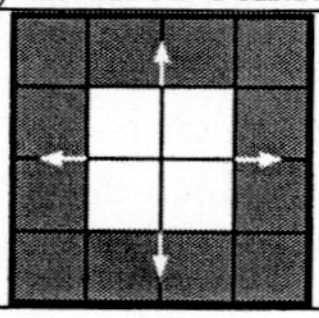	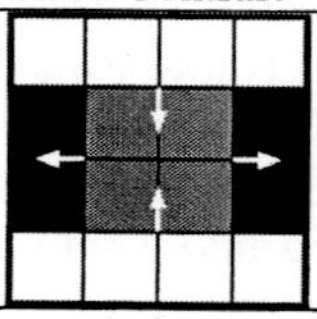
s_2	1	-1	0
s_3	1	1	0
s_4	1	1	1

Fig. 3. The Effect of Contrast Changes to the Scores of the Similarity Measures

The values of s_2 can range from -1 to 1 (see Fig. 3). In case of $s_2 = 1$ and $s_2 = -1$ the model and the image object are identical. If s_2 is equal to one then all vectors in the model and the corresponding image vectors have the same direction (see Fig. 3a and Fig. 3b). If s_2 is equal to "-1" then all the image vectors have exactly opposite directions as the model vectors. This means that only the contrast between the model and the image is changed (see Fig. 3a and Fig. 3c). The similarity values for these image constellations are also shown in Fig. 3.

The above described global contrast changes can be excluded by computing the absolute value of s_2:

$$s_3 = \left|\frac{1}{n}\sum_{k=1}^{n}\frac{\vec{m}_k \cdot \vec{i}_k}{\|\vec{m}_k\| \cdot \|\vec{i}_k\|}\right| \quad (4)$$

Sometimes the contrast is not inversed in all but only in some image pixels (see Fig. 3d). That means that the contrast between the model and the image is inversed locally. If the absolute value of each normalized dot product is determined before summing up the single values then the similarity measure is also invariant against local contrast changes:

$$s_4 = \frac{1}{n}\sum_{k=1}^{n}\frac{|\vec{m}_k \cdot \vec{i}_k|}{\|\vec{m}_k\| \cdot \|\vec{i}_k\|} \tag{5}$$

4.4 Discussion of the Measures

The advantage of the similarity measures in equation (3) to (5) is their invariance against illumination and contrast changes. This is achieved by normalizing the direction vectors to the length of one. But what happens to homogeneous or almost homogeneous areas?

Pixels in homogeneous areas have no direction vectors because there are no changes in grey values. Normalizing a zero vector is not possible because the length of this vector is zero and the division by zero is not defined. We can overcome this problem if we define that the dot product of a zero vector and any other vector is also zero. This definition can be extended to almost homogeneous areas if all direction vectors with a gradient less than the threshold l_{min} are equalized to zero vectors:

$$\frac{1}{\|\vec{i}_k\|} = \begin{cases} 0, & \|\vec{i}_k\| \leq l_{min} \\ \frac{1}{\|\vec{i}_k\|}, & \text{in all other cases} \end{cases} \tag{6}$$

If $l_{min} = 0$ then we will consider any small variation in the gradient. Otherwise we neglect small variation in the gradient of the image up to l_{min}.

We like to note that our assumption is that for identity we want to get the similarity value "1" and for diversity we want to get the similarity value "0".

In case we considered homogeneous areas in the model then for these pixels the gradient will be zero. If we sum up over these pixels with the value of zero and divide the resulting sum by n the final similarity value will never reach the value "1". The similarity value will differ from the value "1" depending on the number of the values of zero in the model. That means that we have to ensure that our model never includes homogenous or nearly homogenous areas.

4.5 Occlusion and Touching of Objects

Note that the similarity measure also indicates the amount of occlusion: If some parts of an object are occluded then the direction vectors of the model and the image will differ. This leads to a less value of the dot product. Thus the similarity score decreases as much as the model instance in the image is occluded. For example, if there is no noise in the image and an object in the image is occluded by 30% the similarity score cannot exceed the value of "0.7". Otherwise, if the image is noisy, the similarity score will approximately be "0.7".

In case, two objects in the image touch each other, either the contrast of the model and the image objects can be inversed in the corresponding regions or there are no edges which match with model edges. In the first case we can apply the similarity measure s_4, which ignores local contrast changes. The second case can be treated as if the objects are occluded.

4.6 Scaling and Rotation

In almost all practical tasks the model will differ from the scale and rotation of the objects in the image. Therefore the model pixels $\vec{p}_k = (t_k, u_k)^T$ and the direction vectors $\vec{m}_k = (v, w)^T$ have to be transformed with a matrix A to:

$$\vec{p}'_k = A \cdot \vec{p}_k \\ \vec{m}'_k = A \cdot \vec{m}_k \tag{7}$$

If φ denotes the angle of rotation and r the scaling factor the matrix may look like the following:

$$A = \begin{pmatrix} a_{11} & a_{12} \\ a_{21} & a_{22} \end{pmatrix} = \begin{pmatrix} r\cos\varphi & -r\sin\varphi \\ r\sin\varphi & r\cos\varphi \end{pmatrix} \tag{8}$$

5 Implementation in the Software Package CaseRec

We developed the case-based object recognition system *CaseRec* which is based on the similarity measure described in Section 4. The following subsections present an overview of how the case-based object recognition was realized if a contour case and an image are given. The case base is filled up with cases obtained by our program CACM [3]. Note that the case description is only comprised of the contour point coordinates, the case ID and that the grey values of the contour points are fixed to the value one.

5.1 Determining the Low Level Feature Representations

For the image and the case pixels have to be calculated the direction vectors. We use the Sobel-operator to transform the image and the case into the necessary representation. Since the calculation is based on the 8-neighboorhood of a pixel we exclude the margin pixels and set their directions to the zero vector.

Each case is a data file which contains the case ID and the coordinates of the contour pixels. In order to determine the corresponding direction vectors we create a binary case image based on this set of pixels. The case image consists of black background and white object pixels. The object pixels are defined as all pixels of the area inside the contour and the contour pixels itself. Note that also the area inside the object has white object pixels. Since our matching is only based on the contour we only calculate the direction vectors along the given object contour. Because the underlying image is binary there is no noise in the direction vector and therefore the vectors are really orthogonal to the edge.

5.2 Translation of the Case

Usually the area which includes the contour is small compared to the image matrix. Therefore, we only consider a part of the image, called *matching window*, which has the size of the surrounding box of the contour area. The similarity measure S is calculated between the contour and the corresponding image pixels inside this matching window.

During the matching process the matching window is pixelwise shifted over the whole image. Let the center of the contour be the origin of the contour, then $q = (x, y)$ denotes the image pixel, which is equal to the origin of the contour. In each Translation q the similarity measure $S(q)$ between the case and the matching window is calculated. Note, that there will be a border effect where the case can only be partially matched against the image. In the recent version of our program we match the case only on that image positions where the window fully fits to the image.

5.3 Speed up the Computation Time

The object recognition process includes three different transformations of the case image against the input image: translation, rotation and scaling. Given the range of rotation and scaling we have to determine the similarity at each pixel on each possible rotation and scale. This requires much time and therefore we included two procedures into our matching process to speed up the computation time. The current method of choice is to use image pyramids and to introduce a minimal value of similarity.

5.3.1 Image Pyramids

Image pyramids are applied for various tasks in image processing [8]. Each pyramid level concludes the information of the next lowest level, beginning with the original image on the bottom. The image generation in each level combines a decimation filter to reduce the image extensions with a function that assigns the grey values to the pixels. In general the image width and the image length are halved level by level. Thus the image of the new level only contains a quarter of the pixels of the image it is generated from. The corresponding pixel to (x,y) in the generated level is defined as the pixel $(2x,2y)$ in the basic image.

In Gaussian pyramids the weighted average of a 5x5 window around the pixels in the basic level is taken [8]. The nearer a pixel to the center of the 5x5-window is, the more its grey value influences the new grey value. The Laplacian Pyramid [8] is based on the Gaussian pyramid: The images of two adjacent levels are subtracted after the image of the higher level is expanded to the size of the image of the lower level.

We implemented a simple and fast pyramid generation method to our system: The image is separated into 2x2-sized blocks. Each block represents a pixel in the next resolution level and the corresponding grey value is determined by averaging all grey values of the block.

The number of levels is restricted by the demand that the main image contents in the different pyramid levels must remain. The matching procedure will be as faster as lower the image size is. Note that you can only match cases and images with the same resolution, i.e. the same pyramid level. After matching the case against the image in the highest pyramid level the approximate position, scale and orientation of each object in the image will be known. So in the next levels the search is focussed on the regions around these objects.

5.3.2 Minimal Value of Similarity

To speed up the calculation time for the whole image we introduce a termination criterion for each iteratively carried out matching process. We demand that the similarity between the model and the image in the actual matching window must reach a predefined minimal value s_{min} after having inspected j case points. If this is not the case the matching process is terminated in the actual matching window.

$$s_j = \frac{1}{n} \sum_{k=1}^{j} \frac{\vec{m}_k \cdot \vec{i}_k}{\|\vec{m}_k\| \cdot \|\vec{i}_k\|} \qquad (9)$$

$$s_j < s_{min} - 1 + \frac{j}{n} \Rightarrow break \qquad (10)$$

5.4 Rotation and Scaling

With the equations (7) and (8) we presented a possibility to scale and rotate a given case. Applying these formulas to the pixel positions of the case lead to floating point coordinates. Since rounding of the coordinates sums up to a high error in pixel positions, we divided the transformation procedure into two parts: First we determine the new pixel positions by selecting some representative contour pixels from the whole set. After transforming these representatives with the Equation (7), we interpolate between the pixels by using a first order polynom. In the second part the corresponding direction vectors are created as described in Section 5.1.

5.5 Summary

Finally we can say:

1. As more objects are included, the evaluation will take more time.
2. Matching in lower resolution levels will be faster than in high resolution levels.
3. As higher the threshold of minimal similarity (s_{min}) is as faster the evaluation will be.
4. The range of scaling and rotation parameters influences the evaluation time as well as the number of steps in scaling and rotation.

Note that the parameters should be chosen to ensure that useful results will still be obtained even when the evaluation takes more time

6 Test of the Algorithm

6.1 Material

Our program was tested against known synthetic shapes. We obtained the expected results for similarity and dissimilarity of objects as described in Section 4.

Here we want to report more comprehensive results about case quality and recognition performance of CaseRec. Therefore we used the test image shown in Fig. 4a for our study. For presentation purposes we gave each object a number. The tag ub6 means that this is an object of the type ulocaldium botrytis and the number 6 means that it is sixth object in the image (see Fig. 4b).

6.2 Cases

With the help of our program CACM [3] the 16 shapes were extracted and the respective prototypes were learnt. In Fig. 5 we can see the similarity relation between the 16 shapes in form of a dendrogram. We intuitively chose two clusters from the dendrogram for our evaluation. Fig. 5 shows the prototypes generated by the program CACM [3] and the names of the objects that are in the clusters.

In order to test the case quality and the recognition performance we matched these prototypes against the objects of the corresponding clusters.

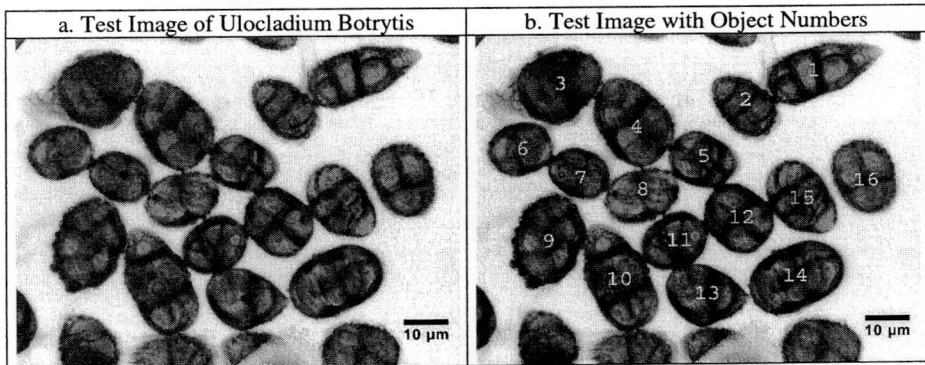

Fig. 4. Image with the Test Objects, Object Numbers

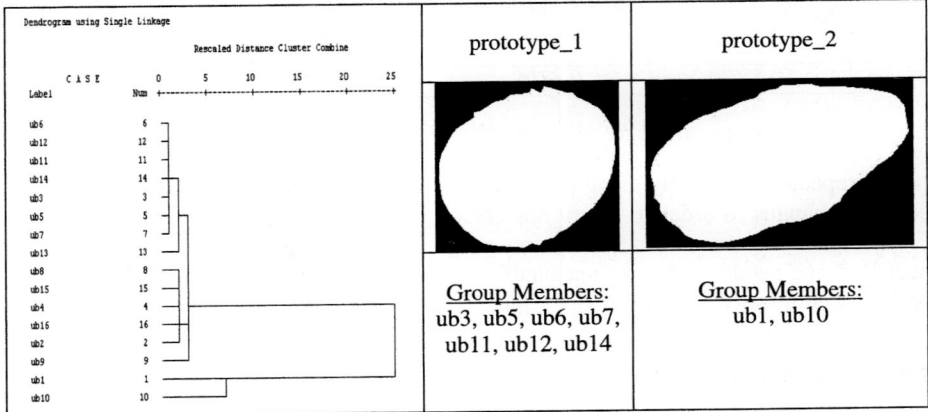

Fig. 5. Dendrogram, resulting Prototypes and Group Members

7 Results

7.1 Discussion of Prototype_1

The prototype_1 (see Fig. 5) was constructed based on the shapes of seven objects. We matched this prototype against the original image using all rotations from 0° to 360° in steps of 1°. The scaling factor ranged from 0.7 to 1.1 using steps of 0.01. We applied the similarity measure s_3 that is only invariant to global contrast changes. Fig. 6 shows the best matches we reached for each object that was used to create the prototype_1. We obtained scores between 0.7619 and 0.9231. This is a rather wide range in the recognition score since the original shapes show high similarity (see the dendrogram in Fig. 5) and since it also seems that the Prototype_1 matches the objects well (see Fig. 6a to 6g). Nevertheless, from Fig. 6 we can see that the objects with low scores often touch other objects. Remember that in the touched regions the contrast between the prototype and the object may be inversed (see Section 4.5). Since the similarity measure s_3 is sensitive to local contrast changes the wide range of scores is explainable.

	a. ub03	b. ub05	c. ub06	d. ub07
s_3	0.7619	0.7908	0.9148	0.8355
s_4	0.8396	0.8788	0.9164	0.8897
	e. ub11	f. ub12	g. ub14	
s_3	0.7830	0.7907	0.9231	
s_4	0.8576	0.8816	0.9274	

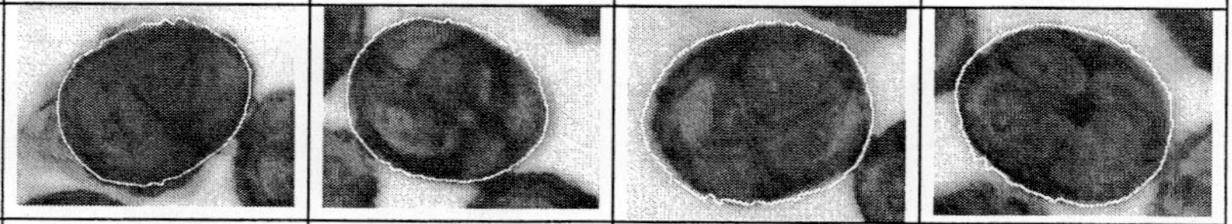

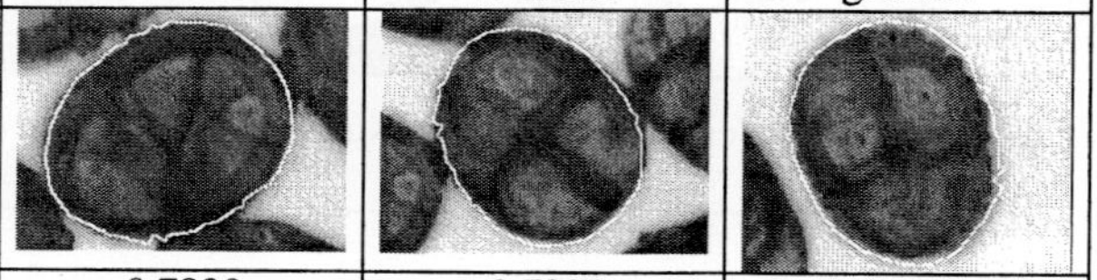

Fig. 6. Results of Matching the Prototype_1

We repeated the test by using the similarity measure s_4 that is also invariant to local contrast changes in order to verify our presumption that we will obtain better results. From Fig. 6 we can see that the scores range from 0.839 to 0.9274 now. As we expected, these results are more reasonable. Therefore we can conclude that we should prefer the similarity measure s_4.

7.2 Discussion of Prototype_2

Looking at the original image of ulocladium botrytis (Fig. 5) the shapes of the objects ub1 and ub10 seem to have similar appearance. The question we want to answer in this subsection is: Can we verify this human feeling with our procedures?

From the objective viewpoint of the dendrogram in Fig. 5 it appears as our human feeling misleads us in this matter, since these two shapes get linked together at a high dissimilarity value. Therefore we carried out two experiments. First, we created a prototype_2 of these two shapes (see Fig. 7a) and matched this prototype_2 against the two objects. Second we took the original shapes of the two objects as prototypes (see Fig. 7a and 7b) and matched with them.

The result in Fig. 8a and 8b show that the prototype_2 matches the object ub1 with a score of 0.8432 and object ub10 with a score of 0.6844. By matching the objects against themselves we obtained a score of 0.8432 for the object ub1 and a score of 0.8020 for the object ub10.

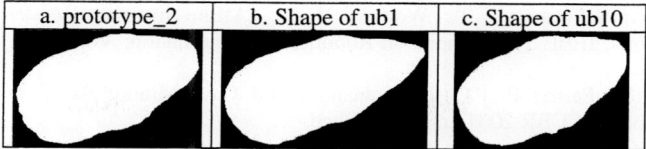

Fig. 7. Prototype_2 and the shapes he is generated from.

Matching with Prototype_2		Matching with the Object Shape	
a. **ub01**	b. **ub10**	c. **ub01**	d. **ub10**
$s_3=0.8432$	$s_3=0.6844$	$s_3=0.8904$	$s_3=0.8020$
$s_4=0.8919$	$s_4=0.8425$	$s_4=0.9302$	$s_4=0.9199$

Fig. 8. Experimental Results

8 Conclusions

In this paper we have proposed a case-based object recognition system. Such a system is necessary when objects of interest should be detected on a complex background, objects are overlapping or touching and thresholding-based image segmentation methods are not useful. There are many applications in biotechnology where a single case for an object is not enough for the recognition process instead of there is a set of cases describing the various appearances of an object required.

We have described our study to similarity measures for case-based object recognition that can work under illumination invariances, occlusion and clutter. The first implementation of the matcher has been presented and tested on a test data set. Implementation details were given as well as results of the matching process.

Further work will be done to improve the similarity measure. It is necessary that the similarity measure can give information about the different types of situations such as occlusion, touching objects or objects fragments. Furthermore we will develop an index structure which allows to further speed up the matching process.

Acknowledgement

The project "Development of methods and techniques for the image-acquisition and computer-aided analysis of biologically dangerous substances BIOGEFA" is sponsored by the German Ministry of Economy BMWI under the grant number 16IN0147.

References

1. Chen, Q. and Petriu, E. M.: "Optical Character Recognition for Model-Based Object Recognition Applications"; Proc. HAVE 2003 - IEEE Intl. Workshop on Haptic, Audio and Visual Environments and their Applications, pp. 77-82, Ottawa, ON, Canada, Sept. 2003.

2. Lamdan,Y.; Schwartz, J. T.; Wolfson H. J.: „Affine Invariant Model-Based Object Recognition"; IEEE Transactions on Robotics and automation; Vol. 5, pp. 578-589, Oct. 1990.
3. Jänichen, S.; Perner P.: "Case Acquisition and Case Mining for Case-Based Object Recognition", ECCBR 2004, to be published.
4. Brown, L.G.: "A survey of image registration techniques"; ACM Computing Survey, Vol. 24 (4); pp. 325-376; 1992.
5. Huttenlocher, D. P.; Klanderman, G. A.; Rucklidge, W. J.: "Comparing images using the Hausdorff distance"; IEEE Transactions on Pattern analysis and Machine Intelligence; Vol. 15 (1), pp. 850-863; September 1993.
6. Olson, C. F.; Huttenlocher, D. P.: "Automatic Target Recognition by Matching Oriented Edge Pixels", IEEE Transactions on Image Processing; Vol. 6 (1), pp. 103-113, 1997.
7. Latecki, L. J.; Lakämper, R.: "Shape Similarity Measure Based on Correspondence of Visual Parts"; IEEE Transactions on Pattern Analysis and Machine Intelligence; Vol. 22 (10), pp. 1185-1190; Oct. 2000.
8. Burt, Peter J.; Adelson, Edward H.: "The Laplacian Pyramid as a Compact Image Code"; IEEE Transactions on Communications, COM-31 pp.532-540, Apr. 1983

Explanations and Case-Based Reasoning: Foundational Issues

Thomas R. Roth-Berghofer[1,2]

[1] Knowledge-Based Systems Group, Department of Computer Science, University of Kaiserslautern, P.O. Box 3049, 67653 Kaiserslautern, Germany
[2] Knowledge Management Department
German Research Center for Artificial Intelligence DFKI GmbH, Erwin-Schrödinger-Straße 57, 67663 Kaiserslautern, Germany
thomas.roth-berghofer@dfki.uni-kl.de

Abstract. By design, Case-Based Reasoning (CBR) systems do not need deep general knowledge. In contrast to (rule-based) expert systems, CBR systems can already be used with just some initial knowledge. Further knowledge can then be added manually or learned over time. CBR systems are not addressing a special group of users. Expert systems, on the other hand, are intended to solve problems similar to human experts. Because of the complexity and difficulty of building and using expert systems, research in this area addressed generating explanations right from the beginning. But for knowledge-intensive CBR applications, the demand for explanations is also growing. This paper is a first pass on examining issues concerning explanations produced by CBR systems from the knowledge containers perspective. It discusses what naturally can be explained by each of the four knowledge containers (vocabulary, similarity measures, adaptation knowledge, and case base) in relation to scientific, conceptual, and cognitive explanations.

1 Introduction

Case-Based Reasoning (CBR) systems, especially in today's commercial contexts, do not have deep general knowledge. One of the strengths of CBR is that it is best applicable when there is no model available or a model is too hard to acquire and when cases are available or easy to generate. The downside is that, obviously, model-based explanations are just not possible to give. But this does not necessarily mean that a CBR system cannot provide good explanations.

In his book 'Visual Explanations' [31], Edward Tufte invites the reader to '*enter the cognitive paradise of explanation, a sparkling and exuberant world, intensely relevant to the design of information.*' The author addresses the human reader. But – because Artificial Intelligence (AI) is all about simulating human intelligence, and Case-Based Reasoning is all about simulating a major aspect of human problem solving ability – we as AI researchers should take Tufte's words especially to heart.

In AI, we are striving (not only but also) for the goal that AI systems discover explanations themselves and that they represent them appropriately in order to communicate with their users. Until that goal is reached, we should at least provide such a system with pre-formulated explanation and representation templates, to support human users in their interaction with the system. In contrast to commercial expert systems in the 1980s, commercial Case-Based Reasoning systems were never marketed as potential replacement to human experts [17], although case-based expert systems exist. CBR tools such as CBRWORKS and EMPOLIS ORENGE[1], or Kaidara Advisor[2] were designed as parts of interactive decision support systems. Their explanation capabilities are rudimentary, yes, but do CBR systems per se need as much explanation capabilities as expert systems?

Looking at all the efforts, already invested in explanation research, I think, we have just rattled at the gates of the above mentioned cognitive paradise. This paper tries to get a glimpse of what is behind those gates and shed some light on explanations in Case-Based Reasoning. It addresses foundational issues of explanations that CBR systems principally can provide, on the basis of the knowledge containers metaphor. The notion of knowledge containers, introduced by Richter [18] in 1995, is widely acknowledged and of great use in CBR system development, application, and maintenance [3, 21]. It helps to ask questions on how to structure available knowledge in order to 'feed' a case-based reasoner properly with knowledge.

In the next section, we will have a look at explanations in Philosophy of Science and revisit some of Roger Schank's work on explanation in AI. Section 3 recapitulates categories of explanations and major quality criteria for explanations. In Section 4, the knowledge containers are examined with respect to their explanatory power, before the explanation categories of Section 3 are related to the knowledge containers in Section 5.

2 What Is an Explanation?

In Philosophy of Science, the main kind of explanation discussed are *scientific explanations*. Scientific explanations answer why-questions [24]: Can some fact E (the *explanandum*) be derived from other facts A with the help of general laws L (the *explanans* $L \cup A$)?

There is an ongoing debate on the definition and semantics of scientific explanations which goes well beyond the scope of this paper. It is certainly domain dependent, how relevant explanations are that answer why-questions on the basis of laws of nature. One should also be aware of the distinction between (cause giving) explanations and (reason giving) justifications [24]. Explanation-seeking why-questions ask *why an explanandum event occurred*, i.e., for its cause or reason for being ('Seinsgrund'). Reason-seeking why-questions ask *why it is reasonable to believe that the explanandum event has occurred or will occur*. They seek the reason for believing ('Vernunftgrund'). Whatever kind of why-question

---

[1] http://www.empolis.com
[2] http://www.kaidara.com

is to be answered in a knowledge-based system depends in the end on the goals of the respective system and its application domain.

In real world situations, explanations are often literally false due to moral, pedagogical, and other context-dependent reasons [7]. Such explanations are designed to satisfy the questioner (at least temporarily). Nevertheless, they do not necessarily fulfill the purpose the questioner expects them to. For example, imagine the situation where a child asks her parents about where babies come from. The explanation most probably will not answer the question, it will just make the questioner stop asking. The adequacy of explanations as well as of justifications is dependent on pragmatically given background knowledge. What counts as a good explanation in a certain situation is determined by context-dependent criteria [7]. In Section 3, we will have a closer look at such quality criteria.

According to Roger Schank, a famous cognitive psychologist and computer scientist who considerably contributed to the early phase of Case-Based Reasoning research, explanations are considered the most common method used by humans to support decisions [23]. Their main purpose is to explain a solution and the path that led to the solution, and to explain how the respective system works as well as how to handle the system. Explanations, therefore, must be *inclusive* as well as *instructive*.

As soon as a system explains its own actions not only to those who inquire about how the system works, but also to itself, the system becomes an *understanding system* according to Schank's spectrum of understanding. The spectrum ranges from *making sense* over *cognitive understanding* to *complete empathy* [23]. In this spectrum, work on computer understanding can only reasonably claim the left half of the spectrum, i.e., from making sense to cognitive understanding, as its proper domain. I think this is still true today and will not change in the near future, if ever.

Schank distinguishes three classes of things that humans explain [22]: the physical world, the social world, and individual patterns of behavior. The three classes together with the above mentioned spectrum of understanding can help deciding what reasonably can be explained by a computer. Most explanations certainly can be given with respect to the physical world, providing scientific explanations. In a world of software agents, recognizing, identifying, and explaining individual patterns of agent behavior becomes more and more important.

But the purpose of explaining is not only a technical one. The (human) user is also interested in how much trust he or she can have in a system. An obvious approach to increasing the confidence in a system's result is to output explanations as part of the result [15]. Belief in a system can be increased not only by the quality of its output but, more importantly, by evidence of how it was derived [29]. In recent work, Doyle et al. [8] address not only the point of credibility, they also demand that knowledge-based systems, such as expert systems and Case-Based Reasoning systems, need to justify and be accountable for their predictions, giving the user a sense of control over the system [30].

3 Explanation in Expert Systems

Expert Systems are programs designed to solve problems similar to a human expert in a particular, well-defined domain. The ability to explain the solution and the reasoning process that led to the solution is another characteristic of so-called First-Generation expert systems. It is seen as an important activity for any knowledge-based system as it satisfies the user's need to decide whether to accept or reject a recommendation.

The explanations of First-Generation expert systems were often found unsatisfactory and the dialogues unnatural [17], i.e., explanations often were nothing more than (badly) paraphrased rules, important aspects were missing, or too much information was given. In order to improve on dialogues, Second-Generation expert systems focused on context, goals and actions, methods and justifications to support explanations, together with an even richer knowledge representation. But what kinds of explanations are of interest and what makes an explanation good?

3.1 Useful Kinds of Explanation

According to Spieker [27], there are five useful kinds of explanations in the context of expert systems:

- *Conceptual Explanations* are of the form 'What is ...?' or 'What is the meaning of ...?'. The goal of this kind of explanation is to map unknown concepts to known ones.
- *Why-explanations* describe the cause or the justifications for a fact or the occurence of an event. Again, one has to clearly distinguish between causes and justifications. Whereas the first concept is causal in nature and not symmetric, the latter only provides evidence for what has been asked for.
- *How-explanations* are a special case of why-explanations, describing processes that lead to an event by providing a causal chain. How-questions ask for an explanation of the function of a device.
- The goal of *Purpose-explanations* is to describe the purpose of a fact or object. Typical questions are of the form 'What is ... for?' or 'What is the purpose of ...?'.
- *Cognitive Explanations* are also a special case of why-explanations. Cognitive explanations explain or predict the behavior of 'intelligent systems' on the basis of known goals, beliefs, constraints, and rationality assumptions.

The first four categories of explanations describe variations of scientific explanations, which answer questions based on laws of nature, thus explaining the physical world. Expert systems answer such questions by using the knowledge contained in their (static) knowledge base. Cognitive explanations, on the other hand, reflect a system-related view. They deal with the processing of the system. In a way, cognitive explanations explain the social world and individual patterns of behavior. We will come back to these kinds of explanations in Section 5.

3.2 Aspects of Good Explanations

Five aspects of good explanation in a knowledge-based system are deemed important and fall into three classes [30]. The first requirement is concerned with how the explanations are generated. The second and third are requirements on the explanations themselves. The fourth and fifth concern the effect of an explanation facility on the construction and execution of an expert system.

- *Fidelity.* The explanation must be an accurate representation of what the expert system does. Therefore, the explanations must be based on the same knowledge that the system uses for reasoning.
- *Understandability.* The generated explanations must be understandable, i.e., conceptually as well as regarding its content. According to Spieker [27], they also should be innovative with respect to the knowledge of the user. Explanations, generally, should not contain already known information apart from knowledge required for argumentation. They must be relevant with respect to the goals and intentions of the users at an appropriate level of abstraction. And last, but not least, explanations must be convincing, i.e., explanations which are based on assumptions accepted by the user should be preferred. Swartout and Moore [30] call those factors involved in understandability *terminology, user sensitivity, abstraction,* and *summarization.* They further identfied the factors *perspectives, feedback,* and *linguistic competence.* The system should be able to explain its knowledge from different perspectives and should allow for follow-up questions if the user indicates that he or she does not understand (part of) an explanation. The explanations should sound 'natural' and adhere to linguistic principles and constraints.
- *Sufficiency.* The system has to know what it is talking about. Enough knowledge must be represented in the system to answer the questions users have.
- *Low construction overhead.* Explanation must either impose a light load on the construction of an expert system, or any load that is imposed should be rewarded, for example, by easing some other phase of the expert system's life cycle.
- *Efficiency.* The explanation facility should not degrade the run time efficiency of the expert system.

Studies indicate that novice users prefer higher-level explanations mixed with background information and low level explanations, whereas experts tend to prefer low-level explanations [8]. Novice users also tend to prefer explanations that justify results (why-explanations), while experts are more interested in anomalies and tend to prefer explanations that explain the reasoning trace (how-explanations). But, according to Cawsey [6], there is no simple relation between the level of user expertise and the level of detail described, and appropriate user models are hard to develop. Therefore, Swartout and Moore [30] suggest to use stereotypical user models where the level of detail is customized to each stereotype.

4 Explanations in Case-Based Reasoning Systems

Doyle et al. recently reviewed CBR systems with respect to their explanation capabilities [8]. All reviewed systems contain rich background knowledge. But what, in principle, can CBR systems explain with respect to the knowledge containers?

Artificial Neural Network systems cannot explain their decisions because knowledge is not available explicitly. Knowledge is compiled into the structure of the neural net. Rule-based systems, e.g. expert systems, can refer to their rules. But even experienced users often have problems following those explanations. In contrast to expert systems, case-based reasoners can present cases to the user *to provide compelling support for the system's conclusions*, as pointed out by Leake [10]. But cases are not the only source of knowledge in a CBR system and cases cannot provide provide information about how they were selected, i.e., they cannot give cognitive explanations.

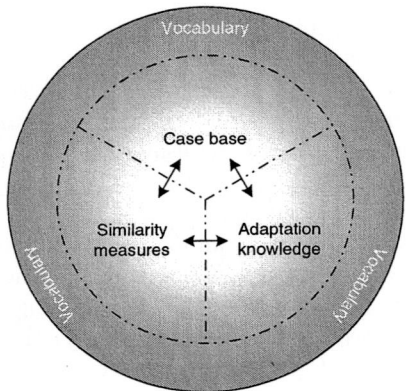

Fig. 1. The four knowledge containers of a CBR system

4.1 The Knowledge Containers Revisited

Knowledge-based systems store knowledge explicitly to use it for problem-solving. Part of the knowledge is represented directly and another part can be derived using methods of inference. For CBR systems, Richter [18] introduced the notion of *knowledge containers* that contain and structure the knowledge of a case-based reasoner. A knowledge container is a collection of knowledge that is relevant to many tasks rather than to one. Prominent knowledge containers in rule-based systems, for instance, are *facts* and *rules*. For CBR systems, Richter describes four such knowledge containers: *vocabulary*, *similarity measures*, *solution transformation* (also called *adaptation knowledge*), and *case base*. They are depicted in Fig. 1.

The *vocabulary knowledge container* covers everything that defines the system, e.g., attributes, predicates, and the structure of the domain schema. Thus the vocabulary forms the basis for all of the other three containers. The knowledge that defines how the most useful case is retrieved and by what means the similarity is calculated, is held by the *similarity measures* container. The *adaptation knowledge* container covers the knowledge for translating a prior solution to fit a given query and the *case base* stores the experience of the CBR system in the form of cases.

The structure of the knowledge of CBR systems is a major advantage of CBR compared with expert systems [11]. It reduces the knowledge acquisition bottleneck to a large degree by forcing attention to issues on the relation between cases, the level of abstractions to encode them, how to generalize them to new problems, etc. Cases are acquired relatively easily in contrast to general knowledge.

Another advantage is that each knowledge container can be changed locally. Changes in one container have little effect on the other containers. For example, adding new cases to the case base does not change the similarity measures. This property helps in maintaining the knowledge of case-based reasoners [21]. Of course, changing one knowledge container will have some impact on the other knowledge containers, but the knowledge containers view helps keeping changes local.

The flexibility to decide pragmatically which container holds which knowledge, is a third advantage, because, in principle, each container can carry almost all available knowledge, but that does not mean that it is advisable [18]. For instance, when the case base contains all potential cases, neither a similarity measure (the identity function would suffice) nor adaptation knowledge would be needed. In fact, a traditional database could be used. The other extreme would be to have a complete model of adaptation. Starting with some arbitrary case and adapting it to solve the current problem, no case base – better, a case base containing only one arbitrary case – and no similarity measure would be needed. In fact, this resembles a model-based reasoner.

Based on the knowledge container view, I will now try to show what a CBR system can explain quite naturally. In the following, I assume an attribute-value representation as is found most commonly in commercial as well as in research CBR shells.

4.2 The Case Base: The Main Source for Explanations?

Cases often are said to be self-explaining. This is probably true if we look at help-desk applications (e.g., [26],[25], or [9]) or hotline scenarios (e.g., [12] or [21]) where prior experience is reused and cases contain problem as well as solution descriptions. But if we look at e-commerce scenarios where complex products are sold such as Electronic Designs [28], the statement is highly questionable. Here, more complex explanation strategies are needed [13].

The two scenarios show two types of cases which, according to Richter [19], are called cases of *rule-type* and cases of *constraint-type*. For cases of rule-type it is known a priori which of the attributes are the problem attributes and which of them are the solution attributes. This distinction is determined at design time of the CBR system. In contrast, cases of constraint-type have no subdivision into problem and solution attributes. Which of the attributes describe the problem situation and which of them describe the solution is determined at run time of the application. Here, the subdivision into problem description and solution is only known a posteriori.

Watson [32] adds two other dimensions of case types: *homogeneous* vs. *heterogeneous* and *episodic* vs. *prototypical* cases. Homogeneous cases all have the same attributes that are easily determined. The set of attributes remains fixed. Real estate is a good example domain. In contrast, heterogeneous cases have different attributes but may share some (e.g., patient cases from a hospital or cases of a help-desk support system). A full set of attributes is hard to elicit. Such applications may have to learn new attributes throughout their lifetime.

The other important distinction is the source of the cases. Episodic cases are records of events such as insurance claims, equipment faults, or patient files. These kinds of cases may easily be converted from existing data in a bottom-up approach. In Textual Case-Based Reasoning [12], documents are transformed into structured cases. This transformation process reduces, in general, the richness of the semantic structure of a document, resulting in an index, the case, that represents the document. Here, the document is the explanation of the corresponding case. Prototypical cases are designed as examples of events, for instance, typical symptoms, or a typical tax fraud. They are designed top-down by experts and require knowledge elicitation.

All of the case types have an impact on what explanations are possible to be constructed. Finding the optimal case, i.e., the case that solves a user's problem, is the goal of the reasoning process. Thus, the resulting case cannot answer explicitly why it was selected or how. Those explanations can only be provided by the other three knowledge containers.

4.3 The Vocabulary: What Is the CBR System Talking About?

Commercial CBR system shells such as EMPOLIS ORENGE or those available from Kaidara employ an object-oriented or frame-like approach in order to capture necessary domain knowledge in a domain model or domain schema. The entities of the model, often called concepts, represent objects or facts about objects of the real world. Specialization of concepts is described by the *is-a* relation (e.g., a car is a vehicle). Properties of a super-concept are *inherited* by its sub-concept. The other important relation is the *has-part/part-of* relation, which decomposes a complex object into its simpler parts (e.g., a car has wheels/wheels are part of a car).

The two structuring techniques, inheritance and decomposition, allow for answering such questions as 'What is the structure of a case?', 'Where is the case's class situated in the domain schema?', 'What other classes could I ask for?', 'Tell me about the parts of the case?', and 'Which parts of the case are specific to the case's class, and which of the parts are inherited?'.

Each attribute (slot, facet) of a concept can only contain values of a certain class limited by type constraints or range restrictions. The values may be of simple or complex type. Simple types are, for example, strings or numerical values, whereas complex types themselves are decomposable. This property allows for explanations in response to questions such as 'What are allowed values for this slot?' and, thus, for 'What could I have entered instead?'. For simple types, such questions are often answered in advance by providing drop down menus, where the user just selects the desired values from a certain range of values. For complex types, more elaborate selection and explanation processes are required.

In general, the domain model should be enriched with comments about the model's structure and about design decisions. Those could be posed to users who want to understand the intentions behind a given domain model. In many domains, the user knows about the values that he or she may enter or select to fill a slot, but in knowledge-intensive scenarios, the user often is at a loss. In those situations the user does not know enough to choose between alternatives, e.g., between two graphics cards for a new PC. In general, it surely holds that the more elaborate a model is, the more explanatory power it has.

The vocabulary can be further divided into subcontainers [20]: input, output, and retrieval attributes. Input attributes are used to trigger completion rules, which set the values of dependent retrieval attributes. Those attributes are used by the retrieval process. Output attributes contain the result values. Each attribute can play one or all of the three roles at once. Again, the substructure can help to structure our thinking about the knowledge contained in the vocabulary.

Exploring the vocabulary using such standards as Topic Maps[3] with an appropriate browser can help make the user more familiar with the application domain addressed by a given CBR system. Topic Maps are used to organize and visualize topics and associations (relationships) between them. They are optimized to support the navigation in an information space.

4.4 Similarity Measures: Domain and Utility Knowledge

The similarity measures knowledge container provides the means to determine the degree of similarity between a query and a case. In [20], Richter describes two subcontainers, the *local measures* and the *amalgamation function*. Each local measure compares one attribute of a case. Local measures contain domain knowledge (e.g., similarity of car colors) while the amalgamation function is task oriented and contains utility knowledge (relevances for the task, e.g., the importance of the attribute car color vs. the attributes manufacturer and horse power in a used car trading scenario).

A local measure can be used to explain how the values of one attribute are related to each other. It can explain relations between portions of the vocabulary. An amalgamation function, e.g., the weighted sum of local similarity values, can then explain the importance or relevance of an attribute based on the weight vector.

Dependencies between attributes are often expressed using completion rules, which are filling in missing attribute values depending on the values of other

---

[3] See [16] for an introduction.

attributes. For example, in an apartment recommendation system, the attribute 'area' depends on the width and length of the respective apartment. A completion rule could easily compute the missing values.

The local-global principle [20] can not only be employed as a guideline for comparing or contrasting cases in order to develop appropriate similarity measures. With the local-global principle, one naturally can derive explanations related to the decomposition hierarchy, dealing with detailed attribute explanations as well as with higher level explanations.

Similarity measures with their inherent utility knowledge are useful for justifying how and why the CBR system derived a particular list of results.

4.5 Adaptation Knowledge: The More the Better!

Solutions obtained from the case base using similarity measures may not be sufficient. This can be due to ill-formed similarity measures or to simply the fact that no better solution is in the case base. In this situation, the solution is adapted to better fit the user's demands.

Adaptation knowledge, often represented by rules, requires the most thorough understanding of the domain to be available and it requires the most formal representation to be applicable. Hence, as soon as adaptation knowledge is available, obviously, a lot more can be explained by the CBR system. In commercial scenarios, adaptation rules play only a tangential role. But, 'there is little known about a systematic improvement of adaptation rules' [20].

Table 1. Knowledge containers and their contribution to supporting explanations

Knowledge container	contributes to
Vocabulary	conceptual explanations, why-explanations, how-explanations, and purpose explanations
Similarity measures	why-explanations, how-explanations, purpose explanations, and cognitive explanations
Adaptation knowledge	why-explanations, how-explanations, and cognitive explanations
Case base	(provides context for explanations)

5 Relating Knowledge Containers to Explanations

In Section 3, we briefly described five categories of explanations. In the following, I will discuss which kind of questions could be answered by using primarily the knowledge of a particular knowledge container. Table 1 briefly summarizes to which kind of explanation each knowledge container contributes mainly.

Generally, a question can either address the CBR application (i.e., how to use the system), or it can be related to its content (i.e., its knowledge). Questions regarding the CBR application are beyond the scope of this paper. They commonly are answered by means of documentation, frequently asked questions, and user communities.

Case-Based Reasoning approaches usually are classified using three categories: *Conversational*, *Structural*, and *Textual Case-Based Reasoning* [3]. *Conversational CBR* is a form of interactive Case-Based Reasoning. This approach is very useful in domains with many simple problems that must repeatedly be solved. Conversational CBR systems, in general, contain little domain knowledge (in machine processible form). Thus, I will not regard it in the following.

Structural CBR relies on cases described with attributes and corresponding values. Structural CBR systems organize attributes in different ways, e.g., as flat attribute lists, as relational tables, or in an object-oriented way. The structural approach is useful in domains where additional knowledge such as complex similarity measures must be used in order to get good results, and where the domain model is easy to acquire.

Textual Case-Based Reasoning systems aim at managing information contained in semi-structured documents and providing means for content-oriented retrieval. A domain model determines the structure of the cases, and a preprocessor fills the cases from the texts. Hence, Textual CBR is Structural CBR at its core where semi-structured texts are transformed into a structured representation. The textual approach is useful in domains where large collections of know-how documents already exist and the intended user is able to immediately make use of the knowledge contained in the respective documents.

5.1 Conceptual Explanations

Conceptual explanations answer questions regarding the semantics of concepts. They mainly address the vocabulary knowledge container. In Structural CBR systems, often object-oriented modeling is employed. The class structure with its inheritance relation and its decomposition structure provide further conceptual explanations. In systems such as CREEK [1, 2], where general (domain-dependent) knowledge is represented as semantic network, much more detailed conceptual explanations can be given[4].

In Textual CBR, as mentioned above, well written documents are to some degree self-explaining, giving at least clues where to look also for more information on the topics described by this document. Due to the fact that Textual CBR is Structural CBR at its core, there is a lot of additional knowledge available that is necessary for transforming a text into a case structure. In order to identify the concepts of the domain model, for example, synonyms and antonyms, different ways of writing, abbreviations, etc. are modelled. They map words or phrases

---

[4] In CREEK, explanations are generated to explain reasoning steps or to justify conclusions to the user, and, more important, for the internal use of the reasoner.

to concepts of the domain schema[5]. Thus, explanations of concepts could be supported by providing contextual information using the transformation information.

5.2 Why-, How-, and Purpose-Explanations

Why-explanations as well as how- and purpose-explanations are scientific explanations (as described in Section 3). Questions expecting those kinds of answers, in general, can only be answered by systems that have an elaborate model of reality, i.e., that have a detailed domain model, rich in classes, attributes, and predicates. Hence, the vocabulary knowledge container with its static knowledge provides most of the knowledge for scientific explanations.

The similarity knowledge container contributes additional domain and utility knowledge. Utility knowledge may help to select the correct level of detail because it contains knowledge about the relevance of attributes. Even more explanatory value can be provided by the adaptation knowledge because, in order to adapt a prior solution to a new situation, complex knowledge is necessary.

The case base can only provide indirect or contextual knowledge. It may be used to enrich model-based explanations.

5.3 Cognitive Explanations

In my opinion and from my experience with the development and maintenance of (commercial) CBR applications, cognitive explanations are the most important kind of explanations. Most users ask such questions as 'Why did the CBR system suggest these results?'. Explanations provided, for example, by EMPOLIS ORENGE use coloring schemes in order to markup concepts identified in the query and the case together with the degree of matching (cf. [28]). But there is more to explain. The similarity measures knowledge container, including completion rules, provide the starting point to explain the match between query and case on different levels of granularity. Together with available adaptation knowledge, the relations between result cases can be explored along different dimensions. This could help the user in developing a mental image of the competence of the CBR system and, thus, building up trust in the CBR system.

6 Conclusions and Future Research Directions

The four knowledge containers provide the major portion of knowledge necessary for CBR systems for constructing explanations. But it may be helpful to add an additional knowledge container for explanatory knowledge, as the knowledge required for reasoning need not be the same as for explaining (even though explanations should be based on the knowledge used for reasoning, as stated

---

[5] In EMPOLIS ORENGE, such knowledge is provided by the analysis model, a part of the domain model (see Appendix A of [21] for further information).

earlier by the 'fidelity principle' of good explanations). Remember that to have understandable explanations one needs to use the users' own terms. Using two knowledge bases is one of the main architectures found in second-generation expert system explanation [30]. Such an additional knowledge container may lessen the burden of explanation generation and could improve the explanation capabilities of a CBR system.

Improving explanation capabilities of knowledge-intensive Case-Based Reasoning systems currently is an important research direction. In domains where the user easily gets lost in the information space, he or she must have trust in the application that is intended to support his or her decisions – a point that was emphasized several times in this paper.

The issue of trustworthiness and trust, credibility, and confidence in computer systems, in general, is also an important issue in the upcoming Semantic Web [4], *an extension of the current web in which information is given well-defined meaning, better enabling computers and people to work in cooperation* [5]. The Semantic Web currently is not an application, it is an infrastructure on which many different applications will be developed. There are already initiatives on increasing trust by exchanging proofs/explanations in standardized formats between (logic-based) inference engines [14], but what about CBR systems. How could CBR systems be integrated in such a 'Web of Trust'? What does a 'CBR proof' look like?

There is currently also revived interest in the development and research of explanations produced by expert systems. For example, Wollny [33] examined the problem of explaining solutions found by cooperating expert systems. An *explanation comment* is attached to each partial solution of the distributed problem solving process and submitted to the expert system, which is interacting with the user. This system then provides an explanation for the whole solution. Perhaps, some of the research results could be transferred to CBR.

This paper is, as stated at the beginning, just a first pass on foundational issues regarding explanations from a knowledge container perspective. The presented ideas will be elaborated in future work.

Acknowledgments

I thank Rainer Maximini for inspiring me to write this paper. I also thank the anonymous reviewers. Their suggestions and comments greatly contributed to improve the preliminary versions of this paper. It was not possible to discuss in this paper all the issues they have highlighted, but this will be helpful for future work.

References

1. Agnar Aamodt. Explanation-driven case-based reasoning. In Klaus-Dieter Althoff Stefan Wess and Michal Richter, editors, *Topics in Case-Based Reasoning*, Berlin, 1994. Springer-Verlag.

2. Agnar Aamodt. A knowledge representation system for integration of general and case-specific knowledge. In *Proceedings from IEEE TAI-94, International Conference on Tools with Artificial Intelligence*, pages 836–839, New Orleans, 1994.
3. Ralph Bergmann, Klaus-Dieter Althoff, Sean Breen, Mehmet Göker, Michel Manago, Ralph Traphöner, and Stefan Wess. *Developing Industrial Case-Based Resoning Applications: The INRECA Methodology.* Lecture Notes in Artificial Intelligence LNAI 1612. Springer-Verlag, Berlin, second edition, 2003.
4. Tim Berners-Lee. What the semantic web can represent, 1998.
http://www.w3.org/DesignIssues/RDFnot.html [Last access: 2002-07-09].
5. Tim Berners-Lee, James Hendler, and Ora Lassila. The semantic web: A new form of web content that is meaningful to computers will unleash a revolution of new possibilities. *ScientificAmerican.com*, May 2001.
http://www.scientificamerican.com/article.cfm?articleID=
00048144-10D2-1C70-84A9809EC588EF21 [Last access: 2004-04-29].
6. Alison Cawsey. User modelling in interactive explanations. *Journal of User Modelling and User Adapted Interaction*, 3(1):1–25, 1993.
7. Daniel Cohnitz. Explanations are like salted peanuts. In Ansgar Beckermann and Christian Nimtz, editors, *Proceedings of the Fourth International Congress of the Society for Analytic Philosophy*, 2000.
http://www.gap-im-netz.de/gap4Konf/Proceedings4/titel.htm
[Last access: 2004-03-11].
8. Dónal Doyle, Alexey Tsymbal, and Pádraig Cunningham. A review of explanation and explanation in case-based reasoning. Technical Report TCD-CS-2003-41, Trinity College Dublin, 2003.
9. Mehmet Göker, Thomas Roth-Berghofer, Ralph Bergmann, Thomas Pantleon, Ralph Traphöner, Stefan Wess, and Wolfgang Wilke. The development of HOMER – a case-based CAD/CAM help-desk support tool. In Barry Smyth and Pádraig Cunningham, editors, *Advances in Case-Based Reasoning, Proceedings of the 4th European Workshop, EWCBR'98, Dublin, Ireland*, pages 346–357, Berlin, 1998. Springer-Verlag.
10. David Leake. CBR in context: The present and the future. In David Leake, editor, *Case-Based Reasoning: Experiences, Lessons, and Future Directions*, pages 3–30, Menlo Park, CA, Cambridge, MA, 1996. AAAI Press/MIT Press.
11. Mario Lenz, Brigitte Bartsch-Spörl, Hans-Dieter Burkhard, and Stefan Wess, editors. *Case-Based Reasoning Technology: From Foundations to Applications.* Lecture Notes in Artificial Intelligence. Springer-Verlag, Berlin, 1998.
12. Mario Lenz, André Hübner, and Mirjam Kunze. *Textual CBR*, chapter 5, pages 115–137. Lecture Notes in Artificial Intelligence. Springer-Verlag, Berlin, 1998.
13. Rainer Maximini, Andrea Fressmann, and Martin Schaaf. Explanation service for complex CBR applications. 2004. See this volume.
14. Deborah L. McGuinness and Paulo Pinheiro da Silva. Infrastructure for web explanations. In Dieter Fensel, Katia Sycara, and John Mylopoulos, editors, *The Semantic Web — ISWC 2003*, 2003.
15. Johanna D. Moore and William R. Swartout. Explanation in expert systems: A survey. Research Report RR-88-228, University of Southern California, Marina Del Rey, CA, 1988.
16. Steve Pepper. The TAO of Topic Maps. 2004.
http://www.ontopia.net/topicmaps/materials/tao.html
[Last access: 2004-06-03].
17. Debbie Richards. Knowledge-based system explanation: The ripple-down rules alternative. *Knowledge and Information Systems*, 5(20):2–25, 2003.

18. Michael M. Richter. The knowledge contained in similarity measures. Invited Talk at the First International Conference on Case-Based Reasoning, ICCBR'95, Sesimbra, Portugal, 1995. http://wwwagr.informatik.uni-kl.de/~lsa/CBR/Richtericcbr95remarks.html [Last access: 2002-10-18].
19. Michael M. Richter. Generalized planning and information retrieval. Technical report, University of Kaiserslautern, Artificial Intelligence – Knowledge-based Systems Group, 1997.
20. Michael M. Richter. Knowledge containers. In Ian Watson, editor, *Readings in Case-Based Reasoning*. Morgan Kaufmann Publishers, 2003.
21. Thomas R. Roth-Berghofer. *Knowledge Maintenance of Case-Based Reasoning Systems – The SIAM Methodology*, volume 262 of *Dissertationen zur Künstlichen Intelligenz*. Akademische Verlagsgesellschaft Aka GmbH / IOS Press, Berlin, Germany, 2003.
22. Roger C. Schank. Explanation: A first pass. In Janet L. Kolodner and Christopher K. Riesbeck, editors, *Experience, Memory, and Reasoning*, pages 139–165, Hillsdale, NJ, 1986. Lawrence Erlbaum Associates.
23. Roger C. Schank. *Explanation Patterns: Understanding Mechanically and Creatively*. Lawrence Erlbaum Associates, Hillsdale, NJ, 1986.
24. Gerhard Schurz. Scientific explanation: A critical survey. IPS-Preprint 1, Department of Philosophy, University of Salzburg, 1993.
25. Evangelos Simoudis. Using case-based retrieval for customer technical support. *IEEE Expert*, 7(5):7–12, October 1992.
26. Evangelos Simoudis and James S. Miller. The application of CBR to help desk applications. In *Proceedings of the DARPA Workshop on Case-Based Reasoning*, pages 25–36, Washington, DC, 1991.
27. Peter Spieker. *Natürlichsprachliche Erklärungen in technischen Expertensystemen*. Dissertation, University of Kaiserslautern, 1991.
28. Marco Spinelli and Martin Schaaf. Towards explanations for CBR-based applications. In Andreas Hotho and Gerd Stumme, editors, *Proceedings of the LLWA Workshop 2003*, pages 229–233, Karlsruhe, Germany, 2003. AIFB Karlsruhe.
29. William R. Swartout. XPLAIN: A system for creating and explaining expert consulting programs. *Artificial Intelligence*, 21(3), 1983.
30. William R. Swartout and Johanna D. Moore. Explanation in second generation expert systems. In J. David, J. Krivine, and R. Simmons, editors, *Second Generation Expert Systems*, pages 543–585, Berlin, 1993. Springer Verlag.
31. Edward R. Tufte. *Visual Explanations*. Graphics Press, Cheshire, Connecticut, 1997.
32. Ian Watson. Workshop on automating the construction of case-based reasoners at IJCAI'99, 1999. http://www.ai-cbr.org/ijcai99/workshop.html [Last access: 2003-02-09].
33. Stefan Wollny. *Erklärungsfähigkeit kooperierender regelbasierter Expertensysteme zum diagnostischen Problemlösen*. PhD thesis, Technische Universität Berlin, 2003.

MINLP Based Retrieval of Generalized Cases

Alexander Tartakovski[1], Martin Schaaf[2],
Rainer Maximini[1], and Ralph Bergmann[1]

[1] University of Trier,
Department of Business Information Systems II
54286 Trier, Germany
{tartakov,rmaximini,bergmann}@wi2.uni-trier.de
[2] University of Hildesheim,
Institute for Mathematics and Applied Computer Science,
Data and Knowledge Management Group,
31113 Hildesheim, Germany
schaaf@dwm.uni-hildesheim.de

Abstract. The concept of generalized cases has been proven useful when searching for configurable and flexible products, for instance, reusable components in the area of electronic design automation. This paper addresses the similarity assessment and retrieval problem for case bases consisting of traditional and generalized cases. While approaches presented earlier were restricted to continuous domains, this paper addresses generalized cases defined over mixed, continuous and discrete, domains. It extends the view on the similarity assessment as a nonlinear optimization problem (NLP) towards a mixed integer nonlinear optimization problem (MINLP), which is an actual research topic in mathematical optimization. This is an important step because most real world applications require mixed domains for the case description. Furthermore, we introduce two optimization-based retrieval methods that operate on a previously created index structure, which restricts the retrieval response time significantly.

Keywords: generalized cases, mixed integer nonlinear programming, kd-trees

1 Introduction

The smallest experience item in Case-Based Reasoning (CBR) is called a *case*. When applying the structural CBR approach, each case is described by a finite and structured set of attribute-value pairs that characterize the problem and the solution. Hence, a single case can be considered as a point in the space defined by the Cartesian product of the problem space $\mathbb{P}$ and solution space $\mathbb{S}$. Newer applications of CBR motivated a new concept called *generalized cases* [1], [2]. In contrast to a traditional case, a generalized case does not cover only a point of the case space but a whole subspace. This allows the representation of complex and configurable products, for instance, reusable electronic design components, in a very natural and efficient way. Generalized cases provide a set of solutions to a set of closely related problems and can be viewed as an implicit representation of a (possibly infinite) set of traditional point cases.

The concept of generalized cases implies the extension of similarity measures as well. In [2] the similarity between a query and a generalized case has been defined as the similarity between the query and the most similar point-case contained in the generalized case.

Previous work, e.g. [3], focuses on generalized cases defined over continuous attribute domains by considering the similarity assessment problem as a kind of Nonlinear Programm (NLP), which is well known in mathematical optimization. In contrast to these approaches, the work presented here addresses the similarity assessment and retrieval problem for generalized cases defined over mixed, discrete and continuous, attribute domains, which are typical for most real world applications.

The concepts presented here were developed in the context of the project *IPQ: IP Qualification for Efficient Design Reuse*[1] founded by the German Ministry of Education and Research (BMBF), which aims at the improvement of electronic design processes by reusing already existing design components called *Intellectual Properties* (IPs) [4]. Nowadays, IPs are offered by specialized vendors via the Internet. For such large IP assets, we developed a CBR-based retrieval solution [5]. Physically, IPs are descriptions that can be later synthesized to hardware. They are usually configurable to some degree, e.g. IPs with flexible bus width or frequency, and recommend themselves to be represented as generalized cases.

In section 2 we introduce an optimization-based approach to solve the similarity assessment problem. In section 3 we present two index-based approaches to improve the retrieval for generalized cases and point cases defined over mixed, continuous and discrete, domains.

2 Optimization Based Similarity Assessment

In this section we characterize a relationship between the similarity assessment problem for generalized cases and the optimization problem in mathematics. Furthermore, we describe how to solve the similarity assessment problem for generalized cases defined over continuous domains. Afterwards, we present a new approach to solve the similarity assessment problem for generalized cases defined over mixed domains.

2.1 Similarity Assessment as Optimization Problem

For the retrieval of generalized cases, the similarity between a problem and a generalized case must be determined. A natural way is to extend a traditional similarity measure as follows [6]:

---

[1] IPQ Project(12/2000-11/2003). Partners: AMD, Frauenhofer Institute for Integrated Circuits, FZI Karlsruhe, Infineon Technologies, Siemens, Sciworx, Empolis, Thomson Multi Media, TU Chemniz, University of Hildesheim, University of Kaiserslautern, and University of Padeborn. See www.ip-qualifikation.de

$$sim^*(q, GC) := max\{sim(q, c) | c \in GC\} \qquad (1)$$

According to this definition, the value of the extended similarity function $sim^*(q, GC)$ is equal to the similarity $sim(q, c)$ between a query q and the most similar point case c contained in the generalized case GC.

Due to the fact that the similarity assessment problem can be viewed as a specific optimization problem, we describe the relationship between both problems as in [6]. An optimization problem is the maximization or minimization of some objective function, often under restrictions given through equalities and inequalities. In general, optimization problems are defined as follows:

$$\begin{aligned} \max_{x} \; & f(x) \\ s.t. \; & x \in F \end{aligned} \qquad (2)$$

with f an *objective function* and F a set of feasible solutions *(feasible set)*, implicit defined through constraints.

By defining an objective function $f(x) := sim(q, x)$ and the feasible set $F := GC$ we transform a similarity assessment problem to a specific optimization problem.

In mathematical optimization several classes of optimization problems are known. They differ in computational complexity, problem solution methods and problem formulation. Therefore, it is important to find out the class and formulation of an optimization problem by deriving it from a similarity assessment problem. These classes and formulations differ for generalized cases defined over continuous domains and for generalized cases defined over mixed domains. This will be further elaborated in the following two sections.

2.2 Similarity Assessment for Continuous Domains

Generalized cases defined over continuous domains are restricted to connected sets in the case space spanned by continuous attributes. A single generalized case can be represented through equality and inequality constraints. The general form is:

$$\begin{aligned} GC = \{ x \in \mathbb{R}^n | & c_1(x) \geq 0 \wedge \ldots \wedge c_k(x) \geq 0 \\ & \wedge c_{k+1}(x) = 0 \wedge \ldots \wedge c_l(x) = 0 \} \end{aligned} \qquad (3)$$

The constraint functions c_i are not restricted to be linear, they can also be nonlinear.

For refining the similarity assessment as an optimization problem, we regard a similarity function sim. Although the aggregation function is commonly a weighted average, which is a linear function, the local similarities are mostly nonlinear. Consequently, the global similarity function sim is nonlinear as well. Nonlinearity of the similarity function together with the nonlinearity of the generalized cases determine the class of optimization problems we are going to derive. It is a nonlinear optimization problem (NLP) [7] having a general form as follows:

$$\begin{aligned}
&\max_{x} f(x) \\
&\text{s.t.} \quad c_1(x) \geq 0, \\
&\qquad \ldots \\
&\qquad c_k(x) \geq 0, \\
&\qquad c_{k+1}(x) = 0, \\
&\qquad \ldots \\
&\qquad c_l(x) = 0, \\
&\qquad x \in \mathbb{R}^n
\end{aligned} \qquad (4)$$

This optimization problem has a nonlinear objective function and nonlinear constraints. By replacing the objective function f with $sim(q,x)$ (with constant q), we receive the desired representation of the similarity assessment problem as optimization problem. The constraint set can be taken directly from the specification of the generalized case itself.

2.3 Similarity Assessment for Mixed Domains

For mixed domains, the formulation of an optimization problem is much more complex. The most difficult issue is handling discrete attributes. In this section we explain mixed integer nonlinear optimization problem (MINLP) and present a formulation of similarity assessment as MINLP problem.

Example from the IPQ Project. For illustrating the concepts presented in this paper, we will use an example from the design of electronic circuits (see above). The discrete cosine transformation IP (DCT IP) is a frequently reused design component because it implements an algorithm widely used for MPEG-2 encoders/decoders. The parameters of this IP are clock frequency, chip area, bus width, and subword size. There are dependencies between these parameters defining the feasible design space. For simplification and without loss of generality, we can restrict the description of DCT IPs to the attributes shown in the following table:

Table 1. Selected parameters of the example IP

parameter		description
frequency	f	The clock frequency that can be applied to the IP. (continuous)
area	a	The chip area the synthesized IP will fit on. (continuous)
width	w	Number of bits per input/output word. Determines the accuracy of the DCT. Allowed values are 6, 7, ..., 16. (discrete)
subword	s	Number of bits calculated per clock tick. Changing this design space parameter may have a positive influence on one quality of the design while having a negative impact on another. Allowed values are 1, 2, 4, 8 and no-pipe. (discrete)

The dependencies between the parameters follow:

$$f \leq \begin{cases} -0.66w + 115 & if\ s = 1 \\ -1.94w + 118 & if\ s = 2 \\ -1.74w + 88 & if\ s = 4 \\ -0.96w + 54 & if\ s = 8 \\ -2.76w + 57 & if\ s = no-pipe \end{cases} \qquad (5)$$

$$a \geq \begin{cases} 1081w^2 + 2885w + 10064 & if\ s = 1 \\ 692w^2 + 2436w + 4367 & if\ s = 2 \\ 532w^2 + 1676w + 2794 & if\ s = 4 \\ 416w^2 + 1594w + 2413 & if\ s = 8 \\ 194w^2 + 2076w + 278 & if\ s = no-pipe \end{cases} \qquad (6)$$

This IP can be viewed as a single generalized case with parameterized attributes f, a, w, and s.

Mixed Integer Nonlinear Optimization Problem. The formulation of the assessment problem for generalized cases defined over mixed discrete and continuous domain is beyond the scope of NLP. The reason is a combinatorial character of the assessment problem which is not covered through an NLP. Therefore we need to use a generalization of NLP called mixed integer nonlinear program (MINLP) [8], which covers nonlinear and integer programming. A general formulation of this problem follows:

$$\begin{aligned} & \min_{x,y} f(x,y) \\ & s.t.\ c_1(x,y) \geq 0, \\ & \quad \ldots \\ & \quad c_k(x,y) \geq 0, \\ & \quad c_{k+1}(x,y) = 0, \\ & \quad \ldots \\ & \quad c_l(x,y) = 0, \\ & \quad x \in \mathbb{R}^m, y \in \mathbb{Z}^n \end{aligned} \qquad (7)$$

The main difference to NLP is that for the objective function f and the constraints a continuous part x and an integer part y is distinguished.

MINLP is harder than NLP since it has, additionally, a combinatorial character. The handling of this problem is one of the actual research topics in mathematical optimization [9]. However, since few years there are several industrial solvers available handling MINLPs.

Similarity Assessment for Generalized Cases with Mixed Integer and Continuous Domains as MINLP. Now we are going to explain a formulation of MINLP for the example of the DCT-IP. In general, the formulation consists of two parts: from modelling of a feasible set and from modelling of the objective function. We start with the first one.

Since a feasible set of MINLP is defined through equalities and inequalities the following dependencies must be transformed:

$$\begin{aligned} f &\leq -0.66w + 115 \; if \; s = 1 \\ f &\leq -1.94w + 118 \; if \; s = 2 \\ &\ldots \end{aligned} \qquad (8)$$

We define in place of the variable s with a domain $T(s) = \{1, 2, 4, 8, no-pipe\}$ $|T(s)|$ new variables:

$$s_1, s_2, s_4, s_8, s_{no-pipe} \in \mathbb{Z}$$

and a set of constraints:

$$s_1 \geq 0, s_1 \leq 1, s_2 \geq 0, s_2 \leq 1, \ldots \qquad (9)$$

Each new variable represents a single attribute value of the variable s. So, if some new variable $s_v = 1$ it implies that $s = v$ and contrary if $s = v$ then $s_v = 1$. Since the variable s can have only one value at a given time, a new additional constraint should be defined:

$$s_1 + s_2 + s_4 + s_8 + s_{no-pipe} = 1 \qquad (10)$$

Every valid assignment of variables $s_1...s_{no-pipe}$ implies a single value for the variable s and every assignment of variable s implies a valid assignment of variables $s_1...s_{no-pipe}$. Example:

$$s = 4 \Leftrightarrow \begin{pmatrix} s_1 \\ s_2 \\ s_4 \\ s_8 \\ s_{no-pipe} \end{pmatrix} = \begin{pmatrix} 0 \\ 0 \\ 1 \\ 0 \\ 0 \end{pmatrix} \qquad (11)$$

Now, it is simple to formulate the dependencies (8) as inequalities:

$$\begin{aligned} s_1(-0.66w + 115 - f) &\geq 0 \\ s_2(-1.94w + 118 - f) &\geq 0 \\ &\ldots \end{aligned} \qquad (12)$$

For $s_1 = 1$ the first inequality is "switched on" and the other inequalities are "switched off", since $s_2 = s_4 = s_8 = 0$.

The feasible set of MINLP is given through the set of constraints (12), (9), (10) and additional constraints depending on the attribute a (chip area):

$$\begin{aligned}
s_1(-0.66w + 115 - f) &\geq 0 \\
s_2(-1.94w + 118 - f) &\geq 0 \\
&\vdots \\
s_1(-1081w^2 - 2885w - 10064 + a) &\geq 0 \\
s_2(-692w^2 - 2436w - 4367 + a) &\geq 0 \\
&\vdots \\
s_1 &\geq 0 \\
-s_1 &\geq -1 \\
s_2 &\geq 0 \\
-s_2 &\geq -1 \\
&\vdots \\
s_1 + s_2 + s_4 + s_8 + s_{no-pipe} &= 1 \\
w &\geq 6 \\
w &\leq 16
\end{aligned} \qquad (13)$$

$f, a \in \mathbb{R}$ and $w, s_1, s_2, s_4, s_8, s_{no-pipe} \in \mathbb{Z}$

We proceed with the objective function f. Because of the introduction of new binary variables the formulation of the function f becomes more complex. To define the objective function we first define the similarity function given by local similarities and an aggregation function Φ:

$$sim(q, c) := \Phi(sim_f(q_f, c_f), sim_w(q_w, c_w), sim_a(q_a, c_a), sim_s(q_s, c_s))$$

Consequently, the objective function can be defined as follows:

$$\begin{aligned}
f_q(f, w, a, s_1, \ldots, s_{no-pipe}) := \Phi\Big(& sim_f(q_f, f), sim_w(q_w, w), \\
& sim_a(q_a, a), \big(s_1 sim_s(q_s, 1) + s_2 sim_s(q_s, 2) + s_4 sim_s(q_s, 4) \\
& + s_8 sim_s(q_s, 8) + s_{no-pipe} sim_s(q_s, no-pipe)\big)\Big)
\end{aligned} \qquad (14)$$

The idea, here, is based on the following fact:

$$sim_s(q_s, c_s) = \big(s_1 sim_s(q_s, 1) + s_2 sim_s(q_s, 2) + s_4 sim_s(q_s, 4)$$
$$+ s_8 sim_s(q_s, 8) + s_{no-pipe} sim_s(q_s, no-pipe)\big)$$

Revisiting the example (11) again and assuming that $s_1 = 0, s_2 = 0, s_4 = 1, s_8 = 0$ and $s_{no-pipe} = 0$ is part of some valid assignment according to the constraint set (13):

$$\big(s_1 sim_s(q_s, 1) + s_2 sim_s(q_s, 2) + s_4 sim_s(q_s, 4)$$
$$+ s_8 sim_s(q_s, 8) + s_{no-pipe} sim_s(q_s, no-pipe)\big) =$$

$$\big(0 sim_s(q_s,1) + 0 sim_s(q_s,2) + 1 sim_s(q_s,4)$$
$$+ 0 sim_s(q_s,8) + 0 sim_s(q_s, no-pipe)\big) = sim_s(q_s,4)$$

The objective function (14) together with the feasible set (13) define the MINLP, its solution provides the similarity between the query q and the example generalized case.

Normally, MINLP problems are not solved exactly but approximately.

There are several commercial solver on the market for MINLP problems, e.g. GAMS/Baron [9], Xpress-SLP, and MINLP.

3 Retrieval

Because of the high calculation complexity of the assessment problem for generalized cases it is very important to develop index-based retrieval approaches. The overall strategy is to build an index structure in advance, which is later used for improving the response time of the retrieval. The step when building the index structure will be denoted as *offline phase*, the retrieval step as *online phase*. Hence, most of the calculation complexity is shifted from the online to the offline phase. For building and integrating index structures, we developed two new methods, a similarity based method presented in section 3.1 and a kd-tree based method, which will be introduced in section 3.2.

3.1 Similarity Based Retrieval Method

Because of the high complexity of the assessment problem for generalized cases we developed a retrieval method that is based on a fix similarity measure for building an index structure.

A main step of this approach, is partitioning of a problem space $\mathbb{P}$ into some simple subspaces. An example of a such simple subspace is a hyperrectangle that has faces parallel to the coordinate planes. Queries are points of exactly one of the subspaces, but it is unknown which one and where exactly.

Furthermore, we define for a subspace Sub and a generalized case GC two similarity bounds:

$$Similarity_{min}(Sub, GC) := \quad (15)$$
$$\min_{s \in Sub} sim^*(s, GC) = \min_{s \in Sub} \max_{g \in GC} sim(s,g)$$

and

$$Similarity_{max}(Sub, GC) := \quad (16)$$
$$\max_{s \in Sub} sim^*(s, GC) = \max_{s \in Sub} \max_{g \in GC} sim(s,g)$$

Consider the subspace Sub and the generalize case $gc5$ in figure 1. The query q' belonging to the subspace Sub has a lowest similarity to generalized case $gc5$

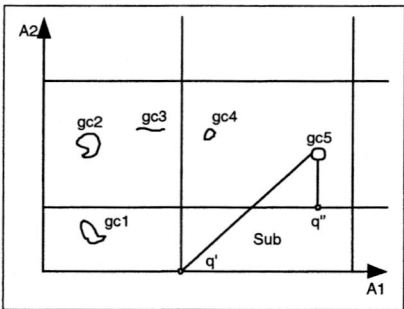

Fig. 1. Similarity bounds

from all queries of this subspace. Exactly this similarity value is provided by the function $Similarity_{min}(Sub, gc5)$. The query q'' belonging to the subspace Sub has a highest similarity to generalized case $gc5$ from all queries of this subspace. This similarity value is provided by the function $Similarity_{max}(Sub, gc57)$. If these bounds are known and some query is inside the subspace Sub in the online phase we can guarantee that its similarity to the generalized case $gc5$ lies within the bounds $Similarity_{min}(Sub, gc5)$ and $Similarity_{max}(Sub, gc5)$.

Based on this fact, a retrieval approach can be simply constructed. The first idea is to calculate, in the offline phase, similarity bounds for all subspaces and all generalized cases. Furthermore, it is necessary to derive a partial order on generalized cases in terms of similarity for every single subspace and all generalized cases. The partial order is defined as follows:

$$\bigwedge_{\substack{gc_1, gc_2 \in CB, \\ Sub \in \mathbb{P}}} gc_1 < gc_2 \Leftrightarrow Similarity_{max}(Sub, gc_1) < Similarity_{min}(Sub, gc_2)$$

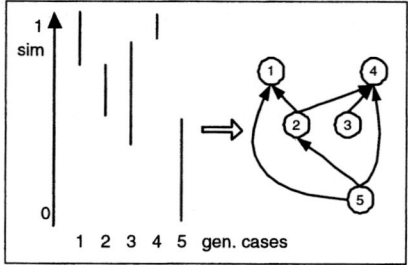

Fig. 2. Similarity intervals and partial order

Figure 2 illustrates the calculated similarity bounds for a single subspace and the generalized cases $gc1$ to $gc5$. Furthermore, Figure 2 shows the resulting partial order. For every query of the online phase, we only need to check to which subspace it belongs to. After this check we know immediately the partial order and the similarity bounds for all generalized cases. When searching for the n

best nearest neighbours, we can exclude all cases having n or more successors because it is guaranteed that at least n cases are more similar. Finally we have to perform linear retrieval on the rest of the cases.

This method can be significantly improved if we bound the size of the retrieval set before building the index structure. The customer is normally interested in at most $10-20$ cases in a retrieval set. Consequently, for a single subspace we have only to remember all generalized cases with fewer predecessors than the desired maximum size of the retrieval set. This improvement reduces significantly the size of information, which should be saved with every single subspace. Therefore, we can produce a much more detailed partition of the problem space and reduce the online complexity. The reason for this significant improvement is the fact that the cardinality-bound of a retrieval set is usually much lower than the size of the case base.

A further improvement can be achieved by using the technique of decision trees. The problem space can be partitioned recursively by choosing attributes and attribute values and building new subspaces with borders on the chosen values. For every gained subspace similarity bounds to all generalized cases and a partial order can be calculated. Based on this data the termination criterion can be specified (e.g. size of non dropped cases, degree of deviation of partial order from linear order and so forth). The main algorithm schema for building an index structure is as follows:

INPUT: Case Base CB, similarity measure sim,
   maximum size of a retrieval set

OUTPUT: A Retrieval Tree

1. create a root node R,
   assign a whole problem space P to it,
   assign all general cases CB to it.
2. select a leaf L with assigned subspace Sub
   and assigned subset $SubCB \subseteq CB$ of cases,
   STOP if termination criterion is valid.
3. select some attribute A of the subspace Sub.
4. determine a cutting point p on selected attribute A
   Condition: there is some point $t \in Sub$
   having attribute value $t_A = p$.
5. create two constraints $A \leq p$ and $A > p$.
6. create two new leafs L_1 and L_2,
   assign $Sub_1 = \{t \in Sub | t_A \leq p\}$ to L_1
   and $Sub_2 = \{t \in Sub | t_A > p\}$ to L_2.
7. calculate $\forall GC \in SubCB$:
   $Similarity_{min}(Sub_1, GC)$,
   $Similarity_{max}(Sub_1, GC)$,
   $Similarity_{min}(Sub_2, GC)$,
   $Similarity_{max}(Sub_2, GC)$.

8. based on the similarity bounds calculate the partial order O_1 and O_2 on generalized cases with respect to Sub_1 and Sub_2.
9. for Sub_1 (Sub_2): drop all cases having equal or more successors as the maximum size of a retrieval set, the rest of generalized cases becomes $SubCB_1$ ($SubCB_2$).
10. assign $SubCB_1$, O_1 to L_1 and $SubCB_2$, O_2 to L_2, delete the assignment of $SubCB$ to L.
11. set a node L as a predecessor of L_1 and L_2. (L is no longer a leaf, now).
12. GOTO 2

The result of this algorithm is a tree with leaves having assigned significant cases and partial orders on them.

For every query in the online phase the subspace where the query belongs to, can be effectively determined. We have to start with a root node and then follow the path of subspaces including the query. The rest is an execution of linear retrieval of cases assigned to the leaf determined.

Computation of MAX/MAX and MIN/MAX-Problems. In the description of this approach we didn't discuss a computation of max/max and min/max problems. In contrast to max/max problems, min/max problems are complex. Hence we start with the simple case first.

Consider the definition of upper similarity bound (16), the max/max problem was given as follows:

$$\max_{s \in Sub} \max_{g \in GC} sim(s, g) \qquad (17)$$

A subspace Sub and a generalized case GC are both located in the problem space P, i.e. $Sub \subseteq P$ and $GC \subseteq P$. Regard a space $P \times P$. Furthermore, imagine that the subspace Sub is located in the first space of a Cartesian product and the generalized case GC in the second space of a Cartesian product. The following optimization problem in general form is then equivalent to the max/max problem (17):

$$\begin{aligned} \max_x \ & sim((x_1, \ldots, x_n), (x_{n+1}, \ldots, x_{2n})) \\ s.t. \ & (x_1, \ldots, x_n) \in Sub, \\ & (x_{n+1}, \ldots, x_{2n}) \in GC, \\ & x \in \mathbb{P}^2 \end{aligned} \qquad (18)$$

The consequence is that the max/max problem can be formulated as a common max problem in double dimensioned space. Since the max/max problem can be formulated as NLP or MINLP, we mention again that this kind of problems can be solved for the majority of cases only approximately. In our approach we have chosen an upper approximation.

The treatment of the min/max problem is much more complex. We were not able to find publications tackling this problem in general. Although there is some work on handling special min/max problems (e.g. in [10]) these approaches are not applicable here. Our idea is not to solve this problem exactly but approximately by estimating a lower bound of the objective function. By estimating upper bound for max/max problem and lower bound for min/max problem the index structure stays consistent, i.e. no cases are excluded that belong to exact retrieval set. Figure 3 shows the relaxed similarity bounds. The figure shows that

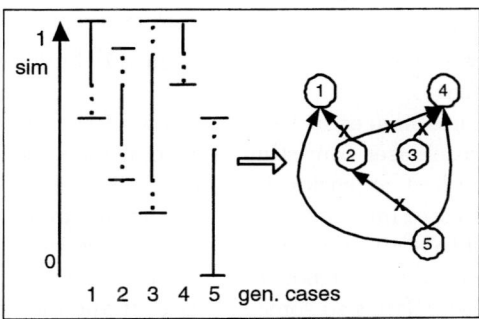

Fig. 3. Relaxation of Similarity Bounds

some intervals that didn't overlap before are overlapping now. Consequently, the ordering between the corresponding generalized cases is not valid anymore. Furthermore, this relaxation doesn't lead to new ordering relationships, so no cases can be excluded, that wouldn't be excluded by exact calculation of bounds.

The simplest way to estimate a lower bound for min/max problem is to solve min/min problem, since:

$$\forall Sub, GC \subseteq P : \\ \min_{s \in Sub} \min_{g \in GC} sim(s, g) < \min_{s \in Sub} \max_{g \in GC} sim(s, g) \tag{19}$$

The handling of the min/min problem is exactly the same as the handling of the max/max problem. It can be formulated as a common min problem in double dimensioned space.

The other possibility to estimate a lower bound for the min/max problem by a known feasible point c in the generalized case is to calculate:

$$\min_{s \in Sub} sim(s, c) \tag{20}$$

Also, here it holds:

$$\forall Sub, GC \subseteq P, c \in GC : \\ \min_{s \in Sub} sim(s, c) < \min_{s \in Sub} \max_{g \in GC} sim(s, g) \tag{21}$$

In both cases the min problem has to be approximated through the lower bound.

3.2 Kd-Tree Based Retrieval Method

Another method to reduce the computational complexity of the retrieval adopts the idea of the kd-trees [11]. The key characteristic of this method is building the index structure independent from the similarity measure.

The traditional kd-tree based retrieval consists of two major steps - building a kd-tree in the offline phase and using this tree for searching during the online phase. For the retrieval of generalized cases these parts will be adapted and extended.

Building a kd-Tree. The following algorithm [11] builds the kd-tree variant for common case bases.

While there are no changes in the main flow of the algorithm necessary to create kd-trees for case bases consisting of generalized cases, two methods have to be extended. The first extension is made in the function *Partition*, which partitions the set of cases into subsets. This function contains a test checking if a given case belongs to a given subspace of the description space. This check is quite simple for point cases, but not for generalized cases.

A generalized case belongs to some subspace if and only if their intersection is not empty. E.g. for generalized case GC represented through $GC = \bigcup_{i=1}^{n} g_i$ with g_i closed connected sets it should be checked if there is some $i \in [1, n]$ with $g_i \cap Subspace \neq \emptyset$.

The feasibility problem, that is, finding a point in the intersection of finitely many sets, is discussed in various areas of sciences. It is well researched and for many cases efficient to solve. Therefore, the test in the function *Partition* should be extended to solve a feasibility problem for the given generalized case and the given subspace.

The function *split* in the traditional algorithm interrupts the split process if a current subspace includes fewer cases as a given limit. Since several generalized cases can overlap, it's not always possible to achieve the limit, therefore the split process should be stopped if, after several attempts, no successful split occurs.

Searching Similar Generalized Cases Using a k-d Tree. There are no major changes necessary for the online phase. Since a case base contains generalized and point cases, sim^* should be calculated instead of sim in this part of the method. The search algorithm, BOB and BWB tests remain the same.

4 Related Work and Summary

The idea of generalized cases is not new and has been already discussed in the area of instance-based learning and in earlier works on CBR [12]. Although not explicitly mentioned, some CBR-based applications adopt the idea of generalizing cases and provide proprietary solutions, often restricted to the particular application domain. For an overview, see [13]. The term generalized case has been introduced in [1], which provides a formal and systematic view using constraints to express the dependencies between several attributes. Based in this, we

INPUT: Case Base CB

OUTPUT: A kd-tree

```
 1. IF NOT Split?(CB) THEN RETURN MakeBucket(CB)
 2. ELSE
 3.         Discriminator := SelectAttribute(CB)
 4.         IF OrderedValueRange(Discriminator) THEN
 5.            Value := SelectValue(CB, Discriminator)
 6.            RETURN MakeInternalOrderedNode(Discriminator, Value,
                  CreateTree (Partition_<(Discriminator, Value, CB)),
                  CreateTree (Partition_>(Discriminator, Value, CB)),
                  CreateTree (Partition_=(Discriminator, Value, CB)),
                  CreateTree (Partition_unknown(Discriminator, Value, CB)))
 7.         ELSE
 8.            RETURN MakeInternalUnorderedNode(Discriminator,
                  CreateTree (Partition_1(Discriminator, CB)), ...,
                  CreateTree (Partition_m(Discriminator, CB)),
                  CreateTree (Partition_unknown(Discriminator, CB)))
 9.         ENDIF
10. ENDIF
```

developed the first index based method for generalized cases defined over mixed, continuous and discrete, domains [14]. The idea of this approach is to transform generalized cases by sampling them into point cases and using fast traditional retrieval engines.

In this paper we presented the formulation of the similarity assessment problem for generalized cases with mixed domains as a special optimization problem MINLP. Because of the computational complexity, we introduced two optimization-based retrieval methods that operate on a previously created index structure. The first retrieval method takes the similarity measure into account, while the second one is based on kd-trees. First experiments have shown that both optimization techniques improve the response time of CBR-based applications with generalized cases significantly. However, generating the required index-structures can be time consuming but this is done only once for static case bases.

References

1. Bergmann, R., Vollrath, I., Wahlmann, T.: Generalized cases and their application to electronic design. In E. Melis (Hrsg.) 7th German Workshop on Case-Based Reasoning (1999)
2. Bergmann, R.: Experience management. Springer-Verlag Berlin Heidelberg New York (2002)
3. Mougouie, B., Bergmann, R.: Similarity assessment for generalized cases by optimization methods. In S.Craw and A.Preece (Hrsg.) European Conference on Case-Based Reasoning (ECCBR'02). Lecture Notes in Artificial Intelligence, Springer (2002)

4. Lewis, J.: Intellectual property (ip) components. Artisan Components, Inc., web page, http://www.artisan.com (1997, Accessed 28 Oct 1998)
5. Schaaf, M., Maximini, R., Bergmann, R., Tautz, C., Traphöner, R.: Supporting electronic design reuse by integrating quality-criteria into cbr-based ip selection. Proceedings 6th European Conference on Case Based Reasoning (September 2002)
6. Bergmann, R., Vollrath, I.: Generalized cases: Representation and steps towards e.cient similarity assessment. KI-99 (1999)
7. Bazaraa, M.S., Sherali, H.D., Shetty, C.M.: Nonlinear programming, theory and algorithms. Wiley (1993)
8. Leyffer, S.: Deterministic methods for mixed integer nonlinear programming. PhD Thesis, Department of Mathematics and Computer Science, University of Dundee (1993)
9. Tawarmalani, M., Sahinidis, N.: Convexification and global optimization in continuous and mixed-integer nonlinear programming: Theory, algorithms, software, and applications. Kluwer Academic Publishers, Boston MA (2002)
10. Horst, R., Tuy, H.: Global optimization: Deterministic approaches. 2nd rev. Edition, Springer, Berlin, Germany (1993)
11. Wess, S., Altho., K.D., Derwand, G.: Using k-d trees to improve the retrieval step in case-based reasoning. University of Kaiserslautern (1993)
12. Kolodner, J.L.: Retrieval and organizational strategies in conceptual memory. PhD thesis, Yale University (1980)
13. Maximini, K., Maximini, R., Bergmann, R.: An investigation of generalized cases: Theory, algorithms, software, and applications. Proceedings of 5th International Conference on Case Base Reasoning (ICCBR'03), June 2003 in Trondheim, Norway. Editors: Kevin D. Ashley, Derek G. Briddge (2003)
14. Maximini, R., Tartakovski, A., Bergmann, R.: Investigating different methods for efficient retrieval of generalized cases. In Reimer U., Abecker A., Staab S., Stumme G.(Hrsg). WM2003: Professionelles Wissensmanagement-Erfahrungen und Visionen (2003)

Case-Based Relational Learning of Expressive Phrasing in Classical Music

Asmir Tobudic[1] and Gerhard Widmer[1,2]

[1] Austrian Research Institute for Artificial Intelligence, Vienna
[2] Department of Medical Cybernetics and Artificial Intelligence,
Medical University of Vienna
{asmir,gerhard}@oefai.at

Abstract. An application of relational case-based learning to the task of expressive music performance is presented. We briefly recapitulate the relational case-based learner DISTALL and empirically show that DISTALL outperforms a straightforward propositional k-NN on the music task. A set distance measure based on maximal matching - incorporated in DISTALL - is discussed in more detail and especially the problem associated with its 'penalty part': the distance between a large and a small set is mainly determined by their difference in cardinality. We introduce a method for systematically varying the influence of the penalty on the overall distance measure and experimentally test different variants of it. Interestingly, it turns out that the variants with high influence of penalty clearly perform better than the others on our music task.

Keywords: relational case-based learning, case-based reasoning, music

1 Introduction

Case-based learning for expressive performance has been demonstrated before in the domain of expressive phrasing in jazz [2,6], where the promise of CBR was shown, but the evaluation was mostly qualitative and based on relatively small numbers of phrases. In previous work we presented what to our knowledge is the first large-scaled quantitative evaluation of case-based learning for expressive performance (against a high-class concert pianist) [12]. An case-based learning system was presented which was able to recognize performance patterns at various levels of musical abstraction (hierarchically nested phrases) and apply them to new pieces (phrases) by analogy to known performances. While the experimental results in this difficult domain were far from being truly satisfying, some of the resulting expressive performances sounded indeed musically sensible[1].

One obvious limitation of the presented system was the simple attribute-value representation used to characterize phrases, which did not permit the

---

[1] A recording of one of the system's expressive performances won second prize at the International Computer Piano Performance Rendering Contest (RENCON'02) in Tokyo in September 2002, behind a rule-based rendering system that had been carefully tuned by hand.

learner to refer to details of the internal structure of the phrases, nor to their broader musical *context*. These problems can be partly overcome by applying a relational representation for phrase description. We briefly recapitulate the relational case-based learning algorithm DISTALL [13], and show how it is indeed able to outperform the straightforward propositional k-nearest neighbor on the 'expressive-performance' task. In the relational setting, where examples are mostly represented as sets of facts, the distance measure between two sets of elements is a crucial part of each case-based learner. DISTALL's rather intuitive set distance measure based on maximal matching (first proposed in [9]) was shown to work well on a number of tasks [10, 13]. One of the problems with this set distance measure is that the distance between two sets with (largely) different cardinalities is mainly determined through a 'penalty' - the difference in cardinalities of both sets. It is thus not clear if the sets should be first scaled in some way to the approximately same cardinalities, e.g. by weighting their elements. In this work we present an experimental study of the impact of varying influence of penalty to the overall results. It turns out that the retention of a high penalty influence is indeed effective: variants of distance measures with high penalty influence produced clearly better results on our data set than the others.

This paper is organized as follows: Section 2 introduces the notion of expressive music performance and its representation via performance curves. We also show how hierarchically nested musical phrases are represented in first-order logic, and how complex tempo and dynamics curves can be decomposed into well-defined training cases for the case-based learning algorithm. Section 2 is a recapitulation of material already published in [13]. Section 3 briefly describes our relational case-based learner DISTALL. Experimental results achieved with DISTALL on the expressive performance learning task and its comparison with a straightforward propositional k-NN are given in Section 4. Experiments with various degrees of penalty influence for the set distance measure based on maximal matching are reported and discussed in Section 5. Section 6 concludes.

2 Real-World Task: Learning to Play Music Expressively

Expressive music performance is the art of shaping a musical piece by continuously varying important parameters like tempo, loudness, etc. while playing a piece. Instead of playing a piece of music with constant tempo or loudness, (skilled) performers rather speed up at some places, slow down at others, stress certain notes or passages etc. The way this 'should be' done is not specified precisely in the written score[2], but at the same time it is absolutely essential for the music to sound alive. The aim of this work is learning predictive models of two of the most important expressive parameters: *timing* (tempo variations) and *dynamics* (loudness variations).

The tempo and loudness variations can be represented as curves which quantify the variations of these parameters for each note relative to some reference

---

[2] The *score* is the music as actually printed.

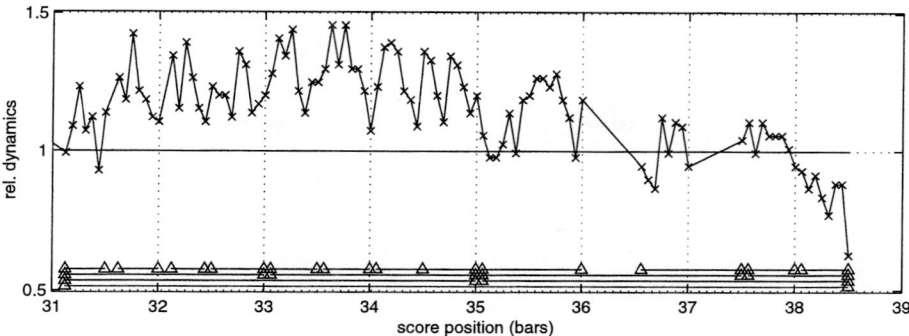

Fig. 1. Dynamics curve (relating to melody notes) of performance of Mozart Sonata KV.279, 1st movement, mm. 31–38, by a Viennese concert pianist.

value (e.g. average loudness or tempo of the same piece). Figure 1 shows a *dynamics curve* of a small part of the Mozart piano Sonata K.279 (C major), 1st movement, as played by a Viennese concert pianist (computed from recordings on a Bösendorfer SE290 computer-monitored grand piano[3]). Each point represents the relative loudness with which a particular melody note was played (relative to an average loudness of the piece); a purely mechanical (unexpressive) rendition of the piece would correspond to a flat horizontal line at $y = 1.0$. Tempo variations can be represented in an analogous way.

A careful examination of the figure reveals some trends in the dynamics curve. For instance, one can notice an up-down, *crescendo-decrescendo* tendency over the presented part of the piece and relatively consistent smaller up-down patterns embedded in it. This is not an accident since we chose to show a part of the piece which is a musically meaningful unit: a high-level *phrase*. This phrase contains a number of lower-level phrases, which are apparently also 'shaped' by the performer. The hierarchical, four-level phrase structure of this passage is indicated by four levels of brackets at the bottom of the figure. The aim of our work is the automatic induction of tempo and dynamics strategies, at different levels of the phrase structure, from large amounts of real performances by concert pianists. The heart of our system, the relational case-based learning algorithm described below, recognizes similar phrases from the training set and applies their expressive patterns to a new (test) piece. In this section we will describe the steps which precede and succeed the actual learning: First we show how hierarchically nested phrases are represented in first-order logic. We then show how complex tempo and dynamics curves as measured in real performances can be decomposed into well-defined training cases for the learner. Finally, we discuss

---

[3] The SE290 is a full concert grand piano with a special mechanism that measures every key and pedal movement with high precision and stores this information in a format similar to MIDI. From these measurements, and from a comparison with the notes in the written score, the tempo and dynamics curves corresponding to the performances can be computed.

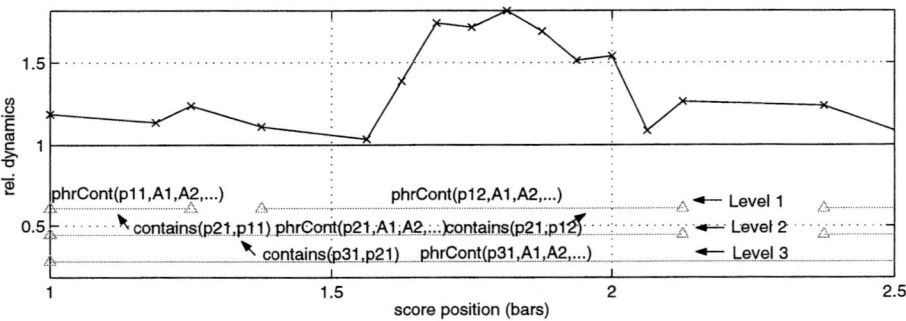

Fig. 2. Phrase representation used by our relational case-based learning algorithm.

the last step: at prediction time, the shapes predicted by the learner for nested phrases at different levels must be combined into a final performance curve that can be used to produce a computer-generated 'expressive' performance.

2.1 Representing Musical Phrases in First-Order Logic

Phrases are segments of music heard and interpreted as coherent units; they are important structural building blocks of music. Phrases are organized hierarchically: smaller phrases are grouped into higher-level phrases, which are in turn grouped together, constituting a musical context at a higher level of abstraction etc. The phrases and relations between them can be naturally represented in first-order logic.

Consider Figure 2. It shows the dynamics curve corresponding to a small portion (2.5 bars) of a Mozart sonata performance, along with the piece's underlying phrase structure. For all scores in our data set phrases are organized at four hierarchical levels, based on a manual phrase structure analysis. The musical content of each phrase is encoded in the predicate $phrCont(Id, A1, A2, ...)$. Id is the phrase identifier and $A1, A2,...$ are attributes that describe very basic phrase properties like the length of a phrase, melodic intervals between the starting and ending notes, information about where the highest melodic point (the 'apex') of the phrase is, the harmonic progression between start, apex, and end, etc. Relations between phrases are specified via the predicate $contains(Id1, Id2)$, which states that the bigger phrase $Id1$ contains the smaller one $Id2$. Note that smaller phrases (consisting only of a few melody notes) are described in detail by the predicate $phrCont$. For the bigger phrases – containing maybe several bars – the high-level attributes in $phrCont$ are not sufficient for a full description. But having links to the lower-lever phrases through the $contains$ predicate and their detailed description in terms of $phrCont$, we can also obtain detailed insight into the contents of bigger phrases.

Predicates $phrCont$ and $contains$ encode a partial description of the musical score. What is still needed in order to learn are the training examples, i.e. for each phrase in the training set, we need to know how it was played by a musician.

This information is given in the predicate *phrShape(Id, Coeffs)*, where *Coeffs* encode information about the way the phrase was played by a pianist. This is computed from the tempo and dynamics curves, as described in the following section.

2.2 Deriving the Training Cases: Multilevel Decomposition of Performance Curves

Given a complex tempo or dynamics curve (see Figure 1) and the underlying phrase structure, we need to calculate the most likely contribution of each phrase to the overall observed expression curve, i.e., we need to decompose the complex curve into basic expressive phrase 'shapes'. As approximation functions to represent these shapes we decided to use the class of second-degree polynomials (i.e., functions of the form $y = ax^2 + bx + c$), because there is ample evidence from research in musicology that high-level tempo and dynamics are well characterized by quadratic or parabolic functions [14]. Decomposing a given expression curve is an iterative process, where each step deals with a specific level of the phrase structure: for each phrase at a given level, we compute the polynomial that best fits the part of the curve that corresponds to this phrase, and 'subtract' the tempo or dynamics deviations 'explained' by the approximation. The curve that remains after this subtraction is then used in the next level of the process. We start with the highest given level of phrasing and move to the lowest. As tempo and dynamics curves are lists of multiplicative factors (relative to a default tempo), 'subtracting' the effects predicted by a fitted curve from an existing curve simply means dividing the y values on the curve by the respective values of the approximation curve.

Figure 3 illustrates the result of the decomposition process on the last part (mm.31–38) of the Mozart Sonata K.279, 1st movement, 1st section. The four-level phrase structure our music analyst assigned to the piece is indicated by the four levels of brackets at the bottom of the plot. The elementary phrase shapes (at four levels of hierarchy) obtained after decomposition are plotted in gray.

We end up with a training example for each phrase in the training set – a predicate *phrShape(Id, Coeff)*, where *Coeff* = $\{a, b, c\}$ are the coefficients of the polynomial fitted to the part of the performance curve associated with the phrase.

2.3 Combining Multi-level Phrase Predictions

Input to the learning algorithm are the (relational) representation of the musical scores plus the training examples (i.e. timing and dynamics polynomials), for each phrase in the training set. Given a test piece the learner assigns the shape of the most similar phrase from the training set to each phrase in the test piece. In order to produce final tempo and dynamics curves, the shapes predicted for phrases at different levels must be combined. This is simply the inverse of the curve decomposition problem. Given a new piece to produce a performance for, the system starts with an initial 'flat' expression curve (i.e., a list of 1.0

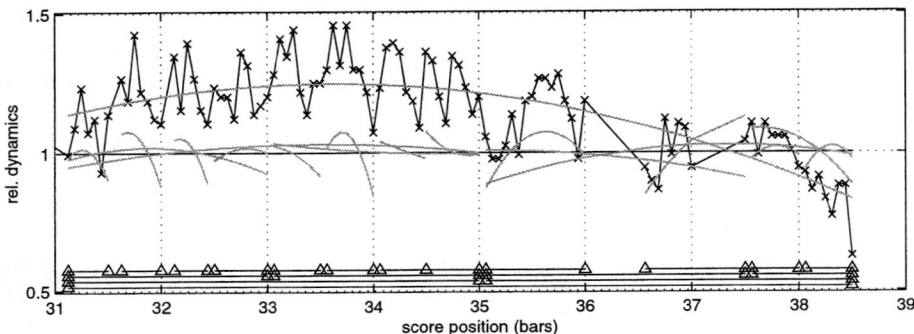

Fig. 3. Multilevel decomposition of dynamics curve of performance of Mozart Sonata K.279:1:1, mm.31-38.: original dynamics curve plus the second-order polynomial shapes giving the best fit at four levels of phrase structure.

values) and then successively multiplies the current value by the multi-level phrase predictions.

3 DISTALL and Set Distance Measure Based on Maximal Matching

The following section gives a brief overview of the relational case-based learner DISTALL. The interested reader is referred to [13] for a more detailed description.

3.1 The Relational Case-Based Learner DISTALL

DISTALL can be regarded as the continuation of the line of research initiated in [1], where a clustering algorithm together with its similarity measure was presented. This work was later improved in [5], in the context of the relational instance-based learning algorithm RIBL. The main idea behind RIBL's similarity measure is that the similarity between two objects is determined by the similarity of their attributes and the similarity of the objects related to them. The similarity of the related objects depends in turn on their attributes and related objects. The same idea is employed by DISTALL. Figure 4 depicts the basic principle of DISTALL (DIstance on SeTs of Appropriate Linkage Level).

In the example, we are interested in the distance between objects Ob_1 and Ob_2. It is calculated as the distance between two sets of FOL-literals: between the set of all literals from the background knowledge also containing object identifier Ob_1 as one of the arguments, and the set of all literals containing object identifier Ob_2. Most elements of these two sets will typically be literals which describe basics properties of objects Ob_1 and Ob_2 (putting this in the context of our music example from section 2.1, objects Ob_1 and Ob_2 would represent two phrases and literals describing their basic musical properties would

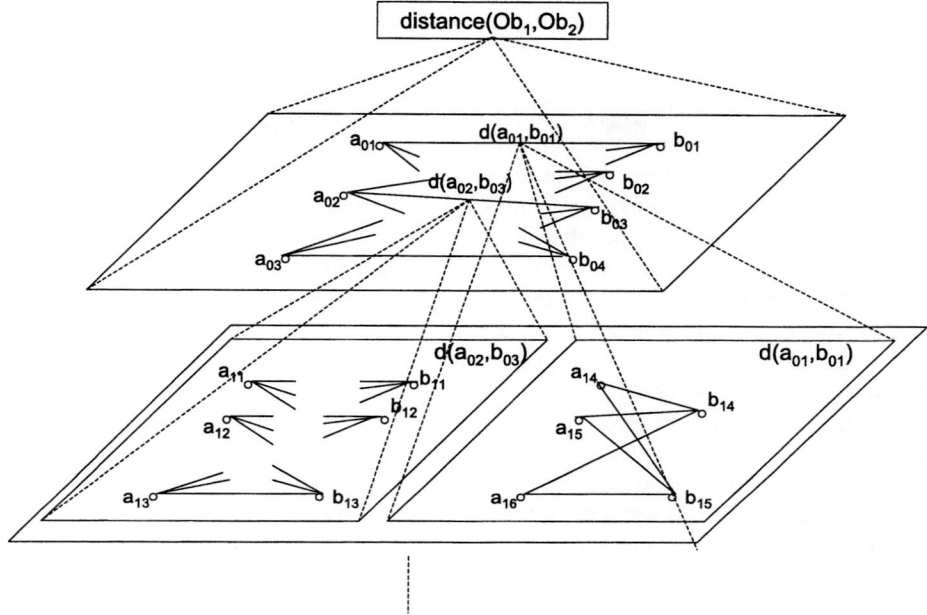

Fig. 4. Basic principle of DISTALL's similarity measure.

be predicates *phrCont*). The distance between such literals can be defined in a straightforward way, e.g., as the Euclidean or Manhattan distance defined over the literals' arguments (or set to 1 if the literals have different functors). But there may also be literals which state relations of objects Ob_1 and Ob_2 to some other objects (these would be *contains* predicates in our music example). In the figure 4 these are literals a_{01}, a_{02}, b_{01} and b_{03}. The distance between such literals is calculated as the set distance between sets of literals from the background knowledge which have the same object identifiers as one of the arguments. The procedure continues recursively, until a user defined depth is reached. At the lowest level, the distance between objects is calculated as the distance between discrete values. From the above it is apparent that a distance measure between *sets of elements* is essential for our learner. It is discussed in the following.

3.2 Set Distance Based on Maximal Matching

Given a normalized (i.e. in interval [0,1]) distance measure between individual points, the distance between two sets of points A and B based on maximal matching is proposed in [9] as:

$$d^m(A, B) = \min_{r \in MM(A,B)} \left\{ \sum_{(x,y) \in r} d(x,y) + \frac{|\#A - \#B|}{2} \right\} \quad (1)$$

where $MM(A, B)$ is the set of all possible maximal matchings between A and B, and $d(x, y)$ are distances between individual matched points.

Stated informally, one wants to maximally match elements from one set with the elements of the other and achieve the minimal possible distance. A penalty for each element of one set which does not match to any element of the other is also added (second term in the formula). In [9] it has been shown that such a metric satisfies the reflexivity, similarity and triangle inequality relations and can be calculated in time polynomial in $\#A$ and $\#B$ [4].

Although rather intuitive, the set distance measure based on maximal matching has two main weaknesses. The first is its computational infeasibility. As stated above, examples in FOL are describes as sets of facts, where, for typical learning tasks, it is not uncommon for examples to have fifty or more facts. Computing the distance between such two examples would have a time complexity of 100^3. For IBL and clustering tasks distances between each pair of examples have to be calculated, with databases typically containing tens of thousands of examples. For this reason DISTALL does not apply the set distance measure directly, but splits initial sets into hierarchically nested subsets (see Figure 4). The computational cost is kept small by applying the distance measure to subsets only, each having a small number of elements (see [13] for details).

The second problem of the presented distance measure is that the distance between a large and a small set is largely determined by their difference in cardinality, i.e. if $A >> B$, then $d^m(A, B) \approx |\#A - \#B|/2$. In order to avoid that, methods for weighting elements in sets are proposed (see [9] for details): E.g. one could assign a weight $W[A](a)$ to each element a in smaller set A and define a size of a set (or virtual cardinality) as: $size(A) = \sum_{a \in A} W[A](a)$. If the weights are chosen appropriately, the sets can be scaled to the same virtual cardinality thus reducing (or eliminating) the penalty part in formula 1. Still it is not clear if the set distance measure should be more influenced by the 'point' distances between already matched set points or by the fact that there is a number of points in one set which do not match any of the points in the other set. For example, suppose there are three families A, B_1 and B_2. Family A consists of mother, father and a child, the same as family B_1. It turns out that each member of family A is rather dissimilar from corresponding person from family B_1. Family B_2 has five children but mother, father and one of the children from B_2 are rather similar to the appropriate members from A. Which family, B_1 or B_2 is more similar to family A?

This question is subject of our experiments in section 5. We gradually vary the influence of the penalty part to the overall distance between two sets (from 0 to the full influence given by equation 1) and test the learning performance of each variant of the distance measure on our music task.

---

[4] Technically, finding a maximal matching and achieving the minimal possible distance between A and B is accomplished by finding a solution to the maximum flow minimal weight problem of adequately constructed transport network (see [7] for more information on the concept of transport networks) and has complexity cubic in $\#A$ and $\#B$.

Table 1. Mozart sonata sections used in experiments (to be read as <sonataName>: <movement>:<section>); *notes* refers to 'melody' notes.

sonata section	notes	phrases at level			
		1	2	3	4
kv279:1:1 fast 4/4	391	50	19	9	5
kv279:1:2 fast 4/4	638	79	36	14	5
kv280:1:1 fast 3/4	406	42	19	12	4
kv280:1:2 fast 3/4	590	65	34	17	6
kv280:2:1 slow 6/8	94	23	12	6	3
kv280:2:2 slow 6/8	154	37	18	8	4
kv280:3:1 fast 3/8	277	28	19	8	4
kv280:3:2 fast 3/8	379	40	29	13	5
kv282:1:1 slow 4/4	165	24	10	5	2
kv282:1:2 slow 4/4	213	29	12	6	3
kv282:1:3 slow 4/4	31	4	2	1	1
kv283:1:1 fast 3/4	379	53	23	10	5
kv283:1:2 fast 3/4	428	59	32	13	6
kv283:3:1 fast 3/8	326	53	30	12	3
kv283:3:2 fast 3/8	558	79	47	19	6
kv332:2 slow 4/4	477	49	23	12	4
Total:	5506	714	365	165	66

4 Experiments: Relational vs. Propositional Learning

In the following we present detailed empirical results achieved with DISTALL on a complex real-world dataset derived from piano performances of classical music. We also provide a comparison with a straightforward propositional *k*-NN. Note that in the experiments we present in this section we do not intend to learn performance curves as close to the pianist's curves as possible (see [12] for this type of problem). Rather, we want to investigate if employing a richer relational representation adds some performance gain compared with a simpler propositional representation.

4.1 The Data

The data used for the experiments was derived from performances of Mozart piano sonatas by a Viennese concert pianist on a Bösendorfer SE 290 computer-controlled grand piano. A multi-level phrase structure analysis of the musical score was carried out manually by a musicologist. Phrase structure was marked at four hierarchical levels; three of these were finally used in the experiments. The sonatas are divided into sections, which can be regarded as coherent pieces. The resulting set of annotated pieces is summarized in Table 1. The pieces and performances are quite complex and different in character; automatically learning expressive strategies from them is a challenging task.

Table 2. Results, by sonata sections, of cross-validation experiment with DISTALL ($k=1$). Measures subscripted with D refer to the 'default' (mechanical, inexpressive) performance, those with L to the performance produced by the learner. The cases where DISTALL is better than the default are printed in bold.

	dynamics					tempo				
	MSE_D	MSE_L	MAE_D	MAE_L	$Corr_L$	MSE_D	MSE_L	MAE_D	MAE_L	$Corr_L$
kv279:1:1	.0341	**.0173**	.1571	**.0929**	.7093	.0161	.0189	.0879	**.0820**	.4482
kv279:1:2	.0282	.0314	.1394	**.1243**	.6162	.0106	.0151	.0720	.0799	.4691
kv280:1:1	.0264	**.0143**	.1332	**.0895**	.7289	.0136	**.0062**	.0802	**.0526**	.7952
kv280:1:2	.0240	.0380	.1259	.1363	.4394	.0125	.0160	.0793	**.0752**	.4983
kv280:2:1	.1534	**.0655**	.3493	**.2022**	.7569	.0310	.0326	.1128	**.1025**	.6360
kv280:2:2	.1405	**.0534**	.3170	**.1854**	.7951	.0323	.0427	.1269	.1293	.5206
kv280:3:1	.0293	**.0125**	.1452	**.0809**	.7575	.0188	**.0104**	.0953	**.0629**	.6971
kv280:3:2	.0187	.0274	.1124	.1151	.4816	.0196	**.0157**	.1033	**.0884**	.5862
kv282:1:1	.0956	**.0297**	.2519	**.1228**	.8367	.0151	.0172	.0905	**.0700**	.4718
kv282:1:2	.0781	**.0397**	.2277	**.1436**	.7839	.0090	.0284	.0741	.0974	.3435
kv282:1:3	.1047	**.0520**	.2496	**.1867**	.7134	.0938	**.0388**	.2236	**.1269**	.8400
kv283:1:1	.0255	**.0236**	.1379	**.0985**	.7377	.0094	.0115	.0664	.0756	.4106
kv283:1:2	.0333	**.0183**	.1560	**.0948**	.7506	.0097	**.0092**	.0691	**.0651**	.5860
kv283:3:1	.0345	**.0099**	.1482	**.0715**	.8818	.0116	**.0077**	.0696	**.0534**	.6847
kv283:3:2	.0371	**.0192**	.1572	**.1002**	.7358	.0100	.0153	.0745	.0757	.4099
kv332:2	.0845	.0869	.2476	**.2398**	.4059	.0146	.0492	.0718	.1498	.2582
WMean	.0437	**.0310**	.1664	**.1225**	.6603	.0141	.0182	.0811	.0823	.5089

4.2 A Quantitative Evaluation of DISTALL

A systematic *leave-one-piece-out* cross-validation experiment was carried out. Each of the 16 sections was once set aside as a test piece, while the remaining 15 pieces were used for learning. DISTALL uses one nearest neighbor for prediction.

The expressive shapes for each phrase in a test piece were predicted by DIS-TALL and then combined into a final tempo and dynamics curve, as described in section 2.3. The experiment setup is similar to the one already published in [13]. The evaluation procedure is somewhat different. What was compared in [13] was the tempo or dynamics curve produced by the learner with the curve corresponding to the pianist's actual performance. This is somewhat unfair, since the learner was given not the actual performance curves but an *approximation*, namely the polynomials fitted to the curve at various phrase levels. Correctly predicting these is the best the learner could hope to achieve. Thus, in this work we use the following performance measures: the *mean squared error* of the system's prediction on the piece relative to the *approximation* curve – i.e., the curve implied by the three levels of quadratic functions – of the actual expression curve produced by the pianist. ($MSE = \sum_{i=1}^{n}(pred(n_i) - expr(n_i))^2/n$), the *mean absolute error* ($MAE = \sum_{i=1}^{n}|pred(n_i) - expr(n_i)|/n$), and the *correlation* between predicted and 'approximated' curve. MSE and MAE were also computed for a *default* curve that would correspond to a purely mechanical, unexpressive performance (i.e., an expression curve consisting of all 1's). That allows us to judge if learning is really better than just doing nothing. The results of the experiment are summarized in table 2, where each row gives the results obtained on the respective test piece when all others were used for training. The last row ($WMean$) shows the weighted mean performance over all pieces (individual results weighted by the relative length of the pieces).

We are interested in cases where the *relative errors* (i.e., MSE_L/MSE_D and MAE_L/MAE_D) are less than 1.0, that is, where the curves predicted by the learner are closer to the approximation of the pianist's performance than a purely mechanical rendition. In the dynamics dimension, this is the case in 12 out of 16 cases for MSE, and in 14 out of 16 for MAE. The results for tempo are worse: in only 6 cases for MSE and 10 for MAE is learning better than no learning.

On some pieces DISTALL is able to predict expressive curves which are surprisingly close to the approximations of the pianist's ones – witness, e.g., the correlation of 0.88 in kv283:3:1 for dynamics[5]. On the other hand, DISTALL performs poorly on some pieces, especially on those that are rather different in character from all other pieces in the training set (e.g. correlation of 0.26 by kv332:2 for tempo).

4.3 DISTALL vs. Propositional *k*-NN

One desirable property of relational learners is performing as well on propositional data as the 'native' propositional learners [4, 5]. Being generalizations of the propositional *k*-NN, DISTALL shows this property. It is however interesting to compare the performance of DISTALL, given the relational data representation, with the performance of the standard propositional *k*-NN[6], since it has been shown that a richer relational representation need not always be a guarantee for better generalization performance [4]. We can represent phrases in propositional logic by describing each phrase in the data set with the attributes $A1, A2, ...$ from the predicate *phrCont*($Id, A1, A2, ...$) together with the 'target' polynomial coefficients *Coeffs* from the predicate *phrShape*($Id, Coeffs$). By doing so we lose information about hierarchical relations between phrases and obtain an attribute-value representation which can be used by the *k*-NN algorithm. Table 3 shows the performance of *k*-NN on our learning task in terms of weighted mean errors over all test pieces. The equivalent results for DISTALL are repeated from table 2 (last row).

DISTALL performs better than propositional *k*-NN in both domains (reducing the errors and increasing the correlation), the only exception being MSE for tempo. Although meaningful, comparing such high-level error measures is somewhat unfair. The actual task for both learner is to predict elementary phrasal shapes and not the composite performance curves. One mispredicted shape at

---

[5] Such a high correlation between predicted and observed curves is even more surprising taking into account that kv283:3:1 is a fairly long piece with over 90 hierarchically nested phrases containing over 320 melody notes.
[6] For a detailed study where propositional *k*-NN is optimized on our learning problem see [12].

Table 3. Comparison between standard k-NN and DISTALL. The table shows weighted mean errors over all test pieces. Measures subscripted with D refer to the 'default' (mechanical, inexpressive) performance, those with L to the performance produced by the learner. The results for DISTALL are repeated from table 2 (last row).

	dynamics					tempo				
	MSE_D	MSE_L	MAE_D	MAE_L	$Corr_L$	MSE_D	MSE_L	MAE_D	MAE_L	$Corr_L$
propositional k-NN	.0437	.0335	.1664	.1309	.6369	.0141	.0177	.0811	.0878	.4628
DISTALL	.0437	.0310	.1664	.1225	.6603	.0141	.0182	.0811	.0823	.5089

Table 4. Comparison between propositional k-NN and DISTALL at the level of phrases. The table shows absolute numbers and percentages of the phrases where the predictions of both learners are equal and where one learner is closer to the actual phrase shape than the other. Both learner use one nearest neighbor for prediction.

	dynamics (%)			tempo (%)		
	MSE	MAE	CORR	MSE	MAE	CORR
equal	697 (56%)	697 (56%)	697 (56%)	697 (56%)	697 (56%)	697 (56%)
prop. closer	240 (19%)	243 (20%)	259 (21%)	249 (20%)	252 (20%)	241 (19%)
DISTALL closer	305 (25%)	302 (24%)	286 (23%)	296 (24%)	293 (24%)	304 (25%)

the highest level can 'ruin' the whole composite curve even if all other shapes at lower levels are predicted perfectly. For this reason it is instructive to compare the learners' performance directly at the phrase level.

The following experiment was performed. The *leave-one-piece-out* cross-validation procedure stayed the same as in the previous section, but now we compare predictions of propositional k-NN and DISTALL with the 'real' phrase shapes, i.e. those obtained by decomposing tempo and dynamics curves played by the pianist. We then check whose prediction was closer to the actual shape (again in terms of MSE, MAE and correlation). That gives us much more test cases (1240 phrases instead of 16 pieces) and thus more detailed insight into differences between the algorithms. The results are given in table 4.

A first look at table 4 reveals that both learners predict the same shapes in a lot of cases – more than 55% of the test set. For the second half however, DISTALL predicts shapes which are closer to the pianist's (i.e., lower MSE and MAE, higher correlation) in more cases than vice versa.

5 Expreriment: Influence of the Mismatch Penalty on the Overall Set Distance Measure

In this section we experimentally examine the influence of the penalty part of the set distance (see section 3.2). We introduce a parameter penalty influence (*penInfl*) which allows us to control the influence of the penalty part in the formula 1 as follows:

The parameter *penInfl* can be varied in the range [0,1]. Before computing the set distance, the elements of the smaller set are weighted according to the

Table 5. Comparison between variants of set distance measure based on maximal matching with different influences of penalty part (see section 3.2). The table shows weighted mean errors over all test pieces. Measures subscripted with D refer to the 'default' (mechanical, inexpressive) performance, those with L to the performance produced by the learner.

$penInfl$	dynamics					tempo				
	MSE_D	MSE_L	MAE_D	MAE_L	$Corr_L$	MSE_D	MSE_L	MAE_D	MAE_L	$Corr_L$
0	.0437	.0376	.1664	.1391	.6091	.0141	.0303	.0811	.1186	.3203
0.2	.0437	.0378	.1664	.1374	.6297	.0141	.0286	.0811	.1107	.3313
0.4	.0437	.0347	.1664	.1306	.6481	.0141	.0253	.0811	.1002	.4043
0.6	.0437	.0350	.1664	.1292	.6514	.0141	.0223	.0811	.0936	.4563
0.8	.0437	.0319	.1664	.1226	.6687	.0141	.0200	.0811	.0865	.4736
1	.0437	.0310	.1664	.1225	.6603	.0141	.0182	.0811	.0823	.5089

formula $w = R + (1 - R) * penInfl$, where $R = max(\#A, \#B)/min(\#A, \#B)$. By setting $penInfl = 0$ (we want to neglect the penalty part), each element of the smaller set is assigned a weight $w = R$. In this case both sets have the same 'virtual cardinality' and each matching of the smaller set to one element of the bigger set is weighted with $w = R$. In setting $penInfl = 1$ elements of the smaller set are weighted $w = 1$ and formula 1 applies. For values of $penInfl$ between 0 and 1, the weights are linearly spread in the range $(R,1)$ (e.g. if $\#A = 2$, $\#B = 4$ and $penInfl = 0.5$, each element of A would be weighted $w = 1.5$ and 'virtual cardinality' of A would be 3).

For each value of $penInfl$ in the range [0,1] with step size 0.2 we repeated the same *leave-one-piece-out* cross-validation experiment from section 4.2. The learning performance of each variant of the distance measure in terms of weighted mean errors over all test pieces is given in table 5. Interestingly, it turns out that the variants of the distance measure with high penalty influence perform clearly better on our learning task than those with reduced influence of penalty. The learners' performances in terms of each error measure (lower MSE and MAE, higher correlation) get monotonically better with increasing values of parameter $penInfl$. Although the learning performance increases in both domains, the gain in the tempo domain is more dramatic (e.g. mean correlation of 0.36 vs. 0.24 for variants $penInfl = 1$ and $penInfl = 0$ respectively). It seems that variants with high penalty basically 'filter out' phrases with different structure (e.g. phrases with a (largely) different number of smaller phrases) and choose the nearest phrase based on 'fine tuning' from the subset of phrases with approximately the same structure. Still it is not clear if this strategy is effective on datasets with even larger differences in cardinalities between examples.

6 Conclusion

We have presented an application of cased-base reasoning on a complex learning task from the domain of classical music: learning to apply musically 'sensible' tempo and dynamics variations to a piece of music at different levels of the phrase hierarchy. The problem was modelled as a multi-level decomposition and prediction task. We showed how hierarchically nested phrases can be naturally described in first-order logic and briefly presented the relational case-based learner DISTALL which can be seen as a generalization of k-NN learner for data described in FOL. Experimental analysis showed that our approach is in general viable. In addition to quantitative evaluations, listening to the performances produced by the learner provides additional qualitative insight. Some of DISTALL's performances - although being the result of purely automated learning with no additional knowledge about music - sound indeed musically sensible. We hope to demonstrate some interesting sound examples at the conference. Experimental results also showed that DISTALL outperforms a straightforward, propositional k-NN learner on the music task.

The set distance measure based on maximal matching, incorporated in DISTALL, was discussed in more detail. Specially, the problem of high influence of the penalty by assigning the distance to sets with largely different cardinalities was discussed. We presented a way to systematically vary the influence of the penalty part on the overall set distance measure. Interestingly, experimental results showed that variants of the set distance measure with high penalty influence perform better than those with reduced influence of penalty. Future experiments should show if reducing influence of penalty is more effective on datasets with examples with larger differences in cardinalities than our music dataset.

Future work with DISTALL could also have an impact on musicology. The rather poor results in the tempo domain (see section 4.2) suggest that other types of approximation functions may be worth trying, which might lead to better phrase-level tempo models.

Acknowledgments

This research is supported by a START Research Prize by the Austrian Federal Government (project no. Y99-INF). The Austrian Research Institute for Artificial Intelligence acknowledges basic financial support by the Austrian Federal Ministry for Education, Science, and Culture, and the Federal Ministry of Transport, Innovation, and Technology. Thanks to Werner Goebl for performing the harmonic and phrase structure analysis of the Mozart sonatas.

References

1. Bisson, G. (1992). Learning in FOL with a Similarity Measure. In *Proceedings of the 10th AAAI*, 1992.
2. Arcos, J.L. and López de Mántaras (2001). An Interactive CBR Approach for Generating Expressive Music. *Journal of Applied Intelligence* 14(1), 115–129.
3. De Raedt, L. (1992). *Interactive Theory Revision: an Inductive Logic Programming Approach*. Academic Press.
4. Dzeroski S., Schulze-Kremer, Heidtke K.R., Siems K., Wettschereck D., and Blockeel H. (1998). Diterpene structure elucidation from 13C NMR spectra with inductive logic programming. *Applied Artificial Intelligence: Special Issue on First-Order Knowledge Discovery in Databases*, 12(5):363-384, July August 1998.

5. Emde, D. and Wettschereck, D. (1996). Relational Instance-Base Learning. In *Proceedings of the Thirteen International Conference on Machine Learning (ICML'96)*, pages 122-130. Morgan Kaufmann, San Mateo.
6. López de Mántaras, R. and Arcos, J.L. (2002). AI and Music: From Composition to Expressive Performances. *AI Magazine* 23(3), 43–57.
7. Mehlhorn, K. (1984). Graph algorithms and NP-completeness, volume 2 of *Data structures and algorithms*, Springer Verlag.
8. Muggleton, S. H. and Feng C. (1990). Efficient Induction of Logic Programs. In *Proceedings of the First Conference on Algorithmic Learning Theory*,Tokyo.
9. Ramon, J. and Bruynooghe, M (1998). A Framework for defining distances between first-order logic objects. In D. Page, (ed.), *Proceedings of the 8th International Conference on Inductive Logic Programming*, volume 1446 of Lecture Notes in Artificial Intelligence, pages 271–280. Springer-Verlag.
10. Ramon, J. and Bruynooghe, M. (2000). A polynomial time computable metric between point sets. Report CW 301, Department of Computer Science, K.U.Leuven, Leuven, Belgium.
11. Rouveirol, C. (1992). Extensions of inversion of resolution applied to theory completion. In S. Muggleton, (ed.), *Inductive Logic Programming*. Academic Press, London.
12. Tobudic, A. and Widmer, G. (2003). Playing Mozart Phrase By Phrase. In *Proceedings of 5th International Conference on Case-Based Reasoning (ICCBR'03)*, Trondheim, Norway. Berlin: Springer Verlag.
13. Tobudic, A. and Widmer, G. (2003). Relational IBL in Music with a New Structural Similarity Measure. In *Proceeding of 9th International Conference on Inductive Logic Programming (ILP'03)*. Szeged, Hungary. Berlin: Springer Verlag.
14. Todd, N. McA. (1992). The Dynamics of Dynamics: A Model of Musical Expression. *Journal of the Acoustical Society of America* 91, 3540–3550.
15. Widmer, G. and Tobudic, A. (2003). Playing Mozart by Analogy: Learning Multi-Level Timing and Dynamics Strategies. *Journal of New Musical Research*, 32(3), 259-268.

CBRFlow: Enabling Adaptive Workflow Management Through Conversational Case-Based Reasoning

Barbara Weber[1], Werner Wild[2], and Ruth Breu[1]

[1] Quality Engineering Research Group / Institute of Computer Science
University of Innsbruck – Technikerstraße 13, 6020 Innsbruck, Austria
{Barbara.Weber,Ruth.Breu}@uibk.ac.at
[2] Evolution Consulting
Jahnstraße 26, 6020 Innsbruck, Austria
werner.wild@evolution.at

Abstract. In this paper we propose an architecture for an adaptive workflow management system (WFMS) and present the research prototype CBRFlow. CBRFlow extends workflow execution with conversational case-based reasoning (CCBR) to adapt the predefined workflow model to changing circumstances and to provide the WFMS with learning capabilities. Business rules within the predefined workflow model are annotated during run-time with context-specific information in the form of cases using the CCBR sub-system. When case reuse becomes frequent, the cases are manually refactored into rules to foster automatic execution. This feedback supports continuous process improvement, resulting in more manageable and more efficient business processes over time.

1 Introduction

Workflow management systems (WFMS) are frequently used to control the execution of business processes and to improve their efficiency and productivity. To date, WFMS have been applied to fairly static environments in which the execution of activities follows a highly predictable path. However, today's business is characterized by ever-changing requirements and unpredictable environments (e.g., due to global competition). Traditional WFMS do not address the needs of the majority of processes [1] and it is widely recognized that more flexibility is needed to overcome these drawbacks [2-5].

Due to this limited flexibility companies have often been restricted to respond quickly to changing circumstances and thus could not always realize the expected cost savings. When WFMS do not allow for changes or handle them in a too rigid manner, users are forced to circumvent the system to do their work properly. Bypassing the system results in a lack of efficiency and missing traceability. Additionally, the knowledge needed to complete the work is lost as it is not recorded in the system and therefore cannot be reused efficiently when similar problems arise in the future.

Due to the significant modeling time needed, workflow models are often obsolete right after their specification is "completed". Not all eventualities and possible deviations can be considered in advance, as requirements change or evolve over time, and exceptions or ad-hoc events may arise. In order to efficiently support the management of business processes, WFMS must be flexible at run-time so that necessary modifications can be made when they arise. The need for flexibility and adaptability in WFMS is addressed by adaptive workflow management research (e.g., WIDE [3], ADEPT$_{flex}$ [5], METEOR [6]).

In this paper we present CBRFlow, a research prototype which extends workflow execution with CCBR. CCBR is used to adapt the predefined workflow model to changing circumstances and to provide the WFMS with incremental learning capabilities. Business rules within the workflow model are annotated with context-specific information in the form of cases using the CCBR sub-system.

After providing a background on workflow management, business rules, hybrid CBR, and CCBR in Section 2, we describe the adaptive approach to workflow management on which CBRFlow is based in Section 3. Section 4 outlines CBRFlow's architecture, related work is discussed in Section 5, followed by conclusions and further studies in Section 6.

2 Background

2.1 Workflow Management

Workflow management involves the modeling, the execution and the monitoring of workflows [7]. During *workflow modeling* an abstract representation of a business process is created to specify which tasks are executed and in what order. A workflow model thus includes functions (i.e., activities), their dependencies, organizational entities that execute these functions and business objects which provide the functions with data. *Workflow execution* and *control* of the automated parts of a business process are supported by a WFMS. Each business case is handled by a newly created workflow instance. *Workflow monitoring* provides status information about running workflows; it supports the evaluation of business processes and fosters continuous process improvement.

2.2 Business Rules

Business rules can be defined as statements about how the business is done, i.e., about guidelines and restrictions with respect to states and processes in an organization [8]. Business rules can be formalized and modeled using ECA (event-condition-action) rules [9]. Within workflow management, business rules are used for activity enactment (i.e., to model the control flow), monitoring and exception handling.

2.3 Conversational Case-Based Reasoning

A CCBR system can be characterized as an interactive system that, via a mixed-initiative dialogue, guides users through a question-answering sequence in a case retrieval context. CCBR is an extension to the CBR paradigm, in which a user is actively involved in the inference process [10]. Allen defines a mixed-initiative dialogue as follows [11]: *"At any one time, one agent might have the initiative – the interaction – while the other works to assist it, contributing to the interactions as required. At other times, the roles are reversed...".*

Traditional CBR requires the user to provide a complete a priori specification of the problem for retrieval and knowledge about the relevance of each feature for problem solving. In CCBR, the system assists the user to find relevant cases by presenting a set of questions to assess a situation. The system guides the users, who, however, can also supply already known information on their initiative. *"The distinguishing benefit of conversational case-based reasoning [...] is that users are not required to initially provide a complete description of their problem. Instead, users enter text partially describing their problem and the system assists in further elaborating the problem during a conversation, which ends when the user selects a solution to apply"* [12].

2.4 Hybrid CBR

Hybrid CBR is the combination of case-based reasoning with other reasoning techniques like rule-based reasoning (e.g., GREBE [13], CABARET [14]). The combination of rules and cases is useful for reasoning in a variety of domains because of their complementary strengths [15-17]. Rules represent the general knowledge of a domain, while cases are able to utilize specific knowledge of previously experienced concrete problem situations. In general, rules capture broad trends in a domain, while cases are good at covering an underlying rule in more detail and at filling in small pockets of exceptions to the rules. The declarative knowledge encoded in rules can be adapted to changing environments by cases, without necessarily requiring the rules to be rewritten at every new turn of events [18].

3 Adaptive Approach to Workflow Management

CBRFlow builds upon the idea of integrating CCBR and workflow management to support run-time modifications to a predefined workflow model and to provide incremental learning capabilities. Figure 1 illustrates the adaptive approach to workflow management on which CBRFlow is based.

During workflow modeling an initial computerized representation of an organization's business processes is created and business rules are used to model the control flow between activities.

At run-time an instance of the workflow model is created and the process is executed as specified in the workflow model. Workflows are evaluated during execution by the workflow user and when run-time changes to the workflow model become necessary due to exceptions or changing requirements, the user annotates the business rules within the workflow model with context-specific information in the form of cases.

This recently gained knowledge is immediately available for reuse without explicitly changing the workflow model. When the process knowledge encoded in the cases becomes well-established, the workflow modeler should abstract these cases to rules, thus updating the underlying model explicitly by using the gained knowledge from within the CCBR-subsystem. The system and the organization continuously learn how to handle new situations in a better way as more and more experience is gained and the knowledge is readily available for reuse. This approach supports many of the principles and values advocated by Agile and Lean Software Development as discussed in [19, 20].

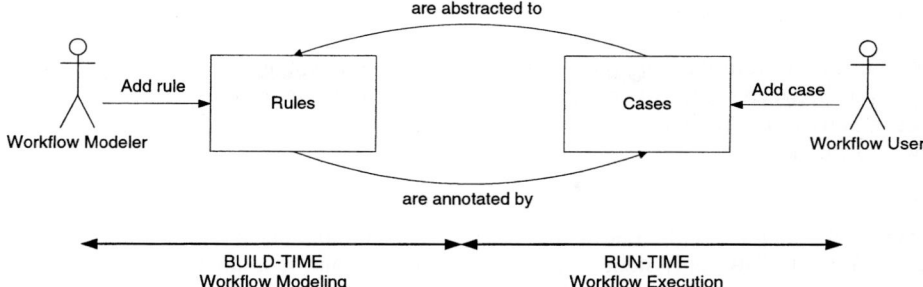

Fig. 1. CBRFlow's adaptive approach to workflow management

In CBRFlow rule-based reasoning has precedence over case-based reasoning. CCBR is only used when there is no domain knowledge specified in the form of rules, when changes must be performed or when exceptions arise, and to continuously improve the execution of an organization's business processes.

The application of such a hybrid CCBR approach offers several advantages for business process management compared to a pure rule-based approach. When modeling a business process it is not always possible to predefine a workflow in every detail as the business environment is continuously changing, as not all information might be available or as getting this information is prohibitively costly or time-consuming, thus making a pure rule-based approach infeasible. Only those aspects of a business process that create clear business benefits and for which enough knowledge is available are covered in or added to the initial workflow model. The detailed modeling of a business process is delayed until enough knowledge is available and uncertainty can be resolved. Cases are then used to deviate from the workflow model during run-time in order to adapt to altered circumstances. The knowledge about these modifications is collected and stored as cases. In most situations, the cases cannot be reused in a fully automated way, because a lot of adaptation knowledge is necessary to execute the workflow correctly. The users must therefore actively be involved in the inference process. CCBR provides the users with past experiences and supports their decision-making. If it becomes obvious that a specific change was more than a one-time ad-hoc deviation, it might be useful to abstract the information stored in the cases as one or more rules in order to allow full automation.

4 Architecture

In this section we present the architecture of the research prototype CBRFlow. First, the workflow building blocks are described (see Section 4.1), followed by an overview of the navigation of the Agent (i.e., representation of a workflow instance) through the workflow (see Section 4.2) and an outline of the core components and their collaborations (see Section 4.3). Finally, the implementation of the prototype is illustrated using an example from the travel domain (see Section 4.4).

4.1 Workflow Building Blocks

Workflow. Within CBRFlow a workflow is described as a set of nodes and the connections between them. It consists of a start node, a finite set of routing nodes, a finite set of activity nodes and an end node. Agent Instructions are used for the connections between nodes.

Start Node, End Node and Agent Instructions. Each workflow contains a single start node and a single end node. The start node indicates the beginning of a workflow. It is the only node without a predecessor and it is always followed by a routing node (i.e., containing an Agent Instruction with a reference to the first routing node). The end node is the only node without a successor and the predecessor of an end node is always a routing node. This provides for a placeholder if cases have to be added.

Agent Instructions are used to connect the nodes and to control the Agents (see also Section 4.2). They consist of an operation code, which specifies the class of the Agent Instruction and up to two parameters, depending on the Agent Instruction. A detailed description of the Agent Instruction Set can be found in [21].

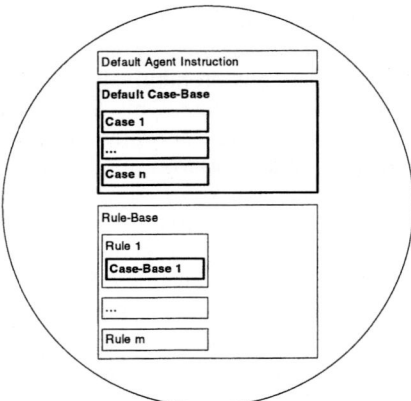

Fig. 2. Structure of a routing node

Routing Node. Routing nodes include the routing information and are responsible for routing the Agent from one activity to the next or to the end node. The decision of where to route an Agent next is made by using the node's routing information and the data provided by the Agent (see also Section 4.2). A routing node is always followed by at least one activity node or by the end node. Each routing node has a Rule-Base, a Default Case-Base, and a Default Agent Instruction as illustrated in Figure 2.

The *Rule-Base* contains all business rules that are relevant for this routing node. A business rule is specified in the form "IF Condition THEN Agent Instruction". *Case-Bases* are used at two locations in the process definition: a Default Case-Base is part of a routing node and is used when no rule fires. Additionally, a Case-Base can be attached to any business rule to implicitly update this rule. Each case C in the Case-Base consists of a set of question-answer pairs $(QA_1..QA_n)$ and a set of actions

$(A_1..A_n)$. For each action, an Agent Instruction is specified. The case structure has been adapted from NaCoDAE [22]. The internal representation of a case within CBRFlow is illustrated in Figure 3.

```
<CASE ID="c15" TITLE="No hotel needed" DESCRIPTION "No hotel needed because
private accommodation is available.">
  <QAPAIRS>
    <QAPAIR QUESTION="Private accommodation available?" ANSWER="Yes"/>
    <QAPAIR QUESTION="Distance from conference center?" ANSWER="Very short"/>
  </QAPAIRS>
  <ACTIONSSET>
    <ACTION ID="A1" DESCRIPTION="">
      <AGENTINSTRUCTION OPCODE="JMP" PARAM1="RN4"/>
    </ACTION>
  </ACTIONSET>
</CASE>
```

Fig. 3. XML-representation of a case

The *Default Agent Instruction* specifies what to do when no rule fires and no cases are available.

Activity Nodes. Activity nodes are used to perform tasks such as using interactive applications or web services (see [21]). An activity node has an In-Queue to let Agents wait until processing can continue. After finishing an activity, the Agent is put into the Out-Queue, if the execution was successful, or in case of an error, into the Error-Queue and a state object is added to the Agent's status for further analysis in the next routing node(s).

4.2 Navigation Between Nodes

The connection between nodes is implemented by Agent Instructions. To move the Agent forward from one node to another, each node contains information about its successor(s) in the form of a Default Agent Instruction. Only the end node does not specify a successor. At each node the Agent is provided with the information needed to know where to go next. As the Agent is about to leave a node, the Default Agent Instruction is fetched and the action specified by the Default Agent Instruction is performed. In general, this is done in the form of a JMP instruction, which contains a reference to the next node and can be interpreted as a simplified ECA-rule (Event-Condition-Action-rule) with an empty condition part.

The Rule-Base within the routing node facilitates decision-based routing of the Agent and enables selecting one out of several possible succeeding nodes. The Rule-Base contains the relevant business rules for this routing node. If a rule fires during workflow execution, the Agent Instruction of the fired rule (i.e., action part) is executed.

In contrast to rules, cases are not applied automatically but require user interaction. Cases can be applied by the workflow user when exceptions arise or annotations to the predefined workflow model become necessary. CBRFlow applies the standard CCBR problem-solving process for case retrieval as described in [22, 23] except for the following deviation. In contrast to standard CCBR, the users do not need to input a problem description. As all cases in the case-base could be relevant for the users, the system initially presents the questions of the complete set of cases to the users on their demand. They can then retrieve similar cases by answering some of the displayed questions in any order they prefer, i.e., by submitting a query Q which consists of a set of answered questions $(QA_1..QA_m)$ to the system. Finally, the users can select a similar case for reuse. As proposed by [22], similarity is calculated by dividing the number of shared observations minus the number of conflicting observations by the total number of observations in this case (see Equation 1).

$$sim(Q,C) = \frac{same(Q_{qa}, C_{qa}) - diff(Q_{qa}, C_{qa})}{|C_{qa}|} \quad (1)$$

The Agent Instruction specified in the action part of the case is then executed by the Agent.

When no rule fires or no rule is available, the Agent fetches the Agent Instruction from the Default Case-Base or, if that case-base is empty, from the Default Agent Instruction.

4.3 Core Components and Their Collaborations

Figure 4 shows the main architectural components: the Workflow Enactment Service, the CCBR system, the User Portal, the Configuration Tool and the Business Process Repository, and the collaborations between them. It further illustrates how the architecture of CBRFlow can be mapped to the reference model of the Workflow Management Coalition (see also [21]).

The *Workflow Enactment Service (WES)* is responsible for the execution and control of workflows based on a predefined workflow model. The *Conversational Case-Based Reasoning* (CCBR) system is used to implicitly update the workflow model during run-time to allow for dynamic changes. The *User Portal* is a graphical user interface and facilitates the interaction of the user with the Workflow Enactment Service. During workflow modeling, the *Configuration Tool* is used to create a computerized model of a business process and stores it in the *Business Process Repository (BPR)*.

The applications and the data persistency (Business Object Repository) are not part of CBRFlow, but are provided by external systems. CBRFlow provides a process layer, which is built on top of existing applications to support their orchestration and underneath the presentation layer, which provides the user interface. The responsibilities of the different layers and their collaborations are detailed below (Figure 5).

The *presentation layer,* consisting of the User Portal, provides the user interface for the users of the WFMS. The screen display and the user interactions are the only components that are handled on the client machine. A To-Do-List metaphor is used in the User Portal, listing all pending activities grouped by the users' roles.

The *process layer* separates business logic from presentation, the applications and data storage. It is responsible for controlling and executing workflows and includes the Workflow Enactment Service, the Business Process Repository and the CCBR system.

CBRFlow: Enabling Adaptive Workflow Management   441

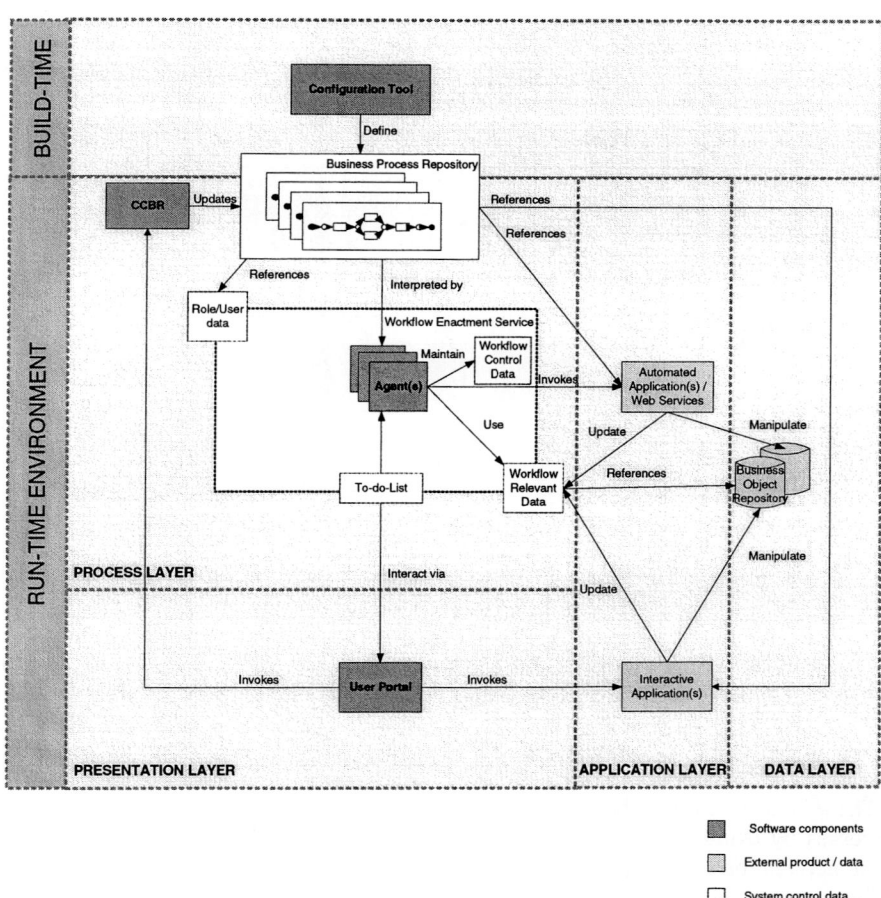

Fig. 4. Architectural mapping to the reference model of the Workflow Management Coalition

The execution of a workflow is triggered by an external event (e.g., a request for a new conference trip) or a message received containing some Business Object(s) to work on. Then, the Workflow Enactment Service instantiates the corresponding workflow definition from the Business Process Repository by creating an Agent to control the execution of the workflow instance. The Agent is set onto the starting point of the selected workflow and follows the flow as specified in the workflow definition (see Section 4.2). Deviations from the workflow model can be made using CCBR. After completing the workflow, the Agent is removed from the workflow enactment service and its execution history is kept for future reference, analysis and auditing.

The process layer interacts with the presentation layer by assigning work to specified roles (i.e., by updating the presentation layer's To-Do-Lists of the users holding these roles). The process layer communicates with the application layer by invoking applications automatically (e.g., by using Web Services) or as requested by the user.

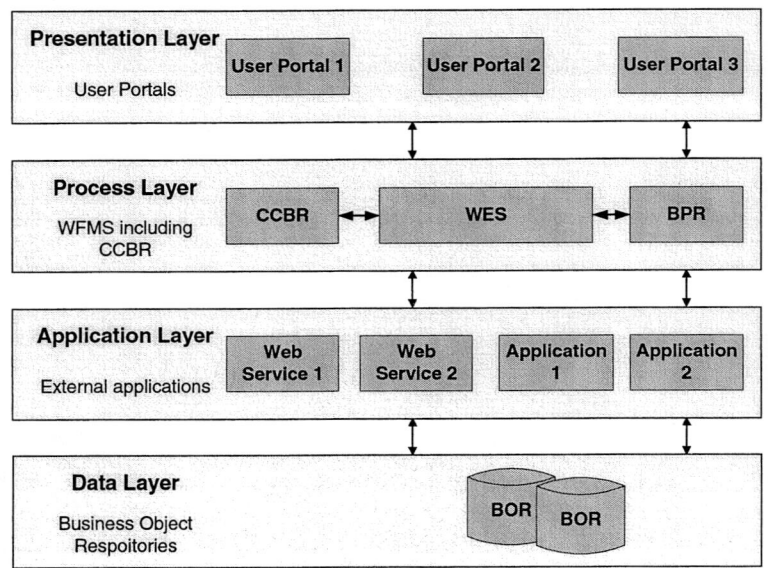

Fig. 5. CBRFlow's 4-Layer architecture

The *application layer* is responsible for providing services and executing applications. The application layer communicates with the data layer by requesting the Business Objects required for the completion of the tasks. The Business Objects are modified by the services and applications and are finally handed back to the data layer for persistency.

The *data layer* allows the separation of data management from the applications and processes by using a *Business Object Repository (BOR)*, which provides persistency to the applications' data. The data layer can also be used to provide persistency to the WFMS, e.g., to workflow models, Agents and the Agent's history.

4.4 Example

Based on the previously elaborated architecture the research prototype CBRFlow has been developed to demonstrate how CCBR can be applied to support run-time changes to the workflow model to increase flexibility and adaptability. The implementation of the research prototype is illustrated by a simplified example from the travel domain.

4.4.1 The Travel Planning Process

Figure 6 illustrates the travel planning process of ProcessGuru Inc., a fictitious corporation. It represents how ProcessGuru Inc. does the planning of a trip to a conference. The travel planning process consists of the following five tasks: choose destination, book a flight, book a hotel, and check public transportation schedules or book a rental car. After choosing the destination, a flight is booked, then the hotel is booked and finally, depending on the availability of public transportation, the schedules are checked, or a rental car is booked.

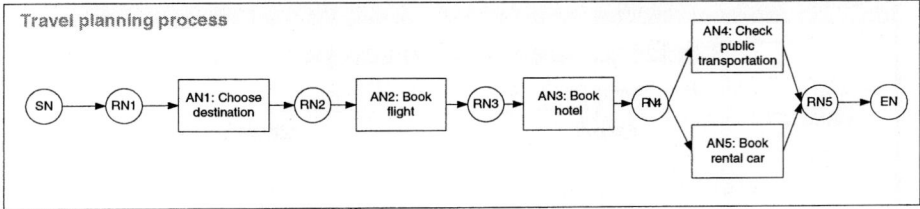

Fig. 6. Travel Planning Process Example

4.4.2 The Implementation

During workflow execution, all workflow users communicate with the workflow enactment service via their respective User Portal. The User Portal allows them to (1) login to the Workflow Enactment Service (2) select an Agent to execute an activity, and to (3) perform changes to a workflow instance represented by the selected Agent. The execution of the travel planning process is illustrated by observing one workflow user at work.

Login
The workflow user starts the User Portal on her PC and logs in using her credentials. The User Portal opens and all open activities for all of her roles are listed in her To-Do-List.

Select an Agent and Execute Activity
The left panel of the User Portal shows all pending activities grouped by the user's roles (like in Figure 7). Currently, there is only a single open task listed for the "Book hotel role". To execute the "Book hotel" activity the user double-clicks the Agent waiting for the "Book hotel" activity and the corresponding application is invoked. After completion, the Agent is added to the Out-Queue of the activity node AN3 and is routed via RN4 – as no public transportation is available - to the "Book rental car" activity.

Perform Change by Adding a New Case
When planning a new conference journey the workflow user selects the "Book hotel" activity for execution. However, because a friend lives near the conference center, no hotel is needed; she wants to skip the activity and stay at the private accommodation. Therefore she has to make a change to the workflow and adds a new case to the casebase (see Figure 7).

She specifies the problem, enters a set of observations and a solution to the problem. The problem part of the case details why the predefined workflow model cannot be applied. Each observation represents a reason why things should be done differently than specified in the workflow model and describes a condition under which the case is applicable. By adding observations the system is taught the relevant attributes for applying this case. In the future, accessing this case again and deciding, if it is an effective solution, can help her and the other workflow users when a similar situation arises. The solution part specifies the alternate execution path, e.g., the user skips the "Book hotel" activity.

The newly added case is then applied, the "Book hotel" activity is skipped and the Agent is forwarded directly to routing node RN4. Knowing that no public transporta-

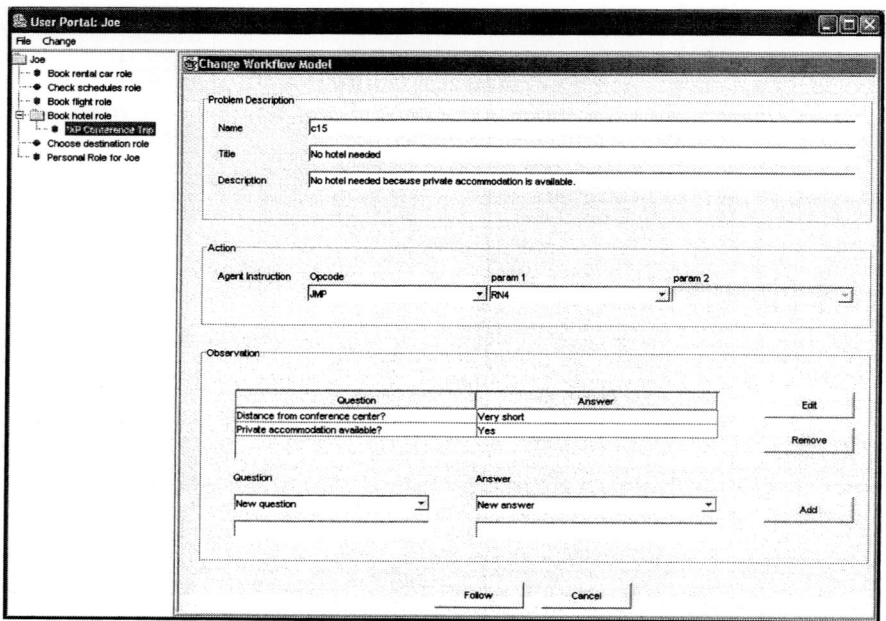

Fig. 7. Perform a change to the workflow model by adding a new case

tion is available, the user performs the activity "Book rental car" and the travel planning process is then finalized.

In a traditional WFMS without support for run-time change, the user would have had to circumvent the system. The user could have aborted the running workflow instance and handled the situation outside the WFMS. As an alternative, the user could have executed the workflow instance following its predefined execution path and have made a reservation for the hotel - even though the user is sleeping at a friend's home – and then have cancelled the hotel reservation after completing the workflow instance.

In a WFMS that supports ad-hoc changes, the user could have easily skipped the activity "Book hotel", but as no learning would have taken place, the knowledge about the less expensive alternative of sleeping at a friend's home would have been lost and could not have been reused in similar situations in the future.

Perform a Change by Reusing a Similar Case

During a later execution of the travel planning process, a new entry is added for the "Book hotel" role in the user's To-Do-List. As cases exist for the previous routing node, the Agent is marked with an asterisk and the user examines the case-base by single clicking the Agent. A mixed-initiative dialogue is then initiated by the system and the user can retrieve similar cases by answering some of the questions in any order preferred. Similar cases can then be applied directly without change or after case adaptation.

Abstract Cases to Rules
When the "Book hotel" activity is skipped more often due to the availability of private accommodation, the WFMS sends a notification to the workflow modeler to perform the suggested case abstraction. The case abstraction itself is currently a manual task and not implemented in CBRFlow. To get an overview of the cases in the Case-Base, the workflow modeler examines them and reflects about which rules could be abstracted from the retrieved case(s). Cooperating with the domain experts and the frontline workers the workflow modeler then defines a set of rules, adds them to the Rule-Base and removes the corresponding case(s) from the Case-Base.

5 Related Work

This paper is based on the idea of integrating workflow management and case-based reasoning. In related work CBR has been applied to support workflow modeling [24, 25], to the configuration of complex core processes [26], to the handling of exceptions [6] and for the composition of Web Services [27].

METEOR [6] models organizational processes with justified ECA-rules and supports the handling of exceptions by using CBR. When no rule fires or any other exception occurs the WFMS tries to derive a capable exception handler, and, if no handler is found, CBR is used to retrieve similar cases to reuse the information about previous exceptions. Human interaction is only necessary if no acceptable solution can be automatically derived.

Our approach uses CBR not only for the handling of exceptions, but empowers the user to implicitly update the workflow model to changing requirements at run-time without demanding an exception generated by the system. CBR can not only be applied when no rule fires, but also to annotate a rule with cases in order to make deviations from that rule. The decision whether to reuse a case is not automated, but is always left to the user. Therefore, when business processes must be executed in an (almost) fully automated way, the application of CCBR might be infeasible. CBRFlow requires the users to be problem solvers, not just process followers as they are entitled to deviate from the predefined workflow model.

In WorkBrain [26], CBR is used for the configuration of complex core processes using process components. Due to the long configuration time needed this approach is most suitable for long-running, complex core processes. WorkBrain does not provide support for workflow adaptation, as CBR is only used at entry time.

DWMSS (document-based workflow modeling support system) uses a CBR approach to support workflow modeling [24]. Existing know-how about the business processes, stored as cases, is reused for the modeling of new workflows. Similarly, [25] propose the application of CBR for the retrieval and reuse of workflow models.

CBR has also been applied for the composition of Web Services, i.e., for service recovery based on user requirements [27].

Related work also includes AI planning, adaptive workflow management and Organizational Memory Information Systems (OMIS). AI planning, especially mixed-initiative case-based planning (e.g., NaCoDAE/HTN [28], MI-CBP [29], SiN [30] and HICAP [31]), can be seen as complementary to our approach as we primarily focus on the execution of workflows and not on modeling or planning.

Adaptive workflow management research suggests exception handling mechanisms and (ad hoc) run-time modifications to the predefined workflow model in order to provide adaptability and flexibility. Expected exceptions are handled by ECA-rules [3, 6, 32] while unexpected exceptions are either handled by supporting dynamic (ad-hoc) modifications to the workflow model [3, 5] or using knowledge-based approaches [6, 32, 33]. All of these systems rely on a predefined workflow model and try to avoid user interactions.

While adaptive workflows cover both well and low structured parts of business processes, Organizational Memory Information Systems (OMIS) are suitable for knowledge intensive workflows (weakly structured) and are often used to provide additional process information to the users in order to support them during the execution of activities (e.g., KnowMore [34], DECOR [35], FRODO [36]).

6 Conclusions and Further Studies

This paper presents an architecture for an adaptive WFMS. The application of case-based reasoning to workflow management relaxes the strict separation between build-time and run-time and supports run-time modifications to the workflow model. This immediate feedback resolves uncertainty, and permits rapid incorporation of the results of the learning processes into subsequent workflow executions. CBRFlow's underlying approach allows the application of many of the values and principles advocated by agile and lean software development [20].

Ongoing work includes an industrial strength implementation of this prototype in the logistics domain and research on how to balance the trade-offs between flexibility and security. Additionally, clear criteria for the decision when to stop the initial modeling should be defined and guidelines for abstracting frequently reused cases into rules should be developed to support both the user and the workflow modeler. In order to free the case-base from obsolete knowledge, an aging or MRU (most recently used) factor should be implemented into the CCBR sub-system and be evaluated.

References

1. Shet, A.; Georgakopoulos, D.; Joosten, S.; Rusinkiewicz, M.; Scacchi, W.; Wilden, J.; Wolf, A.: Report from the NSF Workshop on Workflow and Process Automation in Information Systems., University of Georgia, October 1996.
2. Sadiq, W.; Marjanovic, O.; Orlowska, M. E.: Managing Change and Time in Dynamic Workflow Processes. In: International Journal of Cooperative Information Systems 9 (2000) 1 & 2, pp. 93-116.
3. Casati, F.; Ceri, C.; Pernici, B.; Pozzi, G.: Workflow Evolution. In: Data and Knowledge Engineering 24 (1998) 3, pp. 211-238.
4. Alonso, G.; Agrawal, D.; El Abbadi, A.; Mohan, C.: Functionality and Limitations of Current Workflow Management Systems. In: IEEE Expert, Special Issue on Cooperative Information Systems 1997.
5. Reichert, M.; Dadam, P.: ADEPTflex – Supporting Dynamic Changes of Workflows Without Loosing Control. In: Journal of Intelligent Information Systems, Special Issue on Workflow Management 10 (1998) 2, pp. 93-129.
6. Luo, Z.; Shet, A.; Kochut, K.; Miller, J.: Exception Handling in Workflow Systems. In: Applied Intelligence 13 (2000) 2, pp. 125-147.

7. Gadatsch, A.: Management von Geschäftsprozessen, Methoden und Werkzeuge für die IT-Praxis: Eine Einführung für Studenten und Praktiker, 2. Auflage, Vieweg Verlag, Braunschweig, Wiesbaden 2002.
8. Herbst, H.: Business Rule-Oriented Conceptual Modeling. Contributions to Management Science. Springer-Verlag, 1997.
9. Chiu, D.K.W.; Chan, W.C.W.; Lam, G.K.W.; Cheung, S.C.: An Event Driven Approach to Customer Relationship Management in e-Brokerage Industry. In: Proceedings of the 36th Annual Hawaii International Conference on System Sciences, p. 182a.
10. Aha, D. W.; Muñoz-Avila, H.: Introduction: Interactive Case-Based Reasoning. In: Applied Intelligence 14 (2001) 1, pp. 7-8.
11. Allen, J.: Mixed-Initiative Interaction. In: IEEE Intelligent Systems 14 (1999) 5, pp. 14-16.
12. Aha, D. W.; Maney, T.; and Breslow, L. A.: Supporting dialogue inferencing in conversational case-based reasoning. In: Proceedings of EWCBR-98, Springer, Berlin 1998, pp. 262-273.
13. Branting, L.K.; Porter, B.W.: Rules and precedents as complementary warrants. In: Proceedings of the Ninth National Conference on Artificial Intelligence (AAAI-91), MIT Press, Anaheim, CA 1991, pp. 3-9.
14. Rissland, E.L; Skalak, D.E.: CABARET: Rule Interpretation in a Hybrid Architecture. International Journal of Man-Machine Studies. 34 (6) 1991, pp. 839-887.
15. Leake, D. B. (ed.): Case-Based Reasoning: Experiences, Lessons, and Future Directions. AAAI Press / The MIT Press, Menlo Park 1996.
16. Watson, I.; Marir, F.: Case-Based Reasoning: A Review. In: The Knowledge Engineering Review 9 (1994) 4, pp. 327-354.
17. Slade, S.: Case-based reasoning: A research paradigm. In: AI Magazine 12 (1991) 1, pp. 42-55.
18. Marling, C.; Sqalli M.; Rissland, E.; Muñoz-Avila, H.; Aha, D. W: Case-Based Reasoning Integrations. In: AI Magazine 23 (2002) 1, pp. 69-85.
19. Weber, B.; Wild, W.: Agile Approach To Workflow Modeling. In: Proceedings of Modellierung 2004, Marburg, Germany (23.-26. März 2004), S. 187-201.
20. Weber B.; Werner, W.: Application of Lean and Agile Principles to Workflow Management. In: Proceedings of the Fifth International Conference on Extreme Programming and Agile Processes in Software Engineering, Springer, Berlin 2004.
21. Weber, B.: Integration of Workflow Management and Case-Based Reasoning: Supporting Business Process Management through an Adaptive Workflow Management System. Dissertation, Innsbruck 2003.
22. Aha, D. W.; Breslow, L. A.; Muñoz-Avila, H.: Conversational Case-Based Reasoning. In: Applied Intelligence 14 (2001) 1, pp. 9-32.
23. Gupta, K.; Aha, D. W.: Causal query elaboration in conversational case-based reasoning. In: Proceedings of the Fifteenth Conference of the Florida AI Research Society. AAAI Press, Pensacola Beach, FL 2002.
24. Kim, J.; Suh, W; Lee, H.: Document-based workflow modeling: a case-based reasoning approach. In: Expert Systems with Applications 23 (2002) 2, pp. 77-93.
25. Madhusudan, T.; Zhao, J.L.: A Case-based Framework for Workflow Model Management. Netherlands, June, 2003. Accepted at the 3rd Business Process Management Conference.
26. Wargitsch, C.: Ein Beitrag zur Integration von Workflow- und Wissensmanagement unter besonderer Berücksichtigung komplexer Geschäftsprozesse. Dissertation, Erlangen, Nürnberg 1998.
27. Limthanmaphon, B.; Zhang, Y.: Web Service Composition with Case-based Reasoning, Proceedings of 15th Australasian Database Conferences (ADC2003), Feb. 2002, Australia.
28. Muñoz-Avila, H.; McFarlane, D.; Aha, D.W., Ballas, J.; Breslow, L.A.; Nau, D.: Using guidelines to constrain interactive case-based HTN planning. In: Proceedings of the Third International Conference on Case-Based Reasoning, Springer, Munich 1999, pp. 288-302.

29. Veloso, M.; Mulvehill, A.M.; Cox, M.T.: Rationale-supported mixed-initiative case-based planning. In: Proceedings of the Ninth conference on Innovative Applications of Artificial Intelligence. Providence, AAAI Press, RI 1997, pp. 1072-1077.
30. Muñoz-Avila, H.; Aha, D.W.; Nau D. S.; Breslow, L.A.; Weber, R.; Yamal, F.: SiN: Integrating Case-based Reasoning with Task Decomposition. In: Proc. IJCAI-2001, AAAI Press, pp. 99-104.
31. Muñoz-Avila, H.; Gupta, K.; Aha, D.W.; Nau, D.S.: Knowledge Based Project Planning. In: Dieng-Kunz R.; Matta, N. (eds.): Knowledge Management and Organizational Memories. Kluwer Academic Publishers, July 2002.
32. Hwang, S.; Tang, J.: Consulting past exceptions to facilitate workflow exception handling. In: Decision Support Systems 37 (2004) 1, pp. 49-69.
33. Klein, M.; Dellarocas, C.: A Knowledge-based Approach to Handling Exceptions in Workflow Systems. In: Computer Supported Cooperative Work 9 (2000) 3-4, pp. 399–412.
34. Abecker, A.; Bernardi, A.; Hinkelmann, K.; Kühn, O.; Sintek, M.: Context-Aware, Proactive Delivery of Task-Specific Knowledge: The KnowMore Project. In: Int. Journal on Information Systems Frontiers 2 (2000) 3/4, pp. 139-162.
35. Abecker, A.; et al.: Enabling Workflow-Embedded OM Access With the DECOR Toolkit. In: Rose Dieng-Kuntz and Nada Matta (eds.): Knowledge Management and Organizational Memories. Kluwer Academic Publishers, July 2002.
36. Abecker, A.; Bernardi, van Elst, L.: Agent technology for distributed organizational memories. In: Proc. ICEIS-03, Vol. 2, pp. 3-10.

CASEP2: Hybrid Case-Based Reasoning System for Sequence Processing

Farida Zehraoui, Rushed Kanawati, and Sylvie Salotti

LIPN-CNRS, UMR 7030, Université Paris 13, 99,
Av Jean Baptiste Clément 93430 Villetaneuse, France
{rushed.kanawati,sylvie.salotti,farida.zehraoui}@lipn.univ-paris13.fr

Abstract. We present in this paper a hybrid neuro-symbolic system called "CASEP2", which combines the case-based reasoning with an adequate artificial neural network "M-SOM-ART" for sequence classification or prediction task. In CASEP2, we present a new case modelling by dynamic covariance matrices. This model takes into account the temporal dynamics contained in the sequences and allows to avoid problems related to the comparison of different length sequences. In the CBR cycle, one neural network is used during the retrieval phase for indexing the case base and another is used during the reuse phase in order to provide the target case solution.

1 Introduction

This work reports on the problem of sequence classification or prediction and case base maintenance using hybrid neuro-symbolic systems (case-based reasoning (CBR) and artificial neural network (ANN)). The classification task associates one class to each case and the prediction task consists in predicting a future value of the sequence using its past values.

Our study is motivated by an application, which consists in predicting user behaviour in an e-commerce Web site. Past experiences are provided from the site users' Web log files. This application is characterized by the huge amount of data; the temporal aspect of these data; the presence of noise and real time constraints (we must do the sequence processing before the end of the user navigation in the site). In addition, background knowledge is not available.

The use of case-based reasoning for sequence processing introduces some aspects that don not exist in the processing of "attribute-value" data.

These aspects concern mainly the case representation. The case can be represented by a succession of instants (or points) or by relations between temporal intervals [11]. In addition, the sequences can be very long and with different lengths. The choice of the case granularity is necessary. The case is represented by the whole sequence [19] or by a part of the sequence (sub-sequence) [9].

Moreover, the huge amount of data and the presence of noise in these data associated to the real time constraints make the case base maintenance of the CBR system necessary. In this paper, we present a hybrid system "CASEP2" for sequence classification (or prediction) task. In this system, a new case representation, which takes into account temporal aspect of the sequences is presented. A new neural network adapted to sequence processing is used in the retrieval and the reuse phases of the CBR cycle. In the retrieval phase, the ANN indexes the case base by dividing it into several parts, which is considered as a form of case base maintenance. In the reuse phase, the ANN provides the target cases solutions and preserves learned knowledge from the sub-sequence processing in the same sequence. The first ANN is also used to provide the solutions without using the CBR component.

The paper is organized as follows. Section 2 addresses the sequence processing using CBR and hybrid neuro-CBR systems. Section 3 details CASEP2 system. Section 4 compares our approach to some related work. Section 5 shows our experimental results. Section 5 presents the current state of our work and future work.

2 Related Work

Most of CBR systems consider episodes as distinct in time. However, temporal relationships may exist between parameters in a case and they are generally ignored. Some CBR works have addressed sequence processing. We can classify these works according to the case representation that they have used.

In a first classification, we distinguish the cases that are represented by succession of instants (or points) from those represented by relations between temporal intervals. The representation based on succession of instants was used in several fields like the information research field [10] and the forest fire forecasting field [19]. The representation with interval relations is proposed in [11]. It is a new representation, which is more "rich" than the first one. A case represents different relations between temporal intervals. These relations use the Allen temporal logic. The point representation of a case takes into account the temporal information contained in the case in a simple manner. This representation was used successfully in several fields. The representation of case with relations between temporal intervals is a new approach that is not often used. This approach is certainly more complex than the first one, but makes the representation of more precise information in a case possible. The complexity of case structure can represent some inconvenient, especially when we have huge amount of data with time constraints, as in our application. However, we think that this representation is interesting and can be useful in fields where the point representation of a case can fail.

A second classification distinguishes works where the case represents the whole sequence from those where the case is a sub-sequence. Several works have used the representation of a case with the whole sequence, let's mention the REBECAS system [19] for forest fire forecasting, the Radix system [4], which is a web navigation advisor and the recommender system PADIM [6]. The representation of a case with the sub-sequence was introduced in the recommendation approach BROADWAY [9]. Different applications of this approach use this representation; let's mention the BROADWAYV1 system [10] and the BeCBKB system [13], which is a query refiner. The CASEP system [25, 22] used for sequence prediction and the COBRA system [17] that predicts the user actions in a web site, also use this representation. The representation of a case with a whole sequence allows avoiding an additional storage of more precise knowledge. However, in the majority of the systems that use this representation, no lesson is learned from the different reasoning cycles done during the sequence evolution, as in the REBECAS system, where the addition of the complete sequences to the case base is the only operation done to update the knowledge of the system. Moreover, the retrieval of a whole sequence is time consuming. The representation of a case with sub-sequences can require more memory capacity if the whole sequences and the cases are kept in the memory. The advantage of this representation is that, for each reasoning step, useful knowledge is learned by the system. The different reasoning steps are taken into consideration during the sequence evolution, as in Broadway [9] and CASEP [25, 22], can allow improving the system results in order to reduce the source cases retrieval time and to avoid the preceding failures.

Most of the systems described above do not consider the problems of case base maintenance in the CBR system[1] and the control of the size and the content of the system memory. In CASEP system [25, 22], maintenance measurements are associated to the cases in order to take into account the presence of noise in data and to reduce the case base. This leads to improve CBR system results. But in this system, cases are represented by sub-sequences with a fixed length. This presents limitation in several applications. The reduction of the case base is not important enough to satisfy real time constraints. In order to improve the system results and efficiency, we propose the hybrid neuro-CBR system CASEP2.

Neuro-symbolic hybrid systems can be classified according to the degree or the mode of integration of the neural and the symbolic components.

The integration degree represents the degree of communication and the information flow between the components [18]. The communication can be done using files (loosely coupled systems); shared memory and data structures (tightly coupled systems); or functions (total integration). The components integration mode represents the way in which the symbolic and the neural components are configured in relation to each other and to the overall system. Four integration modes are proposed in [18, 8, 7]: chainprocessing, subprocessing, metaprocessing and coprocessing.

In chainprocessing mode, one of the modules (either symbolic or neural) can be the main processor while the other takes a charge of pre-processing or post-processing. In subprocessing mode, one of the two modules is subordinated to the other, which acts as the main problem solver. In metaprocessing mode, one module is the base level problem solver and the other plays a metalevel role (such as monotoring, control, or performance improvement) towards the first. In coprocessing, the symbolic and the neural modules are equal partners in the problem solving process.

Many hybrid neuro-CBR systems are proposed in the literature. Among the systems, which use the subprocessing mode, we can distinguish those in which the

---

[1] A description of the case base maintenance problem can be found in [25].

main processor is the neural module, like PROBIS system [15, 16] that integrates a CBR module and an incremental neural network containing prototype (ARN2), from those in which the main processor is the CBR module. Let's mention, for example, the CBR system proposed in [3] that uses a radial bases functions neural network (RBF) in the reuse phase of the CBR cycle; the CBR system proposed in [5], which is an extension of the preceding system, uses two different neural networks: Growing Cell Structure (GCS) for indexing the cases in the retrieval phase and an RBF network in the reuse phase; and a CBR system proposed in [12] that uses LVQ3 neural network in the retrieval phase.

Among the systems which use the coprocessing mode, let's mention the system proposed in [20] in which the two modules (ANN and CBR) cooperate to provide a prediction. When the two predictors give close values, the system returns the predicted value. When the provided results are considerably different, the system indicates that the decision cannot be made by the system and that the intervention of experts is necessary for the rejected cases.

These models are used in different real applications like a psychotrope-induced comas, plastic modelling injection process, ocean temperature prediction, ...etc. The majority of the described systems do not process the temporal data. In [3, 5], the systems perform the prediction task in a complex field where the data are temporal sequences, but this temporal aspect of the data was taken into account only by representing the cases by temporal windows with fixed length. This could be restrictive in many applications. We propose a hybrid neuro-CBR system CASEP2 where the temporal aspect of data is taken into account by using a new case modelling and an adequate ANN. A maintenance strategy is also proposed in order to process the great amount of data and the noise contained in these data.

3 CASEP2 Specification

In CASEP2 (see the figure 1), a neural network M-SOM-ART [24, 23] indexes the cases of the case base and provides some target cases solutions without using the CBR component. Another ANN performs classifications (or predictions) in the reuse phase of the CBR component. The case base is divided into several parts. Each part is indexed by a neuron except one called atypical part [15, 16]. This one contains cases added to the case base during the use mode of the system.

CASEP2 functions according to two modes:

- *Off line construction mode:* the neural network is trained. It builds prototypes and indexes the case base by dividing it into several parts and by linking each part (except one) to a neuron. A reduction of the case base is also done.
- *On line use mode:* when a new target case is presented to the system, a neuron is activated in the ANN. If the confidence associated to the neuron class or prediction value (the target case solution) is greater than a threshold β, this solution is returned by the system and the CBR component is not used. Else the CBR component is used. If the activated neuron is linked to

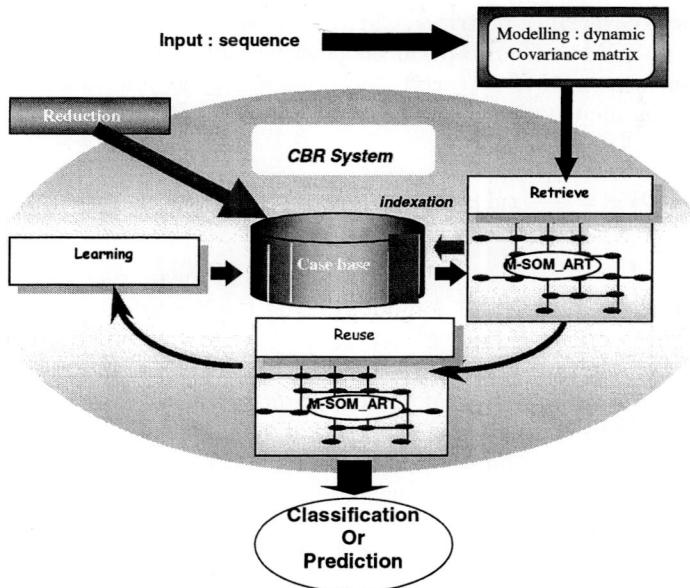

Fig. 1. CASEP2 architecture.

a part of the case base, then a search for similar cases to the target case is done in this part. Else, the search is done in the atypical part. Cases are added to the case base during the use mode of the system. These cases are used for the ANN training during the construction phase.

The CBR cycle phases are described below.

3.1 Artificial Neural Network Description

The neural network used in CASEP2 is the M-SOM-ART [24, 23] network which has the following properties:

- performs classification (or prediction) and clustering tasks;
- processes temporal sequences;
- has plasticity and stability properties.

This network is a temporal growing neural network which integrates a self-organizing map (SOM) [14] in an Adaptive Resonance Theory (ART) paradigm [2]. This paradigm incorporates in SOM stability and plasticity properties. The stability concerns the preservation of previously learned knowledge and the plasticity concerns the adaptation to any change in the input environment.

The ART paradigm controls the neural network evolution by introducing a vigilance test, which verifies if the activated neuron is rather close to the input. The temporal aspect of the data is taken into account by modelling sequences using dynamic covariance matrices. Clusters of cases are formed and indexed by prototypes. M-SOM-ART also performs classification (or prediction) task.

The input sequence $X = (x(i) \in R^n)$ $(1 \leq i \leq p_X)$ is modelled using its associated dynamic covariance matrix $COV_X \in R^n \times R^n$ defined as follows [24, 23]:

$$COV_X = \frac{1}{p_X}[x(1)x(1)^T + \sum_{i=2}^{p_X}(x(i) - \bar{x}(i))(x(i) - \bar{x}(i))^T]$$

where $\bar{x}(t) = \frac{1}{t}\sum_{i=1}^{t} x(i)$ $(t \geq 2)$ is the dynamic mean vector associated to $x(t) \in R^n$ in the sequence and computed using the precedents and the current vectors $\{x(i)\}$, $(1 \leq i \leq t)$, and x^T represents the transposed vector of x.

This model allows representing the position (because the mean vector is introduced in the computation of the covariance matrix) and the shape of the cloud of points representing the sequence. A dynamic mean vector is introduced in the covariance matrix computation in order to take into account the order of the vectors in the sequence. All sequences models have the same dimension.

The distance between a covariance matrix $COV_X = (x_{ij})$, $1 \leq i,j \leq n$ and neuron weights $W_c = (w_{ij}^c)$, $1 \leq i,j \leq n$ is the Frobenius matricial distance (fd) given by:

$$fd(COV_X, W_c) = [tr(COV_X - W_c)^T(COV_X - W_c)]^{1/2} = [\sum_i \sum_j (x_{ij} - w_{ij}^c)^2]^{1/2}$$

where $tr(M)$ is the trace of the matrix M and X^T is the transposed of the vector X.

The M-SOM-ART learning algorithm is described in Algorithm 3.1.

The choice of this network is based on its properties. It performs sequence clustering task for indexing the case base and classification (or prediction) task for providing target cases solutions. The temporal aspect of the data is taken into account and the stability-plasticity properties are very important for a long time use of the system.

3.2 General Description

For sake of clarification, we start by introducing some notations used later in the paper. A sequence q represents an ordered set of states (in our application, a sequence represents a user's navigation in a site).

A state $E_q^j = (v_i)$, $1 \leq i \leq n$ of the sequence q is characterized by the values v_i $(1 \leq i \leq n)$ of n characteristics c_i $(1 \leq i \leq n)$ and by its position j in the sequence q (a state is an n-dimensional feature vector). In our application, a state represents a page.

The presented problem consists in providing the value s_i of a property S of the states succeeding the current state of the sequence (this property can represent, for example, a predicted characteristic of the following sequence states or a classification of a sequence). In our application, it represents the classification of the site user in one of the two classes {buyer, non buyer}.

Algorithm 3.1 M-SOM-ART learning algorithm.
1. Initialise the set A of neurons to contain one unit c_1.
   Initialise the time parameter t: $t = 0$.
   Initialise the connection set C, $C \subset A \times A$ to the empty set: $C = \emptyset$.
2. Present an input signal $X = (x(i))$ $(1 \le i \le p_X)$, $x(i) \in R^n$
3. Model the input X by its associated dynamic covariance matrix:

$$COV_X = \frac{1}{p_X}[x(1)x(1)^T + \sum_{i=2}^{p_X}(x(i) - \bar{x}(i))(x(i) - \bar{x}(i))^T]$$

   Initialise the reference vector W_{c1} of the first unit c_1 to the dynamic covariance matrix of the first input signal.
4. Determine the winner $s(X) \in A$ by:

$$s(X) = \arg\min_{c \in A} fd(COV_X, W_r)$$

   where fd is the Frobenius distance.
5. Subject the winner $s(X)$ to the vigilance test:
   - **If** ($\frac{1}{1+fd(cov_x, s(X))} \ge \rho$) : $\rho \in [0, 1]$ is the vigilance parameter, adapt each unit c_r according to:

$$\Delta W_r = \epsilon(t) h_{rs}[COV_X - W_{c_r}]$$

   $\epsilon(t)$ is the learning rate, σ is the standard deviation of the Gaussian, σ_i and h_{rs} is the neighbourhood function.
   - **else** add a new unit r in the neighbourhood of the closest neuron to the input in the perimeter of the map, initialise its reference vector W_r by: $W_r = COV_X$.
6. Increase the time parameter t: $t = t + 1$
7. If $(t \le t_{max})$, continue with step 2.
   If $(t = t_{max})$ label each unit using a majority vote on the labels of the inputs that have activated these units.

Case Structure

In CASEP2, any sequence $q(m) = (E_{jq})$, $1 \le j \le m$ is modelled by a dynamic covariance matrix cov_q given by:

$$cov_q(m) = \frac{1}{p}[E_{1q}E_{1q}^T + \sum_{j=2}^{m}(E_{jq} - \bar{q}(j))(E_{jq} - \bar{q}(j))^T]$$

Where $\bar{q}(j)$ represents the dynamic mean vector of the sequence's states and X^T represents the transposed of the vector X.

The problem part of the case is defined by the dynamic covariance matrix associated to the sequence and the solution part is the sequence class (or the predicted value).

The target case problem part represents the current sequence[2], which is also modelled by a dynamic covariance matrix.

---

[2] A sequence is formed at each presentation of a new state, the current sequence is a sub-sequence (a part of the site user navigation) of the whole final sequence.

This model is given by the M-SOM-ART neural network. It allows representing each sequence and its sub-sequences by matrices with the same dimension. This avoids sub-sequences extractions. In addition, in the current sequence $q(m+1)$ corresponding to the target case, the new covariance matrix $cov_{q(m+1)}$ can be computed using the previous one $cov_{q(m)}$ associated to the same sequence $q(m)$ at each presentation of a new state as follows:

$$cov_{q(m+1)} = \frac{m}{m+1} cov_{q(m)} + \frac{1}{m+1}[(E_{(m+1)q} - \bar{q}(m+1))(E_{(m+1)q} - \bar{q}(m+1))^T]$$

Memory Organization

CASEP2 contains a simple indexing system that contains two levels of memory (see figure2):

- Memory that contains prototypical cases (prototypes): it is used during the retrieval phase as an indexing system in order to decrease retrieval time. Each prototype is represented by one neuron, which can index a set of cases (a part of the case base) and can provide target cases solutions. Not all the neurons are linked to the case base.
- Memory that contains real cases (the case base): It is partitioned into several parts by the neural network. The cases are organized into parts of similar cases. Each part, apart one (the atypical part), is linked to a neuron. The atypical part contains the cases added to the case base during the use mode of the system.

The use of the neural network improves the retrieval efficiency. The use of the case base can allow to obtain more precise results than those obtained using only the neural network, which retains just the representative cases (the prototypes).

3.3 Construction Mode

In this phase, the neural network is trained, the construction of the case base and its reduction are done.

CASEP2 Initialisation

Initially, the case base is empty. A training dataset is used for adding cases to the case base and for forming clusters linked to the ANN. This training base contains a set of sequences. These sequences are modelled using dynamic covariance matrices. At the last step of the ANN training phase, the case base is formed. For each presentation of a sequence, one neuron is activated.

Each activated neuron is associated to one part of the case base. Each case that activates a neuron is added to a part linked to this neuron. Maintenance measurements [25] are initialised and associated to the cases added to the case base.

CASEP2 Updating

After the system initialisation, it is used for providing classifications (or predictions) in the use mode. During this mode, cases are added to the atypical part

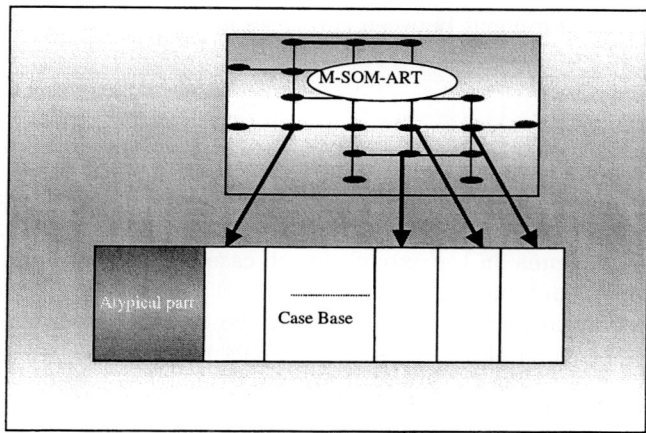

Fig. 2. Memory organisation.

of the case base. This allows their use to provide target cases solutions just after their addition to the system (this makes the system incremental in real time).

When the size of this part is grater than a threshold γ (γ is a system parameter), the system is updated in the construction mode where a training of the neural network is done using the cases contained in the atypical part. Some cases are added to the existing parts and other parts are formed.

Reduction Phase

In this phase, a case base reduction is done in the same way that in CASEP system [25, 22]. Not useful cases are removed from the case base. This allows controlling the contents of the case base. The removal of obsolete cases can also be considered when the system is used for a long time.

3.4 Use Mode

For each presentation of a new state in the current sequence, a new sequence is formed and modelled by a covariance matrix. One neuron is then activated in the neural network.

If the solution confidence associated to the activated neuron is greater than a threshold β, the solution is returned by the system.

Else the CBR component is used. We describe below the CBR cycle in CASEP2.

Retrieve

Several cases are retrieved from the case base.

- If the activated neuron is linked to a part of the case base, a search is done in this part.
- Else the search is done in the atypical part of the case base.

The similarity measurement between two cases modelled by the covariance matrices cov_{q_1} and cov_{q_2} is inversaly proportional to the Frobenius distance, it is given by:

$$similarity(cov_{q_1}, cov_{q_2}) = \frac{1}{1 + fd(cov_{q_1}, cov_{q_2})}$$

The α most similar[3] cases to the target case, such that their similarity to the target case is greater than a similarity threshold, are retrieved. This threshold is variable and depends on the extent of each case [25]. This allows to take into account the noise contained in the data.

For the classification task, if one part of the case base contains only cases belonging to the same class, the search in this part can be avoided and the solution is given by the ANN.

Reuse

In this phase, another M-SOM-ART neural network is used in order to perform classification (or prediction) task. This network use the α retrieved cases as training dataset. Then a class (or a predicted value) is provided for the target case. In order to obtain a neural network with reasonable size (this is necessary for satisfying the real time constraint), M-SOM-ART is initialised for each presentation of a new sequence (corresponding to a new site user's navigation in our application). In the same sequence, the same ANN is used until its end. This allows reusing learned knowledge from previous processing done in the same sequence to provide the current case solution.

Learning

In this phase, the cases are added to the system when the solution is not correct[4] (or do not satisfy some conditions[5]). The update of the maintenance measurements associated to the retrieved cases and the initialisation of these measurements for the added cases are done in the same way as in CASEP [25]. The atypical part contains the learned cases, which can be used in the system just after their addition to the case base, this makes the system incremental in real time.

4 Discussion

In CASEP2, modules are tightly integrated since both CBR and ANN modules communicate using shared memory. Moreover the principal processing is ensured by the CBR component and the two M-SOM-ART neural networks are subprocessors. The first M-SOM-ART network indexes the case base while the second one provides the sequences classification (or prediction) in the reuse phase. We

---

[3] If the number of the retrieved cases is less than α, these cases are used in the reuse phase. If no case is retrieved, the solution is provided by the ANN.
[4] In our application the solution is not correct if the provided class is false.
[5] These conditions can be the belonging to an interval around the solution.

can also view the first M-SOM-ART and the CBR component as co-processors because they both participate to provide the target cases solutions.

In CASEP2, we use the same memory structure as that proposed in PROBIS system [16], but this one does not process the temporal data and the used neural network is different from those used in CASEP2. Moreover the addition of cases is not done in the same manner. In [3, 5], the authors use the neural networks in the different CBR cycle phases to process temporal data, but this temporal aspect is taken into account by defining temporal windows with fixed length to represent the cases. This can limit the systems use in several applications. In CASEP2, no restriction is imposed for the sequence length in the case representation. The temporal data processing is done by an adequate neural network that have the stability and the plasticity properties, which are important for a long-term use of the system. In addition, this network is used in the cases adaptation and takes into account the precedent processing done in the same sequence. The memory organization is not the same as that of CASEP2 (this concerns mainly the atypical part). The ANN used for the case indexation is the GCS, which is a growing SOM that do not take into account the temporal aspect of the data and that do not assure the preservation of old knowledge. In these systems an RBF neural network is used in the reuse phase but do not take into account the temporal aspect of data.

Concerning case representation, in CASEP2 the cases are represented by a succession of instants. They represent sub-sequences with different lengths. We propose a new model of sequences, which takes into account the points (states) distribution and their order in the sequence. In CASEP, the cases have a fixed length and a case base maintenance consists in associating measurements to the cases and in reducing the case base. In CASEP2, we have also used the same measurements and we have performed a case base reduction, but we have, in addition to this, divided the case base into several parts. This leads to improve the system efficiency.

In CASEP, the reuse task consists in computing a confidence associated to each class. A more adequate method is used in CASEP2 since we use M-SOM-ART neural network, which classifies sequences and preserves the preceding processing done in the same sequence.

In CASEP2, the CBR system provides training data sets for the two neural networks; allows the use of the learned cases just after their addition to the case base (this can not be done if the neural network is used alone); and can provide more precise results since concrete cases are used for giving the target cases solutions (in the M-SOM-ART network only prototypes are stored).

5   Experimental Results

We have performed several experiments on log files of an e-commerce Web site, where approximately 3000 navigations are registered every day. More precisely, the behaviour of each site user is described by the information about the succession of pages that he has visited. This succession of pages represents the temporal

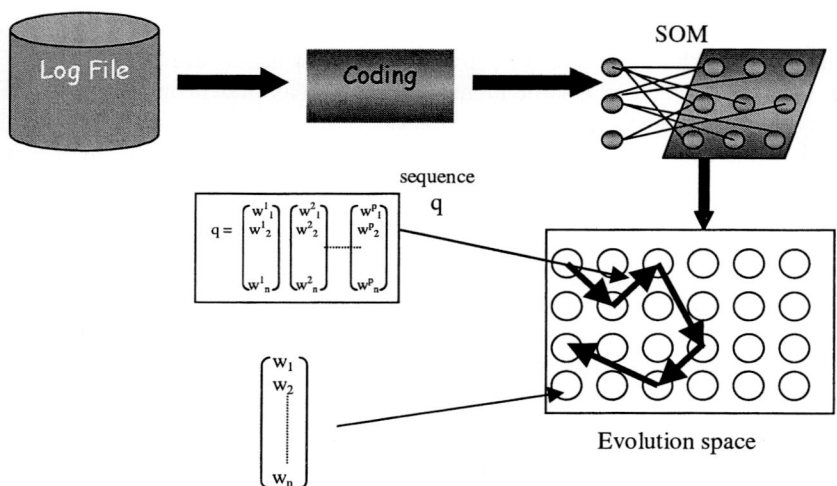

Fig. 3. Data processing.

aspect of the data. Since the log file contains noise, different processing are done before the use of CASEP2 (see figure3).

The data are first filtered in order to remove a part of noise. Then, they are coded using quasi-behavioural matrices [21]. The principle of this coding is to calculate for each page its frequency of precedence and succession over all the other pages and to regroup these frequencies in one matrix. Data are then processed using SOM network in order to obtain an evolution space. The navigation pages are then represented by the weights of the map neurons. The navigation is represented by the succession of these vectors (corresponding to the succession of pages). Navigation lengths are variable.

The goal of the experiments is to classify the site user in one of the two classes {buyer, non-buyer} using CASEP2.

In the experiments, we have used two bases. The first one contains 3000 sequences, it is used in the construction mode in order to initialise the case base. The second one contains 10000 sequences, it is used in the use mode. The buyer sequences represents less than 10% of all the sequences in the two bases.

In order to evaluate CASEP2 system, we have compared its results in the use phase to those obtained using CASEP and M-SOM-ART neural network. In the first experiments, CASEP2 (CASEP2V1 in the tables 1, 2, 3) uses the CBR module to provide the classifications (the neural network is just used to index the case base and in the retrieval phase of the CBR system). In the second ones, CASEP2 uses the M-SOM-ART network for providing target cases solutions without using the CBR component when the confidence associated to the provided class is greater than a threshold β. If this confidence is lower than β, the CBR component is used (the values of β are 0.6, 0.7, and 0.8 corresponding to CASEP2V2(0.6), CASEP2V2(0.7), and CASEP2V2(0.8) in the tables 1, 2, 3). To compare these systems, we have used the following metrics:

- *Recall:* represents the ratio of the number of the correct classifications to the number of queries.
- *Precision:* represents the ratio of the number of the correct classifications to the number of all classifications.
- *Classification rate:* represents the ratio of the number of the classifications to the number of queries.

Preliminary results are shown in the tables 1, 2, 3. Table 1 shows that CASEP2V2 (CASEP2V2(0.6) and CASEP2V2(0.7)) gives better global results than M-SOM-ART and CASEP because it uses the neural network and the CBR components to provide the target cases solutions. The global result increases in CASEP2 with the increasing of the use of the neural network (when the threshold β increases, the neural network use frequency decreases). CASEP2 and M-SOM-ART provide solutions for all target cases, this is not the case for CASEP. Their recall results are better than those of CASEP.

Table 1. Total results comparison.

	CASEP	M-SOM-ART	CASEP2-V2(0.6)	CASEP2-V2(0.7)	CASEP2-V2(0.8)	CASEP2-V1
Classification rate	76,62%	100%	100%	100%	100%	100%
Recall	61%	86,49 %	87,3%	86,82%	84,02%	79,8%
Precision	80%	86,49 %	87,3%	86,82%	84,02%	79,8%

Table 2. Buyer class results comparison.

	CASEP	M-SOM-ART	CASEP2-V2(0.6)	CASEP2-V2(0.7)	CASEP2-V2(0.8)	CASEP2-V1
Recall	43,69%	70,73 %	69,05%	70,33%	75,39%	76,87%
Precision	87,62%	80,76 %	84,77%	82,23%	71,57%	62,60%

Table 3. Non-buyer class results comparison.

	CASEP	M-SOM-ART	CASEP2-V2(0.6)	CASEP2-V2(0.7)	CASEP2-V2(0.8)	CASEP2-V1
Recall	70,61%	93,02%	94,86%	93,70%	87,59%	80,97%
Precision	77,24%	88,46%	88,09%	88,40%	89,58%	89,42%

Tables 2 and 3 show that the increasing of the neural network use in CASEP2 increases the detection of the most frequent class (the non-buyer class) and the increasing of the CBR use improves the rare class (buyer class) detection.

Concerning the system efficiency, CASEP2 processes sequences in less time than CASEP (because the case base is divided into several parts and there is no cases extraction) and the neural nework M-SOM-ART is more efficient than CASEP2. In CASEP2, the increasing of the neural network frequency use increases the efficiency of the system.

These results show that the CBR component can recognize the rare class better than the neural network alone, which better recognizes the most frequent class. In these experiments, one of the CBR or the neural network is used to provide target case solutions.

6 Conclusion and Future Work

We have presented a hybrid neuro-CBR system used for a sequence classification (or prediction) task. A new case model and different interactions between an adequate neural networks and the CBR system are presented. We have performed some experiments on an e-commerce web site. More experiments will be done in different applications and for the prediction task. The similarity measurement used in CASEP2 is based on the Frobenius matricial distance described above. More suitable distances can be used to compare covariance matrices. They use the sphericity measure [1] and are especially conceived for covariance matrices comparison. In future work, we will use these distances to define new similarity measurements between cases.

References

1. F. Bimbot and L. Mathan. Text-free speaker recognition using an arithmetic harmonic sphericity measure. In *Eurospeech'93*, volume 1, pages 169–172, Berlin, Germany, 1993.
2. G.A. Carpenter and S.Grossberg. The art of adaptive pattern recognition by a self-organizing neural network. *IEEE Computer*, 21(3):77–88, march 1988.
3. J.M. Corchado and B. Lees. Adaptation of cases for case based forecasting with neural network support. In Tharam S. Dillon Sankar K. Pal and Daniel S. Yeung, editors, *Soft Computing in Case Based Reasoning*, pages 293–319, March 2000.
4. S. F. Corvaisier, A. Mille, and J. M. Pinon. Information retrieval on the world wide web using a decision making system. *Actes de la 5eme conférence sur la Recherche d'Informations Assistée par Ordinateur sur Internet (RIAO'97), Centre des hautes études internationales d'Informatique, Montréal*, pages 285–295, 1997.
5. F. Fdez-Riverola and J.M. Corchado. Using instance-based reasoning systems for changing environments forecasting. In *Workshop on Applying case-based reasoning to time series prediction*, pages 219–228, Trondheim, Norway, June 2003.
6. B. Fuchs, A. Mille, and B. Chiron. Operator decision aiding by adaptation of supervision strategies. *Case-Based Reasoning Research and Development, proceedings of the 1st International Conference on Case-Based Reasoning (ICCBR'95), LNAI*, 1010:23–32, 1995.
7. M. Hilario, Y. Lallement, and F. Alexandre. Neurosymbolic integration: Unified versus hybrid approaches. In *The European Symposium On Artificial Neural Networks*, Brussels, Belgium, 1995.
8. M. Hilario, C. Pellegrini, and F. Alexandre. Modular integration of connectionist and symbolic processing in knowledge-based systems. In *Proceedings International Symposium on Integrating Knowledge and Neural Heuristics*, Pensacola Beach, Florida, USA, May 1994.

9. M. Jaczynski. *Modèle et plate-forme à objets pour l'indexation par situations comportementales: application à l'assistance à la navigation sur le Web.* Thèse de doctorat, Université de Nice-Sophia Antipolis, 1998.
10. M. Jaczynski and B. Trousse. *www* assisted browsing by reusing past navigations of a group of users. *Proceedings of EWCBR'98, LNAI*, 1488:160–171, 1998.
11. M D. Jaere, A. Aamodt, and P. Skalle. Representing temporal knowledge for case-based prediction. *ECCBR'02*, 2002.
12. G. Jha, S.C. Hui, and S. Foo. A hybrid case-based reasoning and neural network approach to online intelligent fault diagnosis. In *Pro. 3rd International ICSC Symposia on Intelligent Industrial Automation (IIA'99) and Soft Computing (SOCO'99)*, pages 376–381, Genoa, Italy, 1999.
13. R. Kanawati, M. Jaczynski, B. Trousse, and J. M. Andreoli. Applying the broadway recommendation computation approach for implementing a query refinement service in the *cbkb* meta search engine. *Actes de RàPC'99 Raisonnement á Partir de Cas, Plaiseau*, pages 17–26, 1999.
14. T. Kohonen. *Self-Organizing Maps*, volume 30 of *Springer Series in Information Sciences*. Springer, Berlin, Heidelberg, 1995. (Second Extended Edition 1997).
15. M. Malek. *Un modèle hybride de mémoire pour le raisonnement à partir de cas.* Thèse de doctorat, Université J. Fourrier, 1996.
16. M. Malek. Hybrid approaches for integrating neural networks and case based reasoning: From loosely coupled to tightly coupled models. In Tharam S. Dillon Sankar K. Pal and Daniel S. Yeung, editors, *Soft Computing in Case Based Reasoning*, pages 73–94, March 2000.
17. M. Malek and R. Kanawati. Cobra: A cbr-based approach for predicting users actions in web site. 3rd *International Conference on Case-based Resoning ICCBR'01.*, pages 336–346, 2001.
18. K. McGarry, S. Wermter, and J. MacIntyre. Hybrid neural systems: From simple coupling to fully integrated neural networks. *Neural Computing Surveys*, 2:62–93, 1999.
19. S. Rougegrez-Loriette. *Prédiction de processus à partir de comportement observé: le système REBECAS.* Thèse de doctorat, Institut Blaise Pascal, 1994.
20. C. K. Shin and A.C. Park. Towards integration of memory based learning and neural networks. In Tharam S. Dillon Sankar K. Pal and Daniel S. Yeung, editors, *Soft Computing in Case Based Reasoning*, volume 1, pages 95–114, March 2000.
21. A. Zeboulon, Y. Bennani, and K. Benabdeslem. Hybrid connectionist approach for knowledge discovery from web navigation patterns. In *Proceedings of ACS/IEEE International Conference on Computer Systems and Applications*, Tunisia, July 2003.
22. F. Zehraoui. Cbr system for sequence prediction "casep". In *Workshop on Applying case-based reasoning to time series prediction*, pages 260–269, Trondheim, Norway, June 2003.
23. F. Zehraoui and Y. Bennani. M-som-art: Growing self organizing map for sequences clustering and classification. In *16th European Conference on Artificial Intelligence (ECAI2004)*, Valancia, Spain, August 2004.
24. F. Zehraoui and Y. Bennani. Som-art: Incorporation des propriétés de plasticité et de stabilité dans une carte auto-organisatrice. In *Atelier FDC: Fouille de Données Complexes dans un processus d'extraction de connaissances (EGC 2004)*, pages 169–180, Clermont-Ferrand, Janvier 2004.
25. F. Zehraoui, R. Kanawati, and S. Salotti. Case base maintenance for improving prediction quality. In *The 6th International Conference on Case-Based Reasoning (ICCBR-2003)*, pages 703–717, Trondheim, Norway, June 2003.

Improving the Quality of Solutions in Domain Evolving Environments

Josep Lluís Arcos

IIIA, Artificial Intelligence Research Institute
CSIC, Spanish Council for Scientific Research
Campus UAB, 08193 Bellaterra, Catalonia, Spain
arcos@iiia.csic.es, http://www.iiia.csic.es

Abstract. The development of industrial case-based reasoning systems that have to operate within a continually evolving environment, is a challenging problem. Industrial applications require of robust and competent systems. When the problem domain is evolving, the solutions provided by the system can easily become wrong. In this paper we present an algorithm for dealing with real-world domains where case solutions are evolving along the time. Specifically, the algorithm deals with what we call the *innovation problem*: the continuous improvements on the components that are part of case solutions. We will show how the use of the proposed algorithm improves significantly the quality of solutions in a deployed engineering design system.

1 Introduction

The development of industrial case-based reasoning systems that have to operate within a continually evolving environment, is a challenging problem. Industrial applications require of robust and competent systems. When the problem domain is evolving, the solutions provided by the system can easily become wrong.

In this context, *sustained* case-based reasoning systems [2] are strongly needed. The goal of sustained case-based reasoning systems is to learn continuously from the experience of solving problems. As is argued in [1], a sustained case-based reasoning system requires of an underlying deep knowledge model of the domain, as well as a problem solving mechanism that has to make use of it.

Two main evolving directions can be identified in problem domains. The first one is the change on the type of problems: new types of problems may become important and previously important problems may become irrelevant. The second one is the change on the type of solutions: the same type of problems that were previously solved using a specific domain solution may require a new domain solution to be solved.

Examples of case-based reasoning tasks that have to deal with evolving solutions are design and configuration tasks. Real-world design systems have to incorporate functionalities for dealing with the use of new design components or the improvement of previously existing components. We call this design problem the *innovation problem*.

A strategy for solving the innovation problem is to incorporate maintenance processes into the case-based reasoning applications [11, 8, 10]. The most usual techniques used for catching up the changes in the domain environment are case maintenance techniques for reorganizing the case base. Deletion polices are examples of strategies used for dealing with cases with obsolete solutions.

The success of any CBR system is not only motivated by the case base quality. The success of any CBR system depends also on all its knowledge containers [9] and, specially, on the similarity or retrieval knowledge and on the adaptation knowledge. A used policy in design or configuration problems is the improvement of the adaptation knowledge by incorporating rules for component substitution: when a new component is introduced in the solution designs substituting a previous existing component, a new rule is incorporated in the adaptation knowledge.

Nevertheless, not all solution changes can be reduced to the incorporation of new components. One type of the changes is the improvement of a pre-existing component. The main problem with these improvements is that the improvements are usually based on problem specific requirements. That is, there are only experimental evidences of the improvement and not a general theory. Then, a system that has to deal with this incomplete model, could use a case-based reasoning approach. This is the motivation of our proposal, dealing with problem-based improvements for improving the quality of other problem solutions.

In this paper we will present a proposal for dealing with problem domains with evolving solutions concentrating the efforts on the retrieval and the reuse steps. Our goal is to develop an *innovative aware* CBR algorithm, i.e. a CBR algorithm where the retrieval and reuse phases are not degraded by the periodical incorporation of innovations in the problem solutions. We will show how the analysis of solution changes in customary problems – problems that are periodically solved by the system – can be used for improving the quality of solutions in occasional problems – problems that are rarely solved by the system.

We have tested the proposed algorithm in *T-Air*, a deployed engineering design system. *T-Air* is a case-based reasoning application developed for aiding engineers in the design of gas treatment plants [4]. The main problem in designing gas treatment plants is that the diversity of possible problems is as high as the diversity of industrial processes but there are only experimental models for few of them. The knowledge acquired by engineers with their practical experience is essential for solving new problems. The innovation problem in *T-Air* is due to the continuous improvements on the equipment used in the design of gas treatment plants. In this paper we will report the significant improvement of solution quality when using our proposed algorithm.

This paper is organized as follows: In section 2 we present the innovation problem and propose the innovation aware CBR algorithm. In section 3 we exemplify the incorporation of the proposed algorithm in a deployed application an report the results of the experiments performed. The paper ends with a description of the current status of the work and the planned future work.

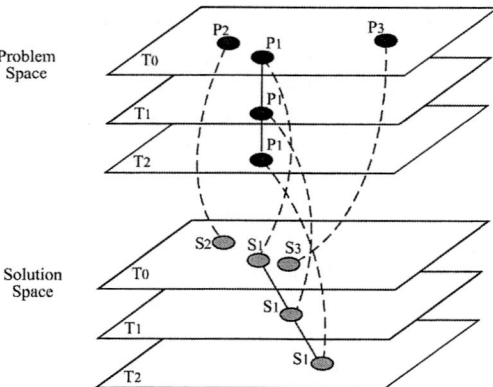

Fig. 1. An Extension of the classical problem and solution CBR spaces for dealing with time factor.

2 The Innovation Aware Problem

The goal of a sustained CBR system is to not degrade the quality of the solutions generated taking into account that the domain environment may evolve. A first naive strategy for solving this problem can be to only use recently solved cases (for instance, including the case date into the similarity measure). Nevertheless, as we will see below this naif approach is not enough.

In a given case base, we can classify the cases into two categories: *customary problems* and *occasional problems*. Customary problems are problems that are periodically solved by the system. Occasional problems are problems that are rarely solved by the system. In customary problems, the strategy of only focusing on recent solutions can be appropriate. The main problem rises with occasional problems: when a new occasional target problem has to be solved, usually only old solutions can be found in the case base. Then, a CBR inference system that is just reusing these old solutions may generate solutions with a low quality, i.e. solutions that may cause the distrust in the system.

Let us illustrate the evolving environment problem using the scheme of the Figure 1. There is a customary problem P_1 that was solved at times T_0, T_1, T_2. Each time the problem was solved, a small innovation was applied to the solution. Whenever a new P_1 target problem has to be solved, it is clear that we can take, as a basis for the reuse, the most recent solution stored in the case-base.

Now let us assume that there is an occasional problem P_2 that was solved at T_0 (see Figure 1), when a new P_2 target problem arises at T_2, we have two alternative cases to consider: S_2 solved at T_0 or S_1 solved at T_2. Using as a criterion the problem similarity, S_2 is the solution designed for the closest problem. Nevertheless, because problems P_1 and P_2 are very similar and P_2 has been solved recently, it can be more feasible to consider S_1 as a candidate for reuse (i.e using the case date when assessing similarity). Taking the last alternative, we are imposing a more powerful adaptation mechanism.

Finally, in the figure, we have another occasional problem P_3 that was solved at T_0. P_3 is a problem far from the other problems P_1 and P_2 but that has a solution S_3 close to the other solutions. When a new P_3 target problem comes to the system, P_1 and P_2 will not be retrieved. Thus, the closest solution is S_3. Nevertheless, taking into account that S_3 was designed at T_0, the solution we can reuse from S_3 will possibly not include recent innovations. Then, taking into account similar solutions more recently i.e. solved (solution S_1 that has been solved at T_2) we can improve the quality of the solution by tuning the solution taking into account the innovations introduced in S_1.

From these simple examples, it is clear that the innovation problem has to be dealt in the CBR inference procedure. Below we will present a variant of the classical CBR inference cycle [3] that incorporates an additional retrieval and reuse steps on the space of solutions.

An alternative approach to deal with the innovation problem could be by implementing a learning module able to incorporate new knowledge into the adaptation model. This approach has the difficulty of managing with the usual incomplete model of the domain and has not been addressed in this paper.

Moreover, it is important to remark that whether we apply deletion policies in the case base, the performance for occasional problems could be affected because we can loose the knowledge about innovation changes. For instance, in our previous example from Figure 1, if we only keep the solution S_1 at time T_2 – deleting the solutions at times T_0 and T_1 – the relationship between the solutions S_3 and S_1 could be not established.

Before describing our innovation aware algorithm for dealing with evolving solutions, we will introduce some basic notation: a case c_i is defined as a tripled $c_i = (p_i, s_i, t)$ where p_i is the problem description, s_i is the solution, and t is the date when c_i was solved. Moreover, we assume that there exists a similarity measure $Sim_p(p_i, p_j)$ between problem descriptions for retrieving and ranking the cases more similar to a new target problem. We say that two cases c_i, c_j are *innovation variants* when their problems p_i, p_j are equivalent ($Sim_p(p_i, p_j) = 1$) and their solutions s_i, s_j are different. Finally, we also assume that exists a similarity measure $Sim_s(s_i, s_j)$ between case solutions.

2.1 The Innovation Aware Algorithm

We propose to incorporate an additional retrieval and adaptation step into the usual CBR inference cycle: after retrieving and reusing the most similar cases for generating the solution of a new target problem – when the reused cases are not recent – we propose to refine the solution generated by looking for recentness paths on the solution space. Our CBR inference algorithm (see Figure 2) is then divided into four phases:

1. Retrieving similar cases using Sim_p: given a new problem p, the first phase uses the Sim_p similarity measure on problem descriptions for retrieving and ranking similar cases (noted C). This phase models the usual retrieval step. Because we are not taking into account the solution date, all the cases with an equivalent problem description will be grouped with the same similarity.

Procedure IN-AW(p , t)
(1)   C = P-Retrieval(p)
(2)   ⟨ s , t' ⟩ = Reuse(p , C)
       if (t - t' < δ) then
          return s
       else
(3)   S = S-Retrieval(s, t')
(4)   s' = Inn-Reuse(s, S)
          return s'
       end if

Fig. 2. The innovation aware algorithm. A first a retrieval step on the problem space; then a reuse step on solutions; next a retrieval step on the solution space; and finally a reuse step on the innovation path.

2. First solution proposal: a first solution s for problem p is constructed by reusing solutions of previously retrieved cases C. We say that s is a solution for time context t', where t' is calculated from the dates of cases C. When the most similar cases are recent (we use a fixed δ parameter), the solution S is proposed as final solution and next phases are skipped. Otherwise,
3. Retrieving similar solutions using Sim_s: the goal of the third phase is to retrieve the customary problems S' with a similar solution to s (using Sim_s) solved near t' (using a fixed threshold γ). Only problems with additional solutions more recent than t' are considered–i.e. cases that gather solutions with innovation variants.
4. Applying innovation variants: the goal of the last phase is to apply innovation variants to s. This phase requires domain specific policies for identifying the relevant solution changes.

The threshold parameters δ and γ have to be determined for each domain problem. In the current implementation of the IN-AW algorithm we have manually tuned their values for the use in their *T-Air* application.

3   The Application in an Industrial System

We incorporated the innovation aware CBR algorithm in *T-Air*, a case-based reasoning application developed for aiding engineers in the design of gas treatment plants[4]. The gas treatment is required in many and diverse industrial processes such as the control of the atmospheric pollution due to corrosive residual gases which contain vapours, mists, and dusts of industrial origin. Examples of gas treatments are the absorption of gases and vapours such as SO_2, CLH, or CL_2; the absorption of NO_x with recovering of HNO_3; the absorption of drops and fogs such as PO_4H_3 or $ClNH_4$; dust removal in metallic oxides; and elimination of odours from organic origin.

The main problem in designing gas treatment plants is that the diversity of possible problems is as high as the diversity of industrial processes but there are

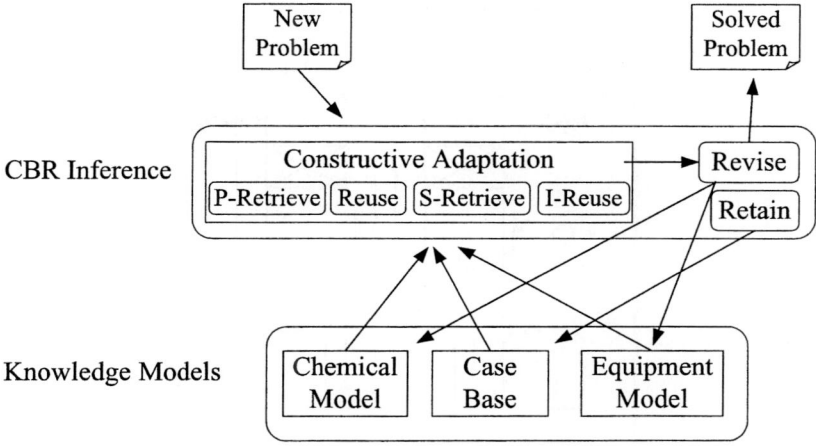

Fig. 3. *T-Air* functional Architecture.

only experimental models for few of them. The knowledge acquired by engineers with their practical experience is the main tool used for solving new problems.

3.1 General Architecture

The *T-Air* architecture is based on three knowledge models and three reasoning modules (see Figure 3). The first knowledge model is the *Chemical Model* and is the basis for determining the similarity between a gas composition in a new problem and those treated previously and stored in the case base. Moreover, since we are mixing a polluted gas with a washing liquid, we also have modeled the properties of the washing liquids, the compatibility among gases and liquids, and some chemical reactions involved.

The second knowledge model is the *Equipment Model*. The equipment model describes the components used in gas treatment plants (gas-washing units, pumps, fans, tanks, and accessories). Each equipment has involved a collection of working parameters. The relationships among these working parameters are modeled by means of a collection of equations, a collection of constraints about their maximum and minimum values, and a collection of safety conditions expressed as heuristics.

Finally, the last knowledge model holds the *Case Base*. T-Air uses a highly structured representation of cases. A case is represented as a complex structure embodying four different kinds of knowledge: the *Input Knowledge*, a *Chemical Case-Model*, the solution *Flow Sheet*, and *Annotations*.

The *Input Knowledge* embodies data about the customer such as the industrial sector it belongs or the industrial process that originates the polluting gas; data about the working conditions of the installation such as temperature or gas flow; data about the composition and concentration of input polluted gas; and data about the desired concentration in the output emission. The *Chemical*

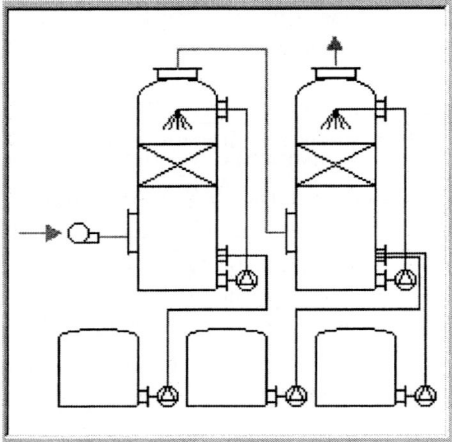

Fig. 4. An example of a simple flow sheet generated by *T-Air* with two scrubbers. each of them with a centrifugal pump that sucks the washing liquids from three tanks to the scrubbers, and one fan at the beginning of the process.

Case-Model embodies a graph structure, generated by *T-Air* using the chemical model, modeling the main characteristics of the input gas. The chemical case-model extends the input knowledge and fixes the thresholds for the working conditions, the main issues to be analyzed, and the kind of gas treatment required. The *Flow Sheet* component describes the solution designed for cleaning a polluted gas. As shown graphically in Figure 4, the flow sheet specifies a collection of required equipment (mainly scrubbers, pumps, tanks, and fans), the design and working parameters for each equipment, and the topology of the installation (the gas circuit and the liquid circuits). The flow sheet is also represented as a graph structure. Finally, *Annotations* are meta-information that, when an external factor influences the solution, describe the reasons for a given solution decision – examples of s annotations are the design decisions forced by the user requirements such as the washing liquid, over-dimensionated parameters because of security reasons, or spatial requirements.

The inference in *T-Air* is performed by three modules (see Figure 3): the *Constructive Adaptation* module, the *Revision* module, and the *Retention* module. The main inference is performed by the constructive adaptation module and will be described in the next subsection.

Because the chemical knowledge required for covering all the potential problems is extremely huge, the approach followed was to only model the knowledge related with the initial case base. This design decision had two main consequences: i) the system required a *Revision* module where the engineers are able to correct the system solution, and ii) the system required a mechanism for gradually built up the chemical knowledge when it is required. Moreover, the engineer have a complete control over the plant parameters (the system only prevents safety violations). The approach we have adopted is close to work of capturing expert design knowledge through "concept mapping" [6]: when the engineer is analyzing a problem involving a gas not previously covered, the engineer uses the navigation interactive capabilities of *T-Air* for determining the possible characteristics of the gas and improves the chemical knowledge of the system by means of completing the information.

An important issue during the development of the system was to provide useful navigation tools for inspecting the chemical knowledge and the case base. This requirement is crucial when the engineer is trying to design the solution for a problem that is not covered by the knowledge of the system.

The retention module is the responsible of storing all the problems solved and manages the indexing structure. Cases are stored in an external database and accessed by SQL queries.

3.2 Inference Process

The *T-Air* inference process has been implemented using *constructive adaptation* [7], a generative technique for reuse in CBR systems. A solution in *T-Air* is constructed by combining and adapting several previously solved designs. We use the input knowledge and chemical knowledge (stored in the chemical case-models) as the basis for determining the similarity between a new problem and those treated previously and stored in the case base. The Chemical Model and the Equipment Model are used in the adaptation stage for assessing the working parameters of each equipment of the flow-sheet. The design of a solution in *T-Air* is organized in four task levels:

a) selecting the class of chemical process to be realized;
b) selecting the major equipments to be used – and their inter-connections;
c) assessing the values for the parameters of each equipment; and
d) adding auxiliary equipment.

Task levels a) and b) are mainly related with retrieval mechanisms. Tasks levels c) and d) are mainly related with adaptation mechanisms.

The innovation problem in *T-Air* is due to the continuous improvements on the equipment used in the design of gas treatment plants. Specifically, the innovation in the scrubbers (the gas washing elements) that are the core elements in a gas treatment plant. It is not usual to incorporate new models of scrubbers. The usual procedure is to apply innovations to the current models. For instance, an innovation on the scrubber cover can decrease the pressure drop– i.e. increase the washing efficiency. Moreover, because there are many washing parameters estimated experimentally, the behavior and the in-site measurements of the deployed gas treatment plants is also a source of knowledge continuously incorporated into future designs. In *T-Air*, the innovation problem decreases the quality of proposed solutions. Because the *T-Air* system has a revision step, the first consequence is that engineers have to spend more efforts in verifying and correcting the proposed solutions. Moreover, each time the engineer has to correct a lot of equipment parameters, the trust in the system decreases.

When designing gas treatment plants two classes of problems can be identified: customary designs and occasional designs. Customary designs – for instance the gas treatment inside wastewater treatment plants – are good examples for tracking the innovations introduced in scrubbers. Solutions for occasional designs have to be tuned with customary designs. Otherwise, the quality of a solution for an occasional design may become very low.

The innovation aware algorithm is only relevant for *T-Air* tasks levels b) and c): the selection of the major equipments to be used and the assessment of the values for the parameters of each equipment.

3.3 Maintenance Policies

As it was argued in section 3.1, due to the impossibility of covering all the chemical knowledge, we only modeled the knowledge required by the cases present in the case base. Thus, the first maintenance component was designed for refining the similarity knowledge. The maintenance of the chemical similarity hierarchy can be performed graphically by adding new leaves or refining intermediate nodes. Moreover, each node in the hierarchy has associated a set of *perspectives* that locally determine the set of 'important' input data. Perspectives [5] is a mechanism developed to describe declarative biases for case retrieval in structured and complex representations of cases. This mechanism is also very powerful for assessing similarities among case solutions where, as in design tasks, solutions are also represented as complex and structured representations. *T-Air* performs automatic subsumption tests for restricting the incorporation of a new perspective that can conflict with the pre-existing ones.

The second maintenance policy implemented in the *T-Air* system was the deletion of problems with obsolete solutions. Because we had all the designs performed by TECNIUM from 1989, some of the solutions provided are now obsolete. The system provides automatic tools for identifying divergent solutions for the same problems and options for manually eliminate cases (useful for problems with non-standard solutions). Moreover, the user can mark a new solution as a 'non-standard solution' and then, the solved problem will not be considered as a case.

The third maintenance policy in *T-Air* was incorporated in the adaptation knowledge. One of the components of the adaptation knowledge is the list of obsolete components. The engineers manually introduce the new components and their corresponding obsoletes. Unfortunately, only auxiliary equipment become obsolete.

Finally, the innovation aware algorithm was introduced for dealing with the improvements of gas-washing units. In the next section we will describe the experiments performed for assessing the use of the innovation aware algorithm in *T-Air*.

3.4 Experimentation

The goal of the experimentation was to compare the quality of solutions provided by *T-Air* using the innovation aware algorithm regarding the correct solutions

Table 1. Summay of experimentation results.

	Main Equipments		Parameter Ass.	
	Inn.	err.	Inn.	err.
Standard Algorithm	0.0 %	25.0 %	0.0 %	83.3 %
IN-AW Algorithm	21.6 %	8.3 %	75.0 %	18.3 %

and the solutions proposed without the innovation aware algorithm. We say that the quality of a solution is preserved when the solution proposed by the innovation aware algorithm prevents the manually revision of the solution.

For testing the performance of the innovation aware algorithm we experimented with a case base of 900 design solutions. These 900 cases are the performed installations since 1997 (the last seven years). Then, the worst situation for the T-Air system is to propose a new solution for an occasional problem based on a solution of 7 years old.

From the case base we selected as testing problems 60 occasional designs – 20 from 2001, 20 from 2002, and 20 from 2003. All the testing problems had as similar cases designs with at least 4 years old. An important remark is that we tested each problem using only the cases older than the problem – i.e problems from 2001 were tested only with cases from 1997 to 2001.

We analyzed the quality of the solutions at two different task levels: the selection of the main plant components and structure (task level b) and the selection of equipment working parameters (task level c). Errors performed at task level b) are critical because the system is proposing an inappropriate type of solution. Errors performed at task level c) are less critical for the chemical process involved, but they increase the analysis cost because the design has to be revised by a more qualified engineer.

Performance at 'Main Equipments' Task Level. The IN-AW algorithm proposed a different design solution for 13 problems (representing the 21.6 %). Two of the proposed solutions were not justified by the case base content. After the experimentation, this situation was easily corrected by refining the equipment model. Moreover, there were three problems with better solutions that were not identified (the error percentage representing both situations is 8.3 %). When T-Air is not able to identify the best solution for a given problem, the inference algorithm behaves like in the standard CBR algorithm. The improvement of quality of solutions at this level was not high but this is coherent with the fact that the design improvements occur mainly in the equipment parameters.

Performance at 'Parameter Assessment' Task Level. The important difference between the IN-AW algorithm and the standard CBR algorithm arisen in this task level. IN-AW proposed different parameter values in 45 of the test problems (representing the 75 %). All the proposed parameter values were correct improvements – comparing with the standard CBR algorithm. The error of 18.3 % arose when comparing the differences with the real solutions. The difference is motivated by the conservative policy we chose when reusing innovation variants: only those innovation variants with a high confidence degree are applied. The consequence is that in those cases the solution proposed by the IN-AW algorithm represents an intermediate point between the solution provided by the standard CBR algorithm and the engineer solution – i.e. the quality of the solution was improved but the optimal was not reached.

4 Conclusions

We presented a CBR algorithm for dealing with problem domains with evolving solutions concentrating the efforts on the retrieval and the reuse steps. The algorithm has been developed for design and configuration tasks, where a solution has a complex and structured representation and is usually constructed with the contribution of different cases. The *innovative aware* CBR algorithm manages the periodically incorporation of innovations in the problem solutions avoiding the decreasing of the system performance. The solution provided incorporates an additional retrieval and adaptation step into the usual CBR inference cycle for capturing the innovations performed in customary problems and applying them to the solutions of occasional problems.

We incorporated the innovation aware algorithm in *T-Air*, a deployed application for aiding engineers in the design of gas treatment plants. The experiments we performed with occasional problems demonstrated the utility of the algorithm: the quality of the solutions provided by *T-Air* were improved. This effect was clearly significant at the 'Parameter Assessment' task level where the percentage of solutions improved is the 75 %.

When the performance of the system degrades, the psychological effect on the users is the lack of trust. An important contribution of the algorithm is that increased the trust of the users in the *T-Air* application.

In the current implementation of the IN-AW algorithm we have manually tuned the values of the recency thresholds δ and γ for their use in the *T-Air* application. As a future work we plan to investigate the use of variable recency thresholds.

Although the use of learning techniques for acquiring adaptation knowledge is a hard task in incomplete domain models, it can be an interesting complement to our proposed algorithm. Future research will continue in this direction.

Acknowledgements

The author thanks Ramom López de Mántaras and Enric Plaza for their helpful and stimulating suggestions in the elaboration of this research. The research reported in this paper has been partially supported by the Spanish Ministry of Science and Technology under the project TIC 2003-07776-C2-02, EU-FEDER funds, and the company TECNIUM. Any possible mistake or error in the description of the working principles of chemical gas treatment is the sole responsibility of the author.

References

1. Agnar Aamodt. A computational model of knowledge-intensive learning and problem solving. In Bob Wielinga et al., editor, *Current Trends in Knowledge Acquisition*. IOS Press, 1990.
2. Agnar Aamodt. Knowledge-intensive case-based reasoning and sustained learning. In Luigia Aiello, editor, *Proceedings of the 9th European Conference on Artificial Intelligence*, pages 1–6. Pitman Publishing, 1990.
3. Agnar Aamodt and Enric Plaza. Case-based reasoning: Foundational issues, methodological variations, and system approaches. *Artificial Intelligence Communications*, 7(1):39–59, 1994. online at http://www.iiia.csic.es/People/enric/AICom_ToC.html
4. Josep Lluís Arcos. T-air: A case-based reasoning system for designing chemical absorption plants. In David W. Aha and Ian Watson, editors, *Case-Based Reasoning Research and Development*, number 2080 in Lecture Notes in Artificial Intelligence, pages 576–588. Springer-Verlag, 2001.
5. Josep Lluís Arcos and Ramon López de Mántaras. Perspectives: a declarative bias mechanism for case retrieval. In David Leake and Enric Plaza, editors, *Case-Based Reasoning. Research and Development*, number 1266 in Lecture Notes in Artificial Intelligence, pages 279–290. Springer-Verlag, 1997.
6. David B. Leake and David C. Wilson. Combining cbr with interactive knowledge acquisition, manipulation and reuse. In *Proceedings of the Third International Conference on Case-Based Reasoning (ICCBR-99)*, pages "218–232", Berlin, 1999. Springer-Verlag.
7. Enric Plaza and Josep Ll. Arcos. Constructive adaptation. In Susan Craw and Alun Preece, editors, *Advances in Case-Based Reasoning*, number 2416 in Lecture Notes in Artificial Intelligence, pages 306–320. Springer-Verlag, 2002.
8. Thomas Reinartz, Ioannis Iglezakis, and Thomas Roth-Berghofer. Review and restore for case-based maintenance. *Computational Intelligence*, 17(2):214–234, 2001.
9. Michael M. Richter. Introduction. In M. Lenz, B. Bartsch-Spörl, H.D. Burkhard, and S. Wess, editors, *CBR Technology: From Foundations to Applications*, pages 1–15. Springer-Verlag, 1998.
10. Barry Smyth and Elizabeth McKenna. Competence models and the maintenance problem. *Computational Intelligence*, 17(2):235–249, 2001.
11. David C. Wilson and David B. Leake. Maintaining case-based reasoners: Dimensions and directions. *Computational Intelligence*, 17(2):196–213, 2001.

PlayMaker:
An Application of Case-Based Reasoning to Air Traffic Control Plays

Kenneth R. Allendoerfer and Rosina Weber

Drexel University, College of Information Science and Technology
Philadelphia, PA 19104, USA
{kenneth.allendoerfer,rosina.weber}@drexel.edu

Abstract. When events such as severe weather or congestion interfere with the normal flow of air traffic, air traffic controllers may implement plays that reroute one or more traffic flows. Currently, plays are assessed and selected based on controllers' experience using the National Playbook, a collection of plays that have worked in the past. This paper introduces PlayMaker, a CBR prototype that replicates the Playbook and models how controllers select plays. This paper describes the PlayMaker design, a model validation, and discusses developments necessary for a full-scale CBR tool for this application.

1 Introduction

The Air Traffic Control System Command Center (ATCSCC) is responsible for establishing nationwide responses to situations that affect air traffic control (ATC) operations [1]. Controllers at the ATCSCC develop and communicate plans to local ATC facilities for implementation. Over time, the ATCSCC has collected these plans, called *plays*, to standardize them and make them easier to communicate. In this paper, we describe the development and performance of PlayMaker, a CBR prototype designed to represent and recommend ATC plays.

1.1 ATC National Playbook

Every day, thousands of aircraft follow routes between their departure and arrival airports. Routes are *roads in the sky* that minimize flight time between airports and balance overall congestion. For example, not every aircraft flying from the northeastern United States to Florida can fly precisely the same route because of congestion and capacity. Instead, there are many routes between cities but some are more direct and desirable than others. Controllers at the ATCSCC continually monitor the routes and intervene when situations disrupt the normal flow.

Bad weather and congestion are the most common situations requiring controller intervention. Large aircraft can fly safely through nearly any weather, but small aircraft cannot, and all pilots prefer to avoid bad weather if possible. When bad weather interferes with normal routes, controllers reroute traffic to avoid it. They select new routes based on where the bad weather is located, the route's original path, and conditions in areas where the aircraft may be sent. For example, if a storm interferes with traffic headed from the northeastern United States to Florida, controllers may reroute traffic to the west over the Appalachian Mountains. However, if the Appalachian routes are already congested, controllers may reroute some aircraft over the Atlantic Ocean. However, aircraft that are not equipped for flight over water would need to be rerouted even farther west or delayed on the ground until the congestion eases or the storm weakens. Other situations that may affect flows include military operations, equipment outages, and national emergencies.

Over time, controllers have identified numerous recurring situations and have collected their solutions into plays. A play contains the reroutes that are necessary to handle a situation. Figure 1 shows a play called Snowbird 5, which reroutes southbound traffic away from the Carolina coast and over the Appalachian Mountains. The reroutes in a play have been selected and negotiated with stakeholders to minimize their impact on airlines, airports, and ATC facilities.

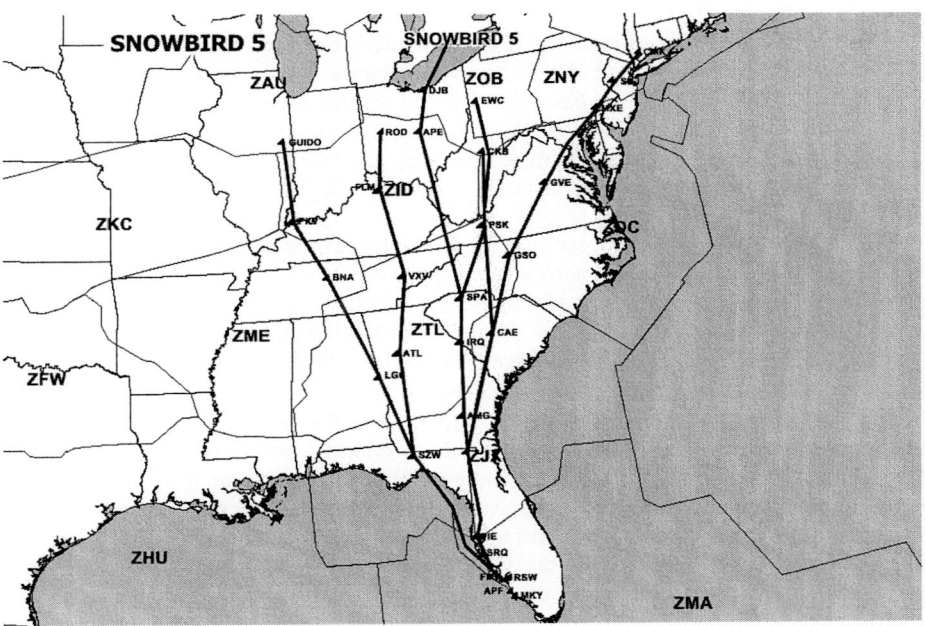

Fig. 1. A map showing the play known as Snowbird 5. Dark lines show routes of southbound traffic heading for western Florida. Note that traffic is avoiding the Carolina coast where an event, typically weather, is occurring. From the National Playbook [2]

When a situation arises that requires reroutes, controllers select and initiate the play that they believe is best for the situation and the overall ATC system. Controllers then contact system stakeholders such as the airlines, local ATC facilities, and the military to inform them which play has been selected. There is some negotiation during these discussions but ultimately, the decision regarding which play to implement comes from the ATCSCC. Because the plays are published ahead of time, the communication burden is much lower than if controllers had to communicate every reroute to every stakeholder individually. The ATCSCC has collected their plays into the National Playbook, which is available online and updated regularly [2].

1.2 Motivating Problem

First, the National Playbook is currently maintained manually. As of early 2004, there are over 130 plays in the Playbook and many are only subtly different. Controllers and other stakeholders must rely on their knowledge of how plays performed in the past to identify the best one for the current situation. This requires extensive training and experience. A system that could recommend plays could potentially assist less-experienced personnel and could be used as a training tool.

Second, many current controllers were hired shortly after the 1981 strike when President Ronald Reagan fired more than 11,000 controllers. Because of this, many experienced controllers will be eligible to retire starting about 2006. With the possibility of such a large number of retirements imminent, there is a need to begin capturing the collective knowledge of these experts in a form that could be used by a new generation of controllers.

Third, when a play is selected, it is disseminated to stakeholders such as airlines. When a play involves substantial reroutes, which cause delays, annoy customers, and cost money, stakeholders increasingly demand explanations and justifications. In addition, the ATCSCC is interested in increasing the transparency and accountability of its processes. When controllers implement a play, it would be beneficial if a system could retrieve concrete examples of occasions when the play worked well to serve as justification.

Finally, novel situations do occasionally arise for which no play exists. A system that could process similarities across many previous events might be able to detect similarities that humans might not immediately identify. A system that could suggest candidate plays could help organize, focus, and expedite the play design process. A system that could represent the creative process by which experts design new plays would be relevant to cognitive science in general.

The prototype described in this paper, PlayMaker, addresses the first three of these goals; we have intentionally left the process of developing new plays to later versions. We selected to implement PlayMaker using CBR because it seemed to fit the procedures and practices already used by controllers. Patterns and regularities between situations became apparent over time and controllers recorded them for use later as plays. This is very analogous to the CBR cycle [3] and should provide good face validity and acceptance from the users. CBR systems can provide explanations by analogy which would be required for any operational use of PlayMaker. A more advanced version of PlayMaker using CBR could be designed to derive new plays and thereby meet all the goals.

1.3 Past Research

ATC is widely studied in AI because of its complexity, the expertise of its workers, and its safety and economic implications. Bonzano and Cunningham [4] and Bonzano, Cunningham, and Meckiff [5] have developed several CBR systems to support ATC decision making. They focused on identifying and avoiding conflicts, which is a critical aspect of tactical ATC. A conflict occurs when two or more trajectories bring aircraft closer than allowed. The most important controller tactical task is to identify potential conflicts and resolve the situation before safety is jeopardized. Bonzano, Cunningham, and Meckiff [5] created a CBR system that was able to provide good resolutions to several types of conflicts.

However, their system targeted reasoning at a tactical level, not strategic. Strategic controllers do not identify or resolve conflicts. They do not work at the individual flight level; they work with whole flows of traffic. In tactical ATC, a controller sees a conflict and immediately takes action to change one or both trajectories. It is not a negotiation; a controller gives commands directly to pilots that are specific to the conflict at hand. In strategic ATC, however, all stakeholders know the possible actions long ahead of time because plays already have been negotiated, validated, and disseminated. The task, then, is to identify which known action best applies to the current situation and inform others of the decision. The amount of tailoring is intentionally minimized.

Recent research in the field of highway traffic operations centers, which respond to events like accidents and congestion, is related to the strategic ATC task. Logi and Ritchie [6] have developed an innovative decision support system for managing highway congestion across multiple jurisdictions. In their system, intelligent agents develop solutions to problems and then negotiate to develop cooperative overall responses.

Logi and Richie's [6] approach might apply to strategic ATC as well because there are many similarities between the domains. But unlike the highway traffic situations, the ATCSCC does not truly negotiate plays in real time. Instead, controllers select from a collection of pre-determined plays. Some real-time modifications may occur but only when absolutely necessary. The plays are designed to minimize impact to stakeholders and to be as straightforward as possible to implement. Dissemination is a major obstacle for strategic ATC. There may be thousands of flights already in progress. There are hundreds of ATC facilities that may need to learn about the change. Without having a pre-determined Playbook, it may be impossible to reach all stakeholders with accurate and timely information. The Logi and Ritchie [6] approach may be useful when modeling the play design process but less so when modeling how plays are used and implemented.

We know of no research in the AI literature that examines how controllers assess and select strategic plays. Because these strategic decisions may affect hundreds of flights and thousands of passengers, the economic importance of these decisions is clear. Because of important differences between related literature and our area of interest, we believe a different approach is warranted. In particular, we hope to develop an intelligent system that closely matches current strategic ATC practice and that has good face validity for the controllers.

2 PlayMaker Design

PlayMaker is a feature-vector CBR system that we prototyped using the Esteem CBR shell [7]. We conceptualize it as a recommendation system that examines existing plays and suggests ones that may be useful for the current situation. It does not generate new reroutes nor does it attempt, at this point, to adapt existing plays. In this section, we describe the features and the similarity metric we used to develop the prototype. In section 4, we propose a more complete implementation of PlayMaker and discuss the changes that would be necessary to create a system for deployment.

2.1 Case Description

We developed a set of features that describe situations that cause controllers to institute plays by interviewing a supervisory ATC specialist from Jacksonville Air Route Traffic Control Center. Each of these is described in the following paragraphs.

Location is the most important feature of a strategic ATC situation. Location determines which routes are affected and which must be changed. Location determines where rerouted traffic can be sent. It determines which facilities must implement the play and it is one factor that determines how bad a situation is. For the purpose of the prototype, we have defined Location as two features, *East-West* and *North-South*, according to a grid of the United States. One unit on the grid represents approximately 50 nautical miles, with 0, 0 located over northern Kansas. We selected this system to avoid the complexities of latitude-longitude geometry. An operational implementation of PlayMaker would require proper geometry and a more sophisticated method for specifying locations (see section 4).

Severity describes the level of operational impact of a situation. For the purpose of selecting plays, controllers do not need to distinguish between causes of events. A thunderstorm that airplanes cannot fly through is the same severity as a military operation that airplanes are not allowed to fly through. The feature Severity, then, describes a situation in terms of the portion of aircraft that would normally fly through an area that cannot because of the event. A low score means that most airplanes that normally come through an area still can. For example, if certain navigation beacons are out of service, older aircraft might not be able to fly through the area whereas newer aircraft would still be able to. In this case, the event is considered low Severity. On the other hand, a military operation might require that all civilian aircraft avoid the area—a complete roadblock. This would receive a high score because all aircraft must be rerouted. As coded in our prototype, each case receives a Severity score between 1 (almost no aircraft must be rerouted) to 5 (all aircraft must be rerouted).

Direction of Majority describes the predominant flow through the affected area. Plays are usually developed for traffic coming from one general direction. This is coded in the prototype according to compass directions: N, NE, E, SE, S, SW, W, NW.

Time of Day describes when the situation is occurring. Controllers may implement different plays (or no play at all) depending on when a situation occurs because traffic levels change throughout the day. Our domain expert explained that situations occurring during the heavier daytime hours are sometimes handled differently than if the same event occurred in the evening or overnight. A play designed for a daytime situation would not be appropriate for an overnight situation and vice versa. In the prototype, we have broken the day into three categories: 0000 to 0659, 0700 to 1859, and 1900 to 2359.

Effect on Major Facilities describes how many major facilities are affected by the situation. Because of the interdependencies of the ATC system, a situation may have effects all over the country but events that affect major facilities deserve special consideration. If two plays could address the same situation equally well, controllers would like to select the play with the least effect on major facilities. For the purpose of our prototype, we defined major facilities as New York (known to controllers as ZNY), Washington (ZDC), and Indianapolis (ZID) as major due to the number of large cities that they serve and their high traffic volumes. We focused on these areas because our case base focuses on these areas. A full implementation of PlayMaker would require including major facilities from across the country. As coded in the prototype, the feature can vary from 0 (no major facilities affected) to 3 (ZNY, ZDC, and ZID affected).

2.2 Similarity Assessment

The prototype uses a weighted similarity metric based on priorities elicited from our domain expert and aimed at the intended use of the system. The most important index features, according to our domain expert, are the Direction of Majority and the two Location features. If a retrieved case is not a close match on these three features, it will very likely not be an appropriate play. The Severity, Time of Day, and Effect on Major Facilities features are more useful when selecting among several good candidates. These judgments of operational importance by our expert were used to determine the weights for the similarity metric. The matching features and weights are shown in Table 1.

The features Location, Severity, and Effect on Major Facilities use the Absolute Fuzzy Range numeric matching function provided by Esteem [7], which returns a number between 0 and 1 according to the formula MAX (0, ABS(value2-value1)/Range). This allows the retrieval of cases whose values are close to the original. This is especially important for Location because of the imprecision of the method we used to specify location. Time of Day uses the Exact text matching function of Esteem, which returns a 0 or 1 if the text matches precisely. Direction of Majority uses the Partial, Case Indifferent text matching function of Esteem, which returns a value between 0 and 1, depending on the number of differences in the letters. This allows directions "NE" and "N" to be treated more similarly than "S" and "N."

Table 1. Features, matching functions, and weights of the playmaker similarity metric

Feature	Type of Feature Matching*	Weight
Location East-West	Absolute Fuzzy Range: 3	0.190
Location North-South	Absolute Fuzzy Range: 3	0.190
Severity	Absolute Fuzzy Range: 2	0.095
Time of Day	Exact	0.048
Direction of Majority	Partial (case indifferent)	0.381
Effect on Major Facilities	Absolute Fuzzy Range: 1	0.095

* The types of feature matching are functions defined in Esteem® [7]

2.3 Cases

For our prototype, we selected 20 plays from 135 available in the National Playbook [2]. We focused on plays affecting the southeastern United States because our ATC domain expert was most knowledgeable about this area and its traffic flows. A full implementation of PlayMaker would require input from multiple controllers who work in various parts of the country.

In CBR, a case is a representation of an experience including a situation and a solution. In ATC, a play is representation of a solution only. To build the cases for PlayMaker, we interviewed a domain expert about each play to determine the situations to which it applied. Our domain expert examined each play and described the situations where it is normally used. This process resulted in 32 cases based on 20 plays because several plays could be applied to multiple situations. For example, the *Florida to NE 1* play can only be applied to situations occurring during the day whereas the *Florida to NE 2* can be applied to situations occurring in the day, evening, or overnight. We created cases for each situation to which a play can be applied. We then presented all the situations to our expert and asked him to characterize each based on the features.

Example. Northbound traffic from Florida follows a path that takes them from the east coast of Florida, off the coast of Georgia and South Carolina, then over North Carolina, Virginia, Maryland and Delaware. Today, however, a strong storm will reach North Carolina and Virginia at about 10:00 am, closing the area to traffic. Controllers at the ATCSCC look at the weather forecast and choose a play to address the situation. A likely choice is a play called *Florida to NE 3* that reroutes this traffic west over the Appalachians and Ohio River Valley. This play is quite severe and affects hundreds of flights. A representation of this situation as a case in PlayMaker is shown in Table 2.

Table 2. An example problem situation described using the PlayMaker features

Feature	Value	Comments
Location East-West	16	These Location values yield the southeast of Virginia and the northeast of North Carolina.
Location North-South	-2	
Severity	5	No traffic may come through the area
Time of Day	0700 to 1859	Storm forecast to arrive at 10:00 am
Direction of Majority	N	Northbound traffic primarily
Effect on Major Facilities	2	New York and Washington are both affected

3 Prototype Validation

We performed a validation of the PlayMaker prototype by comparing its responses to novel situations to those of an ATC domain expert. Our goal is to assess whether the Playmaker model can make recommendations like a human expert.

3.1 Methodology

The dataset we used included all the cases we coded in the Playmaker and a set of 6 new situations (first column Table 3) that we designed to test the prototype. Because our case base included only cases in the south and southeastern United States, we developed our test situations from this region as well. We constructed six test situations using the following procedure. First, we identified several general locations that were represented in our case base: the Carolinas, the Mid-Atlantic, the Appalachians, and Dallas. We identified one or two cases in each location and changed one or more features. We developed a verbal description of the situation and presented these to our expert. We also developed PlayMaker target cases for each situation and entered these in the PlayMaker prototype.

Table 3. Test situastions and recommend plays from the domain expert and PlayMaker

Test Situation	Domain Expert	PlayMaker: Top 3 retrievals (with ties)	Sim. Score
1. Hurricane out in the Atlantic Ocean. Effects (heavy rain, high winds) will start being felt in the Outer Banks of North Carolina around 1000 today.	There is no play in the playbook for this situation. It would be negotiated.	Inland Atlantic Route – Northbound	65
		MGM 1 – Morning	62
		Florida to NE3 - Morning	58
		Florida to NE3 - Evening	58
1.1 Move location of Test Situation 1 to near Wilmington, NC. All other features identical.	Florida to NE 1	Florida to NE 1 - Morning	65
		Inland Atlantic Route – Northbound	65
		Florida to NE 2 - Morning	62
2. Strong thunderstorms north and northeast of Dallas starting around 1500 today.	DFW East 1	DFW East 1 – Morning	80
		DFW East 1 – Evening	75
		Florida to NE 2 - Morning	42
3. Moderate storms over southern North Carolina and all of South Carolina, affecting north and southbound routes, starting around 2000 tonight and continuing until 0300 tomorrow.	Florida to NE 2	Florida to NE 1 - Morning	63
		Inland Atlantic Route – Northbound	60
		Florida to NE 2 - Evening	58
4. Two navaids out of service along J75 from 0000 tonight until 0600 tomorrow.	No J75 1 or No J75 3, depending on the level of congestion in ZDC.	A761	79
		Inland Atlantic Route – Southbound	79
		No J75 3	73
		No J75 1	73
		No WHITE/No WAVEY	73
5. Very heavy congestion expected all day today along northbound routes in ZDC.	Florida to NE 3	Inland Atlantic Route - Northbound	90
		Snowbird 7	65
		Florida to NE 3 - Morning	58
6. Moderate weather affecting all Appalachian Mountain areas all day today, coupled with heavy congestion in ZDC during the day.	Florida to NE 3	Inland Atlantic Route	65
		MGM 1 – Morning	58
		MGM 1 - Evening	53

3.2 Results

The full validation results are presented in Table 3. For four of the six test situations, the play recommended by the domain expert was also one of the top three plays retrieved by PlayMaker. However, the similarity scores on PlayMaker were low (58-80% match). This indicates that while our case base and metrics are on the right track, more work is needed to increase the similarity scores for the top retrieved cases. In particular, because of their importance to the match, small discrepancies or inconsistencies in the features Location and Direction of Majority have major effects on the score. For example, on Test Situation 2, changing Direction of Majority from W to SW (which would be another reasonable interpretation of the direction) changes the similarity score from 80% to 65%. More precision in specifying these features is necessary.

Mismatches. The two cases where PlayMaker did not match the expert's recommendations at all reveal two interesting complexities of the system that must be incorporated in later versions.

First, Test Situation 1 was unexpectedly difficult for PlayMaker to handle. We unintentionally created a situation for which controllers in the field do not use a Playbook play. In the test situation, controllers at the ATCSCC would develop an ad hoc play to precisely address the situation rather than institute a stored play. PlayMaker, on the other hand, retrieved several cases that seem to fit. The similarity scores were low but were in the range of our other test situations.

To continue within the validation, we modified Test Situation 1 and moved it several units southwest to Wilmington, NC. This modification is listed as Test Situation 1.1 in Table 3. In this case, the domain expert recommended the same play as PlayMaker. The most important factor, then, appears to be the location of Test Situation 1. When this situation affects the Outer Banks, controllers do not use a Playbook play but do when the same situation occurs farther south. For this situation, our Location features and similarity metric (which uses a the Fuzzy Range function provided by Esteem) are not precise enough to make this distinction easily. Apparently, in some locations, small differences are important but in other areas, they are not.

The best way to make PlayMaker handle Test Situation 1 is to improve the precision of Location and increase the overall retrieval threshold. Because so many of our similarity scores were generally low, we set a low threshold (50%) in order to retrieve at least a few cases. However, in situations like Test Situation 1, it appears that small differences in Location can be operationally significant. Better representations of Location would provide higher match scores and allow us to increase our threshold. Because no stored cases would be similar to Test Situation 1, PlayMaker's retrieved cases would fall below the threshold and PlayMaker would essentially respond "No Play."

The second mismatch, Test Situation 6, was more complex than our set of features and similarity metric could handle. We could specify either the location of the storm (Appalachian Mountains) or the location of the congestion (ZDC) but not both. As such, PlayMaker's best match avoided the storms in the Appalachians but rerouted the traffic directly into ZDC, which would compound an already bad situation there. The expert recognized this complexity and selected a play that reroutes some of the traffic through the weather in the Appalachians and avoids the most congested areas of ZDC. This is allowable because the severity of the weather was moderate. Future versions of PlayMaker should provide some way to handle multiple simultaneous situations within a single case.

4 Future Work

The PlayMaker prototype presents a first step toward developing a CBR system to replicate the process of using plays in the ATC National Playbook. While it does not demonstrate the complete concept, it helps demonstrate that the idea is feasible and makes clear the areas that need urgent attention. It was not worthwhile to start directly developing the system from scratch without before having this first assessment. The next steps will consist of the development of a prototype developed from scratch to this application including all elements required to demonstrate the feasibility of transitioning the tool for deployment.

4.1 Improvements to Features

First, the representation of Location is very crude. We created a two-dimensional grid and used it to represent an entire event location. In the actual operation, however, an event could be a three-dimensional weather system hundreds of miles long and changing over time. Characterizing such a complex event using our Location features lacks a great deal of information and makes the feature susceptible to error when coding cases or presenting them to experts.

An operational version of PlayMaker would allow users to specify locations as polygons, using latitude-longitude geometry, and would contain altitude and movement parameters. This is similar to how controllers define what they call Flow Constrained Areas in their automation system. In Figure 2, we illustrate how such a feature might look.

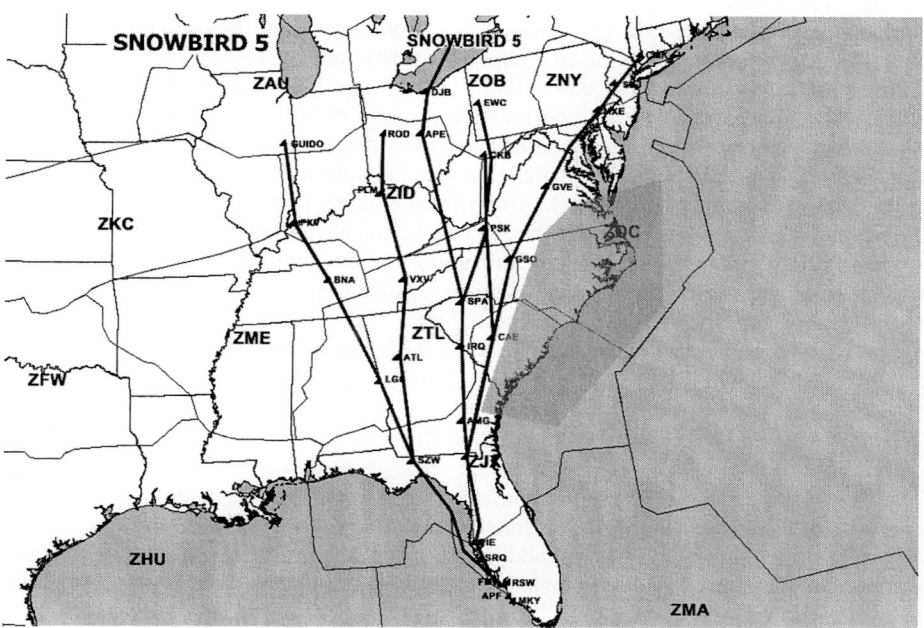

Fig. 2. A map showing the play known as Snowbird 5 with a more complex and precise representation of Location, shown as a gray polygon

The next version of PlayMaker should represent this feature with graphs. Consequently, we will need to employ graph matching methods [8] to assess the similarity between these locations. This would allow much more accurate matching of locations than the current method which is very subjective and error prone.

Second, we must similarly add precision to the Direction of the Majority metric. Currently, an entire set of complex routes must be distilled to a single direction. This is subjective and introduces mistakes. For example, the play known as *No WHITE No WAVEY* is generally southbound but its routes are actually sometimes southbound, sometimes southeast, and sometimes southwest bound.

When the situation is entered into PlayMaker, the user would need to judge how to characterize the flows. Because of the importance of the Direction feature, a small discrepancy on this feature can have a major effect on the match. A better method is to characterize the flows according to categories rather than directions. For example, instead of categorizing traffic coming to Florida as southbound, it could be characterized as *East Coast Florida Arrivals*. This more closely matches how controllers talk about this feature and it would reduce the chance of discrepancy or error.

Third, the system must be able to represent complex situations. In particular, it must be able to represent situations with multiple event locations. For example, our Test Situation 6 had two locations (Appalachian Mountains and ZDC) and PlayMaker could not provide a useful recommendation. One way to implement this improvement is to specify a list of events (e.g., primary, secondary) events based on their severity. For example, in Test Situation 6, the storm would be the primary event because few aircraft could use the area. The congestion over ZDC would be a secondary event.

Finally, current controller automation tools can model traffic flows and can compute which traffic would be affected by a situation in a given three-dimensional location. PlayMaker could use these to compute Severity rather than having to ask experts to estimate it. Examining our cases, there was not a wide range of responses and it seemed that our expert was not confident making the severity judgments. The Severity feature would still represent the same aspect of the situation. That is, how much of the traffic that normally traverses the area will be able to do so when the event occurs? Severity, in this case, could change from a categorical feature to a proportion. Additionally, we may investigate the benefit of incorporating fuzzy labels into this representation. Given the presence of uncertainty in the acquisition of the feature, we may rely on the use of fuzzy rules as employed by Bandini and Manzoni [9]. Main and Dillon [10] have already combined fuzzy and crisp values using a retrieval method based on neural networks. We shall examine its extension also to combine graph-based features.

4.2 Improvements to the Case Base

The PlayMaker case base currently contains only a small portion of the existing cases and is focused on the southeastern United States. Expanding the case base to include all areas of the country may reveal additional insights about the features and similarity assessment. This will involve knowledge elicitation sessions with controllers working in numerous different areas.

In addition, our case base was developed by using the existing plays and asking an expert to describe the situations to which the play applies. An alternative method might be to use ATCSCC records of real situations. This would significantly increase the size of the case base because a play may be used for many situations. By basing the case base on real situations rather than typical ones, we might remove some of the subjectivity inherent in determining the characteristics of a typical situation.

4.3 Adaptation

PlayMaker currently contains no methods for adaptation but a system that could derive new plays from existing ones likely would be useful. The difficulty is that the current method by which plays are designed is extremely complex and not well understood. By involving experts in the CBR adaptation process itself, we could leverage their rich knowledge knowledge of the airspace, existing traffic flows, and political and economic implications of different decisions. For example, experts could be asked to manually adapt recommended plays in PlayMaker which would help us understand their process.

Deriving new plays requires understanding the effects of reroutes on the overall system. As it stands, PlayMaker uses only plays that have already been designed and agreed upon by controllers and stakeholders. Any recommended play is internally sound because it would not exist in PlayMaker otherwise. In this way, PlayMaker reflects the knowledge of the experts without explicitly containing it. For derived plays, however, no such assurance would exist because the derived plays would not exist in the Playbook and would not have undergone the negotiation and validation process. To make use of an already successful manual process, PlayMaker could be built to derive plays offline without waiting for situations to occur and present the derived plays to the controllers and stakeholders. The experts could then negotiate and improve the play as needed and enter the final play into PlayMaker. In this way, derived plays would continue to have some assurance of validity without modeling all aspects of the play development process.

4.4 Maintenance

Watson [11] discusses methods for maintaining CBR systems when they are fielded. If PlayMaker were fielded, it could quickly develop a large base of actual cases because a play is implemented almost every day during the summer. As Watson discusses, redundant cases will need to be identified and eliminated. In addition, as traffic flows in the ATC system change, plays and their associated cases will become obsolete and will require modification or removal. For example, when a new airline moves into an airport (or goes out of business), the volume and characteristics of routes from that airport change. Affected plays may need to be reviewed and revised to reflect the new traffic flows. Once adaptation is included in PlayMaker, adaptation rules will also need to be monitored and refined over time as well.

5 Conclusions

Though this is an initial study, it suggests that the PlayMaker concept is promising. To create a useful system that can recommend plays, next enhancements should focus on improving the case base and the index features. Then, enhancements should seek to add adaptation functions to move the tool toward supporting the design of new plays.

Finally, PlayMaker highlights some of the complexities associated with converting information that is already in a case-like form into a CBR system. The experts who designed the plays in the Playbook did not include all their knowledge and experience in the plays. They still hold deep knowledge about the history of individual plays, the past success of plays, and the implications of plays that is not captured in the Playbook itself. Interviewing the experts reveals some of these complexities but others remain undocumented, as the mismatches we encountered demonstrate. Perhaps by encouraging the experts to document their cases in different ways, future versions of PlayMaker can be improved.

Acknowledgements

We wish to thank Kotb (Sam) Elbialy and Pieter Linden, Master's students in the College of Information Science and Technology at Drexel University, for their assistance conceptualizing the features of PlayMaker. We also wish to thank David Conley of the Federal Aviation Administration for serving as our ATC domain expert. Rosina Weber is supported in part by the National Institute for Systems Test and Productivity at USF under the USA Space and Naval Warfare Systems Command grant no. N00039-02-C-3244, for 2130 032 L0, 2002.

References

1. National Research Council: Flight to the Future: Human Factors in Air Traffic Control. National Academy Press, Washington, DC (1997)
2. Federal Aviation Administration: Air Traffic Control System Command Center National Severe Weather Playbook. Retrieved February 29, 2004 from the World Wide Web: http://www.fly.faa.gov/PLAYBOOK/pbindex.html. (2004)
3. Aamodt, A., Plaza, E.: Case-Based Reasoning: Foundational Issues, Methodological Variations, and System Approaches. Artificial Intelligence Communications 7 (1994) 39-59
4. Bonzano, A., Cunningham, P.: Hierarchical CBR for Multiple Aircraft Conflict Resolution in Air Traffic Control. Proceedings of the European Conference on Artificial Intelligence, Vol. 13. John Wiley and Sons, Hoboken, NJ (1998) 58-62
5. Bonzano, A., Cunningham, P., Meckiff, C.: ISAC: A CBR System for Decision Support in Air Traffic Control. In: Smith, I., and Faltings, B. (eds.): Advances in Case-Based Reasoning. Lecture Notes in Artificial Intelligence, Vol. 1186. Springer-Verlag, Berlin Heidelberg New York (1996) 44-57
6. Logi, F., Ritchie, S. G.: A Multi-Agent Architecture for Cooperative Inter-Jurisdictional Traffic Congestion Management. Transportation Research Part C 10 (2002) 507-527
7. Esteem Software Incorporated: Esteem Version 1.4. Stottler Henke Associates, San Mateo, CA. (1994)
8. Bunke, H., Messmer, B.: Recent Advances in Graph Matching. International Journal of Pattern Recognition and Artificial Intelligence 11 (1997) 169-203
9. Bandini, S., S. Manzoni, S.: Application of Fuzzy Indexing and Retrieval In Case Based Reasoning For Design. In: Proceedings of the 16th ACM SAC Symposium on Applied Computing. ACM Press, New York, NY (2001) 462-466
10. Main, J., Dillon, T: A Neuro-Fuzzy Methodology for Case Retrieval and an Object-Oriented Case Schema for Structuring Case Bases and their Application to Fashion Footwear Design. In: Pal, S. K., Dillon, T. S., Yeung, D. S., (eds.): Soft Computing in Case Based Reasoning. Springer-Verlag, London (2001)
11. Watson, I. A Case Study of Maintenance of a Commercially Fielded Case-Based Reasoning System. Computational Intelligence 17 (2001) 386-398

Case-Based Collaborative Web Search

Evelyn Balfe and Barry Smyth

Smart Media Institute, Department of Computer Science,
University College Dublin, Belfield, Dublin 4, Ireland
{Evelyn.Balfe,Barry.Smyth}@ucd.ie [*]

Abstract. Web search is typically memory-less, in the sense that each new search query is considered afresh and 'solved' from scratch. We believe that this reflects the strong information retrieval bias that has influenced the development of Web search engines. In this paper we argue for the value of a fresh approach to Web search, one that is founded on the notion of reuse and that seeks to exploit past search histories to answer future search queries. We describe a novel case-based technique and evaluate it using live-user data. We show that it can deliver significant performance benefits when compared to alternative strategies including meta-search.

1 Introduction

Today, Web search engines are critical components of the Internet infrastructure that drives the information economy. Every day approximately 60 terabytes of new content is added to the World-Wide Web [1]. Daily Google alone receives more than 200 million queries for its 4 billion or so indexed pages. Unfortunately, a significant portion of searchers are frustrated and disappointed by the performance of search engines when it comes to their ability to deliver the right result at the right time. One important reason for this is that the information retrieval techniques that form the core of Web search engines are not so well suited to the reality of Web search; not surprising given that many of these techniques were originally developed for specialised search tasks by expert users, over limited document collections. As a result, these shortcomings lead to the following inter-related problems:

- *The Coverage Problem*: the continued growth of the Web means that no single search engine can hope to provide complete coverage [2].
- *The Indexing Problem*: the heterogeneous nature of Web documents and the lack of any reliable quality control makes for an indexing nightmare [3].
- *The Ranking Problem*: ranking results on the basis of weighted overlaps with query terms has proven to be unsatisfactory in Web search [4,5].
- *The Query Problem*: the preponderance of poorly formed, vague queries means that most searches are under-specified to begin with [6].

---

[*] The support of the Informatics Research Initiative of Enterprise Ireland is gratefully acknowledged.

Recent years have seen a number of key developments in Web search, many of which are designed to take specific advantage of the unique characteristics of the Web, and the particular way that Web users search for information. For instance, early on, researchers recognised the advantages of combining the results of many individual search engines to produce meta-search engines with improved coverage and accuracy characteristics [7]. More recently, methods have been developed to incorporate information about the Web's topology, specifically regarding the connectivity of individual pages as a way to recognise and rank authoritative pages (see for example, [4, 5]). Others have looked at how clustering techniques can be used to organise a flat list of results into a more structured collection of topical clusters [8]; while this does not solve the query problem, it at least helps the search engine to separate out the different meanings of a vague query into collections of topically related results.

It is perhaps not surprising to note that these developments have all tended to adopt a traditional information retrieval perspective in the sense that they seek to improve the manner in which documents are represented, retrieved or ranked, by focusing at the level of an individual search session. They view Web search as *memory-less*, with each new search treated as a novel problem for the Web search engine to solve. Specifically they ignore regularities in the query-page mappings that are strong indicators for the value of a case-based perspective.

Such a case-based perspective emphasises a reuse-oriented approach, rather than a from-scratch approach, to Web search. Thus, in this paper we propose a *case-based* approach that is *query-centric* rather than document-centric, one that exploits repetition within the query history and regularities within the result-space. We have already shown how the I-SPY search engine can deliver significant precision and recall improvements by reusing past search sessions to re-rank new result-lists [9–11], even though this previous work has focused on only the very simplest approach to reuse, by exploiting exact matches between new queries and the queries associated with past search sessions. This earlier work could not really be viewed as case-based in a true sense. Indeed reviewers and other commentators have often expressed concern about the degree of query repetition that might be available in practice and how this will ultimately limit the benefits offered by I-SPY. As a response, the central contribution of this paper is a more general approach to reuse in Web search. The new approach is informed by a true case-based reasoning perspective, in that it leverages partial matches between queries and that it extends I-SPY's reuse-based ranking technique to exploit the search histories associated with these partial matches. We show that this technique can deliver significant performance improvements in live-user trials when compared to alternatives such as the standard version of I-SPY or meta-search.

2 Related Work

Primarily, this work has been motivated by the need to improve the way that Web search engines cope with vague user queries. Our basic approach has been to introduce a form of context into search by mining the query-selection patterns of a community of like-minded users, and then to reuse these patterns to solve new search problems for this community. Now we are expanding this approach to include CBR techniques with the aim of enhancing our improved search technique.

Vague queries are often problematic because they lack context; the query 'jaguar' does not help to distinguish between automobile, wildlife or operating system pages, any of which might be relevant to the searcher. One way, therefore, to improve a vague query is to expand it by including additional context terms. This can be done according to two basic approaches: either by explicitly establishing context up-front [12] or by implicitly inferring context from the search environment. The most reliable method of attaining context is explicitly from the user. Unfortunately users cannot be depended upon to actually provide this information. It is for this reason that context is often automatically inferred. This usually occurs by analysing a user's behaviour either during or prior to search (see [13] and [14]).

Primarily our work looks at methods to reuse past search queries and their associated result selections in order to re-rank future result-lists. A related idea has been explored by [15]. This work describes how the use of past queries can improve automatic query expansion by using automatic feedback from the top documents returned in a result list. Another area of related research—query-log analysis—resonates well with our approach, in the sense that it considers the value of historical search session information contained within query logs. Briefly, [16] look for correlations between query terms and document terms that can be mined from a search engine's query log. The basic idea is that, if a set of documents is often selected for the same queries, then the terms in these documents must be strongly linked to the terms in the queries. These correlated document terms serve as candidate expansion terms as part of a query-expansion technique, rather than as a result-ranking technique. Nevertheless, the idea of mining query logs is certainly in the spirit of what we are doing within I-SPY and its variations.

In this paper we are investigating the integration of the above techniques with a CBR approach. Previously, most CBR techniques have tended to focus on particular application domains for textual CBR rather than the broader area of Web search. For example in the area of information retrieval tasks, the work of Rissland [17] looks at the application of CBR to legal information retrieval and Burke et al. [18] describe a case-based approach to question-answering tasks. Similarly, in recent years there has been considerable research looking at how CBR techniques can deal with less structured textual cases. This has led to a range of so-called *textual CBR* techniques [19].In the context of Web search, one particularly relevant piece of work concerns the *Broadway* recommender system [20], and specifically the Broadway-QR query refinement technique that uses case-based techniques to reuse past query refinements in order to recommend new refinements. Briefly, Broadway's cases reference a precise experience within a search session and include a problem description (made up of a sequence of behavioural elements including a sequence of recent queries), a solution (a new query refinement configuration), and an evaluation (based on historical explicit user satisfaction ratings when this case was previously recommended). The work of [21] apply CBR techniques to Web search in a different way. Very briefly, their *PersonalSearcher* agent combines user profiling and textual case-based reasoning to dynamically filter Web documents according to a user's learned preferences.

3 Principles of Case-Based Collaborative Search

Our case-based approach to Web search has developed out of the I-SPY project (ispy.ucd.ie). As we will see, I-SPY is a meta-search engine with a difference: it records past search sessions, both the queries submitted and the result pages selected, and uses these search histories to re-rank results based on the selection patterns of past users. In its original form, I-SPY would not be described as a case-based approach to Web search because past search sessions are reused based on exact query matches only. We will describe how this can be readily extended to deliver a case-based approach by incorporating a more sophisticated query reuse model and a new result ranking metric.

3.1 I-SPY

I-SPY implements an approach to Web search that we refer to as *collaborative search* because of the way in which it takes advantage of the search histories of other users, ideally a community of like-minded users. The I-SPY implementation of collaborative search does not implement a new search engine per se. Instead it operates in the mode of a meta-search engine or result post-processor, combining the results of underlying search engines as shown in Figure 1.

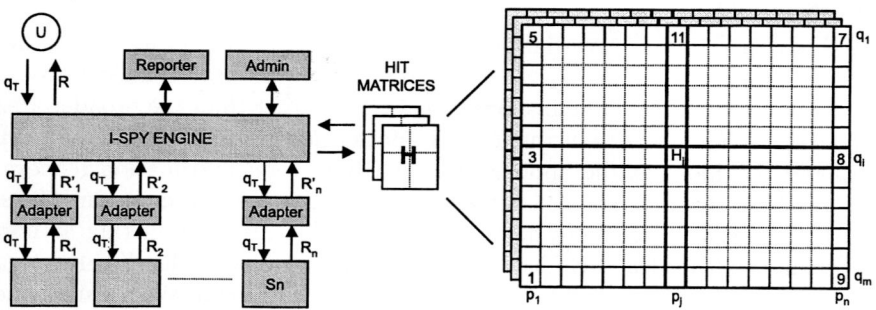

Fig. 1. The I-SPY system architecture.

The Hit-Matrix. I-SPY's central contribution takes the form of a *hit-matrix*, H, which is a record of the results selected in past search sessions. Each time a user selects page p_j for query q_i the value of H_{ij} is incremented. Thus, H_{ij} can be viewed as the number of times that p_j has been selected as a result for query q_i, for example Figure 1 shows that for a query, q_1 and a page, p_1, the value of H_{11} is 5. The row of H that corresponds to query q_i, provides a complete account of the relative number of all page selections for this query over all search sessions that have used this query. In reality, the hit values for query-page pairs will decay over time, as a way of coping with changing selection patterns as well as new and out-of-date pages, but details of this decay function are not necessary for what concerns us here.

Query Reuse. When a user submits a new target query, q_T, I-SPY adapts this query for each underlying search engine and combines their individual results lists by using a standard meta-search ranking metric that gives priority to high-ranking results that appear in the result-lists of multiple search engines. In addition, however, I-SPY also generates a second result-list, this one made up of all those pages from the hit-matrix row, corresponding to q_T, that have a non-zero value. These pages have been previously selected for the query q_T; obviously if q_T has never before occurred then this second result-list will be empty. Assuming it is not empty, however, the results are scored according to the relevance metric shown in Equation 1. This metric computes the number of selections received by a page p_j for the query q_T, relative to the total number of page selections that have occurred for q_T. For example, a relevance of 0.4 for p_j and q_T means that 40% of the page selections from result-lists for q_T have been for this page, p_j. I-SPY's key innovation is this ability to exploit the hit-matrix as a *direct* source of relevancy information; after all, the hit-matrix entries reflect concrete relevancy judgments by users with respect to query-page mappings. Most search engines, on the other hand, rely on *indirect* relevancy judgments based on overlaps between query and page terms.

$$Relevance(p_j, q_T) = \frac{H_{Tj}}{\sum_{\forall j} H_{Tj}} \qquad (1)$$

Collaborative Search. Although relatively simple, the above approach works remarkably well as long as the query-space is limited to a relatively narrow and uniform context. One of the fundamental ideas of I-SPY, and the reason for the term 'collaborative search', is that a hit-matrix should be populated with queries and selections from a community of users operating within a specific domain of interest. As such, I-SPY facilitates the creation of multiple hit-matrices to offer different communities of users access to a search service that is adapted for their query-space and its preferred pages. For example, a motoring Web site might configure a hit-matrix for its users. I-SPY facilitates this through a simple forms interface and in doing so, provides the Web site with access to a search interface that is associated with this new hit-matrix. As visitors to this site use its search service, their queries and page selections will populate the hit-matrix and I-SPY's ranking metric will help to disambiguate vague queries by promoting previously preferred pages for repeated queries. The query 'jaguar' is likely to result in the prioritisation of pages related to the car manufacturer rather than sites related to wildlife or the Apple operating system: previous searches for this term are far more likely to result in the selection of these car pages since the users will have been searching from a motoring Web site.

3.2 A Case-Based Perspective

The benefits of I-SPY notwithstanding, its exact-match approach to query reuse exacerbates the sparseness of the hit-matrix, and must be viewed as a potentially limiting factor. Arguments can be forwarded regarding the prevalence of short queries in Web search and the large volume of query traffic, and how these are likely to lead to a significant degree of query repetition, a fact that is born out by query log analysis. However, in the main, the fact that an I-SPY user with the first-time query 'java inventor' cannot benefit from the past selections of searches under the queries 'inventor java' or 'creator java' or even 'java language' is, at best, an opportunity missed. Of course to a case-based reasoning researcher this limitation is needless and the solution is self evident: instead of relying on exact-match query-reuse, partial query matches should be accommodated so that a broader range of past search histories can influence the final result-list returned to the user.

Search Histories as Cases. This case-based perspective considers each row of the hit-matrix to be an individual case, c_i, or, equivalently, a $k + 1$-tuple made up of the query component (a set of query terms) plus k result-pairs, each with a page id, p_i, and an associated relevance value, r_i, computed from the hit-matrix (see Equation 2). The *problem specification* part of the case (see Equation 3) corresponds to the query terms. The *solution* part of the case (see Equation 4) corresponds to the result-pairs; that is, the set of page selections that have been accumulated as a result of past uses of the corresponding query. The *target problem* is, of course, represented by the target query terms.

$$c_i = (q_i, (p_1, r_1), ..., (p_k, r_k)) \qquad (2)$$

$$Spec(c_i) = q_i \qquad (3)$$

$$Sol(c_i) = ((p_1, r_1), ..., (p_k, r_k)) \qquad (4)$$

$$Rel(p_j, c_i) = r_j \text{ if } (p_j, r_j) \in Sol(c_i); = 0, otherwise. \qquad (5)$$

Similarity-Based Query Reuse. Case similarity, then, means being able to measure query-query similarity, and the most obvious metric is the simple term overlap metric shown in Equation 6. During the retrieval stage, it allows our case-based system to rank-order past search cases according to their similarity to the target query so that all, or a subset of, the similar cases might be reused during result ranking.

$$Sim(q_T, c_i) = \frac{|q_T \cap Spec(c_i)|}{|q_T \cup Spec(c_i)|} \quad (6)$$

Similarity-Based Result Ranking. If multiple similar cases are available for a target query, then there are multiple search histories (case solutions) to inform the result ranking. We must consider how to extend I-SPY's relevance metric, which assumes single page occurrences and single page relevance values. Now the same page may recur in multiple case solutions, each with a different relevance value. For example, the page *www.sun.com* may have a high relevance value (let's say, 0.8) for a past query 'java language' but it may have a lower relevance for another past query 'java' (let's say, 0.33). The question is: how can these relevance values be combined to produce a single relevance score for this page relative to the target query, 'java inventor'? We propose a normalised weighted relevance metric that combines individual relevance scores for individual page-query combinations. This is achieved using the weighted sum of the individual relevance scores, such that each score is weighted by the similarity of its corresponding query to the target query. Thus, in our example above, the relevance of the page *www.sun.com* is 0.516: the sum of 0.264 (that is, 0.8 page relevance to query 'java language' multiplied by the 0.33 query similarity between this query and the target, 'java inventor') and 0.165 (0.33*0.5 for the past query, 'java'), divided by 0.83, the sum of the query similarities. Equation 7 provides the details of this weighted relevance metric with respect to a page p_j, a target query q_T, and a set of retrieved similar cases $c_1, ..., c_n$ $Exists(p_j, c_i)$ is simply a flag that is set to 1 when p_i is one of the result pages represented in the solution of case c_i, and $\text{Rel}(p_j,c_i)$ is the relevance score for p_j in c_i (see 5).

$$WRel(p_j, q_T, c_1, ..., c_n) = \frac{\sum_{i=1...n} Rel(p_j, c_i) \bullet Sim(q_T, c_i))}{\sum_{i=1...n} Exists(p_j, c_i) \bullet Sim(q_T, c_i)} \quad (7)$$

3.3 Discussion

The collaborative search idea implemented in I-SPY is novel, in an IR context at least, because of its adoption of query-reuse techniques. However, its limited form of query-reuse appears naive from a case-based perspective, because reuse is limited to exact matches only. We have described how to remove this limitation by assuming a fairly standard case-based perspective.

Of course this case-based approach is not without its pitfalls. For example, the simple model of query similarities permits the retrieval of unrelated cases; a case corresponding to the past query 'ethernet inventor' could be retrieved, for instance, in response to the target query 'java inventor' because it has a non-zero similarity, even though its solution part is unlikely to be useful. We must bear this in mind during the evaluation. If this scenario turns out to be commonplace then it could degrade result-list quality significantly, because irrelevant results will be actively promoted by the case-based system. One standard solution would be to threshold retrieval so that only the best matching cases are selected, rather than all cases with a non-zero similarity to the target query; limiting retrieval to cases with a query similarity above 0.5 would prevent the specific problem above. But of course this can also work against us, by preventing the retrieval of some appropriate cases with low query similarity. For example, the 0.5 similarity threshold would prevent the relevant 'java language' case from being retrieved. Regardless, the hope is that such spurious query matches, while they will inevitably occur, will be infrequent and diluted by more numerous appropriate matches.

4 Evaluation

In this section we will explore the practical benefits of our new case-based approach. We will use live-user search data and compare case-based performance to the performance of both the standard I-SPY system and a standard meta-search engine. Our central hypothesis is that the case-based approach will result in significant improvements in search performance. We believe that result precision will improve with our new ranking metric, as it allows us to leverage the selection histories of a greater range of related search sessions. We believe that result recall will also improve because these related search sessions are likely to contribute new relevant results to the result-list, results that would not have been retrieved by the target query on its own. Finally, we expect that these benefits will easily outweigh any problems that might occur from spurious query matches.

4.1 Data-Set

The data used in this evaluation was collected during a live-user experiment that involved 92 computer science students from the Department of Computer Science at University College Dublin and took place in October 2003. The original experiment was designed to evaluate the benefits of the standard I-SPY system, relative to a standard meta-search engine, in the context of a fact-finding or question-answering exercise. To frame the search task, we developed a set of 25 general knowledge AI and computer science questions, each requiring the student to find out a particular fact (time, place, person's name, system name etc.).

The students were randomly divided into two groups. Group 1 contained 45 students and Group 2 contained the remaining 47. Group 1 served as the *training group* for I-SPY, in the sense that their search histories were used to populate the I-SPY hit-matrix but no re-ranking occurred for their search results. This group also served as a control against which to judge the search behaviour of the second group of users, who served as the *test group*. In total the Group 1 users produced 1049 individual queries and selected a combined total of 1046 pages, while the Group 2 users used 1705 queries and selected 1624 pages.

In summary, the data from this earlier live-user experiment provides the following key information to form the basis of our current evaluation: the queries submitted by each user; the pages that they selected from the subsequent result-lists; the position of these pages within the result-list; the pages where they located a correct answer to a particular question; and the hit-matrix produced by the Group 1 users. From this data we can build a case-base (essentially the Group 1 hit-matrix), a set of test problems (the Group 2 queries), and a set of correct solutions to these problems (the pages that are known to contain the correct answer to a particular question). Accordingly, we can "re-run" the live-user experiment by responding to Group 2 queries with the new result-lists that are recommended by the case-based version of I-SPY (CB), and we can evaluate the quality of these result-lists with reference to our known set of correct pages, comparing the outcome to the standard I-SPY and meta-search performance results. We actually evaluate 5 different variations of CB, each with a different minimum similarity threshold (0, 0.25, 0.5, 0.75, 1) during case retrieval to limit the range of retrieval cases.

4.2 Overall Accuracy

Perhaps the most basic measure of search engine accuracy concerns its ability to return a single relevant result in its result-list; we will look at more refined measures that focus on the number of relevant results and their positions in due course. To measure the overall accuracy for each search engine (CB, I-SPY and Meta), we compare each of the full result-lists returned by these search engines (including the 5 CB variations), for the 1705 test queries, to the list of known correct results associated with these queries. We compute the percentage of result-lists that contain at least one correct result.

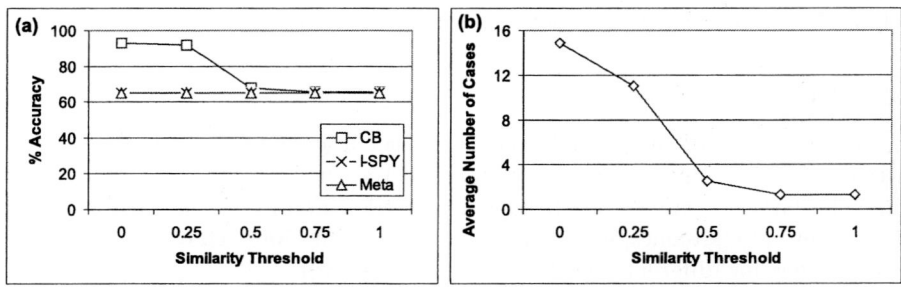

Fig. 2. (a) Overall Accuracy (b) Average number of cases.

The results are presented in Figure 2(a) as a graph of overall accuracy against similarity threshold. Each plot corresponds to a single search engine. The plots for I-SPY and Meta remain flat at 65%; they are unaffected by variations in the CB similarity threshold. The results clearly show the accuracy benefits of the case-based method: at a similarity threshold >0, it returns a correct result page in 93% of sessions, and in 92% of sessions with the similarity threshold >0.25. This is a relative improvement of 43% over I-SPY and Meta for CB. The benefit here is derived from the fact that CB is able to include additional pages beyond those found by the underlying search engines in the result-lists returned for a given query. These additional results come from the result-lists contained within the similar cases. In contrast, Meta and I-SPY are effectively limited to those results returned by the underlying search engines; I-SPY simply reorders the Meta results using its relevance metric. The CB benefit proves that CB's additional pages are frequently relevant to the target query.

It is interesting to note how the CB accuracy drops off sharply with increasing similarity threshold. From a purely CBR perspective this appears strange at first glance. Increasing the similarity threshold will improve the average similarity of the cases being retrieved and we are conditioned to expect that this is likely to improve any 'solution' that is derived from these cases. Not so in our case-based view of search however, because the number of cases retrieved and the diversity of the results, is likely to be important. When we plot the average number of similar cases retrieved, for a typical query, across the different similarity thresholds (see Figure 2(b)) we can see that there is a sharp drop in cases between the 0.25 and 0.5 thresholds. At the 0 and 0.25 thresholds, 15 and 11 cases, respectively, are being retrieved for a target query, but this falls off to 2.5 for the 0.5 threshold and then 1.3 cases beyond this. At the higher thresholds there are simply not enough similar cases to make a meaningful additional contribution to the result-lists offered by the meta-search and so the benefits enjoyed by CB are fractional. So, even though low similarity thresholds may permit the reuse of unrelated search sessions (e.g., 'inventor java' would be considered similar to 'inventor ethernet'), we find that the benefits of a greater number and variety of reusable cases easily outweighs any problems due to inappropriate retrievals, which our weighted relevance metric will tend to discount anyway.

4.3 Precision vs. Recall

The standard objective test of search engine accuracy is the precision and recall test: the former computes the percentage of returned results that are relevant while the latter computes the percentage of relevant results that are returned. We measure the percentage precision and recall values for each of the techniques under review for different result-list sizes (k=5 to 30).

The results are presented as precision and recall graphs, for each of the four similarity thresholds, in Figure 3(a&b). Each graph presents the precision (or recall) plot for the 5 variations of CB, along with I-SPY and Meta, for different sizes of result-lists, k. As expected we find that precision tends to fall-off with increasing result-list sizes; typically the number of relevant results is much less than k, and the majority of these relevant results should be positioned near the top of result-lists. The critical point is that, once again the performance benefits due to the case-based approach are clear, especially at low similarity thresholds.

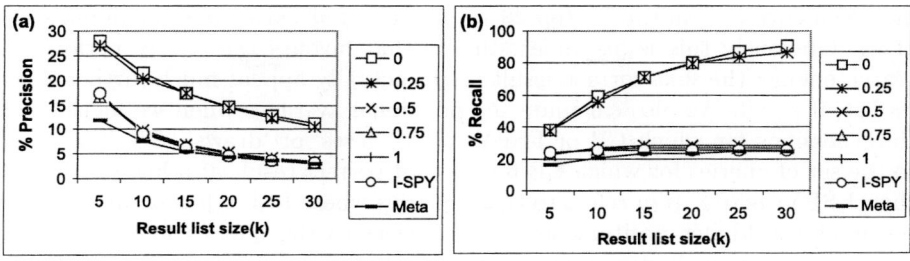

Fig. 3. (a) Precision (b) Recall

For example, in Figure 3(a) we see that CB precision varies between nearly 28% (at $k = 5$ and for a similarity threshold >0) to 11% (at $k = 30$ for the same threshold). This is compared to precision values of between 17% and 3% for I-SPY, and values between 12% and 3% for Meta. These results indicate that CB benefits from a precision improvement of between 60% and 258%, relative to I-SPY at the similarity threshold >0 level; similar benefits are indicated for a similarity threshold >0.25. These precision improvements are even greater (between 130% and 265%) when measured relative to Meta.

The recall results tell a similar story. The recall for CB (at similarity thresholds of >0 and >0.25) grows from approximately 37% ($k = 5$) to just over 91% ($k = 30$). At the same result-list sizes I-SPY's recall only grows from 23% to 25% and Meta's recall, from 16% to 25%. Obviously the CB method is locating a far greater portion of the relevant pages than I-SPY or Meta and it is gaining access to these additional relevant pages from the result-lists of its similar queries.

Once again we see that the CB benefits tend to fall away as the similarity threshold increases, and for thresholds >0.5 and beyond only minor precision and recall improvements are achieved (in the order of 7-12%). As discussed in the previous section, this can be readily explained by the sharp drop in similar cases for similarity thresholds of 0.5 and higher.

4.4 Winners & Losers

It is well known that result position is a major influencing factor on the behaviour of Web searchers, and various analyses of Web search behaviours have highlighted how users are reluctant to venture beyond the first few results [22], regardless of how many are returned by a search engine; our own analysis indicates that up to 90% of result selections occur for the top 5 result positions [10]. Hence in this final experiment we investigate the position of relevant results within the result-lists returned by the various search engines.

This time we confine our analysis to I-SPY, Meta and the CB variation with a similarity threshold >0. We also confine our result-lists to 20 results. For each result-list produced for a particular query, we note the position of its first correct result and average this across each search engine. If a search engine does not include a correct result in its top 20, then it is penalised with a positional score of 21. Obviously this is an underestimate that favours the poorly performing search engine: the first correct result might actually appear much further down its list, if at all. We also calculate the positional averages when we focus in on those sessions for which CB or I-SPY 'wins', 'loses' or 'draws': *CB Win* refers to the set of queries for which CB has its first correct result at a higher position than I-SPY; *I-SPY Win* refers to those queries where I-SPY has its first correct result at the higher position, and *Draw* refers to the queries for which both methods have their first correct result at the same position in the top 20.

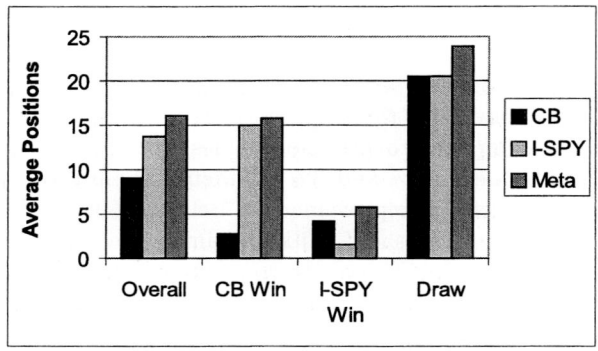

Fig. 4. Average Position of the First Correct Answer

The results are presented in Figure 4 as four groups of bar-charts, one for each scenario. Once again it is clear that there is a significant benefit to the CB method. Overall, its first correct results are found, on average, at position 9, compared to 13.7 and 16.1 for I-SPY and Meta. In CB Win, which occurs 43.4% of the time, the average CB position is only 2.8, compared to 14.9 and 15.7 for I-SPY and Meta respectively. In I-SPY Win—which happens only 23.4% of the time—its top correct result is at position 1.6, beating CB's position of 4.1. When both search techniques draw the average position is the same at 20.53. So, from a positional viewpoint, CB does as good as, or better, than I-SPY 76.4% of the time, and when it does better it does a lot better with a positional difference of 12.1 (2.8 vs. 14.9). Only 23% of the time does I-SPY produce a higher correct result than CB, and in these situations the positional difference is minor— 1.6 vs. 4.1—with both techniques delivering the correct result within the top 5.

5 Discussion

Finally, before concluding it is worthwhile addressing a number of issues, that have been raised during the development of this work. The first concerns the ability of unreliable users to manipulate result rankings, and the importance of user reliability, trust and authority in general. The second concerns how the further processing of result-lists is likely to impact on overall search engine efficiency.

5.1 User Reliability, Trust and Authority

Traditional Web search engines are open to abuse and it is relatively easy for content creators to manipulate a search engine's index by loading a page with preferred keywords and index terms regardless of the page's topic. Even Google's link-based indexing has been subject to abuse as authors create dummy networks to build up the PageRank of target pages. Our collaborative search technique is also open to abuse if determined users (or agents) repeatedly select target pages to give the impression of user selections. In short, the case-based and standard versions of I-SPY are obviously dependent on the reliability of users and their selections. Currently we are exploring a number of options to protect I-SPY from malicious activity. A potentially useful example of this is a simple coping strategy that discounts sequences of selections. Related work concerned with protecting collaborative filtering recommenders from rogue users is also a potentially fruitful option (see [23]).

Our current implementations of collaborative search make no attempt to identify or track individual users. Instead, the activity of community members is stored and combined in the hit-matrix in an anonymous fashion. This anonymity is considered to be an advantage in today's somewhat paranoid Internet world of profiling, cookies and spam. However, it would be interesting to consider tracking individual users in order to explore the hypothesis that different members of a community are likely to be more or less reliable sources of result recommendations. For instance, David McSherry's selections for the query 'CBR' are likely to be more authoritative than the selections of a first year computer science student for the same query. All of this currently forms the basis of our future work programme.

5.2 Efficiency Concerns

So far we have not considered the efficiency implications of our case-based method. At first glance it may seem that this approach adds yet another layer of computational complexity to a world where instant search responses are demanded. However, this is not necessarily the case. In fact our case-based and standard versions of I-SPY can be configured to deliver faster results than the underlying search engines. To achieve this we compile the two sets of results— one set from the underlying search engines (the *remote results*) and one set from the similar cases or hit-matrix (the *local results*)—in parallel. The second set is computed locally and, because it is taken from a hit-matrix that records only previously selected results, this computation can be performed far faster than a search of a full index by a traditional search engine. Thus, the local results can be returned to the user almost immediately and, what is more, these local results are likely to be better candidates than the remote results anyway, because, they have been considered relevant in the past.

6 Conclusions

Web search has traditionally been the domain of information retrieval research and most Web search engines are based on a foundation of IR techniques. There are obvious similarities between the structure of a case-based reasoning system and Web search. Nevertheless, the case-based reasoning community has largely steered clear of Web search as an application domain. We believe that this is a missed opportunity and in this paper we have argued that the reuse-based philosophy of CBR has much to offer.

We have described a case-based Web search engine that is designed to operate with existing search engines in a post-processing mode. Cases are past search sessions with queries as problem specifications and result selections as solutions, and the basic idea is to reuse past search sessions as a source of relevant results. We have described a straightforward approach to case similarity and retrieval, and introduced a relevance-based ranking metric for scoring recommended results from similar cases. We have reported on a comprehensive evaluation, comparing our case-based approach to a more restricted reuse-based approach and to a traditional meta-search engine, using usage data from a live-user trial. The results are promising. They show that the case-based method enjoys improved overall accuracy as well as enhanced precision and recall characteristics. It is interesting to note that the greatest benefits appear to occur under the least stringent case similarity conditions, and that, even though some retrievals may not be appropriate, allowing for the retrieval of a broad range of search cases appears to provide for the best result coverage and result ranking.

Future work will build upon the current evaluation and we hope to avail of larger logs as the basis for a more robust test of case-based Web search. In addition, we will investigate alternative techniques that could cluster queries from logs in order to improve the search performance of the I-SPY system.

References

1. Roush, W.: Search Beyond Google. MIT Technology Review (2004) 34–45
2. Lawrence, S., Giles, C.L.: Accessibility of Information on the Web. Nature **400(6740)** (1999) 107–109
3. Lawrence, S., Giles, C.L.: Searching the World Wide Web. Science **280(5360)** (1999) 98–100
4. Brin, S., Page, L.: The Anatomy of a Large-Scale Web Search Engine. In: Proceedings of the 7th International World-Wide Web Conference. Volume 30., Networks and ISDN Systems (1998) 107–117
5. Kleinberg, J.M.: Authoritative Sources in a Hyperlinked Environment. In: Proceedings of the 9th Annual ACM-SIAM Symposium on Discrete Algorithms, AAAI Press (1998) 668–677
6. Lawrence, S., Giles, C.L.: Context and Page Analysis for Improved Web Search. IEEE Internet Computing **2(4)** (1998) 38–46
7. Selberg, E., Etzioni, O.: Multi-service search and comparison using the MetaCrawler. In: Proceedings of the 4th International World-Wide Web Conference, Darmstadt, Germany (1995)

8. Zamir, O., Etzioni, O.: Grouper: a dynamic clustering interface to Web search results. Computer Networks (Amsterdam, Netherlands: 1999) **31** (1999) 1361–1374
9. Smyth, B., Balfe, E., Briggs, P., Coyle, M., Freyne, J.: Collaborative Web Search. In: Proceedings of the 18th International Joint Conference on Artificial Intelligence, IJCAI-03, Morgan Kaufmann (2003) 1417–1419 Acapulco, Mexico.
10. Freyne, J., Smyth, B., Coyle, M., Balfe, E., Briggs, P.: Further Experiments on Collaborative Ranking in Community-Based Web Search. AI Review: An International Science and Engineering Journal (In Press)
11. Smyth, B., Freyne, J., Coyle, M., Briggs, P., Balfe, E.: I-SPY: Anonymous, Community-Based Personalization by Collaborative Web Search. In: Proceedings of the 23rd SGAI International Conference on Innovative Techniques and Applications of Artificial Intelligence, Springer (2003) 367–380 Cambridge, UK.
12. Glover, E., Lawrence, S., Gordon, M.D., Birmingham, W.P., Giles, C.L.: Web Search - Your Way. Communications of the ACM **44(12)** (2001) 97–102
13. Budzik, J., Hammond, K.: User Interactions with Everyday Applications as Context for Just-In-Time Information Access. In: Proceedings of the 5th International Conference on Intelligent User Interfaces, ACM Press (2000) 44–51
14. Lieberman, H.: Letizia: An agent that assists web browsing. In Mellish, C., ed.: Proceedings of the International Joint Conference on Artificial Intelligence, IJCAI'95, Morgan Kaufman Publishers (1995) 924–929 Montreal, Canada.
15. Fitzpatrick, L., Dent, M.: Automatic Feedback Using Past Queries: Social Searching? In: Proceedings of the 20th Annual International ACM SIGIR Conference on Research and Development in Information Retrieval, ACM Press (1997) 306–313
16. Cui, H., Wen, J.R., Nie, J.Y., Ma, W.Y.: Probabilistic Query Expansion Using Query Logs. In: Proceedings of the 11th International Conference on World Wide Web. (2002) 325–332
17. Rissland, E.L., Daniels, J.J.: A hybrid CBR-IR Approach to Legal Information Retrieval. In: Proceedings of the 5th international conference on Artificial intelligence and law, ACM Press (1995) 52–61
18. Burke, R., Hammond, K., Kulyukin, V., Tomuro, S., Schoenberg, S.: Question Answering from Frequently-Asked Question Files: Experiences with the FAQ Finder System. AI Magazine **18(2)** (1997) 57–66
19. Lenz, M., Ashley, K.: AAAI Workshop on Textual Case-Based Reasoning (1999) AAAI Technical Report WS-98-12.
20. Kanawati, R., Jaczynski, M., Trousse, B., J-M, A.: Applying the Broadway Recommendation Computation Approach for Implementing a Query Refinement Service in the CBKB Meta-search Engine. In: Conférence Française sur le Raisonnement á Partir de Cas (RáPC'99). (1999)
21. Godoy, D., Amandi, A.: PersonalSearcher: An Intelligent Agent for Searching Web Pages. In Monard, M.C., Sichman, J.S., eds.: IBERAMIA-SBIA. Volume 1952., Springer (2000) 62–72
22. Jansen, B.J., Spink, A., Bateman, J., Saracevic, T.: Real Life Information Retrieval: A Study of User Queries on the Web. SIGIR Forum **32** (1998) 5–17
23. O'Mahony, M.P., Hurley, N.J., Silvestre, G.C.: Collaborative Filtering Safe and Sound? In Zhong, N., Ras, Z.W., Tsumoto, S., Suzuki, E., eds.: ISMIS. Volume 2871., Springer (2003) 506–510

Case Based Reasoning and Production Process Design: The Case of P-Truck Curing

Stefania Bandini, Ettore Colombo, Fabio Sartori, and Giuseppe Vizzari

Dipartimento di Informatica, Sistemistica e Comunicazione
Università degli Studi di Milano–Bicocca
Via Bicocca degli Arcimboldi 8, 20126 Milano, Italy
{bandini,ettore.colombo,fabio.sartori,giuseppe.vizzari}@disco.unimib.it

Abstract. This paper describes P–Truck Curing, a Case Based Reasoning system supporting the design of the curing phase for truck tyre production. The design of this process provides a trade–off between an optimal curing degree, to avoid imperfections in the final product, and the reduction of costs, related to thermal energy employed in the curing. Expert curing process designers store information about past episodes and exploit it to define new ones, without starting from scratch. A CBR system is thus a suitable approach to model this problem solving method: case structure, similarity and adaptation functions and a general system overview will be described. This work has been developed in the context of the P–Truck project, whose goal is the development of an integrated Knowledge Management (KM) system to support the Business Unit Truck of Pirelli Tyres in the design and manufacture of truck tyres.

1 Introduction

The work presented in this paper has been developed in the wider context of the P-Truck project, whose goal is the development of an integrated Knowledge Management system to support the Business Unit Truck of Pirelli Tyres in the design and manufacture of truck tyres. In particular this paper will describe a part of the system supporting the design of the curing process, the last phase of tyres production process.

A truck tyre is composed of both rubber compounds and metallic reinforcements: the former are responsible for all the thermal and mechanical properties of the tyre; on the other hand, metallic reinforcements give it the necessary rigidity. The P-Truck Project goal is to support Pirelli's experts in their decision making process related to different phases of the tyre cycle of life, that includes:

– Design of rubber compounds: a rubber compound is a blend of different ingredients, chosen with the goal of achieving required performances (e.g. tensile strength, resistance to fatigue). The designer determines the composition of the blend, identifying ingredients to be adopted and their amounts;
– Mixing: ingredients must be mixed in order to obtain a homogeneous blend. Machineries, timings and many other parameters of this stage must be suitably defined by the mixing process designer;

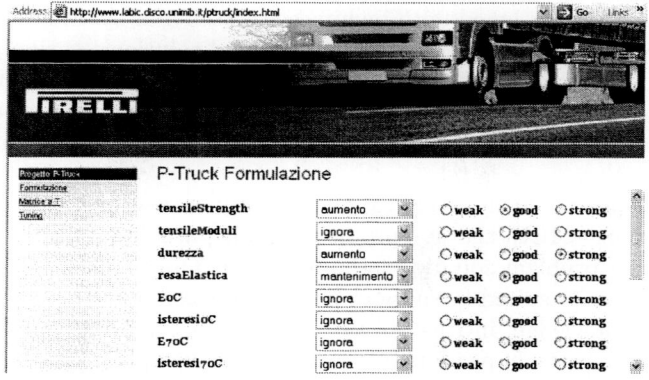

Fig. 1. A screen–shot of P–Truck Compounding.

- Semi–manufactured production: metallic reinforcements are added to rubber compounds, in order to obtain the different parts the tyre will be composed of;
- Assembly: semi–manufactured parts are assembled into a semi–finished product, in jargon called *green–tyre*;
- Curing: the green tyre is "cooked" in order to give it the required thermal–mechanical features.

Four knowledge–based systems supporting the experts' decision–making process in some of those phases have been developed; a screen–shot of the uniform user–interface is shown in Figure 1. These systems are based on different problem solving methods (e.g. rule–based, case–based), reflecting experts' decision–making process in the main phases of the process above described (i.e. design of rubber compounds, mixing and curing).

It is important to note that, although the problem solving strategy is typically diversified, the knowledge–base exploited by different modules is the same. In fact truck tyre production steps are highly correlated (e.g. most of them are related to the same rubber compounds). Thus, while the problem–solving strategy is distributed, it has been decided to design and implement a centralized knowledge–base: each module accesses it in order to create a dynamic view of knowledge needed to work. This choice, that resulted in the development of a specific knowledge elicitation tool (KEPT [5]), has allowed to build a complete and consistent knowledge model, devoted to represent complex knowledge structures concerning both case–based and rule–based modules of P–Truck. In particular, this paper will describe the design choices adopted in the development of *P–Truck Curing*, a case–based system that supports experts in their decision making process about the curing of tyres.

Problem analysis began with meetings and interviews with expert curing process designers, also referred to as curing technologists. Early stages of knowledge acquisition made clear that any of these experts uses to store information related to curing processes, designed both by himself/herself and by other technologists. These notes concern incidental problems, adopted solutions, variants of process and results, both positive and negative, about tyre curing. When a technologist has to design a new curing process he/she uses these information and his/her experience to define its details, without starting from scratch or using formally well–defined rules.

This approach to the design of the right curing process is very similar to Case Based Reasoning (CBR), that is a problem solving paradigm suitable to deal with domains whose problem solving methods have not been fully understood and modelled. Naturally suited to support the preservation and reuse of experiential and episodic knowledge, intrinsically stored into cases, CBR has been adopted for many KM systems, in particular for manufacturing applications (e.g. see [3, 4, 8]). Some of these systems concern the process design problem and, among these, several works concerning chemical processes have been proposed (e.g. see [12, 13, 16, 17]): the aim of these systems is the definition of the process structure (the flow-sheet of the chemical process, a sequence of phases to be performed). Another CBR system tackling a curing process design scenario is Clavier [11]. This system supports expert in the decision of autoclave loading for the curing of graphite–threaded composite materials. Even if the goal of P–Truck Curing is similar to Clavier (i.e. to obtain optimal curing degree of processed materials and to minimize costs) the latter is mainly focused on choosing the optimal placement of parts to be cured inside the autoclave. P–Truck Curing instead focuses on an optimal definition of curing phases features (e.g. timing, energy), in a generally fixed process structure.

According to [1], the CBR cycle of P–Truck Curing, given a problem and a case base of solved problems, can be summarized as follows (see Figure 2): the system receives a description of the problem to be solved, made up of a list of performances to be achieved and the type of machinery to be adopted for the curing process. Then, it retrieves a sequence of past cases with a similar description, chooses one of them and tries to modify its solution in order to derive a new curing process.

The following Section will describe the results of the knowledge acquisition campaign, while Section 3 will show the representation of a case in P–Truck Curing, highlighting the most significant attributes involved in the decisional process of a curing technologist. Then, the paper will focus on how the attributes were used to build a similarity function among cases to be used in the retrieval phase. In Section 5 a brief explanation of how adaptation has been intended will be supplied. Section 6 will briefly describe system architecture, and finally conclusions and future works related to P–Truck Curing will be briefly introduced.

2 Curing Process Description

Vulcanization is a chemical process of treating crude rubber or similar plastic material to give it desired properties, such as elasticity, strength, and stability. In particular, tyre vulcanization is often referred to as curing, and it is during

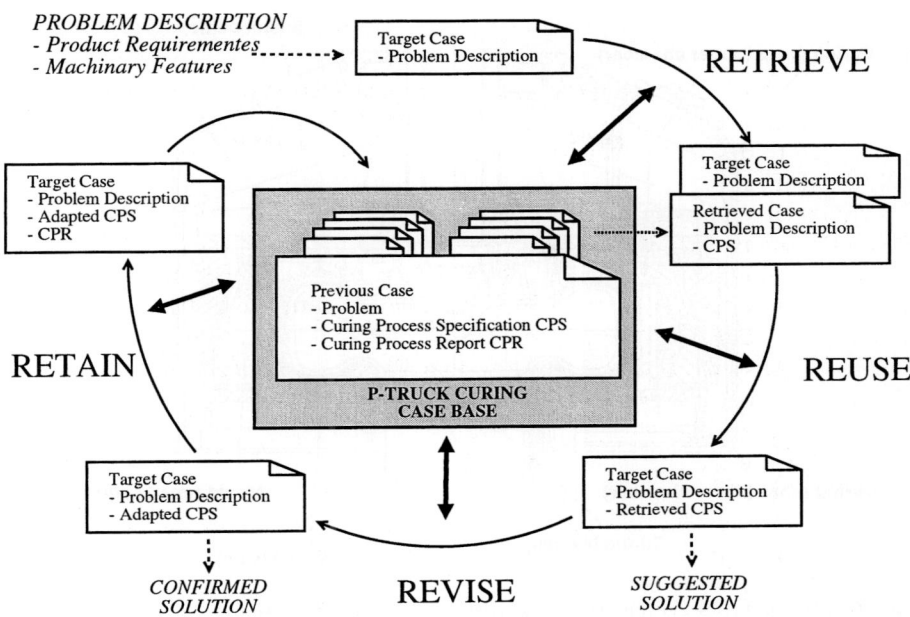

Fig. 2. The P–Truck Curing CBR cycle.

this process that the tread impression, brand, and information on the kind of tyre are printed on the green–tyre, in order to give it the desired shape and appearance. The green–tyre is made up of different rubber compounds, steel reinforcements and other components. During the curing process it undergoes a thermal treatment that activates reactions between polymers (i.e natural or synthetic rubber) and sulphur molecules, that bind themselves and create a lattice. A correct and uniform degree of cure is thus a crucial factor influencing tyre performances (for instance handling on wet or dry surface, fuel saving, dimensional stability and mileage, fatigue and abrasion resistance).

The process takes place inside a machinery called curing press; its main components are the mould, the bladder and a pipe system to supply heating fluids. A sketch of a curing press is shown in Figure 3. Thermal energy is supplied to the mould, containing the green–tyre carcass, in a different way according to the curing press type: it may derive from hot steam surrounding the mould or from its direct contact with heated platens. The green–tyre must be pressed to the mould in order to impress the tread and other information on it. An internal pressure must thus be applied to the carcass, and therefore the bladder must be inflated during the process. The inflating fluid may also contribute to the thermal treatment, if it is a good heat conductor.

The curing process thus provides different phases of external or internal heating, and internal inflation of the green–tyre carcass. To design a curing process the technologist evaluates the characteristics of the green–tyre, that is the output

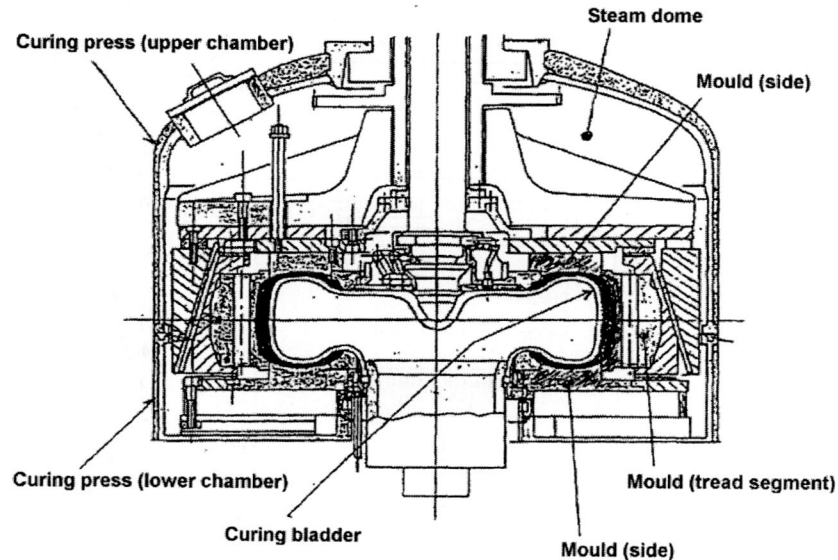

Fig. 3. Curing press sketch: this is a vertical section of a steam–dome curing press, highlighting mould, bladder and other components.

of the last phase before the curing and the kind of machinery to be used, then, for every step of the process, he decides starting instant and duration, temperature and pressure of the involved fluids. Variants to standard procedures can also be suggested (for instance to slightly modify the typical value of factory dependent parameters).

Production tests that can be performed are essentially normal curing processes, but thermocouples are inserted in the green–tyre to monitor its temperature while it is being vulcanized. By doing so an indication on the curing degree in different points of the tyre can be obtained. Results of this test are used by the technologist to guarantee the satisfaction of requirements and constraints, give comments on the obtained product or highlight possible anomalies and imperfections on the tyre.

3 Case Structure

Describing a problem is one of main activities in the definition of a CBR system: the choice of significant attributes is essential for the definition of a suitable similarity function among cases, that is fundamental in order to retrieve past situations similar to the current one. A problem C is usually viewed as a n–tuple of features $C = \{f_1, f_2, \ldots, f_n\}$. This structure may be fixed or variable [6], depending on the complexity of the involved knowledge. P–Truck Curing provides a fixed structure for case representation, since knowledge acquisition sessions have highlighted that curing process technologists do not change the set of significant attributes from the similarity calculus point of view.

The technologist stores all the information about new processes in a *curing process specification (CPS)*. Each CPS concerns one and only one process, summarizing all the choices made by the technologist about it. Curing is a crucial phase: since it is the last one, an error during its execution or an improper design would cause the failure of the whole production process, and, consequently, loss of time and money. The task of these experts is very difficult, as they have to design the curing process in order to obtain an optimal degree of curing, minimizing costs and avoiding imperfections in the final product. A short curing process may not guarantee a good degree of curing, but a long one will be very expensive, requiring a lot of thermal energy and perhaps could even produce imperfections in the cured tyre. Moreover the tyre thickness is different in distinct points (e.g. the tread is quite thicker than the side), but the curing degree should be as uniform as possible.

At the end of the process, the technologist carries out activities needed to produce a *curing process report (CPR)*, a document containing information related to process results.

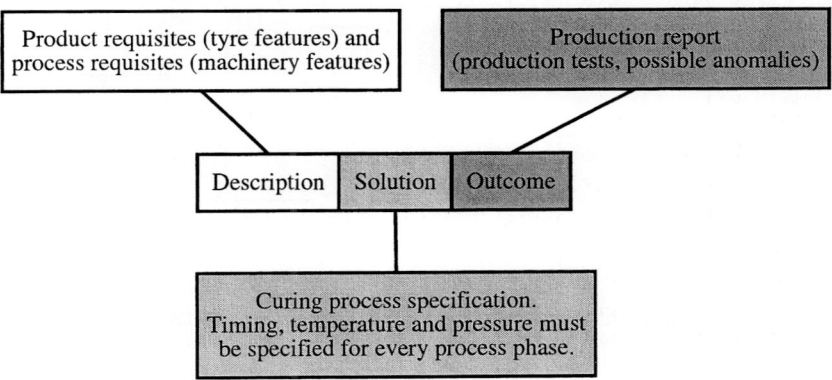

Fig. 4. Case parts: information related to case description, solution and outcome is illustrated.

Figure 4 shows high–level P–Truck Curing case composition, built according to the typical case structure [14]; more precisely:

- *case description* is made up of the evaluation of final product requisites and machinery features (type, temperature of fluids and so on) to be used in order to satisfy them;
- *case solution* is the CPS;
- *case outcome* is the CPR.

A tree–structure was adopted for case representation as it is more suitable to describe complex knowledge structures, given the possibility to model hierarchies. Many concepts described in the previous Section can be linked with *is–a* and *part–of* relations that would be lost in a flat structure. Moreover this is a modular representation, allowing flexible management of related information (e.g. in terms of case structure modification) and the definition of composite and efficient retrieval algorithms (e.g. different case parts, represented by distinct sub–trees, may be handled in a different way). For more details on this kind of case representation in the context of P–Truck see [15].

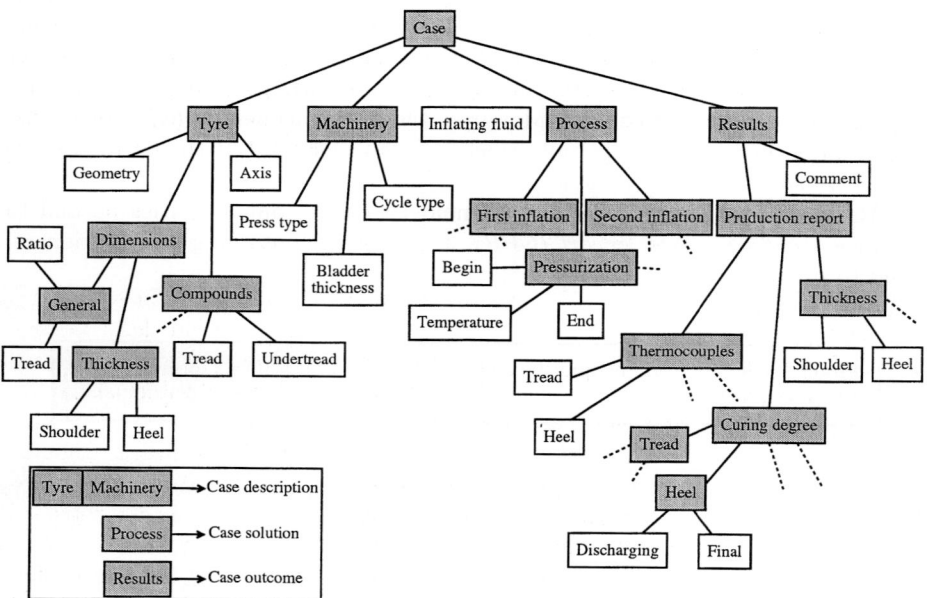

Fig. 5. Case structure: the diagram shows a partial view of the tree–structure related to a case.

Figure 5 illustrates a partial view of the tree–structure representing the case in P–Truck Curing: in particular there are four sub–trees, respectively related to the description of tyre, machinery, curing process and obtained results. A tree inner node, named *category* (i.e. gray filled boxes), represents a collection of *attributes*, which are drawn as tree leaves (i.e. white filled boxes). Note that a category can be made up of other categories too. The tyre is described in terms of its dimensions (e.g. thickness in specific points of its section, width of the tread), usage (e.g. tractive axis, drive axis), morphological features and components (i.e. blends related to its composing parts). The machinery is mainly characterized by its type and the type of the inflating fluid while the process contains information related the starting instant, duration and other parameters of various phases of the curing process. Results contain information related to the tests described in the previous Section and an evaluation of the expert on the process outcome.

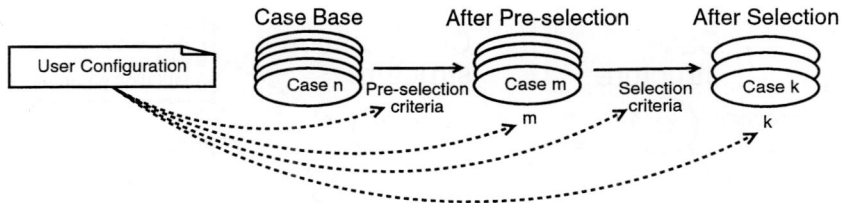

Fig. 6. Retrieval in P–Truck Curing.

The case structure illustrated in this section is not variable at the present, so that the classical *Nearest Neighbor Algorithm* [9] has been adopted to build a similarity function for the retrieval phase of the system, that will be the subject of the next section.

4 Similarity and Retrieval

One of the main steps in a CBR system is the retrieval phase, whose result is a subset of the case–base. Its elements are cases whose problem description is considered *similar* to the one concerning the new problem. Designing P–Truck Curing, it has been introduced a two step retrieval to increase system flexibility, configurability and maintenance in the system.

In Figure 6 there is a description of the two step retrieval designed for P–Truck Curing. This approach is very similar to MAC/FAC [10] (Many Are Called, Few Are Chosen), a psychologically founded model of similarity–based retrieval. In fact the first phase, named *Pre–selection*, has been defined to select from the case base only those cases having a rate of similarity higher than a particular threshold and whose feature values verify some relations with new problem ones. Pre–selection phase can be considered something more than a traditional Indexing because it involves particular relations among features in addition to equality. In the following phase, named *Selection*, the system only works on the set of cases obtained by the Pre–selection, computing their actual similarity to the current one. Whenever the Pre–selection phase returns cases with different solutions to the same problem, Selection can choose the best case, basing on the interpretation and the comparison of reported results (e.g. rates of curing and tyre dimensions at the end of curing process).

Using two different steps to retrieve analogous cases allows to employ different similarity criteria. In fact, even if currently Pre–selection and Selection are completed following the same approach (i.e. comparison of attribute values and categories), it would be possible to exploit a structural similarity measurement in the first phase. In this way, retrieval shows a subset of the case base both as possible solutions and as possible starting points for the adaptation process.

During the knowledge acquisition campaign, with the help of curing experts, an order of importance among attributes and categories has been identified. Nonetheless, for a complete definition of the *similarity function*, in addition

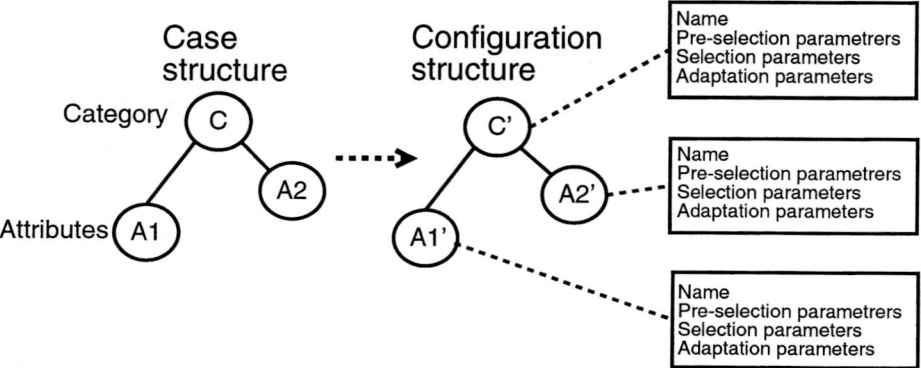

Fig. 7. The structure of the configuration.

to weights, for each node of the tree case structure, a function indicating how to calculate the distance among two analogous nodes in the case–space must be specified. Thus, the rate of similarity of a past case to the current one is recursively calculated starting from the root of the structure: for each category the rate of similarity is obtained aggregating the contribute of each sub–node. When a sub–node is an attribute, the evaluation of the similarity consists in a comparison function (e.g. euclidean distance) of attribute values.

Since more than one end-user can access P–Truck Curing and that each of them may have a different point of view with reference to the similarity function, it has been decided to allow them to specify a personal configuration of the similarity function. This means that for each node of the tree case structure the user can decide weights and functions to be considered when measuring distances in the case space, for both Pre–selection and Selection phases. Figure 7 shows a draft of this configuration structure.

Collections of functions have been designed in order to measure the distance between two feature values. An attribute value can belong to different kind of sets, that could be non-ordered or ordered, continuous or discrete. For the interpretation and comparison of curing results and for the management of categories (both in Pre–selection and in Selection), other collections of functions have been defined.

The number of cases considered in Pre–selection and Selection can be configured by the user (parameters m and k in Figure 6), and these values are also included in the configuration structure. The level of configurability, obtained with the adoption of these solutions, increases the quality of P–Truck as a Knowledge Management system: for instance a curing technologist can obtain an indication of other experts' point of view on case similarity. Moreover this configurability allows high level of system maintenance: in fact it is easy to modify the importance of an attribute or a category, varying the associated weight, or even changing parts of the similarity function, associated to a node of the case structure.

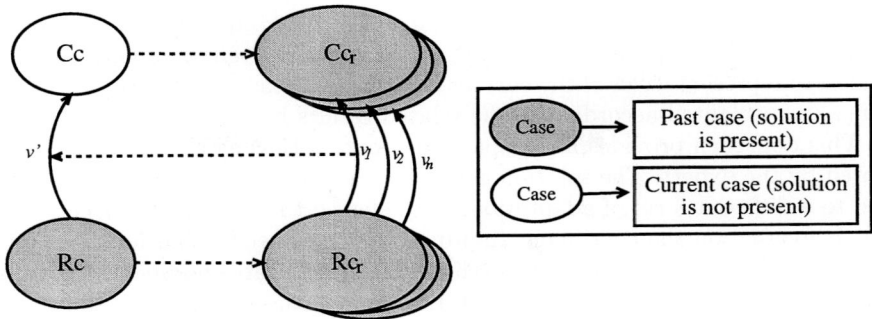

Fig. 8. Couples of past cases representing the current and the retrieved one can be used to adapt the retrieved solution.

5 Adaptation

The adaptation phase in P–Truck Curing guides the designer towards the determination of a good solution to curing process design problem (i.e. time scheduling of curing steps) even if there are no identical problems already solved among the available cases. The approach that was adopted in order to adapt the solution of an old case to a new one is influenced by the limited procedural knowledge that is available with reference to this specific activity. As previously specified, a green–tyre is a composite object, and even if some basic principles are known (e.g. thicker parts of a tyre require more energy to reach an optimal curing degree), to compose them in order to obtain a globally optimal process result is a very complex task. For instance, different tyre parts could require a completely different process modification (i.e. sidewalls are thinner and thus require less energy, while shoulders are thicker and require more), and some components have not a clear influence on the global result (e.g. metallic parts). Nonetheless the adopted approach aims to supply to the designer an indication of how to adapt the retrieved solution to the current case according to past experiences.

It has been considered that, as the current case and the retrieved one have different descriptions, maybe the case base contained other couples of cases presenting the same (or significantly similar) differences among the related descriptions. In other words we may find cases that could act as *representatives* respectively for the current case and the retrieved one. The difference between the related solutions (vector v_i) is an indication of how to modify the solution of the retrieved case Rc in order to adapt it to the situation described in the current case Cc, that is the v' vector. The idea behind this choice, in the framework of a substitutional adaptation (see, e.g., [18]), is that the same difference in problem descriptions indicates that the solutions of the current case and the retrieved one should present a difference similar to those related to the representatives of these cases. Figure 8 shows that this approach provides a passage from the current couple $< Cc, Rc >$ to couples of past cases $< Cc_r, Rc_r >$. The adaptation vector v' represents the modification that must be applied to the solution of case Rc to obtain the solution to the current problem. In this approach vector v' is obtained through an aggregation of $v_1 \ldots v_n$, differences among solutions related to representatives of the current and retrieved cases; currently an average of $v_1 \ldots v_n$ weighted according to the related results has been adopted.

This approach provides an adaptation proposal that can be modified or accepted by the expert. The solution generally undergoes a test whose results can lead to a different form of adaptation, also referred to as solution correction [7], that is focused on the continuous improvement of a specific solution. While the previously described adaptation mechanism can indicate modifications for all parts of case solution (e.g. timings but also temperatures, pressures, and so on), this phase only focuses on the duration of various steps of the curing process. The idea is that, according to the results, these timings can be changed in order to obtain a better curing process. The modification will be higher for processes which brought to poor results, while successful processes will not be substantially changed. The direction of these modifications (increase or decrease process duration) is related to different factors such as costs (i.e. longer processes require more energy and decrease the tyre production rate) and curing degree (too short processes do not bring to an optimal curing degree).

Both of these mechanisms are user–configurable: for instance the concept of representative involves a sort of similarity metric that can be modified by the user as shown in Section 4. Moreover the modifications to process duration related to the solution improvement are also configurable.

6 System Overview

The computer system implementing a support for the design of curing processes is a component of an integrated KM project, shortly described in the introduction. To introduce such a composite system in an important business unit of a company like Pirelli, several non–functional requirements must be taken into account.

System components must coexist and also interact with each other, if needed, and with the current information system, that contains particular data needed by those modules. This kind of access should only be performed when necessary, to keep limited the impact on the existing information system and supported procedures.

The development of this kind of computer systems requires an active involvement of domain experts, whose time is very valuable. The knowledge acquisition campaign must thus be carefully planned, in order to be effective and not excessively divert experts from their day–to–day activities. Various phases of analysis, design and development of different system components have been necessarily carried out in different times, by various groups, and using disparate approaches (e.g. rule–based and case–based).

Finally, Pirelli is a multinational corporation and users can be situated in different locations, and might need to access P–Truck modules through the net-

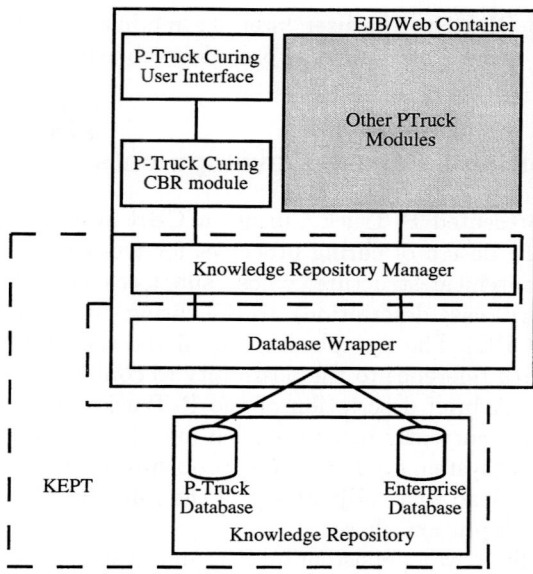

Fig. 9. High level system architecture: this is a diagram showing main system components and collaborations.

work, possibly using a PC without the chance to install additional programs: therefore the adoption of a web–based user interface is almost mandatory.

The adopted platform and architecture must thus provide a high degree of flexibility and extensibility, allowing the integration of heterogeneous components, and a separation between business and presentation logic, that must be web–oriented. The J2EE platform supports the development of heterogeneous components (Enterprise Java Beans), that can be integrated through the use of standard technologies (e.g. Remote Method Invocation, CORBA, XML), providing support for database access and web–based user interface development. It meets all the previously expressed requirements and was thus adopted for the development of the P–Truck system.

A diagram showing a high level view of system architecture is shown in Figure 9. The module implementing the CBR system is separated from the user interface manager and from the database access component, a module that acts as a gateway to the case base, physically stored in Pirelli's enterprise database and in P–Truck private one. Pieces of information related to cases are already available in the existing information system, but some specific data is required by P–Truck system modules. For security and confidentiality reasons it was chosen not to use the existing database management system (DBMS) to store this data, but to install another one dedicated to the P–Truck system. The Database Wrapper does not directly offer services to users, but is meant as a support for other application modules. In particular it is shared by all components requiring an access to the data storage facilities, and represents a uniform and centralized access to the two DBMSs. The user interface module is based on JavaServer Pages and servlet technology, and thus provides web accessibility to the Curing module.

7 Conclusion and Future Developments

This paper has presented P–Truck Curing, a CBR system supporting expert technologists in the design of curing processes for truck tyres. The case is represented in a hierarchical structure, whose sub–trees are related to tyre and available machinery (case description), to the curing process (CPS), and to the obtained results (CPR). The two–phase retrieval and the adaptation mechanism were described, with reference to the possibility to configure both of these steps of the CBR cycle. A brief description of the P–Truck Curing system was also given. The system is currently being installed in order to start a test campaign. An evaluation of the system on day–to–day problems, performed by curing technologists, will likely lead to an adjustment of the configurable aspects related to the retrieval and adaptation phases.

This system will allow a persistent and organized storage of evenly described cases, shared and accessible by different users. It will be integrated into Pirelli's information system, but it will represent a dedicated module specifically developed taking into account curing technologists' needs.

One of the main reasons to adopt a CBR approach was the similarity to the expert problem solving method, but it also seemed suitable because knowledge on the domain is not exhaustive. A future analysis of the case base, possibly with the support of data mining techniques (e.g. see [2]), could thus represent an instrument for a deeper study of relationships between elements of the case description and process features.

A correct and systematic use of this system will also allow an incremental learning, typical of a CBR approach. This also means that the system will not necessarily be able to help experts when a new strategy or technology is introduced in curing process design. Anyway, as long as the case description is valid, the system is ready to receive manually designed cases, related to those innovations, and allow their reuse. Moreover the flexibility of the adopted tree–structure for case representation allows to modify it in order to keep it up–to–date with changes in curing technology.

References

1. Aamodt, A. and Plaza, E., *Case–Based Reasoning: Foundational Issues, Methodological Variations, and System Approaches*, AI Communications, Vol. 7, No. 1, pp. 39-59, 1994.
2. Aamodt, A. and Langseth, H. *Integrating Bayesian networks into knowledge-intensive CBR*, In Aha, D., Daniels J., (eds.) American Association for Artificial Intelligence, Case-based reasoning integrations; Papers from the AAAI workshop, Technical Report WS-98-15, AAAI Press, ISBN 1-57735-068-5, pp 1–6, Menlo Park, 1998.

3. Bandini, S. and Manzoni, S. *Application of fuzzy indexing and retrieval in case based reasoning for design*, Proceedings of the 2001 ACM symposium on Applied computing, ACM Press, New York, 2001.
4. Bandini, S., Manzoni, S. and Simone, C., *Tuning Production Processes through a Case Based Reasoning Approach*, In Craw, S., Preece, A. (eds.) Advances in Case Based Reasoning, LNCS 2416, Springer-Verlag, Berlin Heidelberg New York, pp. 475-489, 2002.
5. Bandini, S., Manzoni, S. and Sartori, F. *Knowledge Maintenance and Sharing in the KM Context: the Case of P-Truck*, AI*IA 2003: Advances in Artificial Intelligence, LNAI 2829, Springer-Verlag, Berlin Heidelberg New York, pp. 499-510 , 2003.
6. Bergmann, R. and Stahl, A., *Similarity Measures for Object–Oriented Case Representations*, LNAI 1488, Springer-Verlag, pp. 25-36, 1998.
7. Craw, S., Jarmulak, J. and Rowe, R., *Using Case-Base Data to Learn Adaptation Knowledge for Design*, Proceedings of the 17th International Joint Conference on Artificial Intelligence (IJCAI 01), Morgan Kaufmann, Seattle, pp. 1011–1016, 2001.
8. Craw, S., Wiratunga, N. and Rowe, R., *Case Based Design for Tablet Formulation*, Proceedings of the 4th European Workshop on Case Based Reasoning, Springer-Verlag, Berlin, pp. 358-369, 1998.
9. Finnie, G.R. and Sun, Z., *Similarity and Metrics in Case-Based Reasoning*, International Journal of Intelligent Systems, Vol. 17, No. 3, pp. 273-287, 2002.
10. Forbus, K., Gentner, D. and Law, K.,*MAC/FAC: A model of Similarity-based Retrieval*, Cognitive Science, Vol. 19, No. 2, pp 141-205, 1995.
11. Hennessy, D., and Hinkle, D., *Applying case-based reasoning to autoclave loading*, IEEE Expert, Vol. 7 , No. 5 , pp. 21-26, 1992.
12. Herbeaux, O., and Mille, A., *ACCELERE: a case–based design assistant for closed cell rubber industry*, Knowledge–Based Systems, Vol. 12, pp. 231–238, Elsevier Science, 1999.
13. King, J. M. P., Bañares–Alcántara, R. and Zainuddin, A. M., *Minimising environmental impact using CBR: An azeotropic distillation case study*, Environmental Modelling and Software, Vol. 14, No. 5, pp. 359-366, Elsevier Science Ltd., 1999.
14. Kolodner, J., *Case Based Reasoning*, Morgan Kaufmann Pu., San Mateo (CA), 1993.
15. Manzoni, S. and Mereghetti, P., *A Tree Structured Case Base for the System P–Truck Tuning*, Proceedings of UK CBR workshop at ES 2002, pp. 17–26, University of Paisley, 2002.
16. Seuranen, T., Pajula, E. and Hurme, M., *Applying CBR and Object Database Techniques in Chemical Process Design*, in D. W. Aha, I. Watson (Eds.), Case–Based Reasoning Research and Development, LNAI 2080, Springer-Verlag, pp. 731-743, 2001.
17. Surma, J., Braunschweig, B., *Case–Base Retrieval in Process–Engineering: Supporting Design by Reusing Flowsheets*, Engineering Applications of Artificial Intelligence, Vol. 9, No. 4, pp. 385-391, Elsevier Science Ltd., 1996.
18. Wilke, W., Bergmann, R., *Techniques and Knowledge Used for Adaptation During CaseBased Problem Solving*, Tasks and Methods in Applied Artificial Intelligence, LNAI 1416, Springer-Verlag, pp. 497-505, 1998.

An Architecture for Case-Based Personalised Search[*]
Research Paper

Keith Bradley[1] and Barry Smyth[1,2]

[1] Smart Media Institute, University College Dublin, Dublin, Ireland
{Keith.Bradley,Barry.Smyth}@ucd.ie
[2] ChangingWorlds, Trintech Building, South County Business Park,
Leopardstown, Dublin 18, Ireland
Barry.Smyth@ChangingWorlds.com

Abstract. Traditional search techniques frequently fail the average user in their quest for online information. Recommender systems attempt to address this problem by discovering the context in which the search occurs. Though effective, these systems are often hampered by the brevity of typical user queries. In this paper we describe CASPER, an online recruitment search engine which combines similarity-based search with a client-side personalisation technique. In particular we argue that CASPER's personalisation strategy is effective in determining retrieval relevance in the face of incomplete queries.

Keywords: case-based search, personalisation, incomplete queries.

1 Introduction

As the Web expands, it's becoming progressively more difficult for its users to find the information they want. Most use search engines to cope with the vast volumes of information currently available. These search engines often rely on traditional database or information-retrieval inspired strategies to fulfill search requests. Users often find it difficult to cope with these technologies as most have little experience in their use and may not be very knowledgeable about the domain within which they are searching. This often results in short, ambiguous and incomplete search queries that are lacking in information [19]. All of this is exacerbated by the limited screen real estate of modern mobile web-enabled devices and the reluctance of users to venture beyond the first two or three results presented to them. Recommender systems have emerged as one possible solution to this problem. By combining ideas from machine learning, user profiling and case-based reasoning, recommender systems promise more focused, intelligent and proactive search that is better adapted to the needs of the individual.

In section 2 we review some popular recommendation strategies adopted by recommender systems. In section 3 we present our own experience with

---

[*] The support of the Informatics Research Initiative of Enterprise Ireland is gratefully acknowledged

CASPER, an online recruitment search engine. CASPER comprises two sub systems: a content-free Automated Collaborative Filtering (CASPER ACF) [14, 15] system and a two-stage personalisation client that combines case-based search with a diversity aware personalisation technique (CASPER PCR). We focus on this personalisation client, in particular we argue that its personalisation strategy is effective in determining retrieval relevance in the face of incomplete queries and benefits from increased privacy compared to other approaches. Section 4 describes a live user trial of the system and the experimental analysis of the accuracy of the predictions made by CASPER PCR. Finally, we present our conclusions in section 5.

2 Background

The emergence of recommender systems has heralded an attempt to improve the quality of search results by determining the context within which the search takes place. There are two main sources of information available to a recommender system and hence two main approaches to improving the relevance of search results in the face of vague queries. Understanding the context of the query itself can reduce the ambiguity of incomplete queries and allow searches to be more focussed. Alternatively knowing more about the user can provide us with valuable preference information.

2.1 Query Context

Contextual information about the query may be obtained explicitly, through interaction with users, or implicitly, by observing their natural behaviour.

Explicit Context. One way to capture explicit context is to force users to search within a specific context. For example, category-based search engines such as Yahoo (*http://www.yahoo.com*) improve their search by limiting the set of documents to which a query is compared. These pre-defined categories provide context for the query but recommendations are necessarily restricted to a small percentage of the total available due to the tedious nature of authoring categories. CiteSeer [9] uses a similar approach by limiting its search to scientific papers. Its document index is built automatically by crawling the web for scientific articles in various formats and by taking advantage of the cross-referencing common to scientific documents. Categories are used in Inquirius 2 [8] not to restrict search but rather to enhance a query. Upon selection of a search category, a set of words associated with that category are added to the user's query. For example choosing the *'research paper'* category adds terms frequently found in research papers such as *'abstract'* and *'references'*. A full search of the web is then performed with this enhanced query.

Implicit Context. Of course users are loathe to expend time and effort providing extra information for their searches. In addition differences in knowledge and vocabulary between users and indexers may prove frustrating. In order for these approaches to be successful users must know which category or search engine is appropriate to their search and must be willing to provide additional information. Ideally we would like to infer search context implicitly from user behaviour. Two popular approaches to implicitly acquiring context focus on individualised and personalised search techniques.

People often search for information to assist them in some task. Knowing more about this task would provide a great source of context for the search. Just-in-time recommenders such as Watson [3] and PIMA [2] continuously build term-based representations of documents the user is working with in other applications such as Microsoft Word or Internet Explorer. Documents from the web with similar representations are then suggested to the user as they work. These terms may also be used to enhance a user-generated query or in Watson's case to retrieve documents with an opposing viewpoint to that expressed in the current work. The Remembrance Agent(RA) [17] and Margin Notes [16] use word co-occurrence to retrieve documents related to one being viewed in an Emacs editor and a web browser respectively. All these approaches produce task-sensitive recommendations and go some way to dealing with the over specification issues of more traditional systems. These approaches largely ignore the other main source of information, namely the user. Users represent a vast repository of information and preferences which, though generally unstated, vastly effect how recommendations are received. The second approach, personalisation, attempts to divine these user preferences and produce recommendations relevant to a given user.

2.2 User Relevance

Query context provides valuable information to enhance the accuracy of a query but it does not necessarily address the relevance of information to the user. Relevance information is really just another type of context, but one that reflects a user's personal preferences rather than immediate task requirements. Once again, relevance information is typically acquired either by explicit questioning of the user or implicitly by observing user interaction with a system. This information is used to create a user profile, essentially a set of beliefs about the user [4].

Explicit Relevance Information. User feedback on recommendations is a popular source of explicit relevance information. For instance, PTV [20], a TV program recommender augments an initial keyword-based user profile by allowing users to rate its recommendations as either interesting or uninteresting. This feedback is used to enhance the user's profile, ensuring that it grows and adapts over time to match the user's changing preferences. Although highly successful, recommendations are limited to a narrow set of items similar to those already liked by the user. New items must also be categorised in such a way that they can be compared to the existing profile elements.

Collaborative recommenders seek to avoid these problems by focussing on similarities between people rather than items. People with similar sets of likes and dislikes are selected to act as *recommendation partners* for each other. It is assumed that if two people share many liked items in their profiles then any unshared items liked by either user should make good recommendations to the other. This obviates the need for complex profiles since all that needs to be recorded is an identifier for each profile element. Group Lens [18] used an automatic technique known as Automated Collaborative Filtering (ACF) to filter Usenet News. Profiles were built based on which news items a user had read. Sufficient similarity between profiles identified recommendation partners whose unshared profile elements could then be used as recommendations for each other.

Collaborative approaches have many benefits but suffer if insufficient recommendation partners are available. Smart Radio [1], a music recommender, tackles this sparsity problem by changing the way user profiles are used. Instead of individual songs, its user profiles are based on collections or programmes of songs created by other users. Relevance feedback is collected in a similar style to PTV and programmes of songs are recommended using ACF in a similar manner to Group Lens. Recommendation partners are identified not just on the basis of shared music programmes however, but also on shared individual songs. In this way two users may be found to have similar tastes despite never having listened to the same music programmes thus increasing the chances of finding recommendation partners. The weaknesses of both content-based and content-free approaches can be overcome by using a hybrid of both. PTV uses collaborative recommendation to compliment its content-based recommendation strategy by using ACF to identify recommendation partners. TV programs liked by one partner but not yet discovered by the other can then be used as recommendations.

Implicit Relevance Information. The reluctance of users to provide explicit preference information has led to various methods of inferring this information implicitly by monitoring the behaviour of users as they interact with the system. Since most recommenders are web-based, one of the most obvious sources of information about user behaviour is the activity logs of the web server. The PageGather algorithm [13] finds groups of pages that often occur together in user visits by mining the activity logs of a web server. These groups of pages are taken to represent coherent topics in the mind of users and web pages based on these topics are automatically generated and placed in the web site.

Often however it is difficult to extract useful information from these logs. One of the most common indicators of interest suggested is the length of time a user spends reading a page. Though some researchers such as Morita and Shinoda [10] and Konstan [7] found a strong correlation between user interest and read-time, others had only limited success [6, 5]. One obvious problem is that although web logs can tell us the length of time between users requesting pages, they cannot guarantee that the intervening time was actually spent reading the page. In addition it can be difficult to identify the actions belonging to individual users unless a web site supports user tracking. Assumptions must therefore be made about the actual time spent reading a document. Oard and Kim [6] argue that additional behaviours such as marking or using an item should be used to supplement basic read time predictions.

CASPER's collaborative recommendation component, CASPER ACF, also infers user preferences from various actions recorded by a web server log. In this case actions such as saving a job advertisement, applying for a job online, or even basic measures such as the number of times a user revisited a job were found to better indicate user interest than the read time data. Recent work [11] comparing recommendations between two TV programme recommenders: PTV, and Físchlar has shown that implicit ratings can be more accurate than explicit. O'Sullivan et. al showed that explicit ratings in PTV were less accurate in predicting user interest than those obtained implicitly from Físchlar. One of the main differences between the two systems was that while PTV provided a web-based set of results, Físchlar actually allowed users to immediately watch the recommended items. The study concluded that explicit ratings systems that were disjointed from the act of consuming the info item suffered compared to implicit systems where user actions were directly linked to consuming the item.

3 System Architecture

CASPER PCR is a two-stage recruitment search engine. It recommends jobs that are not only similar to the target query, but also relevant to the person performing the search. User relevance is determined by CASPER PCR based on a user's interaction history as shown in Figure 1.

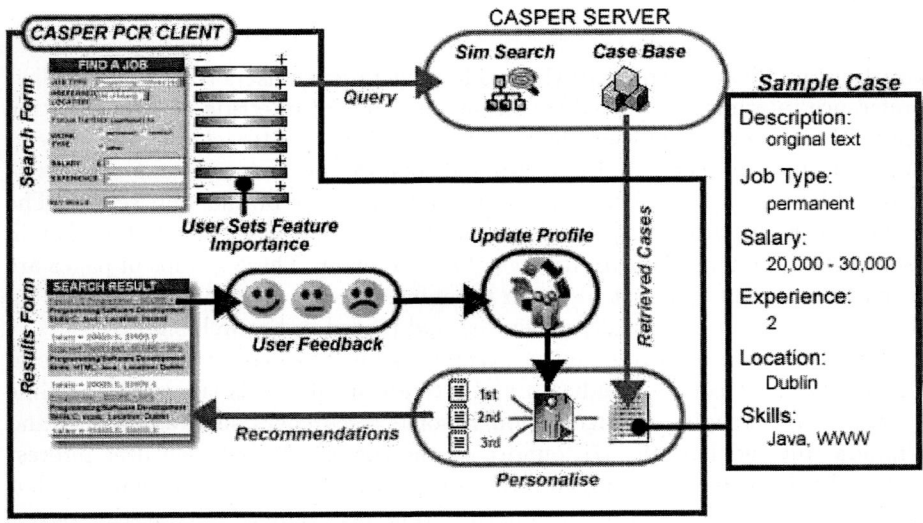

Fig. 1. CASPER PCR architecture.

During the first stage of retrieval, job cases are ranked on the server according to their similarity to the query using a standard similarity metric, which calculates a similarity score between query features and corresponding job case features; each case is made up of a fixed set of features such as *job type*, *location*, *salary*, etc. This means that, unlike traditional search engines, relevant jobs can be identified even though they share no features with the original user query. This retrieval algorithm is presented in Table 1. When presented with a target query t, CasperCB-Recommend treats it as a case and compares it to every other case cc in its case base C. The global similarity (GlobalSim) for each candidate case cc to t is calculated and the best n candidate cases are selected as a result set R. In order to compute GlobalSim each feature f of t is compared to the corresponding feature f of cc. A variety of local similarity functions (LocalSim) are employed to compute the similarity between different feature values. Finally the weight associated with that feature is applied to normalise the LocalSim result.

Table 1. Similarity-based recommendation in CASPER.

t: target query, C: case base, n: #results, R: result set, cc: candidate case, f: case feature, $w(f)$: weight associated with feature f, G: Global Similarity Score
1. define CasperCB-Recommend(t, C, n)
2. begin
3.   Loop $\forall\ cc \in C$
4. $G := $ getGlobalSim(t, cc)
5. $R := $ insertBest(R, cc, G, n)
6.   End Loop
7.   return R
8. end
1. define *getGlobalSim*(t, cc)
2. begin
3.   Loop $\forall f \in cc$
4. $G := G+$ getLocalSim$(t_f, cc_f, w(f))$
5.   End Loop
6.   return G
7. end

As it stands this retrieval approach is still ignorant of the implicit needs of individual users, and therefore the retrieval results are not personalised. This motivates the need for a second stage of retrieval capable of personalising the retrieval results. It reorders the results according to their relevance to the user by comparing them to the user's learned search profile. Each profile specifies the job cases that the user has liked or disliked based on past feedback. Each stage-one result is associated with a relevance score by comparing it to the most similar user profile cases. For instance if the result is similar to many positive profile cases it gets a high relevance score, while if it is similar to negative cases it gets a low score. Thus, priority is given to jobs that are similar to the target query and relevant to the user. If a user has previously liked jobs in the Dublin area, then the second retrieval stage will prioritise job cases from these locations in the future, even if the user does not specify a location constraint in a query.

Table 2. The two-stage personalisation process - PCR Recommend.

P: profile, t: target query, C: case base, n: # results, k: # profile elements used in classification, K: set of profile elements nearest to result, R: result set, cc_i: i^{th} case of R, p_j: j^{th} element of P
1. define PCR-Recommend(P, t, C, n, k)
2. begin
3. $R := PCR - Personalise(P, CasperCB - Recommend(t, C, n), k)$
4.   return R
5. end
1. define PCR-Personalise(P, R, k)
2. begin
3.   Loop to $\|R\|$
4.   PCR-Classify(cc_i, P, k)
5.   end Loop
6. $R :=$ Sort descending classification (R)
7.   return R
8. end
1. define PCR-Classify(cc_i, P, k)
2. begin
3. $K := CasperCB - Recommend(t, P, k)$
3.   Loop $\forall\ cc_i \in K$
4.   Loop $\forall\ p_j \in P$
5. $R := getGlobalSim(cc_i, p_j)$
6.   end Loop
7.   end Loop
8. $R :=$ Sort descending classification $*(R)$
9.   return R
10. end

We view this personalisation phase as the second stage of the CASPER recommendation process, a client-side process, emphasising personalised information ordering. An overview of the entire recommendation process *PCR-Recommend* is shown in Table 2. Results R, obtained from the initial server-side recommender *CasperCB-Recommend* are re-ordered in the second stage client side process *PCR-Personalise* according to their relevance to the user. This is achieved by comparing each result $cc \in R$ to the user's learned search profile P. Each profile specifies the job cases that the user has previously liked or disliked based on past feedback. Each stage-one result is associated with a relevance score by comparing it to the k most similar user profile cases K. Since we are comparing job cases with job cases we again use *CasperCB-Recommend* to select these profile elements. We have chosen to implement personalisation as the second stage of our recommender system using the results obtained from the first stage as our set of candidate cases. However, the personalisation methods described here are generally applicable and not limited to operating on the results of a similarity based search. The algorithms described here will personalise any set of feature-based cases if suitable similarity functions are available. However, this approach adds particular value when used as a second stage process since the first stage algorithm filters un-interesting cases thus allowing the personalisation process to focus on cases that have a higher likelihood of utility to the user.

4 Evaluation

Crucial to the success of this system is the effectiveness of personalisation in dealing with incomplete queries. Previous trials [12] using simulated users yielded positive results and will not be discussed further here beyond saying that the results obtained were in broad agreement with our current evaluation. We now focus on a user study that compares user interest ratings predicted by our personalisation algorithm with those obtained from a standard similarity search and actual user interest ratings.

4.1 Setup

Eleven people were asked to describe their ideal job in terms of 5 features: *salary, key skills, location, required experience* and whether it was *permanent* or *contract*. These preferences were used as a query to a standard similarity based search engine that retrieved 15 jobs similar to the query and 15 jobs least similar to the query. The similarity scores generated by this search, which ranged from 0 (being a poor match for their query) to 1 (being a perfect match for their query), are equivalent to predictions of user interest in a particular job. The users were then asked to rate each of the 30 retrieved jobs again between 0 and 1. These ratings show the actual level of interest in a particular job or its relevance to the user and allow us to judge the effectiveness of any predictions made.

In order to simulate incomplete queries each feature of the original search query was taken in turn to represent an incomplete query with only one feature. Each candidate job was compared to this target query and a predicted interest rating generated based solely on its similarity to the query in terms of that feature. For example Table 3 shows a target query and a job candidate. If *salary* was used as an incomplete single-featured query then the candidate job would be taken to be a perfect match since its *salary* is identical to the desired target, regardless of its other features. This process was then repeated for each of the 5 features that make up a job description.

Table 3. A target query and a candidate job.

Feature	Target	Candidate
Type:	Permanent	Contract
Salary:	35000	35000
Location:	Dublin	London
Min Exp:	2	3
Skills:	HTML, Java	COBOL

Of course incomplete queries may contain more than one feature. We therefore repeated the above procedure for all possible combinations of 2, 3 and 4 features (*2F,3F* and *4F* respectively). For example taking Salary and Location as a possible 2-featured query the candidate in Table 3 would be considered only 50% relevant since although the salaries are identical the locations are vastly different. These similarity-based incomplete queries provide benchmarks for the effectiveness of our personalisation strategy.

This process resulted in 5 different sets of prediction scores

1. 1F: relevance predictions made using only one feature in the similarity computation *(5 queries with different choices of feature were possible)*
2. 2F: relevance predictions made using only two features in the similarity computation *(10 queries with different combinations of two features were possible)*
3. 3F: relevance predictions made using only three features in the similarity computation *(10 queries with different combinations of three features were possible)*
4. 4F: relevance predictions made using only four features in the similarity computation *(5 queries with different combinations of 4 features were possible)*
5. 5F: relevance predictions made using all five features in the similarity computation. This is equivalent to a similarity-based search with a full query. *(1 query with a combination of 5 features was possible)*

Rather than analysing a variety of methods we focus on the most successful methods from previous work [12] Specifically we use a weighted similarity (WS) metric to emphasise candidate jobs similar to those previously liked by the user and de-emphasise those similar to previously disliked items as represented by the user profile. Profiles themselves are made up of the three most highly rated and three least highly rated jobs extracted from the set of candidate cases. The remaining 24 jobs were then available for use as retrieval candidates.

Each of the remaining 24 jobs was presented to the personalisation algorithm in effect acting as a queryless recommender. The predicted relevancy score was then compared to each of the relevancy predictions made by the incomplete similarity-based queries(1F-4F), the full featured similarity query (5F) and the actual relevancy figures given by the users(USC). This process was repeated for all eleven users and the results averaged.

4.2 Prediction Error

Initially we examined the ability of the personalisation client to correctly predict user interest in all the available candidate cases. Figure 2 shows the mean absolute error for each approach, averaged across all users. Absolute error is defined as the absolute difference between the user's actual rating for a job and the predicted relevance score generated by the various prediction algorithms. Errors may vary between 0 and 1 since user ratings are limited to this range. The mean absolute error for a given user denotes the mean difference between all predictions made and the actual user rating. This is then averaged across all users to give the results shown in Figure 2. The personalisation strategy denoted by WS achieved an error of only 17% compared to the full feature (5F) search which had an error of 25%. As the number of features used in the query were reduced the associated error increased as one would expect until the one feature (1F) error reached 33%.

The error suffered by each of the incomplete query methods was highly dependant on which features were used in the query. For example the candidate in Table 3 would be deemed highly relevant if *salary* alone was used as a query despite the fact that it is a very poor match for the user's overall criteria. This would result in a very high error. If *skills* alone were used as the basis of a query then the candidate would have a very low predicted relevance resulting in a low error. Since we cannot guarantee which feature or combination of features will be chosen it is worth noting that worst mean absolute error when averaged over all users using just one feature in a query was 48%.

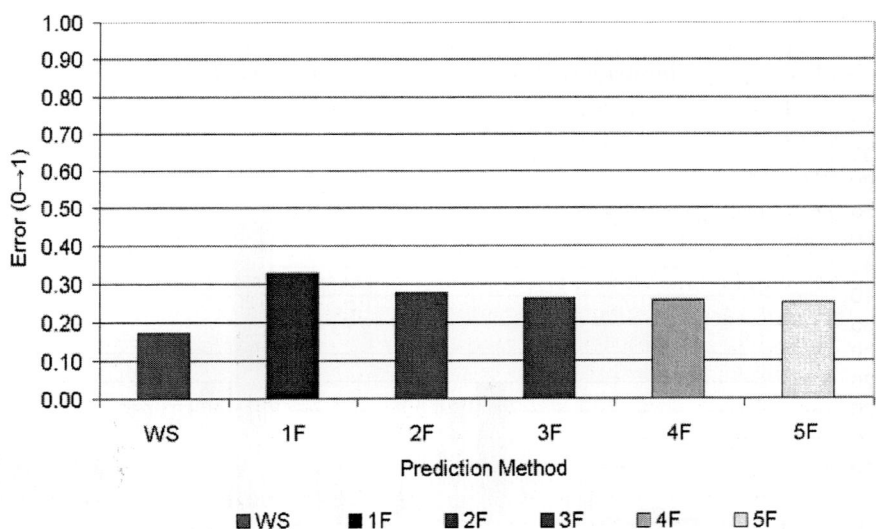

Fig. 2. Mean absolute error for all predictions averaged over all users.

In addition to looking at the mean absolute error we also analysed the mean distribution of errors over all the recommendations made by a particular algorithm. These results are again averaged over all eleven users. Figure 3 shows the mean distribution of all errors made by our personalisation algorithm shown here as the lighter bars.

The horizontal axis indicates the error of a particular recommendation while the vertical axis denotes the frequency of occurrence of that error. Errors were not normalised so as to distinguish between overestimation and underestimation of user ratings. Critical to the success of any recommender is its ability to correctly identify items the user will feel strongly about. Figure 3 therefore

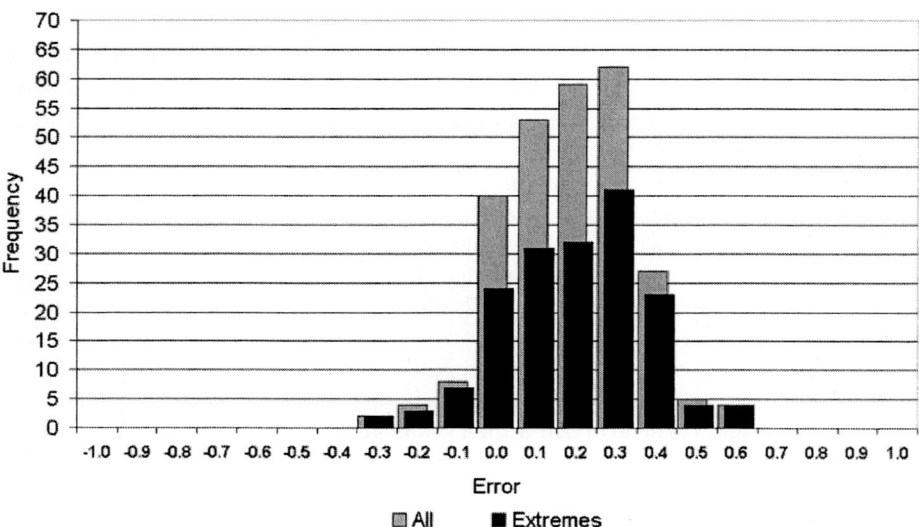

Fig. 3. Error distribution for personalisation algorithm averaged across all users.

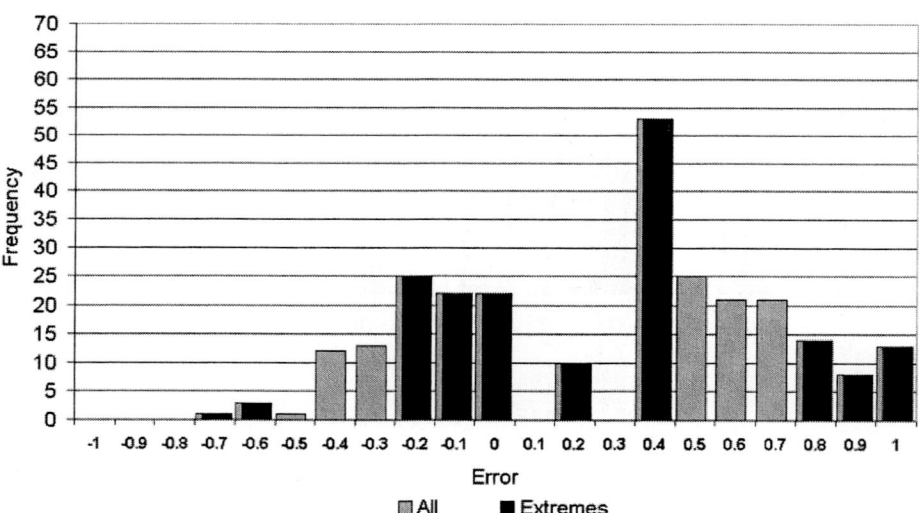

Fig. 4. Error distribution for a single-featured query averaged across all users.

also shows, as darker shaded bars, the error distribution when dealing with *'extreme'* items which the user rated either greater than 0.6 or less than 0.2. Again the results show that the personalisation method is equally adept at predicting extreme ratings.

By contrast the results for single featured queries showed a much flatter curve. Again the quality of the results obtained varied depending on which feature was used as a basis for the query. Figure 4 shows the mean distribution of errors for one of the single-featured queries. In addition to the more frequent occurrence of larger errors denoted by the lighter bars, the darker bars indicate that the worst errors, those furthest from zero occurred for items with extreme ratings. In other words this approach is more likely to make a bad error when recommending items the user feels strongly about.

4.3 Relevance of Top 5

Studies have shown that most users rarely look beyond the first few results presented to them [19]. This is exacerbated by the limited screen display common to many popular mobile devices. We therefore focused on the relevancy of the top 5 recommendations made using each prediction method. Figure 5 shows the mean relevancy of the top 5 recommendations averaged across all users. The various combinations of features used in the incomplete queries resulted in multiple sets of top 5 answers.

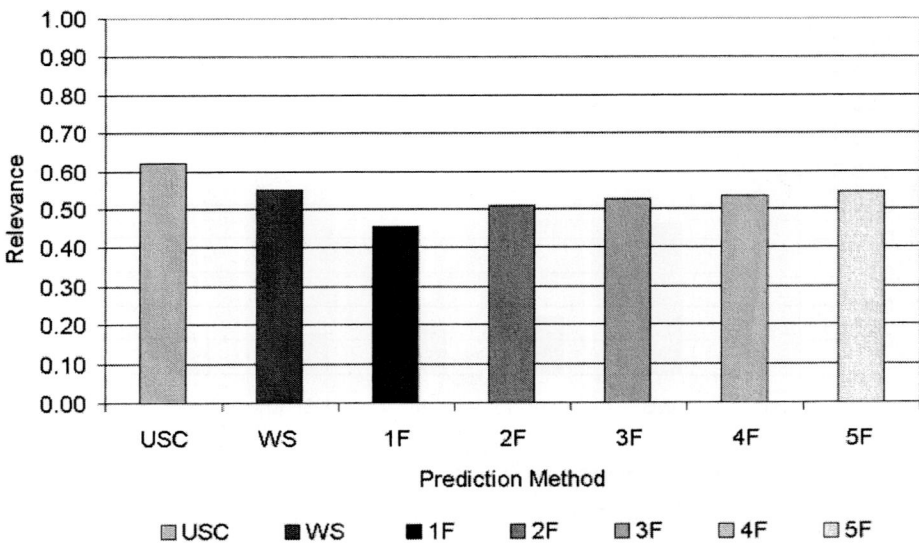

Fig. 5. Average Relevance of Recommendations in the Top 5.

For example each of the five one-featured queries resulted in a different top 5 set. In Figure 5 1F therefore represents the mean relevancy in each of these top five sets averaged over all 5 possible sets. Likewise 2F,3F and 4F represent the mean relevancy of all possible top 5 sets generated by two-featured, three-featured and four-featured queries averaged over the number of possible sets in each case. Our personalisation method produced one set of top 5 results shown here as WS. The actual mean relevance of the user's preferred top 5 is also shown here as USC in order to provide a benchmark. Our personalisation method acting effectively as a queryless recommender again outperformed the incomplete query methods with an average relevance of 0.55 although at higher numbers of features these techniques approached the relevancy of WS with scores of 0.53 and 0.54.

The mean relevancy of the incomplete query methods are again dependant on which combination of features are used. Depending on which combination of features are used the resulting relevance can be up to 17% worse than the WS. Interestingly it is also possible to do up to 3% better than WS using some combinations of features. Unfortunately there is no guaranteed way to identify these features in advance nor are they static across users since user preference and knowledge will determine which features are chosen. By comparison WS failed to include the most relevant case in its top 5 recommendations for only 3 out of the 11 users tested. We feel that this trade-off is acceptable given the other benefits of the WS approach.

This mean view of relevancy hides other negative characteristics of incomplete query methods, namely the worst possible recommendation that can occur in the top 5. Figure 6 shows the least relevant result that occurred in the top 5 recommendations averaged across all users.

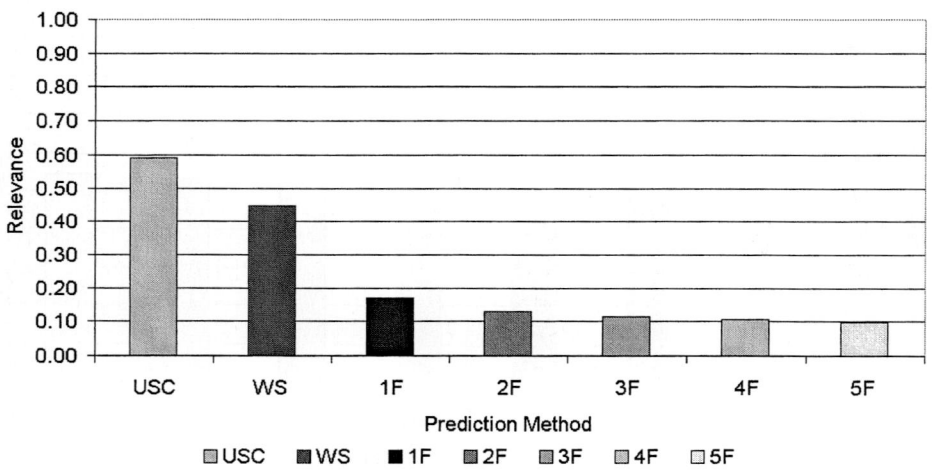

Fig. 6. Least Relevant Recommendation in the Top 5.

The least relevant result in the user's top 5 ratings is again included as a benchmark and denoted here by USC. WS maintains a high level of relevancy with a minimum relevancy of 0.45, while the incomplete query methods allow extremely poor recommendations to be presented, some as low as 0.1. Even the standard similarity method (5F) performs poorly, presenting the user with jobs with as low a relevancy as 0.1.

5 Conclusion

People are much more likely to be antagonised by incorrect or irrelevant results in their top recommendations particularly where bandwidth and screen size are at a premium. We have shown that, when a limited number of recommendations are required, incomplete or short queries run a high risk of including irrelevant recommendations. We argue that the guarantee of high relevance provided by personalisation techniques coupled with their ability to make predictions based on small queries, provides a better method of identifying relevant information for our users.

We are currently analysing the effect of result diversity on incomplete queries. By increasing the diversity of the result set generated with short or incomplete queries we hope to overcome the poor accuracy characteristics of the incomplete query methods. We plan to compare this approach with the improvements gained using personalisation and analyse the effect of combining both personalisation and diversity into an overall quality metric.

References

1. Hayes, C., Cunningham, P., Clerkin, P., Grimaldi, M.: Programme-driven music radio. In Proceedings of the 15th European Conference on Artificial Intelligence, ECAI'2002, Lyon, France, IOS Press (2002) 633–637.
2. Budzik, J., Hammond, K., Marlow, C., Scheinkman, A.: Anticipating information needs: Everyday applications as interfaces to internet information sources. In Proceedings of the 1998 World Conference on the WWW, Internet, and Intranet, Orlando, Florida, USA, November 7-12, 1998, AACE Press. (1998).
3. Jay, B., Kristian, H.: Watson: Anticipating and contextualizing information needs. In Proceedings of the 62nd Annual Meeting of the American Society for Information Science, Medford, NJ, Oct 31-Nov 4, 1999, Information Today, Inc. (1999) 727–740.
4. Kay., J.: Vive la difference!individualized interaction with users. In C. Mellish, editor, Proceedning of the 14th International Joint Conference on Artificial Intelligence, San Mateo, CA, 1995, Morgan Kaufmann. (1995) 978–984.
5. Kelly, D., Belkin, N.J.: Reading time, scrolling and interaction: Exploring implicit sources of user preference for relevance feedback. In Proceedings of the 24th Annual International ACM Conference on Research and Development in Information Retrieval (SIGIR '01), New Orleans, LA. (2001) 408–409.
6. Kim, J., Oard, D., Romanik, K.: Using implicit feedback for user modeling in internet and intranet searching. Technical Report 00-01, College of Library and Information Services (CLIS), University of Maryland at College Park. (2000).
7. Konstan, J.A., Miller, B.N., Maltz, D., Herlocker, J.L., Gordon, L.R., Riedl, J.: Grouplens: applying collaborative filtering to usenet news. In Communications of the ACM, v.40 n.3, March. (1997) 77–87.
8. Lawrence, S., Giles, C.L.: Inquirus, the NECI meta search engine. In Proceedings of the Seventh International World Wide Web Conference, Brisbane, Australia, 1998. Elsevier Science. (1998) 95–105.
9. Lawrence, S., Giles, C.L., Bollacker, K.: Digital libraries and autonomous citation indexing. IEEE Computer, 32(6). (1999) 67–71.
10. Morita, M., Shinoda, Y.: Information filtering based on user behaviour analysis and best match text retrieval. In Croft, W.B., van Rijsbergen, C.J., editors, Proceedings of the 17th Annual International ACM-SIGIR Conference on Research and Development in Information Retrieval. Dublin, Ireland, 3-6 July 1994 (Special Issue of the SIGIR Forum), ACM/Springer, 1994. (1994) 272–281.

11. O'Sullivan, D., Wilson, D., Smyth, B.: Explicit vs. implicit profiling – a case-study in electronic programme guides. In Proceedings of the 18th International Joint Conference on Artificial Intelligence (IJCAI-03), Acapulco, Mexico. (2003) 1351-.
12. Bradley, K., Smyth, B.: Personalized Information Ordering: A Case Study in Online Recruitment. In the Journal of Knowledge-based Systems, 16. (2003) 269-275.
13. Perkowitz. M., Etzioni, O.: Adaptive web sites: Automatically synthesizing web pages. In AAAI/IAAI,(1998) 27–732.
14. Rafter, R., Bradley, K., Smyth, B.: Automated collaborative filtering applications for online recruitment services. In Proceedings of the International Conference on Adaptive Hypermedia and Adaptive Web-Based Systems(AH 2000), Trento, Italy, August 28-30, 2000. Lecture Notes in Computer Science, 1892. (2000) 363–368.
15. Rafter, R., Bradley, K., Smyth, B.: Personalised retrieval for online recruitment services. In Proceedings of the BCS-IRSG 22nd Annual Colloquium on Information Retrieval, Sidney Sussex College, Cambridge, England. (2000) 151–163.
16. Rhodes, B.J.: Margin notes: Building contextually aware associative memory. In Proceedings of the 5th International Conference on Intelligent User Interfaces (IUI '00), New Orleans, LA, United States, January 9-12, 2000, ACM Press. (2000) 219 – 224.
17. Rhodes, B.J., Starner, T.: The Remembrance Agent: A continuously running automated information retrieval system. In the Proceedings of PAAM 96, London, UK, April 1996. (1996) 487–495
18. Sarwar, B.M., Konstan, J.A., Borchers, A., Herlocker, J.L., Miller, B.N., Riedl, J.: Using filtering agents to improve prediction quality in the grouplens research collaborative filtering system. In Computer Supported Cooperative Work (1998) 345–354.
19. Silverstein, C., Henzinger, M.R., Marais, H., Moricz, M.: Analysis of a very large web search engine query log. SIGIR Forum, 33(1). (1999) 6–12.
20. Smyth, B., Cotter, P.: A personalised tv listings service for the digital tv age. In the Journal of Knowledge-Based Systems, 13(2-3) (2000) 53–59.

Quantifying the Ocean's CO2 Budget with a CoHeL-IBR System

Juan M. Corchado[1], Jim Aiken[2], Emilio S. Corchado[3],
Nathalie Lefevre[4], and Tim Smyth[2]

[1] Departamento Informática y Automática, Universidad de Salamanca
Plaza de la Merced s/n, 37008, Salamanca, Spain
corchado@usal.es
[2] Centre for Air-Sea Interactions and fluxes, Plymouth Marine Laboratory,
Prospect Place, Plymouth, PL1 3 DH, UK
ja@mail.pml.ac.uk
[3] Departamento de Ingeniería Civil, Escuela Politécnica Superior
Universidad de Burgos.
C/ Francisco de Vitoria s/n, 09006, Burgos, Spain
escorchado@ubu.es
[4] School of Environmental Sciences, University of East Anglia
Norwich, NR4 7TJ, UK
n.lefevre@ueaS.ac.uk

Abstract. By improving accuracy in the quantification of the ocean's CO_2 budget, a more precise estimation can be made of the terrestrial fraction of global CO_2 budget and its subsequent effect on climate change. First steps have been taken towards this from an environmental and economic point of view, by using an instance based reasoning system, which incorporates a novel clustering and retrieval method - a Cooperative Maximum Likelihood Hebbian Learning model (CoHeL). This paper reviews the problems of measuring the ocean's CO_2 budget and presents the CoHeL model developed and outlines the IBR system developed to resolve the problem.

1 Introduction

This paper presents the results obtained with an instance based reasoning system (IBR) developed to estimate the ocean-atmosphere partial pressure of CO_2 (pCO_2) from information extracted from satellite pictures, wind direction and strength and other parameters such as water temperature, salinity and fluorescence. The final goal of our project is to construct a model that calculates the exchange rate and the global budgets of CO_2, between the ocean and the atmosphere. An understanding of the natural sources and sinks of atmospheric carbon dioxide is necessary for predicting future atmospheric loading and its consequences for global climate. Present estimates of emissions and uptake do not balance, and although some have attributed the imbalance to a terrestrial sink, the magnitude of the oceanic sink remains undefined [7]. The rapid increase in atmospheric CO_2 resulting from atmospheric changes in the carbon cycle has stimulated a great deal of interest. Important decisions need to be made about future tolerable levels of atmospheric CO_2 content, as well as the lead and fossil fuel usage strategies that will permit us to achieve our environmental goals. The solution to these types of problems requires the use of dynamic systems, capable of incorporating new knowledge and facilitating the monitoring and estimation work carried out by oceanographers [14].

Case based reasoning (CBR) and IBR systems have been successfully used in several domains such as diagnosis, prediction, control and planning [13] [5] [18]. However, a major problem with these systems is the difficulty of case retrieval and case matching when the number of cases increases; large case bases are difficult to handle and require efficient indexing mechanisms and optimised retrieval algorithms. Moreover, there are very few standard techniques for automating their construction, since each problem may be represented by a different data set and requires a customised solution. Based on recent successful experiments with this technology [6] an instance based reasoning system has been developed for estimating the partial pressure of CO_2 in the ocean. The IBR system developed incorporates a novel Cooperative Maximum Likelihood Hebbian Learning model for the data clustering and retrieval and a radial-bases function neural network for instance adaptation and forecast, which is an extension and an improvement of the one presented in [6].

This paper reviews a method that can be used for the automation of IBR systems especially developed for estimating the partial pressure of CO_2 in an area of the Pacific ocean from Latitude 22,6°S to 24°S and Longitude 70°W to 72°W, which corresponds to a water mass situated off the Chile coasts of "Mejillones" and "Antofagasta". The Cooperative Maximum Likelihood Hebbian Learning (CoHeL) method is a novel approach that features both selection, in which the aim is to visualize and extract information from complex, and highly dynamic data. The model proposed is a mixture of factor analysis and exploratory projection pursuit [8] based on a family of cost functions proposed by Fyfe and Corchado [9] which maximizes the likelihood of identifying a specific distribution in the data while minimizing the effect of outliers [9] [16]. It employs cooperative lateral connections derived from the Rectified Gaussian Distribution [3] [15] in order to enforce a more sparse representation in each weight vector. This method is used for the clustering of instances, and during the retrieval stage of the IBR cycle, the adaptation step is carried out using a radial basis function network while the revision stage is manually carried out by an oceanographer (since the specific aim of this project is to construct a tool for oceanographers). Finally, the system is updated continuously with data obtained from the afore mentioned satellites and sensors.

First, the present paper will describe the oceanographic problem that defines the framework of our research, then the CoHeL method, used to automate the retrieval stage of the IBR systems, will be described. A presentation will then be made of the instance based reasoning model and finally, the results of the experiments will be described.

2 Ocean-Atmosphere Interaction

The oceans contain approximately 50 times more CO_2 in dissolved forms than the atmosphere, while the land biosphere including the biota and soil carbon contains about 3 times as much carbon (in CO_2 form) as the atmosphere [17]. The CO_2 concentration in the atmosphere is governed primarily by the exchange of CO_2 with these two dynamic reservoirs. Since the beginning of the industrial era, about 2000 billion tons of carbon have been released into the atmosphere as CO_2 from various industrial sources including fossil fuel combustion and cement production. At present, atmospheric CO_2 content is increasing at an annual rate of about 3 billion tons which corresponds to one half of the annual emission rate of approximately 6 billion tons from fossil fuel combustion. Whether the missing CO_2 is mainly absorbed by the oceans or by the land and their ecosystems have been debated extensively over the past decade. It is important, therefore, to fully understand the nature of the physical, chemical and biological processes which govern the oceanic sink/source conditions for atmospheric CO2 [11] [17].

New satellite sensors: ENVISAT, Aqua and other new Earth Observation satellites herald a new era in marine Earth Observation. Satellite-borne instruments provide high-precision, high-resolution data on atmosphere, ocean boundary layer properties and ocean biogeochemical variables, daily, globally, and in the long term. All these new sources of information have changed our approach to oceanography and the data generated needs to be fully exploited. Wind stress, wave breaking and the damping of turbulence and ripples by surface slicks, all affect the air-sea exchange of CO_2. These processes are closely linked to the "roughness" of the sea surface, which can be measured by satellite radars and microwave radiometers. Sea surface roughness consists of a hierarchy of smaller waves upon larger waves (photograph, left, and close-up, below). Different sensors give subtly different measurements of this roughness. Our final aim is to model both the open ocean and shelf seas, and it is believed that by assimilating Earth Observation (EO) data into artificial intelligence models these problems may be solved. EO data (both for assimilation and for validation) are vital for the successful development of reliable models that can describe the complex physical and biogeochemical interactions involved in marine carbon cycling. Satellite information is vital for the construction of oceanographic models, and in this case, to produce estimates of air-sea fluxes of CO_2 with much higher spatial and temporal resolution, using artificial intelligence models than can be achieved realistically by direct *in situ* sampling of upper ocean CO_2.

The systems have been tested in a number of cruises carried out off Chile during the austral summer of 2000, such as the one shown in Figure 1. The oceanographic cruises had several purposes including the calibration of new satellites and sensors, evaluation of the model proposed, etc. During the cruise, data was obtained *in situ* from temperature, chlorophyll, fluorescence and salinity sensors, and satellite images were also obtained. Partial pressure of CO_2 (pCO_2) was also calculated in real time. This data was used to calibrate satellite sensors and to feed the IBR system, with the intention of developing a model that may allow, in the future, the calculation of pCO_2 values from satellite images rather than from *in situ* cruises.

3 CoHeL Model

The Cooperative Maximum Likelihood Hebbian Learning (CoHel) method used during the retrieval stage of an IBR system is closely related to factor analysis and exploratory projection pursuit. It is a neural model based on the Negative Feedback artificial neural network, which has been extended by the combination of two differ-

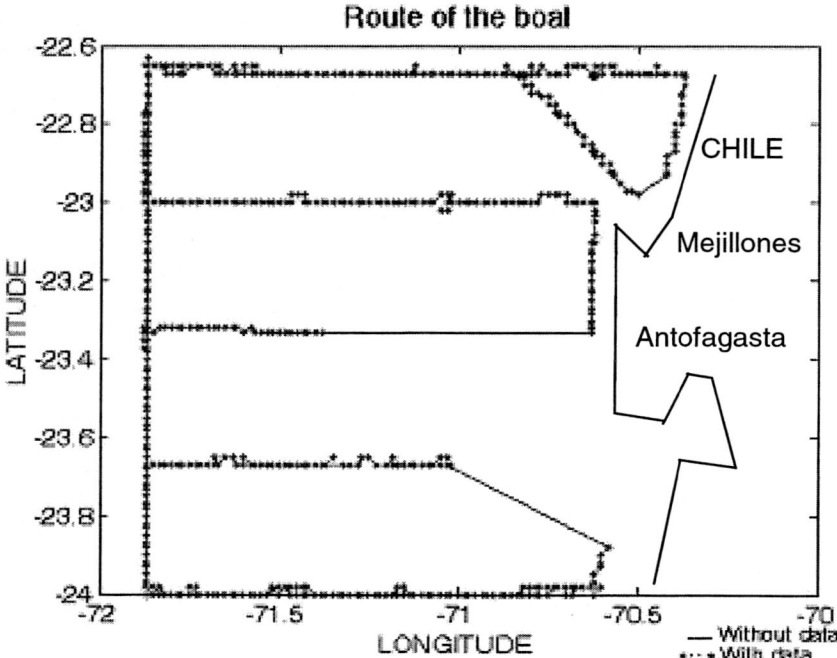

Fig. 1. Cruise track in the Pacific waters.

ent techniques. As mentioned before, this method is an extension and an improvement of the Maximum Likelihood Hebbian Learning (MLHL) method presented in [6]. This is a more robust method, based on a more solid mathematical formulation and that enforces a more sparse representation due to the use of cooperative lateral connections among the output neurons of the neural net, which also guaranties a faster convergence and clustering.

In this case, after selecting a cost function from a family of cost functions which identify different distributions - this method is called Maximum-Likelihood Hebbian learning [4][9] - cooperative lateral connections derived from the Rectified Gaussian Distribution [15] were added to the Maximum-Likelihood method which enforced a greater sparsity in the weight vectors. To understand the proposed method is necessary to review the concepts presented in the following sections.

3.1 The Negative Feedback Neural Network

First, we shall present the Negative Feedback Network, which is the basis of the Maximum-Likelihood model. Feedback is said to exist in a system whenever the output of an element in the system partially influences the input applied to that particular element. It is used in this case to maintain the equilibrium on the weight vectors.

Consider an N-dimensional input vector, $\mathbf{x}$, and a M-dimensional output vector, $\mathbf{y}$, with W_{ij} being the weight linking input j to output i and let η be the learning rate. The initial situation is that there is no activation at all in the network. The input data is fed forward via weights from the input neurons (the x-values) to the output neurons (the y-values) where a linear summation is performed to give the activation of the output neuron. We can express this as:

$$y_i = \sum_{j=1}^{N} W_{ij} x_j, \forall i \qquad (1)$$

The activation is fed back through the same weights and subtracted from the inputs (where the inhibition takes place):

$$e_j = x_j - \sum_{i=1}^{M} W_{ij} y_i, \forall j \qquad (2)$$

After that simple Hebbian learning is performed between input and outputs:

$$\Delta W_{ij} = \eta e_j y_i \qquad (3)$$

The effect of the negative feedback is to stabilise the learning in the network. Because of this, it is not necessary to normalise or clip the weights to get convergence to a stable solution.

Note that this algorithm is clearly equivalent to Oja's Subspace Algorithm [12] since if we substitute Equation 2 in Equation 3 we get:

$$\Delta W_{ij} = \eta e_j y_i = \eta \left(x_j - \sum_k W_{kj} y_k \right) y_i \qquad (4)$$

This network is capable of finding the principal components of the input data in a manner that is equivalent to Oja's Subspace algorithm [12], and so the weights will not find the actual Principal Components but a basis of the Subspace spanned by these components. Since the model is equivalent to Oja's Subspace algorithm, we might legitimately ask what we gain by using the negative feedback in such a way. Writing the algorithm like this gives us a model of the process which allows us to envisage different models which would otherwise be impossible [9].

Factor Analysis is a technique similar to PCA in that it attempts to explain the data set in terms of a smaller number of underlying factors. However Factor Analysis begins with a specific model and then attempts to explain the data by finding parameters which best fit this model to the data. Charles and Fyfe [2] have linked a constrained version of the Negative Feedback network to Factor Analysis. The constraint put on the network was a rectification of either the weights or the outputs (or both). Thus if the weight update resulted in negative weights, those weights were set to zero; if the feed forward mechanism gives a negative output, this was set to zero. We will use the notation $[t]^+$ for this rectification: if t<0, t is set to 0; if t>0, t is unchanged.

3.2 ε-Insensitive Hebbian Learning

It has been shown that the nonlinear PCA rule

$$\Delta W_{ij} = \eta \left(x_j f(y_i) - f(y_i) \sum_k W_{kj} f(y_k) \right) \qquad (5)$$

can be derived as an approximation to the best non-linear compression of the data. Thus we may start with a cost function

$$J(W) = 1^T E\{(x - Wf(W^T x))^2\} \quad (6)$$

which we minimise to get the rule(5). Fyfe and MacDonald [10] used the residual in the linear version of (6) to define a cost function of the residual

$$J = f_1(\mathbf{e}) = f_1(\mathbf{x} - W\mathbf{y}) \quad (7)$$

where $f_1 = \|\cdot\|^2$ is the (squared) Euclidean norm in the standard linear or nonlinear PCA rule. With this choice of $f_1(\ )$, the cost function is minimized with respect to any set of samples from the data set on the assumption that the residuals are chosen independently and identically distributed from a standard Gaussian distribution. We may show that the minimization of J is equivalent to minimizing the negative log probability of the residual, **e**, if **e** is Gaussian. Let:

$$p(\mathbf{e}) = \frac{1}{Z} \exp(-\mathbf{e}^2) \quad (8)$$

The factor Z normalizes the integral of $p(\mathbf{y})$ to unity.

Then we can denote a general cost function associated with this network as

$$J = -\log p(\mathbf{e}) = (\mathbf{e})^2 + K \quad (9)$$

where K is a constant. Therefore performing gradient descent on J we have

$$\Delta W \propto -\frac{\partial J}{\partial W} = -\frac{\partial J}{\partial \mathbf{e}} \frac{\partial \mathbf{e}}{\partial W} \approx \mathbf{y}(2\mathbf{e})^T \quad (10)$$

where a less important term has been has been discarded. In general, the minimisation of such a cost function may be thought to make the probability of the residuals more dependent on the probability density function (pdf) of the residuals [16]. Thus if the probability density function of the residuals is known, this knowledge could be used to determine the optimal cost function. Fyfe and MacDonald [10] investigated this with the (one dimensional) function:

$$p(\mathbf{e}) = \frac{1}{2+\varepsilon} \exp(-|\mathbf{e}|_\varepsilon) \quad (11)$$

where

$$|\mathbf{e}|_\varepsilon = \begin{cases} 0\_ \forall |\mathbf{e}| < \varepsilon \\ |\mathbf{e}| - \varepsilon \_ otherwise \end{cases} \quad (12)$$

with ε being a small scalar ≥ 0. Fyfe and Corchado [9] described this in terms of noise in the data set. However we feel that it is more appropriate to state that, with this model of the pdf of the residual, the optimal $f_1(\ )$ function is the ε-insensitive cost function:

$$f_1(\mathbf{e}) = |\mathbf{e}|_\varepsilon \quad (13)$$

In the case of the Negative Feedback Network, the learning rule is

$$\Delta W \propto -\frac{\partial J}{\partial W} = -\frac{\partial f_1(\mathbf{e})}{\partial \mathbf{e}} \frac{\partial \mathbf{e}}{\partial W} \quad (14)$$

which gives:

$$\Delta W_{ij} = \begin{cases} 0 \_ \text{if } |e_j| < \varepsilon \\ \eta y_i (\text{sign}(e_j)) \text{otherwise} \end{cases} \quad (15)$$

The difference with the common Hebb learning rule is that the sign of the residual is used instead of the value of the residual. Because this learning rule is insensitive to the magnitude of the input vectors x, the rule is less sensitive to outliers than the usual rule based on mean squared error. This change from viewing the difference after feedback as simply a residual rather than an error will permit us later to consider a family of cost functions each member of which is optimal for a particular probability density function associated with the residual.

3.3 A Family of Learning Rules

Now the ε-insensitive learning rule is clearly only one of a possible family of learning rules which are suggested by the family of exponential distributions. Let the residual after feedback have probability density function

$$p(\mathbf{e}) = \frac{1}{Z} \exp(-|\mathbf{e}|^p) \quad (16)$$

Then we can denote a general cost function associated with this network as

$$J = -\log p(\mathbf{e}) = |\mathbf{e}|^p + K \quad (17)$$

where K is a constant. Therefore performing gradient descent on J we have

$$\Delta W \propto -\frac{\partial J}{\partial W} = -\frac{\partial J}{\partial \mathbf{e}} \frac{\partial \mathbf{e}}{\partial W} \approx y(p|\mathbf{e}|^{p-1} \text{sign}(\mathbf{e}))^T \quad (18)$$

where T denotes the transpose of a vector. We would expect that for leptokurtotic residuals (more kurtotic than a Gaussian distribution), values of p<2 would be appropriate, while for platykurtotic residuals (less kurtotic than a Gaussian), values of p>2 would be appropriate. It is a common belief in the ICA community that it is less important to get exactly the correct distribution when searching for a specific source than it is to use a model with an approximately correct distribution i.e. all supergaussian signals can be retrieved using a generic leptokurtotic distribution and all subgaussian signals can be retrieved using a generic platykurtotic distribution. The experiments [3] tend to support this belief to some extent but we often find accuracy and speed of convergence are improved when we are accurate in our choice of p.

Therefore the network operation is:

Feedforward: $$y_i = \sum_{j=1}^{N} W_{ij} x_j, \forall_i \quad (19)$$

Feedback: $$e_j = x_j - \sum_{i=1}^{M} W_{ij} y_i \quad (20)$$

Weight change: $$\Delta W_{ij} = \eta . y_i . \text{sign}(e_j) |e_j|^{p-1} \quad (21)$$

Corchado and Fyfe [3] described their rule as performing a type of PCA, but this is not strictly true since only the original (Oja) ordinary Hebbian rule actually performs

PCA. It might be more appropriate to link this family of learning rules to Principal Factor Analysis since this method makes an assumption about the noise in a data set and then removes the assumed noise from the covariance structure of the data before performing a PCA. We are doing something similar here in that we are basing our PCA-type rule on the assumed distribution of the residual. By maximising the likelihood of the residual with respect to the actual distribution, we are matching the learning rule to the pdf of the residual.

This method has been linked to the standard statistical method of Exploratory Projection Pursuit (EPP) [8]: EPP also gives a linear projection of a data set but chooses to project the data onto a set of basis vectors which best reveal the interesting structure in the data; interestingness is usually defined in terms of how far the distribution is from the Gaussian distribution.

3.4 Rectified Gaussian Distribution

The Rectified Gaussian Distribution [15] is a modification of the standard Gaussian distribution in which the variables are constrained to be non-negative, enabling the use of non-convex energy functions. The multivariate normal distribution can be defined in terms of an energy or cost function in that, if realised samples are taken far from the distribution's mean, they will be deemed to have high energy and this will be equated to low probability. More formally, we may define the standard Gaussian distribution by:

$$p(\mathbf{y}) = Z^{-1} e^{-\beta E(\mathbf{y})}, \tag{22}$$

$$E(\mathbf{y}) = \frac{1}{2} \mathbf{y}^T \mathbf{A} \mathbf{y} - \mathbf{b}^T \mathbf{y} \tag{23}$$

The quadratic energy function $E(\mathbf{y})$ is defined by the vector **B** and the symmetric matrix **A**. The parameter $\beta = 1/T$ is an inverse temperature. Lowering the temperature concentrates the distribution at the minimum of the energy function.

One advantage of this formalisation is that it allows us to visualise regions of high or low probability in terms of energy and hence to view movement to low energy regions as movement to regions of high probability.

The quadratic energy function $E(\mathbf{y})$ can have different types of curvature depending on the matrix **A**. Consider the situation in which the distribution of the firing of the outputs of our neural network follows a Rectified Gaussian Distribution. Then it is possible to identify values of **A** which give increasingly sparse firings and in the extreme, a single neuron will respond to the whole data set. Two examples of the Rectified Gaussian Distribution are the competitive and cooperative distributions. The modes of the competitive distribution are well-separated by regions of low probability. The modes of the cooperative distribution are closely spaced along a non-linear continuous manifold. Our experiments focus on a network based on the use of the cooperative distribution.

Neither distribution can be accurately approximated by a single standard Gaussian. Using the Rectified Gaussian, it is possible to represent both discrete and continuous variability in a way that a standard Gaussian cannot.

Not all energy functions can be used in the Rectified Gaussian Distribution. The sorts of energy function that can be used are only those where the matrix A has the property:

$$\mathbf{y}^T \mathbf{A} \mathbf{y} > 0 \text{ for all } \mathbf{y} : y_i > 0, i = 1...N \tag{24}$$

where N is the dimensionality of y. This condition is called co-positivity. This property blocks the directions in which the energy diverges to negative infinity. The cooperative distribution in the case of N variables is defined by:

$$A_{ij} = \delta_{ij} + \frac{1}{N} - \frac{4}{N}\cos\left(\frac{2\pi}{N}(i-j)\right) \tag{25}$$

$$b_i = 1 \tag{26}$$

where δ_{ij} is the Kronecker delta and i and j represent the identifiers of output neuron. To speed learning up, the matrix **A** can be simplified [3] to:

$$A_{ij} = \left(\delta_{ij} - \cos(2\pi(i-j)/N)\right) \tag{27}$$

The matrix **A** is used to modify the response to the data based on the relation between the distances between the outputs. The outputs are thought of as located on a ring ("wraparound"). Note that the modes of the Rectified Gaussian are the minima of the energy function, subject to non-negativity constraints. The modes of the distribution characterize much of its behaviour at low temperature. Finding the modes of a Rectified Gaussian is a problem in quadratic programming. However we will use what is probably the simplest algorithm, the projected gradient method, consisting of a gradient step followed by a rectification:

$$y_i(t+1) = [y_i(t) + \tau(b - Ay)]^+ \tag{28}$$

where the rectification [ ]$^+$ is necessary to ensure that the y-values keep to the positive quadrant. If the step size τ is chosen correctly, this algorithm can probably be shown to converge to a stationary point of the energy function [1].

In practice, this stationary point is generally a local minimum. The mode of the distribution can be approached by gradient descent on the derivative of the energy function with respect to **y**. This is:

$$\Delta \mathbf{y} \propto -\frac{\partial E}{\partial \mathbf{y}} = -(\mathbf{A}\mathbf{y} - \mathbf{b}) = \mathbf{b} - \mathbf{A}\mathbf{y} ; \tag{29}$$

which is used as in Equation 28.

Now the rectification in Equation 28 is identical to the rectification which Corchado and Fyfe [3] used in the Maximum-Likelihood Network. Thus we will use this movement towards the mode in the Factor Analysis version of the Maximum-Likelihood Network before training the weights as previously. The net result will be shown to be a network which can find the independent factors of a data set but do so in a way which captures some type of global ordering in the data set.

We use the standard Maximum-Likelihood Network but now with a lateral connection (which acts after the feed forward but before the feedback). Thus we have

Feedforward: $$y_i = \sum_{j=1}^{N} W_{ij} x_j, \forall i \tag{30}$$

Lateral Activation Passing: $$y_i(t+1) = [y_i(t) + \tau(b - Ay)]^+ \quad (31)$$

Feedback: $$e_j = x_j - \sum_{i=1}^{M} W_{ij} y_i, \quad \forall j \quad (32)$$

Weight change: $$\Delta W_{ij} = \eta . y_i . sign(e_j) | e_j |^{p-1} \quad (33)$$

Where the parameter τ represents the strength of the lateral connections.

4 A CoHeL-IBR System for Calculating the Exchange Rate of CO_2

An IBR system has been constructed for obtaining the value of the exchange rate or surface partial pressure of CO_2 (pCO_2) in oceanographic waters from biological parameters and satellite information. The IBR system uses the Cooperative Maximum Likelihood Hebbian Learning Model for clustering the Instance-base and for the retrieval of the instances most similar to the "problem instance", due to its topology preserving properties. The selected instances are used during the reuse stage to train a radial function neural network [5] [9], that provides the value of the pCO_2 for a given point and the result is evaluated by an oceanographer. The learning (retain stage) is carried out by updating the instance base, updating the weights of the radial basis function network and by re-calling the Cooperative Maximum Likelihood Hebbian Learning Model for the clustering of the data.

Table 1. Instance attributes.

Instance Field	Measurement
JD	Serial day of the year
LAT	Latitude
LONG	Longitude
SST	Temperature
S	Salinity
WS	Wind strength
WD	Wind direction
Fluo_calibrated	fluorescence calibrated with chlorophyll
SW pCO2	surface partial pressure of CO2

Applying equations 30 to 33 to the instance-base, the algorithm automatically groups the instances into clusters, grouping together those of similar structure. This technique is a classification and visualisation tool for high dimensional data on a low dimensional display. One of the advantages of this technique is that it is an unsupervised method so we do not need to have any information about the data beforehand. When a new instance is presented to the IBR system, it is identified as belonging to a particular type by applying equation 30 to it. Each stored instance contains information relating to a specific situation.

Table 1 presents the values used to define the problem. Where JD, LAT, LONG, SST, S, WS, WD, Fluo_calibrated and SW represent the problem description and pCO2 is the value that the IBR system has to identify from the problem descriptor.

These values for a given point can be obtained from cruises using sensors or from satellite images. Initially the system was tested *in situ* during the cruise carried out in Pacific waters. The instance-base of the system was fed with 85% of the instances recorded during the cruise (over 85.000 instances). The other 15%, homogeneously spread along the cruise track, was left in order to test the system after the cruse was completed.

The results obtained were very accurate, with an average error of 7,4%, which is less than the error provided by the other techniques we used to evaluate the IBR system. Table 2 presents the average error obtained with the CoHeL-IBR system, with the MLHL-IBR system [6], a Radial-basis Function Neural Network, a Multi-layer Perceptron Neural Network, a Growing Cell Structures Neural Network and a K-nearest neighbour algorithm.

Starting from the error series generated by the different models, the Kruskall-Wallis test has been carried out. Since the P-value is less than 0,01, there is a statistically significant difference between the models at the 99,0% confidence level. Table 3 shows a multiple comparison procedure (Mann-Withney test) used to determine which models are significantly different from the others. The asterisk indicates that these pairs show statistically significant differences at the 99.0% confidence level. Table 3 shows that the IBR system presents statistically significant differences from the other models. The proposed model generates the best results of all the tested techniques. Figure 3 presents the error obtained in 40 cases in with the system was tested. These cases have been randomly obtained from the testing data set (15% of the whole data set), the other 85% of the data set was used to create the model.

Table 2. Average error obtained with the IBR system and other methods.

Method	Average Error
CoHeL-IBR system	7,4%
MLHL-IBR system	8,2%
Radial-basis Function Network	9,8%
Multi-layer Perceptron	10,1%
Growing Cell Structures	16,2%
K-nearest neighbour	13,6%

Table 3. Mann-Withney test results.

	CoHeL-IBR	MLHL-IBR	RB	M	GCS	KN
CoHeL-IBR						
MLHL-IBR	*					
RBF	*	*				
MLP	*	*	=			
GCS	*	*	*	*		
KNN	*	*	*	=	*	

The final goal of the project is to calculate the value of pCO2 from satellite images, such as the ones shown in Figure 2. Most of the values of the parameters presented in Table 1 can be directly obtained from such photographs and others may be extracted with some well-known calculation. In this case, the CoHeL-IBR system was tested with data extracted from satellite images of the area in which the cruise took place, such as the ones presented in Figure 2. Problem instances (vectors with the values of: JD, LAT, LONG, SST, S, WS, WD, Fluo_calibrated and SW) were constructed, along the cruise track from such images and were fed into the CoHeL-IBR system, in order for it to obtain the value of the pCO_2. In this case the average error of the CoHeL-IBR system was slightly higher, but still very accurate compared with the results obtained with the other techniques. Oceanographers have also consider these results to be highly significant. The second column of Table 4 shows these results. Then problem instances were obtained from the same photographs, but from points outside the cruise tracks, and similar results were obtained, as shown in the third column of Table 4.

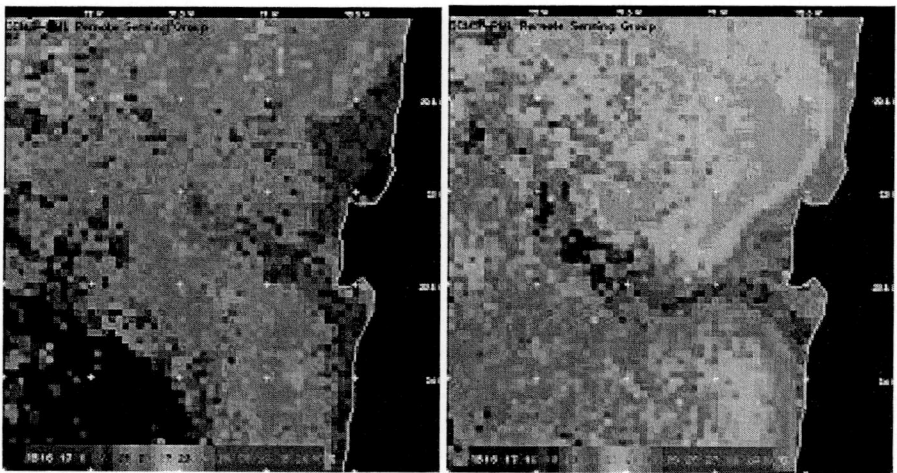

Fig. 2. Processed NOAA Satellite images, showing temperature values, obtained at one week intervals.

Table 4. Average error obtained with the IBR system and other methods on Satellite data.

Method	Average error (Track data)	Average error (Out side track data)
CoHeL-IBR	9,7%	10,3%
MLHL-IBR	12,3%	13,9%
RBF	13,1%	14,5%
MLP	15,2%	14,7%
GCS	18,9%	18,8%
KNN	17,2%	18,1%

5 Conclusions and Future Work

The CoHeL-IBR system presented is able to produce a forecast with an acceptable degree of accuracy. The final constructed tool constitutes the first system developed for calculating the pCO_2 *in situ* and from satellite images. The IBR system incorporates a novel clustering technique capable of indexing huge instance-bases in an unsupervised way and of successfully retrieving instances with a similar structure, which is vital for constructing a model with a radial basis function neural network.

The Cooperative Maximum Likelihood Hebbian Learning Model has also performed better that other algorithms, due to its fast convergence and clustering abilities. It enforces a more sparse representation due to the use of cooperative lateral connections among the output neurons of the neural net. With this technique, the retrieval of the best matching instance is a very simple operation using the proposed method and presents no major computational obstacles. The proposed method is both advantageous in the creation of and retrieval from instance bases but is also important in its own right in the unsupervised investigation of interesting structure in high dimensional data sets. The results obtained in both experiments are very encouraging and the model presents great potential. The experiments carried out have allowed us to determine the efficiency of the model when the data used to create the instance-base and the problem instances is reliable. It has also been shown the potential of the model to automate the resolution of the problem with the help of satellite photographs. In this case, the error may be due to calibration imbalances, lack of definition of the photographs, presence of clouds, errors in the wind measures, etc. These are some of the problems that have to be solved in the framework of this project. Table 4 also shows the generalization capabilities of the proposed model, since it is even able to generate reasonable results in an extended area, when the instance-base has only been constructed with data from one part of the area. More experiments need to be carried out for the model validation and techniques to facilitate the revision of the solution have to be obtained. The uncertainty and the dynamism of oceanographic systems have to be taken into consideration and techniques for monitoring such factors need to be incorporated into the system. The proposed model is a first step towards the resolution of this complex problem, which still requires a great deal more work and research.

References

1. Bertsekas D.P. (1995) Nonlinear Programming. Athena Scientific, Belmont, MA, 1995.
2. Charles D. and Fyfe C. (1998) Modeling Multiple Cause Structure Using Rectification Constraints. Network: Computation in Neural Systems, 9:167-182.
3. Corchado E. and Fyfe C. (2003) Orientation Selection Using Maximum Likelihood Hebbian Learning, International Journal of Knowledge-Based Intelligent Engineering Systems Volume 7 Number 2, April 2003.
4. Corchado E., MacDonald D. and Fyfe C. (2004) Maximum and Minimum Likelihood Hebbian Learning for Exploratory Projection Pursuit, Data mining and Knowledge Discovery, Kluwer Academic Publishing, (In press).
5. Corchado J. M. and Lees B. (2001) A hybrid case-based model for forecasting. Applied Artificial Intelligence: An International Journal Vol 15, no. 2, pp 105-127.

6. Corchado J. M., Corchado E. S., Aiken J., Fyfe C., Fdez-Riverola F. and Glez-Bedia M. (2003) Maximum Likelihood Hebbian Learning Based Retrieval Method for CBR Systems. 5th International Conference on Case-Based Reasoning, Trondheim, Norway, June 23 to 26, 2003. Springer-Verlag
7. Finnegan W. G., Pitter R. L. and Young L. G. (1991) Atmospheric Environment. A25, 2531-2534.
8. Freedman J. and Tukey J. (1974) A Projection Pursuit Algorithm for Exploratory Data Analysis. IEEE Transaction on Computers, (23): 881-890, 1974.
9. Fyfe C. and Corchado E. S. (2002) Maximum Likelihood Hebbian Rules. European Symposium on Artificial Neural Networks. 2002.
10. Fyfe C. and MacDonald D. (2002), ε-Insensitive Hebbian learning, Neuro Computing, 2002
11. Lefevre N., Aiken J., Rutllant J., Daneri G., Lavender S. and Smyth T. (2002) Observations of pCO2 in the coastal upwelling off Chile: Sapatial and temporal extrapolation using satellite data. Journal of Geophysical research. Vol. 107, no. 0
12. Oja E. (1989) Neural Networks, Principal Components and Subspaces, International Journal of Neural Systems, 1:61-68.
13. Pal S. K., Dillon T. S. and Yeung D. S. (2000) Soft Computing in Case-based Reasoning. (eds.). Springer Verlag, London, U.K.
14. Sarmiento J. L. and Dender M. (1994) Carbon biogeochemistry and climate change. Photosynthesis Research, Vol. 39, 209-234.
15. Seung H.S., Socci N.D. and Lee D. (1998) The Rectified Gaussian Distribution, Advances in Neural Information Processing Systems, 10.
16. Smola A.J. and Scholkopf B. (1998) A Tutorial on Support Vector Regression. Technical Report NC2-TR-1998-030, NeuroCOLT2 Technical Report Series.
17. Takahashi T., Olafsson J., Goddard J. G., Chipman D. W. and Sutherland S. C. (1993) Seasonal Variation of CO_2 and nutrients in the High-latitude surface oceans: a comparative study. Global biochemical Cycles. Vol. 7, no. 4. pp 843-878.
18. Watson I. and Marir F. (1994) Case-Based Reasoning: A Review. Cambridge University Press, 1994. The knowledge Engineering Review. Vol. 9. Nº3.

Development of CBR-BDI Agents: A Tourist Guide Application

Juan M. Corchado[1], Juan Pavón[2], Emilio S. Corchado[3], and Luis F. Castillo[1]

[1] Dep. Informática y Automática, Universidad de Salamanca
Plaza de la Merced s/n, 37008, Salamanca, Spain
corchado@usal.es
http://gsii.usal.es/

[2] Dep. Sistemas Informáticos y Programación, Universidad Complutense Madrid
Ciudad Universitaria s/n, 28040, Madrid, Spain

[3] Department of Civil Engineering, University of Burgos, Spain
C/ Francisco de Vitoria s/n, 09006, Burgos, Spain

Abstract. In this paper we present an agent-based application of a wireless tourist guide that combines the Beliefs-Desires-Intentions approach with learning capabilities of Case Base Reasoning techniques. This application shows how to develop adaptive agents with a goal driven design and a decision process built on a CBR architecture. The resulting agent architecture has been validated by real users who have used the tourist guide application, on a mobile device, and can be generalized for the development of other personalized services.

1 Introduction

Over the last few years, multi-agent systems (MAS) have emerged as an interesting paradigm for constructing distributed and dynamic open systems. MAS have been successfully applied in fields such as electronic commerce, medicine, oceanography, trading market, electronic auctions, production intelligent control, robotics, information retrieval, etc. The telecommunication industry expects a new expansion with the development of UMTS and third generation phone systems. The new challenges of this field require new technology that facilitate the construction of more dynamic, *intelligent*, flexible and open applications, capable of working in a real time environment. MAS solutions intend to cope with the requirements of this kind of systems. Although commercial agent technology today is not yet prepared for such demand, it is improving continuously and substantially. The proposal presented in this paper is an example of its possibilities and how it has been adopted for the development of a real application.

Agents are usually classified depending on the set of capabilities that they support, such as autonomy, reactivity, proactivity, social ability, reasoning, learning, and mobility, among others [23]. In this work we are mainly interested in the development of deliberative agents using case-based reasoning (CBR) systems, as a way to implement adaptive systems in open and dynamic environments. Agents in this context must be able to reply to events, take the initiative according to their goals, communicate with other agents, interact with users, and make use of past experiences to find the best plans to achieve goals.

Deliberative agents are usually based on a BDI model [20], which considers agents as having certain *mental attitudes*: Beliefs, Desires, and Intentions (BDI). Under this model, agents have a *mental state* that consists of informational, motivational, and deliberative states respectively. Beliefs represent the information about the environment, the internal state the agent may hold, and the actions it may perform. The agent will try to achieve a set of goals, and will respond to certain events.

A BDI architecture has the advantage that it is intuitive and relatively simple to identify the process of decision-making and how to perform it. Furthermore, the notions of belief, desire and intention are easy to understand. On the other hand, its main drawback lies in finding a mechanism that permits its efficient implementation. Most approaches use multi-modal logic for the formalisation and construction of such agents, but they are not always completely axiomatised or they are not computationally efficient (see, for instance, dMARS [10], PRS [17], JACK [5], JAM [14], and AgentSpeak(L) [19]). Rao and Georgeff [20] state that the problem lies in the great distance between the powerful logic for BDI systems and practical systems. Another problem is that this type of agents have difficulties to implement learning capabilities, as these would require constantly adding, modifying or eliminating beliefs, desires and intentions. As most agent applications have highly dynamic environments, we consider that it would be convenient to have a reasoning mechanism that would enable the agent to learn and adapt in real time, while the computer program is executing, avoiding the need to recompile such an agent whenever the environment changes.

Taking into account previous works [12, 8], we propose the use of a case-based reasoning (CBR) system for the development of deliberative agents. The proposed method starts by identifying agent roles and goals, in a similar way as in AAII/BDI methodology [20], but the design and implementation of the agent architecture follows the form of CBR systems, which facilitates learning and adaptation, and therefore a greater degree of autonomy than with a pure BDI architecture. This is made by mapping the three mental attitudes of BDI agents into the information manipulated by a CBR system. This direct mapping between the agent conceptualisation and its implementation is the main difference with respect to other proposals that have also tried to combine BDI and CBR [16, 4, 22, 18].

The proposed agent architecture has been validated with the implementation of a multi-agent system (MAS) that provides tourist guide services through mobile devices. This application shows how to develop adaptive agents with a goal driven design and a decision process built on a CBR architecture. The system has been validated by users who have used it when visiting the city of Salamanca. The system is able to program a tourist route, and modify it according to the conditions of the places to visit and the available time for the tourist. Because of its design, the services of the tourist guide agent can be easily extended (e.g. to recommend restaurants in the area of the tourist route), and support a high degree of scalability in the number of users.

The rest of the paper is organized as follows. Section 2 describes the wireless tourist guide application and its main components, basically three types of agents, one of them of deliberative nature, which will be used later to show the application of the CBR-BDI agent architecture. This agent architecture is described in Section 3. Implementation details are provided in Section 4. Finally, in the conclusions, we present some of the evaluation results when using this application.

2 The Wireless Tourist Guide System

The tourism industry is one of the major resources of income in Spain and the services offer in this sector is continuously updated and improved. This strategic sector has attracted the attention of the telecommunication operators, who are investing in new tools, services and market research. In this framework, and with the support of a telecommunications partner, a Tourist Guide application, called *TOURIST GUIDE-USAL*, has been developed as a MAS. With this system we wanted to show the feasibility and reliability of this technology, and that fully-functional systems may be constructed within the time restrictions imposed by the industry.

TOURIST GUIDE-USAL agents assist potential tourists in the organization of their tourist routes and enable them to modify their schedules on the move using wireless communication systems. This system has been constructed using an engineering framework developed to design and implement an agent-based tool, as well as integrating existing state of the art in order to create an open, flexible, global anticipatory system with mobile access for the promotion and management of inland and cultural tourism, which will be user-friendly, cost-effective and secure. The system has been standardized to run in any mobile device and is interlingua.

The integrated, multi-platform computer system is composed of a guide agent (*Planner Agent*) that assesses the tourists and help them to identify tourist routes in a city with a given visiting period of time and under a number of restrictions related to cost, tourist interest, etc. There is one assistant agent for each user of the system, the *Performer Agents*. Each user willing to use the system has to register and solicit one of these agents. Finally, there is a third type of agent, the *Tracker agent*, which maintains updated information about the monuments, the restaurants, public transport conditions, etc. This agent maintains horizontally and vertically compiled information on hotel accommodation, restaurants, the commercial sector and transport, in order to meet the needs of the potential visitor on an individually customized basis, and responds to requests for information, reservations and purchases in the precise moment that they are expressed.

The user may decide whether to install the corresponding *Performer Agent* on a mobile phone or PDA, or run it on the server and interact with it via its mobile device. The first choice supposes a reduction of the cost, since the tourist can interact with his agent as much as needed at no cost because it is installed in the wireless device. Nevertheless, the agent will have to contact regularly with the *Planner Agent*.

Fig. 1 describes the system architecture from a very high abstraction level. Users may interact either with their *performer agents* installed in their wireless devices or in an internet server. The *performer agents* interact with the planner agent looking for plans, and the *tracker agent* interacts with the *planner agent* to exchange information. The *planner agent* is the only CBR-BDI agent in this architecture. The *performer agents* can be considered assistant agents and the *tracker agent* is a reactive agent. The focus in this paper is on the *planner agent*.

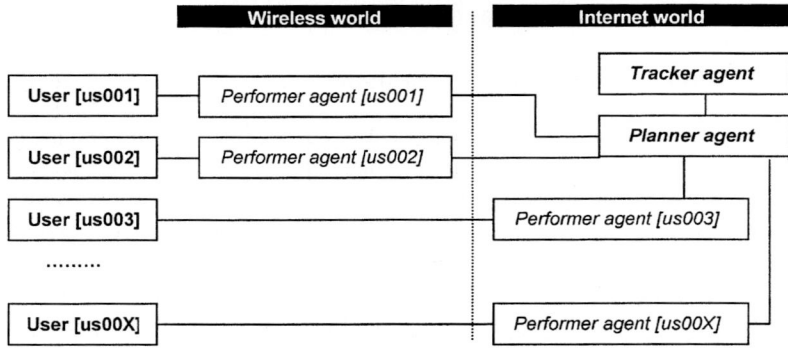

Fig. 1. CBR/Agent integration diagram

3 Case-Based Reasoning Systems and Deliberative Agents

Case-based reasoning (CBR) systems solve new problems by adapting solutions that have been used in the past. Fig. 2 shows a classical CBR reasoning cycle that consists of four sequential phases: retrieve, reuse, revise, and retain [1]. Very often, an additional activity, revision of the expert's knowledge, is required because the memory can change as new cases may appear during this process. Each of these activities can be automated, which implies that the whole reasoning process can be automated to a certain extent [9]. According to this, agents implemented using CBR systems could reason autonomously and therefore adapt themselves to environmental changes.

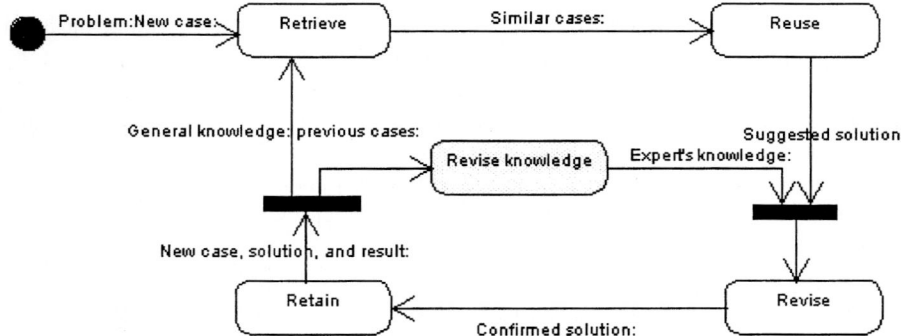

Fig. 2. UML activity diagram describing a CBR life-cycle

On the other hand, as most agent architectures are based on the BDI model, if we are able to establish a relationship between cases, the CBR life-cycle, and the mental attitudes of BDI agents, we can provide a model that facilitates the implementation of the BDI agents using the reasoning cycle of a CBR system, with all its advantages.

Our proposal defines a direct mapping from the concept of an agent to the reasoning model, paying special attention to two elements. First, how the mapping should allow a direct and straightforward implementation of the agent. And second, how the agent is able to learn and evolve with the environmental changes. In this model, the CBR system is completely integrated into the agents' architecture, which differs with the above-mentioned works, in which the agents see the CBR system as just a reasoning tool. Our proposal is also concerned with the agent's implementation and presents a "formalism" which is easy to implement, in which the reasoning process is based on the concept of *intention*. In this model, intentions are cases, which have to be retrieved, reused, revised and retained. To achieve both goals, the structure of the CBR system has been designed around the concept of a *case*. A case is made of three components: the problem, the solution, and the result obtained when the proposed solution is applied. The problem defines the situation of the environment at a given moment. The solution is the set of states that are undergone by the environment as a consequence of the actions that have been carried out inside it. And the result shows the situation of the environment once the problem has been solved. This can be expressed as follows [8]:

Case: <Problem, Solution, Result>
   Problem: initial_state
   Solution: sequence of <action, [intermediate_state]>
   Result: final_state

BDI agent (beliefs, desires, intentions)
   Belief: state
   Desire: set of <final_state>
   Intention: sequence of <action>

In a BDI agent, each state is considered as a belief; the objective to be reached may also be a belief. The intentions are plans of actions that the agent has to carry out in order to achieve its objectives, so an intention is an ordered set of actions; each change from state to state is made after carrying out an action (the agent remembers the action carried out in the past when it was in a specified state, and the subsequent result). A desire will be any of the final states reached in the past (if the agent has to deal with a situation, which is similar to a past one, it will try to achieve a similar result to the previously obtained result).

The relationship between CBR systems and BDI agents can be established implementing cases as beliefs, intentions and desires which led to the resolution of the problem. This relationship is shown in Fig. 3. When the *agent starts to solve a new problem*, with the intention of *achieving a goal*, it begins a new **CBR reasoning cycle**, which will help to **obtain the solution**. The **retrieval, reuse and revise stages of the CBR system** facilitate the construction of the *agent plan*. The *agent's knowledge-base* is the **case-base of the CBR system** that stores the **cases of** *past believes, desires and intentions*. The *agents* work in dynamic environments and their *knowledge-base* has to be adapted and updated continuously by the **retain stage of the CBR system**.

Based on this relationship, agents (conceptual level) can be implemented using CBR systems (implementation level). This means, a mapping of agents into CBR systems. The advantage of this approach is that a problem can be easily conceptualised in terms of agents and then implemented in the form of a CBR system. So once the beliefs, desires and intentions of an agent are identified, they can be mapped into a CBR system.

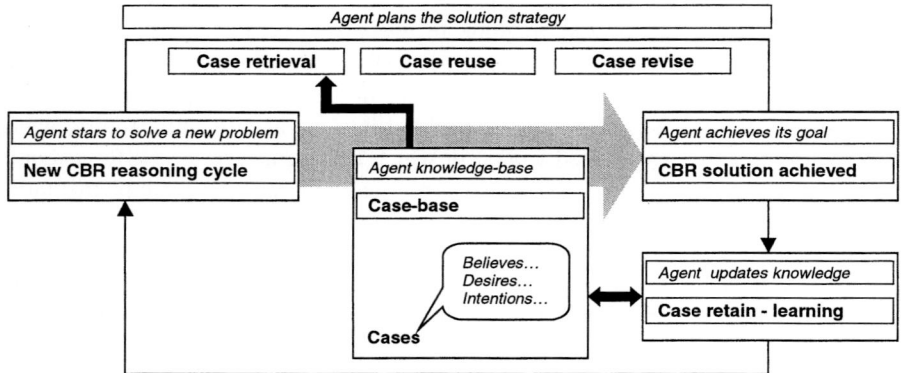

Fig. 3. CBR/Agent integration diagram

4 CBR-BDI Agent Development: The Planner Agent

In this paper we are concerned with the design and implementation of deliberative agents following the principles described in the previous section. Here we start by considering that deliberative agents have already being identified in the system, with their roles, responsibilities and services (the basic organization of agents in this system was already depicted in section 2). We focus, therefore, on the design of the *Planner Agent*, the only deliberative agent in this system, by using the principles described in the previous section.

To set up an agent using the CBR-BDI agent architecture we need to identify an initial set of beliefs, desires and intentions and include them in the case-base of the agent in the form of cases. Then, a number of metrics for the retrieval, reuse, revise and retain steps has to be defined. Besides, rules that describe the Expert's knowledge must be established, if available. Once the agent has been initialised it starts the reasoning process and the four steps of the CBR system are run sequentially and continuously until its goal is achieved (or there is enough evidence for a failure situation).

Fig. 4 shows the AUML (Agent Unified Modeling Language) class diagram of the *Planner Agent* (Agent UML is a modelling language that extends UML; more information at www.auml.org). In these types of diagrams, the roles and goals of the agents are represented as *Capabilities* that may change with the time. In particular, the roles of the *Planner Agent* are (i) to update the believes and intentions, which are stored in the form of cases, (ii) to identify those believes and intentions that can be used to generate a plan n, and (iii) to provide adequate plans to the *Performer Agent* given a number of conditions. These roles allow the agent to generate the closest to the

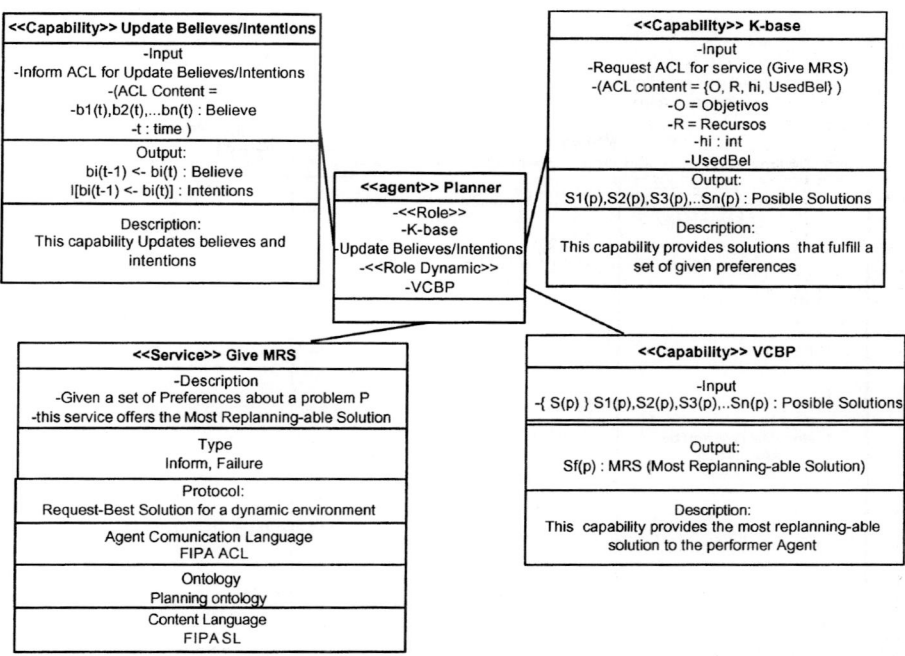

Fig. 4. Planner Agent class diagram in AUML

optimum plan, which in this case has also to be the most replan-able solution. In this context, when the *Performer Agent* asks for a tourist route, given a number of constraints such as the money the tourist is willing to spend, the number of monuments to visit, the type of restaurants to eat, the time availability for the holiday, etc. the Planner Agent generates a plan that fulfils such conditions. This plan is easy to modify at execution time if the user changes of mind. The Planner Agent is a CBR-BDI agent, where the role (i) is carried out during the Retain stage of the CBR life cycle, role (ii) is the Retrieval step, and role (iii) is the Reuse stage.

The *Performer agents*, are assistant agents. Each of them is associated to one user and contact the *Planner Agent* to request a plan. These agents may be in waiting mode, waiting for a request from the user, may ask to the *Planner Agent* for a plan, or request a modification in a plan (replanning) to the *Planner Agent*. The *Tracker Agent* is always looking for changes in the visiting conditions of the different sites, and keeps a record of them. The *Planner Agent* regularly contacts the *Tracker Agent* looking for changes in the environment. Fig. 5 shows the collaboration of these agents with a sequence diagram.

4.1 Implementation of the CBR System for the Planner Agent

The *Planner Agent* uses a CBR system for reasoning and generating its plans. This agent has three roles:

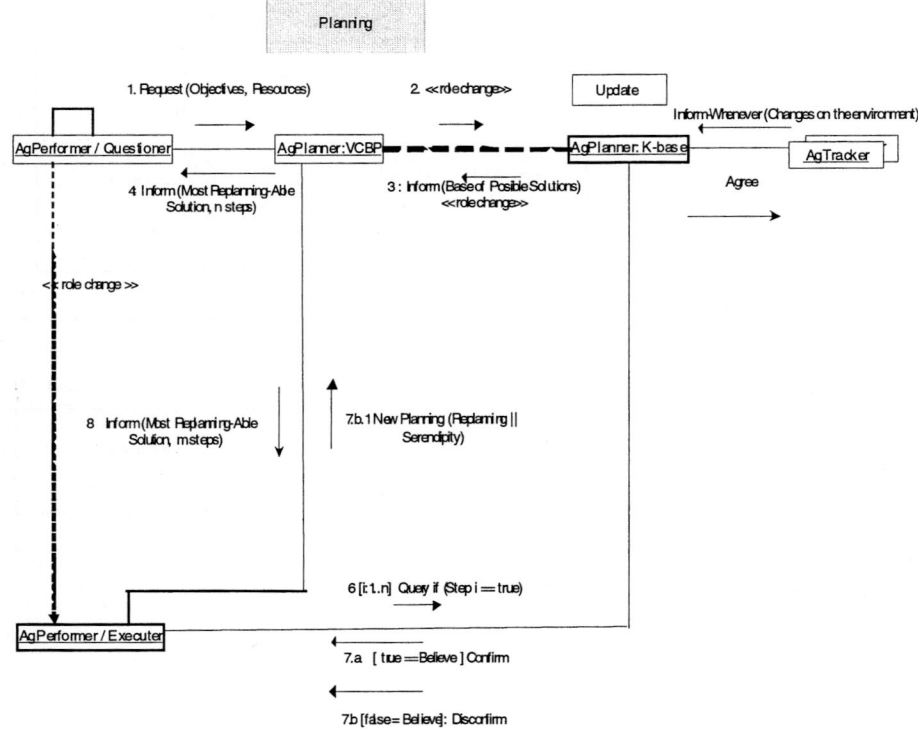

Fig. 5. Collaboration among agents in the tourist guide application

- To identify those believes and intentions that can be used to generate a plan.
- To provide adequate plans to the *Performer Agent* given a number of conditions.
- To update the believes and intentions, which are stored in the form of cases.

These roles are carried out sequentially and correspond with the retrieval, reuse, and retain stages of a CBR system. The reasoning cycle has been constructed using a variational calculus based strategy [12].

The retrieval stage must be carried out using a method that guarantees the retrieval of a reasonably small number of cases that are related to the current problem case. We have experimented with a number of different retrieval methods such as Sparse Kernel Principal Component Analysis [8] or a K-nearest neighbour algorithm based strategy [12]. The best results have been obtained with a variational calculus based strategy, as shown below.

Planning can be defined as the construction of a course of actions to achieve a specified set of goals in response to a given situation. The classical generative planning process consists mainly of a search through the space of possible operators to solve a given problem, but for most practical problems this search is intractable. Given that typical planning may require a great deal of effort without achieving very good results, several researchers have pursued a more synergistic approach through generative and case-based planning [4]. In this context, case indexation strategy facilitates and speeds up the planning process substantially.

A case in case-based planning consists of a problem (initial situation and set of goals) and its plan. Given a new problem, the objective of the retrieval and reuse phase is to select a case or a number of cases from the case-base whose problem description is most similar to the description of the new problem and to adapt it/them to the new situation. In case-based reasoning, two different approaches to reuse can be distinguished: transformational and derivational adaptation. Transformational adaptation methods usually consist of a set of domain dependent concepts which modifies the solution directly obtained in the retrieved case. For derivational adaptation, the retrieved solution is not modified directly, but is used to guide the planner to find the solution.

There are different ways to integrate generative and case-based planning: PRODIGY [7, 21], PARIS [2, 13], and Variational Calculus Based Planner (VCBP) [11], which is the method proposed for the resolution of the case-study. These planners may be used in the development of deliberative agent-based systems. In PRODIGY and PARIS the workload imposed on the generative planner depends on the amount of modification that is required to adapt the retrieved cases. Looking at the structure, we can say that PARIS is a *domain-independent* case-based planner while PRODIGY is *domain semi-dependent*. On the other hand, although VCBP is domain dependent, it introduces a new interesting strategy to efficiently deal with the adaptation stage.

Variational Calculus-based Planner (VCBP) guarantees the planning and re-planning of the intentions in execution time. This planning strategy is divided into two steps:

1. identify cases that are similar to the problem case (retrieval stage), and
2. adapt them to the problem case (reuse stage), which correspond to the two roles of the Planner Agent.

Variational calculus automates the reasoning cycle of the BDI agents, and guarantees the identification of an efficient plan, closed to the optimum. Although different types of planning mechanisms can be found in the literature, none of them allows the replanning in execution time, and agents inhabit changing environments in which replanning in execution time is required if goals are to be achieved successfully in real-time.

Some of the planning techniques developed for case-based reasoning systems to select the appropriate solution to a given problem do not have mechanisms to deal with the changes in the environment. For instance, Corchado and Laza [8] and Knobolock *et al.* [15] introduce a kind of plan schema that needs to be reprogrammed over time, when the planning domain changes. Bergmann and Wilke [3], and Camacho *et al.* [6] propose an architecture that tries to be more flexible, in which, if new information has to be introduced from the environment to the system, it is only necessary to change the planning domain instead of reprogramming the plan schema by hand. This architecture allows building plans that contain steps with no detailed information. This is useful because if no specific information is supplied, the solution can handle planning generic operators, plans that are not influenced by unexpected changes.

Now, to find out if the abstract proposed plan is adequate it is necessary to put it into practice in a real domain. This operation requires a great amount of computational time and resources which may be a disadvantage, in for example, web related problems. The flexibility of this approach increases the time spent in applying the abstract solution to the real problem, which is a handicap for real time systems. The proposed solution, a variational calculus based planner, deals adequately with environmental real-time problem changes without applying a reprogramming strategy and without the disadvantages shown in the works mentioned before, because the technique used can replan in execution time.

5 Results and Conclusions

Development times in the telecommunication industry have been drastically reduced. In the last decade a standard project used to have a development period of 8 to 15 months, and now this period has been reduced to 3 to 5 months. This requires an experimented development team, the use of a reliable technology, and knowledge of the problem domain (or at least the capacity of learning fast). The CBR-BDI agents that are proposed in this paper facilitate the construction of distributed wireless system for mobile devices and may be adapted for different problem domains, within the constrains imposed by the industry. The developed infrastructure includes tools for generating CBR-BDI autonomous agents that can reason, learn and communicate with the users and with other agents, a simple communication protocol based on the FIPA ACL standards, and a number of established processes that facilitate the analysis and design of a MAS using AUML.

The proposed system has been used to improve an agent based system developed for guiding tourists around the city of Salamanca (Spain). As mentioned before, the tourists may use a mobile device to contact their agents and to indicate their preferences (monuments to visit, visits duration, dinner time, amount of money to spend, etc.). There are different types of **cases**. The cases store information about the environment, for example the opening and closing times of monument. This type of information can be seen as an agent believe, for example, The Museum of Contemporary Art opens from 9:00 to 14:00 and from to 16:30 to 20:00. Cases may also be previous successful routes (plans), as shown in Fig. 6(a), that includes the monuments to visit, the time to spend visiting each monument, information about the cost of the visit, the time required for going to one place to another, the characteristics of the route (museum route, family route, university route, roman route, gothic route, etc.), etc. Once a tourist contacts the system he has to describe his profile, to select the type of visit in which he is interested in, to determine how much money he wants to spend and for how long, and the type of restaurants he, she or a family like more. This information is used to construct the **problem case**. Then the reasoning mechanism of the planning agent generates the plan. This reasoning mechanism is the previously mentioned CBR system using VCBP [11, 12]. Fig. 6(b) shows a graphical view of a generated plan.

Development of CBR-BDI Agents: A Tourist Guide Application   557

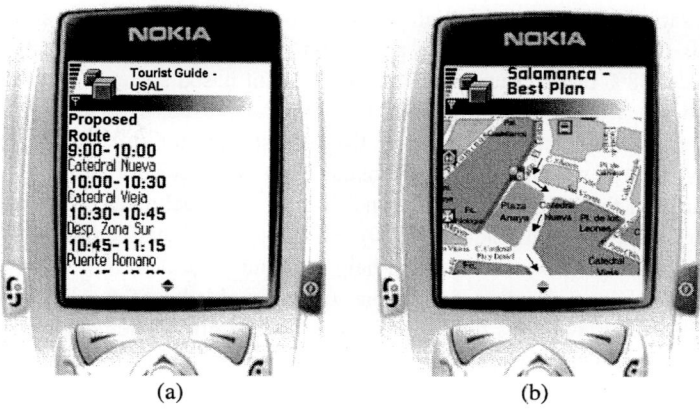

Fig. 6. System overview.

The initial system was tested from the 1st of May to the 15th of September 2003. The case base was initially filled with information collected from the 1st of February to the 25th of June 2003. Local tourist guides provided the agent with a number of standard routes. Three hotels of the City offered the option to their 6217 guests to use the help of the agent or a professional tourist guide, 14% of them decided to use the agent based system and 23% of them used the help of a tourist guide. The rest of the tourists visited the city by themselves. During this period the *Planner agent* stored in its memory 1630 instances of tourist circuits, which covered a wide range of all the most common options that offers the City of Salamanca. The system was tested during 135 days and the results obtained were very encouraging. In this experiment the agent intentions were related to a one-day route (a maximum of 12 hours). On the arrival to the hotel the tourists were asked to evaluate their visit and the route. Table 1 shows the responses given by the tourists after their visit. The tourists that used the help of the agent-based tourist guide provided the answer directly to the agent.

Table 1. Tourists evaluation.

	%	Evaluation - degree of satisfaction				
Tourists that…		8-10	6-8	4-6	0-4	No answer
Used the help of the agent	14%	(55,9%)	(4,7%)	(2,4%)	(0,7%)	(36,3%)
Used the help of a tourist guide	23%	(62,7%)	(19,6%)	(8,9%)	(1%)	(7,8%)
Did not use any of the previous	63%	(16,7%)	(8,3%)	(1,2%)	(0,2%)	(78,8%)

Table 1 shows the degree of satisfaction of the tourists. As it can be seen, the degree of satisfaction of the tourist that used the help of a professional tourist guide is higher that in the other two cases. Nevertheless, the percentage of the tourists whose degree of satisfaction was very high (between 8 and 10) is very similar in the case of the tourists that use the help of the agent and in the case of the tourists that use the tourist guide. 38% of the tourists that used the agent based system let us know that the system did not work successfully due to technical reasons (possibly the server was down, there was a lack of coverage, the tourist did not use the wireless system adequately, etc.) If we take this into consideration, we can say that most of the tourist (92%) that used the help of the agent and did not have technical problems had a high or very high degree of satisfaction (6-10). This degree of satisfaction is higher that the one of the tourist (82,3%) that used the help of a tourist guides.

The CBR-BDI architecture solves one of the problems of the BDI (deliberative) agent architectures, which is the lack of learning capability. The reasoning cycle of the CBR systems helps the agents to solve problems, facilitate its adaptation to changes in the environment and to identify new possible solutions. New cases are continuously introduced and older ones are eliminated. The CBR component of the architecture provides a straight and efficient way for the manipulation of the agents knowledge and past experiences. The proposal presented in this paper reduces the gap that exists between the formalization and the implementation of BDI agents.

Acknowledgements

This work has been supported by the MCyT projects TEL99-0335-C04-03, SEC2000-0249 and TIC2003-07369-C02-02.

References

1. Aamodt A. and Plaza E. (1994). Case-Based Reasoning: foundational Issues, Methodological Variations, and System Approaches, AICOM. Vol. 7. No 1, March.
2. Bergmann, R. and W. Wilke (1995). Learning abstract planning cases. In N. Lavrac and S. Wrobel (Eds.), Machine Learning: ECML-95, 8th European Conference on Machine Learning, Heraclion, Greece, April 1995. Number 912 in Lecture Notes in Artificial Intelligence, pp. 55-76. Berlin, Springer
3. Bergmann, R. and W. Wilke (1996). On the role of abstraction in case-based reasoning. Lecture Notes in Artificial Intelligence, 1186, pp. 28-43. Springer Verlag.
4. Bergmann, R., Muñoz-Ávila, H., Veloso, M. and Melis, E. (1998). CBR Applied to Planning. In Lenz, M. Bartsch-Sporl, B., Burkhard, H. and Wess, S. (Eds.) Case-Based Reasoning Technology: From Foundations to Applications. Lecture Notes in Computer Science 1400, pp. 169-200. Springer 1998, ISBN 3-540-64572-1.
5. Busetta, P., Ronnquist, R., Hodgson, A., Lucas A. (1999). JACK Intelligent Agents Components for Intelligent Agents in Java. Technical report, Agent Oriented Software Pty. Ltd, Melbourne, Australia, 1998.
6. Camacho D., Borrajo D. And Molina J. M. (2001) Intelligence Travell Planning: a multiagent planing system to solve web problems in the e-turism domain. International Journal on Autonomous agens and Multiagent systems. 4(4) pp 385-390. December.

7. Carbonell J.G., Knoblock C. A., Minton S. (1991). Prodigy: An integrated architecture for planning and learning. In K. VanLenh (Ed.), Architectures for Intelligence, pp.241-278. Lawrence Erlbaum Associates, Publishers.
8. Corchado J. M. And Laza R. (2003). Constructing Deliberative Agents with Case-based Reasoning Technology, International Journal of Intelligent Systems. Vol 18, No. 12, December.
9. Corchado J. M. and Lees B. (2001). A Hybrid Case-based Model for Forecasting. Applied Artificial Intelligence. Vol 15, no. 2, pp.105-127.
10. D'Iverno, M., Kinny, D., Luck, M., and Wooldridge, M. (1997). A Formal Specification of dMARS. In: Intelligent Agents IV, Agent Theories, Architectures, and Languages, 4th International Workshop, ATAL '97, Providence, Rhode Island, USA, July 24-26, 1997, Proceedings. Lecture Notes in Computer Science 1365, Springer Verlag, pp. 155-176.
11. Glez-Bedia M. and Corchado J. M. (2002) A planning strategy based on variational calculus for deliberative agents. Computing and Information Systems Journal. Vol 10, No 1, 2002. ISBN: 1352-9404, pp: 2-14.
12. Glez-Bedia M., Corchado J. M., Corchado E. S. and Fyfe C. (2002) Analytical Model for Constructing Deliberative Agents, Engineering Intelligent Systems, Vol 3: pp. 173-185.
13. Holte, R. C., T. Mkadmi, R. M. Zimmer, and A. J. MacDonald (1995). Speeding up problem solving by abstraction: A graph-oriented approach. Technical report, University of Ottawa, Ontario, Canada.
14. Huber, M. (1999). A BDI-Theoretic Mobile Agent Architecture. AGENTS '99. Proceedings of the Third Annual Conference on Autonomous Agents, May 1-5, 1999, Seattle, WA, USA. ACM, pp. 236-243.
15. Knobolock C. A., Minton S., Ambite J. L., Muslea M., Oh J. and Frank M. (2001). Mixed-initiative, multisource information assistants. 10th International world wide web conference (WWW10). ACM Press. May 1-5,pp.145-163.
16. Martín F. J., Plaza E., Arcos J.L. (1999). Knowledge and experience reuse through communications among competent (peer) agents. International Journal of Software Engineering and Knowledge Engineering, Vol. 9, No. 3, 319-341.
17. Myers, K. (1996). A Procedural Knowledge Approach to Task-Level Control. Proceedings of the Third International Conference on Artificial Intelligence Planning Systems,, pp. 158-165.
18. Olivia C., Chang C. F., Enguix C.F. and Ghose A.K. (1999). Case-Based BDI Agents: An Effective Approach for Intelligent Search on the World Wide Web, AAAI Spring Symposium on Intelligent Agents, 22-24 March 1999, Stanford University, USA.
19. Rao, A. S. (1996). AgentSpeak(L): BDI Agents speak out in a logical computable language. Agents Breaking Away, 7th European Workshop on Modelling Autonomous Agents in a Multi-Agent World, Eindhoven, The Netherlands, January 22-25, 1996, Proceedings. Lecture Notes in Computer Science 1038, Springer Verlag, pp. 42-55.
20. Rao, A. S. and Georgeff, M. P. (1995). BDI Agents: From Theory to Practice. First International Conference on Multi-Agent Systems (ICMAS-95). San Franciso, USA.
21. Veloso, M. M. (1994). Planning and Learning by Analogical Reasoning. Number 886 in Lectures Notes in Computer Science. Berlin, Springer.
22. Wendler J. and Lenz M. (1998). CBR for Dynamic Situation Assessment in an Agent-Oriented
Setting. Proc. AAAI-98 Workshop on CBR Integrations. Madison (USA) 1998.
23. Wooldridge, M. and Jennings, N. R. (1995) Agent Theories, Architectures, and Languages: a Survey. In: Wooldridge and Jennings, editors, Intelligent Agents, Springer-Verlag, pp. 1-22.

Improving Recommendation Ranking by Learning Personal Feature Weights*

Lorcan Coyle and Pádraig Cunningham

Department of Computer Science
Trinity College Dublin
{Lorcan.Coyle,Padraig.Cunningham}@cs.tcd.ie

Abstract. The ranking of offers is an issue in e-commerce that has received a lot of attention in Case-Based Reasoning research. In the absence of a sales assistant, it is important to provide a facility that will bring suitable products and services to the attention of the customer. In this paper we present such a facility that is part of a Personal Travel Assistant (PTA) for booking flights online. The PTA returns a large number of offers (24 on average) and it is important to rank them to bring the most suitable to the fore. This ranking is done based on similarity to previously accepted offers. It is a characteristic of this domain that the case-base of accepted offers will be small, so the learning of appropriate feature weights is a particular challenge. We describe a process for learning personalised feature weights and present an evaluation that shows its effectiveness.

1 Introduction

A particular challenge for e-commerce is to provide mechanisms that substitute for the ways in which the human sales assistant facilitates the sales process. An important component of this is the ability to identify the customer's preferences and highlight products and services that will satisfy the customer's requirements and preferences. This is particularly true in the travel domain. A dialog with a good old-fashioned business travel agent would contain phrases like; *"I presume you will want to go out on the first flight.", "You will want to return on the Friday evening.", "You will not want a stopover in Heathrow."* Ideally, an online Personal Travel Assistant will learn these preferences as well.

In this paper we describe such a system that uses CBR to rank offers returned in response to a travel request [6]. There are two types of cases in this system; session-cases and offer-cases. Session-cases represent previous user-interactions or sessions with the system and offer-cases represent individual travel offers. Session-cases can be viewed as request-offer pairs; the problem component of the case is made up of a previous travel request with some additional contextual information; the solution com-

---

* The support of the Informatics Research Initiative of Enterprise Ireland and the support of Science Foundation Ireland under grant No. 02/IN.1/I1111 are gratefully acknowledged.

ponent is a reference to the selected offer (which is an offer-case) in response to that request. The idea behind this is that a user's preferences are encoded implicitly in the accepted offers to particular requests and that similar requests will lead to similar selections of offers. So the ranking is a two-stage process. The first stage is to find a previous session that contains a similar request to the current travel request. This session is assumed to be relevant to the user's current context. In the second stage, the current offers are ranked based on their similarity to the offer component of the retrieved session-case. This session-based recommendation approach is analogous to that used in Ricci et al.'s *DieToRecs* system [10]. Both systems rank presented items based on their similarity to items selected in response to similar queries in the past (twofold similarity) [11]. However, DieToRecs differs from our system in that it uses a mixed-initiative approach to elicit user preferences whereas we determine these preferences implicitly. We incorporate these preferences into the similarity measures used in the recommendation process. Some users will be very price conscious, others will be adverse to stopovers or long stopover times, and others will have preferences on departure times. Rather than ask users to weight the importance of these criteria we choose to learn this from past behaviour. There are two reasons for this, first, it places less cognitive load on the user. Second, it avoids the problem of asking users to assign numeric weights to criteria – a skill at which people are notoriously poor.

We use techniques along the lines of introspective learning as described in the past by Bonzano et al. [2], Branting [4] and Stahl [13, 14]. Introspective learning refers to an approach to learning problem solving knowledge by monitoring the run-time progress of a particular problem solver. The approach used here is failure-driven in the sense that an attempt is made to improve feature weights only in the case of a recommendation failure. This is done by decreasing the weights of unmatching features and increasing the weights of matching features. This will tend to push down the recommendation scores of offers that are not being taken up and pull up the scores of ones that are selected.

Section 2 discusses a number of feature weighting algorithms where user feedback drives learning. Section 3 describes our Personal Travel Assistant application and how CBR is used to recommend flights to users. In Section 4 we give a description of our feature weight learning algorithm. Section 5 presents results that show that weight learning improves recommendation accuracy. We discuss some future work in Section 6 and draw our conclusions in Section 7.

2 Feature Weighting Based on User Feedback

There are a number of systems that use user feedback to assist in problem solving episodes. Mixed initiative CBR and conversational CBR systems use feedback to direct a search through a problem space, e.g. [5, 9, 12, 11]. Some learners attempt to incorporate a level of *utility* [1] into the similarity measures by looking at case order feedback [2, 4, 13, 14]. Utility is indicative of adaptability or usefulness to the current problem. We hope that by incorporating utility into the similarity measure in this way we will improve and personalise recommendations in our system.

Bonzano's et al ISAC system uses a form of *introspective learning* to improve its retrieval mechanism. Feature weights are updated in order to optimise problem solving performance. Stahl [13, 14] describes a *similarity teacher* that has knowledge of the utility function of what the system is trying to learn. This teacher goes through every retrieved set of cases and uses its utility function to calculate a similarity error. By minimising this error on a feature by feature basis, he attempts to learn the best feature weights for the problem-at-hand. Branting describes a method of learning feature weights by looking at customer selections from sets of presented items. This method is called *LCW* (learning customer weights), and involves boosting the ranking order of selected items by altering the feature weights. These techniques are broadly similar; in each of these approaches there is an attempt to learn a utility function by altering feature weights to improve retrieval accuracy. The learning techniques themselves are also similar, using a combination of failure and success-driven approaches.

Our system uses implicit user feedback – the final selection of an item for purchase by the user – to drive the learning process. It is a failure driven approach; if the system is making good recommendations there is no attempt to improve the retrieval mechanism. Because we only use the selection of a single item by the user as our retrieval mechanism we cannot look at the overall case order feedback as Stahl does, instead we use a technique more closely aligned with Branting's work. We also examine ideas from Bonzano's work with relation to the issue of contextual features. The fundamental differences between our work and other work in the area are:

- There is no a priori knowledge about the items being recommended (apart from their expected structure) as the items are being retrieved in real time. All that is known is that all items will completely satisfy the user's initial query.
- Each user of the system acts as her own similarity teacher and the learnt feature weights are stored in her personal profile.
- Learning is attempted on both stages of the recommendation process; session retrieval and final offer recommendation.

These techniques all concern introspective learning of feature weights, but there are alternative techniques available which we intend to evaluate with further work, e.g. feature selection rather than feature weighting. There has also been work done on the problem of learning local similarity measures – the similarity measure for each individual feature – e.g. [15], but in this work we have confined ourselves to the learning of the feature weights.

3 Recommending Travel Offers

The main purpose of the PTA is to take a user's request for flights, contract with real online flights brokers for travel solutions and recommend the best of these to the user. Since the flights come in from real, external sources, their details cannot be known in advance. For the purposes of a demonstration, consider the plight of a user making a request for a holiday trip from Dublin to Rome. On making the request the user is faced with choosing flights from a set of forty-nine offers (twenty-four outgoing and twenty-five return flights). The following list of feature value possibilities illustrates the diversity of the outgoing offers set:

- Two carriers
- Two destination airports (Ciampino and DaVinci)
- Price ranging from €52 to €112
- Departing as early as 06:30 and arriving as late as 23:45
- Single flight trips and two hop trips. Among the multiple-hop set (of which there are twenty-three in this set) there are the following additional choices:
    o   Four possible stopover airports
    o   Stopover times ranging from two hours up to 12:30 hours

The size of this set is not atypical of the scenarios encountered by users of the PTA. In fact our users have average return-set sizes of more than 24 offers. Some requests yield much larger sets, e.g. London to Milan - 79 offers; Dublin to London - 73 offers. With this degree of freedom the idea that a single feature would override all others and offer the user the ability to manually search the set by sorting by a single feature is inadequate. This is why a recommender system is needed to reduce the offer set to a more manageable size. The remainder of this section describes the recommendation process in the PTA.

The PTA makes recommendations by looking at interactions the user has had with the system in the past. By using the selections the user made in similar sessions in the past we hope to make good recommendations in future sessions. To do this we need to store information about the user's habits. After every successful user interaction with the PTA (i.e. after the user has selected a flight and is forwarded on to the booking page), we record data about the request (e.g. origin, destination, departure date) in the form of a session-case. We also store a reference to the offer that was selected by the user. In this way, the request features represent the problem, and the selected offer the solution of the session-case. We represent offers as cases in the second stage of the recommendation process (offer-ranking). This allows us to rank the current set of offers based on their similarity to the offer-case referenced in the retrieved session-case.

We will illustrate the recommendation process by describing the steps taken in an example where a user makes a request for a flight from Dublin to Rome. The user logs into the PTA and submits a form containing details of the origin, destination, dates of travel and number of tickets required. The PTA decomposes this request into its constituent parts and forwards these on to a number of online travel brokers. It then composes the responses into a number of travel offers. These offers make up the current offer case-base.

At the same time, the PTA searches the user's session case-base for the session with the most similar request to the current one. It then uses the selected offer from that session to rank the offers in the current offer case-base. In this example, the retrieved session contained a request for a trip to Milan made by the user two months earlier. In that previous session, the user selected a cheap two-hop trip via London Stansted with a short stopover time. Therefore, the PTA will tend to recommend similar offers from the current offer case-base, e.g. cheap flights with a short stopover, preferably in Stansted.

Both stages use CBR and as such are dependant on the definition of good similarity measures. Traditionally, CBR systems have depended on domain experts to design similarity measures. However we have implemented a process whereby our users "teach" the system their personal preferences which are incorporated into both the session case-base and the similarity measures.

Unless the user constantly selects offers on the basis of a single feature (which we observe not to be true) it is important to gauge the relative importance of feature similarities in order to offer better recommendations. We describe the relative importance of features using feature weights in the similarity measure and describe our technique to learn them in the following section.

In summary, the recommendation process follows two stages:
i. Context-Matching: Finding the session with the most similar request from the user's session case-base and retrieving the selected offer from that session
ii. Offer-Ranking: Using that offer to rank the offers in the current session. The highest ranked offers are then presented to the user

4 Personalising Recommendations – Learning Feature Weights

As mentioned in Section 3, the recommendation process involves two similarity measures. We begin by describing our algorithm for learning feature weights for the second stage of recommendation, i.e. offer-ranking. The similarity between a previously selected offer, S and a current offer, C is given by the sum of the similarities of their constituent features (σ_f) multiplied by their respective weights:

$$Sim(S,C) = \sum_{f \in F} w_f \times \sigma_f(sf, cf) \qquad (1)$$

Where F is the set of features that can occur in a case. We infer the relative importance of features by comparing our predicted recommendations with the actual selections of the users. When we run the recommendation process on a set of offers, we end up with an ordering across the set. By comparing the eventual selection of a preferred offer by the user with this ordering we can generate a recommendation error, E_{rec} as follows:

$$E_{rec} = \frac{index - 1}{N - 1} \qquad \forall N : N > 1 \qquad (2)$$

Where N is the size of the offer set and *index* is defined as the ranking of the offer the user selected. However, if the offer is ranked equally with other offers, *index* is the lowest ranking of the equals (e.g. if the selected offer is ranked equal third with four other offers *index* is six – two higher ranked plus four equal ranked offers). In this way, a recommendation error of 0 would indicate that the recommender system recommended the selected offer above all other offers; this is to encourage the PTA to minimize the number of offers it must present to the user. Sessions with return flights have two retrieval accuracies, one for the outgoing and one for the return offers. The overall retrieval error for a user, E_{user} is the mean of their recommendation errors.

Table 1. Table 1 shows the selected offer from the previous session (S) and two of the offers from the current offer set (C_1 and C_2). C_1 was recommended above C_2 but the user selected C_2. Our algorithm should alter the feature weights so that C_2 would be ranked above C_1 if the recommendation process were executed again.

	S	C_1	C_2
Trip Details	Dublin->Milan	Dublin->Rome	Dublin->Rome
Price	€50	€60	€85
Stopover location	London Stansted	London Stansted	London Stansted
Stopover Time	125 minutes	240 minutes	150 minutes
Selected	N/A	not selected	selected

To improve our recommendation accuracy we must alter the feature weights in such a way as to ensure that the selected case is ranked higher than the other offers. To this end we calculate the local similarity difference, $\Delta\sigma_f$ for cases ranked lower than index. The local similarity difference for the feature of a case (c_i) is the difference between its local similarity score and that of the selected case. We then find out which cases ($w_{learn}(C_1) = true$) could be ranked lower if we altered the feature weights:

$$w_{learn}(C_i) = false \text{ if } \Delta\sigma_f <= 0 \;\forall f \in C_i \quad (3)$$

$$\text{where } \Delta\sigma_f = \sigma_f(s, C_{index}) - \sigma_f(s, c_i) \quad (4)$$

The local similarities and similarity differences for the example in the last section are shown below in Fig 1. We are now faced with the decision of which case to use to drive learning. We have achieved good results when using the highest ranked learnable case (i.e. with $w_{learn}(C_1) = true$) to drive learning. Returning to our example scenario, we can use offer C_1 to improve the ranking of C_2 with respect to C_1. We use the following equations to change the weights on price and stopover time:

$$w_f = w_f \times increment \quad \text{if } \Delta\sigma_f > 0 \quad (5)$$
$$w_f = w_f / increment \quad \text{if } \Delta\sigma_f < 0$$

The *increment* parameter was set to 1.1 in the results presented here. Weights are then normalised and the whole process is repeated until the algorithm passes an iteration limit or one of the following stopping criteria is met:

$$index == 1 \quad (6a)$$
$$w_{learn}(C_i) == false \;\forall i < index \quad (6b)$$

Criterion 6a indicates that we have reached the overall optimal solution and that no further learning is necessary; criterion 6b indicates that no further improvement is possible. As we iterate through the algorithm we check for an improvement (i.e. a reduction) in *index*. If this occurs we save the feature weights as the current best. When one of the stopping criteria is met, we save the current best weights for that session (session-weights).

There are two ways we can use these session-weights. The PTA could store a single set of weights for each user (user-weights) and could incorporate the session-weights

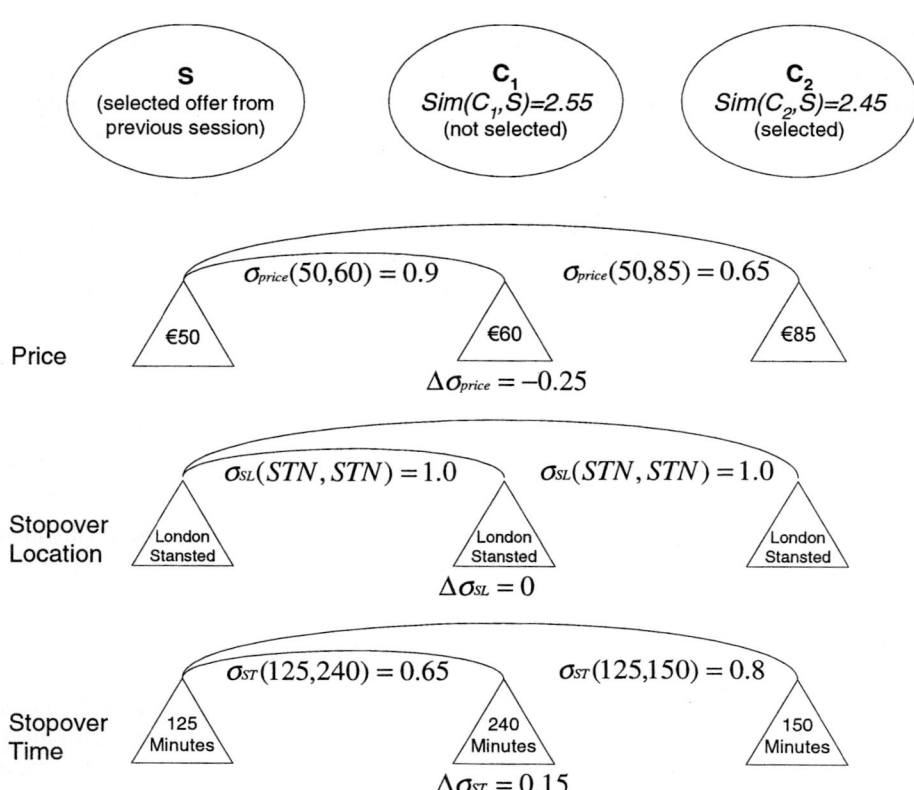

Fig. 1. This figure shows the local similarity scores for the Dublin to Rome example. Details are shown for the features price, stopover location and stopover time. In this example the user selected the second highest recommended feature so *index* is 2. The similarity differences for case C_1 are shown beneath its feature values, i.e. $\Delta\sigma_{price}$=-0.25.

into the user weights after every completed session. Alternatively, it could store a reference to these session-weights with the session-case in such a way that the ranking preferences are viewed as part of the context of the session. We have performed experiments that confirm that it is better to store session-weights with each session-case than to store user-weights for each user (these results are presented in Section 5). This reflects the fact that people have different ranking and selection criteria under different contexts.

Learning the Request Similarity Measure
We use a different similarity measure for finding the most similar previous request. We intend to apply the same learning techniques for this similarity measure. However there is a fundamental difference in how this learning is driven. As we use a failure driven approach, we can only trigger learning on the request similarity measure when we are unable to learn an optimal set of feature weights in the offer recommendation stage, i.e. when we are unable to find a set of feature weights such that *index* = 1.

When this occurs, we believe that the problem is not with the learning algorithm but with the most similar request; i.e. that the context of the most similar request was different from the context of the current request. We search through the user's sessions to see if there was another session that would have yielded a better recommendation and attempt to alter the request feature weights to improve the recommendation score of the selected offer. This mechanism is more computationally expensive than simply learning feature weights at the offer granularity, and care must be taken to ensure that a change in the measure does not affect the accuracy of earlier sessions. We are currently in the process of implementing this algorithm and so have no results to present at this point.

5 Results

The PTA has been up and running since December 2003, but due to the nature of the domain, there is a dearth of sessions. This is because the average user will only make a few requests every year. To overcome this, we created a number of travel scenarios and asked people to complete them using the system. One such scenario was to make plans for a holiday to one of a list of destinations for any duration between five days and fourteen days. These scenarios were chosen to guarantee a large number of possible solutions with diversity in the offer sets. Each user was given six scenarios to complete.

The emphasis on this evaluation was to make the data as realistic as possible. With this in mind, users were given the freedom to choose their own destination and were allowed to reject a whole set of offers and make a totally new request if they were not happy with any of the offer set. The key point to note is that selected offers were considered by the user to be the genuinely preferred offer from the presented set. Many users had also completed sessions on their own initiative, and purchased real offers. These "real" sessions are included in our evaluations.

We use an offline-technique to evaluate our approach to feature weight learning. This involves simulating interactions with the system using the PTA's history of user-interactions. In the first evaluation, we go through every session in the history and calculate a set of session-weights using the techniques outlined in Section 4. We store these weights with the session-case.

The evaluation proceeds as follows: we use a leave-one-out approach whereby we remove one session from the user's session case-base and treat it as a new (unseen) session. This session contains a travel-request and a set of offers that were viewed by the user as well as her eventual selection of a preferred offer. We retrieve the most similar session-case from the user's session case-base. With the referenced offer-case and the optimal set of session weights that we learnt for that session we can calculate a ranking order on the current set of offers. By comparing this ordering with the user's actual selection we calculate a recommendation error for that session. We do this for every case in the user's session case-base and calculate an average recommendation error for each user. We plot the recommendation accuracies against a baseline accuracy for each user of the system in Fig 2. The baseline is calculated by using the same techniques as above except that we do not use session weights but weight features equally in the ranking process. Fig 2 shows that the recommendation process using learnt session-weights is significantly more accurate than using equal weights for every feature.

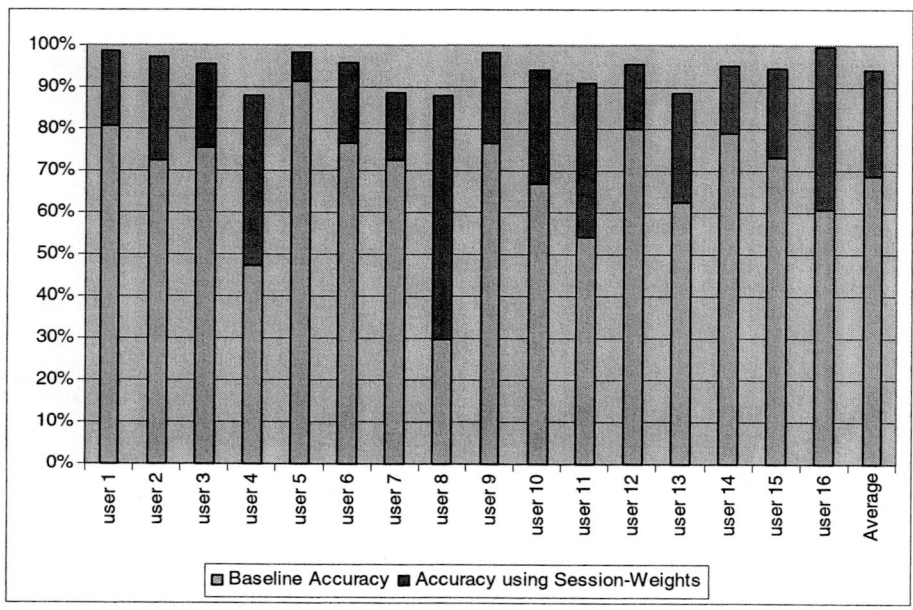

Fig. 2. A comparison of the baseline recommendation accuracy against the session-weight recommendation accuracy for each of the sixteen users. The average accuracies of all users are shown in the far right column. The improvement in accuracy is statistically significant at the 99.99% confidence level.

Our second evaluation assesses the value of user-weights in the recommendation process. User-weights are an amalgamation of session-weights and provide a better level of generalization. The user-weights are the average of each user's session-weights as calculated in the previous evaluation. A comparison of the recommendation accuracies in the previous evaluation (i.e. baseline and session-weight recommendation accuracies) against user-weights is shown in Fig 3. This shows that session-weights offer a significant improvement in recommendation accuracy over user-weights. We see the fact that session-weights are more valuable than user-weights as proof of over-generalization and a confirmation of our premise that context is an important element in this domain.

Over-Fitting
It is important at this point to mention the problem of over-fitting. Previous research has shown that feature weighting algorithms tend to over-fit the data [8]. We believe that over-fitting is unavoidable in this domain due to the lack of data. However, our leave-one-out evaluation shows that the learned weights are still better that the starting

position of equal weights. As more data is collected, we intend to perform an evaluation of the level of over-fitting that is occurring in our algorithm and to attempt to minimise it.

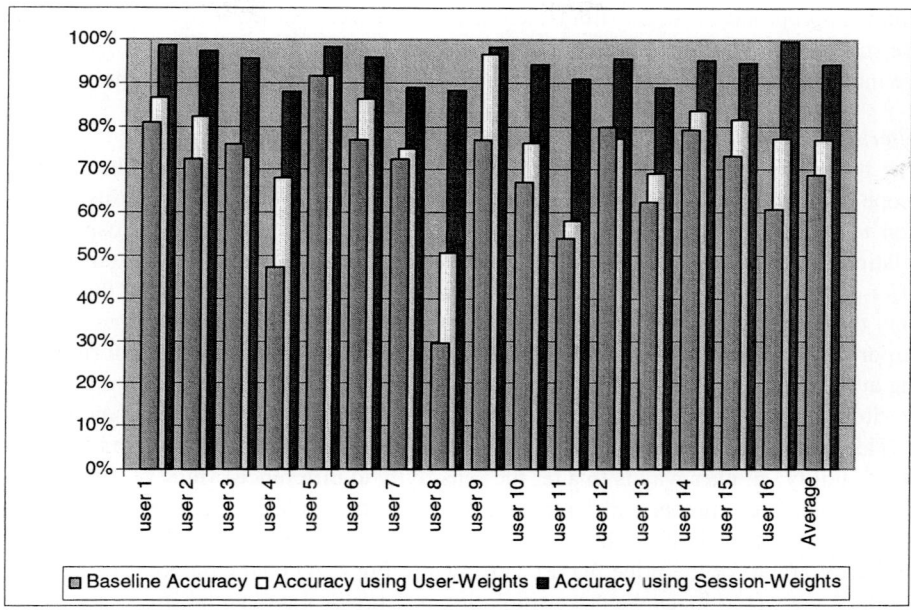

Fig. 3. A comparison of the baseline recommendation accuracy, the session-weight recommendation accuracy and the user-weight recommendation accuracy for each of the sixteen users. The average accuracies of all users are shown in the far right column. The improvement of learning session-weights over user-weights is statistically significant at the 99.99% confidence level.

6 Future Work

We intend to develop our approach to making good recommendations to users of our PTA system. We are currently implementing the mechanism for learning the request feature weights and hope to use this to further improve our recommendations. We intend to implement further techniques including Collaborative CBR and learning the local similarity measure (in the same manner as work done by Stahl [15]).

Collaborative CBR
Because of the lack of session information, we intend to investigate collaborative techniques to improve our recommendations. When a user makes a request, and the retrieved session's similarity score is below a threshold, we look to the user's neighbours for a better match. If a similar request is found from a neighbour's session case-base we use their experience to recommend offers from the user's current session. This is especially useful for new users.

The main issue with this approach is the determination of a user's neighbours. We intend to do this by comparing the feature weights of each of the users and group users together by virtue of the similarity between their weights. We will strengthen these groupings if collaboration leads to good recommendations and vice versa. This solution is appropriate for users with a rich history and well learned weights; however we are still faced with the problem of determining neighbours for new users. To solve this we intend to allow new users access to the collective case-base of the system.

Altering the Similarity Measure
The focus of this paper has been on the learning of feature weights, but there is also scope to learn local similarity measures. In fact this is also happening in this evaluation to a small extent. The PTA uses a taxonomy difference function to capture the relationships between geographical locations (the origin and destination features in the offer-cases use this representation). However, due to the configuration of this taxonomy there will never be diversity in similarity among the set of current offers, since all airports in a city are at the same level in the taxonomy. To allow us to perform learning at this level, we reorder the taxonomy by boosting the selected feature value above its siblings, thus incorporating a measure of utility into the local similarity function.

This is only one example of how local similarity functions can be altered to incorporate utility; another way is to alter the sensitivity to difference. Many of the features in this domain use numeric difference as the basis for similarity calculations, by altering the user's sensitivity to difference we can implement further personalisation. The similarity graph for the price feature is shown in Fig 4; by changing point {200, 0} to {100, 0} we would focus the price similarity measure on cases with differences of less than €100. A more in depth description of our representation of similarity measures is given in [7].

7 Conclusions

This paper described our approach to learning personalized feature weights in an online travel recommendation system. The key motivation in developing a good recommender system is to combine good recommendations with a low cognitive load on the user. We have achieved good recommendation results by implementing personalised profiles, with learning algorithms specific to each user. We minimise cognitive load by using implicit feedback to drive this learning. Our recommendation process is based on Case-Based Reasoning, and we learn a user's profile in two ways; by adding cases to their case-base with every interaction, and by learning optimal sets of feature weights for each interaction.

Our motivation for learning in this way is that users enter each interaction with a different context. In the offer recommendation process, the defining context is the request itself, it is clear that a user's preferences with respect to a long haul flight will be quite different than for a short trip, e.g. price may become less important, and comfort may be the defining feature. It is these preferences that we are trying to learn. We have performed evaluations of our techniques with real users of the system that show a highly significant improvement in recommendation accuracy with our learning algorithms.

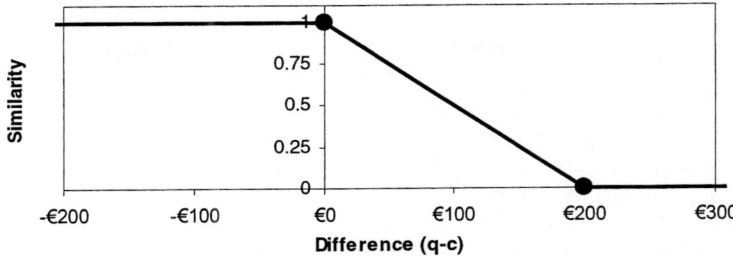

Fig. 4. Fig 4 shows the relationship between a difference in price between S and C. A difference of greater than €200 results in a similarity of zero.

One interpretation of our techniques is that they are geared towards reducing the return set size in response to a request. If we present a subset of the total number of offers we cannot offer a guarantee that our system will present the most suitable offer in the first retrieval. For this reason we see the potential for our techniques to operate in parallel with other recommendation strategies such as comparison-based recommendation [9] and diversity boosting [3] in a mature recommendation system.

References

1. Bergmann, R., Richter, M. M., Schmitt, S., Stahl, A., Vollrath, I. (2001). Utility-Oriented Matching: A New Research Direction for Case-Based Reasoning. Proceedings of the 9th German Workshop on Case-Based Reasoning, GWCBR'01, Baden-Baden, Germany. In: H.-P. Schnurr, S. Staab, R. Studer, G. Stumme, Y. Sure (Hrsg.): Professionelles Wissensmanagement. Shaker Verlag. pp. 264-274.
2. Bonzano, A., Cunningham, P., Smyth, B. (1997) Using introspective learning to improve retrieval in CBR: A case study in air traffic control. Proceedings of the 2nd International Conference on Case Based Reasoning (ICCBR-97), David B. Leake, Enric Plaza (Eds.), LNCS 1266 Springer pp 291-302 1997.
3. Bradley K. & Smyth B. (2001). Improving Recommendation Diversity. Proceedings of the Twelfth Irish Conference on Artificial Intelligence and Cognitive Science, D. O'Connor (ed.) pp85-94, 2001.
4. Branting, L. K. (2003). Learning Feature Weights from Customer Return-Set Selections. The Journal of Knowledge and Information Systems (KAIS) 6(2) March (2004)
5. Burke, R., Hammond, K., & Young, B. (1997). The FindMe Approach to Assisted Browsing. IEEE Expert, 12(4), pages 32-40, 1997.
6. Coyle, L., Cunningham, P. & Hayes, C. A Case-Based Personal Travel Assistant for Elaborating User Requirements and Assessing Offers. Proceedings of the 6th European Conference, ECCBR 2002, Susan Craw, Alun Preece (eds.). LNAI Vol. 2416 pp. 505-518, Springer-Verlag 2002.
7. Coyle, L., Doyle, D., & Cunningham, P. (2004) Representing Similarity for CBR in XML. To appear in the proceedings of the 7th European Conference on Case Based Reasoning, ECCBR 2004.

8. Kohavi, R., Langley, P., Yun, Y., The Utility of Feature Weighting in Nearest-Neighbor Algorithms. , 9th European Conference on Machine Learning ECML-97, Prague, Czech Republic. Poster session.
9. McGinty, L., & Smyth, B. (2002). Comparison-Based Recommendation. Proceedings of the 6th European Conference, ECCBR 2002, Susan Craw, Alun Preece (eds.). LNAI Vol. 2416, pp 575-589, Springer-Verlag, 2002.
10. Ricci, F., Mirzadeh, N. & Venturini, A. (2002). ITR: a case-based travel advisory system. Proceedings of the 6th European Conference, ECCBR 2002, Susan Craw, Alun Preece (Eds.). LNAI Vol. 2416, pp 613-627, Springer-Verlag, 2002.
11. Ricci, F., Venturini, A., Cavada, D., Mirzadeh, N., Blaas, D. & Nones, M. (2003). Produce Recommendation with Iteractive Query Management and Twofold Similarity. Proceedings of the 5th International Conference on Case-Based Reasoning, ICCBR 2003, Kevin D. Ashley, Derek G. Bridge (Eds.). LNCS Vol. 2689, pp479-493 Springer 2003.
12. Shimazu, H. (2001). ExpertClerk: Navigating Shoppers' Buying Process with the Combination of Asking and Proposing. Proceedings of the 17th International Joint Conference on Artificial Intelligence, IJCAI-01, Seattle, Washington, USA.
13. Stahl, A. (2001). Learning Feature Weights from Case Order Feedback. Proceedings of the 4th International Conference on Case-Based Reasoning, ICCBR 2001, David W. Aha, Ian Watson (Eds.). LNCS Vol. 2080 pp502-516 Springer 2001
14. Stahl, A. (2002). Defining similarity measures: Top-Down vs. bottom-up. Proceedings of the 6th European Conference, ECCBR 2002, Susan Craw, Alun Preece (Eds.). LNAI Vol. 2416, pp 406-420, Springer-Verlag, 2002.
15. Stahl, A., Gabel, T. (2003). Using Evolution Programs to Learn Local Similarity Measures. Proceedings of the 5th International Conference on Case-Based Reasoning, ICCBR 2003, Kevin D. Ashley, Derek G. Bridge (Eds.). LNCS Vol. 2689, pp 537-551, Springer 2003.

Investigating Graphs in Textual Case-Based Reasoning

Colleen Cunningham, Rosina Weber, Jason M. Proctor,
Caleb Fowler, and Michael Murphy

College of Information Science & Technology, Drexel University, Philadelphia, PA 19104
{cmc38,rw37,jp338,clf29,mpm37}@drexel.edu

Abstract. Textual case-based reasoning (TCBR) provides the ability to reason with domain-specific knowledge when experiences exist in text. Ideally, we would like to find an inexpensive way to automatically, efficiently, and accurately represent textual documents as cases. One of the challenges, however, is that current automated methods that manipulate text are not always useful because they are either expensive (based on natural language processing) or they do not take into account word order and negation (based on statistics) when interpreting textual sources. Recently, Schenker et al. [1] introduced an algorithm to convert textual documents into graphs that conserves and conveys the order and structure of the source text in the graph representation. Unfortunately, the resulting graphs cannot be used as cases because they do not take domain knowledge into consideration. Thus, the goal of this study is to investigate the potential benefit, if any, of this new algorithm to TCBR. For this purpose, we conducted an experiment to evaluate variations of the algorithm for TCBR. We discuss the potential contribution of this algorithm to existing TCBR approaches.

1 Introduction

Textual case-based reasoning (TCBR) extracts cases from textual documents whenever knowledge is contained in texts. There are extremely critical tasks and domains where tasks could be automated if text presented recognizable patterns and clear structure. Some examples of relevant domains include help desks [2], customer support [3], intelligent tutoring [4] and law [5]. In the legal domain alone, reasoning from text provides the ability to, for example: predict the outcome of legal cases [6]; construct legal argumentation [7][8], perform jurisprudence research [9], interpret and apply the facts of one case to a new case [8][10], and sentencing [11][12].

In fact, finding legal precedents is central to how the legal system in the US operates. Given the potential issues with acting upon incomplete information (e.g. poorly constructed arguments, misinterpretation and application of the law, erroneous decisions), it would be desirable if the methods used for jurisprudence research had high recall and precision. Recall is the ratio of useful documents that are retrieved to the total number of useful documents that exist [13]. Precision is a ratio of the number of useful documents that are retrieved to the total number of documents that are retrieved [13]. The most widely used technique for finding similar documents is Information Retrieval (IR), which is based on term frequency and measured in terms of recall and precision. IR in the legal domain is not adequate because term frequencies do not take into account domain-specific knowledge, therefore they only recall approximately 25% of relevant documents [14].

Unlike either IR or clustering methods [15], case-based reasoning (CBR) replicates reasoning by analogy to retrieve relevant cases based upon domain-specific knowledge [2][16]. CBR determines similarities between a current event and a past event similar to the manner in which people reason by using analogies. Furthermore, when using domain-specific knowledge to retrieve useful cases, one would expect that recall and precision would improve [9]. One of the challenges in TCBR, however, is finding an automated method to manipulate textual knowledge that takes into consideration order and negation [17] when interpreting the text.

Interestingly, recent developments in Graph Theory relate to text representation [1]. Graphs are mathematical representations that consist of vertexes (nodes) and edges (arcs), which offer a number of advantages over traditional feature vector approaches [18] - the most significant is the ability to create rich representations of cases [19]. Furthermore, unlike vector representations, the structure and word order of the original document can be retained. By definition, graph structures apply to representations that capture relationships between any two elements, as well as allowing an unlimited number of elements to be added or deleted at will [20]. This flexibility of the representation allows CBR cases to capture previously unforeseen information without the need to reconfigure the case base.

When the graphs are unlabeled or their labels are not fixed, the only applicable similarity methods are ones that search for identical subgraphs. This is the well-known subgraph isomorphism problem, which is NP-complete [21]. For this reason and for the nature of CBR similarity, we target case graphs that have fixed labels. This search is polynomial [1]. Additionally, because the fixed labels embed meaning, the similarity assessment is domain-specific. Although being polynomial, graph representations do have a significant computational cost. Fortunately, there are a number of methods and techniques aimed at reducing this problem [18].

There are promising developments in Graph Theory related not only to reduced complexity but also to text representation. In Schenker et al. [1], the authors proposed an algorithm to automatically convert textual documents (i.e. web pages) into graphs. Additionally, they have also demonstrated how to cluster the resulting graphs by using a variation of the k-means algorithm and by using the maximum common subgraph to measure similarity [22].

Given the successful use of graphs to represent web documents [1], the purpose of this paper is to examine the benefits of the algorithm presented in [1] for representing textual documents as case graphs in TCBR. Section 2 presents two algorithms to convert textual documents: the one proposed by Schenker et al. [1], to convert textual documents into graphs, henceforth referred to as Text-to-Graph (TtG); and our proposed variant that converts textual documents into case graphs, henceforth referred to as Text-to-Case-Graph (TtCG). Section 3 presents the experimental study we conducted to compare these algorithms with a feature vector CBR prototype and a human expert. We then discuss the potential impact of our findings on related work in Section 4. Finally, the conclusion and potential future work are presented in Section 5.

2 Graphs in Textual Case-Based Reasoning

Graphs are data structures that allow the easy implementation of algorithms. Therefore, it would be desirable to have textual content represented in graphs. The challenge is to determine a method for the conversion that preserves meaning while keeping graphs at a manageable size. If the goal is to compare graphs by searching for isomorphic subgraphs, this search is NP-complete. However, if the purpose is to assess distance by comparing graphs with fixed labels, then this search is polynomial [1]. In this section, we present the original algorithm presented in [1], TtG; and our proposed variant, TtCG, that represents a first attempt to convert textual documents into case graphs.

2.1 From Textual Documents to Graphs

In Schenker et al. [1], the authors introduced an algorithm to automatically convert textual web documents into graphs, Text-to-Graph (TtG). In the TtG approach, the unique words (excluding stop words) that appear in the web document are mapped to vertexes on the graph. Each vertex is then labeled with the unique word that it represents. The directed edges on the graph are drawn from the vertex that represents one word to the vertex that represented the word that immediately follows the first word. The edges are then labeled with the structural section in which the two words appeared. The TtG approach has several implied benefits to textual case-based reasoning. First, the structure and word order of the original document would be retained. Additionally, the TtG approach would reduce the amount of time required by knowledge engineers to encode representation of the textual sources.

Although the TtG approach does retain the word order and structure of the original text, it does not take into account negation. Furthermore, according to Aha [23], CBR is richer when it considers the relative importance of features; however, the TtG approach neither identifies features nor their relative importance. The creators of TtG [1] used a clustering algorithm to group similar textual documents together. It does not indicate the commonalities between the documents within a cluster. The ability to identify features and their relevance on a graph would mean that textual sources could automatically be converted to cases for CBR without the added expense of the time that it would take a knowledge engineer to manually represent a text as a case.

2.2 From Textual Documents to Case Graphs

We propose a variant of the TtG, which aims at converting textual documents into *case graphs*. Case graphs are representation formalisms that use graphs to represent situated experiences. Given that the essence of case-based reasoning is similarity, case graphs must be amenable to have their similarity assessed against other case graphs in conformity with the CBR hypotheses. Therefore, similarity is not a domain independent process, but one whose main goal is to replicate domain-specific similarity. For these reasons, our first attempt to create an algorithm to create case graphs from unrestricted data makes use of a list of potential domain-dependent indexes, which we call *signifiers*. Signifiers can be single words or expressions that we can guarantee play a role in the description of the situated experience. In cases that describe personal injury claims, for example, the occurrence of the term chiropractor is a predictive index. Consequently, our algorithm differs from the one introduced in Schenker et al. [1] in that it preserves the signifiers independent of the level of their occurrence in the source text.

The use of the signifiers allows for the use of traditional graph distance techniques to be used for case-based reasoning. Without the signifiers, we could not use graph distance techniques because they are not suitable to replicate similarity assessment.

2.3 Graph Distance Algorithms

Several graph distance techniques rely on finding the maximum common subgraph (MCS) [22]. The maximum common subgraph of two graphs is the set of all linked nodes that the two have in common.

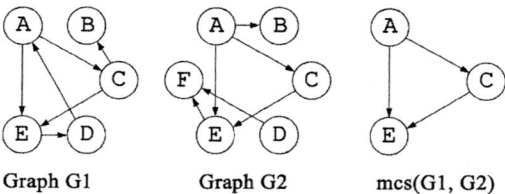

Fig. 1. MCS example

In Figure 1, the nodes of the graphs are labeled A, B, C, etc.; these would be words in the graph representation of a document. The arrows indicate word order in the original text. For instance, the document represented by graph G1 in the figure has at least two occurrences of word A, one of which is followed by word C and the other by word E. Note that words B and D appear in both graphs, but they are connected differently, so are not part of the MCS.

Collectively, distance techniques that use MCS are called MCS-based techniques. In [22], the authors also refer to one particular distance formula as *MCS*. In order to distinguish MCS-based techniques from this formula, we refer to the formula as BLG (Bunke Largest Graph). We use BLG [25] and WGU [26], which require finding the maximum common subgraph.

BLG distance is determined by dividing the size (number of vertexes plus number of edges, denoted by |...| in the equations below) of the maximum common subgraph by the size of the larger of the two graphs being compared, and then subtracting the quotient from 1 as shown in Equation 1.

$$d_{BLG}(G_1, G_2) = 1 - \frac{|mcs(G_1, G_2)|}{max(|G_1|, |G_2|)} \quad (1)$$

Unlike the BLG distance, WGU (Wallis Graph Union) distance is not sensitive to graphs of disparate sizes. The WGU distance is determined by dividing the size of the maximum common subgraph by the sum of the sizes of the two graphs being considered minus the size of the MCS (so those nodes are not counted twice), and then subtracting the quotient from 1, as shown in Equation 2.

$$d_{WGU}(G_1, G_2) = 1 - \frac{|mcs(G_1, G_2)|}{|G_1| + |G_2| - |mcs(G_1, G_2)|} \quad (2)$$

The range for both the BLG and WGU distances is from 0.0 (identical) to 1.0 (MCS is null – the graphs have no nodes in common). For example, referring to the graphs in

Figure 1 above, |G1| = 5 vertexes + 6 edges = 11; similarly, |G2| = 12, and |mcs(G1, G2)| = 6. The BLG distance between G1 and G2 is 1 - (6/12) = 0.5, but the WGU distance is 1 - (6/17) = 0.647.

3 Experimental Study

Our hypothesis is that using an algorithm to convert textual documents into graphs is beneficial to textual case-based reasoning. We tested our hypothesis using precision and recall for four different approaches to manipulate text and retrieve relevant documents: domain expert, feature vector CBR, the TtG algorithm and the TtCG approach. The domain expert's assessment was the baseline for the analysis.

This section describes the methods that were used to manipulate and represent the textual documents as well as the techniques that were used to assess the similarity between documents; the dataset; and how our chosen metrics, precision and recall, were computed. Subsections 3.6 and 3.7 present the results and the discussion, respectively. Table 1 summarizes the methodologies.

Table 1. Summary of approaches used in the experiment

	Domain Expert (DE)	Feature Vector CBR	TtG	TtCG
Source Text	Claim summary documents	Claim summary documents	Claim summary documents	Claim summary documents
Representation Method	DE	DE chose features and identified their values	TtG algorithm to automatically convert texts into graphs	TtCG algorithm to automatically convert texts into graphs
Representation Formalism	Mind of DE	Feature vectors	Graphs	Graphs
Similarity Assessment	DE judgment	Inferred and weighted nearest neighbor	MCS-based distance algorithms	MCS-based distance algorithms

3.1 Domain Expert Method

Text Manipulation/Representation. The domain expert was asked to read a collection of claim summary documents in order to identify the similar documents in the collection. In this case, there was not a formal representation of the documents.

Similarity Assessment. Based upon experience, the domain expert manually assessed the similarity between the claim summary documents. This method represents the baseline for subsequent analysis.

3.2 Feature Vector CBR

Text Manipulation/Representation. The domain expert reviewed the claim summary documents in order to identify the features that should be used to build the case base. Knowledge engineers then used the features that the expert identified in order to represent the documents as cases within the case base. An example of the identified features and their values for case 1 is shown in Table 2. Additionally, the knowledge engineers worked very closely with the domain expert in order to assign weights to each feature in order to capture the relative importance of each feature. This was a very challenging effort.

Table 2. Feature values in case 1

Question	Values
Was the incident reported?	yes
How soon was the incident reported?	same day
How old is plaintiff?	76
How many personnel injury lawsuits has the plaintiff filed before this complaint?	0
Was the plaintiff employed on the day of the incident?	no
Does the plaintiff have a criminal history that includes crimes of falsehood?	no
Did plaintiff have surgery as a result of the (alleged) incident?	no
How much did the plaintiff spend on medical bills?	4595
Does the plaintiff have pre-existing injuries in the same area as alleged in the current lawsuit?	yes
Is there a loss of consortium or per quod claim?	yes
Was plaintiff treated exclusively by a chiropractor?	no
Is there a permanent loss claim?	no
Is the injury claimed soft-tissue in nature?	yes
What is the plaintiff's annual income?	not available
How many days of work did the plaintiff miss due to the incident?	not available
Are there fact witnesses (other than plaintiff)?	yes
Case number	1
Case file	case1

Similarity Assessment. For the feature vector CBR, the similarity step was designed in a trial-and-error effort. We started by using the feedback feature weighting algorithm gradient descent, but the individual similarities between different values changed based on a variety of reasons. For example, a permanent injury is a predictive index only when the plaintiff is below a certain age. Consequently, we had to use a number of rules to assign weights whenever conditions changed, and we were limited by the shell we used.

3.3 Textual Documents to Graphs

Text Manipulation/Representation. The TtG method was used to convert the claim summary documents into graphs. It was not possible to use the algorithm in its exact original form because the claim summary documents did not consistently have three structural sections that were common across all documents. We modified the TtG method of representing textual documents as graphs for the claim summary documents by defining two *sections* – titles and text – instead of TtG's three (titles, text, and hypertext links), but kept other steps as similar as possible (see Section 2). Stop words were culled from the document, then the remaining ordered list of words was stemmed using Porter's algorithm [24]. Each unique term in the resulting list was added as a vertex in the graph representation, with its occurrence count as an attribute of the vertex. Directed edges were created between the vertexes representing words that were adjacent in the document, where adjacency crosses stop words but not numerals or *breaking* punctuation (period, question mark, exclamation point, colon, semicolon, parentheses, brackets, and single and double quotation marks). The edges were labeled with the section (title or text) in which the adjacent vertexes appeared. As with the vertexes, the count of adjacent occurrences was an attribute. Finally, the graphs were pruned to only include vertexes which occurred with a minimum frequency (specified at run-time).

Similarity Assessment. We used the techniques described in Subsection 2.3 to compute the distance between the resulting graphs.

3.4 Textual Documents to Case Graphs

Text Manipulation/Representation. As a further test of the potential benefit of a graph-based representation to TCBR, we modified the TtG method above to enhance the graphs using some domain knowledge. Based on the feature list provided by the expert, we identified ten *signifier* words, which represent expressions that are meaningful in the domain and thus may indicate the similarity between documents. These signifier words were never removed from the graph regardless of the frequency with which they actually occurred in the document. Dates and other numbers (usually monetary values) were also considered important to the expert, so we included month-names in the list of feature signifiers, and modified the methods that prepare the word list not to exclude numbers. This TtCG method was a first step towards adapting the graph-based work to textual CBR. We have introduced one aspect only as a preliminary amendment. Further adjustments remain for future work.

Similarity Assessment. The methods for the similarity assessment for the TtCG approach were identical to the methods used with the TtG approach. It should be noted, however, that unlike the case for the TtG representation, the features were also taken into consideration when computing the maximum common subgraph for the TtCG representation.

3.5 Precision and Recall

The precision was computed by dividing the number of useful (i.e. relevant) documents by the total number of documents that were retrieved. We did not, therefore, explore the ordering of the retrieved documents. The recall was computed by dividing the number of useful documents by the total number of relevant documents in the collection. The average precision and average recall were then computed by taking the averages of individual precision and recall values. It should be noted that the precision and recall for cases 9, 10 and 23 were not included when computing the averages because the domain expert stated that there were no similar documents in the collection for those specific cases.

3.6 Dataset

The data consisted of twenty-six claim summary documents from a law firm handling insurance cases. Insurance companies create these documents for insurance claims where there are legal questions or where the claimant has retained legal counsel.

Cases are usually loosely related because law firms tend to specialize in the types of cases they handle. However, we do not know about the specifics of the dataset except for what the methods used in the study revealed. The number of words range from 942 (case 27) to 9192 (case 17) with a mean of 3886.8, a median of 3898 (interpolated), and a standard deviation of 2151.8. Cases are numbered consecutively except for 8 and 19, which were missing. Finally, we used the same dataset for each of the methodologies discussed in the previous subsection.

3.7 Results

With respect to our hypothesis, our preliminary finding is that the use of an algorithm to convert textual documents into graphs is potentially beneficial to textual case-based reasoning. Table 3 shows the resulting precision and recall for the different approaches in our study. When comparing the different methods in our study to the baseline, we concluded that the TtG method alone can reach levels comparable to the alternative approaches tested. Besides, the performance of the TtCG method suggests that graph-based approaches can be tailored to domain specific tasks, potentially becoming significant to TCBR.

Table 3. Average observed precision and recall

	DE	Feature Vector CBR	TtG		TtCG	
			BLG	WGU	BLG	WGU
Precision	100%	16.3%	21.1%	21.4%	21.6%	21.6%
Recall	100%	33.3%	42.0%	44.2%	42.8%	46.7%

For reference, we compared the precision and recall values in Table 3 with the average values that could be obtained by random selection of the same number of similar documents for each cell in Table 5. These average probability values for precision and recall are presented in Table 4.

Table 4. Average probabilities for precision and recall

	DE	Feature Vector CBR	TtG		TtCG	
			BLG	WGU	BLG	WGU
Precision	n/a	.082	.089	.08.9	.08.9	.08.9
Recall	n/a	.237	.136	.130	.148	.153

The generally low values are an indication of the sparseness of the original dataset. On average, the domain expert selected 2.2 claim summary documents as being similar to any given document. When the observed values in Table 3 are compared with the random probabilities in Table 4 using paired-samples t tests, the scores for the feature vector CBR are not statistically different at $p < 0.05$, but the scores for all graph methods are. This disparity is primarily because the feature vector CBR selected more similar documents than the graph methods – its baseline probabilities indicated higher recall and lower precision than the graph methods.

For the TtG method, the BLG and WGU distance methods produced very similar results; for N=235 pairs, Pearson's $r=0.967$, $p<0.01$. For the TtCG approach, the correlation between BLG and WGU distances was also very similar ($r=0.970$, $p<0.01$). We tested BLG and WGU measures between TtG and TtCG, and found $r=0.979$ and $r=0.982$, respectively with $p<0.01$ in both cases. Our results confirmed that the WGU distance technique is more accurate than the BLG technique when the sizes of the graphs vary widely [26].

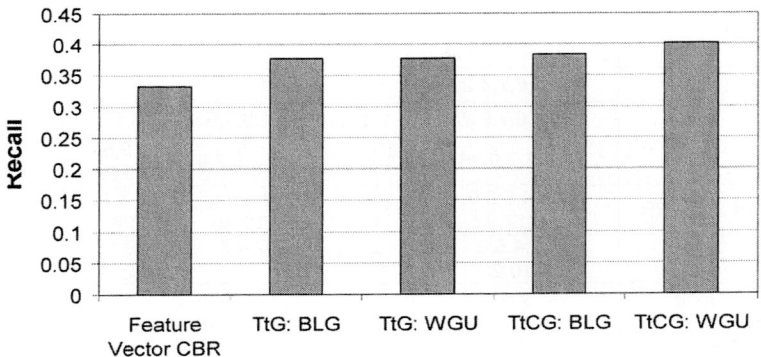

Fig. 2. Average recall obtained by the methods

Given the relevance of recall to the legal domain, Figure 2 compares the recall rates across the methods in our study. Although there is not a substantial difference among the graph-based methods, they performed noticeably better than the feature vector CBR.

Table 5 describes the results of the similarity assessments from the study. The table lists case numbers that were considered to be similar to the target case. In the columns designated for the graph-based methods, the table includes results from both of the distance measures that were used in the study.

The metrics in our study were precision and recall, which represent measures of retrieval accuracy. Ideally, we would like to find a way to automatically and accurately represent textual documents as cases. Therefore, we should also consider the potential reduction in the knowledge engineering requirements that a graph-based approach would facilitate. We did not measure the knowledge engineering effort because of its subjectivity. However, this is another implied characteristic that substantiates the potential benefit of this approach to TCBR.

3.8 Discussion

As expected, the TtCG method yielded an improvement over the original TtG method. The improvement, however, was only a slight improvement. We believe that the reason that the improvement was not more pronounced was because our preliminary adjustment to the TtG approach did not account for the relative importance of the features. Additionally, a major drawback of the signifier list was that it did not account for the range of synonyms and other semantic constructs, which an expert can interpret but a word-by-word analysis may not detect. This is an area for future research.

Table 5. Similar documents found by different methods

#	Domain Expert	Feature Vector CBR	TtG Method		TtCG Method	
			BLG	WGU	BLG	MGU
1	5,17	3,4,5,7,9	3,4,5	3,4,5	3,4,5	3,4,5
2	3,4	14,15,16,17,18,20	3,4,7,9,20	3,4,7,9,20	4,7,9,20	1,3,4,7,9,20
3	2,4	1,4,5,6,7,9	1,4,5,12	1,2,5,12	1,4,5,12	1,2,5,7,12
4	2,3	1,3,5,6,7,9,22	1,5	1	1,5	1
5	1,17	1,3,4,6,7,9,22	1,3,4,10	1,3,4,9	1,3,4,10	1,3,4,9
6	13	3,4,5,7,9,26	1,2,5,7,9	1,3,5,7,9	1,2,5,7,9,26	1,5,7,9,21,26
7	24,25,26,28	1,3,4,5,6,9,10,17,22	1,2,4,12,28	1,4,11,12,28	1,2,4,28	1,4,11,12,28
9	None	1,3,4,5,6,7,10,22	2,5,6,16	2,4,5,6	2,6,16,26	2,4,5,6,16,21,26
10	None	7,9	1,3,4,5	1,4,5,7,9	1,3,4,5	1,4,5,7,9
11	12,21,27	12	7,13,21,28	7,13,21,28	7,13,21,27,28	7,13,21,27,28
12	11,21,27	11	1,3,4,5,7	1,3,4,7	1,3,4,5,7	1,3,7,28
13	6	26	11,21	11,21	11,21	11,21,26,27
14	18	2,15,16,17,18,20,23,27	18,25	18,25	18,25	18,25
15	22	2,14,16,17,18,20,23,26,27	1,5,23,24	5,23,24	1,5,23,24	5,23,24,26
16	20	2,14,15,17,18,20,23,24,27	18,20,25	18,20,25	9,18,20,25	14,18,20,25
17	1,5	2,7,14,15,16,18,20,23,26,27	1,4,5,12	1,4,5,12,23	1,4,5,12,15	1,4,5,12,15,23
18	14	2,14,15,16,17,20,23,24,27	14,25	14,25	14,25	14,25
20	16	2,14,15,16,17,18,23,24,27	2,16,24	2,16,25	2,16,24	2,16,25
21	11,12,27	18	13,25	13,16,25,26	11,13,25,26	13,16,25,26
22	15	4,5,7,9	2,7,9,20	9,21	2,7,9,20,23	9,20,23
23	None	14,15,16,17,18,20,24,26,27	5,15,24,26	5,15,26	5,9,15,24,26	5,9,15,26
24	7,25,26,28	16,18,20,23,26,27	15,20	2,15,16	1,4,5,15,20	2,15,26
25	7,24,26,28	None	14,16,18,21	14,16,18	14,16,18	14,16,18
26	7,24,25,28	6,13,15,17,18,23,24,27,28	6,9,16,21,23	6,9,21,23	6,9,16,21,23	9,16,21,23,27
27	11,12,21	14,15,16,17,18,20,23,24,26	14,18,21	14,18,21	14,18,21	14,18,21,26
28	7,24,25,26	15,17,23,26	2,7,12	7,11,12	2,7	7,11,12

The results suggest other peculiarities of the legal domain. While feature vector systems are commonly used in a variety of tasks, when trying to use this representation to model the similarities between claim summary documents, we faced several difficulties. In part, the problems stemmed from the limitations of using a shell, but more significant were the number of exceptions learned in the knowledge elicitation sessions. For example, the features designated for annual income and the number of days the plaintiff was out of work become irrelevant when the plaintiff is not employed. In the legal domain, for example, this could mean finding one additional jurisprudence that may change the outcome of a legal case.

4 Impact of Graph-Based Method on Related Work

In TCBR, the representation of the text source is key because it is used as the basis for computing the similarity between cases, which ultimately determines which cases are retrieved. As such, the primary focus within TCBR has been on identifying features that can be used to index the cases. Since the first TCBR workshop [27], progress has been made to add domain-specific thesaurus [28][29], assign indexing concepts to texts [29], add linguistic knowledge in order to deal with negation [5] and use latent semantic analysis to extract semantic similarity of words and phrases [30] in order to build more meaningful representations.

Building CBR systems from textual knowledge has involved very expensive and manual efforts [7], basic text retrieval using information retrieval (IR) techniques [31], Information Extraction (IE) techniques [16], Natural Language Processing (NLP) techniques and Machine Learning techniques [32]. Although fast and easy to use, the disadvantage of using the IR approach is that feature vectors do not take into consideration the word order of the text, the structure of the text, negation, the semantic meaning of words and phrases. Instead, IR is a domain-independent approach that is based merely on statistics. IE, on the other hand, involves building templates that can be used for meaningful pattern matching [9]. However, developing the extraction rules that are used in IE is a very labor-intensive and expensive task that requires large training data or domain knowledge. Furthermore, pattern-matching techniques are only good for semi-structured texts that have a limited number of phrases [5]. NLP is a technique that parses the text based upon grammar. Unfortunately, textual documents, particularly technical documents, do not always contain grammatically correct sentences [28].

A graph-based method could overcome some of the issues with the previously discussed approaches. The use of graphs in TCBR in the legal domain is not new. For example, Branting [33] used graphs to determine case precedents. A graph-based approach, however, could contribute to the work of Gupta and Aha [3] by providing the ability to automatically identify unknown attributes (i.e. feature value pairs). Additionally, the graph-based approach could contribute to the work of Brüninghaus and Ashley [32][29][5] by eliminating words that are not a part of the factors used to build relationships between features in order to reduce the required knowledge engineering efforts. Furthermore, unlike NLP techniques, which are computationally too inefficient for processing large amounts of data [34], both the graph-based algorithm [22] and, in principle, the adapted algorithm are computationally efficient. NLP also requires a complete dictionary of terms a priori, which is not often practical. The adapted algorithm, on the other hand, can use a partial list that identifies the relationships between features in computing the similarity between cases. One of the immediate benefits of the TtG algorithm is that, unlike Weber's approach [35], the TtCG algorithm can be used with unstructured text. This represents a clear advantage over template mining techniques and a potential contribution of the TtG algorithm to TCBR.

5 Conclusions and Future Work

In this study, we examined one step towards developing an algorithm to convert textual documents into case graphs. This is a first step in the investigation of the potential usefulness of graphs for textual case-based reasoning. We compared the precision and recall rates that were obtained using different methods. Specifically, our proposed variant, the TtCG algorithm, yielded better precision and recall rates when compared to the results of both the TtG algorithm and the feature vector CBR.

Though not explicitly measured, the incorporation of any automated approach to the TCBR process impacts its cost because it reduces its required engineering effort. Given the expected reduction in engineering requirements in conjunction with a potential improvement in the levels of accuracy, we conclude that there is sufficient motivation for continuing to study graph-based approaches to textual CBR.

Furthermore, our proposed approach does not require source text to be structured. This point is particularly important in the legal domain because the structure of the legal documents varies from one jurisdiction to another, and even between courts within the same jurisdiction. While the preliminary results seem promising, there are, however, further additional adjustments that should be made in future work.

We have also learned from investigating the use of graphs in TCBR that graph distance techniques from Graph Theory are not suitable for assessing similarity between case graphs. This is because they are not designed to incorporate domain specific aspects that guide similarity assessment, e.g. representing varying relative importance.

We used case graphs with fixed labels in order to facilitate similarity assessment by using domain specific information. Using fixed labels has the additional benefit of reducing complexity given that distance algorithms applied to graphs with fixed labels are polynomial and not NP-complete [1].

Although our TtCG method shows some potential to represent textual documents as case graphs, our method does not address negation. Negation, however, is important in the legal domain as well as in other domains such as medicine. Moreover, in order to conform to the CBR hypotheses, it is desirable to incorporate the relative importance of indexes on the graph. Furthermore, graphs have the powerful ability to represent concepts that are described in relationships. Therefore, it would be useful to capture the domain-specific relationships that exist between features and represent them in graphs. All of these abilities would further capture the richness of a domain in the representation, which would potentially improve the recall, and represent an inexpensive means towards automatically, accurately and efficiently converting textual documents into case graphs. Therefore, we intend to incorporate negation, relationships between features, the relative importance of each feature and domain-specific rules in a future study.

Acknowledgements. We would like to thank Drs. Abe Kandel and Adam Schenker for allowing us to use their algorithm in this study. We also would like to thank Dr. Bunke, Dr. Kandel, and Dr. Last for inciting the use of their methods for case-based reasoning. Thanks to Zane Reynolds for his help with his implementation and helpful comments. We are also indebted to Attorney Lisa Green for contributing her domain expertise to this study. We would also like to express our gratitude to Daniella Goral for assisting in the cleansing of the documents. Dr. Rosina Weber is supported in part by the National Institute for Systems Test and Productivity at USF under the USA Space and Naval Warfare Systems Command grant no. N00039-02-C-3244, for 2130 032 L0, 2002.

References

1. Schenker, A., Last, M., Bunke, H., Kandel, A.: Clustering of Web Documents using a Graph Model. In: Antonacopoulos, A. and Hu, J. (eds.): *Web Document Analysis: Challenges and Opportunities* (2003) 1-16
2. Lenz, M.: *Defining Knowledge Layers for Textual Case-Based Reasoning.* In: B. Smyth, P. Cunningham (eds.): Advances in Case-Based Reasoning, Lecture Notes in Artificial Intelligence, Vol. 1488. Springer-Verlag, Berlin Heidelberg New York (1998) 298-309
3. Gupta, K. M. and Aha, D. W.: Towards Acquiring Case Indexing Taxonomies from Text. In: Barr, V. and Markov, Z. (eds.): Proceedings of the Seventeenth Annual Conference of the International Florida Artificial Intelligence Research Society. AAAI Press, Menlo Park, CA (2004) 172 – 177
4. Ashley, K. and Aleven, V.: Toward an Intelligent Tutoring System for Teaching Law Students. In: Proceedings of International Conf. on AI and Law. ACM Press, New York (1991) 42-52
5. Brüninghaus, S. and Ashley, K. D.: The Role of Information Extraction for Textual CBR. In: Aha, D.W. and Watson, I. (eds.): *Case-Based Reasoning Research and Development,* Lecture Notes in Artificial Intelligence, Vol. 2080. Springer-Verlag, Berlin Heidelberg New York (2001) 74-89
6. Brüninghaus, S., and Ashley, K. D.: Combining Model-Based and Case-Based Reasoning for Predicting the Outcomes of Legal Cases. Bridge, D., Ashley, K. D. (eds.): Case-Based Reasoning Research and Development. Lecture Notes in Artificial Intelligence, Vol. 2689. Springer-Verlag, Berlin Heidelberg New York (2003) 65-79
7. Ashley, K. D.: Modeling Legal Argument: reasoning with cases and hypotheticals. A Bradford book. The MIT Press, Cambridge, Massachussetts (1990)
8. Rissland, E.L., Ashley, K.D., Loui, R.P.: AI and Law: A fruitful synergy. Artificial Intelligence 150 (2003) 1 – 15
9. Weber, R.: Intelligent Jurisprudence Research. Doctoral dissertation, Department of Production Engineering, Federal University of Santa Catarina, Brazil. (1998) Available online: http://www.pages.drexel.edu/~rw37/dissertation.zip
10. Ashley, K. D. and Rissland, E. L.: Law, Learning and Representation. Artificial Intelligence 150 (2003) 17-58
11. Bain, W.: (1986). Case-based reasoning: A computer model of subjective assessment. Ph. D. dissertation, Department of Computer Science, Yale University.
12. Bain, W.: Judge. In: Inside Case-Based Reasoning. Riesbeck, C. K. and Schank, R.C. (eds.): Erlbaum, Northvale, NJ (1989)
13. Salton, G.: Dynamic Information and Library Processing. Prentice-Hall, Inc. Englewood Cliffs, New Jersey (1975)
14. Blair, D. and Maron, M.: Full-text information retrieval: further analysis and clarification. 1990. Information Processing and Management 26, 3 (1990) 437-447
15. Ghosh-Roy, R., Habiballah, I.O., Stonham, T.J. and Irving, M.R.: On-line legal aid: Markov chain model for efficient retrieval of legal documents. Image and Vision Computing 16 (1998) 941-946
16. Weber, R., Martins, A., and Barcia, R.: On legal texts and cases. In: Lenz, M. and Ashley, K. (eds.): Textual Case-Based Reasoning: Papers from the AAAI-98 Workshop (Technical Report WS-98-12). AAAI Press, Menlo Park, CA (1998) 40-50

17. Ashley, K.: Progress in Text-Based Case-Based Reasoning. Invited Talk at the Third International Conference on Case-Based Reasoning. Seeon, Germany. (1999)
18. Bunke, H.: Recent Developments in Graph Matching. In: Proceedings of the 15th International Conference on Pattern Recognition, Vol. 2. IEEE Computer Society Press, Los Alamitos, CA (2000) 117 – 124
19. Gebhardt, F., Vob, A., Grather, W. & Schmidt-Belz, B.: Reasoning with complex cases. Kluwer Academic, Boston, MA (1997)
20. Sanders, K., Kettler, B., Hendler, J.: The case for graph-structured representations. In: Leake, D. and Plaza, E. (eds.): Case-Based Reasoning Research and Development, Lecture Notes in Artificial Intelligence, Vol. 1266. Springer-Verlag, Berlin Heidelberg New York (1997) Available online: http://citeseer.nj.nec.com/sanders97case.html
21. Garey, M. R. and Johnson, D.S.: Computers and Intractability. W. H. Freeman and Company, New York (1979)
22. Schenker, A., Last, M., Bunke, H., Kandel, A.: Comparison of Distance Measures for Graph-based Clustering of Documents. In: Hancock, E. and Vento, M. (eds.): Lecture Notes in Computer Science, Vol. 2726 (2003) 202–213
23. Aha, D. W.: Feature weighting for lazy learning algorithms. In: H. Liu and H. Motoda (eds.): Feature Extraction, Construction and Selection: A Data Mining Perspective. Kluwer, Norwell, MA, (1998) 13-32
24. Porter, M.: An Algorithm for Suffix Stripping. Program 14, 3 (1980) 130–137. Available online: http://www.tartarus.org/~martin/PorterStemmer/ (retrieved 25 Feb 2004)
25. Bunke, H. and Shearer, K.: A Graph Distance Metric Based on the Maximal Common Subgraph. *Pattern Recognition Letters* 19 (1998) 255–259
26. Wallis, W.D., Shoubridge P., Kraetz, M., Ray, D.: Graph Distances using Graph Union. *Pattern Recognition Letters* 22 (2001) 701–704.
27. Lenz, M. and Ashley, K. (eds.): Textual Case-Based Reasoning: Papers from the AAAI-98 Workshop (Technical Report WS-98-12). AAAI Press, Menlo Park, CA (1998)
28. Lenz, M.: Managing the Knowledge Contained in Technical Documents. In: Proceedings of the Second International Conference on Practical Aspects of Knowledge Management (PAKM98). October 29-30, Basel, Switzerland. (1998)
29. Brüninghaus, S. and Ashley, K. D.: Bootstrapping Case Base Development with Annotated Case Summaries. In: Althoff, K.D., Bergmann, R. and Branting, L.K. (eds.): *Case-Based Reasoning Research and Applications.* Lecture Notes in Computer Science, Vol. 1650. Springer-Verlag, Berlin Heidelberg New York (1999) 59-73
30. Foltz, P. W., Laham, D., and Landauer, T. K.: Automated Essay Scoring: Applications to Educational Technology. In: Collis, B. and Oliver, R. (eds.): Proceedings of EdMedia. (1999)
31. Leake, D., and Wilson, D.: Combining CBR with Interactive Knowledge Acquisition, Manipulation and Reuse. In: Althoff, K.D., Bergmann, R. and Branting, L.K. (eds.): Case-Based Reasoning Research and Applications. Lecture Notes in Computer Science, Vol. 1650. Springer-Verlag, Berlin Heidelberg New York (1999) 203-217
32. Brüninghaus, S. and Ashley, K. D.: How Machine Learning Can Be Beneficial for Textual Case-Based Reasoning. In: Proceedings of the AAAI-98/ICML-98 Workshop on Learning for Text Categorization (AAAI Technical Report WS-98-05) (1998) 71-74
33. Branting, L.K.: A reduction-graph model of precedent in legal analysis. Aritificial Intelligence 150 (2003) 59-95
34. Lenz, M. and Glintschert, A.: On Texts, Cases, and Concepts. In: Proceedings of XPS-99:Knowledge-Based Systems. Lecture Notes in Computer Science, Vol. 1570. Springer-Verlag, Berlin Heidelberg New York (1999) 148-156
35. Weber, R.: Intelligent Jurisprudence Research: a new concept. In: Bing, J., Jones, A. J. I., and Gordon, T. F. (eds.): Proceedings of the Seventh International Conference on Artificial Intelligence and Law. ACM Press, New York (1999) 164-172

A Case Study of Structure Processing to Generate a Case Base*

Hector Gómez-Gauchía, Belén Díaz-Agudo, and Pedro A. González-Calero

Dep. Sistemas Informáticos y Programación
Universidad Complutense de Madrid, Spain
`{hector,belend,pedro}@sip.ucm.es`

Abstract. Although Case-based Reasoning is supposed to alleviate the well known knowledge acquisition bottleneck for knowledge-based systems, case acquisition remains an expensive process. In this paper we present a semiautomatic methodology for building an ontology-based organization of the Case Base and to populate it with cases extracted from structured documents. The methodology is analyzed through the case study of a help desk system.

1 Introduction

The case study we tackle is the building of a Help-Desk system for the Customer Service Department of a software company. The feasibility study suggests us using a case based reasoning (CBR) approach. More specifically, it results to be useful to complement the specific knowledge contained in the cases with two ontologies. The first is a lightweight ontology representing the general and static domain knowledge, and the latter, called CBROnto, has the knowledge to represent the case structure and the CBR processes (mainly similarity assessment for retrieval and adaptation).

Knowledge acquisition and, more specifically, building the case base is an expensive task. This still is a bottleneck in CBR development. Almost all the current case generation approaches are from databases, where records are clustered to get representative and generalized cases. These approaches apply several theories,such as rough set, fuzzy logic, genetic algorithms, knowledge discovery or data mining. Our source of knowledge it is not a database, but text documents. In [7] we have used IR techniques and structure processing to select relevant concepts and building the ontology that defines the vocabulary to describe cases. The next step taken is the automatic acquisition of the case base from semi-structured text documents in XML format and the vocabulary of the lightweight ontology.

Our line of work during the last years has been the research of different techniques and approaches to build Knowledge Intensive CBR (KI-CBR) systems: integrated Knowledge Based Systems that combine case specific knowledge with models of general terminological domain knowledge [3,5,6]. Our environment

---

* Supported by the Spanish Committee of Science & Technology (TIC2002-01961)

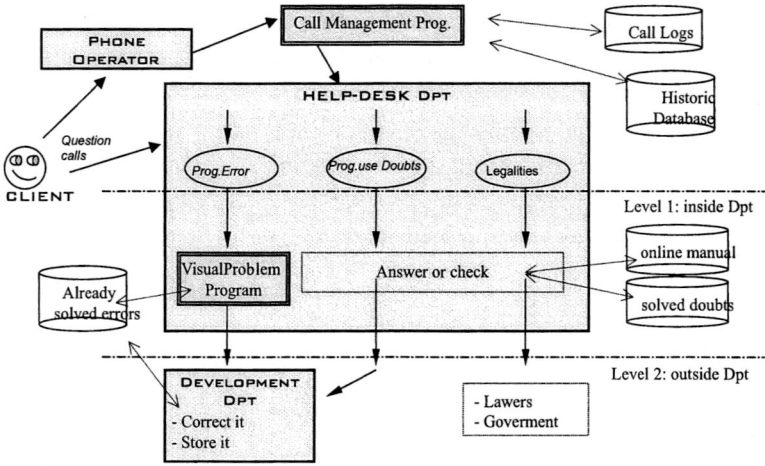

Fig. 1. Problem Domain Scenario. Workflow of questions and answers

COLIBRI (Cases and Ontology Libraries Integration for Building Reasoning Infrastructures) assists during the design of knowledge intensive CBR (KI-CBR) systems. Like in previous works we use Description Logic based languages (DLs) that are commonly used to implement ontologies, and have been proven to be useful to formalize aspects of representation and reasoning in CBR systems [10, 3, 4]. In this paper we apply our research results to a real case study.

Our solution proposes processing the structure of the documents to define the case structure, and using the content of the different sections to populate the case base. This is made in several steps. We describe in this paper the whole process because all phases are interrelated: the problem domain scenario, the ontology building, the case generation and the reasoning process.

2 Problem Domain Scenario

The project is for a software company, GoldenSoft in Spain. It needed a computer support for a very intense human work of the Department of Client Attention, or Help-Desk. Help desks are groups that provide service support to a company's products.

GoldenSoft is one of the main local software companies developing software for the management of small and medium size companies. It sells five complex integrated applications for invoicing, accounting, payroll, teller machines and taxes. The Help-Desk supports the phone calls with questions about these applications.

One of the keys of its success is the Help-Desk department with ten technicians that are trained during a year before they are ready to answer calls. They attend two hundred calls a day about complex problems of several kind of topics, mainly program errors, application use, legal or computer user related issues. Some of these questions take even hours to be solved. In the Fig. 1 are depicted the main elements of this department and how it relates with the rest of related elements: development department, the client, the phone operator that uses the call management program, the kind of topics and the sources of knowledge. There are two levels of problem treatment, when the first one doesn't solve the question, it goes into the second level.

As sources of knowledge we have the technicians, the users, the application developers and several written materials (Fig. 1) that technicians use to solve the calls:

- phone call logs
- a historic database that records only keywords about the problems and solutions of the solved client calls.
- semi-structured documentation like application help-manuals
- unstructured summaries of their past solved problems

Our first attempt was using as cases, both the call logs and the summaries of the past solved problems. Although it would be expected that they were relevant and useful to be used as the cases (like in [11]), there was not the reality in our case study. The call logs were not relevant for us because they had only business data of each call received requesting a solution to a problem. Regarding the informal documentation of the technicians solved problems, it has interesting information but very limited to a small set of problems. The historic database keywords are used in a refinement phase of the case base. The on-line Help Manuals is the main source of knowledge as it has several good characteristics for our purpose, namely:

- We consider as relevant topics those that are consulted most frequently by the clients, so they are the *concepts*. We can say that the whole domain concepts are in them, because the rest are not considered in the manuals.
- They have sections of the whole functionality of the application that are almost all the problems that clients consult.
- They have the steps to perform the functionality; these are the solutions to the problems.
- The experts, developers and clients know all the important terms used in the manuals in the specialized domains, so we can say that there is a consensus of the meaning, something very valuable when we are building an ontology.

The application of CBR to help desk applications was already present since the beginning of CBR ([11]). CBR is appropriate in these domains because problems recur and when they do so they utilize the same solutions. Our CBR system is a Help-Desk that give solutions to requests posted by the users of the applications that the company sells. The users interact with the system in a conversation until they get a satisfactory solution. The requests are written in natural language with a vocabulary restricted by the domain ontology that is described in the next section.

3 The Proposed Approach

The case generation is dictated by four issues: the knowledge representation approach used in the cases, the organization of the domain knowledge ontology, the kind of reasoning tasks we want to apply and the overall purpose of the system.

In our project, the cases and the ontology are modeled with DLs. The reasoning tasks are related with conversational CBR because they include continuous interaction with the user, although we use a structured case representation (see section 4). The overall purpose of the system is a Help-Desk application. These topics are described briefly before the case generation process is detailed. To simplify the explanation we separate the cases and the ontology, although they are interrelated in the DLs representation.

3.1 Description Logics

DLs are considered one of the most important knowledge representation formalism unifying and giving a logical basis to the well known traditions of Frame-based systems, Semantic Networks and KL-ONE-like languages, Object-Oriented representations, Semantic data models, and Type systems. They are characterized by its expressiveness and clearly defined semantics. DLs capture the meaning of the data by concentrating on entities (grouped into classes or concepts) related by relationships. This intuition is shared by formalisms such as semantic data models, semantic networks or frame systems. More important than the DLs representational characteristics are its reasoning mechanisms. The most important characteristic is the checking of inconsistencies and the organization of the concepts on a taxonomy that the system automatically builds from the concept definitions. This is possible because of the clear and precise semantic of concept definitions that save the user from putting the concepts in the correct place of the hierarchy (as is the case in frame systems, which provide inheritance but not classification).

DL reasoning mechanisms are based on *subsumption*, to determine whether a description –concept or relation– is more general than another, and *instance recognition*, to determine the concepts that an individual satisfies and the relations that a tuple of individuals satisfies. Subsumption supports classification, i.e., the ability of automatically classifying a new description within a –semi–lattice of previously classified descriptions; and instance recognition supports completion, i.e., the ability of drawing logical consequences of assertions about individuals, based on those descriptions they are recognized as instances of. Contradiction detection, both for descriptions and assertions about individuals, completes the basic set of reasoning mechanisms provided by DLs systems.

3.2 Ontology Construction

The use of an incremental domain model within an ontology, that integrates the case base prevents of typical problems when dealing with natural language

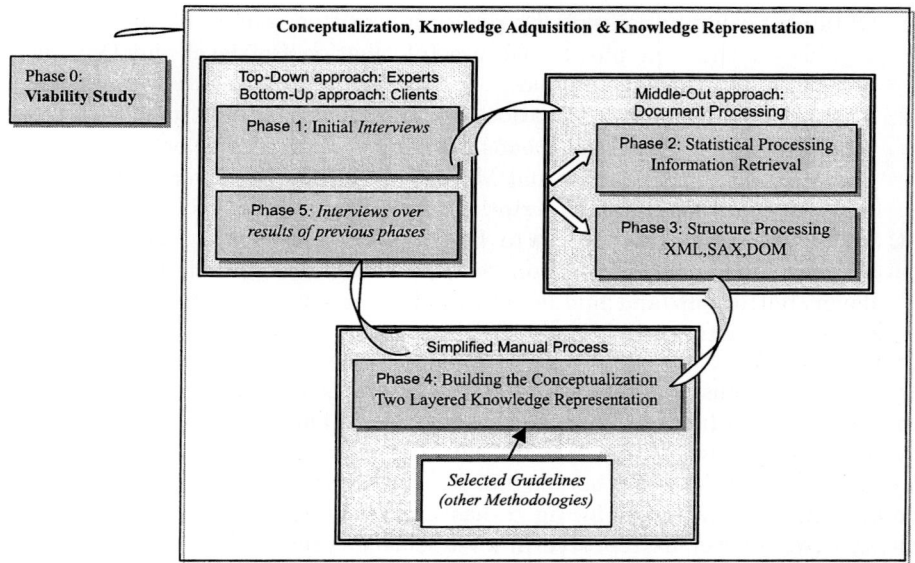

Fig. 2. Lightweight Ontology Methodology summary: Refinement Cycle

texts. For example, we avoid the typical situation where a common language verb means different actions in different domains (same with nouns). Another example is that, to obtain a good retrieval quality, the matching must be accurate. To do this we need synonyms and generic and concrete concepts to cover those used by the clients and technicians in their usual conversations. It is not possible to generate automatically these words because they are not always synonyms in the real natural language, English or Spanish, but only in the user jargon.

To make the ontology of the KI-CBR system we reviewed, in [7], some of the most representative methodologies to build ontologies and identified good guidelines that we may apply in the adequate phase of the proposed methodology as it is shown in Fig. 2. The current methodologies to build ontologies follow a wide range of theories, approaches and scopes of their application. After doing the survey of methodologies and starting the conceptualization phase, we found several problems applying them:

1. The lack of understanding of the domain terms and the lack of experts.
2. The need to facilitate the ontology definition, using a formal representation language, by domain experts that are not computer experts. In this article we call them users.
3. The need to structure the whole process of guidelines, tasks and support materials.

To solve them we, as knowledge engineers, use theoretical paradigms already tested in other areas of research. We propose the following solutions to face up these problems:

1. Obtaining relevant concepts by processing written sources of knowledge, as a guide for the next phases. We use Information Retrieval and Document Structure processing techniques.
2. To support human communication through conceptual structures we propose representing knowledge by means of two layers: a user layer with an easy graphical language, Conceptual Maps, and an internal layer with a formal representation language, Description Logics.
3. To define a refinement cycle to build up the ontology in an incremental manner. The cycle is based on the three main conceptual strategies, top-down, bottom-up and middle-out, applied in different phases, including a final phase with a manual task by the user.

In [7] we discuss the first stages of the knowledge engineering approach, i.e. the conceptualization of the knowledge acquisition and the knowledge representation of a lightweight ontology. We have defined a pragmatic methodology as a complement to other methodologies. It has a cycle with five phases. The proposed methodology, shown in Fig. 2, has three main tasks, which group the five phases. These tasks are repeated in a refinement cycle until all the participants reach a consensus of the ontology semantics. The tasks are based on the source of information and its treatment:

1. *Interviews*, with the clients in a bottom-up style and with the experts in a top-down style. It includes phase one, the initial conceptualization, and phase five, the refinement of the ontology obtained in previous phases.
2. *Document Processing* of the written documentation to extract the most relevant terms, this is the middle-out strategy. Depending on the nature of documents, a statistical processing, phase two, or a document structure processing, phase three, is applied.
3. *Simplified Manual Building* of the ontology in a two-layered representation taking as the basis the relevant concepts obtained in the previous tasks. This is phase four. The selected guidelines of the studied methodologies in the survey are applied in this task. The user only works with the informal graphical representation, leaving the formal layer internal to be used by the KI-CBR system.

We have implemented the domain ontology using the last release of the PROTEGE-2000 ontology editor that was developed at Stanford University shown in Fig. 3. Protégé 2.0.1[9] can manage ontologies in OWL[2], a new standard that has recently reached a high relevance. Reasoning is done by the DLs inference engine RACER[8] that communicates PROTEGE using a DIG interface[1] in OWL DF version.

3.3 Case Representation

There are different approaches to case representation and, related to that, different techniques for Case Based Reasoning: the textual CBR approach, the

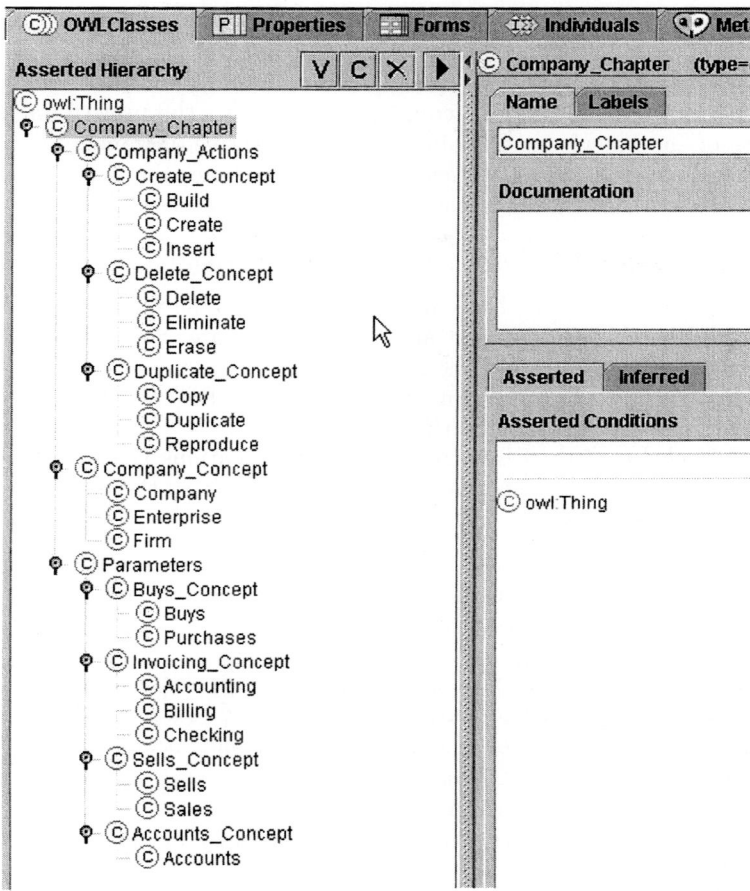

Fig. 3. Partial ontology with PROTEGE (OWL format)

conversational CBR approach, and the structural CBR approach. In the textual CBR approach, cases are represented in free-text form. In the conversational CBR approach, cases are lists of questions and answers. For every case, there can be different questions. In the structural CBR approach, the developer of the case-based solution decides ahead of time what features will be relevant when describing a case and then stores the cases according to them.

We propose structural CBR with conversations during the reasoning tasks. We represent cases within complex case representation structures instead of lists of questions and answers as Conversational CBR does.

Our structural CBR approach relies on cases that are described with attributes and values that are pre-defined, and structured in object-oriented manner. This structural CBR approach is useful in domains like the one we are considering where additional knowledge, beside cases, must be used in order to produce good results. The domain ontology insures that new cases are of high quality and the maintenance effort is low. Within the defined case structures we deal with texts that are used directly (without adaptation) as the case solutions. This approach eases case acquisition, and allows the user to immediately make use of the knowledge contained in the respective documents. The use of structures to describe cases (instead of texts) overcomes the main drawback of textual CBR systems that retrieve a large number of cases that are irrelevant.

Case Vocabulary. We need to represent three different aspects:

- The *case structure*, it is the skeleton that supports the rest of the knowledge. It should be able to represent any kind of structure. We use the CBROnto [3, 4, 6] that is described in the next section.
- The *reasoning tasks* need terms that allow the CBR system to perform its tasks. These are provided by the CBROnto too.
- The *knowledge of the cases* to describe the situations that they represent. This is to fill the case structure with the terms from the domain ontology described in Figure 3.

That way CBR processes will reason with both, domain and CBR terms. The issue of case representation includes deciding the type and the structure of the domain knowledge within the cases.

Case Structure. We work with structured case representation where individuals are concept instances and concepts are organized in a hierarchy with inheritance. In our approach, cases are linked within a semantic network of domain knowledge. Cases in the case base won't have, in general, the same structure. This way the designer could define different types of cases.

We facilitate the case structure authoring tasks by proposing a framework to represent cases that is based on the DLs instance definition language and the CBROnto terminology. Besides, we define a reasoning system, based on generic CBR Problem Solving Methods, that works with such representations [6]. CBROnto provides a semantic CBR terminology to define case structures and expresses domain terminology in CBR terms using classification.

CBROnto provides a *primitive* concept **CASE**. We will call *case-type* concepts the **CASE** subconcepts. That way, cases can be represented as instances of the case-type concepts. Besides, the concrete cases (**CASE** instances) may add other proper features to the fixed structure inherited through the case-type concepts.

The designer will define case-type concepts to represent the new types of cases. The CBROnto vocabulary is used to guide the definition of these concepts by providing CBR semantically important terms, such as `has-description`, `has-solution`, `has-result`, `similarityMeasure`, `weight`, `has-part`, `goal`, `precondition`, or `description-property`, among others.

Figure 4 illustrates how the slots of a case are implemented using the CBROnto representation framework. The domain specific concepts (like *Company-Chapter*, *Company-Actions*, *Duplicate-Concept*, and *Create-Concept*) are concepts from the domain model (see figure 3) and are obtained from the documents (as we describe in section 3.4).

We use, directly or through the subconcept hierarchy, an instance of the concept CASE-DESCRIPTION to represent the description of a case. The has-description relation links a CASE instance with the individual representing the description of this case. It outlines the problem that is solved in this case by referencing the ontology concepts through the domain slots. This description is used by the CBR reasoning tasks to index and retrieve the cases. The different levels of abstraction in the description allows having cases that are part of other cases. For example, the description of the case c1 is made of individuals c11, c12, c13, c14 that are cases themselves (subconcepts of *case*).

The solution of a case is represented as an instance of the CASE-SOLUTION concept. The has-solution relation links a CASE instance with the CASE-SOLUTION individual representing its solution. As we have described in section 4, in this application we deal with texts that are used directly, i.e. without adaptation, as the case solutions. The text indicates what to do to solve the problem.

The domain slot *loosely-related-references* links a description with other chapters where the description concepts are mentioned as secondary topics in the text body. It is used to offer related sources of information about the problem.

To finish with the case main parts, the result of a case might include components as the success or failure of the case, the explanation of a failure, or links to other possible solutions.

Our representational framework allows complex structures and does not restrict the possible relations among the parts of a case, facilitates the definition of cases having different structures. The case instances may be related with other individuals, and in particular with other case instances, i.e. a case can be related with cases that are cases themselves.

We deal with different levels of abstraction, where there are small and detailed cases that can be grouped using a description to get a more complex and general case. For example, a very general description like "a problem with enterprises" may relate a whole chapter of the manual that is composed by several dozens of sections. Each of them maybe composed by several subsections with several cases each. If, on the contrary, we have a very detailed and specific description, it relates only a simple case, that is very small, representing just a subsection of a subsection of a chapter. As we described in Section 3.3 we use the COLIBRI/CBROnto mechanism that is able to reason with cases in different level of abstraction.

Reasoning Process. The system interacts with the user through a conversation. Questions are not stored but they are automatically generated from the case structure using DLs reasoning mechanisms. The process begins when the user writes the description of the problem that is analyzed to create a generic description of a case. Cases with similar descriptions are retrieved. Similarity is based on the semantics found on the domain ontology. The system searches in the ontology the relevant terms of the question.

In the example shown in Figure 5 the user poses a very abstract and vague description (step 2). *Enterprise* is the only relevant word found in the ontology. The system relates *enterprise* with its synonym *company* (step 3). Then the sys-

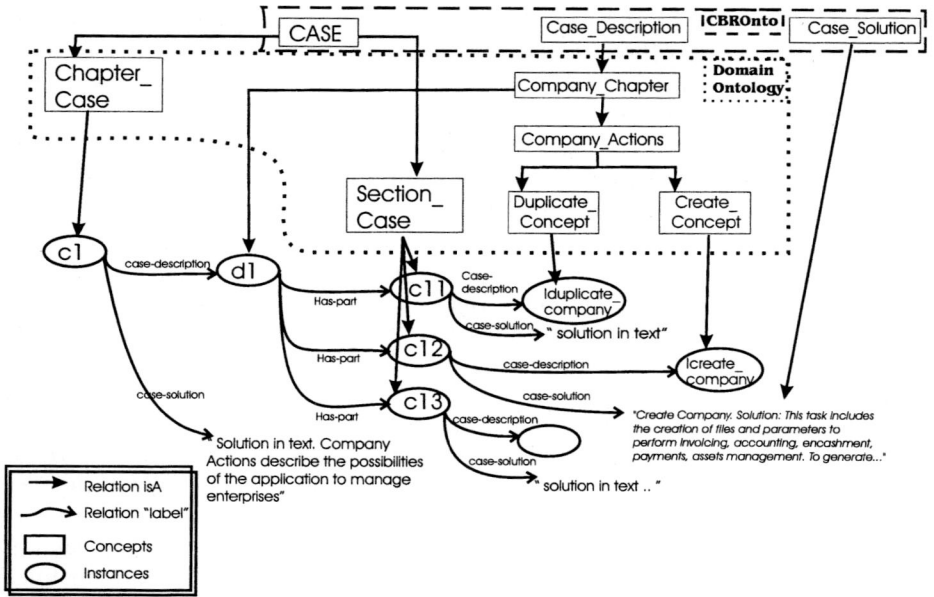

Fig. 4. Case representation structure

tem retrieves cases that are related with either of these concepts. In our example, only the *company chapter* case is retrieved (step 4). The system shows the text of the slot `solution` in the retrieved case, that is a brief description of the general functionality related with companies. In this stage the case is still very abstract and general. The system detects this situation, because the case has other cases as its components, and asks the user a more detailed specification in order to give other useful advise (step 8). As the user explains that her problem is related with the *creation* of a new company, the system travel through the ontology to retrieve the cases related with `create`. Then, the current case solution (step 13) is displayed. To refine the solution the system tries again to obtain from the user a more detailed problem description. The system consults the ontology, and, by the related concepts with the *company* concept, finds *parameters*, that is a part-of concept. It retrieves the cases under the concepts *parameters* and *company*, and shows the solution (step 18). This solutions satisfies the user (step 20). Before finishing, the system offers the possibility to get some related information in other chapters indicated by the slot *loosely related references*. Afterwards it retrieves cases of the chapters mentioned in this slot and shows the *solution* slots content to the user (step 21). There is still the possibility of giving more information by retrieving cases following the slots of more abstract or more specific concepts of those in the user description of the case, starting the reasoning cycle again.

In this process we can see one of the advantages of using DL's: the fact that cases are linked semantically allows to combine cases in many different manners. This is done in order to build an original solution to a new problem. Some cases

1. (shown to user) *Please write a description of your problem*
2. (user) *I have a problem with a new enterprise*
3. (system)   S= get-direct-instances(get-parent(enterprise))
                S= {Company, Enterprise, ..
4. (system)   retrieve(S)
               Result: c1 (instance of Chapter-Case) its description is d1 (instance of Company_Chapter)
               get-parent(get-filler(c1,case-description))= Company_Chapter
5. (system)   get-filler(c1, case-solution)
6. (shown to user) *"Company Chapter. Solution: Company Actions describe the possibilities of the application to manage enterprises..."*
7. (system)   SB= get-filler(get-filler(c1,case-description), has-part))
               SB={c11,c12,c13,c14}
               (get-parent(get-filler(c11,case-description)))∪
               (get-parent(get-filler(c12,case-description))) ∪
               (get-parent(get-filler(c13,case-description))) =
               { Duplicate_Concept, Create_Concept, Delete_Concept }
8. (shown to user) *If you describe more your query I can be more specific? Might be a problem with some of the tasks : Create, Duplicate, Delete?*
9. (user)   Yes, my problem is in the insertion of a new enterprise
10. (system)   S= get-direct-instances(get-parent(insertion))
                S= {insert, create, ..
11. (system)   retrieve(create)
                Result: c12 (instance of Section_Case) its description is icreate_company (instance of Create_Concept)
12. (system)   get-filler(c12, case-solution)
13. (shown to user) *"Create Company. Solution: This task includes the creation of files and parameters to perform invoicing, accounting, encashment, payments, assets management. To generate..."*
14. (shown to user) *Is your problem solved?*
15. (user)   No
16. (shown to user) *Please, describe your problem*
17. (user)   *I have problems with the parameters of the enterprise*
18. (system)   retrieve (parameters) ∩ retrieve(create)
19. (shown to user) *Solution: ... Is your problem solved?*
20. (user) Yes
21. (shown to user) *Do you need more help, like any related information with the topic?*
22. (user) Yes
......

Fig. 5. Example of user interaction

of the solution are associated with concepts that has semantic relationships with the actual problem description concepts. Therefore this new solution was not part of the knowledge used to generate the case base, but deduced from the semantics of the descriptions.

3.4 Case Generation Process

Authoring cases is a very expensive task, there have been many projects to generate them automatically with several well-known problems such as: incompleteness, obtaining cases with a partial coverage of the domain; lack of precision and efficiency. This last issue refers to facts such as cases that are not representative of the real stereotyped situations and generation of irrelevant, inaccurate or inconsistent cases. We made an effort to overcome these problems in our approach.

Since CBROnto and the domain ontology contain all the concepts and relationships or slots that maybe used to build the cases, the case generation will consist on filling the case structure with the correct knowledge. To perform this consists on the creation of the right instances of the adequate concepts and their relationships with other instances.

As we have described in Section 2, from the several written materials available the useful sources of knowledge have been the on-line help manuals and the historic database. Each application has its help manual with 27 chapters,each of them in a separate file in Microsoft Word format. After their study, we delimited the problem to processing the online manuals because these characteristics:

- The user questions, i.e. our problem domain, about the functionality of the applications are the 80 % of the call topics.
- The help manual covers the functionality of the applications.
- The description of the problems in the questions is mainly related to the chapter titles of the manuals or, if it is more detailed, to the section or subsection titles.
- The content of the chapters and the sections represent the solutions to the problems.

The overall process has two main tasks:the first one is, for each element in the document structure -chapter, section, sub section- to find the right place in the ontology through a semantic navigation process guided by the concepts in the title of the element. The second one has two subtasks, one is to create the instances of those concepts and the other is to create the relationships with related concepts by an assignation of these instances to the roles or slots of the correct instances of the related concepts. This last subtask needs to know the roles where to create the relationships that are in the ontologies. It is guided by the roles or slots defined in the ontologies depending on the type of concept.

We describe this process with an example of the description and solution slots, whose final result is depicted in the Fig. 4. Although this is an oversimplification, it gives an overview of the process:

At the beginning of the chapter we get its title that is looked up in the domain ontology `"concept-synonyms, concept?"`. It is correct because *Company-Chapter* exists. After that, two instances are created: an instance d1 of that title `"add-concept-assertion"` and an instance c1of *Chapter-Case*. Then both are linked by the *Case-Description* slot of the latter `"(define-primitive-role define-primitive-attribute)"`. It is created a *Case-Solution* of c1 with the text found following the title until the next section title. This text is considered the solution of that case at very abstract level.

The process with the section or a subsection is very similar to the chapter one. The section title is looked up in the domain ontology, *Company-Actions* is found. Because the section has subsections, the process continues walking down the document structure until the first subsection title is found, *Duplicated-concept*, it is looked up in the domain ontology. Then, since this case has not more subcases, this title is the most detailed description of it and is assigned to the slot *Case-Description* of a newly created instance c11 of *Section-Case*. And c11 is subcase of d1, so c11 is linked to it using the slot *has-part*. The *Loosely related References* slot is filled when concepts of titles of one chapter or section, appear in other chapters or sections titles.

There is a preprocess of the documents to transform them to an adequate XML format, we use the program Doc2net from Logictran. To transverse the XML document structure we process the tags with a parser JAXP. And the reasoning tasks of the ontologies are performed with COLIBRI/CBROnto that calls a DL's reasoner, Racer. The functions between parenthesis are of Racer.

There is a subsequent refinement phase that takes into account the problem of precision and efficiency of cases. Using the historic database as a log of real topics of the users questions, we filter those generated cases that never have been consulted and put them on a secondary case base. It still maybe used when the main case base fails.

4 Conclusions and Further Work

In this paper we describe our experience with a real case study: a CBR Help-Desk system where the specific knowledge in the cases is complemented with general conceptual structures.

Using IR techniques we have defined a lightweight ontology that is used as the terminology around which the case base is embedded. In this paper we mainly tackle the task of the automatic acquisition of the case base from semi-structured text documents in XML format and the vocabulary of the lightweight domain ontology.

We have used COLIBRI to assist during the design of the knowledge intensive CBR system. We have used Protégé 2.0.1 to edit and export ontologies to OWL, a new standard based on Description Logics, that eases the reasoning tasks, and have been proven to be useful to formalize aspects of representation and reasoning in CBR systems.

Our solution proposes processing the structure of the documents to define the case structure, and using the content of the different sections to populate the case base. We have made an effort to overcome the main problems associated with case authoring, mainly incompleteness, obtaining cases with a partial coverage of the domain; lack of precision and efficiency.

We facilitate the case structure authoring tasks by proposing a framework to represent cases that is based on the DLs instance definition language and the CBROnto terminology. Besides, we define a reasoning system that works with such representations. CBROnto provides a semantic CBR terminology to define cases structures and expresses (using classification) domain terminology in CBR terms.

CBROnto and the domain ontology contain all the concepts and relationships or slots that maybe used to build the cases. The case generation will consist on filling the case structure with the correct knowledge. To perform this consists on the creation of the right instances of the adequate concepts and their relationships with other instances.

DLs reasoning mechanisms helps the system to dynamically define the questions of a conversation with the user during the CBR processes.

As further work, we first want to include learning in the CBR cycle. This new process will allow the inclusion of new cases based on the new problems solved by the system and the conversations with the user. Besides we want to formally give results about the completeness and precision of the case base, that have been informally proved by now.

References

1. Bechhofer, S., Moller, R. and Crowther, P. 2003. "The DIG Description Logic Interface", Description Logics 2003, CEUR Workshop Proceedings.
2. Bechhofer, S., van Harmelen, F., Hendler, J., Horrocks, I., McGuinness, D., Patel-Schneider, P.F., and Stein, A., "OWL Web Ontology Language Reference", "W3C http://www.w3.org/TR/2004/REC-owl-ref-20040210/", February 2004.
3. Díaz-Agudo, B., González-Calero, P.A., 2000: "An Architecture for Knowledge Intensive CBR Systems". In *Advances in Case-Based Reasoning (EWCBR 2000)* (Blanzieri, E., Portinale, L., eds.), Springer-Verlag.
4. Díaz-Agudo, B., González-Calero, P.A., 2001: "A Declarative Similarity Framework for Knowledge Intensive CBR". In *Procs. of the (ICCBR 2001)*.
5. Díaz Agudo, B., González Calero, P.A., 2002. "CBROnto: A Task/Method Ontology for CBR", Procs. of the 15th International FLAIRS 2002 Conference, ISBN: 1-57735-141-X, AAAI Press, USA
6. Díaz Agudo, B., González Calero, P.A., 2003. Knowledge Intensive CBR through Ontologies. *Expert Update* Vol. 6, 1, pp. 44-54 British Computer Society ISSN: 1465-4091
7. Gómez Gauchía, H., Díaz Agudo, B., González Calero, P.A., 2004. "A Pragmatic Methodology for Conceptualization with two layered Knowledge Representation: a case study." submitted to 12th International Conference on Conceptual Structures: Conceptual Structures at Work.
8. Volker Haarslev and Ralf Möller, 2003. "RACER User s Guide and Reference Manual Version 1.7.7", Concordia University and Univ. of Appl. Sciences in Wedel.
9. J. Gennari and M. A. Musen and R. W. Fergerson and W. E. Grosso and M. Crubézy and H. Eriksson and N. F. Noy and S. W. Tu, The Evolution of Protégé: An Environment for Knowledge-Based Systems Development, Stanford University, 2002.
10. Salotti S. & Ventos V., 1998: "Study and Formalization of a CBR System using a Description Logic". In *Advances in CBR (EWCBR'98)* (Smyth B. & Cunningham P., eds.), Springer-Verlag.
11. Simoudis E., Miller, J., 1991. The Application of CBR to Help Desk Applications. Proceedings of the DARPA Case-Based Reasoning Workshop, 1991.

TempoExpress, a CBR Approach to Musical Tempo Transformations

Maarten Grachten, Josep Lluís Arcos, and Ramon López de Mántaras

IIIA, Artificial Intelligence Research Institute,
CSIC, Spanish Council for Scientific Research,
Campus UAB, 08193 Bellaterra, Catalonia, Spain
{maarten,arcos,mantaras}@iiia.csic.es
http://www.iiia.csic.es

Abstract. In this paper, we describe a CBR system for applying musically acceptable tempo transformations to monophonic audio recordings of musical performances. Within the tempo transformation process, the expressivity of the performance is adjusted in such a way that the result sounds natural for the new tempo. A case base of previously performed melodies is used to infer the appropriate expressivity. Tempo transformation is one of the audio post-processing tasks manually done in audio-labs. Automatizing this process may, therefore, be of industrial interest.

1 Introduction

In this paper we describe a CBR system, *TempoExpress*, that automatically performs musically acceptable tempo transformations. This paper significantly extends previous work [1], that addressed the process of performance annotation, a basic step to construct the cases needed in the CBR system described now.

The problem of changing the tempo of a musical performance is not as trivial as it may seem. When a musician performs a musical piece at different tempos, the performances are not just time-scaled versions of each other, as if the same performance were played back at different speeds. Together with the changes of tempo, variations in musical expression are made [3]. Such variations do not only affect the timing of the notes, but can involve for example the addition or deletion of ornamentations, or the consolidation/fragmentation of notes. Apart from the tempo, other domain specific factors seem to play an important role in the way a melody is performed, such as meter, and phrase structure.

Tempo transformation is one of the audio post-processing tasks manually done in audio-labs. Automatizing this process may, therefore, be of industrial interest.

In section 2, we will present the overall structure of *TempoExpress*. In section 3, we briefly explain the processes involved in case and problem representation. Section 4 describes the crucial problem solving phases of the CBR mechanism, retrieval and reuse. In section 5, some initial results are presented. Conclusions and future work are presented in section 6.

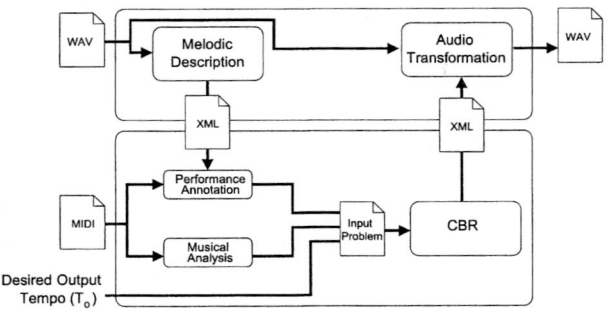

Fig. 1. Overview of the basic *TempoExpress* components

2 Overview of *TempoExpress*

TempoExpress consists of three main parts and two additional parts. The main parts are the melodic description module, the CBR problem solving module, and the audio transformation module. The additional parts are the performance annotation module and the musical analysis module (see figure 1). The melodic description module generates a melodic description of the input recording, that represents information about the performance on a musical level. This information is used together with the score of the performed melody (as a MIDI file), and the desired tempo of the output performance, to construct an input problem. CBR is then applied to obtain a solution for the problem in the form of a melodic description of the new performance. The audio transformation produces an audio file, based on the original audio and the new melodic description.

Since the main information in the input problem and the cases (the melodic material of the score and the annotated performance) is of sequential nature, we apply edit distance techniques in the retrieval step, as a means to assess similarities between the cases and the input problem. In the reuse step we employ constructive adaptation [13], a reuse method for synthetic tasks. This method constructs a solution to a problem by searching the space of partial solutions for a complete solution that satisfies the solution requirements of the problem.

2.1 Melodic Description and Audio Transformation

The melodic description and audio transformation are not part of the research reported here. These processes are being implemented within a common research project by members of the Music Technology Group (MTG) of the Pompeu Fabra University, using signal spectral modeling techniques (see [6] for a detailed description). The output of the melodic description process (and input of the audio transformation process), is a description of the audio in *XML* format, that adheres to (and extends) the *MPEG7* standard for multimedia description [5]. This description includes information about the starting and ending of notes, their pitches and amplitudes.

3 Case/Problem Representation

In this section, we will explain the various aspects of the construction of cases from available information. To construct a case, a score (in MIDI format) is needed. This score is represented internally as a sequence of note objects, with the basic attributes like pitch, duration and temporal position. This score is analyzed automatically to obtain a more abstract representation of the melody, called I/R representation. This procedure is explained in subsection 3.1. Furthermore, an input performance at a particular tempo is needed. The performance is not stored literally, but rather a *performance annotation* is constructed to describe how the elements from the performance relate to the elements from the score. This procedure is explained in detail in [1], and is briefly reminded in subsection 3.2. The performance annotation is stored as a solution, associated to a particular input description that applies to the performance (in our case, the tempo of the performance). Lastly, the desired output tempo is also included as a part of the problem description, specifying what the solution should be like.

3.1 Music Analysis

To prepare cases, as well as the input problem, music analysis is performed on the musical score that was provided. The analysis is used in the problem solving process, for example to segment musical phrases into smaller groups of notes, and to perform retrieval of cases. The musical analysis is based on a model for melodic structure, that is explained below.

The Implication/Realization Model. Narmour [11, 12] has proposed a theory of perception and cognition of melodies, the Implication/Realization model, or I/R model. According to this theory, the perception of a melody continuously causes listeners to generate expectations of how the melody will continue. The sources of those expectations are two-fold: both innate and learned. The innate sources are 'hard-wired' into our brain and peripheral nervous system, according to Narmour, whereas learned factors are due to exposure to music as a cultural phenomenon, and familiarity with musical styles and pieces in particular. The innate expectation mechanism is closely related to the *gestalt theory* for visual perception [9]. Gestalt theory states that perceptual elements are (in the process of perception) grouped together to form a single perceived whole (a 'gestalt'). This grouping follows certain principles (*gestalt principles*). The most important principles are *proximity* (two elements are perceived as a whole when they are perceptually close), *similarity* (two elements are perceived as a whole when they have similar perceptual features, e.g. color or form, in visual perception), and *good continuation* (two elements are perceived as a whole if one is a 'good' or 'natural' continuation of the other). Narmour claims that similar principles hold for the perception of melodic sequences. In his theory, these principles take the form of *implications*: Any two consecutively perceived notes constitute a melodic interval, and if this interval is not conceived as complete, or closed, it is an *implicative interval*, an interval that implies a subsequent interval with certain characteristics. In other words, some notes are more likely to follow the two

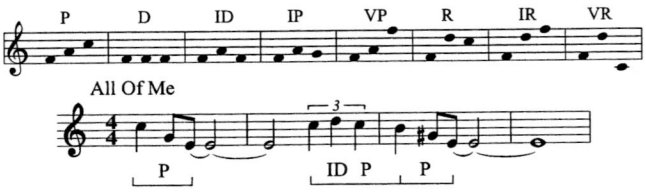

Fig. 2. Top: Eight of the basic structures of the I/R model. Bottom: First measures of All of Me, annotated with I/R structures

heard notes than others. Two main principles concern *registral direction* and *intervallic difference*. The principle of registral direction states that small intervals imply an interval in the same registral direction (a small upward interval implies another upward interval, and analogous for downward intervals), and large intervals imply a change in registral direction (a large upward interval implies a downward interval and analogous for downward intervals). The principle of intervallic difference states that a small (five semitones or less) interval implies a similarly-sized interval (plus or minus 2 semitones), and a large intervals (seven semitones or more) implies a smaller interval. The definitions of 'small', 'large', and 'similarly sized' intervals are specified by the I/R model [11].

Based on these two principles, melodic patterns can be identified that either satisfy or violate the implication as predicted by the principles. Such patterns are called *structures* and labeled to denote characteristics in terms of registral direction and intervallic difference. Eight such structures are shown in figure 2(top). For example, the P structure ('Process') is a small interval followed by another small interval (of similar size), thus satisfying both the registral direction principle and the intervallic difference principle. Similarly the IP ('Intervallic Process') structure satisfies intervallic difference, but violates registral direction.

Additional principles are assumed to hold, one of which concerns *closure*, which states that the implication of an interval is inhibited when a melody changes in direction, or when a small interval is followed by a large interval. Other factors also determine closure, like metrical position (strong metrical positions contribute to closure, rhythm (notes with a long duration contribute to closure), and harmony (resolution of dissonance into consonance contributes to closure). The closure in each of these dimensions add up to the total closure. The occurrence (and degree) of closure at a given point in the melody determines where the structures start and end. For example, on a note where strong closure appears (e.g. closure in meter, harmony and rhythm at the same time), the interval between that note and the next will not be perceived as implicative, and therefore there is no structure describing that interval. When no closure occurs at all, every interval implies a new interval, and since the structures describe two subsequent intervals, this causes a *chaining*, or overlapping of structures.

We have designed an algorithm to automate the annotation of melodies with their corresponding I/R analyses. The algorithm implements most of the 'innate' processes mentioned before. The learned processes, being less well-defined by the I/R model, are currently not included. Nevertheless, we believe that the resulting analysis have a reasonable degree of validity, since the analyses generated for melodic examples given in [11] were in many cases identical to the analyses proposed by Narmour. An example analysis is shown in figure 2(bottom). This example shows various degrees of structure chaining: the first two structures (P and ID) are not chained, due to strong closure (meter and rhythm); the second pair of structures (ID and P) are strongly chained (sharing two notes, one interval), because closure is inhibited by 'ongoing' rhythms (like triplets); the last pair of structures (P and P) are chained by one note, because of weak closure (only in meter).

3.2 Performance Annotation

In addition to the score and its musical analysis, the cases in the case base, as well as the problem specification, contain a performance of that score by a musician. The raw format of the performance is an audio file. Using the melodic description mechanism described in section 2.1, we obtain a melodic description of the audio, in XML format. This description contains a sequence of note descriptors, that describe the features like start and end times, pitch, energy of the notes, as they were detected in the audio file. In order to be informative, the sequence of note descriptors is to be mapped to the notes in the score, since this mapping expresses how the score was performed. For example, it allows us to say that a particular note was lengthened or shortened, or played early or late.

But the mapping between score notes and performed notes does not necessarily consist of just 1-to-1 mappings. Especially in jazz performances, which is the area on which we will focus, performers often favor a 'liberal' interpretation of the score. This does not only involve changes in expressive features (like lengthening/shortening durations) of the score elements as they are performed, but also omitting or adding notes. Thus, one can normally not assume that the performance contains a corresponding element for every note of the score, neither that every element in the performance corresponds to a note of the score. Taking these performance liberties into account, a description of a musical performance could take the form of a sequence of *performance events*, that represent the phenomena like note deletions or additions that occured in the performance.

From this perspective the edit distance [10] is very useful, since performance events can be mapped in a very natural way to edit operations for sequences of score and performance elements. A performance annotation can then be obtained in the form of a sequence of performance events, by constructing the optimal alignment between a score and a performance, using the edit distance. The set of performance events/edit operations we use is a slight revision of the set proposed by Arcos et al. [1]. It includes:

Transformation Representing the reproduction of a score note, possibly with several kinds of transformations, such as change of pitch, duration and temporal position

Insertion Representing the occurrence of a performance note that does not correspond to any score note

Ornamentation A special case of insertion, where the inserted note (or possibly more than one) has very short duration, and is played as a lead-in to the next note

Deletion Representing the occurrence of a score note that does not correspond to any performance note

Fragmentation Representing the reproduction of a score note by playing two or more shorter notes (adding up to the same total duration)

Consolidation Representing the reproduction of two or more score notes by playing a single longer note (whose duration equals the sum of the score note durations)

We defined the costs of these operations as functions of the note attributes (pitch, duration and onset). However, rather than fixing the relative importance of the attributes (as in [1]), we parametrized the cost functions to be able to control the importance of each of the note attributes in each of the cost functions, and the relative costs of edit operations. This setup enables us to tune the performance annotation algorithm to produce annotations that correspond to intuitive human judgment. We have used a genetic algorithm [8] to tune the parameters of the cost functions, which substantially improved the accuracy of annotation over untuned settings.

4 Problem Solving

In this section, we will explain the steps taken to transform the performance presented as input into a performance of the same score at a different tempo. The first step is the retrieval of relevant cases from the case base. In the second step, the retrieved cases are selectively used to obtain a new sequence of performance events. This sequence can then be used to modify the XML description of the performance. Based on this modified description, the original audio file is transformed to obtain the final audio of the performance at the desired tempo.

4.1 Retrieval

The goal of the retrieval step is to form a pool of relevant cases, that can possibly be used in the reuse step. This done in the following three steps: firstly, cases that don't have performances at both the input tempo and output tempo are filtered out; secondly, those cases are retrieved from the case base that have phrases that are I/R-similar to the input phrase; lastly, the retrieved phrases are segmented. The three steps are described below.

Case Filtering by Tempo. In the first step, the case base is searched for cases that have performances both at the tempo the input performance was played, and the tempo that was specified in the problem description as the desired output tempo. The matching of tempos need not be exact, since we assume that there are no drastic changes in performance due to tempo within small tempo ranges. For example, a performance played at 127 beats per minute (bpm) may serve as an example case if we want to construct a performance at 125 bpm.

I/R Based Retrieval. In the second step, the cases selected in step 1 are assessed for melodic similarity to the score specified in the problem description. In this step, the primary goal is to rule out the cases that belong to different styles of music. For example, if the score in the problem description is a ballad, we want to avoid using a bebop theme as an example case. Note that the classification of musical style based on just melodic information (or derived representations) is far from being an established issue. Nevertheless, there is some evidence [7] that the comparison of melodic material at different levels of abstraction yields different degrees of discriminatory power. For example comparing on the most concrete level (comparing individual notes) is a good way to find out which melodies in a set are nearly identical to a particular target melody. But if the set of melodies does not contain a melody nearly identical to the target, the similarity values using this measure are not very informative, since they are highly concentrated in a single value. On the other hand, comparisons based on more abstract descriptions of the melody (e.g. melodic contour, or I/R analyses), tend to produce a distribution of similarity values that is spread out through the spectrum more equally. Thus, these measures tell us in a more informative way *how* similar two melodies are (with respect to the other melodies in the set), even if they are considerably different. As a consequence, a melodic similarity measure based on an abstract representation of the melody seems a more promising approach to separate different musical styles.

We use the I/R analysis of the melodies to assess similarities. The measure used is an edit distance. The edit distance measures the minimal cost of transforming one sequence of objects into another, given a set of edit operations (like insertion, deletion, and replacement), and associated costs. We have defined edit operations and their corresponding costs for sequences of I/R structures (see [7] for more details). The case base is ranked according to similarity with the target melody, and the subset of cases with similarity values above a certain threshold are selected. The resulting set of cases will contain phrases that are roughly similar to the input score.

Segmentation. In this step, the melodies that were retrieved in the second step are segmented. The motivation for this twofold. Firstly, using complete melodic phrases as the working unit for adaptation is inconvenient, since a successful adaptation will then require that the case base contains phrases that are nearly identical as a whole to the input phrase. Searching for similar phrase *segments* will increase the probability of finding a good match. Secondly, the segmentation is motivated by the intuition that the way a particular note is performed does not only depend of the attributes of the note in isolation, but also on the musical context of the note. Therefore, rather than trying to reuse solutions in a note-by-note fashion, it seems more reasonable to perform the reuse segment by segment. This implies that the performance of a retrieved note is only reused for a note of the input phrase if their musical contexts are similar.

Melodic segmentation has been addressed in a number of studies (e.g. [16][2]), with the aim of detecting smaller musical structures (like motifs) within a phrase. Many of them take a data driven approach, using information like note interonset intervals (IOI) and metrical positions to determine the segment boundaries. Our

Fig. 3. Segmentation of the first phrase of 'All of Me', according to I/R structures. The segments correspond to single I/R structures, or sequences of structures if they are strongly chained (see subsection 3.1)

method of segmentation is based on the I/R representation of the melodies. This may seem quite different from the approach mentioned above, but in essence it is similar. The melodies are split at every point where the overlap of two I/R structures is less than two notes (see subsection 3.1). This overlap is determined by the level of closure, which is on its turn determined by factors like metrical posisiton and IOI. The resulting segments usually correspond to the musical motifs that constitute the musical phrase, and are used as the units for the stepwise construction of the output performance. As an example, figure 3 displays the segmentation of the first phrase of 'All of Me' (the complete phrase is shown in figure 2).

4.2 Reuse

In the reuse step a performance of the input score is constructed at the desired tempo, based on the input performance and the set of retrieved phrase segments. This step is realized using constructive adaptation [13], a technique for reuse that constructs a solution by a best-first search through the space of partial solutions. In this subsection, we will first explain briefly how the reuse step can in general be realized as best-first search, and then we will explain how we implemented the functions necessary to make the search-algorithm operational in the context of performance transformation.

In constructive adaptation, partial solutions of the problem are represented as states. Furthermore, a function HG must be defined for generating a set of successor states for a given state. The state space that emerges from this function and the state that represents the empty solution (generated by a function Initial-State), is then searched for a complete solution that satisfies certain constraints (through a function Goal-Test). The resulting state is transformed to a real solution by a function SAC. The order of expansion of states is controlled by a function HO that orders the states in a best-first manner. The search process is expressed in pseudo code below.

We explain our implementations of the functions Initial-State, HG, HO, Goal-Test, and SAC below.

Initial-State. The function Initial-State returns a state that is used as the starting point for the search. It takes the input problem description (the score, analysis, input-performance, and desired output tempo) as an argument. In our case, the state contains a sequence of score segments, and a slot for storing the corresponding performance segments (none of which is filled in the initial state, obviously). Furthermore, there is a slot that stores the quality of the

```
Initialize OS = (list (Initial-State Pi))
Function CA(OS)
    Case (null OS) then No-Solution
    Case (Goal-Test (first OS)) then (SAC (first OS))
    Case else
        Let SS = (HG (first OS))
        Let OS = (HO (append SS (rest OS)))
        (CA OS)
```

Fig. 4. The search process of constructive adaptation expressed in pseudo code. Functions HG and HO are Hypotheses Generation and Hypotheses Ordering. Variables OS and SS are the lists of Open States and Successor States. The function SAC maps the solution state into the configuration of the solution. The function Initial-State maps the input problem description Pi into a state. From Plaza and Arcos [13]

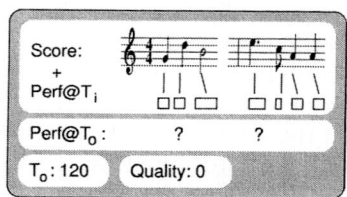

Fig. 5. Example of an initial state in Constructive Adaptation. T_i is the tempo of the input performance; T_o is the desired output tempo

partially constructed performance, as a number. We will explain the derivation of this number in the next subsection. Figure 5 shows the initial state for a short musical fragment (containing two segments).

Hypothesis-Generation (HG). The Hypothesis-Generation function takes a state as an argument and tries to find a sequence performance events for one of the unprocessed score segments in the state. We will illustrate this procedure step by step, using the first segment of the initial state in figure 5 as an example. The steps are presented graphically in figure 7 (at the last page of this paper).

The *first step* is to find the segment in the pool of retrieved melodic segments that is most similar to the input score segment. The similarity is assessed by calculating the edit distance between the segments (the edit distance now operates on notes rather than on I/R structures, to have a finer grained similarity assessment). A mapping between the input score segment and the best matching retrieved segment is made.

In the *second step*, the performance annotation events (see subsection 3.2 and [1]) corresponding to the relevant tempos are extracted from the retrieved segment case and the input problem specification (both the input tempo T_i and the output tempo T_o for the retrieved segment case, and just T_i from the input problem specification).

The *third step* consists in relating the annotation events of the retrieved segment to the notes of the input segment, according to the mapping between the input segment and the retrieved segment, that was constructed in the first step. For the notes in the input segment that were mapped to one or more notes in the retrieved segment, we now obtain the tempo transformation from T_i to T_o that was realized for the corresponding notes in the retrieved segment. It is also possible that some notes of the input segment could not be matched to any notes of the retrieved segment. For such notes, the retrieved segment can not be used to obtain annotation events for the output performance. Currently, these gaps are filled up by directly transforming the annotation events of the input performance (at tempo T_i) to fit the output tempo T_o (by scaling the duration of the events to fit the tempo). In the future, more sophisticated heuristics may be used.

In the *fourth step*, the annotation events for the performance of the input score at tempo T_o are generated. This is done in a note by note fashion, using rules that specify which annotation events can be inferred for the output performance of the input score at T_o, based on annotation events of the input performance, and the annotation events of the retrieved performances (at T_i and T_o). To illustrate this, let us explain the inference of the Fragmentation event for the last note of the input score segment (B)in figure 7. This note was matched to the last two notes (A, A) of the retrieved segment. These two notes were played at tempo T_i as a single long note (denoted by the Consolidation event), and played separately at tempo T_o. The note of the input segment was also played as a single note at T_i (denoted by a Transformation event rather than a Consolidation event, since it corresponds to only one note in the score). To imitate the effect of the tempo transformation of the retrieved segment (one note at tempo T_i and two notes at tempo T_o), the note in the input segment is played as two shorter notes at tempo T_o, which is denoted by a Fragmentation event (F).

In this way, adaptation rules were defined, that describe how the tempo transformation of retrieved elements can be translated to the current case. In figure 7, two such rules are shown. If the antecedent part matches the constellation of annotation events, the tempo transformation in the consequent part can be applied. It can occur that the set of rules contains no applicable rule for a particular constellation, in particular when the performances at T_i of the retrieved note and the input note are too different. For example, if the score note is played as a Transformation event, but the retrieved note is deleted in the performance at T_i, then the performances are too different to make an obvious translation. In this case, the annotation events from the input performance are transformed in the same way as in the case where no corresponding note from the retrieved segment could be found (see the third step of this subsection).

The mismatch between the input segment and the retrieved segment and the inability to find a matching adaptation rule obstructs the use of case knowledge to solve the problem and forces *TempoExpress* to resort to default mechanisms. This will affect the quality of the solution. To reflect this, the value of the quality slot of the state (see figure 5) is calculated as the number of input score notes for which annotation events could be inferred from retrieved cases, divided by the total number of notes processed so far (that is, the sum of all notes in the processed input segments, including the current input segment).

Hypothesis-Ordering (HO). The Hypothesis-Ordering function takes a list of states (each one with its partial solution) and orders them so that the states with the most promising partial solutions come first. For this ordering, the quality value of the states is used. In our current implementation, the quality value is only determined by one factor, roughly the availability of appropriate cases. Another factor that should ideally influence the quality of the states is the 'coherence' of the solution. For example, if the notes at the end of one segment were anticipated in time (as a possible effect of a Transformation event), then anticipation of the first notes of the next segment will not have the typical effect of surprise, since the listener will experience the performance as being shifted forward in time, instead of hearing a note earlier than expected. We are currently incorporating the detection and evaluation of such phenomena into the Hypothesis-Ordering function, so that this functionality will soon be available.

Goal-Test. The Goal-Test function is called on the best state of an ordered list of states to test if the solution of that state is complete and satisfies the constraints imposed upon the desired solution. The completeness of the solution is tested by checking if all segments of the input score have a corresponding segment in the performance annotation for the output tempo. The constraints on the solution are imposed by requiring a minimal quality value of the state. In our case, where the quality value represents the ratio of notes for which annotation events were obtained using retrieved cases (a value between 0 and 1), the quality value is required to be superior or equal to 0.8.

State-to-Solution (SAC). The State-to-Solution function takes the state that passed the goal-test and returns a solution to the input problem. This step consists in building a complete performance annotation from the annotation events for the score segments (basically concatenation of the events). The new performance annotation is used to adapt the XML description of the original audio file, by changing attribute values, and possibly deleting and inserting new note descriptors. Finally, the audio transformation module (which is under development) generates a new audio file, based on the new XML description.

4.3 Retain

When the solution that was generated is satisfying to the listener, and when the quality of the solution is high (that is, default adaptation operations have been scarcely used, or not at all), it is retained as a case that includes the input score, the input performance, and the newly generated performance.

5 Results

Although the *TempoExpress* is operational, there are some components that need improvement. In particular, the case base is still of limited size (it contains ten different phrases from three different songs, played at approximately ten different tempos). Nevertheless, some good results were obtained for some melodies. We

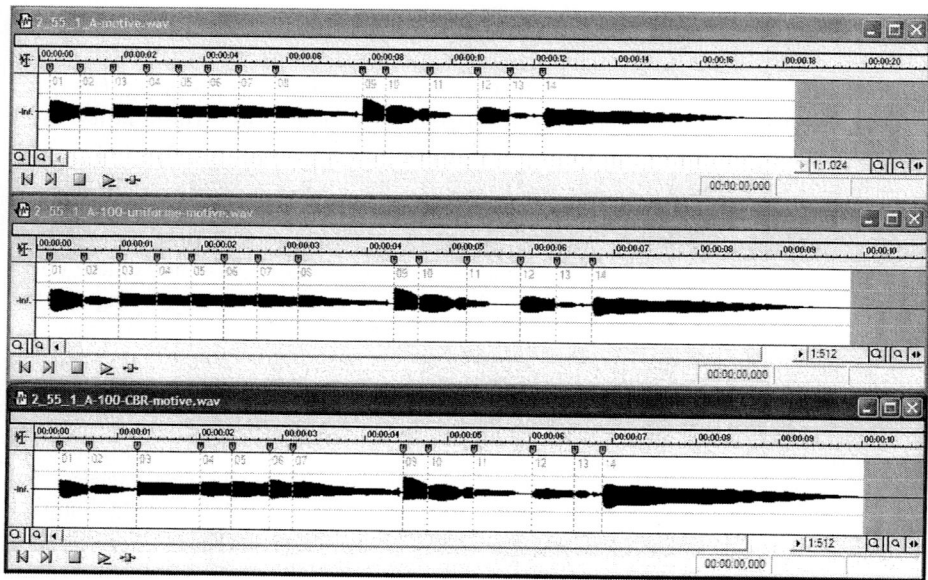

Fig. 6. Audio signals of a part of the first phrase of *Once I Loved*. The upper view shows original sound file (55 bpm), the middle view shows a tempo transformation by uniform time stretching, and the lower view shows a tempo transformation using the CBR system. The vertical lines indicate the positions of the note onsets

have performed a tempo transformation of a phrase from *Once I Loved* (A.C. Jobim). The original performance of the phrase was at a tempo of 55 beats per minute (bpm), and using the CBR system, the performance was transformed to a tempo of 100 bpm. For comparison, the tempo transformation was also realized using uniform time stretching of the original sound file (i.e. the durations of all notes in the original performance are lengthened by a single scaling factor, while leaving the pitches of the notes unchanged). Figure 6 shows the audio signals of the original sound, and the two transformations. Notable differences between the two transformations occur in the notes 3 to 9 (the numbered vertical lines in the views indicate the start of the notes). Note that in the CBR transformation, the eighth note is missing, due to a consolidation. Furthermore, those notes have considerable variations of duration in the CBR transformation, whereas they are more regularly played in the uniformly time stretched version (as in the original), making the latter sound somewhat mechanical at the faster tempo. Slight changes in the dynamics can also be observed, e.g in note 1 and 12. The sound files from the example are publicly available in mp3 format, through the world-wide web[1].

---

[1] http://www.iiia.csic.es/~maarten/cbr/tempo-transformation

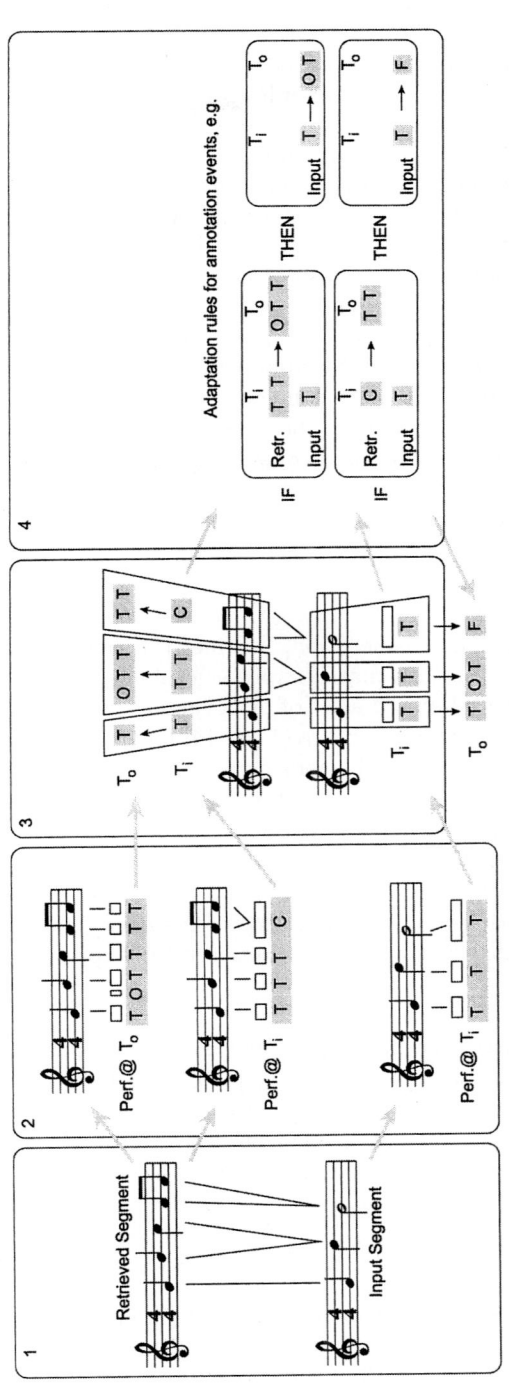

Fig. 7. The process of hypothesis generation. In step 1, a mapping is made between the input score segment and the most similar segment from the pool of retrieved segments. In step 2, the performance annotations for the tempos T_i and T_o are collected. In step 3, the performance annotation events are grouped according to the mapping between the input score and retrieved score. In step 4, the annotation events are processed through a set of rules to obtain the annotation events for a performance at tempo T_o of the input score segment

6 Conclusions and Future Work

In this paper, we have described *TempoExpress*, an application for applying musically acceptable tempo transformations to monophonic audio recordings of musical performances. *TempoExpress* has a rich description of the musical expressivity of the performances, that includes not only timing deviations of performed score notes, but also represents more rigorous kinds of expressivity such as note ornamentation, and consolidation. Within the tempo transformation process, the expressivity of the performance is adjusted in such a way that the result sounds natural for the new tempo. A case base of previously performed melodies is used to infer the appropriate expressivity.

Future work includes elaborating the reuse step, to put more musical constraints on the way in which partial solutions can be combined. Also, we intend to add more cases to the case base, to broaden the range of problems that can be satisfyingly solved by the system. Finally, a more thorough evaluation of the results is necessary. This could be done for example by quantitatively comparing transformed performances to performances at the final tempo by a musician, or by a blinded evaluation of performances by a panel.

6.1 Related Work

In the field of expressive music performance generation, Widmer [17] has taken a data mining approach to discover rules that match expressive phenomena to musical patterns. Friberg et al. [4] have proposed a set of performance rules that was constructed with the help of musical experts. Serra et al. [14] have applied a CBR approach to expressive music performance. They designed *SaxEx*, a system for adding expressiveness to inexpressive performances of melodies. Some design choices in *TempoExpress* were adapted from this application. Suzuki has recently presented *Kagurame*, a CBR system for the expressive performance of a musical score [15]. All of the above approaches either generate expressive performances only based on a score, or apply a transformation to an inexpressive performance (*SaxEx*). Thus, as opposed to *TempoExpress*, they don't consider any expressive information as input to the system.

Acknowledgments. This research has been partially supported by the Spanish Ministry of Science and Technology under the project TIC 2003-07776-C2-02 "CBR-ProMusic: Content-based Music Processing using CBR" and EU-FEDER funds. The authors acknowledge the Music Technology Group of the Pompeu Fabra University for providing the melodic description and audio transformation modules.

References

1. J. Ll. Arcos, M. Grachten, and R. López de Mántaras. Extracting performer's behaviors to annotate cases in a CBR system for musical tempo transformations. In *Proceedings of the Fifth International Conference on Case-Based Reasoning (ICCBR-03)*, 2003.

2. E. Cambouropoulos. Melodic cue abstraction, similarity and category formation: a formal model. *Music Perception*, 18(3):347–370, 2001.
3. P. Desain and H. Honing. Tempo curves considered harmful. In "Time in contemporary musical thought" J. D. Kramer (ed.), Contemporary Music Review. 7(2), 1993.
4. A. Friberg. Generative rules for music performance: A formal description of a rule system. *Computer Music Journal*, 15 (2):56–71, 1991.
5. E. Gómez, F. Gouyon, P. Herrera, and X. Amatriain. Using and enhancing the current mpeg-7 standard for a music content processing tool. In *Proceedings of Audio Engineering Society, 114th Convention*, Amsterdam, The Netherlands, 2003.
6. E. Gómez, A. Klapuri, and B. Meudic. Melody description and extraction in the context of music content processing. *Journal of New Music Research*, 32(1), 2003.
7. M. Grachten, J. Ll. Arcos, and R. López de Mántaras. A comparison of different approaches to melodic similarity, 2002. Second International Conference on Music and Artificial Intelligence (ICMAI).
8. M. Grachten, J. Ll. Arcos, and R. López de Mántaras. Evolutionary optimization of music performance annotation. In *CMMR 2004*, Lecture Notes in Computer Science. Springer, 2004. To appear.
9. K. Koffka. *Principles of Gestalt Psychology*. Routledge & Kegan Paul, London, 1935.
10. V. I. Levenshtein. Binary codes capable of correcting deletions, insertions and reversals. *Soviet Physics Doklady*, 10:707–710, 1966.
11. E. Narmour. *The Analysis and cognition of basic melodic structures : the implication-realization model*. University of Chicago Press, 1990.
12. E. Narmour. *The Analysis and cognition of melodic complexity: the implication-realization model*. University of Chicago Press, 1992.
13. E. Plaza and J. Ll. Arcos. Constructive adaptation. In Susan Craw and Alun Preece, editors, *Advances in Case-Based Reasoning*, number 2416 in Lecture Notes in Artificial Intelligence, pages 306–320. Springer-Verlag, 2002.
14. X. Serra, R. Lopez de Mantaras, and J. Ll. Arcos. Saxex : a case-based reasoning system for generating expressive musical performances. In *Proceedings of the International Computer Music Conference 1997*, pages 329–336, 1997.
15. T. Suzuki. The second phase development of case based performance rendering system "Kagurame". In *Working Notes of the IJCAI-03 Rencon Workshop*, pages 23–31, 2003.
16. D. Temperley. *The Cognition of Basic Musical Structures*. MIT Press, Cambridge, Mass., 2001.
17. G. Widmer. Machine discoveries: A few simple, robust local expression principles. *Journal of New Music Research*, 31(1):37–50, 2002.

Case Acquisition and Case Mining for Case-Based Object Recognition

Silke Jänichen and Petra Perner

Institute of Computer Vision and applied Computer Sciences,
IBaI, Körnerstr. 10, 04107 Leipzig
ibaiperner@aol.com
www.ibai-institut.de

Abstract. Model-based image recognition requires a general model of the object that should be detected in an image. In many applications such models are not known a-priori instead of they must be learnt from examples. Real world applications such as the recognition of biological objects in images cannot be solved by one general model but a lot of different models are necessary in order to handle the natural variations of the appearance of the objects of a certain class. Therefore we are talking about case-based object recognition. In this paper we describe how the shape of an object can be extracted from images and input into a case description. These acquired cases we mine for more general shapes so that at the end a case base of shapes can be constructed and applied for case-based object recognition.

Keywords: Case Acquisition, Case Mining, Case-Based Object Recognition

1 Introduction

Model-based object recognition is used to detect objects of interest on a complex background where thresholding-based image segmentation methods fail. The basis for such a recognition method is a good model of the object that should be recognized. Usually this method is applied to applications where the general appearance of the object is known or can be directly extracted from the image content. New applications such as biomedical applications require object recognition methods for segmentation but the object of interest is of great variation in appearance and cannot be modeled by a single model. A set of cases is necessary which describes the variation in appearance of the object on different abstraction levels so that it is possible to detect an object with a sufficiently high recognition score. That is the point where case-based object recognition comes in charge. Such a method is based on a case base filled up with different appearance cases of the objects of one class. A case is comprised of the contour points of an object and the case ID. The recognition is done by retrieving similar cases from the case base and matching these cases against the image. Objects whose pixel points match the case points with a high recognition score are marked in the actual image.

Related work is described in Section 2. The image material used for this study is presented in Section 3. We describe how image information can be extracted from an image and mapped into a case description in Section 4. In order to learn groups of shapes that can be generalized by a more general shape we pair-wise align and rescale the shapes and calculate the dissimilarity between the shape instances, see Section 5. Based on the pair-wise dissimilarity values we cluster the shape instances into groups (see Section 6) and calculate prototypes for each group (see Section 7). These prototypes are then stored into the case base of the case-based object recognition system [26] and they are used for object recognition in new images. Results on the acquisition and learning process are given in Section 8. Finally we give conclusions in Section 9. The presented methods are implemented in our program named *CACM* Version 1.0.

2 Related Work

The acquisition of object shapes from real images is still an essential problem of image segmentation. For automated image segmentation often low-level methods, such as edge detection [2] and region growing [3], [4], are used to extract the outline of objects from an image. Low-level methods yield good results if the objects have conspicuous boundaries and are not occluded. In the case of complex backgrounds and occluded or noisy objects, the shape acquisition may result in strong distorted and incorrect cases.

Therefore segmentation is often performed manually at the cost of a very subjective, time-consuming procedure. Landmark coordinates [5], [6], [7], [8] can be assigned by an expert to some biologically significant points of an organism. If there are objects with an absence of anatomical landmarks, it is a common procedure to determine landmark points according to the defined mathematical or geometrical properties of the objects. However in some applications it is impossible or insufficient to describe the shape of an object only by means of these landmarks because important characteristics of the shape might be lost. To increase the total of landmarks it is usual to trace the complete outline of an object manually and subsequently determine corresponding points on each shape [10]. New semi-automatic approaches were developed [11], [12] for interactive image segmentation. These approaches use live-wire segmentation algorithms which are based on a graph search to locate mathematically optimal boundaries in the image. If the user moves the mouse cursor in the proximity of an object edge, the labeled outline is automatically adjusted to the boundary.

Based on an acquired set of shape instances it is usually desirable to describe and compare deformations and distances between these shapes. The problems of shape spaces and distances have been intensively studied by Kendall [5] and Bookstein [6] in a statistical theory of shape. All of them assume that point correspondences between two sets of landmarks are already known. However at the beginning of many applications this condition is not hold and various approaches are made to determine corresponding points for the automated generation of statistical shape models. Hill et al. [10] presented an interesting framework for the automated landmark identification on a set of two-dimensional, polygonal shapes. They assume that all acquired shapes are similar so that, proportionately, the arc path-lengths between consecutive points are equal. Bookstein [13] applied landmark methods to continuous contours represented as thin-plate splines, but his approach is not completely automatic. The Softassign Procrustes Matching algorithm [15] solves the correspondence problem using deterministic annealing. This algorithm works robust with respect to outlier identification and noise, but is it also a computationally-expensive procedure. Belongie et al. [14] found correspondences between points on the basis of the shape context descriptor. Latecki et al. [17] used a tangent space representation of shapes to determine correspondences of visually significant parts and to define a shape similarity measure.

Another interesting method was presented by Mokhtarian et al. [18] who calculate a similarity measure between two exemplars based on their maxima in the curvature scale-space. But especially in cases of noisy or distorted cases the analysis of these feature-based shape representations is problematic.

3 Material Used for This Study

The materials we used for our study are fungal strains that are naturally 3-D objects but that are acquired in a 2-D image. These objects have a great variance in the appearance of the shape of the object because of their nature and the imaging constraints. Six fungal strains representing species with different spore types were used for the study. Table 1 shows one of the acquired images for each fungal strain.

Table 1. Images of Six Different Fungi Strains

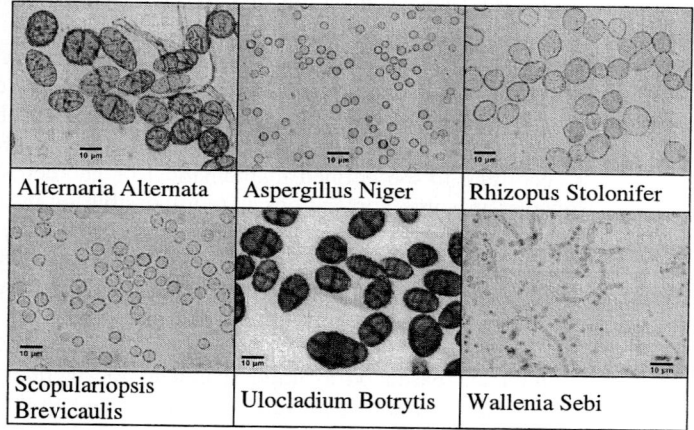

Alternaria Alternata	Aspergillus Niger	Rhizopus Stolonifer
Scopulariopsis Brevicaulis	Ulocladium Botrytis	Wallenia Sebi

The strains were obtained from the fungal stock collection of the Institute of Microbiology, University of Jena/ Germany and from the culture collection of JenaBios GmbH. All strains were cultured in Petri dishes on 2% malt extract agar (Merck) at 24°C in an incubation chamber for at least 14 days. For microscopy fungal spores were scrapped off from the agar surface and placed on a microscopic slide in a drop of lactic acid. Naturally hyaline spores were additionally stained with lactophenol cotton blue (Merck). A database of images from the spores of these species was produced.

4 Acquisition of Shape Cases

Case-based object recognition can be done based on the case model or based on the case contour. We are considering the contour of an object S but not the appearance of the object inside the contour. Therefore we want to elicit from the real image the object shape S_C represented by a set of n_{S_C} boundary points $s_i(x, y)$, $i = 1, 2, \ldots, n_{S_C}$.

We obtain the set of boundary pixels by implementing into our program a function that allows the user to mark the contour S_C of an object S by moving the mouse cursor of the computer or by moving an electronic pen over a digitizer tablet. Notice that the sampled points are not required to be landmark coordinates or curvature extrema. The user starts labeling the contour S_C of object S at an arbitrary pixel $s_i(x,y)$, $i = 1,2,\ldots,j,\ldots,n_{S_C}$ of the contour S_C. After having traced the complete object the labeling ends at a pixel $s_j(x,y)$ in the 8-neighbourhood of $s_i(x,y)$. To obtain the complete set S_C of all boundary pixels we need to ensure that the contour is closed which means $s_j(x,y)$ is a direct neighbour of $s_i(x,y)$. Therefore we insert missing boundary pixels using the Bresenham [20] procedure. Figure 1 presents a screenshot from our program *CACM* with three labeled shapes of the strain Ulocladium Botrytis with their coordinates on the right side of the screenshot.

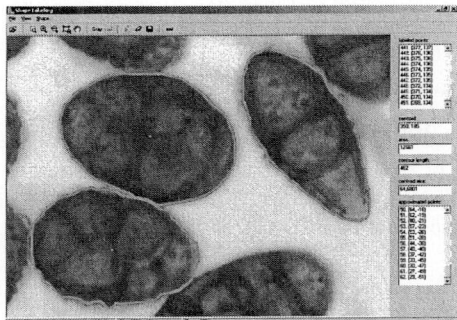

Fig. 1. Labeled and Approximated Shapes with Coordinates

It might be very difficult to exactly determine and meet every boundary pixel of an object when manually labeling the contour of an object. The quantization of a continuous image constitutes a reduction in resolution which causes considerable image distortion (Moiré effect). Furthermore the contour of an object in a digitized image may be blurred which means the contour is extended over a set of pixels with decreasing grey values. In fact image digitization and human imprecision always implies small error rates in the object shapes. Therefore in the next step our intention is to introduce into the program procedures that help the user to find the right boundary of an object and that speed up the labeling process.

As a result of the labeling process we obtain the set S_C of n_{S_C} ordered, connected points that describes the boundary of the object S. Having labeled the contour S_C of the object S its boundary pixels are still defined by their absolute position in the 2-D matrix of the original image. In order to describe and compare the shapes of objects it is useful to specify a common coordinate system that is invariant under translation and scale. Therefore we transform the contour such that the centroid is at the origin and the maximal distance of the contour points from the origin is one. In a following approximation of the contour we reduce this set of pixels to a sufficiently large number of pixels that will speed up the succeeding computation time of the alignment and clustering process. The number of the pixels in this set will be influenced by the chosen order of the polygon and the allowed approximation error. For the polygonal approximation we used the approach based on the area/length ratio of Wall and Daniellson [21] because it is a very fast and simple algorithm without time-consuming mathematic operations.

5 Shape Alignment and Similarity Calculation

5.1 Theory of Procrustes Alignment

The aim of the alignment process is to compare the shapes of two objects in order to define a measure of similarity between them. Consider two shape instances P and O defined by the point-sets $p_i \in R^2$, $i = 1,2,...,N_1$ and $o_j \in R^2$, $j = 1,2,...,N_2$ respectively. The basic task of aligning two shapes consists of transforming one of them (say P) so that it fits in some optimal way the other one (say O). Generally the shape instance $P = \{p_i(x,y)\}_{i=1...N_1}$ is said to be aligned to the shape instance $O = \{o_j(x,y)\}_{j=1...N_2}$ if a distance $d_{min}(P,O)$ between the two shapes can not be decreased by applying a transformation ψ to P. Various alignment approaches are known [16], [24], [2], [25]. They differ in the kind of mapping (similarity [2], rigid [9], affine [10]) and the chosen similarity measure [1]. For the similarity measure between P and O we use Procrustes distance [22]:

$$d(P,O) = \sum_{i=1}^{N_{PO}} \left\| \frac{(p_i - \mu_P)}{\sigma_P} - R(\theta)\frac{(o_i - \mu_O)}{\sigma_O} \right\|^2 \quad (1)$$

where $R(\theta)$ is the rotation matrix, μ_P and μ_O are the centroids of the object P and O respectively, σ_P and σ_O are the sums of squared distances of each point-set from the centroids and N_{PO} is the number of point correspondences between the point-sets P and O. Thus the point correspondences are required for calculating the Procrustes distance. Generally this method is applied to centered shape instances represented by sets of landmark coordinates. Each of these shapes is rescaled so that the sum of squared distances of all landmarks to the centroid is identical ($\sigma_P = \sigma_O$). Then it is possible to compute a similarity transformation based on these centred pre-shapes. Finally the Procrustes average shape and Procrustes residuals can be evaluated.

5.2 Our Approach to Shape Alignment

We are considering a set of shape instances where differences in the translation and the scale were already eliminated. To compare the shape of these two instances we still have to eliminate differences in the rotation. The measure of similarity is based on the Procrustes distance between all points of P and their correspondences in O. As it can be seen from equation (1) the Procrustes distance requires the knowledge of point correspondences between the shapes P and O. Therefore we are confronted with the following problems:

1. In our application we use an approximation of the manually labeled set of contour points instead of a predefined number of landmark coordinates. Therefore we can not guarantee that all shape instances are defined by an identical number of contour points.
2. The point correspondences between the two shapes instances P and O are completely unknown.
3. We have no information about point outliers.

The outline of our approach to shape alignment is as follows: For every pair of points $\{p_i, o_j\} \in P \times O$ we calculate the similarity transformation ψ_{ij} that aligns these two points. The transformation ψ_{ij} is applied to all points in P to obtain the transformed shape instance P' which is defined by the point-set $p'_k \in R^2$, $k = 1,2,...,N_1$. For every point p'_k we define the nearest neighbour $NN(p'_k)$ in O as the point correspondence of p'_k. Note that we do not enforce one-to-one point correspondences. One point in O can have more than one point correspondences or even not a single point correspondence in P. The sum of squared distances $d(P',O)$ between every pair of point correspondents is calculated. In addition to that we define the quantity $\sqrt{\frac{1}{N_1} d(P',O)}$ as the mean alignment error $\bar{\varepsilon}(P',O)$:

$$\bar{\varepsilon}(P',O) = \sqrt{\frac{1}{N_1} d(P',O)} \qquad (2)$$

with:

$$d(P',O) = \sum_{k=1}^{N_1} (p'_k - NN(p'_k))^2 \qquad (3)$$

If the distance $d(P',O)$ is smaller then all earlier calculated distances $d_{min}(P,O)$ is set to $d(P',O)$, $\bar{\varepsilon}_{min}(P,O)$ is set to $\bar{\varepsilon}(P',O)$ and ψ_{min} is set to ψ_{ij}. After having iteratively aligned every possible pair of points $\{p_i, o_j\} \in P \times O$ we may estimate the dissimilarity between the shape instances P and O based on the value of the minimum mean alignment error $\bar{\varepsilon}_{min}(P,O)$. To ensure that our final measure of dissimilarity ranges from 0 to 1 we normalize the measure $\bar{\varepsilon}_{min}(P,O)$ to a predefined maximum distance T:

$$\bar{\varepsilon}'_{min}(P,O) = \frac{\bar{\varepsilon}_{min}(P,O)}{T} \qquad (4)$$

If $\bar{\varepsilon}_{min}(P,O) = 0$ then the shape instance P is identical with the shape instance O. With an increasing value of $\bar{\varepsilon}_{min}(P,O)$ the shape instance P is less similar to shape instance O. If $\bar{\varepsilon}_{min}(P,O) > T$ then the term $\frac{\bar{\varepsilon}_{min}(P,O)}{T}$ is automatically set to value one.

It is obvious that the constant T has a direct influence to the value of the resulting score. The parameter T can be defined by the user in the setting dialog of our program *CACM*. For our calculations we set T to 35% of the mean distance of all contour points to the centroid. Our investigations showed that this value leads to good results. Figure 2 shows pair-wise aligned shape instances and calculated values of the dissimilarity measure. It can be seen that in case of identity the shapes are superposed. With an increasing value of dissimilarity we can see the increasing deviation of the two shapes.

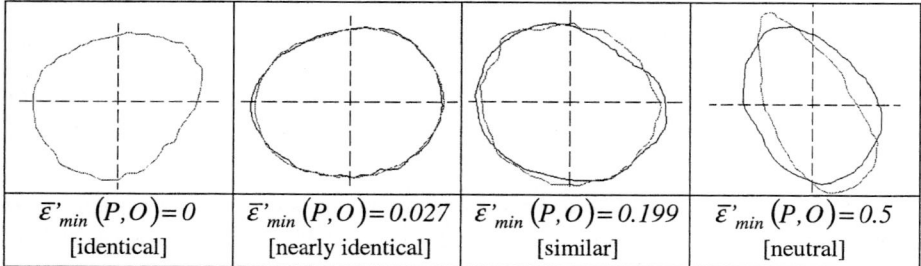

$\bar{\varepsilon}'_{min}(P,O)=0$	$\bar{\varepsilon}'_{min}(P,O)=0.027$	$\bar{\varepsilon}'_{min}(P,O)=0.199$	$\bar{\varepsilon}'_{min}(P,O)=0.5$
[identical]	[nearly identical]	[similar]	[neutral]

Fig. 2. Aligned Shape Instances of Strain Ulocladium Botrytis with Distances

6 Clustering

The alignment of every possible pair of objects in our database leads us to $N \times N$ pair-wise dissimilarity measures between N cases. These distances can be collected in a matrix where each row and each column corresponds to an instance of our dataset. The dissimilarity measure $\bar{\varepsilon}'_{min}(P,O)$ between shape instance P and shape instance O will be entered into the cell where the row of P and the column of O intersect. This results in a squared symmetric matrix with diagonal elements equal to value zero since the dissimilarity between an instance and itself is zero.

This matrix is the input for the hierarchical cluster analysis [23]. It depends on the selected clustering method how the instances are merged together into groups. After having investigated different hierarchical clustering methods we chose single linkage (nearest neighbour) where the linkage is done at the minimum distance between the two most similar cases of two different clusters.

The result of the hierarchical cluster analysis can be graphically represented by a dendogram. The dendogram is drawn on a proximity scale to show the clustering and the proximities at which the cases are merged together. The merging is done with increasing distances until all cases are combined in only one cluster. The distance at which two cases are merged in the same cluster is called the cophenetic proximity measure [27]. Note that the cophenetic proximity measure $d_C(P,O)$ between two cases P and O is not identical with the dissimilarity measure $\bar{\varepsilon}'_{min}(P,O)$ between these two cases.

Table 2 presents the merging steps and the cophenetic proximity measures for clustering eight instances of strain Ulocladium Botrytis using Single Linkage.

Table 2. Merging Steps with Cophenetic Proximity Measure

Merging Step	Case1	Case2	Cophenetic Proximity Measure
1	ub_6	ub_7	0,0110
2	ub_5	ub_7	0,0162
3	ub_2	ub_4	0,0500
4	ub_3	ub_6	0,0579
5	ub_4	ub_5	0,0583
6	ub_1	ub_8	0,2489
7	ub_8	ub_2	0,2634

The graphical output of this table is presented in the dendogram in Figure 3.

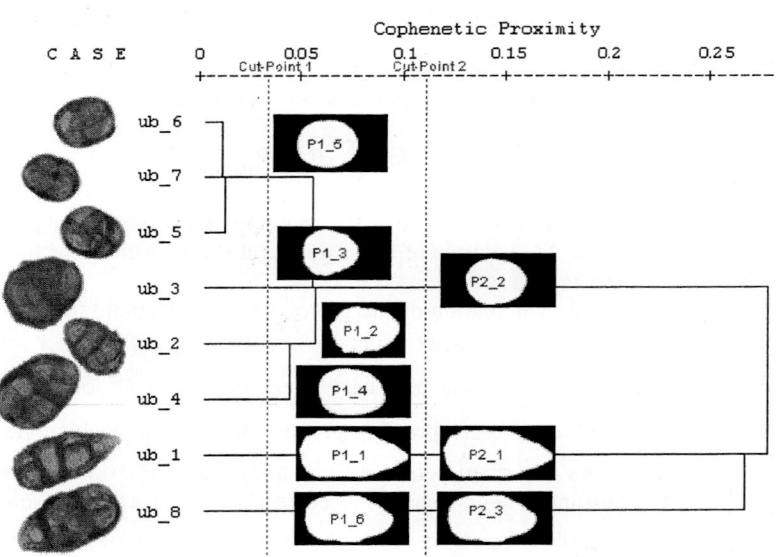

Fig. 3. Dendogram of Eight Instances of Strain Ulocladium Botrytis Using Single Linkage

In the dendogram in Figure 3 we marked two exemplary cut-points at different distances. A cut-point is a virtual vertical line in the dendogram. The horizontal position of this line marks the cophenetic proximity measure at which the cases were split into several clusters. The level of the cut-point has a direct influence on the resulting number of clusters and the number of prototypes. As smaller the level is as more groups are created. That means the prototypes are more specialized which will result in matches with higher scores. As higher the chosen cophenetic proximity measure of a cut-point is as fewer models have to be created. The models are more general and the inner-class variance inside a cluster is higher. In general this will result to matches with lower scores.

7 Prototype Calculation

We have divided our set of N shape instances $\{P_1, P_2, ..., P_N\}$ into k clusters $C_1, C_2, ..., C_k$. Each cluster C_i, $i = 1, 2, ..., k$ consists of a subset of n_i shape cases. For each cluster we need to compute a prototype $\bar{\mu}$ that will be the representative of the cluster. The full Procrustes estimate [7] of the mean shape is obtained by minimizing (over $\bar{\mu}$) the sum of squared full Procrustes distances d_f^2 from each instance P_j, $j = 1, 2, ..., n_i$ to an unknown unit size mean configuration $\bar{\mu}$, i.e.

$$[\bar{\mu}] = \arg \inf_{\bar{\mu}} \sum_{j=1}^{n_i} d_f(P_j, \bar{\mu})^2 \qquad (5)$$

We have implemented and tested two different approaches of computing a prototype for the cluster. In the first approach we compared the similarity measures of all shape instances $\{P_1, P_2, ..., P_j\}$ included in the same cluster C_i, $i = 1, 2, ..., k$. As the prototype we chose the median shape $P_{median}(C_i)$ of that cluster that is the shape instance which has the minimum distance to all other shape instances:

$$[\bar{\mu}] = P_{median}(C_i) = \arg \inf \sum_{j=1}^{n_i} d(P_j, P_{median})^2 \qquad (6)$$

The main advantage of this solution is that the prototype represents a natural shape instance out of that cluster. An example of using a natural shape instance as the prototype of a cluster is shown in Figure 5a.

Another approach for the calculation of the prototype is to calculate the arithmetic mean of the shape instances of a cluster. Suppose a cluster C_i including a set of n_i shape instances $\{P_1, P_2, ..., P_{n_i}\}$. In the best case every point $p \in R^2$ of a shape instance $P_j \in C_i$ has exactly $n_i - 1$ corresponding points, one point on each single shape instance of that cluster. As described before we can not guarantee a one-to-one point mapping. We are confronted with one-to-n correspondences where each point $p_m \in R^2$, $m = 1, 2, ..., N_1$ of P_j can have zero, one or even more then n_i point correspondences. In worst cases this may result in strong distortions in the prototype contour (See Figure 4b).

To improve the results of the calculations for the arithmetic mean of corresponding points we reject all contour points as outliers of the prototype where at least 80% of all individuals of that cluster do not have a point correspondence. In general this approach leads to a better representation of the mean contour for all instances in one cluster. The comparison of Figure 4b and 4d shows that the sharp edges shown in Figure 4b are eliminated after rejecting the outlier.

Figure 5a shows the median shape and Figure 5b shows the arithmetic mean as two different kinds of prototypes representing a cluster which consists of only two shape instances. The prototype in Figure 5a is identical with one individual out of that cluster. In comparison the prototype in Figure 5b is not a natural shape instance but it is a better representative for both members in that cluster. In addition to that we would favour the mean shape as prototype for the cluster since it appears visually smoother. With our program *CACM* it is possible to calculate both types of prototypes – the median of shapes and the arithmetic mean. Each prototype can be exported as an image, where the contour pixels are labeled by the grey level one and the background pixels are labeled by zero, and as a list of coordinates of the contour points.

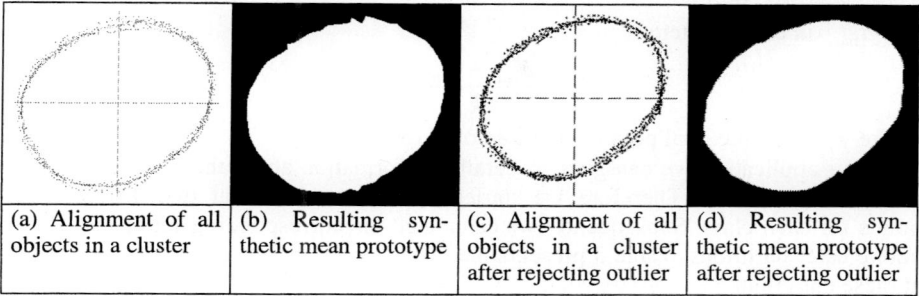

| (a) Alignment of all objects in a cluster | (b) Resulting synthetic mean prototype | (c) Alignment of all objects in a cluster after rejecting outlier | (d) Resulting synthetic mean prototype after rejecting outlier |

Fig. 4. Aligned Shapes and Mean Shape of a Single Cluster before and after Rejecting Outlier

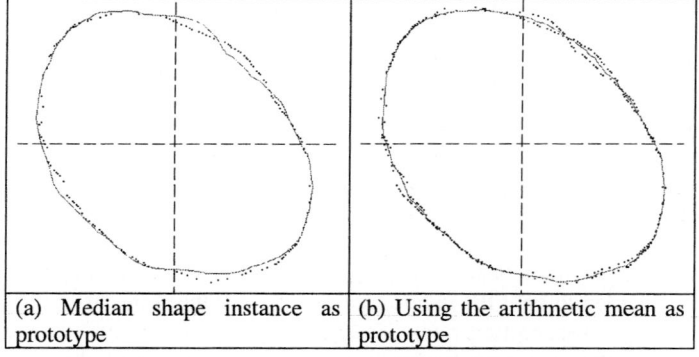

| (a) Median shape instance as prototype | (b) Using the arithmetic mean as prototype |

Fig. 5. Median of Shapes in a Cluster and Arithmetic Mean of the Shapes

8 Results

We have tested our approach on six different airborne fungi spores. Some digitized sample images for the analyzed spores are presented in Table 1. We have labeled a total of 60 objects for each of the six fungi strains. In the following registration process we have aligned every single object with all objects of the same strain to calculate the pair-wise similarity values. As a result we obtain six similarity matrices, one for each analyzed fungi strain. These matrices are the input for the following hierarchical cluster analysis. The outcome of this process was a dendogram for each of the six fungi strains.

Now we need to define a cut-point on each dendogram to obtain the groups of the shapes. As described earlier the choice of the right position for a cut-point is a central issue and it directly influences the recognition rate and performance. Visual the dendograms impart only some limited information about the best position of the cut-point. This is one of the main disadvantages of classical hierarchical clustering methods. The algorithms only create clusters but do not explain why they were established. It is not possible to draw direct conclusions about the quality of the clusters from the classification hierarchy.

If it is possible to specify the number of clusters in advance we can calculate the position of the cut-point d_w by taking the minimal and the maximal distance d_{min} and d_{max} in each cluster:

$$d_w = \frac{d_{max} - d_{min}}{k} \quad (7)$$

where k is the maximal possible number of clusters.

In our application we can give no detailed information about the expected number of resulting clusters. Therefore we started our investigations at two different cut-points for each class. Subsequently we calculated the corresponding set of models for both cluster partitions. Table 3 presents the resulting number of models for each class at these cut-points.

Table 3. Number of Models on Two Different Cut-Points

Classes	$d_w(1)$	Number of Models	$d_w(2)$	Number of Models
Alternaria Alternata	0,045	23	0,031	34
Aspergillus Niger	0,017	5	0,029	3
Rhizopus Stolonifer	0,027	22	0,037	16
Scopulariopsis Brevicaulis	0,063	8	0,050	10
Ulocladium Botrytis	0,025	24	0,020	30
Wallenia Sebi	0,158	7	0,065	17

Both case bases of models were applied to our case-based object recognition system [26]. We decided to split the dendograms at the distances of cut-point (2) because it results in the best recognition rates. The models from these clusters were incorporated as cases into the case base. Figure 6 shows exemplary the resulting case base for the class Rhizopus Stolonifer on cut-point (2).

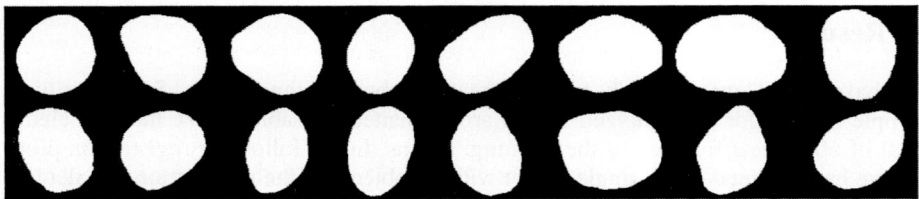

Fig. 6. Case Base of Models for Strain Rhizopus Stolonifer Representing the 16 Resulting Clusters

In fact, we know little about the accuracy of these models at the moment. Therefore in the next step our intention is to introduce into the program procedures that improve the information gathering procedure and to develop an incremental clustering procedure [23].

9 Conclusions

The recognition of objects in images can be done based on a model-based recognition procedure. That requires a model from the objects which should be recognized. Natural objects have a great variation in shape that makes it not easy to specify a model by hand. Therefore it is necessary to have a computerized procedure that helps to acquire the model from the real objects. We have proposed a method for the acquisition of contour instances and learning of general shape models. We use Procrustes similarity measure for aligning and determining the similarity between different shapes. Based on the calculated similarity measure we create clusters of similar shapes by using single linkage method. The mean shape or the median of the cluster is calculated and taken as prototype of the cluster. The methods are implemented in the program *CACM Version 1.0* which runs on a Windows PC. Further research will be to improve the information gathering procedure and to develop an incremental clustering procedure.

Acknowledgement

The project "Development of methods and techniques for the image-acquisition and computer-aided analysis of biologically dangerous substances BIOGEFA" is sponsored by the German Ministry of Economy BMWA under the grant number 16IN0147.

References

1. R.C. Veltkamp, Shape Matching: Similarity Measures and Algorithms, Shape Modelling International, pp. 188-197, 2001
2. A. Rangarajan, H. Chui and F.L. Bookstein, The Softassign Procrustes Matching Algorithm, Proc. Information Processing in Medical Imaging, pp. 29-42, 1997
3. M. Kass, A. Witkin, and D. Terzopoulos, Snakes: Active contour models, In 1st International Conference on Computer Vision, pp. 259-268, London, 1987
4. D.-C. Cheng, A. Schmidt-Trucksäss, K.-S. Cheng, H. Burkhardt, Using Snakes to Detect the Intimal and Aventitial Layers of the Common Carotid Artery Wall in Sonographic Images, Computer Methods and Programs in Biomedicine 67, pp. 27-37, 2002
5. D.G. Kendall, A Survey of the Statistical Theory of Shape, Statistical Science, Vol. 4, No. 2, pp. 87-120, 1989
6. F.L. Bookstein, Size and Shape Spaces for Landmark Data in Two Dimensions, Statistical Science, Vol. 1, No. 2, pp. 181-242, 1986
7. I.L.Dryden and K.V.Mardia, Statistical Shape Analysis, John Wiley & Sons Inc., 1998
8. T.F. Cootes and C.J. Taylor, A Mixture Model for Representing Shape Variation, Image and Vision Computing 17, No.8, pp. 567-574, 1999
9. J. Feldmar and N. Ayache, Rigid, Affine and Locally Affine Registration of Free-Form Surfaces, The International Journal of Computer Vision, Vol. 18, No. 3, pp. 99-119, 1996
10. A. Hill, C.J. Taylor and A.D. Brett, A Framework for Automatic Landmark Identification Using a New Method of Nonrigid Correspondence, IEEE Transactions on Pattern Analysis and Machine Intelligence, Vol. 22, No. 3, pp. 241-251, 2000
11. E.N. Mortensen and W.A. Barrett, Intelligent Scissors for Image Composition, In Computer Graphics Proceedings, pp. 191-198, 1995

12. T. Haenselmann and W. Effelsberg, Wavelet-Based Semi-Automatic Live-Wire Segmentation, Proceedings of the SPIE Human Vision and Electronic Imaging VII, Vol. 4662, pp. 260-269, 2003
13. F.L. Bookstein, Landmark Methods for Forms without Landmarks: Morphometrics of Group Differences in Outline Shape, Medical Image Analysis, Vol. 1, No. 3, pp. 225-244, 1997
14. S. Belongie, J. Malik and J. Puzicha, Shape Matching and Object Recognition Using Shape Contexts, IEEE Transactions on Pattern Analysis and Machine Intelligence, Vol. 24, No. 24, pp. 509-522, 2002
15. A. Rangarajan, H. Chui and F.L. Bookstein, The Softassign Procrustes Matching Algorithm, Proc. Information Processing in Medical Imaging, pp. 29-42, 1997
16. D. Huttenlocher, G. Klanderman and W. Rucklidge, Comparing Images Using the Hausdorff Distance, IEEE Trans. Pattern Analysis and Machine Intelligence, Vol. 15, No. 9, pp. 850-863, 1993
17. L.J. Latecki and R. Lakämper, Shape Similarity Measure Based on Correspondence of Visual Parts, IEEE Transactions on Pattern Analysis and Machine Intelligence, Vol. 22, No. 10, pp. 1185-1190, 2000
18. F. Mokhtarian, S. Abbasi and J. Kittler, Efficient and Robust Retrieval by Shape Content through Curvature Scale Space, In Proc. International Workshop on Image Databases and Multimedia Search, pp. 35-42, 1996
19. P Besl and N. McKay, A Method for Registration of 3-D Shapes, IEEE Trans. Pattern Analysis and Machine Intelligence, Vol. 14, No. 2, pp. 239-256, 1992
20. M. Petrou and P. Bosdogianni, Image Processing – The Fundamentals, John Wiley & Sons Inc., 1999
21. K. Wall and P.-E. Daniellson, A Fast Sequential Method For Polygonal Approximation of Digitized Curves, Comput. Graph. Image Process. 28, pp. 220-227, 1984
22. S.R. Lele and J.T. Richtsmeier, An Invariant Approach to Statistical Analysis of Shapes, Chapman & Hall / CRC 2001
23. P. Perner, Data Mining on Multimedia Data, Springer Verlag Berlin, 1998
24. H. Alt and L.J. Guibas, Discrete Geometric Shapes: Matching, Interpolation and Approximation, Handbook of Computational Geometry eds. J.-R.Sack and J. Urrutia, Elsevier Science Publishers B.V., pp. 121-153, 1996
25. S. Sclaroff and A. Pentland, Modal Matching for Correspondence and Recognition, IEEE Trans. Pattern Analysis and Machine Intelligence, Vol. 17, No. 6, pp. 545-561, 1995
26. P. Perner and A. Bühring, Case-Based Object Recognition, ECCBR 2004, accepted
27. A.K. Jain and R.C. Dubes, Algorithms for Clustering Data, Prentice-Hall Inc., 1988

Appendix: Notation

S	object in an image
S_C	contour of object S
n_{S_C}	number of pixels defining the contour of object S
$s_i(x, y)$, $i = 1,2,...,n_{S_C}$	pixel on the contour of object S
P, O	shape instances, defined by the point-sets $p_i \in R^2$, $i = 1,2,...,N_1$ and $o_j \in R^2$, $j = 1,2,...,N_2$ respectively
P'	transformed shape instance, defined by the point-set $p'_k \in R^2$, $k = 1,2,...,N_1$

ψ	similarity transformation function
$R(\theta)$	rotation matrix
$\mu_P(x,y)$	centroid of the shape instance P
σ_P	sum of squared distances of each point in P and $\mu_P(x,y)$
N_{PO}	number of point correspondences between P and O
$NN(p)$	nearest neighbour of a point
$\bar{\varepsilon}(P,O)$	mean alignment error between P and O
$\bar{\varepsilon}_{min}(P,O)$	minimum mean alignment error between P and O
$\bar{\varepsilon}'_{min}(P,O)$	dissimilarity measure between shape instances P and O
T	predefined maximum threshold distance between shapes
N	number of shape instances $\{P_1, P_2, \ldots, P_N\}$
k	number of resulting clusters
$C_i, i=1,2,\ldots,k$	cluster, comprises a subset of n_i shape instances
$\bar{\mu}_i$	prototype, representative shape instance of the cluster C_i
$P_{median}(C_i)$	median shape of cluster C_i
$d(P,O)$	distance function between two shape instances P and O
d_f^2	squared full Procrustes distance
d_w	position of the cut-point on the proximity scale

Criteria of Good Project Network Generator and Its Fulfillment Using a Dynamic CBR Approach

Hyun Woo Kim[1] and Kyoung Jun Lee[2,*]

[1] Graduate School of Management, KAIST
Cheongryangri-dong, Dongdaemun-Ku, Seoul, Korea
Kimhyunu@kgsm.kaist.ac.kr
[2] School of Business, Kyung Hee University
Hoegi-Dong, Dongdaemun-Ku, Seoul, Korea
klee@khu.ac.kr

Abstract. Most project-based industries such as construction, shipbuilding, and software development etc. should generate and manage project network for successful project planning. We suggest a set of criteria of good project network generator such as network generation efficiency, quality of network, and economics of system development. For the efficiency of the planning, the first criterion, we decided to take a CBR approach. However, using only previous cases is insufficient to generate a proper network for a new project. By embedding rules and constraints in the case-based system, we could improve the quality of the project network: the second criterion. The integration of CBR approach and the knowledge-based approach makes feasible the development of the project network generator and improves the quality of the network by mutual enhancement through crosschecking the knowledge and cases in the development and maintenance stages. For some complex project network planning, a single-case assumed project network generation methodology is refined into Dynamic Leveled Multiple Case approach. The methodology contributes again the efficiency and effectiveness of project network generation and reduces the efforts of the system development.

1 Introduction

Generation, verification, and modification of construction project schedule networks in the PERT-CPM chart are the essential tasks for successful project planning and management in the construction industry. Because a project network consists of hundreds of activities and precedence relationships, project planning is a time-consuming and knowledge-intensive task. To compete with other companies for a contract, it is critical for a construction company to quickly generate a good and consistent project plan.

To generate a project network, much domain knowledge, experience and the control knowledge are needed. The domain knowledge describes the domain world and the available actions to the planner. The control knowledge indicates how the planner will achieve its goals; it controls the planner's search for a plan. In other words, control knowledge is prescriptive, whereas domain knowledge is descriptive. So the project manager responsible for generating project network should have much domain

---

* Corresponding Author

knowledge, control knowledge and time. Especially in the construction domain, the generation of project network is a time consuming task. It takes a couple of days for generating the simplest construction project network such as project network for APT (apartment) construction although the 5 years experienced construction manager worked. We need the project network generation system to respond to management's requirements quickly and flexibly, to reduce time to generate network, and to improve quality of network. The quality of network can be measured by technical soundness, satisfaction of due date, and resource efficiency. To achieve these objectives, system contains much knowledge.

In the area of project planning, there had been a lot of research and developments on project scheduling methods and management techniques assuming that a project network is given to the project manager. However, since the earliest research prototype CONSTRUCTION PLANEX [1], there has only been a limited amount of research to automate or support the project network generation using knowledge-based techniques, such as GHOST [5], SIPE-2 [2], and HISCHED [6]. To generate a plan by these systems, the users have to input a lot of activities' information since these systems are not designed to utilize past cases.

Most of the previous systems were not designed to use past cases; so, their users had the burden of inputting vast amounts of information, or their developers had to provide this knowledge for the systems. OARPLAN [7], a model-based planning system, does use past cases, but the user has to input the precedence relationships between activities. In contrast to these systems, the system that we developed for this project doesn't require the users to input any precedence relationships because the system uses past cases containing these precedence constraints and adaptation knowledge. Zhang and Maher [8] used a CBR method for the structural design of buildings. They claimed that CBR as a design model is intuitively appealing because much of the design knowledge comes through the experience of multiple, individual design situations. The same holds true in the construction planning situation.

To select an approach among these alternatives, we need a set of criteria to evaluate a project network generation system. Therefore, in this paper, we first suggest the set of criteria of good project network generator.

2 Criteria of Good Project Network Generator

In this section, we discuss about the criteria of good project network generator. Some of the criteria are related to the system itself and the other criteria are related to the project network. The system relating criteria are classified into the efficiency feature and the implementation feature. The efficiency feature can be evaluated by time for network generation. The implementation feature can be evaluated by the cost. The project network relating criteria can be evaluated by the quality of project network. Though there is much variation in the characteristics of project network depending on the specific features of the domains such as construction, shipbuilding, and SW development etc., we can generalize and define a project network as follows.

A project networks is a set of activities and their interrelated precedence relationships to start and finish a project. Generating a project network, whether it is done by human or computer, is a function of project requirement, project-related domain knowledge, and domain-independent commonsense knowledge. The project requirement in other word project specification consists of the function requirement given by client and the engineering requirement. The project-related domain knowledge includes the work breakdown structure, the activity selection knowledge and the precedence knowledge. The domain independent commonsense knowledge means network principles kept to compose a sound network structure of the project. This knowledge is necessary in project network evaluation as well as generation.

2.1 Efficiency of Project Network Generation

The efficiency can be evaluated from two viewpoints. The one is the total generation time for project network that can be used in real field. Generally, the project manager can understand required activities and their precedence relations with only the project network for the project management. So, even if the generated project network has no error, the project network generator's operator has to customize the system generating project network in the cognitive view point. Efficiency should therefore be evaluated by the total time of the system generation time and the customizing time.

Another evaluation method is comparing the pure system time of alternatives those generate same quality of project network if they have same input.

2.2 Effectiveness of the Project Network Generator

Is It the Well-Formed Project Network?

This question is concerned with the structure of project network. There is the principle for project network structure. We call the project network as a well-formed project network if the project network satisfies the principle.

One is there should be no isolated part in the project network. Every part in project network is necessary to achieve the goal of project. In this viewpoint, it is not difficult to conclude that they should be tightly coupled by relationship. If there is any part should be isolated, it means the project network contains another project. And it should be divided into another project network.

Another requirement is that there should be no cycled relationship. An example of a cycled relationship is that 'B' activity has to start after 'A' activity, 'C' activity has to start after 'B' activity, but 'A' activity has to start after 'C 'activity. Even though it is a logic error, we can find it without checking and fix it up temporary by removing a relationship with heuristic algorithm.

The other is the optional principle. There should be only one start and end node. It is helpful when we analyze project network with CPM method and interpret the result. Especially in the construction domain, this principle is a strong custom.

Is It the Valid Network?

This criterion is interested in the conformity of activity. In other word, this criterion evaluate that the project network generator decides correctly about what activities are required according to the project specification. If the project network includes only the necessary activities, then we call it as a valid project network. The evaluation result of this criterion is largely dependent on the degree of detail in the input project specification. The issue in this research is how to maximize the conformity of activity without detail project specification such as CAD data.

Is It the Verified Network?
This criterion is concerned with the relationship between activities. If there is no violation of critical precedence constraints then we call it the verified project network.

2.3 Economics of Development of Project Network Generator

The system development cost is very important evaluation criterion for the project network generation system. As we have reviewed, the project network generator is a typical knowledge based system generating the proper project network for a new project using domain knowledge and the commonsense knowledge. Therefore we can evaluate which alternative is better by comparing the development cost in the knowledge based system development perspective. The cost consists of the knowledge acquisition cost and the inference engine development cost.

3 Case and Knowledge Based Project Network Generator

Network generation by case and knowledge is inspired by an expert's generation method and adapted for efficiency and effectiveness. The reasons why we adapt case approach is currently the expert start with the most similar past network to get a new project network quickly and to use the implicit knowledge in the past project network. We have understood that if we would use a similar past project network, we could generate a new initial project network without much knowledge and time. In other words, the case based approach could be very helpful to generating a new project network efficiently if we could modify the retrieved past project network by system.

This is the reason why we have integrated the knowledge approach. Currently most of experts finish generating a new project network by modification of the selected past project network with their domain knowledge gained from experience. Through this process, a new project network is being generated. The project network can be represented formally. So we had represented the project network using frames for machine understanding and we had identified the required adaptation knowledge. And, we have acquired and represented the knowledge by constraints and rules. We have comprehended that case based approach helps to generate project network efficiently and the knowledge based modification make the quality of project network higher.

We could get initial project network by past case retrieval. And we use rules to analysis the difference between the new project and the selected case. The project network generator modifies the initial project network with the set of operators for activity modification. Next it uses a set of knowledge that is represented by constraint to satisfy the precedence constraints between activities. We call the constraint type knowledge as precedence constraint. We have implemented several construction project network generators using case and knowledge based methodology.

3.1 Procedure of Case and Knowledge Based Project Network Generation

The first step is project specification analysis. In this step, we can reduce the search space by the case base filtering with the result of analysis. It needs almost new generating effort if we would modify a project network for concrete framed building to a project network for still beam framed building. For this reason, we have introduced the project specification analysis process with case base filtering function.

The second step is project network retrieval under the least modification principle.. The output of the project network generator is not the project itself but the project network for the project. By this viewpoint, we use the amount of modification effort as a similarity measure. It means that a project network needs the least modification efforts is the most similar project network. An obvious question that arises here is how to calculate the amount of modification effort before the adaptation is performed.

The third step is the project network modification by addition or deletion of activities. The most of initial project network have discrepancies with the new project. We fill the gap.

The fourth step is activity's features modification such as activities' duration and assigned resource.

The fifth step is network analysis and constraint satisfaction. In this step, we have the modified project network for the new project. We analyze the project network with PERT/CPM. By this task, we can get the earliest start time (ES), the earliest finish time (EF), the latest start time (LS) and the latest finish time (LF). We check the set of precedence constraints. If there are any violated precedence constraints, then we fix up the project network.

Finally, the network will be executed and customized by the project manager. The executed project network will be restored to case base.

3.2 Case Representation

A case consists of a design specification and project network. The project network consists of hundreds of activities and relationships. We use a frame-based representation scheme for representing design specification and project network. For this representation, we used the expert system tool UNIK-FRAME [3], which was developed by KAIST. A project frame has the slots such as the name, address, start date, due date, ground type, topography, and construction area. A project can have more than one building.

3.3 Project Network Retrieval Under the Least Modification Principle

We retrieve the most similar case under the least modification principle. The amount of modifications required can be calculated before the adaptation process is performed by the following process. If it is different the new projects specification with a past case's, then this discrepancy is added to the discrepancy list. After finished the comparison, the system run the forward rule inference to identify what the modifications are required to fill gap in between the past project network and the new project network. The result of rule inference is represented by the set of primitive operators for modification such as add, delete, replication, add-replication and reduce-replication. We can count how many modifying actions will be required for each operator. The distance between the new project and the past project is the sum of modifying actions counting in the previous process. The past project that has the least distance is the most similar case for the new project.

Distance = $\Sigma dist(X_{Ni}, X_{Pi})$
    X_{Ni}: ith specification for the new project
    X_{Pi}: ith specification for the past project in case base
    $dist(X_{Ni}, X_{Pi})$: Distance function

If Xi is the interior finish work and the new project(X_{Ni}) is stone finish and the past project(X_{Pi}) is no interior, then the distance function calculates the distance value and returns through the following step:

Step1: Identify the Set of Required Primitive Operators
In this case, the operator set is as following. Operator set = {add interior frame, add attach stone}

Step2: Calculate the Number of Modifying Actions
For executing the [add interior frame] operator, it should add the interior framing activity. To add an activity to project network, it has to create a proper activity and give several relationships to the new activity. The relationships can be generated by converting the related precedence constraints. If we would count the number of action for [add interior frame], it needs one of modifying action for activity creation, and add the number of the related precedence constraints to the total number of modifying actions. We could formalize the number of modification action for each network modification operators as follows.

ADD
Activity node addition: $count(A_N^*)$
New Relationship addition: $count(Con(A_i:A_N^*)) + count(Con(A_N^*: A_j))$ actions
A_N^*: set of newly added activities to the project network
A_i: set of activities which are predecessor to A_N^*
A_j: set of activities which are successor to A_N^*
$Con(A_1, A_2)$: set of precedence constraints which the predecessor is in set A_1 and the successor is in set A_2
$count(S)$: function for counting the number of set S

DELETE
Activity node deletion: $count(A_S^*)$
Connected Relationship deletion: $count(Con(A_i: A_S^*)) + count(Con(A_S^*:A_j))$ actions
New Relationship addition: $count(Con(A_i: A_i^C)) + count(Con(A_j^C:A_j))$ actions
A_S^*: set of deleting activities from the project network
A_i: set of activities which are predecessor to A_S^*
A_j: set of activities which are successor to A_S^*
A^C: complementary set of A
$Con(A_1, A_2)$: set of precedence constraints which the predecessor is in set A_1 and the successor is in set A_2
$count(S)$: function for counting the number of set S

REPLACE
Activity node addition (1 action) and activity node deletion (1 action)

ADD_REPLICATION
Activity node addition (1 action) and relationship addition (1 action)

REDUCE_REPLICATION
Activity node deletion (1 action) and relationship deletion (1 action)

Step3: Repeat Step 2 for Other Operators and Summation the Results

3.4 Knowledge Based Project Network Modification

We could get the list of discrepancies between the new project network and the past project network when we calculate the modification effort for the project network retrieval. And we could get the set of primitive operators for filling gap in between the past project network and the new project network by rule based inference. We design five primitive operators to modify project network. The first operator is the ADD operator. If the retrieved project network is without interior but the new project is stone interior then we have to add necessary activities into the retrieved project network. The procedure for executing the ADD operator is described as below Figure 1(a).

Notation for Procedure of Operators

act_i – activities included in selected project network

A_i, A_j: set of activities

$R(A_i : A_j)$ – set of relationships between the predecessor is in the set A_i and the successor is in the set A_j

$W(act_i)$ - act_i's work breakdown structure considered as a class of activities

F_{Ni} - the i th information of new project

F_{Si} - the i th information of selected project

W_{Fi} – set of work breakdown structure codes related with F_{Ni} and F_{Si}

W_{FSi} – set of work breakdown structure codes related with F_{Si}

W_{FNi} – set of work breakdown structure codes related with F_{Ni}

A^* - set of activities with W_{Fi} WBS ; $\{act_i \mid W(act_i) \in W_{Fi}\}$

A_S^* - set of activities with W_{FSi} WBS ; $\{act_i \mid W(act_i) \in W_{FSi}\}$

A_N^* - set of activities with W_{FNi} WBS ; $\{act_i \mid W(act_i) \in W_{FNi}\}$

act^*_{FSi} - last activity in A^*

$Con(A_1, A_2)$: set of precedence constraints which the predecessor is in set A_1 and the successor is in set A_2

The second operator is DELETE operator. The DELETE operator is needed at the situation to the contrary of the ADD's. The procedure for executing DELETE operator is described in Figure 1(b).

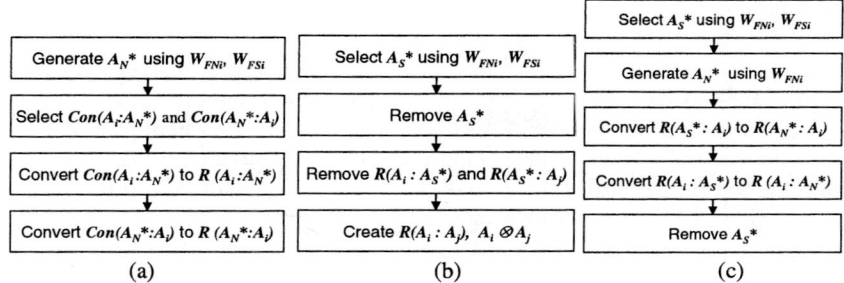

Fig. 1. ADD (a), DELETE (b), and REPLACE (c) operator

The third operator is REPLACE operator. If the retrieved project network with aluminum interior but the new project is stone interior then we have to delete unnecessary activities and add necessary activities into the retrieved project network. But some of these modifications can be finished by replacement. In this case, we don't have to consider relationship modification. So we can reduce the modification efforts. The procedure for executing REPLACE operator is described in Figure 1(c).

The fourth operator is ADD-REPLICATION operator. If the retrieved project network is 18th floor but the new project is 20th floor then we have to add 19th and 20th activities into the retrieved project network as in Figure 2.

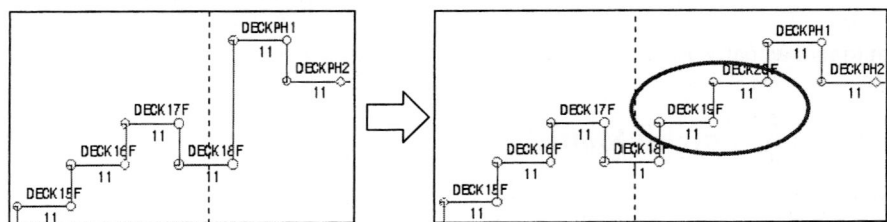

Fig. 2. ADD-REPLICATION operator

The last operator is REDUCE-REPLICATION operator. The REDUCE-REPLICATION operator is needed at the situation to the contrary of the ADD-REPLICATION's. The procedure for executing ADD-REPLICATION and REDUCE-REPLICATION operator is described in Figure 3.

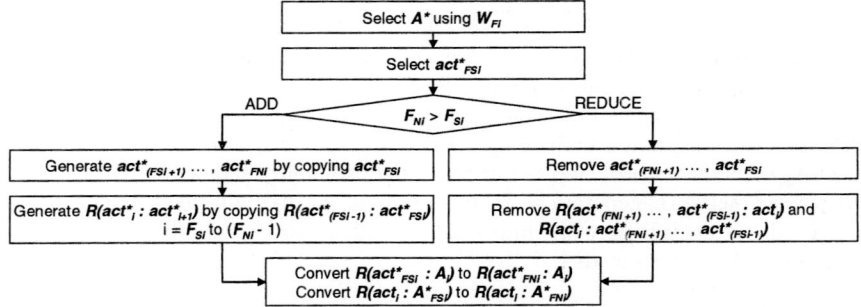

Fig. 3. ADD-REPLICATION and REDUCE-REPLICATION operator

3.5 Implementation of FASTRAK-APT

We have developed the apartment building project network generator FASTRAK-APT with case and knowledge approach [4] in 1996. First, the system user inputs the project specification. Second, the FASTRAK-APT generates a new project network and the operator reflects his or her intention by interaction with the FASTRAK-APT. Finally, the operator modifies the activities' row, font, or color with project network viewers such as PERTware or Primavera.

FASTRAK-APT has been proved to reduce the effort required for generating an initial project plan from seven person-days to one person-day. The cost of updating a plan, which occurs every three months on a project, has been also reduced from 2 person-days to half a person-day. The running time of the system is about 5 minutes for a building from case loading to adaptation (a 20-floor building has about 500 activities and 700 precedence relationships).

The plans generated by FASTRAK-APT have been proved by human experts to be sound technically and have even satisfied more constraints than the cases prepared by domain experts. Therefore, the generated and executed project networks were used for enhancing the case base, and the refined case base helped improve the quality of generated plans.

The case approach great helps to reduce the development cost. The FASTRAK-APT had 430 precedence constraints and 50 cases when it had started. If we did not use a CBR approach, we would have to gather more precedence constraints, up to 13,203 ($_{163}C_2$) for FASTRAK-APT theoretically. If we didn't adopt knowledge based adaptation, actually the project network auto generation was impossible.

4 Dynamic Leveled Multiple Case Approach

Although the methodology used for FASTRAK-APT satisfies the criteria of good project network generator, it has problems to be generalized into other domains. For example, in the office building construction, the structures of project networks are very much different according to the construction method of each project while in the apartment building construction the structures of project networks are similar to each other. If we use the adaptation of a single case, we need much knowledge for network adaptation or large number of cases for various project network structures, which leads to low efficiency and development economy.

The analysis of the past cases of office building project networks found that the project networks can be divided into several subnetworks and each subnetwork also can be divided into several lower subnetworks. We could represent a project network by a subnetwork hierarchical structure. We also found that if we divide the project networks with a proper level then the subnetworks are expected to be modified with a small amount of adaptation knowledge. By adding only a new type of knowledge for connecting the subnetworks, we can improve the efficiency and economy of the case-based project network generation. In this section, we explain such a methodology which divides a project network into multiple subnetworks, modifies and integrates them into a new project network.

4.1 Dynamic Leveled Multiple Cases Approach

For most of large project networks in the domains such as construction and software development, a project network is composed of subnetworks that are also composed of subnetworks. In such domain, we may have three kinds of strategy for utilizing project networks: maximization, minimization, and middle-level strategy. Maximization strategy (Figure 4) uses a past case as a whole project and corresponds to the single case approach as in FASTRAK-APT. This strategy is inefficient and not economical when the shape of the project network structure is various.

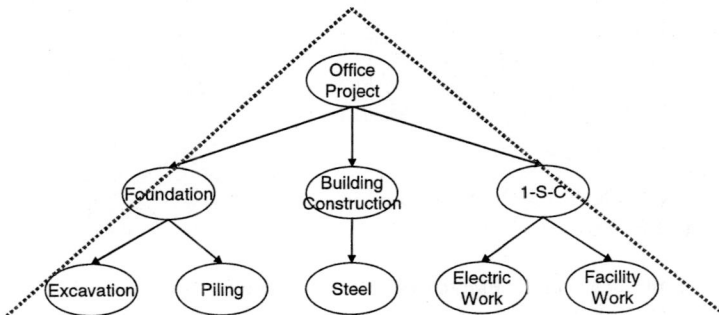

Fig. 4. Maximization strategy

Minimization strategy (Figure 5) creates a new project networking by retrieving subnetworks at most primitive level and synthesizing them into a whole network and can be called a static leveled multiple cases approach. Using the primitive level subnetworks contribute to the efficiency and economics of project network generator by reducing the variety of project network structures. However, in this approach, synthesizing many primitive level subnetworks depends on the network synthesis knowledge therefore the quality of the project network depends on this knowledge. Furthermore, when we create a project network which is almost the same as the executed and validated one in the case base, we should retrieve the primitive level cases and synthesize them into one network. This approach can be used in generating a bridge construction project composed of simple relationships among subnetworks.

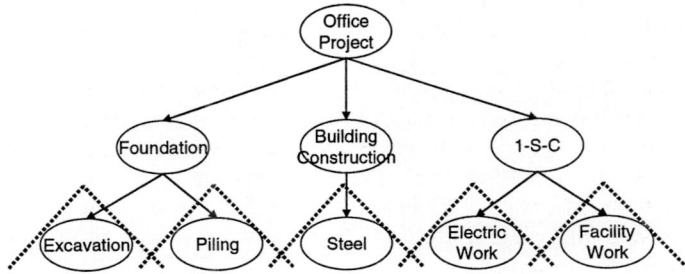

Fig. 5. Minimization strategy

Middle level strategy (Figure 6) is acquiring the subnetworks in case base at a proper level for minimizing the network synthesis and modification efforts and described as a dynamic leveled multiple case approach. Using this strategy solves the problem of efficiency and economics resulting from the variety of project networks. By varying the subnetwork level from the high level to the low level for minimizing modification knowledge the strategy removes the flaws of static leveled multiple cases approach and reduces the risk that determines the effectiveness of project network generation.

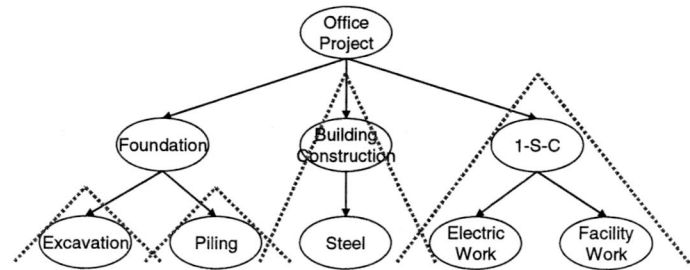

Fig. 6. Middle level strategy

Network Breakdown Structure
To implement Dynamic Leveled Multiple Case (DLMC) approach we need information on the subnetworks that a specific case has and a Network Breakdown Structure for fast retrieval of subnetworks as in Figure 7. Network Breakdown Structure is stored in the case base with past project information and project networks and provides subnetwork information when a project network generator demands subnetwork information in case base.

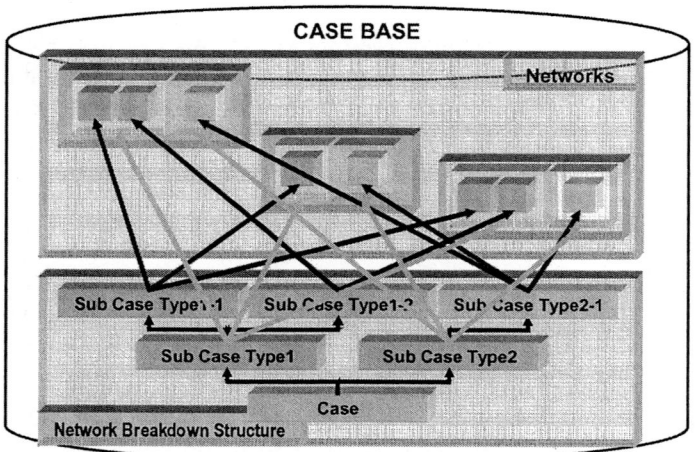

Fig. 7. Network Breakdown Structure

4.2 Procedure for Dynamic Leveled Multiple Cases Approach

The First Step: The Project Specification Analysis

In this step, we not only reduce the search space by filtering but also generate NBS for the new project with meta NBS. Meta NBS describes the relationship among subnetworks in a whole project network and consists of AND, OR, XOR (exclusive OR), and replication nodes. As in Figure 8, a project must include a Foundation, a Building Construction, and a Finalizing. Here Building Construction subnetworks can be included multiple times and should select either concrete structure or steel structure. Finalizing can include Electric Work or Facility Work or both.

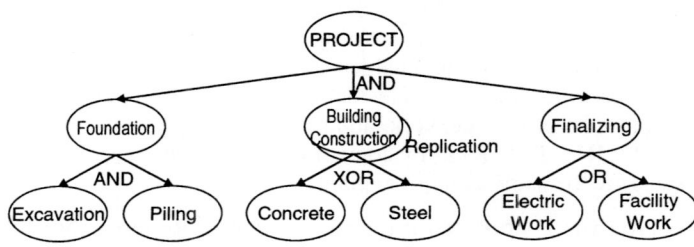

Fig. 8. Meta NBS

Analyzing a project specification with rule-based inference produces a network breakdown structure necessary for a new project network. The following rule states that if a construction method is "top-down-concrete" or "bottom-up-concrete" then we need to select "concrete" rather than "steel".

(fwd-rule NBS-gen-001   (office   ^construction-method << '"top-down-concrete"
                                                           '"bottom-up-concrete" >>)
-->
            (new-value   'concrete   'instance-num   1)
            (new-value   'steel   'instance-num   0))

Using the rules in the above, when a project network has both a "concrete"-type tower and a "steel"-type tower, we can produce a Network Breakdown Structure which is proper for a new project (Figure 9).

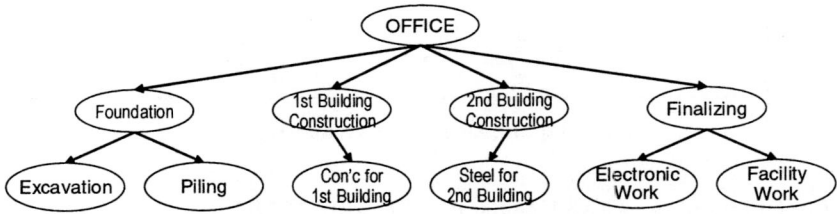

Fig. 9. Generated Network Breakdown Structure

The Second Step: The Dynamic Leveled Multiple Sub-network Retrieval

The criteria for selecting subnetworks depend on the network modification efforts and the network synthesis efforts. Calculating modification effort is described in a previous section. Synthesis effort is calculated in such a way similar to that of adding a new activity. Therefore, the calculation of synthesis efforts is as follows: Synthesis effort: count(Con($A_{NS}^C : A_{NS}$) $\cup$ Con($A_{NS} : A_{NS}^C$)) where A_{NS} is the set of activities included in newly selected subnetwork. The level of subnetworks retrieved is determined so that the calculated efforts for modification and synthesis can be minimized.

The Third Step: Subnetwork Modifications by Addition or Deletion of Activities
This step is the same as that explained in section 3.

The Fourth Step: Initial Project Network Generation by Subnetworks Synthesis
Synthesizing new subnetworks into a new project network is implemented by converting the precedence relationship knowledge into precedence relationship between activities in the subnetwork and other selected activities (Figure 10). To combine 'Piling' sub-network to the project network, add sub-network {A3, A4, R3} and generate relationships {R13, R14, R16, R17} by converting the related precedence constraints.

The next steps are the same as those explained in section 3.

The Fifth Step: Activity Features (Duration and Assigned Resource) Modification

The Sixth Step: Network Analysis and Constraint Satisfaction

The Final Step: Network Executed, Customized, and Restored into Case Base

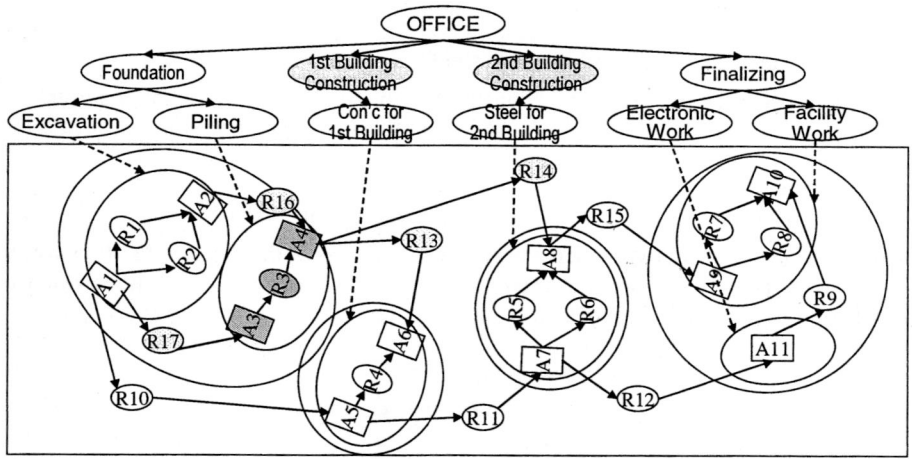

Fig. 10. Subnetwork synthesis

4.3 Implementation of FASTRAK-OFFICE with DLMC

We have developed the office building project network generator (FASTRAK-OFFICE, Figure 11) using the dynamic leveled multiple cases approach. The FASTRAK-OFFICE had 236 precedence constraints, 25 analysis rules for generating NBS and with only 5 full past project network when it had started even the office project network is more complex then the apartment project network. If we had developed it with the single case approach then we had to gather more precedence constraints in the worst case 12,090 constraints would be needed ($_{156}C_2$) with only 5 full past project network, and gather more past project networks up to 3,360 networks with only 236 precedence constraints.

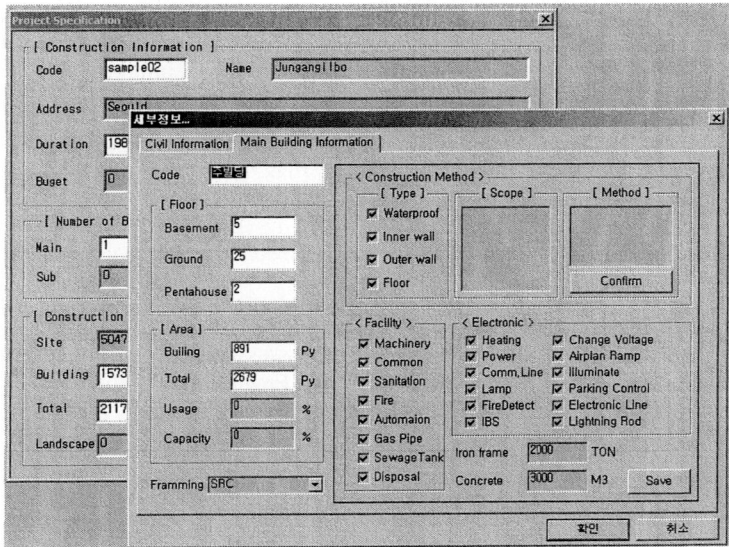

Fig. 11. User interface for inputting the project specifications

5 Conclusion

Most of project-based industries such as construction, shipbuilding, and software development etc. should generate and manage project network for successful project planning. In this paper, we suggested a set of criteria of good project network generator such as network generation efficiency, the quality of the network, and economics of system development. For the efficiency of the planning, the first criterion, we decided to take a case-based approach. However, using only previous cases is insufficient to generate a proper network for a new project. By embedding rules and constraints in the case-based system, we could improve the quality of the project network: the second criterion. Interestingly, we found that the integration of CBR approach and the knowledge-based approach makes feasible the development of the project network generator and improves the quality of the network by mutual enhancement through crosschecking the knowledge and cases in then development and maintenance stages. However, for some complex project network planning, we had to refine a single-case assumed project network generation methodology into Dynamic Leveled Multiple Case (DLMC) approach. The DLMC methodology contributes again to the efficiency and effectiveness of project network generation and reduces the system development effort.

References

1. Hendrickson, C.; Zozaya-Gorostiza, C.; Rehak, D.; Baracco-Miller, E.; and Lim, P. 1987. An Expert System for Construction Planning. Journal of Computing in Civil Engineering 1(4): 253–269.
2. Kartam, N.; Levitt, R.; and Wilkins, D. 1991. Extending Artificial Intelligence Techniques for Hierarchical Planning. Journal of Computing in Civil Engineering 5(4): 464–477.
3. Lee, J. K. 1994. UNIK User's Manual (in Korean), Intelligent Information Systems Laboratory, Korea Advanced Institute of Science and Technology, Seoul, Korea.
4. Lee, K., Kim, H., Lee, J., and Kim, T., "Case- and Constraint-Based Project Planning for Apartment Construction", AI Magazine, vol.19, no.1, pp.13-24, Spring, 1998.
5. Navinchandra, D.; Sriram, D.; and Logcher, R. 1988. GHOST: Project Network Generator. Journal of Computing in Civil Engineering 2(3): 239–254.
6. Ory, S., and Abraham, W. 1995. Knowledge-Based System for Construction Planning of High-Rise Buildings. Journal of Construction Engineering and Management 121(2): 172–182.
7. Winstanley, G.; Chacon, M.; and Levitt, R. 1993. Model-Based Planning: Scaled-Up Construction Application. Journal of Computing in Civil Engineering 7(2): 199–217.
8. Zhang, D., and Maher, M. 1995. Case-Based Reasoning for the Structural Design of Buildings. Paper presented at the Industrial and Engineering Applications of Artificial Intelligence and Expert Systems (IEA/AIE) 95, 6–8 June, Melbourne, Australia.

Integrated CBR Framework for Quality Designing and Scheduling in Steel Industry

Jonghan Kim[1], Deokhyun Seong[2], Sungwon Jung[3], and Jinwoo Park[3]

[1] Production Managemant Research Team, RIST, San 32, Hyoja-Dong, Nam-Gu,
Pohang City, 790-330 Kyungbuk, Korea
kjh@rist.re.kr
[2] School of Business Administration, Pukyong National University,
599-1 Daeyon-Dong, Namgu, Pusan 608-737, Korea
dhsung@pknu.ac.kr
[3] Department of Industrial Engineering, Seoul National University,
San 56-1, Shillim-Dong, Kwanak-Gu, Seoul, 151-742, Korea
jsw25@ultra.ac.kr, autofact@snu.ac.kr

Abstract. In the steel industry, quality designing is related to the determination of mechanical properties of the final products and operational conditions according to the specifications that a customer requests. It involves the utilization of metallurgical knowledge and field experience in the industry. On the other hand, the production scheduling for steel making is a large-scale, multi-objective, grouping and sequencing problem with various restrictions. Traditionally, these two problems have been handled separately. However, the rapid development of information techniques has enabled the simultaneous solution of these two problems. In this paper, we develop an integrated case based reasoning framework for quality designing and scheduling. As proposed, the case base is established with proper case representation scheme, similar cases are retrieved and selected using fuzzy techniques, and finally the selected cases are put into the production process using the scheduling technique. The experimental results show good performance to the quality designing and scheduling of steel products. The framework developed is expected to be applied to other process industries.

1 Introduction

In the steel industry, quality designing for new orders is performed according to the chemical components, operational conditions, and restrictions of the manufacturing facilities. The designing implies the determination of the specifications based on the design standards, design data applied in the past, and the designers' experience. Usually, most orders in steel making companies are designed from prototype designs already prepared, while the remaining orders require particular specification such as extraordinary sizes or product properties. The problem implicated in the steel quality design for each individual customer order to achieve the desired mechanical properties is not merely a one-off application of a specific formula or an algorithm. To make the best decision, the knowledge and experience acquired in the field should be utilized in addition to the mechanical constraints and standards. Literature on steel quality design practice indicates that the designing decision is generally based on practical experience and falls short of using easily understandable and systematic methods.

The production scheduling for steel making is a large-scale, multi-objective, grouping and sequencing problem with various restrictions. There are several factors that restrict production scheduling: product quality specifications, process efficiency, and delivery. Therefore, the relationship of scheduling problems conflicts with these objectives. These quality and scheduling problems are significant in the steel industry that produces formulated products through chemical and physical operations among constituents of the steel products. These types of problems, such as quality designing and scheduling, are usually tackled using artificial intelligence techniques, combinational optimization methods, and heuristic algorithms because of the nature of the problem with mutually conflicting objectives. Traditionally, these two problems have been handled separately. However, the rapid development of information techniques has enabled the simultaneous solution of these two problems. Since the problems of quality design and scheduling are actually interrelated, more cost benefits are gained if problems are solved simultaneously.

In this paper, we develop an integrated framework for quality design and scheduling in the steel making process. This framework is based on case-based reasoning (CBR) for quality design and the bin-packing algorithms and cost-benefit analysis for scheduling. The remainder of this paper is organized as follows. The quality design and scheduling problems in steel products are described and previous research is discussed in Section 2. In section 3, we suggest the integrated model for quality designing and scheduling. Finally, the experimental results are presented in Section 4, and concluding remarks in Section 5.

2 Quality Designing and Scheduling Problem

2.1 Steel Products and Production Processes

Fig.1 shows the production process of wire rod and bar in a steel making company. The first step is the steel making process through Electric Arc Furnace

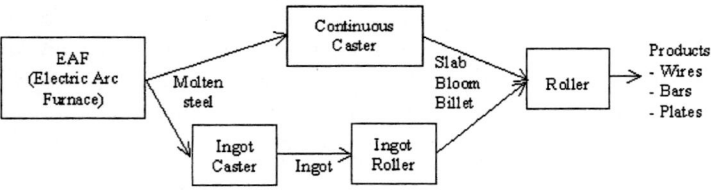

Fig. 1. Production process of plates, wires and bars

(EAF). In EAF, the composition of chemical elements, such as carbon, manganese, silicon, copper, and nickel, is determined and that of other elements is controlled. The molten steel goes through the caster to make billets. Some special products that can not be produced via the continuous caster are processed to the batch process as ingot or bloom making. After casting, the in-process materials, called semi-finished products, go through the rollers to make the final products.

2.2 Quality Designing Problem

The quality of a steel product is usually expressed in terms of yield point, tensile strength, elongation, and other mechanical properties. These are determined by a number of factors as shown in Fig.2. Since the effect of these factors on the steel quality has not been clearly examined, no analytical, quality designing model has ever been developed. Hence the aim of this study to develop a CBR-based model for quality designing.

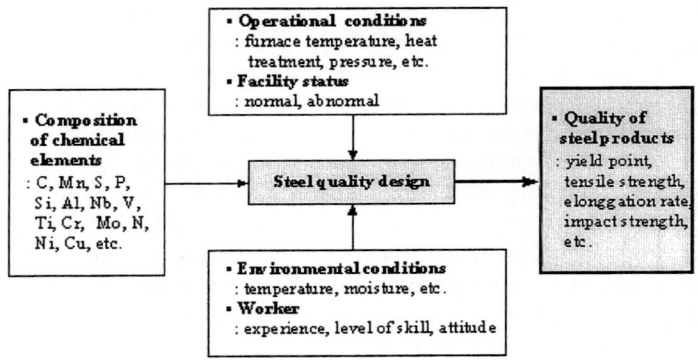

Fig. 2. Factors influencing the quality of steel products

The quality design works may differ according to the client requirements. If there exists a pre-established standard which satisfies the requirement, there is no need to deviate from the standard. If there are two or more pre-established standards, the design is somewhat difficult since choosing the best alternative involves consideration for the cost of manufacturing, previously established scheduling, and sales information. If there is no pre-established standard, a new quality standard should be established using metallurgical knowledge and previous experience. Usually, the quality designing in practice has been manually performed by steel quality designers with comprehensive metallurgical knowledge and more than five years of experience.

2.3 Scheduling Problem

The EAF capacity shown in Fig.1 is usually bigger than the quantity of individual customer order, i.e., one EAF batch should fulfill several customer orders.

Obviously, the orders included in the same batch must have the same composition of chemical elements. The discrepancy between capacity and size of received orders causes the problem of lot sizing and scheduling to accomplish the optimum process operation. This is the reason why we combine the CBR model with scheduling.

2.4 Previous Research

In early '80s, Leslie [8] surveys physical metallurgy models to solve the quality design problem which are limited to some specific ranges of products. VerDuin [15] adopts the statistical methods for the quality design problem. He provides the relationship between the input parameters and the resulting quality properties. However, because of its statistical nature, his approach cannot give the exact relationship to predict the quality properties.

Iwata and Obama [4] develop a quality design expert system (QEDS) that provides valid designs for shaped-steel products. Regardless of his frontier effort for using the expert systems, his results are lacks of considering the operational situation and design adaptation. Omura et al. [12] introduce the quality and process design expert system for steel plates by case-based reasoning. However, they needed a clear definition of similarity for case retrieval and scheduling. Suh et al. [13] present a case-based expert system approach for assisting design engineers and their results are proven to have good applicability. But they fail to consider operational problems such as production flexibility, lot size, and cost.

Recently, the increasing attention has been given to CBR and several tutorials and philosophical investigations are found [5, 7]. CBR has been used successfully in various domains such as diagnosis, prediction, control, and planning. Major concern with these applications is the difficulty in case retrieval and case matching when the number of cases increases [9]. To overcome this difficulty, Bayesian distance measures [6] and some heterogeneous difference metrics [16] are proposed as new similarity measures for case retrieval.

Scheduling methods for each of the steel making processes have also been proposed by many researchers [3, 14]. They develop the scheduling algorithm for the limited process among the integrated steel making processes because the model integration is hard to be achieved. Moreover, combining the quality designing and scheduling is known to be very hard because they are interrelated with.

3 Framework for Integration of Quality Design and Scheduling

A new CBR system for "Steel QUAlity design and Production" called CBR-SQUAP, is developed. The overall framework of the system is illustrated in Fig.3. In this paper, we have employed a CBR and a variant bin-packing algorithm.

A session of a CBR task begins with identification of a new problem. Whenever a customer order is received, CBR-SQUAP searches for the most similar prior case among those in the case base. If we can find a case that entirely matches the new problem, it is passed to the designers to formulate a quality design for the new case. If not, the retrieved one must be adjusted to the new one. As a result, the process is performed partly by the system (CBR-SQUAP) and partly by human designers. The resulting design is released to the scheduling module and processed to the production plant. Once the product is made according to the quality design and scheduling, the quality of the product is examined, and the unique modified case is added to the case base for future use.

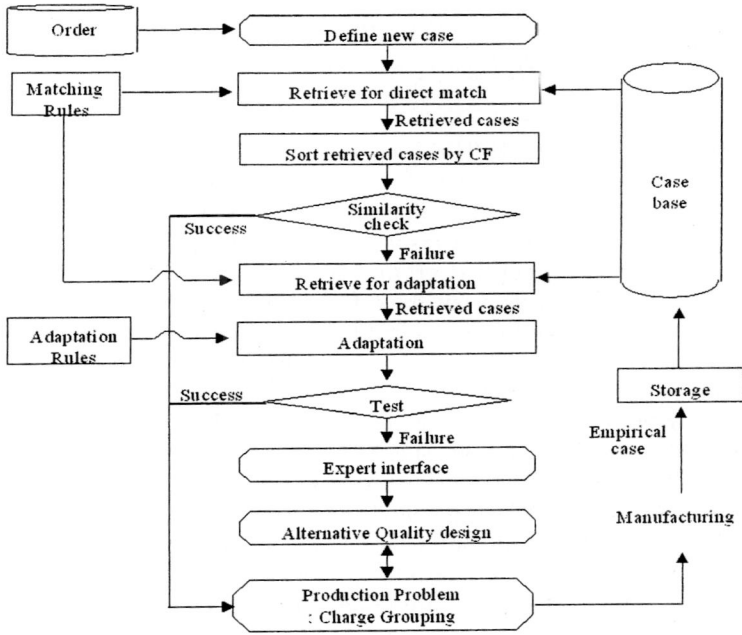

Fig. 3. The framework of CBR-SQUAP

3.1 Case Representation

A case can be defined in terms of the problem description and the potential solutions to the problem. The problem portion describes the mechanical properties of the product; yield point, tensile strength, elongation rate, and impact resistance. The solution part generates the design parameters as determined by the designer or customer. Among the various design parameters, only seventeen chemical compositions are taken into account in designing steel quality. The combination of product category and the serial number serves as the primary key while the product categories are usage, specification, class, and size. The represented usage is based on the classification scheme. To represent cases, four types of tables have been designed as shown in Table 1.

3.2 Retrieval

The retrieval tries to select the most similar cases to the problem among the stored ones. The CBR-SQUAP borrows three methods; induction, nearest neigh-

Table 1. Case representation

Tables	Attributes	Fields
Domain category	Subgroup ID and serial number	Usage, specification class, size, serial number
Problem part	Yield point, tensile strength, elonga-tion rate, hardness, roughness, impact resistance	Lower and upper limits, mode
Solution part	Chemical elements: C, Mn, S, Si, P, Ti, Cu, Mo, N, Al, Nb, V, Ni, Cr, B, Ca, Co	Lower and upper limits, mode
Production & Sales Part	Process Plan, Heat treatment, Cost, Frequency of Orders	2nd Steelmaking process plan, heat treatment, cost

bor, and template retrieval [1]. However, in this paper a new hybrid retrieval is developed that combines the above three and fuzzy theory[10].

For a given new problem, the induction method is first applied and a group of similar cases are identified as a result. Using the domain category table, only the cases stored in the identified group are considered as possible candidates to the new problem because they have the same mechanical properties. The fuzzy nearest neighbor method is applied to these selected cases to filter out the dissimilar ones. Every case in the group is compared with the new problem, and its similarity is calculated. Cases whose similarity is greater than a predetermined threshold are retrieved. If only a single case is retrieved, then it is transferred to the next stage as the matched one. If more than one case is retrieved, the case with a wider range of chemical elements is selected. This is described in detail in the next section. When no cases are retrieved, it means that we have a completely new problem, and the fuzzy nearest neighbor is applied again with the similarity set at a lower predetermined threshold. The following fuzzification method and statistical adaptation are applied to quality design and scheduling.

Fuzzification. The values expressing the mechanical property of a case are considered as "fuzzy" because the mechanical properties of the products differ from the same design. It is accepted that such randomness can be well represented by fuzzy membership functions. We assume that a membership function exists that can well describe the mechanical property of a case. However, the mechanical properties that the customers require are rather non-fuzzy because their values are usually expressed in acceptable ranges, i.e. upper and lower limits. When the inspected property of a product after production falls within the acceptable range, the requirement is fulfilled and the product is delivered. Otherwise, the product is rejected. Therefore, the fuzzy membership function, μ, of a new case, c, for each value of mechanical property, x, can be simply represented by the following uniform function,

$$\mu_c(x) = \begin{cases} 1 & c_{jl} \leq x \leq c_{ju} \\ 0 & elsewhere \end{cases} \quad (1)$$

where c_{jl} and c_{ju} are the lower and upper limits, respectively, of the jth property of case c.

Fuzzy Adaptability. Several fuzzy similarity indices are generally used to indicate the degree to which two fuzzy sets are equal or similar [10]. In this paper, fuzzy adaptability is defined below.

Definition 1. *If a design of a new case is delivered from the design of a prior case, then the two cases are adaptable.*

Let p_{ij} be the jth property of prior case p_i, c_j be the jth property of new case c, and P_{ij} and C_j be the fuzzy sets whose elements are the products described by p_{ij} and c_j, respectively. Also, let $\mu_{P_{ij}}$ and μ_{C_j} be the corresponding membership functions. Here, $\mu_{P_{ij}}$ forms any type of function while μ_{C_j} forms a uniform function. Putting the two functions together, as shown in Fig.4, the shaded area represents the similarity between the two cases. The fuzzy adaptability index should be able to reflect this similarity and the shaded area can be a good indicator for it.

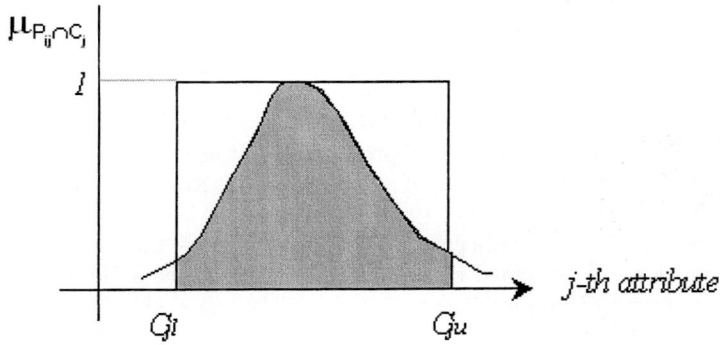

Fig. 4. The membership function and the intersection

In this paper, the adaptability index between P_{ij} and C_j, $ADAP(P_{ij}, C_j)$ is computed using the following equation, where the area of intersection is assumed to be normal from the prior cases.

$$ADAP(P_{ij}, C_j) = \frac{\int_x \mu_{P_{ij} \cap C_j}(x)}{\int_x \mu_{P_{ij}}(x)} \quad (2)$$

Since we deal with n mechanical properties with different importance among them, the weighted adaptability index between P_i and C, $ADAP(P_i, C)$, is defined as

$$ADAP(P_i, C) = \sum_j w_j \cdot ADAP(P_{ij}, C_j), \, for \, i \subseteq \{1, 2, 3, ..., N\} \quad (3)$$

where $\sum_j w_j = 1$, w_j is the weight of jth property and N is the number of prior cases that are contained in the same class with new case c.

The adaptability index takes a value of [0, 1] and its characteristics are observed.

i) $ADAP(P_i, C) = 1$ if and only if $P_i \subseteq C$. This means that all the products produced with the prior case possibly satisfy the requirements of the new case. Therefore, the design contained in the jth property of the solution part of P_i can be directly used for the new case without any modification.

ii) $0 < ADAP(P_i, C) < 1$ if and only if $P_i \cap C \subseteq P_i$. Prior cases with sufficiently high values of $ADAP(P_i, C)$ can be candidates for adaptation for the new case.

iii) $ADAP(P_i, C) = 0$ if and only if $P_i \cap C = \phi$. The case cannot be adapted to the new case.

Decision Making. An adaptability index indicates the degree to which a prior case satisfies the new case. Therefore, we retrieve the prior cases that provide the highest adaptability index. If this value is greater than or equal to a predetermined threshold, 1, then the prior cases are delivered for the new case.

If there are several prior cases with the same adaptability, an additional criterion is necessary to choose a single case from among them. Now, we define the coefficient of flexibility (CF) that is the weighted sum of the range of the attributes of the solution part.

$$CF(P_i j) = p_{iju} - p_{ijl}, \text{ for } j = 1, 2, 3, ..., n \qquad (4)$$

$$CF(P_i) = \sum_j \{w_j \cdot CF(P_{ij}/n)\}, \text{ for } i = 1, 2, 3, ..., N \qquad (5)$$

where $\sum_j w_j = 1$, n is the number of properties that are used in the adaptability computation and N is the number of prior cases that are contained in the same class with new case c.

If the coefficient of flexibility for P_i, $CF(P_i)$, is large, this indicates that the product can be easily assigned to some batch in the process. The past case not only satisfies customer requirements but also maximizes the flexibility of operation. If there are several prior cases with the same adaptability, then the case with the highest CF is selected. Here, the weight of the jth property of solution part, w_j, should be determined by the relationships between manufacturing cost and the difficulty of operation. However, no closed form equation about the relationship exists. In this paper, we form these weights from the inverse of $p_{ija} = (p_{iju} - p_{ijl})/2$ and normalize.

3.3 Adaptation

A new method of *transformational adaptation* has been developed among the proposed methods in [2]. All the retrieved cases have very similar mechanical properties to the new problem except one. We first examine the statistical correlation between the ignored mechanical property and chemical elements. If they are correlated, then the chemical component is determined by regression using all the retrieved cases. While using this method, care should be exercised when the ignored property has the opposite correlation with that of other chemical elements. Solving this type of case is difficult, even in metallurgical sciences, and is beyond the scope of this research. If it is discovered that the specification of the chemical elements does not show any significant relationship with the ignored property, they can be simply set by taking the average of those utilized in the retrieved cases.

3.4 Scheduling

Finally, the retrieved case is delivered to the production process. In case of batch production like the steel making process, the delivered case needs to be inserted smoothly into the in-process batch. This becomes the scheduling problem, especially the optimal lot sizing. In this paper, we develop a variant bin-packing algorithm that is composed of a revised non-decreasing best-fit rule and cost-benefit analysis procedure for for the lot sizing problem arising from the steel making process [11]. The main objective is to minimize the slack capacity in batch where the retrieved case needs to be joined together. In reality, the performance of CBR-SQUAP partly depends upon the scheduling module because the designed case is realized through the actual production.

3.5 Case Retain

Case retaining is a procedure for storing new experience in a case base for future use. Once a new quality design is made from a retrieved one, the new design is checked and compared with previous cases in terms of mechanical properties and percentages of chemical elements. The similarity between p_{ij} and c_j, $SIM(P_{ij}, C_i)$, is similar to the adaptability index. $SIM(P_{ij}, C_i)$, is computed using the following equation.

$$SIM(P_{ij}, C_i) = \frac{2 \int_x \mu_{P_{ij} \cap C_j}(x)}{\int_x \mu_{P_{ij}}(x) + \int_x \mu_{C_j}(x)} \quad (6)$$

The index takes a value of [0, 1]. Some extreme cases of this fuzzy similarity index can be observed. The similarity between p_i and c, $SIM(P_i, C)$, is computed using the following equation,

$$SIM(P_i, C) = \sum_j \{w_j \cdot SIM(P_{ij}, C_j)\}, \quad i = 1, 2, 3, ..., N \quad (7)$$

Let $SIM(P, C) = \underset{i=1,..,N}{Max} SIM(P_i, C)$. If the maximum similarity, $SIM(P, C)$, is less than a predetermined value, then the new case is stored as an case. Otherwise, it is not stored in case base at once.

4 Experimental Results

The proposed scheme has been implemented onto the quality designing process of steel products obtained from one of the steel manufacturing companies in Korea, namely Changwon Specialty Steel Company. This company has gathered a large amount of data (about 200 cases for each product category) and its case base currently hold 4,577 cases. Also, as shown in Tables 2 and 3, a new case is represented as explained in Section 3 while the cases stored in a case base have the same representation scheme.

Table 2. Domain category of new case

Classification	Attribute	Value	Characteristic
Domain category	Usage	STS-300	Stainless Steel (Ni, Cr)
	Specification class	W	Wire
	Size	0.5	5mm

Table 3. Problem part of new case

Classification	Weight	Lower Bound	Upper Bound
Yield point (YP) (Kg/mm^2)	1/3	200	300
Tensile strength (TS) (Kg/mm^2)	2/9	530	600
Elongation (EL) (mm/mm)	2/9	50	70
Roughness (R)	1/9	70	90
Hardness (HARD)	1/9	100	215

To retrieve the similar cases with a new case, we must first calculate five kinds of fuzzy adaptability indices. A triangular form about the distribution of each mechanical element is proven to be well fitted in our experimental model. On the other hand, the distribution of each mechanical attribute of a new case is assumed to be uniform because we have only lower and upper abounds. Hence, there would be eight possible situations that can arise when we calculate the fuzzy adaptability index P_i and C.

SubGroup ID	Seial Num.	YP_L	YP_U	YP_A	TS_L	TS_U	TS_A	EL_L	EL_U	EL_A	R_L	R_U	ADAP (YP,C)	ADAP (TS,C)	ADAP (EL,C)	ADAP (R,C)	ADAP (Hard.,C)	ADAP (Pi, C)
New Case		200	300		530	600		50	70		70	90						
Weight			1.5			1			1			0.5						
Cases																		
STS_300	2	210	260	232.5	540	580	560	50	70	60	70	90	1.00	1.00	1.00	1.00	1.00	1.00
STS_300	1	200	300	250	530	600	565	50	70	60	70	90	1.00	1.00	1.00	1.00	1.00	1.00
STS_300	3	210	280	242.5	540	580	550	50	70	55	60	90	1.00	1.00	1.00	0.78	1.00	0.98
STS_300	4	210	310	257.5	540	585	562.5	40	70	55	70	90	0.98	1.00	0.78	1.00	1.00	0.94
STS_300	5	170	280	225	540	580	550	45	70	55	70	90	0.85	1.00	0.90	1.00	1.00	0.93
STS_300	6	200	240	220	520	580	550	40	70	55	60	90	1.00	0.94	0.78	0.78	1.00	0.91

Fig. 5. Calculating the weigted total fuzzy adaptability

Fig.5 shows a module of our developed system for calculating the weighted total fuzzy adaptability. P_{ij}_L, P_{ij}_U, and P_{ij}_A represent the lower and upper bounds, and average for each mechanical element, P_{ij}. For example, ADAP(YP,C) means the fuzzy adaptability index between the Yield Point and a new case. Two rows, NewCase and Weight, show the problem parts of a new case, and the following rows also represent the problem parts of matched cases stored in a case base. As a result, fuzzy adaptability index of each mechanical element, ADAP(P_{ij},C), is shown on the right, and the weighted total fuzzy adaptability, ADAP(P_i,C), is shown on the last column.

SuBGroup ID	Seial Num.	YP_L	YP_U	YP_A	TS_L	TS_U	TS_A	EL_L	EL_U	EL_A	R_L	R_U	ADAP (Pi, C)	CF
New Case		200	300		530	600		50	70		70	90		
Weight			1.5			1			1			0.5		
Cases														
STS_300	2	210	260	232.5	540	580	560	50	70	60	70	90	1.00	1.86
STS_300	1	200	300	250	530	600	565	50	70	60	70	90	1.00	1.15
STS_300	3	210	280	242.5	540	580	550	50	70	55	60	90	0.98	1.87
STS_300	4	210	310	257.5	540	585	562.5	40	70	55	70	90	0.94	1.83
STS_300	5	170	280	225	540	580	550	45	70	55	70	90	0.93	0.80
STS_300	6	200	240	220	520	580	550	40	70	55	60	90	0.91	1.87

Fig. 6. The example of the adaptability indices and CF

SuBGroup ID	Seial Num.	ADAP(Pi, C)\EI	CF	C_L	C_U	C_A	Si_L	Si_U	Si_A	Mn_L	Mn_U	Mn_A	P_L	P_U	P_A	S_L	S_U
New Case																	
Weight					0.3			0.3			0.5			1			0.5
Cases																	
STS_300	2	1.00	1.86	0	0.035	0.018	0	0.75	0.375	0	2	1	0	0.045	0.023	0	0.03
STS_300	1	1.00	1.15	0	0.03	0.015	0	0.25	0.125	1	2.5	1.75	0	0.03	0.015	0	0.03
STS_300	4	0.99	1.83	0	0.03	0.015	0	1	0.5	0	2	1	0	0.045	0.023	0	0.03
STS_300	3	0.97	1.87	0	0.08	0.04	0	1	0.5	0	2	1	0	0.045	0.023	0	0.03
STS_300	6	0.95	1.87	0	0.03	0.015	0	1	0.5	0	2	1	0	0.045	0.023	0	0.03
STS_300	7	0.95	1.90	0	0.08	0.04	0	0.75	0.375	0	2	1	0	0.045	0.023	0	0.03
STS_300	9	0.95	1.92	0	0.08	0.04	0	1	0.5	0	2	1	0	0.2	0.100	0.1	0.15

Fig. 7. The example of the designed quality corresponding to the new case

We have retrieved two cases that have the same maximum adaptability. The coefficient of flexibility (CF) is calculated, and the last two columns in Fig.6 show the adaptability indices and CF in descending order. So, the designer can select the best one from the retrieved cases and designs the new case using the retrieved one. In this example, a case among the candidates which have the largest CF is chosen, and the quality designing is done using the selected case. The right columns in Fig.7 show the designed quality, which are represented by the specification of each chemical element.

As explained above, if we have one or more retrieved cases, it is not complicated. However, the problem becomes more complicated if no case is retrieved, which means $SIM(P,C) = \underset{i=1,..,N}{Max} ADAP(P_i, C) < 1$. In order for a problem to have no case retrieved, we can change the lower bound of elongation from 55 to 50. The fuzzy adaptability index is recalculated when the infeasible mechanical element, elongation, is excluded. The notation $ADAP(P_i, C)\backslash EL$ of the last column of table 4 means the fuzzy adaptability index when elongation is excluded. Twenty-seven prior cases are retrieved if we set $ADAP(P_i, C)\backslash EL \geq 0.9$ The correlation coefficients between elongation and the chemical components are drawn using the above 26 retrieved cases. Among the chemical components, only Si, Mn, and Co are selected as having the great relationship with EL. (In the experiment, the threshold is set to be 0.5). This implies that the values of

Table 4. The result of statistical analysis

Components	Correlation	Cases that have $ADAP(P_i, C)\backslash EL = 1$			Designed quality		
		Lower Bound	Mode	Upper Bound	Lower Bound	Mode	Upper Bound
EL	1	50	63	70	**55**	**63**	**70**
C	0.118	0	0.0162	0.033	0	0.0162	0.033
Si	**-0.813**	0	0.25	0.5	*0*	*0.24*	*0.49*
Mn	**0.556**	0.5	1.38	2.25	*0.51*	*1.42*	*2.31*
P	-0.124	0	0.019	0.38	0	0.019	0.38
S	-0.096	0	0.02	0.03	0	0.02	0.03
Ni	0.032	9.5	11	12.5	9.5	11	12.5
Cr	0.02	17.8	18.9	20	17.8	18.9	20
Mo	0.074	1	1.4	1.8	1	1.4	1.8
Cu	-0.108	0	0.15	0.3	0	0.15	0.3
Al	na	na	na	na	na	na	na
V	na	na	na	na	na	na	na
Ti	-0.067	0	0	0	0	0	0
Co	**0.556**	0	0.050	0.100	*0*	*0.051*	*0.103*
Nb	na	na	na	na	na	na	na
N	0.184	0	0.045	0.09	0	0.045	0.09
B	na	na	na	na	na	na	na
Ca	na	na	na	na	na	na	na

selected three mechanical properties are geared with elongation. For example, Si will probably decrease as elongation increases while Mn and Co will increase.

Table 4 shows the designed quality of a new case. As shown in this table, only the lower bound of EL is assumed to increase from 50 to 55 while mode and upper bounds are assumed to remain constant. Then the average of EL is changed from 61 to 62.67 that is 2.7% increase. The correlation analysis gives theoretical backup of changing the values of Si, Mn, and Co proportionally to the correlated direction. In this experiment, the lower and upper bounds and mode of Si decrease about 2.7% from the original values while those values of Mn and Co increases 2.7%.

In case where no significant correlation is found between the excluded property and the chemical components, then the process would have to handled manually. But this matter shall not be discussed here as it is out of the scope of this paper.

The designed case should be put into the production process. To integrate the quality designing and the scheduling, all of the retrieved cases are passed to the scheduling module in descending order of the fuzzy adaptability and coefficient of flexibility. This means that usually we can have the feasible lot sizing using the next best retrieved case if we fail to make batch with the best retrieved case. As a result, it improves the performance of scheduling based on the bin packing heuristics even if all the information about the retrieved cases, including those that are not among the best ones, are forwarded. The performance of bin-packing heuristics largely depends upon the number of feasible sets. The more the retrieved cases delivered to the production process, the easier the scheduling module. Thus, we can obtain a "good" feasible solution to the lot sizing problem with bin-packing heuristics.

Table 5 shows two orders that have different design specifications; Order 1 is for (STS_400,1) and Order 2 is for (STS_400,2). The quantity of each order is 15 and 20 tons, respectively, and the capacity of a furnace is 35 tons. Therefore, each order is processed to the furnace separately because of different design specifications. In this case, the planning inventory of each order should be 20 tons and 15 tons for Order 1 and Order 2, respectively. However, if the alternative design criterion for Order 2 is set as (STS_400,1) by quality design module, then two orders can be combined into one batch at the furnace, and no planned inventory results. Less planned inventory leads to reduce the amount of scrapped products, which saves cost substantially. On average, about 40% of the planned inventory is scrapped, and they are sold at extremely low price.

Table 5. Specifications and designed alternatives

Order No	Design Specification	Order Quantity	Alternative Designed Specification	Order Frequency
1	STS_400,1	15	na	2 months
2	STS_400,2	20	STS_400,1	2 years

Experiments showed that 89% among 3,000 orders received had only one retrieved case while 10% had multiple retrieved cases. The remaining 1% hade no retrieved case and the proposed scheme was able to produce a solution for overcoming this kind of problem.

5 Conclusion and Further Research

In this paper, we propose an integrated framework for quality designing and scheduling applied in steel making companies. This framework is based on the case-based reasoning for quality designing and a bin-packing algorithm for scheduling. To design the quality of steel products, the process is carried out sequentially in the following order of case representation, retrieval using fuzzy adaptation, and storing the selected new case. The designed case is passed onto the production process. To make the production process smoother when handling a new design, it should be included in the in-process batch, which in turns causes brings lot sizing. The ultimate objective of the proposed framework is to integrate the entire quality designing and scheduling processes. The proposed framework had been implemented in actual steel making processed and the result showed good performance.

The CBR-SQUAP showed that the repetitive quality designing and adaptation can be performed very quickly on Windows XP and able to produce results that can save about 1.8 millon dollars a year than before.This saving comes from several factors; minimization of the planned inventory, which reduces the amount of scrapped products, and increased productivity as a result of increased lot size combined properly. Moreover, the time consumed in carrying out our operation with a PC does not even exceed 10 minutes. Finally, we are planning on the extending the approach provided here in several respects, one immediate concern is case merging in case base and the case retain procedures minimize memory storage.

References

1. Aamodt, A., and Plaza, E.: Case-based reasoning: foundational issues, methodological variations, and system approach. AI Communications. **7** (1), 39-59(1994)
2. Hanney, K., Keane, T., Smyth B., and Cunningham, P.: What kind of adaptation do CBR systems need? : A review of current practice. In: Proceedings of the 1995 AAAI Fall symposium, 1995, pp128-146
3. Hyungwoo, P., Yushin H., and Sooyoung C.: An efficient scheduling algorithm for the hot coil making in the steel mini-mill. Production Planning and Control **13** (3), 298-306 (2002)
4. Iwata, Y. and Obama, N.: QDES: Quality-design expert system for steel product. In: Proceedings of the 3rd innovative application of AI conference, 1991, pp177-191
5. Kolodner, J.: *Case-Based Reasoning* (Morgan Kaufmann, San Francisco, California 1993)
6. Kontkanen, P., Lathinen J., Myllymaki P., and Tirri H.: An unsupervised Bayesian distance measure. In: Proceedings of the 5th European Workshop on Case-Based Reasoning, EWCBR2000, 2000, pp148-160
7. Leake, D.: *Case-Based Reasoning: Experiences, Lessons, and Future Directions* (AAAI Press, Menlo Park, California 1996)
8. Leslie, W.: *The physical metallurgy of steels* (McGraw-Hill 1981)
9. Juan C., Emilio C., Jim A., and Colin F.: Maximum likelihood Hebbian learning based retrieval method for CBR systems. In: Proceedings of the 5th international conference on case-based reasoning, ICCBR 2003, 2003, pp107-121
10. Mukaidono, A., and Masao, E.: *Fuzzy logic for beginners* (World Scientific Pub Co. 2001)
11. Nemhauser, L., and Wolsey, A.: *Integer and combinatorial optimization* (John Wiley & Sons 1988)
12. Omura, K., Watanabe, T., Konishi, M., Shosaki, N., and Maeoka, K.: Application of expert system for quality design and process design of steel products. In: Proceedings of the IEEE symposium on engineering techniques and factory automating, 2004, pp92-98
13. Suh, M.S., Jhee, W.C., Ko, Y.K., Lee, A.: A case-based expert system approach for quality design. Expert Systems with Applications **15**, 181-190 (1998)
14. Tang, L.X., Lue, P.B., Liu, J.Y., and Fang, L.: Steel-making process scheduling using Lagrangian relaxation. International Journal of Production Research **40** (1), 55-70 (2002)
15. VerDuin, W.H.: Role of integrated AI technologies in product formulation. ISA Transactions **31**(2), 151-157 (1992)
16. Wilson, D. and Martinez, T.: Improved heterogeneous distance functions. Journal of Artificial Intelligence Research **6**, 1-34 (1997)

RHENE: A Case Retrieval System for Hemodialysis Cases with Dynamically Monitored Parameters

Stefania Montani[1], Luigi Portinale[1], Riccardo Bellazzi[2], and Giorgio Leonardi[2]

[1] Dipartimento di Informatica, Università del Piemonte Orientale,
Spalto Marengo 33, 15100 Alessandria, Italy
{stefania,portinal}@unipmn.it
[2] Dipartimento di Informatica e Sistemistica, Università di Pavia
Via Ferrata 1, 27100 Pavia, Italy
riccardo.bellazzi@unipv.it giorgio@aim.unipv.it

Abstract. In this paper, we present a case-based retrieval system called RHENE (**R**etrieval of **HE**modialysis in **NE**phrological disorders) working in the domain of patients affected by nephropatologies and treated with hemodialysis. Defining a dialysis session as a case, retrieval of past similar cases has to operate both on static and on dynamic (time-dependent) features, since most of the monitoring variables of a dialysis session are time series. In RHENE, retrieval relies upon a multi-step procedure. In particular, a preliminary grouping/classification step, based on static features, reduces the retrieval search space. Intra-class retrieval then takes place by considering time-dependent features, and is articulated as follows: (1) "locally" similar cases (considering one feature at a time) are extracted and the intersection of the retrieved sets is computed; (2) "global" similarity is computed - as a weighted average of local distances - and the best cases are listed. The main goal of the paper is to present an approach for efficiently implementing step (2), by taking into account specific information regarding the final application. We concentrate on a classical dimensionality reduction technique for time series allowing for efficient indexing, namely Discrete Fourier Transform (DFT). Thanks to specific index structures (i.e. *k-d trees*) range queries (on local feature similarity) can be efficiently performed on our case base; as mentioned above, results of such local queries are then suitably combined, allowing the physician to examine the most similar stored dialysis sessions with respect to the current one and to assess the quality of the overall hemodialysis service,

1 Introduction

Health Care Organizations (HCO) have nowadays evolved into complex enterprises, in which the management of knowledge and information resources is a key success factor in order to improve their efficacy and efficiency. Unfortunately, although HCO are data-rich organizations, their capability of managing implicit (i.e. operative) knowledge is still very poor: the day-by-day collection of patients' clinical data, of health care provider actions (e.g. exams, drug deliveries, surgeries) and of health care processes data (admissions, discharge, exams request) is not often followed by a thorough analysis of such kind of information. Thanks to the Knowledge Management (KM) perspective [5], on the other hand, it is now clear that implicit knowledge may be effectively used to change organizational settings and to maintain and retrieve unstructured situation-action information [13]. In recent years, Case-Based Reasoning (CBR) has become widely accepted as a useful computational instrument for KM; the retrieval and reuse of past data and the possibility of retaining new information fit the KM objectives of keeping, increasing and reusing knowledge with particular attention to decision making support [5].

In medical applications, in particular, analogical reasoning is typically applied for decision making: physicians actually reason by recalling past situations, afforded by themselves or by some colleague and this kind of process is often biased by the tendency of recalling only the most recent cases. The CBR methodology could be of great help, since it enables an automatic retrieval of *all relevant* past situation-action patterns (including the oldest ones), as well as the retrieval of the other physicians' expertise, embedded into concrete examples [12].

Despite CBR appears to be an appropriate technique to support medical decisions, its exploitation in this field has not been as successful as in other domains; probably the weakness resides in the difficulties of implementing the adaptation step of the CBR cycle [1], adaptation being strongly application-dependent. As a matter of fact, the definition of a (possibly general) framework for performing adaptation in medical problems is a challenging task. Moreover, physicians would not easily accept a therapy/diagnosis automatically produced by a decision support system. On the other hand, a pure retrieval system, able to extract relevant knowledge, but that leaves the user the responsibility of providing an interpretation of the current case and of proposing a solution, seems much more suitable in this context.

The goal of this paper is to present RHENE[1] (Retrieval of **HE**modialysis in **NE**phrological disorders) a case-based system, developed in order to investigate the application of retrieval techniques in a time-dependent clinical domain: the management of End Stage Renal Disease (ESRD) patients treated with hemodialysis. Even though the system concentrates only on case retrieval, its architecture is non-trivial. In particular, a multi-step procedure is implemented, where retrieval itself is anticipated by a *grouping/classification* phase. Classification provides a reduction of the retrieval search space, by identifying relevant subparts of the case base. In particular, the procedure can be automatic (the system implements a k-Nearest Neighbour (k-NN) approach on a subset of the case features), or user driven (the physician explicitly selects on which subparts of the library s/he wants to concentrate the attention).

Intra-class *retrieval* is then performed. Retrieval is in turn structured in a multi-step fashion: *local similarity* is first taken into account, by allowing the selection of a subset of very relevant features, on which a range query (one

---

[1] RENE in Italian means *kidney*.

in each feature's direction) is executed. The intersection of the locally similar cases is then computed, thus extracting the cases that satisfy the request of being within all the specified ranges of similarity contemporaneously. Clearly this is a strong requirement, but results can be finely tuned by varying the range parameters. *Global similarity* is then computed, as a weighted average of local similarities in the space of all the case features (including classification ones). In this way, the best cases are identified and ranked.

In particular, since in the hemodialysis domain most of the case features are in the form of time series, the (local) retrieval step requires a pre-processing phase; in this phase dimensionality reduction techniques are applied to, in order to speed up the retrieval process itself, while maintaining sufficient information about the series and avoiding false dismissals[2].

Finally, retrieval takes advantage of an index structure, built on the series coefficients, that allows to avoid exhaustive search. A range query algorithm directly operating on the index has been implemented [14].

The paper is organized as follows: section 2 provides some details about the application domain, while section 3 addresses the technical aspects of our approach, by describing the basic RHENE architecture with some examples of useful retrieval of dialysis sessions; conclusions are discussed in section 4.

2 Hemodialysis Treatment for ESRD

ESRD is a severe chronic condition that corresponds to the final stage of kidney failure. Without medical intervention, ESRD leads to death. Hemodialysis is the most widely used treatment method for ESRD; it relies on an electromechanical device, called hemodialyzer, which, thanks to an extracorporal blood circuit, is able to clear the patient's blood from metabolites, to re-establish acid-base equilibrium and to remove water in excess. On average, hemodialysis patients are treated for four hours three times a week. Each single treatment is called a hemodialysis (or simply a dialysis) session. Hemodialyzers typically allow to collect several variables during a session, most of which are in the form of time series (see Table 1); a few are recorded in the form of single data points (see Table 2 for some of them). As regards time series, in the current technical settings the sampling time ranges from 1 min to 15 min.

The most important analysis is to evaluate the agreement of the dialysis session to the prescribed therapy plan; in fact, sessions are classified as: **type 1**, positive session that agree to the therapy plan without external (from hospital attendants) intervention; **type 2**, positive session after attendants' intervention; **type 3**, negative session that fail to adhere to the therapy plan. In this context, the application of case-based retrieval techniques seems particularly suitable for hemodialysis efficiency assessment. In particular, defining a dialysis session as a case, it is possible to retrieve cases with the same outcome, or, more in detail, to

---

[2] As we will clarify in the following, since we execute retrieval in a transformed (reduced) feature space, we must assure that distance computation on the transformed space never overestimate actual distance.

Table 1. Monitoring variables for hemodialysis, collected as time series.

Variable name	Abbreviation
Venous Pressure	VP
Blood Bulk Flow	QB
Arterial Pressure	AP
Systolic Pressure	SP
Diastolic Pressure	DP
Cardiac Frequency	CF
Hemoglobin	Hb
Hematic Volume	HV
Output Pressure of dialyzer	OP
Dialysate Conductivity	DC

Table 2. Monitoring variables for hemodialysis, collected as single data points (one per session).

Variable name	Abbreviation
Weight Before Session	WB
Weight Loss	WL
Dry Weight	DW
Vascular Access	VA
Dialysis Time duration	T

look for similar situations - typically patterns corresponding to persistent failures over time. It is then possible to highlight if these patterns are repeated over the same patient or over different ones and what solutions have been provided in those cases, in terms of dialysis prescription (i.e. the prescribed flow rates at the beginning of dialysis).

3 RHENE: A Case Retrieval System for ESRD

3.1 Basic Architecture

As previously observed, in our application, a dialysis session is interpreted as a case. The case structure involves two categories of features:

- *static features*, representing: (i) general information about the patient such as age class, sex, type of the disease that caused ESRD; (ii) long-term varying data about the patient, that can be approximately considered as static within an interval of a few weeks/months (e.g. several laboratory exams); finally (iii) general information about the dialysis session and the dialysis targets such as the dry weight - i.e. the desired weight at the end of a dialysis session, the vascular access, the dialysis duration and the additional pharmacological treatments (see Table 2);
- *dynamic (time-dependent) features* which are the information automatically recorded within a dialysis session in the form of time series with different sampling times (see Table 1).

Moreover, each case records the *outcome* of the session, following the classification outlined in section 2 (type 1, 2 and 3).

Case structure is described by the Entity-Relationship diagram of figure 1; time invariant information about each patient and the whole dialysis session are mantained in the PATIENT and SESSION_STATIC entities respectively, while time series information are maintained in the SESSION_DYNAMIC$_i$ entities corresponding to session dynamic feetures. Note that the case outcome is a static information and it is therefore stored in the SESSION_STATIC entity.

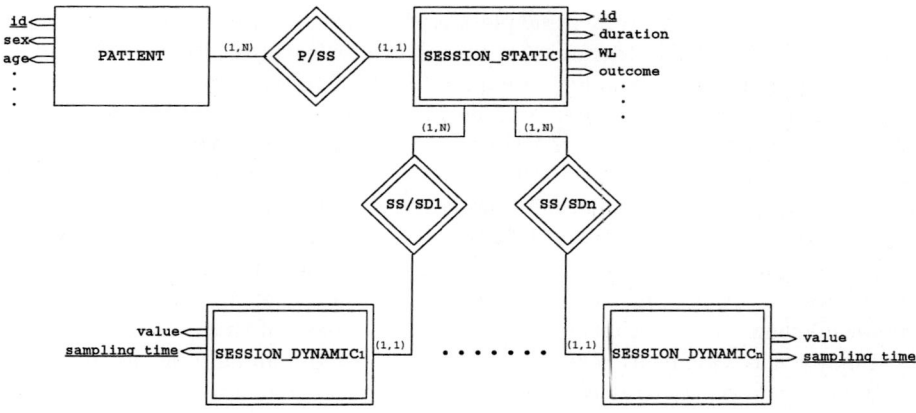

Fig. 1. Case structuring in RHENE.

Since static features provide both a general characterization of the patient and of the dialysis session as a whole, they provide the context under which to evaluate the results of the dialysis, based on the interpretation of all the relevant measured parameters (both static and dynamic). Following some classical CBR literature [7], defining the context for retrieval corresponds to the so-called *situation assessment* step of CBR. Therefore, it is quite natural to structure case retrieval as a two-step procedure, articulated as follows:

1. **Grouping/Classification.** Produces the relevant context under which to base retrieval; a classification step can be important if the physician needs to restrict attention only to particular subsets of the whole case base.
2. **Retrieval.** Takes place on the restricted case base possibly produced by the classification step (intra-class retrieval); in our system, it is in turn a two-step procedure: first a local retrieval in the space of each single dynamic feature is performed, by exploiting a range query on the corresponding index, finally local retrievals are suitably combined, in order to produce the set of most similar cases to the current one.

In the following, we will motivate and detail our approach, with particular emphasis on intra-class retrieval.

3.2 Grouping/Classification

The classification step is implemented relying on static features alone. Target classes can be both implicit or explicit. In the first situation, there is no need to explicitly identify a set of predefined classes, so this phase implements a kind of "grouping" operation; a k-NN step is used, in order to restrict the case library. This makes sense for example when a grouping is required at the PATIENT entity level; static features of the patient are used in order to obtain (through *k-NN retrieval*) the set of most similar patient: only cases related to such patients are then used in intra-class retrieval.

This approach can be in principle adopted also when considering both patient and session static features (or session static features alone); however, in this case it is more reasonable to exploit a set of predefined explicit classes[3]. The explicit target classes can be identified in the different diseases patients are affected with or in particular characterizations of patients concerning age, sex, weight, life style or in characterization of sessions concering duration, drug treatments, hemodialysis treatment modality, etc... Cases belonging to the same class as the input case are identified this time through *k-NN classification* and they will be used as the search space for the subsequent retrieval step. In other words, we classify the input case through *k-NN* and then we perform retrieval by considering only the case library restricted to cases of that particular class.

Finally, the classification step can also be realized manually by the physician if s/he wants to directly restrict her/his attention to particular cases; for instance s/he can be interested only in cases belonging to the same patient in the latest month, or only in cases of patients following a given diet, etc...

In order to implement this step, in RHENE we resort to the standard Heterogeneous Euclidean-Overlap Metric (HEOM) [15], with the use of distance tables in case of nominal features.

3.3 Intra-class Retrieval

Intra-class retrieval is the core of our methodology. At the beginning of the consultation, the physician has the possibility of choosing a set of dynamic features (that are in the form of time series) on which to ground the retrieval; this allows her/him to focus the attention on a subset of features that s/he considers relevant for the analysis s/he's going to perform. The requirement implemented by the system is that the retrieved cases must have a required level of similarity for every selected feature. For each one of the selected dynamic features (a subset of those listed in Table 1), we work on *local similarity*, i.e. we look for the most similar cases to the input case relatively to the dimension represented by the feature at hand. Local results are then combined and a set of complete cases is returned, ranked by global similarity with respect to the target one (see below).

A wide literature exists about similarity-based retrieval of time series. Several different approaches have been proposed (see the survey in [6]), but most are based on the common premise of dimensionality reduction. The reduction of the time series dimensionality should adopt a transform that preserves the distance between two time series or understimates it. In the latter case a post-processing step is required to filter out the so-called "false alarms"; the requirement is never to overstimate the distance, so that no "false dismissals" can exist [6]. A widely used transform is the Discrete Fourier Transform (DFT) [2].

DFT maps time series to the frequency domain. DFT application for dimensionality reduction stems from the observation that, for the majority of real-world time series, the first (1-3) Fourier coefficients carry the most meaningful information and the remaining ones can be safely discarded. Moreover, Parseval's

---

[3] Indeed, if we perform *k*-NN retrieval on session static feature, too few cases will be kept as search space, unless to consider large values for *k*.

theorem [10] guarantees that the distance in the frequency domain is the same as in the time domain, when resorting to any similarity measure that can be expressed as the Euclidean distance between feature vectors in the feature space. In particular, resorting only to the first Fourier coefficients can understimate the real distance, but never overestimates it.

In our system, we implemented DFT as a means for dimensionality reduction, exploiting the Euclidean distance as a similarity measure (in particular, in presence of missing data, we set the distance equal to its maximum value, i.e. to the feature range). The choice of DFT is motivated by the observation that DFT is a standard technique. Moreover, DFT offers the possibility of relying on well known index structures, without studying ad hoc solutions and avoiding exhaustive search. In particular, we have implemented an index belonging to the family of k-d trees and a range query algorithm directly operating on k-d trees themselves [14].

Note that, if every distance is in the range $[0,1]$ independently of the considered feature f, it becomes more natural to characterize a range query, and we can exploit a set of parameters $0 \leq s_i \leq 1$ as the distance thresholds for the various range queries concerning the dynamic features of our cases.

In order to make the distance scale independent with respect to the series values, we operate as follows. Given two time series $X = \{x_1, \ldots x_r\}$ and $Y = \{y_1, \ldots y_q\}$, a parametric distance measure can be defined by considering an integer parameter p (if $p = 2$ we get the standard Euclidean distance):

$$D(X, Y, p) = \left(\sum_{j=1}^{\min(r,q)} |x_j - y_j|^p \right)^{\frac{1}{p}}$$

Distance can then be normalized over the range $RANGE_f$ of the corresponding feature f:

$$D_f(X, Y, p) = \left(\frac{1}{m} \sum_{j=1}^{m} \left| \frac{x_j - y_j}{RANGE_f} \right|^p \right)^{\frac{1}{p}} = \frac{D(X, Y, p)}{m^{\frac{1}{p}} RANGE_f}$$

with $m = \min(r, q)$.

In details, given a query case C_Q, intra-class retrieval starts by considering each single dynamic feature f that the physician has selected for her/his analysis; let T_f be the k-d tree index for feature f, Q_f the query series (i.e. the time series relative to feature f in case C_Q) and s the distance threshold for the range query (obviously, for a non-selected feature it is sufficient to apply the same mechanism and to perform the range query with $s = 1$). The following steps are then implemented: since the dialysis device has starting and ending phases during which monitored data are meaningless, the query series Q_f is first validated by removing head and tail data corresponding to noisy values; in this way all the considered time series are aligned to the first valid point. After that, Q_f is reduced through DFT by considering a predefined number of coefficients[4]

---

[4] The number of DFT coefficients to consider is a tunable parameter of the system.

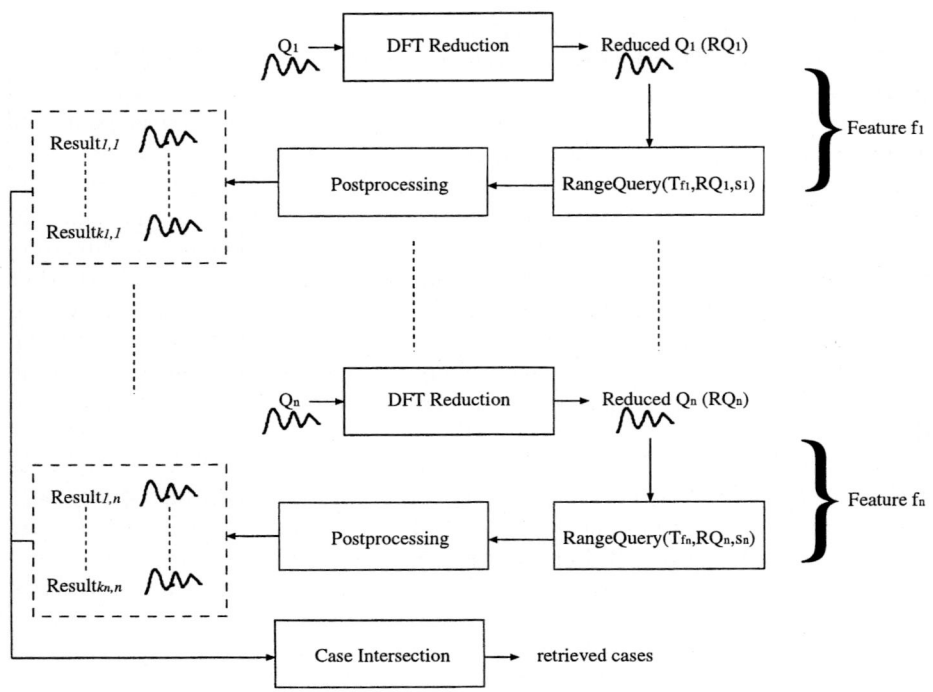

Fig. 2. Block scheme for local retrieval.

(usually from 3 to 6). We are then able to perform a range query on T_f using the reduced Q_f and the threshold s; this returns a set of time series (relative to feature f) having a distance from Q_f that may be less than s (due to Parseval's theorem we are only guaranteed that no indexed time series whose distance is actually less than s has been missed). We then need a post-processing of the results, where actual distance with respect to Q_f is computed.

The whole process is performed for every dynamic feature that has been selected for local retrieval and finally only cases that have been retrieved in every feature direction are returned (case intersection). Figure 2 depicts this mechanism. As a matter of fact, the case intersection step first extracts from the case library the whole case to which the series belongs and then perform the intersection of the obtained set of cases. In this way we are guaranteed that returned cases have a distance less than the threshold for every considered dynamic feature (as mentioned above).

Since we are finally interested in obtaining the best cases in terms of global distance with respect to C_Q, we compute such a global measure as a weighted average of feature (local) distances for every returned case:

$$D(C, C_Q) = \frac{\sum_{i=1}^{n} w_i D_{f_i}(X_{C,i}, Y_{Q,i}, p)}{\sum_{i=1}^{n} w_i}$$

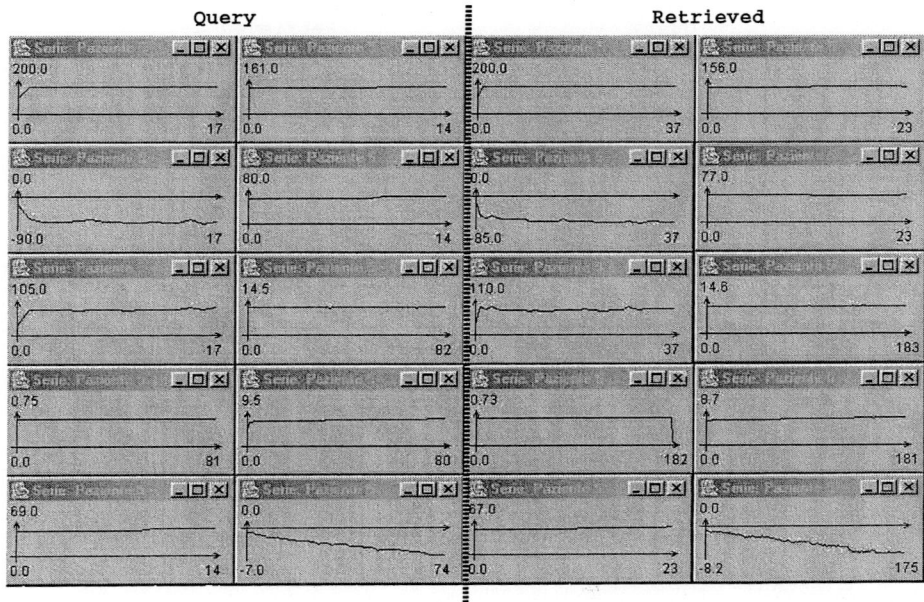

Fig. 3. Example of retrieval of signals of a dialysis session: query case (on the left), best retrieved case (on the right). Parameters in both cases are shown in the same position (e.g. top left series of the query case corresponds to top left series of the retrieved one and so on); numbers on the ordinate of each graphic represent maximum or minimum value of the time series.

where C is a retrieved case, C_Q the query case, $X_{C,i}$ and $Y_{Q,i}$ are the time series (values) of the feature f_i in case C and C_Q respectively and w_i is the weight representing the importance of feature f_i; the latter is another tunable parameter of the system available to the physician for biasing the order of presentation with more emphasis on a particular set of features (usually those selected for local retrieval, since they represent the features on which to base the analysis of the results).

3.4 Some Retrieval Examples

We tested the retrieval system on a set of data coming from the Nephrology and Dialysis Unit of the Vigevano Hospital. The data set comprises 45 different patients with more that 200 dialysis sessions for each patient and with 10 different monitored signals (the time series features of Table 1) for each session.

As a first example, we have considered a case (patient #5, dialysis #72) in which, even though the outcome is classified as succesfull (i.e. type 1), a more subtle analysis reveals some sub-optimal behaviors in the monitored parameters.

In particular, the patient suffers from hypertension. Hypertension, in turn, may cause alterations in the hematic volume (HV) reduction. In a good session

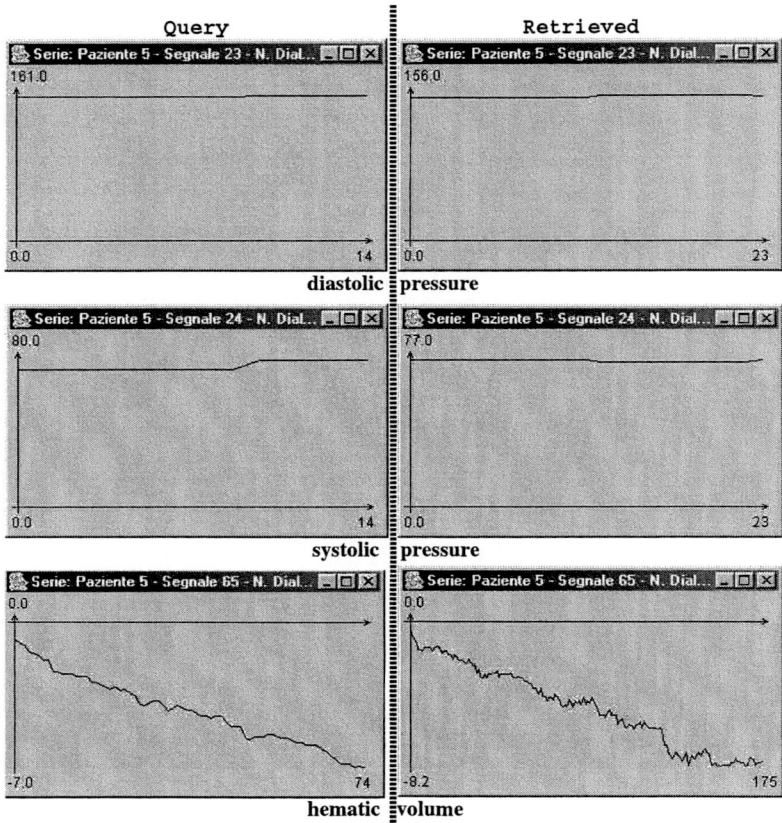

Fig. 4. Diastolic, systolic pressure and hematic volume retrieval (cfr. fig. 3).

HV fits a model where, after a short period of exponential decrease, a linear decrease follows; hypertension may inhibit the exponential pattern, and lead to a slower reduction of the HV, that fits a linear model since the beginning of the session. As a matter of fact, in the case at hand this situation holds. Figure 3 shows on the left (first two columns) all the signals of the query case (patient #5, dialysis #72). Figure 4 (always on the left) highlights on the diastolic pressure (DP) and systolic pressure (SP) as well as on the HV.

Retrieval was performed by asking for a high similarity (distance threshold equal to 0.15) with respect to DP, SP, blood bulk flow (QB) and HV; QB is the first shown signal (top-left) of the cases in figure 3 and has been considered as an important contextual factor of the retrieval. In correspondence to these very relevant features, we also set the highest weights to be used for global similarity calculation.

The right part of figure 3 shows an overview of the first retrieved case (patient #5, dialysis #36), while figure 4 (on the right) details the situation of the DP,

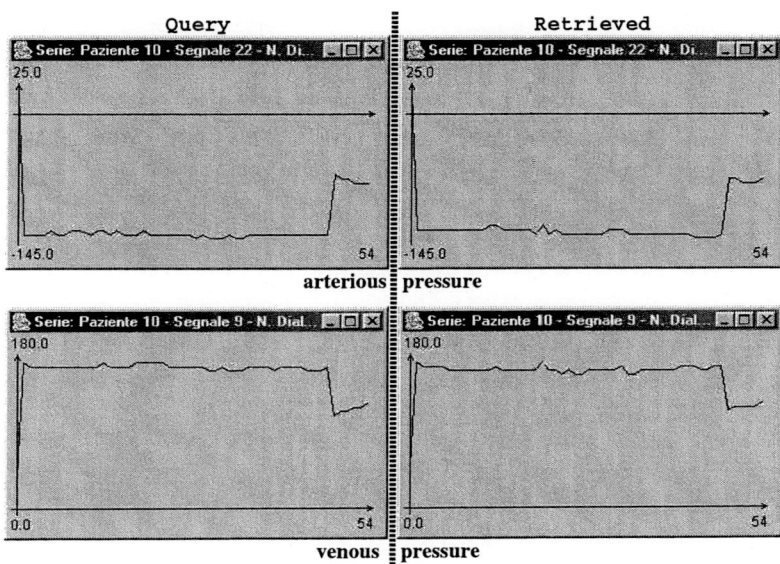

Fig. 5. Arterious and venous pressure retrieval in the second example.

SP and HV features. These time series behaviors look very similar in the two cases (see figure 4): in particular, hypertension is present in both situations; moreover, even though less data points are available for the query case with respect to the retrieved one, it is clear that the HV decreases linearly, missing the initial exponential pattern.

Observe that also the retrieved case was labeled as successful by the physician. Actually, it seems that the outcome definition is based just on a macroscopic observation of (a subset of) the features. On the other hand, our system allows to obtain a deeper insight of the situation, highlighting types of anomalies which, if they don't lead to an immediate dialysis failure, could produce poor therapeutic results in the long run.

As a second example, we have considered a case (patient #10, dialysis #71) in which some alterations in the extra-corporeal blood circuit took place. This kind of problems (typically due to an occlusion of the patient's fistulae) are indicated by a sudden increase of the arterious pressure (AP) around the end of the session, and by a corresponding decrease of the venous pressure (VP). Retrieval has been conducted by requiring a high similarity for AP and VP, and by assigning them the highest weights. Figure 5 details the values of AP and VP for the query case and for the best retrieved one; the overview is not provided due to lack of space.

Observe that, while the query case was labeled as succesfull (type 1 outcome), the retrieved case has a type 2 outcome (i.e. succesfull after nurse intervention). In particular, the nurse provided the patient with a diuretic drug, to compensate hypotension.

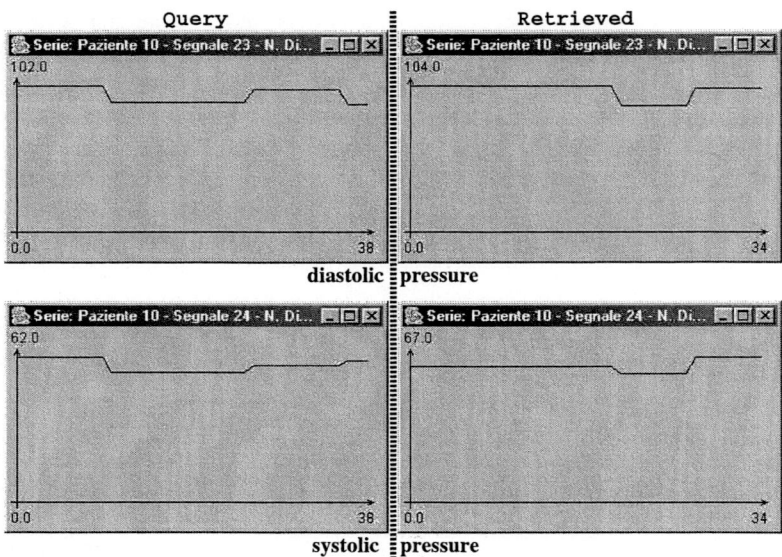

Fig. 6. Diastolic and systolic pressure retrieval in the second example.

This result has led us to consider the values of DP and SP (see figure 6): as a matter of fact, the values are low in both cases (in particular, the final increase in the retrieved case corresponds to the drug effect). The information provided by the retrieval procedure can thus warn the physician to pay particular attention to hypotension for this patient, since in the past a medical intervention was required, in a situation that is extremely similar to the current one.

In conclusion, our tool provides results that allow to better assess the dialisys efficiency, and that can indicate directions for further analyses and considerations.

4 Conclusions and Future Works

In this paper, we have described an application of case-based retrieval in a time-dependent clinical domain: the treatment of ESRD patients. Despite only the first phase of the CBR cycle is implemented, the system architecture is non-trivial, as retrieval is articulated as a multi-step procedure. Moreover, since most of the case features are in the form of time series, dimensionality reduction (based on DFT) and indexing techniques (based on k-d trees) have been relied upon.

The system is provided with a user-friendly graphical interface, which allows the physician to tune the retrieval parameters (e.g. ranges and importance of the features), in order to focus her/his attention on different aspects of the dialysis sessions. Moreover, s/he can choose whether to visualize the overall case structure, or to concentrate the retrieval on a single feature. In this way, the tool proves to be a flexible means for realizing an explorative analysis of the patient's data: it allows to look for similar situations (typically patterns corresponding to persistent failures over time), understanding if these patterns are repeated over the same patient or over different ones, and retrieving what solutions have been provided in those cases, in terms of dialysis prescription (i.e. the prescribed flow rates at the beginning of dialysis). This information can be adopted by the physician to characterize the current patient and to identify the best therapy adjustments to be implemented. A possible improvement we are working on is to add more interaction between the physician and the system during the retrieval session; this will allow the system to relax or constrain the actual query, depending on the results obtained at each step. Useful suggestions about the strategy to adopt can be provided by similar work currently developed in the area of recommender systems [11].

Moreover, the system could be relied upon for quality assessment, i.e. to assess the performance of the overall hemodialysis service at hand and to isolate the reasons of failures. Technically speaking, quality assessment requires to fulfil two tasks: (1) retrieve similar time series within the process data, in order to assess the frequency of particular patterns, (2) discover relationships between the time patterns of the process data and the performance outcomes. Clearly, our tool would be suitable for task (1), but it could also be embedded within a more complex tool, able to summarize the dialysis sessions from a clinical quality viewpoint (see e.g. [3]).

The system version described in this paper is still a prototype, that retrieves the data from ad hoc files. From the technical viewpoint, in the future we plan to interface it with a commercial DBMS. In this way, the DBMS into which dialysis variables are stored by the hemodialyzer would directly be used as the case repository, making the system easy to be integrated into clinical practice.

At present, we have implemented dimensionality reduction through DFT and we resort to a k-d tree as an index structure where range queries can be directly performed. We are currently studying the possibility of adopting alternative methods such as Discrete Wavelets Transform (DWT) [4] or Piecewise Constant Approximation (PCA) [8, 9].

Moreover, we are also evaluating the option of substituting the k-d tree index structure with TV-trees [14], an organization able to efficiently access data in very large dimensional spaces (this would allow us to resort to a larger number of coefficients to represent a time series, thus speeding up retrieval[5]). An efficient algorithm for k-NN queries on TV-trees is described in [14]. Note that performing a k-NN query (and thus providing only the parameter k) is more intuitive for a physician with respect to working with range queries. As a matter of fact, in this case a range (a number between 0 and 1) has to be specified for *each* feature, and range values don't have an immediate mapping to the physical interpretation of the features themselves. The request to specify the ranges from one side allows a fine tuning of the retrieval results, but on the other hand sometimes forces the physician to make several tests before finding a really suitable value, that guarantees a non empty intersection of the different query results.

---

[5] Postprocessing time may be significantly reduced.

Finally, we plan to make an extensive testing and evaluation of our approach, working on new real patients' data coming from the Nephrology and Dialysis Unit of the Vigevano Hospital in Italy.

Acknowledgments

We are very grateful to Dr. Roberto Bellazzi of the Dialysis Unit of the Vigevano Hospital for having made available the set of cases. We also thanks the anonymous referees for their useful suggestions.

References

1. A. Aamodt and E. Plaza. Case-based reasoning: Foundational issues, methodological variations and system approaches. *AI Communications*, 7(1):39–59, 1994.
2. R. Agrawal, C. Faloutsos, and A.N. Swami. Efficient similarity search in sequence databases. In D. Lomet, editor, *Proc. 4th Int. Conf. of Foundations of Data Organization and Algorithms*, pages 69–84. Springer-Verlag, 1993.
3. R. Bellazzi, C. Larizza, P. Magni, and R. Bellazzi. Quality assessment of dialysis services through temporal data mining. In *Proceedings 9th Conference on Artificial Intelligence in Medicine Europe*, Cyprus, 2003.
4. K.P. Chan and A.W.C. Fu. Efficient time series matching by wavelets. In *Proc. ICDE 99*, pages 126–133, 1999.
5. R. Van der Spek and A. Spijkervet. Knowledge management: dealing intelligently with knowledge. In L.C. Wilcox J. Liebowitz, editor, *Knowledge Mangement and its Integrative Elements*. CRC Press, 1997.
6. M.L. Hetland. A survey of recent methods for efficient retrieval of similar time sequences. In H. Bunke M. Last, A. Kandel, editor, *Data Mining in Time Series Databases*. World Scientific, 2003.
7. D.B. Leake J.L. Kolodner. A tutorial introduction to CBR. In *Case Based Reasoning: Experiences, Lessons and Future Directions*, pages 31–65. AAAI Press, 1996.
8. E. Keogh. A fast and robust method for pattern matching in time series databases. In *Proc. Int. Conf. on Tools with Artificial Intelligence*, 1997.
9. E. Keogh, K. Chakrabarti, M. Pazzani, and S. Mehrotra. Dimensionality reduction for fast similarity search in large time series databases. *Knowledge and Information Systems*, 3(3):263–286, 2000.
10. A.V. Oppenheim and R.W. Shafer. *Digital signal processing*. Prentice-Hall, 1975.
11. F. Ricci, A. Venturini, D. Cavada, N. Mirzadeh, D. Blaas, and M. Nones. Product recommendation with interactive query management and twofold similarity. In *Proceedings ICCBR'03, LNAI 2689*, pages 479–493, Trondheim, 2003.
12. R. Schmidt, S. Montani, R. Belazzi, L. Portinale, and L. Gierl. Case-Based Reasoning for medical knowldge-based systems. *International Journal of Medical Informatics*, 64:355–367, 2001.
13. M. Stefanelli. The socio-organizational age of artificial intelligence in medicine. *Artificial Intelligence in Medicine*, 23(1):25–47, 2001.
14. V.S. Subrahmanian. *Principles of Multimedia Database Systems*. Morgan Kaufmann, 1998.
15. D.R. Wilson and T.R. Martinez. Improved heterogeneous distance functions. *Journal of Artificial Intelligence Research*, 6:1–34, 1997.

A Case-Based Classification of Respiratory Sinus Arrhythmia

Markus Nilsson and Peter Funk

Mälardalen University
Department of Computer Science and Engineering
S:ta Ursulas väg 2A
P.O. Box 883, SE-721 23 Västerås, Sweden
{markus.nilsson,Peter.Funk}@mdh.se

Abstract. Respiratory Sinus Arrhythmia has until now been analysed manually by reviewing long time series of heart rate measurements. Patterns are identified in the analysis of the measurements. We propose a design for a classification system of Respiratory Sinus Arrhythmia by time series analysis of heart and respiration measurements. The classification uses Case-Based Reasoning and Rule-Based Reasoning in a Multi-Modal architecture. The system is in use as a research tool in psychophysiological medicine, and will be available as a decision support system for treatment personnel.

1 Introduction

This paper describes a system for pattern classification of Respiratory Sinus Arrhythmia (RSA). The patterns are classified with Case-Based Reasoning (CBR) and Rule-Based Reasoning (RBR) using physiological time series measurements. The system is developed to be a decision support system for treatment personnel, as well as a research tool in psychophysiological medicine. The next paragraph defines RSA and put it into clinical context.

Respiratory Sinus Arrhythmia is described as centrally modulated cardiac vagal and sympathetic efferent activities associated with respiration [3]. RSA occurs because the heart rate, i.e. the number of beats per minute, is variable. This Heart Rate Variability (HRV) is an effect of inhibitions on the sympathetic and parasympathetic systems while breathing. The sympathetic and the parasympathetic systems, which are a part of the autonomous nervous system, have different activity levels during different stages of the respiration cycle [9]. That is, RSA is a sinusoid pattern of the heart rate associated with the breathing. The pattern is directly connected to the state of the respiration of a normal healthy person, i.e. without cardiac and pulmonary dysfunctions. The pulse increases dramatically on an inhalation and decreases in the same fashion on an exhalation. This is illustrated in figure 3 in section 2.2.

Physicians detect irregular heart rate patterns by analysing the RSA. Some of the irregularities are dysfunctions caused by physiological and/or psychological stress. A common diagnostic method for detecting dysfunctions in RSA is to

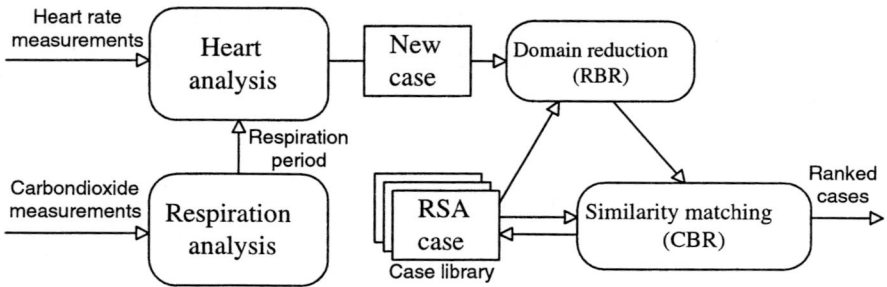

Fig. 1. A design for a classification system of Respiratory Sinus Arrhythmia.

manually analyse sampled heart rate measurements together with an analysis of the measurements' frequency spectrum [4, 3, 9]. The dysfunctions are treated with cognitive behavioural sessions with psychologists, and with biofeedback training [8].

Time-series analysis in medical Case-Based Reasoning has previously been studied by Montani et al. [11, 12], where they integrated CBR, RBR and Model-Based Reasoning (MBR) in a Multi-Modal Reasoning (MMR) platform for managing, i.e. suggesting insulin therapy, for type 1 diabetic patients. Another CBR system which analyses time series is ICONS [17]. ICONS forecasts kidney functions by an extended CBR cycle which abstracts states from measurements and predicts trends from the states. Other related medical CBR systems are The Auguste project [10], Bichindaritz's CARE-PARTNER [2] and MNAOMIA [1], and Perner et al.'s airborne fungi detection system [16]. Further information of these systems can be found in Nilsson and Sollenborn's survey on medical CBR [14]. CBR in the medical domain was first pioneered in the late 1980's. Some of the early systems are PROTOS [5] and CASEY [6].

We propose a MMR system design for the classification of RSA, where CBR matches physiological parameters and RBR reduces the domain of cases. A system design for the classification of RSA is introduced in the next section. We evaluate the proposed system in section 3, and conclude the paper in section 4.

2 System Architecture

A classification system for RSA is naturally divided into two initial analytical stages. Each stage analyses time series measurements. The first stage analyses the respiration and the second stage analyses the heart measurements. Cases are thereafter created based on the findings in the analysis processes. Rules limit the number of cases for the matching procedure to compare to, and the cases that pass the filter are matched and ranked. The design is illustrated in figure 1. The system is a revised version of the two later parts of the design described in [13], the first part is processed in the hardware. Each part of the figure is described in the remainder of this section. The respiration analysis is described in subsection 2.1, followed by heart analysis, domain reduction, case matching and finally the user interface.

As RSA is quantified during a breath (a respiration cycle), a respiration analysis precedes the heart analysis. The respiration analysis locates when the respiration occurs and passes that information to the heart analysis.

2.1 Respiration Analysis

A breath begins, by definition, on an inhalation. Hence, the respiration cycle starts when an exhalation stops and inhalation begins. Capnograph [7] measurements are used to pinpoint the beginning and end of the respiration cycle. The capnograph is a non invasive method, and measures the contents of carbon dioxide (CO_2) in exhaled air. Capnograph measurements are depicted in figure 2.

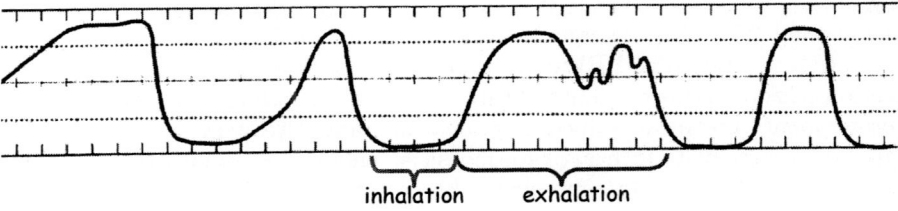

Fig. 2. Capnography measurements illustrating the respiration cycle, divided into inhalation and exhalation. The picture is adapted from [7].

Finding either the beginning or the end of the respiration cycle is actually sufficient to determine the entire respiration cycle, since the end of a respiration cycle marks the beginning of the next. A new breath starts, in the ideal case, when the level of CO_2 dramatically drops from circa 5% to just above 0%, followed by a steadily low level. This low level of CO_2 occurs during the entire inhalation. The level of CO_2 never reaches 0% because the surrounding air naturally contains CO_2, and it is also difficult to vacate the measuring sensor from all gases, even with a pump driven device.

A rough estimate of the respiration period is calculated by searching for a local maximum followed by a local minimum. The maximum represents the exhalation and the minimum the inhalation. A simulated annealing algorithm is then used on the first order derivates of the CO_2 measurements to find an approximate position between the maximum and minimum. The position is where the exhalation stops and the inhalation starts, i.e. where the respiration cycle begins.

Two points are identified, the first as the beginning and the second as the end of the respiration cycle. The samples in the respiration period are shifted in time due to lag in the sensor and additional delays associated with capnography measurements. A major delay is the transportation of CO_2 from the measur-

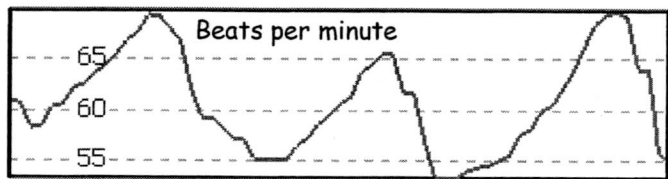

Fig. 3. The heart rate variability, i.e. the oscillating effect of the heart can easily be seen in these heart rate measurements.

ing point to the sensor. The CO_2 is sucked through a tube with a pump. The corrected measurements are then sent to the heart analysis as seen in figure 1.

2.2 Heart Analysis

Physicians observe both the HRV and the frequency spectrum of the HRV when they classify RSA. The beginning and the end of a HRV period is based on the respiration analysis. The HRV period span over the same time period as the respiration period, and is calculated from heart rate measurements. The heart rate measurements are mean-valued electrocardiogram (ECG) measurements. The conversion from ECG to heart rate measurements are automatically computed in the hardware[1]. HRV measurements are depicted in figure 3.

$$\sum_{i=1}^{n}\left(HR(i) - \frac{\sum_{j=1}^{n} HR(j)}{n}\right) = 0 \qquad (1)$$

The frequency spectrum is calculated when the samples for the HRV have been collected. However, some pre-processing is required before a frequency spectrum can be calculated. The physicians are only interested in the oscillation of the sequence of samples, HR, that make up the HRV, when they observe the frequency spectrum. The sample sequence has to be shifted to oscillate around its own mean value, as seen in equation 1. If not, a large portion of the lower end of the frequency spectrum is mixed with non relevant oscillations due to the nature of the heart rate samples. The heart rate samples are always positive numbers with a range of about 50-90 beats per minute, which unintentionally create large sine waves, or low frequencies within the measurement sequence.

The output sample rate from the hardware sensors is 2 Hz; and a normal breath is in the range of 6-12 seconds. Hence, there are usually too few samples in the HRV to make any useful frequency transformation. The solution is to pad, or to add, the sample sequence with zeroes. Padding with zeroes does not affect the frequency distribution in the spectrum. The sample sequence is padded to 2048 samples. The samples are then transformed to the frequency spectrum using a Fast Fourier Transformation (FFT). The length, or power value, of each

---

[1] The AirPas and cStress hardware environments from PBM StressMedicine are used to measure physiological parameters.

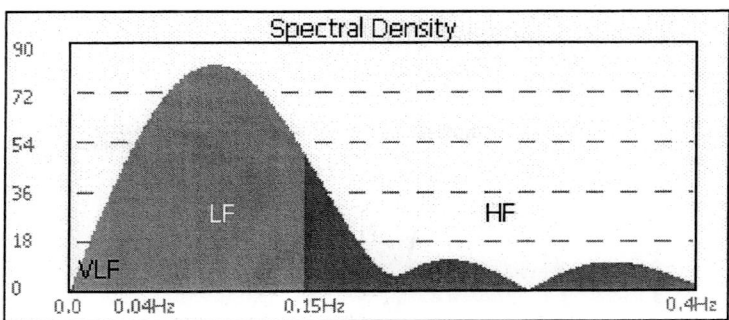

Fig. 4. A frequency spectrum of a typical RSA. Physicians are only interested in the range from 0 to $0.4Hz$. The spectrum is divided into three major frequency bands. Very Low Frequencies (VLF), Low Frequencies (LF) and High Frequencies (HF), as various physiological variables appear within these individual bands.

frequency is calculated from the FFT's output of complex numbers, see equation 2, and figure 4.

$$Power(f) = \sqrt[2]{FFTreal(f)^2 + FFTimg(f)^2} \qquad (2)$$

Physicians study additional parameters in their classification of RSA. The additional parameters are notch patterns and peak-to-valley differences in the heart rate measurements. The peak-to-valley value is the ΔY difference of the maximum and minimum heart rate sample values. Notches are irregular dips in the otherwise smooth heart rate oscillation. The notches have different significances depending on where they occur. Both peak-to-valley and notches are calculated.

2.3 Cases and Domain Reduction

Cases contain all above described parameters and measurements, with one addition, first order derivates of the heart rate measurements are also included. A case is represented by 17 features, 10 of which are actively used in the matching process. Five features contain time-series or other sequences, they are the CO_2 measurements, heart rate measurements, first order derivates of the heart rate measurements, the power and frequency table of the FFT. The remaining 7 structure the Case, such as the RSA class, a couple of variables to speed up the matching process. Sample frequencies for both heart rate and CO_2 is also included, and finally a second classification of RSA. The second classification is based on another quantification approach for RSA [4] and is not of interest for this paper.

A case belongs to one of the stereotypical classes of RSA identified in [18]. A class can contain an arbitrary number of example cases. The classes are clustered into larger groups, the clustering criterion is based on the number of notches the heart rate measurement contains[2]. A notch is a smaller or larger dip in the heart rate pattern, as illustrated in figure 5.

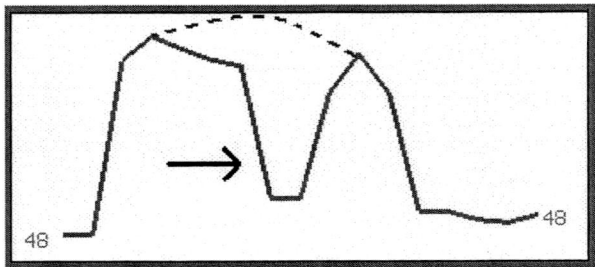

Fig. 5. The arrow marks a notch in the heart rate pattern. The rules concluded this is a notch due to the steep fall of the heart rate in the middle of the sequence. The dotted line marks a, would be normal, i.e. non-dysfunctional, RSA pattern.

A class is not limited to one group. An RSA class may end up in several clusters. Rules trigger new cases for notches. One rule indicates whether there is a change in the direction of the heart rate signal, i.e. starts falling after an inclination and vice versa. Another rule monitors the acceleration of any changes and a third decides if the change is big enough to be considered a notch or if it merely is a part of the naturally oscillation. The rules do also consider where the dips occur before they are concluded as notches. The number of notches for the entire sequence of heart rate measurements is calculated. This determines which cluster of classes the matching procedure is to use. The current clusters are illustrated in figure 6.

2.4 Case Similarities

A new case is matched with stored cases by calculating the similarity of the heart rate measurements and the heart rate frequency spectrum. The new case is matched with all cases in all the classes of the local cluster, as can be seen in figure 6.

The frequency match calculates the distance between two frequency vectors by comparing the spectral density of each individual frequency. This is calculated throughout the entire length of the vector, i.e. all the elements in the vector. The power, i.e. amplitude, corresponding to each frequency is normalized against the maximum power (largest power value in the vector) in order to be in the range of $0 - 1$. The difference between the stored and the new case's frequency powers are weighted, and the difference is accumulated. The total difference between the vectors is then normalized to become the similarity distance. A similarity distance of 0 represents two identical frequency vectors. A pseudo code follows:

---

[2] Stereotypical classes and their clusters may change whenever new knowledge from psychophysiological research is available.

A Case-Based Classification of Respiratory Sinus Arrhythmia

```
similarity_distance = 0

/* for all frequencies */
FOR (frequency = 1 TO number_of_frequencies)
  /* Normalize the powers (range 0-1) for the stored case */
  IF (maximum_power > 0)
    power_storedcase = frequency / maximum_power_storedvector
  ELSE power_storedcase = 0
  ENDIF

  /* Normalize the powers (range 0-1) for the new case */
  IF (maximum_power > 0)
    power_newcase = frequency / maximum_power_newvector
  ELSE power_newcase = 0
  ENDIF

  /* calculate the weighted difference between the two
     frequencies and accumulate the differences */
  IF (power_storedcase > power_newcase)
    similarity_distance += (power_storedcase-power_newcase)*weight
  ELSE
    similarity_distance += (power_newcase-power_storedcase)*weight
  ENDIF
ENDFOR

/* normalize the similarity for the vector (range 0-1) */
similarity_distance /= frequencies
```

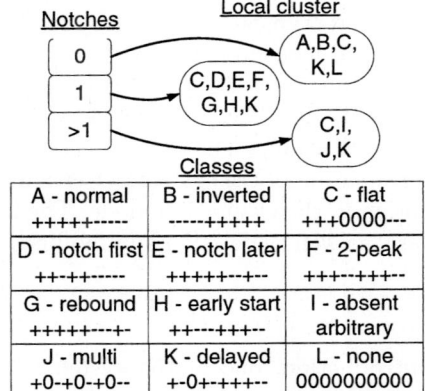

Fig. 6. The local clusters and the corresponding stereotypical classes of RSA. Each RSA class is described with its typical structure in the form of first order derivates. + is an increase in the heart rate, - a decrease and 0 is status quo. The RSA patterns are visualised with examples of sample sequences and corresponding frequencies in [18].

A sequence of heart rate measurements is not constant in length unlike the frequency vector. This is due to the variable time of an individual breath, and the heart rate measurements are coupled with the respiration cycle. The heart rate measurements are matched by their first order derivates. Changes within the heart rate pattern are easier to find if two vectors with first order derivates are used instead of the original measurements.

The derivates of the new case are interpolated to match the number of derivates in the stored case, if they do not contain equal number of samples. The distance is calculated for every pair of derivates and compiled to a normalised similarity distance for the entire heart rate sequence, much like the frequency similarity measurement.

The similarities of the measurements and the spectrum are merged to one similarity distance for the entire case, $similarity\ distance = frequency\ dist. \times derivate\ dist.$ The cases are ranked based on the similarity distance, lower value equals closer match. The list is then purged from duplicate cases of the same class, as there is often several example cases of the same class appearing in a sequence. As an example, a list of cases indicating the following RSA classes 3, 3, 3, 3, 9, 9, 1, 1, 1, 1, 2 is transformed to 3, 9, 1, 2.

The relevant cases, with the closest similarity, are finally presented to the user. The frequency and derivate similarity distances are also available to the user.

2.5 Case Library

The case library consists of approximately 50 cases. These 50 cases represents the existing 12 stereotypical classes of RSA [18]. Each class is represented with several example cases. The examples are distributed that the more common classes has more examples than the rare occurring classes.

There is no adaptation of the cases in the system, since the solution domain consists (currently) of 12 stereotypical classes of RSA. The RSA classification tries to label the physiological measurements with a single integer, i.e. this solution domain is not suited for adaptation, and is typical for problem domains that are not well understood [19]. The system has several operational modes: classification, evaluation and learning. The system classifies RSA patterns in the classification mode. An evaluation of the system performance compared to a user is added to the classification in the evaluation mode. The learning mode accepts new cases to the case base, as well as deletion and modification of existing cases.

2.6 User Interface

As mentioned in the introduction, one of the systems tasks is to serve as a research tool for researchers in psychophysiology. Hence, a windowed environment was chosen to display the measurements. The user can freely choose what measurements or parameters he/she wants to work with, as well as enabling different operational modes. A screenshot of the system is displayed in figure 7. The screenshot illustrates the complexity of classifying RSA.

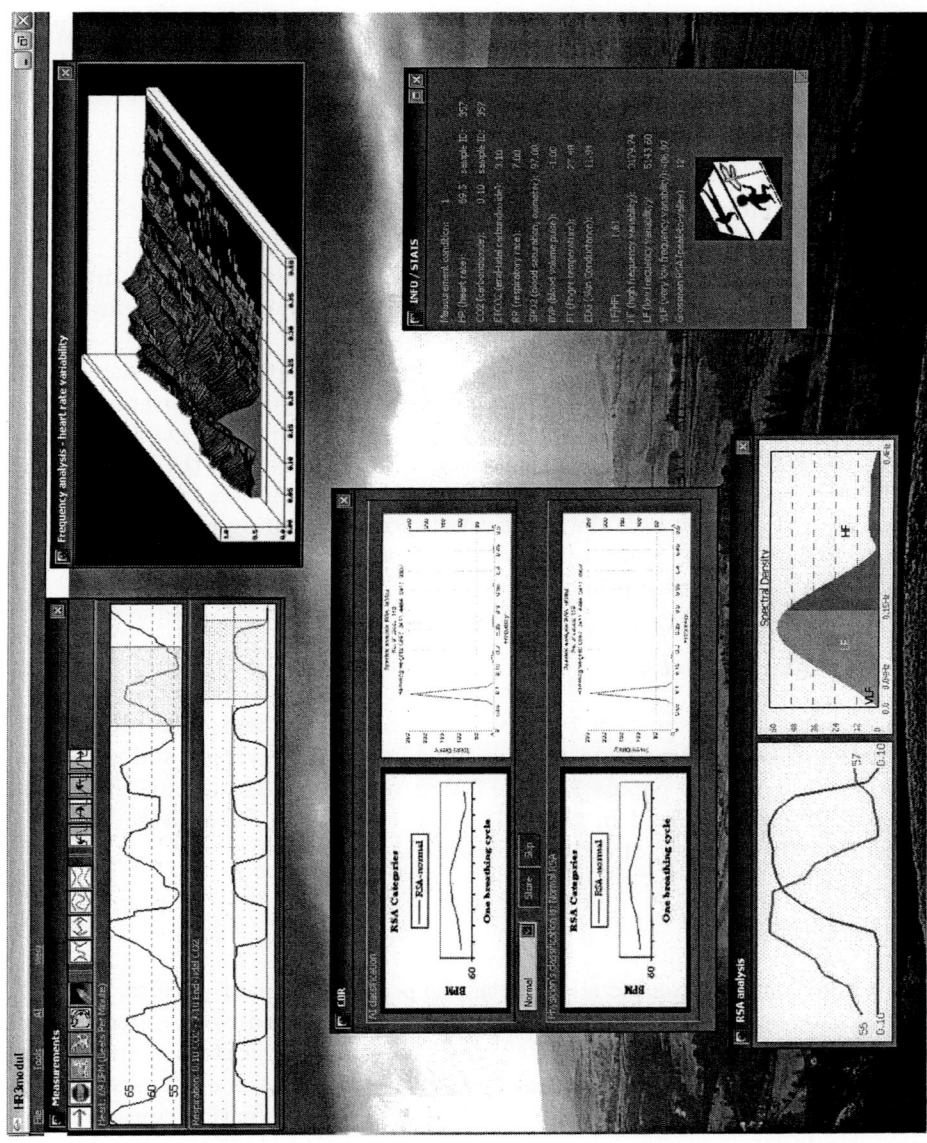

Fig. 7. A screenshot of the application christened HR3modul. HR3modul is a tool for classification of Respiratory Sinus Arrhythmia. The top left shows heart rate, CO_2, and end-tidal CO_2 measurements. Below the measurements is a classification, and at the bottom an RSA period that is being classified. The top right shows a frequency spectrum for each analysed RSA and below it shows additional information physicians/clinicians find useful.

The system is currently implemented in C++ as an application for the Windows platform. The application uses OpenGL to display graphics, as by doing this it is easier to port the application to other platforms in the future, due to OpenGL's OS independent interface.

3 Evaluation

This section contains a first evaluation of the RSA classification. The first evaluation was also the first time leading experts in the field of psychophysiology came in contact with the system.

The case-base was initialized with stereotypical cases produced by domain experts. The cases are described in [18]. The cases are supposed to cover all known classifications of RSA, i.e. cover the entire domain. Additional cases were also added to the case library. The additional cases belong to one of the stereotypical classes, and were added to facilitate an easier matching process. An example of an additional case is where the heart rate is constant during the entire respiration cycle, i.e., $\forall_i(s_i \in S : s_i = 0)$ after the conversion in equation 1. There exist no frequencies in a straight line.

3.1 Evaluation Data Set

A data set of approximately 100 pre-recorded measurements was used in the evaluation. The measurements were recorded in a cStress system, and were measured from a normal population of 17 year olds. Pre-recorded measurements are parsed and simulated in the HR3modul system as if they were real-time measurements streamed directly from hardware.

3.2 Results

The evaluation was conducted with the help of the domain experts. Cases of special interest for an accurate classification were pushed to the case library. An evaluation mode was enabled when the case library contained enough example cases of RSA. The evaluation mode collects statistics of the accuracy of the classification system. The case library used in the evaluation consists of approximately 50 cases. The cases represent the existing stereotypical classes of RSA.

However, as this was the first time the physicians had an opportunity to view every individual RSA, i.e. the HRV per respiration cycle; new patterns of RSA were discovered. This invalidates the notion of total domain coverage by the cases in the case library, since the new RSA patterns do not fit into any of the stereotypical classes described in section 3. The new patterns are for the most parts deviations of similar existing patterns. A first hint from the physiologists points towards a reorganisation of the class structure; super classes with subclasses as an addition to totally new patterns.

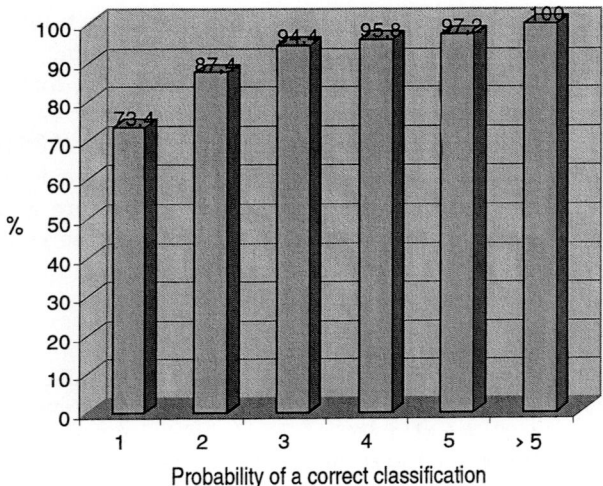

Fig. 8. Evaluation of the classification system. The columns represent the probability of an accurate classification, ranging from the same classification as an expert in the first attempt to the correct classification in the 5th attempt. All attempts beyond the 5th are summarised in the rightmost column.

Nevertheless, statistics were collected from the evaluation. A summary of the statistics are presented in figure 8. The figure represents the accuracy, i.e. similarity, of the classification system in a comparison with a domain expert. The leftmost column represents the probability that the first RSA class suggested by the system is the same as the expert would choose. The second column from the left represents the probability that the expert's choice of class is the same as either the first or the second RSA class suggested by the system. The rest of the columns proceed in the same manner, from left to right. All statistics of the similarities beyond the 5th suggested class have been summarised into the rightmost column.

4 Conclusions

We have presented a MMR design for the classification of RSA. The design uses two analytical stages of time series measurements from the heart and from exhaled air. The analytical stages process the time series measurements so they will conform into cases, for later similarity comparisons. A RBR stage limits the number of RSA classes that have to be considered in the matching, and a CBR stage makes a similarity match with the cases from the remaining RSA classes.

The MMR design for the classification of RSA seems to be reliable, as 19 out of 20 cases in the evaluation data set were among the three top most suggested classes. But the spread of the accuracy also suggests that it would be beneficial of using a differential diagnosis in the future, if the accuracy do not reach 100%.

The evaluation also showed that even the experts benefit from the system, as they discovered new patterns of RSA while using the system.

The algorithm for calculating the similarity is sufficient for the time being. But some sort of improvement will probably be necessary as the case library grows. An interesting approach is to reduce the dimensions of the time-series features by for instance using the D-HS^T indexing [15], as it is specially suited for temporal time-series. Adaptation might also be a future issue as the case library is adapted for super classes and subclasses. A case could possible be adapted from a super class to fit a subclass or vice versa.

References

1. Isabelle Bichindaritz. Mnaomia: Improvingcase-based reasoning for an application in psychiatry. In *Artificial Intelligence in Medicine: Applications of Current Technologies*, pages 14–20. AAAI, 1996.
2. Isabelle Bichindaritz, Emin Kansu, and Keith M. Sullivan. Case-based reasoning in care-partner: Gathering evidence for evidence-based medical practice. In *Advances in CBR: 4th European Workshop*, pages 334–345. ECCBR'98, September 1998.
3. Tuan Pham Dinh, Helene Perrault, Pascale Calabrese, Andre Eberhard, and Gila Benchetrit. New statical method for detection and quantification of respiratory sinus arrhytmia. *IEEE Transactions on Biomedical Engineering*, 46(9):1161–1165, September 1999.
4. P. Grossman and J. Van Beek et al. A comparison of three quantification methods for estimation of respiratory sinus arrhytmia. *Psychophysiology*, 27(6):702–714, November 1990.
5. Ellis Raymond Bareiss jr. *PROTOS: A unified approach to concept representation, classification and, learning*. UMI Dissertation Services, 300 North Zeeb Road, P.O. Box 1346, Ann Arbor, Michigan 48106-1346, USA, 1988.
6. Phyllis Koton. *Using Experience in Learning and Problem Solving*. MIT Press, 1988.
7. Bernard Landis and Patricia M.Romano. A scoring system for capnogram biofeedback: Preliminary findings. *Applied Psychophysiology and Biofeedback*, 23(2):75–91, 1998.
8. Paul M. Lehrer, Evgeny Vaschillo, and Bronya Vaschillo. Resonant frequency biofeedback training to increase cardiac variability: Rationale and manual for training. *Applied Psychophysiology and Biofeedback*, 25(3):177–191, 2000.
9. Marek Malik and John Camm et al. Heart rate variability - standards of measurement, physiological interpretation, and clinical use. *European Heart Journal*, 17:354–381, March 1996.
10. Cindy Marling and Peter Whitehouse. Case-based reasoning in the care of alzheimer's disease patients. In *Case-Based Research and Development*, pages 702–715. ICCBR'01, July/August 2001.
11. Stefania Montani, Paolo Magni, Riccardo Bellazzi, Cristiana Larizza, Abdul V. Roudsari, and Ewart R. Carson. Integrating model-based decision support in a multi-modal reasoning system for managing type 1 diabetic patients. *Artificial Intelligence in Medicine*, 29:131–151, 2003.
12. Stefania Montani, Paolo Magni, Abdul V. Roudsari, Ewart R. Carson, and Riccardo Bellazzi. Integrating different methodologies for insulin therapy support in type 1 diabetic patients. In *Artificial Intelligence in Medicine*, pages 121–130. AIME'01, July 2001.

13. Markus Nilsson, Peter Funk, and Mikael Sollenborn. Complex measurement classification in medical applications using a case-based approach. In *Workshop proceedings: Case-Based Reasoning in the Health Sciences*, pages 63–72. International Conference on Case-Based Reasoning, June 2003.
14. Markus Nilsson and Mikael Sollenborn. Advancements and trends in medical case-based reasoning: An overview of systems and system development. In *Proceedings of the 17th International FLAIRS Conference*, pages 178–183, May 2004.
15. David Patterson, Mykola Galushka, and Niall Rooney. An effective indexing and retrieval approach for temporal cases. In *Proceedings of the 17th International FLAIRS Conference*, pages 190–195, May 2004.
16. P. Perner, T. Günther, H. Perner, G. Fiss, and R. Ernst. Health monitoring by an image interpretation system - a system for airborne fungi identification. In *Medical Data Analysis*, volume 2868 of *Lecture Notes in Computer Science*, pages 62–74, 2003.
17. Rainer Schmidt and Lothar Gierl. Temporal abstractions and case-based reasoning for medical course data: Two prognostic applications. In *Machine Learning and Data Mining in Pattern Recognition*, volume 2123 of *Lecture Notes in Computer Science*, pages 23–34, 2001.
18. Bo von Schéele. *Classification Systems for RSA, ETCO2 and other physiological parameters*. PBM Stressmedicine, Heden 110, 821 31 Bollnäs, Sweden, 1999.
19. Ian Watson. *Applying Case-Based Reasoning: Techniques for Enterprise Systems*. Morgan Kaufmann Publishers Inc, 340 Pine St, 6th floor, San Fransisco, CA 94104, USA, 1997.

Fault Diagnosis of Industrial Robots Using Acoustic Signals and Case-Based Reasoning

Erik Olsson[1], Peter Funk[1], and Marcus Bengtsson[2]

[1] Department of Computer Science and Engineering
Mälardalen University, Västerås, Sweden
{erik.olsson,peter.funk}@mdh.se
[2] Department of Innovation, Design and Product Development
Mälardalen University, Västerås, Sweden
marcus.bengtsson@mdh.se

Abstract. In industrial manufacturing rigorous testing is used to ensure that the delivered products meet their specifications. Mechanical maladjustment or faults often show their presence through abnormal acoustic signals. This is the same case in robot assembly - the application domain addressed in this paper. Manual diagnosis based on sound requires extensive experience, and usually such experience is acquired at the cost of reduced production efficiency or degraded product quality due to mistakes in judgments. The acquired experience is also difficult to preserve and transfer and it often gets lost if the corresponding personnel leave the task of testing. We propose herein a Case-Based Reasoning approach to collect, preserve and reuse the available experience for robot diagnosis. This solution enables fast experience transfer and more reliable and informed testing. Sounds from normal and faulty robots are recorded and stored in a case library together with their diagnosis results. Given an unclassified sound signal, the relevant cases are retrieved from the case library as reference for deciding the fault class of the new case. Adding new classified sound profiles to the case library improves the system's performance. So far the developed system has been applied to the testing environment for industrial robots. The preliminary results demonstrate that our system is valuable in this application scenario in that it can preserve and transfer the related experience among technicians and shortens the overall testing time.

1 Introduction

Mechanical faults in industrial robots often show their presence through abnormal acoustic signals compared with the normal ones. Correct classification of the robot sound may be a very critical part of the end-test. An incorrect classification of the sound can result in the delivery of a faulty robot to the customer. A technician needs rich experience to make a reliable diagnosis of robots. The importance of fault detection based on sound is confirmed by a current activity of Volkswagen which sells CDs containing recordings of different faults in equipments to aid technicians in classifying audible faults. The use of sound and vibration measurements for the purpose of fault detection in end-testing of industrial equipments is today most commonly practiced by gearbox manufacturers. The measurements are shown graphically and analysed manually by a technician via careful observations of the measurements (normal/high amplitude level, frequency distribution etc.). Some toolbox systems exist (e.g. Math Lab or more sound and vibration profiled tools such as the Plato toolbox [6]) that offer a variety of aids enabling experts to analyse and visualise data in different ways. Some additional modules are offered able to classify a measurement as pass/failure or compare it with a library of faults. These systems are semiautomatic, large and run on PC computers. Some diagnostic systems use neural nets, such as Dexter [7] employing probabilistic neural net for classification.

We propose the use of a Case-Based Reasoning (CBR) system resorting to a nearest neighbour approach for a lightweight solution of recognising and diagnosing audible faults in industrial robots. Sound is recorded with a microphone and compared with previous recordings; similar cases are retrieved and shown to the user with correspondence to relevant diagnosis results in history. A prototype system for this purpose has been developed.

AI techniques such as Case-Based Reasoning (CBR) have some advantages in this category of applications. The fundamental idea of CBR – applying old knowledge of problem solving to solve new problems is very feasible for industrial applications. Implementing this technique in industrial applications preserves experience that would be often lost if skilled personnel leave their employments. The system aids technicians in making a correct diagnosis of industrial robots based on earlier classifications of similar sounds. It also eases the knowledge acquisition bottleneck [1].

This paper gives an overview of the CBR system for robotic fault classification and describes the implemented prototype system as well as some initial evaluation results. The system is able to successfully diagnose faults in an industrial robot based on sound recordings (4 recordings from faulty robots and 20 recordings from normal robots are used in the evaluation). The system elicits classifiable features from the sound recordings and makes a diagnosis according to prior knowledge.

The paper is organized as follows. Section 2 gives a brief overview of the sound classification technique. Section 3 describes the model used in this paper to classify sound recordings. Sections 4, 5 and 6 describe the implementation of the prototype classification system based on the model. Section 7 discusses system evaluation with a case study. Section 8 gives an experimental comparison of FFT and wavelet analysis and finally section 9 concludes this paper with summary and conclusions.

2 Classifying Sound Recordings

This section gives short background knowledge for sound classification and outlines some of the methods and techniques used to filter, analyse and classify sound recordings.

2.1 Filtering and Pre-processing

Filtering is used to eliminate unwanted components in the signal by removing noise and distortions. A number of different techniques, such as adaptive filters, wavelet analysis and time domain averaging have been developed for signal filtering and noise reduction (see [2, 3]). The filtering process may be complicated in some scenarios because of heavy background noise. After a successful pre-processing the signal will have an increased Signal to Noise Ratio (SNR), which makes it more amenable for further processing such as feature extraction.

2.2 Features and Feature Vector

When experienced technicians are classifying robot sound they listen for abnormalities in the sound. An indication of an abnormal sound can be the presence or absence of certain acoustic features. Using feature vector as the signature for sound is a well-adopted method to detect and identify faults in machinery. It is also commonly used in CBR systems. A simplified example for feature vector from a sound profile is shown below where the elements above the sign "—" are signal amplitude values and those under "—" denote the corresponding frequencies.

$$\left[\frac{max\_value\ 45}{300\ HZ}, \frac{max\_value\ 18}{520\ HZ}, \frac{max\_value\ 89.6}{745\ HZ} \right] \quad (1)$$

The adoption of frequency-based features in this context is motivated by the awareness of resonant frequency of each mechanical part that depends on its mass and rigidity. Hence the faults occurring in different parts will result in different frequency spectra. Experienced technicians often listen for such features on an intuitive basis in order to propose a diagnosis in terms of his/her experience. However technicians may not always be able to point out these features that he/she uses to classify sounds.

Wavelet analysis [4] is a powerful technique for filtering out noises and transforming analogue signals to frequency diagrams. It is hence adopted in our research to establish frequency-dependent features from polluted acoustic signals collected from environments with strong background noise. Extraction of sound features based on wavelet will be detailed in section 4.2.

2.3 Classification Process

A number of different methods are available for the classification of machine sound. The selection of classification method is based on the nature of the task. A simple classification may only require a single test with a threshold (e.g. amplitude above or below 10) for a complete classification.

A different approach to the classification of feature vectors is to use Artificial Neural Nets (ANN). Reliable classification using the ANN approach requires prior training of the network with a sufficient number of classified examples. Moreover, once a new important case is recognized, the old network has to be retrained in order to assimilate this new acquired experience. However, in our task of robot fault diagnosis, sufficient samples of classified sound recordings required for training are frequently not available.

3 Case-Based Categorization of Machine Sound

This section gives an overview and introduction to the case-based classification of machine sound. The different steps, pre-processing, feature identification and classification are described in sections 4, 5 and 6, respectively. Sound is obtained from the robot to be diagnosed via a microphone as shown at the top left in Fig. 1. The sound is recorded to a computer and the recording is taken as input to the pre-processing step. The pre-processing component in Fig. 1 is responsible for filtering and removal of unwanted noise. It also extracts period information from the sound.

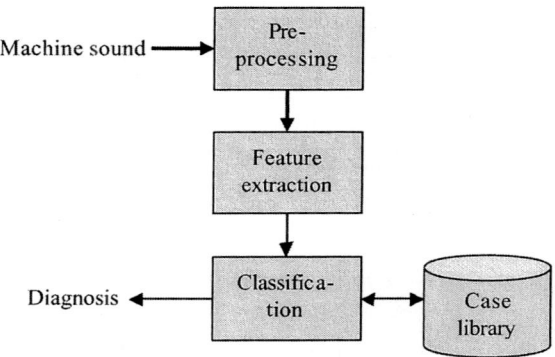

Fig. 1. Schematic picture of the system

In the feature identification process, the system uses a two-pass model, first identifying features and then creating a vector with the extracted features. Once the features are identified, the system classifies the feature vector. The classification is based on previously classified measurements (case library) in Fig. 1. After a new sound has been classified it is added to the case library. The classification process will be described in section 6. A diagnosis based on the result of the classification is shown to the technician. In the research prototype a ranked list of the most similar cases based on a nearest neighbour function is presented as decision support to the technician.

3.1 Comparison to the OSA-CBM Architecture

The design of the system described in this paper has some similarities with the Open System Architecture for Condition Based Maintenance (OSA-CBM) [9]. This architecture is seen as a proposed standard for Condition Based Maintenance (CBM) system which is recommended to consist of seven modules [10], including sensors, signal processing, condition monitoring, diagnosis, prognosis, decision support, and presentation (see Fig. 2). In the system presented in this paper the microphone can be regarded as a sensor module. The pre-processing and feature extraction components play the role of signal processing. The classification (with the case-library) component performs both condition monitoring and diagnosis as it can both detect deviations in the sound profiles and classify different sound profiles into different fault modes.

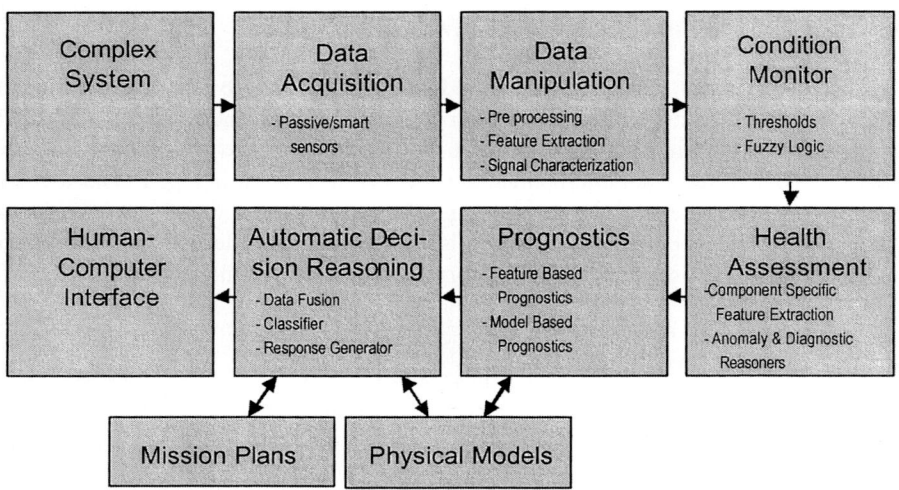

Fig. 2. The standard OSA-CBM architecture proposed in [9]

4 Pre-processing

Robot sound typically contains unwanted noise. The presence of a fault is often indicated by the presence, or increase in impulsive elements in the sound. The detection of these impulsive sound elements can be hard. This is owing to the mixture of signals from normal running of the robot and from various sporadic background noises normally existing within an industrial environment. Before a classification attempt is made, the machine sound is pre-processed in order to remove as much unwanted noise as possible. In this system wavelets are used to purify the raw signal and transform the incoming sound into a series of wavelet coefficients. Selected wavelet values are then used as features.

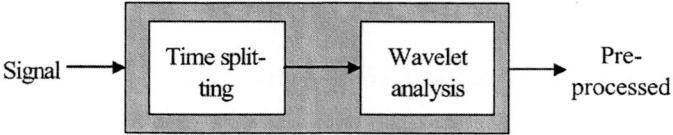

Fig. 3. Pre-processing of the signal in the system

Fig. 3 shows the pre-processing process. It contains two steps; splitting and wavelet analysis. In the first step the signal is split to windows of discrete time steps. The length of each window can be arbitrary. Each window is then sent to the wavelet analysis algorithm (step #2). The output from the wavelet analysis and from the pre-processing step is a series of wavelet values. Below, the function of each step is further explained.

4.1 Time Splitting

Only a part of the input signal can be analysed each time conducting the wavelet algorithm. Due to this fact the signal is divided into windows of discrete time steps. The length of each window can be arbitrary but its data size must be 2^n where n>=2. This is due to the way the wavelet packet algorithm is implemented.

4.2 The Discrete Wavelet Transform

Wavelet transforms are popular in many engineering and computing fields for solving real-life application problems. Wavelets can model irregular data patterns, such as impulse sound elements better than the Fourier transform (see chapter 8). The signal $f(t)$ will be represented as a weighted sum of the wavelets $\psi(t)$ and the scaling function $\varphi(t)$ by

$$f(t) = A_1 \varphi(t) + A_2 \psi(t) + \sum_{\substack{n \in +Z, \\ m \in Z}} A_{n,m} \psi(2^n t - m) \qquad (1)$$

where $\psi(t)$ is the mother wavelet and $\varphi(t)$ is the scaling function.

In principle a wavelet function can be any function witch positive and negative areas canceling out. That means a wavelet function has to meet the following condition:

$$\int_{-\infty}^{\infty} \psi(t) dt = 0 \qquad (2)$$

Dilations and translations of the mother wavelet function define an orthogonal basis of the wavelets as expressed by

$$\psi_{(sl)}(t) = 2^{\frac{-s}{2}} \psi(2^{-s} t - l) \qquad (3)$$

where variables s and l are integers that scale and dilate the mother function $\psi(t)$ to generate other wavelets belonging to the Daubechies wavelet family. The scale index s indicates the wavelet's width, and the location index l gives its position. The mother function is rescaled, or "dilated" by powers of two and translated by integers. To span the data domain at different resolutions, the analyzing wavelet is used in a scaling equation as following

$$\varphi(t) = \sum_{k=-1}^{N-2} (-1)^k c_{k+1} \psi(2t + k) \qquad (4)$$

where $\varphi(t)$ is the scaling function for the mother function $\psi(t)$, and c_k are the wavelet data values.

The coefficients $\{c_0, \ldots, c_n\}$ can be seen as a filter. The filter or coefficients are placed in a transformation matrix, which is applied to a raw data vector (see Fig.4). The coefficients are ordered using two dominant patterns, one works as a smoothing filter (like a moving average), and the other works to bring out the "detail" information from the data.

The wavelet coefficient matrix is applied to the input data vector. The matrix is applied in a hierarchical algorithm, sometimes called a pyramidal algorithm. The wavelet data values are arranged so that odd rows contain an ordering of wavelet data values that act as the smoothing filter, and the even rows contain an ordering of wavelet coefficients with different signs that act to bring out the data's detail. The matrix is first applied to the original, full-length vector. Fig. 4 shows an example of a data vector consisting of 8 samples. The samples can be any type of data; sensor signals from various process applications, stock market curves etc. In this paper the samples are acoustic signals from a gearbox of an industrial robot.

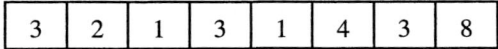

Fig. 4. Original signal consisting of 8 samples

The data vector is smoothed and decimated by half and the matrix is applied again (see Fig. 5).

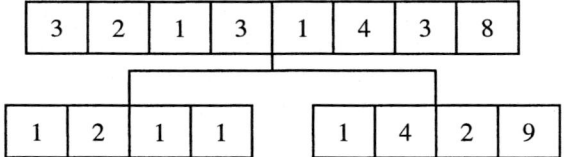

Fig. 5. Smoothed data vectors

Then the smoothed, halved vector is smoothed, and halved again, and the matrix applied once more. This process continues until a trivial number of "smooth-smooth-smooth..." data remain (see Fig 6).

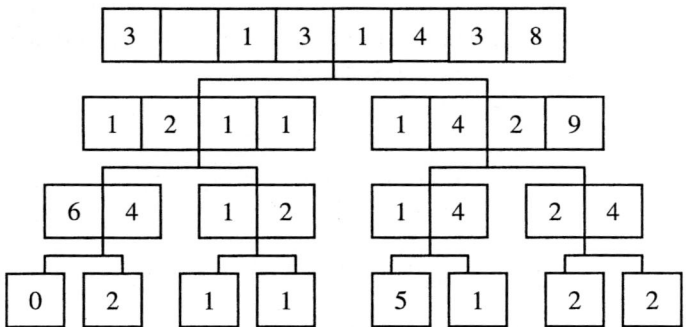

Fig. 6. The result of the pyramidal algorithm

This system uses the wavelet packet transform algorithm. It is a computer implementation of the Discrete Wavelet Transform (DWT). It uses the Daubecies mother wavelet, scaling function and wavelet coefficients [11].

The result of the pyramidal algorithm is a tree of smoothed data values (see Fig. 6). Each collection of smoothed data values (node in the tree) can be seen as a "time-frequency-packet". Each "time-frequency-packet" can be seen as a filtered version of the original data samples. As an example, the left "packet" in Fig. 5 can be seen as a low pass filtered version of the original data and the right "packet" in Fig. 5 can be seen as a high pass filtered version of the original data. The leaves of the tree can be seen as high and low pass units of length 2^0.

The depth of the tree is determined from the length of the input data. If the input data are of length 2^n the depth of the tree will be n. A suitable collection of "time-frequency-packets" can be selected by taking a cross section of the tree at an arbitrary depth. Each sibling in the cross section of the tree is spanning the entire time of the original data set. This means that going deeper in the tree produces at better resolution in frequency but a poorer resolution in time. The best compromise between time and frequency resolution is to take a cross section in the tree were the length of each sibling is the same as the number of siblings in the cross section. At a given depth n and with original data size S, the length of a sibling (or leaf) is $S/2^n$ and the number of siblings is 2^n.

The wavelet packet algorithm offers the basis for the Pre-processing process. The input signal is first divided into windows of discrete time steps. Each window is then passed to the wavelet packet algorithm resulting in a wavelet "packet tree" as pictured in Fig 6. The wavelet data values from a cross section of the wavelet packet tree are then passed to the Feature Extraction process.

5 Feature Extraction Process

It is necessary to find a suitable form in which to represent and compress the sound data while storing enough information to be able to classify the sound correctly. The feature extraction component uses a two-pass model to achieve this. First, wavelet data values obtained from pre-processing are fed as inputs to the feature extraction component which extracts features from these coefficients (left box in Fig. 7). The extracted features are then stored in a feature vector (right box in Fig. 7).

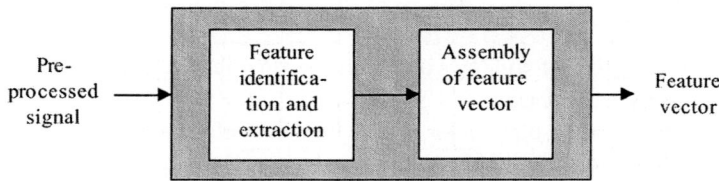

Fig. 7. Feature identification in the system

5.1 Feature Identification

Our system uses normalized wavelet data values as features. The values are selected from a cross-section of the wavelet packet tree. Gear defects often show their presence as sharp peaks or dips in the sound. Such peaks or dips can be spotted in some dominant wavelet data values in certain packets in the cross section of the wavelet packet tree. The feature extraction component examines the wavelet data values and extracts one dominant value from each packet in a cross section at an arbitrary depth. In Fig. 8 the grey area shows a cross section at level 2 in the tree. The chosen coefficients are those that are marked as bold. They are chosen because they are the dominant values in each packet in that cross section.

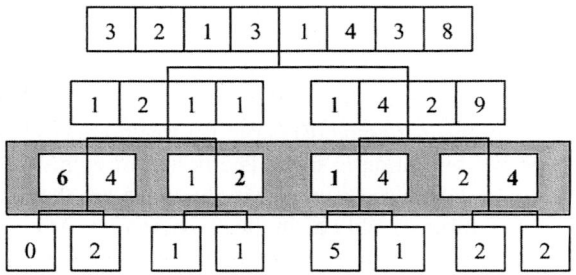

Fig. 8. Feature identification from wavelet data values

5.2 Assembly of a Feature Vector

A feature vector is assembled from these dominant wavelet values. A feature vector forms a cross section of wavelet data values at level n in the wavelet packet tree containing 2^n features. This system is dynamic and can assemble vectors from all depths of the tree. The feature vector assembled from Fig. 8 is **[6, 2, 1, 4]**.

In order to purify sounds from various sporadic background noises normally existing within an industrial environment - several cross sections of the wavelet packet tree from a series of windows are passed from the Pre-processing component to the feature extraction component. The amount of cross sections passed to feature extraction is dependent on the length of the recorded sound and the size of the window. We denote the vector produced from window i by X_i. Then a mean vector $\bar{x}$ is calculated by

$$\bar{x} = \frac{(X_1 + X_2 + ... + X_w)}{w} \qquad (6)$$

Here w is the number of windows and $\bar{x}$ is the final feature vector that will used as condition description of a case.

Apart from the final feature vector, a case contains information about the robot being diagnosed. Typical information contained in a case is the serial number, model number of the robot and a field that can be manually filled with expert's classification. Each case also contains a weight vector of the same dimension as the feature vector. The weight vector is used to adjust and suppress unwanted features in the feature vector in the matching process (explained in the next section). A typical case data structure is displayed in Fig 9. The data structure can be extended to contain more information if wanted. Other useful information could be graphs of the sound, the sound itself etc.

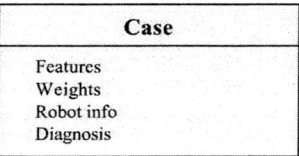

Fig. 9. Data structure for stored cases in the case library

6 Fault Classification

When a feature vector for a new case is assembled from the robot sound, it is compared with known cases that were previously stored in the case library. The comparison is called matching and is based on a nearest neighbour algorithm.

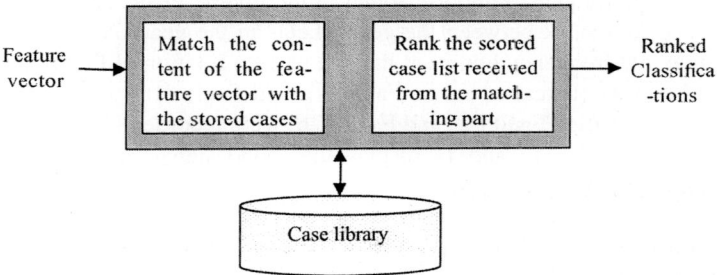

Fig. 10. Case-based classification as decision support

The matching algorithm calculates the Euclidian distance between the case that is to be classified and those cases previously stored in the case library. The distance function uses the feature vectors along with a set of weights defined on the features. Such weights c_j are incorporated into the distance calculation, as indicated in (7), to reflect different importance of different features.

$$\sum_{j=1}^{d}\left|a_j - b_j\right| * c_j, a,b,c \in \Re^d \qquad (7)$$

The classification of robot sound is based on the above matching function. The result of matching yields a scored list of the most similar cases. This list can be presented to responsible technicians as decision support for their further evaluation. An alternative is to derive a voting score for every class involved in the retrieved list of similar cases and then the final decision is settled upon the class exhibiting the highest voting score [13].

It is worthwhile to mention that the performance of our CBR system is improved each time when a new classified case is injected into the case library. The system can thereafter be tested with sounds from other robots previously classified by experts so as to estimate its accuracy. If the accuracy is estimated to be adequate, this CBR system can then be applied to diagnosing robot faults for practical usage.

7 Evaluation

Sounds from 20 robots have been recorded. All recordings were obtained during the end-test of the robots. The end-test involves a separate axis test. In the separate axis test, all axes on the robot were individually tested. Each individual axis was tested twice – with and without a payload attached to it. A microphone was mounted close to the axis of the industrial robot that was going to be measured. The robot was set to separate axis tests and the signals from axis 4 has been chosen for analysis

Ten recordings were performed on robots not equipped with payloads and 10 recordings were performed on robots equipped with payloads. The sound from a robot equipped with a payload differs a bit from that without a payload.

Two types of faults have been recorded, hereafter called Fault #1 and Fault #2. Fault #1 is caused by a notch on the big gear wheel in the gearbox of axis 4. It is characterized by a low frequency impulse sound in the middle of the rotation of the axis. Fault #2 is due to a slack between the gear wheels in the gearbox. This fault can be heard as a few low frequency bumps at the end of each rotation of the robot arm. Two robots with Fault #1 (hereafter called Fault #1a and Fault #1b) and two robots with Fault #2 (hereafter called Fault #2a and Fault #2b) were recorded.

Below, Figs. 11, 12, 13 and 14 display the sound signals gathered from robots Fault #1a, #1b, #2a, and #2b respectively. The black plots show s the unfiltered original sound profiles and the wavelet filtered sounds are represented by grey plots. The span of the frequency of the filtered sounds is from 384Hz to 512Hz.

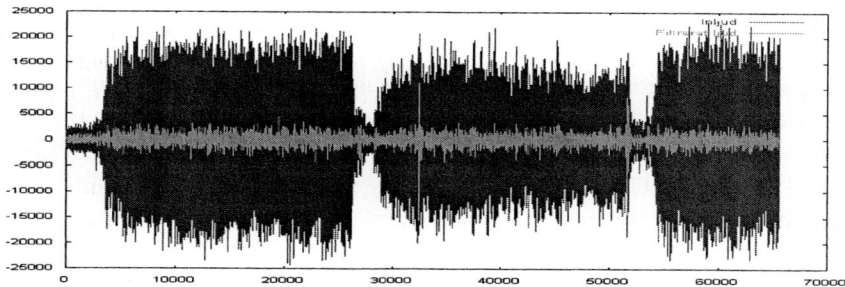

Fig. 11. Sound signals for robot Fault #1a

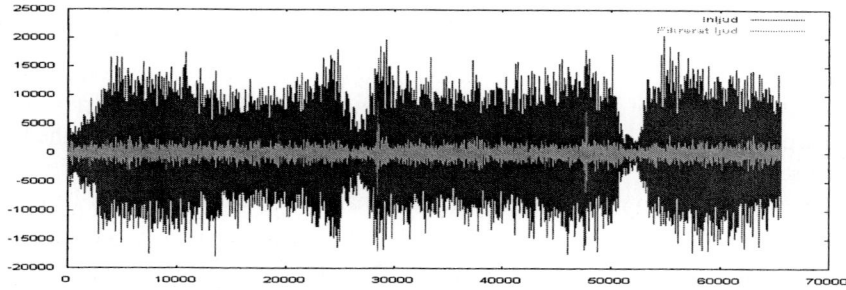

Fig. 12. Sound signals for robot Fault #1b

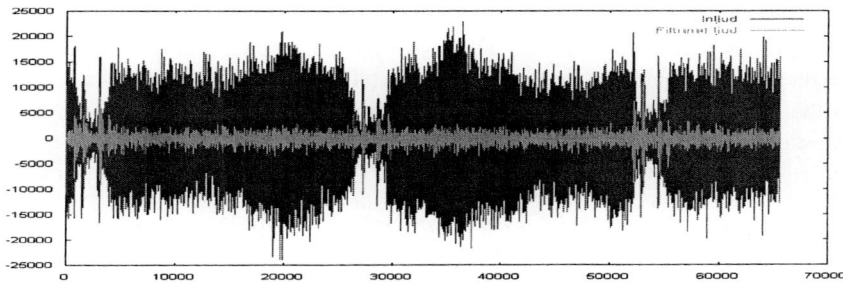

Fig. 13. Sound signals for robot Fault #2a

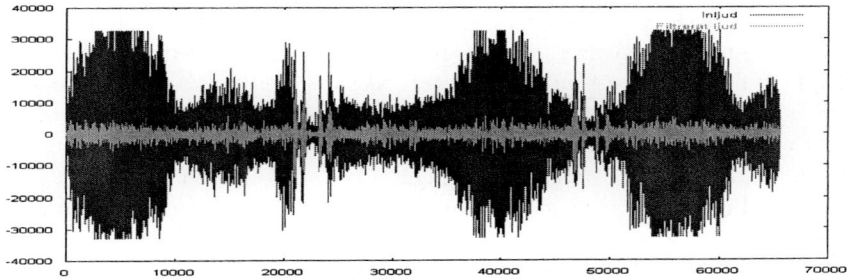

Fig. 14. Sound signals for robot Fault #2b

All recordings were analysed in the system and transformed to cases and inserted into the case library. Because of dramatic differences between sounds with and without payloads, recordings in both situations were collected and added to the case library. The number of features extracted equals 64.

The cases were first manually analysed. The cases from normal robots were compared to other cases from faulty recordings. The analysis betrays that feature 4 seems a strong attribute for distinguishing abnormality from normal ones. This is obvious to perceive by observing the following two figures. Fig. 15 shows the distribution of feature 4 extracted from the sound signals of the robots not equipped with payloads. Fig. 16 shows the distribution of feature 4 for the robots equipped with payloads. The feature in both figures is a normalised absolute value of the dominant wavelet coefficient at a frequency between 384Hz and 512Hz. Likewise we can use the same method to assess the discriminating capabilities of other features.

Example of Case Retrieval

In Fig. 11 the sound of the notch can be seen as two repeated prominent peaks in the filtered sound in the middle of the figure. The frequency of the filtered sound spans from 384 HZ to 512 Hz. This figure also indicates three successive rotations of the robot arm. A feature vector with 64 features is assembled from the sound and matched with the previously inserted cases in the case library. Table 1 illustrates a ranked list of the most similar cases retrieved. As can be seen form table 1, a previously diagnosed notch fault is regarded to be the closest to the current recording, thus making the strongest recommendation for diagnosis as Fault #1a. The cases ranked as the second candidate (case #3) and the third candidate (case #10) comes from normal recordings in the case library.

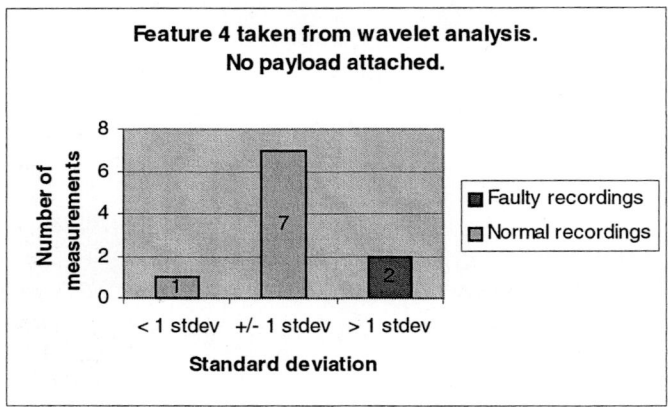

Fig. 15. Distribution of feature 4 for robots not equipped with a payload

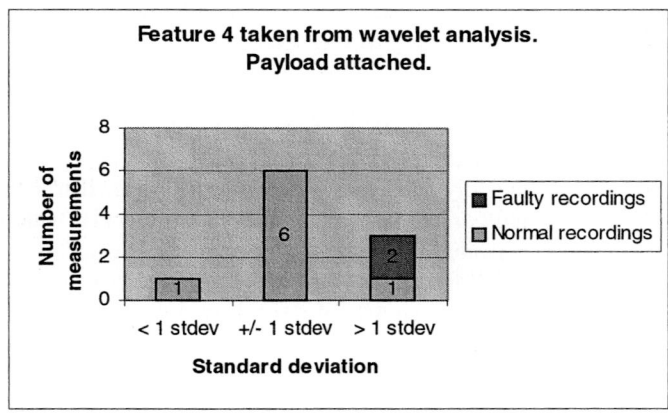

Fig. 16. Distribution of feature 4 for robots equipped with a payload

Table 1. The three most similar cases in the case library

Case name	Similarity degree	Case ranking
Fault #1a	99.1%	1.
Normal case #3	84.1%	2.
Normal case #10	83.2%	3.

The above matching and classification process involves prior specification of the weights for individual features by means of available background knowledge and/or preliminary analysis of extracted features from pre-diagnosed sound recordings (as what is done in Figs. 15 and 16). One other method for weighting is to automate the process using machine learning technique [12]. The matching process can also be extended with a neural net classifier.

8 How About FFT in This Context

FFT analysis is another common method for feature extraction from signals and it has been shown to be useful in some classification tasks. In this section the performance of FFT is highlighted to explain why it is not employed in our context. An FFT analysis with a Hanning window of length 512 was conducted on the recordings. The FFT–spectrum was broken down into 64 features and a feature vector was assembled from the features as described in section 5. A manual analysis of the FFT-spectrum and of the feature vectors was made in order to find out if any difference between faulty and normal recordings in the frequency spectrum could be spotted. Figs. 17 and 18 show the results of a standard deviation calculation for feature 4 in the feature vectors.

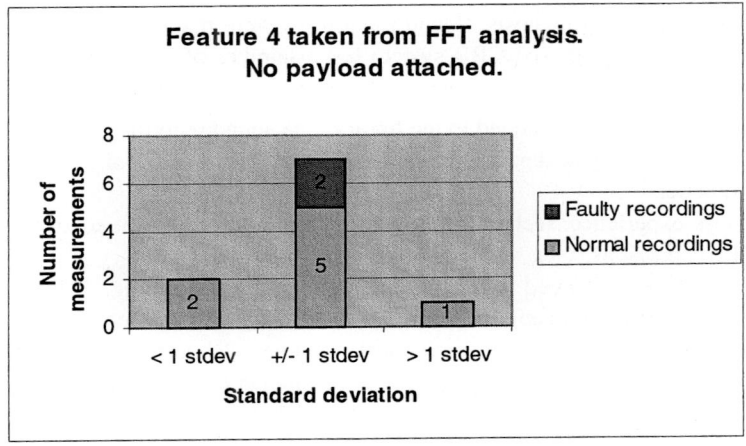

Fig. 17. Distribution of feature 4 for robots not equipped with a payload

As can be seen in the distributions in Figs. 17 and 18, feature values from faulty recordings end up amongst those from normal recordings, making it impossible to separate features between faulty and normal signals. This is true when performing suchlike analysis on any other features. The connotation is that FFT does not offer well distinguishable features for case-based classification in our context. Unlike wavelet analysis, FFT does not clean raw signals and thus is not able to discriminate different kinds of robot sounds that are overwhelmed by even stronger background noise.

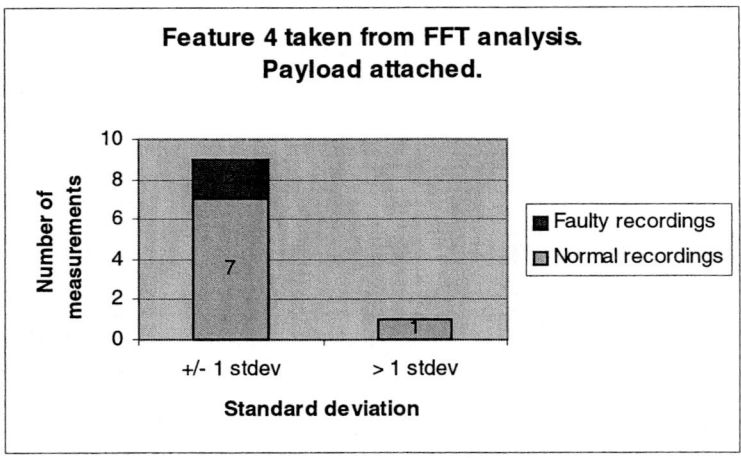

Fig. 18. Distribution of feature 4 for robots equipped with a payload

9 Conclusions

Case-Based Reasoning is a feasible method to identify faults based on sound recordings in robot fault diagnosis. Sound recordings were made under realistic industrial conditions. The proposed CBR system has a number of benefits as an industrial diagnostic tool:

- New cases are easy to be added to the library, one sound recording is sufficient.
- The method is easily accepted by technicians and is seen as a tool enabling them to perform better.
- It transfers experience; technicians are able to listen to different sounds and make manual comparisons.
- The system does not need to be "complete" from the beginning. A list of similar sounds and their classifications can be shown to technicians as decision support.
- System performance increases continuously. If a new "abnormal" sound is recorded but cannot be classified by the system, the technician contributes to the system experience by classifying the sound after the fault has been identified and corrected.

In the validation we have shown that one recording is sufficient for identification of a similar sound in the case library. Also a straightforward feature vector extracted from the original sound recording is sufficient for good results in the matching based on nearest neighbour algorithm. The feature vector and matching process has good potential for improvement. The selected features in the tests are peak wavelet values. Potential users have been interviewed and their reaction to our research prototype tool is very positive and they all consider that it would improve their performance and productivity.

References

1. Aamodt A., Plaza E.: Case-Based Reasoning: Foundational Issues, Methodological Variations, and System Approaches. Artificial Intelligence Com. Vol 7:1, pp. 39-59. IOS Press (1994).
2. Lee S. K., White P. R.: The Enhancement Of Impulse Noise And Vibration Signals For Fault Detection In Rotating and Reciprocating Machinery. Journal of Sound and Vibration (1998), pp. 485-505
3. Lin J.: Feature Extraction of Machine Sound using Wavelet and Its Application in Fault Diagnosis. NDT&E International 34 (2001), pp 25-30.
4. Bachman G. Fourier and Wavelet Analysis. New York, Springer (2000). ISBN:387-98899
5. Nilsson M., Funk P., Sollenborn M.: Complex Measurement in Medical Applications Using a Case-Based Approach. ICCBR (2003).
6. Intelligent Noise/Vibration Measurement and Analysis http://www.abd.uk.com/ 2004-01.
7. Kevin P. Logan, Prognostic Software Agents for Machinery Health Monitoring, MACSEA Ltd. http://www.dexteragents.com/pdf/dexter_wp1a.pdf, (2002).
8. Zhao Z et al: Application of principal component analysis in gear fault diagnosis. Modal Analysis, Modeling, Diagnostics, and Control - Analytical and Experimental, 1991, p 159-163
9. Thurston, M. G., An Open Standard for Web-Based Condition-Based Maintenance Systems. AUTOTESTCON Proceedings (2001). USA, Valley Forge, PA, pp. 401-415.
10. Bengtsson, M., Standardization Issues in Condition Based Maintenance. COMADEM - Proceedings of the 16th International Congress (2003). Växjö University, Sweden. Edited by Shrivastav, O. and Al-Najjar, B. Växjö University Press, ISBN 91-7636-376-7.
11. I. Daubechies, "Orthonormal Bases of Compactly Supported Wavelets," *Comm. Pure Appl. Math.,* Vol 41, 1988, pp. 906-966.
12. A. Stahl, Learning Feature Weights from Case Order Feedback, in: Proceedings of the 4th International Conference on Case-Based Reasoning, Springer, 2001.
13. E. Olsson, P. Funk and N. Xiong, Fault Diagnosis in Industry Using Sensor Readings and Case-Based Reasoning, accepted for publication by Journal of Intelligent and Fuzzy Systems, IOS Press.

A Case-Based Approach to Managing Geo-spatial Imagery Tasks*

Dympna O'Sullivan[1], Eoin McLoughlin[1], Michela Bertolotto[1], and David C. Wilson[2]

[1] Smart Media Institute, Department of Computer Science, University College Dublin,
Belfield, Dublin 4, Ireland
{dymphna.osullivan,eoin.A.mcloughlin,michela.bertolotto}@ucd.ie
[2] Department of Software and Information Systems
University of North Carolina at Charlotte, USA
davils@uncc.edu

Abstract. Advances in technology for digital image capture and storage have caused an information overload problem in the geo-sciences. This has compounded existing image retrieval problems whereby most image matching is performed using content-based image retrieval techniques. The biggest problem in this field is the so-called *semantic gap* - the mismatch between the capabilities of current content-based image retrieval systems and the user needs. One way of addressing this problem is to develop context-based image retrieval methods. Context-based retrieval relies on knowledge about why image contents are important in a particular area and how specific images have been used to address particular tasks. We are developing a case-based knowledge-management retrieval system that employs a task-centric approach to capturing and reusing user context. This is achieved through image annotation and adaptive content presentation. In this paper we present an extension of a previous implementation of our approach and a thorough evaluation of our application.

1 Introduction

The explosive development of communication technologies has brought information overload problems into focus. The Geo-Spatial domain parallels many other application areas in that progress in digital image capture techniques has not only resulted in more available data but also in more complex imagery. As a result it has now become necessary to concentrate on developing intelligent techniques and applications to manage geo-spatial imagery tasks. The majority of current image retrieval techniques retrieve images by similarity of appearance, using features such as color, texture or shape. In order to bridge this gap, applications that can unite information about underlying visual data with contextual information provided by users as they complete specified tasks are required. It is necessary to capture user or human expertise and proficiency in order to understand why relevant information was selected and also how it was employed in the context of a specific user task. This approach would make possible the capture and reuse of best-practice examples thereby dramatically reducing both the time and effort required to carry out new tasks. Such an approach also

---

* The support of the Research Innovation Fund initiative of Enterprise Ireland is gratefully acknowledged.

has beneficial repercussions from a knowledge management standpoint in that contextual knowledge pertaining to particular tasks may now be stored and reused as a resource for support, training and preserving organizational knowledge assets.

Our approach to the development of such a system incorporates sketch-based querying for image retrieval and image manipulation and annotation tools for emphasizing and organizing relevant aspects of task-relevant imagery. Case-based techniques are then applied to form a knowledge base from previously issued queries. The knowledge base can be exploited to improve future context-based query processing by retrieving appropriate previous task experiences and also to build organizational memory through experience capture. We have developed an approach for knowledge management of geo-spatial imagery, however we believe the approach is a general one and would scale well to other domains or other types of image sets.

From a case-based standpoint our research focuses on case knowledge acquisition and case knowledge reuse where a case is represented by a complete user task including all interactions with the system in the course of carrying out the task. We collect information in relation to particular imagery and to how the data has been employed to address specific domain tasks. We have extended the system to make use of real-time audio and video capture for acquiring user task context. The uploaded files are represented by media icons that can replay the annotations and these icons vary in transparency depending on their similarity to the current task. The system has also been expanded to allow the user to upload and view relevant documents from the Internet and to link to other documents that may be useful in fulfilling their task. We have provided new adaptive interfaces that change content presentation dynamically in response to user actions to reflect current context. The amassed contextual knowledge is reused in support of some similar tasks. We have achieved the goal of capturing important contextual information by situating intelligent support for gathering it inside a flexible task environment. It is considered imperative that the information should be collected implicitly to shield the users from the burden of explicit knowledge engineering.

Adopting this method of collecting contextual information by observing and interpreting user actions (as they proceed with domain specific tasks), allows correlations or associations between complex imagery to be made without using content-based image analysis. The tools developed to monitor and record user actions can be interpreted differently depending on perspective. From a system perspective the tools are present to capture fine-grained task knowledge that improves the ability of the application to make pro-active context-based recommendations to similar users. From a user's perspective the tools support them in carrying out their task by making it easier for them to select and highlight relevant features, to store insights and to summarize aspects of their work. Such an environment forms a lucid and well-structured foundation for users to report verdicts and conclusions as may be required of them in a typical work-related situation.

This paper presents the current implementation of our case-based retrieval application. The paper begins with a brief discussion of related research in Section 2, and it continues with a description of the image library interaction that provides a baseline for contextual knowledge capture in Section 3. In section 4 we describe the annotation tools available for image manipulation and capturing user experiences. We then go on to describe how we combine image retrieval techniques with previous user tasks to calculate annotation-based retrieval. Section 6 outlines an evaluation of the system. We conclude with a description of future work.

2 Background and Related Research

In our research we are focusing on managing large quantities of geo-spatial information available in raster format, primarily digital aerial photos. We have used some pre-existing techniques such as those described in [1] to provide a system that performs efficient geo-spatial database indexing and retrieval. As part of a general effort in intelligent geo-spatial information systems, we are developing case-based knowledge management support for libraries of geo-spatial imagery. This research draws on a substantial body of work in case-based knowledge management [2, 3, 4, 5, 6, 7]. Our image retrieval system provides support for natural user sketch-based interaction. Sketches provide a more intuitive method of communication with a spatial information system as demonstrated by existing systems such as Spatial-Query-By-Sketch [8].

The approach of locating intelligent support tools within task environments has been exploited in similar systems [9,10]. Our approach to knowledge capture parallels research performed in capturing rationale in aerospace design [11] and automotive design feasibility analysis [12]; however, the emphasis here is on making use of self-directed annotations provided by users as a means of task analysis support, rather than prompting users for particular kinds of choices.

3 System Overview

Geo-spatial information represents the location, shape and relationships among geographic features and associated artifacts. Typically, such imagery will also include metadata information, such as: time and date of image acquisition, image location, usually expressed in hierarchically arranged geographic entities. As a baseline for interaction with the system we have developed an image query mechanism that can incorporate image metadata information, textual user task descriptions and user sketches for image retrieval. In this paper we focus on image retrieval using only metadata and semantic information (annotation text).

The system is based on a three-tier architecture: client, server and database. The front end of the system consists of the clients with the back end of the system composed of the server and database. The server is capable of communicating with multiple clients simultaneously and also has access to the geo-spatial data and associated metadata. The client and server communicate using the TCP/IP protocol and this model allows for remote access over the World Wide Web.

When a user logs in they are directed to an interface that enables them to search directly for images that correspond to their current task needs. A typical task-based query to our image repository is a straightforward request to a geo-spatial image database (metadata, textual task description and sketch). The metadata component of the query is used to filter the result set by retrieving any images that correspond to the specific criteria outlined. From this subset of images any sketches and textual task information supplied is used to further constrain the result set. The resulting information can be returned as a list of matching imagery or a list of previous similar user sessions. The query process is illustrated in Fig. 1 below.

For example a user from the urban planning domain might be interested in building a shopping center in Boston, USA, and wish to view recent images of possible

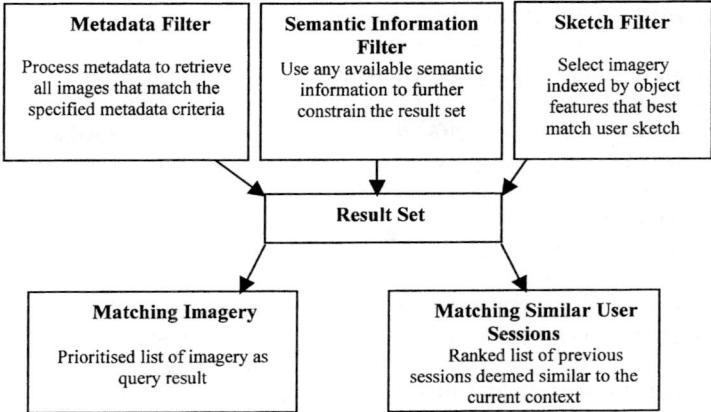

Fig. 1. Query Process

building sites and related areas. The user could outline a metadata query specifying a location in which they are interested and a small scale value as the areas they are interested in viewing are quite large when compared to other developments. They could express their query by means of a sketch, outlining undeveloped areas of land that are bordered by residential developments and good infrastructure. They could also verbalize their task description by entering a textual representation of it. For example in this case they could specify that they are interested in developing a new shopping center and in retrieving images of relatively large areas of undeveloped land of low elevation with good infrastructure that borders residential areas. The interfaces we have developed for outlining metadata, sketch and task queries are shown below in Fig. 2.

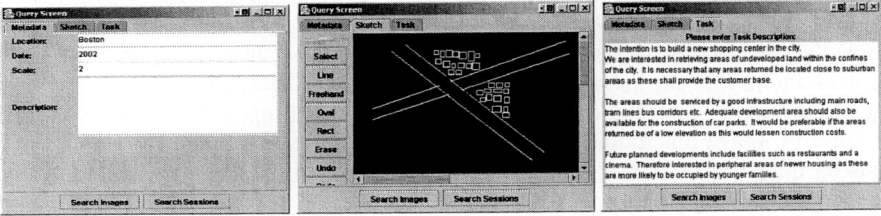

Fig. 2. Query Screens

Users may search for relevant information in one of two ways. Firstly they may perform a basic image retrieval search whereby individual images that match their search criteria are returned. Secondly they may search the case-base of previous user's work. We refer to the complete process of a user interacting with the system with the aim of carrying out a specified task as a user "session". In a typical interaction, the system can capture sketches and geo-spatial queries posed by the user, the results that were found to be useful as well as all the user's annotations of the results. All of the contextual knowledge required to address the task goal can thus be captured as an experience case or session, thus enabling an increasingly powerful cycle of proactive support with case-based suggestions based on task context. The procedure and resulting screens involved in searching the case-base for similar user sessions is described in detail in the following sections.

If a user chooses to perform a basic image retrieval search then the resulting matching images are returned as a ranked list of thumbnails with an associated matching percentage score. A subset of the most relevant metadata for each image is available as tool tip text when mousing over the image. The user can browse the images retrieved in the results screen and select any images that are relevant to the task at hand for further manipulation. As the user selects imagery from the results screen the matching image scores are recalculated dynamically using a combination of the current users task context and any annotations that may have previously been uploaded to the particular image as new parameters for similarity matching. The interface is then redrawn to reflect the updated task context. All the selected images are then collected in the current user context and made available for task specific manipulation and annotation.

4 Capturing User Context and Task Knowledge for Retrieval

As part of our effort to capture task knowledge with the ultimate goal of performing more effective image retrieval by employing annotations we have developed tools for direct image manipulation. The tools assist the user in organizing information about relevant imagery and their task. These insights are then captured in a form the system may use to perform better similarity matching. The tools for direct image manipulation include filters, transformation, highlighting, sketching, post-it type and multimedia annotations. They allow the user to identify regions of interest that can be linked to clarifications, rationale and other types of annotations. The manipulations and annotations do not alter the underlying raster or geo-spatial data, rather they are layered to provide a task-specific view. This enables the capture and refinement of more general task-based ideas and rationale. To illustrate our annotation tools, we return to the shopping center example. After retrieving and selecting imagery of Boston (Section 3) the user can then annotate each image using a substantial set of tools as shown in Fig. 3 and trigger the knowledge acquisition process. The tools are a subset of what might typically be found in a fully-fledged image-processing suite. We have selected the kinds of image manipulations that would be most useful in helping to analyze and focus on image features (e.g., high-pass filtering). All of the sketching manipulations can be performed in a variety of colors and brush styles. The architecture has also been designed to facilitate the addition of new types of image tools as the need arises. The user can then go on to add personal media annotations to the image as a whole or to particular highlighted image aspects. Currently, the system supports annotation by text, audio and video, though retrieval is focused on text. A facility is in place that allows users to upload web documents as annotations. This allows further context to be extracted by following HTML links. The system integrates real-time audio and video capture as well as compression. A wide variety of compression formats are supported, including QuickTime, Mpeg and H.263. All textual, audio and video annotations can be previewed before being incorporated as part of the knowledge base and once recorded, can be saved and uploaded to the image context as a knowledge parcel associated with the task in question.

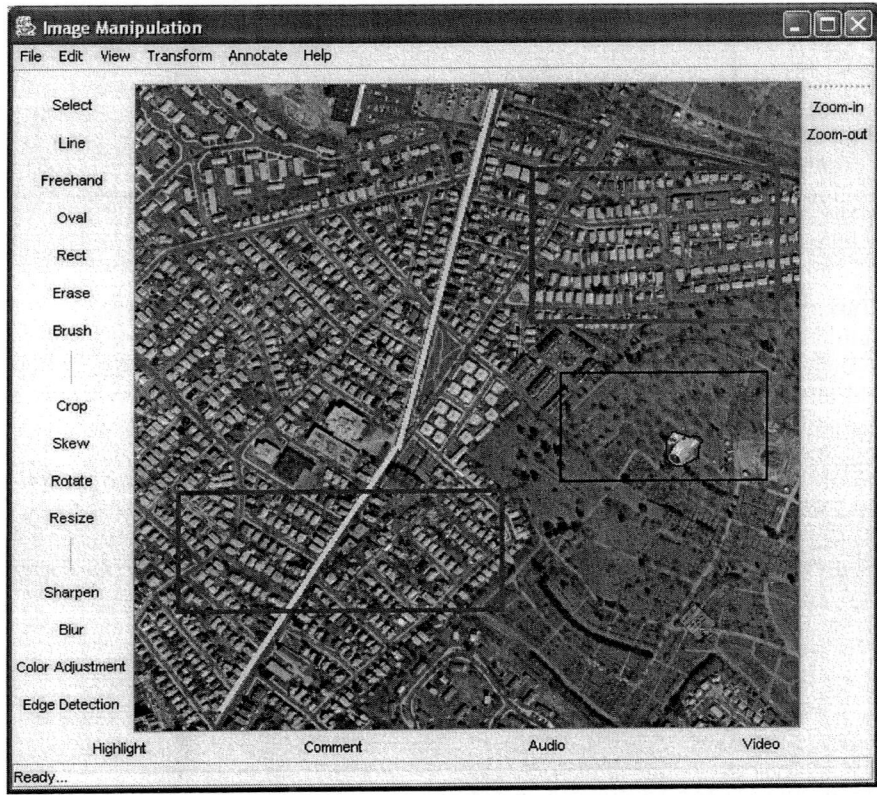

Fig. 3. Image Manipulation

Returning to our shopping center example, in Fig. 3, the user has made use of the transformation and annotation tools in carrying out their task. They have circled and highlighted some residential areas, indicating their awareness that the area would provide a large customer base. They have highlighted a large road running through the heart of the image showing interest in the infrastructure of the area as outlined in their task description. The user has also uploaded a video file to an undeveloped area peripheral to the residential area indicating the feasibility of development in this area. They may have recorded this video while they were carrying out their task or this may have been an existing file that they had in their possession containing information specific to urban development. The textual and media annotations are represented by icons, which are painted on the image. If the user mouses over any of these icons the region associated with the annotation is emphasized by a rectangle drawn around the icon. This is shown by the dark rectangle around the camera icon in Fig. 3. The user can click on any of these icons to display a pop-up description. The system also supports annotation by cut, copy and paste between a given image and other images in the dataset, as well as images in any application that supports clipboard functionality for the given operating system. A user's entire process of image interaction in the system is stored as an encapsulated session case in the case-base. Note that a session can be saved and re-opened to continue processing later.

5 Annotation Based Retrieval

Capturing task-based knowledge enables a powerful cycle of proactive support. Such a system allows us to facilitate knowledge sharing by retrieving potentially relevant knowledge from other experiences. Currently, we are focusing our annotation-based retrieval on textual annotations. We use information retrieval metrics (e.g., [13]) as a basis for similarity. We presume that image retrieval is taking place towards some goal in the context of an overall workflow and given a textual representation of the task context, we can match previously annotated session images to the current context.

Task descriptions could be provided by the user directly. Since we expect our system to be used in the context of an overall workflow, we have designed the system to link directly with upstream task descriptions, as they are provided to the user. This could allow for multiple users to share the same context for cooperative tasks. The task-based retrieval employs indexes in three separate spaces - Annotation Index, Image Index and Session Index. For a full description of our similarity indices please refer to [14]. Theses indices are used in two different types of retrieval - image retrieval and session retrieval.

Task-based image retrieval serves two purposes. First, task-based similarity can be used directly to access annotated images in the image library. Second, it can be integrated with similarities from the other types of query information, such as by image content, to provide a more refined overall metric for retrieval. In either case, the resulting images are presented through the same type of interface for consistent interaction. In searching for relevant images, all retrieved images must initially pass a metadata filter. For the images that pass the metadata filter similarity is computed by calculating similarity in both the image index and the annotations index. The final image score is an average of overall image and individual annotation similarities.

As the system builds up encapsulated user interactions, another type of retrieval is enabled, retrieving entire previous task-based sessions. This enables a current user to look for the previous image analysis tasks that are most similar to the current task both to find relevant imagery and to examine the decisions and rationale that went into addressing the earlier task. One challenge in retrieving previous sessions has been how to present an entire session to the user in a manner that is compact enough to allow multiple results to be viewed simultaneously while still providing enough information for the user to discriminate potential relevancy. Fig. 4 shows an example of our results for retrieved sessions, displayed in a newly designed interface. In order to keep session listings small and still provide enough discriminatory information, each session result is summarized to include the following:

- Percent similarity score
- The most discriminating query information (if more than one) for the session (since we have captured which results were actually used, we know which queries were most fruitful)
- The most important annotations (words, phrases, media buttons that play any audio or video clips uploaded during the session and are deemed to have high similarity to the current user's context)
- Thumbnail versions of the most important images (images that have been annotated as part of the similar users context and bear relevance to the current users task and have been ranked accordingly)

By providing a relative ranking for session elements, we can tailor the session view to a reasonable amount of available space for displaying results.

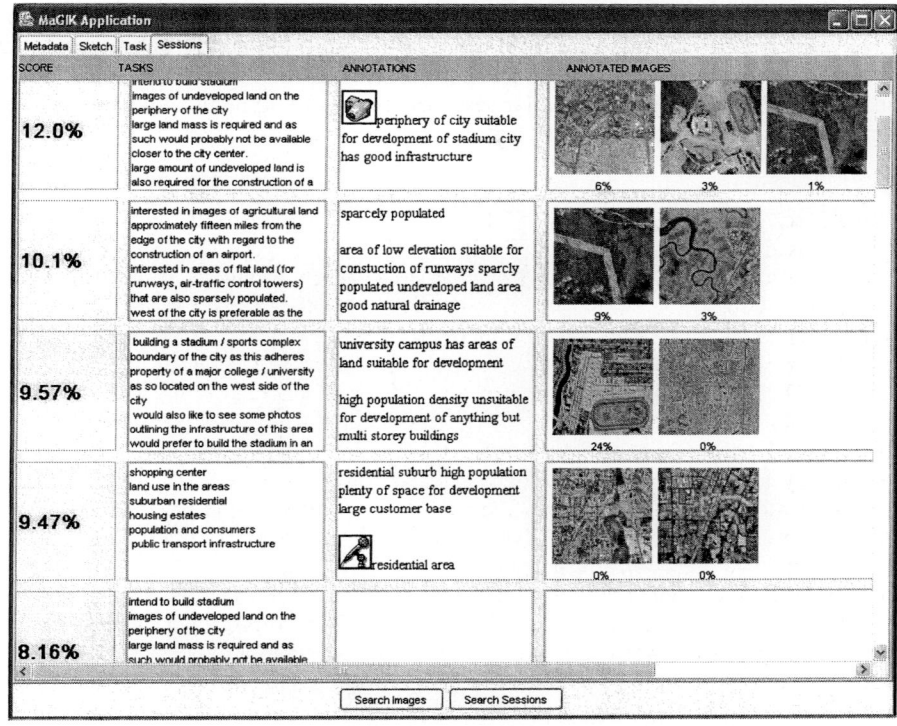

Fig. 4. Similar Sessions

In searching for relevant sessions, similarity is computed by calculating matching scores for all of the individual elements of which a session is composed. The preliminary similarity score is calculated in a vector space across all retrieved sessions, where the text for each session is composed of the task description, annotations and user metadata query information. The total number of images annotated and browsed in each similar session as a fraction of the total number of images returned is then computed. The final session score is a weighted sum of session similarity and proportion of annotated and browsed images.

The proportion of annotated and browsed images provide a measure of the relative usefulness of a given session and they are given a parameterized weighting relative (currently lower) to the session index similarity component. The scores for the individual images annotated or browsed in a similar session are calculated by comparing any textual annotations made to those images during that session with the metadata and textual task description entered by the current user.

If the user wishes to view the annotations made to an image returned in a similar session, they may do so by clicking on the thumbnail, which brings up the image and all its annotations in the image manipulation screen as shown in Fig. 5. Here the user has an opportunity to view sketching annotations, a video file and read a textual comment uploaded as part of the similar session. When displayed on these session images, the icons representing the textual and media annotations have different levels of transparency depending on their similarity to the current users context. All textual annotations may be displayed in a web browser thereby giving the user the opportunity to read annotations uploaded from the World Wide Web and to link to any other relevant or contextual material from those documents. If the current user select a session for closer examination the similar sessions scores vary dynamically based on this interaction.

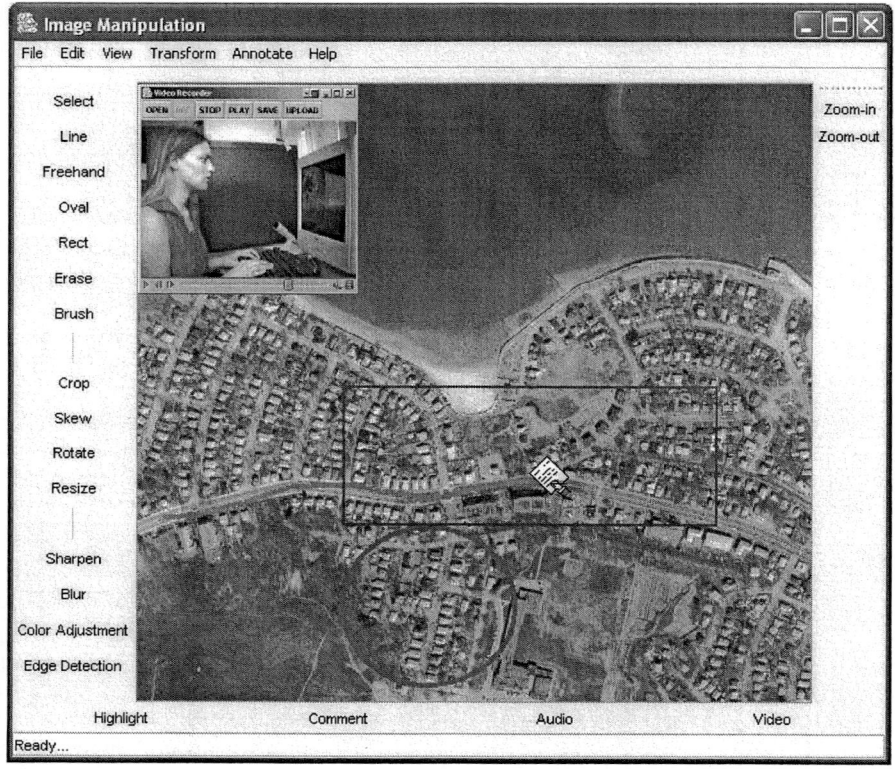

Fig. 5. Viewing Annotations

For example if our user browses the annotations of another user or annotates images that another user has already found useful in the context of their task, the scores assigned to the sessions will increase as the current user proceeds with their own task. The interface is then redrawn to reflect this context. Conversely session scores will decrease if associated queries, annotations, or images are ignored by our current user. The user may further annotate images from similar sessions if they wish and/or retain the previous users annotations by adding them to their current session image context. Once the user saves the desired previous/new annotations, all of these annotations are transferred to the current users view of the image. The user may perform many different queries and annotate or manipulate many images during the course of a session, and these are all saved as part of the users profile when they exit the application.

Because the knowledge management system is tightly coupled with the tasks that the user is performing, the system also has the capacity to make proactive recommendations in a natural and unobtrusive manner by monitoring the user's current task context. Based on increments in the geo-spatial image information accessed and annotations provided, the system can correspondingly anticipate and update what previous experiential knowledge would be relevant at that stage, making it available to the user. If a user decides to incorporate the work of another user as part of their own session, this knowledge is implicitly captured by the system and the scores associated with that session as well as the reused annotations are updated to reflect this recycling process. The knowledge is provided unobtrusively, so that it need only be accessed when required. Thus the process of knowledge retrieval does not distract from the task at hand, yet makes relevant knowledge available just-in-time.

6 Evaluation

In the evaluation phase of our work we tested with a dataset of 1600 annotated images. The dataset contained images from the astronomy domain and had been annotated by expert users in the field. In order to evaluate the system we conducted experiments to test both the image and session retrieval capabilities of the application. In investigating image retrieval we were most interested in showing that by including contextual annotations for retrieval the system can better match individual images to specified user tasks. In testing session retrieval we were interested in showing that the system is capable of capturing and deciphering fine-grained task specific knowledge. We were aiming to show that proactive recommendations made by the system based on the acquired knowledge could facilitate effective knowledge sharing.

6.1 Image Retrieval Evaluation

In order to evaluate image retrieval we applied clustering techniques to our annotated image library. The dataset contained 1600 annotated images and was clustered into five categories for evaluation. The categories were created by examining the semantic content of the annotations associated with the images and the images divided up accordingly. There was some overlap between images in different categories. These categories were "Telescope", "Mars", "Nebula", "Comet" and "Manned Space Exploration". The images were clustered so that there were 505 images in the Telescope category, 152 images in the Mars category, 285 images in the Nebula category, 130 in the Comet category and 77 images in the Manned Space Exploration category. The remaining images were clustered together into an "Other" category.

To perform this evaluation we outlined three different task descriptions in each of the five original categories. These task descriptions can be viewed as sub-clusters of the original partitions. An example of a task description in the Manned Space Exploration category was "Interested in the work carried out on the construction of the International Space Station for research into manned space exploration".

The fifteen queries were entered into the system as task descriptions and the top 100 images and their matching scores for each of the fifteen were recorded. A trial was then carried out to distinguish which images were correctly classified.

If an image was returned in response to a sub-category task description and was also in the original umbrella cluster we considered that image to be correctly classified. For example if an image had been classified as belonging to the Telescope category and was returned in response to a query " Interested in retrieving images taken by the Hubble space telescope for research into star formation" then this image was considered to be correctly classified. The table below shows how many images in the top 100 images returned in response to each query were considered correctly categorized.

Table 1. Image Retrieval Results

Category	% Images Correctly Classified
Telescope	74
Mars	61
Nebula	62
Comet	53
Exploration	58

As a second phase of our image retrieval evaluation we conducted a relative comparison of average positive and average negative scores for retrieved images. For this experiment we again made use of the clusters and sub-clusters described above. The purpose of this experiment was not to test our algorithms for calculating percent similarity scores rather the aim was to demonstrate that in response to a particular query the scores of those images correctly classified is on average much higher than the scores of those incorrectly classified. In carrying out this experiment we calculated the average score of all images that were correctly classified and the average score of all images that were incorrectly categorized for the top 100 images returned. The scores used here were the percentage matching similarity scores returned along with an image in response to a user task description. In this instance the matching scores for returned images tended to be quite low. Due to the large size of the image library and very broad clusters this was to be expected. We considered it more important that the more relevant images be ranked higher in the returned results. In a returned set of 100 images a user is unlikely to view more than 10 images so if the relative positive scores are higher than the relative negative scores then it is improbable that a user will inspect an image that has been incorrectly classified.

The results of this test are shown in the graphs in Fig. 6 below. The average positive scores for the returned images are represented by the darker columns, and the average negative scores by the lighter columns. In general the average positive scores are higher than the average negative scores. This means that in relative terms, for a result set of 100, there are more images present that are relevant to the task description entered by the user than images that are not relevant.

6.2 Session Retrieval Evaluation

In order to evaluate session retrieval we applied the same clustering techniques to our annotated image library as we did for image retrieval. For this analysis the dataset also contained 1600 annotated images and no user sessions had been created prior to evaluation. The dataset was clustered into the same five categories for evaluation - "Telescope", "Mars", "Nebula", "Comet" and "Manned Space Exploration". However

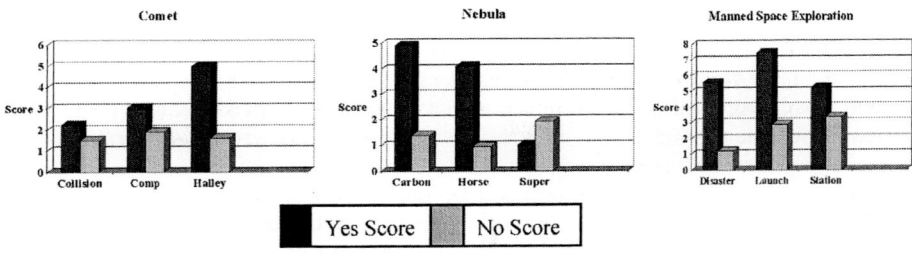

Fig. 6. Average Positive Scores v Average Negative Scores

in this instance we did not limit the clusters to 100 images as testing session retrieval is a much more subjective task.

Once the dataset was portioned we automatically created fifteen user sessions (i.e. fifteen cases in our case base). The user sessions were created by outlining three different task descriptions in each of the five clustered categories. An example of a task description in the Mars category was "Interested in retrieving imagery of the planet Mars that shows that there may once have been or is now water on the planet. Especially interested in images that depict sedimentary rock".

The fifteen sessions were created by entering task descriptions such as the one above. Image searches were performed on the 1600 annotated images using these fifteen task descriptions as queries. From the returned images the top five most relevant images were selected for annotation. These five images were then annotated with their original annotation from the annotated dataset. The original annotation was used for a number of reasons. Firstly it was the most complete description of the image available having been provided by an expert user. Also by including it we are simulating the behaviour of an expert user utilizing the application to carry out a specified task. It was possible to use this annotation for creating user sessions as there were no pre-existing user sessions in the case-base and therefore even though the annotation would have been included in the image index for retrieval it would not yet have been included in the session index. Each user session created was then saved to include the task query, the resulting images, the images selected for annotation and the annotations applied to each image as an encapsulated case in the knowledge base. This process was repeated for the fifteen user sessions. When the fifteen user sessions had been added the annotations were indexed and included for retrieval.

Once user sessions had been created and the annotations had been indexed, the next step of the evaluation was to assess how effectively the system performs Session Retrieval. We referred once again to the five clusters in the dataset and created generic task descriptions relating to each of the five outlined categories. An example of a generic task description for the Nebula category was "Interested in the gaseous content of nebulae i.e. what are the relative amounts of various gases (hydrogen, helium, oxygen, nitrogen) present". Once a generic task description had been outlined for each category they were entered as queries to the system and a search for similar sessions performed. The desired outcome was that the generic task description would best match the three more specific cases already assigned to that cluster. If this was not the case we should have been able to explain why such discrepancies occurred.

As in our image retrieval evaluation this test was a relative comparison of returned sessions and once again the session matching scores were quite low the large number of images in the dataset and a relatively small number of user sessions in the knowledge base. The aim of the test was to demonstrate that in response to a particular query the scores of those sessions correctly classified should on average be much higher than the scores of those incorrectly classified. If this is the case, then if the system was being used on a large scale with a greater numbers of sessions users of the system would be unlikely to access sessions returned in the wrong categories as these sessions would overall have lower matching scores.

When analysing the sessions returned in response to the generic task descriptions we did not set a threshold on the number of sessions returned. Instead for consistency in our calculations all fifteen session were returned for each query. For the returned sessions for each query we calculated the average percentage "Case in Cluster" score and the average percentage "Case not in Cluster" score. The average percentage "Case in Cluster" score was calculated by averaging the scores associated with each of the three sessions of more specific task description (that fell with the bounds of the more generic task description). The average percentage "Case not in Cluster" score was the average score associated with all other returned sessions. Even though the three generated sessions within each cluster were not always returned as the top three sessions, the average percentage "Case in Cluster" score was always higher than the average percentage "Case not in Cluster" score. This demonstrates that on a larger scale the system would be more likely to return sessions from the correct categories than the incorrect categories.

For some of the different categories the "Case in Cluster" and "Case not in Cluster" scores are shown in the graphs in Fig. 7 below. The lighter dots represent the three sessions (sub-categories) that are relevant to the particular category while the darker dots represent all other sessions returned.

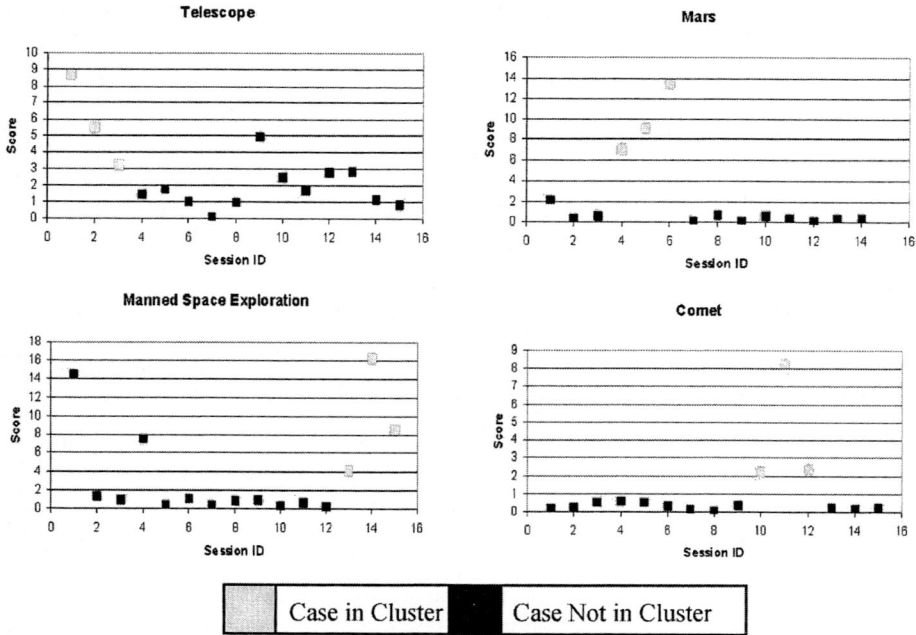

Fig. 7. Evaluating Similar Sessions

We then repeated the session retrieval evaluation using humans to judge the relevancy of the results returned by the system. The subjects entered the generic task descriptions and were asked to choose and place the top three most relevant sessions from the results. In 85% of cases the subjects agreed with the results returned by the system. These results are very promising as they demonstrate that the system is proficient at retrieving similar sessions based on current user context. The results show the application we have developed can be used to address specific tasks in many fields that rely on image analysis. Users of a system such as this one could benefit from the type functionality offered by this application as it can reduce both the time and effort required to carry out new tasks by facilitating the sharing of contextual knowledge.

7 Conclusions

We have introduced our approach to developing a case-based knowledge management system for geo-spatial imagery. The system makes use of knowledge capture techniques to capture human expertise and then attempts to understand this task-specific context and to convert the knowledge into a format that the system can reuse. Our evaluation shows system implementation performing as expected thus far; we continue to test the system further as development proceeds. We are currently in the process of transferring the system to the mobile platform and we are investigating the possibility of adding other resources such as speech to text in order to facilitate media retrieval and to capture more fine-grained task context. We plan to further investigate implicit knowledge acquisition techniques by extracting information from more subtle user actions, for example, click stream data. We also note that our system has much wider potential applications beyond geo-spatial imagery, such as medical imagery, and we expect that such techniques will prove valuable in many fields that rely on image analysis.

References

1. Shekhar, S., Chawla, S., Ravada, S., Fetterer. A., Liu, X., and Lu, C.: Spatial databases: Accomplishments and research needs. IEEE Transactions on Knowledge and Data Engineering (TKDE), (1900) 11(1): 45-55
2. Minor, M., and Staab, S.: In Proceedings of the German Workshop on Experience Management GI-Edition - Lecture Notes in Informatics (LNI), Bonner Köllen Verlag, P-10 (2002)
3. Aha, D., Becerra-Fernandez, I., Maurer, F., and Mu͂noz-Avila, H.: Proceedings of the AAAI-99 Workshop on Exploring Synergies of Knowledge Management and Case-Based Reasoning. AAAI Press (1999)
4. Becerra-Fernandez, I. and Aha, D.: Case-based problem solving for knowledge management systems. In Proceedings of the Twelfth Annual Florida Artificial Intelligence Research Symposium, AAAI (1999) 219-223
5. Kitano, H., and Shimazu, H.: The experience sharing architecture: A case study in corporate-wide case-based software quality control. In Leake, D., ed., Case-Based Reasoning: Experiences, Lessons, and Future Directions. Menlo Park, CA: AAAI Press (1996) 235-268
6. Aarts, R.: A CBR architecture for project knowledge management. In Proceedings of the Fourth European Workshop on Case-Based Reasoning, Springer Verlag (1998) 414- 424

7. Klahr, P.: Knowledge management on a global scale. In Gaines, B. Musen, M., and Uthurusamy, R., eds., Proceedings of the 1997 AAAI Spring Symposium on Artificial Intelligence in Knowledge Management, (1997) 82-85
8. Egenhofer, M. J.: Spatial-query-by-sketch. In M. Burnett and W. Citrin eds, VL'96, IEEE Symposium on Visual Languages, Boulder, CO (1996) 60-67
9. Budzik, J., Hammond, K. and Birnbaum. L.: Information access in context. Knowledge Based Systems 14(1-2), (2001) 37-53
10. Lieberman. H.: Letizia: An agent that assists web browsing. In Proceedings of the Thirteenth International Joint Conference on Artificial Intelligence, San Francisco, CA, Morgan Kaufmann (1995)
11. Leake, D. B., and Wilson, D. C.: A case-based framework for interactive capture and reuse of design knowledge. Applied Intelligence 14(1) (2001)
12. Leake, D.; Birnbaum, L.; Hammond, K.; Marlow, C.; and Yang, H.: Integrating information resources: A case study of engineering design support. In Proceedings of the Third International Conference on Case-Based Reasoning, (1999) 482-496
13. Salton, G., and McGill, M.: Introduction to modern information retrieval. New York, McGraw-Hill (1983)
14. O'Sullivan, D., McLoughlin, E., Wilson, D. C., and Bertolotto, M.: Capturing Task Knowledge for GeoSpatial Imagery, Proceedings K-CAP 2003 (Second International Conference on Knowledge Capture), Florida, USA, ACM press (2003) 78-87

Analysing Similarity Essence for Case Based Recommendation*

Derry O'Sullivan[1], Barry Smyth[1], and David C. Wilson[2]

[1] Smart Media Institute
University College Dublin
{dermot.osullivan,barry.smyth}@ucd.ie
[2] Department of Software and Information Systems
University of North Carolina at Charlotte
davils@uncc.edu

Abstract. Initial successes in the area of recommender systems have led to considerable early optimism. However as a research community, we are still in the early days of our understanding of these applications and their capabilities. Evaluation metrics continue to be refined but we still need to account for the relative contributions of the various knowledge elements that play a part in the recommendation process. In this paper, we make a fine-grained analysis of a successful case-based recommendation approach, providing an ablation study of similarity knowledge and similarity metric contributions to improved system performance. In particular, we extend our earlier analyses to examine how measures of *interestingness* can be used to identify and analyse relative contributions of segments of similarity knowledge. We gauge the strengths and weaknesses of knowledge components and discuss future work as well as implications for research in the area.

1 Introduction

Recommender systems reflect a coming together of technologies and ideas from a number of areas including information retrieval, user profiling and machine learning. The job of a recommender system is to seek to gain a deep understanding of a particular user's information needs and to provide them with a short-list of targeted recommendations that satisfy these needs. Recommender systems first began to appear in the late 1990's as a response to the growing problem of information overload [1] and the paradigm has provided a rich source of inspiration for researchers. The intervening years have brought with them an abundance of algorithmic developments that have led to a variety of different basic recommendation techniques and strategies [1] and, most recently, to the development of a range of hybrid strategies [2].

Movie recommenders – made famous by the likes of EachMovie [3] and MovieLens [4] – are an example of the quintessential recommender system, recommending movies to users based on their viewing preferences. They provide a

---

* The support of the Informatics Research Initiative of Enterprise Ireland is gratefully acknowledged.

good backdrop to describe two of the most fundamental of recommendation approaches: content-based recommendation and collaborative filtering. The former relies on the availability of meta-data that captures the essence of items available for recommendation – movie descriptions that include genre, actor and director information – taking advantage of similarity assessment techniques to match a target user's profile to a set of recommendable items [5, 6]. Indeed content-based methods resonate well with many case-based reasoning approaches to similarity assessment, retrieval, profiling and relevance feedback, and this has in turn led to the development of a range of case-based recommenders [7, 8]. In contrast, collaborative filtering (CF) techniques provide an alternative strategy if meta-data descriptions are inadequate, unavailable or when behavioural information about the actions of users is plentiful [4, 6]. Suitable items are chosen for recommendation not because their description matches them with a target user, but rather because these items have been liked by users who are similar to the target user; a collaborative filtering movie recommender 'knows' nothing about a movie's genre or actors or its director, but it 'knows' that other users have liked this movie and that these users are similar to the target user in the sense that they, and the target user, have liked and disliked many of the same movies in the past. Thus, as a general characterisation, we find that content-based methods rely on item-item [9] and item-user [10] similarities whereas collaborative filtering methods rely on user-user similarities [4].

In our previous research, we have investigated and developed a range of content-based, collaborative and hybrid (combination) recommendation techniques [11, 12]. More recently, however, we have explored the relationship between content-based and collaborative techniques and, in particular, we have demonstrated how ratings-based collaborative filtering profiles can be mined to provide a rich source of item-item similarity knowledge so that case-based recommendation techniques (similarity assessment and recommendation ranking) might be used to enhance a traditional collaborative filtering approach. The result has been a significant improvement in recommendation accuracy across a wide range of standard data-sets [11–13]. Like many researchers we find ourselves with a range of important questions left unanswered. While the traditional 'recommendation accuracy' evaluation has provided us with a high-level understanding of recommender performance, gaps remain when it comes to our detailed understanding of the computational strengths and weaknesses of our specific technique and its component elements and knowledge sources. Hence, in this paper we provide a more fine-grained analysis of our work focusing on a knowledge-level analysis of the similarity knowledge elements that underpin our recommendation approach.

This paper describes the results of a comprehensive ablation study that seeks to identify the key sources of competence and performance that exist within our system, by manipulating the similarity knowledge and ranking functions used during recommendation. This includes a detailed analysis of our similarity knowledge as it is mined from ratings-based profiles. Some commentators have asked the question as to whether our recommendation power stems from all of this knowledge or just a small set of the rules; we know that previous work in case-based reasoning [14] has highlighted how, oftentimes, the power of a case-base stems from just a small subset of identifiable cases. In previously related work [13], we disassembled the similarity knowledge and recommendation ranking sections of our algorithm and analysed their contribution to the overall recommendation algorithm; results showed that the quality and amount of similarity knowledge and the dominance of certain ranking criteria are important factors in recommendation quality. Further ablation possibilities were found by this research and so – as part of an ongoing ablation study – we continue this line of research by looking at a variety of different ways to characterize the quality of *interestingness* of our similarity knowledge as a precursor to eliminating low-quality rules. The results are somewhat surprising: while learned similarity knowledge varies from low to high quality it appears that the majority of this knowledge is making a unique competence contribution. Eliminating even the low quality similarity knowledge has a marked affect on recommendation performance. The details of our study are discussed in Sections 3 and 4, but first we provide an overview of our own case-based recommendation strategy and how it exploits similarity knowledge mined from ratings-based profiles.

2 Mining Similarity Knowledge for Case Based Recommendation

Our recent work in case-based recommendation has applied data mining techniques to derive similarity knowledge in order to ameliorate similarity coverage problems that arise for systems employing ratings-based user profiles as cases. Issues of similarity coverage arise from the relative sparsity of ratings overlap between average user profiles. Our case-based approach addresses the sparsity problem by first applying data-mining techniques to a set of ratings-based user profiles in order to derive similarity knowledge in the form of rules that relate items. As we will see in the following subsections, these item-item rules, and their associated probabilities, are used to increase the density of the user-item ratings matrix by leveraging similarities between profile cases to reduce ratings sparsity. Due to space constraints, and to avoid repetition, these sections provide only a technical summary of our case-based technique and the interested reader is referred to [11, 12] for additional detail. Examples in the following discussion are taken from the PTVPlus television programme recommendation domain.

2.1 Association Rule Mining

The Apriori algorithm [15] is a well-known data-mining technique that can be used to efficiently discover similarity knowledge from PTVPlus profile cases (consisting of sets of television shows and user-defined ratings) by finding frequently occurring associations between rated profile items (television programmes), and by assigning confidence scores to the associations. These association rules indicate which items can be considered to be similar, and their associated confidences can be used as a proxy for their level of similarity. In turn, these *direct* rules can be chained together to produce additional *indirect* associations and similarities in order to further elaborate the item-item similarity matrix. When mining association rules, confidence and support values are used to constrain exponentially large candidate rule sets by setting appropriate thresholds. The Apriori algorithm is designed to efficiently process a database of transactions to discover well-supported association rules by finding the set of most frequently co-occurring items [11].

We should emphasize that data mining using the Apriori algorithm is one of many possible approaches to generating additional similarity knowledge; we have simply chosen data Apriori as a reasonable initial technique to demonstrate the feasibility of our new recommendation strategy. Alternative possibilities include Singular Value Decomposition (SVD) [16], Latent Semantic Indexing (LSI) [17], and Principal Component Analysis (PCA) [18]. Indeed, it is worth highlighting that SVD and PCA methods have already been used in the past to address the sparsity problem [16, 18], although they have not been used to generate similarity knowledge.

2.2 Direct and Item-Item Similarities

By treating PTVPlus user profiles as transactions and the rated programmes therein as itemsets, the Apriori algorithm can be used to derive a set of programme-programme association rules with confidence values serving as similarity scores. For example, in PTVPlus we might find the rule *Friends* $\Rightarrow$ *ER* with a confidence of 37%, allowing us to conclude a similarity of 0.37 between *Friends* and *ER* to fill the appropriate slot in our similarity matrix. These direct associations can be chained together to further improve similarity coverage. For example, discovering rules $A \Rightarrow B$ and $B \Rightarrow C$ may indicate that A and C are also related and the strength of their relationship can be estimated by combining their individual confidence values (see [11] for further details). Experiments in this paper use a maximal combination model to calculate indirect rule confidences.

2.3 Recommendation Strategy

The recommendation strategy consists of two basic steps:

1. The target profile, t is compared to each profile case, $c \in C$, to select the k most similar cases.
2. The items contained within these selected cases (but absent in the target profile) are ranked according to the relevance to the target, and the r most relevant items are returned as recommendations.

Profile Matching: The profile similarity metric (Equation 1) is computed as the weighted-sum of the similarities between items in the target and source profile cases (weights are not currently used but could represent what exact preference a user displays for an item). If there is a direct correspondence between an item in the source, c_i, and the target, t_j, then maximal similarity is assumed (Equation 2). However, direct correspondences are rare and so the similarity value of the source profile item is computed as the mean similarity between this item and the n most similar items in the target profile case $(t_1, ..., t_n)$ (Equation 3).

$$PSim(t, c, n) = \sum_{c_i \epsilon c} w_i \cdot ISim(t, c_i, n) \qquad (1)$$

$$ISim(t, c_i, n) = 1 \ \ if \ \exists \, t_j = c_i \qquad (2)$$

$$ISim(t, c_i, n) = \frac{\sum_{j=1..n} sim(t_j, c_i)}{n} \qquad (3)$$

Recommendation Ranking: Once the k most similar profile cases ($\hat{C}$) to the target have been identified, their items are combined and ranked for recommendation using three criteria. We prioritise items that (1) have a high similarity to the target profile case, (2) occur in many of the retrieved profile cases, and (3) are recommended by profiles most similar to the target. Accordingly we compute the *relevance* of an item, c_i, from a retrieved profile case, c, with respect to the target profile, t, as shown in Equation 4; where $C' \subseteq \hat{C}$ is the set of retrieved profile cases that contain c_i.

$$Rel(t, c_i, \hat{C}) = ISim(t, c_i, k) \cdot \frac{|C'|}{|\hat{C}|} \cdot \sum_{c \epsilon C'} PSim(t, c, k) \qquad (4)$$

Finally, the top-N ranked items are returned for recommendation; for these experiments, we have selected an N value of 10 recommendations.

3   A Fine-Grained Ablation Study

Our previous work has shown that the above approach is quite successful in addressing the sparsity problem to produce (1) higher-quality recommendations and (2) better orderings of recommendation results, especially when compared to traditional collaborative filtering approaches, even though it is driven by the same ratings-based knowledge source [11, 12]. Intuitively, we expect that the main contributing success factors are to be found in the derived similarity knowledge that provides additional similarity coverage, and in the ranking metric that applies the derived knowledge for ordering recommendations; thus emphasising the need for analysis of similarity essence in such techniques. Each of these components, however, can be analysed at a deeper level, and here we are interested in characterizing the relative contributions of their constituent elements. We do so by performing ablation studies on these components that significantly extend earlier work reported in [13]. This analysis may provide a clearer view of the essential strengths of the approach, as well as insights that would be useful in developing more effective recommendation systems.

The ranking metric provides a natural breakdown for analysis in its component factors and the possibilities for their interaction. Here we analyse the contributions of the individual factors and their possible combinations toward good recommendation ranking. It is more difficult to characterize the relative contributions of the derived similarity knowledge components. At an atomic level, the additional similarity knowledge consists of item associations, and we adopt the view that selectively testing the contribution of clusters of such associations, based on a measure of their reliability, can provide insight into the power of the applied whole. We are particularly interested in segmenting similarity knowledge by proposed measures of interestingness [19]. It is hoped that by analysing the similarity knowledge contribution, we can optimize the derivation and usage of such knowledge. Thus we propose comprehensive real-world tests that individually focus on:

- The importance of the quality of the mined similarity knowledge relative to recommendation accuracy;
- The overall importance of the similarity knowledge combined with different ranking factors relative to recommendation accuracy.

3.1 Interestingness Pruning

Despite the usage of reasonable support and confidence thresholds in association rule mining, many of the discovered association rules might be obvious, redundant or useless [15]. Research on association rules has shown that further pruning can be utilized using a number of interestingness measures based on both users responding to a particular rule and a statistical analysis of the rules [19]. We have analysed a number of measures and found the following to be most relevant to our research; each $rule(A \Rightarrow B)$ denotes a relationship between 2 television programmes where if A occurs in a profile, then B may occur with certain probabilities (support & confidence as discovered by the Apriori algorithm):

- **Reliability:** The bigger the value of the reliability measure, the more assured we can be that the rule is accurate as regards its probabilities:

$$Reliability(A \Rightarrow B) = |P(A \wedge B)/P(A) - P(B)| = |P(B|A) - P(B)| \quad (5)$$

- **Lift:** Tells us how much better the rule predicts the consequent than the random prediction:

$$Lift(A \Rightarrow B) = P(B|A)/P(B) \quad (6)$$

- **Interest:** The interest of a rule measures how dependent A and B are by computing:

$$Interest(A \Rightarrow B) = support(A \Rightarrow B)/(support(A) * support(B)) \quad (7)$$

- **Cosine:** Similar to *Interest*; measures how dependent A and B are by computing:

$$Cosine(A \Rightarrow B) = support(A \Rightarrow B)/\sqrt{(support(A) * support(B))} \quad (8)$$

Using these measures, we can trim the number of rules available in the hope that higher quality similarity knowledge will result; we also are interested in determining what evidence exists for using these interestingness measures as a new basis for similarity knowledge that is a potential replacement for rule confidence as an estimate of item-item similarity.

3.2 Datasets

We conducted our experiments using a dataset from the television domain; PTV-Plus is an established online recommender system deployed in the television listings domain [6]. Operated commercially by ChangingWorlds (www.changingworlds.com), PTVPlus uses its recommendation engine to generate a set of TV programme recommendations for a target user, based on their profiled interests, and it presents these recommendations in the form of a personalized programme guide. We use the standard PTVPlus dataset consisting of 622 user profiles, extracting a list of positively rated programmes from each profile for use in our system, for example:

"Friends", "Frasier", "24", "Cheers", "The Simpsons", "ER"

In the following experiments, we have ignored the negative ratings and also the rating values themselves.

3.3 Algorithms

We use a number of different algorithms in testing the aforementioned recommender strategies:

1. *NOSIM* - System run with only collaborative filtering style similarity knowledge (diagonal matrix of item-item relationships)- this serves as a baseline comparator;
2. *DR* - our case-based approach using direct similarity knowledge with all recommendation ranking criteria;
3. *INDR* - our case-based approach using indirect similarity knowledge with all recommendation ranking criteria.

We also run variants of *DR* and *INDR* which use a subset of the recommendation ranking criterion (example *C1&2-INDR* is *INDR* but only uses criteria (1) & (2) in recommendation ranking). This will allow us to see the effect of the recommendation ranking criteria in overall recommendation accuracy as well as ranking accuracy.

3.4 Method and Metrics

The dataset is split into test and training subsets using a 30:70 split. Using the Apriori [15] technique, we generated rules from the training data and then analysed these rules to see how well the similarity knowledge fits the test dataset

[11]; we do this by counting the percentage of profiles that a given rule 'fits' in the sense that the antecedent and consequent (both rule items) are both in the profile. To see the effect of rule accuracy on the overall quality of system recommendations, we sort rules by how well they fit the test dataset, placing them into bins of rules less than 10% accurate, less than 20% accurate and so on, up to less than 70% accurate (highest rule accuracy seen on test dataset).

Our initial ablation analysis research [13] pruned rules by further analysis using the test dataset; here we also prune using interestingness measures (see Section 3.1) as a new approach to selectively cut away un-'interesting' rules. We are also interested in testing the quality and ranking of our techniques; taking the full association ruleset (direct rules) created from the training dataset and extended to a indirect ruleset. Using the different algorithms described earlier, we then tested both recommendation quality and ranking quality of the system. In evaluating recommendation accuracy, our primary accuracy metric measures the percentage of test profile items that are present in a user's recommended set; this is equivalent to the standard recall metric used in information retrieval. So, for example, if all of the items in a user's test profile are contained within their recommended set a maximum recall of 100% is achieved.

Recall: The proportion of items in the user's test profile that are recommended, averaged over all users.

In general recall is a strong measure of recommendation accuracy and it should be noted that in our evaluation it serves as a *lower-bound* on real recommendation accuracy. This is because the only way that we can judge a recommendation to be relevant is if it exists in the user's test profile, which of course represents only a limited subset of those recommendations that are truly relevant to the user. With this in mind we also introduce a weaker notion of recommendation accuracy, which we call *hit rate*. The basic idea is that a given set of recommendations has at least some measurable value of usefulness to a user when it contains at least one recommendation from the user's test profile. A maximum hit rate of 100% indicates that a given algorithm always makes at least one relevant recommendation (present within the user's test profile) per recommendation session.

Hit Rate: The proportion of users for which at least one item from the user's test profile is recommended.

To test our ranking functions, we look for correlations between the rank of an item and its recommendation success over all profiles. Programmes are ranked by recommendation list position and sorted into ranking bins (0 - 1.0 in 0.1 increments). For example, if we have a list of 20 recommendations then these are distributed across the 10 bins with 2 recommendations in each. We repeat this binning for each recommendation list produced from a profile and calculate the percentage of correct recommendations in each bin. We are looking for a strong positive correlation between the success percentage in a bin and the ranking value of that bin; higher ranking values should lead to higher percentages of correct recommendations.

4 Results

We conduct two experimental studies: the first analyses the relative contributions of clusters of similarity knowledge, and the second examines the relative contributions of factors in recommendation ranking.

4.1 Similarity Knowledge

The association rules that comprise the similarity knowledge are categorised by their data-set accuracy (percentage of profiles that a given rule fits as discussed above) and clustered into bins at decimal percentage levels. Experimental runs are then made with progressively increasing levels of similarity knowledge by augmenting the current set of associations with those from the next higher set. At each level, system accuracy is measured in order to determine the relative uplift in accuracy provided by the additional knowledge. Figure 1 shows the results for Recall and Hit Rate.

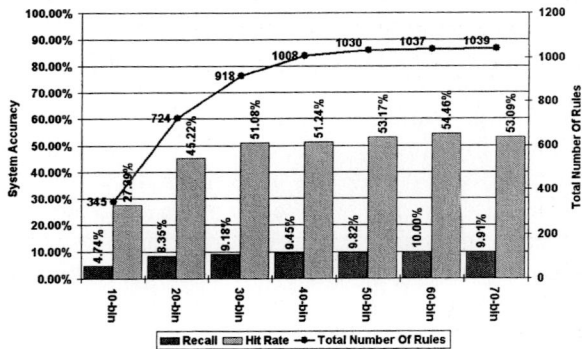

Fig. 1. Rule Binning Accuracy

At first glance, the results show a natural trend of increasing accuracy as similarity knowledge fit increases, as expected. However, closer inspection reveals a few surprises. For both Recall and Hit Rate measures, the uplift provided by adding additional associations levels off rapidly, so that the relative contribution of additional associations is fairly small above the 30%-bin level. This is mainly due to the fact that the number of rules added after the 30%-bin level is relatively small (121 extra rules out of a full 1039 rule-set offers only slight (within 3%) accuracy improvements). This results indicates that a large quantity of weak association rules is sufficient for good overall accuracy with a small number of high quality rules adding only small performance increase although sacrificing efficiency.

We also wanted to note the effect of interestingness measures both in rule pruning and also in usage as similarity indicators themselves. Firstly, we calculated interestingness scores for all rules by generating direct rules from the training data and then using the various formulae shown in Section 3.1. We normalised the interestingness scores and used these to sort the rules; we again created bins of rules - this time removing rules below a certain interestingness threshold - and used the confidence scores for these rules as similarity knowledge. The results for this experiment can be seen in Figures 2 and 3; for example, *lift33* denotes the accuracy seen when using the lift measure to eliminate rules below a 33% threshold and using the resulting rules and their confidences as similarity knowledge for recommendation. We can see that accuracy falls off drastically as interestingness thresholds increase (fewer rules, and therefore less similarity knowledge, is made available to the system). However, if we compare these results to the previous graphs from a rule perspective (e.g. comparing *reliability33* with 285 rules to *10-bin* with 345 rules), we can see that in certain cases, higher recall and hit rate accuracies are seen with fewer rules, indicating that interestingness approaches are a valid method towards improving the quality of similarity knowledge available to the recommender. It is also noted that, from a interestingness measure standpoint, trimming the rules by 50% does not reflect on system accuracy in a similar manner (*reliability66* achieves more than 50% accuracy of its full reliability set counterpart *reliability* with only 4% of its similarity knowledge); this demonstrates that pruning using such measures allows fewer higher quality rules to achieve a relatively high accuracy with the bonus of dropping a large number of weaker rules.

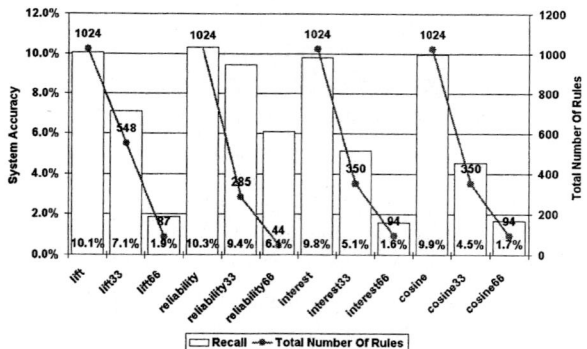

Fig. 2. Recall using Interestingness Pruning

We were also interested in seeing the effect of using interestingness values directly instead of confidence scores as similarity indicators. Figures 4 and 5 indicates the performance of such approaches; for example, *reliabilitypure66* denotes accuracy seen using rules with a reliability value over 0.66 (and also using the reliability value as similarity information). Slightly higher accuracies are seen across the board (compared to DR/INDR/CF) and we again note that cutting rules affects recommender performance greatly. We also see that comparing by rule amounts confirms the validity of using interestingness measures in pruning.

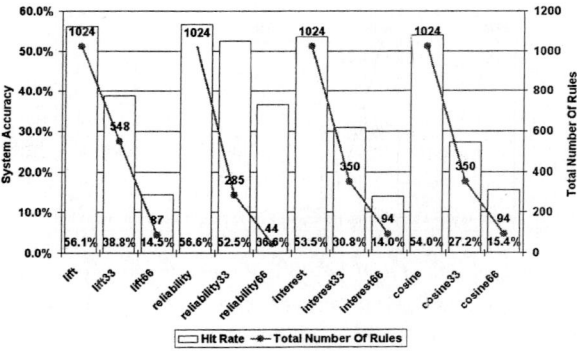

Fig. 3. Hit Rate using Interestingness Pruning

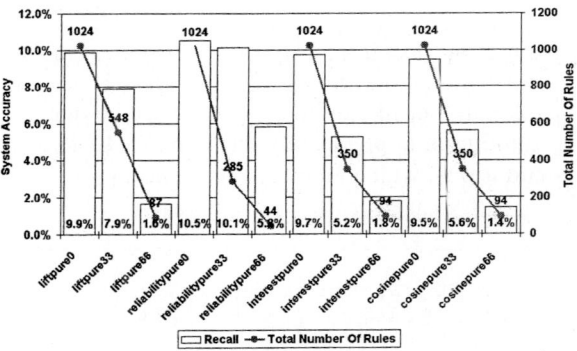

Fig. 4. Recall using Interestingness Measures

From the standpoint of implementing recommender systems, these results indicate that it may be possible to achieve a significant boost in performance with a smaller proportion of the knowledge discovered. This has obvious implications regarding efficiency; having the ability to provide high quality recommendations with a relatively small amount of similarity knowledge.

4.2 Recommendation Ranking

Rankings and accuracies were computed for each combination of the three factors in the item ranking criteria:

- C_1 - Item similarity to target profile
- C_2 - Item frequency across retrieved profiles
- C_3 - Similarity of item profile to target profile

These combinations were computed both for direct and indirect similarity knowledge. Accuracies were measured in terms of Recall, Hit Rate, and Rank Binning Correlation (as described in Section 3.4). In terms of system accuracy, Figures 6

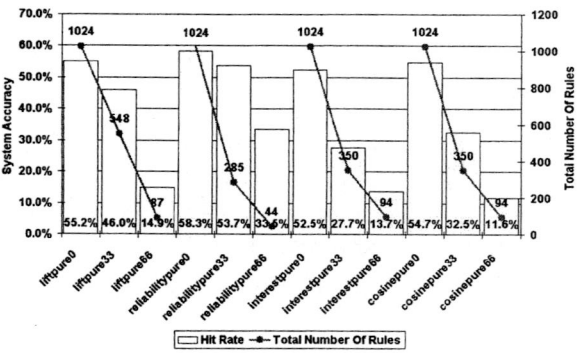

Fig. 5. Hit Rate using Interestingness Measures

and 7 show the results for Recall and Hit Rate. Ranking makes a difference in system accuracy, since the similarity metric provides the top k similar profiles from which a variable number of candidate items may be derived for recommendation. After the ranking is applied, only the top N (10 here) items are taken as actual recommendations, which can impact accuracy.

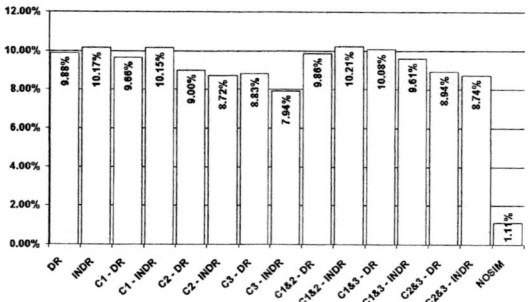

Fig. 6. Recall for various ranking combinations

Employing similarity knowledge is clearly beneficial in all combinations, compared to the NOSIM baseline. Across all combinations, direct and indirect modes perform similarly, with minor variations. This is consistent with earlier comparisons between direct and indirect modes [11, 12], but it is verified here across the finer-grained analysis, showing that each of the ranking criteria provides similar benefit across direct and indirect modes. Individually, C_1 outperforms the others, with C_2 outperforming C_3 in most conditions. In combination, it can be seen that C_1 is more consistent. Combining C_1 with the others tends to result in an improvement, while combining another with C_1 (rather than using C_1 alone) tends to result in a degradation of performance. The differences between the best performances are very small indeed, but it is worth noting that, while a

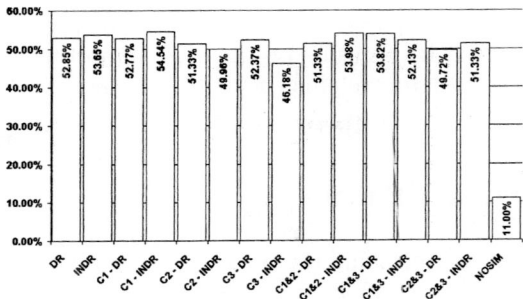

Fig. 7. Hit Rate for various ranking combinations

single performing combination is not apparent, the standard mode of system operation (combining all 3 criteria) is consistently within 1% of the best, and the best performing combination consistently involves C_1.

In terms of rank binning correlations, shown in Figure 8, we again find that indirect and direct modes show similar overall results. Most of the combinations provide very good and highly comparable rankings. The notable exceptions are C_2 and, intriguingly, the standard system combination of all 3. Again C_1 appears in the best combinations. Overall, we find that C_1 is the most consistent indicator of good ranking performance, and that while the standard system combination of all 3 criteria is consistent in the overall ranking for providing accuracy, it is not as consistent in ordering the final recommendation set. In terms of implementing recommender systems, it may be worth focusing on C_1 for recommendation ranking.

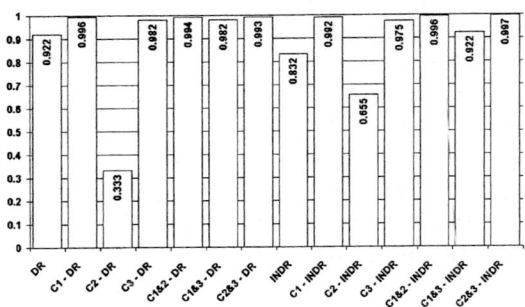

Fig. 8. Rank Binning Correlation for various ranking combinations

Overall, these results indicate that the success of our approach may be based more on underlying finer-grained critical success factors than have previously been thought. By refining the similarity knowledge to eliminate possible interference in the associations, we might hope to improve performance further, or at least to improve efficiency by streamlining the similarity knowledge set for a given performance level. By focusing on the most important ranking criteria, it may also be possible to improve efficiency while maintaining the same level of performance.

5 Conclusions and Future Work

Evaluation is the key to unlocking the secrets of recommender systems and recommender systems research is characterised by a strong evaluation mind-set, at least on the surface. However, we believe that the time is right to move beyond the traditional system-level evaluation, which seeks to learn about a recommender system's high-level performance properties, to look at the contributions of individual component technologies. To this end we have described a fine-grained ablation study of our own case-based recommendation approach. This study has concentrated on understanding the contribution of the similarity knowledge and recommendation ranking components of a recommender system and it has revealed a number of interesting and surprising results.

Case-based reasoning researchers have, in the past, highlighted how the case-base knowledge container is prone to redundancy – that many cases can be pruned without loss of performance. We have asked this question of the similarity knowledge container but found a different answer. While our similarity knowledge is varied in terms of the predicted quality of individual similarity rules, we do not find high degrees of knowledge redundancy or overlap and, in fact, even weak similarity rules are found to play an important role in recommendation. Separately, we have examined the contributions made by the different criteria used in recommendation ranking. The results suggest that certain criteria dominate while other play an insignificant role; criteria involving comparison with the target user enjoy higher accuracy which seems logical from a recommendation perspective. Such analysis allows us to preserve ranking accuracy and improve efficiency concurrently.

This paper serves as a source of further evaluation detail on our own work and we believe that the results have implications for the recommender research community in the main. But, perhaps more importantly, we hope that this paper will act as a call for other researchers to provide their own ablation studies so that our community can better understand the implications of past, present and future recommender systems' developments.

References

1. Resnick, P., Varian, H.R.: Recommender Systems. Communications of the ACM **40** (1997) 56–58
2. Burke, R.: Hybrid Recommender Systems: Survey and Experiments. User Modeling and User-Adapted Interaction **12** (2002) 331–370
3. McJones, P.: Eachmovie Collaborative Filtering Dataset, DEC Systems Research Center, http://www.research.compaq.com/src/eachmovie/ (1997)

4. Konstan, J.A., Miller, B.N., et al: Grouplens: Applying Collaborative Filtering to Usenet News. Communications of the ACM **40** (1997) 77–87
5. Rosenstein, M., Lochbaum, C.: Recommending from Content: Preliminary Results from an E-Commerce Experiment. In: CHI '00, ACM Press (2000) 291–292
6. Smyth, B., Cotter, P.: Personalized Electronic Programme Guides. Artificial Intelligence Magazine **22** (2001) 89–98
7. Hayes, C., Cunningham, P., Smyth, B.: A Case-Based View of Automated Collaborative Filtering. In: 4th International Conference on Case-Based Reasoning. Volume 2080., Springer (2001) 234–248
8. Burke, R.: A case-based reasoning approach to collaborative filtering. In: Proceedings of EWCBR-00, Springer (2000) 370–379
9. Sarwar, B., Karypis, G., et al: Item-based Collaborative Filtering Recommendation Algorithms. In: Proceedings of the 10th International WWW Conference, ACM Press (2001) 285–295
10. Sarwar, B., Karypis, G., et al: Analysis of Recommendation Algorithms for E-Commerce. In: Proceedings of the 2nd ACM Conference on Electronic Commerce, ACM Press (2000) 158–167
11. O'Sullivan, D., Wilson, D., Smyth, B.: Using Collaborative Filtering Data in Case-based Recommendation. In Haller, S.M., Simmons, G., eds.: Proceedings of the 15th International FLAIRS Conference, AAAI Press (2002) 121 – 128
12. O'Sullivan, D., Wilson, D., Smyth, B.: Preserving Recommender Accuracy and Diversity in Sparse Datasets. In Russell, I., Haller, S., eds.: Proceedings of the 16th International FLAIRS Conference, AAAI Press (2003) 139 – 144
13. O'Sullivan, D., Smyth, B., Wilson, D.: In-Depth Analysis of Similarity Knowledge and Metric Contributions to Recommender Performance. In: Proceedings of the 17th International FLAIRS Conference, In Press. (2004)
14. McKenna, E., Smyth, B.: Competence-Guided Case-Base Editing Techniques. In Blanzieri, E., Portinale, L., eds.: Proceedings of EWCBR-00. Volume 1898., Springer (2000) 186–197
15. Agrawal, R., Mannila, H., et al: Fast Discovery of Association Rules. In Fayyad, U.M., et al, eds.: Advances in Knowledge Discovery and Data Mining. MIT Press (1996) 307–328
16. Goldberg, K., Roeder, T., et al: Eigentaste: A Constant Time Collaborative Filtering Algorithm. Information Retrieval Journal **4** (2001) 133–151
17. Foltz, P.W.: Using Latent Semantic Indexing for Information Filtering. In: Conference on Office Information Systems, ACM Press (1990) 40–47
18. Honda, K., Sugiura, N., et al: Collaborative Filtering Using Principal Component Analysis and Fuzzy Clustering. In Zhong, N., et al, eds.: Web Intelligence: Research and Development, WI 2001. Volume 2198., Springer (2001) 394–402
19. Tan, P.N., Kumar, V., et al: Selecting the Right Interestingness Measure for Association Patterns. In: Proceedings of the 8th ACM SIGKDD Conference. (2002) 32–41

Satellite Health Monitoring Using CBR Framework

Kiran Kumar Penta and Deepak Khemani

Dept of Computer Science & Engineering, IIT Madras, India
mail_kiranp@yahoo.com, khemani@iitm.ac.in

Abstract. Satellite health monitoring is a specialized task usually carried out by human experts. In this paper, we address the task of monitoring by defining it as an anomaly and event detection task cast in Case Based Reasoning framework. We discuss how each CBR step is achieved in a time series domain such as the Satellite health monitoring. In the process, we define the case structure in a time series domain, discuss measures of distance between cases and address other issues such as building initial Case Base and determining similarity threshold. We briefly describe the system that we have built, and end the paper with a discussion on possible extensions to current work.

1 Introduction

Complex systems such as satellites are monitored by tracking values of several on-board parameters. The sensed values of various parameters are down-linked from the satellite to the ground monitoring centers at a frequent, regular intervals. Such down-linked data is called *telemetry*. In this work, we try to address some of the issues in online Satellite Health Monitoring (SHM). Though the primary focus remains on SHM, the design that we suggest is also applicable to similar sensor based health monitoring domains. In this paper, we refer to the system that is being monitored as the 'source system'.

Automated Health Monitoring System

In many critical systems, one needs to monitor the functioning of the system closely. A lot of monitoring is currently done by humans. Monitoring by humans can happen at different levels of expertise. When a surgeon looks at some plots, or a design engineer looks at operational parameters in a machine, their conclusions are based on deep understanding of the underlying system. Emulating this level of monitoring would require a model based approach. On the other hand people lacking such deep understanding have to rely on shallow knowledge such as rules and cases. Rules themselves need to be articulated by experts, but cases can be acquired by observation.

We adopt a case base approach in which the monitoring program is an apprentice to the human expert. The program remembers actions taken by the expert along with the context defined by the data, and attempts to replicate them in similar contexts. If the current scenario is not present in the case memory, then the system flags it as an anomaly.

2   Related Work

Several rule based expert systems have been developed for automated health monitoring.

TIGER

Tiger is probably the most popular among diagnostic tools in this kind of domains where, a complex system is monitored by observing values of several sensory parameters [1]. Tiger is used in monitoring Gas-Turbines.

Tiger system basically consists of a set of rule based diagnostic tools handling faults at different levels. At the first level is a high speed rule based system the KHEOPS, which is primarily a limit-checking system. However, since KHEOPS allows one to express different conditions for limits, the limits used within Tiger go beyond normal limit checking. For example, different limits can be set based on the turbine's operating state. Though KHEOPS allows checks at any point of time with respect to the underlying system state, tracking evolution of parameter values too is important. This kind of reasoning is done at second level using a rule based temporal reasoner LxTeT. In LxTeT, each rule is a set of event patterns and the temporal constraints between them with respect to the context. Much complex reasoning for diagnosis is done at the third level using causal reasoning mechanisms combined with the first principles model of the underlying system. This is achieved using a formalism CA-EN. All the three tools are integrated using a Fault-Manager.

A drawback with Tiger is that each rule at every layer needs to be articulated by the expert. With several possible scenarios in complex systems, it is difficult to elicit all rules that the trend might follow. One example is, the influence of the Sun on the satellites. The Sun unlike the discrete devices, influences the satellite system gradually. Moreover, the influence varies gradually with seasons of the year. Eliciting several such continuous influences in to crisp rules is difficult.

COGNATE

Hunter and McIntosh describe a system **COGNATE** [2] that relies on the knowledge entered by experts to detect *events* in a multi channel time series data. An *event*, represents a particular process in the underlying source system. In the context of COGNATE, the source system is the health of a newly born baby.

Conventional knowledge acquisition normally includes sessions in which the expert is presented with a typical problem and comments are captured on how he arrives at an interpretation. However, it is much more difficult to talk about temporal patterns. For this reason, the authors developed a tool, *time series work-bench* that displays time series data and enables the expert to mark particular intervals and attach a symbolic description to each interval.

However, the knowledge acquisition from human experts is usually very difficult. The process of identifying an event to be monitored, capturing instances of such event and eliciting common patterns in collected instances to frame rules, is too human intensive. This shortcoming in rule based system can be over come if rules can be acquired automatically.

Automatic Rule Acquisition

Yiari *et al.* propose a fault detection methods for spacecrafts based on an automated rule acquisition scheme [3]. Their method is based on time series pattern clustering and association rule mining, first proposed by Das *et al.* [4]. The process may be briefly outlined in the following steps:

Using the event classes generated by clustering algorithm, time series data is discretized. Then the *Association rule mining* [5] is used to extract rules from the resultant encoded time series. Various rule evaluating measures such as J-measure are used to obtain a set of important rules. The set of rules thus generated can be regarded as a kind of qualitative model of the source system. These rules are used for health monitoring of spacecrafts in real time. Streaming telemetry data is passed through the process of discretization, and the resultant sequence is matched with the antecedent of each rule. Consequent of the matching rule is to be expected in the data yet to come.

3 The CBR System Design

It has been shown by Keogh *et al.* that the rule acquisition from streaming time series is very difficult [6]. We approached the problem using the CBR [7–9] approach and implemented a simplified version of CBR, the Instance Based Learning (IBL). In this model, the concept of interest is implicitly represented by a set of instances that exemplify the concept. A previously unseen query instance is classified according to its similarity to stored instances. The four most important aspects of this design are:

- The Case Structure/Schema
- The Measure of Distance between Cases
- The Reasoning process
- The Case Base

Case Structure

In traditional CBR systems, each case is a set of attribute-value pairs. In SHM kind of applications, the data available is streaming values, -the telemetry. In such systems, unlike other domains, the trend in parameters over a period of time is a better indicator of the source system state than values at any one point of time. That is, we have attribute-trend pairs instead of attribute-value pairs.

For a parameter, the values are not really independent of values from adjacent time points. The value at each time point is determined by it preceding values and influences the values that follow. That is, each value remains relevant at least till its influence lasts. This determines the length of the trend to be considered. The duration of influence is different for different parameters.

Closely related to the issue of length is the question of sampling rate. In most systems, attributes are sampled so frequently that several consecutive values are repetitive. From the stand point of observing meaningful patterns, high frequency of repetitions is not very useful and often indicate over sampling of original data. [10]. Usual approach for reducing redundancy is to reduce the sampling rate. Again the sampling rate is very much dependent on the parameter being monitored.

Table 1. Sample Case Schema in satellite domain

Attribute Id	Length of time series	Attribute sampling rate	lower bound	upper bound
1511	5400	30	-5	70
1464	1000	2	0	60
1467	5400	60	0	50

The set of attribute-trend pairs is popularly known as Multi Attribute Time Series or Multi Variate Time Series (MVTS). Accordingly, we identify that the *problem* part of case in SHM can be seen as MVTS sequence where each sequence corresponds to values of a parameter. In the past, MVTS sequences (also referred as *multi sequence* from now on) has been defined to be a set of sequences, each of same length. However, in SHM, different lengths of history to be considered for each parameter and the different sampling rates, makes each sequence in the MVTS to be of different sizes. An example *problem* part of a case structure is given in Table 1.

MVTS Distance

The measures of distance between time series sequences has been well studied in past [11–15]. Time series distance computation has received so much attention because, one of the most important steps in mining time series data is the search for similar sequences. This problem of search for similar time series sequences is non-trivial because of the inherent high dimensionality of large sequences. The challenge is to devise a distance measure that most aptly captures the notion of similarity between sequences and also allows fast calculation, and quick search.

We define the distance between two multi sequences as the average distance between constituent sequences. That is, if $d_l(R_i, Q_i)$ is locally the distance between two sequences R_i and Q_i, the global distance d_g, between multi sequences **R**, **Q** may be defined as:

$$d_g(\boldsymbol{R}, \boldsymbol{Q}) = \frac{1}{k} \sum_{i=1}^{k} d_l(R_i, Q_i) \qquad (1)$$

where, k is the number of sequences that constitute the each of the multi sequences $\boldsymbol{R}$ and $\boldsymbol{Q}$.

An advantage by defining d_g as in equation 1 is that, it is feasible to use different distance measures d_l for comparing different sequences as long as computed distances by each of them is comparable to each other. It is also possible to incorporate the factor of importance to each sequence by way of assigning different weights for different parameters. The most important property is that, the multi sequence distance measure d_g satisfies the triangle inequality if the sequence distance measure d_l satisfies triangle inequality. Triangle inequality is an important property, which several search techniques use in searching the data fast.

Euclidean Based MVTS Distance: A sequence of length n can be seen as a point in n-dimensional coordinate space. Hence similarity between two sequences has traditionally been defined as a function of Euclidean distance between them. Euclidean distance d_{e_1} between sequences R and Q, each of length n is defined as,

$$d_{e_1}(R, Q) = \sqrt{\sum_{i=1}^{n} (r_i - q_i)^2} \qquad (2)$$

One can replace d_l in equation 1 by d_{e_1} to get an euclidean distance based global distance d_g. But this may some times result in unintuitive results as contributions by each sequence to the global sum might be incomparable. Contribution mismatch arises due to two reasons, the lengths of constituent sequences might be different or the values of the sequences might be from different ranges.

In order to make the contributions of each parameter towards the global distance comparable, the sequence distances need to be scaled for them to fall into a uniform range. Among several ways to scale, one way to normalize is to divide the local distance d_{e_1} by number of elements in the sequence and the range of the sequence. The resultant sequence distance measure d_e is given in equation 3.

$$d_e(R, Q) = \frac{1}{n\delta} \sqrt{\sum_{i=1}^{n} (r_i - q_i)^2} \qquad (3)$$

δ is the range of values the parameter can take,
and n is the number of elements in each sequence R, Q.

Substituting d_e for d_l in d_g, one can get d_{g_e} the equation for multi sequence distance based on simple euclidean distance, as given in equation 4.

$$d_{g_e}(\boldsymbol{R}, \boldsymbol{Q}) = \frac{1}{k} \sum_{i=1}^{k} d_e(R_i, Q_i) \qquad (4)$$

Observe that the global distance as calculated in equation 4 will always be in the range [0, 1]. This allows one to define multi sequence similarity too in terms of the distance, as given in equation 5. Having a measure for similarity, one can define a threshold based notion of multi sequences being *similar*. Given a similarity threshold ϵ, two multi sequences may be said to be *similar* if the similarity between them is beyond ϵ.

$$sim_e(\boldsymbol{R}, \boldsymbol{Q}) = 1 - d_{g_e} \qquad (5)$$

Though there are several other distance measures such as the warp distance, correlation and feature based measures to compute distance between sequences, we preferred the usage of euclidean distance based similarity measure. In several instances, this simple distance measure has proved it efficiency compared to much complex measures [16]. Warp distance is very slow to be computed. More over many other sequence distance measures such as correlation, warp distance do not satisfy triangle inequality.

The CBR Process

CBR is a methodology that helps the expert to reuse experiences. Experience stored and retrieved are in the form of *cases*. Underlying philosophy of CBR is that *similar problems have similar solutions* and *problems are often similar*. The *solution* part of a stored case is assumed applicable to a new situation, if the *problem* parts match. An overview of the CBR system that we developed is given in Figure 1. CBR at an abstract level can be seen as a cycle of four steps:

- **Retrieve** the most similar case or cases
- **Reuse** the knowledge in the retrieved case to solve the problem
- **Revise** the proposed solution
- **Retain** the new experience, likely to be useful for future problem solving

Case Extractor: As data streams, the case extractor constructs case from the telemetry. In our current implementation, this is not done online but data is read from files to simulate such a behaviour. The time at which the case is picked is called the *case point*. Using case structure as the template, a case is constructed from the data, looking back wards from the *case point*. For each attribute, the 'length' specified in the structure is divided into windows of size 'sampling rate' and only one value from each window is picked. Thus if l is the length of an attribute specified in the schema and if n is its sampling rate, the time series corresponding to that attribute will be of length l/n. Time series data in satellite domain is highly noisy. Noise needs to be removed to observe any meaningful patterns in the data. Averaging is a widely acknowledged technique to clean noise from data. In our current implementation, the value representing each window is an average of all values in that window.

Retrieve: The search routine takes a query case and a similarity threshold as inputs and retrieves all those instances in the Case Base that are closer to

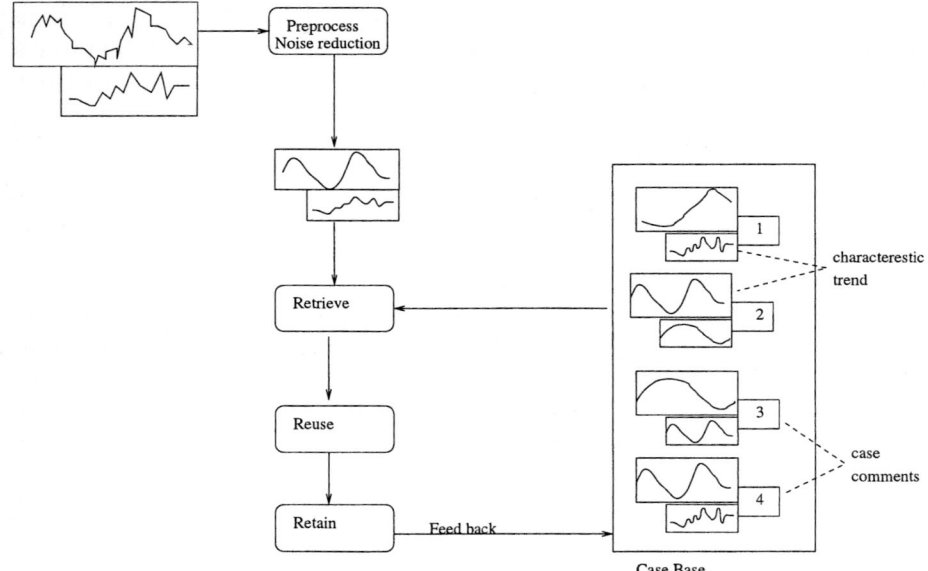

Fig. 1. Overview of the CBR system

the query by a similarity greater than the similarity threshold. To speed up the search, we propose to use the GEMINI framework. The GEneric Multimedia INdexIng (GEMINI) was proposed by Faloutsos *et al.* to index time series sequences [12]. GEMINI framework exploits dimensionality reduction of time series and the triangle inequality of the distance measure to search faster. With the usage of euclidean based MVTS distance, the GEMINI framework can be extended to search multi sequences.

Reuse: Goal of the system that we are building is to automate the SHM. The two most common activities carried out by human agent while monitoring health are *anomaly detection* and *event detection*.

Anomaly Detection: Anomaly detection (AD) corresponds to identifying if the given query is abnormal. In the CBR setting, a query case can be said to be anomalous if its similarity with all the cases in the Case Base is less than the similarity threshold ϵ.

Event Detection: Event detection corresponds to identifying if some known, interesting trend is occurring that requires human attention. Again in CBR setting, this corresponds to finding if there is an instance in Case Base that is similar to the query case by a similarity greater than the threshold and is marked as an event to be notified.

Retain: The performance of a CBR system is critically dependent on how representative its Case Base is. Adding new cases and modifying the existing

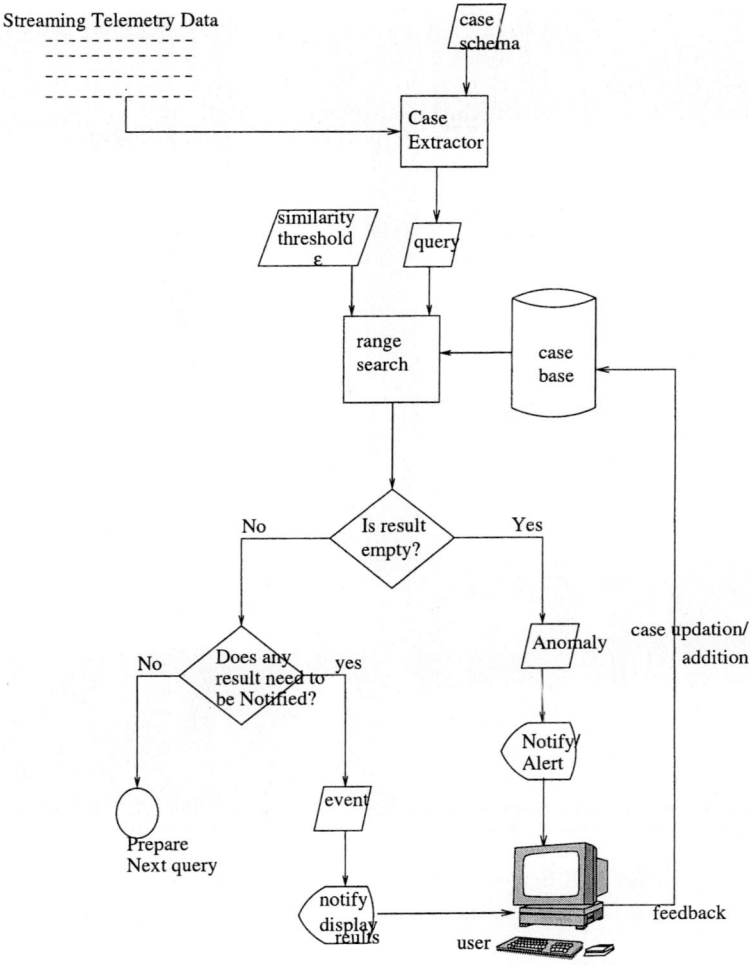

Fig. 2. Flow Chart for Anomaly/Event Detection

cases are the ways in which the Case Base is made richer with experience. When an event is notified, CBR displays the matching instances too. This allows the human agent to browse through the past episodes that might contain clues as to how to approach the current situation. The comments field in the retrieved cases serves the purpose of hinting the action to be taken. If the expert feels that the comments are not appropriate any more, he may modify the comments field and store the case back in Case Base. On the other hand, if the matched sequences themselves are not satisfactory, he may add the query case to the Case Base along with comments. Similarly, when an anomalous case is seen, it is invariably added to the Case Base, along with appropriate comments for the sake of reminding on being recalled later.

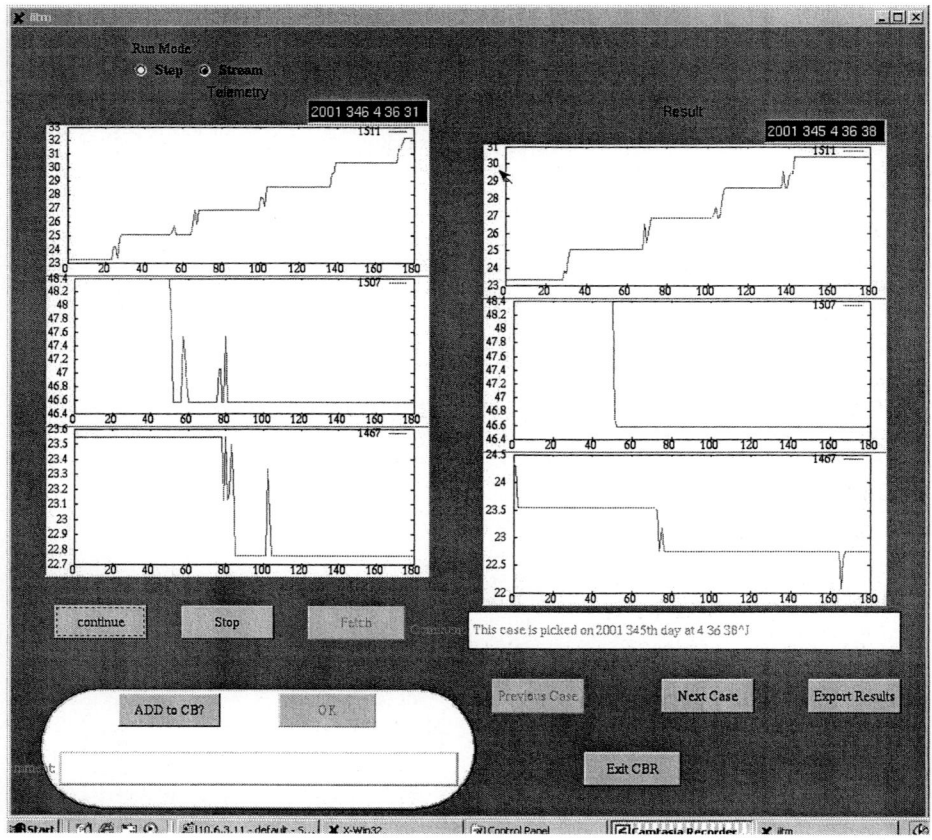

Fig. 3. A Screen shot of the prototype CBR system

The complete CBR process flow for anomaly/event detection is shown in Figure 2. Figure 3 shows a screen shot of the prototype health monitoring system that we developed. Plots on the left side of the figure reperesent a simulation of streaming telemetry data. Plots on the right side is one of the instances picked from the Case Base. The matching instances from Case Base can be browsed and the text box below the results window displays the comments associated with each instance. On the left side below the query plot is a provision for the query to be added to the Case Base. Figure 4 illustrates the system identifying an anomalous instance.

Initializing the Case Base: Once the CBR system is deployed, *Retaining* is the step by which the repository of normal behavior is built case after case. However, it is desirable to have the Case Base existing before the system is initialized. In SHM kind of domain, usually there is a large amount of archived telemetry data. Typically, most of the data reflects normal behavior of the satellite.

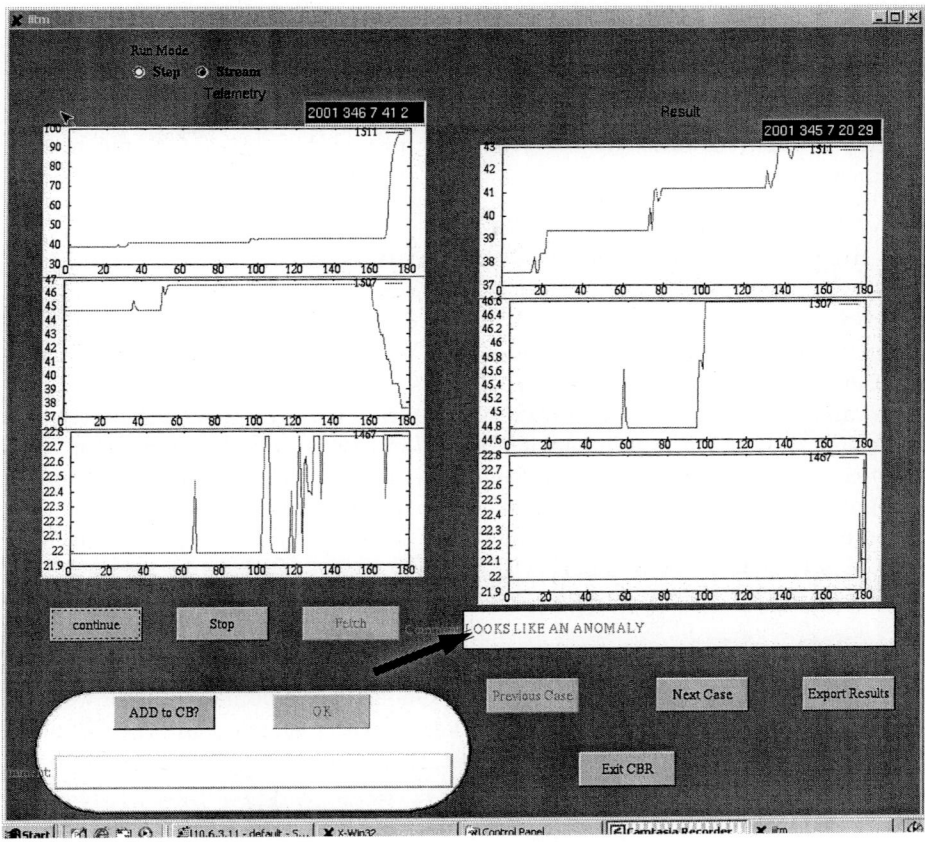

Fig. 4. Identifying an anomalous scenario

We implemented a naive auto case builder using the CBR frame work itself. Input to the auto case builder is the normal days' telemetry from past and the similarity threshold ϵ. The case extractor picks cases at regular intervals from the archive, reduces the noise and prepares *potential cases*. The frequency at which the cases need to be picked from the archive is currently user defined. An alternative is to pick cases from random points. The search routine matches the *potential case* with the cases in the Case Base already built and determines its similarity with the best matching case. If the similarity is more than ϵ, the *potential case* is ignored. Otherwise, the *potential case* is added automatically to the Case Base as a new case. The comments field of the newly added case is left blank while adding to the Case Base. With this naive approach, though the case when picked later does not suggest solution, it captures the normal behavior of the source system.

A potential disadvantage with this set up is that, the comments field in the cases from the seed Case Base is empty. Hence on being recalled later when queried, the time stamped case will not contain much information than just being able to say that a similar pattern occurred in past. However, since the normal case any way does not generate alarms(Refer Figure 2), it might be acceptable to have cases with null comments field. Another drawback with this scheme is that, the order of presenting the normal data influences which cases get included in the Case Base.

4 Similarity Threshold Determination

The two most important tasks that a human does while monitoring health are the anomaly detection and the event detection. We conducted experiments to evaluate the anomaly/event detection capabilities of the monitoring system at different similarity thresholds. Two important criterion to evaluate an anomaly/event detection system is the number of *False Alarms*(FA) and the number of *False Dismissals*(FD) it generates. False dismissal corresponds to an anomaly being not recognized by the algorithm. False alarm corresponds to the algorithm branding a non anomalous instance to be anomalous. General objective of the monitoring system is to reduce the number of FA and FD.

Data Sets

We ran our experiments in two domains. One is a real domain, where we used thermal data from satellites, while the other is an artificial domain, the Cylinder-Bell-Funnel (CBF). In the following subsections, we give a brief introduction to each domain.

Synthetic Domain – CBF: The CBF has originally been used by Kadous ([17]) as a 3 class classification problem. The domain constitutes three functions, one each to generate Cylinder(C), Bell(B), Funnel(F) classes. This can easily be extended to generate a 3^k class MVTS domain, where k is the number of sequences that make up each MVTS instance. We chose this synthetic domain as CBF functions typify real world time series domain in several respects.

The MVTS instances, each made of four sequences is considered as the test data. Since each sequence can be either C/B/F, the total number of possible classes with such as specification is 3^4. An instance belonging to the class Cylinder-Cylinder-Funnel-Bell is shown in Figure 5. To run the experiment, three case bases were created with random instances of MVTS:

- A case base U with 1000 random instances is created such that, it contains all instances of the possible 3^4 classes
- A case base Q with 100 random instances is created such that it contains instances of only some randomly picked classes (in this run, twelve classes were randomly picked)
- And a case base E of size 1000 random instances is created such that, it contains instances of only those classes that were not generated for Q

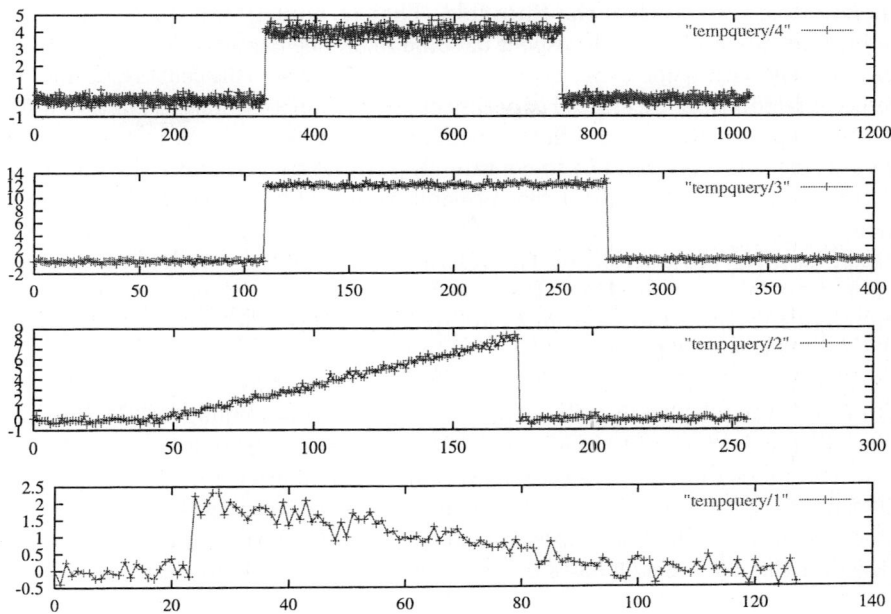

Fig. 5. Instance of a Multi sequence in CBF domain with 4 sequences

Satellite Domain – Thermal Parameters During Eclipse: Proper functioning of several devices on-board a satellite is dependent on ambient temperature. Hence some of the important parameters that are monitored relate to temperature at different places on-board a satellite. One of the factors that influence temperature is the *Sun*. The sun follows a cycle with a period of 24 hours. Hence, usually the temperature profiles of various parameters have a predictable trend periodic with solar cycle. However, there are some times in an year during which the sun remains eclipsed to the satellite resulting in rapid fall of on-board temperatures during that time. In such a case it might be required to switch the on-board heaters ON to maintain temperatures. Since the eclipse induces drastic swings in the temperature, monitoring thermal parameters during that time is an important task for monitoring agents. Hence, we chose the eclipse time temperature values as test bed to evaluate the anomaly detection abilities of the proposed monitoring system.

We have defined a case structure with three thermal parameters. A case base E of normal day's trends is created from a day on which there is no eclipse. Similarly, a case base U of eclipse day's trends is created. Browsing through various eclipse times on other days, a query base Q containing 100 instances of eclipse time trends is created.

The Experiment

Given a similarity threshold ϵ, a multi sequence may be said to be anomalous with respect to a given reference base if its similarity with every instance from reference base is less than the threshold. That is, a query multi sequence might be branded anomalous with respect to some reference base, while it might not be an anomaly with some other reference base. Exploiting this feature of anomaly detection definition, we carried experiments to evaluate the discrimination ability of the proposed system at different similarity thresholds. In both the domains, we prepared the case base U to contain all possible trends, while the query base Q was prepared with only a few possible trends. Case base E was prepared such that it contains no trends that are present in Q. The idea is that, when instances of Q are queried on the reference base U the number of anomalies amount to false alarms(**FA**). The number of instances that are marked non-anomalous when instances from Q are queried on the reference base E amount to false dismissals(**FD**).

The resultant FD and FA for different similarity thresholds ϵ are shown in plots 6, 7. With increasing threshold, the FD decreases while the FA increases. The ideal system would have a zero FD and zero FA. But it can be observed from the plots that this is not achieved at any similarity threshold. Moreover, the similarity threshold is domain dependent. Hence we suggest that one should choose a suitable similarity threshold to handle false alarms and false dismissals, based on the asymmetric costs involved in the domain of concern.

5 The Advantages and Disadvantages of the Proposed System

Salient features of the proposed system include, its human like reasoning, continuous learning and aiding in recall of past actions. The system also provides an easy interface to capture and share knowledge of different experts at the monitoring station. The design provides enough flexibility to replace any of the techniques employed at each stage of the CBR with suitable alternatives. The system is designed to actively seeks cases from telemetry and prompt the expert, unlike traditional CBR systems which usually run on the human initiative.

One problem with current approach is that, the knowledge gained for one satellite can not be easily applied to monitor other satellites. Another is that, the query structure is fixed statically at the system design phase, while expert might sometimes wish to frame query structure dynamically.

6 Conclusions

In this paper, we have described prototype of a CBR based Satellite Health Monitoring System. In the process, we have extended the traditional definition of MVTS to include variable length sequences and defined an Euclidean based distance metric for MVTS instances. The health monitoring task has been approached as an anomaly/event detection task set in a CBR framework. We have also addressed other relavent issues such as assisting the expert in determining similarity threshold, building a initial case base of normal satellite behaviour.

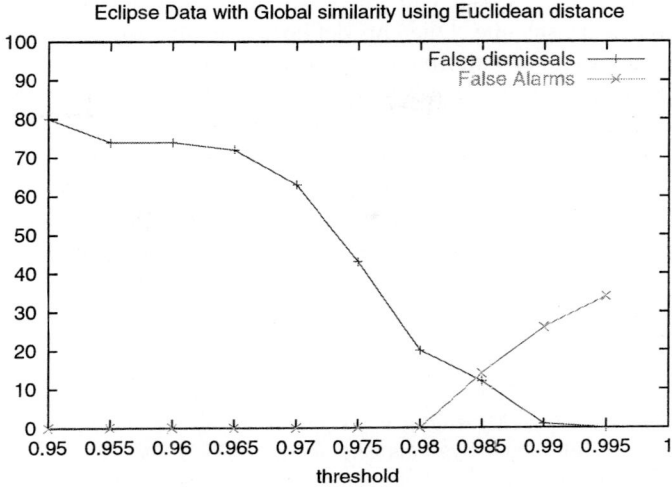

Fig. 6. FD and FA at different similarity thresholds

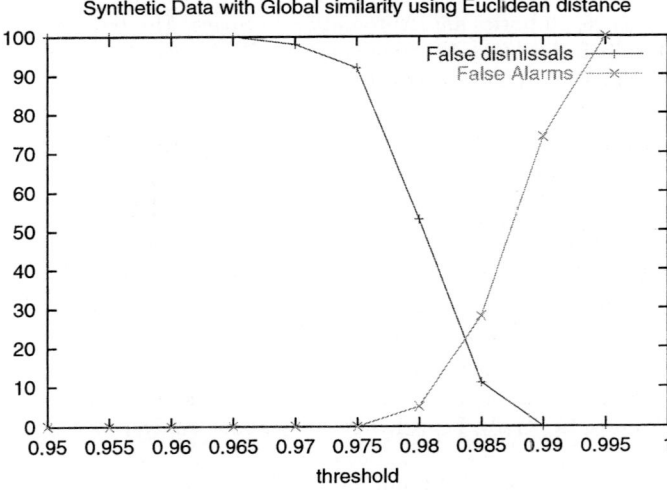

Fig. 7. FD and FA at different similarity thresholds

Current work can be extended in several ways.

- MVTS Distance measure: Several authors have observed that the Euclidean distance is too brittle with noise and small variations in trends along the time axis. Warp distance is a better measure but slow to compute. Recently, there have been efforts to speed up computing warp distance and also define index when using such a distance [18]. One can compare performance trade offs of using faster distance measure against better matching distance measure.

– Building Seed Case Base: Currently, we build initial Case Base using a naive acquisition scheme. One can define better measures of surprisingness to choose a case. For example, Silberschatz and Tuzhilin observe that actionability is an important criterion to make a pattern interesting [19]. Accordingly, picking cases around an action event (in SHM domain this might correspond to a command given) might result in a richer seed case base.
– Other issues: Some other issues such as considering the asymmetric costs of FA and FD while deciding the similarity threshold, the frequency at which query case from telemetry should be picked etc too need to be studied further.

References

1. Aguilar, J., Bousson, K., Dousson, C., Ghallab, M., Guasch, A., Milne, R., Nicol, C., Quevedo, J., Trave-Massuyes, L.: Tiger: real-time situation assessment of dynamic systems. Intelligent Systems Engineering (1994) 103–124
2. Hunter, J., McIntosh, N.: Knowledge-based event detection in complex time series data. In: AIMDM:Joint European Conference on Artificial Intelligence in Medicine and Medical Decision Making, Springer Verlag (1999)
3. Yairi, T., Kato, Y., Hori, K.: Fault detection by mining association rules from house-keeping data. In: Proceedings of the 6th International Symposium on Artificial Intelligence, Robotics and Automation in Space, Montreal, Canada (2001)
4. Das, G., Lin, K.I., Mannila, H., Renganathan, G., Smyth, P.: Rule discovery from time series. In: Proceedings of the 4th Int'l Conference on Knowledge Discovery and Data Mining., New York (1998) 16–22
5. Agrawal, R., Imielinski, T., Swami, A.: Mining association rules between sets of items in large databases. In: Proceedings of the ACM SIGMOD Conference. (1993)
6. Lin, J., Keogh, E., Truppel, W.: Clustering of streaming time series is meaningless. In: Proceedings of the 8th ACM SIGMOD workshop on Research Issues in data mining and knowledg discovery, San Diego, California (2003)
7. Kolodner, J.: Case-Based Reasoning. Morgan Kaufmann (1993)
8. Aamodt, A., Plaza, E.: Case-based reasoning: Foundational issues, methodological variations, and system approaches. AI Communications (**7:1**) 39–59
9. David, B.L.: Cbr in context: The present and future. Leake D., ed. Case-Based Reasoning: Experiences, Lessons and Future Directions (1996)
10. Daw, C., Finney, C., Tracy, E.: A review of symbolic analysis of experimental data (2001)
11. Agrawal, R., Faloutsos, C., Swami, A.: Efficient similarity search in sequence databases. In: Proceedings of the 4th International Conference on Foundations of Data Organization and Algorithms, Chicago, IL (1993) 69–84
12. Faloutsos, C., Ranganathan, M., Manolopoulos, Y.: Fast subsequence matching in time series databases. In: Proceedings of ACM SIGMOD Conference, Minneapolis (1994)
13. Keogh, E., Pazzani, M.: An enhaced representation of time series that allows fast and accurate classification, clustering and relevance feedback. In: Proceedings of the 4th International Conference on Knowledge Discovery and Data Mining, New York (1998) 239–241
14. Berndt, D., Clifford, J.: Finding patterns in time series: A dynamic programming approach (1996)

15. Rafiei, D.: On similarity-based queries for time-series data. In: Proceedings of the 15th IEEE Intl. Conf. on Data Engineering., Sydney, Australia (1999) 410–417
16. Keogh, E., Kasetty, S.: On the need for time series data mining benchmarks: A survey and empirical demonstration. In: ACM SIGKDD, Edmonton, Alberta, Canada (2002)
17. Kadous, M.W.: Learning comprehensible descriptions of multivariate time series. In: Proceedings of the ICML, Morgan-Kaufmann (1999)
18. Keogh, E.: Exact indexing of dynamic time warping. In: Proceedings of the 28th VLDB Conference, HKN, China (2002)
19. Silberschatz, A., A.Tuzhilin: What makes patterns interesting in knowledge discovery systems. IEEE Trans. On Knowledge and Data Engineering **8** (1996) 970–974

Extending a Fault Dictionary Towards a Case Based Reasoning System for Linear Electronic Analog Circuits Diagnosis

Carles Pous, Joan Colomer, and Joaquim Melendez

Institut d'Informàtica i Aplicacions, Universitat de Girona
Avda. Lluís Santaló s/n. Edifici P-4,
17071 Girona, Spain
{carles,colomer,quimmel}@eia.udg.es

Abstract. There are plenty of methods proposed for analog electronic circuit diagnosis, but the most popular ones are the fault dictionary techniques. Admitting more cases in a fault dictionary can be seen as a natural development towards a CBR system. The proposal of this paper is to extend the fault dictionary towards a Case Based Reasoning system. The case base memory, retrieval, reuse, revise and retain tasks are described. Special attention to the learning process is taken. An application example on a biquadratic filter is shown. The faults considered are parametric, permanent, independent and simple, although the methodology could be extrapolated for catastrophic and multiple fault diagnosis. Also, the method is focused and tested only on passive faulty components. Nevertheless, it can be extended to cover active devices as well.

1 Introduction

As circuits become daily more complex and larger, more complexity in test design is needed. The total cost of the circuits is augmented by a significant percentage due to costs in the test stage [1], [2], [3] and the time the test takes. According to [4], the high quality analogue tests are the most expensive in terms of both test development costs and test implementation. In the commercial market, up to 80% of the test costs are on account of the analogue functions that typically occupy only around 10% of the chip area.

Test and diagnosis techniques for digital circuits have been successfully developed and automated. But, this is not yet the situation for analog circuits [5]. There are plenty of proposals for testing analog circuits, although the most popular are the fault dictionary techniques. But Artificial Intelligence (AI) techniques have been a major research topic over the last decades. In [6] a good review of AI techniques applied to electronic circuits is given. The main advantage of these techniques is that they can cope with new situations because they can learn from faults that have not been previously predicted.

One of the major interests when designing diagnosis system is focused on its learning capability. It can be said that a diagnosis system is learning if its percentage of success increases when diagnosing. This happens because the diagnosis system gains knowledge about the circuit. As fault dictionaries can not learn from new situations, this paper proposes a methodology to extend a fault dictionary towards a CBR-system. It is straightforward to use the dictionary table as a case base only with slight modifications [7].

Next section gives a short introduction to fault dictionaries and their limitations. Section 3 proposes the CBR system construction methodology and its cycles. Section 4 shows the results obtained applying the method to a biquadratic filter. Some conclusions are given in the last section.

2   Fault Dictionaries and Their Limitations

Although new techniques have been introduced into the industry, fault dictionaries were by far the most widely used technique for testing circuits in the past and continue to be today. They are simple and work quite well for fault detection. They are completely based on quantitative calculations. Once the universe of faults to be detected is defined (Fault 1, Fault 2, ..., Fault m), selected characteristics of the measured or simulated output are obtained from the system for each considered fault and stored in a table. This set of output characteristics is known as *Fault signature*. The groups of fault signatures considered constitute the *Fault dictionary*. Hence, there are basically two steps: first, it is necessary to obtain the fault signatures to build the dictionary; and second, the most similar fault signature to the new situation presented is extracted. The comparison is typically performed using the neighborhood criterion, obtaining distances, minimizing certain indexes, and so on. The more similar dictionary signature to the new presented situation is extracted. Also, it is possible to find failures that produce the same symptoms. They constitute an *ambiguity group*, [8]. This concept should be considered when deciding the type of measures to take and where they will be taken from to obtain a high degree of circuit diagnosibility.

The dictionary can be generated by simulating the most likely circuit faults before the test or by obtaining real measures from a prototype circuit. This simulation allows to define the stimuli set and the signatures of the responses to be stored in order to detect and/or isolate the faults. The test for the faulty circuit is done using the same stimuli used when building the dictionary. The simulation provides us with a set of responses related with each fault.

A lot of methods corresponding to these techniques can be found in the literature. As example, let us take the dictionary proposed in [9] that is based on the response to a saturated ramp input. The ramp has a rise time t_r and a saturation value V_{SAT}.

The parameters used to characterize the faults are:

- *Steady state* (V_{est}): Final value at which the output tends to.
- *Overshoot (SP)*: Defined as

$$SP = \frac{V_{\max} - V_{est}}{V_{est}} 100 \qquad (1)$$

where V_{max} is the maximum amplitude value reached at the output.

- *Rising time (t_r)*: Time used by the output to rise from the 10% to 90% of the steady state value.
- *Delay time (t_d)*: Interval of time between the instant that the input and the output get to the 50% of the steady state value.

The main drawbacks of fault dictionary techniques are the lack in detection for the non-considered faults and the tolerances effect. Only the pre-simulated faults will be detected and located. Tolerances produce deviations of the considered universe of fault signatures. These discrepancies can produce a wrong diagnosis. Of course, storing more cases is going to improve the percentage of diagnosis successes. But, generating random faulty cases using the Monte-Carlo algorithm and storing these new cases spoil the dictionary performance. Hence, there is a compromise between fault coverage and dictionary length.

3 The CBR-System

Case Based Reasoning is an approach to problem solving that is able to use specific knowledge of previous experiences [10]. A new problem will be solved by matching it with a similar past situation. If the problem is solved, this new situation will be retained in order to solve the new ones. In case of diagnosis, solving the problem means that the CBR-system proposes a solution satisfactory enough to identify the new fault.

It has several advantages with respect to other machine learning schemes: First of all it is easier to obtain rules and there is no bottleneck waiting for expert knowledge to be acquired. On the other hand, it is quite intuitive in certain tasks, such as diagnosis. At the same time it tolerates lazy learning schemes which means that the CBR-system can take advantage of these techniques that are well-known and permanently updated.

One of the main drawbacks is to know when to stop training. If the case base is oversized, its efficiency falls. This is known as *the utility problem*. Hence, a good policy for the training and maintenance tasks is necessary. Another problem common to machine learning methods is how to train the system. The order in which the new cases are selected is very important, making the method more or less efficient and the case base size bigger or smaller. With this in mind, data mining techniques can be applied in order to help with data treatment and case base maintenance. That is, reducing the case base size, eliminating redundant attributes or for a new case retaining decision. A method like the well-known ten-fold cross-validation has to be applied when testing the case base efficiency. In our case, we have decided to build several independent sets $\{S_1, S_2, ..., S_n\}$ of randomly generated exemplars corresponding to a N number of cases for each component, with faults uniformly distributed between $\pm 70\%$. The CBR-system is trained with several series $\{T_1, T_2, ..., T_m\}$ of these sets randomly sorted in order to obtain a case base that performs better.

There are four "containers" which can carry knowledge [11] in a CBR-system: the vocabulary, the similarity measure, the case base and the solution transformation. The methodology proposed in this paper focuses on the case base knowledge container, where the learning is performed keeping new cases, when necessary, and forgetting noisy exemplars. The method could be classified as a multi-edit technique, since is a mixture and modification of two existing ones. The following subsections describe how the CBR-system is designed, compressing its main tasks.

3.1 Case Base Memory

The case structure is chosen to be the same used in the fault dictionary techniques, simply introducing a slight difference in the information about the fault. The proposed structure is shown in Figure 1. One part of the case is directly related with the measures taken from the circuit at one or several nodes. They could be temporal, frequency or static measures. This numeric part will be used to retrieve the most similar cases. The second part of the case contains information about the fault diagnosis.

Case Num	Meas. 1	Meas. 2	...	Meas. n	Class	Compo	Devi	Hierarchy
Case i	M_{1i}	M_{2i}	...	M_{ni}	Class i	Compo i	X%	$L_j.M_j$

Measures. Numeric Part — Fault. Qualitative Part

Fig. 1. Case Structure

Observe that the field *Class* has been maintained. As a reference, the classes associated with the faults considered in the classical dictionary (±20% and ±50%) are taken. When a fault has a deviation that does not correspond exactly to one of the original ones, the associated class will be the same given to the closest possible deviations considered as references. For example, if a fault is $R + 40\%$, its associated class will be the same as $R + 50\%$. But if a fault is $R + 35\%$, its corresponding class will be the same as $R + 20\%$. This *Class* field is not used for classification purposes. It is only used in particular steps to help in the maintenance task explained later on in this paper.

Concerning the other three qualitative fields, one of them has the faulty component location (*Compo*); the second contains the characterization of the fault (*Devi*) corresponding to the % of deviation from the *Compo* nominal value. When there are deviations of the components smaller than the tolerance, the circuit is considered to be not faulty. This is known as the nominal case (*Compo* = *Nom*).

The third field (*Hierarchy*) has additional information about the component, for example at level L_i and the module M_j to which the component belongs. Case base hierarchy is defined considering several levels depending on circuit complexity [12]. Therefore, the diagnosis result could be more or less precise depending on the retrieved qualitative parts, according to Figure 2. The last level corresponds to the faulty component deviation. The next upper level is defined as the component level. At this point, the system will only be able to diagnose which component is wrong, but not the fault deviation. Also, it is possible that certain faults can only be located just at a certain module, but not deep inside it. So, going to upper levels, the circuit is divided into modules. The number of module levels depends on the circuit complexity.

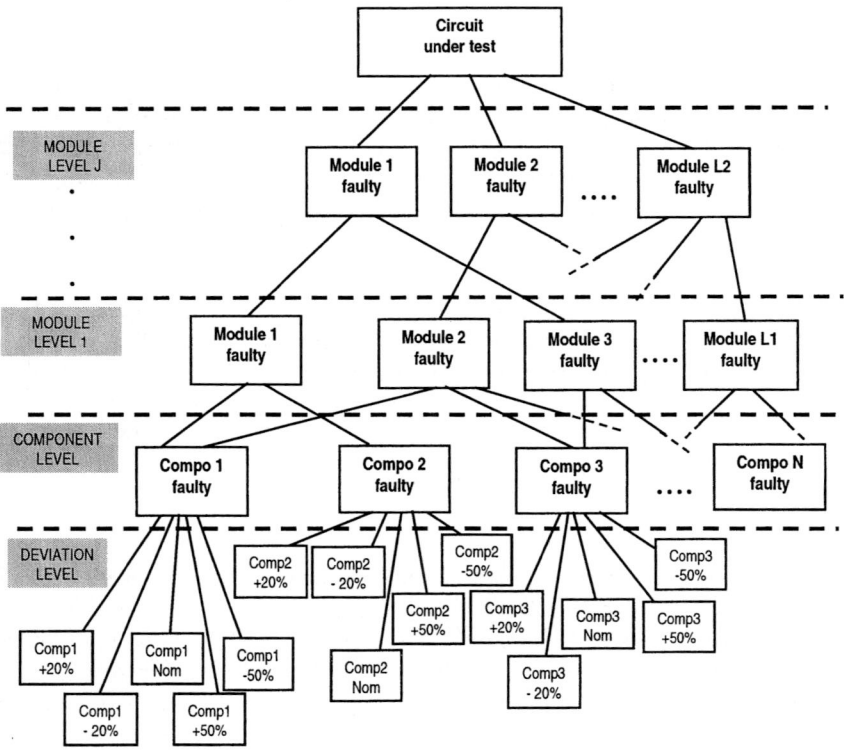

Fig. 2. General Case hierarchy

It is necessary to have certain knowledge on the circuit topology in order to build the case base hierarchy. For small circuits it can be done simply by inspection. For large circuits the method proposed in [13] can be used.

3.2 Retrieve

It is necessary to define a metric function and the number of cases to retrieve from the case base. Since the proposed CBR-system uses numerical data corresponding to the measures, we deal with continuous linear attributes; that is, attributes that can be any real number. Therefore, from among all possible distance functions [14], the normalized Euclidean distance has been chosen. Attributes Normalization is necessary because of their different order of magnitude. For example the measures can be μsec, and amplitudes that corresponds to a magnitude of a fraction of $Volts$ or even $Volts$.

So, the distance between to instances is calculated as shown in equation 2

$$E(\vec{x}\,\vec{y}) = \sqrt{\sum_{i=1}^{m} \alpha_i \left(\frac{x_i - y_i}{range_i}\right)^2} \qquad (2)$$

where $\vec{x}$ and $\vec{y}$ are the vector instances to be compared, x_i and y_i are the corresponding attribute value i, and m is the number of attributes. $range_i$ is the difference between the maximum and minimum value of the attribute i. At first instance, all the attributes are considered to be equally important, hence the weight α_i given to each of them is 1. Of course each particular circuit will require a more in-depth study on how the attributes influence on the retrieval and the final diagnosis.

The number of cases k to retrieve from the case base will be related to the value of k that produces the best diagnosis results. Normally it is a small odd number. In general, the more noisy the data is, the greater the optimal value of k. In our experiments, a value of $k = 3$ produces the best results. Taking a bigger value produces confusion in the diagnosis because of the extraction of cases corresponding to other different faults to be diagnosed.

3.3 Reuse

Once $k - nearest$ cases are extracted, they are used to propose a possible diagnosis. The proposal is to use the qualitative part of the extracted cases to derive a possible solution. Several situations can be given. If the *Compo* field of all the k extracted cases is the same, then the proposed solution is compounded using the *Compo* field of one of them and the average deviation of the extracted cases in the *Devi* field and the same module M_i and level L_j (Figure 3).

If the *Compo* is different, the proposed solution will have a *Compo* made up of the different components, and each of them with its corresponding deviation in *Devi*. *Hierarchy* will contain the common module M_n or several if different, and the first common level L_m. The case adaptation is carried out completely in the reuse task. It uses the past case solution instead of the past method that constructed the solution (transformational reuse) [15].

At the same time it has to be taken into account that the nominal case (when there are deviations of the circuit components smaller than 10%) does not have any faulty component. Therefore, a label in the *Compo* field with a value *Nom* indicates that this case belongs to the *Nominal* situation.

3.4 Revise and Retain

Once the solution to the new presented case is proposed, it has to be revised. If the solution is considered correct and accurate enough, it is not necessary to

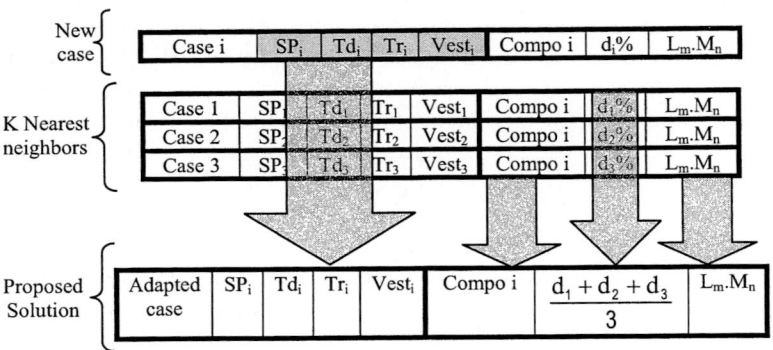

Fig. 3. With the same *Compo* field adaptation

retain the new case. On the other hand, if it is considered to be incorrect or with poor accuracy, the new case will be retained in the case memory. The revision analyzes how the cases that constitute the adapted solution are performing the diagnosis. Hence it is supposed that the new case diagnosis is known by the user for its revision, which allows a decision to be made about when it should be retained. When the CBR-system is testing circuits with unknown faults, there is no revision task, since the proposed diagnosis can not be contrasted with the correct one. The reasoning follows the flow diagram in Figure 4. When it is decided that the new case should be introduced, it is finally retained if the selected learning algorithm applied decides it. The algorithm can be any one used in the machine learning schemes, although the best results obtained by the authors from several tested algorithms were performed by the DROP and the All-KNN algorithms. There are 8 possible situations considered when revising while training:

1. The *Compo* field of the k extracted cases is equal to the new case, and the average deviation calculated has an error of less than 10%. This threshold is selected because this is the magnitude of the considered tolerances and an error of the same magnitude can be tolerated. The proposed solution is the correct one, and the case memory is enough to diagnose the new case. Hence, it is not necessary to retain the new case.
2. The *Compo* field of the k extracted cases is equal to the new case, but the average deviation has an error bigger than 10%. The present solution is considered to be not performing well and, the new case has to be introduced, if the corresponding learning algorithm allows it.
3. The *Compo* field of the k extracted cases are equal between them, but different from the new case. If the *Compo* field of the extracted cases does not belong to the nominal diagnosis, the new case should not be introduced. This case will be an isolated case among all cases belonging to another type of fault. Its introduction worsens the diagnosis of that type of fault.

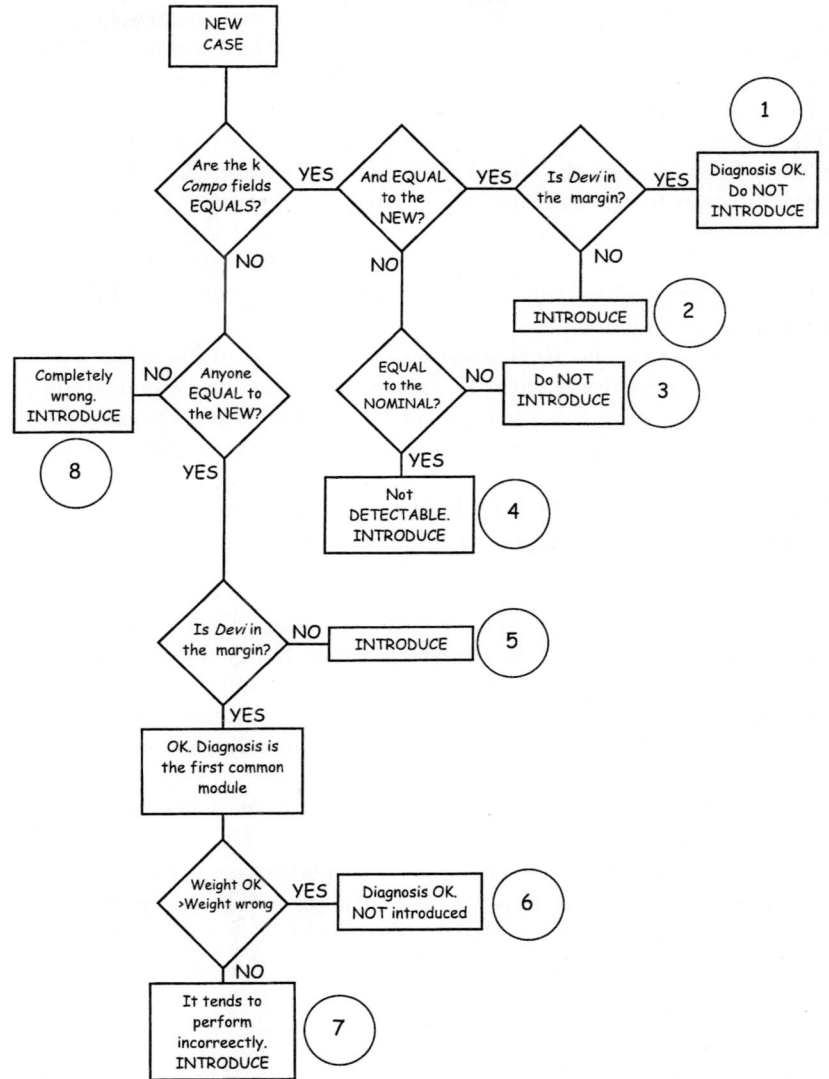

Fig. 4. Revision task flow diagram

4. The *Compo* field of the k extracted cases are equal between them, but different from the new case. If the *Compo* field of the extracted cases belongs to the nominal diagnosis, the new case should be introduced, because it is not detectable. Of course its introduction is going to spoil the diagnosis of nominal cases a little, but it is preferable to have false alarms to not detecting faults. Hence, the case will be retained, if the learning algorithm decides that the new case is not going to disturb others.

5. There is at least one, but not all of the k extracted cases with the *Compo* field equal to the *Compo* field of the new case. If the *Devi* field of these cases is out of the tolerated range, the case should be retained, after the learning algorithm approval.
6. There is at least one, but not all of them, of the k extracted cases with the *Compo* field equal to the *Compo* field of the new case. The *Devi* field of that cases belongs to the tolerated error range. In this case the diagnosis of the corresponding first common block is correct. But if the sum of the weights associated to these cases is higher than the sum of the weights of the rest of the extracted cases, the case memory tends to be correct. Hence, the new case is not retained.
7. In the same way as the previous situation, if the sum of the weights associated with the extracted cases with the same *Compo* field and equal to the *Compo* field of the new case is lower than the sum of the rest of the extracted cases, the case memory tends to be wrong. In these conditions, the new case is not introduced.
8. There is a *Compo* field of the k extracted cases equal to the *Compo* field of the new case. The diagnosis in these conditions is clearly wrong, and the new case should be retained.

In order to keep new cases on the case base, the DROP4 (Decremental Reduction by Optimization Procedure, version 4) is firstly used [16]. After taking the decision that a new case should be stored, the DROP4 algorithm is run. According to this algorithm, if this case is not going to disturb other cases diagnosis it will be finally introduced. This is evaluated using the *associate* concept described in the DROP4 algorithm.

But DROP4 tends to retain border points in order to reduce the number of instances to keep while it preserves the success ratio. Of course, if center points are deleted, diagnosis with less than a certain percentage error will be difficult. In spite of the case base size growing, when the algorithm in Figure 4 is applied, if a decision to keep the new instances is made, the case will be introduced even if its retention is going to spoil the classification of other cases (All-KNN). This algorithm has shown better diagnosis results.

3.5 Forgetting Noisy Exemplars

To avoid the *utility problem* factor, a maintenance of the case base memory is proposed. It is very similar to the IB3 ([17]) algorithm used when dropping cases. In fact, it uses the same criterion for removing cases, that is, when the performance of a particular case drops below a certain established value with a certain confidence index, the case is considered to be spoiling the diagnosis and it will be deleted. The confidence limit used is the one defined by the success probability of a Bernoulli process and given in Eq. 3 [18].

$$\frac{p + \frac{z^2}{2n} \pm z\sqrt{\frac{p(1-p)}{n} + \frac{z^2}{4n^2}}}{1 + \frac{z^2}{n}} \qquad (3)$$

In the equation, z is the confidence index, p is the proportion of instances that are of this class, and n is the number of the previously processed instances. The sign $\pm$ gives the lower and upper bounds. When the number of trials increases, the bound interval shrinks and approaches the true probability. Equation Eq. 3 with a particular confidence level z is used to forget cases. If the lower bound of the success probability for a particular case L_{si} is below the upper bound of the probability U_{ci} then the case belongs to this class, the case will be considered to be removed. In this sense, the *Class* field is used for comparing how the case is performing according to exemplars of its class, as IB3 does. The bigger the confidence z is taken, the sooner the instances are marked for removal.

IB3 normally takes a confidence index $C_{max} = z = 0.9$ for acceptance and $C_{min} = z = 0.7$ for rejecting. Note that accepting an instance is made more difficult than removing it. This is because exemplars with poor performance only contribute a little to the classification correctness, and they will probably be replaced by a new similar one during future training. In the present paper the algorithm is used only for removing noisy cases. several values of confidence, from 0.3 to 0.9 have been tested. The maximum performance is obtained for $C = z = 0.9$ as the confidence level to forget cases. Hence it is better for our system to forget irrelevant cases faster.

The following section shows the results obtained by applying the method to a biquadratic filter.

4 Results on a Real Circuit

After the description of the CBR-system, it was applied to the biquadratic filter circuit. It is shown in Figure 5, with the component values $R_1 = R_6 = 2.7K$, $R_2 = 1K$, $R_3 = 10K$, $R_4 = 1.5K$, $R_5 = 12K$, $C_1 = C_2 = 10nF$. This circuit is extensively used as a benchmark [19], [9].

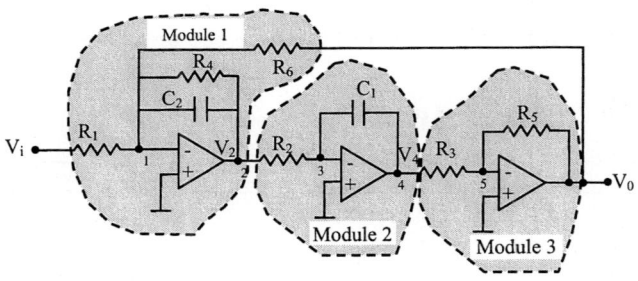

Fig. 5. Biquadratic filter under test

A tolerance of 10% is considered as normal for each component. Therefore, a component is considered faulty when it has a deviation greater than 10% from its nominal value. The circuit is linear and only parametric faults on the passive components are taken into account.

The case structure and case base hierarchy are defined as previously explained. For the learning process and maintenance, the multi-edit algorithm described in the previous sections is applied. The case revision and retention tasks are performed following the algorithm in Figure 4. On the other hand, the algorithm similar to the IB3 is used for forgetting noisy exemplars. Let's see some numerical examples demonstrating how the proposed method works.

Consider for the fault dictionary construction that deviations of $\pm 20\%$ and $\pm 50\%$ for each component compound the universe of faults. Also, let us take the saturated ramp input with values $t_r = 100~\mu sec$ and $V_{SAT} = 1V$ as the fault dictionary method selected. The simulated measures at the output V_0 produce a dictionary with 33 cases (32 faults + nominal). The faults for R_2, R_3 and C_1 are grouped because they produce exactly the same measures, forming an *ambiguity group*. The biquadratic filter is a small circuit that can be divided into 3 blocks by inspection, ($M1$, $M2$, $M3$), belonging to the same hierarchy level $L1$. As example, component R_1 belongs to level L_1 and module M_1, while component R_5 belongs to the same level but to module M_3.

Figure 6 depicts a case corresponding to fault at R_5 with a deviation of -43%, using the measures derived from the saturated ramp method.

Case Num	SP	Td	Tr	Vest	Class	Compo	Devi	Hierarchy
Case i	SP_i	Td_i	Tr_i	$Vest_i$	20	R5	-43%	$L_1.M_3$

Measures. Numeric Part   Fault. Qualitative Part

Fig. 6. Case Structure for the fault $R_1 - 43\%$

First of all, let us concentrate on the retaining procedure described in Figure 4. Examples corresponding to each type of decision considering $k = 3$ neighbors to extract are displayed. The weights are calculated using the exponential kernel with $w_k = 0.2$.

Consider the results given in Table 1, where the measures are normalized.

Table 1. Case of a type 1 decision (Figure 4)

	SP	t_d	t_r	V_{est}	Class	Compo	Devi	Weight
New Case	0.5099	0.5152	2.2353	1.3024	4	R_1	-54.64	-
Neighbor 1	0.5411	0.5252	2.2059	1.2593	4	R_1	-54.55	0.5167
Neighbor 2	0.5162	0.4545	2.2353	1.1525	4	R_1	-50.00	0.3765
Neighbor 3	0.5546	0.4545	2.2353	1.0466	4	R_1	-43.19	0.2000

The $k = 3$ neighbors all correspond to *Compo* 1, the same *Compo* field as the new case. As proposed by the algorithm in Figure 4, the average deviation should be obtained and compared to the new case. The average deviation of the

3 neighbors is $Devi = -49.25\%$, comparing this with the deviation of the new case gives an error estimation of 9.86%. Since the error is less than 10%, the case is supposed to be correctly estimated, and therefore it is not necessary to introduce it into the case base.

Suppose now, that the situation of Table 2 is given

Table 2. Case of a type 5 decision (Figure 4)

	SP	t_d	t_r	V_{est}	Class	Compo	Devi	Weight
New Case	0.3474	0.8182	2.4118	0.5702	7	R_2	64.4636	-
Neighbor 1	0.4234	0.7576	2.3529	0.5798	5	R_2	24.5949	0.6063
Neighbor 2	0.4670	0.6364	2.2941	0.5623	7	R_2	48.3634	0.3374
Neighbor 3	0.4694	0.5152	2.2647	0.4918	1	R_1	13.7863	0.2000

In this situation there are some retrieved cases, but not all of them have the same *Compo* field as the new case. Neighbor 1 and Neighbor 2 correspond to *Compo* 2, giving an average deviation of $Devi = 36.48\%$. It is clear that the new case is *Compo* 2 but with a deviation far from the proposed one. Hence, the case will be introduced, if it does not disturb the other case base members.

According to the algorithm for forgetting noisy exemplars, the maximum performance is obtained for $C \approx 0.9$ as the confidence level to forget cases. Hence it is better for our system to forget irrelevant cases faster.

Figure 7 demonstrates how the process is learning while training. It has been obtained for 150 training sets randomly sorted. The curves show the diagnosis results obtained for one of the best sorted combination of training sets. Each training set is compound by 10 faults for each component considering deviations from 0 to 70% (a total of 80 new case per train) randomly generated by means of the Monte-Carlo algorithm.

Precision success stands for the cases that are diagnosed correctly (component and deviation with an error $< 10\%$). On the other hand, *Component success* represents the percentage of cases that are only correct at locating the component (deviation with an error $> 10\%$). Cases with neither component nor deviation are correct are considered in the Figure 7 as *Wrong*. *Success with overlap* contains the percentage of faults that provides the correct diagnosis only at the faulty module. The sum of all these types of successes is given in Figure 7 by *Total success*. At last, the *Data base size* during training is shown in the last graphic of the same figure. The first value displayed in each graphic of Figure 7 corresponds to the diagnostic values obtained by the classic fault dictionary. At the beginning, the total of correct cases increases abruptly. This fact is due to the multiple cases being taken instead of one as a neighbor in the diagnosis. Therefore, it is more probable to extract the correct class between them, but there will be overlapping with the other neighbors. The increase is therefore due to the percentage of the correct module detection rising (second row second column plot in Figure 7). As the training advances, the case base substitutes component and module success diagnosis by increasing the average of precision diagnosis.

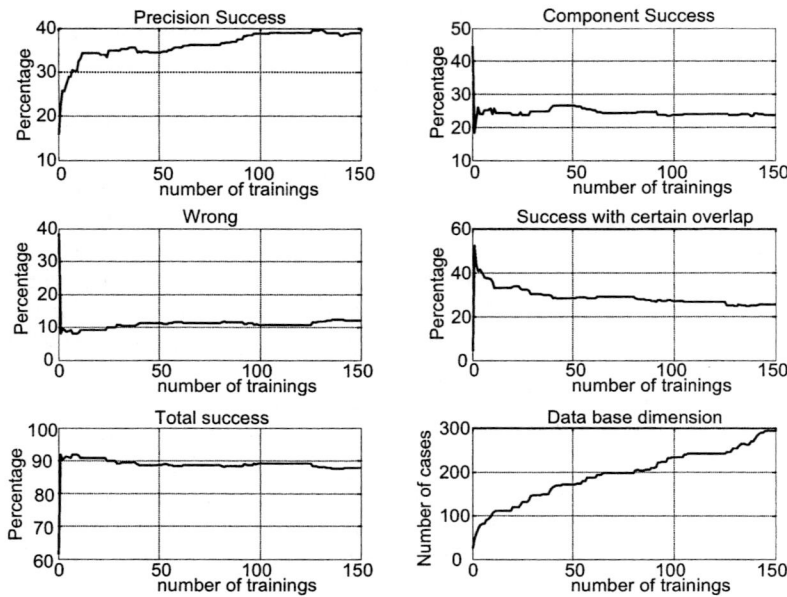

Fig. 7. Analysis sorting the train sets

On the other hand, another important factor to observe is that the number of cases continuously increases. Observe that the system classifies correctly (including the deviation), almost the 40% of tested new cases. If the situations in which at least the correct component or its corresponding module is diagnosed, almost 90% of the new tested cases are rightly located and identified. These percentages show that better results are obtained comparing with the fault dictionary. Table 3 shows the detailed results stopping the training at set number 132.

Table 3. Performance for non previously considered faults. CBR

Method	OK diagnosed	Component OK	Module OK	Wrong	Case Base size
Fault dictionary	17%	46.375%	0%	36.625%	25
DROP4 retain	39.375%	23.25%	25.625%	11.75%	263
All-KNN retain	49.40%	20.25%	19.80%	10.37%	742

5 Conclusions

A new methodology for building a CBR system for analog electronic circuits diagnosis has been developed. The proposed CBR-system is based on fault dictionaries, taking advantage of its case structure and provided signatures, and completed with learning and maintenance tasks. The classic dictionary with a faults universe of ±20% and ±50% serves as an initial case base. Of course the type of measures to select is circuit dependent.

About the case base maintenance, a multi-edit algorithm based on DROP4 or All-KNN for adding and IB3 with $C = z = 0.9$ confidence index for deleting cases has been proposed. The method works quite well improving substantially the percentage of success with precision as shown in Table 3. Of course taken more measures at other nodes will decrease the number of ambiguities and more faults will be distinguishable, as it will happen with the classical dictionaries or other methodologies. But comparing the success rate for the studied methods all of them in the same conditions (taking measures only at the output), the CBR system proposed presents a higher percentage of success identifying the parameter values.

For the biquadratic filter circuit, the results have shown that the method improves the diagnosis provided by the fault dictionary. For a set of 100 faults for each component corresponding to deviations compressed in the range of ±70%, the classic dictionary has a success rate of 17% while using the proposed multi-edit technique increases it to 39.375%. Also, the incorrect diagnostics decrease from 27% to 11.75%. A transition of success rates from the component success rate to the precise success rate can be observed, meaning that the system is more precise when diagnosing. The increase in the case base size is not dramatic. The classic dictionary has 25 cases while the multi-edit technique produces a case base of 263. The confidence index selected for forgetting is $C = z = 0.9$. This index shows the best results after several simulations. A case that is performing badly can quickly be deleted because it will be substituted by another training case that can perform better. If the cases are introduced even though they have a bad influence on the classification of other cases already contained in the base, the system performs even better. In this situation, success with precision is increased up to 49.40% using the same test set. The case base reaches saturation as well, but the training can be truncated at training 63. The system performance is improved at expenses of increasing the case base size to 742.

References

1. Chandramouli, R., Pateras, S.: Testing system on a chip. IEEE Spectrum (1996) 42–47
2. Milor, L., Sangiovanni-Vicentelli, A.: Minimizing production test time to detect faults in analog circuits. IEEE Trans. On Computer-Aided Design of IC **13** (1994) 796–807
3. Murray, B., Hayes, J.: Testing ICs: Getting to the core of the problem. IEEE Design and Test (1996) 32–38
4. Pang, J., Starzyk, J.: Fault diagnosis in mixed-signal low testability system. International Journal of Circuit Theory and Applications (2002) 487–510
5. Fanni, A., Giua, A., Marchesi, M., Montisci, A.: A neural network diagnosis approach for analog circuits. Applied Intelligence 2 (1999) 169–186
6. Fenton, B., McGinnity, M., Maguire, L.: Fault diagnosis of electronic systems using artificial intelligence. IEEE Instrumentation and Measurement (2002) 16–20

7. Sheppard, J.W., Simpson, W.R.: Research Perspectives and Case Studies in Systems Test and Diagnosis. Volume 13 of Frontiers in Electronic Testing. Kluwer (1998) Chapter 5. Inducing Inference Models from Case Data.ISBN 0-7923-8263-3.
8. Stenbakken, G., Souders, T., Stewart, G.: Ambiguity groups and testability. IEEE Transactions on Instrumentation and Measurement **38** (1989) 941–947
9. Balivada, A., Chen, J., Abraham, J.: Analog testing with time response parameters. IEEE Design and Test of computers (1996) 18–25
10. Lopez de Mantaras, R., Plaza, E.: Case-based reasoning: An overview. AI Communications (1997) 21–29
11. Richter, M.: The knowledge contained in similarity measures. remarks on the invited talk given at ICCBR'95 (Sesimbra, Portugal, October 25, 1995) http://www.cbr-web.org/documents/Richtericcbr95remarks.html.
12. Voorakaranam, R., Chakrabarti, S., Hou, J., Gomes, A., Cherubal, S., Chatterjee, A.: Hierarchical specification-driven analog fault modeling for efficient fault simulation and diagnosis. International Test Conference (1997) 903–912
13. Sangiovanni-Vicentelli, A., Chen, L., Chua, L.: An efficient heuristic cluster algorithm for tearing large-scale networks. IEEE Transactions on Circuits and Systems **cas-24** (1977) 709–717
14. Wilson, D.R., Martinez, T.R.: Improved heterogeneous distance functions. Journal of Artificial Intelligence Research (1997) 1–34
15. Aamodt, A., Plaza, E.: Case-based reasoning: Foundationalu issues, methodological variations and system approaches. AI Communications (1994) 39–59
16. Wilson, D., Martinez, T.: Reduction techniques for instance-based learning algorithms. Machine Learning **38** (2000) 257–286
17. Aha, D.W., Kibler, D., Albert, M.: Instance based learning algorithms. Machine Learning. **6** (1991) 37–66
18. Witten, I.H., Frank, E.: Data Mining. Practical Machine Learning Tools and Techniques with Java Implementations. Data Management Systems. Morgan Kaufmann Publishers (2000) ISBN 1-55860-552-5.
19. Kaminska, B., Arabi, K., Goteti, P., Huertas, J., Kim, B., Rueda, A., Soma, M.: Analog and mixed signal benchmark circuits. first release. IEEE Mixed Signal Testing Technical Activity Committee ITC97 (1997) 183–190

Dynamic Critiquing

James Reilly, Kevin McCarthy, Lorraine McGinty, and Barry Smyth

Adaptive Information Cluster*, Smart Media Institute,
Department of Computer Science, University College Dublin (UCD), Ireland
{james.d.reilly,kevin.mccarthy,lorraine.mcginty,barry.smyth}@ucd.ie

Abstract. Critiquing is a powerful style of feedback for case-based recommender systems. Instead of providing detailed feature values, users indicate a directional preference for a feature. For example, a user might ask for a 'less expensive' restaurant in a restaurant recommender; 'less expensive' is a critique over the *price* feature. The value of critiquing is that it is generally applicable over a wide range of domains and it is an effective means of focusing search. To date critiquing approaches have usually been limited to single-feature critiques, and this ultimately limits the degree to which a given critique can eliminate unsuitable cases. In this paper we propose extending the critiquing concept to cater for the possibility of *compound critiques* – critiques over multiple case features. We describe a technique for automatically generating useful compound critiques and demonstrate how this can significantly improve the performance of a conversational recommender system. We also argue that this generalised form of critiquing offers explanatory benefits by helping the user to better understand the structure of the recommendation space.

1 Introduction

Conversational recommender systems are a response to the fact that in many information seeking scenarios it is unlikely that the user will provide enough requirements information to uniquely identify what it is that she is looking for. As such, conversational recommender systems assume that a user's initial query is merely a starting point for search, perhaps even an unreliable starting point, and the job of the recommender system is to help the user to refine her initial query as part of an extended system-user interaction (see for example, [1, 9, 16, 18]). Thus, a typical session with a conversational recommender system usually takes the form of a series of *recommend-review-revise* cycles: the user is presented with one or more item recommendations; she provides some form of feedback regarding the suitability of these items; and the recommender updates its user-model according to this feedback and proceeds to the next recommendation cycle. The hope of course is that after a small number of cycles the recommender will have sufficient information to recommend a suitable item to the user.

---
* This material is based on works supported by Science Foundation Ireland under Grant No. 03/IN.3/I361

Research in the area of recommender systems to date has focused on various aspects of the conversational recommender system architecture, with a number of researchers exploring different options when it comes to the recommend, review and revise stages of each cycle. Briefly, researchers have explored a variety of ways to select items for recommendation, recently moving beyond straightforward similarity-based approaches towards more sophisticated techniques that incorporate factors such as item diversity into the retrieval process [2, 8, 12, 16, 18]. In turn, there are many ways in which a user can review a set of recommendations and a variety of different forms of feedback have been proposed [17]. Finally, other recent work has looked at how user feedback can be exploited to update the recommender's model of the user's requirements [9].

In this paper we focus on the use of a popular form of feedback in conversational recommender systems: *critiquing*. The basic idea was first introduced by Burke *et al.* [3–5] and proposes a form of feedback that expresses what might be termed a *directional preference* over a particular item feature. Entree is the quintessential recommender system that employs critiquing (also sometimes referred to as *tweaking*). Entree is a restaurant recommender, and each time a restaurant is suggested it allows the user to provide feedback in the form of a *critique* or *tweak*. Each tweak is a constraint over the value-space of a particular restaurant feature. For example, the user might indicate that they are looking for a *less expensive* restaurant or a *more formal* setting. These are two individual tweaks: the former on the *price* feature and the latter on the *setting* feature. The advantage of critiquing is that it is a fairly lightweight form of feedback, in the sense that the user does not need to provide specific value information for a feature, while at the same time helping the recommender to narrow its search focus quite significantly [10, 11].

This standard form of critiquing *normally* operates at the level of individual features and this limits its ability to narrow the search focus. At the same time it seems that users often think more naturally about combinations of features. For example, in the PC domain a user might be looking for a PC that is similar to the one shown but that has more memory at a lower price; this is an example of a *compound critique* over the *memory* and *price* features of a PC case. Intuitively compound critiques appear to have the ability to improve the efficiency of conversational recommender systems, by focusing search in the direction of multiple, simultaneous feature constraints; of course they are not limited to two features and in theory compound critiques could be created to operate over all of the features of a case, although this might impact on a user's ability to understand the critique.

This is not to say that the idea of compound critiques is novel. In fact, the seminal work of [4] refers to critiques for manipulating multiple features. They give the example of the 'sportier' critique, in a car recommender, which increases engine size and acceleration and allows for a greater price. This is a compound critique but it has been fixed by the system designer. We believe that a more flexible approach is required because the appropriateness of a particular compound critique will very much depend on the remaining cases that are available.

For example, if, during the course of the recommender session, a car-buyer has focused on large family cars then it is unlikely that many 'sporty' cars will exist in the remaining cases and the 'sportier' critique may no longer be valid. However, a new compound critique – lower engine size, greater fuel economy and a higher eco-rating – might now be useful. The point is that compound critiques should be generated on the fly with reference to the remaining cases and this is the starting point for our work. In this paper we will describe and evaluate different approaches to automatically creating and prioritising compound critiques. Specifically, in Section 2.2 we will describe how the Apriori algorithm[7, 15] can be used to generate and grade candidate compound critiques, and in Section 3 we will demonstrate how the availability of these selected critiques can reduce the average number of recommendation cycles needed by up to 40%.

2 Dynamic Compound Critiquing

In this work we will assume a conversational recommender system in the image of Entree. Each recommendation session will be commenced by an initial user query and this will result in the retrieval of the most similar case available for the first recommendation cycle. The user will have the opportunity to accept this case, thereby ending the recommendation session, or to critique this case. When she critiques the case, the critique in question acts as a filter over the remaining cases, and the case chosen for the next cycle is that case which is compatible with the critique and which is maximally similar to the previously recommended case.

To critique a case the user will be presented with a range of single-feature (*unit*) critiques plus a set of compound critiques that have been chosen because of their ability to carve-up the remaining cases. In this section we will describe in detail how these compound critiques are generated and selected during each cycle by looking for frequently occurring patterns of critiques within the remaining cases; we refer to our approach as *dynamic critiquing*.

2.1 Critique Patterns – A Precursor to Discovery

Let us assume that our recommender system is currently engaged in a recommendation session with a user, and that a new case has been returned as part of the current cycle. Each case that remains in the case-base can be compared to this new case to generate a so-called *critique pattern*. This pattern essentially recasts each case in the case-base in terms of the unit critiques that apply to each of its features when compared to the current case.

Figure 1 illustrates what we mean with the aid of an example. It shows the current case that has been selected for recommendation to the user as part of the current cycle and also a case from the case-base. The current case describes a 1.4GHz, desktop PC with 512Mb of RAM, a 14" monitor and a 40Gb hard-drive, all for 1500 euro. The comparison case, from the case-base, describes a 900MHz, desktop with 512MB or RAM, a 12" monitor and a 30Gb hard-drive for 3000

	Current Case	Case c from CB	Critique Pattern
Manufacturer	Compaq	Sony	!=
Monitor (inches)	14"	12"	<
Memory (MB)	512	512	=
Hard-Disk (GB)	40	30	<
Processor	Pentium 3	Pentium 3	=
Speed (Mhz)	1400	900	<
Type	Desktop	Desktop	=
Price (Euro)	1500	3000	>

Fig. 1. Illustrating how a critique pattern is generated.

euro. The resulting critique pattern reflects the differences between these two cases in terms of individual feature critiques. For example, the critique pattern shown includes a "<" critique for processor speed – we will refer to this as [Speed <] – because the comparison case has a slower processor than the current recommended case. Similarly, the pattern includes the critique [Price >] because the comparison case is more expensive than the current case. So, prior to the discovery process, and after a case has been selected for the current cycle, it is necessary to generate a critique pattern for every case in the case-base relative to the current case. These patterns serve as the source of compound critiques.

2.2 Discovering Compound Critiques

The key to exploiting compound critiques relies on our ability to recognise useful recurring subsets of critiques within the potentially large collection of critique patterns (the *pattern-base*). Our intuition is that certain subsets will tend to recur throughout the pattern-base. For example, we might find that 50% of the remaining cases have a smaller screen-size but a larger hard-disk size than the current case; that is, 50% of the critique patterns contain the sub-pattern $\{[Monitor <],[Hard-Disk >]\}$. If this critique is applicable to the user – if she is in fact looking for smaller screens and larger hard-disks – then its application will immediately filter out half of the remaining cases, thus better focusing the search for a suitable case during the next cycle. Presumably, neither of the individual critiques that make up this compound critique would wield the same discriminatory power on their own.

The problem at hand then is how to recognise and collate these recurring critique patterns within the pattern-base. This is similar to the so-called *market basket analysis*, which aims to find regularities in the shopping behaviour of customers [7]: each critique pattern corresponds to the shopping basket for a single customer, and the individual critiques correspond to the items in this basket. Many data-mining algorithms try to find sets of items that are frequently purchased together, and so our proposal is to use similar techniques to find sets of critiques that frequently occur together. Ordinarily this is a challenging problem, largely because of the combinatorics involved: a typical supermarket will have several thousand different products and this can lead to a combinatoric explosion in the number of possible groups of recurring items. This problem is not so acute in our critiquing scenario because there are only a limited number of possible critiques. For instance, each numeric feature can have a "<" or a ">" critique and each nominal feature can have a "=" or a "! =" critique, so there are only $2n$ possible critiques in a case-base where the cases are made up of n individual features.

In addition, efficient algorithms do exist for restricting the search-space of possibilities so that only a subset of all of the possible compound critiques needs to be checked. One such algorithm is the well-known Apriori algorithm [7, 15], which characterises these recurring item subsets as association rules of the form $A \rightarrow B$ – from the presence of a certain set of critiques (A) one can infer the presence of certain other critiques (B). For example, one might learn that from the presence of the critique, $[Monitor <]$, we can infer the presence of $[Hard - Disk >]$ with a high degree of probability; in other words the pattern $\{[Monitor <],[Hard - Disk >]\}$ is commonplace.

Apriori measures the importance of a rule in terms of its *support* and *confidence*. The support of a rule, $A \rightarrow B$, is the percentage of patterns for which the rule is correct; that is, the number of patterns that contain both A and B divided by the total number of patterns. Confidence, on the other hand, is a measure of the number of patterns in which the rule is correct relative to the number of patterns in which the rule is applicable; that is, the number of patterns that contain both A and B divided by the number of patterns containing A. For instance, we would find that the rule $[Monitor <] \rightarrow [Hard - Disk >]$ has a support of 0.1 if there are a total of 100 critique patterns but only 10 of them contain $[Monitor <]$ and $[Hard-Disk >]$. Likewise, the confidence of this rule would be 0.4 if 25 of the critique patterns contain only $[Monitor <]$. Unfortunately a detailed account of Apriori is beyond the scope of this paper but, very briefly, Apriori is a multi-pass algorithm, where in the kth pass all large itemsets of cardinality k are computed. Initially *frequent itemsets* are determined. These are sets of items that have at least a predefined minimum support. Then, during each new pass those itemsets that exceed the minimum support threshold are extended. Apriori is efficient because it exploits the simple observation that no superset of an infrequent itemset can be frequent to prune away candidate itemsets.

Our specific proposal is to use Apriori, during each recommendation cycle, to generate a collection of compound critiques (frequent itemsets over the pattern-base), and to then select a subset of these compound critiques so that they may be presented to the user as alternative critiquing options.

2.3 Grading Compound Critiques

During any particular cycle a large number of compound critiques, of varying sizes, may be discovered. Of course it is not feasible to present all of these to the user so we must look to choose a select subset. Which subset we choose is likely to have a significant bearing on the degree to which the compound critiques may prove to be successful at reducing session length. There are two main criteria in this regard:

- We would like to present compound critiques that are likely to be applicable to the user, in the sense that they are likely to constrain the remaining cases in the direction of their target case. In this way there is a good chance that these compound critiques will be selected over any of the unit critiques.
- We would like to present compound critiques that will filter out large numbers of cases so that there is a greater chance that the target case will be retrieved in the next cycle.

The first of these criteria is difficult to cater for since it is unlikely to be at all clear exactly what target case the user is seeking. That said, it is a good bet that certain features of their target case may be inferred from the feedback provided during previous cycles. For example, if the user reliably looks for cheaper PCs then compound critiques that contain $[Price <]$ may be good candidates. The second criterion is more straightforward to address. The support of a compound critique is a direct measure of its ability to filter out few or many cases. A compound critique with a low support value means that it is present in a small proportion of critique patterns and thus it is only applicable to a few remaining cases. If applied the critique will therefore eliminate many cases from consideration.

It is worth noting that there is a tension between the use of support as a grading metric for compound critiques and the way that it will influence the above criteria. While low-support critiques will eliminate many cases, these critiques seem less likely to lead to the target case, all things being equal. Conversely, preferring high-support critiques will increase the chance that the critiques will lead to the target case, but these critiques will fail to eliminate many cases from consideration.

3 Evaluation

At this point we have described how our dynamic critiquing technique applies Apriori within a standard critiquing-based, conversational recommender system in order to identify sets of compound critiques that may be presented to the user during each cycle. Ultimately we are doing this in the hope that compound critiques will be selected in favor of unit critiques and that they will help to reduce the number of cycles needed to satisfy the user. In this section we will evaluate this in the context of a PC recommender and we will look at a number of key issues including: the number of compound critiques that are generated during a typical cycle; the size of these critiques and the size of the critiques that are selected for presentation to the user; the application frequency of compound critiques during a typical cycle; and finally, the impact of dynamic critiquing on session length.

3.1 Setup

Algorithmic Variations. The basic dynamic critiquing approach is fixed: compound critiques are generated during each cycle (with a minimum support threshold of 0.25). However, we will examine three variations on this theme, each distinguished according to how the set of top 5 critiques is chosen for presentation to the user during the current cycle: (1) LS - the top 5 critiques with the lowest support are chosen; (2) HS - the top 5 critiques with the highest support are chosen; (3) RAND - A random set of 5 critiques are chosen. So the above provide three system variations based on dynamic critiquing and in addition we also include a standard, unit critiquing approach (STD) as a benchmark.

Dataset. The well-known PC dataset is used as a source of case and query data [9, 13]. This dataset consists of 120 PC cases each described in terms of 8 features including *type, manufacturer, processor, memory*, etc. This dataset is available for download at *www.cs.ucd.ie/staff/lmcginty/PCdataset.zip*

Methodology. We adopt a similar leave-one-out methodology to [9–11]. Specifically, each case (*base*) in the case-base is temporarily removed and used in two ways. First it serves as the basis for a set of queries constructed by taking random subsets of its features. We focus on subsets of 1, 3 and 5 features to allow us to distinguish between hard, moderate and easy queries, respectively. Second, we select the case that is most similar to the original base. These cases serve as the recommendation *targets* for the experiments. Thus, the base represents the ideal query for a 'user', the generated query is the initial query that the 'user' provides to the recommender, and the target is the best available case for the 'user', based on their ideal. Each generated query is a test problem for the recommender, and in each recommendation cycle the 'user' picks a critique that is compatible with the known target case; that is, a critique that, when applied to the remaining cases, results in the target case being left in the filtered set of cases. In a typical cycle there may be a number of critiques (unit and compound) that satisfy this condition and the actual one chosen depends on the system being used: LS picks the critique with the lowest support with ties broken by a random choice, HS picks the one with the highest support with ties broken by a random choice, and RAND picks a random critique. Each leave-one-out pass through the case-base is repeated 30 times and recommendation sessions terminate when the target case is returned.

3.2 How Many Compound Critiques?

Perhaps the first question to explore concerns the number of compound critiques that can be generated during a recommendation cycle. Obviously this will depend on a number of factors including: the current recommended case; the number of cases that are available in the cycle; and the variation that exists among these cases.

To form a general picture of how critique generation was influenced by the number of cases we recorded the number of compound critiques generated during each cycle along with the number of cases that were available during that cycle. The results are presented in Figure 2 as a graph of the average number of critiques versus the different numbers of cases. They indicate a general trend towards fewer compound critiques as the number of available cases decreases. Initially, for large numbers of cases (between 120 and 110), the number of generated critiques falls off quickly from a high of over 200, and then is seen to stabalise around the 100 level. Obviously the actual number of compound critiques generated per cycle is significant and typically there are more critiques than cases due to the combinatorics of critique generation. Remember we select only 5 of these critiques per cycle for presentation to the user so it will be interesting to investigate how the different policies (LS, HS and RAND) vary in terms of their ability to influence recommendation efficiency.

Fig. 2. Graph of the average number of critiques generated versus the different numbers of cases available.

3.3 Critique Size

Early on in this work we were concerned that the size of compound critiques would be an important issue: that compound critiques containing many features would be routinely generated, and that these critiques would be too complex to present to any user. There are 8 features per PC case and thus a compound critique can have a size of between 2 and 8, but presenting compound critiques with, for example, 5 or 6 separate features would make for a user-interface nightmare.

To understand the size-range of the critiques being generated we first counted the number of critiques generated for each of the 8 different sizes across an entire leave-one-out pass through the case-base. The results are presented in Figure 3 and they show that the majority of compound critiques are actually quite short. For instance, 66% of critiques contain either 2 or 3 features and less than 2.5% contain more than 5 features. This indicates that there is a significant degree of variation between the PC cases; if these cases were more homogeneous then larger critiques would have been commonplace.

As a follow-up experiment on the issue of critique size, we also looked at the average size of the compound critiques that are being presented to the user as part of the recommendation cycle, for each of the different critiquing strategies. The results are shown in Figure 4 as a graph of the average compound

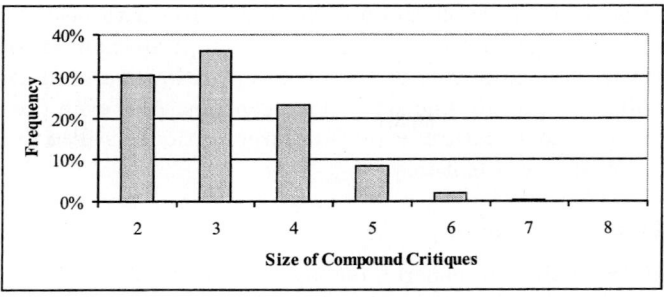

Fig. 3. Results showing the frequency of sizes of compound critiques.

critique size presented during a cycle versus the maximum generation threshold, t; terminating Apriori at the $t + 1^{th}$ iteration will limit all itemsets (compound critiques) to be no greater than t in size. The results show that the compound critiques chosen by the HS strategy are unaffected by the maximum generation threshold; the top 5 HS critiques have an average size of about 2.12 regardless of the generation threshold. Of course this is to be expected since critiques with a high support value are likely to be small; high support means that the critique is common across the available cases and this is more likely if the compound critique contains few features. Thus, preferring compound critiques with high support is tantamount to preferring small compound critiques. Conversely, the average size of the compound critiques selected by the LS strategy are larger by up to 76% (an average size of 3.7) when the maximum generation threshold is set to its maximum value of 8. When we look at the average size of compound critiques that are actually selected by the 'user' in our experiments we find that they too follow the pattern presented in Figure 4 and are virtually identical to the sizes shown.

In summary then, our initial concerns about the generation of large compound critiques, and the problems that this might cause, appear to be unfounded.

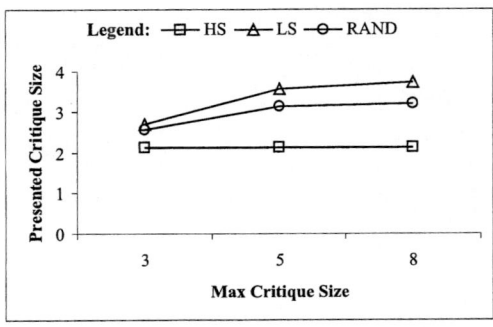

Fig. 4. Graph of the average compound critique size presented during a cycle versus the maximum generation threshold.

First of all, it is always possible to limit the size of the critiques, at generation-time, by prematurely halting Apriori after an appropriate number of iterations. Secondly, even without imposing this limit, large critiques are unlikely to occur unless the available cases are unusually homogeneous. And even the LS critique selection strategy, which naturally favours large critiques still only selects critiques with at most 3 or 4 features.

3.4 Application Frequency

So far we have seen that, in general, our dynamic critiquing technique tends to produce large numbers of compound critiques in a typical cycle. We have also found most of these critiques to contain between 2 and 4 features and the HS selection strategy tends to prefer small critiques while the LS strategy prefers the larger critiques. Given that in our experiment we are returning 5 compound critiques per cycle to the user the next logical question is whether these critiques tend to be chosen.

Figure 5 presents a graph of the probability that a compound critique will be chosen by the 'user' at each cycle in a recommendation session. We compute the probability that a compound critique will be chosen in cycle k by calculating the proportion of times that a compound critique was selected in a kth cycle throughout our experiment. Figure 5 plots these probability distributions for each dynamic critiquing strategy for up to the 20th recommendation cycle. The results are as predicted in Section 2.3 where we suggested that compound critiques would be more likely to be chosen under the HS strategy than under the LS strategy. Figure 5 indicates that compound critiques are chosen under the HS strategy between 55% and 86% of the time. Under the LS strategy they are chosen between only 33% and 40% and under RAND they are chosen about 15% of the time.

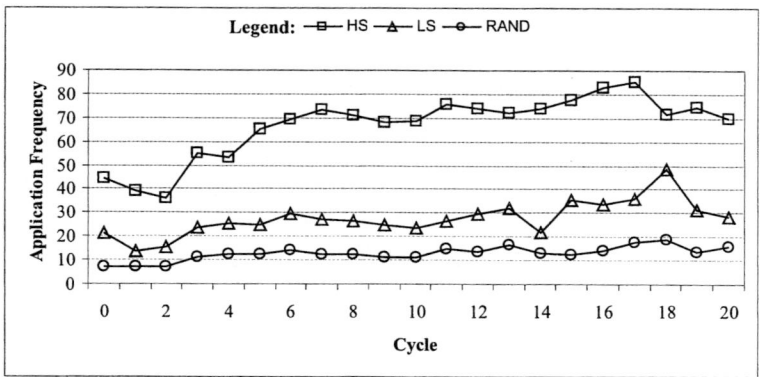

Fig. 5. Results showing the probability that a compound critique will be selected for each of the strategies evaluated.

3.5 Recommendation Efficiency

Our basic assumption is that the application of a compound critique should help to focus search more efficiently than the application of a unit critique and therefore reduce the length of recommendation sessions. We now know that the HS strategy leads to the frequent application of small compound critiques whereas the LS strategy leads to the less frequent application of large critiques. Which, if either, of these strategies leads to a reduction in session length remains to be seen. To test this we compare the performance of each of our four strategies on the PC case-base according to the leave-one-out test methodology described above.

For each recommendation session we record the number of cycles required before the target case is retrieved, and we average these values for each system. The summary results are presented in Figure 6 as a bar-chart with each bar showing the average session length for each of the four test systems measured across all test queries. Clearly, there is an advantage to the dynamic critiquing approach, with all three variations out-performing the standard critiquing system on average. However, the scale of this advantage is very much dependent on the variation of dynamic critiquing that is used. For example, the HS variation provides only a very minor advantage, reducing average session length from 5.89 cycles to 5.68 cycles, a relative reduction of less than 4%. This is to be expected as the HS system prefers compound critiques with high support values and these critiques, by definition, will not serve to filter cases greatly upon their application. The advantage is far more striking when we look at the LS system, which uses a complementary strategy that prefers critiques with low support values, critiques that are likely to constrain the cases for the next cycle. The LS variation reduces session length to 3.8, a reduction of nearly 36% relative to STD. The RAND variation occupies the middle-ground offering relative reductions of almost 16%.

It is also worth investigating how recommendation efficiency is influenced by initial query length, as a measure of query difficulty. To do this we recomputed the session length averages above by separating out the queries of various sizes.

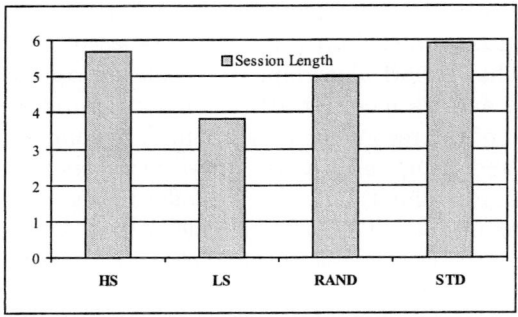

Fig. 6. Evaluation results illustrating the average session lengths recorded for each of the systems compared.

The results are presented in Figure 7. Figure 7(a) shows a graph of average session length against initial query length. Once again the results are very clear, pointing to a significant advantage for LS, but little or no advantage for HS. As expected the average session length falls with increasing initial query length but it is interesting to note that the scale of any advantage due to dynamic critiquing appears to be greater for the more difficult (smaller) initial queries. Figure 7(b) shows the results for the relative improvements realised over STD for all of the strategies evaluated. For example, for difficult queries (with a single specified feature) we find that LS enjoys a session length reduction of just over 40%, relative to STD. This falls to almost 32% for the moderate queries (containing 3 specified features) and falls again to just under 26% for the relatively easy queries with 5 fully specified features. This is to be expected perhaps since the easier queries naturally result in shorter sessions and thus there are fewer opportunities for compound critiques to be chosen, and hence fewer opportunities for their benefit to be felt.

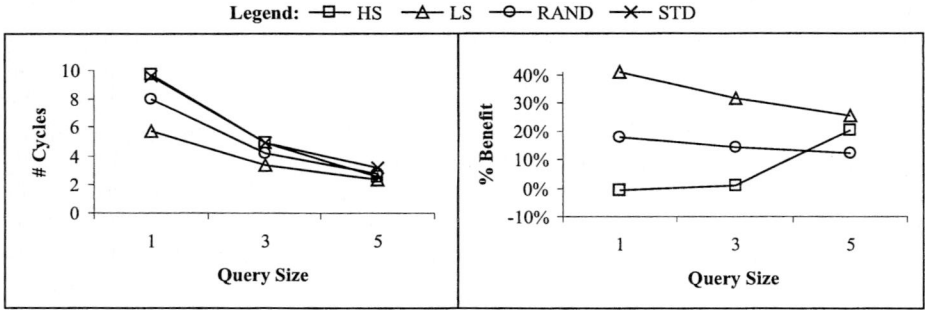

Fig. 7. Recommendation Efficiency Results.

4 Discussion

In summary then, dynamic critiquing (LS strategy) appears to offer significant performance benefits when compared to standard critiquing. We believe that it can be readily incorporated into standard case-based conversational recommender systems. The Apriori algorithm is an efficient approach to compound critique generation and its inclusion does not add appreciably to the overall computational load of the recommender system. For example, in our evaluation system, the compound critiques for a typical cycle are generated in an average of 46ms (on a 2.8 GHz Pentium 4) and, as such, offer no significant computational burden to the recommender. This does not mean that Apriori will necessarily scale well for very large case-bases, but we believe that it will remain computationally tractable for typical case-bases sizes. After all, Apriori is designed for large-scale data-based mining running into the millions of transactions and thousands of unique items and case-bases with hundreds or even thousands of cases and only tens of features do not present a significant challenge.

In addition to the performance advantages of dynamic critiquing it is also worth considering what we might term its 'explanatory benefits'. Recently a number of researchers have argued for the need for improved interaction between system and user, with many arguing that recommender systems must provide some form of explanation to the user in order to help her understand the reason behind recommendations [14, 6]. We believe that compound critiques have a role to play in this regard. Unlike unit critiques, compound critiques help users to understand some of the common interactions that exist between groups of features. For example, in the PC domain, the compound critique $[Speed >], [Memory >], [Price >]$ tells the user that faster processors, more memory, and higher prices go hand-in-hand, and by tagging this critique with its support value we can inform the user about the proportion of remaining cases that satisfy this critique. We believe that in many recommender domains, where the user is likely to have incomplete knowledge about the finer details of the feature-space, that compound critiques will help to effectively map out this space. For this reason we believe that users will actually find it easier to work with compound critiques than unit critiques and this may, for example, help the user to make fewer critiquing errors. For instance, with standard critiquing in the PC domain a user might naively select the $[Price <]$ unit critique in the mistaken belief that this may deliver a cheaper PC that satisfies all of their other requirements. However, reducing price in this way may lead to a reduction in memory that the user might not find acceptable and, as a result, she will have to backtrack. This problem is less likely to occur if the compound critique $[Price <], [Memory <]$ is presented because the user will come to understand the implications of a price-drop prior to selecting any critique. Of course all of these findings need to be validated in real-user trials.

A further research issue relates to the cognitive load associated with asking the user to evaluate more that one feature at a time. While we are confident that savings in processing time and session length will outweigh the cognitive burden placed on the user, supportive evaluations have yet to be carried out. Once again, a real-user study is necessary here.

5 Conclusions

Critiquing is an important mode of user feedback that is ideally suited to many case-based recommendation scenarios. It is straightforward to implement, easy for users to understand and use, and it has been shown to be effective at guiding conversational recommender systems. To date the standard form of critiquing has been largely limited to single-feature critiques, what we have called unit critiques. In this paper we have suggested the use of compound critiques to constrain multiple features simultaneously. We have described a technique called dynamic critiquing, which is capable of automatically and efficiently generating compound critiques during each recommendation cycle. And as part of each cycle a subset of these new critiques is presented to the user, along with the standard unit critiques. We have evaluated our technique using the well-known PC data-set and compared different strategies for selecting a suitable subset of critiques. Our experiments indicate that significant performance improvements are possible: the LS dynamic critiquing strategy, which prefers low-support critiques, has the ability to reduce session length by up to 40% compared to standard critiquing.

In summary then, the idea of using compound critiques is a general one that is likely to be just as applicable as standard critiquing across a wide range of recommendation scenarios. The use of compound critiques clearly has the potential to improve recommendation efficiency and dynamic critiquing provides an efficient approach to generating suitable compound critiques in conversational recommender systems. We further suggest that these compound critiques may confer an explanatory advantage on a recommender system by helping the user to appreciate the dependancies that exist between features and cases. Together these advantages establish compound critiquing as a powerful new interaction modality for case-based conversational recommender systems.

References

1. D.W. Aha and K.M. Gupta. Causal Query Elaboration in Conversational Case-Based Reasoning. In S. Haller and G. Simmons, editors, *Proceedings of the Fifteenth International FLAIRS Conference*, pages 95–100. AAAI Press, 2002. Pensacola Beach, Florida, USA.
2. D. Bridge. Product Recommendation Systems: A New Direction. In D. Aha and I. Watson, editors, *Workshop on CBR in Electronic Commerce at The International Conference on Case-Based Reasoning (ICCBR-01)*, 2001. Vancouver, Canada.
3. R. Burke. Interactive Critiquing for Catalog Navigation in E-Commerce. *Artificial Intelligence Review*, 18(3-4):245–267, 2002.
4. R. Burke, K. Hammond, and B. Young. Knowledge-based navigation of complex information spaces. In *Proceedings of the Thirteenth National Conference on Artificial Intelligence*, pages 462–468. AAAI Press/MIT Press, 1996. Portland, OR.
5. R. Burke, K. Hammond, and B.C. Young. The FindMe Approach to Assisted Browsing. *Journal of IEEE Expert*, 12(4):32–40, 1997.
6. P. Cunningham, D. Doyle, and J. Loughrey. An Evaluation of the Usefulness of Case-Based Explanation. In K. Ashley and D. Bridge, editors, *Case-Based Reasoning Research and Development. LNAI, Vol. 2689.*, pages 191–199. Springer-Verlag, 2003. Berlin.
7. Z. Hu, W.N. Chin, and M. Takeichi. Calculating a New Data Mining Algorithm for Market Basket Analysis. *Lecture Notes in Computer Science*, 1753:169–175, 2000.
8. A. Kohlmaier, S. Schmitt, and R. Bergmann. Evaluation of a Similarity-based Approach to Customer-adaptive Electronic Sales Dialogs. In S. Weibelzahl, D. Chin, and G. Weber, editors, *Empirical Evaluation of Adaptive Systems. Proceedings of the workshop held at the 8th International Conference on User Modelling*, pages 40–50, 2001. Sonthofen, Germany.
9. L. McGinty and B. Smyth. Comparison-Based Recommendation. In Susan Craw, editor, *Proceedings of the Sixth European Conference on Case-Based Reasoning (ECCBR-02)*, pages 575–589. Springer, 2002. Aberdeen, Scotland.
10. L. McGinty and B. Smyth. On The Role of Diversity in Conversational Recommender Systems. In D. Bridge and K. Ashley, editors, *Proceedings of the Fifth International Conference on Case-Based Reasoning (ICCBR-03)*, pages 276–290. Springer, 2003. Troindheim, Norway.

11. L. McGinty and B. Smyth. Tweaking Critiquing. In *Proceedings of the Workshop on Personalization and Web Techniques at the International Joint Conference on Artificial Intelligence (IJCAI-03)*, pages 20–27. Morgan-Kaufmann, 2003. Acapulco, Mexico.
12. D. McSherry. Diversity-Conscious Retrieval. In Susan Craw, editor, *Proceedings of the Sixth European Conference on Case-Based Reasoning (ECCBR-02)*, pages 219–233. Springer, 2002. Aberdeen, Scotland.
13. D. McSherry. Balancing User Satisfaction and Cognitive Load in Coverage-Optimised Retrieval. In Preece A. Macintosh A. Coenen, F., editor, *Research and Development in Intelligent Systems XX. Proceedings of AI-2003*, pages 381–394. Springer-Verlag, 2003. Cambridge, UK.
14. D. McSherry. Explanation of Retrieval Mismatches in Recommender System Dialogues. . In *Proceedings of the ICCBR-03 Workshop on Mixed-Initiative Case-Based Reasoning*, pages 191–199, 2003. Trondheim, Norway.
15. R. Srikant H. Toivonen R. Agrawal, H. Mannila and A. Inkeri Verkamo. Fast Discovery of Association Rules in Large Databases. *Advances in Knowledge Discovery and Data Mining*, pages 307–328, 1996.
16. H. Shimazu. ExpertClerk : Navigating Shoppers' Buying Process with the Combination of Asking and Proposing. In Bernhard Nebel, editor, *Proceedings of the Seventeenth International Joint Conference on Artificial Intelligence (IJCAI-01)*, pages 1443–1448. Morgan Kaufmann, 2001. Seattle, Washington, USA.
17. B. Smyth and L. McGinty. An Analysis of Feedback Strategies in Conversational Recommender Systems. In P. Cunningham, editor, *Proceedings of the Fourteenth National Conference on Artificial Intelligence and Cognitive Science (AICS-2003)*, pages 211–216, 2003. Dublin, Ireland.
18. B. Smyth and L. McGinty. The Power of Suggestion. In *Proceedings of the International Joint Conference on Artificial Intelligence (IJCAI-03)*, pages 127–138. Morgan-Kaufmann, 2003. Acapulco, Mexico.

Using CBR for Semantic Analysis of Software Specifications

Nuno Seco[1], Paulo Gomes[2], and Francisco C. Pereira[2]

[1] Department of Computer Science, University College Dublin,
Dublin 4, Ireland
nuno.seco@ucd.ie

[2] CISUC – Centro de Informática e Sistemas da Universidade de Coimbra,
Departamento de Engenharia Informática, Universidade de Coimbra,
3030 Coimbra, Portugal
{pgomes,camara}@dei.uc.pt

Abstract. Helping software designers in their task implies the development of tools with intelligent capabilities. One such capability is the integration of natural language understanding in CASE tools, thus improving the designer/tool communication. In this paper, we present a CBR approach for the generation of UML class diagrams from natural language text. This approach is implemented in a CASE tool, with the goal of helping the software designer create the first system model. We describe the natural language conversion module and give an overview of the tool in which it is integrated. Experimental results for retrieval and adaptation mechanisms are also presented.

1 Introduction

Design is a complex task involving several types of reasoning mechanisms and knowledge types [1]. In software design this holds true, especially if we think of software design as a way of computationally modelling part of the real world. Two designers have different views about the same system, and consequently, two different designs will emerge. This is just an example of the difficulties associated with software design. CASE (Computer Aided Software Engineering) tools were developed some decades ago to help the designer in the modelling of software systems. Many of these tools are only graphical editors that help the designer create diagrams that represent the system being modelled. Giving these tools capabilities beyond simple editing skills is a goal that must be attained in order to relieve the designer from boring or time consuming tasks. Another way to improve CASE tools is to integrate modules that can suggest new alternative designs or that can improve the interface between man and machine. We are interested in the second type of modules, with the main focus on developing natural language processing modules that can help the designer communicate with the CASE tool.

We are developing a CASE tool with several functions that go beyond the usual editing skills. One of the functions of this tool, is to translate a textual description of the system being developed, to the formalism used by the CASE tool. This process implies at least three steps: morphological analysis, syntactic analysis, and semantic analysis. The morphological analysis identifies the lexical category of each word. The syntactic analysis creates the parse tree of the text being analyzed, which represents the syntactic relations between the different text elements. Finally, semantic analysis associates semantic meaning to text elements and converts them into the formalism used in our CASE tool. For the first and second steps, there are well established methods to perform these analysis, stemming from the Natural Language Processing (NLP, [2,3]) community. The semantic analysis is domain dependant and requires well developed approaches to cope with the immensity of natural language. In this paper, we propose a new approach to sematic analysis of texts, and how to convert them into a software specification language.

Case-Based Reasoning (CBR, [4,5]) is generally described as a reasoning paradigm from the Artificial Intelligence area, but we think that CBR is more than that. We view CBR as a methodology to develop Knowledge-Based systems [6]. The main idea of CBR is to reuse experience to solve new problems. This experience is in the form of cases and is stored in a case base, ready for being reused. CBR is especially useful when no domain model is available, which is the specific case of our NLP task. Another characteristic of a CBR system, is that it can learn new cases, and thus evolve in time. This is a very interesting property, not only enabling the system to gradually cover the problem space, but also to adapt to the users of the system (individually).

In this paper, we present a CBR approach to semantic analysis of texts, and to the conversion of these texts into UML (Unified Modelling Language, [7]). UML is the design language used by the CASE tool that we are developing (called REBUILDER [8]) and in which this approach is implemented. The module that implements this approach is called NOESIS (**N**atural Language **O**riented **E**ngineering **S**ystem for **I**nteractive **S**pecifications) and it converts natural language text (in English) into UML class diagrams. The huge number of syntactical and semantic relations that exist in natural language, makes the development of a theory to translate every sentence (or just a representative portion of the possible sentences) very hard. This is one of the reasons why we think that CBR is an appropriate approach to this problem. Another advantage of a CBR approach, is that the system evolves in time adapting to the user modelling preferences.

The next section describes the basics of NLP, detailing the steps of an NLP module. Section 3 describes the CASE tool in which NOESIS is integrated. The NOESIS module is detailed in section 4. In section 5, we focus on the NLP steps of the conversion process and on the case representation, retrieval and adaptation mechanisms. Section 6 presents experimental work done with NOESIS. In section 7, our approach is compared with other similar approaches and some final remarks about our work are made.

2 Natural Language Processing

One of the primary goals of the AI community has been the development of computer systems capable of processing and understanding natural language. The field of NLP has roots that date to the early 1940s [2], nevertheless the goal is still far from being attained in a satisfactory manner. Many processing paradigms have been developed since then, but recently there has been a strong tendency to use empirical (corpus based) methods over rational methods, using hand-coded rules [9]. The preference for empirical methods is mainly due to the fact that developing rational systems requires a great deal of human effort and patience compared to statistical and machine learning methods.

When dealing with natural language one must be aware of the types of knowledge used in processing and understanding natural language. Systems that intend to process and understand natural language should be aware of these categories and should try to embed them into their reasoning mechanism. Though it is possible for some categories to be omitted, for example a system that deals with written text probably does not need phonetical and phonological knowledge, the role played by these categories should be present when constructing NLP systems. As stated in [2], we can identify six distinct knowledge categories:

Phonetics and Phonology Deals with the recognition of sounds and how these sounds map on to words.
Morphology Studies how words are structured and how they can be transformed, possibly by concatenation of prefixes or suffixes, into other words. Morphological knowledge also involves the correct identification of word classes (verbs, nouns, adjectives, adverbs, pronouns, ...).
Syntax Knowledge of syntax enables the construction of valid phrases and sentences. The rules used to construct a valid sentence are often defined in a grammar. Syntax plays an important role in the comprehension of language, the way words are ordered, grouped and related together to form sentences influences the way we interpret those sentences [2].
Semantics After the identification of valid word forms and sentences there is the need of assigning a meaning to these units. The selection of the correct meaning is a difficult task even for humans. This uncertainty with regard to interpretation is normally referenced to as semantic ambiguity. Ambiguity arises when a word has multiple meanings.
Pragmatics Pragmatic knowledge is concerned with the way language is used in order achieve certain goals.
Discourse The last category is knowledge of discourse. This category deals with aspects of how units larger than single utterances or sentences are constructed. This kind of knowledge allows the resolution of certain linguistic phenomenon such as anaphor.

3 REBUILDER

NOESIS is integrated into a larger system named REBUILDER, an Intelligent CASE (Computer Aided Software Engineering) tool. The main goals of RE-

BUILDER are: to create and manage a repository of software designs, and to provide cognitive functionalities capable of aiding the software designer modeling a system. NOESIS is one of these functionalities, allowing the designer to create the first version of the UML design out of natural language text.

Figure 1 shows the architecture of REBUILDER. It comprises four main modules: the UML editor, the knowledge base manager, the knowledge base (KB), and the CBR engine. It also shows the two different user types: software designers and KB administrators. Software designers use REBUILDER as a CASE tool with reuse capabilities. A KB administrator has the function of keeping the KB updated and consistent. The UML editor is the interface between REBUILDER and the software designer, while the KB manager is the interface between the KB administrator and the system.

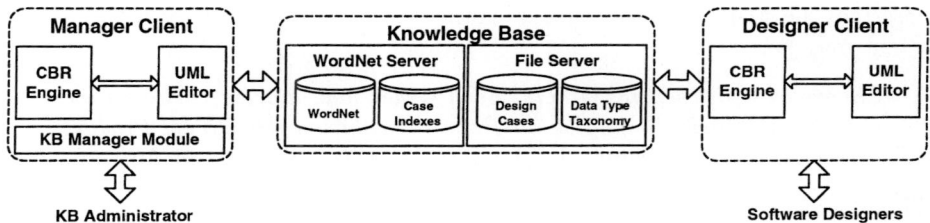

Fig. 1. REBUILDER's Architecture.

The UML editor is the front-end of REBUILDER and the environment used by the software designer. It provides the user with a graphical editor for all UML diagrams. Besides the usual editor functionalities, there are also cognitive actions, which are the extra functionalities provided by the CBR engine and the KB Manager (in the case of a KB administrator).

The KB comprises four distinct parts: the case library which stores the cases of previous software designs, or regarding NOESIS, it stores text cases; an index memory that is used for efficient case retrieval; the data type taxonomy, which is an ontology of the data types used by the system; and WordNet [7], which is a general purpose ontology. The KB Manager module is used by the administrator to manage the KB, keeping it consistent and updated.

The CBR Engine is the reasoning part of REBUILDER. As the name shows, it uses the CBR paradigm to establish a reasoning framework. This module comprises seven different parts: Retrieval, Design Composition, Design Patterns, Analogy, Verification, Learning, and NOESIS. The Retrieval sub-module retrieves cases from the case library based on the similarity with the target problem. Design Composition modifies old cases to create new solutions. It can take pieces of one or more cases to build a new solution by composition of these pieces. The Design Patterns sub-module, uses software design patterns and CBR for generation of new designs. Analogy establishes a mapping between problem and selected cases, which is then used to build a new design by knowledge transfer between the selected case and the target problem. Case Verification checks the coherence and consistency of the cases created or modified by the system. It revises a solution generated by REBUILDER before it is shown to the software designer. The learning sub-module represents the retain phase, where the system learns new cases. The cases generated by REBUILDER are stored in the case library and indexed using a memory structure. The last module is NOESIS, which is the focus of this paper.

4 NOESIS

NOESIS aims at helping the designer create the initial UML class diagram. Consequently the diagram may be submitted to the other reasoning modules completing and elaborating the initial model. The text used as input to NOESIS describes the structural requirements of the desired software. An example of such a text may be:

> *Clients can post several Orders. Each Order may include various Products. Some Products may be on Promotion during the Order. Products can be Books or Clothing. All Books must be associated to an Author.*

These texts are subject to some peculiarities and simplifications [10], which somewhat eases the difficulty of understanding them. Of these peculiarities, **explicitness** is probably one of the most simplifying ones. It is useful to reduce to a minimum the amount of unexpressed information in the requirements, avoiding future disputes of what the software should or should not do between the designer and the customer.

NOESIS, as any other NLP system, is aware of the knowledge categories identified in section 2. However, due to the specific nature of the problem some categories were omitted. Phonetic and phonological knowledge is absent because the requirements will be fed to NOESIS in the form of digital texts. The other knowledge category omitted was pragmatic knowledge. Because we assume that these texts are explicit, and that hidden implicit information is usually avoided.

Figure 2 illustrates the main modules that comprise the NLP engine of NOESIS and the process of translating a sentence. The system receives as its input a sentence in natural language representing a requirement. Sentences from the original text are sent one by one to the NLP engine for processing. Each word in the sentence is tagged with a label that identifies the grammatical class of that word. The tagged sentence is then fed to a syntactic parser, which derives the possible parse trees that the sentence can have. One of these parse trees is then chosen as the best derivation and is sent to the case based semantic analyzer, which outputs an UML class diagram. This diagram corresponds to a partial representation of the input requirement. These partial diagrams will have to be merged together before presenting a candidate solution to the user.

The first step to be executed during morphological analysis is to run a Part-Of-Speech Tagger on the sentence being processed. A Part-Of-Speech Tagger is responsible for lexically classifying each word in a sentence. The tagger used

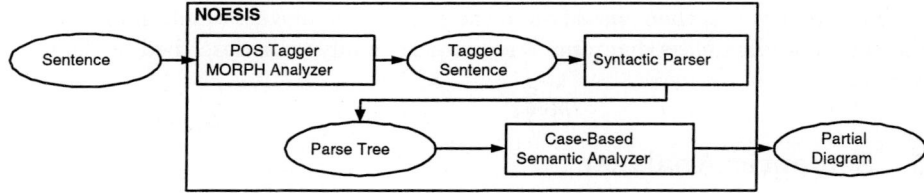

Fig. 2. NOESIS's Architecture.

in NOESIS is a stochastic tagger called QTAG[1]. QTAG [11] uses a Hidden Markov Model for selecting the tags to assign to each word. If the sentence is successfully tagged and all nouns and verbs exist in the WordNet lexicon, then the tagged sentence is passed on to the next analyzer. Otherwise, the sentence will undergo morphological processing in order to identify inflected words. These inflections are removed from the sentence and the tagger is asked to process the sentence again. If the sentence is still not correctly tagged, then the user may tag the problematic word manually. Consider the first sentence of the example text given above, the words are tagged in following manner:

Clients=NOUN can=AUXVERB post=VERB several=ADJECTIVE orders=NOUN.

The goal of the syntactic parser is to discover all valid syntactic parse trees for a given sentence. The parser is coupled with a grammar that states the rules that can be used for constructing sentences. The grammar used in NOESIS was adapted from [12] and is a context free grammar for the English language. The parsing algorithm that was implemented is based on dynamic programming and is known as the Earley algorithm [13]. After the derivation of the parse trees only one is used for semantic analysis. Returning to our example sentence, the syntactic parser would generate the derivation presented in figure 3.

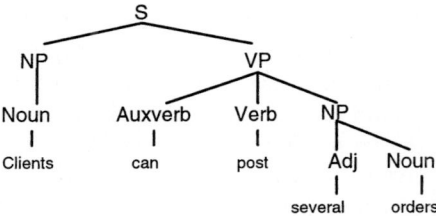

Fig. 3. Syntactic derivation of an example sentence.

---

[1] The tagger has been developed at Corpus Research in Birmingham. More information can be obtained at http://www.clg.bham.ac.uk/tagger.html

The parse tree is then passed on to the semantic analyzer, which shall produce the corresponding class diagram. The semantic analyzer is described in the next section.

5 Semantic Analyzer

A semantic analyzer receives a syntactic parse tree as input, and generates a class diagram that models the requirement text. Our analyzer uses a case based reasoning mechanism to produce a valid diagram.

5.1 Cases, The Case Library and Indexes

Previous requirements are stored and indexed as cases in the case library. Cases in NOESIS are composed of a single parse tree (the leaves are the words of the sentence), a corresponding class diagram and a mapping tuple that establishes the coupling between nouns in the sentence and the entities in the diagram. These cases are then indexed according to the verbs present in the sentence. Each verb is attributed a synset[2] from WordNet, then an index representing the case is created and attached to the corresponding synset node in WordNet. The use of verbs for indexing has to do with the fact that the verb provides a relational and semantic framework for its sentence [7]. Basically, the verb occupies a core position in the sentence, and no valid sentence may exist with out a verb. Another justification for the attachment of cases to verb synset nodes is associated with performance reasons. There are much more nouns than verbs in the English language [7], which means that searching the WordNet noun graph is much more demanding than searching the verb graph. The types of relations used to connect noun synsets are hypernym and meronym relations. In respect to verb synsets, meronym relations do not exist, these are replaced by entailment relations (specific verb clustering relations were also added) [7].

Attaching indexes to WordNet helps in the evaluation of semantic similarity, but syntax is also a very important facet in the interpretation of a sentence. In order to close this gap, we have created a second structure that is also used for indexing. This means that every index is simultaneously attached to these two different structures. Figure 4 shows how this syntactic indexing tree is organized. The root of the tree has no syntactic meaning, it simply exists for the sake of simplicity on the algorithms that use these data structures. Imagine that the nodes $s1$ and $s2$ correspond to the parse trees in figure 5, these trees could represent the syntactic derivation of the sentences "Book that flight." and "John ate the pizza.", respectively. As can be seen each node of the tree of figure 4 syntactically subsumes every other descending node, this kind of structure facilitates the assessment of syntactic similarity. We say that $s1$ subsumes $s2$ when every branch of $s1$ is contained in $s2$. This indexation tree is dynamically rearranged when new cases are added to the case base.

---

[2] A synset identifies the intended meaning for the word.

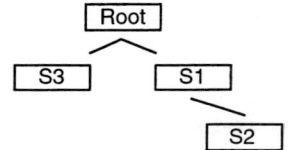

Fig. 4. Syntactic index tree.

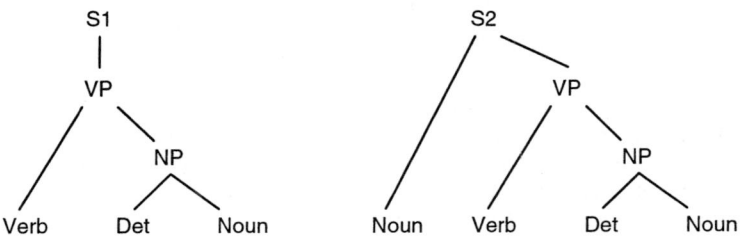

Fig. 5. Example parse trees.

5.2 Retrieval

Our retrieval algorithm consists of two substeps as encountered in [5]. We first look for relevant candidates through the use of indexes and then choose the most promising candidate that maximizes our similarity-assessment metric.

The first substep takes advantage of the implemented indexation scheme, where both WordNet and the syntactic index tree can be used. This flexibility enables the implementation of several algorithms that use both structures simultaneously or individually (giving preference either to semantics or syntax).

Four retrieval algorithms were implemented, combining the use of these structures. The implementation uses a spreading activation algorithm that expands the search to neighboring nodes until some final condition is met, ending the search. All algorithms start by using a list of entry points into the relevant structure(s). The synsets of the verbs are used as entry points into WordNet. Concerning the syntactic index tree, the entry point is the node representing the same syntactic derivation as our target sentence, or if no such node exists, a list of entry points is created containing nodes that immediately subsume and are subsumed by our target sentence. The four algorithms used by NOESIS are:

1. **Semantic Retrieval** – Only uses the WordNet verb graph.
2. **Syntactic Retrieval** – Only uses the syntactic index tree.
3. **Semantic Filtering Retrieval** – Uses the syntactic index tree, but eliminates indexes that have a semantic distance above some user defined threshold. The semantic distance between two synsets is given by the minimum number of arcs between them in the WordNet graph.
4. **Conjunctive Retrieval** – Uses both structures simultaneously. Intersecting indexes that are reached during the search on both structures. These indexes are considered valid and may be returned.

5.3 Similarity Assessment

The second substep ranks each of the cases returned by the retrieval algorithm. The cases returned by the retrieval algorithms comprise a parse tree. This parse tree is then used for similarity assessment. We use four different criterions as the basis for ranking cases:

- Syntactic Similarity is given by:

$$\frac{\frac{\#\ intersect(target,\ source)}{\#\ nodes(target)} + \frac{\#\ intersect(target,\ source)}{\#\ nodes(source)}}{2} \quad (1)$$

Where *intersect* computes a list of nodes that are syntactically common in both parse trees and *nodes* returns a list of nodes contained in the tree. Basically, it computes the similarity between the target and source parse trees.
- Semantic Similarity is given by:

$$\frac{dist(nouns(target), nouns(source)) + dist(verbs(target), verbs(source))}{2 \times MSL} \quad (2)$$

Where *dist* computes the semantic distance between noun synsets or verb synsets. *nouns* and *verbs* return a list of the nouns or verbs contained in the parse tree. MSL (Maximum Search Length) defines the maximum number of arcs that the search may transverse, if the distance can not be computed the value of the MSL is returned. This formula assesses the conceptual distance between concepts in sentences using WordNet as an ontology, which is used for computing distances between concepts.
- Contextual Similarity is given by:

$$\begin{cases} 1 & \text{if } source \text{ belongs to a text from which a sentence was previously used} \\ 0 & \text{otherwise} \end{cases} \quad (3)$$

The idea behind this similarity metric, is that if a sentence from the same text as the one being evaluated, has already been used, then it should have a higher similarity. This way, we are trying to give preference to sentences from the same text.
- Discourse Similarity is given by:

$$\frac{1}{(sentenceNumber(target) - sentenceNumber(source))^2 + 1} \quad (4)$$

Where *sentencenumber* returns the absolute position of the sentence in the original text. This metric assesses the similarity of sentences relative to their position in the text they are part of. Assuming that text sentences have a coherent structure.

All equations (1, 2, 3, 4) are normalized yielding values between [0..1]. After the calculation of each of these components a weighted sum is used to evaluate the overall similarity between the target tree and the source tree. Cases are then ranked and the case that maximizes (5) is chosen for reuse.

$$Sim(target, source) = \omega_1 \cdot SyntacticSimilarity + \omega_2 \cdot SemanticSimilarity + \\ \omega_3 \cdot ContextSimilarity + \omega_4 \cdot DiscourseSimilarity \quad (5)$$

Assume that a case represented in figure 6 is retrieved and selected, according to the similarity metric, as the best candidate for our example problem sentence. Note that the case is composed of a syntactic derivation tree, an UML diagram and a mapping tuple as was mentioned in sectionCasesSection. In the next section, we show how this case is adapted to the problem domain.

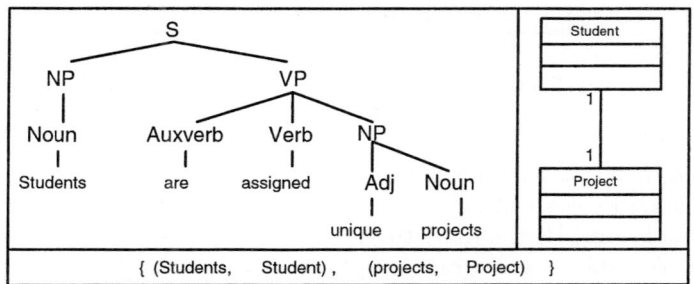

Fig. 6. Example of a case stored in the Case Library.

5.4 Adaptation

After all sentences of the target text have been mapped with a similar source sentence, the adaptation phase begins. Adaptation starts by loading the actual diagrams, specified by the selected cases into memory. Then the names of the entities from the source diagrams are replaced with the nouns encountered in the target sentence. This substitution of names is possible because each case holds the mapping (see section 5.1) between the sentence nouns and the diagram entities, this mapping is denoted by:

$$\Upsilon : Source_{sentence} \longrightarrow Source_{diagram} \qquad (6)$$

Having defined the correspondence function between nouns and entities, we need a function that can map nouns from the target sentence with the nouns that appear in the source sentence. A simple algorithm was used to accomplish this task, basically the isomorphism between nouns is established based on their relative positions in each sentence. This means that the first noun in one sentence will be isomorphic to the first noun of the second sentence and so on. The correspondence is denoted by:

$$\Gamma : Target_{sentence} \longrightarrow Source_{sentence} \qquad (7)$$

Obtaining a diagram for the target sentence is now a matter of discovering the mappings between $Target_{sentence}$ and $Source_{diagram}$, this is easily accomplished by applying formula (8) and replacing the names of the entities in the diagram with the nouns in the sentence.

$$\Upsilon \circ \Gamma : Target_{sentence} \longrightarrow Source_{diagram} \qquad (8)$$

Considering the case chosen in the previous section as the best case for our problem sentence and applying transformation (8) we obtain the diagram of figure 7.

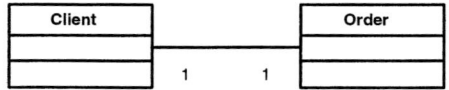

Fig. 7. Generated diagram for the sentence "Clients can post several orders".

It should be noted that this partial diagram is not totally correct, the multiplicity of the Order association end should be * and not 1, which was transferred from the source case. Hence, this situation must be corrected in the Retain phase (next section) if this new diagram is to be stored as a case.

Applying the above process yields a set of partial diagrams. There will be as many diagrams as target sentences. It will frequently occur that each diagram will have entities with the same name (some simple inflections may exist), these entities are then merged, resulting in a single diagram, which is presented to the user.

5.5 Retain

The suggested diagram may be altered by user modifications. If there were many modifications on the suggested diagram, this may indicate a lack of coverage of the case base. Which opens the possibility of retaining this new case for future use, if the user recognizes the same lack of coverage he/she may submit the case to the case library. The administrator must then decide if the submitted case is or not worth being made available for retrieval.

6 Preliminary Experimental Studies

In this section we present some results of preliminary experimentations. The aim of these experiments is to compare the output of NOESIS's solution with one of a software designer. We are aware of the subjectivity involved in these experiments, since the ideal environment for testing NOESIS is in a real software production environment.

The results presented are based on a case base compromising 62 cases, which correspond to 12 different texts (an average of 4 sentences per text). A set of 22 problems (an average of 3 sentence per problem) were used for testing the overall accuracy of the system.

For each problem text, a corresponding class diagram was designed by a software designer. The same problems were given to NOESIS and the two solutions were compared using a class diagram comparison metric. This metric returns a

Table 1. Weight configurations for formula 5.

ω	C01	C02	C03	C04	C05	C06	C07	C08	C09	C10	C11	C12	C13	C14	C15
ω_1	1	0	0	0	0.5	0.5	0.5	0	0	0	0.33	0.33	0.33	0	0.25
ω_2	0	1	0	0	0.5	0	0	0.5	0.5	0	0.33	0.33	0	0.33	0.25
ω_3	0	0	1	0	0	0.5	0	0.5	0	0.5	0.33	0	0.33	0.33	0.25
ω_4	0	0	0	1	0	0	0.5	0	0.5	0.5	0	0.33	0.33	0.33	0.25

number ranging from 0 to 1, where 1 represents an identical match and 0 two completely different diagrams. This metric is actually part of a larger evaluation system, which computes the similarity between two packages (each package may contain a diagram and several other packages), a detailed explanation can be found in [14].

The four retrieval algorithms presented in section 5.2 along with a set of weight configurations of formula 5 were combined resulting in 60 different configurations. (see table 1). The Semantic Filtering Retrieval algorithm was used with a predefined threshold of 5 (see section 5.2). Each problem was solved using each of the configurations presented in table 1.

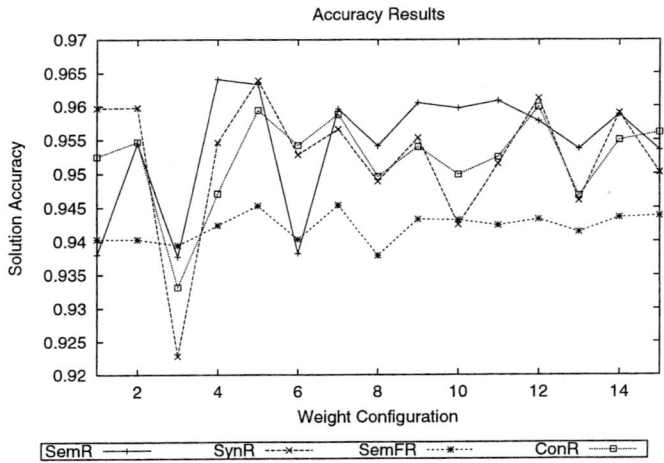

Fig. 8. Average Accuracy of Solutions. SemR - Semantic Retrieval; SynR - Syntactic Retrieval; SemFR - Semantic Filtering Retrieval; ConR - Conjunctive Retrieval.

Figure 8 shows the average accuracy of the generated solutions using each of the configurations presented previously.

These results show us that configuration C03 (where only context is used for similarity assessment) has inferior accuracy for all retrieval algorithms. The Semantic Filtering Retrieval algorithm performs worse than all other algorithms, this may be caused by the low threshold value used. This plot may also indicate that the adaptation mechanism, independent of the retrieval algorithm, is able to adapt the retrieved cases to the target situation. Nevertheless, the accuracy values are high, being in the range of 92% to 96.5% (see table 2).

Table 2. Analysis of accuracy results for the retrieval algorithms (in percentage).

Algorithm	Average	Standard Deviation	Confidence Interval (95%)
SynR	95.43	0.91	[94.97, 95.89]
SemR	95.23	1.01	[94.72, 95.74]
SemFR	94.21	0.22	[94.10, 94.32]
ConR	95.22	0.67	[94.89, 95.56]

The computation time of each retrieval algorithm was also assessed, results are shown in table 3. Configuration C15 was used in these experiment since it is the only configuration that uses all the four similarity criteria. Each algorithm was run 10 times for each one of the 22 problems. These results show that, although the syntactic retrieval has the best accuracy results, it's computation time is one of the most time demanding. The semantic retrieval has the worst results, which can be explained by WordNet dimensions, where it can have to search to many nodes until it reaches the desired ones. The other two retrieval algorithms have the best results, showing that there is a trade-off between computational efficiency and accuracy.

Table 3. Analysis of computation time results for the retrieval algorithms (in seconds).

Algorithm	Average	Standard Deviation	Confidence Interval (95%)
SynR	7.42	0.73	[6.99, 7.86]
SemR	10.99	0.66	[10.60, 11.38]
SemFR	4.65	0.31	[4.46, 4.83]
ConR	5.58	0.72	[5.16, 6.01]

7 Related Work

Hoppenbrouwers et al. [15] use a methodology often used in Information Extraction [16], where textual elements are semantically tagged and are put together by filling predefined template slots. The filled templates are then translated into an initial model that the user may modify.

In [17] another approach is proposed for the generation of object-oriented specifications from natural language. Their approach is based on a formal definition of relations between linguistic and object-oriented conceptual structures. A set of linguistic patterns is defined along with a function that translates these patterns into predicate logic. A similar mapping is established between conceptual patterns and set theory. Finally an equivalence function is defined between predicate logic and set theory, enabling the transformation of natural language texts into a conceptual model.

CIRCE [10] is a web-based environment for aiding natural language requirements gathering, elicitation, selection and validation. A central component of this system, used for the creation of the models, is a glossary describing and classifying all the domain and system-specific terms used in the requirements text, each term is associated with a set of tags. This glossary is manually or semi-manually built for the domain to be modelled. When a text is processed, words are tagged with the aid of the predefined glossary. Afterwards a set of rules, denoted as MAS (Model Action and Substitution) rules, are used for recognizing the tagged text, resulting in a forest of parse trees, with which the system can build several types of models.

NOESIS differs from these systems basically because of its learning capabilities. The retention of new cases allows NOESIS to learn new modelling patterns and adapt itself to the users linguistic practice. Nevertheless NOESIS still needs predefined linguistic knowledge in order to produce conceptual models. The linguistic knowledge used in this initial prototype is a very reduced subset of the actual necessary knowledge.

8 Conclusions and Future Work

This paper presents a CBR approach for the translation of natural language into UML class diagrams, which is implemented in a CASE tool. One advantage of using CBR to perform semantic analysis of sentences, is that CBR does not need a domain theory. In software design is very difficult to come up with a domain theory, since the designer is modelling part of the real world. Another advantage of CBR, is that it enables learning of new knowledge in the form of cases. Not only can the system evolve in time, but it can also learn the designers' modelling preferences. In NOESIS, cases reflect these modelling preferences, enabling a continuous learning of the system. The adaptation mechanisms used, are crucial in the solution generation, since they are able to combine and adapt several different cases.

The experimental results shown in section 6 are not conclusive, but they do motivate further research in using CBR as the main reasoning mechanism for translation of software descriptions into class diagrams. This work has raised several issues that can be tackled or improved. One of these issues is extending the system to deal with attributes and methods, which is going to be the next step in NOESIS development. Another improvement is to establish a case base maintenance policy capable of dealing with the rapid increase of the number of cases in the case base.

References

1. Tong, C., Sriram, D.: Artificial Intelligence in Engineering Design. Volume I. Academic Press (1992)
2. Daniel Jurafsky, J.H.M.: Speech and Language Processing. Prentice Hall (2000)

3. Manning, C., Schütze, H. In: Foundations of Statistical Natural Language Processing. The MIT Press, Cambridge, US (1999)
4. Aamodt, A., Plaza, E.: Case–based reasoning: Foundational issues, methodological variations, and system approaches. AI Communications **7** (1994) 39–59
5. Kolodner, J.: Case-Based Reasoning. Morgan Kaufmann, San Mateo, California (1993)
6. Althoff, K.D.: Case-based reasoning. In Chang, S.K., ed.: Handbook on Software Engineering and Knowledge Engineering. Volume 1., World Scientific (2001) 549–588
7. Miller, G., Beckwith, R., Fellbaum, C., Gross, D., Miller, K.J.: Introduction to wordnet: an on-line lexical database. International Journal of Lexicography **3** (1990) 235 – 244
8. Gomes, P., Pereira, F.C., Paiva, P., Seco, N., Carreiro, P., Ferreira, J.L., Bento, C.: Case retrieval of software designs using wordnet. In Harmelen, F.v., ed.: European Conference on Artificial Intelligence (ECAI'02), Lyon, France, IOS Press, Amsterdam (2002)
9. Eric Brill, R.J.M.: An overview of empirical natural language processing. AI Magazine **18** (1997) 13–24
10. Ambriola, V., Gervasi, V.: Processing natural language requirements. In: Proc. of the 12th International Conference on Automated Software Engineering, Los Alamitos, IEEE Computer Society Press (1997) 36–45
11. Tufis, D., Mason, O.: Tagging romanian texts: a case study for qtag, a language independent probabilistic tagger. Proceedings of the First International Conference on Language Resources and Evaluation (LREC) (1998) 589–596
12. Oliveira, A.: Relatório técnico-cientifico, textstorm - leitura e análise automática de textos (2000)
13. Earley, J.: An efficient context-free parsing algorithm. Communications of the ACM **13** (1970) 94–102
14. Gomes, P., Pereira, F.C., Paiva, P., Seco, N., Carreiro, P., Ferreira, J.L., Bento, C.: Experiments on case-based retrieval of software designs. In: European Conference on Case-Based Reasoning (ECCBR'02), Aberdeen, Scotland (2002)
15. Hoppenbrouwers, J., van den Heuvel, W., Hoppenbrouwers, S., Weigand, H., de Troyer, O.: The grammalizer: A case tool based on textual analysis (1997)
16. Wilks, Y., Cowie, J. In: Information Extraction. In R. Dale, H. Moisl and H. Somers (eds.) Handbook of Natural Language Processing. Marcel Dekker (2000) 241–260
17. Juristo, N., Morant, J.L., Moreno, A.M.: A formal approach for generating oo specifications from natural language. The Journal of Systems and Software **48** (1999) 139–153

An Indexing Scheme for Case-Based Manufacturing Vision Development

Chengbo Wang[1], John Johansen[1], and James T. Luxhøj[2]

[1] Center for Industrial Production, Aalborg University, Fibigerstræde 16,
9220, Aalborg, Denmark
{chengbo,jj}@iprod.auc.dk

[2] Department of Industrial and Systems Engineering, Rutgers University,
96 Frelinghuysen Road, Piscataway, New Jersey 08854-8018, USA
jluxhoj@rci.rutgers.edu

Abstract. This paper focuses on one critical element, indexing – retaining and representing knowledge in an applied case-based reasoning (CBR) model for supporting strategic manufacturing vision development (CBRM). Manufacturing vision (MV) is a kind of knowledge management concept and process concerned with the competence improvement of an enterprise's manufacturing system. There are two types of cases within the CBRM – an event case (EC) and a general supportive case (GSC). We designed one set of indexing vocabulary for the two types of cases, but a different indexing representation structure for each of them. In this paper, after the background introduction of the MV, the CBRM and the indexing challenges of the MV cases, we present the structure and content of the index vocabulary and the two indexing representation structures, then illustrate briefly the indexing of cases with two examples. We also summarize the methods, primary conclusions of test runs with the indexing scheme. Further research work to refine the index vocabulary is discussed as well.

1 Introduction

Indexing, as a knowledge categorization and representation method, plays a critical role in a case-based reasoning (CBR) system in organizing the case information into the case base for retention and for subsequent retrieval. The "indexing problem" is a key problem in case-based reasoning [1].

To be more particular, indexes are composed by the features describing that in which circumstances a case might be found useful by a reasoner [3]. Indexes must be both abstract and concrete enough for effective performance of a CBR system.

Our work for indexing aroused in the development of a CBR model for manufacturing vision (MV) development (CBRM) [4]. The CBRM is an application of the CBR methodology in the field of manufacturing strategy development. It is briefly introduced together with MV in the next section. Its target is to help an enterprise to find and establish a competitive manufacturing portfolio (namely MV) to assure its healthy survival and success in the fiercely competitive marketplace.

Nevertheless, in the domain of strategy on manufacturing and the relationship of its sub-systems, the contents and contexts of the available cases and their application environment are very complicated. When trying to find a previous similar case to deal with a new problem, there could be numerous properties possible to be used for reminding, but which of them are the ones that could be unequivocal and recognizable enough to help select the previous cases really needed? And how to describe the content and formulate the structure of the index vocabulary to make it easier to be understood and applied by practitioners in real world operations? These are the challenging tasks for a CBR model aimed at the domain of manufacturing strategy formulation.

As noted by Kolodner [3], it is perhaps impossible to obtain a complete covering index vocabulary regarding all the aspects of a CBR system concerned domain; what we can and should endeavor towards is a functional working set of indexes to cluster and to represent the case knowledge.

Based on the categorization of the two different types of cases in our research – EC and GSC (detailed in the next section), in order for clustering the domain knowledge for MV development, we created one set of index vocabulary but expressed in two different types of indexing structure. The index vocabulary is termed by us as the indexing matrix for MV development (IM-MVD), which is expressed in the form of a relational table containing the so called feature-value pairs in CBR terminology. One type of indexing structure is the changeable-slot indexing structure (CSIEC) representation for the majority of ECs. Another is the fixed-slot indexing structure (FSGSC) representation for GSCs and some ECs.

This paper is structured in this way: in next section are the general backgrounds regarding MV and CBR's application in MV research – the CBRM, as well as the cases and case base and the indexing challenges. Then the methodology and the introduction of the designed index vocabulary – IM-MVD are presented; particularly, the nominal group technique used to conduct the creation process is also briefly described in this section. After which the index representation structures of CSIEC and FSGSC are also illustrated. Following them are the test run methods of the index vocabulary and the primary conclusions. The paper is finalized by a presentation of the future research.

2 General Fundamental Backgrounds

In this section, the background and basic concepts regarding the manufacturing vision (MV) and the CBR model for MV development – CBRM, the cases/case base and the indexing challenges within the model are briefly illustrated.

2.1 Conception of MV and CBRM

Within recent two decades, the expedited changing industrial conditions and the global competition environment have brought tremendous pressure to the manufacturing enterprises. Responding to these challenges, every enterprise needs to set up a robust strategy in manufacturing to help achieve the general corporate mission. The competitive advantage is to be achieved, when manufacturing decisions are created with a holistic view to synthesize the strengths within the organization towards the realization of corporate strategy [5] [6] [7].

To address the problem of competent manufacturing strength generation, a quite new concept, manufacturing vision (MV), was put forward by some researchers [8], [9]. MV is defined as a company specific, commonly shared, holistic picture of the way in which future manufacturing in the company will function [8]. It links the corporate strategy to the production system design. It identifies the methods and ways to ensure that enterprises stay competitive in a changing environment, and responds to the rapid change in technological and global competition. The concept of MV and its development process, function dynamically in enabling and supporting the enterprise achieving its corporate strategy and maintaining its competitive advantages in the global economic environment. In order to grasp and collaborate the creative ideas and knowledge of the employees and management of a company for the setup of a MV, Riis and Johansen [8] proposed a process, which consists of five phases; Maslen and Platts [9] have also suggested relevant methods for a MV creation.

Nevertheless, the research around MV is in an early stage, there is still a lack of generic tools easily understandable and extensively applicable to help run the entire MV development process effectively and efficiently.

Case-Based Reasoning (CBR), as both a methodology for modeling the reasoning and thinking of human being, and a methodology to support the construction of intelligent computer systems [10], has its special effective property to tackle the complex/open/real world problems, such as MV development.

As noted by Althoff and Bartsch-Spoerl [11], quite often, classical Artificial Intelligence (AI) approaches cannot be used in complex, open and real world domains; under these conditions CBR may be the only chance to provide effective support. Many aspects involved in improving an enterprise's manufacturing system competence belong to this category. Besides, compared with other techniques, CBR still has some further advantages [10] [12] as an approach to incremental, sustained learning: reduce the knowledge acquisition effort; require less maintenance effort; improve over time and adapt to changes in the environment; high user acceptance.

Based on the understanding of the MV's development process and the methodology/application of CBR, we have designed a CBR model for MV development – CBRM, the details of the contents and structure of CBRM are provided in Wang, Luxhøj and Johansen [4].

2.2 The Cases and Case Base for the CBRM and Their Indexing Challenges

In order to make the CBRM effective, the knowledge storage – case base must be filled by representative cases that contain the relevant previous knowledge that could be used for solving new problems. These cases' information will facilitate to synthesize the manufacturing portfolio of competitive advantages for supporting an enterprise to survive and succeed. The cases are collected and codified from literatures and practical case reports, as well as the ones generated by the CBRM after the model execution in practice.

Considering the practical conditions of the obtained cases and the application of cases in the knowledge domain of MV, we divide the cases in the case base into two categories: an event case (EC) and a general supportive case (GSC).

An EC is the kind of case that holds the information regarding the real world concrete strategic and tactical activities performed by organizations to eliminate their weakness, to improve competence, to enhance their strength, etc. The content of an EC normally consists of the following parts: the problem description, including the present problems faced by the firm and/or the future targets to achieve; the solutions, including the countermeasures to deal with the current problems in a long-term strategic view, and the means to improve the competences for achieving future targets; the outcome or anticipated outcome by implementing the case solutions, if possible; and the action plans to implement the activities for realizing the strategic tasks, when available.

A GSC is the kind of case that holds the information regarding the generalized best techniques and practices in operations, so called 'best practices', which could be integrated into a new MV and also be the inspiring stars for arousing new ideas. The content of a GSC consists of the problems and/or the environment description for the functioning of the practically proven or the researchers proposed good practices/techniques; the description of the certain best practices/techniques; the consequences of using the practices/techniques; and the ways to apply them, when available.

The major differences between ECs and GSCs are: an EC is only a "good experience" for a certain enterprise, and if another organization desires to use it, normally they must make an adaptation; while, a GSC is globally applicable in similar industrial situations. Typically, a GSC has far less content than an EC, and it is also more focused on a certain aspect of manufacturing.

Before the cases can be used in the model's processing to generate an applicable MV, one must index them for retention into the case base and so that the CBRM can retrieve them during the processing.

Although there are some index paradigms for CBR system application, such as the Universal Index Frame (UIF) from Schank and Osgood [3] [13], and CreekL from Aamodt [2], there is not a concrete index vocabulary existing that could be directly used in the domain of MV development to describe the complicated contextual and content situation. Meanwhile, the contents of the available cases are also quite complex with disparate information in them. This brings many challenges for creating guidelines, i.e., index vocabulary that will instruct the indexing work of a practitioner in charge of knowledge acquisition and retention within the field.

Concerning all the factors in practice and the structure of the software (Intellix Desiner 4.1 from Intellix A/S, Denmark) used in support of case retrieval and retention, we decide to develop one set of focused index vocabulary, namely IM-MVD, for the manufacturing strategy related areas; and based on the understanding of the frame representation structure [14] [15] [16] [17], we use the slot-filler expression format in representing the cases, with two types of indexing representation structure – CSIEC and FSGSC. In the IM-MVD, the aspects and their condition descriptions for MV decision areas appear as feature-value pairs that are a commonly adopted effective and efficient approach in commercial usage [18]. For the indexing representation, the slot is stuffed by the feature in IM-MVD, and the filler stuffed by the value.

In the next sections, the creation methodology and detailed structure and contents of the index vocabulary and the indexing representation structures, as well as the example indexing scheme on both of the two types of cases are described.

3 Creating the Index Vocabulary – IM-MVD and Applying the Indexing Scheme

3.1 Methodology for IM-MVD Creation

The theoretical background of the creation of the indexing vocabulary comes from the functional approach and the reminding approach [3]. According to the understanding from the description about the two approaches by Kolodner, the functional approach is to check and analyze the contents and structures of a set of available cases obtained either from literature and/or directly from practices, try to discern what each case can be used for and the ways it needs to be indexed to make it easier identified when in need; the reminding approach is to examine the reminding points that commonly exist among domain experts who know exactly the contexts and contents of the certain cases, and can choose and determine the similar aspects between the current and previous conditions, the experts recall which kinds of aspects and related condition descriptions are important to judge similarity in the corresponding circumstances.

Here in this research, we made an extension on the reminding approach. When using it, besides asking the experts to recall the most likely popping out aspects and related possible condition descriptions regarding the actual cases, we emphasize that the aspects could be from hypothetical cases with the relevant solutions generated by their expertise, i.e., to ask them first to form hypothetical cases that could happen, and then to tease out the points of reminding; in this way, the experts could have more space to play with the full use of their domain knowledge and expertise, and the index vocabulary could also be enriched.

Procedurally, the indexing vocabulary creation is fulfilled through three phases:

The first phase involves extensive search of the relevant literature and case reports, comparing them, then abstracting the representative aspects and condition descriptions within the decision areas of MV focused by this research, i.e., find the relevant case features and value descriptions that could be predictive and representative. This step is in accordance with the functional approach.

The second phase involves using the extended reminding approach through a technique called nominal group (briefly described in the next sub-section), to gain another set of possible features and values from the experts' view.

The third phase is to triangulate, modify, practically combine and synthesize the features and values gained from the two approaches to form a workable index vocabulary table – the IM-MVD.

According to Kolodner [3], developing an index vocabulary is an incremental pragmatic process. Thus, the approach of maturing by testing is used to make this prototyping index vocabulary more towards high degree of representative ability.

3.2 Nominal Group Technique (NGT)

The nominal group technique is used to identify and solve problems by collecting and sharing individual opinions. It is a process for a group of people who become a group in name only when they are using the technique; at the time that the group uses the technique they avoid the normal problems of a few individuals doing all the talking, the rest listening, and very few people taking the time to actually think about the issue at hand [19] [20] [21]. The NGT helps to overcome these common problems often encountered in small group meetings organized for the purpose of generating ideas and problem solving. By NGT, individuals can be more creative and everyone is given a structured opportunity to participate.

The NGT herein used is adapted in order to reduce the time consumed and to improve the efficiency during the group sessions, which is called as a modified nominal group technique (MNGT). Details about MNGT session are provided in Wang [22].

3.3 Details of the IM-MVD

In the following, we introduce the index vocabulary – IM-MVD.

The IM-MVD can be regarded as a kind of authority file. An authority file contains a set of controlled vocabulary, i.e., it is a set of specially designated items used during indexing [23]. When the end user desires to index the real world stories into case base, they will walk through the items in the IM-MVD to pick out the representative ones to compose a set of distinctive indexes. Also, we apply the IM-MVD as instruction on the knowledge acquisition work in gathering information and formulating the contents of cases.

As stated before, the IM-MVD is acquired through the codifying of the results from both the functional approach and the extended reminding approach. Nevertheless, when performing indexing on a certain case, not all of these features/values will be needed, i.e., not all of them will be used for one certain case. Their existence in the IM-MVD is forming a resource for combining some of them as a portfolio at the time when indexing an individual case into case base.

Within the CBR community, there are some certain principles for index determination [3] [18]: indexes should be predictive for certain circumstances; the predictions should be useful for identifying the usage of the case; indexes should be abstract enough to cover various situations; indexes should be concrete enough for easy and accurate retrieval against a new problem situation. During the generation of the IM-MVD, we attempted to follow these principles.

In general, the content of a case for MV can be clustered into three main parts, the first part is the situation description, i.e. the occurring circumstances and the contextual domain; the second part is the description of the concrete countermeasures, i.e., case solutions; the third part is the outcomes of the implemented solutions, and the action plans. The case index vocabulary focuses on these three aspects to make the representation accurate to support effective and efficient retention and retrieval.

Table 1 is an example format of the IM-MVD, the first column is the classification of the general categories clustering the issues within the domain of a MV, i.e., general organizational profile, hard factors and soft factors [4]; the second column includes the detailed decision areas of a manufacturing system focused on by the CBRM; the third column includes the features used for indexing cases that correspond to the concretized aspects within a certain decision area of manufacturing system; the fourth column lists the value-describing prepositions (VDPs) that indicate the type of time horizon of the values indexing the case information consisting of the is-condition (IS_C) and the to-be-condition (TB_C). IS_C means the actual state the indexed case is in; TB_C means the future state the indexed case will approach. When users index the practical cases, they could use either IS_C or TB_C to represent the information in seeking to make case indexes more inclusive and expressive. The columns starting from the fifth column are the possible values of the relevant features.

Table 1. The example format of IM-MVD

General categories	Concerned decision areas	Features and values — Features	Value describing preposition (VDP)	Alternative feature value 1	Alternative feature value 2	...
General profile	GENERAL	Type of enterprise	IS_C / TB_C	manufacturing	manufacturing, batch production	...
		Annual revenue	IS_C/ TB_C	USD 50M	USD 100M	...
		Enterprise history	IS_C / TB_C	founded in 19th century	founded in 1962	...
		Organizational diversity	IS_C / TB_C	single BU	multi BUs	...
		Geographical scope	IS_C / TB_C	single place	multi-places	...
		Product structure	IS_C / TB_C	complex	simple	...
Hard factors	LOCATION	Factory location	IS_C / TB_C	ecological unharmful	transportation opportunities well assured	...
		Local infrastructure	IS_C / TB_C	incomplete	completed and supportive	...
		Industrial Complexes	IS_C / TB_C	unpleasant to the local people	friendly to local people	...
	:	:	:	:	:	...
	:	Current and planned tansporting-MH equipments	IS_C / TB_C	space arranged and layouted	routine designed and leaned	...
		:	:	:	:	
Soft factors	:	:	:	:	:	

To ensure the consistency of indexing between different users, there are some rules to be followed while applying the VDP: 1) Indexing for retention: for the target, use TB_C; for the strategic approaches and other relevant information about manufacturing system, use IS_C; if the IS_C description is not possible and the information is available to describe the to-be situation, apply TB_C; if both TB_C and IS_C apply, then use IS_C. 2) For indexing a new case information for retrieval of previous cases, follow the same rule.

In the IM-MVD, the user is also provided the possibility to add more values and features into the vocabulary in case of new findings that can be done by using the reminding approach [3] run in a MNGT session.

For a particular feature, its value could have two different properties: open-end description and close-end description. Open-end values refer to those that are different while not necessarily opposite, and the numbers of alternatives could be as many as available; and could be multiple choices for the same feature, in this condition, the feature-value pairs will be respectively listed. Since close-end values are those that hold the mutually exclusive alternative values, the number of alternative values will be less. The open-end and close-end value types are just used for the research aim of classifying the possible alternative value descriptions. In practice, the user-oriented IM-MVD table will not list this property.

The focused manufacturing decision areas within the IM-MVD include the process and layout design, location, capacity management, time management, inventory management, quality, human resource management (HRM), workforce organization and culture, plus the general profile of a case entity. The aspects within these decision areas are features, and their situation or state descriptions are feature values. The features and values form the detailed contents of the IM-MVD accommodating the various practical case conditions.

In the case base of the CBRM, two types of information of a case are stored. One type is the indexed abstracted information; another type is the concrete description of the context and content of a case. The IM-MVD is the guideline to link the two types of information. Whether an EC or a GSC in the case base of CBRM, all that exists is their abstracted index information, i.e., in the CBRM case base, the retrieved "cases" are only the names of the cases, not the concrete contents. The main knowledge body of cases will be stored in another library, in which cases will be described in the form of natural language expressed in a standardized structured format. We would like to call this name-case-base as meta-case-base. It is connected by an embedding frame model designed using Visual Basic (VB) 6.0, to the real case-body library [24].

The procedural flow chart of applying the IM-MVD to index knowledge source in the CBRM is as shown in Figure 1.

3.4 Example Indexation by Applying the IM-MVD

Using the CSIEC representation structure to index EC. The following is an example of using the CSIEC, applying the IM-MVD vocabulary items, to index a part of the information from a test EC, which is formulated through both the literature and our practical experience. The majority of ECs within the CBRM have different features and various values; the case base composed by this type of cases is a kind of heterogeneous case base, according to Watson [18]. For those ECs with the same features but different values, use FSGSC to index them, which is normally used for GSCs within this research.

An Indexing Scheme for Case-Based Manufacturing Vision Development

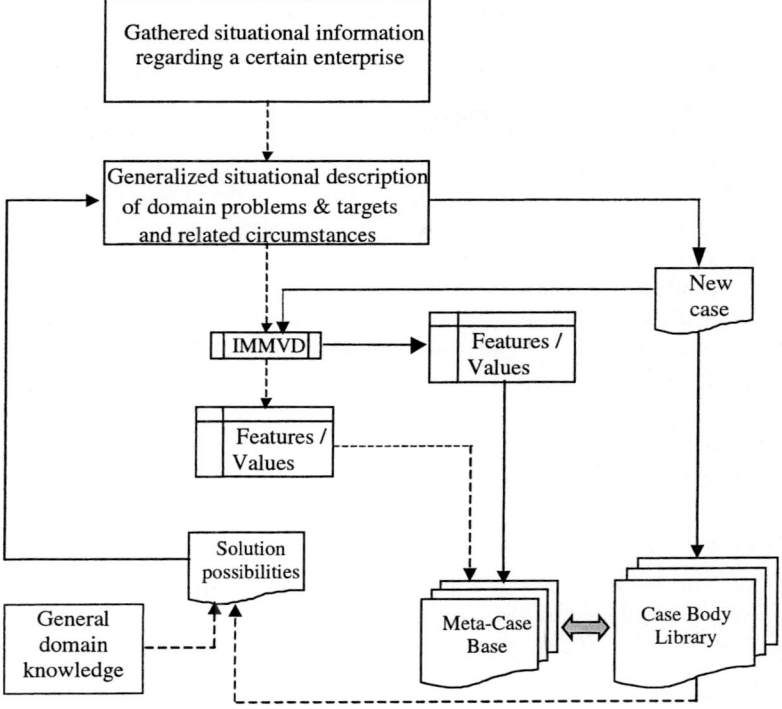

Fig. 1. The functional flow of applying IM-MVD

The part of case information is as follows:

Manufacturing process appeared much older, although the manufacturing machinery was about only 10 years old.

Numbers of current employees are more than needed for the same production volume compared with the competitors, this means either the full potential of the production system is not explored or the people are surplus over the technological structure and infrastructure need.

Planning and control on production system is not in harmony, semi-finished goods often sit for several days waiting for complementary parts, which are out of stock, resulting the final assembly has lots of discontinuities. This reflects the technological and production control information systems function ineffectively and inefficiently.

Figure 2 is the example of indexes on the case information.

EC-xyz

Changeable slot	VDP	Filler
Processing technology vs. up to date standard	IS_C	inferior
Stage on life span of machines	IS_C	in the medium of machine life span
Material and information flows within or outside of the enterprise and its physical structure	IS_C	ineffective and inefficient, not well planed
Capacity of employees	IS_C	more than needed
Manufacturing process attributes	TB_C	well throughput time control

Fig. 2. Example indexing using CSIEC

The indexes are input to the CBRM and stored in the EC division for case retention and retrieval.

Using FSGSC representation structure to index GSC. The FSGSC uses the same features but various value descriptions for different cases, the case base composed by this type of cases is a kind of homogeneous case base, according to Watson [18].

When indexing a GSC, the features in the IM-MVD could also be used as lower level value descriptions while necessary; we cluster this condition in the additional column of FSGSC, called as a sub-filler. In Figure 3, we use the indexes on a quality problem as an example to show the FSGSC indexing representation.

The indexes will also be input into case base and stored in the GSC division.

Case-qi		
Core problem aspect	Scrap level	Very high
Focused points	Inspection and control methods	Does not exist

Fig. 3. Example indexing using FSGSC

4 Testing the Indexing Approaches

4.1 Test Method

The IM-MVD has completed test runs within academic circles, both in Denmark and the USA. The tests were performed by different indexers with dissimilar theoretical and empirical backgrounds.

The procedure is composed of the following three phases:

1) indexing a case story by going through the items in the IM-MVD, 2) then doing case retrieval work based on the indexes, 3) checking the effectiveness of the indexing based on the comparison of the retrieved results.

4.2 Test Results

In Table 2, we summarize the indexes from different indexers and the retrieved results by using them; the indexers did the indexing by following the IM-MVD. For the same indexing contents of the testing case, the indexers have determined different numbers of indexed items. What the results show is that for the situation with more items indexed, the retrieved case numbers are less.

Table 2. Indexation results by different indexers

Indexer	1	2	3	4	5
Indexed item numbers	30	30	24	58	75
Retrieved case numbers	5	6	6	3	1

Figure 4 visualizes the relationship between the indexed item numbers and the retrieved case numbers; the dotted lines are the trends of each curve.

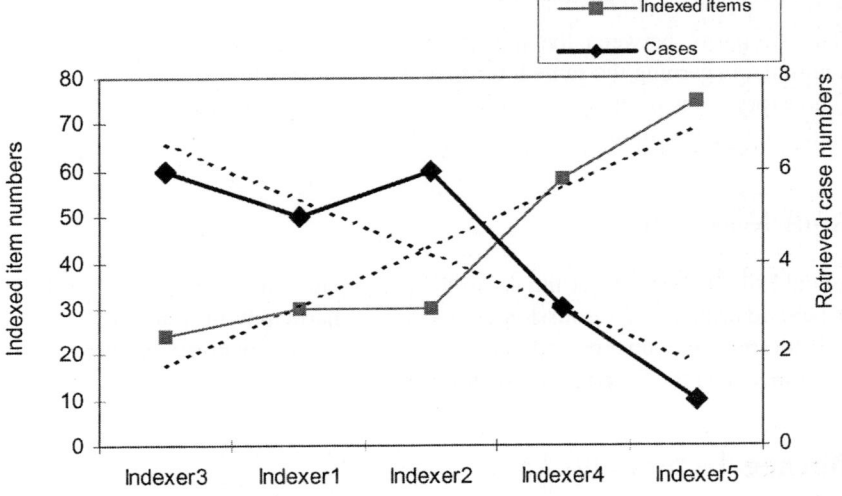

Fig. 4. Relationship between the indexed item numbers and retrieved case numbers

5 Primary Conclusions

By checking carefully on the indexes, we found that indexer4 and indexer5 had more detailed indexed items, while the other indexers have ignored some of the details. The most significant issue is that, among the top three ranked retrieved cases by using the different indexes, there is always one same case existing – ec5 in common.

In fact, ec5 provided the most important and appropriate information when later creating the MV solutions regarding the problems identified in the testing case. This means the index vocabulary has a tolerant property to be inclusive for finding the relevant cases to avoid the information loss.

Here, it is reasonable to say that the IM-MVD will support the CBRM being more robust and effective as well as efficient to be applied for a creative MV's generation. Of course, there is still much modification and refinement work awaiting.

Generally, the structures and contents of indexing of this model as well as the processing procedure are intentionally simple, although it will require some patience to complete the indexing by going through the index vocabulary. By using the IM-MVD, including the pre-training, it takes around half a day for a person who is not familiar with the process but having the relevant domain knowledge of an MV, to index a case into CBRM. Meanwhile, the person should have a clear understanding of the information to be indexed in advance.

6 Future Research

Workable as the IM-MVD is, it still has weak points that need further effort to improve. Later, during the CBRM's further application in academia and case companies, the following points will have the opportunity to be refined:

1. The similarity between the indexed items from different indexers shall be increased, concerning the same information to be indexed on;
2. The expressions of the feature values shall be refined to make them more accurate and to avoid any ambiguity in understanding.

Acknowledgement

We would like to extend our thanks to the participants in Denmark and the USA for their beneficial informal discussion and/or formal participation in the testing sessions and all the relevant support; and also to the anonymous reviewers for their constructive comments on the former version of this paper.

References

1. Aamodt, A. and Plaza E.: Case-Based Reasoning: Foundational Issues, Methodologies Variations, and System Approaches. AI Communication, IOS Press, Vol. 7: 1 (1994) 39-59
2. Aamodt, A.: Knowledge Representation System for Integration of General and Case-Specific Knowledge. Proceedings from IEEE TAI-94, International Conference on Tools with Artificial Intelligence, New Orleans (1994) 836-839
3. Kolodner, J. L.: Case- Based Reasoning. Morgan Kaufmann Publishers (1993)
4. Wang, C., Luxhøj J. T. and Johansen, J.: A Case-Based Reasoning Model (CBRM) for Supporting Strategic Manufacturing Vision Development. Proceedings of Hawaii International Conference on Business, Honolulu, Hawaii, USA, June (2003)

5. Skinner, W.: Manufacturing: Missing Link in Manufacturing Strategy. Harvard Business Review, May-June (1969) 136-145
6. Hill, T.: Manufacturing Strategy: The Strategic Management of the Manufacturing Function. Macmillan, Pitman Publishing (1996)
7. Brown, S.: Strategic Manufacturing for Competitive Advantage Transforming Operations from Shop Floor to Strategy. Prentice Hall (1996)
8. Riis, J. O. and Johansen J.: Developing a Manufacturing Vision. International Working Conference on Strategic Manufacturing, Aalborg, Denmark, August (2001)
9. Maslen, R. and Platts, K. W.: Manufacturing Vision and Competitiveness. Integrated Manufacturing Systems, Vol. 8, No. 5 (1997) 313-322
10. Bergmann, R.: Introduction to Case-Based Reasoning. University of Kaiserlautern. At http://www.cbr-Web.org/CBR-Web/cbrintro/, July (1998)
11. Althoff, K.-D. and Bartsch-Spörl, B.: Decision Support for Case-Based Application. Special Issues on Case-Based Decision Support, in: Wirtschaftinformatic, Vol. 38 (1996)
12. Luxhøj, J. T.: Case-Based Reasoning (CBR): An Overview. Lecture Notes. Center for Industrial Production, Aalborg University, September (2001)
13. Burke, R. and Kass, A.: Refining the Universal Indexing Frame to Support Retrieval of Tutorial Stories. In AAAI Workshop on Indexing and Reuse in Multimedia Systems. AAAI (1994) 1-11
14. Mulholland, P.: Introduction to Ontologies. Technical Report. Knowledge Media Institute, The Open University, UK.
At http://216.239.51.104/search?q=cache:aRcDLuMGpNUJ:rich-odl.open.ac.uk/docs/onto-intro-v2.pdf (1999)
15. Gonzalez, A. J. and Dankel, D. D.: The Engineering of Knowledge-Based Systems: Theory and Practice. Prentice-Hall, Inc (1993)
16. Marshall D.: Artificial intelligence II. Lecture Note. At http://www.cs.cf.ac.uk /Dave/AI2/ AI_notes.html (1997)
17. Turban, E.: Decision Support and Expert Systems. Mackmillan Publishing Company, New York (1988)
18. Watson, I.: Applying Case-Based Reasoning: Techniques for Enterprise Systems. Morgan Kaufmann Publisher (1997)
19. Extension to Communities (EtC): Tips For Nominal Group Process. Iowa State University. At: http://www.extension.iastate.edu/communities/tools/decisions/ nominal.html (2002)
20. Delbecq, A. L., Van de Ven, A. H. and Gustafson, D. H.: Group Techniques for Program Planning, a Guide to Nominal Group Technique and Delphi Processes. Scott Foreman (1975).
21. Delbecq, A. L., and Van de Ven, A. H.: A Group Process Model for Identification and Program Planning. Journal of Applied Behavioural Sciences, 7 (1971) 466-492
22. Wang, C.: Concepts Refinement through Modified Nominal Group Technique (MNGT). Technical Report. Centre for Industrial Production, Aalborg University, March (2003).
23. Bradshaw, R.: Indexing Guidelines for the ADAM Database. At: http://adam.ac.uk/adam/ reports/indexing/, (Found in 2003 on Internet)
24. Wang, C., Luxhøj J. T. and Johansen, J.: A Knowledge Management System Prototype for Manufacturing Vision. Unpublished Paper. Centre for Industrial Production, Aalborg University, November (2003)

Feature Selection and Generalisation for Retrieval of Textual Cases

Nirmalie Wiratunga[1], Ivan Koychev[2], and Stewart Massie[1]

[1] School of Computing, The Robert Gordon University,
Aberdeen AB25 1HG, Scotland, UK
{nw, sm}@comp.rgu.ac.uk
[2] Smart Web Technologies Centre, The Robert Gordon University,
Aberdeen AB25 1HG, Scotland, UK
ik@comp.rgu.ac.uk

Abstract. Textual CBR systems solve problems by reusing experiences that are in textual form. Knowledge-rich comparison of textual cases remains an important challenge for these systems. However mapping text data into a structured case representation requires a significant knowledge engineering effort. In this paper we look at automated acquisition of the case indexing vocabulary as a two step process involving feature selection followed by feature generalisation. Boosted decision stumps are employed as a means to select features that are predictive and relatively orthogonal. Association rule induction is employed to capture feature co-occurrence patterns. Generalised features are constructed by applying these rules. Essentially, rules preserve implicit semantic relationships between features and applying them has the desired effect of bringing together cases that would have otherwise been overlooked during case retrieval. Experiments with four textual data sets show significant improvement in retrieval accuracy whenever generalised features are used. The results further suggest that boosted decision stumps with generalised features to be a promising combination.

1 Introduction

Past problem solving experiences captured in textual form present an interesting challenge to CBR system development. This is because experiences in unstructured form containing free text must first be mapped into structured cases before they can be meaningfully compared and reused for future problem solving. Textual CBR (TCBR) involves reuse of experiences that are in text form [14]. Unlike Information Retrieval approaches TCBR aims to develop case representation mechanisms that can better support knowledge-rich comparison of cases.

TCBR systems often access a variety of knowledge sources (e.g. domain specific thesauri, natural language parsers etc.) to establish an indexing vocabulary [5]. The general aim is to facilitate structured case representation and enhance retrieval. In this paper we investigate how introspective learning can be employed to automate the acquisition of the case indexing vocabulary [13]. We present techniques that are generally applicable when textual experiences are pre-classified according to the types of problems they solve. Essentially we shall exploit implicit knowledge already existing in text documents to discover keywords that on their own or as a set in combination with others, are predictive of the problem class. The case indexing vocabulary will constitute just these selected keywords and so this process can be viewed as dimension reduction or feature selection.

Feature selection techniques employed by machine learning algorithms for supervised learning tasks such as classification are known to successfully improve accuracy, efficiency and comprehension of learned concepts [12]. Typically these techniques have been applied in problem domains consisting of structured cases. They have also been employed by CBR systems to identify relevant features for building an index for case retrieval [11]. A feature selection technique can be categorised as either being a filter or a wrapper approach. The wrapper approach uses feedback from the final learning algorithm to guide the search for the set of features. Generally this feedback ensures selection of a good set of features tailored for the learning algorithm but has the disadvantage of being time consuming because feedback involves learner accuracy ascertained from cross-validation runs. Filters are seen as data pre-processors and generally do not require feedback from the final learner. As a result they tend to be faster, scaling better to large datasets. Selection techniques presented in this paper fall under filter approaches which are particularly suited to processing of medium to large text collections.

In classification problems a *good* feature is one that is predictive of the problem class on its own or in combination with other features. Selection according to the performance of a combination of features is particularly useful for text data because there is often the need to identify similar meaning words that are used interchangeably (synonyms) and the same word being used with different meaning (polysemies). In both situations similar cases can be overlooked during retrieval if these semantic relationships are ignored. This paper introduces a novel feature selection technique that discovers and preserves semantic relationships in the case representation as part of the selection process. Boosted decision stumps are used for feature selection and semantic relationships are captured using association rule induction.

Section 2 describes the commonly used information gain based feature selection technique which is then used by the boosted feature selection technique in Section 3. The Apriori association rule learner is discussed in Section 4 and is employed as a means to capture semantic relationships between features. In Section 5, induced rules are utilised to form a generalised document representation and in doing so introduces novel ways of combining it with feature selection. Experimental results are reported on four textual classification tasks in Section 6. An overview of case representation and indexing issues in textual CBR research and how techniques presented in this paper relate to existing ones are discussed in Section 7, followed by conclusions in Section 8.

2 Feature Selection with Information Gain

We first introduce the notation used in this paper to assist presentation of the different feature selection techniques. Let $\mathcal{D}$ be the set of all labelled documents, $\mathcal{W}$ the set of all features which are essentially words. A document d is a pair $(\vec{x}, y)$, where $\vec{x} = (x_1, \ldots, x_{|\mathcal{W}|})$ is a binary valued feature vector corresponding to the presence or absence of words in $\mathcal{W}$; and y is d's class label [18]. The experiments in this paper use binary class domains so y is either 0 (negative class) or 1 (positive class). Let $\mathcal{S}$ be the training subset containing labelled documents $\{d_1, \ldots, d_n\}$.

The main aim of feature selection is to reduce $|\mathcal{W}|$ to a smaller feature subset size m by selecting features ranked according to some goodness criteria. The selected m features then form a new binary-valued feature vector $\vec{x}'$ and a corresponding reduced word vocabulary set $\mathcal{W}'$, where $\mathcal{W}' \subset \mathcal{W}$ and $|\mathcal{W}'| \ll |\mathcal{W}|$. The new representation of document d with $\mathcal{W}'$ is a pair $(\vec{x}', y)$.

A feature's discriminatory power is a useful gauge of its goodness and is commonly ascertained using the information gain (IG) score ([17], [16]).

$$IG(X,Y) = \sum_{x \in 0,1} \sum_{y \in 0,1} P(X=x, Y=y).log_2 \frac{P(X=x, Y=y)}{P(X=x).P(Y=y)}$$

Here the probabilities are estimated from $\mathcal{S}$ using m-estimates [15]. The information gain based ranking and selection of features is the base line algorithm used in this paper and we will refer to it as BASE (Figure 1).

m = feature subset size
BASE
    Foreach $w_i \in \mathcal{W}$
        calculate IG score using $\mathcal{S}$
    sort $\mathcal{W}$ in decreasing order of IG scores
    $\mathcal{W}' = \{w_1, \ldots, w_m\}$
    Return $\mathcal{W}'$

Fig. 1. Feature selection with IG based ranking.

A feature goodness score like IG reflects a feature's ability to discriminate between classes. A possible shortfall with BASE is that selected features although having high scores may exercise their discriminatory power in similar ways. Consider documents from two mailing lists about computer hardware, one list containing messages about solving PC problems and the other dedicated to Apple Macs. An example of the top ranked words might be: "centris", "quadra", "eisa", "bus", "client", "server" etc. Here both "centris" and "quadra" are likely to suggest a hidden concept such as machine type. Similarly "eisa" and "bus" are likely to co-occur in similar documents an possibly relate to an implicit concept like internal architecture, while "client" and "server" are also features that can be viewed as belonging to a further implicit concept such as process communication. Ideally we would like to explicate these semantic relationships but firstly we need to ensure that as many of the hidden concepts are captured by at least a single representative discriminatory feature. This means that if we were restricted to select just three out of the six words a useful selection might be: "quadra", "eisa" and "server" to cover each of the hidden concepts; instead of just the top three "centris", "quadra" and "eisa". What this example is highlighting is that selecting just the top ranked features with BASE can result in a feature set that is not particularly representative of hidden concepts thereby having a detrimental effect on case comparison. In the following section we combine IG based feature selection with boosting as a first step towards dealing with this problem.

3 Feature Selection with Boosted Decision Stumps

Boosting is known to improve the performance of learning algorithms particularly with tasks that exhibit varying degrees of difficulty [9]. The general idea of boosting is to iteratively generate several (weak) learners, with each learner biased by the training set error in the previous iteration or trial. Each learner works hard at solving training instances that were incorrectly classified in previous iterations. This is achieved by associating weights with instances in the training set and updating these weights at each trial. Weights of instances correctly solved by the most recent learner are decreased, and this has the effect of increasing weights of incorrectly classified instances. It means that at the next trial the learner is forced to work harder at solving these difficult instances. In order to classify a new test instance, the votes of each learner are combined to form a majority vote. Each vote is typically weighted by learner accuracy because it makes sense to trust those learners that have a higher accuracy on the training set.

An interesting approach to feature selection is to use boosting with a one-level decision tree, known as a decision stump, as the learning algorithm ([6], [8]). Constructing such a learner involves selecting a single feature, based on its ability to discriminate between classes [10]. For this purpose decision stumps are typically formed from features with high information gain. An example of two decision stumps from the binary classed computer hardware domain appear in Figure 2. Here a "+" denotes documents from the Apple mailing list and "-" the PC mailing list. With the "centris" stump the left leaf is formed by documents in which "centris" is present and the right leaf contains documents where it is absent. Predicting the class of a test document using this decision stump involves traversing the left or right branch leading to a leaf depending on the presence or absence of "centris" and labelling the document with the majority class at that leaf. Similar explanations hold for the stump having "bus" as the splitting feature. The stump error on the training set (err) is the percentage of the number of minority class documents in both branches.

Since a decision stump partitions the domain based on the values of a single feature, the set of stumps generated with boosting form the set of selected features. Therefore with m boosted iterations a set of m features are selected and these form the reduced feature subset $\mathcal{W}'$. The BOOST feature selection technique is shown in Figure 3. At each boosted iteration the feature with highest IG is selected forming the stump for the training set $\mathcal{S}$. Initially all n documents are assigned the same weight of $1/n$. With each trial these weights are updated so that the weights of correctly classified examples are reduced according to the error of the stumps. In practice once weights are updated, they need to be re-normalised so that their sum remains one. The impact of updated weights will be reflected in the IG scores where the prior and conditional probabilities are calculated on weighted documents, and this in turn will influence the feature selected in the next iteration when forming the stump. The boosting mechanism adopted here is similar to AdaBoost.M1 [9], the only difference being that updating of document weights is based on the error of the committee of stumps learned thus far, instead of the error of the most recent decision stump. With initial stumps containing features with higher IG scores the committee approach to updating document weights enables stumps from earlier iterations to exert a greater influence on feature selection.

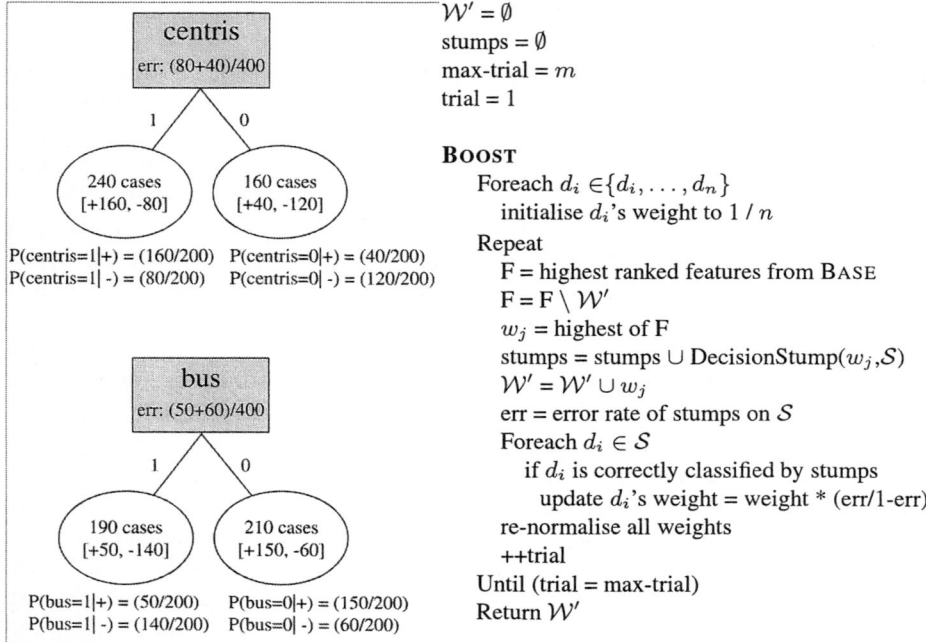

Fig. 2. Decision stumps.   Fig. 3. Feature selection with boosted stumps.

Features that are discriminatory in similar ways have less opportunity to be selected with BOOST. However, with most tasks, information about which features co-occur with selected features can provide useful knowledge for case similarity, particularly in the presence of hidden concepts. In the next section we use an association rule learner to identify co-occurring features for selected features. A generalised feature space formed by applying these learned rules to selected features provides a richer case representation which in turn will enrich case comparison.

4 Feature Generalisation with Association Rule Induction

Apriori [1] is a well known association rule induction algorithm introduced for the market-basket analysis domain where one wishes to find regularities in people's shopping behaviour. It generates rules of the form H ← B, where the rule body B is a conjunction of items, and the rule head H is a single item. Association rules are discovered in two stages. Firstly Apriori identifies sets of items that frequently co-occur, i.e. above a given minimum threshold. It then generates rules from these itemsets ensuring frequency and accuracy are above minimum thresholds.

4.1 Rule Generation and Selection

An obvious analogy exists between frequently occurring itemsets in shopping transactions and frequently occurring words in a set of documents. This means that rules can be

```
+r1:centri<- print    (6.5%,  17.2%,  0.3%)
+r2:centri<- card     (6.6%,  25.4%,  1.1%)
+r3:centri<- fpu      (5.5%,  24.5%,  0.8%)
+r4:centri<- iisi     (7.7%,  14.5%,  0.1%)
+r5:centri<- simm     (9.0%,  16.3%,  0.3%)
+r6:centri<- quadra  (10.8%,  24.0%,  1.5%)
+r7:centri<- lc       (9.0%,  16.3%,  0.3%)

-r1:bus <- local      (7.7%,  46.4%,  3.0%)
-r2:bus <- standard  (10.3%,  31.5%,  1.2%)
-r3:bus <- window    (13.6%,  29.5%,  1.2%)
-r4:bus <- id        (20.5%,  28.3%,  1.7%)
-r5:bus <- drive     (29.6%,  31.7%,  4.8%)
-r6:bus <- id local   (9.0%,  42.0%,  2.7%)
-r7:bus <- drive local (10.3%, 37.0%, 2.1%)
```

Fig. 4. Example list of rules from the hardware domain.

used to predict the presence of the head feature given that all the features in the body are present in the document. This means that a case satisfying the body even when the head feature is absent, will be considered closer to other cases that actually have the head feature present. Figure 4 lists two sets of rules generated for the hardware mailing list domain. The first rule set corresponds to rules generated with "centris" as the rule head and the other set with "bus" as the head. The class of documents from which these rules were induced are indicated by the rule prefix. This is important because co-occurrences of features are a signature of a particular class of documents.

In order to tie in a set of rules to a class it is necessary to constrain rule generation so that a rule's body contains features that are predictive of the same class as the rule's head, and learning is restricted to documents from this class. The predictive class of features is estimated according to class conditional probabilities. Going back to Figure 2, if "centris" is to be used as the head feature of the rule then the higher conditional probability, $P(centris = 1|+)$ indicates that it is most likely to appear in documents from the positive class. If instead "bus" is the head feature then the higher conditional probability $P(bus = 1|-)$ suggests the negative class.

An informed rule selection strategy is necessary because Apriori typically will generate many rules [3]. The percentages in Figure 4 are the coverage, accuracy and information gain for each generated rule. Generally the first two measures are used by Apriori during rule generation to prune the search space. Here coverage (or frequency) is the percentage of documents in which a rule is applicable; and confidence (or accuracy) is the proportion of documents in which the rule prediction is correct. The third measures the gain in information due to the rule's body, and indicates how well the body is able to predict the presence or absence of the head feature. It is this measure that we have found most informative when selecting the K best rules from those generated. The three best rules predictive of each of the two head features (i.e. "centris", "bus") according to information gain are in bold.

4.2 Feature Generalisation

The objective of applying learned association rules is to improve case comparison by providing a more generalised case representation. Good generalisation will have the desired effect of bringing cases that are semantically related closer to each other that previously would have been incorrectly treated as being further apart. Association rules are able to capture implicit relationships (e.g. like synonyms) that exist between features. When these rules are applied they have the effect of squashing these features, which can be viewed as feature generalisation.

For a feature $w_i \in \mathcal{W}$, let $\mathcal{R}_i$ be the set of association rules induced with w_i as the head feature, where $r_{ij} : w_i \leftarrow B_j$. Here the rule body B_j is a conjunction of features from $\mathcal{W} \setminus \{w_i\}$ and when true implies the presence of the head feature w_i. Given a document's initial representation $d = (\vec{x}, y)$ (i.e. using all features in $\mathcal{W}$), the generalised representation $d = (\vec{x}'', y)$ is obtained by applying $r_{ij} : x_i \leftarrow x_{i1} \wedge \ldots \wedge x_{in_j}$ where $x_{ik} \neq x_i$, giving;

$$x_i'' = \begin{cases} 1 & \text{if } x_i = 1 \\ 1 & \text{if } (\bigwedge_{k=1}^{n_j} x_{ik}) = 1 \\ 0 & \text{otherwise} \end{cases}$$

All this means is that x_i'' is instantiated with value 1 if either the head of the rule or its body is true, and is 0 otherwise. Consequently, the generalised new document representation $\vec{x}''$ tends to be less sparse than $\vec{x}$, because 0 values are likely to have their values flipped to 1. Essentially $\vec{x}''$ remains a binary valued feature vector, whose values indicate the presence or absence of a feature w'', where $w'' \in \mathcal{W}''$, but $\mathcal{W}'' \not\subset \mathcal{W}$, since these features no longer correspond to presence or absence of single words.

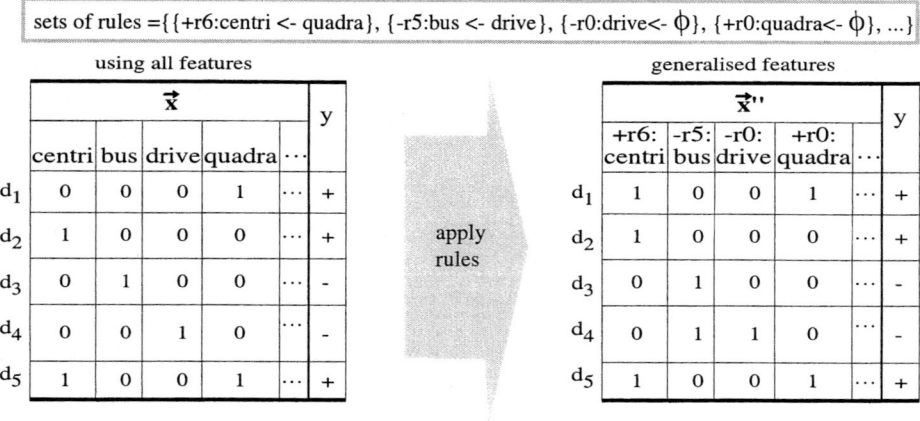

Fig. 5. Example of generalisation with rules.

Figure 5 illustrates how rules are used to generalise feature vectors. Here two forms of five trivial feature vectors are shown. The left table shows values for each vector using all the features in $\mathcal{W} = \{$"centri", "bus", "drive", "quadra",...$\}$, with the y column showing the document class. The right table shows the effect of generalisation after the sets of rules are applied. For sake of simplicity we use only the single best rule from each of the rule sets $\{\mathcal{R}_{centri}, \mathcal{R}_{bus}, \mathcal{R}_{drive}, \mathcal{R}_{quadra} \ldots\}$; listed at the top of the figure. The first two rule sets contain a complete rule each: $\mathcal{R}_{centri} = \{+r6 : centri \leftarrow quadra\}$, $\mathcal{R}_{bus} = \{-r5 : bus \leftarrow drive\}$. So for example any rule from $\mathcal{R}_{centri}$ (e.g. $+r6 : centri$) is applied to the left table's "centri" column on any document from the positive class, while rules from $\mathcal{R}_{bus}$ are applied to the "bus" column on any document from the negative class. The right table is the result of applying these rule sets. The other two rule sets: $\mathcal{R}_{drive}$ and $\mathcal{R}_{quadra}$ contain rules that have empty bodies. Such rules are not uncommon and indicate that Apriori was unable to find rules above specified minimum thresholds. Applying empty rules amounts to unchanged values, i.e. no generalisation takes place.

5   Combining Feature Selection with Generalisation

An obvious manner in which to perform generalisation is after feature selection. In Figure 6 BASEGEN does exactly this using BASE first to form $\mathcal{W}'$. It then uses $\mathcal{W}'$ as a handle on ruleset generation, where a ruleset $\mathcal{R}_i$ is generated for each selected feature $w_i' \in \mathcal{W}'$. This restricts the number of generated rule sets to m, so $|\mathcal{W}''| = |\mathcal{W}'|$. Here a rule $r_{ij} \in \mathcal{R}_i$ is of the form $r_{ij} : w_i' \leftarrow B_j$, where the rule body B_j is still a conjunction of features in $\mathcal{W} \setminus \{w_i'\}$, but the head now applies to a selected feature in $\mathcal{W}'$, where $\mathcal{W}' \subset \mathcal{W}$.

Interestingly we can also combine feature generalisation with boosted feature selection so that the boosted search for the best set of features is influenced at each itera-

```
W″ = ∅; W′ = ∅
BASEGEN
    call BASE to form W′
    Foreach dᵢ ∈ S
        Foreach wⱼ ∈ {W′ ∩ W}
            x″ᵢⱼ = generalise(xᵢⱼ, wⱼ)
            w″ⱼ = new generalised feature
            W″ = W″ ∪ w″ⱼ
    Return W″

generalise(x, w)
    R = select-rules(w)
    apply each rule in R
    generalising x to x″
    Return x″

select-rules(w)
    R = rules with w as rule head
    sort R decreasing order of rule IG
    break ties with coverage
    retain the best K in R
    Return R
```

```
W″ = ∅; W′ = ∅; stumps = ∅
max-trial = m
trial = 1

BOOSTGEN
    ⋮
    Repeat
        F = highest ranked features from BASE
        F = F \ W′
        wⱼ = highest of F
        W′ = W′ ∪ wⱼ
        Foreach dᵢ ∈ S
            x″ᵢⱼ = generalise(xᵢⱼ, wⱼ)
            w″ⱼ = new generalised feature
            stumps = stumps ∪ DecisionStump(w″ⱼ, S)
            W″ = W″ ∪ w″ⱼ
            err = error rate of stumps on S
        ⋮
        ++trial
    Until (trial = max-trial)
    Return W″
```

Fig. 6. Generalisation after feature selection.   **Fig. 7.** Generalisation with boosted selection.

tion by the generalisation of the feature selected in the previous iteration. BOOSTGEN achieves this as shown in Figure 7. It calls *generalise* before forming the decision stump, as a result the decision stump is formed by splitting the training set according to the new generalised feature.

Generalisation after feature selection is attractive because generated rules will contain rule bodies that bring in features from the larger feature pool $\mathcal{W}$. In this manner both BASEGEN and BOOSTGEN are able to link selected features from $\mathcal{W}'$ with other less frequently used features. This may be seen as supplementing selected features in $\mathcal{W}'$ with background knowledge from $\mathcal{W}$. Additionally BOOSTGEN's boosted feature selection will tend to discover generalised features that are less likely to have overlapping semantic relationships with other generalised features.

6 Evaluation

Feature selection and generalisation techniques enable the mapping of textual documents into structured cases with which the case base is formed. Different case representations are formed using the 4 algorithms presented in this paper:

1. BASE, feature selection using the standard IG ranking (Figure 1);
2. BOOST, feature selection with boosting (Figure 3);
3. BASEGEN, generalisation after feature selection (Figure 6); and
4. BOOSTGEN, generalisation in combination with boosting (Figure 7)

The case retrieval performance using test set accuracy with 3 nearest neighbours is used to compare the above algorithms. A modified case similarity metric is used to refrain from treating the absence of words in the same way as the presence of words. This is because the presence of a word in documents is intuitively more important for measuring their similarity, than its absence. We accomplish this affect by weighting the similarity in non-present words by the inverse of the feature subset size. What this means is that as increasing number of features are used to represent documents, the influence of similarity due to the absence of similar words is reduced.

Textual cases were formed by pre-processing documents by firstly removing stop words (common words) and special characters such as quote marks, commas and full stops (except for "!", "@", "%", "$" because they have been found to be discriminative for some domains [17]). Remaining words are reduced to their stem using the Porter's algorithm. Essentially, $\mathcal{W}$ is formed by all word-stems ($|\mathcal{W}| \approx 8000$) remaining after document pre-processing. For our experiments we use pre-processed documents from the following text corpuses:

- **LingSpam** dataset has been formed to study the problem of spam. It contains 2893 email messages, of which 83% are non-spam messages related to linguistics, and rest are spam [17].
- **20 Newsgroups** dataset is a corpus of about 20,000 Usenet news postings into 20 different newsgroups. One thousand messages from each of the twenty newsgroups were chosen at random and partitioned by newsgroup name [15]. For our experiments we use three sub-corpuses, where the messages from two newsgroups are combined to form a binary classification as follows: Religion and Politics (RelPol); Apple Mac and PC Hardware (MacPc); and Space and Medical Science (SpcMed).

We created equal sized disjoint training and test sets, where each set contains 20% of documents randomly selected from the original corpus, preserving class distribution in the original corpus. For repeated trials, 15 such train test splits are formed. Significance is reported from a paired one tailed t-test with 99% confidence. The graphs show averaged accuracy on test set with increasing number of selected features.

6.1 Results

The general behaviour of all four algorithms with the LingSpam corpus indicate an initial steep rise in accuracy (upto 20 features) after which there is hardly any improvement with increasing numbers of features (see Figure 8). The generalisation achieved with BASEGEN has resulted in a small but significant increase in accuracy over BASE, while BOOST has only managed a slight improvement. However, BOOSTGEN's generalisation combined with boosting has significantly outperformed the other algorithms, achieving the highest accuracy approaching 99%. The overall accuracy results suggest that this domain is relatively easy because BASE achieves 93.6% accuracy with only five features and improves this accuracy to over 97% with twenty features and above. The reason for this is due to the nature of the LingSpam corpus, where there are a few very discriminatory features from non spam messages that are sufficient to differentiate spam messages.

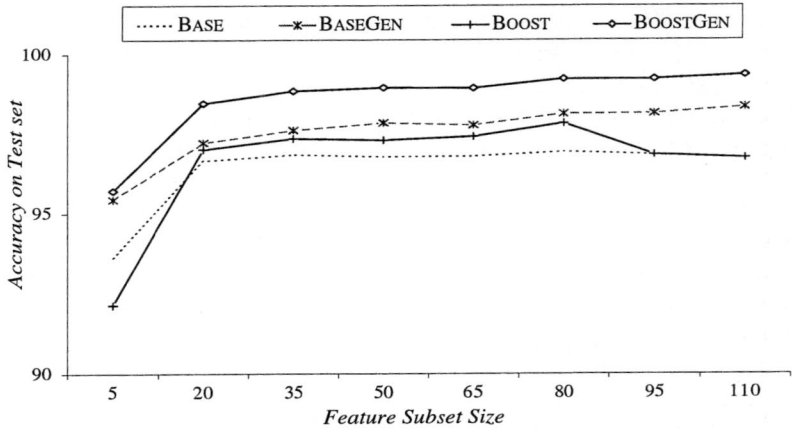

Fig. 8. Accuracy results for LingSpam.

Figure 9 shows the results with the RelPol task. Compared to LingSpam the classification of documents in to Religion and Politics seems to present a harder task because overall accuracy is lower. BOOST results are comparable to BASE where boosted feature selection shows improved accuracy with relatively smaller feature subset sizes. As before algorithms employing generalisation (BASEGEN and BOOSTGEN) outperform those without generalisation (BASE and BOOST), with BOOSTGEN having significantly improved performance over all other algorithms (including BASEGEN).

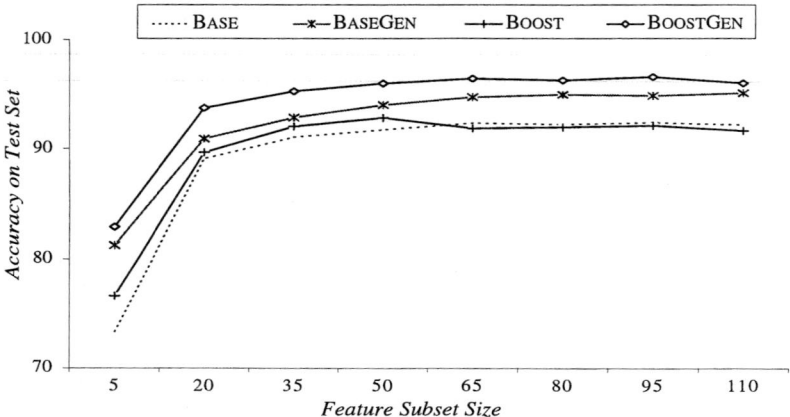

Fig. 9. Accuracy results for RelPol.

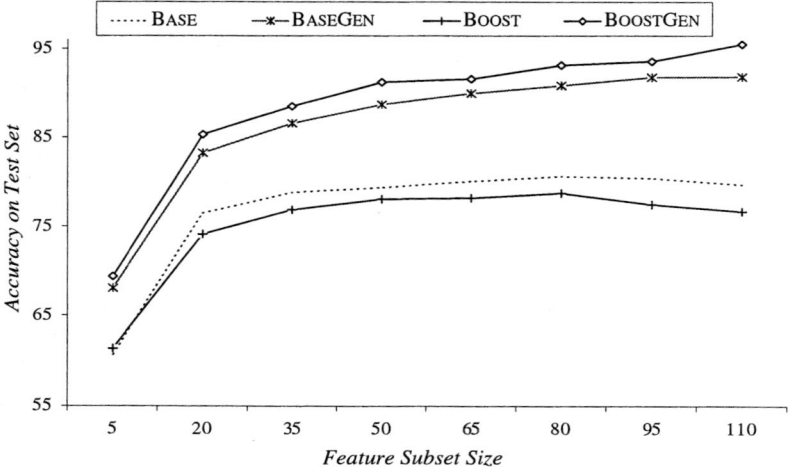

Fig. 10. Accuracy results for MacPc.

The results from the MacPc classification task appear in Figure 10. This task is expected to be the hardest, because similar terminology (e.g. monitor, hard drive) can be used in reference to both PC and Apple Mac hardware. Additionally the same hardware problem can be applicable in both mailing lists resulting in cross posting of the same message. Although boosting on its own has not improved accuracy, boosting combined with generalisation (BOOSTGEN) is significantly better than all other algorithms including BASEGEN at all feature subset sizes. Interestingly the accuracies for algorithms using generalisation (BASEGEN and BOOSTGEN) continue to rise with increasing feature subset sizes. The poor performance of BOOST can be explained by the relatively low discriminatory power of features in this domain. In fact selecting the most discriminatory feature followed by boosting of incorrectly classified documents can be harmful,

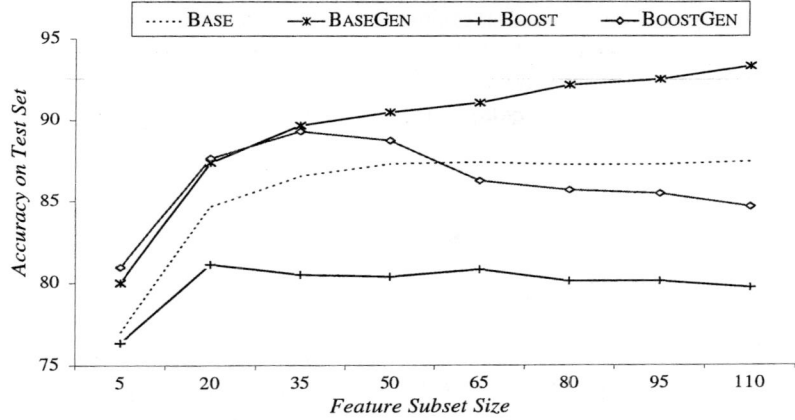

Fig. 11. Accuracy results for SpcMed.

because updating of document weights prevents discovery of supportive features in subsequent boosted iterations.

A similar significant increase in classification accuracy with generalisation compared to without it is seen with the SpcMed domain (see Figure 11). Noticeably the overall winner here is BASEGEN having done significantly better than BOOSTGEN for the first time. Furthermore, boosting is not helpful and its performance is significantly worse than BASE. Closer examination of BOOST's results indicate over-fitting behaviour, because the accuracy on training set is higher than that of BASE's accuracy on training set, but this gain is not reflected in test set accuracy. The generalisation used in BOOSTGEN maintains comparable performance to BASEGEN with up to 35 features, after which accuracy drops quickly as more features are used and over-fitting from boosting takes effect.

6.2 Evaluation Summary

The results from the significance tests are summarised in Table 1. The first two columns convey the gain with boosting (BOOST vs. BASE and BOOSTGEN vs. BASEGEN); and the other two the gain with generalisation (BASEGEN vs. BASE and BOOSTGEN vs. BOOST). Overall feature generalisation improves algorithm performance significantly

Table 1. Results summary according to significance.

	Boosting		Generalisation	
Data Set	BOOST vs. BASE	BOOSTGEN vs. BASEGEN	BASEGEN vs. BASE	BOOSTGEN vs. BOOST
LingSpam	no diff.	✓	✓	✓
RelPol	no diff.	✓	✓	✓
MacPc	×	✓	✓	✓
SciMed	×	×	✓	✓

It is worth noting that generalisation is able to continuously improve accuracy with increasing feature subset sizes with all domains, making it clearly more robust to overfitting. Generally boosting is not helpful on its own, but BOOSTGEN combining boosting with generalisation achieves significant improvement over all other algorithms in 3 out of 4 domains.

7 Related Work

Current practice in TCBR system development show that the indexing vocabulary and similarity knowledge containers are typically acquired manually [19]. This is not surprising because of the ambiguous nature of free text. Although NLP tools can be applied to analyse free text they are often too brittle partly because they tend to analyse text from a purely linguistic point of view. Instead a piecemeal approach involving increasing levels of knowledge intensive containers have been identified as the basis for TCBR system development [13]. Generally these levels are broadly seen as connected with the case representation vocabulary or the similarity measure. Tools such as stemming, stop word removal and domain specific dictionaries form less intensive knowledge levels and are mostly automated. Acquiring semantic relationships between words typically form higher knowledge levels and are harder to automate and remain an important challenge.

The difficulty with acquiring an appropriate indexing vocabulary and the need for structured case representation within the law domain is discussed in [4]. The SMILE system adopts a fine-grained sentence level class, whereby sentences are manually categorised into classes. It is interesting to note that although our approach does not explicitly assign classes at the sentence level, we also found it necessary to automatically link induced rules to applicable document classes. SMILE employs a decision tree based index scheme to partition the case base, but this is only possible after case sentences are manually marked-up (with words specified in a domain specific thesauri) to mitigate the synonym problem. We believe that our approach to feature generalisation with association rules helps automate the extraction of synonym relationships, provided that these relationships are already implicit in the textual case base.

Association rules have previously been used to reduce sparseness of initial user rating tables in collaborative recommendation [2]. Unlike traditional correlation based approaches Apriori is able to capture statistics about co-occurring features efficiently because it exploits the fact that no superset of an infrequent itemset can be frequent. Work presented in this paper combines feature selection with rule induction providing a useful strategy to manage rule generation and selection. Additionally the boosting in our approach attempts to capture features that tend to be orthogonal and with which hidden concepts can be discovered by exploiting rules generated by Apriori.

The aims of feature generalisation discussed in this paper are similar to those of Latent Semantic Indexing (LSI); a popular dimension reduction technique for text data. It uses singular value decomposition to map the word based feature vector representation into a lower dimensional latent space of artificial features [6]. Recently LSI was also integrated with textual case retrieval, where case similarity is computed on the basis of the lower dimensional case representation [7]. Unlike LSI our approach to feature vector generalisation explicitly captures hidden semantic relationships by way of association rules, enabling easier interpretation of generalised features during case comparison. Still it will be intriguing to see how the feature selection and generalisation techniques introduced in this paper compare with LSI based case representation.

8 Conclusions

The idea of feature generalisation and combining this with feature selection to form structured cases for textual retrieval is a novel contribution of this paper. Feature generalisation helps tone down ambiguities that exist in free text by capturing semantic relationships and incorporating these in the case representation. This enables a much better comparison of cases.

The two main approaches presented in this paper are feature selection with boosting and feature generalisation with association rules. Essentially feature selection helps with identifying discriminatory features while feature generalisation captures semantic relationships. Overall case representation with generalisation significantly improved accuracy over algorithms without generalisation, and promises great potential for automated acquisition of both the indexing vocabulary and the similarity containers. The effect of boosting is mixed where on its own gives modest improvement or even harmful in some domains, where it is more prone to over-fitting. Further research is needed to understand the relationship between types of problem domains and boosting performance. However the best results in 3 of the 4 test domains were obtained by the combination of generalisation with boosting.

An interesting observation is that with feature selection and generalisation a more effective case retrieval is achieved even with a relatively small set of features. This is attractive because smaller vocabularies can effectively be used to build concise indices that are understandable and easier to interpret.

Acknowledgements

We thank Susan Craw, Rob Lothian and Dietrich Wettschereck for helpful discussions on this work.

References

1. Agrawal, R., Mannila, H., Srikant, R., Toivonen, H., Verkamo, A.: Fast discovery of association rules. In *Advances in Knowledge Discovery and Data Mining*, 307–327. AAAI/MIT Press (1995)
2. Alvarez, W., Ruiz, C.: Collaborative recommendation via adaptive association rule mining. In *Proceedings of the International Workshop on Web Mining for E-Commerce* (2000) 35–41
3. Borgelt, C., Kruse, R.: Induction of association rules: Apriori implementation. In *Proceedings of the 14th Conference on Computational Statistics* (2002)
4. Bruninghaus, S., Ashley, K.: Bootstrapping case base development with annotated case summaries. In *Proceedings of the Second International Conference on Case-Based Reasoning, ICCBR'99* (1999) 59–73

5. Bruninghaus, S., Ashley, K.: The role of information extraction for textual CBR. In *Proceedings of the 4th International Conference on Case-Based Reasoning, ICCBR'01* (2001) 74–89
6. Cai, L., Hofmann, T.: Text categorisation by boosting automatically extracted concepts. In *Proceedings of the 26th Annual International ACM SIGIR Conference on Research and Development in Information Retrieval* (2003) 182–189
7. Chakraborti, S., Ambati, S., Balaraman, V., Khemani, D.: Integrating knowledge sources and acquiring vocabulary for textual CBR. In *Proceedings of the 8th UK-CBR workshop* (2003) 74–84
8. Das, S.: Filters, wrappers and a boosting based hybrid for feature selection. In *Proceedings of the 18th International Conference on Machine Learning*, Morgan Kaufmann (2001) 74–81
9. Freund, Y., Schapire, R.: Experiments with a new boosting algorithm. In *Proceedings of the Thirteenth International Conference on Machine Learning* (1996)
10. Iba, W., Langley, P.: Induction of one-level decision trees. In *Proceedings of the Ninth International Workshop on Machine Learning* (1992) 233–240
11. Jarmulak, J., Craw, S., Rowe, R.: Genetic algorithms to optimise CBR retrieval. In Enrico Blanzieri and Luigi Portinale, editors, *Proceedings of the 5th European Workshop on Case-Based Reasoning*, Trento, Italy, Springer-Verlag, Berlin (2000) 137–149
12. John, G., Kohavi, R., Pfleger, K.: Irrelevant features and the subset selection problem. In *IML94* (1994) 121–129 Journal version in AIJ.
13. Lenz, M.: Defining knowledge layers for textual CBR. In *Proceedings of the 4th European Workshop on Case-Based Reasoning*, Dublin, Ireland, Springer Verlag (1998)
14. Lenz, M.: Knowledge sources for textual CBR applications. In *In Proceedings of the AAAI-98 Workshop on Textual Case-Based Reasoning*, Menlo Park, CA, AAAI Press (1998) 24–29
15. Mitchell, T.: *Machine Learning*. McGraw-Hill International (1997)
16. Pazzani, M. J., Muramatsu, J., Billsus, D.: Syskill and Webert: Identifying interesting web sites. In *Proceedings of the Thirteenth National Conference on Artificial Intelligence*, Portland, OR (1996) 54–61
17. Sakkis, G., Androutsopoulos, I., Paliouras, G., Karkaletsis, V., Spyropoulos, C., Stamatopoulos, P.: A memory-based approach to anti-spam filtering for mailing lists. *Information Retrieval*, 6 (2003) 49–73
18. Salton, G., McGill, M. J.: An introduction to modern information retrieval. McGraw-Hill (1983)
19. Weber, R., Aha, D. W., Sandhu, N., Munoz-Avila, H.: A textual case-based reasoning framework for knowledge management applications. In *Proceedings of the 9th German Workshop on Case-Based Reasoning. Shaker Verlag.* (2001)

Author Index

Aamodt, Agnar 1
Aha, David W. 211
Aiken, Jim 533
Allendoerfer, Kenneth R. 476
Arcos, Josep Lluís 464, 601
Arshadi, Niloofar 17

Balfe, Evelyn 489
Bandini, Stefania 504
Bellazzi, Riccardo 659
Bello-Tomás, Juan José 32
Bengtsson, Marcus 686
Bergmann, Ralph 404
Bertolotto, Michela 702
Bichindaritz, Isabelle 47
Bogaerts, Steven 62
Bradley, Keith 518
Branting, Karl 77
Breu, Ruth 434
Bridge, Derek 157
Bühring, Angela 375
Burke, Robin 91

Cardoso, Amílcar 257, 272
Castillo, Luis F. 547
Cheetham, William 106
Colombo, Ettore 504
Colomer, Joan 748
Corchado, Emilio S. 533, 547
Corchado, Juan M. 533, 547
Coyle, Lorcan 119, 560
Cunningham, Colleen 573
Cunningham, Pádraig 119, 128, 157, 560

Delany, Sarah Jane 128
Díaz-Agudo, Belén 32, 142, 587
Doyle, Dónal 119, 157

Fowler, Caleb 573
Freßmann, Andrea 302
Funk, Peter 673, 686

Gabel, Thomas 169
Gervás, Pablo 142
Göker, Mehmet H. 16
Gómez-Gauchía, Hector 587

Gomes, Paulo 184, 778
González-Calero, Pedro A. 32, 587
Grachten, Maarten 601
Grech, Alicia 198
Gupta, Kalyan Moy 211

Iglezakis, Ioannis 227

Jänichen, Silke 616
Johansen, John 793
Jung, Sungwon 645
Jurisica, Igor 17

Kanawati, Rushed 449
Khemani, Deepak 732
Kim, Hyun Woo 630
Kim, Jonghan 645
Koychev, Ivan 806

Lamontagne, Luc 242
Lapalme, Guy 242
Leake, David 62
Lee, Kyoung Jun 630
Lefevre, Nathalie 533
Leonardi, Giorgio 659
Lester, James 77
Li, Lei 361
López de Mántaras, Ramon 601
Luxhøj, James T. 793

Macedo, Luís 257, 272
Main, Julie 198
Martin, Francisco J. 287
Massie, Stewart 806
Maximini, Rainer 302, 404
McCarthy, Kevin 763
McGinty, Lorraine 763
McLoughlin, Eoin 702
McSherry, David 317, 331
Melendez, Joaquim 748
Montani, Stefania 659
Moore, Philip 211
Mott, Bradford 77
Murphy, Michael 573

Nilsson, Markus 673

O'Sullivan, Derry   717
O'Sullivan, Dympna   702
Olsson, Erik   686
Ontañón, Santiago   346

Pan, Rong   361
Park, Jinwoo   645
Pavón, Juan   547
Peinado, Federico   142
Penta, Kiran Kumar   732
Pereira, Francisco C.   778
Perner, Petra   375, 616
Plaza, Enric   287, 346
Portinale, Luigi   659
Pous, Carles   748
Price, Joseph   106
Proctor, Jason M.   573

Rahman, Yusof   157
Reilly, James   763
Reinartz, Thomas   227
Roth-Berghofer, Thomas R.   227, 389

Salotti, Sylvie   449

Sartori, Fabio   504
Schaaf, Martin   302, 404
Seco, Nuno   778
Seong, Deokhyun   645
Smyth, Barry   489, 518, 717, 763
Smyth, Tim   533
Stahl, Armin   169

Tartakovski, Alexander   404
Tobudic, Asmir   419

Vizzari, Giuseppe   504

Wang, Chengbo   793
Weber, Barbara   434
Weber, Rosina   476, 573
Widmer, Gerhard   419
Wild, Werner   434
Wilson, David C.   702, 717
Wiratunga, Nirmalie   806

Yang, Qiang   361

Zehraoui, Farida   449

Lecture Notes in Artificial Intelligence (LNAI)

Vol. 3194: R. Camacho, R. King, A. Srinivasan (Eds.), Inductive Logic Programming. XI, 361 pages. 2004.

Vol. 3157: C. Zhang, H. W. Guesgen, W.K. Yeap (Eds.), PRICAI 2004: Trends in Artificial Intelligence. XX, 1023 pages. 2004.

Vol. 3155: P. Funk, P.A. González Calero (Eds.), Advances in Case-Based Reasoning. XIII, 822 pages. 2004.

Vol. 3139: F. Iida, R. Pfeifer, L. Steels, Y. Kuniyoshi (Eds.), Embodied Artificial Intelligence. IX, 331 pages. 2004.

Vol. 3131: V. Torra, Y. Narukawa (Eds.), Modeling Decisions for Artificial Intelligence. XI, 327 pages. 2004.

Vol. 3127: K.E. Wolff, H.D. Pfeiffer, H.S. Delugach (Eds.), Conceptual Structures at Work. XI, 403 pages. 2004.

Vol. 3123: A. Belz, R. Evans, P. Piwek (Eds.), Natural Language Generation. X, 219 pages. 2004.

Vol. 3120: J. Shawe-Taylor, Y. Singer (Eds.), Learning Theory. X, 648 pages. 2004.

Vol. 3097: D. Basin, M. Rusinowitch (Eds.), Automated Reasoning. XII, 493 pages. 2004.

Vol. 3071: A. Omicini, P. Petta, J. Pitt (Eds.), Engineering Societies in the Agents World. XIII, 409 pages. 2004.

Vol. 3070: L. Rutkowski, J. Siekmann, R. Tadeusiewicz, L.A. Zadeh (Eds.), Artificial Intelligence and Soft Computing - ICAISC 2004. XXV, 1208 pages. 2004.

Vol. 3068: E. André, L. Dybkjær, W. Minker, P. Heisterkamp (Eds.), Affective Dialogue Systems. XII, 324 pages. 2004.

Vol. 3067: M. Dastani, J. Dix, A. El Fallah-Seghrouchni (Eds.), Programming Multi-Agent Systems. X, 221 pages. 2004.

Vol. 3066: S. Tsumoto, R. Słowiński, J. Komorowski, J.W. Grzymała-Busse (Eds.), Rough Sets and Current Trends in Computing. XX, 853 pages. 2004.

Vol. 3065: A. Lomuscio, D. Nute (Eds.), Deontic Logic in Computer Science. X, 275 pages. 2004.

Vol. 3060: A.Y. Tawfik, S.D. Goodwin (Eds.), Advances in Artificial Intelligence. XIII, 582 pages. 2004.

Vol. 3056: H. Dai, R. Srikant, C. Zhang (Eds.), Advances in Knowledge Discovery and Data Mining. XIX, 713 pages. 2004.

Vol. 3055: H. Christiansen, M.-S. Hacid, T. Andreasen, H.L. Larsen (Eds.), Flexible Query Answering Systems. X, 500 pages. 2004.

Vol. 3040: R. Conejo, M. Urretavizcaya, J.-L. Pérez-de-la-Cruz (Eds.), Current Topics in Artificial Intelligence. XIV, 689 pages. 2004.

Vol. 3035: M.A. Wimmer (Ed.), Knowledge Management in Electronic Government. XII, 326 pages. 2004.

Vol. 3034: J. Favela, E. Menasalvas, E. Chávez (Eds.), Advances in Web Intelligence. XIII, 227 pages. 2004.

Vol. 3030: P. Giorgini, B. Henderson-Sellers, M. Winikoff (Eds.), Agent-Oriented Information Systems. XIV, 207 pages. 2004.

Vol. 3029: B. Orchard, C. Yang, M. Ali (Eds.), Innovations in Applied Artificial Intelligence. XXI, 1272 pages. 2004.

Vol. 3025: G.A. Vouros, T. Panayiotopoulos (Eds.), Methods and Applications of Artificial Intelligence. XV, 546 pages. 2004.

Vol. 3020: D. Polani, B. Browning, A. Bonarini, K. Yoshida (Eds.), RoboCup 2003: Robot Soccer World Cup VII. XVI, 767 pages. 2004.

Vol. 3012: K. Kurumatani, S.-H. Chen, A. Ohuchi (Eds.), Multi-Agnets for Mass User Support. X, 217 pages. 2004.

Vol. 3010: K.R. Apt, F. Fages, F. Rossi, P. Szeredi, J. Váncza (Eds.), Recent Advances in Constraints. VIII, 285 pages. 2004.

Vol. 2990: J. Leite, A. Omicini, L. Sterling, P. Torroni (Eds.), Declarative Agent Languages and Technologies. XII, 281 pages. 2004.

Vol. 2980: A. Blackwell, K. Marriott, A. Shimojima (Eds.), Diagrammatic Representation and Inference. XV, 448 pages. 2004.

Vol. 2977: G. Di Marzo Serugendo, A. Karageorgos, O.F. Rana, F. Zambonelli (Eds.), Engineering Self-Organising Systems. X, 299 pages. 2004.

Vol. 2972: R. Monroy, G. Arroyo-Figueroa, L.E. Sucar, H. Sossa (Eds.), MICAI 2004: Advances in Artificial Intelligence. XVII, 923 pages. 2004.

Vol. 2969: M. Nickles, M. Rovatsos, G. Weiss (Eds.), Agents and Computational Autonomy. X, 275 pages. 2004.

Vol. 2961: P. Eklund (Ed.), Concept Lattices. IX, 411 pages. 2004.

Vol. 2953: K. Konrad, Model Generation for Natural Language Interpretation and Analysis. XIII, 166 pages. 2004.

Vol. 2934: G. Lindemann, D. Moldt, M. Paolucci (Eds.), Regulated Agent-Based Social Systems. X, 301 pages. 2004.

Vol. 2930: F. Winkler (Ed.), Automated Deduction in Geometry. VII, 231 pages. 2004.

Vol. 2926: L. van Elst, V. Dignum, A. Abecker (Eds.), Agent-Mediated Knowledge Management. XI, 428 pages. 2004.

Vol. 2923: V. Lifschitz, I. Niemelä (Eds.), Logic Programming and Nonmonotonic Reasoning. IX, 365 pages. 2004.

Vol. 2915: A. Camurri, G. Volpe (Eds.), Gesture-Based Communication in Human-Computer Interaction. XIII, 558 pages. 2004.

Vol. 2913: T.M. Pinkston, V.K. Prasanna (Eds.), High Performance Computing - HiPC 2003. XX, 512 pages. 2003.

Vol. 2903: T.D. Gedeon, L.C.C. Fung (Eds.), AI 2003: Advances in Artificial Intelligence. XVI, 1075 pages. 2003.

Vol. 2902: F.M. Pires, S.P. Abreu (Eds.), Progress in Artificial Intelligence. XV, 504 pages. 2003.

Vol. 2892: F. Dau, The Logic System of Concept Graphs with Negation. XI, 213 pages. 2003.

Vol. 2891: J. Lee, M. Barley (Eds.), Intelligent Agents and Multi-Agent Systems. X, 215 pages. 2003.

Vol. 2882: D. Veit, Matchmaking in Electronic Markets. XV, 180 pages. 2003.

Vol. 2871: N. Zhong, Z.W. Raś, S. Tsumoto, E. Suzuki (Eds.), Foundations of Intelligent Systems. XV, 697 pages. 2003.

Vol. 2854: J. Hoffmann, Utilizing Problem Structure in Planing. XIII, 251 pages. 2003.

Vol. 2843: G. Grieser, Y. Tanaka, A. Yamamoto (Eds.), Discovery Science. XII, 504 pages. 2003.

Vol. 2842: R. Gavaldá, K.P. Jantke, E. Takimoto (Eds.), Algorithmic Learning Theory. XI, 313 pages. 2003.

Vol. 2838: N. Lavrač, D. Gamberger, L. Todorovski, H. Blockeel (Eds.), Knowledge Discovery in Databases: PKDD 2003. XVI, 508 pages. 2003.

Vol. 2837: N. Lavrač, D. Gamberger, L. Todorovski, H. Blockeel (Eds.), Machine Learning: ECML 2003. XVI, 504 pages. 2003.

Vol. 2835: T. Horváth, A. Yamamoto (Eds.), Inductive Logic Programming. X, 401 pages. 2003.

Vol. 2821: A. Günter, R. Kruse, B. Neumann (Eds.), KI 2003: Advances in Artificial Intelligence. XII, 662 pages. 2003.

Vol. 2807: V. Matoušek, P. Mautner (Eds.), Text, Speech and Dialogue. XIII, 426 pages. 2003.

Vol. 2801: W. Banzhaf, J. Ziegler, T. Christaller, P. Dittrich, J.T. Kim (Eds.), Advances in Artificial Life. XVI, 905 pages. 2003.

Vol. 2797: O.R. Zaïane, S.J. Simoff, C. Djeraba (Eds.), Mining Multimedia and Complex Data. XII, 281 pages. 2003.

Vol. 2792: T. Rist, R.S. Aylett, D. Ballin, J. Rickel (Eds.), Intelligent Virtual Agents. XV, 364 pages. 2003.

Vol. 2782: M. Klusch, A. Omicini, S. Ossowski, H. Laamanen (Eds.), Cooperative Information Agents VII. XI, 345 pages. 2003.

Vol. 2780: M. Dojat, E. Keravnou, P. Barahona (Eds.), Artificial Intelligence in Medicine. XIII, 388 pages. 2003.

Vol. 2777: B. Schölkopf, M.K. Warmuth (Eds.), Learning Theory and Kernel Machines. XIV, 746 pages. 2003.

Vol. 2752: G.A. Kaminka, P.U. Lima, R. Rojas (Eds.), RoboCup 2002: Robot Soccer World Cup VI. XVI, 498 pages. 2003.

Vol. 2741: F. Baader (Ed.), Automated Deduction – CADE-19. XII, 503 pages. 2003.

Vol. 2705: S. Renals, G. Grefenstette (Eds.), Text- and Speech-Triggered Information Access. VII, 197 pages. 2003.

Vol. 2703: O.R. Zaïane, J. Srivastava, M. Spiliopoulou, B. Masand (Eds.), WEBKDD 2002 - MiningWeb Data for Discovering Usage Patterns and Profiles. IX, 181 pages. 2003.

Vol. 2700: M.T. Pazienza (Ed.), Extraction in the Web Era. XIII, 163 pages. 2003.

Vol. 2699: M.G. Hinchey, J.L. Rash, W.F. Truszkowski, C.A. Rouff, D.F. Gordon-Spears (Eds.), Formal Approaches to Agent-Based Systems. IX, 297 pages. 2002.

Vol. 2691: V. Mařík, J.P. Müller, M. Pechoucek (Eds.), Multi-Agent Systems and Applications III. XIV, 660 pages. 2003.

Vol. 2684: M.V. Butz, O. Sigaud, P. Gérard (Eds.), Anticipatory Behavior in Adaptive Learning Systems. X, 303 pages. 2003.

Vol. 2682: R. Meo, P.L. Lanzi, M. Klemettinen (Eds.), Database Support for Data Mining Applications. XII, 325 pages. 2004.

Vol. 2671: Y. Xiang, B. Chaib-draa (Eds.), Advances in Artificial Intelligence. XIV, 642 pages. 2003.

Vol. 2663: E. Menasalvas, J. Segovia, P.S. Szczepaniak (Eds.), Advances in Web Intelligence. XII, 350 pages. 2003.

Vol. 2661: P.L. Lanzi, W. Stolzmann, S.W. Wilson (Eds.), Learning Classifier Systems. VII, 231 pages. 2003.

Vol. 2654: U. Schmid, Inductive Synthesis of Functional Programs. XXII, 398 pages. 2003.

Vol. 2650: M.-P. Huget (Ed.), Communications in Multi-agent Systems. VIII, 323 pages. 2003.

Vol. 2645: M.A. Wimmer (Ed.), Knowledge Management in Electronic Government. XI, 320 pages. 2003.

Vol. 2639: G. Wang, Q. Liu, Y. Yao, A. Skowron (Eds.), Rough Sets, Fuzzy Sets, Data Mining, and Granular Computing. XVII, 741 pages. 2003.

Vol. 2637: K.-Y. Whang, J. Jeon, K. Shim, J. Srivastava, Advances in Knowledge Discovery and Data Mining. XVIII, 610 pages. 2003.

Vol. 2636: E. Alonso, D. Kudenko, D. Kazakov (Eds.), Adaptive Agents and Multi-Agent Systems. XIV, 323 pages. 2003.

Vol. 2627: B. O'Sullivan (Ed.), Recent Advances in Constraints. X, 201 pages. 2003.

Vol. 2600: S. Mendelson, A.J. Smola (Eds.), Advanced Lectures on Machine Learning. IX, 259 pages. 2003.

Vol. 2592: R. Kowalczyk, J.P. Müller, H. Tianfield, R. Unland (Eds.), Agent Technologies, Infrastructures, Tools, and Applications for E-Services. XVII, 371 pages. 2003.

Vol. 2586: M. Klusch, S. Bergamaschi, P. Edwards, P. Petta (Eds.), Intelligent Information Agents. VI, 275 pages. 2003.

Vol. 2583: S. Matwin, C. Sammut (Eds.), Inductive Logic Programming. X, 351 pages. 2003.

Vol. 2581: J.S. Sichman, F. Bousquet, P. Davidsson (Eds.), Multi-Agent-Based Simulation. X, 195 pages. 2003.

Vol. 2577: P. Petta, R. Tolksdorf, F. Zambonelli (Eds.), Engineering Societies in the Agents World III. X, 285 pages. 2003.

Vol. 2569: D. Karagiannis, U. Reimer (Eds.), Practical Aspects of Knowledge Management. XIII, 648 pages. 2002.